THE HANDBOOK OF COMPARATIVE CRIMINAL LAW

THE HANDBOOK OF

COMPARATIVE CRIMINAL LAW

Edited by KEVIN JON HELLER
AND MARKUS D. DUBBER

STANFORD LAW BOOKS
An Imprint of Stanford University Press
Stanford, California

Stanford University Press
Stanford, California

©2011 by the Board of Trustees of the Leland Stanford Junior University. All rights reserved.

No part of this book may be reproduced or transmitted in any form or by any means, electronic or mechanical, including photocopying and recording, or in any information storage or retrieval system without the prior written permission of Stanford University Press.

Printed in the United States of America on acid-free, archival-quality paper

Library of Congress Cataloging-in-Publication Data

The handbook of comparative criminal law / edited by Kevin Jon Heller and Markus D. Dubber.
  p. cm.
   Includes bibliographical references and index.
   ISBN 978-0-8047-5758-4 (cloth : alk. paper)
   1. Criminal law. 2. Comparative law. 1. Heller, Kevin Jon. II. Dubber, Markus Dirk.
K5015.4.H36 2011
345—dc22   2010020243

Typeset by Westchester Book Group in 10/13.5 Minion.

CONTENTS

Introduction: Comparative Criminal Law   1
Kevin Jon Heller and Markus D. Dubber

Argentina   12
Marcelo Ferrante

Australia   49
Simon Bronitt

Canada   97
Kent Roach

China   137
Wei Luo

Egypt   179
Sadiq Reza

France   209
Catherine Elliott

Germany   252
Thomas Weigend

India   288
Stanley Yeo

Iran   320
Silvia Tellenbach

Israel 352
Itzhak Kugler

Japan 393
John O. Haley

Russia 414
Stephen C. Thaman

South Africa 455
Jonathan Burchell

Spain 488
Carlos Gómez-Jara Díez and Luis E. Chiesa

United Kingdom 531
Andrew J. Ashworth

United States 563
Paul H. Robinson

The Rome Statute of the International Criminal Court 593
Kevin Jon Heller

Index 635

THE HANDBOOK OF

COMPARATIVE CRIMINAL LAW

INTRODUCTION: COMPARATIVE CRIMINAL LAW

Kevin Jon Heller and Markus D. Dubber

The comparative analysis of criminal law can do many things for many people. For the legislator, it can be a source of possible approaches to a specific issue or even to the enterprise of criminal law reform and criminal lawmaking in general. For the judge, it can suggest different solutions to tricky problems of interpretation or common-law adjudication. The theorist can mine the vast stock of principles and rules, of structures and categories, and of questions and answers that can be found in the world's criminal law systems. And the teacher, too, can draw on the positive manifestation of different, or not-so-different, approaches to particular or general questions of criminal law to challenge students' ability to comprehend, to formulate, and eventually to critically analyze black-letter rules that are all too often presented by judicial—or, occasionally, professorial—oracles of law as the manifestations of inexorable logic or, at least, of *stare decisis*.[1]

Oddly, it is precisely this critical potential that may well account for the fact that the comparative study of criminal law traditionally has been neglected. In fact, if not in theory, Anglo-American criminal law continues to be regarded as an exercise of the police power of the state, where the power to police is thought to be closely related, even essential, to the very idea of sovereignty. More particularly, the police power is the modern manifestation at the state level of the deeply rooted power of the householder (*oikonomos, paterfamilias*) over his household (*oikos, familia*).[2] In Blackstone's memorable phrase, "public police or oeconomy" is "the due regulation and domestic order of the kingdom: whereby the individuals of the state, like members of a well-governed family, are bound to

---

Kevin Jon Heller is a Senior Lecturer at Melbourne Law School. His recent publications include "The Cognitive Psychology of Mens Rea," 99 *Journal of Criminal Law and Criminology* 317 (2009), and "Mistake of Legal Element, the Common Law, and Article 32 of the Rome Statute: A Critical Analysis," 6 *Journal of International Criminal Justice* 419 (2008).

Markus D. Dubber is Professor of Law at the University of Toronto. His recent publications include *The Police Power: Patriarchy and the Foundations of American Government* (Columbia University Press, 2005) and *The Sense of Justice: Empathy in Law and Punishment* (New York University Press, 2006).

conform their general behavior to the rules of propriety, good neighborhood, and good manners: and to be decent, industrious, and inoffensive in their respective stations."[3]

As essentially discretionary, and defined by its very indefinability, the police power is incompatible with principled critique. And insofar as a penal police regime is not subject to critical analysis, it has no use for regarding criminal law comparatively.

Comparative analysis fits more comfortably with a conception of criminal law as law, which recognizes and attempts to meet the challenge of a system of state punishment consistent with the state's function of safeguarding and manifesting the autonomy of its constituents under the rule of law (i.e., in a *Rechtsstaat*). It is therefore no surprise that the project of comparative criminal law begins in the wake of the Enlightenment's fundamental critique of state power in general, and of state penal power in particular. P. J. A. Feuerbach, one of the leading figures of Enlightenment criminal law and the generally acknowledged "father" of modern German criminal law, thought the comparative method essential to the project of constructing a critical theory of criminal law. Comparative analysis, in Feuerbach's view, was essential not only to the project of critical criminal law but also to the project of legal theory in general: "Just as the comparison of various tongues produces the philosophy of language, or linguistic science proper, so does a comparison of laws and legal customs of the most varied nations, both those most nearly related to us and those farther removed, create universal legal science, i.e., legal science without qualification, which alone can infuse real and vigorous life into the specific legal science of any particular country."[4]

One need not share Feuerbach's enthusiasm for a universal legal science, or pursue the analogy between language and law that was commonly drawn at the time, to appreciate his insight into the critical potential of comparative analysis. That critical potential can be put to use in various contexts, some more ambitious than others. The least self-conscious and ambitious form of comparative analysis is exemplified by modern American criminal law. At least since the completion of the Model Penal Code in 1962 and the widespread reform of American criminal codes in its wake, American criminal law can no longer be regarded as a common-law subject. Instead, it is a collection of self-standing code-based jurisdictions, dominated by the criminal law systems of the fifty states and the District of Columbia, superimposed on which is the ever-growing body of federal criminal law. In teaching and in scholarship—though decreasingly in judicial opinions, which by necessity concern themselves with the criminal law of the jurisdiction in question—the subject of "American criminal law" survives as a form of domestic or internal comparative criminal law, where norms from various American jurisdictions are compared, contrasted, and (with difficulty) synthesized into a more or less coherent whole. American criminal law teaching and scholarship would benefit from the conscious adoption of a comparative approach that includes both domestic and foreign materials, rather than maintaining the anachronistic image of a unified body of "American criminal law" that contributes to the evolution of a yet larger body of "common law."[5]

An explicit form of international and external comparative analysis is exemplified by the ambitious research project prompted by an early twentieth-century effort to revise the German Penal Code. Although the effort proved unsuccessful—the Code was not significantly reformed until the late 1960s—it generated a sixteen-volume overview of criminal law systems throughout the world.[6]

The frequent reference to foreign criminal law in the jurisprudence of the Canadian Supreme Court falls somewhere in between the two forms of comparative criminal law exemplified by this systematic inquiry into foreign criminal law and the implicit comparativism of contemporary American criminal law. In general, these references are restricted to "common-law" countries, notably England and to a far lesser extent Australia, New Zealand, and the United States,[7] although certain basic concepts of German criminal law have had some influence, indirectly, as disseminated in English-language criminal law scholarship, notably George Fletcher's *Rethinking Criminal Law*.[8] The limitation to Commonwealth countries and the continued special place accorded English criminal law, however, indicates that Canadian criminal law also continues to regard itself as part of the general "common-law" enterprise; in this sense, references to foreign law are less an exercise in comparative criminal law than they are the canvassing of persuasive, though no longer controlling, precedent familiar from centuries of common-law judging.[9]

The emerging enterprise of international criminal law is inherently and explicitly comparative. The broad provisions of the Rome Statute of the International Criminal Court (ICC) leave considerable room for comparative inquiries into the treatment of central questions of criminal liability, including intent and other forms of *mens rea*, accomplice and group liability, inchoate criminality (conspiracy, attempt, solicitation), and the availability of defenses (e.g., self-defense, necessity, duress, superior orders, and ignorance of law). Article 21 of the Rome Statute expressly instructs ICC judges to consult "general principles of law derived by the Court from national laws of legal systems of the world." Because of the often-nebulous quality of international criminal law, judges of the International Criminal Tribunal for the former Yugoslavia (ICTY) and the International Criminal Tribunal for Rwanda (ICTR) have frequently decided cases through such comparative surveys: in *Delalic* (1998),[10] where ICTY judges had to interpret the *mens rea* requirement for murder when charged as a grave breach of the Geneva Conventions; and in *Akayesu* (1998),[11] where ICTR judges examined national criminal law systems to decide what kinds of acts qualify as rape when charged as a crime against humanity.[12]

The rise of international criminal law and the creation of institutions of international criminal law have attracted the attention of criminal law theorists who, like Feuerbach, see an opportunity for the development of a universal, or at least supranational, theory of criminal law.[13] But even without this doctrinal ambition, which reflects an elevated sense of the significance of theorizing (and of the theorizer) in the construction and maintenance of a system of criminal law, criminal law theory can be enriched by taking a comparative perspective. The mere recognition of the existence of well-developed and well-considered alternatives makes room for the consideration not only of new answers to familiar questions, but of new questions as well. Comparative analysis, of course, can also be rewarding as a scholarly end in itself, although the meaningful comparison of even a single doctrinal rule requires careful consideration of the rule's place in the doctrinal system as a whole, along with an inquiry into historical and sociolegal context, notably its interpretation and implementation. To quote Feuerbach once more: "Without knowledge of the real and the existing, without comparison of different legislations, without knowledge of their relation to the various conditions of peoples according to time, climate, and constitution, a priori nonsense is inevitable."[14]

This *Handbook* contains seventeen chapters, sixteen that are country specific—a sample that includes countries in six different continents and covers all of the world's major legal systems—and one that discusses the criminal law applied by the International Criminal Court from a comparative perspective.

Argentina's criminal code, the Código Penal (CP), was adopted in 1921. The CP has been influenced by both the German and the Italian criminal law traditions: the first draft of the CP, the Tejedor Code, was heavily influenced by Feuerbach's Bavarian Criminal Code of 1813, and the 1891 draft code that ultimately led to the current CP was primarily influenced by Giuseppe Zanardelli's Italian Criminal Code of 1889. The current CP was intended "to capture in a simple and pragmatically oriented text the basics of the Tejedor Code and the 1891 draft," and to a significant extent it succeeded: the CP established a simple regime of sanctions, abolished the death penalty, and endorsed straightforward rules of responsibility and definitions of offenses. However, as Marcelo Ferrante notes, the numerous minor reforms and amendments adopted since 1921 have—as is often the case with codes that are updated in piecemeal fashion—"introduced complexity into an otherwise relatively simple text, often affecting the code's systematicity." Ferrante offers a particularly striking example of this in the area of punishment: possessing explosives in Argentina is now subject to longer imprisonment (5 to 15 years) than detonating the explosives and destroying goods or endangering human life (3 to 10 years).

"The history of Australia's criminal law," according to Simon Bronitt, "is bound up in its foundation as a penal colony." Because it was a settled colony, as opposed to a conquered or ceded one, English criminal law applied in Australia. Nevertheless, English criminal law's "tangled mass" of common-law and statutory offenses ultimately made Australia "fertile ground for codification." Today, most states and territories in Australia, which are bound together by Australia's federal system of government, have codified systems of criminal law (the "code jurisdictions"), and even those that do not (the "common-law jurisdictions") have adopted extensive criminal consolidation statutes. The many important substantive differences between the various jurisdictions led Australia—like the United States—to develop a Model Criminal Code. The Code has been received with markedly different degrees of enthusiasm across Australia, however, so fundamental differences remain. For example, although the Code provides that murder requires a perpetrator to act with at least English criminal law's oblique intention, five of Australia's eight jurisdictions continue to criminalize reckless murder.

Like the United States and Australia, Canada has a federal system. Unlike those countries, however, all criminal law in Canada is federal—a direct response, in fact, to the perceived weaknesses of the U.S. system. The federal criminal power in Canada is quite broad, extending to a number of areas that are not traditionally regulated by criminal law, such as tobacco advertising and pollution. But there are important limits, the most important of which is the Canadian Charter of Rights and Freedoms, adopted in 1982. According to Kent Roach, the Charter "has ... emerged as a significant restraint on the criminal law in Canada, with some basic criminal law principles being constitutionalized." Roach provides a number of illuminating examples of how courts have used the Charter to restrain the more punitive tendencies of Canadian criminal law: striking down constructive murder offenses on the ground that the stigma and penalties associated with a murder conviction require proof that the perpetrator subjectively foresaw the likelihood that his or her act would lead to death; holding that criminal negligence requires a much greater departure from the standard of care than ordinary civil negligence; and refusing to apply a statutory definition of duress that is far more restrictive than its common-law counterpart.

China's current criminal code was adopted in 1979, after a thirty-year period in which the Chinese Communist Party ruled the country without a criminal code or comprehensive set of criminal laws. As Wei Luo notes, many of the basic principles of the current code—for example, mental states, foreseeability, and causation—differ from their common-law and civilian counterparts. The code abandons several features of traditional Chinese criminal law, such as its lack of separation between administrative and judicial powers (which permitted a person to be convicted of a crime without a formal judicial proceeding), its willingness to extend the definition of crimes by analogy (which served as a useful tool for political repression), and its reliance on severe penalties for even minor crimes (which was useful to deter crime during times of social instability), but retains the death penalty for nearly seventy offenses, including bribery and embezzlement.

Modern Egyptian criminal law began in 1883 with the creation of national courts and a number of new legal codes. The Penal Code itself, which was modeled along the lines of the Napoleonic Code, was adopted in 1937. Perhaps the most striking aspect of Sadiq Reza's account of Egyptian criminal law is the progressive role that the Supreme Constitutional Court has played in its development: striking down both irrebuttable and rebuttable presumptions of knowledge on the ground that they violated the presumption of innocence; affirming the constitutional status of the voluntary-act requirement by disapproving a status law criminalizing vagabondage; declaring the Penal Code's conspiracy provision unconstitutional as inconsistent with the principle of legality; creating a "fair-notice" mistake-of-law defense; and so on. Unfortunately, as is the case in many criminal law systems, the Egyptian judiciary has proved considerably more deferential when it comes to terrorism offenses, where the president's decisions have largely gone unchallenged.

France finally adopted a new criminal code in 1992, after nearly two centuries of unsuccessful efforts to reform the Napoleonic Code of 1810. Like many criminal law systems, French criminal law normally distinguishes between crimes that require some form of intention and those that do not. Interestingly, though, *le dol éventuel*—where a perpetrator foresees the possibility of a particular result but does not want it to occur—does not satisfy the *mens rea* requirement of a crime that requires a special intent to cause a result forbidden by law. As Catherine Elliott discusses, before the adoption of the new Criminal Code *dol éventuel* was simply treated and punished as a form of negligence. Now, however, that mental state is a *mens rea* in its own right: "deliberately putting someone in danger." A perpetrator who deliberately puts someone in danger—a *mens rea* that lies somewhere between intention and negligence—is either convicted of a separate substantive offense (where there was an immediate risk of death or serious injury) or is sentenced as if he or she committed an aggravated offense of negligence (for crimes such as involuntary homicide and nonfatal offenses against the person).

The German Penal Code has been amended regularly since it was adopted in 1871, but its main structure has remained intact. German criminal law is remarkably systematic, particularly in terms of protecting fundamental interests. The centrality of the right to life in the German legal and philosophic tradition, for example, means that necessity can never justify killing an innocent person—not even in order to save the lives of several innocent people. However, Thomas Weigend makes clear that even German criminal law is willing to deviate from its own principles when the situation demands it. The strict prohibition against applying criminal laws retroactively is a striking example. After the reunification of Germany, East German soldiers who were charged with manslaughter for shooting people who tried to escape from the German Democratic Republic (GDR) often invoked a GDR statute that, under certain circumstances, justified such killings. The Federal Constitutional Court recognized that prohibiting the soldiers from relying on the statute was inconsistent with the principle of nonretroactivity, but prohibited the defense anyway.

Macaulay's Indian Penal Code, which dates from 1860, was inspired by English criminal law, the French Penal Code, and Edward Livingston's Benthamite draft of a Louisiana Penal Code.[15] Particularly noteworthy, as Stanley Yeo points out, is Indian criminal law's comprehensive taxonomy of homicides, which are divided into two categories—culpable homicide amounting to murder and culpable homicide not amounting to murder—and are arranged in descending order of culpability according to the perpetrator's intent to harm or his or her knowledge of the likelihood of death. Culpable homicides amounting to murder include killings in which the perpetrator intended to cause death, intended to cause injury the perpetrator knew would "likely" cause death, intended to cause injury that a reasonable person would have known "most probably" would cause death, or did not intend to cause death but knew that death would be a "virtual certainty." Culpable homicides not amounting to murder include killings in which the perpetrator intended to cause injury that a reasonable person would have known was "likely" to cause death or did not intend to cause death but knew that death was "likely." Finally, killings in which the perpetrator did not intend to cause death and only knew that death would "possibly" result are excluded from the category of culpable homicide entirely and constitute the much less serious crime of "causing death by a rash act." A number of partial defenses are also available under Indian criminal law to reduce culpable homicide amounting to murder to culpable homicide not amounting to murder, such as provocation, excessive self-defense, and consent. Interestingly, and reflective of India's unique caste system, although the existence of adequate provocation is assessed objectively, the standard is "a reasonable man, belonging to the same class of society to which the defendant belongs."

The Islamic Revolution in 1979 led Iran to replace its General Criminal Code of 1926, which had been strongly influenced by the Napoleonic Code, with a new criminal code based exclusively on classical Islamic criminal law. The Iranian Penal Code contains a general part, but—unusually—the principles contained therein do not apply to all the substantive crimes in the special part. Indeed, Silvia Tellenbach shows how the same principle can have a different meaning depending on the offense at issue. *Dolus eventualis* is a striking example: a death that results from an inherently deadly act (such as using a weapon) committed with *dolus eventualis* is regarded as intentional, while an arson that leads to death committed with the same *dolus* is regarded as nonintentional. This is an important difference, because the former crime will be punished by retaliation, while the latter will be punished only by blood money. However, whether to prosecute the perpetrator for homicide at all will be decided solely by the victims of the crime: "The role of the state is limited to conducting proceedings on the demand of the blood avengers."

The general part of Israel's Penal Law, which dated back to the criminal code enacted by the British mandatory legislature, was completely revamped by the Knesset in 1994. A number of features of Amendment no. 39, the vehicle for reform, have proven controversial and have led to judicial resistance. An example Itzhak Kugler discusses is section 20(b), the so-called foresight rule, which provides that the *mens rea* of all intention crimes is satisfied if the person knew that a particular result was almost certain to occur—equivalent to "oblique intention" in English criminal law. Before Amendment no. 39 was adopted, Israeli courts had held that the foresight rule did not apply to the crime of murder, because only persons who intended to cause death deserved the stigma (and accompanying life sentence) of a murder conviction. Amendment no. 39 would seem to eliminate that exception, but a number of courts have held that because murder requires "premeditation" and section 20(b) speaks only of "intention," the traditional exception to the foresight rule continues to apply.

Japan's criminal code, Keihō, celebrated its one hundredth birthday in 2007. Two aspects of Japanese criminal law, clearly interrelated, are worth noting. On the one hand, negligence crimes play an unusually large role in Japanese criminal law, which criminalizes a wide range of conduct, such as negligent driving, that would attract only civil liability in most countries. On the other hand, Japanese criminal law is remarkably lenient: as John O. Haley points out, "[o]nly rarely . . . do convicted offenders receive any significant formal punishment." In part, that is due to Japan's very low crime rate and the fact that more than two-thirds of code violations consist of negligence offenses, which are normally punished with fines instead of incarceration, but it also reflects the significant discretion possessed by police, prosecutors, and judges: the police fail to report 33 percent of all crimes; prosecutors refuse to prosecute 33 percent of their cases; and judges suspend nearly 60 percent of all sentences. It is little wonder, then, that Japan has the lowest per capita incarceration rate of any industrial democracy, including the Nordic countries.

Russia's criminal code, the Ugolovnyy kodeks Rossiyskoy Federatsii (UK), is relatively new, having been adopted in 1996 and amended frequently since, including a comprehensive reform in 2003. One of the more unusual aspects of the UK, in Stephen Thaman's view, is its "socially dangerous act" requirement, according to which an act that does not pose a danger to society is not criminal even if it satisfies all the formal requirements of a particular offense. Although the "socially dangerous act" requirement is a vestige of Soviet criminal law, it now serves to limit the ambit of criminal responsibility instead of, as in the Soviet era, to expand it. And limit it does: Russian criminal law's emphasis on social protection leads to expansive defenses of necessity (permitting an actor to take a "justified risk toward the achievement of socially useful goals") and self-defense (permitting the use of force to defend "social or state interests protected by the law"), among others.

South African criminal law is a true hybrid system that blends, in Jonathan Burchell's words, "Roman-Dutch, English, German, and uniquely South African elements." There is much that is unusual about this system, particularly its insistence that a person does not act with the "guilty mind" that criminal responsibility requires unless he or she subjectively appreciates the unlawfulness of his or her conduct. True mistakes of law are thus always exculpatory in South Africa, even if they are unreasonable or unavoidable. Equally unusual—and equally subjectivizing—is South African criminal law's concept of "non-pathological incapacity," according to which mental disturbance that falls short of insanity can negate not only the *mens rea* of a criminal offense but also criminal capacity itself. A number of courts have relied on "non-pathological incapacity" to acquit defendants who committed serious crimes because of intoxication, provocation, or emotional stress.

Although modern Spanish criminal law dates back to the reform movement of the late eighteenth century—and is thus deeply influenced by Cesare Beccaria's seminal work *Of Crimes and Punishments* (1764)—the current penal code was enacted only in 1995. There are a number of interesting features of Spanish criminal law, such as its categorical rejection of strict liability and its willingness to acquit individuals who use disproportionate force in self-defense. The most interesting aspect, however, has to be the right of victims to pursue civil claims against a defendant within a criminal proceeding. As Carlos Gómez-Jara Díez and Luis E. Chiesa explain, "As private prosecutors, the victims not only charge the defendant with the commission of an offense but also seek monetary relief through restitution, compensation, or indemnification." Indeed, Spanish criminal law provides victims with an incentive to litigate civil and criminal claims simultaneously, because civil courts cannot award damages to victims until a criminal court has determined that a crime was committed.

The criminal law of the United Kingdom is perhaps the most common-law of all the common-law systems: although efforts to codify English criminal law have led to the adoption of a number of important statutory reforms, such as the Theft Act 1968 and the Sexual Offences Act 2003, "the vast majority of rules relating to the general part of the criminal law remain governed by the common law and therefore by judicial decisions." The lack of a comprehensive criminal code explains, at least in part, what Andrew Ashworth describes as English criminal law's "shadowy engagement" with the principle of legality; indeed, as late as 1962 the House of Lords was willing to convict a defendant of "conspiracy to corrupt public morals" even though he could not have known at the time that such a crime existed. More recently, however, that shadowy engagement has begun to blossom into open marriage—the result of Parliament's decision to enact the Human Rights Act 1998, which incorporated the European Convention on Human Rights (ECHR) into English law. The principle of legality enshrined in article 7 of the ECHR has transformed English courts' approach to determining the ambit of common-law offenses, and the ECHR has had a significant impact on English criminal law in general, such as leading courts to "read down" reverse burdens of proof for many defenses into more easily discharged evidentiary burdens. However, on more than one occasion English courts have resisted giving the ECHR domestic effect—upholding, for example, the conviction of a fifteen-year-old boy of raping a child, the most serious child sex offense in English criminal law, despite the fact that such a conviction would almost certainly be impermissible under the ECHR.

The defining feature of criminal law in the United States, in Paul Robinson's account, is that there is no such thing as American criminal law: "there are fifty-two American criminal justice systems"—the fifty states, the federal system, and the District of Columbia—"and each is different from the others in some way." The fragmentation of criminal law in the United States has been minimized somewhat by the promulgation of the 1962 Model Penal Code: a number of states have adopted the Code wholesale, with only minor revisions, while other states have used it to provide the style and form for their statutory (re)codifications. Other states, however, have yet to adopt a modern criminal code, and all efforts to reform the federal code over the last four decades have failed miserably, meaning that the federal code "is not significantly different in form from the alphabetical listing of offenses that was typical of the original American codes in the 1800s." However, modern state criminal codes are remarkably comprehensive, with detailed general and special parts that are "designed to include a comprehensive and self-contained statement of all the rules required to adjudicate all criminal cases."

The Rome Statute of the International Criminal Court was adopted in 1998 and entered into force in 2002. The Rome Statute has been described as a "major step forward for substantive international criminal law," and with good reason: unlike the minimalist statutes of earlier international courts, such as the Nuremberg Tribunal, the ICTR, and the ICTY, the Rome Statute provides detailed definitions of the core international crimes, the possible modes of participation in those crimes, and the permissible grounds for excluding criminal responsibility. The Statute thus represents the international community's most ambitious attempt to create a special and general part of international criminal law. How successful that attempt has been remains to be seen: as Kevin Jon Heller explains, the Rome Statute is based on a complicated and often-unstable hybridization of common law and civil law that leaves open as many questions —including fundamental ones, such as the meaning of "intent"—as it answers.

Rather than present an album of postcards from faraway, and not-so-faraway, criminal law places, never mind an encyclopedic overview of World Criminal Law, this *Handbook* aims to provide a diverse selection of criminal law systems designed to stimulate comparative analysis. The authors of each chapter were asked to address a common set of topics to ensure reasonable comprehensiveness and facilitate comparison among chapters (and systems). At the same time, the list and order of topics were designed to allow for maximum flexibility. Conceptual rigidity is not only inconsistent with the very idea of comparative analysis, but also may result in formulaic summaries that are neither accurate nor particularly interesting. Instead, contributors were encouraged to write the sort of essay they would like to read about an unfamiliar criminal law system. The contributors are not necessarily comparativists by trade; they are leading criminal law scholars who portray a given ("their") criminal law system with a comparative sensibility (i.e., with an eye to facilitating comparative criminal law research).

General principles of criminal liability (the general part of criminal law) receive greater attention than detailed definitions of specific offenses (the special part), which differ considerably, but not necessarily interestingly, from jurisdiction to jurisdiction. In the special part, coverage is largely limited to key offenses like homicide, theft, rape, and victimless crimes.

Although specific topics for fruitful comparison will emerge from perusing the rich and varied contributions to this *Handbook*, some promising issues may include the rationales for punishment (and other sanctions, or "measures"), the scope and shape of the legality principle (*nulla poena sine lege*), the role and design (and existence) of criminal codes, the general structure of the analysis of criminal liability (and the related question of the distinction between justifications and excuses), accounts of *mens rea* (including the distinctions between *dolus* and *culpa*, and between intent and recklessness or negligence), and—in the special part—the scope of criminal law and the sorts of interests and rights the criminal law is designed to protect (*Rechtsgüter*), as well as the continued relevance, if any, of the distinction between "common law" and "civil law" systems or, relatedly, the influence of so-called Anglo-American criminal law, on one hand, and of German criminal law, on the other. Different readers, and different readings, will reveal different points of similarity and contrast, producing an image of convergence or divergence depending on one's point of view and point of focus.

NOTES

1. The pedagogic potential of comparative criminal law is explored in Richard S. Frase, "Main-streaming Comparative Criminal Justice: How to Incorporate Comparative and International Concepts and Materials into Basic Criminal Law and Procedure Courses," 100 *West Virginia Law Review* 773 (1998); Markus D. Dubber, "Criminal Law in Comparative Context," 56 *Journal of Legal Education* 433 (2007).

2. See Markus D. Dubber, *The Police Power: Patriarchy and the Foundations of American Government* (New York: Columbia University Press, 2005).

3. 4 William Blackstone, *Commentaries on the Laws of England* 162 (Chicago: University of Chicago Press, 1979) (1769); see also Jean-Jacques Rousseau, "Discourse on Political Economy," in *On the Social Contract with Geneva Manuscript and Political Economy* 209, 209 (Roger D. Masters ed. & Judith R. Masters trans.) (Boston: Bedford Books, 1978) (1755) ("political economy" derived from "*oikos*, house, and *nomos*, law," extending "the wise and legitimate government of the household for the common good of the whole family" to "the government of the large family which is the State").

4. P. J. A. Feuerbach, *Anselm Feuerbachs kleine Schriften vermischten Inhalts* 163 (1833).

5. For an attempt to implement this approach, see Markus D. Dubber and Mark Kelman, *American Criminal Law: Cases, Statutes, and Comments*, 2d ed. (Foundation Press Thomson/West, 2009).

6. *Vergleichende Darstellung des deutschen und ausländischen Strafrechts: Vorarbeiten zur deutschen Strafrechtsreform*, 16 vols. (1905–1909).

7. See, e.g., R. v. Martineau, [1990] 2 S.C.R. 633 (England, New Zealand, Australia, United States).

8. George P. Fletcher, *Rethinking Criminal Law* (Little, Brown, 1978); see, e.g., R. v. Perka, [1984] 2 S.C.R. 232.

9. For a broader comparative analysis, see BVerfG, 2 BvR 392/07 (26 Feb. 2008) (German Constitutional Court judgment relying on study of criminal incest laws in "twenty Anglo-American, European, and other non-European jurisdictions," prepared by the Max-Planck-Institute for Foreign and International Criminal Law, Freiburg, Germany). The U.S. Supreme Court, to put it mildly, has less enthusiastically embraced comparative analysis in its constitutional criminal law jurisprudence, although this has begun to change. See, e.g., Lawrence v. Texas, 539 U.S. 558, 573, 576 (2003) (discussing European Court of Human Rights [ECtHR] jurisprudence); Atkins v. Virginia, 536 U.S. 304, 317 n. 21 (2002) (considering attitude of "world community" toward execution of mentally retarded offenders).

10. Prosecutor v. Delacic et al., Case No. IT-96-21-A, Judgment (16 Nov. 1998).

11. Prosecutor v. Akayesu, Case No. ICTR-96-4-T, Judgment (2 Sept. 1998).

12. See also ECtHR, M.C. v. Bulgaria, Appl. Nr. 39272/98, paras. 88–100 (4 Dec. 2003) (comparative analysis of European rape law).

13. See, e.g., George P. Fletcher, *The Grammar of Criminal Law: American, Comparative, and International*, vol. 1: *Foundations* (Oxford University Press, 2007).

14. P. J. A. Feuerbach, "Versuch einer Criminaljurisprudenz des Koran," 2 *Bibliothek für die peinliche Rechtswissenschaft und Gesetzkunde* 163, 164 (1800).

15. See generally Barry Wright, "Macaulay's Indian Penal Code: Historical Context and Originating Principles," in *A Model Indian Penal Code* (forthcoming 2011); see also Sanford Kadish, "Codifiers of the Criminal Law: Wechsler's Predecessors," 78 *Columbia Law Review* 1098, 1106–1121 (1978).

ARGENTINA

Marcelo Ferrante

I. Introduction
   A. Historical Sketch
   B. The Constitution and the Criminal Law (Judicial Review and Juries)
   C. Jurisdiction
   D. Legality Principle

II. General Part
   A. Theories of Punishment
   B. Liability Requirements
   C. Defenses

III. Special Part
   A. Structure
   B. Homicide
   C. Sex Offenses
   D. Property Offenses

Marcelo Ferrante is Professor of Law at the Universidad Torcuato Di Tella. His recent publications include "Causation in Criminal Responsibility," 11 *New Criminal Law Review* 470 (2008), and "Recasting the Problem of Resultant Luck," 15 *Legal Theory* 267 (2009).

In writing this chapter I have benefited from the assistance of Guillermo Orce, who wrote first drafts for sections II.A and II.B.3.iii and edited the notes and the selected bibliography. Many thanks to him. I would also like to thank Gustavo Bruzzone, Luis María Bunge Campos, Fernando Córdoba, Leonardo Filippini, Roberto Gargarella, Hernán Gullco, and Pablo Parenti for helpful comments during the preparation of this chapter. The selection of judicial cases I include in this chapter has been influenced by Gullco's selection in Hernán V. Gullco, *Principios de la parte general del derecho penal: Jurisprudencia comentada* (Buenos Aires: Editores del Puerto, 2006).

I. INTRODUCTION

A. Historical Sketch

Argentine criminal law, as we now conceive of it, began in the second half of the nineteenth century with the first attempts at enacting a criminal code under the 1853 constitution.[1] The centerpiece of current Argentine criminal law is the Criminal Code (the Código Penal, or CP), which was enacted by the federal Congress in 1921. The 1921 code put an end to a long period of debates over criminal law reform that the constitution had mandated almost seventy years earlier.

That period had begun with public discussion—within both the federal Congress and the provincial governments—of the first official draft of a national criminal code. This first draft, known as the Tejedor Code after its author, jurist Carlos Tejedor, was heavily influenced by the Bavarian Criminal Code of 1813 drafted by Anselm Ritter von Feuerbach. A deeply modified version of the Tejedor Code was finally enacted as the first national criminal code in 1887. Once enacted, the code underwent several reforms and amendments—typically in the form of special criminal statutes—in only a few years. It seemed that the constitutional ideal of unified legislation through the adoption of stable codes had yet to be achieved. Several alternative criminal codes were thus proposed in those years to the Congress and the executive to replace the 1887 criminal code. One of them, the 1891 Criminal Code Draft, eventually led, in 1903, to an important reform of the 1887 code. The 1891 draft had been influenced primarily by the Italian Criminal Code of 1889, also known as the Zanardelli Code after the then Italian minister of justice, Giuseppe Zanardelli. The code that the Congress enacted in 1921, often referred to as the Moreno Code after Rodolfo Moreno (h), the congressman who led the drafting and enacting process, was meant to capture in a simple and pragmatically oriented text the basics of the Tejedor Code and the 1891 draft.[2] Unlike its immediate antecedents, it was the work of no individual drafter, but the result of a collective drafting process that managed to engage representative members of the different groups whose conflicting views had contributed to the instability of the previous legislative attempts (i.e., scholars with conflicting legal approaches, practitioners, and judges and other officials).

As its salient antecedents suggest—especially the Bavarian Code of 1813 and the Zanardelli Code—the 1921 code (the CP) falls within the liberal codification tradition of the nineteenth century. It is brief and relatively simple. It established a simple regime of sanctions, comprising primarily imprisonment[3] and secondly fines and incapacitation to perform certain activities (like holding official positions or exercising a given profession). The CP indeed marks the abolition of capital punishment in Argentine criminal law.[4] In general, prison terms in the CP were comparatively mild, with a maximum prison term of 25 years—only after a 2004 reform could the maximum imprisonment time mount up to 50 years in the case of the commission of a plurality of crimes (article 55). It introduced a regime of conditional convictions for first-time offenders (articles 26–28) and of freedom on parole (or conditional freedom) for the last third of the sentence (articles 13–17). Its general part was written with a pragmatic eye; besides adopting general rules for the application of the criminal law, including a statute of limitations, it included only a narrow set of simple rules of responsibility, avoiding definitions that might have shown commitment to a particular theoretical position. In particular, it included a list of substantive defenses (article 34), rules of attempt liability (articles 42–44) and of accomplice liability (articles 45–49), and a few rules for the aggregation of convictions and sentences (articles 54–58).

The special part of the CP contained fewer than 250 rules defining crime types and affixing sanctions—typically ranges of punishment, with legal minima and maxima (e.g., from 8 to 25 years' imprisonment for criminal homicide, article 79). Crime types are ordered by the kind of interest affected, starting with personal life and following with bodily integrity, honor or reputation, personal status and identity, basic freedoms (like freedom from sex abuses, freedom of movement, and freedom from intrusion in one's home and other protected places), property, public safety, political order, and other public goods (such as those secured by legal currency and other documents).

The CP is still the centerpiece of Argentine criminal law. In the meantime it has undergone many relatively marginal reforms and amendments,[5] which in the aggregate have introduced complexity in an otherwise relatively simple text, often affecting the code's systematicity—especially by altering its punishment schedule. To cite just one example, possessing explosives is now subject to higher penalties (5 to 15 years' imprisonment, article 189 bis) than making those same explosives explode and thus risking or actually destroying goods or even endangering another person's life (3 to 10 years' imprisonment, or up to 15 years in case of risk of death, article 186). In addition, many special statutes containing criminal clauses—typically introducing new crime types—have been passed in the ninety years since the adoption of the CP.[6] All in all, the CP still rules the basics of the general principles of criminal liability, the definition of most core crimes, and the punishments affixed to them.

B. The Constitution and the Criminal Law (Judicial Review and Juries)

Argentine law is based on its 1853 written constitution, which was modeled after the U.S. Constitution.[7] Very roughly, the Argentine constitution is a nineteenth-century liberal constitution, establishing a government in three branches—though more biased toward the executive than its American model—and a strong set of individual rights of liberal and republican lineage. Laws are passed primarily by the federal Congress, and in the legal domains of common jurisdiction (i.e., civil, commercial, labor, and criminal law) it has done so (observing a constitutional mandate) by adopting national codes. Argentine law thus combines an American-like constitutional law with nonconstitutional legal codes of a civil law tradition.

As is the case under its American model, Argentine constitutional law establishes a system of diffuse judicial review, under which each and every judge, in any judicial case, has the power to evaluate the constitutionality of the applicable law and to refuse to apply it if it is found unconstitutional. My impression is that there have been only a few sustained declarations of unconstitutionality in the domain of substantive criminal law during Argentine constitutional history. Part of this story may be due to a kind of resistance of the courts to declare statutes unconstitutional.

This resistance may be exemplified by introducing another feature of Argentine criminal law that is worth comment. Criminal trials are conducted before professional, life-tenured judges, appointed either by the national government through a complex process in which the three government branches intervene or by a provincial government through variable processes.[8] In striking contrast with this practice, the constitution states that "every criminal trial . . . shall be decided by juries" (article 118). Indeed, under the constitution, an express constitutional task of the Congress is that of "promoting the establishment of the trial by juries" (article 24) by adopting the statutes that such a task may require (article 75, section 12). However, after more than 150 years of constitutional life, no such statute has ever been passed, although many have been proposed. From time to time a criminal case appears in which the defendant moves for a dismissal on the ground that he or she has a constitutional right to be judged by a jury rather than by the professional judge who is hearing his or her case. Courts have invariably rejected such motions, typically on the argument that there is no operational constitutional right to be judged by juries; the constitution has placed no term, and therefore, the argument goes, it is for the Congress to determine the proper time to reform criminal procedures by adopting a regime of trial by juries.[9] That courts are prepared to make this argument even today, after more than 150 years of congressional inactivity on this issue, I take to be a peculiar feature of Argentine practice of judicial review.[10]

C. Jurisdiction

Argentine criminal law is territorial. As affirmed in article 1, section 1, of the CP, the code is applicable to crimes committed, or "whose effects should occur," within Argentine territory, which is conventionally understood to comprise land, jurisdictional waters, and airspace, Argentine boats navigating on international waters, and Argentine aircraft flying through international airspace.

There are two legal exceptions to territorial jurisdiction. The first exception is afforded by article 1, section 2, of the CP: Argentine criminal law is applicable to crimes committed by Argentine "official agents or employees" while discharging their official duties outside Argentine territory. The second exception is provided by article 118 of the constitution, which claims federal jurisdiction over crimes committed "beyond the borders of the Nation, against the Law of Peoples," a clause that is understood as a constitutional commitment to universal jurisdiction for international law crimes.[11]

Another jurisdictional feature that should be of interest has to do with federalism. Argentine constitutional distribution of power between the federal government, on the one hand, and the provinces, on the other, is such that it gives the federal government the task of legislating on substantive issues—including the adoption of, among other codes, a criminal code—while leaving to the provinces the tasks of legislating on procedural issues and of interpreting and applying the substantive laws adopted by the national government. Thus, even though there is only one criminal code that is applicable in every province, there may be as many interpretations of it as there are provinces—but no more than that, because each of the twenty-four provinces has procedural mechanisms to unify the interpretation of the substantive law within the provincial jurisdiction.[12] The impact of this decentralization of the interpretation of a common code has proved less dramatic than it could have been. Still, there are interpretive differences from jurisdiction to jurisdiction, especially in the realm of the special part of the criminal law. For example, under article 163, section 6, of the CP, the misappropriation of "vehicles left on the street or other places of public access" is an aggravated form of theft. Within some jurisdictions a bicycle amounts to a "vehicle" as this term figures in article 163, section 6, whereas in others only motor vehicles count as "vehicles" in the legal sense, on the theory that this was the original meaning of the statute.[13]

D. Legality Principle

Like any other criminal law that is governed by a liberal constitution, Argentine criminal law is subject to the so-called principle of legality. Indeed, the constitution provides for legality together with other liberal guarantees of mostly procedural nature in the first clause of article 18, which states that no one shall ever be punished "without a prior trial based on a statute that is itself prior to the facts of the case on trial." Courts—especially the Supreme Court—have interpreted this clause of the constitution as encompassing essentially four doctrines: (i) the prohibition of *ex post facto* criminal laws (the *lex praevia* requirement); (ii) the prohibition of criminal law sources other than statutes passed by the Congress (the *lex scripta* requirement); (iii) the void-for-vagueness doctrine (the flip side of the *lex certa* requirement); and (iv) the requirement of strict judicial construction (the *lex stricta* requirement). (International treaties on human rights signed by the government during the twentieth century, which have constitutional status since a 1994 constitutional reform, have given textual support to some of these doctrines that the courts had previously inferred only from article 18's nonretroactivity clause.)

These four doctrines do not have the same weight. The judicial practice appears to be that whereas the *lex praevia* requirement is as strict as a rule (a rule, that is, with one exception: the retroactivity of more lenient laws), the other three doctrines work as more or less weak principles that compete with other considerations on a case-by-case basis.

The case *Arancibia-Clavel* is revealing. Defendant Arancibia-Clavel was convicted on murder and conspiracy charges in 2000. He had been an official of the Chilean dictatorship working in Argentina with the support of the local government—his work being kidnapping and murdering opponents of the Chilean dictatorship. The facts of the case had taken place between 1974 and 1978, far beyond the maximum fifteen-year term of the statute of limitations.[14] The court, however, considered the crimes committed by Arancibia-Clavel to be crimes against humanity according to international law and therefore not subject to statutory limitations. The defendant appealed on the claim (among others) that at the time of commission his crimes were subject to the statute of limitations of domestic law—the Argentine Congress approved the International Convention on the Non-applicability of Statutory Limitations to War Crimes and Crimes against Humanity only in 1995. Before that date there was only an unqualified statute of limitations, with no exception made for crimes against humanity. The Supreme Court ultimately affirmed the conviction on the argument that, in holding the statute of limitations inapplicable to the crimes committed by Arancibia-Clavel in the 1970s, the trial court could not validly have applied the 1995 statute approving the International Convention on the Non-applicability of Statutory Limitations to War Crimes and Crimes against Humanity because that would have amounted to an unconstitutional retroactive application of a criminal statute. The statute of limitations was nevertheless inapplicable to the case, the Supreme Court held, in virtue of international law (mostly of nonconventional nature) that was binding on Argentina already in the early 1970s.

The *Arancibia-Clavel* case exemplifies two aspects of the Argentine *lex praevia* requirement that I think are worth emphasizing. The first aspect concerns the requirement's scope. Although Argentine courts have denied that the requirement applies to merely procedural criminal law, they have classed statutes of limitations as nonprocedural criminal law to which the requirement does apply. Thus, in contrast to prevailing American and European case law, Argentine case law is such that the *lex praevia* requirement bars the retroactive extension of the term of a statute of limitations even in cases where the prior limitation term has not expired at the time when the extension is approved.

The second aspect relates to the weight of the *lex praevia* requirement in comparison with the rest of the legality doctrines. Courts are unwilling to tolerate exceptions to the *lex praevia* requirement, other than the legally established exception for more lenient criminal laws,[15] but they are open to considering deviations from the other requirements. Indeed, in cases like *Arancibia-Clavel* and other comparable cases[16] courts take pains to find what the law was at the time of commission, suggesting that there is no room for a judicial exception to the ban on *ex post facto* criminal laws, while they accept that what counts as the law may be norms other than statutes passed by Congress—for example, international nonconventional law—and hence deviate from the *lex scripta* requirement.

Deviations from the *lex scripta* requirement are also found in domains other than the prosecution of crimes against humanity and can be based on reasons other than those related to the Argentine constitutional commitment to international criminal law. They are indeed commonplace in the domain of what we may call regulative criminal law, where the Congress passes blanket criminal statutes—that is, statutes providing for legal punishment for more or less undefined kinds of conduct and delegating to a different authority (typically a regulatory agency in the executive branch) the task of defining the punishable kind of conduct to which the punishment will be affixed. Two examples of this practice are the Drugs Act, in which the Congress delegated to a public health agency within the executive branch the definition of the substances that count as illegal drugs,[17] and the Criminal Exchange Act (Régimen Penal Cambiario), in which sanctions up to 8 years of imprisonment are set for "any act or omission infringing the [executive] regulations on money exchange."[18] In upholding blanket statutes of this kind, Argentine courts reveal that the democratic reasons that give support to the *lex scripta* requirement compete with, and are outweighed by, the reasons that militate in favor of legislative delegation in many, typically technical, fields.[19]

There is a similar trend in case law on the *lex certa* requirement. There seems to be no Supreme Court ruling invalidating a criminal statute on the grounds that its language is vague. Every time a claim that a statutory definition is vague has arrived at the Supreme Court, the court has upheld the statute, arguing that a degree of vagueness in legal language is inescapable, and that it is the business of courts to specify its meaning through interpretation.[20] (When a petition of void for vagueness did prosper—only in low-level courts—it did so together with other, stronger objections, like the fact that the statute criminalized harmless actions or a character trait or personal status, or it had been passed by a government department lacking authority.)[21] Again, then, the reasons to allow courts room to interpret more or less vague legal language have proved to outweigh the reasons grounding the *lex certa* requirement.

A final remark should be made on the local application of the doctrine of strict judicial construction, or the *lex stricta* requirement. There are two contrasting views in comparative criminal law on the *lex stricta* requirement. Both views yield different prescriptions in the scenario in which the language of a statute defining a criminal act is such that it is unclear whether a given case falls under the legal definition. According to the first view, the court should not apply the statute to the case—criminal law, according to this view, applies only when there is no doubt that the Congress approves of its application, as follows from the language of the law. According to the second view, the court should interpret the law and find out whether the unclear case should fall under the statute, in which case it should apply the statute to the unclear case. Under this second view, the *lex stricta* requirement allows for an "extensive" construction of the law and bars only its analogical application, which means the application of a statute to a case that clearly does not fall under the language of the legal definition but should be treated alike on normative grounds. Argentine criminal courts and scholars massively assume that the second view is true.

II. GENERAL PART

A. Theories of Punishment

According to the CP, there are only four types of punishment—two forms of incarceration (reclusion and prison), fines, and the deprivation of rights related to the activity through which the crime was committed (e.g., withdrawal of driving or professional licenses, or incapacitation to hold public official positions). The two forms of incarceration, reclusion and prison, were intended to express a difference in seriousness that manifested itself in the kinds of treatments inmates received under either one. Reclusion, purportedly the harsher of the two, involved somewhat longer incarceration terms and in distant facilities, whereas prison involved incarceration in a local facility. Reclusion was also meant to have a shaming dimension that prison would not have.[22] As a matter of fact, however, reclusion and prison sentences have long been indistinguishable—incarceration at an available correctional facility and under a unified punitive treatment.

Still, the CP includes a number of rules that presuppose a difference between the two forms of incarceration. Thus legal privileges regarding freedom on parole,[23] conditional conviction,[24] and the discounting of time spent under pretrial detention[25] vary from one form of punishment to the other, making things worse for those subject to sentences that the sentencing court happens to label *reclusion* rather than *prison*. In a recent case the Supreme Court affirmed a decision by a sentencing court that had declared unconstitutional the application of one of these rules. In its ruling the Supreme Court stated that because current law on the administration of incarceration sentences makes no distinction of kinds of incarceration, the older CP distinction between prison and reclusion should be considered "virtually abrogated," and with it all the aggravated conditions affixed to reclusion sentences.[26]

After conviction, courts ought to enter a determinate sentence falling within the legal minima and maxima established in the applicable criminal statute—say, between 8 and 25 years' imprisonment for criminal homicide (article 79 CP); between 6 months' and 4 years' imprisonment for a minor sexual abuse, 4 to 10 years for aggravated sexual abuse, and 6 to 15 years for rape (article 119 CP); between 1 month's and 2 years' imprisonment for nonaggravated larceny (article 162 CP); between 1 month and 6 years for nonaggravated robbery (article 164 CP); and the same for the basic forms of swindling and embezzlement (articles 172 and 173 CP). Only occasionally does the code mandate life imprisonment, most saliently for murder (article 80 CP).

The CP makes an exception to the requirement of a determinate sentence in article 52, which mandates an additional "reclusion for an indeterminate period of time" for multirecidivists having four previous sentences (one longer than 3 years) or five previous sentences of any length. (Temporally indeterminate reclusion is mandatory, although courts may once "suspend" it if there are circumstances that make indeterminate reclusion "inconvenient.") Temporally indeterminate reclusion amounts to life imprisonment, with the chance of being released on parole only after 5 years since the expiration of the last prison term to which the convict had been sentenced.[27] In a recent decision, however, the Supreme Court reversed a decision that had imposed temporally indeterminate reclusion on a multirecidivist defendant who had otherwise been sentenced to 2 years' imprisonment for attempted robbery.[28] In a nutshell, the court argued that, lacking proportion to the crime for which the defendant had been convicted, the imposition of indeterminate reclusion—a sort of life imprisonment under another name—was unconstitutionally cruel.

In addition to the regime of sanctions, the CP includes a regime of what have traditionally been called *safety measures*.[29] Briefly, this term means some sort of confinement in mental institutions of mentally insane defendants who are acquitted by reason of insanity.[30] Safety measures do not follow automatically from insanity acquittals; they require a court finding that the defendant poses a danger "for himself or others." In line with that requirement, confinement should not be merely incapacitating but should involve rehabilitative treatments addressed to counteract the condition that justifies the confinement (i.e., the condition grounding the court finding of dangerousness). Also, although there is no time limit for safety measures of this sort, they must cease when that condition disappears.[31]

Rehabilitation or resocialization is the main, legally stated goal of imprisonment sanctions. The source of this legal goal lies in the texts of the International Covenant on

Civil and Political Rights (article 10, section 3) and of the American Convention on Human Rights (article 5, section 6), both with constitutional status by virtue of article 75, section 22, of the constitution. Accordingly, the Imprisonment Administration Act of 1996 organizes incarcerative sanctions that expressly track this goal.[32]

The rehabilitation-organizing goal, however, is of limited force. Under the rehabilitation goal, incarceration is conceived of as a way to administer to inmates some kind of treatment (e.g., psychological, medical, social) that would somehow help them steer clear of criminal activity. However, sensitive to weightier constitutional values, article 5 of the Imprisonment Administration Act affirms that submission to such rehabilitative treatments is not mandatory—according to the Act, only "norms regulating coexistence, discipline, and work" are mandatory within correctional facilities. Thus, under the Act, there is room for nonrehabilitative imprisonment because, when inmates refuse treatment, imprisonment obviously continues, even though in such cases rehabilitation may no longer play any organizing role.

Furthermore, inmates are subject to determinate prison terms, fixed by the sentencing court after conviction. They are released when the prison term determined by the sentencing court expires, rather than when the rehabilitation treatment to which they might have submitted comes to successful completion. In other words, punishment ends, and the convicted person is released, when the time comes, independently of whether resocialization has already been achieved or not.

There is also an apparent inconsistency between the rehabilitation goal and rules mandating life imprisonment, most notably for types of murder crimes (article 80 CP). It is meaningless to claim a resocialization purpose for a sanction that implies removing the convict from social life once and for all. Because the rehabilitation goal has constitutional status, this point would suggest an argument for the unconstitutionality of life imprisonment. The customary answer to this argument stresses the fact that convicts sentenced to life imprisonment may apply for freedom on parole after 35 years in prison,[33] and that hence life imprisonment is just long imprisonment as a matter of fact. (This answer is, however, weakened by the fact that release on parole ultimately rests on a court's discretion.)

A similar argument applies, of course, to the use of death penalty. The death penalty, however, is banned in Argentine law on independent grounds. Article 18 of the 1853 constitution declared the abolition of the death penalty for political reasons, as well as the use of torture. As I mentioned earlier, capital punishment for regular (i.e., nonpolitical) crimes continued on the books until the enactment of the CP in 1921. It was reinstated during two short periods (1971–1972 and 1976–1983) by two military dictatorships. In 1984 Argentina committed itself not to reinstate the death penalty any more by adopting the American Convention on Human Rights.[34] Ten years later the constitution was reformed, and among the reforms the constitutional assembly included article 75, section 22, second paragraph, which gives constitutional status to the international legal commitments stemming from a number of human rights treaties, including the American Convention on Human Rights. The prohibition of this convention on reinstating capital punishment, legally binding since 1984, has thus become a constitutional prohibition since

1994. In line with this legal trend, the death penalty is nowadays not a public issue in Argentina.

Let me conclude this section with a word on actual prison conditions. On average, correctional facilities are in bad or very bad condition, with severe prison overpopulation in some jurisdictions. Litigation on this issue has only recently started to gain momentum. The most salient case involves a collective habeas corpus action on behalf of prison inmates in the province of Buenos Aires, which holds more than twice as many inmates as it is prepared to hold. Most of them are in pretrial detention, many are kept in police jails rather than in appropriate correctional facilities, and there are other problems. The Supreme Court granted certiorari, reversing previous rulings, and enjoined the provincial state to start a process of prison reform that the court will oversee.[35] Achievements after this promising decision are still to come.

B. Liability Requirements

1. Objective/Actus Reus
i. Act

Is there an act requirement in Argentine criminal law? If we construe the act requirement as the prohibition of the criminalization of nonacts of any sort, then the answer is negative. Even though legal crime types regularly pick out kinds of actions, nonactions such as omissions and relations of possession are also criminalized in Argentine criminal law. There is still a normative commitment against the criminalization of some kinds of nonacts, such as personal status, character traits, and the like, and it is this narrower commitment that is sometimes referred to by courts and commentators as the act requirement, or act principle.

It is nevertheless unclear what the legal or constitutional source of such an act requirement might be. There is certainly no explicit rule stating an act requirement of any sort. Case law in this respect is also barely available and of little help. In a salient case in which the act requirement was at stake, a court of appeals found unconstitutional an ordinance allowing for fines and arrest for being a "habitual vagrant" or a "professional of crime." The court cited the act requirement as part of the constitutional principles the ordinance violated, but without stating any constitutional clause as a source.[36]

A constitutional source was mentioned in a case in which a trial court invalidated legal rules denying privileges, like the possibility to be released on parole, to recidivists. Those rules were unconstitutional, the trial court held, because they were a response to the kind of person the offender was, rather than to the particular illicit actions he or she had performed.[37] In this ruling the court cited article 19 of the constitution as the source of a constitutional ban on the criminalization of personal status, character traits, ways of life, and the like, as opposed to the criminalization of individual acts.

In the paragraph pertinent to the court's argument, article 19 of the constitution states as follows: "People's private actions, which in no way offend public morality and order, or affect third parties, are only reserved to God, and free from the authority of the magistrates." It appears to be a settled reading of this clause that it pledges adherence to a fundamental liberal principle in the line of the Millian harm principle.[38] The trial court went further and read the clause as providing for another restriction besides the Millian harm principle: only actions and nothing but actions may be criminalized—and among these, only those that satisfy the restriction of the harm principle.

A recent study on the subject shows that the Supreme Court has never found that such an act requirement is part of article 19, or that it has any other constitutional ground.[39] In the cases in which it evaluated the constitutionality, under article 19 of the constitution, of a criminal statute criminalizing a nonact, namely, the possession of illicit substances, the court considered only whether the criminalized nonact was harmful to others or only—if it was harmful at all—to the defendant. The court ruled that the statute was unconstitutional for violating article 19 when it found that the possession of illicit substances was intended only for self-consumption.[40] Later the same court, but with a different composition, decided not to follow that precedent, partly on the claim that there might be after all some likely harm that the Congress might want to prevent, though indirectly, by the criminalization of the possession of illicit substances, even when intended for self-consumption.[41] These rulings suggest that, in the Supreme Court's view, the fact that the object of the criminalization in the statutes under constitutional scrutiny was a nonact (i.e., a relation of possession) raised no constitutional claim as far as article 19 was concerned.

In sum, there is in Argentine law a normative commitment to a kind of act requirement, with two important qualifications. The first has to do with the requirement's scope. In its Argentine version, the requirement does not amount to a ban on the criminalization of nonacts of any sort, although it does seem to prevent the legal adoption of criminal statutes grounding punitive treatment in personal status, character traits, and ways of life. As a matter of fact, legislation criminalizing the possession of illicit materials (e.g., drugs, stolen goods, weapons, or forgery apparel) has found no legal barrier, judicial or otherwise, even though the criminalized possession relations are not actions.

The second qualification has to do with the weight of the requirement. Since there is no clear legal source for the act requirement, constitutional or otherwise, if a statute criminalizing character traits or personal status were in fact adopted,[42] a judicial declaration of unconstitutionality might not be forthcoming.

> ii. Omission

A kind of nonact whose criminalization survives judicial scrutiny is omissions. There are a few clauses in the special part of the CP that explicitly criminalize omissions. Articles 106 and 108 of the CP are the core examples. Article 108 contains a Bad Samaritan statute, providing for the imposition of a mild sanction (i.e., a fine ranging from 750 to 12,500 Argentine pesos) on those who, "finding a lost child, or a person wounded, crippled or otherwise threatened by a risk of any kind, fail to give the needed help, if it could be given without personal risk, or to immediately warn the authority." Even though this clause has been in the CP since 1921, I am unaware of any prosecution that has ever been conducted for the commission of this offense.

Article 106, on the other hand, criminalizes the behavior of those who fail to help a person whose life or health is at risk, and to whom the agent owes a special duty of care (including explicitly the case in which the agent has caused the victim's need). Sanctions for this offense—commonly referred to as *abandonment of people*, or simply *abandonment*—are relatively high, with prison terms ranging from 2 to 15 years depending on the outcome of the abandonment (risk or injuries, severe injuries, or death), and up to one-third higher when the duty of care is that which holds between parents and children or between spouses.

There are broadly two interpretations of this legal provision of the abandonment crime, which are the flip side of the two opposing answers to the question whether it is possible in Argentine criminal law to convict defendants for their failure to prevent harm under regular result-crime provisions—like those defining homicide (article 79) or bodily injuries (articles 89 to 91)—which are couched in terms of actions and causation.

It is regularly taught in Argentine law schools that one may be convicted as the author of, say, a criminal homicide under article 79 of the CP for letting another person die—rather than killing him or her, as article 79 literally defines—if the agent has a special duty to rescue that person from dying,[43] and even though there is no explicit rule in the CP providing for that possibility.[44] We can call this the broad interpretation of omission liability. The broad interpretation of omission liability stems from the conjunction of the following three ideas: (i) the idea that there are omission cases that are morally on a par with action cases; (ii) the idea that the concepts in whose terms result-crime legal definitions are couched are broad enough to refer not only to actions but also to comparable omissions; and (iii) the idea that the principle of legality—particularly the so-called *lex stricta* requirement—leaves room for the extensive construction of criminal legislation.

In striking contrast with this broad interpretation, courts have rarely used regular result-crime clauses, such as article 79, to convict defendants in omission cases. When rationale for this resistance has been offered, it has been centrally based on the *lex stricta* requirement. Take, for instance, a case in which the defendant, the mother of a nine-month-old baby, failed to prevent her boyfriend from hitting the baby to death.[45] Since it was beyond dispute that the defendant was under the duty to rescue her son, the trial court, following the broad interpretation of omission liability, entered a conviction for homicide. On appeal, however, a state supreme court reversed the homicide conviction on the argument that it was conceptually beyond dispute that whatever the defendant might have done, she did not kill the victim (her boyfriend did). Since article 79 defines homicide as the "killing of another," it could not be that the defendant's behavior amounted to a homicide. For an extensive construction to be called for, it must happen that the case *may* fall under the meaning of the language of the legal definition. If, as in this case, it is undisputable that the legal language of article 79 does not describe the defendant's behavior, then treating her as the author of a homicide under article 79 would be to engage in a kind of analogical application of the law, and that is certainly prohibited by the principle of legality. Or so the court concluded.

This court held what may be called the narrow interpretation of omission liability. Under the narrow interpretation, current Argentine criminal law is such that there is no scenario in which an omission may give rise to a conviction under a regular result-crime definition (e.g., article 79). The narrow interpretation makes room for a simple reading of the omission-crime types of articles 106 to 108. Under this reading, the legal definition of the crime of abandonment of article 106, together with the Bad Samaritan clause of article 108, exhausts the domain of omission liability in Argentine criminal law, at least in regard to legally protected interests like personal life and bodily integrity. Thus defendants who only fail to prevent harm may be convicted only of the commission of the crime of abandonment of article 106 (or, in the absence of a special duty to prevent the pertinent harm, under the Bad Samaritan clause of article 108).

Courts and commentators who hold the broad interpretation of omission liability, in turn, are expected to draw a distinction between committing, on the one hand, an article 79 homicide through an omission, which would be punished with a prison sentence ranging from 8 to 25 years, and, on the other, committing an abandonment followed by death of article 106, third paragraph, with a prison sentence of from 5 to 15 years. The best criterion considers the different mental requirements for the two offenses.[46] Thus, under this view, for an omission to prevent a death to count as a homicide, besides bearing the special duty to rescue or provide life-supporting help, the omitter must have been aware that his or her omission would have the fatal consequence it actually had—if not reveal some other attitudes as well.[47] Article 106, in turn, captures the behavior of the specially obliged agent who knowingly omits helping a victim whose life or health is at risk. Punishment rises, under article 106, second and third paragraphs, with the severity of the harm that actually obtains—and that would have been prevented had the omitter helped the victim—irrespective of whether the omitter believed that any of these outcomes would result from his or her omission. So, unlike homicide by omission, the abandonment followed by death in article 106, third paragraph, would require that the omitter be aware of the fact of his or her omission and only be negligent with regard to the potential outcome.

2. Subjective/Mens Rea/Mental Element

In a recent decision the Supreme Court maintained that a so-called principle of culpability is part of the constitution, and that this principle bans criminal strict liability and may also afford mistake-of-fact and mistake-of-law defenses.[48] In that case the court held that articles 95 and 96 of the CP, which define the crimes of taking part in a fight from which death or injury results, do not violate the constitutional principle of culpability because, as they had been construed by the trial court, the articles require that the defendant knowingly enter the fight and be at least negligent as to the resulting death or injury. As to the constitutional status of the principle of culpability, however, the court gave no supporting argument. It merely based its claim on a 1968 precedent in which, however, the court did not interpret the constitution, but only a federal statute providing for sanctions for tax evasion and related offenses.[49]

The constitutional credentials of the principle of culpability notwithstanding, the fact is that Argentine criminal law does not, in fact, provide for strict liability. Most legal crime definitions, as found in the special part of the CP, pick out only objective properties, like "killing a person" (article 79), "causing bodily injury" (article 89), "shooting a firearm" (article 104), "misappropriating movable property" (article 162), "causing an explosion" (article 186), and "possessing explosives" (article 189 bis). For some of them—and only some of them—there are what may be called *negligence clauses*, that is, legal crime definitions describing the negligent performance of an otherwise objectively described type of action and prescribing reduced punishments for them.[50] For the six aforementioned examples of crimes, only three have corresponding negligence clauses: "negligently causing the death of a person" (article 84), "negligently causing bodily injury" (article 94), and "negligently causing an explosion" (article 189).[51]

As is the case with the criminal codes that served as models of the CP, courts and commentators have interpreted this contrast as establishing that for responsibility under normal, mostly objectively defined, crime types to be warranted, agents must act with a worse-than-negligence mental state—a sort of mental state that is technically called *dolus*. Roughly, for a type of act defined as the "killing of a person," an agent will act with *dolus* if he or she intentionally kills a person—that is, if the killing of a person is the intention that guides his or her conduct—but also if he or she does it knowingly and maybe even recklessly.[52]

Thus, as a matter of fact—if not also as a matter of constitutional obligation—Argentine criminal law demands specific mental states for criminal responsibility to be warranted (i.e., there is no strict criminal liability) and divides its mental-state requirements into two general classes, negligence and *dolus*. *Dolus*, finally, is the default mental-state requirement; negligence is sufficient for liability only under specific and rather exceptional crime types (i.e., those for which there are negligence clauses).

A word on negligence is necessary. Legal clauses establishing negligence criminal responsibility are available only for crime types for which there is also, and primarily, *dolus*-based liability. This fact puts negligence-based criminal liability in a secondary position, in the sense that the case for negligence arises when the case for *dolus* has failed. A negligence conviction thus involves two judgments. The first is positive, the finding of negligence, which is generally assessed by applying a reasonable-agent standard, one that should vary in accordance with the agent's abilities and the position he or she is in.[53] The second is negative, the absence of a mental state amounting to *dolus*.

i. The *Dolus*/Negligence Distinction: The Cognitive Dimension

According to the standard reading of the CP, the *dolus* mental state requires that the agent acts with certain beliefs—namely, he or she must believe that his or her act has (or is likely to have) the objective features that make it an instance of a crime type. More specifically, for an agent to act with *dolus* of, say, criminal homicide, he or she must believe that his or her action is (or is likely to end up being) the killing of another person (i.e., the factual features picked out by the legal definition of the homicide crime type). Notice that the agent need not know that his or her act meets the corresponding legal definition, or any other—indeed, the agent would act with *dolus* even if he or she believed that his or her action was permissible or not criminal at all.

It follows from this that factual mistakes that affect the elements of the crime definition—more precisely, mistakes consisting of the agent's ignorance of one or more features of his or her action in virtue of which the action meets the legal definition of a crime type—are always a defense for every crime type in the CP (except those few that allow for negligence-based liability). A fair translation of the technical name with which

Argentine legal professionals refer to this kind of factual mistake is *crime-type mistake* or simply *type mistake*.

In brief, the doctrine is that type mistakes entail the absence of *dolus*, and therefore the absence of the illicit action the legal definition purports to capture. An action that meets the objective features of a crime-type definition but is performed under a type mistake could warrant criminal responsibility only under a negligence clause, provided that there is a negligence legal clause for that crime type, and that the agent was indeed negligent in performing the action (i.e., flunks the pertinent reasonable-person test).

The rationale of the doctrine lies in the view that the beliefs with which an agent performs an otherwise criminal act affect either the kind of wrong the action does or the agent's degree of culpability or blameworthiness.[54] What I want to stress here is that the doctrine is not premised on any express legal requirement. Rather, it is a reflection of a conceptual stance. Indeed, according to black-letter law (particularly article 34, section 1 CP), "factual mistakes" secure innocence if they are "nonimputable," suggesting that there is a kind of factual mistake (i.e., *imputable* factual mistakes) that would be as incriminating as nonmistaken beliefs. Thus, if we were to favor a view of wrongdoing (or culpability) such that factual mistakes do not mark a difference in kind (as they do under currently prevailing views), we would face no legal constraint on adjusting the standing type-mistake doctrine in order to accommodate our view.

Indeed, it may be claimed that there are reasons to adjust the standing type-mistake doctrine, because it does in fact yield counterintuitive consequences. Notice that the doctrine, under which type mistakes entail the absence of *dolus*, would treat as *dolus* the mental state of a scrupulous agent who is aware of even the most insignificant risk he or she creates, while it would regard as merely negligence the behavior of a brutally inconsiderate agent who cares so little for others that he or she imposes huge risks on everyone without ever noticing it. As noted, article 34, section 1, leaves room for treating the mistake of such an inconsiderate agent as imputable, and therefore as one that is consistent with a finding of *dolus*. Still, there is no principled theory that has been offered giving grounds for this possible reading.[55]

ii. The *Dolus*/Negligence Distinction: The Noncognitive Dimension

The dominant view among courts and commentators is that there is a further, noncognitive dimension of the *dolus*/negligence distinction. Under this dominant view, an agent who, for example, knowingly kills another person acts with *dolus*—that is, meets the mental requirements of the homicide crime type of article 79 of the CP—only if his or her act exhibits some sort of positive attitude toward its being a killing of another person (e.g., if the agent intends his or her action to be a killing of another person) or is at least indifferent to whether it would end up being a killing of another person or not. Although there is no relevant distinction in terms of legal treatment, courts and commentators typically distinguish between the *dolus* case in which the agent acts with the intention to perform the criminal act (often called *first-degree dolus*), on the one hand, and the case in which the agent just foresees the criminal act as a side effect (the case known as *dolus eventualis*), on the other.

If an agent who knowingly kills another person does so without exhibiting such a positive or indifferent attitude (e.g., if he or she sincerely hopes that the death that he or she knows her action makes probable would not eventually ensue), then, under the dominant view, he or she may be convicted only of the commission of a negligent homicide under article 84 of the CP. *Dolus*, even *dolus eventualis*, would thus require a positive or indifferent attitude toward the crime event.

In brief, the dominant view in this domain is, first, that the mental state we should identify as *dolus* has both cognitive and noncognitive factors, and, second, that there exists what normally goes by the name of *conscious negligence*—that is, a mental state we should treat as negligence for legal purposes, which differs from *dolus* only along a noncognitive dimension.

This view, however, is not without its detractors. Against the orthodox view it is often argued that by letting the *dolus*/negligence distinction depend on morally thick concepts such as "indifference" and "positive attitudes" toward harm, it makes room for arbitrariness. It is allegedly easy to disguise one's personal disapproval of a person—of his or her character traits, values, and so on—as a finding of a noncognitive attitude of hostility or indifference that the agent's action expresses.[56]

The most common alternative view that critics propose is that there is nothing like a noncognitive dimension to the *dolus*/negligence divide. Under this alternative view, to *knowingly* kill another person simply *is* to kill another person with *dolus*. Negligence would thus entail that the agent is unaware of the features of his or her action in virtue of which the action objectively satisfies a legal crime definition. Thus what would count as *conscious negligence* under the dominant view would count as *dolus* under this alternative view.

iii. Other Mistakes of Fact

Factual mistakes are also relevant under Argentine criminal law when they affect the instantiation of the objective elements of justificatory defenses, like self-defense or necessity. Cases falling within this category are those in which the agent, whose action meets a legal crime definition, mistakenly believes that some circumstances obtain such that, if they were to obtain, they would justify the performance of the crime. Recurrent examples go like this: the agent mistakenly believes, when deciding to hit another person, that he or she is under a threat of an imminent attack,[57] or that only deadly force will be sufficient to repel the attack.[58] The doctrine is that when the mistake is reasonable, it warrants innocence; however, when the relevant reasonable person in the position of the agent would not have entertained such mistaken beliefs (i.e., the mistake is unreasonable), it grounds only a mitigated conviction. (Argentine legal professionals would put the contrast in different language by calling reasonable mistakes *inevitable* or *invincible* and unreasonable mistakes *evitable* or *vincible*.) Nevertheless, it is disputed what the scope of this mitigation should be. The CP openly deals only with the case in which the mistake is such that the agent "exceeds the limits imposed by law, authority or necessity" (article 35). For this kind of case, the CP establishes that the agent shall be punished with the punishment affixed to the corresponding negligent crime, despite his or her having acted with *dolus*. Some commentators favor the extension of this treatment to all other cases of unreasonable mistake about justificatory circumstances, even if they could not properly be referred to with the language of article 35—for example, the case in which the agent errs about the very occurrence of the attack he or she believes that he or she is repelling with his or her defensive measure.[59]

Others, in contrast, argue that the special mitigation of article 35 holds only for cases of originally justified actions, in which the agent exceeds the limits of a justification that otherwise actually applies. Thus, under this view, the agent who kills a person, unreasonably believing that this person is about to attack him or her, should be convicted of an article 79 homicide with no, or only marginal, mitigation.[60]

Moreover, it is sometimes claimed that the mitigating rule of article 35 may apply even if the excess is not due to a mistaken evaluation. Indeed, the originalist reading of this clause is that for the mitigation to apply, the excess should be determined by an emotional state, like fear or anxiety, not inconsistent with law-abidingness.[61]

iv. Mistakes of Law

The Supreme Court construes the principle of culpability as requiring, as a necessary condition for the imposition of punishment, that the agent has had the actual possibility of adjusting his or her conduct to the demands of the law, which, in turn, would imply that he or she has had the actual, reasonable opportunity to learn that his or her action was illegal.[62] This interpretation gives rise to a mistake-of-law defense with the following scope. When an agent commits a criminal action—that is, an action that meets the objective requirements of a legal crime-type definition and is performed with *dolus*—he or she may still lack culpability if he or she believes that his or her act is legal by virtue of a reasonable (again, the local term is typically *inevitable* or *invincible*) mistake of law. Unreasonable (or evitable or vincible) mistakes of law ground no, or only marginal, mitigation.

The decisive issue in this domain is the finding of reasonability. Reasonability of mistakes of law is found on a case-by-case basis without an apparent definite set of criteria. Two salient considerations that case law shows are that the standard of reasonability is sensitive to the agent's epistemic abilities,[63] and that reliance on an authoritative source warrants reasonability.[64]

Notice that sometimes mistakes of law, which normally give rise only to that defense (i.e., they warrant nonculpability only if the mistake is reasonable), may in turn determine that the agent ignores a feature of his or her act by virtue of which the act meets the objective requirements of a crime type, and therefore may amount to type mistakes (i.e., mistakes that entail the absence of *dolus* even if the mistake is unreasonable). This occurs when elements in the crime-type definition are such that knowing them requires legal information. Common examples involve requirements such as that a misappropriated thing "belongs to another person" (in larceny cases),[65] that the action violates a particular duty (in embezzlement cases),[66] or that the substance possessed bears the status of an illegal drug (in drug-related offenses).[67]

3. *Theories of Liability*
   i. Inchoate Crimes: Attempts

There is liability for failed attempts in Argentine criminal law. The CP includes a general regime of attempt liability with three simple clauses: the first defines what counts as a criminal attempt (article 42); the second introduces the availability of a defense of abandonment (article 43); and the third states the applicable punishment rules (article 44).

According to the legal definition, an agent is liable for committing a criminal attempt if, acting "with the purpose" of accomplishing a definite crime, he or she "starts to execute" that crime and fails, or otherwise is not responsible for the corresponding result. Two remarks on this definition are worth making.

First, attempt liability under Argentine criminal law is broad with regard to the types of crimes involved—if something amounts to a crime (from killing a person to falsely writing a check), then starting to perpetrate it may give rise to attempt liability. That is, there are in principle no crime types exempted from the doctrine of attempt liability. However, the "with the purpose" requirement suggests, if literally construed, a restriction for all types of crimes that may be accomplished without the agent acting with the purpose of accomplishing them. As I noted earlier, most crime types in Argentine criminal law do not require that the agent acts with the intention or purpose of accomplishing the relevant type. Thus, for example, one may be liable for an accomplished criminal homicide under article 79 of the CP even if the killing of the victim is not something that the agent intends, but merely foresees as a side effect (the case of *dolus eventualis*). But under the literal construction of the "with the purpose" clause, if the victim does not eventually die, the agent is not liable for an attempted homicide unless he or she acted with the purpose of killing the victim.

Courts tend to favor this literal construction of the "with the purpose" clause.[68] Still, highly influential commentators, such as current Supreme Court justice Eugenio Raúl Zaffaroni and current attorney general Esteban Righi, have famously objected to the literal reading.[69] Take Righi's version of the objection. In its best light, his objection is that the "with the purpose" restriction is groundless, for it hits on a mental state—the purpose to accomplish the criminal act—that is morally on a par with other mental states, particularly other positive attitudes toward the possibility of accomplishing the criminal act, that do not amount to purpose or intention. Thus, the objection goes, we should read the "with the purpose" clause broadly to include all those morally similar mental states, as courts do with accomplished crimes, where they treat as *dolus* not only the purposeful commission of the crime but also the knowing commission of the crime when accompanied with some sort of positive attitude toward the possibility of accomplishing the pertinent criminal act.[70]

The second point I shall make concerns the concept of perpetration or execution. As usual in comparative criminal law, attempt liability raises the issue of the distinction between the *preparation* of a crime (that which comes close to, but is not yet, an attempt) and the *perpetration* of that crime (that which is already a criminal attempt). Comparative criminal law shows that the existing criteria vary from jurisdiction to jurisdiction and across time. It is hard to tell, however, what the dominant criterion is in Argentine criminal law. There is no indication whatsoever in the CP or in any other piece of criminal legislation of what this criterion should be, and so it has been left entirely to the courts to determine. But there is no comprehensive study available of what the behavior of the courts has been in this regard. Casual evidence indicates that even though there is a huge amount of diversity from court to court, there may be something like a tendency to adopt formal tests of execution (according to which there is perpetration only if the agent starts doing something we may properly refer to with the language of the legal definition of a crime type) or last-act tests (according to which there is perpetration when the agent does the act *immediately before* the act we would properly refer to with the language of the legal definition of a crime type).[71]

I turn now to the abandonment defense. The abandonment rule in article 43 of the CP has given rise to two issues. The first issue is what sort of behavior may count as an abandonment; the second is under what conditions a piece of behavior of that sort is "voluntary," as this term figures in article 43. As to the first issue, commentators usually distinguish between (i) the case in which the agent, having started to perpetrate a crime, fails to complete the acts that were necessary, in his or her view, for him or her to accomplish the crime and (ii) the case in which the agent, having done everything he or she deemed necessary to accomplish the crime, somehow prevents the criminal harm from obtaining. The distinction is relevant, for although no one disputes that (i) is a case of abandonment under article 43, there are arguments against extending the defense to (ii). A prominent Argentine criminal law scholar, Marcelo Sancinetti, has famously argued that we may extend the abandonment defense to cases such as (ii) only when the preventing measure the agent resorts to leaves no residual risk. Otherwise, the argument goes, we would introduce an arbitrary punitive difference.[72] In brief, the point is this. Suppose that agent A poisons her enemy V at t_1 intending to kill V, and later, at t_2, before V dies, A gives V an antidote that has a low probability of saving V. If we extend the abandonment defense to cases of sort (ii), then in the foregoing case we would have that A should be exempted from punishment if the antidote happens to save V from dying. Now consider an alternative case that is as close to the previous case as it can be except for the fact that the poison and the antidote are given in reverse order. Thus, suppose that A* gives V* the antidote at t_1 and then poisons V* at t_2, intending to kill him. The antidote may have immunized V* against the poison with a very low probability. In this alternative scenario we would have that if the antidote luckily saves V*, A* will be convicted of attempting to murder V*. What accounts for the difference in punitive treatment of A and A* is just the temporal order of poison and antidote, and there seems to be no good reason to make a mere temporal difference ground such a dramatic penal discrimination.

As to the "voluntary" requirement, courts have massively construed the requirement as demanding more than we do in normal parlance to call an act *voluntary*. Indeed, according to judicial case law, an act (or omission) will count as a voluntary abandonment depending on which reasons the agent takes as his or her motive to abandon the crime. Particularly, if the reason is either the prospect of being caught or the prospect of failing, courts will find the abandonment nonvoluntary and consequently will deny the defense.[73]

Finally, I turn to the legal regime of sanctions for attempts. With one exception, attempts are systematically punished more leniently than the corresponding accomplished crimes. The general rule is that attempts are to be punished with a sanction that ranges from one-half to two-thirds of the sanction that would have been imposed had the agent accomplished his or her crime—or, if the corresponding accomplished crime would have led to life imprisonment, article 44 CP establishes that the punishment for the attempt should range between 10 and 20 years of imprisonment. Two deviations from this rule are worth noting.

First, for the crime of smuggling goods into and out of the country, as regulated in articles 863 to 873 of the National Customs Code,[74] there is no reduction of punishment for attempted smuggling, which is punished as severely as the corresponding accomplished smuggling crime. The rationale often given for this equal treatment of attempted and accomplished smuggling crimes seems to be pragmatic rather than moral. Indeed, it turns on the fact that there is practically no prosecution at all of accomplished smugglings, for smuggling cases are detected at the border by the customs official who frustrates the smuggling by detecting it.[75]

Second, article 44 of the CP allows for an *impossibility defense* by stating that courts may further reduce sanctions, and even altogether exempt agents from punishment, "if the crime were impossible." To predicate of an attempt to commit a criminal action that it is an "impossible crime" (rather than a garden-variety criminal attempt) in the sense of article 44 of the CP, courts engage in an assessment of the action's *efficacy* (the Spanish term is *idoneidad*, which itself is a translation of the German *Tauglichkeit*), or the capacity of the pertinent kind of action to bring about the corresponding accomplished crime. Therefore, if the action is *too inefficacious*, it would be considered an impossible crime, and its agent would typically be exempted from punishment—moreover, an acquittal would typically be entered. But there is no precision at all, either in courts' decisions or among commentators, about what sort of assessment the efficacy assessment is, or about what makes an inefficacious attempt too inefficacious to be punished. The most I can tell is that the common scenario in which courts engage in assessments of this sort is prosecutions for the crime of swindling, understood as obtaining property by false pretenses, as defined in article 172 of the CP. In this domain, a casual review of decisions shows that courts predominantly hold something like a reasonability standard, according to which an attempt at deceiving would be too inefficacious—and hence would give rise, if at all, to an impossible crime of swindling—if no reasonable person in the position of the victim would be deceived by it.

ii. Complicity

Accomplice liability in Argentine criminal law is ruled by articles 45 to 49 of the CP. The law distinguishes between several classes of parties to a crime but imposes only two punitive schemes. Besides principals or perpetrators, the law distinguishes instigators, first-degree accomplices, second-degree accomplices, and accessories after the fact. Article 45 parties (perpetrators, instigators, and first-degree accomplices) are to be punished with the sanction established for the kind of crime they take part in, whereas article 46 parties (second-degree accomplices and accessories after the fact) are subject to diminished sanctions—between one-half and two-thirds of the sanctions established for the principal.

The CP's text suggests a relatively thin criterion to distinguish principals from other parties. The legal distinction seems to be "taking part in the execution" of the crime. However, case law reveals that a thicker notion actually drives court decisions. Among the leading cases the well-known *Causa 13* stands out, the case in which five members of the military juntas that ruled the country during the 1976–1983 dictatorship were tried and convicted of the commission of a representative set of the thousands of crimes against humanity committed by the de facto government during those years.[76] The defendants had been commanders in chief of the national armed forces, and they were tried for a number of murders, tortures, kidnappings, robberies, and other crimes that had been *directly perpetrated* by officials operating within the forces each of the defendants commanded. The term *directly perpetrated* here refers to the performance of the physical doings over the victims' bodies (or physical property, in the case of robberies) that are sufficient for there to be an instance of murder, torture, false imprisonment, robbery, and so on. The trial court—in a decision later confirmed on appeal by the Supreme Court—found the defendants guilty as principals of (many) of the crimes with which they had been charged. The theory was that even though they did not "take part in the execution" of the crimes in the thin sense of direct perpetration, they nevertheless exercised the kind of control over the perpetration of the crimes that is characteristic of direct perpetrators and, moreover, is the reason that we normally treat direct perpetrators as principals. More specifically, the court applied to the case a variation of the innocent-instrumentality doctrine, or the doctrine of indirect agency, according to which a nonperpetrator may be regarded a principal to a crime when the crime is directly perpetrated by an innocent agent (e.g., one who would be exonerated by acting under a relevant mistake) and the nonperpetrator controls the behavior of the innocent agent by manipulating the grounds of his or her innocence (e.g., by creating the mistake). The innocence of the instrumentality, the court argued, is not essential to the indirect-agency doctrine. What is germane to the doctrine is the relation of control that links the indirect agent and the innocent perpetrator's behavior. The defendants in the *Causa 13* case were found to be principals because they exerted the same kind of control over the behavior of the direct perpetrators, even when these perpetrators had been—as they typically were—perfectly guilty of the crimes they directly executed. The relation of control was secured by a complex set of facts, among which the following stand out: the defendants designed the plan that the direct perpetrators would then follow; the defendants controlled the hierarchical organization (i.e., an entire armed force and related departments of government) within which the direct perpetrators acted; the direct perpetrators were interchangeable (i.e., if one would not do his part, there would be another to replace him); and the defendants provided the direct perpetrators with everything they needed to commit the crimes, especially securing them the required secrecy and impunity conditions.

In general, then, anyone who fails to bear this kind of (direct or indirect) control over at least a part of the execution of a crime would not count as its perpetrator (or coperpetrator)—at most, he or she would count as an accomplice of one sort or another. As far as the *actus reus* requirement is concerned, it takes very little for an action to ground accomplice liability. The law seems to be that it suffices that the action in any way favors, assists, or facilitates the doing of the principal. Thus, for instance, the Cámara Nacional de Casación Penal (the highest-level federal court for criminal matters) recently confirmed a conviction of a defendant as an accomplice to a robbery for giving the principal mere "moral support"—which he did, according to the decision, by hanging out with the principal while he was picking out an appropriate victim from the crowd, and running away with the principal once he accomplished the robbery.[77]

There is no certainty about how to distinguish between first-degree accomplices and second-degree accomplices. The explicit rule is that every assistant to a crime is a second-degree accomplice unless the help he or she provides is such that the perpetrator could not have committed the crime without it. Notice the source of vagueness in this rule: if "the crime" is identified in a fine-grained fashion—that is, taking into account every factual aspect of it—almost every help would count as first-degree complicity, for without it the crime would be other (it would lack one of its factual aspects). If, in contrast, "the crime" is identified coarsely—say, by taking into account only its crime-making aspects—then almost every assistance would ground only second-degree complicity, for there will typically be alternative ways to commit a crime of the same type.

Accomplice liability in Argentine criminal law is derivative in nature, and this manifests itself in the following two rules. According to article 47, accomplices may be punished only if the principal *executes* the crime that the accomplice has assisted. It is not necessary that the principal accomplish the crime—although if he or she only attempts the crime, both the principal and the accomplice sanctions are reduced pursuant to the attempt-liability punitive scheme.[78] But if the principal changes his or her mind during the preparation stage, there will be no accomplice liability. This rule is often referred to as the rule of *external dependence*.

The core of the second rule, or the rule of *internal dependence*, is that accomplices are responsible for the type of crime they actually help commit—that is, in the paradigmatic case, the crime that the principal actually commits with the accomplice's help. The CP explicitly deals with two nonparadigmatic scenarios: the case of excess in the principal's doing (accomplices are not responsible for a crime they did not know that the principal would commit with their help),[79] and the case of attenuating and aggravating personal factors (accomplice liability includes every aggravating factor principals and accomplices are aware of, even if they are personal factors like parental relations or emotional states that correspond to only one of them, whereas attenuating personal factors apply only to the party to which they personally correspond).[80] There is a third nonparadigmatic scenario the code does not explicitly deal with, and over which there has been some discussion. This scenario obtains when the principal is exonerated by a defense that does not apply to the accomplice (e.g., the principal, but not the accomplice, acts under a relevant mistake or under agent-relative justificatory circumstances). The mainstream view is that because accomplice liability derives from principal liability in the sense that accomplices are responsible for the crime the principal commits, if there is no crime that the principal commits, there is no accomplice liability. This view has been challenged on the argument that it assumes a defective conception of the foundation of accomplice liability. If the reason that complicity is illicit is that it is a way of contributing to the victim's harm, it should not matter whether the principal's doing is technically a crime or not. In the absence of an explicit legal rule to the contrary, accomplice liability should apply in this scenario.[81]

iii. Corporate Criminal Liability

There is no kind of corporate criminal liability in current Argentine criminal law. Most Argentine scholars and court decisions stay loyal to the ancient motto *Societas delinquere non potest* (corporations are incapable of committing crimes). This view was openly articulated in a recent dissenting opinion by Supreme Court justice Zaffaroni.[82] In that case a trial court had dismissed the petition by the prosecution to bring a corporation to stand trial as a codefendant in proceedings in which the manager of that company was facing smuggling charges. The prosecution eventually filed a certiorari, which the Supreme Court denied. In his dissenting opinion, Justice Zaffaroni argued that the trial court's ruling should be affirmed on its merits because, he maintained, allowing corporations to face criminal sanctions would run against the constitution.

Zaffaroni's argument is rather poor because it is grounded in two feeble, if not outright false, premises. The first is that the constitution endorses a strong act requirement or act principle—a proposition for which, we have seen, there seem to be no solid grounds.[83] The second premise is that there is nothing like an action of a corporation—that only individuals act. This proposition improperly confuses the fairly strong idea that collective actions are *reducible* to individual actions with the dubious (if not straightforwardly false) claim that there are not collective actions.

In 2006 a commission appointed by the government released a draft of a proposed statute updating and reforming the CP.[84] The drafted new code—which, by the way, the executive did not send to the Congress—did include a rule establishing a form of corporate criminal liability. Although the proposed rule is problematic, as the following remarks will show, the very fact that the commission addressed the issue, thus opening the discussion on the role of corporate criminal responsibility, deserves recognition.

The proposed rule falls within the model of vicarious corporate liability, establishing that a corporation may be held liable for the deeds of people representing it or otherwise acting in its name or interest or to its benefit. However, it is widely argued in the comparative literature on the issue that vicarious models of corporate liability of the kind of the proposed rule are improperly overinclusive. First, not every corporation is large enough to be considered an independent entity from its owners or agents. Holding the corporation jointly liable with its individual agents could thus be utterly pointless.

Second, and crucially, vicarious models of that sort allow for corporate criminal liability even when the corporation is adequately structured in a way that does not encourage or promote the wrongdoing of its agents. A wiser alternative would be to devise the liability regime so as to allow for corporate punishment only upon a finding that the corporation's structure is such that it makes the corporation somehow prone to criminal activity by its agents.

Let me make a final remark on the scheme of sanctions proposed. The rule includes a wide catalogue of sanctions (together with fines, the publication of the conviction and sentence, suspension for up to three years and withdrawal of state registration, and other measures). In general, they exhibit the characteristically expressive nature of criminal punishment, thus contrasting with mere administrative fines. Some of them, however, have been challenged, especially the withdrawal (or long suspension) of state registration, which would amount to a sort of death penalty for corporations.

C. Defenses

1. Introduction (Necessity and Self-Defense)

There is no legal classification of defenses in the CP. It contains only a broad, indiscriminate list of general defenses, including insanity, duress, exercise of an outweighing right or duty, necessity (or choice of evils), and self-defense and defense of others (article 34), together with a number of special clauses establishing specific defenses for specific crime types—for example, special defenses for abortion (article 86 CP) and for property offenses (article 185 CP). Despite this indiscriminating legal treatment, it is a scholarly practice, also reflected in judicial parlance, to classify defenses as justifications and excuses, as is customary in the criminal law literature of continental Europe, depending on whether they affect the illicit character of the behavior (i.e., they render permissible what is generally illicit) or affect the agent's responsibility for an illicit behavior (culpability).

In general, the CP's regulation is couched in broad terms, leaving ample room for judicial interpretation. Take, for instance, the legal formulation of two core defenses, necessity and self-defense. The necessity defense is recognized in article 34, section 3, which reads that "he who causes an evil to prevent another imminent and larger evil" shall not be punished. The only qualification that the CP adds is that to be eligible for the defense, the agent must be "alien to" the larger evil the lesser evil would prevent. Beyond this, there is no explicit clue about how to rank evils, or about whether any difference in value between the conflicting evils (even a minimal difference) would be enough to grant the necessity permission.

The situation is similar with the other star justificatory defense, self-defense. According to the CP's article 34, section 6, self-defense applies when the defending measure is "rationally necessary" "to repel" an "illegitimate aggression," provided there has been no provocation from the defending agent. Crucial issues, such as which interests may be protected with self-defense, or whether there is a general duty to retreat, or whether the defending force should be proportional to the risk the aggression imposes, are left to the judiciary to determine. Despite the fact that these rules have been on the books since 1921, there appears to be no clear pattern of cases translating such vague standards into a relatively precise doctrine. In what follows I comment on a brief selection of issues that, I believe, might be of comparative interest.

2. Insanity

Three features of the Argentine insanity doctrine are worth highlighting. The first has to do with the scope of the inabilities that ground a declaration of innocence by virtue of insanity. The declaration of insanity requires that the agent is unable either (i) to "understand the criminality of the act" or (ii) to "direct his actions" in accordance with a proper understanding. The inability of the second sort is at stake in cases in which the defendant, who is otherwise able to understand the criminality of his or her act, claims to have been moved by an "irresistible impulse." Casual evidence shows that this version of the defense seldom leads to innocence findings.[85]

The second feature has to do with the source of the inabilities leading to insanity. According to the legal text (article 34, section 1), the inability to understand the criminality of the act or to control behavior according to a proper understanding should be due to the agent's "insufficient mental abilities" or to "morbid alterations thereof." This clause has raised the issue whether the mental condition that results in the required inability should be such that it counts as a mental disease—so that an otherwise "mentally healthy" person who is as unable to understand the criminality of the act or to control the act according to proper understanding as a mentally insane person is would nevertheless not be eligible for the defense. The traditional tendency among courts to opt for the more restrictive position has changed in the last decades in favor of an approach that focuses on the inabilities independently of its "morbid" causes. Or so it is claimed.[86]

The third feature I want to highlight is that there is no general provision for the case of *diminished capacity* to understand the criminality or to control behavior comparable to the general provision for the absence of such abilities. Not that such diminished capacity is of no significance in Argentine criminal law. The CP contains a rule attenuating punishment of criminal homicide and bodily injuries when they are caused by a "violent emotional reaction" for which there are "excusing circumstances."[87] This rule applies precisely in cases in which the agent's capacity to make his or her behavior track moral and legal reasons not to kill (or injure) others is severely diminished by virtue of "excusing circumstances" (e.g., circumstances that both explain the reaction and for which the agent is not responsible).[88]

3. Outweighing Rights

Article 34, section 4, of the CP makes it explicit that the exercise of a right may justify an otherwise criminal action. This clause has opened the door to a number of attempts at justifying actions falling under crime definitions, most noteworthily by appeal to freedom of speech.[89] Take the following two groups of cases.

Freedom of speech has been regularly offered as a justification in criminal libel cases. Defamation and slander are criminal offenses under articles 109 and 110 of the CP. Taken at face value, the law is such that any derogatory comment concerning another person, be it the expression of an opinion or a statement of fact, would meet at least the more general crime type of defamation. (The more specific crime type of slander requires the false assertion that another person has committed a crime.)

Prosecution for libel is typically triggered by media reports on the behavior of officials and other public figures.[90] In a 1987 decision the Supreme Court ruled that the constitutional protection of freedom of speech was such that, in the domain of statements of fact on issues of public interest and concerning public figures, there could be no legal responsibility whatsoever unless the person affected by a defamatory statement proved that the statement was false, and that its author asserted it knowing it to be false or at least being reckless about its falsity.[91] Applying this doctrine, criminal courts have progressively tended ever since to dismiss cases of defamation or slander in which the prosecution fails to prove such highly demanding mental requirements.[92]

Defendants have also claimed justification under freedom of speech in recent instances of prosecution for picketing on public streets in protest against governmental decisions or policies. The charge normally was that of "obstructing the normal functioning of land, water or air transportation," an offense under article 194 of the CP. The specific right claimed is the right to a public forum as part of the constitutionally protected freedom of speech. (Depending on what the protest was about, the public forum argument was sometimes accompanied by a claim to a justification under the necessity defense.) In this domain, the prevailing tendency among the courts has been against granting justification based on this right.[93]

4. Specific Defenses

A final interesting feature of the Argentine regime of defenses appears in the regulations on abortion.[94] As a matter of positive criminal law, abortion is a crime in Argentine criminal law—a relatively minor crime, as far as sanctions are concerned—even when it is performed during the first stage of pregnancy. There is an ongoing discussion about whether such a broad prohibition is constitutional, but there has been no judicial ruling in any direction yet.

The CP also contains, in article 86, a number of specific defenses for abortion. According to this rule, a medically performed abortion, if the woman consents, is legally permissible if the pregnancy would affect the life or health of the woman (article 86.1) or is the consequence of sexual abuse (article 86.2). Taken at face value, article 86 has a huge potential to secure an extensive range of permissible abortions—think of the possibility of construing the notion of health broadly in article 86.1 or extending the sexual abuse permissibility clause of article 86.2 to any other pregnancy for which the woman lacks responsibility (e.g., failures of contraception methods). However, after nearly ninety years since the adoption of the rule, the dominant reading is as narrow as it can be—and even narrower. Indeed, exploiting an ambiguity in the text of the sexual abuse permissibility clause, anti-abortionists have favored the peculiar reading that for an abortion to be permissible when the pregnancy is due to sexual abuse, the woman must also be mentally challenged.[95] The availability of this reading within the legal profession has brought about the unfortunate consequence of doctors' reluctance to perform abortions in cases of pregnancies stemming from sexual abuses when they are unaccompanied by a mental disorder.

III. SPECIAL PART

A. Structure

The special part of a national criminal law such as the Argentine law is too vast to cover in a chapter like this. The CP has nearly 250 special-part clauses, to which are added no less than 70 special statutes that include special-part clauses. Throughout this chapter I have made reference to many of the aspects of the special part of Argentine criminal law that might be of comparative interest—its general structure, its scheme of sanctions—and I have provided a number of examples of its crime types. To conclude this chapter I will add a brief note on the regulation of just three groups of core crimes—criminal homicides, sex offenses, and property offenses.

B. Homicide

Homicides are regulated in articles 79 through 84 of the CP. Article 79 criminalizes the conduct of "killing of a person" (other than the agent) and establishes for it a sanction of imprisonment for from 8 to 25 years. This basic or simple homicide crime type requires the default *dolus* mental state.[96] In the absence of *dolus*, homicides are still punishable by virtue of article 84 of the CP, which criminalizes the behavior of "negligently causing the death of a person." Sanctions for these negligent homicides range between 6 months' and 5 years' imprisonment and the suspension for up to 10 years of rights related to the activity that led to the killing (e.g., withdrawal of driving permits or professional licenses).

Article 80 lists a number of aggravating factors that, if they concur with an intentional homicide, lead to mandatory life imprisonment. The set of aggravating factors is quite diverse. It includes motivations like killing out of greed, pleasure, racial or religious hate, or for a price or a promise of compensation. Placing the killing in an otherwise criminal plan is also a listed aggravating factor—for example, when the killing is intended "to prepare, facilitate, complete, or hide another crime," or when it is meant by the agent to secure "the produce" obtained from another offense, or impunity for the agent or another putative defendant (as in killing a witness of a crime) (article 80, section 7). Other factors involve complexes of objective and subjective elements, such as killing treacherously (conventionally understood as killing a defenseless victim by taking advantage of the victim's defenselessness), with cruelty (both listed under article 80, section 2), or "with the premeditated intervention of two or more people" (article 80, section 6). In the same category we may include the killing of security officers when it is motivated by the fact that the victim holds that office (article 80, section 8), or killing by a security officer when it is done by abusing the agent's office (article 80, section 9). Finally, some aggravating factors refer to merely objective features, such as the identity of the victim (e.g., close relatives, article 80, section 1) or the nature of the risk created (e.g., by highly risky means, article 80, section 5).

Two further rules are worth highlighting. The first is in article 81.1(b) of the CP, which establishes a punishment of 1 to 6 years' imprisonment for the case of an action that meets two more basic crime types—a nonaggravated causing of bodily injuries (defined in article 89 and punished with 1 month's to 1 year's imprisonment) and a negligent homicide under article 84. If the general rules for aggregating convictions (articles 54 and 55 CP) are applied to this case, in the absence of the article 81.1(b) rule the case would lead to two convictions (one for the article 89 bodily injuries and one for the article 84 negligent homicide), but the sanction should fall within the minimum and maximum affixed to the negligent homicide (prison for from 6 months to 5 years). Since this combination of crimes appears quite often in the practice of criminal law, article 81.1(b) makes the charge simpler and raises a little the sanction that would otherwise apply. There are similar rules concerning negligent homicides and crimes other than nonaggravated bodily injuries, such as abortion (article 85), rape and other sex abuses (article 124), and robbery (article 165).

Second, article 83 criminalizes instigating or assisting somebody else's suicide, which is to be punished with a prison term ranging from 1 to 4 years whatever the outcome of the suicidal attempt. There has been no prosecution for this crime type that I am aware of, but there is still something to be said about its interpretation. Helping terminal patients end their suffering with high doses of painkilling drugs, with the known consequence of an anticipated death, is an everyday medical practice. It seems safe to characterize these cases as instances of assisted suicide. The absence of prosecution in spite of the letter of the law suggests that one of the following two readings of article 83 might be at work. According to the first, "to instigate" and "to assist," as these verbs are used in article 83, require that the agent *intends* the patient to kill himself or herself—and that would not be the intention guiding the physician's conduct, who would only foresee the patient's death as a side effect of the painkilling treatment. Under the second reading, the physician's behavior does meet article 83's crime definition, but it also meets the conditions of a justifying defense—one that is dependent on the right of the patient to finish his or her life as he or she sees fit.

C. Sex Offenses

Sex offenses in the Argentine CP were subjected to a major reform in 1999. The regulation is now relatively complex—comprising articles 119 through 132 of the CP—but its basics are simple to grasp. The core crime type is defined in article 119 as the action of "sexually abusing a person," which is to be read as the imposition of any action charged with sexual meaning on a person who does not validly consent to it, as characteristically happens, according to the statutory language, (i) when the victim is less than thirteen years old; (ii) when the agent makes use of violence, threats, or coercion or abusively exploits a hierarchical relationship; or (iii) when the agent takes advantage of the fact that the victim cannot freely consent. The amount of punishment imposed for article 119 sexual abuses varies depending on the nature of the sexual behavior—starting at 6 months' to 4 years' imprisonment in the basic case, 10 years when the abuse involves "a gravely outrageous sexual subjugation," and up to 15 years when it involves penetration. Punishment may be even harsher if any of a long list of aggravating circumstances is involved, ranging from the identity of the agent to the kind of harmful consequences that the abuse produces in the victim. In the worst scenario—when the victim dies as a consequence of the abuse—the punishment is mandatory life imprisonment (article 124).

The CP deals with child sex abuse essentially in the following way. Any kind of sexual intercourse with a child under thirteen is treated as an instance of article 119 sex abuse. Sexual intercourse with children under sixteen is otherwise criminal only if the agent "exploits the sexual immaturity of the victim" (article 120). This offense carries a prison term ranging from 3 to 6 years. Harsher sanctions are established for a crime that article

125 of the CP couches in terms of "promoting or facilitating the corruption of people under eighteen" (with punishment raising up to 15 years' imprisonment in the case of victims under thirteen). It is hard to tell with certainty what "corruption" means here. There are two things we can learn from court decisions and legal comments. First, sexual corruption presupposes a range of appropriate or normal, sexual developing paths. To corrupt a child would be to take the child away from such a normal path—for example, to inculcate in a child a taste for abusive sexual relationships. Second, sexual intercourse is neither necessary nor sufficient for an instance of this crime to obtain.

The CP also criminalizes some forms of conduct related to prostitution and to pornography and obscenity (articles 125 bis to 129 CP), but neither prostitution nor pornography are criminalized activities by themselves. In the case of prostitution-related offenses, what is criminalized is getting people involved in prostitution by intimidating, coercive, or straightforwardly violent means, or, in the absence of such forms of manipulation, when the person involved is less than eighteen years old. Similarly in the case of pornography, it is the involvement of people under eighteen that is defined as criminal, along with the exposition of pornography to nonconsenting persons.

D. Property Offenses

Four crime types form the core of the Argentine regime of property offenses: criminal damage (article 183), larceny (article 162), fraud or obtaining by deception (article 172), and embezzlement (article 173 section 7). There are many other property offenses, of course—for example, robberies (articles 164 to 167 bis), extortions (articles 168 to 171), and specific forms of frauds and embezzlements (articles 173 to 175)—but I will limit my commentary to the four core crimes.

The simplest of the four is criminal damage under article 183—a simple result crime defined in terms of causing any kind of setback to tangible property belonging (even partially) to another person. Punishment is relatively mild (a prison term of from 15 days to 1 year), which may increase to 4 years' imprisonment in case any of a number of aggravating circumstances is involved (article 184).

The other three types of offenses deal with the misappropriation of property. In Argentine criminal law, though, there is nothing like an umbrella type of theft under which every case of misappropriation might fall. The three core offenses thus have characteristic punitive lacunae. Article 162 defines the larceny offense, which is couched in terms of the misappropriation of somebody else's movable property. Although the requirement of movable property has been often construed extensively—as in the case of the misappropriation of electricity—the appropriation requirement is typically interpreted narrowly as demanding that the agent *takes away* the stolen thing from its legitimate holder—something to which the appropriation language does not seem to commit us. Punishment for larceny ranges from 1 month's to 2 years' imprisonment but can be up to 8 years' imprisonment if aggravating circumstances are involved (articles 163 and 163 bis). Robberies, which are conceived of as specially aggravated forms of larceny, are punished with prison terms ranging from 1 month to 25 years (articles 164 to 167 bis).

In contrast to the larceny offense, article 172 (frauds) and article 173, section 7 (embezzlements), have no restriction on the kind of property involved. The CP does not provide an explicit definition of fraud. Instead, article 172 lists a number of examples of what it takes to be cases in which one commits fraud against another. Still, there seems to be no dispute among courts and commentators that for an action to satisfy the notion of fraud that article 172 captures, the action must be (i) a kind of deception (not merely an instance of lying) (ii) that causes a person mistakenly to believe that there are reasons to transfer property of any kind (e.g., to make a payment or to deliver valuable goods) when there are no such reasons, and (iii) the deceived person, acting on the basis of his or her mistaken beliefs, makes the transfer, and thus he or she (or somebody else) gets harmed.

Article 173, section 7, defines in very general terms a kind of fraudulent behavior that does not fall under the model of fraud as obtaining by deception. In order to contrast these two models, local legal professionals tend to use different terms to refer to each of the two kinds of conduct—obtaining by deception is referred to with the Spanish word *estafa* (which I am translating here as *fraud*), while the kind that meets the article 173, section 7, model is referred to as *defraudación* (which I am translating here as *embezzlement*).

Article 173, section 7, captures the behavior of an agent who bears special duties to act on behalf of another person—particularly on behalf of another person's property interests—and, by violating any such duty, harms the property interests he or she was obliged to advance or protect. This crime type often figures among the charges in the prosecution of executive officers of corporations for offenses committed against the interests of the corporation or its stockholders. Unlike larceny and fraud, which require the *dolus* default mental state, article 173, section 7, requires more—it demands that the agent acts guided by the intention "to draw an illegitimate economic advantage, or to produce harm." Both basic forms of fraud and embezzlement are punished with sanctions that range from 1 month's to 6 years' imprisonment.

SELECTED BIBLIOGRAPHY

Bacigalupo, Enrique. *Derecho penal: Parte general*. 2d ed. Buenos Aires: Hammurabi, 1999.
Gargarella, Roberto. *El derecho a la protesta, el primer derecho*. Buenos Aires: Ad Hoc, 2005.
Gullco, Hernán Víctor. *Principios de la parte general del derecho penal: Jurisprudencia comentada*. Buenos Aires: Editores del Puerto, 2006.
Imaz, Esteban, and Ricardo E. Rey. *El recurso extraordinario*. 3d ed. Buenos Aires: Abeledo Perrot, 2000.
Jiménez de Asúa, Luis. *Tratado de derecho penal*. 7 vols. Buenos Aires: Losada, 1964–1970.
Levaggi, Abelardo. *Historia del derecho penal argentino*. Buenos Aires: Perrot, 1978.
Magariños, Hector M. *Los límites de la ley penal en función del principio constitucional de acto*. Buenos Aires: Ad Hoc, 2008.

Maier, Julio B. J. *Derecho procesal penal*. 2d ed. 2 vols. Buenos Aires: Editores del Puerto, 1996–2003.
Moreno (h), Rodolfo. *El Código Penal y sus antecedentes*. 6 vols. Buenos Aires: H. A. Tommassi, 1922.
Nino, Carlos S. *Fundamentos de derecho constitucional*. Buenos Aires: Astrea, 1992.
———. *Radical Evil on Trial*. New Haven, CT: Yale University Press, 1996.
Núñez, Ricardo C. *Derecho penal argentino*. 3 vols. Buenos Aires: Editorial Bibliográfica Argentina, 1959.
Palermo, Omar. *La legítima defensa: Una revisión normativista*. Buenos Aires: Hammurabi, 2007.
Sancinetti, Marcelo A. *Casos de derecho penal*. 3d ed. Buenos Aires: Hammurabi, 2005.
———. *Fundamentación subjetiva del ilícito y desistimiento de la tentativa*. Bogotá: Temis, 1995.
———. *Teoría del delito y disvalor de acción*. Buenos Aires: Hammurabi, 1991.
Sancinetti, Marcelo A., and Marcelo Ferrante. *El derecho penal en la protección de los derechos humanos*. Buenos Aires: Hammurabi, 1999.
Soler, Sebastián. *Derecho penal argentino*. 4th ed. 5 vols. Buenos Aires: Tipográfica Editora Argentina, 1989.
Tau Anzoátegui, Víctor. *La codificación en la Argentina (1810–1870)*. Buenos Aires: Imprenta de la Universidad, 1977.
Zaffaroni, Eugenio Raúl. *Tratado de derecho penal: Parte general*. 5 vols. Buenos Aires: Ediar, 1987.
Zaffaroni, Eugenio Raúl, Alejandro Alagia, and Alejandro Slokar. *Manual de derecho penal: Parte general*. Buenos Aires: Ediar, 2005.

NOTES

1. This does not mean that there was no criminal law before that period. Historians distinguish an Indian and colonial criminal law, before 1810, and the criminal law of the preconstitutional period (1810–1853). Two distinctive features of these criminal laws were the multiplicity of legal sources and the discretionary power of the judicial authorities—two features that the constitution was intended to change. See, e.g., Abelardo Levaggi, *Historia del derecho penal argentino* (Buenos Aires: Editorial Perrot, 1978); and Eugenio Raúl Zaffaroni, *Tratado de derecho penal: Parte general* (Buenos Aires: Ediar, 1987), vol. 1, 403–458.

2. See Rodolfo Moreno (h), *El Código Penal y sus Antecedentes*, 6 vols. (Buenos Aires: H. A. Tommassi, 1922).

3. Originally the CP established two different kinds of imprisonment, prison and reclusion. The practical significance of the difference, however, has now disappeared. See infra section II.A.

4. See, however, infra section II.A.

5. A dictatorial government introduced a major reform of the CP in 1967. This reform was later repealed after the return to democracy in 1973, was virtually reinstated in 1976 by a new military dictatorship, and was finally abrogated in 1984 when Argentina last returned to democracy. See, e.g., Zaffaroni, supra n. 1, vol. 1, 450–455.

6. Unsystematic research reveals that no less than seventy statutes of this sort are currently in force.

7. For an overview in comparative perspective, see, e.g., Carlos S. Nino, *Fundamentos de derecho constitucional* (Buenos Aires: Astrea, 1992).

8. There is one exception. Only a few years ago, in 2004, one of the twenty-four Argentine provinces, Córdoba, adopted a form of jury trial for criminal matters.

9. The leading case is still "Loveira v. Mulhall," Corte Suprema de Justicia de la Nación (CSJN), *Fallos* 115:92 (1911).

10. On the issue of jury trials in Argentine criminal law, see, e.g., Julio B. J. Maier, *Derecho procesal penal*, 2d ed., vol. 1 (Buenos Aires: Editores del Puerto, 1996), 775–793.

11. See, e.g., "Peyrú," CSJN, *Fallos* 318:108 (1995) (dismissing petition for prosecution of crimes committed in Chile on the argument that they were not crimes against the law of nations).

12. The federal judiciary may intervene in a judicial case of provincial jurisdiction only through an appeal to the Supreme Court of Justice of the Nation (CSJN), after the case has been conclusively decided by the provincial judiciary, and only when the interpretation of the constitution or some other piece of federal law is at stake. See, e.g., Esteban Imaz and Ricardo E. Rey, *El recurso extraordinario*, 3d ed. (Buenos Aires: Abeledo-Perrot, 2000).

13. See, e.g., "Vílchez," Cámara Nacional de Casación Penal (CNCP), *La Ley* (*LL*) 2001-E:778.

14. I am simplifying here. The Argentine statute of limitations for criminal prosecutions is complex, with terms ranging from 2 to 15 years depending on the punishment legally determined for the type of crime committed, and with a complex regime of extensions and suspensions. See articles 62–64 and 67 CP.

15. See article 2 CP.

16. See, e.g., "Priebke," CSJN, *Fallos* 318:2148 (1995) (also declaring inapplicable the statute of limitations, but in an extradition case); "Simón," CSJN, *Fallos* 328:2056 (2005) (invalidating statutes that barred prosecution for state crimes committed during the 1976–1983 dictatorship).

17. Law No. 23.737, *Anales de la Legislación Argentina* (*ADLA*) XLIX-D:3692 (1989).

18. Law No. 19.359, art. 1(f), *ADLA* XXXII-A:2 (1972).

19. See, e.g., "Cristalux," CSJN, *Fallos* 329:1053 (2006); "Ayerza," CSJN, *Fallos* 321:824 (1998) (Justice Petracchi dissenting).

20. See, e.g., "Mussotto," CSJN, *Fallos* 310:1909 (1987) (upholding criminal statute punishing "reproducing obscene materials" in spite of the recognized vagueness of the term *obscene*).

21. See, e.g., "Antúnez-García," Cámara de Apelaciones en lo Criminal y Correccional (CCC) (City of Buenos Aires), *LL* 1986 C:251 (invalidating penal norms for the City of Buenos Aires passed by the chief of police in the late nineteenth century but still in force a century later).

22. See, e.g., Sebastián Soler, *Derecho penal argentino*, 4th. ed., vol. 2 (Buenos Aires: Tipográfica Editora Argentina, 1989), 429.

23. See article 13 CP.

24. See article 26 CP.

25. See article 24 CP.
26. See "Méndez," CSJN, *Fallos* 328:137 (2005).
27. See article 53 CP.
28. See "Gramajo," CSJN, *Fallos* 329:3680 (2006).
29. See article 34, section 1, second and third paragraphs CP.
30. On insanity in Argentine criminal law, see infra section II.C.2.
31. See also articles 16–20 Drugs Act, supra n. 17 (specifying safety measures for cases of drug addiction).
32. Law No. 24.660, *ADLA* LVI-C:3375 (1996).
33. See article 13 CP.
34. See article 4, American Convention on Human Rights.
35. See "Verbitsky," CSJN, *Fallos* 328:1146 (2005).
36. See "Antúnez García," CCC (City of Buenos Aires), *LL* 1986-C:251.
37. See "Schmidt," TOC No. 23 (City of Buenos Aires) (1994) (unpublished decision; on file with author).
38. See, e.g., Nino, supra n. 7, 304–327.
39. See Héctor Mario Magariños, *Los límites de la ley penal en función del principio constitucional de acto* (Buenos Aires: Ad Hoc, 2008) (defending the same reading).
40. See "Bazterrica," CSJN, *Fallos* 308:1392 (1986).
41. See "Montalvo," CSJN, *Fallos* 313:1347 (1990).
42. Indeed, between the 1920s and the 1940s several drafts of a so-called Dangerous Person Act were proposed for the consideration of the Congress, intending one way or another to criminalize people on account of their allegedly dangerous status. Fortunately, the Congress never passed any of them, presumably because of a widespread sense that such regimes clashed with basic constitutional values. See, e.g., Zaffaroni, supra n. 1, vol. 1, 433–436.
43. I do not mean to suggest that the homicide offense is the only crime type for which this construction is available. The homicide offense serves here only as an example. The same construction is, in principle, available for any other type of offense.
44. The Argentine CP thus differs from other comparable criminal codes that do contain such a general rule, e.g., the German criminal code: § 13, StGB.
45. See "Cabral," SCJ (Buenos Aires), *JA* 1995-I:396 (reversing a homicide conviction).
46. See, e.g., Marcelo A. Sancinetti, *Teoría del delito y disvalor de acción* (Buenos Aires: Hammurabi, 1991), 233–240.
47. That will depend on the favored general theory of the mental requirements for criminal liability under the CP. See infra section II.B.2.
48. See "Antiñir," CSJN, *Fallos* 329:2367 (2006).
49. The precedent is "Parafina del Plata," CSJN, *Fallos* 271:297 (1968).
50. The language with which the CP refers to what is normally called negligence is unnecessarily complex. A translation of such legal language would go like this: to do so and so (e.g., kill another person, cause bodily injury) "through imprudence, negligence, or lack of due skill in the agent's art or profession, or by violating applicable regulations or duties of care." Some commentators have tried to find insight in the apparent legal distinctions as describing different kinds of negligence, but the dominant view is that these distinctions are pointless.

51. Reductions in punishment are dramatic. A simple criminal homicide is punishable with prison terms ranging from 8 to 25 years. Prison terms for negligent homicide range from 6 months to 5 years. Sanctions for intentional infliction of bodily injuries range from 1 month to 10 years of imprisonment. In the case of negligently caused bodily injuries, sanctions vary from a mild fine to a prison term of 3 years.

52. For more precisions, see infra sections II.B.2.i and ii.

53. See, e.g., "Navarro," CSJN, *Fallos* 324:2133 (2001) (reversing a conviction of a number of defendants in a case of negligent homicide for not distinguishing the different reasonability standards applicable to each defendant, who were physicians of different experience and held different institutional positions within the hospital where the victim died.)

54. The dominant view among criminal law professionals seems to be the former one, because this is the mainstream position in legal education. Indeed, massively used textbooks, such as Zaffaroni, supra n. 1, Enrique Bacigalupo, *Derecho penal: Parte general*, 2d ed. (Buenos Aires: Hammurabi, 1999), and Marcelo A. Sancinetti, *Casos de derecho penal*, 3d ed. (Buenos Aires: Hammurabi, 2005), draw on the conception of German legal scholar Hans Welzel, under which the dolus/negligence distinction tracks a qualitative difference in wrongdoing. See, e.g., Hans Welzel, *Das neue Bild des Strafrechtssystems: Eine Einführung in die finale Handlungslehre*, 4th ed. (Göttingen: O. Schwartz, 1961). Still, classic textbooks like Soler, supra n. 22, and Ricardo C. Núñez, *Derecho penal argentino*, 3 vols. (Buenos Aires: Editorial Bibliográfica Argentina, 1959), massively used in legal education up to the 1980s, deploy a conception according to which mental states influence culpability rather than wrongdoing.

55. See, however, Marcelo A. Sancinetti, *Dogmática del hecho punible y ley penal* (Buenos Aires: Ad Hoc, 2003), 133 (suggesting this possibility).

56. See Sancinetti, supra n. 46, 172–181.

57. See, e.g., "Insaurralde" CCC (Santa Fe), *LL* 1975-A:182 (acquitting a defendant who hit the victim, reasonably but mistakenly believing that the victim was about to attack him).

58. See, e.g., "Arce," CCC (City of Buenos Aires), *LL* 2004-B:715 (finding that the defendant unreasonably believed that shooting was necessary to defend himself against an actual attack).

59. See, e.g., Enrique Bacigalupo, "Sistema del error sobre la antijuridicidad en el Código Penal," *Nuevo Pensamiento Penal* 1 (1972): 45.

60. See, e.g., Zaffaroni, supra n. 1, vol. 4, 230–231.

61. See, e.g., Moreno (h), supra n. 2, vol. 3, 309.

62. See "Krill," CSJN, *Fallos* 316:1239 (1993).

63. See, e.g., "Chanampa," CCCFed. (City of Buenos Aires), *JA* 1995-III:199.

64. See "Fernández," CSJN, *Fallos* 315:2817 (1992).

65. Article 162 CP.

66. See, e.g., "Mass," CCC (City of Buenos Aires), *JA* 1990-II:207 (rejecting type-mistake theory and endorsing unreasonable mistake of law in affirming conviction for embezzlement of public property by an official in violation of a judicial injunction, under article 260 CP).

67. See, e.g., "Gebauer," CSJN, *Fallos* 323:407 (2000) (reversing a conviction for drug commerce, which requires dolus, when the defendant's mistake, which consisted in his false belief that the substance he sold did not count as an illegal drug, had been characterized as a type mistake, and therefore one that entails the absence of *dolus*).

68. See Esteban Righi, "El dolo eventual en la tentativa," *Nuevo Pensamiento Penal* 1 (1972): 303–307 (reviewing judicial case law as of 1973); and Hernán V. Gullco, *Principios de la parte general del derecho penal: Jurisprudencia comentada* (Buenos Aires: Editores del Puerto, 2006), 221–223 (reviewing recent court decisions).

69. See Eugenio R. Zaffaroni, Alejandro Alagia, and Alejandro Slokar, *Manual de derecho penal: Parte general* (Buenos Aires: Ediar, 2005), 646–647; and Righi, supra n. 68.

70. See supra section II.B.2.

71. As an example of the formal stance, take a case in which a court of appeals found that a taxi driver who had secretly altered the meter so that it would record an excessive fare and was on the street waiting for a passenger to appear was not yet perpetrating a fraud—he has only prepared to start perpetrating one if a passenger appeared. See "F.V.V.," CCC (City of Buenos Aires) *JA* 2004-I:13. The last-act test may be exemplified by another case in which another panel of the same court found the defendant guilty of attempted robbery, even though he had not yet started to steal or remove any good (he had only broken the side window of a car). See "Mendoza," CCC (City of Buenos Aires) *JA* 1992-I:48. As I said in the text, these relatively narrow criteria appear to be a probably dominant tendency. Broader criteria are also held, though less often, even among courts within the same national jurisdiction. Take, e.g., a case in which a panel of the national appeals court for economic criminal affairs affirmed a conviction for attempted smuggling when the defendant had been arrested while he was at the bar of an international airport, holding a flight ticket for a flight that would depart three hours later and a bag containing cocaine. See "Campistol Espinosa," CPEcon. *JA* 2007-I:13.

72. See Marcelo A. Sancinetti, *Fundamentación subjetiva del ilícito y desistimiento de la tentativa* (Bogotá: Temis, 1995), 84–89, elaborating on an argument by Günther Jakobs, "Rücktritt als Tatänderung versus allgemeines Nachtatverhalten," *Zeitschrift für die gesamte Strafrechtswissenschaft* 104 (1992): 82.

73. See, e.g., "Wasser," CNCP, *LL* 2003-E:6 (the defendant was about to cross a customs check point at an international airport with several packages of cocaine hidden under his shirt when he noticed that passengers were being frisked by customs officers—something he had not previously considered. So he ran away—not very far, for he was immediately arrested and charged with attempted smuggling. The court denied the defense of abandonment on the ground that it had been nonvoluntary, because the reason for Wasser to abandon had been the prospect of being caught when frisked).

74. Law No. 22.415, *ADLA* XLI-A:1325 (1981).

75. See "Steiger," CNCP, *JA* 2002-II:55 (rejecting defendant's claim that the equal treatment of attempted and accomplished smuggling crimes is unconstitutional).

76. See "Causa originariamente instruida por el Consejo Supremo de las Fuerzas Armadas en cumplimiento del decreto 158/83 del Poder Ejecutivo Nacional," CSJN, *Fallos* 309:5 (1986). For the legal history of this case, see, e.g., Carlos S. Nino, *Radical Evil on Trial* (New Haven, CT: Yale University Press, 1996); and Marcelo A. Sancinetti and

Marcelo Ferrante, *El derecho penal en la protección de los derechos humanos* (Buenos Aires: Hammurabi, 1999).

77. See "Cabaña," CNCP, *JA* 2004-II:822.
78. See supra section II.B.3.i.
79. Article 47 CP.
80. Article 48 CP.
81. See Sancinetti, supra n. 46, 759–808.
82. See "Fly Machine," CSJN, *Fallos* 329:1974 (2006) (Zaffaroni dissenting).
83. See supra section II.B.1.i. Justice Zaffaroni claims in addition that human rights international treaties—if not the constitution—do explicitly require actions and omissions as preconditions of punishment. But this proposition, though true, is irrelevant. Human rights treaties ground duties with respect to the imposition of punishment on human beings, not corporations.
84. See the proposed draft at derechopenalonline, http://www.derechopenalonline.com/derecho.php?Ibid=43,289,0,0,1,0 (accessed July 29, 2008).
85. See, e.g., "Villadoniga," TOC No. 23 (City of Buenos Aires) (1995) (unpublished decision; on file with author).
86. See Gullco, supra n. 68, 293–300, who traces the changing wave to a dissenting opinion by Judge Jorge Frías Caballero in a 1965 case.
87. See article 81, section 1.a CP, for the attenuation of criminal homicide, and article 93 CP for the corresponding attenuation of bodily injuries.
88. There is still an unsolved question this rule has raised: whether there are good reasons to confine this partial excuse to the domain of violent corporal attacks (homicidal and otherwise) rather than extending it to every possible crime.
89. Freedom of speech is a constitutional right in Argentine law in the double sense of its being recognized by the original constitution (articles 14 and 32 of the constitution) and its being protected by international treaties having constitutional status by virtue of article 75, section 22, of the constitution (i.e. the American Convention on Human Rights and the International Covenant on Civil and Political Rights).
90. There is no official prosecution for these crimes—indeed, for defamation and slander, together with three other relatively minor and personal offenses, only the individual affected by the offense has standing to prosecute. See article 73 CP.
91. The case is "Costa v. Ciudad de Buenos Aires," CSJN, *Fallos* 310:508 (1987). The court expressly applied to the Argentine constitutional clause of freedom of speech the U.S. Supreme Court interpretation of the First Amendment to the U.S. Constitution adopted in *New York Times v. Sullivan*, 376 U.S. 254 (1964).
92. This tendency is no more than that—a tendency. Evidence of that is the recent decision of the Inter-American Court of Human Rights in the case "Kimel v. Argentina," in which the court found that Argentina had violated Kimel's freedom of speech by convicting him under the criminal law of defamation, disregarding the *Costa* doctrine. See http://www.corteidh.or.cr/docs/casos/articulos/seriec_177_esp.pdf. This international ruling may serve to consolidate the tendency into a generally applied law.
93. See, e.g., "Alais," CNCP, *JA* 2004-III:274 (reversing an appellate decision that had dismissed the prosecution of a case under article 194 CP). See also Roberto Gargarella, *El*

derecho a la protesta, el primer derecho (Buenos Aires: Ad Hoc, 2005) (favoring justification).

94. Articles 85–88 CP.

95. The ambiguity in the text is best explained as a poor translation from its Swiss source. See Soler, supra n. 22, vol. 3, 113–115. For the antiabortionist reading, see Núñez, supra n. 54, vol. 1, 390–393.

96. See supra section II.B.2.

AUSTRALIA

Simon Bronitt

I. Introduction
   A. Historical Sketch
   B. Jurisdiction
   C. Legality Principle
   D. Sources of Criminal Law
   E. Process

II. General Part
   A. Theories of Punishment
   B. Liability Requirements
   C. Defences
   D. Justifications
   E. Excuses
   F. Sanctions

III. Special Part
   A. Structure
   B. Homicide
   C. Sex Offences
   D. Theft and Fraud
   E. "Victimless" Crimes
   F. Terrorism

Simon Bronitt is Director of the Australian Research Council Centre of Excellence in Policing and Security and Professor at Griffith University. His recent publications include (with Bernadette McSherry) *Principles of Criminal Law*, 3d ed. (Sydney: Thomson Reuters, 2010), and (with Stephen Bottomley) *Law in Context*, 3d ed. (Sydney: Federation Press, 2006).

I. INTRODUCTION

A. Historical Sketch

The history of Australia's criminal law is bound up in its foundation as a penal colony. The colony was first claimed by the British Crown in 1770 by Captain James Cook, and the first permanent European settlement was established in 1788. The reason for the establishment of the colony was Britain's urgent need to transport convicts following the loss of its thirteen colonies as a result of the American War of Independence.

The colony of New South Wales was established as a penal settlement in January 1788. Because it was a settled colony, as distinct from a conquered or ceded one, the criminal law that applied was the inherited laws of England.[1] This principle, however, was subject to a significant qualification. As Blackstone pointed out, "[C]olonists carry with them only so much of the English law, as is applicable to their own situation and the condition of an infant colony."[2]

The theory of *terra nullius*, which applied the legal fiction that lands of Australia were uninhabited,[3] denied legal recognition to Aboriginal customary laws. The doctrine remained unchallenged until the High Court of Australia's decision in *Mabo*[4] in 1992, although this decision extended only to property rights and the recognition of native title.[5] The traditional position in relation to criminal law has not changed. Consequently, Aboriginal customary law is not a source of law, although in some (but not all) jurisdictions it may be considered as a matter relevant to sentencing.[6]

The criminal law inherited from England was a tangled mass of common law and statutory offences. The difficulty of stating with confidence which laws had been received prompted local legislatures to enact their own criminal laws, provided they were not repugnant with the laws of England. By the mid-nineteenth century[7] the difficulties in accessing and applying common law rules made the new colonies fertile ground for codification.[8] Consolidation of the criminal law thus became a major preoccupation in the mid-nineteenth century, and numerous commissions were established to review portions of the criminal law with a view to reducing it to statutory form.[9]

Today most jurisdictions in Australia work under a codified system of criminal law. In Australia, codes based on a draft by Samuel Griffith (who subsequently became the first chief justice of the High Court) were enacted in Queensland (1899), Western Australia (1902, reenacted and compiled in 1913), Tasmania (1924), and the Northern Territory (1983).[10] The criminal code drafted for Queensland, the "Griffith Code," has been influential, not only in Australian code states, but also in other overseas common law jurisdictions.[11] The federal jurisdiction, the Australian Capital Territory, and Norfolk Island have adopted criminal codes based on the Australian Model Criminal Code (see discussion below). The remaining jurisdictions, the so-called common law jurisdictions, are a mixture of common law offences and statutory provisions that create new offences, clarify definitions, and deal with sentencing and procedural matters.[12]

The history of the twentieth century in Australia was marked by the advent and steady expansion of federal criminal law. The amalgamation of the Australian colonies into a

Commonwealth in 1901 did alter the framework just described even though the constitution did not grant power to the new federal Parliament to enact criminal laws. The federal Parliament can only enact laws that are directly supported by or incidental to a head of power in the Commonwealth Constitution.

The expansion of the scope of federal criminal law in the course of the twentieth century has witnessed a significant part of drug law in Australia being federalized: federal trafficking offences are based on powers contained in the Commonwealth Constitution to enact legislation relating to customs[13] and external affairs.[14] In relation to the latter, the numerous international United Nations treaties relating to the suppression of drugs have provided the constitutional basis for enacting an ever-expanding range of drug offences and law-enforcement and confiscation powers. The external-affairs power in the Constitution has also provided the constitutional basis for enacting crimes against humanity into federal law.[15] More recently the defence power in the constitution has provided the basis for the terrorism offences enacted after 9/11, although the states have also referred their powers to legislate in this field to the Commonwealth under s 51(xxxvii).[16] The federal Parliament retains the power to legislate directly for the territories, a power that was exercised most recently to override the controversial voluntary euthanasia laws in the Northern Territory.[17]

This distribution of legislative power between the Commonwealth, states, and territories promotes considerable diversity in approaches to the criminal law in Australia. However, two factors have promoted some degree of conformity in the criminal law: first, the High Court, as the ultimate appellate court[18] in matters of federal, state, and territory law, has promoted consistency in the core definitions in the criminal law; second, since 1990 the governments of Australia have sought to promote harmonization of criminal laws through the Model Criminal Code project. Like the U.S. Model Penal Code, it has provided a template for codification and development of general principles and common offence definitions.[19] The harmonization project, however, is hampered by "law and order" politics at the state level, which produces significant differences in the degrees of enthusiasm for adoption of the Model Criminal Code across Australia.

B. Jurisdiction

A general thesis of the common law is that criminal offences are territorial in nature, in the sense of being bound to a defined geographic territory.[20] This is reflected in the statutory presumption (albeit rebuttable) that offences do not have extraterritorial effect.[21] The tests of territoriality developed by courts and legislatures in Australia provide the legal framework within which jurisdiction is determined. Only rarely is jurisdiction an issue in the courtroom. When it is disputed, the determination of jurisdiction is a question for the tribunal of fact: "When an issue is raised as to locality of the offence the jury may have to decide the issue in order to determine whether the conduct charged falls within the territorial ambit of the law of the forum."[22]

The leading High Court decision *Ward v The Queen* (1980) 142 CLR 308 settled the common law principles governing criminal jurisdiction. The accused, standing on the bank of the Murray River in Victoria, shot and killed his victim, who was standing on the opposite bank in New South Wales. The accused was tried and convicted of murder in Victoria. On appeal, the accused challenged the jurisdiction, and the High Court considered that the question of jurisdiction fell to be determined by (1) the place where the conduct causing death initiated (the *initiatory theory*) or (2) the place where the consequences of that conduct occurred (*the terminatory theory*).[23] Although under international law, either of these approaches suffices for granting criminal jurisdiction, the High Court in the context of these facts favored the terminatory theory. Accordingly, the court held that New South Wales rather than Victoria had jurisdiction to try the accused for murder.

The common law has, however, been subjected to extensive statutory modification, with many legislatures adopting a broader and more flexible test based on "territorial nexus." In Queensland and Western Australia the legislatures have adopted a composite test, fusing the so-called initiatory and terminatory theories.[24] Other jurisdictions, such as the Australian Capital Territory, New South Wales, and South Australia, have supplemented the common law with a statutory test of jurisdiction based on "territorial nexus" or "geographical nexus."[25]

A more modern scheme for determining jurisdiction was proposed in the Model Criminal Code and has been applied to federal criminal offences.[26] Under the model scheme a default test applies where the offence provision does not expressly address jurisdiction: in these cases jurisdiction applies where the "conduct" or "a result" required by the offence occurs wholly or partly in Australia. This territorial test is supplemented by four nongeographic bases for jurisdiction of varying breadth. These bases, described as categories A through D, do not require the crime to be connected to the territory. Category A covers Australian citizens or body corporates anywhere in the world, subject to a foreign law defence.[27] Category B covers Australian citizens, body corporates and residents anywhere in the world, subject to a foreign law defence.[28] Category C covers anyone anywhere regardless of citizenship or residence, subject to a foreign law defence.[29] Category D covers anyone anywhere regardless of citizenship or residence, with no foreign law defence. Jurisdiction extends overseas because of the citizenship or resident status of the accused and/or the nature of the offence, not because of any geographic or territorial connection with Australia. The Model Criminal Code's scheme aims to "provide for more certainty about the geographical reach of various offences and will turn the mind of the legislature to this very important issue in all contexts."[30]

There are generally no statute of limitations provisions in Australia that require a prosecution to be instituted within a prescribed period.[31]

C. Legality Principle

A key idea inherent in the rule of law is that no person may be punished except for a breach of law established in the ordinary manner before the courts. These values are reflected in the twin maxims *nullum crimen sine lege* (no crime without law) and *nulla poena sine lege* (no punishment without law).[32] In the absence of an entrenched national bill of rights, legislatures in Australia have the power to enact retrospective criminal laws.[33] Although two maxims lack constitutional status, they nevertheless find expression through a common law presumption against the retrospective application of penal laws.[34]

Also, the presumption finds expression in the two Australian jurisdictions that have enacted human rights legislation.[35]

Departures from this presumption are exceptional. Recent examples include the retrospective terrorist offences enacted in the aftermath of the Bali bombings in Indonesia in 2002 that killed eighty-eight Australians. To make these terrorist acts criminal under Australian law, the Federal Parliament inserted part 5.4 into the Criminal Code (Cth). Division 115, titled "Harming Australians," created a range of extraterritorial "offences against the person," including murder, manslaughter, and causing serious injury to Australian citizens or residents. From a review of the parliamentary debates, it is clear that the legislature intended these offences to have retrospective operation.[36]

D. Sources of Criminal Law

1. Legislature

Even in those common law jurisdictions that have not adopted a code, the bulk of offences in the criminal law are statutory. Reflecting the wide array of regulatory functions performed by the modern criminal law, the legislature now favors detailed statutory offences that clearly articulate the *actus reus* (physical elements) and *mens rea* (fault elements) and possible defences. Offence and penalty provisions cover diverse regulatory fields, ranging from occupational health and safety to environmental protection offences. However, many key offences (such as murder) and defences (such as provocation) continue to be defined and developed through case law.

In codified systems, such as the federal criminal law, the general principles of responsibilities are contained in the General Part of the Criminal Code (chapter 2), which applies to all offences whether or not contained in the code (see below). These principles not only guide how courts should interpret offences but also have a significant impact on the framing and drafting of legislation. Codes have the potential to produce higher degrees of conceptual and definitional consistency, although these provisions do not seem to have stemmed the legislative trend of creating offences that dispense with *mens rea* and impose strict liability.

Offences may also be enacted under delegated legislation in the form of local bylaws that apply to specific places or at prescribed times.

2. Judiciary

As noted earlier, the appellate courts have played a significant role in fashioning and developing the general principles of the criminal law. Many of the leading decisions of the High Court on causation, intention, recklessness, and defences have influenced the statutory definitions adopted in the Model Criminal Code. The High Court, as noted earlier, has sought to promote uniformity between the common law concepts, developed through cases, and the meaning and scope of equivalent statutory concepts. The High Court does not have an inherent jurisdiction to declare new offences. The High Court also draws on a range of decisions of related common law jurisdictions, including the Privy Council, the House of Lords, and the Supreme Court of Canada, although these decisions now have only persuasive rather than binding authority.[37]

3. Executive

The executive has no power to declare conduct unlawful—there is a general prohibition on such bills of attainder.[38] However, legislation may provide the executive (typically in the form of the Governor-General or relevant minister of the Crown) with the power to proscribe particular things or organizations. For the purpose of the federal terrorism offences, the Governor-General can specify that an organization is a "terrorist organization" when the minister is satisfied on reasonable grounds that it is directly or indirectly engaged in, preparing, planning, assisting in, or fostering the doing of a terrorist act or that the organization advocates the doing of a terrorist act (whether or not a terrorist act has occurred or will occur).[39]

4. Scholars

The influence of legal academics on the development of the criminal law in Australia has been significant, though indirect. The appointment of professional law teachers to full-time university positions began in earnest after World War II, marking the commencement of an academic rather than simply a trade-school model of legal training in Australia. Through the establishment of a specialized Australian journal (*Criminal Law Journal*) and law reports (*Australian Criminal Reports*), the legal academy has provided significant intellectual and scholarly resources for the development of criminal law doctrine. Its role in law reform is particularly noteworthy; leading academics, such as Ian Leader-Elliott, have played a key role in the development of the Model Criminal Code and its associated commentaries. Appellate courts, including the High Court, make regular use of scholarly writing and research in their judgments. Leading senior members of the bar also play an important role in authoring leading texts (e.g., Odgers).

E. Process

1. Adversarial/Inquisitorial

The Australian criminal justice system is based on an adversarial or accusatorial model. This model, inherited from England, requires that the party who alleges or *avers* must prove the matter, which, in the criminal context, means proving the guilt of the defendant beyond reasonable doubt.[40] The principles underscoring the adversarial or accusatorial model are reflected in many of the applicable rules of procedure and evidence, including the presumption of innocence[41] and the privilege against self-incrimination.[42] The judge's role is to ensure that the trial is conducted according to law, and that the defendant is not subjected to an unfair trial.[43]

Under the adversarial or accusatorial model the trial judge does not exercise direct control or supervision over the conduct of law enforcement officials or the prosecution. However, the judge may exert influence indirectly through pretrial processes and during the trial itself through the application of discretion to exclude improperly or illegally obtained evidence[44] or to grant a stay of proceedings on the grounds of an abuse of process.[45] Although this model is said to be a fundamental feature of the Australian criminal justice system, the last two decades have witnessed significant modifications. For example, although victims are not party to the proceedings, they have come to play an increasingly visible and active role through victim impact statements during sentencing hearings and as participants in restorative justice conferences. Also, the advent of case management, introduced to address issues of delay and promote cost-effectiveness, has required more active involvement of trial judges to clarify the matters in dispute during the pre-trial phase, with the additional anticipated effect of encouraging early pleas of guilt where appropriate.[46]

2. Jury/Written Opinions

Reflecting the condition of New South Wales as a penal settlement in the late eighteenth century, the institution of juries—both grand and petty—was not part of the received legal inheritance from England. Juries were impractical because most early inhabitants of the colony were convicted felons and thus were legally excluded from sitting on juries. The function of the jury was instead performed by a panel of military officers or benches of justices of the peace. The political campaign by Emancipists to establish trial by jury in New South Wales became an important symbolic and practical marker of the transition from a penal colony to representative self-government.[47] By the mid-nineteenth century the jury had established itself as a regular feature of the Australian criminal justice system for serious matters.

As in England, the grand jury was either abolished or fell into disuse in the late nineteenth century and was replaced by a preliminary hearing or committal conducted before magistrates. At this pretrial hearing the prosecutor must present a prima facie case against the defendant in order to commence the prosecution in the superior court before a jury. The committal has evolved as a procedural filter to ensure that a person is not put to trial by jury without sufficient evidence. However, discharging a defendant on the grounds of insufficient evidence is not the committal's sole function. As noted by the High Court in *Barton v The Queen*,[48] the committal also provides the defence with an opportunity to gain relatively precise knowledge of the prosecution's case, to hear the Crown witnesses give evidence on oath, and to test that evidence by cross-examination. In some jurisdictions there is also a power to waive the right to a jury trial and elect trial by a judge alone.[49]

Today the jury plays a relatively small but nevertheless significant role—trials by jury constitute less than 1 percent of criminal proceedings. In relation to federal criminal proceedings, the constitution provides a guarantee of a jury trial in the following terms: "[T]rial on indictment of any offence against any law of the Commonwealth shall be by jury."[50] Although this guarantee is expressed in mandatory terms, most federal criminal trials in Australia do not trigger its operation because the High Court has consistently held that the Commonwealth Parliament can avoid this obligation by simply labeling the offence a "summary" offence.[51]

II. GENERAL PART

A. Theories of Punishment

Ideas about the nature and aims of punishment may be broadly grouped into theories that are retributive (promoting just deserts) or utilitarian (promoting general or specific deterrence, prevention, rehabilitation, or incapacitation).[52] At common law, the various purposes of sentencing are found scattered in judicial dicta of the appellate courts, which often conflict. As the chief justice of New South Wales, the Honourable J. J. Spigelman, has noted: "The requirements of deterrence, rehabilitation, denunciation, punishment and restorative justice do not point in the same direction. Specifically, the requirements of justice, in the sense of just deserts, and of mercy, often conflict. Yet we live in a society which values both justice and mercy."[53]

The late twentieth century witnessed a growing acceptance of theories and processes based on the principles of restorative justice, which, as noted above, provide a broader range of diversionary options and prospects for offender and victim restoration. The Australian Capital Territory has adopted a comprehensive statute that defines the objects and procedures governing restorative-justice processes.[54] Its objects are to

- enhance the rights of victims of offences by providing restorative justice as a way of empowering victims to make decisions about how to repair the harm done by offences;[55]
- set up a system of restorative justice that brings together victims, offenders, and their personal supporters in a carefully managed, safe environment;[56]
- ensure that the interests of victims of offences are given high priority in the administration of restorative justice under this Act;[57]
- enable access to restorative justice at every stage of the criminal justice process without substituting for the criminal justice system or changing the normal process of criminal justice;[58]
- and enable agencies that have a role in the criminal justice system to refer offences for restorative justice.[59]

To promote consistency, the aims and principles guiding the exercise of sentencing discretion have been cast in legislative form, although these provisions merely supplement the common law governing sentencing. A common provision directs judges to consider a range of factors, including whether the sentence is "just" and would serve the goals of rehabilitation, deterrence, denunciation, and community protection (although the specific purposes differ between jurisdictions).[60] Other jurisdictions do not expressly identify the aims of sentencing, such as the federal sentencing provisions in the Crimes Act 1914 (Cth), although they do provide a list of factors relevant to the exercise of sentencing discretion.[61]

B. Liability Requirements

The common law adheres to the time-honoured Latin maxim *actus non facit reum, nisi mens sit rea*, which, roughly translated, means "an act does not make a person guilty unless his or her mind is also guilty." According to this approach, behavior is broken down into two parts: the *actus reus* or physical element (which may include an act, an omission, or even a state of affairs) and the *mens rea* or fault element (which may include intention, knowledge, recklessness, or even negligence) that accompanies that physical element.

The precise scope and meaning of these elements varies between common law and codified systems. The importance of these two elements is reflected in chapter 2 of the Model Criminal Code, which proposed the following formulation:

3.1 Elements

(1) An offence consists of physical elements and fault elements.

(2) However, the law that creates the offence may provide that there is no fault element for one or more physical elements.

(3) The law that creates the offence may provide different fault elements for different physical elements.

3.2 Establishing guilt in respect of offences

In order for a person to be found guilty of committing an offence the following must be proved:

(a) the existence of such physical elements as are, under the law creating the offence, relevant to establishing guilt;

(b) in respect of each such physical element for which a fault element is required, one of the fault elements for the physical element.

1. Objective/Actus Reus

i. Act

At common law the physical element of the offence is usually said to comprise an act, an omission, or a state of affairs.[62] A similar approach was proposed in chapter 2 of the Model Criminal Code. As implemented in section 4.1(1) of the Criminal Code (Cth), the physical element of an offence is defined as comprising (a) conduct; or (b) a result of conduct; or (c) a circumstance in which conduct, or a result of conduct, occurs. Under section 4.1(2), "conduct" is given an extended definition that includes an act, an omission to perform an act, or a state of affairs.

At common law there is a requirement that conduct must be voluntary in the sense that it is willed in order to ground criminal responsibility.[63] Accordingly, evidence of automatism will cast doubt on whether the conduct was voluntary and support a verdict of not guilty. The codes have been interpreted in a consistent manner: conduct can be a physical element only if it is voluntary. The Criminal Code (Cth) expressly states that a physical element "must be a product of the will of the person whose conduct it is."[64]

ii. Omission

At common law, reflecting the position in England, there is no liability for an omission in the absence of an express or implied duty to act.[65] Although there is no general duty to prevent a crime or to come to the aid of others, the legislature in some jurisdictions has enacted special statutory duties to provide "necessaries."[66] In the Northern Territory there is a duty to rescue or provide help to a person whose life may be endangered if it is not provided.[67]

The Model Criminal Code proposed the codification assistance of the common law approach, recognizing that an omission liability is exceptional. Section 4.3 of the Criminal Code (Cth) provides that an omission to perform an act can be a physical element only if it is expressly or impliedly provided for by law.

Without further legislative elaboration, the circumstances where "law" implies a duty to perform an act will be determined by the facts of each case.[68] Case law suggests that the duties to perform acts may be implied by statute or the general common law, as well as the legal status or relationship between the parties.[69] Even in the absence of this legal status or relationship, the courts have held that a defendant may voluntarily assume a duty or responsibility to intervene arising from the facts of a particular case.[70]

iii. Status

Criminalizing status, like liability for omissions, is said to be exceptional. However, there are no legislative or constitutional prohibitions of offences that proscribe a state of affairs, or perhaps more precisely, a state of "being" rather than conduct. Many of these offences are minor in nature, relating to being drunk and disorderly in a public place or vagrancy. Although these are usually summary offences, other status offences, such as being "knowingly concerned" in the importation of illicit drugs or being a member of a proscribed terrorist organization, carry a maximum penalty of life imprisonment.[71]

2. Subjective/Mens Rea/Mental Element
i. Intent

Australia strongly subscribes to an orthodox subjectivist approach to fault. The distinguished British judge Lord Irvine of Lairg has remarked that, compared with England, "Australian criminal law has more rigorously followed the subjective path when approaching questions of *mens rea*."[72] His assessment is based largely on the High Court's decision in 1963 not to follow the objective approach to intent taken by the English House of Lords.[73] This strong commitment to subjective models of fault is reflected in the common law presumption that the legislature intended that all offences require proof of intent, although this presumption may be rebutted in certain circumstances.[74] A similar presumption applies in the Model Criminal Code.[75]

The older requirement of "malice" has been removed from most statutes. Where it is retained, the courts interpret the provision as simply requiring proof of recklessness.[76] The Model Criminal Code's approach to intention, which is reflected in the definitions applied in the federal criminal law, has adopted the broader definition of intention that encompasses oblique or indirect intention. Under section 5.2 of the Criminal Code (Cth):

(1) A person has intention with respect to conduct if he or she means to engage in that conduct.

(2) A person has intention with respect to a circumstance if he or she believes that it exists or will exist.

(3) A person has intention with respect to a result if he or she means to bring it about or is aware that it will occur in the ordinary course of events.[77]

In New South Wales the term *malice* has recently been removed from the Crimes Act 1900 (NSW).[78] Motive is distinguished from intention, although some offences incorporate specific motives as part of the fault element.[79] A beneficent motive (e.g., to relieve suffering of a terminal cancer patient) will not negate the defendant's intention to kill and hence liability for murder.[80] The difficulty of determining intention or knowledge was recognized by Justice Kirby in *Peters v The Queen* (1998):

> Absent a comprehensive and reliable confession, it is usually impossible for the prosecution actually to get into the mind of the accused and to demonstrate exactly what it finds was there at the time of the criminal act. Necessarily, therefore, intention must ordinarily be inferred from all of the evidence admitted at the trial. . . . It is a search, by the process of inference from the evidence, to discover the intention which, subjectively, the accused actually had.[81]

ii. Recklessness

Like intention, the definition of recklessness has been refined in the context of murder under the common law.[82] Murder by recklessness requires a high degree of foresight based on the foresight of the probability of death or grievous bodily harm.[83] The Australian Capital Territory, New South Wales, South Australia, Tasmania, and Victoria include recklessness as one of the fault elements for murder by contrast; recklessness is not sufficient for murder under the codes in Queensland, the Northern Territory, and Western Australia.[84] Such a high degree of foresight based on probability is not required for other offences, where recklessness is typically satisfied by foresight of the possibility of particular circumstances existing or results occurring.

The Model Criminal Code proposed that recklessness be defined in terms of awareness of a substantial risk that is known to be unjustifiable. In including a requirement that the risk taking must be "unjustifiable," the Australian drafters have been influenced by the approach adopted in the U.S. Model Penal Code.[85] In relation to both circumstances and results, the defendant must be aware of a substantial risk that the circumstance exists or will exist, or that the result will occur, and that the risk-taking is unjustifiable.[86] Under the federal Criminal Code, if recklessness is a fault element for a physical element of an offence, proof of intention, knowledge, or recklessness will satisfy that fault element.[87]

iii. Negligence

The fault required for negligence is based on the objective standard of the reasonable person.[88] The most serious offence of criminal negligence is manslaughter, which is recognized in all Australian jurisdictions.[89] Negligence under the common law is defined in terms of a great falling short of the standard of care that a reasonable person would have exercised, involving "such a high risk that death or grievous bodily harm would follow that the doing of the act merited criminal punishment."[90] This common law formulation—the *Nydam* test—was incorporated into the Model Criminal Code and now finds statutory expression in the Criminal Code (Cth), section 5.5.

3. Theories of Liability
   i. Inchoate Crimes
      a. Attempt

The common law relating to attempt in Australia was inherited from England and is recognized by statute in most jurisdictions.[91] In all Australian jurisdictions an attempt to commit a crime is a distinct offence. The source of the definition of an attempt, its application, and the penalty imposed vary between Australian jurisdictions. Despite these variations, the actual substances of the common law and statutory definitions are similar. The general trend, following England, has been toward a more flexible, context-dependent formulation of the test of criminal attempt based on the formulation "more than merely preparatory."[92] An influential definition under common law was formulated by Justice Murphy, who held that

> criminal attempt is committed if it is proven that the accused had at all material times the guilty intent to commit a recognized crime and it is proven that at the same time he did an act or acts (which in appropriate circumstances would include omissions) which are seen to be sufficiently proximate to the commission of the said crime and not seen to be merely preparatory to it.[93]

This formulation was adapted for the Model Criminal Code and finds expression in section 11.1 of the federal Criminal Code (Cth). Other jurisdictions have adopted similar formulations based on the "more than merely preparatory" test.[94]

In Australia, as in England, there was considerable controversy over whether factual or physical impossibility constituted a bar to a conviction for criminal attempt following the House of Lords decision in *Haughton v Smith* [1975] AC 476.[95] Except for South Australia, which continues to apply this discredited English decision, it is no longer a bar to a conviction that the offence was physically impossible to complete.[96] This approach to impossibility is reflected in the Model Criminal Code, which finds expression in section 11.1 of the Criminal Code (Cth).[97]

There are, in addition to the provisions dealing with the general doctrine, specific attempt offences such as attempted murder.[98]

b. Conspiracy

All Australian jurisdictions criminalize conspiracy to commit certain crimes as a distinct offence, inheriting the relevant legal principles from England. The common law applies in most jurisdictions, although it is supplemented by legislative provisions in some jurisdictions defining the physical and fault elements, as well as a number of procedural and penalty provisions.[99] Section 11.5(2) of the Criminal Code (Cth) follows the common law definition based on agreement and intention but also elevates the "overt-act" requirement to a physical element of the offence:

(2) For the person to be guilty [of conspiracy]:

 (a) the person must have entered into an agreement with one or more other persons; and

 (b) the person and at least one other party to the agreement must have intended that an offence would be committed pursuant to the agreement; and

 (c) the person or at least one other party to the agreement must have committed an overt act pursuant to the agreement.

The controversial extension of the common law in England in *Shaw v DPP* [1962] AC 220 to include conspiracies to corrupt public morals or outrage public decency (which are not distinct offences) has not been followed by the courts or legislatures in Australia.[100] Conspiracies to defraud and pervert the course of justice, however, are recognized in Australia and are commonly prosecuted.[101]

   ii. Complicity

The law of complicity in Australia is largely a matter of common law. Although statutes in some jurisdictions have defined and clarified the procedural and sentencing rules governing the trial and punishment of accessories,[102] the physical and fault elements of accessory liability, and defences such as withdrawal, have been developed by the courts. The leading case is the High Court decision in *Giorgianni*,[103] in which the court held that aiding, abetting, counselling or procuring required that the defendant must intentionally assist or encourage the commission of an offence by the principal offender, with knowledge of the essential matters that constitute the offence. Recklessness or wilful blindness will not suffice for liability.

The common law has further extended liability of accessories through the doctrine of common purpose (which broadly equates with the doctrine of "joint criminal enterprise" in England). The defendant can be liable for offences committed by others during the course of a common criminal venture. This extends to offences that (a) fall within the contemplation of the parties as a possible incident of the original criminal venture, or (b) are merely foreseen as a possible incident of the original criminal venture. The latter is often called *extended common purpose*. This is a form of "reckless accessoryship" that may be contrasted with the narrower scope of aiding and abetting liability in *Giorgianni* and is justified as a broader form of liability intended to deter group-based or gang-related criminality.[104] There is some variation between the approach taken in the common law and under codes. With the exception of the Northern Territory, which follows the common law approach,[105] the code jurisdictions depart from the common law approach to common purpose. In Queensland, Tasmania, and Western Australia, the codes retain the nineteenth-century approach to criminal fault, adopting an objective test in assessing whether the crime committed by the principal offender was a probable consequence of carrying out the common purpose.[106]

Under the Model Criminal Code, complicity and common purpose have been preserved, although the doctrines have been melded into a single provision. The drafters of the Model Criminal Code intended no fundamental change to common law principles governing accessory liability.[107] The Criminal Code (Cth) provides:

11.2 Complicity and common purpose

   (1) A person who aids, abets, counsels or procures the commission of an offence by another person is taken to have committed that offence and is punishable accordingly.

   (2) For the person to be guilty:

      (a) the person's conduct must have in fact aided, abetted, counselled or procured the commission of the offence by the other person; and

      (b) the offence must have been committed by the other person.

(3) For the person to be guilty, the person must have intended that:
   (a) his or her conduct would aid, abet, counsel or procure the commission of any offence (including its fault elements) of the type the other person committed; or
   (b) his or her conduct would aid, abet, counsel or procure the commission of an offence and have been reckless about the commission of the offence (including its fault elements) that the other person in fact committed.

It is clear from the drafting committee's reports and authoritative commentaries that section 11.2(3)(b) serves as the basis for common purpose.[108] The reformulation was not intended to modify the established common law position that accessory liability is derivative in nature. At the trial of the accessory, there must be proof of the principal's guilt, although there is no requirement to obtain a conviction of the principal before the trial of the accessory (see 11.2(5)).

There is a further related common law doctrine of "acting in concert," which is a form of joint principal liability applying where two or more persons jointly act in the furtherance of an offence. The leading High Court case is *Osland*, which emphasized that concert liability is imposed on the basis that those who act in concert are to be treated as being "causatively jointly responsible for the commission of the crime."[109] Unlike aiding and abetting, liability is primary (as a principal) rather than derivative.

Withdrawal by an accessory may also negate liability. Under the common law test, the scope and basis of withdrawal remain unclear. In some decisions the importance of "timely communication" of the intention to abandon the common purpose was emphasized, with much turning on the facts of the particular case. Thus a direction on withdrawal should emphasize that "where practicable and reasonable it ought to be by communication, verbal or otherwise, that will serve unequivocal notice upon the other party to the common unlawful cause."[110]

The Model Criminal Code has adopted a simplified test based on a crime-prevention rationale. In the Criminal Code (Cth) subsections 11.2(4)(a)–(b) provides that a person cannot be found guilty where he or she terminates his or her involvement and takes all reasonable steps to prevent the commission of the offence.

iii. Corporate Criminal Liability

A corporation is considered a legal person and, as such, may be criminally liable to the same extent as a natural person.[111] Under the common law there appears to be one qualification: a corporation cannot be tried for an offence that can be punished only by imprisonment.[112] In some jurisdictions this qualification has been reversed by statute. For example, section 161(2) of the Legislation Act 2001 (Australian Capital Territory) states that "a provision of law that creates an offence can apply to a corporation even though contravention of the provision is punishable by imprisonment (with or without another penalty)." Section 161(3) then sets out the maximum penalty units that can be ordered by a court against a corporation where the penalty for the offence is a period of imprisonment only.

Under the common law there is some uncertainty about how the fault element is attributed to the corporation. Using principles of vicarious liability, the courts have held corporations liable for the criminal conduct of their employees.[113] An adaption of vicarious liability applied in the English decision *Tesco v Nattrass* [1972] AC 153 has been widely followed in Australia.[114] Under this doctrine, a corporation can be criminally liable if its "directing mind" (typically the board of directors of the corporation) satisfied the requisite fault element. This approach has been subject to extensive academic criticism in Australia. Brent Fisse and John Braithwaite have observed:

> This compromised form of vicarious liability is doubly unsatisfactory because the compromise is struck in a way that makes it difficult to establish corporate criminal liability against large companies. Offences committed on behalf of large concerns are often visible only at the level of middle management whereas the *Tesco* principle requires proof of fault of a top-level manager. By contrast, fault on the part of a top-level manager is much easier to prove in the context of small companies.[115]

A new scheme of corporate criminality has been included in the federal Criminal Code. Section 12.1 confirms that the Code applies to bodies corporate in the same way as to individuals and that a body corporate may be found guilty of any offence, including one punishable by imprisonment. Section 12.2 states that the physical element of an offence may be attributed to a corporation where an employee, agent, or officer committed the physical element while acting within the actual or apparent scope of his or her employment. This is similar to the principle of vicarious liability. But if the relevant offence contains a fault element, section 12.3 requires that intention, knowledge, or recklessness must also be attributed to the corporation.

Departing from the *Tesco* principle, section 12.3(1) states that a fault element will be attributed where the corporation "expressly, tacitly or impliedly authorized or permitted the commission of the offence." Section 12.3(2) then lists four ways in which this authorization or permission may be established:

- proving that the body corporate's board of directors intentionally, knowingly, or recklessly carried out the relevant conduct, or expressly, tacitly, or impliedly authorized or permitted the commission of the offence; or

- proving that a high managerial agent of the body corporate intentionally, knowingly, or recklessly engaged in the relevant conduct, or expressly, tacitly, or impliedly authorized or permitted the commission of the offence; or

- proving that a corporate culture existed within the body corporate that directed, encouraged, tolerated, or led to noncompliance with the relevant provision; or

- proving that the body corporate failed to create and maintain a corporate culture that required compliance with the relevant provision.

4. Causation

The principles governing causation are entirely based on the common law, developed primarily in relation to homicide. Although viewed as a general principle of the criminal law, these doctrines have not been addressed in Australian codifications or consolidation statutes. The Model Criminal Code is surprisingly silent on the meaning of causation, although chapter 2, dealing with the general principles of criminal responsibility, covers other fundamental concepts, such as voluntariness. Although causation is a common element of offences, such as murder and assault, the governing principles tend to reveal themselves only in cases where the defendant adduces some evidence that disputes causation, for example, arguing that there is a *novus actus interveniens* (intervening conduct or external event).

In addition to homicide cases, causation plays a significant role in relation to offences that have dispensed with fault, that is, crimes of strict or absolute liability. In Australia the courts have been prepared to recognize a special common law defence based on "external intervention" for strict and absolute offences. The defence was set out by Chief Justice Bray in *Mayer v Marchant* (1973) 5 SASR 567: "It is a defence to any criminal charge to show that the forbidden conduct occurred as the result of an act of a stranger, or as the result of non-human activity, over which the defendant had no control and against which he or she could not reasonably have been expected to guard."

Causation is a question of fact for the jury.[116] In homicide cases juries are instructed to apply their "common sense" in determining whether a defendant's conduct caused the death of a victim.[117] Although causation is said to be a matter of common sense, it has a distinctive legal meaning, and the courts have developed a number of tests in order to assess whether the conduct caused the requisite result or consequence. These may be broadly defined as the reasonable foreseeability test, the substantial cause test, and the natural consequence test. Each test has found favor at different times, although the preponderance of authority now favors the substantial cause test, but it is not unusual for the courts to refer to these tests interchangeably. What appears clear, however, is that another test, the "but for" test of causation, should not be applied.[118] The law of causation under the common law remains unsettled. As Justice McHugh observed in the leading case dealing with causation in the context of murder: "Judicial and academic efforts to achieve a coherent theory of common law causation have not met with significant success. Perhaps the nature of the subject matter when combined with the lawyer's need to couple issues of factual causation with culpability make achievement of a coherent theory virtually impossible."[119]

C. Defences

1. Types of Defence

Australian common law, like its English counterpart, does not have a refined typology of defences. Academics debate the distinction between justifications and excuses, although the difference has no practical import. It is commonly said that claims of justification negate wrongdoing, whereas in relation to excuses, the defendant's conduct remains wrongful, although liability is not attributed.[120] The distinction is unstable, and as noted in section D below, defences like necessity have been rationalized both as a justification and as an excuse. The Model Criminal Code has not employed this distinction, simply setting out the general defences that apply in "circumstances in which there is no criminal responsibility." The Code groups these defences of general application under the following divisions:

- circumstances involving lack of capacity (age incapacity; mental impairment);
- intoxication;
- circumstances involving mistake or ignorance;
- circumstances involving external factors (which include intervening conduct or event; duress; sudden or extraordinary emergency; self-defence; lawful authority).

Defences that apply to a more limited class of offences are dealt with elsewhere in the Code and in other laws.

2. Burden of Proof

The meaning of the burden of proof is governed by the common law. The most significant burden of proof is the *legal* or *persuasive burden*. In criminal cases, consistent with the position in English law, the general rule is that the prosecution bears the legal burden of proving all the elements of the crime and rebutting any defences to the criminal standard of beyond reasonable doubt.[121] Since the codes of the Northern Territory, Queensland, Tasmania, and Western Australia are silent on the question of burden of proof, it has been held that the common law applies.[122] The codification of these rules by section 13.1 of the Criminal Code (Cth) simply restates the common law position without further elaboration.

There are several exceptions to this rule: where the defence raises evidence of insanity, it bears both the legal and evidential burden of proof to establish that defence on the standard of the balance of probabilities. Parliament may also modify the burden of proof, specifically placing the onus on the defence to raise and prove the existence of exculpatory matters on the balance of probabilities. Under section 13.4 of the Criminal Code (Cth), a burden of proof that a law imposes on the defendant is a legal burden only if the law expressly

(a) specifies that the burden of proof in relation to the matter in question is a legal burden; or

(b) requires the defendant to prove the matter; or

(c) creates a presumption that the matter exists unless the contrary is proved.

D. Justifications

1. Necessity

The defence of necessity involves a claim by the defendant that he or she was compelled to do what he or she did by reason of some extraordinary emergency. Both justification and excuse have been used as rationales for the defence. The accused's behavior in a situation of necessity is not unlawful because the law may be broken to avoid a greater harm than would occur by compliance with it—breaking the law is the lesser evil. This is sometimes referred to as the *greater-good* or *lesser-evil* principle. The common law governs the defence in New South Wales, South Australia, and Victoria. Interestingly, the common law also appears to apply in Tasmania because the Criminal Code (Tas) is silent about the defence, and pursuant to section 8, the common law governing defences continues to apply. The two leading Australian cases on necessity are *R v Davidson* [1969] VR 667 and *R v Loughnan* [1981] VR 443.

In the former case the accused was charged with unlawfully using an instrument to procure a miscarriage. Justice Menhennit stated that the defence of necessity was applicable in determining whether a therapeutic abortion was lawful or unlawful within the meaning of the statutory offence. Menhennit ruled that for the defence to be made out, the accused must have believed on reasonable grounds that his actions were necessary to preserve the woman from serious danger to her life or her physical or mental health and that they were not out of proportion to the danger to be averted. Although *Davidson* is only a trial ruling at first instance, it continues to provide the lawful basis for performing an abortion in Australia, which remains an offence in all but one jurisdiction.[123]

In the *Loughnan* case the accused was charged with escaping from prison. He raised the issue of necessity, claiming that he had committed the offence to avoid being killed by his fellow prisoners. The Victorian Full Court, consisting of Chief Justice Young, Justice King, and Justice Crockett, was prepared to recognize a defence of necessity but held that it had not been made out on the facts. In *R v Loughnan* [1981] VR 443 Young and King summarized (at 448) the elements of the defence of necessity as follows:

- the criminal conduct must have been done only in order to avoid certain consequences which would have inflicted irreparable evil upon the accused or upon others whom he was bound to protect;
- the defendant must honestly believe on reasonable grounds that he or she was placed in a situation of imminent peril;
- the conduct of the defendant must not be out of proportion to the peril to be avoided.

In other jurisdictions the claim of necessity is subsumed under a defence of sudden or extraordinary emergency.[124] Although this defence is formulated differently, its core concepts substantially mirror the common law defence. This approach has been favored by the drafters of the Model Criminal Code, formulating in place of necessity a defence of sudden or extraordinary emergency that is available in relation to all offences, including homicide.[125] Under section 10.3(2) of the Criminal Code (Cth), the defence applies if the following conditions are satisfied: the defendant reasonably believed that first, circumstances of sudden or extraordinary emergency existed; second, committing the offence was the only reasonable way to deal with the emergency; and third, the conduct was a reasonable response to the emergency. The term *sudden or extraordinary emergency* is not further defined. Unlike the common law defence of necessity, which restricts the defences to murder cases, there appear to be no restrictions on the availability of the defence of sudden or extraordinary emergency.[126]

All jurisdictions impose an objective standard in relation to necessity. Under the common law the accused's response to the situation of imminent peril is measured against the reaction of a reasonable or ordinary person in the position of the accused. Section 33 of the Criminal Code (N.T.) expressly refers to "an ordinary person similarly circumstanced." Section 10.3 of the Criminal Code (Cth) and section 41 of the Criminal Code (ACT) avoid any mention of an ordinary person test by requiring that the accused reasonably believed that his or her conduct was a reasonable response to the emergency. As with the defence of duress, the accused bears the evidential burden in relation to necessity, while the legal burden is placed on the prosecution to negate any evidence of necessity beyond reasonable doubt.

2. Self-Defence

The definition of self-defence varies across Australian jurisdictions. The defence of self-defence is available to crimes involving the use of or threat of force to the person, such as murder and assault, and it results in a complete acquittal. It may also be raised in relation to the protection of personal property, although this is more restricted, especially under the codes. The leading High Court decision dealing with self-defence under the common law is *Zecevic v DPP (Vic)* (1987), in which Justices Wilson, Dawson, and Toohey set out the requirements for self-defence as follows:

> The question to be asked in the end is quite simple. It is whether the accused believed upon reasonable grounds that it was necessary in self-defence to do what he did. If he had that belief and there were reasonable grounds for it, or if the jury is left in reasonable doubt about the matter, then he is entitled to an acquittal. Stated in this form, the question is one of general application and is not limited to cases of homicide.[127]

This case significantly subsumed within the test of reasonableness the previously separate elements of the defence relating to proportionality, the unlawfulness of the attack, and the duty to retreat. After *Zecevic*, these are merely evidential factors relevant to determining whether the defendant believed on reasonable grounds that it was necessary to do what he or she did.

Section 10.4(2) of the Criminal Code (Cth) contains a simplified test that also contains these two requirements:

10.4 Self-defence

(1) A person is not criminally responsible for an offence if he or she carries out the conduct constituting the offence in self-defence.

(2) A person carries out conduct in self-defence if and only if he or she believes the conduct is necessary:

   (a) to defend himself or herself or another person; or

   (b) to prevent or terminate the unlawful imprisonment of himself or herself or another person; or

   (c) to protect property from unlawful appropriation, destruction, damage or interference; or

   (d) to prevent criminal trespass to any land or premises; or

(e) to remove from any land or premises a person who is committing criminal trespass;

and the conduct is a reasonable response in the circumstances as he or she perceives them.

This simplified version of the test of self-defence has been mirrored in the legislative provisions of the Australian Capital Territory and the Northern Territory.[128] Although New South Wales law is generally not codified, in 2001 the Crimes Act 1900 (NSW) was amended, applying the codified defence included in the Model Criminal Code. Under section 418 of the Crimes Act 1900 (NSW), a person carries out conduct in self-defence if

- the person believes the conduct is necessary to defend himself or herself or another person; and
- the conduct is a reasonable response in the circumstances as he or she perceives them.

The older formulations of the defence in the Queensland and Western Australian criminal codes contain the core element of "reasonable necessity" with additional rules that outline the limits of permissible force. The Criminal Code Act (Cth) follows the Queensland and Western Australian approach and excludes self-defence in cases where the defendant is responding to lawful conduct and he or she knew that the conduct was lawful.[129]

The most significant limitation to the scope of self-defence under the Model Criminal Code relates to the use of force to protect property. Under section 10.4(3) of the Criminal Code Act (Cth), the defence does not apply where the defendant uses force that involves the intentional infliction of death or really serious injury

(a) to protect property; or

(b) to prevent criminal trespass; or

(c) to remove a person who is committing criminal trespass.

For almost a decade between 1978 and 1987, the common law of Australia recognized a partial defence of excessive force in self-defence, which operated to reduce the verdict of murder to manslaughter in cases where the force used was disproportionate or excessive.[130] Because of the complexity of the jury directions, the majority of the High Court reversed its position and abolished the defence in *Viro* in *Zecevic v DPP* (1987) 162 CLR 645.[131]

The legislatures in New South Wales, Victoria, and South Australia have since reintroduced excessive self-defence as a defence to murder.[132] The Model Criminal Code recommended against the inclusion of excessive self-defence, and the Criminal Code (Cth) does not contain such a provision.[133]

3. Consent

Consent is not a defence of general application in the common law or under the codes in Australia. In relation to specific offences, however, such as assault or rape, consent negates liability. This is not because consent is a defence strictly speaking, but rather that lack of consent must be proved as an element of the offence. Thus consent to a common assault renders the act lawful.[134] This element of non-consent is inherent in the notion of assault and rape. The common law and the codes reflect the general principle that consent, subject to some qualification, negates liability for offences against the person. The Supreme Court of Queensland commented in *Schloss v Maguire* (1897) 89 LJ 21: "[T]he term assault of itself involves the notion of want of consent. An assault with consent is not an assault at all."[135] Consent may be express or implied.[136] It must be freely given and must not be induced by fraud, force or threats.[137] The situation in relation to aggravated assaults, such as assault occasioning actual bodily harm, differs quite markedly from consent as it relates to common assault. A number of English cases set out the general rule that a victim cannot consent to activities that are intended to cause, or will probably cause, him or her actual bodily harm unless it is in the public interest (relating to well-established categories, such as lawful sports and reasonable surgical interference).[138] There are no decisions in Australian common law jurisdictions directly addressing these public interest limitations on consent. In *Lergesner v Carroll* (1989) 49 A Crim R 51 the Queensland Court of Criminal Appeal held that consent may negate liability for assault occasioning actual bodily harm. It has been argued that in Queensland, because of formulation in the Criminal Code (Qld), the public interest limitations to consent apply only to acts involving the infliction (or likely infliction) of serious injury or grievous bodily harm.[139]

The law relating to consent in the context of sexual offences has been extensively reformed and is discussed in section III in this chapter.

4. Superior Orders

The common law does not recognize superior orders as a justification or excuse. The federal statutory defence of superior orders contained in section 268.116 of the Criminal Code (Cth) is discussed in section II.E.6 in this chapter.

E. Excuses

1. Mistake/Ignorance of Law or Fact

The defence of honest and reasonable mistake of fact is sometimes referred to as the *Proudman v Dayman* defence.[140] The defence applies to offences of strict liability in which criminal responsibility may be established by proof of the physical element alone. Where the crime is one requiring proof of fault, consistent with the principle applied in *DPP v Morgan*,[141] the mistake need only be genuine or honest rather than reasonable.

Justice Dixon in *Proudman v Dayman* (1941) 67 CLR 536 framed the defence as follows: "As a general rule an honest and reasonable belief in a state of facts which, if they existed, would make the defendant's act innocent affords an excuse for doing what would otherwise be an offence".[142]

To negate liability, the mistake must be one of fact and not of law.[143] The defence remains available in cases of "mixed" mistakes of fact and law.[144] This common law position that a mistake of law, or indeed ignorance of law, affords no excuse is reflected in the Criminal Code (Cth).[145]

A mistake of law occurs where the defendant is mistaken about the legal effect or legal significance of facts known to him or her,[146] or where the mistaken person believed that the act in question was lawful either because it was unregulated or because the requirements of law had been satisfied.[147] The High Court has confirmed that reliance on official advice does not convert a mistake of law into one of fact.[148]

The proposition that ignorance or mistake of law is no excuse is deceptive in its simplicity because there are many other defences that permit mistaken beliefs in the legality of the defendant's actions to excuse wrongdoing. These defences include the claim of right, due diligence, and lawful excuse.[149]

In code jurisdictions the defence of mistake of fact is now governed by legislation. Although there are some differences, there is a high degree of convergence between common law and code jurisdictions.[150] In the Australian Capital Territory and Tasmania the defence is available only where no offence would have been committed on the facts as they were believed to be (which is similar to the position at common law). In the Northern Territory, Queensland and Western Australia, however, the defence is broader in enabling a mistaken belief to lead to a conviction for a lesser offence or even an acquittal. In these jurisdictions, if an accused honestly and reasonably believed in facts that would render him or her guilty of a lesser offence or liable to a lower penalty, then he or she can be convicted of that lesser offence or given a lower penalty.

The *Model Criminal Code, Chapters 1 and 2: General Principles of Criminal Responsibility Final Report* (1992) proposed the retention of the *Proudman* defence in relation to strict liability offences. This recommendation was subsequently transposed into section 9.2 of the Criminal Code (Cth):

(1) A person is not criminally responsible for an offence that has a physical element for which there is no fault element if:

   (a) at or before the time of the conduct constituting the physical element, the person considered whether or not facts existed, and is under a mistaken but reasonable belief about those facts; and

   (b) had those facts existed, the conduct would not have constituted an offence.

(2) A person may be regarded as having considered whether or not facts existed if:

   (a) he or she had considered, on a previous occasion, whether those facts existed in the circumstances surrounding that occasion; and

   (b) he or she honestly and reasonably believed that the circumstances surrounding the present occasion were the same, or substantially the same, as those surrounding the previous occasion.

2. Insanity/Diminished Capacity

Australian law bases its defence of insanity or mental impairment on English law as reflected in the *M'Naghten* rules (1843).[151] This test requires the defence to prove on the balance of probabilities that at the time a crime was committed the defendant was acting under the influence of a disease of the mind that made him or her incapable of knowing that the act was wrong. Insanity has been reformulated into a statutory defence in all jurisdictions, although these defences of mental impairment nevertheless reflect the core elements of the *M'Naghten* rules, including the exceptional reversal of the burden of proof.[152]

The term *disease of the mind* means mental illness in the modern law. In *R v Radford* (1985) Chief Justice King of the Supreme Court of South Australia stated:

> The expression "disease of the mind" is synonymous, in my view, with "mental illness." . . . The essential notion appears to be that in order to constitute insanity in the eyes of the law, the malfunction of the mental faculties called "defect of reason" in the *M'Naghten rules*, must result from an underlying pathological infirmity of the mind, be it of long or short duration and be it permanent or temporary, which can be properly termed mental illness, as distinct from the reaction of a healthy mind to extraordinary external stimuli.[153]

This definition has been influential in the code jurisdictions.[154] However, the definitions are not identical. The criminal codes of the Australian Commonwealth and the Australian Capital Territory include "severe personality disorder" within their definitions of mental impairment.[155] However, its inclusion is controversial, and it has been omitted from the definition of mental impairment in the Northern Territory and South Australia.[156]

There are two aspects of the knowledge element in the *M'Naghten* rules: not knowing the "nature and quality" of the act one has done, and not knowing that it was wrong. Justice Dixon offered a trial direction on insanity in *R v Porter* (1933) that was widely followed, especially in relation to the meaning of wrong: "What is meant by 'wrong'? What is meant by wrong is wrong having regard to the everyday standards of reasonable people."[157] This approach has been followed in the statutory formulations of the defence.[158]

The *M'Naghten* rules referred to a "defect of reason" arising from a "disease of the mind," and this formulation is still followed in the New South Wales defence of mental illness. In Queensland and Tasmania the term *mental disease* is used. Some jurisdictions have reformulated the test into a new defence of "mental impairment," following the recommendations of the Model Criminal Code.[159] For example, under the Criminal Code (Cth), the defence is defined as follows:

7.3 Mental impairment

(1) A person is not criminally responsible for an offence if, at the time of carrying out the conduct constituting the offence, the person was suffering from a mental impairment that had the effect that:

(a) the person did not know the nature and quality of the conduct; or

(b) the person did not know that the conduct was wrong (that is, the person could not reason with a moderate degree of sense and composure about whether the conduct, as perceived by reasonable people, was wrong); or

(c) the person was unable to control the conduct.

(2) The question whether the person was suffering from a mental impairment is one of fact.

(3) A person is presumed not to have been suffering from such a mental impairment. The presumption is only displaced if it is proved on the balance of probabilities (by the prosecution or the defence) that the person was suffering from such a mental impairment.

A special verdict of not guilty by reason of insanity or mental impairment renders the defendant liable to indefinite preventive detention in a secure psychiatric facility, although in the modern law there is a wider range of dispositional options, including supervision orders.

Pleas of insanity have become less significant in Australia since the abolition of the death penalty for murder cases and the availability of other avenues for the defence raising mental impairment at trial. There is a presumption of mental capacity in the common law that the accused acted pursuant to an exercise of will.[160] By claiming non-insane automatism, the defence may cast sufficient doubt on whether the conduct was willed or voluntary to justify an acquittal—states of automatism have been induced by consumption of drugs, sleep disorders, epilepsy, concussion, and dissociation arising from acute stress.[161]

All jurisdictions except Victoria and New South Wales also include a further element for mental impairment relating to the capacity to control the defendant's conduct or actions. The Model Criminal Code has also included a "volitional" component in its model defence, and this is reflected in the defence of mental impairment included in 5.7.3 of the Criminal Code (Cth).[162]

3. Intoxication

Intoxication is not, strictly speaking, a defence in Australian law. However, under the common law, the High Court in *R v O'Connor* (1980) held that evidence of intoxication (whether self-induced or not) may be adduced in order to negate the elements of a crime—casting doubt on the existence of the requisite *mens rea* or, in cases of extreme intoxication, the voluntariness of the conduct.[163] The High Court rejected the established English approach, which held that self-induced intoxication may not be raised to exculpate the defendant except in relation to crimes of "specific intent."[164] The English approach, nevertheless, continues to apply in the codes of Queensland, Tasmania, and Western Australia.[165] *O'Connor* remains the law in Victoria.

The drafters of the Model Criminal Code recommended that the approach in *O'Connor* be followed, viewing the division of crimes into those where intoxication is relevant (so-called crimes of specific intent) and those where it is irrelevant (so-called crimes of basic intent) as unprincipled and unworkable.[166] Notwithstanding academic support for *O'Connor* and the absence of evidence that it operated as a "Drunks' Charter,"[167] the legislative trend is firmly against the common law. Section 8.2 of the Criminal Code (Cth) departed from *O'Connor*, providing that self-induced intoxication "cannot be considered in determining whether a fault element of basic intent existed."[168] Evidence of self-induced intoxication may, however, be relevant to the defence of mistake and to determining whether the defendant was mistaken in his or her belief about facts. It also clarified the relevance of intoxication to defences: for defences based on actual knowledge or belief, evidence of intoxication may be considered in determining whether that knowledge or belief existed; and for defences based on reasonable belief, in determining whether that reasonable belief existed, regard must be had to the standard of a reasonable person who is not intoxicated.[169] The Code clarified that in relation to crimes of negligence, the standard of a reasonable person to be applied is that of one who is not intoxicated.[170]

In New South Wales the common law was expressly abolished in 1996. Part 11A was inserted into the Crimes Act 1900 (NSW) and constitutes a mini-code on intoxication. The key provision states that self-induced intoxication may be taken into account only in relation to whether the accused "had the intention to cause the specific result necessary for an offence of specific intent."[171] To assist with offence classification, the Crimes Act 1900 (NSW) diverges from the Criminal Code (Cth) by including a non-exhaustive list of offences as examples of offences of specific intent to which Part 11A applies.[172]

In South Australia the common law has not been expressly abolished. However, changes in 2004 significantly reformed the relevance of intoxication. Where the defendant's "consciousness was (or may have been) impaired by such intoxication to the degree of criminal irresponsibility," in a number of situations the guilt of the defendant is to be "presumed," with consciousness expressly defined as including volition, intention, knowledge, or any other mental state or function relevant to criminal liability.[173] The first presumption reflects the common law position in situations involving "Dutch Courage" cases, where the defendant formed an intention to commit the offence before becoming intoxicated and consumed intoxicants in order to strengthen his or her resolve to commit the offence.[174] The second presumption restricts the relevance of self-induced intoxication generally except where the offence involves foresight by the accused of the consequences of his or her conduct, or an awareness of certain circumstances surrounding his or her conduct.[175] These in effect limit the relevance of intoxication to crimes of specific intent, although this terminology is not used.

4. Duress

The defence of duress operates to excuse a defendant who has committed an offence under a threat of physical harm to himself or herself or to some other person should he or she refuse to comply with the threatener's command.[176] The defence is recognized by the common law in New South Wales, South Australia, and Victoria. The statutory provisions at the federal level and in the Australian Capital Territory and the codes of the Northern Territory, Queensland, Tasmania, and Western Australia largely reflect the common law, albeit with modifications.[177] The crux of the defence is a threat, and as a result, it has not been extended by case-law development or statute to include "duress of circumstances." In Australia, crime induced by exigent circumstances may fall within the defence of necessity, or statutory equivalents, such as sudden or extraordinary emergency (discussed above).

Duress operates as a complete defence. However, there are some limitations on its availability. Under the common law it is not available as a defence to murder and attempted murder, following the English position.[178] The code jurisdictions extend this limitation to other crimes, such as piracy, treason, rape, abduction, robbery, and crimes involving an intention to cause grievous bodily harm.[179] In the Northern Territory the Code adopts the "halfway house" of recognizing that duress in relation to murder operates as a partial defence, reducing liability to manslaughter.[180] The drafters of the Model Criminal Code rejected these policy restrictions on the defence. As a consequence, there are no limits on the availability of duress in the Criminal Code (Cth) and the Australian Capital Territory.[181] The Criminal Code (Cth) defines the defence as follows:

10.2 Duress

(1) A person is not criminally responsible for an offence if he or she carries out the conduct constituting the offence under duress.

(2) A person carries out conduct under duress if and only if he or she reasonably believes that:

(a) a threat has been made that will be carried out unless an offence is committed; and

(b) there is no reasonable way that the threat can be rendered ineffective; and

(c) the conduct is a reasonable response to the threat.

(3) This section does not apply if the threat is made by or on behalf of a person with whom the person under duress is voluntarily associating for the purpose of carrying out conduct of the kind actually carried out.

5. Entrapment

Unlike the position in the United States, where entrapment by state officials bears on the guilt of the accused, Australian courts and legislatures have refused to recognize entrapment as a substantive criminal defence.[182] Police incitement of criminality may, however, trigger judicial discretion to exclude evidence on the grounds of illegality or impropriety or, in extreme cases, may warrant a stay of proceedings on the grounds of an abuse of process.[183] Because there is no general public-interest defence or immunity under the common law that permits the police to break the law in order to enforce it, legislation has been enacted in most jurisdictions to regulate and confer legal immunity for approved controlled operations.[184] Under these laws, law-enforcement and customs officials and civilians (informers) are granted a conditional authorization to engage in the commission of offences, including drug-related ones, and other serious offences. Beyond this legislative scheme, there are judicial dicta, albeit obiter, suggesting that possession and supply of drugs by law-enforcement officials as part of a controlled delivery may fall within the statutory defence of "reasonable excuse" (which has been built into the offence definition of various drug-trafficking offences).[185]

6. Superior Orders

The High Court of Australia confirmed in *A v Hayden (No. 2)* (1984) 156 CLR 532 that there is no defence of superior orders recognized in the common law. The defence of superior orders will always be contentious because of its association with the notorious "Nuremberg" defence. However, most military law systems have allowed some version of this defence provided that the order is not "manifestly unlawful."[186] The Criminal Code (Cth) contains a specific defence of superior orders. The provision expressly precludes this defence for genocide and crimes against humanity (where conceptually it is not a justification). With respect to war crimes, section 268.116(3) provides:

> It is a defence to a war crime that:
>
> (a) the war crime was committed by a person pursuant to an order of a Government or of a superior, whether military or civilian; and
>
> (b) the person was under a legal obligation to obey the order, and
>
> (c) the person did not know that the order was unlawful; and
>
> (d) the order was not manifestly unlawful.

There are also some superior-order-type defences that apply in specific contexts and may be relied on by Australian Defence Force personnel who are subject to orders under a chain of command to use force (including lethal force) to protect critical infrastructure under Part IIIAAA of the Defence Act 1903 (Cth). The reforms have been described as "a hybrid defence melding elements of superior orders, lawful authority and necessity."[187]

The only jurisdiction to adopt a general defence of superior orders was Western Australia. The defence of superior orders was remodeled into a defence of "lawful authority" in the Criminal Code (WA) in 2008, although this change did not alter its essential elements:

> 31. Lawful Authority
>
> (1) A person is not criminally responsible for an act done, or an omission made, in any of the following circumstances—
>
> (a) in execution of the law;
>
> (b) in obedience to the order of a competent authority which the person is bound by law to obey, unless the order is manifestly unlawful.
>
> (2) Whether an order is or is not manifestly unlawful is a question of law.

The Model Criminal Code Committee rejected both the defences of entrapment and superior orders.[188] However, the defence of lawful authority, which is recognized under the Criminal Code (Cth), may be applicable in cases where a general superior order type defence would otherwise have been available. Section 10.5 ("Lawful Authority") of the Criminal Code (Cth) provides that "[a] person is not criminally responsible for an offence if the conduct constituting the offence is justified or excused by or under a law."

F. Sanctions

1. Punishment

Punishment is a matter of state, territory, and federal law. A significant limitation applies to federal prisoners who are held in state and territory prisons. This arises from section 120 of the Australian Constitution, which states: "Every State shall make provision for the detention in its prisons of persons accused or convicted of offences against the laws of the Commonwealth." This section imposes an obligation on the states to accommodate federal prisoners and those accused of crimes against the Commonwealth.[189]

The Australian Constitution vests the judicial power of the Commonwealth in the High Court, in such other federal courts as the Australian Parliament creates, and in such other courts as it invests with federal jurisdiction. Section 77(iii) provides that the Australian Parliament may make laws investing state courts with federal jurisdiction. Specific provision is made under section 68(2) of the Judiciary Act 1903 (Cth) for the exercise of federal criminal jurisdiction by state and territory courts. Sections 68(1) and 79 of the Judiciary Act pick up and apply state and territory procedural laws to federal prosecutions in state and territory courts. In such cases, although the substantive criminal law applied is federal, state and territory procedural laws apply to the sentencing of federal offenders. This gives rise to potential differences in the way in which federal offenders are treated around Australia.[190] The High Court has held that the administration of federal criminal law on a state-by-state basis is valid even though this gives rise to significant differences in the procedures applying to the adjudication of federal offences.[191]

Federal offences typically provide for only two types of sentencing options: fines and imprisonment. A much wider range of options is available at state and territory levels, including community-service orders, periodic detention, and home detention. These procedural options are also picked up and applied in the sentencing of federal offenders. It should be noted that efforts are being made to achieve greater consistency in federal sentencing with the launch of a Commonwealth Sentencing Database for use by judicial officers in 2008. As the Australian Law Reform Commission notes, the number of federal prisoners is relatively small—there were only 672 federal prisoners in custody on 1 March 2006, or less than 3 percent of the total Australian prison population.[192]

2. Quantity/Quality of Punishment

The nature and purpose of sentencing depend on the offender and the offence. Under the common law, general deterrence is accorded less weight when sentencing an offender with a mental illness or intellectual disability, and rehabilitation should be accorded more weight when sentencing a young offender. Identifying one purpose of sentencing or mandating a hierarchy in which the purposes should be considered is an unnecessary fetter on judicial discretion. The High Court emphasized in *Veen v R (No 2)* (1988):

> [S]entencing is not a purely logical exercise, and the troublesome nature of the sentencing discretion arises in large measure from unavoidable difficulty in giving weight to each of the purposes of punishment. The purposes of criminal punishment are various: protection of society, deterrence of the offender and of others who might be tempted to offend, retribution and reform. The purposes overlap and none of them can be considered in isolation from the others when determining what is an appropriate sentence in a particular case. They are guideposts to the appropriate sentence but sometimes they point in different directions.[193]

As noted above, the objects or purposes of sentencing have been placed on a statutory footing in some jurisdictions, although these lists are non-exhaustive.[194]

3. Death Penalty

Capital punishment has been abolished in Australia at state, territory, and Commonwealth levels.[195] Most jurisdictions abolished the death penalty for murder in the 1970s, although it remained available for treason and piracy until the 1980s in some jurisdictions.[196]

III. SPECIAL PART

A. Structure

The criminal law in Australia covers a vast terrain, from serious offences against the person, like homicide, to minor regulatory offences. The more serious offences are contained in the criminal codes or equivalent consolidated criminal statutes in non-code jurisdictions. It is important to recognize that offence provisions and penalties are used to promote compliance in many fields of regulation at state, territory and federal levels.[197] Indeed, it is sometimes difficult to maintain a clear distinction between the civil and the criminal law because there is a range of hybrid provisions that are not strictly "criminal" in terms of requiring a verdict of guilt following a criminal trial but nevertheless may impose a pecuniary penalty.[198] For example, civil penalty provisions in the Corporations Act (Cth) apply to breaches of account-keeping duties and directors' duties. The question of characterization is simply a matter for the legislature, although there are now federal guidelines to assist policy makers in determining how particular regulatory provisions should be framed.[199]

The older common law distinction between offences of treason, felony, and misdemeanor, graded in terms of severity, has been abolished in the Australian Capital Territory, South Australia, Victoria and New South Wales.[200] The code systems did not adopt this tripartite classification. In the Commonwealth, the Australian Capital Territory, Tasmania, and Victoria, crimes are referred to simply as "indictable offences" and "summary offences."[201] The codes simply divide offences into categories: crimes, misdemeanors, and simple offences (and regulatory offences in Western Australia).[202] These distinctions are relevant only to determining the mode of trial, and there is no consistent approach to the classification of specific offences.

After the general part, outlining the principles of responsibility, the Criminal Code (Qld) distributes the specific offences across five parts: offences against public order; offences against the administration of law and justice; acts injurious to the public in general; offences against the person and relating to marriage (which include sexual offences); and offences relating to property and contract. This structure reflects nineteenth-century perspectives on the interests requiring protection by the criminal law: sexual offences are grouped under marriage and family crimes, and computer offences are grouped under property crimes. The consolidated criminal statutes adopted in some states similarly reflect these nineteenth-century perspectives on the hierarchy of crimes; for example, the New South Wales legislation divides the offences into parts (although these have been amended and added to over time): offences against the sovereign; offences against the person; offences relating to public order; offences relating to property; offences relating to transport services; offences relating to corruption; offences relating to blackmail and to forgery; computer offences; offences relating to escape from lawful custody; terrorism; and public justice offences. The parts are not ranked in terms of seriousness.

A different approach to categorization has been adopted in the Model Criminal Code, which has been influential in the drafting of the federal Criminal Code (Cth). The inclusion of chapters on serious drug offences and the grouping of computer offences with criminal damage offences reflect a different conceptualization of the interest being protected.[203] The recognition of crimes against humanity and extraterritorial war crimes reflects the increasing reach and diversity of functions performed by the modern criminal law in Australia.

B. Homicide

1. Murder/Manslaughter

Murder is largely a matter of state and territory law. As noted above, the Federal Parliament cannot enact a law of homicide of general application. However, there are distinct federal homicide provisions in the Criminal Code (Cth). It is an offence to murder a "UN or associated person" under section 71.2. There is also an extraterritorial murder offence called "harming Australians," enacted in the aftermath of the Bali bombings in 2002. This extraordinary retrospective offence makes it an offence to murder an Australian citizen or resident overseas (see section III.F in this chapter).

Murder is governed by common law in Victoria and South Australia. Elsewhere, the elements of the offence have been enacted into statutory form. However, there is considerable diversity in the approaches to defining the fault elements for murder, even in the code jurisdictions. Key differences relate to whether the fault element for murder extends beyond intention to include recklessness, and also to the scope of that concept. In code jurisdictions the offence of murder is limited to intention (to cause death or grievous bodily harm). However, even in these jurisdictions there remains speculation about how broadly intention may be defined.[204]

The common law of murder in Australia is broader than its English counterpart in a number of respects. First, the offence is not limited to intention to kill or inflict grievous bodily harm. The High Court held unanimously in *Crabbe* (1985) that the fault element extends to foresight of probability of death, a subjective mental state that is commonly described as recklessness:

> If an accused knows when he does an act that death or grievous bodily harm is a probable consequence, he does the act expecting that death or grievous bodily harm will be the likely result, for the word "probable" means likely to happen. That state of mind is comparable with an intention to kill or to do grievous bodily harm. . . . [A] person who, without lawful justification or excuse, does an act knowing that it is probable that death or grievous bodily harm will result, is guilty of murder if death in fact results.[205]

However, the High Court in *Crabbe* held that the fault element did not extend further to willful blindness to the possibility that conduct might cause death. New South Wales has enacted a similar form of reckless murder. Under section 18 of the Crimes Act 1900 (NSW), the fault element is also satisfied by "reckless indifference to human life," a term that has been judicially defined more narrowly than under the common law as foresight of probability of death only, not grievous bodily harm.[206]

The other distinctive feature of the law of murder in Australia is the preservation of the felony-murder rule—a form of constructive murder—in most jurisdictions. It should be noted that felony murder was abolished more than fifty years ago by the United Kingdom Parliament, and twenty years ago it was declared by the Canadian Supreme Court to be in violation of the principle of "fundamental justice" in the Canadian Charter of Rights and Fundamental Freedoms.[207] A typical offence formulation is section 18 of the Crimes Act 1900 (NSW), which defines murder as including causing death, inter alia, "done in an attempt to commit, or during or immediately after the commission, by the accused, or some accomplice with him or her, of a crime punishable by imprisonment for life or for 25 years." Although this form of constructive liability is roundly criticized by academics, the arguments in favor of its retention, based on public policy and deterrence, have prevailed in Australia.[208]

2. Provocation

The defence of provocation, under the common law and in statutory form, reduces the charge from murder to manslaughter.[209] Although the formulations vary, the High Court has consistently emphasized that there is a large degree of conformity in the law of provocation, whether it be common law or statutory.[210] In both academic and policy circles the trend has been firmly against provocation. Responding to these criticisms, the High Court in the 1990s modernized the defence, abolishing some of the restrictive elements of the defence that had limited its availability in cases where gender or cultural background was a significant factor.[211] In 1998 the Model Criminal Code Officers Committee recommended that the defence of provocation be abolished on the ground that the defence was gender biased, concluding that it was more appropriate for the differences in culpability between types of homicide to be reflected in the sentencing process. The defence attracted controversy when the High Court held that persistent homosexual advances could amount to provocative conduct.[212] To address the problematic use of provocation in such cases,[213] some jurisdictions have enacted provisions to exclude nonviolent sexual advances from forming the basis of the defence.[214] In 2003 Tasmania became the first Australian jurisdiction to abolish the defence of provocation, followed by Victoria in 2005.[215]

C. Sex Offences

The law governing sexual offences has been extensively modified by statute in Australia.[216] There are several distinctive features of rape and sexual assault law. Some of the code jurisdictions construe rape as a crime of strict liability, in which the defendant may raise a mistaken belief in consent as a defence provided that it is honest and reasonable.[217] The common law jurisdictions follow the approach of the English House of Lords in *Morgan*, where proof of intent or recklessness will be negated by an honest (albeit unreasonable) belief in consent.[218]

Reform of the *mens rea* for rape has not been a primary concern in Australia. Rather, law reform efforts have focused on redefining consent as "free agreement" and identifying the specific circumstances where consent may be negated. Section 5.2.3(2) of the Model Criminal Code contains a list of examples where there is no consent, including, for example, where the person submits to the act because of force or the fear of force or because the person is unlawfully detained and where the person is asleep or unconscious or is so affected by alcohol or another drug as to be incapable of consenting.

In many jurisdictions, following extensive law reform and community consultation, the discriminatory rules of evidence have been abolished or repealed, with modification to the rules relating to corroboration, past sexual history, and recent complaint.[219] The marital rape immunity was rejected as part of the common law of Australia by the High Court in 1992, reflecting the legislative trend firmly in favor of repeal in the preceding decades.[220]

There is an extensive range of related sexual offences, dealing with incest, sexual intercourse with minors, and persons with mental impairment, as well as sexual indecency.[221] Reforms to homosexual offences are discussed in section III.E in this chapter.

D. Theft and Fraud

The law of theft is statutory in all jurisdictions. The traditional terminology of larceny has been abandoned in all jurisdictions except New South Wales, which continues to apply the common law definition. To avoid the complexity and modernize the terminology, the Theft Act model from the United Kingdom has been adopted either in whole or in part in most Australian jurisdictions.[222] Unlike larceny, the emphasis is on a core offence of theft or stealing that requires the dishonest appropriation of property belonging to another with an intention to permanently deprive. The offence functions as a mini-code in these jurisdictions, although these provisions have generated their own extensive case law and commentary, particularly in relation to the interpretation of key definitions such as dishonesty. The offence of theft is distinguished from fraud offences, such as obtaining property or services by deception. There are a number of specific offences dealing with credit-card and identify theft fraud to address the difficulties straining the offence to cover deceptions directed to machines.[223]

E. "Victimless" Crimes

The concept of "victimless" crime is not a formal legal category used to determine whether behavior should be criminalized. Indeed, the modern criminal law in Australia, as elsewhere, is used extensively to regulate behavior that presents little or no identifiable risk to others (or, indeed, the defendant). Self-harming behavior (such as recreational drug use) and consensual sex between a sex worker and a client have been criminalized in many jurisdictions in Australia. However, there have been reforms to these areas, with many jurisdictions decriminalizing or legalizing such behavior. Significantly, the case for reform in the fields of recreational drug use and sex work has been motivated primarily by public policy concerns (for example, recognition that criminalization contributes to the spread of HIV infection and other lethal diseases).

In the field of consensual sexual relations, homosexual conduct between adult males in private was historically criminalized by offences of sodomy, acts of gross indecency between consenting adult males, and indecency offences. From the 1970s onward, this position was modified in many jurisdictions in Australia. By the early 1990s only two jurisdictions, Tasmania and Western Australia, continued to maintain (though not enforce) these "homosexual" offences. In *Toonen v Australia* (1994) 1 PLPR 50, the compatibility of these laws with the right to privacy under the International Covenant on Civil and Political Rights (ICCPR) was challenged. The United Nations Human Rights Committee held that the existence of these offences violated the rights of privacy protected under article 17 of the ICCPR, largely following the approach taken by the European Court of Human Rights.[224] The subsequent failure to immediately repeal these laws in Tasmania led the Federal Parliament, relying on its external-affairs power under the constitution, to enact a right to privacy in relation to sexual conduct for adults. The Human Rights (Sexual Conduct) Act 1994 (Cth) renders inoperative any Commonwealth, state or territory law that constitutes an arbitrary interference with sexual conduct between adults in private. In the absence of a constitutional bill of rights, this provision is one of the few federal laws protecting human rights—in this case the right to sexual privacy— that can influence the scope of Commonwealth, state or territory criminal law in Australia.[225]

F. Terrorism

In the wake of 9/11, the federal government moved swiftly, as did the United States, to enact a package of counterterrorism laws. The resulting 2002 reforms were not preceded by any systematic governmental or independent review of the adequacy of existing criminal laws. There was no consideration of whether minor adaptation (with sentence enhancement for crimes with a terrorist motive) could achieve a result more consistent with the existing fabric of Australian criminal laws. It has been suggested that the new terror legislation was created "on the cheap" in Australia with "off-the-shelf" solutions drawn from the United Kingdom's terrorism legislation.[226] Not only were key definitions borrowed from the U.K., but also new legal measures, such as control orders and preventive detention, were swiftly enacted following the Madrid and London bombings.[227] The core definition of "terrorist act," which triggers many of the counterterrorism powers and forms an element of a number of the terrorism offences in the Criminal Code (Cth), was drawn directly from the Terrorism Act 2000 (UK). The offences are definitionally and geographically far reaching, with many of the offences having extraterritorial and even retrospective effect.

A good example of jurisdictional overreach is the legal response to the Bali bombings that killed eighty-eight Australians on 12 October 2002. The bombings exacted a swift legislative response, even though the events occurred on foreign soil. A new part was inserted into the Criminal Code (Cth). Division 104 is titled "Harming Australians" and creates a range of extraterritorial offences against the person, including murder, manslaughter, and causing serious injury to Australian citizens or residents of Australia.[228] The most serious offence, murder, adopts the maximum penalty of life imprisonment. Although the perpetrators of the Bali bombings have been prosecuted and executed under terrorism laws in Indonesia, the symbolic importance of legislating to safeguard Australians overseas from harm proved to be politically irresistible.

In relation to these reforms, the Australian government has demonstrated an alarming willingness to depart both from its own guidelines governing the creation of new offences and from the presumptions in favor of fault that lie at the heart of the Criminal Code

(Cth). Indeed, strict liability and reversal of onus provisions have become the rule rather than the exception in relation to terrorism offences, reflecting the wider trends toward the normalization of extraordinary powers in the "War on Terror."[229]

SELECTED BIBLIOGRAPHY

Attorney-General's Department. *A Guide to Framing Commonwealth Offences, Civil Penalties and Enforcement Powers*. 2004.

Attorney-General's Department in association with the Australian Institute of Judicial Administration. *The Commonwealth Criminal Code: A Guide for Practitioners*. 2002.

Bronitt, Simon, and Bernadette McSherry. *Principles of Criminal Law*. 3d ed. Sydney: Thomson Reuters, 2010.

Brown, David, David Farrier, Sandra Egger, Luke McNamara, and Alex Steel. *Criminal Laws: Materials and Commentary on Criminal Law and Process in New South Wales*. 4th ed. Sydney: Federation Press, 2006.

Colvin, Eric, Suzie Linden, and John McKechnie. *Criminal Law in Queensland and Western Australia*. 4th ed. Chatswood, NSW: LexisNexis Butterworths, 2005.

Findlay, Mark, Stephen Odgers, and Stanley Yeo. *Australian Criminal Justice*. 4th ed. South Melbourne, Austalia: Oxford University Press, 2009.

McSherry, Bernadette, and Bronwyn Naylor. *Australian Criminal Laws: Critical Perspectives*. South Melbourne, Austalia: Oxford University Press, 2004.

Odgers, Stephen. *Principles of Federal Criminal Law*. Pyrmont, NSW: Law Book Co., 2007.

NOTES

1. For a historical account of the legal effect of this distinction, see William Blackstone, *Commentaries on the Laws of England*, originally published by the Clarendon Press at Oxford, 1765–1769 (New York: Clarendon Press, 1983), bk. 1, ch. 4, 106–108.

2. Ibid.

3. A position affirmed by the Privy Council in *Cooper v Stuart* (1889) 14 App Cas 286.

4. *Mabo & Others v State of Queensland (No. 2)* (1992) 175 CLR 1.

5. For a contrary view exploring the potential effect of *Mabo* on the criminal law, see Ron Levy, "Native Title and the Criminal Law: The Defence of Galarrwuy Yunupingu," *Indigenous Law Bulletin* 4, no. 13 (1998): 10; and Richard Edney, "Linkages: *Mabo* and the Sentencing of Indigenous Offenders," *International Journal of Punishment and Sentencing* 1 (2005): 28.

6. In November 2006 the Federal Parliament inserted s 16A(2A) into the Crimes Act 1914 (Cth), which precluded customary law or cultural factors when considering sentencing for Commonwealth offences. See also Simon Bronitt and Bernadette McSherry, *Principles of Criminal Laws*, 3d ed. (Sydney: Thomson Reuters, 2010), 157–158.

7. For the first half of the nineteenth century, the reform movement focused on ensuring many of the fundamental institutions of British justice, such as trial by jury. See David Neal, *The Rule of Law in a Penal Colony: Law and Power in Early New South Wales* (Sydney: Cambridge University Press, 1991), 167–187.

8. The drafter of the Queensland Criminal Code, Sir Samuel Griffith, thought it "strange to the ordinary mind" that a great branch of the law should not be reduced to writing, and that the desirability of a code required no argument. Samuel Griffith, *Explanatory Letter to Draft of a Code of Criminal Law* (Brisbane: Government of Queensland, 1897), iv.

9. The impact of the New South Wales Law Reform Commission and the Criminal Law Commissioners in the United Kingdom on reforming criminal law and procedure are reviewed in Gregory Woods, *A History of Criminal Law in New South Wales: The Colonial Period, 1788–1900* (Sydney: Federation Press, 2002).

10. Criminal Code Act 1899 (Qld); Schedule to Appendix of the Criminal Code Act Compilation Act 1913 (WA); Criminal Code Act 1924 (Tas); and Criminal Code Act 1983 (NT). The Griffith Code was also adopted in the protectorates of Papua (1902) and New Guinea (1921).

11. Alberto Cadoppi, "The Zanardelli Code and Codification in the Countries of the Common Law," *James Cook University Law Review* 7 (2000): 177 (including India, Jamaica, New York, and England.)

12. The so-called common law jurisdictions of New South Wales, South Australia, and Victoria have more or less extensive criminal consolidation statutes: see Crimes Act 1900 (NSW); Criminal Law Consolidation Act 1935 (SA); and Crimes Act 1958 (Vic). See also Bronitt and McSherry, above n. 6, 84, noting the distinct cultures of the common law and code jurisdictions and the High Court's concern to promote convergence, wherever statutory language permitted, in the interpretation of common concepts such as provocation, and discussing *Masciantonio v The Queen* (1995) 183 CLR 58: 66.

13. Australian Constitution s 90.

14. Ibid., s 51(xxix).

15. See *Polyukhovich v Commonwealth* (1991) 172 CLR 501 (upholding validity of war-crimes legislation); *XYZ v Commonwealth* [2006] HCA 25 (13 June 2006) (upholding validity of child sex-tourism offences).

16. See *Thomas v Mowbray* (2007) 237 ALR 194 for a discussion of the federal powers to enact legislation in the field of counterterrorism.

17. Rights of the Terminally Ill Act 1995 (NT), repealed by the Euthanasia Laws Act 1997 (Cth) sch 1.

18. See Australian Constitution ss 73, 74.

19. In 1990 the Standing Committee of Attorneys-General (SCAG) placed on its agenda the question of the development of a uniform criminal code for Australian jurisdictions. The SCAG established the Model Criminal Code Officers Committee (MCCOC) to draft a Model Criminal Code for the Commonwealth, which would provide the model for codes adopted in the states and territories. The general part of the Code has been enacted as the Criminal Code Act 1995 (Cth).

20. *Thompson v The Queen* (1989) 169 CLR 1: 33 (Deane J). See generally Bronitt and McSherry, above n. 6, 98–103.

21. The presumption that criminal offences do not have extraterritorial effect may be rebutted expressly or impliedly: *Pearce v Florenca* (1976) 135 CLR 507; *Treacy v DPP* [1971] AC 537: 561 per Lord Diplock.

22. *Thompson v The Queen* (1989) 169 CLR 1 at 22, per Brennan J. Where the issue of

jurisdiction is raised, the jury should be directed to return a special verdict on that issue before considering guilt. See further Alan Leaver, *Investigating Crime* (Sydney: LBC, 1997), 38–39.

23. These theories and the authorities cited supporting them are discussed in David Lanham, *Cross-Border Criminal Law* (Melbourne: FT Law and Tax Asia Pacific, 1997), ch. 1.

24. Criminal Code 1899 (Qld) s 12; Schedule to Appendix of the Criminal Code Act Compilation Act 1913 (WA) s 12.

25. Criminal Code 2002 (ACT) pt 2.7; Crimes Act 1900 (NSW) s 10C; Criminal Law Consolidation Act 1935 (SA) s 5G.

26. Criminal Code Act 1995 (Cth) div 15, ss 15.1–15.4.

27. Ibid., s 15.1(2).

28. Ibid., s 15.2(2).

29. Ibid., s 15.3(2).

30. Explanatory Memorandum, Criminal Code Amendment (Theft, Fraud, Bribery and Related Offences) Bill 1999 (Cth): 5.

31. No provisions of the relevant state statute of limitations acts are expressed to apply to criminal proceedings, although unreasonable delay balanced against actual prejudice and the public interest may provide a basis for the trial court to grant a stay of proceedings on the grounds of an abuse of process: *Jago v District Court (NSW)* (1989) 168 CLR 23.

32. See Bronitt and McSherry, above n. 6, 8 and 111.

33. See *Polyukhovich v Commonwealth* (1991) 172 CLR 501, where the High Court upheld the validity of the retrospective provisions of the War Crimes Act 1945 (Cth) on the ground that it did not usurp judicial power and did not offend the doctrine of separation of powers. It also held that as the legislation was within the Federal external affairs power and was not *ultra vires*. *Polyukovich* was affirmed in *Nicholas v The Queen* (1998) 193 CLR 173. See also *R v Kidman* (1915) 20 CLR 425.

34. See generally Dennis Pearce and Robert Geddes, *Statutory Interpretation in Australia*, 6th ed. (Sydney: Butterworths, 2006), ch. 10, 250–257. In *Rodway v The Queen* (1990) 169 CLR 515 at 518 it was held that "[t]he rule at common law is that a statute ought not be given a retrospective operation where to do so would affect an existing right or obligation unless the language of the statute expressly or by necessary implication requires such construction."

35. Human Rights Act 2004 (ACT) s 25; Charter of Human Rights and Responsibilities Act 2006 (Vic) s 27. Under this model of human rights legislation, courts are placed under a duty to interpret legislative provisions to be consistent with these rights, or, if this is not possible, to make a declaration of incompatibility. Upholding the principle of parliamentary supremacy, the courts do not have the power to invalidate legislation on the grounds of inconsistency with the enumerated human rights.

36. See Explanatory Memorandum, Criminal Code Amendment (Offences against Australians) Bill 2002 (Cth).

37. Appeals in criminal matters to the Privy Council from state courts were effectively abolished by the Privy Council (Limitation of Appeals) Act 1968 (Cth), the Privy Council (Appeals from the High Court) Act 1975 (Cth), and finally by the Australia Act 1986 (Cth) (with enabling legislation from each state).

38. See *Polyukhovich v Commonwealth* (1991) 172 CLR 501: 536 (Mason CJ).

39. Criminal Code (Cth) s 102.1(2).

40. Evidence Act 1977 (Qld) s 10; Evidence Act 2008 (Vic) s 128(3)(a); Evidence Act 1906 (WA) ss 11, 24; Evidence Act 1939 (NT) s 10; Evidence Act 1995 (Cth) s 128(2)(a); Evidence Act 1995 (NSW) s 128(2)(a); Evidence Act 2001 (Tas) s 128.

41. See Bronitt and McSherry, above n. 6, 130–136. The presumption is also contained in human rights legislation: see Human Rights Act 2004 (ACT) s 22; and Charter of Human Rights and Responsibilities Act 2006 (Vic) s 25.

42. The fundamental common law rule has been reaffirmed by the High Court on several occasions: see *Weissensteiner v R* (1993) 178 CLR 217; and *Petty and Maiden v R* (1991) 173 CLR 95. It is also reflected in legislative form in some jurisdictions; see, for example, Evidence Act 1995 (NSW) s 128. The scope of the privilege, however, differs across jurisdictions. In some jurisdictions there is a prohibition on both the judge and the prosecution against commenting on the defendant's failure to testify: Crimes Act 1958 (Vic) s 399(3); Evidence Act 1939 (NT) s 9(3). In others the prohibition applies only to the prosecutor and not to the judge: Evidence Act 2001 (Tas) s20; Evidence Act 1929 (SA) s 18(1)(b); Evidence Act 1995 (Cth) s20; Evidence Act 1995 (NSW) s 20; Evidence Act 1906 (WA) s 8(1)(c). In Queensland no such provision exists.

43. The right to a fair trial was discussed in *Jago v District Court (NSW)* (1989) 168 CLR 23 and *Dietrich v The Queen* (1992) 177 CLR 292. See also Bronitt and McSherry, above n. 6, 124–126.

44. See, e.g., Evidence Act 1995 (NSW) s 138.

45. See, e.g., *Watson v Attorney-General (NSW)* (1987) 8 NSWLR 685.

46. See, e.g., Criminal Procedure Act 1986 (NSW) div 3, ss 134–149.

47. Neal, above n. 7, ch. 7. The first civil jury was empanelled in the Supreme Court of New South Wales in 1830 for an action of trespass arising from a malicious prosecution. The conclusion of the trial was marked, somewhat comically, by a stern judicial admonishment to members of the jury for passing notes to each other ridiculing the proceedings. One note described the juror's irritation of sitting through the "blundering prose of a superannuated old wig"; see *Hall v Rossi* [1830] NSWSC 16 (15 March 1830).

48. (1980) 147 CLR 75.

49. Supreme Court Act 1933 (ACT) s 68B; Criminal Procedure Act 1986 (NSW) s 132; Criminal Procedure Act 2004 (WA) s 118; Juries Act 1927 (SA) s 7.

50. *Australian Constitution* s 80. See generally James Stellios, "The Constitutional Jury—'A Bulwark of Liberty'?" *Sydney Law Review* 27 (2005): 113.

51. See, e.g., *R v Federal Court of Bankruptcy: Ex parte Lowenstein* (1938) 59 CLR 556; and *Kingswell v The Queen* (1985) 159 CLR 264. See generally Bronitt and McSherry, above n. 6, 95 and 98 (for indictable versus summary offences).

52. For other theories of punishment, see Bronitt and McSherry, above n. 6, 17–33.

53. J. J. Spigelman, "Judging Today," Address to the Local Courts of New South Wales 2003 Annual Conference, 2 July 2003.

54. Crimes (Restorative Justice) Act 2004 (ACT).

55. Ibid., s 6(a).

56. Ibid., s 6(b).

57. Ibid., s 6(c).

58. Ibid., s 6(d).

59. Ibid., s 6(e).

60. The aims of sentencing are identified in Crimes (Sentencing) Act 2005 (ACT) s 7; Crimes (Sentencing Procedure) Act 1999 (NSW) s 3A; and Penalties and Sentences Act 1992 (Qld) s 3. Cf. Criminal Law (Sentencing) Act 1988 (SA) s 10; Sentencing Act 1997 (Tas) s 3; Sentencing Act 1991 (Vic) s 5(1); and Sentencing Act (NT) s 5.

61. Crimes Act 1914 (Cth) pt IB, ss 16–22A. See generally Australian Law Reform Commission, *Same Crime, Same Time: Sentencing of Federal Offenders,* Report no. 103 (Sydney: ALRC, 2006).

62. See Bronitt and McSherry, above n. 6, 185–187.

63. *Ryan v The Queen* (1967) 121 CLR 205. See also Bronitt and McSherry, above n. 6, 187.

64. Section 4.2(3) of the Criminal Code (Cth) includes examples of conduct that is not voluntary, including spasms and acts performed during sleep or impaired consciousness.

65. *R v Instan* [1893] 1 QB 450; (1893) 17 Cox CC 602; *R v Russell* [1933] VLR 59; *R v Miller* [1983] 2 AC 1.

66. Crimes Act 1900 (NSW) s 44; Criminal Code (NT) s 183; Criminal Code 1899 (Qld) s 285; Criminal Law Consolidation Act 1935 (SA) s 30; Criminal Code 1924 (Tas) s 144; Schedule to Appendix of the Criminal Code Act Compilation Act 1913 (WA) s 262.

67. Criminal Code (NT) s 155. There are also statutory duties to assist police officers in effecting an arrest, preventing crime, or quelling disorder; see, e.g., Criminal Code (Tas) ss 28–34.

68. Under the Criminal Code (Cth) dictionary, law means "a law of the Commonwealth, and includes this Code."

69. For an example in the family relationship context, see *R v Clarke* [1959] VR 645.

70. *R v Taktak* (1988) 14 NSWLR 226.

71. Crimes (Traffic in Narcotics Drugs and Psychotropic Substances) Act 1990 (Cth) s 6(2)(ba); Criminal Code (Cth) s 102.3.

72. Lord Irvine of Lairg, Lord Chancellor, "Intention, Recklessness and Moral Blameworthiness: Reflections on the English and Australian Law of Criminal Culpability," *Sydney Law Review* 23 (2001) : 7.

73. See *Parker v R* (1963) 111 CLR 610, refusing to follow the approach of the English House of Lords in *DPP v Smith* [1961] AC 290.

74. *He Kaw Teh v R* (1985) 157 CLR 523. See generally Bronitt and McSherry, above n. 6, 200–201. Less prominence has been given to the meaning and scope of intention partly because the offence of murder, both at common law and in statutory form, is satisfied by recklessness, as well as by an intention to kill or inflict grievous bodily harm.

75. See Criminal Code (Cth) s 5.6, which states that where there is no express fault element, intention is required for the conduct element of an offence. In relation to the physical elements of circumstance or result, the lesser fault element of recklessness suffices.

76. *R v Coleman* (1990) 19 NSWLR 467: 475; *R v Stokes* (1990) 51 A Crim R 25: 40.

77. Also reflected in Criminal Code 2002 (ACT) s 18.

78. Crimes Amendment Act 2007 (NSW) s 3 and Sch 1[2]. The Crimes Act 1900

(NSW) does not define fault elements, although under s 4A "if an element of an offence is recklessness, that element may also be established by proof of intention or knowledge."

79. Recent examples of offences incorporating particular motives are those enacted to deal with terrorism. The key offences criminalize perpetrating a terrorist act or issuing a threat of action "with the intention of advancing a political, religious or ideological cause"; see s 100.1 of the Criminal Code (Cth).

80. However, this type of motive may be taken into account in mitigation of sentence: Margaret Otlowski, "Mercy Killing Cases in the Australian Criminal Justice System," *Criminal Law Journal* 17, no. 1 (1993): 10.

81. *Peters v The Queen* (1998) 192 CLR 493: 551 (Kirby J).

82. For a general discussion of recklessness, see Bronitt and McSherry, above n. 6, 205–209.

83. *R v Crabbe* (1985) 156 CLR 464.

84. Crimes Act 1900 (ACT) s 12(1)(b); Crimes Act 1900 (NSW) s 18(1)(a); Criminal Code (Tas) ss 157(1)(b), (1)(c). See further I. G. Campbell, "Recklessness in Intentional Murder under the Australian Codes," *Criminal Law Journal* 10, no. 1 (1986): 3.

85. Criminal Law Officers' Committee of the Standing Committee of Attorney-Generals (CLOC/SCAG), *Model Criminal Code, Chapters 1 and 2: General Principles of Criminal Responsibility, Final Report* (1992): 27. For a recent essay on the U.S. Model Penal Code, see Paul Robinson and Markus Dubber, "The American Model Penal Code: A Brief Overview," *New Criminal Law Review* 10 (2007): 319.

86. Criminal Code (Cth) s 5.4. The question whether taking a risk is unjustifiable is one of fact: s 5.4(3).

87. Ibid., s 5.4(4).

88. See generally Bronitt and McSherry, above n. 6, 209–212.

89. Crimes Act 1900 (ACT) s 15; Crimes Act 1900 (NSW) s 18(1)(b); Criminal Code (NT) s 163; Criminal Code (Qld) s 303; Criminal Law Consolidation Act 1935 (SA) ss 13, 14; Criminal Code (Tas) s 156(2)(b); Criminal Code (WA) s 280. Negligent manslaughter is a common law offence in Victoria; see *Nydam v The Queen* [1977] VR 430.

90. *Nydam v The Queen* [1977] VR 430: 445 (Full Court, Supreme Court of Victoria).

91. These statutes generally stipulate the procedural and sentencing provisions, which range from the same maximum penalty as that for the completed offence to some fraction depending on the severity of the offence. For a table detailing the wide diversity of approaches to penalties, see Bronitt and McSherry, above n. 6, 448.

92. This formulation is based on the recommendations of the Law Commission in *Attempt and Impossibility in Relation to Attempt, Conspiracy and Incitement*, Report no. 102 (London: HMSO, 1980). In the subsequent enacting legislation, section 1(1) of the Criminal Attempts Act 1981 (UK) applied a test based on "acts more than merely preparatory to the commission of the offence."

93. *Britten v Alpogut* [1987] VR 929: 938.

94. Criminal Code (ACT) s 44(2); Crimes Act 1958 (Vic) s 321N(1); Criminal Code (WA) s 4.

95. The Law Commission of England and Wales has recommended that physical impossibility should be irrelevant to criminal responsibility: Law Commission, *Attempt and Impossibility in Relation to Attempt, Conspiracy and Incitement*, Report no. 102

(London: HMSO, 1980). These recommendations were enacted in section 1(2) of the Criminal Attempts Act 1981 (UK).

96. The test in *Haughton v Smith* [1975] AC 476 was followed by the Supreme Court of South Australia in *R v Collingridge* (1976) 16 SASR117. See Criminal Law Consolidation Act 1935 (SA) s 86E(2)(b).

97. Under the common law it has never been doubted that *legal* impossibility operates as a bar to a conviction for criminal attempt: *Britten v Alpogut* [1987] VR 929: 935 (Murphy J). It remains unsettled whether the statutory formulation dealing with impossibility extends also to legal impossibility, in which case an attempt to commit an imaginary crime would be criminalized. This significant extension of the law was envisaged by the Australian drafting committee, which stated, "The Committee took the view that impossibility arising by reason of matters of fact or law should no longer be a bar to conviction": *Model Criminal Code, Chapters 1 and 2: General Principles of Criminal Responsibility, Final Report* (1992), 83.

98. See Criminal Code (Cth) s 11.5; Crimes Act 1900 (NSW) ss 27–30; Criminal Code (NT) s 165; Criminal Code (Qld) s 306; and Criminal Code (WA) s 283. An example of this approach in relation to other offences includes the preparatory offence relating to burglary, "going equipped with the instruments of housebreaking," enacted in most jurisdictions.

99. For example, these include requiring the consent of the director of public prosecutions or the attorney-general before instituting proceedings: Criminal Code (Cth) s 11.5(8); Criminal Code (ACT) s 48(10); Criminal Code (Qld) ss 541(2), 542(2), 543(2); Crimes Act 1958 (Vic) ss 321(4), 321F(4).

100. See Bronitt and McSherry, above n. 6, 424–426.

101. See *Peters v The Queen* (1998) 192 CLR 493.

102. These reforms are based on the mid-nineteenth-century reforms enacted in the Accessories and Abettors Act 1861 (UK): see Criminal Code (Cth) s 11.2; Criminal Code (ACT) s 45; Crimes Act 1900 (NSW) s 346; Criminal Code (NT) s 12; Criminal Code (Qld) s 7; Criminal Law Consolidation Act 1935 (SA) s 267; Criminal Code (Tas) s 3; Crimes Act 1958 (Vic) s 323; and Criminal Code (WA) s 7.

103. *Giorgianni v The Queen* (1985) 156 CLR 473.

104. Stephen Odgers, "Criminal Cases in the High Court of Australia: *McAuliffe and McAuliffe,*" *Criminal Law Journal* 20, no. 1 (1996): 43.

105. Criminal Code (NT) s 8(1); Criminal Code (Qld) s 8(1); Criminal Code (Tas) s 4; Criminal Code (WA) s 8.

106. The High Court has recently held in *Keenan* [2009] HCA 1 (2 February 2009) that liability under section 8 of the Criminal Code (Qld) requires the offence committed by the principal to be of *such a nature* that it is a probable consequence of embarking on the common purpose. Defining probable consequence has proved challenging: "[O]nce it is accepted that 'probable' does not mean 'on the balance of probabilities' and that it means more than a real or substantial possibility or chance, it is difficult to arrive at a verbal formula for what it does mean and for what the jury may be told. The expression 'a probable consequence' means that the occurrence of the consequence need not be more probable than not, but must be probable as distinct from possible. It must be probable in the sense that it could well happen." *Darkan* [2006] HCA 34: [78]–[79].

107. *Model Criminal Code, Chapters 1 and 2: General Principles of Criminal Responsibility, Final Report* (1992): 86ff.

108. *The Commonwealth Criminal Code: A Guide for Practitioners* (2002), 255, states that the this provision "reformulates the doctrine of common purpose as a form of liability for recklessness." See also the *Model Criminal Code, Chapter 2: General Principles of Criminal Responsibility, Final Report* (1992): 86.

109. (1998) 197 CLR 316: 402 (Callinan J). Joint commission has been placed on a statutory footing in the Criminal Code (Cth), 511.2A.

110. *R v Whitehouse* (1941) 1 WWR 112 (British Columbia, Supreme Court). This direction was affirmed by the High Court in *White v Ridley* (1978) 140 CLR 342.

111. Acts Interpretation Act 1901 (Cth), with equivalents in all other jurisdictions.

112. *R v ICR Haulage Ltd* [1944] KB 551: 556; [1944] 1 All ER 691; *R v Murray Wright Ltd* [1970] NZLR 476: 484 (McCarthy J). For academic arguments against this qualification, see Brent Fisse, *Howard's Criminal Law*, 5th ed. (Sydney: Law Book Company, 1990), 611. For a corporation being subject to a prosecution for manslaughter, see *R v P & O European Ferries (Dover) Ltd* (1991) 93 Cr App R 73; and *DPP (Victoria) Reference No 1 of 1996* [1998] VR 217.

113. See *The King and the Minister for Customs v Australasian Films Limited and Anor* (1921) CLR 195, where the High Court held that a body corporate may be guilty of an offence involving an intent to defraud the revenue where its servant or agent, in the course of his or her employment, engaged in the proscribed conduct and that servant or agent, or a superior, had the necessary intent.

114. *Tesco Supermarkets Ltd v Nattrass* [1972] AC 153. This approach applied in *Tesco* is known variously as the identification rule, the attribution rule, or the alter-ego rule. For applications of this approach, see Bronit and McSherry, above n. 6, 180–185.

115. Brent Fisse and John Braithwaite, *Corporations, Crime and Accountability* (Cambridge: Cambridge University Press, 1993), 47. The authors develop a new model of corporate criminal responsibility based on the idea of organizational blameworthiness. These ideas were largely adopted in the Model Criminal Code, drawing on Brent Fisse's earlier works: "Corporate Criminal Responsibility," *Criminal Law Journal* 15 (1991): 166; and "Criminal Law: The Attribution of Criminal Liability to Corporations; A Statutory Model," *Sydney Law Review* 13 (1991): 277.

116. *R v Evans & Gardiner (No 2)* [1976] VR 523: 527; *R v Pagett* (1983) 76 Cr App R 279: 290–291.

117. *Campbell v The Queen* [1981] WAR 286: 290 (Burt CJ).

118. *Arulthilakan v The Queen* (2003) 203 ALR 259: 268 (Gleeson CJ, Gummow, Hayne, Callinan, and Heydon JJ), 273 (Kirby J).

119. *Royall v The Queen* (1991) 172 CLR 378: 448. For further discussion, see Bronitt and McSherry, above n. 6, 187–196.

120. Traditionally, the common law distinguished between killings that were "justified" and those that were "excused." Pleas of justification focus on the objective circumstances surrounding the act itself, whereas excuses focus on the actor's state of mind: see Bronitt and McSherry, above n. 6, 333–334.

121. *Woolmington v DPP* [1935] AC 462, 482 (Viscount Sankey LC).

122. *R v Packett* (1937) 58 CLR 190, 212 (Dixon J); *R v Mullen* (1938) 59 CLR 124: 132 (Rich J), 136 (Dixon J), 138 (McTiernan J).

123. The crimes of procuring an abortion has been abolished in the Australian Capital Territory: *Crimes (Abolition of Abortion) Act 2002* (ACT). See further Bronitt and McSherry, above n. 6, 549–554; Kerry Petersen, "Abortion: Medicalisation and Legal Gatekeeping," *Journal of Law and Medicine* 7, no. 3 (2000): 267.

124. Criminal Code (Cth) s 10.3; Criminal Code (ACT) s 41; Criminal Code (NT) s 33; Criminal Code (Qld) s 25; Criminal Code (WA) s 25.

125. *Model Criminal Code, Chapters 1 and 2: General Principles of Criminal Responsibility, Final Report* (1992): 67.

126. *R v Dudley and Stephens* (1884) 14 QBD 273. Some academics have doubted the continuing authority of this decision, although no authority is provided for this reversal: J. C. Smith and B. Hogan, *Criminal Law*, 10th ed. (London: Butterworths, 2002), 273–274; J. C. Smith, B. Hogan, and David Ormerod, *Criminal Law*, 11th ed. (Oxford: Oxford University Press, 2005), 322.

127. *Zecevic v DPP (Vic)* (1987) 162 CLR 645: 661. This statement was expressly approved by Mason CJ (654) and Brennan J (666) and was accepted by dissenting judges, Deane and Gaudron JJ.

128. See Criminal Code (ACT) s 42; Crimes Act 1900 (NSW) s 418; Criminal Code (NT) s 29.

129. Criminal Code (Cth) s 10.4(4). This approach is also adopted in the Australian Capital Territory and the Northern Territory codes: Criminal Code (ACT) s 42(3)(b); Criminal Code (NT) s 29(5).

130. The common law defence was first articulated in *Howe* (1958) 100 CLR 448 and clarified in *Viro* (1978) 141 CLR 88: 147. The code states rejected *Howe* from the outset: see *R v Johnson* [1964] QR 1 and *Aleksovski v The Queen* [1979] WAR 1.

131. *Zecevic v DPP (Vic)* (1987) 162 CLR 645: 654 (Wilson, Dawson, and Toohey JJ).

132. See Crimes Act 1900 (NSW) s 421 Crimes Act 1958 (Vic) s 9 AD, and Criminal Law Consolidation Act 1935 (SA) s 15(2).

133. See *Model Criminal Code, Chapter 5—Fatal Offences against the Person*, Discussion Paper (1998), 113.

134. Criminal Code (NT) s 187; Criminal Code (Qld) s 245; Criminal Code (Tas) s 182; Criminal Code (WA) s 222; *R v Donovan* [1934] 2 KB 498; *Attorney-General's Reference (No 6 of 1980)* [1981] QB 715; *R v Brown* [1993] 2 WLR 556.

135. *Schloss v Maguire* (1897) 8 QLJ 21: 22.

136. *Beer v McCann* [1993] 1 Qd R 25: 28–29 (Derrington J); *Carroll v Lergesner* [1991] 1 Qd R 206; *Boughey v The Queen* (1986) 161 CLR 10: 24 (Mason, Wilson, and Deane JJ).

137. *Clarence* (1888) 22 QBD 23 held that the fraud inducing consent must relate to the nature of the act or the identity of the accused. This leading English case has been applied in Australia in the context both of rape and of assault: *Papadimitropoulos v The Queen* (1957) 98 CLR 249; *R v Mobilio* [1991] 1VR 339. The broad principles governing fraud have been restated in the codes: Criminal Code (NT) s 187; Criminal Code (Qld) s 245; Criminal Code (WA) s 222; Criminal Code (Tas) s 2A; *Wooley v Fitzgerald* [1969] Tas SR 65.

138. *R v Coney* (1882) 8 QBD 534 (prizefighting); *R v Donovan* [1934] 2 KB 498 (caning a seventeen-year-old girl for sexual gratification); *Attorney General's Reference*

(No 6 of 1980) [1981] QB 715. Actions that constitute a "good reason" for causing consensual bodily harm include personal adornment such as tattooing, body piercing, and branding; surgery; and rough "horseplay" and violent lawful sports. Consensual sadomasochistic sexual activities have been viewed as not providing a "good reason" for the infliction of bodily harm: *R v Brown* [1993] 2 WLR 556.

139. David Kell, "Consent to Harmful Assaults under the Queensland *Criminal Code*: Time for a Reappraisal?" *Australian Law Journal* 68 (1994): 363.

140. *Proudman v Dayman* (1941) 67 CLR 536.

141. [1976] AC 182.

142. *Proudman v Dayman* (1941) 67 CLR 536: 540.

143. Questions concerning the effect of a statutory provision, the elements of an offence, or whether a person or thing falls within a statutory description are said to be matters of law: *Ianella v French* (1968) 119 CLR 84: 114 (Windeyer J).

144. *R v Thomas* (1937) 59 CLR 279, 306 (Dixon J); *Iannella v French* (1968) 119 CLR 84: 115 (Windeyer J); *Power v Huffa* (1976) 14 SASR 337: 344–345 (Bray CJ), 355 (Zelling J), 356 (Jacobs J).

145. See, for example, Criminal Code (Cth) s 9.3; note, however, the limited defence of mistake or ignorance of subordinate legislation in section 9.4.

146. *Pollard v DPP (Cth)* (1992) 28 NSWLR 659: 678 (Abadee J); *Strathfield Municipal Council v Elvy* (1992) 25 NSWLR 745; *Khammash v Rowbottom* (1989) 51 SASR 172; *Griffin v Marsh* (1994) 34 NSWLR 104.

147. *Von Lieven v Stewart* (1990) 21 NSWLR 52.

148. *Ostrowski v Palmer* [2004] 218 CLR 493, discussed in Bronitt and McSherry, above n. 6, 229–230.

149. See Kumaralingam Amirthalingam, "Ignorance of Law, Criminal Culpability and Moral Innocence: Striking a Balance between Blame and Excuse," *Singapore Journal of Legal Studies* (2002): 302; Bronitt and McSherry, above n. 6, 227–229.

150. Criminal Code (ACT) s 36; Criminal Code (NT) s 32; Criminal Code (Qld) s 24; Criminal Code (Tas) s 14; Criminal Code (WA) s 24.

151. See generally Louis Waller, "McNaughton in the Antipodes," in Donald West and Alexander Walk (eds.), *Daniel McNaughton: His Trial and the Aftermath* (Ashford: Headley Brothers, 1977), 170–185.

152. See Criminal Code (Cth) s 7.3(3).

153. *R v Radford* (1985) 42 SASR 266: 274. This statement was accepted by the High Court in *R v Falconer* (1990) 171 CLR 30: 53 (Mason CJ, Brennan and McHugh JJ), 60 (Deane and Dawson JJ), 85 (Gaudron J).

154. See Criminal Code (Cth) s 7.3(9); Criminal Code (ACT) s 27(2); Criminal Code (NT) s 43A; Criminal Code (WA) s 1.

155. Criminal Code (Cth) s 7.3(1); Criminal Code (ACT) s 27(1).

156. See further Bronitt and McSherry, above n. 6, 244–245.

157. *R v Porter* (1933) 55 CLR 182. This model direction emerged from a jury instruction offered in a case where the High Court had exercised its original jurisdiction in a criminal matter. Dixon J's direction was expressly approved in *Stapleton v The Queen* (1952) 86 CLR 358. Significantly, the definition of wrong in England was further

restricted to knowledge that it was *legally* wrong: see *R v Windle* (1952) 2 QB 826, where Devlin J asserted that "wrong" in the *M'Naghten* rules meant "contrary to law."

158. Wrong is statutorily formulated in the following terms: "[T]he person could not reason with a moderate degree of sense and composure about whether the conduct, as perceived by reasonable people, was wrong": Criminal Code (Cth) s 7.3(1)(b); Criminal Code (ACT) s 28(2); Criminal Code (NT) s 43C(1)(b); Crimes (Mental Impairment and Unfitness to be Tried) Act 1997 (Vic) s 20(1)(b).

159. The relationship between insanity and automatism is discussed in the High Court decision in *R v Falconer* (1990) 171 CLR 30. See Bernadette McSherry, "Automatism in Australia since *Falconer's* Case," *International Bulletin of Law and Mental Health* 6 (1996): 3.

160. *R v Falconer* (1990) 171 CLR 30: 41–42 (Mason CJ, Brennan and McHugh JJ), approving *R v Radford* (1985) 42 SASR 266.

161. For a review of the extensive case law on this issue, see Bronitt and McSherry, above n. 6, 225–241. See also Stanley Yeo, "Clarifying Automatism," *International Journal of Law and Psychiatry* 25 (2002): 445.

162. Criminal Code (Cth) s 7.3(1)(c). Section 16(1)(b) of the Criminal Code (Tas) defines the lack of ability to control as an act or omission "under an impulse which he or she was in substance deprived of any power to resist."

163. *R v O'Connor* (1980) 146 CLR 64.

164. See *DPP v Beard* [1920] AC 479; *DPP v Majewski* [1977] AC 443.

165. See *Criminal Code* (Qld), s 28; Criminal Code (WA), s 28; Criminal Code (Tas), s 17(2).

166. *Model Criminal Code, Chapters 1 and 2: General Principles of Criminal Responsibility, Final Report* (1992): 51.

167. G. Smith, "A Footnote to *O'Connor's* Case," *Criminal Law Journal* 5 (1981): 270; Victorian Law Reform Commission, *Criminal Responsibility: Intention and Gross Intoxication,* Report no. 6 (1986), 19.

168. Reflecting the scheme in the Code, the fault element of basic intent concerns intention that relates to conduct, excluding intention with respect to a circumstance or with respect to a result: Criminal Code (Cth) s 8.1(2). See also Criminal Code (ACT) s 31. See further Bronitt and McSherry, above n. 6, 279–280.

169. Criminal Code (Cth) s 8.4. See also Crimes Act 1900 (NSW) s428F.

170. Criminal Code (Cth) s 8.3.

171. Crimes Act 1900 (NSW) s 428C.

172. Ibid., s 428B.

173. See Criminal Law Consolidation Act 1935 (SA) s 267A(1).

174. Ibid., s 268(1). Similar provisions exist in New South Wales, Crimes Act 1900 (NSW) s 428C. This formulation is based on the approach taken in *Attorney-General (Northern Ireland) v Gallagher* [1963] AC 349.

175. See Criminal Law Consolidation Act 1935 (SA), ss 268(2)–(3).

176. See *R v Hurley* [1967] VR 526: 543 (Smith J); *R v Lawrence* [1980] 1 NSWLR 122; *R v Pakazoff* (1986) 43 SASR 99; *R v Darrington and McGauley* [1980] VR 353; *R v Dawson* [1978] VR 536; *Emery* (1978) 18 A Crim R 49.

177. Criminal Code (Cth) s 10.2; Criminal Code (ACT) s 40; Criminal Code (NT) s 40; Criminal Code (Qld) s 31(4); Criminal Code (Tas) s 20(1); Criminal Code (WA) s 31(4).

178. *R v Howe* [1987] AC 417.

179. See Bronitt and McSherry, above n. 6, 353, table 2, which outlines the crimes where duress is unavailable.

180. See Criminal Code (NT) s 41.

181. Criminal Code (Cth) s 10.2; Criminal Code (ACT) s 40.

182. *A v Hayden* (1984) 156 CLR 532 and *Ridgeway v The Queen* (1995) 184 CLR 19; cf. *Jacobson v. United States*, 112 S. Ct. 1535 (1992). See further Simon Bronitt, "The Law in Undercover Policing: A Comparative Study of Entrapment and Covert Interviewing in Australia, Canada and Europe," *Common Law World Review* 33, no. 1 (2004): 35; and Simon Bronitt, "Entrapment," in Peter Cane and Joanne Conaghan (eds.), *The New Oxford Companion to Law* (Oxford: Oxford University Press, 2008), 381–382.

183. *Ridgeway v The Queen* (1995) 184 CLR 19.

184. See Crimes Amendment (Controlled Operations) Act 1996 (Cth); Measures to Combat Serious and Organised Crime Act 2001 (Cth); Law Enforcement (Controlled Operations) Act 1997 (NSW); Criminal Law (Undercover Operations) Act 1995 (SA); Police Powers and Responsibilities Act 2000 (Qld).

185. See *He Kaw Teh v The Queen* (1985) 157 CLR 523: 588 per Brennan J.

186. See Mark J. Osiel, *Obeying Orders: Atrocity, Military Discipline, and the Laws of War* (New Brunswick, NJ: Transaction Publishers, 1999).

187. See Simon Bronitt and Dale Stephens, "'Flying under the Radar'—The Use of Lethal Force against Hijacked Aircraft: Recent Australian Developments," *Oxford University Commonwealth Law Review* 7, no. 2 (2007): 265, 273.

188. See *Model Criminal Code, Chapters 1 and 2: General Principles of Criminal Responsibility, Final Report* (1992): 73.

189. *R v Turnbull; ex parte Taylor* (1968) 123 CLR 28.

190. For a review of the principles and practices in federal sentencing, see Australian Law Reform Commission, above n. 61. See also Richard Fox and Arie Freiberg, *Sentencing: State and Federal Law in Victoria*, 2d ed. (1999); and Kate Warner, *Sentencing in Tasmania*, 2d ed. (2002).

191. *Williams v The King (No 2)* (1934) 50 CLR 551; *Leeth v Commonwealth* (1991) 174 CLR 455; *Putland v The Queen* (2004) 218 CLR 174.

192. Australian Law Reform Commission, above n. 61, para 1.62.

193. *Veen v R (No 2)* (1988) 164 CLR 465: 476–477 (Mason CJ, Brennan, Dawson, and Toohey JJ).

194. See Crimes (Sentencing Procedure) Act 1999 (NSW) s 3A; Sentencing Act 1991 (Vic) s 5(1); Penalties and Sentences Act 1992 (Qld) s 3; Sentencing Act 1997 (Tas) s 3(e); Sentencing Act 1995 (NT) s 5.

195. The Death Penalty Abolition Act 1973 (Cth) abolished capital punishment for all federal and territory offences, and this was extended by the Crimes Legislation Amendment (Torture Prohibition and Death Penalty Abolition) Act 2010 to all states and terrorities (the state had previously abolished capital punishment); see Crimes

(Amendment) Act 1955 (NSW); Crimes (Death Penalty Abolition) Amendment Act 1985 (NSW); Miscellaneous Acts (Death Penalty Abolition) Amendment Act 1985 (NSW); Criminal Code Amendment Act 1922 (Qld); Statutes Amendment (Capital Punishment Abolition) Act 1976 (SA); Criminal Code Act 1968 (Tas); Crimes (Capital Offences) Act 1975 (Vic); and Acts Amendment (Abolition of Capital Punishment) Act 1984 (WA).

196. The Crimes Amendment (Death Penalty Abolition) Act 1985 (NSW) abolished the death penalty for treason and piracy. Capital punishment was abolished for murder in 1955. The last person hanged in Australia was Ronald Ryan in 1967. For a useful resource, see the NSW Council for Civil Liberties, *The Death Penalty in Australia and Overseas*, Background Paper 2005/3 (2005).

197. See generally Australian Law Reform Commission, *Principled Regulation: Federal Civil and Administrative Penalties in Australia Report No. 95* (2002).

198. As the ALRC notes, these "non-criminal contraventions" or "regulatory contraventions," which are dealt with by using civil penalties and administrative procedures, must be distinguished from "criminal offences": ibid., para. 2.22.

199. Attorney-General's Department, *A Guide to Framing Commonwealth Offences, Civil Penalties and Enforcement Powers* (2004). This guide is available online at http://www.ag.gov.au.

200. Crimes Act 1900 (ACT) s 9; Criminal Law Consolidation Act 1935 (SA) s 5D; Crimes Act 1958 (Vic) s 322B(1); Crimes Act 1900 (NSW) s 580E.

201. The Commonwealth never introduced the distinction, simply dividing crimes into indictable or summary offences: Crimes Act 1914 (Cth), ss 4G–4H.

202. Criminal Code (NT) s 3; Criminal Code (Qld) s 3; Criminal Code (Tas) s 5; Criminal Code (WA) s 3.

203. Under the Criminal Code (Cth), the rationale for cybercrime offences is related to the importance of protection of infrastructure rather than the protection of property and privacy rights of computer users; see Simon Bronitt and Miriam Gani, "Shifting Boundaries of Cybercrime: From Computer Hacking to Cyberterrorism," *Criminal Law Journal* 27 (2003): 303.

204. Uncertainty remains whether this intention may extend to the equivalent state of oblique intention that is satisfied by foresight that death or grievous bodily harm is virtually certain to occur in the ordinary course of events; see Bronitt and McSherry, above n. 6, 175–176.

205. *R v Crabbe* (1985) 156 CLR 464.

206. See *Royall v The Queen* (1990) 172 CLR 378 at 395 (Mason CJ).

207. Homicide Act 1957 (UK) and *R v Vaillancourt* [1987] 2 S.C.R. 636 (Supreme Court of Canada).

208. See Prue Bindon, "The Case for Felony Murder," *Flinders Journal of Law Reform* 9, no. 2 (2006): 149.

209. The common law governs the defence in South Australia and Victoria and is also reflected in the statutory provisions of the Australian Capital Territory, New South Wales, and the Northern Territory: Crimes Act 1900 (ACT) s 13(2); Crimes Act 1900 (NSW) s 23(2); Criminal Code (NT) s 34. The common law has also been held to apply to

the interpretation of provocation under section 304 of the Criminal Code (Qld): *Van Den Hoek v The Queen* (1986) 161 CLR 158: 168 (Mason J).

210. See *Stingel v The Queen* (1990) 171 CLR 312 at 320, and *Masciantonio v The Queen* (1995) 183 CLR 58 at 66.

211. See Ian Leader-Elliott, "Sex, Race and Provocation: In Defence of Stingel," *Criminal Law Journal* 20 (1996): 72; and S. Yeo, "Sex, Ethnicity, Power of Self-Control and Provocation Revisited," *Sydney Law Review* 18 (1996): 304. The leading case on provocation is *Masciantonio v The Queen* (1994) 183 CLR 58.

212. *Green v The Queen* (1997) 191 CLR 334: 347 (Brennan CJ).

213. For data on the use of the defence and the profile of cases, see Judicial Commission of NSW, *Partial Defences to Murder in NSW, 1990–2004* (June 2006), discussed in NSW Parliamentary Library Research Service, *Provocation and Self-Defence in Intimate Partner and Homophobic Homicides—Briefing Paper* (2007).

214. Reforms were enacted in the Australian Capital Territory in 2004 and the Northern Territory in 2006; see, e.g., Crimes Act 1900 (ACT) s 13(3).

215. This reform was based on the recommendation of the Victorian Law Reform Commission, *Defences to Homicide—Final Report* (2004).

216. See Bronitt and McSherry, above n. 6, ch. 11.

217. See Criminal Code (Qld) s 349; Criminal Code (Tas) s 185; and Criminal Code (WA) s 325. See *R v Daniels* (1989) 1 WAR 435.

218. *DPP v Morgan* [1976] AC 182 was followed in New South Wales in *R v McEwan* [1979] 2 NSWLR 926 and affirmed as the correct approach by the High Court in *He Kaw Teh v R* (1985) 157 CLR 523: 592 (Dawson J). See also *R v Brown* [1975] 10 SASR 139; *R v Flannery* [1969] VR 31; and *R v Maes* [1975] VR 541.

219. For a review of these reforms, see Bronitt and McSherry, above n. 6, 674–675.

220. *R v L* (1992) 174 CLR 379. By coincidence, the Australian decision was handed down at the same time as the House of Lords decision in *R v R* [1992] 1 AC 599, which repealed the immunity.

221. See Bronitt and McSherry, above n. 6, 674–689.

222. Theft Act 1968 (UK). See Criminal Code (Cth) s 131.1; Criminal Code (ACT) s 308; Criminal Code (NT) s 210; Criminal Law Consolidation Act 1935 (SA) s 134; Crimes Act 1958 (Vic) s 74.

223. See Bronitt and McSherry, above n. 6, 746–748.

224. *Dudgeon v United Kingdom* [1981] ECHR 7525/76 and *ADT v United Kingdom* [2000] ECHR 35765/97.

225. See further Wayne Morgan, "Identifying Evil for What It Is: Tasmania, Sexual Perversity and the United Nations," *Melbourne University Law Review* 19 (1994): 740.

226. See Simon Bronitt, "Balancing Liberty and Security: Critical Perspectives on Terrorism Law Reform," in Miriam Gani and Penelope Mathew (eds.), *Fresh Perspectives on the "War on Terror"* (2008), ch. 5.

227. In late 2005, in the wake of the London bombings, the Council of Australian Governments agreed to enact powers to impose preventive detention and control orders on a person without charge, trial, or conviction, which were modeled directly on the

measures inserted into the Terrorism Act 2000 (UK). See Anti-Terrorism Act [No 2] 2005 (Cth).

228. Criminal Code (Cth), ss 104.1–101.4.

229. Simon Bronitt and Miriam Gani, "Criminal Codes in the 21st Century: The Paradox of the Liberal Promise," in Bernadette McSherry, Alan Norrie, and Simon Bronitt (eds.), *Regulating Deviance: The Redirection of Criminalisation and the Futures of Criminal Law* (Oxford: Hart Publishing, 2009), 235–260.

CANADA

Kent Roach

I. Introduction
   A. Historical Sketch
   B. Jurisdiction
   C. Legality Principles and Codification
   D. Sources of Criminal Law
   E. Process

II. General Part
   A. Theories of Punishment
   B. Liability Requirements
   C. Defences
   D. Justifications
   E. Excuses
   F. Sanctions

III. Special Part
   A. Structure
   B. Homicide
   C. Sex Offences
   D. Theft and Fraud
   E. "Victimless" Crimes
   F. Terrorism Offences

Kent Roach is Professor of Law and holds the Prichard-Wilson Chair in Law and Public Policy at the University of Toronto. His recent publications include *Criminal Law*, 4th ed. (Irwin Law, 2009), and "Canada," in Craig M. Bradley (ed.), *Criminal Procedure: A Worldwide Study*, 2d ed. (Carolina Academic Press, 2007).

I. INTRODUCTION

Canadian criminal law should be of interest to students of comparative criminal law for a variety of reasons. Although Canada is a federal state, matters of criminal law and procedure are within the exclusive jurisdiction of the federal legislature. Canada has had a national Criminal Code since 1892, but this code is not comprehensive because it does not preclude the development of defences under judge-made common law. It also does not contain systemic definitions and applications of fault elements. Nevertheless, federal jurisdiction has produced an accessible and national body of criminal law with leading texts in both English and French.

In 1982 Canada added a bill of rights, the Canadian Charter of Rights and Freedoms (henceforth the Charter) to its constitution.[1] Although it primarily governs criminal procedure,[2] it has had a significant and surprising impact on both the general and the special parts of the criminal law. For example, the courts have used the Charter to invalidate offences that result in imprisonment but do not require proof of fault. They have also invalidated murder offences that do not require the accused to have subjective knowledge in relation to the victim's death. The Charter has also been interpreted to invalidate restrictive statutory defences that allow the punishment of morally involuntary conduct. The Charter has thus emerged as a significant restraint on the criminal law in Canada, with some basic criminal law principles being constitutionalized.

A. Historical Sketch

The first criminal law in Canada was developed and applied by its indigenous peoples. This law was not written but depended on community practices and oral understandings. It did not distinguish between crime as a matter between the state and the individual and civil wrongs as disputes between individuals. Aboriginal justice did not use imprisonment but relied instead on other forms of punishment, such as reparation and banishment. Although Aboriginal peoples have been subject to colonial criminal law since European settlement, there has been a revived interest in Canada in the last few decades in Aboriginal forms of justice.[3] This interest is related to the fact that Aboriginal peoples are dramatically overrepresented in Canadian prisons and to increased interest in restorative justice.

The British defeat of French forces in Canada in 1763 brought with it the abolition of French criminal law in Canada. English criminal law was preferred because of a desire to enjoy the benefits of "the certainty and lenity of the Criminal Laws of England"[4] and because of concerns about the procedures and punishments used in French criminal law at that time.

B. Jurisdiction

With the union of four colonies into Canada in 1867, a decision was made to depart from the American example and give the central government exclusive jurisdiction over criminal law and procedure.[5] Canada's first prime minister, Sir John A. Macdonald, argued that "it is one of the defects of the United States system, that each separate state has or may have a criminal code of its own" and maintained that "under our Constitution we shall have one body of criminal law, based on the criminal law of England and operating equally throughout British America, so that a British American . . . knows what his rights are in that respect, and what his punishment will be if an offender against the criminal laws of the land."[6] The federal government's jurisdiction over criminal law and procedure has generally been defined broadly to include matters beyond the traditional domain of the criminal law, so long as they have a valid "criminal law purpose" backed by a prohibition and penalty.[7] Laws restricting the advertising of tobacco,[8] requiring licenses for all firearms,[9] prohibiting pollution,[10] and prohibiting the possession of marijuana[11] have all been upheld under the federal criminal law power. This power, however, is not unlimited. Laws with no valid criminal law purpose, such as laws prohibiting the sale of margarine,[12] regulating the content of light beer,[13] or driving without a valid license,[14] have not been sustained under the federal power to enact criminal law.

The provinces and municipalities have the power to impose punishment by fine, penalty, or imprisonment in relation to matters within their jurisdiction. This jurisdiction has sustained a large number of regulatory offences and bylaws relating to matters such as health and safety regulation and traffic safety. The provincial power to enact offences cannot, however, be used to enact criminal laws. Thus provincial laws designed to prohibit the propagation of communism,[15] prostitution,[16] or the performance of abortions outside hospitals[17] have all been struck down as invasions of the exclusive jurisdiction of the federal Parliament to enact criminal law.

C. Legality Principles and Codification

The Canadian Criminal Code was first enacted in 1892. It was based on the work of Sir James Stephen, as well as the 1880 Royal Commission in England that had proposed a criminal code.[18] There was little opposition to the proposed Code in Canada, but one judge of the Supreme Court complained that the Code was not comprehensive and did not systematically address the act or fault requirements of the criminal law.[19] The Code was far from comprehensive: it did not abolish common-law offences and did not even consolidate all statutory criminal law. Nor did it systematically define fault levels or other principles of the criminal law. It preserved "all rules and principles of the common law which render[ed] any circumstances a justification or excuse for any act, or a defence to any charge."[20] Today the Code[21] still does not systematically define fault elements, and several other federal statutes, most notably the Controlled Drugs and Substances Act,[22] also contain criminal offences. The courts continue to exercise their power to invent and proclaim new defences.

In a 1950 decision the Supreme Court of Canada (henceforth the Court) refused to rely on common-law offences on the basis that they "would introduce great uncertainty into the administration of the Criminal Law."[23] A few years later Parliament amended the Criminal Code to abolish common-law offences with the exception of contempt of court. This common-law offence was challenged in 1992 on the basis that codification of all crimes was a principle of fundamental justice protected under section 7 of the Charter. The Court rejected this argument on the basis that Canada had historically used common-law crimes, the common-law crime of contempt of court did not violate the principle of a fixed predetermined law, and the common-law offence was not excessively vague.[24] This was an unfortunate decision because codified offences help provide fair and advance notice to citizens and limit the discretion of law-enforcement officials. The refusal of the courts to require codification as a principle of fundamental justice under the Charter has probably put an end to any movement toward a comprehensive code. Any attempt to define defences in a comprehensive manner in a code would likely be futile, given that the absence of a defence can in appropriate cases be found to violate the Charter.

Most commentators in Canada despair at the present state of the Criminal Code. Every year it is subject to a number of amendments, many of which add new offences, but with little attention to the Code's overall structure and coherence. The Law Reform Commission of Canada conducted extensive work leading to its 1987 proposals for a new Criminal Code of Canada.[25] This proposed Code would have been a radical revision of the present Code, drastically reducing the number of offences and following the model of the U.S. Model Penal Code in establishing general definitions of fault and default fault provisions. Some attempts were made by the federal government to introduce a new general part in the early 1990s, but they were abandoned, largely as a result of criticisms of particular sections.[26] Some feminists were not supportive of the idea of a new general part of the Criminal Code because of fears that it would reflect general principles such as subjective fault that they argued were not developed with the experience of women in mind.[27] Although the Criminal Code grows larger and less coherent each year as a result of ad hoc amendments, there is little likelihood that Canada will soon engage in what most commentators believe is a necessary recodification and simplification of Canadian criminal law.

D. Sources of Criminal Law

1. Legislature

There is a hierarchy of sources of criminal law in Canada. The constitution is the supreme law of the land and limits attempts by legislatures to enact criminal law. Statutory criminal law enacted by Parliament can displace judicially developed common law under the traditional doctrine of legislative supremacy. Thus a defence developed at common law can be abolished by a clear statute. A new complication, however, is the symbiotic relation between the common law and section 7 of the Canadian Charter of Rights and Freedoms. This provision protects the "right to life, liberty and security of the person and the right not to be deprived thereof except in accordance with the principles of fundamental justice." The principles of fundamental justice are often informed by the values of the common law. A common-law defence cannot be abolished by statute if that defence is required by the principles of fundamental justice under section 7 of the Charter. The constitutionalization of select parts of the common law has thus served to augment the considerable power of the judiciary in shaping criminal law.

2. Judiciary

The Charter protects a range of rights subject to section 1, which guarantees rights subject to reasonable limits that are prescribed by law and demonstrably justified in a free and democratic society. The most important right for criminal law is section 7 of the Charter, as described earlier. Section 11 also includes the right "to be presumed innocent until proven guilty according to law in a fair and public hearing by an independent and impartial tribunal"[28] and the right not to be found guilty unless the act or omission "constituted an offence under Canadian or international law or was criminal according to the general principles of law recognized by the community of nations" at the time it was committed.[29] Section 52 provides that the constitution, including the Charter, is the supreme law and that all laws that are inconsistent with the Charter are of no force and effect to the extent of their inconsistency. Finally, section 33 of the Charter allows legislatures to enact laws for a five-year renewable period notwithstanding fundamental freedoms, legal rights, or equality rights as protected under the Charter. This override power, which makes the law valid even if it conflicts with the Charter, has never been used by the federal Parliament, but should it ever be used, it is likely to be used to displace a controversial judicial interpretation of the Charter rights of the accused.

3. Executive

Administrative regulations promulgated by the executive do not play an important role in Canadian criminal law. Some regulations are used to define schedules of prohibited drugs or prohibited firearms, but criminal offences remain defined in legislation. Administrative regulations play a greater role with respect to regulatory offences, with standards of conduct with respect to environmental or health and safety legislation being specified in regulations that are proclaimed by the executive to supplement framework legislation.

4. Scholars

Although Canadian courts are generous in their citation of scholarly work, it would be wrong to classify the work of scholars as a source of Canadian criminal law. Although the Court will at times adopt approaches suggested by a scholar, scholars are often quite critical of the criminal laws enacted by Parliament and of judicial interpretations of those laws or of the common law and the Charter.

E. Process

1. Adversarial/Inquisitorial

The Canadian criminal process is an adversarial process in which the prosecutor generally has to establish all the elements of the offence and disprove any relevant defence beyond a reasonable doubt. The courts, however, have upheld a burden on the accused to prove some defences such as mental disorder on a balance of probabilities.[30] The prosecution and the defence are responsible for presenting their own evidence, including, where appropriate, their own expert evidence. The prosecutor is also generally required under the Charter to disclose all relevant information to the accused before trial,[31] generally without any reciprocal disclosure requirements of the defence. In addition, the courts have indicated that adverse inferences should not be drawn from the pretrial silence of the accused.[32] At trial, the prosecutor cannot comment on the refusal of the accused to testify.

2. Jury/Written Opinions

Section 11(f) of the Charter provides that an accused who faces five years' imprisonment or more is entitled to a right to trial by jury. In practice, however, accused persons who are eligible for trial by jury often elect trial by a judge alone before the lower criminal courts, which decide over 90 percent of all criminal cases in Canada and do not have jurisdiction to sit with a jury. Judges are now generally required to give reasons for their decisions, while juries deliver only their verdicts. It is a criminal offence for jurors to reveal their deliberations,[33] and the Court has affirmed broad common-law protections of juror secrecy as being consistent with the Charter.[34]

II. GENERAL PART

A. Theories of Punishment

The Canadian Criminal Code provides as a "fundamental principle" of sentencing that a sentence "must be proportionate to the gravity of the offence and the degree of responsibility of the offender."[35] The Court has also recognized that "the principle of proportionality in punishment is fundamentally connected to the general principle of criminal liability which holds that the criminal sanction may only be imposed on those actors who possess a morally culpable state of mind."[36] The retributive principle of proportionality attempts to link the amount of punishment with the seriousness of the offence and the offender's degree of culpability. Therefore, it both authorizes and limits punishment. The Court has also recognized that it is a principle of fundamental justice protected under section 7 of the Charter that punishment be proportionate to the moral blameworthiness of the offender, and that those causing harm intentionally should be punished more severely than those causing harm unintentionally.[37] In addition, the right not to be subjected to cruel and unusual punishment protected under section 12 of the Charter has been interpreted as prohibiting punishment that is grossly disproportionate.

Despite the recognition of proportionality as the fundamental principle of sentencing, the Criminal Code recognizes a broad range of sentencing purposes, including denunciation of crime, the specific deterrence of the offender, the general deterrence of others, the separation of offenders from society where necessary, the rehabilitation of offenders, the acknowledgment of the harm done to victims and the community, and reparation for victims and the community.[38] The Court has also drawn a distinction between the punitive purposes of sentencing associated with denunciation, deterrence, and incapacitation and the restorative purposes of sentencing associated with the rehabilitation, restitution, and reintegration of offenders.[39] The restorative purposes of sentencing are generally advanced by a variety of community sanctions, including probation orders and conditional sentences of imprisonment that are served in the community, often under conditions of partial house arrest. The Court has indicated that the 1996 sentencing reforms were designed to reduce reliance on imprisonment for all offenders, but with particular attention to the circumstances of Aboriginal offenders.[40] At the same time, the Court has indicated that the punitive purposes of sentencing associated with imprisonment will become more relevant the more serious the offence.[41]

B. Liability Requirements

In the case of criminal offences, the prosecutor must prove beyond a reasonable doubt that the accused was responsible for a prohibited act or omission (*actus reus*) with a required fault element (*mens rea*). There must also be a coincidence between the *actus reus* and the *mens rea*.

The prohibited-act requirement depends on the particular offence that is charged. If the offence involves prohibited consequences, such as the causing of death, then causation may also have to be established. The legislature often defines the prohibited act broadly, so that it applies to behavior that is associated with a risk of harm.

The fault element also depends on the particular offence charged. Most offences in the Criminal Code contain no explicit fault elements. In such cases courts will read in a fault element, often in accordance with the common-law presumption that criminal offences will require proof of subjective fault unless Parliament indicates an intent to the contrary.[42] The fault element may not necessarily extend to all the elements of the prohibited act. The courts have decided that symmetry between the prohibited act and the fault element is an element of "criminal law theory" but is not a requirement under section 7 of the Charter.[43]

Some defences, such as intoxication, are factors that prevent the prosecutor from establishing fault beyond a reasonable doubt. Other defences, such as self-defence, will prevent the conviction of the accused even if a prohibited act with prohibited fault has been established. Although the classification of a defence as an excuse or justification can affect the judicial interpretation of its ambit, both justifications and excuses have the same legal status as defences that prevent the conviction of the accused. The only partial defence is that of provocation, which reduces murder to manslaughter.

1. Objective/Actus Reus

Given the decision of Parliament to abolish common-law offences except contempt of court,[44] the interpretation of the prohibited act is a matter of statutory interpretation. Courts generally interpret a criminal act in a manner that is designed to advance the statute's purpose and resort to the doctrine of strict construction of the criminal law only if there are reasonable ambiguities in the offence after it has been interpreted in light of its purposes. Federal statutes in Canada are equally authoritative in English and in French, and courts should look at both versions of the statute in determining whether ambiguities can be resolved by the other version of the offence.[45] Courts rarely resort to strict construction even with respect to the most serious criminal offences. For example, the Supreme Court has broadly interpreted references to the killing of a person while committing another offence in the offence of first-degree murder to include killings that were not simultaneous with the commission of the underlying offence[46] or even killings that were closely connected to the commission of the underlying offence against a third party who was not the victim of the killing.[47]

Parliament is generally free to define the prohibited act. The Court has rejected the idea that section 7 of the Charter requires that Parliament use the criminal law only to respond to proven harms. This decision was made in a case that rejected a Charter challenge to the criminal offence of possession of marijuana. The Court left open the possibility that an offence that was arbitrary, irrational, or grossly disproportionate to the state interest would violate the Charter,[48] but so far no offences have been struck down on this basis.

Criminal offences that are defined in a manner that is excessively vague or overbroad will violate the principles of fundamental justice under section 7 of the Charter. The Supreme Court has been cautious about striking down laws as excessively vague. It has stressed that the issue is not whether the law is crystal clear, but whether it "sets real boundaries and delineates a risk zone for criminal sanction."[49] Thus the court has accepted that Parliament can use flexible words such as "reasonable" and "undue." In addition, courts consider the interpretive jurisprudence of previous courts when determining whether a law is unconstitutionally vague or overbroad.[50] Thus a law that may be vague on its face may be saved by the ability of courts to interpret the law and place limits on it. This approach limits the ability of the void-for-vagueness doctrine in serving its stated purposes of ensuring that individuals receive fair notice about possible criminal liability and that limits are placed on law-enforcement discretion.

i. Act

Parliament often defines the prohibited act broadly. For example, there are various offences that make it a completed offence for a person to issue an invitation to a child to engage in sexual touching[51] or to communicate with a child over the Internet for the purpose of facilitating various sexual offences.[52] As discussed earlier, courts interpret criminal acts in a purposive manner and rarely resort to the doctrine of strict construction to narrow the ambit of the offence. In one important case, *R. v. Jobidon*, the Court even expanded an offence beyond the ambit of the words used by Parliament. This case involved the offence of assault, defined by Parliament as the intentional application of force "without the consent of another person."[53] With reference to English common law, the majority of the Court held that consent would be vitiated in cases where adults consented to a fistfight and intentionally caused serious hurt or nontrivial bodily harm. One judge issued a strong dissent that argued that the majority was expanding the statutory offence of assault beyond the clear limits imposed by Parliament and was also coming dangerously close to creating new common-law crimes, again contrary to clear legislation enacted by Parliament.[54] Although the policy of discouraging consensual violence may be sound, the Court's decision ran roughshod over clear statutory language and significantly expanded the crime of assault.

In certain instances courts may find that a prohibited act was not committed because the accused acted in an involuntary manner. The Supreme Court has refused to convict a person of impaired driving where the impairment was caused by involuntarily consuming a drug at a dentist's office, with one judge concluding that "there can be no *actus reus* unless it is the result of a willing mind at liberty to make a definite choice or decision."[55] A person who struck another person while having an epileptic seizure or responding involuntarily to a bee sting or detached retina would likewise be held not to have committed a voluntary criminal act.[56]

ii. Omission

Parliament can define a failure or omission to act as a prohibited wrong for the purposes of criminal liability, but it has been relatively sparing in doing so. Section 215 of the Criminal Code makes it an offence for a parent, spouse, or guardian to fail to provide the necessities of life for his or her child, spouse, or a person under his or her charge. The Supreme Court has held that the fault requirement for this offence is criminal negligence in the form of a marked departure from the standard that society expects from a parent, spouse, or guardian. In reaching this decision, the Court concluded that a subjective fault standard would be inconsistent with the idea that a duty establishes uniform community standards of care.[57]

The failure to act is criminalized in a number of other offences in the Criminal Code and in a greater number of regulatory offences. These offences include breach of a duty to use reasonable care in handling explosives,[58] disobedience to a court order,[59] failure to assist a peace officer when requested,[60] abandoning a child,[61] failing to seek assistance in childbirth,[62] the neglect of animals,[63] and failing to stop when a vehicle is involved in an accident.[64] The Supreme Court has held that the duty to use reasonable care when providing medical treatment was violated when a person donated blood that he knew was infected with HIV.[65]

iii. Status

The Criminal Code generally does not contain status-based crimes. The Supreme Court held that a vagrancy offence that made it illegal for a person previously convicted of a sexual offence to be found loitering in or near a school ground, playground, public park, or bathing area violated the principles of fundamental justice under section 7 of the Charter because the offence was overbroad in relation to Parliament's objective of protecting children from sexual assault. The Court expressed concerns that there was a lack of fair notice to the offender and that the offence was so broad that it delegated unfettered discretion to the police in its enforcement.[66] Parliament responded with a new offence that made it a crime for those convicted of sexual offences with young children to attend places where children are reasonably expected to be present or to seek employment or volunteer positions that will place them in a position of trust or authority with respect to children. The offender is also given specific notice of his or her potential liability under this offence.[67] This new offence demonstrates how the state can advance its interest in protecting children from sexual offenders without relying on overbroad or purely status-based offences.[68]

iv. Causation

Parliament can choose to make questions of causal responsibility relevant when defining an offence as one that causes prohibited consequences. Parliament can also impose its own test of causation for determining whether the accused should be held responsible for causing the proscribed harms.

Causation issues most often arise with respect to causing death. Canadian criminal law generally does not impose overly strict causation requirements. For example, a person may be found responsible for causing death even though the death was caused in part by the victim's own preexisting condition or vulnerability, often termed a "thin skull."[69] In addition, a person may also be found to have caused death even when there is some other operating cause of death, including improper but good-faith treatment of the deceased's injuries[70] or in circumstances in which the deceased's death might have been prevented by resorting to proper treatment.[71]

In *R. v. Smithers*[72] the Supreme Court upheld a manslaughter conviction in a case where the accused kicked the victim in the stomach and the victim died by choking to death on his own vomit because of a malfunctioning epiglottis. The Court held that there was sufficient causation as long as the accused's conduct "was at least a contributing cause of death, outside the *de minimis* range." This broad test of causation has been held to be consistent with the principles of fundamental justice protected under the Charter, in large part on the basis that liability would not be determined on the basis of causation alone but would also require the establishment of objective or subjective fault.[73] In order to make the causation standard more understandable to juries, the Supreme Court in *R. v. Nette*[74] stated that the standard should now be described as a "significant contributing cause" of death. Some judges dissented on the basis that this new formulation raised the test for causation. All the judges, however, agreed that the accused had caused the death of an elderly victim whom he had left hog-tied and alone, despite the fact that the victim's age, asthma, and congestive heart failure might also have played roles in her death.

Although the courts have not imposed overly strict standards of causation, Parliament has created some forms of first-degree murder that require that death be caused by the accused while committing or attempting to commit a serious crime.[75] The Supreme Court has interpreted such offences as requiring a higher test of substantial, as opposed to significant, causation. Even when such a stricter test is applied, however, the accused's act need not be the physical cause of death. For example, an accused who held the victim's legs while another offender strangled her to death was found to have substantially contributed to that death.[76]

Causation issues sometimes arise in nonhomicide cases but will depend on the selection of charges. In one case the accused was given the benefit of a reasonable doubt whether he had infected the victim with HIV by having unprotected sex with her when he knew that he was HIV-positive. He was acquitted of aggravated assault. At the same time, he was convicted of attempted aggravated assault because he had the necessary fault for the assault and had committed the *actus reus* of the attempt by doing something beyond mere preparation with the intent to commit aggravated assault.[77]

2. *Subjective/*Mens Rea*/ Mental Element*
There are no general definitions of fault elements in the Canadian Criminal Code, no provisions for default fault elements, and no general rule that the fault element will apply to all aspects of the *actus reus*, or prohibited act. In the absence of legislative rules, the Supreme Court has articulated some judge-made or common-law presumptions with respect to fault. In 1978 the Court articulated the following presumption: "Where the of-

fence is criminal, the Crown must establish a mental element, namely, that the accused who committed the prohibited act did so intentionally or recklessly, with knowledge of the facts constituting the offence, or with willful blindness towards them. Mere negligence is excluded from the concept of the mental element required for conviction."[78] This common-law presumption of subjective fault can, however, be displaced by a clear legislative intent to use objective or negligence-based forms of fault.

In addition to the common-law presumption of subjective fault, the Supreme Court has also interpreted section 7 of the Charter to embrace some fault requirements. Section 7 of the Charter has been interpreted to require proof of fault, including negligence, with respect to any offence that will result in imprisonment.[79] In 1993 the Court further indicated that section 7 of the Charter would require that the *mens rea* of a crime reflect the stigma attached to the offence and its available penalties, that punishment be proportionate to the moral blameworthiness of the offender, and that those who caused harm intentionally should be punished more severely than those who caused harm unintentionally. In the same case, however, the Court rejected the idea that section 7 of the Charter would require that the fault element relate to all aspects of the prohibited act.[80]

Section 7 of the Charter has been interpreted to require subjective knowledge of the likelihood that the prohibited act will cause death with respect to the offences of murder[81] and attempted murder.[82] The Court has based these pronouncements not on general principles of fault but rather on the stigma and penalties of these specific offences. Similarly, the Court has held that "the stigma and opprobrium" that would accompany convictions of crimes against humanity or war crimes require the Crown to prove that the accused either knew or was willfully blind to the aggravating facts and circumstances that would make a crime constitute a war crime or a crime against humanity.[83] In a subsequent case the Court noted that this interpretation accorded with international criminal law principles, but it also indicated that the slightly lower subjective fault element of recklessness with respect to the conditions that would make a crime constitute a war crime would suffice.[84]

The Court has also interpreted section 7 of the Charter to require that negligence when used as a form of criminal fault that could result in a deprivation of liberty requires proof of a marked departure from reasonable standards of care. This requirement of a marked departure is necessary in order to distinguish criminal from civil negligence. The Court warned that "if every departure from the civil norm is to be criminalized, regardless of the degree, we risk casting the net too widely and branding as criminals persons who are in reality not morally blameworthy. Such an approach risks violating the principle of fundamental justice that the morally innocent not be deprived of liberty."[85]

i. Intent

A variety of forms of subjective fault can be associated with the idea of "intent," including willfulness and purpose. Such high levels of subjective fault are used relatively infrequently, and convictions even for serious offences, such as murder, can be satisfied by slightly lower forms of subjective fault, such as knowledge of the probability of the prohibited act or consequence occurring. Higher forms of *mens rea* based on intent and purposes, however, are used with respect to some forms of participation in crimes and most inchoate offences. For example, a person will be guilty as a party to an offence by assisting the commission of the offence if the person acts "for the purpose of aiding" the principal offender.[86] A person will be guilty of an attempted crime if the person does something beyond mere preparation with the intent to commit the completed offence.[87] High levels of intent are an important restraint on the ambit of inchoate offences and crimes based on participation with others in crime.

Even high fault requirements that an accused have an intent or purpose to commit a crime will not assist a person who intentionally commits a crime because of a praiseworthy or understandable motivation. The Supreme Court has indicated that a person who assists another person to commit a crime because he has been threatened by the principal offender would still be acting with the intent or purpose of assisting in the commission of the crime. In other words, the fault elements of intent or purpose will generally not be negated by circumstances of duress.[88] Thus even the highest forms of subjective fault in Canadian criminal law are generally seen as descriptive of the actual mental state of the accused and are distinguished from deeper questions about what motivated the accused to act in the manner in which he or she did.

ii. Knowledge and Willful Blindness

Knowledge is a common form of subjective *mens rea* that requires proof that the accused knows the probability that the prohibited consequences or circumstances exist. An honest but mistaken belief in the existence of an innocent state of affairs can produce a situation in which the Crown is unable to establish the fault level of knowledge beyond a reasonable doubt. For example, an accused person who possesses illegal drugs while believing that they are an innocent substance would not be guilty of the offence of possession of the drugs because of the absence of guilty knowledge.[89] Although knowledge is a slightly lower form of *mens rea* than intent, it has been held to be constitutionally sufficient even for serious offences such as murder.[90]

A more controversial form of subjective fault is that of willful blindness, which has generally been interpreted as being the equivalent of knowledge. Willful blindness "arises when a person who has become aware of the need for some inquiry declines to make the inquiry because he does not wish to know the truth."[91] Willful blindness can be difficult to distinguish from negligence in the form of a failure to make inquiries about the existence of the prohibited circumstances or consequences when one should make such inquiries. The courts have, however, stressed that the willfully blind accused has made a deliberate decision not to know by closing his or her eyes to the prohibited circumstances or consequences.[92]

iii. Recklessness

Recklessness is a lower form of fault than intent, purpose, knowledge, or willful blindness, but it is applied as a form of subjective fault in Canadian criminal law. The Supreme Court has explained that "recklessness, to form a part of the criminal *mens rea*, must have an element of the subjective. It is found in the attitude of one who, aware that there is danger that his conduct could bring about the result prohibited by the criminal law, nevertheless persists, despite the risk. It is, in other words, the conduct of one who sees the risk and takes the chance."[93] Recklessness is distinguished from knowledge on the basis that the accused need only be aware of the *possibility* of the prohibited consequences or circumstances occurring, as opposed to knowing the *probability* of such eventualities. Recklessness is distinguished from negligence on the basis that the reckless accused must subjectively be aware of the risk of the prohibited consequences or circumstances occurring, whereas negligence can be found if a reasonable person in the accused's position would have been aware of these eventualities even if the accused was not so aware.

    iv. Negligence

After some initial controversy, it is now accepted that negligence can be a sufficient fault requirement in Canadian criminal law. The Supreme Court, however, has distinguished between criminal negligence that is sufficient for criminal liability and ordinary negligence that may be sufficient for civil liability. In several cases the Court has insisted that negligence as a form of criminal fault requires conduct that reveals a marked departure from the standard expected of a reasonable person in the circumstances.[94] Indeed, the Court has insisted on the formulation of "a marked departure from reasonable conduct" even in cases where the underlying offence seemed to have prohibited merely careless use of a firearm[95] or a failure to provide the necessities of life.[96] This approach of requiring a marked departure from reasonable standards has recently been affirmed by the Court as constitutionally required under section 7 of the Charter in order to ensure that the morally innocent not be branded as criminals.[97] A slightly higher standard of a "marked and substantial" departure from standards of reasonable care is required under a specific offence of criminal negligence causing death or bodily harm.[98]

In applying fault standards of negligence, the Supreme Court decided in a 5–4 decision that the standard of the reasonable person should be used without consideration of any of the personal circumstances of the accused, such as age, gender, or education.[99] Such personal characteristics will be considered only if they establish the incapacity of the particular accused to appreciate the nature and quality of the prohibited conduct and consequences. Justice Beverley McLachlin elaborated for the majority of the Court:

> Mental disabilities short of incapacity generally do not suffice to negative criminal liability for criminal negligence. The explanations for why a person fails to advert to the risk inherent in the activity he or she is undertaking are legion. They range from simple absent-mindedness to attributes related to age, education and culture. To permit such a subjective assessment would be "co-extensive with the judgment of each individual, which would be as variable as the length of the foot of each individual", leaving "so vague a line as to afford no rule at all, the degree of judgment belonging to each individual being infinitely various." . . . Provided the capacity to appreciate the risk is present, lack of education, and psychological predispositions serve as no excuse for criminal conduct, although they may be important factors to consider in sentencing.[100]

In contrast to this uniform reasonable-person approach with respect to criminal negligence, the Court has held that reasonable conduct for the purposes of self-defence, provocation, necessity, and duress will be judged on the basis of how a reasonable person of the same age, gender, and relevant past experiences as the accused person would have acted. The only possible reconciliation of these divergent approaches to the reasonable-person standard is that the use of objective standards of fault requires that all individuals live up to minimal standards of socially desirable behavior, while the determination whether a particular accused qualifies for a defence can be done in a manner that is more tailored to the accused's particular characteristics.

3. Theories of Liability

Canadian criminal law generally casts a broad net of criminal liability through general provisions providing for inchoate liability and participation in offences. In addition to these provisions, crimes defined in the special part, for example, crimes relating to support for and participation in terrorism, may also serve a similar function to general crimes that would apply to attempts, counseling, or conspiracies to commit crimes such as murder.

i. Inchoate Crimes

Attempts and conspiracy constitute the main forms of inchoate crimes, but there is also a separate crime of counseling a crime that is not committed.[101] This latter incitement offence typically occurs when a person procures, solicits, or incites another person to commit an offence and when that person refuses to commit the offence. The *actus reus* of this offence must go beyond a simple description of the offence and include active inducement or advocacy of the offence. As an inchoate offence that, by definition, occurs when the completed offence does not occur, it might be expected that this offence would require proof of intent by the accused that the completed offence be committed. Nevertheless, the Supreme Court has interpreted the fault requirement of this incitement offence to be satisfied by an awareness of the unjustified risk that the offence counseled is in fact likely to be committed as a result of the accused's conduct.[102] Thus something less than the intent that the offence be committed is now sufficient for a conviction of the offence of counseling an offence not committed.

a. Attempt

The most common form of inchoate offence is an attempt to commit a offence. The *actus reus* of an attempt is the doing or omitting to do anything beyond mere preparation to commit the offence. The *actus reus* of an attempt need not in itself constitute a crime or even a moral or social mischief.[103] Although section 24(2) of the Criminal Code provides that it is a question of law for the judge whether an act or omission "is or is not mere preparation to commit the offence and too remote to constitute an attempt," the courts have taken a qualitative approach to the distinction between mere preparation and something that can constitute a crime of attempt. Courts will consider the relative proximity of the act to any completed offence but have held that an attempt can be committed even though the completed offence could not occur for some time in the future.[104] In a practical sense, the stronger the evidence of the accused's intent to commit the completed offence, the more willing the courts will be to accept as the *actus reus* an act that is remote from what would be required for the completion of the crime.

Section 24(1) of the Code provides that a person may be guilty of an attempt "whether or not it was possible under the circumstances to commit the offence." The Supreme Court has rejected the idea that the legal impossibility of committing the completed offence should be a defence to an attempt charge. Thus a person could be convicted of attempting to launder the proceeds of a crime even though the money was owned by the government.[105] In reaching this conclusion, the courts have stressed that a person is primarily being punished for his or her intent to commit a crime.

The courts have also stressed that the intent requirements for attempts are high and require proof beyond a reasonable doubt that the accused intended to commit the completed crime.[106] This approach recognizes that a person punished for attempts is primarily being punished for having the intent to commit the completed offence. The Supreme Court has held that the stigma and punishment of attempted murder require as a constitutional minimum that a person have knowledge that death would result.[107] Nevertheless, this decision only establishes the constitutional minimum under which the courts and Parliament cannot go. The offence of attempted murder, like all attempt crimes,[108] is interpreted to require the intent to commit the completed crime.[109]

b. Conspiracy

There is a general offence of conspiring to commit an indictable offence, as well as some offences relating to conspiracy to commit specific offences, such as conspiracy to commit murder.[110] Parliament repealed an offence of conspiracy to effect an unlawful purpose after the Supreme Court indicated a reluctance to recognize conspiracies to commit common-law offences, as opposed to statutory crimes.[111]

The *actus reus* of conspiracy is the agreement to commit an offence, and it is not necessary that any act be done in furtherance of such a meeting of minds.[112] The courts have refused to recognize an offence of attempted conspiracy when no agreement is reached because of a concern about extending the criminal sanction too far.[113] At the same time, the Court has recognized that some cases of unilateral conspiracies where there is no agreement may also constitute the separate offence discussed earlier of counseling a crime that is not committed.

The *mens rea* for conspiracy includes both the intention to agree and the intention to commit the completed crime. The Court has indicated that "the intention cannot be anything else but the will to obtain the object of the agreement."[114] Such a double intent requirement is consistent with the idea that the primary purpose of punishing inchoate crimes is to punish the intent to commit the crime.

ii. Complicity

Section 21(1) of the Criminal Code provides that a person is a party to an offence not only if the person actually commits the offence, but also if he or she does or omits to do anything for the purpose of aiding or abetting any person to commit an offence. The *actus reus* of aiding and abetting is defined broadly and does not actually require attendance at the scene of the crime. Nevertheless, the act requirement is not satisfied in a case in which a person simply observes a crime being committed and takes no step to render aid, assistance, or encouragement to the accused. In 1978 the Supreme Court explained that "[a] person who, aware of a rape taking place in his presence, looks on and does nothing is not, as a matter of law, an accomplice. The classic case is the hardened urbanite who stands in a subway station when an individual is murdered."[115] The *mens rea* of aiding and abetting requires proof of the purpose of aiding the person, as well as knowledge of the offence. Recklessness is not a sufficient form of *mens rea*.[116] At the same time, the requirement of having a purpose to assist the perpetrator can be satisfied even if the accused is threatened and acting under duress and does not desire that the crime be committed.[117]

Section 21(2) applies in those cases where two or more people agree to effect an unlawful purpose such as a robbery, and another crime, such as an assault or a homicide, occurs in the course of carrying out that purpose. Section 21(1) provides that when two or more persons form a common intention to carry out an unlawful purpose and to assist each other, then they are parties to any offence that they knew or ought to have known would be the probable consequence of carrying out the unlawful purpose. This provision first requires the formation of a common unlawful purpose. Although originally of the view that this purpose could be negated by duress,[118] the Supreme Court now holds that a common unlawful purpose can exist even when one of the parties does not desire that the crime occur and is threatened into participation.[119] The second *mens rea* requirement is that the accused either know or ought to know that the commission of a subsequent crime will be a probable consequence of carrying out the unlawful purpose. The objective arm of this *mens rea* requirement is constitutional in most of its applications, and there is no constitutional principle that requires parties to an offence to have the same *mens rea* as the principal offender. Thus offenders could be guilty of assault under section 21(2) on the basis that they ought to have known that their accomplice would commit an assault during the robbery even though the principal offender would be convicted of assault on the basis of subjective fault. The objective arm of section 21(2), however, violates section 7 of the Charter and is of no force and effect if the person is charged with murder, attempted murder, war crimes, or crimes against humanity. The stigma and penalties for these crimes require that each person convicted of these crimes have subjective fault in relation to the prohibited act.[120]

Section 22(1) makes a person a party to an offence where he or she counsels a person to commit an offence and the person counseled afterward becomes a party to the offence. Counseling includes procuring, soliciting, or inciting, even if the person counseled committed the offence in a different manner than was counseled, and even if the person counseled cannot be convicted of the offence, for example, because he or she is under twelve years of age and is not capable of being convicted.[121] Section 22(2) makes a person who counseled another person a party to any other crime that he or she knew or ought to have known was likely to be committed in consequence of the counseling. The objective arm of this section cannot constitutionally be used to convict a person of murder, attempted murder, war crimes, or crimes against humanity for the same reasons discussed earlier in relation to the objective arm of section 21(2).

Both sections 21 and 22 operate to make a person a party to the offence. Section 23 creates a separate offence of being an accessory after the fact in cases where a party receives, comforts, or assists a person for the purpose of enabling that person to escape while knowing that the person being assisted has been a party to an offence. A provision providing that a person could not be convicted of assisting his or her spouse was repealed in 2000.[122] Nevertheless, the offence of accessory after the fact requires the prosecutor to establish both that the accused knew that the person was a party to the offence and that he or she assisted that person for the purpose of enabling him or her to escape.

iii. Corporate Criminal Liability

In 2003 Canada amended its Criminal Code to replace the common law of holding corporations responsible for the fault of their "directing mind" with new statutory provisions to govern the criminal liability of organizations, public bodies, partnerships, trade unions, and associations of persons, as well as corporations. The immediate impetuses for these changes were decisions that restricted a corporation's "directing mind" to those who designed and supervised the implementation of corporate policy, as opposed to those who simply carried out the corporation's policy.[123] Concerns were articulated that restrictive definitions of "directing mind" would render corporate activity in Canada immune from the criminal law, given the high rates of foreign control of corporations in Canada. There was also increased concern about corporate misconduct. The new legislation abolishes the common-law concept of a directing mind and replaces it with the concept of a senior officer, which includes not only those who play an important role in establishing an organization's policies but also those responsible for managing an important part of the organization's activities.[124] Thus the fault of important corporate managers can now be attributed to corporations. The new legislation also defines the representatives of an organization broadly to include agents, contractors, and members, as well as employees.[125] Thus a corporation could be held responsible for the acts of nonemployees such as agents.

Section 22.1 governs organizational fault for negligence-based criminal offences. It imposes liability on the basis that one or more representatives acting within the scope of their authority individually or collectively committed the *actus reus* of the offence and the responsible senior officer or the senior officers collectively committed the *mens rea* by departing "markedly from the standard of care that, in the circumstances, could reasonably be expected to prevent a representative from being a party to the offence." The innovations in this provision are the recognition of the collective commission of an *actus reus* by two or more representatives of an organization and the recognition of a collective fault by all the senior officers of that organization. This provision also recognizes that negligence for the purpose of criminal liability requires a marked departure from a reasonable standard of care. If an organization was charged with a regulatory offence of negligence, as opposed to a criminal offence of negligence, it would have the burden of proving that it was not negligent by establishing on a balance of probabilities a defence of due diligence or a defence of a reasonable but mistaken belief in facts that would have rendered its conduct reasonable.[126] Perhaps for this reason, the new section 22.1 has not yet been used frequently.

Section 22.2 governs organizational fault for subjective fault criminal offences. It provides that a corporation is liable if one of its senior officers (which term now includes important managers) acting within the scope of his or her authority and with the intent at least in part to benefit the organization is (1) a party to the offence; (2) while having the mental element for the offence, directs the work of representatives of the organization so that they commit the offence; or (3) while knowing that a representative is or is about to be a party to the offence, does not take all reasonable measures to stop that representative from being a party to the offence. The innovation here lies mainly in the idea that an organization can be held liable for a subjective fault criminal offence if its senior officer knows that a representative is committing an offence and fails to take all reasonable measures to prevent the commission of the offence. Although the senior officer must know that the offence is being or is about to be committed, the dominant fault requirement here is simply failing to take all reasonable measures to stop the offence. This fault requirement may even be lower than the requirement of a marked departure from a reasonable standard of care required with respect to criminal offences of negligence. The Court has yet to interpret this new measure, which combines subjective and objective fault requirements.

C. Defences

1. Types of Defence

The conceptual distinction between justification and excuse is relevant in Canadian criminal law. The most important application of this distinction is the Supreme Court's recognition of necessity solely as an excuse, as opposed to a justification, for crimes. Excuses are based on a realistic concession to human weaknesses and reject the idea that individuals can decide for themselves between a choice of lesser evils or higher law.[127] The Court has used the concept of an excuse to confine the defences of necessity and duress to exigent circumstances.

This understanding of excuses has also influenced the Court in holding that punishing morally involuntary behavior would violate the principles of fundamental justice protected under section 7 of the Charter.[128] The Court reasoned that "moral involuntariness is also related to the notion that the defence of duress is an excuse." It elaborated that an accused who acted in a morally involuntary manner should be excused because he or she "had no 'real' choice but to commit the offence."[129] An act can be morally involuntary even though the accused had the requisite *actus reus* and *mens rea* and even if the accused cannot be said to be blameless because there were alternatives to breaking the law, albeit unpalatable ones. In other words, morally involuntary behavior includes behavior in exigent circumstances where the accused would have a valid excuse, but not a justification, for breaking the law.

2. Burden of Proof

The accused is generally given the benefit of the existence of a reasonable doubt about a defence. In other words, once a defence such as self-defence, necessity, duress, or provocation is left to the jury, the prosecution must prove beyond a reasonable doubt that the defence does not exist. There are some exceptions to this general rule, but they have to be justified under section 1 of the Charter as a reasonable limit on the presumption of innocence in section 11(d), which has been interpreted to apply to defences, as well as elements of the offence.[130] The exceptions that must be established by the accused on a balance of probabilities include the defence of extreme intoxication to a general-intent offence,[131] the defence of mental disorder,[132] the defence of non-mental-disorder automatism,[133] the defence of entrapment,[134] and the defence of officially induced error.[135] As can be seen, the list of exceptions is long. The presumption of innocence that gives the accused the benefit of a reasonable doubt about the existence of a defence is often honored in its breach.

In addition to the persuasive burden imposed on the accused, evidential burdens are imposed before a defence is left to the jury. In order for a defence to be left to the jury, there must be some evidence that, if believed by the jury, is capable of supporting each required element of the defence.[136] This evidential burden is a matter of law for the trial judge, but it is not seen as a burden of proof that engages concerns about the presumption of innocence.

D. Justifications

1. Necessity

The majority of the Supreme Court in *R. v. Perka*[137] rejected the idea that necessity could ever be a justification. Justice Brian Dickson for the majority stressed the dangers of allowing individuals to decide whether to obey a higher law and the need to confine necessity to exigent and imminent circumstances where the accused would have no realistic choice but to violate the law. Justice Bertha Wilson dissented on this point and argued that it was premature to dismiss necessity as a possible justification in cases where the accused would break a law in pursuit of a higher legal duty. As examples, she cited the destruction of property to save lives or the performance of a surgical operation in order to protect life. As a result of the Court's categorical rejection of necessity as a justification, it would appear that premeditated acts can never qualify for the limited defence of necessity as an excuse.[138]

2. Self-Defence

The statutory provisions in the Criminal Code governing self-defence are notoriously and unnecessarily complex because they attempt to differentiate between different factual circumstances in which an accused acts in self-defence. Section 34(1) provides a justification when a person is unlawfully assaulted without having provoked the assault, or when a person willingly engages in a fight[139] and responds with no more force than is necessary for defence and without an intent to cause death or grievous bodily harm.[140] Section 35 imposes an additional requirement that an accused retreat as far as feasible in situations where the accused without justification assaulted or provoked the other person. Like section 34(1), this provision does not apply if the accused intended to cause death or grievous bodily harm. Section 37 extends the ambit of self-defence to a justification for using force to defend oneself or anyone under one's protection if the accused uses no more force than is necessary to prevent the assault or the repetition of the assault. Unlike section 34(1), section 37 can apply even if the accused provokes an assault and intends to cause death or grievous bodily harm, provided the force was necessary and not excessive.[141]

Section 34(2) provides that an accused who is (1) unlawfully assaulted and causes death or grievous bodily harm is justified if he has (2) a reasonable apprehension of death or grievous bodily harm and (3) believes on reasonable grounds that he cannot otherwise preserve himself from death or grievous bodily harm. The accused must have both a subjective belief and a reasonable basis for the belief that he is being unlawfully assaulted, faces a risk of death or grievous bodily harm, and is unable to preserve himself from such harms except by using force. The accused can be mistaken in these beliefs, but the mistakes must be reasonable. In determining the reasonableness of the mistake, the court may consider the past history and gender of the accused, but cannot consider the accused's intoxication.[142] The reasonable person for purposes of defences will be endowed with relevant characteristics such as gender, age, and relevant experiences even though this is not the case when the reasonable-person standard is used to determine objective fault. The Court has allowed expert evidence of battered woman's syndrome and has concluded that in such cases the ultimate issues are what the accused reasonably believed, given the accused's own experience, history, and perceptions.[143] The fact that the accused is or is not diagnosed with battered woman's syndrome is not a substitute for the determination of the elements of self-defence. At the same time, however, the reasonableness of the accused's belief that she was being assaulted and faced death or grievous bodily harm and that the force was required to escape the threat will be determined by taking into account the accused's age, gender, and relevant experiences.

Self-defence is an all-or-nothing proposition, and there is no partial defence of excessive use of force. In cases where the accused is charged with murder and has the fault and act for murder, this means that the accused will either be convicted of murder or acquitted on the basis of self-defence.

3. Consent

There is no general defence of consent in Canadian criminal law,[144] and the courts have not recognized a principle of fundamental justice that would prohibit the criminalization of all activities between consenting adults. Section 14 of the Criminal Code provides that no person can consent to death so as to relieve a person of criminal liability. In *Rodriguez v. British Columbia*[145] the Supreme Court decided in a 5–4 decision that the offence of assisted suicide did not violate the Charter. Although the Court recognized that the offence could violate the liberty and security of the person who wanted to die, as well as the equality rights of those who wished to end their lives but were not able to do so without assistance because of a debilitating disease, the Court nonetheless held that the offence did not offend the principles of fundamental justice and was justified as a reasonable limit on equality rights because of the social interest in protecting life and vulnerable persons.

Consent does not provide a defence to assault-based offences in cases where serious harm is intended and caused.[146] The Court in *R. v. Jobidon* decided that consent would be vitiated for reasons of public policy. It defended this ruling on the basis that "all criminal law is 'paternalistic' to some degree—top-down guidance is inherent in any prohibitive rule. That the common law has developed a strong resistance to recognizing the validity of consent to the intentional application of force in fist fights and brawls is merely one instance of the criminal law's concern that Canadian citizens treat each other humanely and with respect."[147] There was a strong dissent in this case that relied on the legislative definition of assault as the infliction of force without consent and argued that it was for the legislature to expand the criminal law for policy reasons. In any event, the Court has continued to restrict the ambit of consent as a defence of criminal activity and has held that consent to sex was vitiated by fraud in cases where an accused who knew that he was HIV-positive had unprotected sex.[148] Appellate courts have also held that sexual assault may be committed in cases where people consent to the intentional infliction of bodily harm as part of their sexual activities[149] and have refused to invalidate the offence of incest among adults on the basis of consent.[150] There are specific common-law and statutory rules defining consent in the context of sexual assault offences; these will be discussed in section III.C in this chapter.

E. Excuses

1. Mistake/Ignorance of Law or Fact

Defences of mistake of fact more accurately refer to conditions relating to the accused's perceptions that prevent the prosecution from proving the fault element of the particular offence. For example, a person who possessed illegal drugs but honestly believed that the drugs were a harmless substance would be acquitted because the prosecution could not establish subjective fault.[151]

Section 19 of the Criminal Code provides that "ignorance of the law by a person who commits an offence is not an excuse for committing the offence." This means that an accused who relied on erroneous legal advice from his or her lawyer that a drug had been legalized would not have an excuse. There are some limited exceptions to the general principle that ignorance or mistake of law is not an excuse. One is that the *mens rea* for theft and other property offences requires that a person act without color of right. A mistaken belief in a legal entitlement to property can thus be a defence to theft, arson, or mischief to property.[152]

The Supreme Court has recognized a defence of officially induced error as a limited exception to the principle that ignorance of the law is not an excuse.[153] The accused must establish on a balance of probabilities that he or she considered the legal consequences of his or her actions, that he or she relied on advice from an appropriate official, and that the advice and the reliance on the erroneous advice were reasonable. The reasonableness of the advice and the reliance on it must be determined on an objective basis. A successful defence of officially induced error results in a stay of proceedings, as opposed to an acquittal. Although the Court has recognized this new defence, it rejected it on the facts of the case in question because the accused simply relied on information about administrative practices and did not make positive inquiries or place reasonable reliance on a legal opinion.[154] The defence of officially induced error is a narrow exception to the basic and sometimes harsh principle that ignorance of and mistakes about the law are not an excuse.

2. Insanity/Diminished Capacity

The mental-disorder defence is infrequently raised, in large part because it can result in indeterminate detention for treatment. The accused must establish the defence on a balance of probabilities, and the prosecution can raise the defence only in response to an argument that places the accused's capacity for intent at issue or after the accused has been found to have committed the *actus reus* and *mens rea* of the crime.

The mental-disorder defence in section 16 of the Code is based on the common-law

M'Naghten rules.[155] It requires the accused to have a disease of the mind[156] that renders him or her incapable of appreciating the act's nature and quality, or renders him or her incapable of knowing that the act was wrong. "Disease of the mind" has been defined broadly to include "any illness, disorder or abnormal condition which impairs the human mind and its function, excluding however, self-induced states caused by alcohol or drugs, as well as transitory mental states such as hysteria or concussion."[157]

The determination whether an accused suffers from a disease of the mind can be critical to the disposition of an accused who acts in an involuntary state of automatism. If there is a mental disorder, then the disposition will be "not criminally responsible on account of mental disorder," and the accused will usually be detained pending assessment or treatment. If there is no mental disorder, then the verdict will be acquittal because the prosecution will not be able to establish a voluntary commission of the crime with the necessary fault. A controversial 1992 decision to hold that an accused who killed while he was sleepwalking did not suffer from a disease of the mind led to the acquittal of the accused on the grounds of non-mental-disorder automatism.[158] A few years later, however, the Supreme Court restricted the defence of non-mental-disorder automatism leading to an acquittal by holding that courts should require the accused to establish an automatic state on a balance of probabilities and should presume that a mental disorder was the cause of the automatic state.[159] The Court cited concerns for social protection for these innovations, which have generally been criticized as contrary to the presumption of innocence. A successful sleepwalking defence now produces a verdict that the accused is not criminally responsible by reason of mental disorder.[160]

An accused with a disease of the mind will be held not criminally responsible by reason of mental disorder if the disease renders him or her incapable of appreciating the physical consequences of his or her actions.[161] An inability to have an appropriate emotional response to the act[162] or to appreciate the penal consequences of the act[163] will not be sufficient, even if that inability is related to the accused's mental disorder. The alternative second arm of the mental-disorder defence requires the mental disorder to have caused the accused to be incapable of knowing that his or her actions were wrong. "Wrong" previously was interpreted as being restricted to knowledge that the actions were illegal, but now it is interpreted to include the inability to know that the act would be regarded as morally wrong according to social standards.[164] This arm does not apply to a psychopath or a person following a deviant moral code, provided that the person is capable of knowing that society would regard his or her acts as wrong.[165]

The two arms of the mental-disorder defence are alternatives. A person who believed that he was God killing Satan would not qualify under the first arm because he could appreciate the physical consequences of killing, but would qualify under the second arm because he was incapable of knowing that the action was wrong.[166] As with self-defence, the codified defence is an all-or-nothing proposition: there is no defence of diminished capacity. Evidence of mental disorder can, however, along with other evidence, be considered in determining whether the prosecution has established the requisite *mens rea*.

3. Intoxication

As with the laws concerning insanity, Canada inherited the English common-law rules in *Director of Public Prosecutions v. Beard*[167] that restricted the intoxication defence to cases where intoxication rendered the accused incapable of forming an intent to commit a "specific-intent" offence. Specific-intent offences were offences such as murder and robbery that required the accused to have the intent of achieving some illegal object, such as killing or robbing, beyond the immediate physical act.[168] General-intent offences were offences such as manslaughter and assault that required only an intent to commit an immediate act that in fact caused harm. Despite being criticized in strong dissents as a policy-based legal fiction imposed by the courts,[169] the distinction between specific- and general-intent offences still governs the availability of the intoxication defence in Canada.

In 1996 the Supreme Court rejected as too restrictive the requirement in *Beard* that intoxication render the accused incapable of forming a specific intent, and it redefined the test as whether evidence of intoxication left a reasonable doubt whether the accused had the specific intent. Even when evidence is presented about the accused's capability to form an intent because of intoxication, it should be made clear to the jury that the ultimate issue is whether the prosecution has established the actual intent beyond a reasonable doubt.[170] In order to avoid confusion, the Supreme Court has recently recommended that only the issue of whether the Crown has proven the accused's intent beyond a reasonable doubt should be left to the jury, with no mention of the possibly confusing issue of capacity.[171] This approach follows basic *mens rea* principles and has been relatively uncontroversial.

Much more controversial was a 1994 decision of the Supreme Court in *R. v. Daviault*[172] that held that the categorical denial of the intoxication defence for general-intent offences violated sections 7 and 11(d) of the Charter because it could result in the conviction of an accused who acted in an involuntary state because of extreme intoxication and could substitute the fault of voluntary intoxication for the fault of the particular general-intent offence. The majority of the Court stressed that the defence of extreme intoxication would have to be established by the accused on a balance of probabilities and with expert evidence. It ordered that the accused face a new sexual assault trial on this basis and indicated that Parliament could enact a new intoxication-based offence[173] to provide for social protection if necessary. The decision was extremely controversial, and Parliament quickly responded. It did not enact a new intoxication-based offence. Rather, Parliament enacted sections 33.1–33.3 of the Criminal Code, which declare that it is not a defence to a charge involving assault or interference with bodily integrity that the accused "by reason of self-induced intoxication, lacked the general intent or voluntariness required to commit the offence."[174] The provision also deemed that such self-induced intoxication constituted a marked departure from the reasonable standard of care. This legislation essentially reversed the Court's decision in *Daviault*, with the exception of general-intent offences that do not involve an invasion of bodily integrity. Therefore, the legislation has also been held by lower courts to violate the Charter because it allows for the conviction of a person who acted in an involuntary manner. The lower courts are, however, divided on whether the violation can be justified as a reasonable limit on the accused's Charter rights.[175] The constitutionality of this restriction on the intoxication defence will eventually have to be decided by the Supreme Court, but it is also possible that even if the Court struck down the restriction on the defence, Parliament would reenact it notwithstanding the legal rights in the Charter.[176]

4. Duress and Necessity

As discussed earlier, both necessity and duress are accepted only as defences that excuse the commission of morally involuntary crimes committed in exigent circumstances. A necessity defence requires that there be at least a reasonable doubt that there are (1) imminent peril or danger, (2) no reasonable legal alternative to the commission of the crime, and (3) proportionality between the harm inflicted and the harm avoided. The first two factors require both a subjective belief by the accused and a reasonable basis for that belief, with the reasonable person having the same relevant characteristics and experiences as the accused. The third requirement, proportionality, is judged on a purely objective basis and is somewhat in tension with the idea that necessity operates only as an excuse and not as a justification. Nevertheless, the Supreme Court requires only that the harm inflicted and the harm avoided be "of a comparable gravity" and has declined to create an absolute rule that the offence of murder would be disproportionate to all perils. It did hold, however, that killing was disproportionate to relieving non-life-threatening suffering and pain in a case in which a father killed his severely disabled child before she was scheduled for surgery.[177]

Unlike necessity, which remains a judge-made common-law defence, the defence of duress is partially codified in section 17 of the Criminal Code. The courts have been resistant to the restrictive codification of duress and have held that the statutory defence applies only to those who actually commit the crime while applying a more flexible residual common-law defence to those who are parties to a crime.[178] The common-law defence of duress generally mirrors the necessity defence by requiring (1) an imminent threat of death or bodily harm, (2) no legal way out for the accused or no safe avenue of escape, and (3) proportionality between the harm inflicted and the harm avoided. The courts have employed a modified objective approach that takes into account relevant experiences and characteristics of the accused. In addition, courts have taken a fairly relaxed approach to the proportionality requirement. For example, the common-law duress defence has been accepted as a defence to both murder and attempted murder.[179]

The Court has also held that requirements in the statutory defence in section 17 of the Criminal Code that the accused face "immediate" death or bodily harm from a person who is "present" violate section 7 of the Charter because they allow for the conviction of a person who commits a crime in a morally involuntary manner.[180] The remaining parts of the section 17 defence are also constitutionally suspect because they exclude a person who is a party to a conspiracy or association whereby the person is subject to threats. The courts have rejected a similar "clean-hands" doctrine as inconsistent with the recognition of necessity as an excuse for morally involuntary conduct.[181] Furthermore, section 17 contains a long list of categorically excluded offences, including such less serious offences as arson and robbery. As noted earlier, the courts have interpreted the more generous common-law defence of duress to apply even to the most serious crimes of murder and attempted murder and have refused to exclude killing under the relaxed requirements in the necessity defence that there be proportionality between the threat and the crime committed.[182] Canada's experience with the highly restrictive and unconstitutional defence of duress suggests that defences may be best left to common law and constitutional development by judges, as opposed to more punitive and populist statutes enacted by legislatures.

5. Entrapment

In 1988 the Supreme Court created a new defence of entrapment on the basis of its common-law powers to control an abuse of the court's process. The defence must be established by the accused on a balance of probabilities and results in a stay of proceedings. It applies if the state offers the accused an opportunity to commit a crime without reasonable suspicion that the accused is involved in a crime or without conducting a bona fide inquiry into crime in a high-crime neighborhood.[183] Even if the state has one of these grounds, entrapment will also occur if the state goes beyond providing the accused with an opportunity to commit the crime and actually induces the commission of the crime by engaging in conduct that would induce an average person to commit the crime and would bring the administration of justice into disrepute. The entrapment defence focuses on the objective conduct of the state and is still available to an accused subjectively predisposed to commit the crime.[184]

6. Superior Orders

In *R. v. Finta*[185] the Supreme Court recognized a defence of obedience to superior orders in a 4–3 decision. The case involved a person alleged to have participated in the rounding up of Jews in Hungary during World War II. The Court held that the accused could have a defence of obedience to superior orders if the orders were not manifestly unlawful. Furthermore, even if the orders were manifestly unlawful, the defence would still apply if the accused had no moral choice but to follow the order. This decision was very controversial. In 2000 Parliament enacted the Crimes against Humanity and War Crimes Act.[186] The Act excludes reliance on section 15 of the Criminal Code, which provides that no person shall be convicted of an offence for an act done in obedience to the laws made and enforced by persons in de facto possession of sovereign power in the place where the act occurred. Section 14 of the new Act provides that there is a defence of obedience to superior orders only if the accused was under a legal obligation to obey the orders, the accused did not know that the order was unlawful, and the order was not manifestly unlawful. Orders to commit genocide and crimes against humanity are deemed manifestly unlawful, and the defence of superior orders cannot be based on a belief that encouraged the commission of inhumane acts against a civilian population or an identifiable group of persons.

F. Sanctions

1. Punishment

In 1996 Canada introduced its first codified purposes of sentencing. As mentioned in section II.A in this chapter, the Criminal Code provides that the fundamental principle of sentencing is that a sentence must be proportionate to the gravity of the offence and the offender's degree of moral responsibility.[187] The Code also includes the traditional sentencing purposes of denunciation, specific and general deterrence, separation of offenders from society when necessary, and rehabilitation, as well as the restorative concepts of acknowledgment and reparation of harm done to victims and the community.[188]

Section 12 of the Charter contains a right not to be subjected to cruel and unusual treatment or punishment. The Supreme Court originally interpreted this right in a generous manner and held in 1987 that a mandatory minimum penalty of seven years' imprisonment for importing narcotics was cruel and unusual because it could be applied to a young person importing a small amount of marijuana.[189] In reaching this conclusion, the Court considered not only what was required to punish but also what was required to rehabilitate and deter the offender. In subsequent years the Court has been more deferential to mandatory minimum sentences, upholding a minimum four-year imprisonment term for the negligent infliction of death with a firearm[190] and holding that courts cannot fashion constitutional exemptions from mandatory sentences in exceptional cases.[191] The number of mandatory sentences is growing, but most offences in the Code still allow the judge a full range of sentencing options, including absolute and conditional discharges and community sanctions in the form of probation or conditional sentences of imprisonment and fines.

2. Quantity/Quality of Punishment

Canada has an imprisonment rate of 108 per 100,000 population.[192] It has significant overrepresentation of Aboriginal people in its prisons and likely of African Canadians as well. Aboriginal people make up about 4 percent of the Canadian population but about 18 percent of admissions to federal penitentiaries for those serving two years' imprisonment or more and 24 percent of admissions to provincial facilities for those serving lesser terms of imprisonment.[193] Section 718.2(e) of the Criminal Code is designed to address Aboriginal overrepresentation and instructs judges to consider "all available sanctions other than imprisonment that are reasonable in the circumstances, with particular attention to the circumstances of aboriginal offenders." This provision has been in place since 1996 and has been given a purposive interpretation by the Supreme Court,[194] but it has not reduced Aboriginal overrepresentation in prisons.

3. Death Penalty

Canada has not executed any person since 1962, and the last remaining death penalty for military offences was abolished in 1988. In 2001 the Supreme Court held that extradition to face the death penalty would generally violate the principles of fundamental justice under section 7 of the Charter. The Court stressed the international trend toward abolition, recent experience with wrongful convictions, and concerns about the "death-row phenomenon" as a justification for departing from its prior decisions in 1991 that allowed fugitives to be extradited to the United States to face the death penalty.[195]

III. SPECIAL PART

A. Structure

The Criminal Code does not contain a comprehensive catalogue of all statutory crimes in Canada, but it does contain most crimes. It contains separate sections dealing with offences against public order, terrorism, firearms offences, sexual offences, offences against the person and reputation, and various offences against property. There is no coherent penalty or fault structure in the Code with respect to the differences between crimes against the state, persons, or property.

B. Homicide

1. Murder/Manslaughter

There are three homicide offences: murder, manslaughter, and infanticide. The Supreme Court has struck down constructive or "felony" murder offences that applied to unintended killings committed during another serious crime on the basis that they violated section 7 of the Charter because they did not require the state to establish that the accused knew that the victim was likely to die. Knowledge of death is a constitutionally required minimum fault element, given the stigma and penalty for murder.[196] The Court found that constructive or "felony" murder offences could not be justified as a reasonable limit on Charter rights because the state could pursue its legitimate objective of deterring the use of violence and firearms in the commission of offences through more proportionate means such as stiff penalties for those crimes. However, the Court refused to strike down a sentencing classification of first-degree murder based on the commission of another serious crime at the time of the murder on the basis that the state would still have to prove that the accused knew that the victim was likely to die.[197] Planned and deliberate killings[198] and the killing of various justice system officials in the execution of their duties where the accused knows or is reckless of the victim's status also constitute first-degree murder.[199] All murder convictions result in a mandatory sentence of life imprisonment, but a first-degree murder conviction generally results in ineligibility for parole for twenty-five years.[200]

Manslaughter is an offence that is committed when an accused causes death by an unlawful act or by criminal negligence. In addition to establishing the *mens rea* of the unlawful act, the prosecution must establish that there was objective foresight of nontrivial bodily harm. In a 5–4 decision the Supreme Court rejected the idea that the fault for manslaughter should relate to the *actus reus* of causing death, in large part because of a concern about the need to convict a person of manslaughter who causes the unexpected death of a "thin skull" victim. The same majority of the Court also rejected the idea that the reasonable person used to determine objective fault should have the same characteristics and experiences as the accused because of concerns about applying uniform standards of conduct.[201] In justifying an expansive offence of manslaughter, the majority of the Court noted that the trial judge had complete sentencing discretion. Nevertheless, a four-year mandatory minimum sentence has subsequently been created for manslaughters that occur with firearms, and this sentence has been held to be constitutional.[202]

Manslaughter by criminal negligence requires proof that the accused engaged in a marked and substantial departure from the standard of reasonable care and showed wanton or reckless disregard for the lives and safety of others with respect to both the *actus reus* and the *mens rea*. This requirement of a marked and substantial departure is slightly higher than the requirement of a marked departure that is constitutionally required for all criminal offences that require negligence.[203]

Infanticide is a separate homicide offence punishable by no more than five years' imprisonment and applies when a woman by willful act or omission causes the death of her newborn child when her mind is disturbed by reason of not being fully recovered from childbirth.[204]

2. Provocation

Provocation is a defence that reduces murder to manslaughter. As defined in section 232 of the Criminal Code, provocation requires (1) a wrongful act or insult that would deprive an ordinary person of self-control and (2) that the accused must act on the wrongful act or insult "on the sudden and before there is time for [his or her] passion to cool." Anger alone will not suffice to reduce murder to manslaughter.[205]

The ordinary-person standard is designed to encourage reasonable and nonviolent behavior,[206] but the ordinary person is defined by the courts to be of the same age and gender as the accused and to have the same experiences that are relevant to the provocation in question.[207] There are concerns that this modified reasonable-person or objective approach may diminish the level of self-control expected from the accused and may afford defences in particular to jealous or homophobic males. At the same time, the courts have not been receptive to claims that the cultural or religious background of the accused should be considered in cases where a man kills a wife leaving a relationship. For example, the Ontario Court of Appeal has stressed that

> provocation does not shield an accused who has not lost self-control but has instead acted out of a sense of revenge or a culturally driven sense of the appropriate response to someone's else misconduct. An accused who acts out of a sense of retribution fuelled by a belief system that entitles a husband to punish his wife's perceived infidelity has not lost control, but has taken action that, according to his belief system, is a justified response to the situation.[208]

C. Sex Offences

Sexual offences have been the site of much controversy and change over the last quarter of a century of Canadian criminal law. In 1982 Parliament abolished the offence of rape and replaced it with three new offences of (1) sexual assault, (2) sexual assault with a weapon, threats to a third party or causing bodily harm, and (3) aggravated sexual assault. These offences were modeled after the corresponding assault offences in sections 266–268 of the Code in an attempt to emphasize that sexual assault is a crime of violence. The *actus reus* was broadened from rape to sexual assault, and the new offences, unlike the old offence of rape, applied to both genders and to a man who sexually assaulted his wife.

In 1992 Parliament again reformed the offence of sexual assault by defining consent to mean the voluntary agreement to engage in the sexual activity in question. Parliament provided a "no means no" law that states that there will be no consent if the complainant, having initially consented to engage in sexual activity, expresses by words or conduct a lack of agreement. The law also provides that there will be no consent if the complainant is incapable of consenting, is induced to consent by an abuse of a position of trust, power, or authority, or if a third party purports to provide consent.[209] The *actus reus* of sexual assault occurs if the application of force without consent is in circumstances that are objectively sexual and regardless of whether the accused had a sexual intent.[210] Consent as a matter of *actus reus* is based on the subjective views of the complainant, even if those views are not expressed to the accused. The Court also rejected the idea that there can be implied consent in cases where the woman did not consent but the accused may have perceived that there was consent.[211] Both the judicial and legislative approaches are united in defining the act in a manner designed to maximize the integrity of victims of sexual violence.

The *mens rea* of sexual assault requires an intentional application of force. The 1992 reforms addressed the controversial issue of the accused's mistaken belief in consent by providing that it would not be a defence if the belief arose from the accused's self-induced intoxication, recklessness, or willful blindness,[212] or if "the accused did not take reasonable steps, in the circumstances known to the accused, at the time, to ascertain whether the complainant was consenting."[213] This latter provision changed the law that had previously allowed a defence of honest but unreasonable mistaken belief in consent as an incident of the requirement to prove subjective fault in relation to all aspects of the *actus reus*.[214] This provision has been upheld under the Charter on the basis that the accused is not required to demonstrate that he took all reasonable steps to ascertain whether the complainant consented, and that the obligation to take reasonable steps depends on what circumstances are actually known to the accused.[215] Without reference to this provision, the Supreme Court has indicated that an accused cannot take silence, passivity, or ambiguous conduct as consent and must believe that the complainant has affirmatively communicated consent through words or actions. Once a complainant has expressed an unwillingness to engage in sexual activity, the accused must make certain that the complainant has changed her mind and cannot rely on lapse of time, silence, or ambiguous conduct.[216]

There are other sexual offences in the Code that apply to sexual interference and invitation to sexual touching with respect to children under the age of sixteen. Consent is not a defence, and a mistaken belief that the child is older than sixteen years of age is not valid unless the accused took all reasonable steps to ascertain the child's age.[217] The Criminal Code has recently been amended to raise the age of consent for most sexual offences from fourteen years of age to sixteen years of age while allowing some exceptions for those accused who are less than five years older than the complainant.[218]

D. Theft and Fraud

Theft requires the taking and conversion of anything fraudulently and without color of right, with the intent to deprive the owner of the property temporarily or permanently.[219] The property must be able to be converted in a manner that deprives the victim of the property. Thus confidential information that has not been reduced to a list or other tangible thing has not been considered property for the purpose of theft.[220] Conversion can be accomplished by delivery of goods or the conversion of property to the accused's own use with the intent to deprive the other person of the property.[221] A person may have a color of right if he or she honestly believes that he or she has a legal claim to the property.[222]

Fraud requires the taking of property or services by deceit, falsehood, or other fraudulent means.[223] Fraud requires proof of dishonesty, and dishonesty is judged by the standard of the reasonable person and requires at least the risk of depriving others of what belongs to them.[224] There must also be at least a risk of prejudice to the economic interests of the person defrauded.[225] The accused need not subjectively appreciate the dishonesty of his or her actions, but he or she must have subjective knowledge of the prohibited act and that the act could place the financial interests of the victim at risk.[226] The accused's expectation that his or her superior would ultimately validate fraudulent practices is not a defence.[227]

E. "Victimless" Crimes

In rejecting a Charter challenge to the offence of possession of small amounts of marijuana, the Supreme Court refused to recognize the principle that the criminal law should be used only to respond to harm as a principle of fundamental justice protected under section 7 of the Charter. The Court reached this decision on the basis that there is no consensus that the criminal law should be used only to respond to harm and that harm is not a manageable standard.[228] In any event, the Court also held that there was sufficient harm from the consumption of marijuana that the possession offence was not arbitrary, irrational, or grossly disproportionate so as to violate the principles of fundamental justice. The courts have, however, declared that prohibitions on the possession of marijuana for valid medical reasons would violate section 7 of the Charter, and regulations have been enacted to allow such possession.[229]

In 1993 the Court upheld the offence of assisted suicide, in part to respond to the risk that vulnerable people may be coerced into ending their lives.[230] It will be interesting to see whether this approach is subject to legislative or judicial change as a consequence of Canada's aging population.

The Supreme Court has upheld, under the Charter, laws prohibiting public solicitation for prostitution and the keeping of a bawdy house for the purposes of prostitution as a reasonable response to the public nuisance of prostitution. The majority of the Court stressed the nuisance of street prostitution, but one judge also argued that such laws would protect vulnerable groups who engage in prostitution. Two judges dissented on the basis that the law was overbroad in restricting freedom of expression and association and irrational in punishing the solicitation and the keeping of bawdy houses but not the actual act of prostitution.[231]

Laws against the possession and distribution of obscene material[232] have been upheld as a reasonable limit on the freedom of expression, but only after the law was interpreted not to include explicit sexual activity between adults that was not degrading and humiliating or involved violence.[233] Parliament subsequently enacted a law against pornography depicting those under the age of eighteen years or depicted as being under that age.[234] This offence was also upheld as a reasonable limit on the freedom of expression after the Court suggested that defences related to the possession of such material for legitimate purposes related to the administration of justice, science, medicine, and education be read broadly and that there be exemptions for privately held material created or depicting the accused that did not depict otherwise unlawful activity.[235]

The Supreme Court upheld offences against the willful promotion of hatred against identifiable groups on the basis that they responded to harms and constituted a reasonable limitation on freedom of expression.[236] In all these cases, offences prohibiting expression were upheld largely on the basis of concerns that women, children, and minorities could potentially be harmed by some forms of expression. In other words, what in another era might have been seen as "victimless" crimes were seen as acts that should be criminalized because they responded to potential victimization and the risk of harms to identifiable groups. The Court has been quick to assume that the criminal sanction will protect vulnerable groups that are at risk of being victimized by crime.[237]

F. Terrorism Offences

Shortly after the 9/11 terrorist attacks, Canada enacted a number of new offences against the financing of and participation in terrorist groups and the facilitation of terrorist activities.[238] In 2004 an offence of hoaxing terrorist activities was also added.[239] Section 83.01 was inspired by British legislation and defines terrorist activities broadly to include actions that endanger life or health or safety or that cause serious disruptions to essential services and are intended to intimidate the public or compel a person, government, or organization to act. There is an exemption for protests and strikes that are not intended to endanger life or cause a serious risk to health or safety. There is also a requirement that the state establish that the accused acted for a political, religious, or ideological purpose. Although some judges have upheld the requirement of a political or religious motive on the basis that it applies to violent activities that are not a protected form of expression,[240] one judge has struck out the motive requirement as an unjustified violation of fundamental freedoms.[241] The rejection of the requirement of a political or religious motive in the first terrorism prosecution that used the new offences is unique among countries that have used British legislation as a template for antiterrorism law and can perhaps be explained on the basis of Canada's commitments to multiculturalism, as well as freedom of expression.

Terrorism offences generally require high levels of intent or purpose, perhaps because of concerns that the high stigma and penalties for crimes of terrorism, like those with respect to murder, attempted murder, war crimes, and crimes against humanity, may constitutionally require high forms of subjective fault. At the same time, the new offences also contain interpretive clauses that qualify the fault requirement. For example, section 83.19(2) severely qualifies the fault element of knowingly facilitating a terrorist activity by providing that a person can facilitate a terrorist activity whether or not he or she knows that a particular terrorist activity is facilitated or even whether "any particular terrorist activity was foreseen or planned at the time it was facilitated." Although this offence has been upheld as having a constitutionally sufficient form of fault and as not unconstitutionally vague and overbroad,[242] the remaining fault requirement is far from clear. There are also other interpretive provisions that deem specific actions, including simply entering or remaining in a country for the benefit of a terrorist group, a sufficient *actus reus* for the offence of participating in a terrorist group[243] and specify that evidence such as the use of a name or a symbol associated with a terrorist group is relevant evidence.[244] These provisions are designed to mandate a broad interpretation of terrorist offences and seem to be based on a distrust of the ability of judges to give the offences a sensible interpretation.

The existence of a national criminal code subject to interpretation by the Supreme Court of Canada makes Canadian criminal law more uniform and accessible than criminal law in other federations such as Australia and the United States where the states exercise primary jurisdiction over criminal law. The fact that Canadian law is also accessible on the Internet and equally authoritative in both English and French should make it a frequently consulted source in comparative research into criminal law.

Canadian criminal law is a fertile source to study the strengths and weaknesses of courts and legislatures in making criminal law, as well as their interaction. For example, a comparison between the restrictive and unconstitutional statutory defence of duress and the more generous judge-made common-law defence of duress is instructive in revealing differences between how courts and legislatures make criminal law. The Canadian Criminal Code allows the judiciary much freedom both in interpreting statutory offences and defences and in creating new common-law defences, such as necessity, entrapment, and officially induced error. Since 1982 Canadian courts have had the new tool of a constitutional bill of rights to use in shaping and trimming the criminal law. Although the Charter remains primarily concerned with criminal procedure, it has had a significant impact on substantive criminal law.

The Canadian Supreme Court has interpreted the principles of fundamental justice in section 7 of the Charter to require that all offences that result in imprisonment have some fault elements and to require subjective fault for the offences of murder, attempted murder, and war crimes because of the high stigma and penalties that follow from conviction. Although section 7 of the Charter allows the use of negligence as a form of criminal liability, it requires that the state demonstrate that the accused has engaged in a marked departure from reasonable standards in order to distinguish criminal from civil liability and to ensure that the net of criminal liability is not too broad. Section 7 also prohibits criminal offences that are excessively vague or overbroad. The Court has also found that restrictive defences that punish morally involuntary conduct also violate the principles of fundamental justice under section 7 of the Charter. The Court has also ruled that extradition to face the death penalty would be contrary to the Charter, in large part because of recent revelations about the incidence of wrongful convictions.

The increased role of the courts in shaping criminal law under the Charter is a double-edged sword. The unelected court has been reluctant to constitutionalize subjective fault principles beyond the most serious crimes and has refused to find that important principles, such as the principle that criminal sanctions should be used only to respond to harm or that fault requirements should relate to all the aspects of the *actus reus*, are principles of fundamental justice under section 7 of the Charter. The Court has also become deferential to the increasing number of mandatory minimum penalties that are being enacted to limit the sentencing discretion of judges and has frequently accepted laws that infringe the presumption of innocence or freedom of expression as reasonable limits on those rights. Once the Court has held that a law is consistent with the Charter, it becomes difficult to repeal such "Charter-proof" laws even if they are not necessary or do not constitute wise penal policy. Conversely, Parliament has not been shy about attempting to reverse the Charter rulings of the Court when they are intensely unpopular. For example, Parliament has abolished the Court's recognition of a defence of extreme intoxication for general-intent offences, such as assault or sexual assault.

With the notable exception of populist responses to high-profile crimes, Parliament generally has delegated the task of law reform to the courts. Despite some selective trimming by the courts, the Canadian Criminal Code remains an unwieldy and incoherent code that grows every year as Parliament adds new offences in responses to the anxieties of the day.

SELECTED BIBLIOGRAPHY

Cameron, Jamie, ed. *The Charter's Impact on the Criminal Justice System*. Toronto: Carswell, 1996.

Cameron, Jamie, and James Stribopoulous, eds. *The Charter and Criminal Justice: 25 Years Later*. Toronto: Lexis-Nexis, 2008.

Canadian Criminal Law Review (journal published three times each year devoted to Canadian criminal justice issues).

Colvin, Eric, and Sanjeev Anand. *Principles of Criminal Law*. 3d ed. Toronto: Thomson, 2007.

Criminal Law Quarterly (journal published four times each year devoted to Canadian criminal justice issues).

Roach, Kent. *Criminal Law*. 4th ed. Toronto: Irwin Law, 2009.

Roach, Kent. *Due Process and Victims' Rights: The New Law and Politics of Criminal Justice*. Toronto: University of Toronto Press, 1999.

Stuart, Don. *Canadian Criminal Law*. 5th ed. Toronto: Thomson, 2007.

Stuart, Don. *Charter Justice in Canadian Criminal Law*. 4th ed. Toronto: Thomson, 2005.

Stuart, Don, R. J. Delisle, and Allan Manson, eds. *Towards a Clear and Just Criminal Law*. Toronto: Carswell, 1999.

NOTES

1. Enacted by the Canada Act, 1982 (U.K.), c. 11, Sched. B. The Charter is part 1 of the Constitution Act. The full text of the Charter can be found at Federal Department of Justice of Canada, http://laws.justice.gc.ca/en/charter/index.html.

2. Kent Roach, "Canada," in Craig Bradley, ed., *Criminal Procedure: A Worldwide Study*, 2d ed. (Durham, NC: Carolina Academic Press, 2007).

3. Public Inquiry into the Administration of Justice and Aboriginal People, *Report of the Aboriginal Justice Inquiry*, vol. 1 (Winnipeg: Queens Printer, 1991); Royal Commission on Aboriginal Peoples, *Bridging the Cultural Divide: A Report on Aboriginal People and Criminal Justice* (Ottawa: Supply and Services, 1996).

4. *Quebec Act*, 1774, 14 Geo. 3 c. 83, c. 11 (Eng.).

5. Constitution Act, 1867, s. 91(27).

6. As quoted in M. L. Friedland, "Criminal Justice and the Constitutional Division of Power in Canada," in Friedland, *A Century of Criminal Justice* (Toronto: Carswell, 1984), at 48.

7. *(Re) Dairy Industry Act (Canada) s. 5(a)* [1949] S.C.R. 1. Note that virtually all Supreme Court of Canada opinions are available in English and French at University of Montreal, http://csc.lexum.umontreal.ca/en/.

8. *R. J. R. MacDonald v. Canada (A.G.)* [1995] 3 S.C.R. 199.

9. *Re Firearms Act* [2000] 1 S.C.R. 783.

10. *R. v. Malmo-Levine* [2003] 3 S.C.R. 571.

11. *R. v. Hydro-Quebec* [1997] 3 S.C.R. 213.

12. *(Re) Dairy Industry Act (Canada) s. 5(a)* [1949] S.C.R. 1.

13. *Labatt Breweries v. A-G. Can.* [1980] 1 S.C.R. 914.

14. *Boggs v. The Queen* [1981] 1 S.C.R. 49.

15. *Switzman v. Elbling* [1957] S.C.R. 285.

16. *R. v. Westendorp* [1983] 1 S.C.R. 43.

17. *R. v. Morgentaler* [1993] 3 S.C.R. 463.

18. Desmond Brown, *The Genesis of the Canadian Criminal Code of 1892* (Toronto: University of Toronto Press, 1989), at 142.

19. Letter from Justice Taschereau to Minister of Justice Sir John Thompson, Jan. 20, 1893, in Desmond Brown, ed., *The Birth of a Criminal Code* (Toronto: University of Toronto Press, 1995), at 247.

20. *Criminal Code of Canada* (hereafter *Criminal Code*), S.C. 1892 s. 7 (see now R.S.C. 1985 s. 8(3)).

21. *Criminal Code*, R.S.C. 1985, c-46. The *Code* is available at http://laws.justice.gc.ca/en/C-46?noCookie.

22. S.C. 1996 c. 29.

23. *Frey v. Fedoruk* [1950] S.C.R. 517.

24. *United Nurses of Alberta v. Alberta (Attorney General)* [1992] 1 S.C.R. 901.

25. *Recodifying Criminal Law—Revised and Enlarged Edition* (Ottawa: Law Reform Commission of Canada, 1987).

26. Don Stuart, *Canadian Criminal Law*, 5th ed. (Toronto: Carswell, 2007), at 4–8.

27. Lucinda Vandervort, "To Codify or Not the Principles of Criminal Responsibility," in Don Stuart, R. J. Delisle, and Allan Manson, eds. *Towards a Clear and Just Criminal Law* (Toronto: Carswell, 1999), at 70.

28. Charter of Rights and Freedoms, s. 11(d).

29. *Ibid.* s.11(g).

30. *R. v. Chaulk* [1990] 3 S.C.R. 1303.

31. *R. v. Stinchcombe* [1991] 3 S.C.R. 326.

32. *R. v. François* [1994] 2 S.C.R. 827; *R. v. Lepage* [1995] 1 S.C.R. 654.

33. *Criminal Code* s. 649.

34. *R. v Pan* [2001] 2 S.C.R. 344.

35. *Criminal Code* s. 718.1.

36. *R. v. M (C.A.)* [1996] 1 S.C.R. 500 at para. 41.

37. *R. v. Creighton* [1993] 3 S.C.R. 3.

38. *Criminal Code* s. 718.
39. *R. v. Gladue* [1999] 1 S.C.R. 688; *R. v. Proulx* [2000] 1 S.C.R. 61.
40. *R. v. Gladue* [1999] 1 S.C.R. 688, para. 82.
41. *Ibid.* para. 79.
42. *R. v. Beaver* [1957] S.C.R. 531.
43. *R. v. Creighton* [1993] 3 S.C.R. 3.
44. *Criminal Code* s. 9(a).
45. *R. v. Mac* [2002] 1 S.C.R. 856; *R. v. Lamy* [2002] 1 S.C.R. 860.
46. *R. v. Paré* [1987] 2 S.C.R. 618.
47. *R. v. Russell* [2001] 2 S.C.R. 804.
48. *R. v. Malmo-Levine* [2003] 3 S.C.R. 571.
49. *Canadian Foundation for Children, Youth and the Law v. Canada (A.G.)* [2004] 1 S.C.R. 76 at para. 18.
50. *R. v. Nova Scotia Pharmaceutical Society* [1992] 2 S.C.R. 606; *Canadian Foundation for Children, Youth and the Law v. Canada* [2004] 1 S.C.R. 76.
51. *Criminal Code* s. 152.
52. *Ibid.* s. 172.1.
53. *Ibid.* s. 265(1)(a).
54. *R. v. Jobidon* [1991] 2 S.C.R. 714.
55. *R. v. King* [1962] S.C.R. 746 per Taschereau J. at 749.
56. *R. v. Hundal* [1993] 1 S.C.R. 867.
57. *R. v. Naglik* [1993] 3 S.C.R. 122.
58. *Criminal Code* s. 79.
59. *Ibid.* s. 127(1).
60. *Ibid.* s. 12.
61. *Ibid.* s. 218.
62. *Ibid.* s. 242.
63. *Ibid.* s. 446.
64. *Ibid.* s. 252.
65. *R. v. Thornton* [1993] 2 S.C.R. 445.
66. *R. v. Heywood* [1994] 3 S.C.R. 761.
67. *Criminal Code* s. 161.
68. This new offence has been upheld under the Charter as not excessively vague or overbroad except to the extent that that it prohibits attendance at a community centre where children might not be present. *R. v. Budreo* (2000) 142 C.C.C. (3d) 225 (Ont. C.A.).
69. *Criminal Code* s. 226.
70. *Ibid.* s. 225.
71. *Ibid.* s. 224.
72. [1978] 1 S.C.R. 506 at 519.
73. *R. v. Cribbin* [1994] O.J. No. 477, 89 C.C.C. (3d) 548 (Ont. C.A.).
74. [2001] 3 S.C.R. 488.
75. *Criminal Code* ss. 231(5) and 231(6).
76. *R. v. Harbottle* [1993] 3 S.C.R. 306.
77. *R. v. Williams* [2003] 2 S.C.R. 134.
78. *Sault Ste Marie v. The Queen* [1978] 2 S.C.R. 1299 at 1309.

79. *Re Section 94.2 of the BC Motor Vehicle Act* [1985] 2 S.C.R. 486.; *R. v. Hess* [1990] 2 S.C.R. 906; *R. v. Pontes* [1995] 3 S.C.R. 44.
80. *R. v. Creighton* [1993] 3 S.C.R. 3.
81. *R. v. Martineau* [1990] 2 S.C.R. 633.
82. *R. v. Logan* [1990] 2 S.C.R. 731.
83. *R. v. Finta* [1994] 1 S.C.R. 701.
84. *Canada v. Mugesera* [2005] 2 S.C.R. 100 at paras. 173–176.
85. *R. v. Beatty* 2008 SCC 5 at para. 34.
86. *Criminal Code* s. 21(1)(b).
87. *Ibid*. s. 24; *R. v. Ancio* [1984] 1 S.C.R. 225.
88. *R. v. Hibbert* [1995] 2 S.C.R. 973.
89. *R. v. Beaver* [1957] S.C.R. 531.
90. *R. v. Martineau* [1990] 2 S.C.R. 633.
91. *R. v. Sansregret* [1985] 1 S.C.R. 570, para. 22.
92. *R. v. Jorgensen* [1995] 4 S.C.R. 55 at 106; *R. v. Lagacé* (2003) 181 C.C.C. (3d) 12 (Ont. C.A.); *R. v. Briscoe* 2010 SCC 3,
93. *R. v. Cooper* [1993] 1 S.C.R. 146.
94. *R. v. Tutton* [1989] 1 S.C.R. 1392 per Justice William McIntyre; *R. v. Hundal* [1993] 1 S.C.R. 867; *R. v. Creighton* [1993] 3 S.C.R. 3.
95. *R. v. Finlay* [1993] 3 S.C.R 103; *R. v. Gossett* [1993] 3 S.C.R. 76.
96. *R. v. Naglik* [1993] 3 S.C.R. 122.
97. *R. v. Beatty* 2008 SCC 5.
98. *R. v. J.F.* 2008 SCC 60.
99. *R. v. Creighton* [1993] 3 S.C.R. 3.
100. *Ibid*. para. 137.
101. *Criminal Code* s. 464.
102. *R. v. Hamilton* [2005] 2 S.C.R. 432.
103. *R. v. Cline* [1956] O.R. 539 at 550, 551, 115 C.C.C. 18 at 26, 28 (Ont. C.A.).
104. *R. v. Deutsch* [1986] 2 S.C.R. 2.
105. *United States of America v. Dynar* [1997] 2 S.C.R. 462.
106. *R. v. Ancio* [1984] 1 S.C.R. 225.
107. *R v. Logan* [1990] 2 S.C.R. 731.
108. *R. v. Roach* [2004] O.J. No. 2566, 192 C.C.C. (3d) 557 (Ont. C.A).
109. *R. v. Ancio* [1984] 1 S.C.R. 225.
110. *Criminal Code* s. 465.
111. *R. v. Gralewicz* [1980] 2 S.C.R. 493.
112. *R. v. Cotroni* [1979] 2 S.C.R.256.
113. *R. v. Dery* [2006] 2 S.C.R. 669.
114. *R. v. O'Brien* [1954] S.C.R. 666 at 668.
115. *R. v. Dunlop* [1979] 2 S.C.R. 881 at 898. See also *R. v. Jackson* 2007 SCC 52 at paras. 3 and 9 for a recent affirmation of the principle that mere presence at the scene of a crime that is consistent with innocence will not support a conviction.
116. *R. v. Roach* [2004] O.J. No. 2566, 192 C.C.C. (3d) 557 (Ont. C.A.).
117. *R. v. Hibbert* [1995] 2 S.C.R. 973.
118. *R. v. Paquette* [1977] 2 S.C.R. 189.

119. *R. v. Hibbert* [1995] 2 S.C.R. 973.
120. *R. v. Logan* [1990] 2 S.C.R. 731.
121. *Criminal Code* s. 23.1. This provision also applies to aiding and abetting and being an accessory after the fact.
122. *Criminal Code* s. 23(2).
123. *"The Rhone" v. "The Peter A.B. Widener"* [1993] 1 S.C.R. 497 at 521; *R. v. Safety Kleen Canada Inc.* (1997) 32 O.R. (3d) 493 (Ont. C.A.).
124. In the case of a corporation, the director, the chief executive officer, and the chief financial officer are also defined to be senior officers. *Criminal Code* s. 2.
125. *Ibid.*
126. *R. v. Wholesale Travel Group, Inc.* [1991] 3 S.C.R. 154.
127. *R. v. Perka* [1984] 2 S.C.R. 233; *R. v. Hibbert* [1995] 2 S.C.R. 973.
128. *R. v. Ruzic* [2001] 1 S.C.R. 687.
129. *Ibid.* para 39.
130. *R. v. Whyte* [1988] 2 S.C.R. 3.
131. *R. v. Daviault* [1994] 3 S.C.R. 63.
132. *R. v. Chaulk* [1990] 3 S.C.R. 1303.
133. *R. v. Stone* [1999] 2 S.C.R. 290.
134. *R. v. Mack* [1988] 2 S.C.R. 903.
135. *City of Levis v. Tétreault* [2006] 1 S.C.R. 420.
136. *R. v. Cinous* [2002] 2 S.C.R. 3; *R. v. Fontaine* [2004] 1 S.C.R. 702.
137. [1984] 2 S.C.R. 233.
138. *R. v. Morgentaler* (1985) 52 O.R. (2d) 353, 22 C.C.C. (3d) 353 (Ont. C.A.); rev'd on other grounds [1988] 1 S.C.R 30.
139. *R. v. Paice* [2005] 1 S.C.R. 339.
140. *R. v. Hebert* [1996] 2 S.C.R. 272.
141. *R. v. Grandin* (2001) 95 B.C.L.R. (3d) 78, 154 C.C.C. (3d) 408 (B.C.C.A).
142. *R. v. Reilly* [1984] 2 S.C.R. 396.
143. *R. v. Lavallee* [1990] 1 S.C.R. 852; *R. v. Malott* [1998] 1 S.C.R. 123.
144. Don Stuart, *Canadian Criminal Law*, 5th ed. (Toronto: Carswell, 2007), at 587–608.
145. [1993] 3 S.C.R. 519.
146. *R. v. Jobidon* [1991] 2 S.C.R. 714; *R. v. Paice* [2005] 1 S.C.R. 339. There are exceptions for sporting events such as hockey where the intentional application of force is within the customary rules of the game.
147. *R. v. Jobidon* [1991] 2 S.C.R. 714 at para. 121.
148. *R. v. Cuerrier* [1998] 2 S.C.R. 371.
149. *R. v. Welch* (1995) 101 C.C.C. (3d) 216 (Ont. C.A.), citing *R. v. Brown* [1993] 2 All E.R. 75 (H.L.) with approval.
150. *R. v. F.(C.J.)* (1996) 105 C.C.C. (3d) 435 (N.S.C.A.).
151. *Beaver v. The Queen* [1957] S.C.R. 531.
152. *Criminal Code* ss. 322 and 429.
153. *Levis (City) v. Tétreault* [2006] 1 S.C.R. 420.
154. *Levis (City) v. Tétreault* [2006] 1 S.C.R. 420.
155. *R. v. M'Naghten* (1843) 10 Cl. & Fin. 200, 8 Eng. Rep. 718 (H.L.).

156. Since 1992, s. 16 of the *Criminal Code* refers to a "mental disorder," but this term is defined in s. 2 as a "disease of the mind."

157. *R. v. Cooper* [1980] 1 S.C.R. 1149.

158. *R. v. Parks* [1992] 2 S.C.R. 871.

159. *R. v. Stone* [1999] 2 S.C.R. 290.

160. *R. v. Luedecke* (2008) 236 C.C.C. (3d) 317 (Ont. C.A.).

161. *R. v. Cooper* [1980] 1 S.C.R. 1149.

162. *R. v. Simpson* (1977) 16 O.R. (2d) 129 (Ont. C.A.); *R. v. Kjeldsen* [1981] 2 S.C.R. 617.

163. *R. v. Abbey* [1982] 2 S.C.R. 24.

164. *R. v. Chaulk* [1990] 3 S.C.R. 1303, reversing *R. v. Schwartz* [1977] 1 S.C.R. 673.

165. *R. v. Oommen* [1994] 2 S.C.R. 507.

166. *R. v. Landry* [1991] 1 S.C.R. 99.

167. [1920] A.C. 479 (H.L.).

168. *R. v. George* [1960] S.C.R. 871.

169. *R. v. Leary* [1977] 1 S.C.R. 29; *R. v. Bernard* [1988] 2 S.C.R. 83 per Dickson C.J.C. in dissent.

170. *R. v. Robinson* [1996] 1 S.C.R. 683.

171. *R. v. Daley* [2007] S.C.C. 53 at paras. 101–102. Note that four judges in dissent would have required some instruction on the capacity issue because of the presence of expert evidence on that issue. *Ibid.* para. 128.

172. [1994] 3 S.C.R. 63.

173. Intoxication had been rejected as a defence for offences such as impaired driving that contained an element of intoxication. *R. v. Penno* [1990] 2 S.C.R. 865.

174. *Criminal Code* s. 33.1.

175. Contrast *R. v. Dunn* [1999] O.J. No. 5452, 28 C.R. (5th) 295 (Ont. S.C.J.); *R. v. Brenton* [1999] N.W.T.J. No. 113, 28 C.R. (5th) 308 (N.W.T.S.C.); and *R. v. Jensen* [2000] O.J. no. 4870 aff'd. on other grounds (2005) 27 C.R. (6th) 240, striking the provisions down, and *R. v. Vickberg* [1998] B.C.J. No. 1034, 16 C.R. (5th) 164 (B.C.S.C.), holding that the provision was justified under section 1 of the Charter. See generally Kent Roach, *Criminal Law*, 4th ed. (Toronto: Irwin Law, 2009), at 233–248.

176. On the institutional implications of this judgment, see Kent Roach, "Dialogue or Defiance? Legislative Reversals of Supreme Court Decisions in Canada and the United States," 4 *International Journal of Constitutional Law* 347 (2006).

177. *R. v. Latimer* [2001] 1 S.C.R. 3 at para 41.

178. *R. v. Paquette* [1977] 2 S.C.R. 189; *R. v.Hibbert* [1995] 2 S.C.R. 973.

179. *R. v. Paquette* [1977] 2 S.C.R. 189; *R. v.Hibbert* [1995] 2 S.C.R. 973.

180. *R. v. Ruzic* [2001] 1 S.C.R. 687.

181. *R. v. Perka* [1984] 2 S.C.R. 233.

182. *R. v. Paquette* [1977] 2 S.C.R. 189; *R. v.Hibbert* [1995] 2 S.C.R. 973; *R. v. Latimer* [2001] 1 S.C.R. 3.

183. *R. v. Barnes* [1991] 1 S.C.R. 449.

184. *R. v. Mack* [1988] 2 S.C.R. 903.

185. [1994] 1 S.C.R. 701.

186. S.C. 2000 c. 24.

187. *Criminal Code* s. 718.1.

188. *Ibid.* s. 718.
189. *R. v. Smith* [1987] 1 S.C.R. 1045.
190. *R. v. Morrisey* [2000] 2 S.C.R. 90.
191. *R. v. Ferguson* 2008 SCC 6.
192. Adult Correctional Services in Canada, 2005–2006 (2008) 28(6) Juristat, available at http://www.statcan.gc.ca/pub/85-002-x/2008006/article/10593-eng.htm.
193. *Ibid.* at 1.
194. *R. v. Gladue* [1999] 1 S.C.R. 688; *R. v. Wells* [2000] 1 S.C.R. 207.
195. *United States of America v. Burns* [2001] 1 S.C.R. 283, reversing *Reference re Ng Extradition* [1991] 2 S.C.R. 858.
196. *R. v. Vaillancourt* [1987] 2 S.C.R. 636; *R. v. Martineau* [1990] 2 S.C.R. 633; *R. v. Sit* [1991] 3 S.C.R. 124.
197. *R. v. Luxton* [1990] 2 S.C.R. 711. The list of serious offences has become longer as Parliament has responded to particularly horrific and well-publicized crimes by designating the commission of murder during crimes such as criminal harassment and gang or terrorist offences as first-degree murder. See *Criminal Code* ss. 231(5) to 231(6.2).
198. *Criminal Code* ss. 231(2) and (3).
199. *Ibid.* s. 231(4); *R. v. Collins* (1989) 48 C.C.C. (3d) 343 (Ont. C.A.).
200. In some cases, after fifteen years' imprisonment an offender can apply to a jury, which can declare that person eligible for parole. *Criminal Code* s. 745.6ff. A bill has recently been introduced in Parliament to repeal the ability of those convicted of first degree murder to apply for parole before 25 years. Bill S-6 *Serious Time for the Most Serious Crime Act* adopted by the Senate 29 June 2010.
201. *R. v. Creighton* [1993] 3 S.C.R. 3.
202. *R. v. Morrisey* [2000] 2 S.C.R. 90; *R. v. Ferguson* [2008] 1 S.C.R. 96.
203. *R. v. J.F.* 2008 SCC 60; *R. v. Beatty* 2008 SCC 5.
204. *Criminal Code* s. 233.
205. *R. v. Parent* [2001] 1 S.C.R. 761.
206. *R. v. Hill* [1986] 1 S.C.R. 313.
207. *R. v. Thibert* [1996] 1 S.C.R. 37.
208. *R. v. Humaid* (2006) 37 C.R. (6th) 347 at para. 85 (Ont. C.A.).
209. *Criminal Code* s. 273.1. See also *R. v. Jobidon* [1991] 2 S.C.R. 714, which suggests that consent may be vitiated for reason of public policy where consenting adults intend and cause serious harm to each other. For an application of this concept to consensual violent sexual activities and application of *R. v. Brown* (1993) 97 Cr. App R. 44 (H.L.), see *R. v. Welch* (1995) 25 O.R. (3d) 665, 101 C.C.C. (3d) 216 (Ont. C.A).
210. *R. v. K (B)* [1993] 2 S.C.R. 857; *R. v. Bernier* [1998] 1 S.C.R. 975.
211. *R. v. Ewanchuk* [1999] 1 S.C.R. 330.
212. *R. v. Sansregret* [1985] 1 S.C.R. 570.
213. *Criminal Code* s. 273.2.
214. *Pappajohn v. The Queen* [1980] 2 S.C.R. 120.
215. *R. v. Darrach* (1998) 38 O.R. (3d) 1, 122 C.C.C. (3d) 225 (Ont. C.A.), aff'd on other grounds [2000] 2 S.C.R. 443.
216. *R. v. Ewanchuk* [1999] 1 S.C.R. 330.
217. *Criminal Code* ss. 150.1, 151, and 152.

218. *Ibid.* s. 150.1(2).

219. *Ibid.* s. 322.

220. *R. v. Stewart* [1988] 1 S.C.R. 963. Note, however, that there are many other separate theft-based offences, including the offence of unauthorized use of a computer and theft of telecommunications signals. *Criminal Code* ss. 342.1, 326.

221. *R. v. Milne* [1992] 1 S.C.R. 697.

222. *R. v. Howson* [1966] 2 O.R. 63, 3 C.C.C. 384 (Ont. C.A.).

223. *Criminal Code* s. 380.

224. *R. v. Zlatic* [1993] 2 S.C.R. 29.

225. *R. v. Campbell* [1986] 2 S.C.R. 376.

226. *R. v. Theroux* [1993] 2 S.C.R. 5. As with theft, there are many other separate fraud-based offences, including those related to fraud in relation to fares, insider trading, and issuing a false prospectus. *Criminal Code* ss. 393, 382.1, and 400.

227. *R. v. Lemire* [1965] S.C.R. 174.

228. *R. v. Malmo-Levine* [2003] 3 S.C.R. 571.

229. *R. v. Parker* (2000) 49 O.R. (3d) 481 (Ont. C.A.); *R. v. Hitzig* [2003] O.J. No. 3873 (Ont. C.A.).

230. *Rodriguez v. British Columbia* [1993] 3 S.C.R. 519.

231. *Reference re Section 193 and 195.1(1) (c) of the Criminal Code* [1990] 1 S.C.R. 1123.

232. *Criminal Code* ss. 159 and 163.

233. *R. v. Butler* [1992] 1 S.C.R. 452.

234. *Criminal Code* s. 163.1(4).

235. *R. v. Sharpe* [2001] 1 S.C.R. 45.

236. *R. v. Keegstra* [1990] 3 S.C.R. 697.

237. See generally Kent Roach, *Due Process and Victims' Rights: The New Law and Politics of Criminal Justice* (Toronto: University of Toronto Press, 1999), at ch. 4.

238. *Criminal Code* pt. II.1.

239. *Criminal Code* s. 83.231.

240. *R. v. Fahim Ahmad et al.* (31 March 2009), Ontario CRIMJ (F) 2025/07 (Ont. Sup. Ct.), Ruling No. 12; *United States of America v. Nadarajah* (2009) 95 O.R. (3d) 514 (Ont. Sup.Ct.).

241. *R. v. Khawaja* (2006) 214 C.C.C. (3d) 399 (Ont. Sup. Ct.). See generally Kent Roach, "Terrorism Offences and the *Charter*: A Comment on *R. v. Khawaja*," 11 *Canadian Criminal Law Review* 271 (2007).

242. *R. v. Khawaja* (2006) 214 C.C.C. (3d) 399 (Ont. Sup. Ct.).

243. *Criminal Code* s. 83.18(3). Membership in a terrorist group is not an offence, but participation in a terrorist group for the purpose of enhancing the ability of the group to facilitate or carry out a terrorist activity is an offence. *Ibid.* s. 83.18(1).

244. *Ibid.* s. 83.18(4).

CHINA

Wei Luo

I. Introduction
   A. Historical Sketch
   B. Jurisdiction
   C. Sources of Criminal Law
   D. Unique Criminal Process

II. General Part
   A. Theories of Punishment
   B. Liability Requirements
   C. Defenses
   D. Justifications
   E. Excuses
   F. Sanctions

III. Special Part
   A. Structure
   B. Homicide
   C. Sex Offenses
   D. Theft and Fraud
   E. "Victimless" Crimes
   F. Political Crimes: From Counterrevolution to Endangering State Security

---

Wei Luo is Director of Technical Services and a Lecturer in Law at Washington University in St. Louis. His recent publications include *The Civil Procedure Law and Court Rules of the People's Republic of China* (Hein, 2006) and *Chinese Law and Legal Research* (Hein, 2005).

I. INTRODUCTION

A. Historical Sketch

Throughout Chinese history, nearly every dynasty exerted great effort in creating a comprehensive penal code. This phenomenon was described by Chinese legal history scholars as "paying more attention to criminal law than civil law" (*zhong xing qing min*). Even today the Chinese still regard criminal law as the second most important law after the constitution. Nevertheless, unlike the Soviet Union, which enacted a criminal code within five years of the Bolshevik Revolution,[1] the Chinese Communist Party (CCP) ruled the People's Republic of China (PRC) without a criminal code or a comprehensive set of criminal laws for thirty years in the era of Mao Zedong (1893–1976), from 1949 to 1979. Instead, the government relied on a few principal laws to govern criminal justice, such as the Act for Punishing Counterrevolutionaries of 1951, the Act for the Punishment of Corruption of 1952, the Arrest and Detention Act of 1954, and the Security Administration Punishment Act of 1957.[2] Other provisions related to criminal sanctions were scattered among various acts and regulations, such as the Provisional Act for Punishment of Crimes That Endanger State Currency of 1951 and the Interim Act of Customs.[3] The most significant reason for that reliance appears to be Mao Zedong's preference for rule by man, which allowed him to freely manipulate power, rather than the rule of law, which requires formal process.

After the Cultural Revolution ended in 1976, and particularly after Deng Xiaoping (1904–1997) was restored to power in 1978, the new Chinese leaders started an ambitious campaign to establish a modern legal system and bring the country under the rule of law. To that end, the Legal Affairs Commission of the Standing Committee of the National People's Congress (NPC) and other concerned government agencies resumed drafting of the Criminal Code based on its thirty-third draft done in 1965. In June 1979 the Legal Affairs Commission submitted the final draft to the Second Session of the Fifth NPC for review and deliberation. This Congress adopted the finalized draft on July 1, 1979, and promulgated it on July 6, 1979. The 1979 Criminal Code became effective on January 1, 1980.[4] The 1979 Criminal Code was not amended until March 1997. During this time the NPC and its State Council promulgated twenty-four individual criminal acts or regulations, such as the Decisions of Severely Punishing the Criminals Who Seriously Undermine the Economy, the Decisions of Severely Punishing the Criminals Who Seriously Disturbed the Social Order, the Supplementary Rules of Punishing the Crimes of Smuggling, the Supplementary Rules of Punishing the Crimes of Embezzlement and Bribery, and the Supplementary Rules of Punishing the Crimes of Revealing National Secrets. Various other acts and regulations also contain provisions related to criminal sanctions.

During the seventeen years after the enactment of the 1979 Criminal Code, tremendous changes occurred in the political, economic, and social life of China. New crimes cropped up, and as a result of the emergence of the market economy, a series of new economic crimes surfaced. In December 1996 the NPC's Standing Committee began the process of drafting a new criminal code. On March 6, 1997, the amended Criminal Code was presented to the Fifth Session of the Eighth NPC for review and deliberation. Many delegates suggested revisions and new provisions to the amended draft. The amended draft code was revised in some places, and a few new provisions were added, such as imposing criminal liability on publications that insult or discriminate against ethnic minorities.[5] The revised draft of the amended Criminal Code was finally adopted by the majority of the delegates on March 14, 1997. On October 1, 1997, the new Criminal Code of the PRC became effective.

B. Jurisdiction

Because the PRC is a highly centralized country, the Chinese judicial system, as a branch of the government, is structured like a pyramid: the Supreme People's Court (SPC) sits on top, followed by thirty-one higher courts at the provincial level, a few hundred intermediate courts at the municipal level, and at the bottom thousands of local basic courts at the county/district level.

Each people's court consists of a president, several vice presidents, judges, assistant judges, and registrars. The president of a local court is elected by the local people's congress, while the vice presidents, tribunal chiefs, and adjudicators of a local court are appointed by the standing committees of the local people's congress.[6] Every people's court normally has four tribunals: the criminal tribunal, the civil tribunal, the economic tribunal, and the enforcement tribunal. Each tribunal has a chief judge and several deputy chief judges. The distinction between civil and economic tribunals is that whereas the civil tribunal mainly adjudicates cases involving individuals and their property, the economic tribunal adjudicates cases involving enterprises or economic entities. As economic and commercial activities became more complicated and sophisticated and litigation volume increased dramatically, some local courts, particularly intermediate courts in big cities, created a number of more specialized tribunals, such as the intellectual property tribunal, the real estate tribunal, and the consumer protection tribunal.

In general, the jurisdiction of Chinese courts is subdivided both hierarchically and geographically according to the Criminal Procedure Law and the Civil Procedure Law. The SPC is the highest judicial organ and is responsible for supervising the administration of justice by the people's courts at various levels and the specialized people's courts. It also has the ultimate power to review and change all death penalties entered by lower courts.[7]

Under the principle of "the four levels of courts and at most two trials to conclude a case" (one trial at first instance and one trial on appeal), most criminal litigation is adjudicated in basic people's courts or intermediate people's courts, while higher people's courts and the SPC handle only appeals. Intermediate people's courts review judgments appealed from basic people's courts. The jurisdictions of the four levels of courts are described here, pursuant to the Organic Law of the People's Courts, the Criminal Procedure Law, and the Civil Procedure Law of the PRC.

1. Basic People's Courts
A basic people's court is a court of first instance. It adjudicates criminal or civil cases lodged in the place where the court is located. If a criminal case is very significant or too complicated or the court believes that a defendant could be sentenced to life imprisonment

or death, the basic people's court must transfer the case to its superior intermediate people's court for adjudication.[8]

2. Intermediate People's Courts

An intermediate court can adjudicate civil and criminal cases appealed from a basic people's court. As previously indicated, an intermediate people's court may also hear cases in the first instance. Only an intermediate people's court has jurisdiction to hear criminal cases involving national security, criminal cases in which defendants may be sentenced to life imprisonment or death, and crimes committed by aliens.[9]

3. Higher People's Courts

A higher court can adjudicate civil and criminal cases appealed from an intermediate people's court. A higher people's court can also serve as a court of first instance for prominent criminal and civil cases if these cases will have an impact on the whole province.[10] Every death sentence entered by an intermediate people's court is verified by a higher people's court and approved by the Supreme People's Court.[11]

4. The Supreme People's Court

The Supreme People's Court (SPC) adjudicates all cases appealed from any higher people's court and reviews all death sentences entered by an intermediate court. It may also hear a case in the first instance if the case may have a significant impact on the whole nation.[12] In the history of the PRC, however, the SPC has formed such a special tribunal only once—in 1980 to try the Gang of Four.[13] The SPC also has the power to retry a case that has been tried and decided by a lower court or, if the SPC concludes that there is a mistake in the judgment or in any of the lower court's rulings, to order the lower court to retry the case itself.[14] Since 1949 the SPC has retried only one ordinary criminal case, the case of Liu Yong in December 2003. In that case an intermediate people's court in Liaoning Province tried and sentenced Liu Yong, a notorious crime-ring boss, to death with immediate execution. The Higher People's Court of Liaoning Province then changed the intermediate court's sentence to the death sentence with a two-year suspension of execution. The commutation sparked a controversy in public and Chinese legal circles that led the SPC to decide to retry the case itself. After an open trial the SPC sentenced Liu Yong to death with immediate execution.[15]

C. Sources of Criminal Law

The major source of Chinese criminal law is its 1997 Criminal Code. Before 2000 the NPC normally enacted individual acts to amend or supplement the Criminal Code. For example, on October 30, 1999, the NPC's Standing Committee enacted a law titled "the Decision on Banning Cult Organizations, and Guarding against and Punishing Cult Activities." This pattern began to change in December 1999, when the NPC's Standing Committee enacted its first amendment to the Criminal Code. Between December 1999 and August 2009 the NPC's Standing Committee enacted seven amendments to the Criminal Code. China does not have a criminal law codification equivalent to the United States Code, and there is no Chinese government agency responsible for incorporating these amendments and the criminal law–related pieces of legislation into the Criminal Code.

Besides the Criminal Code, its amendments, and related legislation, legislative and judicial interpretations are another very important source of Chinese criminal law. This is very different than in countries that adopt a governmental structure with three branches (legislative, executive, and judicial), in which the power of statutory interpretation is vested in the judicial branch or in the court system. In 1981 the NPC's Standing Committee passed a resolution to empower the NPC's Standing Committee, the Supreme People's Court and the Supreme People's Procuracy (SPP), and the State Council to promulgate interpretations of the law.[16] These legal interpretations are called "legislative interpretation," "judicial interpretation," and "administrative interpretation," respectively.

The NPC's Standing Committee's power to interpret legislation was later confirmed by the 1982 constitution and the Legislative Law of 2000 (section 4). However, the Standing Committee has not exercised this power very often. As of June 2008 the Standing Committee had issued only about seventeen interpretations, and nine of them interpreted the Criminal Code.

Courts should possess the inherent power to apply law or interpret law in specific cases brought for litigation. However, the SPC has not only issued legal opinions upon specific requests from lower courts but has also proactively promulgated hundreds of judicial interpretations dealing with broader criminal law issues. The Interpretation of How to Apply Law When Adjudicating Theft Cases (11-04-1997), for example, has thirteen articles that deal with a variety of legal issues in the crime of theft.

Because the power of approving a judicial interpretation resides with the Adjudicating Committee of the SPC, which consists of about ten members (some of them not presiding judges but Communist officials), the process of formulating and promulgating a piece of interpretation is much like legislation, especially when a judicial interpretation deals with substantive law. Many Chinese jurists feel that it is inappropriate for the SPC to issue such judicial interpretations to supplement the legislature. Regardless of the legitimacy of the SPC's power to issue judicial interpretations, however, such interpretations constitute a very important source of Chinese law.

According to Chinese constitutional law, the SPP is directly under the National People's Congress and is not within the administrative branch of the government but parallel with the State Council and the Supreme People's Court. The people's procuracies not only prosecute criminals but also have the power to supervise civil and administrative litigations. Therefore, the National People's Congress classified the interpretations issued by the SPP under the judicial interpretation.

Both the SPC and the Supreme People's Procuracy have promulgated numerous judicial interpretations related to criminal issues. They have also often jointly promulgated such judicial interpretations. By August 2009 they had issued about 400 judicial interpretations of the Criminal Code. Despite the jurists' criticisms, many Chinese practitioners find the judicial interpretations very useful, particularly when legislation is vague or too abstract, because these judicial interpretations often function as implementation rules for the statutes.

Because China is a civil law country, its judicial system does not treat previous court opinions as legal precedent in the manner of common-law countries. Nevertheless, in recent years the SPC has asked lower courts to use the opinions delivered, selected, or published by the SPC as references when delivering their own judgments. The SPC usually publishes its opinions in the *Gazette of the SPC* and the *Selected Opinions of People's Courts*.[17]

D. Unique Criminal Process

The current Criminal Procedure Law of the PRC has adopted many basic principles commonly accepted by Western countries, such as formal judicial proceedings and the right to counsel. However, defendants' rights to an attorney and to a formal judicial proceeding are more limited in China. The unique aspects of Chinese criminal process can be characterized as follows.

1. No Presumption of Guilt until Rendering of Judgment

A new article that provides, "No one shall be found guilty without a judgment rendered by a people's court according to law," was added to the Part I General Provisions of the 1996 Criminal Procedure Law (CPL).[18] It was a very significant breakthrough to add this article to China's criminal procedure code because China has a long historical tradition of not separating administrative and judicial powers. In imperial China a magistrate also served as a judge. A person could easily be found guilty without going through a formal judicial proceeding. Between 1949, when the CCP took over China, and 1979, when the first Criminal Procedure Law was promulgated, there was no law that clearly defined and governed the functions of the police, the prosecution, and the judiciary. A few government officials working together could decide to arrest, prosecute, and convict a person. Even after 1979 many people viewed courtroom hearings as a mere formality to convict criminals. Additionally, the Chinese traditional concept has been to give more respect to the rights of the state than to individual rights.

This principle is also a very important prerequisite for the right of defendants to defend themselves before the courts. Some Chinese scholars claim that adding article 12 symbolizes that the Chinese criminal justice system has adopted the "presumption of innocence"; however, most Chinese scholars deem that article 12 does not exactly embrace a "presumption of innocence" but instead adopts the principle of "no judgment without a hearing." The latter view is probably more accurate because the rights of criminal suspects in China to legal counsel and a fair trial are still quite restricted.

2. Limited Right to Defense Counsel

The 1996 CPL enhances the involvement of defense counsel in criminal proceedings by allowing attorneys to provide legal services for criminal suspects during the police investigation of a criminal case and by granting attorneys more rights to present evidence during courtroom trials. Article 96 of the 1996 amended CPL provides, "After receiving the first interrogation from an investigation organ or from the day of receiving a compulsory measure, the criminal suspect may retain a lawyer to provide him with legal advice, to represent him to file a complaint, or to make an accusation on his behalf." Previously, lawyers could not be involved until the case was submitted to the court for trial. This change is very important in protecting the human rights of criminal suspects and easing the anxieties of the suspects' families, both of which are conducive to maintaining social stability. Under the 1996 amended CPL, before a criminal suspect is formally charged, he or she can retain a lawyer to seek legal advice, know what his or her legitimate rights are, and have his or her attorney keep the police in check and make sure that the police do not abuse their power. If the criminal suspect is arrested, he can also have his attorney apply for his release from custody on bail. The earlier involvement of attorneys in criminal proceedings ahead of trial should help prevent fabricated, false, and erroneous criminal charges, and it may also help avoid the illegal activity of extorting confessions by torture. Nevertheless, the involvement of lawyers at the investigation stage remains very limited. Because they are not yet participants in a trial, the lawyers cannot access the case files and evidence gathered by a public security organ. Additionally, in comparison with the American system, a Chinese person suspected of anything but a minor crime still does not have the right to an attorney when he is picked up and questioned for the first time by the police.[19] The CPL also still limits suspects' right to counsel by requiring them to obtain approval from the authorities if there is any state secret involved in their case. In practice, the definition or interpretation of state secret is often broadly interpreted to include cases involving not only military and political matters but also economic matters, religious matters, or anything to do with any state information.

The CPL guarantees the right of criminal suspects to retain defense counsel as soon as police departments recommend that procuracies indict them.[20] In addition, procuracies have the obligation to notify accused persons of their right to retain defense counsel within three days of receiving the prosecution recommendation from the police.[21] The amended law also grants attorneys more rights when they prepare a defense by allowing them to review and duplicate case files and evidence,[22] and by permitting them to collect evidence from witnesses and victims by themselves or to request that relevant people's courts or people's procuracies obtain evidence for them.[23]

The CPL guarantees an accused's right to be defended by an attorney, but the enforcement of that right can be another story, particularly when the Chinese government penalizes political dissidents. When the Chinese government placed Wang Youcai, a leading Chinese prodemocracy activist, on trial for subversion in December 1998, the Chinese authorities used intimidation to prevent Wang Wenjiang, the attorney chosen by Wang Youcai, from going to Hangzhou, where Wang Youcai's trial was to be held.[24] Chinese police can legally hold a person for questioning for up to twenty-four hours without a charge,[25] so they detained Wang Wenjiang repeatedly and consecutively four times in a deliberate effort to prevent him from defending Wang Youcai.[26]

3. Juries versus People's Assessors

The Chinese judicial procedure does not have a jury system like that of common-law countries. Instead, it uses a check-and-balance system called the people's assessor system to make sure that trials and judgments are fair. However, the people's assessor system is very different from the common-law jury system. Under the people's assessor system, the people's assessors (*renmin peishenyuan*) are not selected randomly; instead, they are picked and screened by the local people's courts with the local justice departments, and then the people's courts ask their local people's congresses to confirm their selections.[27] The term of a people's assessor is five years, with unlimited possibility of renewal.[28] People's assessors are nonprofessional adjudicators who sit in a collegiate bench and participate in the decision-making process, acting as a kind of juror and providing representation of the population in both criminal and civil adjudications. This system was introduced in the early 1940s within the territory controlled by the CCP's army[29] and was mentioned expressly in the 1954 and 1978 constitutions, although the 1982 constitution no longer refers to it. The 2006 Amended Organic Law of the People's Courts of 1979 also provides that a collegiate bench for a trial at the first instance may consist of either professional adjudicators and people's assessors or professional adjudicators only.[30] For cases on appeal, however, the collegiate bench does not include people's assessors.

Under the 1979 CPL, when a collegiate bench adjudicated a criminal case of the first instance in a basic people's court or an intermediate people's court, it was composed of one judge and two people's assessors; when it adjudicated a criminal case of the first instance in a higher people's court or the Supreme People's Court, it was composed of one to three judges and two to four people's assessors.[31] After the 1996 amendment, a collegiate bench of a basic or an intermediate people's court can be composed of one judge and two people's assessors or two judges and one people's assessor; a collegiate bench of a higher people's court or the SPC can be composed of three to seven judges or from three to seven judges and people's assessors. This amendment reduced the mandatory number of people's assessors when forming a collegiate bench.

Because it is difficult to find qualified assessors who have legal knowledge, there are not many people who are interested in being people's assessors, and few people's courts like to use them. Some Chinese legal scholars argue that China should put an end to this practice.

4. Lack of Pretrial Discovery Rule

The 1979 CPL required the prosecutor, before trial, to submit all of the prosecution's evidence to the court; the defendants and their counsels would then have an opportunity to review the evidence. Because there was a widespread perception in Chinese legal circles that judges might decide the outcome before going through a trial if they had a chance to review all of the prosecution's evidence,[32] the 1996 CPL changed this practice and only requires the prosecutor to submit "major" evidence to the court.[33] Although the 1996 CPL provides that defense counsel "may" review, copy, and duplicate evidential materials related to the criminal indictments after the indictments are accepted by courts for adjudication,[34] defense counsel can review only whatever evidence is submitted by the prosecutor. Therefore, defense counsels are not able to review all the evidence presented by the prosecutor for trial. "This reform had the unintended consequence that defense counsels receive less advance notice of the prosecution evidence under current law than they did before the 1997 'reform.'"[35] Obviously, this practice curtails a defendant's right to prepare a defense to the charges against him.

II. GENERAL PART

A. Theories of Punishment

As stated in articles 1 and 2 of the 1997 Criminal Code of the PRC, the Criminal Code is formulated to combat all kinds of crimes in order to protect people and property, defend national security, and safeguard the social order. Criminal punishments are the severest compulsory measures imposed on criminals.

Like most other countries, the 1997 Criminal Code of the PRC has adopted the following two basic principles to guide the formulation, interpretation, and enforcement of the Criminal Code.

1. The Principle of Prescribed Punishments for Specific Crimes

Before the 1979 Criminal Code, the Chinese government followed the Chinese tradition of the analogical approach to deal with crimes that were not prescribed in the penal codes. Article 79 of the 1979 Criminal Code stated: "A crime not specifically prescribed under the specific provisions of the present law may be confirmed a crime and sentence rendered in light of the most analogous article under the special provisions of the present law; provided, however, that the case shall be submitted to the Supreme People's Court for its approval."[36]

This provision and the analogical approach were repealed in the 1997 Criminal Code. The principle of determining offenses according to law was adopted and stated in article 3 of the 1997 Criminal Code: "Any act deemed by explicit stipulations of law as a crime shall be convicted and given punishment by law, and any act that no explicit stipulations of law deem a crime shall not be convicted or given punishment."

According to this principle, acts not stipulated in explicit terms as offenses are not offenses. The 1979 Criminal Code had 192 articles, but only 103 specific provisions. Because some provisions were not specific or comprehensive enough, it was very difficult for the trial courts to apply the prescribed criminal penalties to those offenses. In the 1997 Criminal Code, the number of articles in the specific provisions that deal with specific crimes was increased to 345, and those articles more clearly and specifically define the various kinds of crimes, making it possible to abolish the analogical approach.[37] The new approach may provide both more effective legal protection for citizens' personal freedom and rights and a more solid legal foundation for judicial institutions to punish crimes according to law. The legal source for the rule of analogy was one of China's ancient legal traditions. There was also a similar provision in the Qing Code., which was in force between 1644 and 1912.[38] In fact, after the founding of the PRC and before the promulgation of the 1997 Criminal Code—especially during the Cultural Revolution (1966–1976)—the practice of analogical reasoning in the Chinese criminal justice system was rampant. As a result, many innocent Chinese were penalized for political reasons. It is hoped that abolishing the analogical approach will bring this practice to an end and will reconcile Chinese criminal law with the Western legal idea that no one should be convicted of a crime without proof that he committed a specific offense that was clearly recognized as a crime when committed.

2. Matching Punishment with Crime

The principle of matching punishment with crime was established in the 1997 Criminal Code. Article 5 of the 1997 Criminal Code provides that whether severer or lighter punishment is to be meted out should be determined on the basis of the crime committed by the criminal and the criminal responsibility provided by the Criminal Code. This principle is conducive to avoiding inappropriate or different measurements of penalties, such as imposing light punishment for serious crimes or severe punishment for minor crimes (misdemeanors). The practical significance of adopting this principle is that the Chinese government has tried to change another Chinese traditional practice of using severe penalties to stabilize the social order when the crime rate is increasing. Since 1949 the Chinese government has carried out various strike-hard campaigns to combat surging crimes. One of the most notable campaigns was initially advocated by the Central Committee of the CCP in August 1983 and was confirmed by the NPC's Standing Committee when it issued the Decision of Severely Punishing Criminals Who Seriously Disturbed the Social Order in September 1983. The decision required courts to impose severe punishments on criminals and use speedy trial procedures to conclude criminal cases. This strike-hard campaign lasted for three years. Later, many people who were convicted and sentenced during this campaign were found to be either innocent or deserving of a less severe sentence.[39] Unfortunately, the strike-hard campaign of "imposing severe punishment and using speedy trial" is still being deployed. For example, on July 30, 2002, the SPC, the SPP, and the Ministry of Public Security jointly issued the Notice of Strike-Hard on Robbery and the Other Related Crimes to combat the robbery crime wave.

B. Liability Requirements

The Chinese theory of what constitutes a crime that is described in the 1997 Criminal Code is very similar to the theory of common-law jurisdictions. Many legal terms used in the Chinese Criminal Code, such as intention, recklessness, knowledge, negligence, foreseeability, and causation, are very familiar to common-law lawyers.[40] However, how those elements are described and how those elements combine to constitute a crime are very different in Chinese theory and common-law theory.

1. Elements That Constitute a Crime

Under Chinese criminal law theory, the following four basic elements or requisites (*yaojian*) are required to constitute a crime and establish criminal liability: (1) the object of the crime (literally translated from the Chinese term *fanzui keti*) (the type of crime); (2) the objective aspect of the crime (*fanzui keti fangmian*) (the harm caused); (3) the criminal subject (*fanzui zhuti*) (the person who performed the criminal act); and (4) the criminal subject aspect (*fanzui zhuti fanmian*), similar to the term *mens rea* or guilty mind (the person's intention, recklessness, or negligence).[41] If all four elements are satisfied, a person's action constitutes a crime, and the person is criminally liable. If any of the elements are missing or deficient, there is no criminal liability.[42] These four elements/requisites are discussed in detail in mainstream Chinese criminal law textbooks.

2. The Objects of Crimes

The objects of crimes refer to the social orders, values, rights, interests, and the like that are protected by Chinese criminal laws. If an action does not harm any social orders, values, rights, or interests that are protected by Chinese criminal law, the actor should not be punished. Therefore, the objects of crimes referred to by Chinese criminal theory are not offended persons (victims) or properties. The objects of crimes are generally described by article 13 of the 1997 Criminal Code and specifically described in Part 2 Specific Provisions. For example, in offenses involving subverting the political power of the state or overthrowing the socialist system, the object of crime is not the state but political power and the system of the state. Similarly, in robberies and murders, the object of crime is not the victim himself but the victim's right to live and right to property. The crimes of undermining social orders are mostly provided in chapters 3 and 6 of the 1997 Criminal Code, while the crimes of endangering the state's interests are mainly provided in chapters 1–2 and 7–9. Because China has abolished the analogical approach (discussed in section II.A.1 in this chapter), if there is no identifiable specific object, there is no crime.

To determine which specific object of crime is being violated is an important part of deciding which crime has been committed. For example, a person was apprehended while he was stealing 2,000 meters of communication cable used for both civilian and military purposes. The procuracy charged him with the crime of stealing communication cable under article 265 of the 1997 Criminal Code, but the court convicted him of sabotaging the public communication system under article 124 of the 1997 Criminal Code, because the court believed that the object of the crime was endangering public security.

3. *Objective*/Actus Reus
   i. Act

The objective aspects of crime refer to criminal conduct and the harmful consequences caused by criminal conduct. A crime's objective aspect has three related components: criminal conduct, a harmful consequence, and the causal link between the criminal conduct and the harmful consequence. To convict someone of a crime, it must be proved that there is a criminal conduct or action. For example, if Mr. Zhang told his friends that he intended to kill Ms. Chen, but he never put his intention into action, he did not commit a murder.

The second component of the criminal aspect is a harmful consequence, which refers to the consequences usually specified by the Criminal Code. Under Chinese criminal law, criminal liability is imposed only if a substantial harmful consequence resulted, although some offenses do not require any harmful consequences to actually materialize, such as some of the crimes of endangering national security and the crimes of manufacturing and distributing fake and shoddy goods.[43] For example, if a Chinese political dissident used the Internet to post his idea of establishing a party to oppose the Chinese Communist Party, he could be convicted of the crime of endangering state security even if it was impossible to prove that specific damage resulted from his action.

The third crucial component of the criminal aspect is that there must be a causal link between the act or omission and the harmful consequence. Of course, there are exceptions to the causal link, including unavoidable or unforeseeable causes.[44]

   ii. Omission

Articles 13–16 of the 1997 Criminal Code define the general scope of criminal aspects. Criminal conduct refers to acts and nonacts (omissions). Omissions usually refer to certain people who are under certain obligations to react to certain circumstances but fail to react accordingly—an on-duty doctor, for example, who refused to treat a very sick person without proper reasons.

iii. The Subjects of Crime

The subjects of crimes refer to natural persons or legal persons who commit crimes proscribed by the Criminal Code and who are thus liable for those crimes. According to Chinese criminal law, the subject of a crime must be a natural person who is at least fourteen years old and is mentally fit to take legal responsibility,[45] or a legal person (unit) such as a corporation, enterprise, institution, organ, or organization.[46] The legal status of a criminal subject must, therefore, be used to test whether the offender should be charged with a crime or set free. If an offender does not meet the requirements of a criminal subject that are provided in the Criminal Code, that person cannot be found guilty. For example, no one under the age of fourteen can be charged with a crime. In addition, insanity, self-defense, and emergency situation can also be used to protect someone against criminal liability if he or she is indicted. Insanity is defined as the inability to recognize or control one's own conduct.[47] Self-defense and emergency situation are defined in articles 20 and 21 of the 1997 Criminal Code.

iv. Status

The legal status of a criminal subject can also affect that subject's criminal liability. For example, criminal offenders between the ages of fourteen and sixteen are responsible only for serious crimes such as murder, rape, or robbery, and those between fourteen and eighteen are to be given lighter or mitigated punishment.[48] A deaf-mute or a blind person who commits a crime may be given a lesser punishment or a mitigated punishment or may be exempted from punishment entirely.[49]

4. Subjective/*Mens Rea*/*Mental Element*

The literal translation of the Chinese definition of "the subjective aspect of a crime" is "the psychological state of the criminal subject (offender) toward the harmful consequences that may have resulted from his action." This element is used to test whether the criminal subject should be held criminally responsible. In fact, the subjective aspect of crime is very similar to the Western criminal concept of *mens rea*. Under the current Chinese Criminal Code, an offender will be held criminally responsible only when his intentional or negligent act results in harmful consequences to society. In other words, even if a person causes a harmful consequence, he will not be charged with a crime if he did not intend to cause that harmful consequence or was not negligent in causing it. Therefore, there are two major categories of the subjective aspect of crime: (1) intentionally committing a crime, where the person clearly knows that his act will produce harmful consequences and desires or accepts that such consequences will occur,[50] and (2) negligently committing a crime, where the person should have foreseen that his act might cause harmful consequences or foresaw the harmful consequences but believed that those consequences could be avoided.[51]

In addition to the mental states of intention or negligence, some specific offense provisions of the Criminal Code require other, more specific mental states, such as acting for "the purposes of reaping profits" or for "the purposes of retaliation." For example, to find a smuggler guilty of smuggling obscene articles, it must be proved that the smuggler smuggled the obscene articles for the purposes of reaping profits or disseminating these articles.⁵² Similarly, to find someone guilty of sabotaging a business operation, it must be proved that the suspect committed sabotage for the purposes of retaliation, out of spite, or for other personal motives.⁵³

The Chinese Criminal Code also provides that although an act results in harmful consequences, it shall not be deemed a crime if it was caused by unavoidable or unforeseeable causes instead of by intent or negligence.⁵⁴ The term *unavoidable circumstances* is similar to the definition of *force majeure*, and most Chinese criminal law textbooks describe an unavoidable circumstance as one where the occurrence of harmful consequences was beyond the control of the person involved, no matter how hard that person tried to avoid those consequences. For example, a coachman was driving a horse carriage on a street in a normal manner when suddenly an automobile frightened the horse and caused it to run toward pedestrians. The coachman pulled the brake but could not stop the carriage from killing a pedestrian. Because the coachman could not avoid this tragic accident, he would not be criminally liable for killing the pedestrian.

The definition of "unforeseeable circumstances" refers to situations where the actor not only failed to foresee that his actions would result in harmful consequences, but where the actor was also unable to foresee those consequences at the time of his act. In a hypothetical case widely used by several Chinese criminal law websites, Mr. Wang, a middle student 1.6 meters tall, and several of his classmates went to play in a river. Mr. Wang did not know how to swim, so he stayed in the shallow area. Mr. Liu, one of Mr. Wang's classmates, teased Mr. Wang by dragging him from the shallow area into the area where the water was 1.4 meters deep. Mr. Wang went into shock because he could not swim, so Mr. Liu held him with his arms. Soon both of them were submerged by water. Mr. Liu was afraid that he was going to drown, so he pushed Mr. Wang away and swam to the bank. Mr. Wang drowned. If Mr. Liu could prove that he did not know that Mr. Wang could not swim and that he did not and could not foresee that he would not have been able to pull Mr. Wang back to the shallow area, he might not be held liable for intentional murder.

The subjective aspect of crime can also be used to measure an offender's criminal liability. For example, a person who intentionally killed someone would be charged with murder and could be sentenced to a maximum of death, while a person who unintentionally killed someone would be charged with manslaughter and would not be sentenced to more than a seven-year prison term.⁵⁵ Consider the case *Zhang Shuancheng: Manslaughter Due to Negligence*.⁵⁶ In 2004 Zhang Guozheng's son-in-law raped the defendant Zhang Shuancheng's niece and then fled after an arrest warrant was issued. One day in 2005 the defendant went to Zhang Guozheng's home to look for his son-in-law. The defendant and Zhang Guozheng began a fistfight. The defendant used his fists to punch Zhang Guozheng's head and other parts of his body several times. Zhang Guozheng soon felt very sick and died on the way to the hospital. The autopsy showed that Zhang Guozheng had some minor injuries from the fistfight and had died from a heart attack. Zhang Guozheng had a history of heart disease. The defendant was charged with manslaughter due to his negligence. The Hua County People's Court of Henan Province found the defendant guilty of negligent manslaughter because he failed to foresee that his punches on Zhang Guozheng, an older man, could trigger a fatal heart attack. Although the defendant appealed, the

Anyang City Intermediate People's Court of Henan Province affirmed the lower court's holding.

5. Theories of Liability

i. Inchoate Crimes

Inchoate crimes refer to situations in which criminals stop or withdraw from acting in the process of committing crimes. The Chinese Criminal Code divides inchoate crimes into the following three situations.

a. Crime Preparation

Crime preparation refers to an actor who prepares tools and creates conditions necessary to commit a crime. According to Chinese practice, preparing tools to commit a crime includes making and acquiring the tools, while creating conditions for committing a crime includes (1) surveying crime scenes, (2) planning, (3) removing obstacles that hinder the commission of a crime, (4) stalking or approaching victims, (5) being on the way to commit a crime or luring a victim to a crime scene, (6) conspiring with others to commit a crime, or (7) planning to escape after committing a crime or covering up criminal activity. According to the Criminal Code, when imposing criminal liability on someone who prepared to commit a crime, the court should impose a lesser or mitigated punishment relative to the punishment for a completed crime or should exempt the actor from criminal liability entirely.[57]

b. Attempt to Commit a Crime

Attempt to commit a crime refers to a situation where an offender began to commit a crime but could not complete the crime because of reasons beyond the offender's control. The punishment imposed on an offender who attempts to commit a crime is lighter or mitigated in comparison with one who accomplishes a similar crime.[58]

In Chinese criminal justice practice, attempt to commit a crime can be subdivided into two categories: attempt to commit a crime but the action is uncompleted, and attempt to commit a crime but the mission is unaccomplished. The first category refers to a criminal who began to commit a crime but was unable to complete the criminal act. The second category refers to a criminal who attempted to commit a crime and completed the criminal action, but did not accomplish the harmful consequences because of a reason beyond his control. For example, X attempts to murder Y by putting poison into Y's wine glass, but Y accidentally knocks over his wine glass, preventing him from being killed by the poison. Because the second situation is closer to an accomplished crime, the offender's punishment is severer than in the first situation.

c. Discontinuation of a Crime

Discontinuation of a crime refers to cases where, during the process of committing a crime, the offender voluntarily terminates the criminal activity or voluntarily takes action to prevent the harmful consequence from occurring. The Chinese Criminal Code does not impose criminal liability on an offender who successfully discontinues the criminal activity before causing any damage. However, the code does impose a mitigated punishment on an offender if any damage resulted.[59]

ii. Complicity

The Chinese Criminal Code refers to complicity as joint crimes, which means crimes that are deliberately committed by two or more persons as a result of a conspiracy to commit the crimes together.[60] If a crime is negligently committed by two or more persons, however, the crime is not punished as a joint crime, and the persons are individually punished according to the crimes they committed.[61] Therefore, a joint crime must meet the following three conditions:

1. The crime must be committed by two or more persons.
2. The harmful acts and harmful consequences (objective aspects) must be the product of conspiracy between the joint criminals.
3. The joint criminals must have the same criminal objective (subjective aspect).

The code distinguishes between joint criminals according to their roles in a crime and imposes different punishments accordingly. Joint criminals are classified into the following four categories:

1. *Principal offenders*, which refers to persons who organize and lead criminal syndicates in carrying out criminal activities or who play a principal role in a joint crime. The code defines a criminal syndicate as a relatively permanent organization consisting of more than three persons who come together for the purposes of committing crimes. The code also divides principal offenders into two subcategories: *ringleaders*, who are the leaders of a criminal syndicate and who should be punished for all the crimes committed by the syndicate; and *other principal offenders*, who are not the leaders of a criminal syndicate but play leading roles in some of its criminal acts and should thus be punished for those crimes.[62]

2. *Accomplices*, which refers to persons who play a secondary or supplementary role in a joint crime. The code imposes less severe punishment on an accomplice than on a principal offender, depending on the circumstances.[63] An accomplice who plays a secondary role in a joint crime is directly involved in the criminal acts, while an accomplice who plays a supplementary role is indirectly involved in a joint crime by abetting the principal offenders, such as by providing them with information, tools, or a hideout. Their criminal liabilities are thus different.

3. *Coerced offenders*, which refers to persons who are coerced into participating in a crime. The code imposes less severe punishment on a coerced offender than on an accomplice or does not punish a coerced offender at all, depending on the circumstances.[64]

4. *Instigators*, which refers to persons who intentionally instigate others to commit a crime. According to the Criminal Code, an instigator should be punished according to the role that person plays in the joint crime. Instigators who instigate minors (under eighteen years old) should be punished more severely. If the instigated persons fail to commit a crime, the instigators should receive a less severe penalty.[65]

iii. Corporate Criminal Liability

In the PRC the Chinese term *danwei* (unit) has been used as a generic term for corporations, for-profit enterprises, government agencies, nongovernmental organizations, and *shiye danwei* (public institutions founded for public interests and not for profit, which can be founded and supported by central or local government agencies, state-owned enterprises, collectively owned enterprises, or privately owned enterprises, such as the media, museums, schools, hospitals, and research institutions). In China, therefore, corporate crimes are called unit crimes or crimes committed by units.

The 1997 Criminal Code was the first time that Chinese criminal law included units (corporate entities) as criminal subjects and held units criminally liable.[66] Between 1957, when the PRC nationalized private enterprises, and 1978, when China began its economic reform, enterprises, companies, and organizations were either state-owned or collectively owned entities (units). Because of China's highly centralized economic planning, units rarely participated in commercial activities. As a result, few units were held liable for the crimes they committed. Since 1978, however, new kinds of entities have emerged, such as corporations, privately owned business entities, foreign joint ventures, and foreign wholly owned subsidiaries. Even various kinds of state-owned units have been involved in business transactions. The 1987 Customs Act was the first Chinese law to accept the doctrine that units can be criminal subjects. The Act provides that a unit that commits a crime shall be fined, and the responsible persons in charge or those directly responsible shall be punished.[67]

Because it is difficult to determine whether a crime is committed by a unit or by the persons who are in charge of the unit, prosecutors can hold the unit liable for a crime only if they can prove either that the crime was committed in the name of the unit (in other words, the criminal acts were decided or carried out by the unit's governing body, leaders, or authorized personnel) or that the illegal gains resulting from the criminal acts were obtained by the unit. If an organization is incorporated for the purpose of engaging in illegal acts, the company will not be prosecuted under unit crimes but as a criminal syndicate, and the leaders or members of the company will be prosecuted for joint crimes.

6. Causation

Criminal theory in China defines causation as the relationship between the criminal subject's act and the harmful result. Causation must be determined in order to decide whether a crime has been committed and to determine what punishment should be imposed. Of course, an actor cannot normally be held criminally liable for acts that were not illegal or prohibited by law. In other words, an actor may not be held liable criminally for lawful or proper acts even if those acts cause harm.

The degree of an actor's criminal liability also depends on the closeness of the causal relationship between act and result. For example, X inflicted damage on Y's arms, and Y had to be hospitalized. During the hospitalization the hospital caught fire accidentally, and Y had no time to be evacuated and burned to death. Since there was no direct causation between X's infliction of damage on Y and Y's death, X should not be held liable for Y's death. However, if X injured Y's legs and Y could not move by himself to escape the fire, then X may be held liable for X's death because X indirectly caused Y's death.

The Chinese Criminal Code does not specifically prescribe general rules on causation, but some articles of the code use words and phrases related to causation to describe the relationship between acts and harms, such as *yinqi* (causing), *zhishi* (leading to), *zaocheng* (resulting in), and *yiner fasheng* (thus occurred). For example, article 257 of the Criminal Code provides that it is a crime for a person to use violent means to interfere with a marriage, and if such interference causes a victim's death the person could be sentenced to up to seven years' imprisonment. For example, if a father who did not want his daughter to marry violently disturbed his daughter's wedding and his daughter committed suicide because of the humiliation, the father could be convicted under this article. Similarly, although some articles of the code do not specifically use words or phrases related to causation, they nevertheless imply that causation between criminal acts and harmful consequences is required. For example, article 232 provides only that anyone who intentionally commits homicide shall be sentenced to death, life imprisonment, or fixed-term imprisonment of not less than ten years. However, this article implies that the intentional act caused the death of a human being.

C. Defenses

1. Types of defense

The Criminal Code does not have a specific section for "exculpatory defenses," but some articles in section 1, "Crime and Criminal Liabilities," and chapter 2, "Crimes," deal with defenses. Criminal Code defenses are narrowly defined, normally including mental impairment, deaf and blind, justifiable defense, necessity, and superior orders.

2. Burden of Proof

China does not yet have a law on evidence, and neither the Chinese Criminal Code nor the 1996 Criminal Procedure Law specifies whether the defendant or the prosecution has the burden of proof for exculpatory defenses. In general, the prosecution and public security organs have the burden to provide all the evidence used in a criminal proceeding. However, article 35 of the Chinese Criminal Procedure Law provides that a defendant's attorney must provide evidence and opinions that prove that the defendant should be acquitted, exempted from criminal liability, or given a mitigated sentence. In theory, therefore, the burden of collecting evidence, including exculpatory evidence, should be on public security organs, while the burden of proof should be on the prosecution. If a public security organ finds exculpatory evidence, the criminal suspect should not be prosecuted. If the public security organ did not or could not find any exculpatory evidence and the defendant or his attorney raises an exculpatory defense, the defendant should bear the burden of proof.

D. Justifications

In Chinese criminal law theory, the phrase "actions preventing criminal acts" is used to refer to what common-law countries call "justifications." The Chinese phrase is more in line with the concepts of justification used in civil law countries. Under the Chinese Criminal Code, actors who prevent criminal acts from happening may be exempt from criminal liability. Two major kinds of actions can be used for justification: justifiable defense and actions to avoid imminent harm. These justifications are similar to the concepts of self-defense and necessity used in common-law countries.

Article 20 of the Chinese Criminal Code provides that a person, for the purpose of stopping the progress of an illegal encroachment on the interests of the state, the public, or his or another person's body, property, or other rights, may inflict harm on the person who is threatening that encroachment. Such action will be deemed a justifiable defense, and the person will not suffer criminal liability.

Article 20 requires a person who invokes justifiable defense to satisfy the following five tests:

1. *Illegal encroachment.* Justifiable defense can be used only with reference to an action to prevent an illegal encroachment from happening. In other words, no one—including the encroached person or a third party—has the right to stop legal encroachments. Illegal encroachments mainly refer to criminal acts but also refer to illegal acts that do not constitute crimes or are performed by persons who cannot be held criminally liable, such as minors or insane persons. Legal encroachments include encroachments caused by law-enforcement officials or persons who are enforcing the law or carrying out the government's orders, the apprehension of criminals or criminal suspects by citizens, justifiable defenses, and urgent actions to avoid danger.

2. *Illegal encroachment in progress.* Only when an illegal encroachment is in progress or is imminent can justifiable defense be used to prevent that encroachment. The illegal encroachment, in other words, must have begun but must not have been completed. In Chinese criminal justice practice, if a person feels that someone is approaching him with the intent to cause bodily injury or death, he is entitled to resort to force to stop the encroachment.

3. *To protect legitimate interests.* Justifiable defense can be used only to protect a legitimate interest, whether state, public, or personal (including the body and property interests of the person who uses justifiable defense and of third persons). In other words, actions used to protect illegitimate interests cannot be justifiable defenses—two drug rings, for example, that use violence to fight for drug-distribution territories. A person who uses force to protect his interests must also act in good faith. For example, Mr. Chen insulted Mr. Wang verbally with an intention to instigate a fight. Mr. Wang initiated the violence against Mr. Chen, but Mr. Chen then beat up Mr. Wang severely. Obviously, Mr. Chen's action is not justifiable defense.

4. *Against the perpetrator.* Justifiable defense can be used only against the perpetrator who is responsible for the illegal encroachment. The purpose of justifiable defense is to stop criminal perpetrators from hurting others, so the defensive action must be used to counterattack the perpetrator directly. The Chinese Criminal Code does not specify the amount of justifiable defense that can be used against minors or people with limited capability, but there is consensus that limited force should be used against such perpetrators.

5. *Appropriate defense.* Justifiable defenses must be appropriate and should not cause excessive damage to the perpetrators. Article 20 of the Criminal Code also provides that if the action for justifiable defense obviously exceeds what is necessary and causes undue harm, the actor may be investigated for potential criminal liability. However, because the Chinese government and Chinese society encourage people to combat crimes, the code specifically provides that anyone who takes action to stop ongoing physical assault, homicide, robbery, rape, kidnapping, or another life-threatening violent crime should not be investigated even if that person's defensive action causes death or bodily injury to the perpetrator.[68] Therefore, it can be concluded that China adopts a broader standard to test the limit of excessive defensive actions than many other countries. In fact, many Chinese women who killed men attempting to rape them are never charged with any wrongdoing.

1. Necessity (Averting Imminent Harms)

"Averting imminent harms" is the direct translation of the Chinese phrase that describes the concept of necessity (choice of evils). Article 21 of the Criminal Code provides that no person should be investigated who took a damaging action against a smaller interest in order to avert imminent harm to a larger interest. Larger interests include state interests, public interests, and personal bodily and property interests. Personal bodily and property interests include the interests of the person who takes action to avert imminent harm and the interests of third persons who might have suffered the imminent harm.

Article 18 of the Criminal Code requires a person who invokes the necessity defense to satisfy the following four tests:

1. The protected interest must be threatened by imminent peril. The peril must be real and not simply possible. Therefore, the necessity defense should not be applied to perils that may not happen.
2. The protected interests must be legitimate. To prevent people who hold special positions or are engaged in important professions from putting themselves in situations in which they need to act to avert imminent harm to their personal interests, the Criminal Code provides that such people cannot use necessity as a defense.[69]
3. The action must be the only way to avoid the imminent harm.
4. The action that averts the imminent harm must be appropriate. This means that the damaged interest must be smaller than the protected interest.

There are not many cases of averting imminent harms reported in China. Here is one such case published by the Supreme People's Court. On July 28, 2003, the defendant Wang Renxing was driving his fishing boat in the Yangtze River when he found that his neighbor's fishing boat's net was tangled with the steel cable that was fastened to a floating navigation lantern placed by the local transportation administration. While the defendant was trying to help his neighbor untangle the fishing net, his own fishing boat's propeller also became tangled with the steel cable. The defendant could not untangle his boat from the cable and untied the cable from the navigation lantern because he was afraid that his boat might sink. The local transportation administration found that the total damage for repairing the navigation lantern was 1,555 renminbi (RMB, Chinese currency). Later the defendant was charged with the crime of sabotaging public transportation safety under article 108 of the Criminal Code. The Jiangbei District Court of Chongqi City found the defendant guilty of intentionally damaging transportation infrastructure without considering public safety and sentenced the defendant to three years in prison. The defendant appealed to the No. 1 Intermediate Court of Chongqing City. He argued that he should be excused from criminal liability because his actions were necessary to avoid imminent danger. The intermediate court held that the criminal law recognizes necessity as a defense in extreme circumstances and found that it was necessary for the defendant to untie the steel cable to prevent his fishing boat from capsizing. However, the court also found that the defendant failed to take any measures to prevent the navigation lantern from drifting away after his life was no longer in danger and that his failure to act had put other vessels in danger of sailing into the rock. The court thus still sentenced the defendant to three years' imprisonment, but with three years' probation.[70]

   2. Consent

Although the Chinese Criminal Code does not address the issue of consent, Chinese legal scholars believe that a defendant can use the victim's consent to a crime as a defense if the following six conditions are met:

1. The person consenting is the person whose body, rights, or interests were invaded.
2. The person consenting had the full civil capacity to understand his or her consent.
3. The consent was offered by the victim consciously and voluntarily.
4. The scope of the victim's consent was limited to personal interests that the law allows individual citizens to give up. No one has the right to consent to the invasion of state or public interests.
5. The consent was expressed by the victim before the personal interest was invaded.
6. The person who invaded the interest clearly understood that the victim consented and carried out the invasion within the scope of the victim's consent.

As in many countries, assisted suicide for people suffering and dying from incurable diseases is a very controversial issue in China. Since the 1990s Chinese lawmakers have tried several times to legalize this kind of assisted suicide (mercy killing) without success. Because of the absence of legislation, Chinese courts have taken a very conservative position on this issue and normally do not allow consent as a defense in assisted-suicide cases.

The first Chinese assisted-suicide case took place in Hanzhong City, Shanxi Province. In 1986, after a patient who was suffering from an incurable liver disease had passed out several times, her son and daughter took her to a hospital for treatment. Doctor Bu Liansheng told them that their mother was dying and that there was no hope for a cure. The son did not want to see his mother suffer, so he asked the doctor to end his mother's life. The doctor had a nurse inject chlorpromazine into the patient. The next day she died. The doctor and the son were charged with the crime of intentional murder, but the trial court of Hanzhong City Court found them not guilty. The Procuracy of Hanzhong City then appealed. In 1992, after six years of litigation, the Intermediate Court of Hanzhong upheld the trial court's verdict on the basis of the fact that chlorpromazine was not the main cause of the patient's death.[71]

A recent assisted-suicide case, by contrast, led to a conviction. On May 13, 2006, a woman who had been suffering from the skin disease lupus erythematosus for eight years attempted to commit suicide by drinking pesticide. After drinking pesticide, the woman could not bear the pain and begged her husband to end her life immediately. Her husband used a piece of rope to strangle her to death. The husband was then charged with intentional murder. Although the local villagers testified that the wife had asked her husband to commit the mercy killing and petitioned the court to free the husband, the court of Zhengyuan County, Gangsu Province, found the husband guilty of intentional murder and sentenced him to a ten-year prison term.[72]

3. Superior Orders

Although the Criminal Code does not specify that superior orders can be used as an exculpatory defense, most Chinese criminal law textbooks recognize that state functionaries may use superior orders to defend actions that are performed pursuant to orders from their superior and within the scope of their duties. A legitimate defense of superior orders should meet all of the following five conditions:

1. The order given by the superior organ or leader must be within the scope of that organ or leader's powers.
2. The action ordered must be within the responsibilities of the subordinate state functionary who carried out the orders.
3. The procedure involved in giving the order must be consistent with the law.
4. The subordinate who carried out the order must not know that the order was illegal.
5. The execution of the order must not exceed the scope of the order.

E. Excuses

The Chinese Criminal Code expressly provides that only youth, insanity, and diminished capacity may be used as excuses for criminal liability.[73] However, mistake/ignorance of law and entrapment usually may also lead to lighter or mitigated punishments. The Criminal Code also specifies that alcohol-intoxicated persons who commit crimes must be investigated for potential criminal liability.[74]

1. Underage Criminals

According to Chinese law, a Chinese citizen who reaches the age of eighteen becomes an adult and has full legal and civil capacity.[75] However, the Criminal Code provides that anyone who reaches the age of sixteen and commits a crime may be tried as an adult, and those who have reached the age of fourteen but are younger than sixteen and commit murder or other violent crimes may be held criminally responsible.[76] The code allows only underage criminals who are between fourteen and eighteen to be given a lighter or mitigated punishment. Therefore, only criminals who are younger than fourteen may be excused from criminal liability. However, the code also allows the government to lock up underage criminals for education if it deems it necessary.[77]

2. Insanity/Diminished Capacity

Article 18 of the Criminal Code provides that a mentally ill person who causes a harmful consequence may not be held criminally liable if two conditions are satisfied. First, it must be shown that the defendant was psychologically incapable of understanding or controlling his or her conduct when he or she inflicted harm on others. Second, it must be clinically verified that the defendant was insane according to a specified legal procedure. According to article 120 of the Criminal Procedure Law, the medical evaluation of insanity can be carried out only by a psychiatrist from a hospital that is designated by a provincial government. The Criminal Code also mandates that a mentally ill person's family members or guardian be responsible for keeping the person under strict surveillance and arranging for medical treatment. If necessary, the government may force mentally ill persons to receive medical treatment.[78]

Intermittently mentally ill persons who commit a crime when they are in a normal mental state may not escape criminal liability. In other words, if an intermittently mentally ill defendant is shown to be psychologically capable of understanding or controlling his or her conduct when inflicting harm on others, he or she should be held criminally liable.[79] For persons with diminished capacity—those who commit crimes but have not completely lost their ability to understand or control their conduct—the code provides that they may not be excused from criminal liability but may be given a lighter punishment.[80]

F. Sanctions

1. Punishment

According to the Chinese Criminal Code, criminal punishments are divided into principal punishments and supplementary punishments. Principal punishments include public surveillance, criminal detention, fixed-term imprisonment, life imprisonment, and the death penalty.[81] Supplementary punishments include fines, deprivation of political rights, confiscation of property, and deportation (applied to foreigners only).

Only one type of principal punishment may be imposed on an individual criminal, while two or more types of supplementary punishment may be imposed. Normally, the supplementary punishments are imposed with a principal punishment. However, they can also be imposed independently, as with deportation.[82]

Public surveillance (*guanzhi*) is a unique criminal penalty created by the Chinese criminal justice system and is imposed only for minor offenses. Under this penalty, a criminal is not confined in a prison or a place for rehabilitation through labor, but rather is free to live in society while being kept under surveillance by the local public security bureau (local police department). However, the criminal loses his rights of free speech, publication, assembly, and demonstration unless he obtains special permission from the security bureau. He also needs to report his activities regularly to the security bureau and must ask for permission if he meets visitors or changes his domicile. The duration of a public surveillance sentence may be between three months and two years.[83]

Criminal detention (*juyi*) is a penalty imposed for relatively minor offenses. The criminal on whom this penalty is imposed is deprived of freedom but, unlike those serving fixed terms or life sentences, is confined in a detention house by the local public security bureau rather than being put in prison or sent to a place of rehabilitation through labor. The criminal is also permitted to go home for one or two days each month and receives a salary or payment for the work he provides while in detention. The duration of a criminal detention sentence may be between fifteen days and six months.[84]

Fixed-term and life imprisonment are used for offenders convicted of major crimes. Criminals who are sentenced to fixed-term or life imprisonment have to serve their prison terms in prisons or other places (normally labor camps) and must be rehabilitated through labor if their health permits.[85] Fixed-term imprisonment is the most common criminal penalty (depending on the type of crime in question). Terms of fixed-term imprisonment range from six months to fifteen years, with the exception of criminals who are sentenced for multiple crimes, whose terms can be up to twenty years.[86] Life imprisonment is normally used for very serious violent crimes and major economic corruption criminal cases involving government officers. Moreover, many criminals who were originally sentenced to death with a two-year stay of execution have had their sentences commuted to life imprisonment after two years. Criminals sentenced to death with a two-year stay of execution who perform substantial and meritorious service in prisons or labor camps may have their death sentences commuted to fixed-term imprisonment of not less than fifteen years and not more than twenty years.[87]

According to the Criminal Code, the death penalty is imposed only on criminals who commit the most heinous crimes.[88] However, a death sentence should not be imposed on persons who are under eighteen or are pregnant.[89] More issues related to the death penalty are discussed in section II.F.3 in this chapter.

A fine is a penalty that requires criminals to pay cash to the state treasury for their crimes. Fines are used for nonviolent crimes, such as organizing prostitution, abducting and trading women and children, and trading fake and shoddy goods.

Deprivation of political rights is a penalty that deprives a criminal of certain kinds of rights, including (1) the right to vote and to stand for election; (2) the rights of free speech, publication, assembly, organization, and parade and demonstration; (3) the right to hold office in any state organ; and (4) the right to hold a leading position in any state-owned company, enterprise, institution, or organization.[90] The term for a sentence of deprivation of political rights should be not less than one year but not more than five years, with the exception that criminals who are sentenced to life imprisonment or death shall be deprived of their political rights for life.[91] The purpose of depriving death-sentenced criminals of their political rights is to provide the government with a legal ground to prohibit the publication of their writings even after they are executed. The Criminal Code specifically provides that this punishment shall be imposed on criminals who commit the crime of endangering national security (essentially the same as political criminals) as a supplementary punishment.[92] This punishment is also used as a supplementary punishment for intentional murder, rape, arson, bombing, poisoning, and other crimes that undermine public order.[93] It can also be used independently for criminals who commit nonviolent crimes (mainly endangering national security) that do not cause serious consequences.

Confiscation of property is a penalty imposed on criminals who endanger national security, produce and trade fake or shoddy goods, smuggle, forge state currency, commit financial fraud, encroach on property, bribe, and embezzle.[94] The property confiscated is turned over to the state treasury. Confiscation of property is intended not only to punish criminals but also to deprive them of their ability to gain financially from financial power from ongoing criminal activity. The Criminal Code restricts the confiscated property to the property belonging to the criminal and provides that sufficient property should be set aside for the living expenses of the criminal and family members who depend on that person's support.[95]

Deportation can be independently or supplementally applied to foreigners who violate Chinese law.[96] In Chinese criminal justice practice a foreign criminal sentenced to deportation independently will be deported immediately, while a foreign criminal sentenced to deportation as a supplementary punishment will be deported as soon as that person completes serving the principal punishment.

2. Quantity/Quality of Punishment

The Criminal Code provides that the basic principle of measuring punishment is that sentences must be determined according to law and must be based on the facts, nature, circumstances, and consequences of the crime.[97] In other words, after a guilty verdict is delivered, sentencing must be based on the circumstances and consequences of the crime and must be in accordance with the specific provisions of the Criminal Code. For each specific crime, the Criminal Code also lists all possible punishments and provides the permissible ranges of imprisonment.

Chinese criminal law theory divides the circumstances for measuring punishment into statutory circumstances and discretionary circumstances. The statutory circumstances have the following four sentencing outcomes:

1. If the circumstances are at the minimum, no criminal punishment may be imposed.[98]
2. If the circumstances are minor, lighter, mitigated, or no criminal punishment may be imposed, depending on other factors.[99] Mitigated punishment should be lighter than the lowest punishment prescribed by the Criminal Code.[100]
3. If the circumstances are serious, heavier criminal punishment must be imposed.[101]
4. If the circumstances are very serious, the most severe punishment listed among the punishment options or a combination of punishments must be imposed.

The discretionary circumstances are not specifically prescribed by the Criminal Code but have been developed by the courts. Some Chinese criminal law textbooks divide them into the following six categories:

1. *Criminal motivation.* Chinese criminal law holds that a criminal's motivation affects the amount of damage that the person's crime causes to society as a whole.

For example, punishment should be severer for a criminal who steals in order to live a life of luxury than for a criminal who steals in order to survive.

2. *Criminal methods.* Criminals who use cruel or sophisticated methods to commit crimes, such as mutilating a body after a murder, should be punished more severely.

3. *Context of the crime.* Criminals who commit crimes during a state of emergency, such as robbery in an earthquake-recovery area, should receive severer punishment.

4. *Object of the crime.* For example, embezzling or stealing money or materials from an emergency relief fund should be punished more severely than stealing "ordinary" money or materials.

5. *The criminal's previous behavior.* For example, when two thieves who stole goods of the same value are being sentenced, the one who is a professional thief should be punished more severely.

6. *Attitude after committing a crime.* China does not have a plea-bargain system like the United States, but it uses a very popular discretionary practice called *tanbai congkuang kangju congyuan*, which literally means "confession for leniency and stricter punishment for resistance." Under this practice, a criminal who confesses the crime he or she committed and admits guilt should receive a more lenient punishment than a criminal who refuses to confess and denies his or her guilt.

Besides these factors, the courts also consider, when determining sentences, whether criminals are recidivists, surrender to the authorities voluntarily, or identify other criminals. Recidivists who commit new crimes intentionally should receive heavier punishments, while recidivists who commit new crimes unintentionally should not.[102] If a criminal voluntarily surrenders to the authorities and confesses a crime, that person should receive a lighter or mitigated punishment.[103] The scope of voluntary surrender also covers criminals who are under a compulsory measure (such as custody or serving a jail term) and voluntarily confess their crimes even though they are not under investigation.[104] Finally, if a criminal (normally a member of a crime ring) exposes other crimes or criminals to the authorities or provides information crucial to solving a criminal case, that person should be given a lighter or mitigated punishment.[105] If the cracked case is a major one or the criminal who voluntarily surrenders provides particularly crucial information, he or she may be exempt from criminal liability entirely.[106]

3. Death Penalty

China has a very strong tradition of using the death penalty to ensure social order. In the last ten years Chinese legal experts, law-enforcement officers, and the public have engaged in unprecedented debate about the proper severity of criminal punishment. Some people in academic circles have advocated for reducing the number of crimes for which the capital sentence can be imposed, or even abolishing capital punishment. But Chinese judicial bodies and the public are more concerned about worsening public security and believe that it is still too early to adopt such proposals. Considering the fact that the situation—grave public disorder and serious economic crimes—did not warrant a reduction in death sentences, the 1997 Criminal Code neither increased nor decreased the types of death sentences prescribed in the 1979 Criminal Code and other supplementary criminal laws.[107] However, under the 1997 Criminal Code, the maximum punishment for people between sixteen and eighteen years old was reduced from the death sentence with a two-year reprieve[108] to life imprisonment.[109] The amendment reflects China's commitment to the United Nation Convention on the Rights of the Child (1989), which prohibits giving a death sentence to a person less than eighteen years old.

The 1997 Criminal Code has sixty-eight crimes that are punishable by death. Twenty of them are so-called economic offenses, such as bribery and embezzlement of large amounts of money. For example, anyone who commits the crime of graft or bribery may be sentenced to death if the amount of money involved is more than 100,000 RMB (approximately U.S. $14,500).[110] In recent years many Chinese legal scholars have called on the NPC to reduce capital punishment for nonviolent offenses and to consider the possibility of abolishing capital punishment entirely for such offenses. The following summary is based on a book published in China in 2004 that collects twenty-eight essays that advocate abolishing capital punishment:

The conditions for the complete abolition of the death penalty are obviously premature and insufficient, considering the realities of present-day China, although the preservation of the death penalty has received doubts and challenges from many aspects of Chinese society. Because of the common and long-standing retributive nature of the public, it is still impossible for legislators to take radical measures toward the abolition of the death penalty. Moreover, Chinese society remains in a period of transformation, characterized by a high criminal rate and a strong need for public order, which makes legislators believe that it's still necessary to preserve the death penalty in order to strengthen the deterrent function of the punishment. But it should also be noted that the death penalty is definitely a kind of punishment with unavoidable weaknesses. Therefore, the restriction of the death penalty should be advocated strongly, and for the crimes where the stipulations of the death penalty are too severe or may lead to the imbalance of value the death penalty should be annulled at the right time by legislation. At the present time the gradual abolition of the death penalty for nonviolent crimes should be put on the legislative agenda first, and for those nonviolent crimes in which there is no specific person being harmed or there is no potential danger to basic human rights, the death penalty should be annulled by legislation as soon as possible.[111]

One of the crimes for which Chinese criminology scholars have advocated the elimination of the death penalty is the crime of organizing prostitution.[112] Several prostitution organizers have been sentenced and put to death, including several who had not committed violent crimes. On November 17, 1998, for example, the First Intermediate People's Court of Beijing sentenced a woman named Ma Yulan to death because, between June 1996 and September 1997, she hired approximately ten women and arranged for them to provide sex services for profit.[113] On March 1, 1999, only four and one-half months after her sentence, she was executed by shooting.[114] The court found that the case of Ma Yulan was "exceptionally serious" because Ma Yulan and her associates might have made a few hundred thousand RMB in profit from the prostitution. The sentence caused the public to debate whether she deserved the death penalty for the crimes she committed. Because Ma Yulan did not use coercive or deceptive means to force women to engage in prostitution, and because there was no violence toward either the prostitutes or the prostitutes' clients, many people felt that the death sentence was excessive. The public's opinion might have influenced subsequent cases similar to the case of Ma Yulan. In June 2000 the First Intermediate People's Court of Beijing found that Ms. Hu Kaiying, the ringleader, had committed the crime of organizing prostitution and sentenced her to death with a two-year stay of execution.[115] Ms. Hu Kaiying did not appeal the sentence.

Another controversial issue is that the Chinese Criminal Code gives prosecutors and judges significant discretion to determine "if the circumstance is serious or exceptionally serious," thus justifying a severe sentence. The People's Supreme Court has not issued a set of comprehensive sentencing guidelines for lower courts to follow. Rather, it has only issued a few judicial interpretations to guide judges on how to determine whether the circumstances of certain crimes are serious. For the crime of organizing prostitution, the SPC has never given out any directions. Therefore, the First Intermediate People's Court could decide that the criminal circumstances of the case of Ma Yulan were exceptionally serious, and it sentenced her to death.

The current Chinese government's policy toward the death penalty is "keeping death penalty with careful application," as described in the Opinion on Taking Further Steps to Ensure the Quality of Handling Death Penalty Cases According to Law, which was jointly issued by the SPC, the SPP, the Ministry of Public Security, and the Ministry of Justice. Item 4 of this opinion states as follows:

> "Preserving death penalty and strictly controlling the application of death penalty" is the basic principle of our country towards death penalty. Our practicing experiences prove that this principle is absolutely correct and we must continue to carry it out. The policy of "strike hard" shall be understood and implemented fully and accurately. Serious criminals shall be struck hard according to law. For the very small numbers of extremely serious criminals, we shall not hesitate to sentence them to death according to law. Currently, our country still shall not abolish death penalty but shall decrease the application of death penalty gradually. If a criminal can be either sentenced to death or be spared from death sentence, he shall not be sentenced to death. When handling death penalty cases, we shall be very careful and diligent in order to meet the requirements of constructing a harmonized society and maintaining the society's stability. Therefore, we shall ensure that we not only conclude the facts of cases based on evidence but also convict criminals accurately and impose punishment appropriately. Thus, we could reach the goal of killing less and carefully.[116]

In 1979, when the Chinese Criminal Code and the Criminal Procedure Code were promulgated, both laws authorized the SPC to review and approve all death sentences before such sentences were carried out.[117] In 1981, when crime rates were rising rapidly, the Chinese government began a crime-curtailing campaign called "strike hard" (*yanda*). Under this campaign, criminals were detained for speedy investigation and trial, and many criminals were given more severe criminal penalties than the crimes for which they were convicted allowed. One of the measures that the NPC's Standing Committee adopted was to eliminate the SPC's authority to review and approve death sentences for criminals who committed violent crimes, such as murder, robbery, rape, bombing, and arson, and to vest the higher people's courts with final review.[118] In September 1983, when it was revising the Organic Law of People's Courts, the NPC's Standing Committee reiterated its decision to give final review to the higher people's courts.[119] Then, in 1996 and 1997, when the Criminal Procedure Law and the Criminal Code, respectively, were amended, both laws returned final review of death sentences to the SPC.[120] However, the laws also gave the SPC the power to authorize the higher courts to review and approve death sentences if it felt that this was necessary. Indeed, the SPC had delegated its authority several times. In 1991 the SPC gave final review and approval power to the Higher Court of Yunan Province in drug-trafficking cases.[121] In June 1996 the SPC gave the same power to the higher people's courts of Guanxi, Sichuan, Ganshu, and Guizhou provinces. On September 26, 1997, the SPC issued a notice authorizing the higher courts to review and approve death sentences in cases involving the violent crimes mentioned earlier in this paragraph.[122]

In the last twenty-five years the higher people's courts have approved 90 percent of the death sentences they have handled. Therefore, only a few death sentences were changed as a result of the new death-penalty review procedures.[123] Many Chinese criminal scholars criticized the absence of judicial oversight for death sentences approved by the higher people's courts. Several wrongful death-penalty cases have also spurred public debate over the review procedures. Public opinion led the Supreme Court to reassert its final review power over all death sentences. On December 13, 2006, the SPC issued a notice revoking all its delegations of the review power to the higher courts effective January 1, 2007.[124] On February 28, 2007, the SPC also promulgated new rules concerning the death-penalty review procedure.[125]

In 2007, the first year after the SPC reclaimed the right to approve all death sentences, Chinese courts handed down about 30 percent fewer death penalties than in 2006.[126] Moreover, in the first half of 2008, the SPC overturned 15 percent of the death sentences handed down by lower courts.[127]

III. SPECIAL PART

A. Structure

Part Two Specific Provisions of the Criminal Code consists of 350 articles and 413 offenses. These articles and offenses are classified into ten categories and organized in the following ten chapters: (1) crimes of endangering national security, (2) crimes of endangering public security, (3) crimes of undermining the socialist economic order (economic crimes), (4) crimes of infringing on the rights of persons and the democratic rights of citizens (civil rights offenses), (5) crimes of encroaching on property, (6) crimes of disrupting social administration (public order), (7) crimes of endangering national defense interests, (8) crimes of graft and bribery, (9) crimes of dereliction of duty, and (10) crimes of violating duties owed by military servicemen.

Most of the articles in the Specific Provisions of the code describe each offense, identify all the subjective and objective aspects of the offense (criminal motives, actions, and consequences), and prescribe specific criminal penalties. For example, article 305 provides that anyone who gives a false statement at a trial with the motive of framing others or concealing crimes may be sentenced to criminal detention or fixed-term imprisonment of no more than seven years, depending on the circumstances. Some articles simply identify the offense and provide penalties. For example, article 241 provides that anyone who buys and keeps an abducted woman or child may be sentenced to public surveillance or up to three years' imprisonment. Other articles also only identify the offense but do not describe the offense's subjective and objective aspects. Instead, these articles refer to other laws to determine what kinds of acts constitute the proscribed offense. For example, article 344 provides that anyone who violates the provisions of forest law by illegally logging or destroying precious trees may be sentenced to a maximum of seven years' imprisonment.

B. Homicide

1. Murder/Manslaughter

The Criminal Code divides homicide into two types: intentional homicide (murder, article 232) and negligent homicide (involuntary manslaughter, article 233). For murder, the first sentence of article 232 provides that anyone who intentionally commits homicide shall be sentenced to death, life imprisonment, or fixed-term imprisonment of not less than ten years. Although the Criminal Code does not specifically mention that malice aforethought—which includes an unintentional killing that exhibits a willful disregard for life—is required for murder, Chinese practice accepts that it is a necessary element of the crime.

Although Chinese criminal law does not have a Chinese term for manslaughter, the justice system does recognize the concept of manslaughter, because the second sentence of article 232 provides that if the circumstances are minor, the sentence shall be fixed-term imprisonment of not less than three years and not more than ten years. In Chinese practice, such minor circumstances (voluntary manslaughters) may include righteous and indignant killing (see section III.B.2 in this chapter), heat-of-passion killing, assisted suicides, contract killings, suffocating newborn babies (usually referring to mothers who suffocated their own children because of birth defects, birth out of wedlock, or their inability to raise a child), and excessive self-defense. Of course, defendants who argue voluntary manslaughter in order to mitigate their culpability have to prove that the circumstances of their killing are minor.

Chinese criminal law uses the term *negligent homicide* instead of *involuntary manslaughter*. Article 233 of the Criminal Code provides that anyone who negligently kills a person shall be sentenced to fixed-term imprisonment of not less than three years and not more than seven years. Although the Criminal Code does not further divide the category of negligent homicides, Chinese criminal law theory recognizes two kinds of negligent homicides (where there is no intention to kill or cause serious injury): those caused by carelessness and those caused by overconfident negligence. However, as noted earlier in this section, if the unintentional conduct amounts to such gross negligence as to amount to willful or depraved indifference to human life, the state of mind may be considered malice. In this case the charged offense may be murder.

A person between the ages of fourteen and sixteen who commits intentional murder is criminally liable.[128] Although the Criminal Code does not mention the same age group in reference to negligent homicides, the SPC has instructed that this group of youths should not be criminally investigated. Instead, courts should order their parents or guardians to educate and supervise them or have the local government put them in custody for purposes of rehabilitation.[129]

2. Provocation

The Criminal Code does not specify that provocation can be a defense to murder or manslaughter, which may reflect the fact that the Chinese system does not encourage people to take the law into their own hands. However, provocation is often used to reduce the offense of murder to culpable manslaughter or to impose a mitigated punishment. In Chinese practice, provocation may include excessive self-defense killing, righteous and indignant killing, and heat-of-passion killing. Normally, the second sentence of article 232 will be applied so that the circumstances will be considered minor, and the sentence will be fixed-term imprisonment of not less than three years and not more than ten years.

Most Chinese cases involving righteous and indignant killings involve parents killing children who were considered chronic lawbreakers or troublemakers by their local communities or wives killing their husbands because of domestic abuse. For heat-of-passion killing, the defendant must show that the killing was not done because of premeditated intent, the killing was provoked by the victim, and the killing happened while the defendant had lost self-control.

C. Sex Offenses

1. Rape

The Criminal Code defines "rape" as a man's employment of violence, coercion, or other means to have sex with a woman.[130] In Chinese criminal law theory the key issue is proving that the intercourse took place against the victim's will. Violence includes beatings, strangling, physical restraint, and other kinds of physical violence. Coercion includes causing the victim to submit to intercourse through threats to kill or cause bodily harm, disclosing private information or destroying reputation, and abusing official power or other special relationships. Other means refer to means that render the victim so physically or mentally impaired that she is incapable of giving informed consent to intercourse—for example, using a drug to render a woman unconscious or incapacitated and then having sex with her.

When the victim is a woman older than fourteen, the prosecution must show that the male rapist's genital organ penetrated the victim's reproductive organ. This is the traditional Chinese view. However, if the victim is under the age of fourteen, the prosecution need only show that the male rapist's genital organ touched the girl's genital organ.[131]

The Criminal Code does not consider deviate sexual intercourse, such as sodomy or oral sex. These acts, only done to women by force or to minors (girls or boys), will be prosecuted as the crime of sexual abuse according to article 237 of the Criminal Code of 1997. Before 1997 there was a crime called "the crime of hooliganism" provided in article 160 the Criminal Code of 1979. On November 2, 1984, the SPC and the SPP jointly promulgated a judicial interpretation called the Answer to Several Issues on the Specific Application of Handling Hooligan Cases. Item 6 of section 2 of this interpretation provided that anyone who sodomizes a minor, forces sodomy on young boys, or uses violent means to sodomize others repeatedly may be prosecuted under the crime of hooliganism. The Criminal Code of 1997 repealed the crime of hooliganism. Therefore, since 1997, the crimes of men who forced sodomy on other men or young boys older than age fourteen cannot be prosecuted as sex offenses. Some of these offenders were only sanctioned by police for up to fifteen days' detention or were ordered by courts to pay compensation to their victims if the victims brought civil law suits to the courts.

For statutory rape, the Criminal Code provides that anyone who has sexual relations with a girl under the age of fourteen will be prosecuted for rape and should be punished severely even if the sex was consensual.[132] However, the code does not clarify whether the man had to know the age of the minor. In 2003 the Judicial Committee of the SPC instructed that if a man does not know that the girl was under fourteen, there is no serious consequence involved, and the man should not be investigated for criminal liability.[133]

The Criminal Code defines rape victims as women but does not specify that the perpetrators must be men. Nevertheless, according to Chinese criminal law theory and practice, only men can be charged with rape. If the rape is a joint crime, however, a woman who conspires in the rape may be charged as an accomplice.

To protect mentally retarded or ill persons, the Handicap Protection Law provides that anyone who had sex with a mentally retarded or mentally ill person who could not understand her acts may be investigated for the crime of rape.[134] Interestingly enough, the Chinese language of this provision does not indicate the required gender of such a perpetrator or victim.

The Criminal Code provides that a convicted rapist should normally be sentenced to between three and ten years' imprisonment. If one of the following circumstances is present, however, he may be sentenced to more than ten years, to life imprisonment, or to death: (1) the rape was particularly disgusting, (2) multiple rapes, (3) raping a woman in front of many people in a public place, (4) gang rape (raping a woman with at least one other man), and (5) causing severe injury, death, or other serious consequences to the victim(s).[135]

2. Forcible Sexual Abuse or Humiliation of Women or Children
The crime of forcible sexual abuse or humiliation of women refers to the act of a man who subjects a woman to sexual contact other than sexual intercourse or who creates a sexually humiliating situation through the use of forcible compulsion or verbal abuse.[136] Forcible compulsions include violence, coercion, and intoxication. The crime of sexual abuse of children refers to molesting children under the age of fourteen. For that crime, the gender of the victim or the perpetrator is irrelevant.

For the two kinds of sexual-abuse crimes, the criminal penalty is normally no more than five years' imprisonment or criminal detention. If the crimes are committed by a group of men or are carried out before many people in a public place, the criminals may be sentenced to more than a five-year term.

D. Theft and Fraud

1. Theft

Under the Chinese Criminal Code, the crimes of theft and fraud are two of the twelve crimes under chapter 5, "Crime of Property Encroachments." However, the code does not define what constitutes theft and fraud; instead, it simply provides that criminal penalties for those crimes depend on the value of the stolen or swindled property and the circumstances of the particular crime. According to Chinese criminal law theory, theft is defined as the act of secretly stealing property, either multiple times or in large amounts, for the purposes of illegal possession. The criminal subject can be any person older than sixteen. The object of the crimes can be either public or private property. The Criminal Code does not specify whether the property should be movable or tangible, so the crime can involve immovable property and intangible property such as electricity, gas, technologies, trade secrets, and know-how.[137] However, protected property normally does not include real estate. The subjective aspect of theft requires the person to act with the intent to illegally possess the property. "Secretly stealing" refers to stealing property without notice to the property owner; that element distinguishes theft from other property crimes.

To distinguish occasional stealing or petty theft from criminally punishable theft, the code provides that only those who steal property in a large amount or multiple times are criminally liable and are subject to imprisonment of up to three years, detention, public surveillance, or a fine.[138] Therefore, occasional stealing or petty theft is not punishable under the Criminal Code but may be penalized by administrative sanctions such as detention or a fine.

Criminal penalties for the crime of theft are determined on the basis of the value of the stolen property and the circumstances involved. If the stolen amount is relatively large and the circumstances are serious, the sentence may be fixed-term imprisonment of not less than three years and not more than ten years and may additionally (or exclusively) include a fine. If the stolen amount is exceptionally large and the circumstances are extremely serious, the sentence may be fixed-term imprisonment of between ten years and life imprisonment and may additionally (or exclusively) include a fine or confiscation of property.[139] If the stolen property is owned by a financial institution, is an extraordinarily large amount, or includes precious cultural relics and the circumstances are serious, the penalty may include life imprisonment or death.[140] Obviously, this provision is designed to crack down on insider thefts from financial institutions and museums.

The Criminal Code does not specify how many acts of stealing qualify as "multiple times of theft" and does not define what qualify as relatively large amounts, exceptionally large amounts, or extraordinarily large amounts of property. Instead, in 1998, after the new Criminal Code was promulgated, the SPC, the SPP, and the Ministry of Public Security issued a rule interpreting those standards. According to the rule, stealing three times per year is considered "multiple times of theft" for purposes of the Code.[141] The rule also defines "relatively large amount" as 500 to 2,000 RMB, "exceptionally large amount" as 5,000 to 20,000 RMB, and "extraordinarily large amount" as 30,000 to 100,000 RMB.[142] Because of uneven economic development and different crime rates around China, the rule allows local courts, the procuracy, and public security bureaus to jointly formulate and promulgate their own standards for the applicable penalties.

2. Fraud

The crime of fraud refers to using false facts or concealing facts to swindle, for the purpose of illegal possession, either public or private property in a relatively large amount. Article 266 of the Criminal Code addresses general fraud, while section 5 of chapter 3 of the Crimes of Undermining the Socialist Market Economic Order devotes nine articles (articles 192–200) to financial frauds. For the general criminal penalties, the Criminal Code creates the following three tiers of penalties, based on the value of the swindled property:

1. For a relatively large value, the sentence may be fixed-term imprisonment of not more than three years, criminal detention, or public surveillance.
2. For a very large value and very serious circumstances, the sentence may be fixed-term imprisonment of not less than three years and not more than ten years.
3. For an exceptionally large value and extremely serious circumstances, the sentence may be fixed-term imprisonment of between ten years and life imprisonment.[143]

Fines and confiscation of property can be applied independently or jointly with the penalties just listed. As with the crime of theft, the Criminal Code does not specify what constitutes a relatively large value, a very large value, or an exceptionally large value of swindled property. Chinese courts have been applying a judicial interpretation promulgated by the SPC to determine the appropriate sentence.[144]

To help courts determine sentences, the SPC's interpretation also defines what qualify as serious, very serious, and extremely serious circumstances. In addition, the interpretation lists some special circumstances. The listed very serious circumstances include frauds in the area of birth control, marriage fraud, and inciting children to swindle; the listed extremely serious circumstances include organized fraud; swindling materials in short supply; swindling disaster relief, economic aid, and medical materials; wasting swindled property; failing to recover swindled property; using swindled property for illegal activities; a previous fraud conviction; and fraud causing death, mental illness, or serious consequence to the victim. Criminal penalties for financial frauds are very severe. If the amount involved is exceptionally large and the damage done to the interests of the state or individuals is also exceptionally large, the criminal penalty may be life imprisonment or death.[145]

E. "Victimless" Crimes

In China, victimless crimes are normally referred to as crimes with no direct victims. Chinese criminal law theory in this area is underdeveloped. Few articles discuss this topic. Most Chinese criminal law textbooks do not even mention it. By analyzing the

Chinese Criminal Code, we can divide victimless crimes into two major categories: (1) political issues, such as free speech, free association, and free religion; and (2) moral issues, such as gambling, drug abuse, loan-sharking (illegal fund-raising and lending), vagrancy, bigamy, pornography, prostitution, and group sex.

The first category of victimless crimes, involving political issues, can be very controversial. For example, a person who engages in the following activities may be sentenced to imprisonment, criminal detention, public surveillance, or deprivation of political rights: (1) holding an assembly, parade, or demonstration without obtaining a permit from the government,[146] (2) deliberately insulting the Chinese national flag or a national emblem in public by burning, destroying, scraping, scrawling on, or trampling it,[147] and (3) organizing or participating in a superstitious sect, secret society, or cult.

Given the second category of victimless crimes, it can be seen that the Chinese government exercises a great deal of control over people's lives and is willing to promote the state's interest by using the law to regulate or set moral standards. Before the first Criminal Code was promulgated in 1979, adultery was a crime. The current code provides that anyone who is involved in the following activities may be investigated for criminal liability even if the activity in question is consensual or voluntary: (1) gathering a group of people to engage in promiscuous sexual activities,[148] (2) manufacturing, duplicating, publishing, distributing, or disseminating pornographic materials for profit,[149] (3) making a living as a gambler or gathering a group of people to gamble for profit,[150] (4) sheltering people who use narcotics,[151] (5) organizing pornographic shows (such as topless or nude dancers),[152] (6) committing bigamy,[153] and (7) raising funds from the public illegally or without authorization (which normally refers to private citizens contributing cash to set up a fund or offering unsecured loans to others at high interest rates).[154]

F. Political Crimes: From Counterrevolution to Endangering State Security

Some crimes listed under the crimes of endangering state security are controversial because they permit the Chinese government to continue to use the criminal justice system to persecute political dissidents. Before 1979 there was a crime called counterrevolution. That crime was removed from the 1979 Criminal Code[155] but reappeared in the 1997 Criminal Code as the crime of endangering state security.[156] The new crimes have been defined more concretely, but this change does not mean that the CCP regrets what the party has done in the past and does not prevent the prosecution of political dissidents. Wang Hanbin, former vice president of the NPC's Standing Committee, stated the following when he delivered a speech to the delegates at the Fifth Session of the Eighth National People's Congress:

> The provisions related to crimes of counterrevolutions in the criminal law have played a very important role and have been necessary to maintain the state's security, strengthen the political power of the people's democratic dictatorship and defend the socialist system. However, there have been some new situations and problems to apply the provisions of the crimes of counterrevolutions due to the development of the nation's politics, economy and society. It was very difficult to define some offenses of counterrevolutions for the purpose

of keeping the crimes of counterrevolutions. It is more appropriate to apply the crimes of endangering the state's security on some criminal activities than to apply the crimes of counterrevolutions. Therefore, the draft changed the chapter of the crimes of counterrevolutions into the crimes of endangering the state's security.[157]

The 1997 Criminal Code retains the original provisions related to colluding with a foreign state and conspiring to jeopardize the sovereignty, territorial integrity, or security of the motherland,[158] and it provides more specific articles that deal with crimes considered to be the most serious threats to national security. Those crimes include disrupting the motherland,[159] armed rebellion,[160] subverting the government, overthrowing the socialist system,[161] and collaborating with overseas groups, organizations, and persons in a manner likely to endanger the state.[162]

The 1997 Criminal Code adds a new article that prohibits colluding with a foreign institution, organization, or individual to commit the crimes of undermining national unification and security, subverting the political power of the state, or overthrowing the socialist system.[163] This article was added to deal with Chinese who collude with foreign institutions or individuals to engage in the activities of westernizing (*xihua*), splitting the homeland (*fenhua*), or other activities that endanger state security.[164] Thus the Chinese government can continue to prosecute Chinese political dissidents who have connections with foreigners under the new Criminal Code.

According to the case database at Chinalawinfo.com, there were twenty-one cases related to the crimes of endangering state security between 1999 and 2005. However, nine of those cases should not have been prosecuted as criminal cases because the alleged acts involved only promoting different political views or practicing religions that were not approved by the Chinese government. For example, in the 2003 *Case of Huang Jingqiu: The Crime of Subverting the State Power*,[165] Huang published several articles critical of the Chinese government and the Chinese Communist Party on the Internet. He also invited Chinese to join a political party called the Chinese Patriotic and Democratic Party. He was quickly arrested by Chinese authorities, convicted, and sentenced by the Changzhou City People's Intermediate Court of Jiangsu Province to twelve years' imprisonment with four years' deprivation of his political rights. He appealed the judgment, but the Higher People's Court of Jiangsu Province affirmed his conviction and sentence.

NOTES

1. Jerome Cohen, *The Criminal Process in the People's Republic of China, 1949–1963* (Cambridge, MA: Harvard University Press, 1968), 315.

2. Shao-chuan Leng, "Chinese Criminal Code Symposium: Criminal Justice in Post-Mao China; Some Preliminary Observations," *Journal of Criminal Law* 73 (1982): 204. The English translations of the Counterrevolutionaries Act and the Corruption Act can be found in Cohen, *supra* note 1, at 299–311, and their Chinese texts are in *Zhonghua Renmin Zhenfu Faling Huibin* [Collection of Laws and Decrees of the Central People's Government], vol. 2 (1953), at 3–5, and vol. 3 (1954), at 25–28, respectively. The Chinese

texts of the Arrest and Detention Act of 1954 and the Security Administration Punishment Act of 1957 are in *Zhonghua Renmin Gongheguo Fagui Huibian* [Collection of Laws and Regulations of the People's Republic of China] (Beijing: Fa Lu Chu Ban She, 1956–), vol. 1, at 239–242 (1956), and vol. 6, at 245–261 (1957), respectively.

3. *Xing Fa Zong Lun* [General Principles of Criminal Law] (Beijing: Beijing University Press, 1981), 45.

4. *See Xing Fa Zong Lun, supra* note 3, at 50.

5. 1997 Criminal Code of the People's Republic of China [hereinafter Criminal Code], article 250.

6. Organic Law of the People's Courts (amended in 2006), article 35.

7. *Ibid.*; 1996 Criminal Procedure Law of the PRC [hereinafter CPL], articles 13 and 99.

8. Supreme People's Court's Interpretation of the Criminal Procedure Law (1998), article 16.

9. CPL, article 20.

10. *Ibid.* article 21; Civil Procedure Law (1991), article 20.

11. CPL, articles 199 and 200; Criminal Code, article 48.

12. CPL, article 22; Civil Procedure Law (1991), article 21.

13. The Gang of Four was a group of hard-core Communists who dreamed of a China with the most orthodox form of communism. In the mid-1960s they pushed for the total destruction of traditional Chinese culture, which was to be replaced by textbook Communist ideology and culture. They became the leading forces in Mao's Cultural Revolution. After Mao's death in 1976, the members of the Gang of Four were arrested. They were sentenced to death, but later their sentences were reduced to life in prison.

14. CPL, article 205; Civil Procedure Law (1991), article 177.

15. Liu Yong, forty-three, chairman of the board of the Shenyang Jiayang Group, was found guilty of organizing criminal groups, intentional injury, robbery, illegal business operations and illegal possession of firearms, tax evasion, blackmail, and bribery. In one of the most serious allegations, Liu reportedly ordered dozens of his subordinates to beat a cigarette vendor to death. On April 17, 2002, the Intermediate People's Court of Tieling, a city in Liaoning Province, sentenced Liu to death at the first trial. However, the Liaoning Higher People's Court commuted the penalty after a second trial by sentencing Liu to death with two years' reprieve. The commutation was based mainly on an allegation that the police might have tortured Liu into confessing to the killing of the cigarette vendor, which was what had led to the death sentence at the first trial. Because Liu Yong was a notorious criminal ringleader, the commutation sparked anger among the people of his home city and debates among Chinese legal experts. Because this case was widely publicized by the media, the Supreme People's Court decided to retry the case itself. In December 2003 the SPC held a public trial to retry Liu Yong and sentenced him to death with immediate execution. CNN, "Death Penalty for China Crime Boss," December 22, 2003, http://edition.cnn.com/2003/WORLD/asiapcf/12/21/china.mafia.ap/ (accessed August 27, 2004).

16. The Resolution to Enhance the Work of Legal Interpretation by the NPC's Standing Committee on June 6, 1981.

17. *Ren Min Fa Yuan An Li Xuan* [The Selected Opinions of People's Courts] has been published in Chinese by the People's Court Press (Ren Min Fa Yuan Chu Ban She) since 1992.

18. CPL, article 12.

19. In *Miranda v. Arizona*, 384 U.S. 436 (1966), the Supreme Court of the United States set forth the *Miranda* rules. One of the rules requires that a law-enforcement official, when making an arrest, must clearly inform the suspect that he or she has the right to consult with a lawyer and to have the lawyer with him or her during interrogation, without regard to whether it appears that he or she already is aware of this right.

20. CPL, article 33.

21. *Ibid.*

22. *Ibid.* article 36.

23. *Ibid.* article 37.

24. United States, Foreign Broadcast Information Service (China), "Top PRC Dissidents without Lawyers before Trial," FBIS-CHI-98-349 (December 15, 1998).

25. 1997 amended CPL, article 65.

26. *See* United States, Foreign Broadcast Information Service (China), *supra* note 24.

27. Resolution of the Standing Committee of the NPC on the Perfection of the People's Assessor System (*Quan guo ren min dai biao da hui chang wu wei yuan hui guan yu wan shan ren min pei shen yuan zhi du de jue ding*), promulgated on August 28, 2004, articles 7–8.

28. *Ibid.* article 9.

29. *See Xing Fa Zong Lun, supra* note 3, at 23–25.

30. 2006 Amended Organic Law of the People's Courts, article 9.

31. 1979 CPL, article 105.

32. Ira Belkin, "China," in *Criminal Procedure: A Worldwide Study*, ed. Craig M. Bradley (Durham, NC: Carolina Academic Press, 2007), 102-103.

33. 1996 CPL, article 150.

34. *Ibid.* article 36.

35. *See* Belkin, *supra* note 32, at 103.

36. *The Criminal Code of the People's Republic of China*, translated by Chin Kim (Littleton, CO: Fred B. Rothman and Co., 1982), 46.

37. Wang Hanbin, "Guanyu Zhonghua Renmin Gongheguo Xingfa Xiuding De Shuoming" [The Explanations on the Amendment of the Criminal Law of the PRC], *Zhonghua Renmin Gongheguo Quan Guo Ren Min Dai Biao Da Hui Chang Wu Wei Yuan Hui Gong Bao* [*Gazette of the Standing Committee of the National People's Congress of the People's Republic of China*], issue no. 2 (1997): 220.

38. William Jones, "The Criminal Law of the People's Republic of China," *Review of Socialist Law* 6 (1982): 409.

39. For more on the Chinese strike-hard campaigns, see Susan Trevaskes, *Courts and Criminal Justice in Contemporary China* (Lanham, MD: Lexington Books, 2007), ch. 5.

40. Ian Dobinson, "Criminal Law," in *Introduction to Chinese Law*, ed. Wang Chenguang and Zhang Xianchu (Hong Kong: Sweet and Maxwell Asia, 1997), 110–111.

41. *Ibid.* 111.

42. *Ibid.*

43. Criminal Code, articles 102–107, 140.
44. *Ibid.* article 16.
45. *Ibid.* article 17.
46. *Ibid.* article 30. For more about minors' criminal liabilities, consult the relevant specific criminal provisions in the Criminal Code and the other relevant judicial interpretations of the SPC.
47. Criminal Code, article 18.
48. *Ibid.* article 17.
49. *Ibid.* article 19.
50. *Ibid.* article 14.
51. *Ibid.* article 15.
52. *Ibid.* article 152.
53. *Ibid.* article 276.
54. *Ibid.* article 16.
55. *Ibid.* article 233.
56. *Zhang Shuancheng Guoshi Zhi Ren Shiwang An* [The Case of Zhang Shuancheng: Manslaughter Due to Negligence], 62 *Ren Min Fa Yuan An Li Xuan* [Selected Cases of the People's Courts], issue no. 4 (Beijing: People's Court Press, 2008), 48, 49–52. This Chinese case reporter series is edited by the Chinese Practicing Law Institute of the People's Supreme Court and is considered one of the few authoritative publications for Chinese case law.
57. Criminal Code, article 22.
58. *Ibid.* article 23.
59. *Ibid.* article 24.
60. *Ibid.* article 45.
61. *Ibid.*
62. *Ibid.* article 27.
63. *Ibid.* article 28.
64. *Ibid.* article 29.
65. *Ibid.* article 29.
66. *Ibid.* article 30.
67. *Ibid.* article 31.
68. *Ibid.* article 20, paragraph 3.
69. *Ibid.* article 21, paragraph 3.
70. *Wang Renxing Pohuai Jiaotong Sheshi An* [The Case of the Wang Renxing Sabotaging Transportation Device] (Case #295), in *Xingshi Shenban Cangkao (Reference to Criminal Trial)*, issue 38 (Beijing: People's Court Press, 2004), 82–87.
71. This case was widely reported by Chinese media, but the official case report cannot be found. The defendant's brief and documentation related to this case were posted by the defendants' attorney on his blog, http://blog.163.com/luo_shuihe/blog/static/609549292008219101041680/ (accessed August 30, 2009).
72. The official report of this case cannot be found, but the story of this case was reported in the case-law database of Chinacourt.org, http://www.chinacourt.org/public/detail.php?id=250374&k_title=%B0%B2%C0%D6%CB% C0&k_ content=%B0%B2%C0%D6%CB%C0&k_author= (accessed August 30, 2009).

73. Criminal Code, articles 17, 18 and 19.
74. *Ibid.* article 18.
75. 1982 Constitution, article 34; General Principles of Civil Law, article 11.
76. Criminal Code, article 17. The other violent crimes include intentionally causing serious body injuries or death, rape, robbery, narcotics trafficking, arson, bombing, and poisoning.
77. *Ibid.* last paragraph.
78. *Ibid.* article 18.
79. *Ibid.* second paragraph.
80. *Ibid.* third paragraph.
81. *Ibid.* article 33.
82. *Ibid.* articles 33 and 35.
83. *Ibid.* articles 38–41.
84. *Ibid.* articles 42–44.
85. *Ibid.* article 46.
86. *Ibid.* articles 45, 50, and 69.
87. *Ibid.* article 50.
88. *Ibid.* article 48.
89. *Ibid.* article 49.
90. *Ibid.* article 54.
91. *Ibid.* articles 55 and 57.
92. *Ibid.* article 56.
93. *Ibid.*
94. *Ibid.* article 59 and various articles prescribing specific crimes in the code.
95. *Ibid.* article 59.
96. *Ibid.* article 35.
97. *Ibid.* article 61.
98. *Ibid.* article 37.
99. *Ibid.* article 62.
100. *Ibid.* article 63.
101. *Ibid.* article 52.
102. *Ibid.* article 65.
103. *Ibid.* article 67.
104. *Ibid.* second paragraph.
105. *Ibid.* article 68.
106. *Ibid.*
107. *See* Wang, *supra* note 37, at 226–227.
108. 1979 Criminal Code, article 44.
109. Criminal Code, article 48.
110. *Ibid.* article 383.
111. Zhao Binzhi, "Discussion on the Gradual Abolition of Death Penalty for the Non-violent Crimes," in *The Road of the Abolition of the Death Penalty in China*, ed. by Binzhi Zhao (Beijing: Press of Chinese People's Public Security University, 2004), 3. Binzhi Zhao is considered one of the most authoritative Chinese law professors in criminal law. His view reflects mainstream Chinese legal scholars' views on the death penalty.

112. Article 358 of the Criminal Code provides:

Anyone who organizes or forces another person to engage in prostitution shall be sentenced to fixed-term imprisonment of not less than five years nor more than ten years, and may in addition be subject to a fine. In any of the following listed situations, the sentence shall be fixed-term imprisonment of not less than ten years or life imprisonment, and may in addition include a fine or confiscation of property:
  (1) Arranging people to engage in prostitution, where serious circumstances are involved,
  (2) Forcing a minor girl under the age of 14 to engage in prostitution,
  (3) Forcing more than one person to engage in prostitution or repeatedly forcing others to engage in prostitution,
  (4) Forcing another person to engage in prostitution after raping her, or
  (5) Causing serious injuries, death, or some other serious consequences to the person who is forced to engage in prostitution.

Anyone who commits the above listed crimes, where exceptionally serious circumstances are involved, shall be sentenced to life imprisonment or death, and may in addition be subject to confiscation of property.

113. The judgment of the case of Ma Yulan cannot be found in any Chinese published case report, but the case was widely reported by the Chinese media and was discussed in many Chinese law-review articles. One of the websites that reported the story is Chinese Death Penalty Watch, http://www.chinamonitor.org (accessed August 30, 2009).

114. This is another problem with the Chinese criminal justice system. The execution of criminals sentenced to death is too swift and does not leave enough time for the condemned to appeal or seek other judicial remedies. In fact, some innocent people have been wrongfully accused and executed.

115. The *Case of Organizing Prostitution by Hu Kaiying and Others* was also widely reported by the Chinese media and is reported in the case database of Chinalawinfo at http://eol.sdu.edu.cn/eol/data/repository/20070809/U/122/case/showcase9ae9.html?id=4870 (accessed May 11, 2010). According to article 50 of the 1997 Criminal Code, if a person sentenced to death with a stay of execution does not intentionally commit another crime during the period of the stay, his punishment may be commuted to life imprisonment; moreover, as noted in section II.F.1 in this chapter, if he performs substantial meritorious service, his punishment may be commuted to fixed-term imprisonment of not less than fifteen years and not more than twenty years.

116. Opinion on Taking Further Steps to Ensure the Quality of Handling Death Penalty Cases According to Law (*Guan yu jin yi bu yan ge yi fa ban an que bao ban li si xing an jian zhi liang de yi jian*), jointly issued by the SPC, the SPP, the Ministry of Public Security, and the Ministry of Justice on March 9, 2007, item 4. The opinion is available on Chinalawinfo at http://law.chinalawinfo.com/Newlaw2002/SLC/SLC.asp?Db=chl&Gid=89175 (accessed August 30, 2009).

117. 1979 Criminal Code, article 43; 1979 Criminal Procedure Law, articles 144–147.

118. The Decision of the NPC's Standing Committee on the Death Penalty Case Approval Issue, enacted on June 10, 1981.

119. Organic Law of People's Courts (revised 1983), article 13.

120. 1996 Criminal Procedure Law, article 199; and Criminal Code, article 48.

121. The Notice of Authorizing the Higher People's Court of Yunan Province to Approve the Death Penalty Imposed on Some Crimes of Drug Trafficking, promulgated by the Supreme People's Court on June 6, 1991.

122. The Supreme People's Court's Notice Regarding the Authorization of the Higher People's Courts and the Military Court of the Liberation Army to Review and Approve Death Penalties on Certain Crimes, promulgated by the Supreme People's Court on September 26, 1997.

123. "Sixing He Zhunquan: Jianna Huigui" [Death Penalty Review and Approval Right: A Road of Difficult Return], *Democracy and Legal System (Min zu yu fa zhi)* 24 (2006): 20–21.

124. The Supreme People's Court's Decision on the Issue of Uniform Application of Death Penalty Review and Approval of December 13, 2006.

125. On February 28, 2007, the Supreme People's Court promulgated the Rules on Several Issues Related to Death Penalty Review.

126. "China Sees 30% Drop in Death Penalty," *China Daily* (May 10, 2008), http://www.chinadaily.com.cn/china/2008-05/10/content_6675006.htm (accessed August 30, 2009).

127. Xie Chuanjiao, "Top Court Overturns 15% Death Sentences in 1st Half Year," *China Daily* (June 27, 2008), http://www.chinadaily.com.cn/china/2008-06/27/content_6798854.htm (accessed August 30, 2009).

128. Criminal Code, article 17.

129. The Reply of the Research Office of the Supreme People's Court Regarding the Question Whether the Underage Persons between Fourteen and Sixteen Who Commit Negligent Homicides Should Bear Criminal Liabilities (February 9, 1991).

130. Criminal Code, article 236.

131. Interpretation of Several Issues on How to Specifically Apply Law When Handling Rape Cases, jointly issued by the Supreme People's Court, the Supreme People's Procuracy, and the Ministry of Public Security (1984), article 5, item 3.

132. *Ibid.* second paragraph.

133. The Reply of the Supreme People's Court Regarding the Issue of Whether the Actor Who Did Not Know the Minor Girl Is under Fourteen-Years Old and Had a Sexual Intercourse with the Girl Committed the Crime of Rape, issued by the Judicial Committee of the Supreme People's Court of the PRC on January 17, 2003, in reply to an interpretation request from the High People's Court of Liaoning Province.

134. Handicap Protection Law of the PRC (1990), article 52, sentence 5.

135. Criminal Code, article 236, third paragraph.

136. *Ibid.* article 237, first paragraph.

137. Article 265 of the Criminal Code also provides that anyone who, for the purpose of reaping profits, illegally connects other people's communication lines or counterfeits other people's telecommunication codes should be convicted of theft and punished according to article 264.

138. Criminal Code, article 264.

139. *Ibid.*

140. *Ibid.*

141. The Provision Regarding the Standards to Determine the Amounts of Stolen Property Values, jointly issued by the Supreme People's Court, the Supreme People's Procuracy, and the Ministry of Public Security on March 26, 1998.

142. *Ibid.*

143. Criminal Code, article 266.

144. The Interpretation on Several Issues Regarding the Specific Application of Law When Handling Fraud Cases, promulgated by the Supreme People's Court on December 24, 1996.

145. Criminal Code, article 199.

146. *Ibid.* article 296.

147. *Ibid.* article 299.

148. *Ibid.* article 300.

149. *Ibid.* article 363.

150. *Ibid.* article 303.

151. *Ibid.* article 354.

152. *Ibid.* article 365.

153. *Ibid.* articles 258 and 259.

154. *Ibid.* article 176.

155. 1979 Criminal Code, Part II Specific Provisions, Charter 1.

156. *Ibid.*

157. *See* Wang, *supra* note 37, at 222–223.

158. 1979 Criminal Code, article 91; see also Criminal Code, article 102.

159. Criminal Code, article 103.

160. *Ibid.* article 104.

161. *Ibid.* article 105.

162. *Ibid.* article 106.

163. *Ibid.*

164. *See* Wang, *supra* note 37, at 223.

165. *The Case of Huang Jingqiu: The Crime of Subverting the State Power*, Higher People's Court of Jiangsu Province, Su Xing Zhong #309 (December 9, 2004). The judgment can be found at the case database of Chinalawinfo, http://law.chinalawinfo.com/newlaw2002/SLC/SLC.asp?Db=fnl&Gid=117485112 (accessed August 30, 2009).

EGYPT

Sadiq Reza

I. Introduction
   A. Historical Sketch
   B. Jurisdiction
   C. Legality Principle
   D. Sources of Criminal Law
   E. Process

II. General Part
   A. Liability Requirements
   B. Defenses
   C. Justifications
   D. Excuses
   E. Sanctions

III. Special Part
   A. Structure
   B. Homicide
   C. Sex Offenses

Sadiq Reza is Professor of Law at New York Law School. His recent publications include "Islam's Fourth Amendment: Search and Seizure in Islamic Doctrine and Muslim Practice," 40 *Georgetown Journal of International Law* 703 (2009); and "Egypt," in Craig M. Bradley (ed.), *Criminal Procedure: A Worldwide Study* (Carolina Academic Press, 2d ed., 2007).

The author thanks New York Law School for financial support, Amr Shalakany for guidance, and the following individuals and institutions for assistance with research and sources: Peter Bessada, Luna Droubi, Natalie Smolenski, Ned Thimmayya, Nabil Fouda of the Middle East Library for Economic Services (MELES), Amira Heikal and Eihab Seoudi of Legislation and Development Information Systems (LADIS), and the libraries of New York Law School and Harvard Law School. The author dedicates this chapter to the memory of Lesley Wilkins (1944–2007)—the first Bibliographer for the Law of the Islamic World at Harvard Law School, a former president of the Middle East Librarians' Association, an inveterate traveler, and an always cheerful colleague and friend.

D. Theft and Fraud
E. "Victimless" Crimes

I. INTRODUCTION

Criminal law in the Arab Republic of Egypt is governed primarily by a Penal Code, modeled along Napoleonic lines, that was promulgated in 1937 and has been amended periodically since then. Supplementing that code are, among many other laws and regulations, the country's 1979 constitution and interpretations of the Penal Code and the constitution by the courts of several overlapping judicial systems.[1] The most important of these courts for criminal law purposes are the Court of Cassation, which is Egypt's highest court of ordinary civil and criminal justice, and the Supreme Constitutional Court, which considers constitutional questions that arise in any of Egypt's judicial systems—ordinary justice, administrative justice, military justice, and emergency justice.

This chapter focuses on criminal law under the Penal Code and the constitution, as applied and interpreted by the ordinary judiciary and the Supreme Constitutional Court. However, reference will also be made to matters of criminal law that appear in other laws or arise in Egypt's other judicial systems.

A. Historical Sketch

Modern criminal law in Egypt dates from 1883, when a system of national courts was established and several new codes of law were promulgated, all modeled along Napoleonic lines. Criminal law before the 1883 penal code consisted of a mixture of uncodified Islamic law (*sharia*) and periodic and piecemeal criminal legislation (*qanun*s), the latter under Ottoman rule from the sixteenth to the eighteenth centuries and then essentially independent of it in the nineteenth century (although Egypt nominally remained a province of the Ottoman Empire until its collapse in 1923). The 1883 reforms explicitly modernized Egypt's legal system in an effort to strengthen the country internally and vis-à-vis Ottoman and European powers; therefore, they were the culmination of several intersecting developments of the preceding 100 years. Egypt's nineteenth-century leaders, beginning with Governor Muhammad Ali (1805–1848), had increasingly sought to enhance the central government's authority and control over local officials and civilians through penal codes and other legislation; Egyptian intellectuals were increasingly influenced by European law and legal thought, especially French models; the growing presence of Europeans in Egypt itself (primarily for commerce), Egypt's increasing economic dependence on them, and European demands for special legal protections in the country had resulted in the creation in 1876 of a separate system of legal codes and courts for foreigners, modeled along French lines and called the "mixed courts"; and a combination of fiscal problems and a nationalist movement led to political instability that occasioned the British occupation of Egypt in 1882. The 1883 legal reforms, of which Egypt's first modern penal code was a part, thus constituted an explicit assertion of political sovereignty and legal modernity.

The 1883 penal code and other legislation governed only Egyptian nationals; foreigners were still subject only to the jurisdiction of the mixed courts. Egypt regained nominal independence from the British in 1922; a replacement penal code issued in 1937, in connection with the termination of certain foreign privileges; and finally in 1949, when the mixed courts were abolished, the new penal code reached all residents of Egypt. That 1937 code, as amended periodically and interpreted regularly by Egypt's judicial systems, remains in force today.

B. Jurisdiction

The Penal Code authorizes prosecuting the following: (1) anyone who commits a listed offense in the country; (2) anyone who commits in a foreign country an act that makes him or her an accomplice in a listed offense that takes place wholly or partially in Egypt; (3) anyone who commits an offense listed as threatening national security from inside or outside Egypt; (4) anyone who commits one of several specified offenses of forgery or counterfeiting; and (5) any Egyptian national who commits in a foreign country an act that constitutes an offense under both the Code and the law of the country in which the act was committed, unless that person has been prosecuted for the offense in the foreign country and either acquitted or convicted (and, if convicted, has completed the sentence).[2]

An ordinary criminal case can be brought in any one of three places: where the crime was committed, where the defendant resides, or where the defendant was arrested.[3] Attempt crimes may be charged anywhere part of the attempt took place.[4] If a crime is committed outside the country and the defendant neither resides in Egypt nor was arrested there, jurisdiction lies in one of two designated courts in Cairo: the Cairo Criminal Court for felonies and the Abdin Summary Court for misdemeanors and violations.[5] Juvenile courts, created under a 1974 law, try defendants who were under eighteen years old at the time of the offense. Military courts, authorized by the constitution and established by the 1966 Military Justice Law, have jurisdiction over defendants who are members of the armed services, as well as over civilian defendants whose cases the president expressly refers to a military court. "Emergency" state security courts, established pursuant to the 1958 Emergency Law, can hear alleged violations of orders the president issues pursuant to his emergency powers, as well as any criminal offenses the president refers to them.

Prosecutions in the military and emergency courts have been a prominent and controversial feature of Egyptian criminal law in recent decades. The Military Justice Law authorizes civilian referrals in two types of cases—felonies that pertain to state security, and any crimes during a state of emergency[6]—and judicial challenges to such referrals reached the Supreme Constitutional Court on two separate occasions in the 1990s. (The court ruled in the president's favor in the first case and never issued a decision in the second.) Future challenges of this kind are ostensibly foreclosed by a new constitutional provision, adopted in a package of constitutional amendments passed in March 2007, that authorizes the president to refer crimes of "terrorism" to "any judicial body established by the Constitution or the law."[7] Criminal prosecutions also regularly proceed in the state security courts established pursuant to the Emergency Law, which has been in force continuously since 1981 and for all but three of the last fifty years. (The law's most recent extension came in May 2010, for two years.) A presidential decree that was issued in 1981 and was amended in 2004 refers a variety of crimes to these courts, including crimes concerning state security, public incitement, and public demonstrations and gatherings. Moreover, the president's new constitutional authority to refer crimes of terrorism to "any judicial body" includes, by definition, the emergency courts too; constitutional challenges to emergency-court terror prosecutions are also thus presumably foreclosed now.

C. Legality Principle

Egypt's constitution affirms the principle of legality (*la jarimah wa la 'uqubah illa bina'an 'ala qanun*), forbids *ex post facto* punishment, and forbids punishment without a judicial sentence.[8] The Supreme Constitutional Court (SCC) has addressed these principles on a number of occasions. In a 1992 case the SCC considered a military order that sanctioned an army officer who had refused to obey a command during a military campaign. The law pursuant to which the sanction was ordered, which enumerated the sanctions for acts of military insubordination, had not been enacted until after the officer's misconduct. The SCC found that the sanction constituted a criminal punishment and therefore violated the constitution's *ex post facto* clause.[9] In a 1993 case the SCC considered a 1945 law that criminalized and punished persons who were "vagabonds or suspects"; included within this group were persons "notorious for" committing any of a number of listed offenses. The legality principle requires criminal offenses to be clearly defined, the SCC said, and it found that the law at issue violated that requirement, as well as the prohibition of *ex post facto* punishment.[10] The following year the SCC reached the opposite result when considering a customs law that forbade smuggling and listed several specific acts that constituted it. The defendant had challenged on vagueness grounds catchall language that appeared at the end of the provision, which said that smuggling included "any other act designed to evade payment of customs taxes . . . or in contravention of the applicable regulations on prohibited merchandise." The SCC found the language sufficiently clear to satisfy the legality principle since it stated precisely what the legislature aimed to prevent: the avoidance of customs tax.[11]

Article 5 of the Penal Code restates the legality principle and adds two defendant-friendly corollaries on *ex post facto* legislation. First, after an offense is committed but before final judgment in a case, if a new law reduces the sentence for the offense, the defendant faces only the lesser sentence. Second, after final judgment in a case, if a new law decriminalizes the conduct for which the defendant was convicted, the judgment and sentence are vacated.

D. Sources of Criminal Law

1. Legislature

The primary source of substantive criminal law in Egypt is, as noted at the beginning of this chapter, the 1937 Penal Code, as periodically amended and regularly interpreted by the courts. The Code was adopted by what was to become Egypt's parliament, the People's Assembly, and that body alone can amend it. Drug crimes and punishments are set out in supplemental legislation, the Law Combating Drugs and Regulating Their Use and Trade (hereafter Drug Law), which originated as a presidential decree in 1960, was thereafter approved by the People's Assembly (see section I.D.3), and has been amended regularly since. Further penal provisions appear in other statutes, such as the 1961 Law Combating Prostitution, the 1973 Law Forbidding Drinking Alcoholic Beverages, and the 2002 Law Combating Money Laundering. The constitution also contains provisions that govern criminal law, particularly in guarantees that include the legality principle and the presumption of innocence. Other laws that bear on criminal matters include the Code of Criminal Procedure (enacted in 1950), the Emergency Law (1958), the Appeals Law (1959), the Military Justice Law (1966), the Police Authority Law (1971), and the Juvenile Code (1974, rewritten in 1996).

The Penal Code contains over 400 provisions and is divided into four Books.[12] Book 1, "General Provisions," sets out the types of crimes and possible penalties, along with rules of accomplice liability, attempt, defenses, and other matters that fall in modern criminal law's general part (discussed in more detail in section II in this chapter). But that book contains only 76 of the Code's provisions; the remainder of the provisions, and thus the vast majority of them, are in Books 2 through 4, which enumerate specific crimes in three categories and thus constitute the code's special part (discussed in more detail in section III in this chapter). The Code classifies all criminal offenses in three categories: felonies (*jinayat*), which carry punishments that range from three years' imprisonment to death (as well as possible ancillary punishments); misdemeanors (*junah*), which carry jail sentences of up to three years or fines above 100 Egyptian pounds (£E 100) (approximately U.S. $18 as of this writing); and violations (*mukhalafat*), which carry fines of not more than £E 100.[13] These punishments are discussed more fully in section II.E, while specific offenses in the three categories of crime are discussed there and in section III.

2. Judiciary

The Supreme Constitutional Court is the final authority on penal matters insofar as provisions of the constitution bear on them; its decisions bind all branches of the government, including all of Egypt's judiciaries—ordinary, administrative, military, and emergency. The bulk of jurisprudence on criminal law lies, however, in decisions of the Court of Cassation, the country's highest court of ordinary justice (civil and criminal). The Court of Cassation is the second level of appeal in violations and misdemeanors and the only level of appeal in felonies (as noted in section I.E), and it hears only claimed errors of law: failures to apply the law, misapplications of the law, misinterpretations of the law, and legal insufficiency of evidence for conviction. Its decisions thus provide the most plentiful and substantial elaborations and interpretations of the Penal Code. Indeed, as will be seen in later sections, Court of Cassation decisions regularly provide content and detail the Code lacks, such as articulating the necessary elements of specific crimes and even the standard elements of every crime (*actus reus*, *mens rea*, and so on).

3. Executive

Executive decrees supplement the criminal law legislation set out in section I.D.1. Egypt's president has the constitutional authority to issue implementing regulations that do not "modify, obstruct, or prevent" the execution of the law; the president may also delegate that authority to others (Const. Art. 144). Separate constitutional provisions empower the president to issue regulations for the police (Art. 145) and for public services and authorities

(Art. 146). The constitution also authorizes the president to issue decrees that have the force of law in cases of "necessity" or "exceptional circumstances" and with prior authorization by two-thirds of the members of the People's Assembly, and these decrees become laws—and are thereafter called "decree-laws"—if the People's Assembly approves them at its next regular session (Art. 108). The statute on "vagabonds on suspects" that the SCC deemed unconstitutional in 1993 (see section I.C) took effect in 1945 as such a decree-law; so too did the 1960 Drug Law, which continues to govern drug crimes and punishments.[14] Additional executive authority in criminal law can derive from legislation itself; one example is the power, originally statutory and now constitutional, given the president to refer criminal cases to military or emergency courts (discussed in section I.B), and another is article 54 of the Drug Law, which authorizes the president to issue regulations to implement the law's provisions.

4. Scholars

Commentaries on the Penal Code and treatises on criminal law are plentiful in Egypt. How influential these are is not clear; court decisions do not typically cite scholarly works. At least three subsets of Egyptian criminal law scholarship are discernible. One subset annotates the Penal Code with pertinent court decisions and adds explanatory and conceptual material, for instance listing the elements courts have deemed required of particular crimes or of crime generally. In doing so, this scholarship implicitly and explicitly identifies gaps in the Penal Code and other legislation that have been filled by judicial decisions, and provides and organizes the missing content. A second subset of criminal law scholarship explains the Egyptian system in light of the French system that was its model or compares it with other foreign systems. A third compares the contemporary Egyptian regime with "Islamic" criminal law, the remnants of which ended with the first modern code of 1883. Of these three types of scholarship, the first is presumably the type that bears most directly on the work of judges, legislators, and practitioners.

E. Process

Crimes in the two lesser categories—misdemeanors and violations—are tried in single-judge Summary Courts (*mahakim juz'iyyah*), of which there are over 200 throughout the country; these courts also hear minor civil claims.[15] Appeals from these courts go to three-judge panels of the courts of first instance (*mahakim ibtida'iyyah*), which also have trial jurisdiction over major civil claims; when hearing criminal appeals, these courts are called misdemeanor courts of appeal (*mahakim junah al-isti'naf*).[16] Felonies are tried in three-judge criminal courts (*mahakim al-jinayat*), panels for which are drawn from a judicial body that also hears first appeals in major civil cases, the Court of Appeal (*mahkamah al-isti'naf*).[17] Appeals from the felony-trial criminal courts and from the misdemeanor courts of appeal go to the Court of Cassation, where they are decided by panels of five judges.

1. Adversarial/Inquisitorial

Criminal procedure in Egypt remains patterned on the French system, but there are substantial differences. The 1950 Code of Criminal Procedure followed the French model in assigning the duties and powers of pretrial investigation and charging to judicial officers, namely, an examining magistrate and an indicting chamber. Subsequent amendments, however, have given prosecutors the powers of examining magistrates and abolished the indicting chamber. The Code still allows prosecutors to refer cases to examining magistrates if they wish, but in practice prosecutors conduct all pretrial investigations and make all charging decisions. Victims, as well as putative civil plaintiffs (i.e., those alleging financial harm from the defendant's conduct), can initiate criminal prosecutions or join them after they have commenced, as in the French system. Trial procedure also follows the French model, beginning with a preliminary colloquy between the presiding judge and the defendant in which the defendant is informed of the charge and invited to make any statements. The court determines the order of witnesses, and although the parties may question each witness, in practice the parties present their questions to the court and the court asks the witness those questions it allows, along with any questions the court itself wishes to pose. Verdicts must rest only on evidence that is presented at trial, and the court can order a recitation of evidence from the preliminary examination, including statements of the defendant. At trial the defendant need not testify; the court can, however, give the defendant the opportunity to clarify or respond to any issue that arises at trial. After testimony is completed, all parties can present closing statements, after which the court retires to deliberate.

2. Jury/Written Opinions

All criminal trials in Egypt are bench trials; there are no juries. As noted at the beginning of this section, a single judge hears and decides violations and misdemeanors, while three judges do the same for felonies. Felony convictions and sentences require agreement by two of the three judges, except death sentences, which must be unanimous. Verdicts must be issued publicly and in writing, and they must provide reasons for the judgment and for all rulings on motions made by the parties. Verdicts must be signed by the issuing court within eight days of issuance (absent "compelling reasons" for delay); unsigned verdicts of guilt become invalid after thirty days.

3. Presumption of Innocence

The presumption of innocence is guaranteed by the constitution (Art. 67) and has been addressed several times by the Supreme Constitutional Court. In a 1995 case, for instance, the SCC found the guarantee violated by a ministerial decree that forbade the sale of spoiled meat and deemed any meat that did not carry an official butchery seal per se spoiled. The decree established presumptions about both the condition of the meat (the *actus reus* of the crime) and a seller's awareness of that condition (the *mens rea*), the SCC said, and thus violated the presumption of innocence; on that ground, among others, the SCC reversed the conviction of a butcher under the decree. In a 1996 case the SCC found the guarantee violated by a statute that created a rebuttable presumption of knowledge that foreign goods were smuggled when a person was found in possession of such goods without documentation that duty was paid on them. The presumption allowed a conviction without proof of *mens rea*, the SCC said, and the statute was therefore unconstitutional.

4. Burden of Proof

Neither the constitution nor the Penal Code specifies the quantum of the government's burden of proof in criminal cases. Uniformly, though, court decisions and commentary describe that quantum in terms that approximate or replicate the American standard of "proof beyond a reasonable doubt." In its 1993 ruling striking down the law that penalized "vagabonds and suspects," for instance, the SCC said that a criminal conviction requires proof of guilt at a level of "definitiveness and certainty" (*jazm wa yaqin*) that "leaves no reasonable cause for doubt to the contrary" (*la yada'u majalan ma'qulan li shubhah intifa'iha*).[18]

II. GENERAL PART

A. Liability Requirements

1. Objective/Actus Reus

   i. Act

The Penal Code does not directly mention *actus reus* or its equivalent. It does, however, effectively establish a voluntary-act requirement for criminal liability by forbidding punishment for acts that are committed as a result of an offender's unconsciousness, insanity, or mental infirmity, or from the forced or unknowing ingestion of any kind of drugs, or are otherwise not a result of the offender's free will (Art. 62). Court of Cassation opinions and criminal law scholarship also regularly discuss the "material element" (*rukn maddi*) of a crime as both a definitional component of specific crimes and a general liability requirement, and the SCC has declared that element to be a constitutional requirement. In its 1993 ruling striking down the law that penalized "vagabonds and suspects," the SCC said that one of the constitutional flaws of that law was its failure to specify a material element or to require proof of one for a conviction; both requirements, the SCC said, follow from the constitutional guarantee of the legality principle (Const. Art. 66).[19] In a 1996 ruling, elaborating on these and other constitutional requirements of criminal liability, the SCC provided the term *actus reus* in parentheses as the equivalent of the Arabic term "material element," as though to remove any doubt that the concept at issue was the same.[20]

   ii. Omission

The Penal Code does not explicitly address liability for omissions, but a number of provisions establish such liability. Case law and commentary accordingly discuss criminal liability for omissions, which are called "passive" (*salbi*) conduct, as opposed to "affirmative" (*ijabi*) conduct. The SCC has embraced liability for omissions as a general matter; in its 1993 ruling striking down the law on vagabonds and suspects, for instance, the SCC noted that the material-element requirement could be satisfied by designating either affirmative or passive conduct as the basis of liability.

Most of the Code provisions that punish omissions address breaches of explicit or obvious legal duties and bring misdemeanor penalties or less. Among these are duties of government officials to fulfill the obligations of their positions at the time or in the manner required, and duties to care and provide for members of one's family.[21] Other provisions suggest duties that one might consider less common or obvious. For instance, under article 84 of the Penal Code, a person who knows about another's act of treason or other crime of state security but fails to notify law-enforcement authorities faces up to one year of detention and a £E 500 fine unless the offender is the person's spouse or blood relative; these penalties are doubled if the crime occurs during a time of war. Under article 39 of the Drug Law, any person who is apprehended in a place maintained for obtaining drugs (unlawfully) at a time when, with the person's knowledge, drugs are in fact being obtained unlawfully faces a minimum penalty of one year's detention and a fine of £E 1,000 to £E 3,000, unless the person lives in the place or is the spouse or blood relative of the person who maintains the place for obtaining drugs. In other words, according to the latter provision, one has a duty to leave premises that are maintained for unlawful drug use unless one lives on the premises or is married or related to the person who maintains them for that purpose.

iii. Status

The Penal Code does not address status as a permitted or prohibited basis of criminal liability, nor do any of its provisions appear to suggest such liability. Provisions of other criminal statutes have suggested such liability, however, and the SCC has issued rulings that disapprove of it. One such ruling was the SCC's 1993 invalidation of the law on vagabonds and suspects, discussed in previous sections, where the SCC noted the absence of a material element (*actus reus*) for liability as one of the law's constitutional flaws. A second such ruling came in 1996 when the SCC struck down a provision of the 1960 Drug Law that essentially penalized the status of being a habitual offender or accusee: the law authorized courts to commit to a work institution, for a period of one to ten years, anyone who had been convicted or accused "for serious reasons" (*li asbab jaddiyyah*) more than once of any of a list of specified drug crimes. Among the provision's flaws, the SCC said, was that it permitted punishment without proof of a specified *actus reus* or *mens rea*; it thus violated the legality principle.[22]

2. *Subjective/Mens Rea/Mental Element*

Intent elements appear in the definitions of many offenses in the Penal Code, but the Code contains neither definitions of these elements nor even a general *mens rea* requirement. Case law and commentary do, however, discuss criminal intent (*qasd jina'i*) as the necessary "moral element" (*rukn ma'nawi*) that, along with the material element (*actus reus*), must exist for a crime to have been committed. And as with the material element, the SCC has declared that proof of the moral element is a constitutional requirement of criminal liability. In its 1996 ruling striking down the habitual-drug-offender law (discussed in section II.A.1.iii in this chapter), the SCC discussed the moral element along with the material element as a necessary aspect of criminal liability pursuant to the legality principle. As it did with the term *actus reus*, the SCC inserted the term *mens rea* in parentheses as the equivalent of the Arabic term "moral element"; but on the latter point the SCC went further, listing as examples four particular *mens rea* terms in English—felonious intent, malice aforethought, fraudulent intent, and guilty knowledge—and equivalents for them in Arabic.

i. Intent

The Penal Code uses the term "willful" (*'amdan*) to express the most culpable degree of *mens rea* (except when premeditation is added to a willful homicide, as discussed in section III.B.1 in this chapter). The Code does not define the term, but the Court of Cassation has defined willfulness as the intentional commission of the *actus reus* with knowledge of its consequences[23]—that is, what appears to be at least "knowledge" under the American Model Penal Code. Willfulness is the specified *mens rea* for a variety of crimes in the Code—for example, murder (Arts. 231–234), arson (Arts. 252–259), harming beasts of burden (Arts. 355, 357), destroying property (Art. 361), disabling a public utility (Art. 361(*bis*-A)), destroying government documents (Art. 364), and the very first crime listed in the Code, the capital crime of threatening the country's unity or independence (Art. 77).

ii. Recklessness

Although reckless conduct is not expressly defined as such in the Penal Code, it gives rise to criminal liability in various contexts. Under article 244, personal injury resulting from an error that is caused by an offender's "gross breach of duties" carries a penalty of up to two years in jail and a £E 300 fine. The same provision lists two other types of wrongdoing that give rise to liability if personal injury results: (a) using liquor or narcotics and (b) refraining from assisting a crime victim or other person in need when asked and able to assist. That behavior is thus implicitly defined as criminally reckless per se. Moreover, as noted in section II.A.4 in this chapter, the Court of Cassation has defined criminal causation to include foreseeable consequences of actions taken with disregard for potential harm to others and has thus endorsed criminal liability for recklessness generally.

iii. Negligence

Like reckless conduct, negligent conduct is not expressly defined in the Penal Code but can give rise to criminal liability. The Code provision that criminalizes reckless personal injury also criminalizes personal injury that is caused by an offender's "neglect, imprudence, carelessness, or non-observance of the law," and deems it punishable by the lesser penalty of up to one year in jail and a £E 200 fine.[24] Many other crimes in the Code involve negligence, with liability triggered by "neglect," "carelessness," or "error" in a variety of circumstances: for example, in managing public funds or property (Arts. 116(*bis*-A)–116(*bis*-B)), permitting an arrestee to escape (Art. 139), caring for a mentally infirm person who is in one's custody (Arts. 377/3, 378/8), and repairing or maintaining chimneys and other places where fire is used (Art. 378/2). A series of Code provisions also define the crime of "criminally negligent bankruptcy" (*tafalus bi taqsir*) (Arts. 330–333), which carries a penalty of detention for up to two years (Art. 334).

iv. Strict Liability

No Penal Code provision directly addresses strict liability. The Court of Cassation has said, however, that criminal intent generally cannot be presumed or imputed but must be proven—that is, that there is no strict liability; thus the owner of an animal that has injured someone cannot be held criminally liable for the harm absent proof that the owner negligently failed to prevent such harm.[25] But the Court of Cassation has also recognized a presumptive strict liability in at least one category of offenses, so-called immoral or indecent offenses. According to this doctrine, a man who has sexual intercourse with a married woman, punishable by jailing for up to two years under articles 274 and 275 of the Penal Code (see section III.C.2 in this chapter), is presumed to know that the woman is married; and a person who commits the nonforcible sexual assault of someone under the age of eighteen—that is, statutory rape, which is punishable by jailing under article 269 (see section III.C.1 in this chapter)—is presumed to know that the victim is underage. In both cases the defendant can rebut the presumption of knowledge by proving exceptional circumstances that made it impossible for him to learn the victim's status.

3. *Theories of Liability*
   i. Inchoate Crimes
      a. *Attempt*

Attempt is defined as undertaking an act with the intent to commit a felony or misdemeanor, but failing to complete the act for reasons beyond the actor's will.[26] Expressly excluded from this definition is "mere resolution or preparation" to commit a crime.[27] The Court of Cassation has elaborated on this definition and has said that the line between preparation and perpetration is crossed when, provided intent is proven, the offender undertakes an act that "immediately precedes" the *actus reus* and would "inevitably lead to" it.[28] The punishments for attempt crimes are fixed reductions of the penalties for the completed crimes: life imprisonment for offenses that carry the death penalty, aggravated imprisonment for offenses that carry life imprisonment, imprisonment or one-half the designated sentence of aggravated imprisonment for offenses that carry aggravated imprisonment, and detention or one-half the designated sentence of imprisonment for offenses that carry imprisonment.[29]

   b. *Conspiracy*

The Penal Code's conspiracy provision, article 48, was declared unconstitutional by the SCC in 2001, and a replacement provision does not appear to have been promulgated. The provision defined a conspiracy (*ittifaq jina'i*, "criminal agreement") as an agreement between two or more persons to commit a felony or misdemeanor or to undertake preparatory acts toward one. Penalties were set out according to the degree of the contemplated crime and the level of involvement of the offender; all participants, however, were said to be punishable simply for joining the agreement. Among the grounds the SCC listed for striking down the provision was its failure to specify an *actus reus*, which the SCC said violated both the legality principle and the presumption of innocence (Const. Arts. 66 and 67).[30]

   ii. Complicity

Seven articles in the Penal Code address accomplice liability. Article 39 defines a principal perpetrator as one who either commits the crime or, if the crime consists of several discrete acts, intentionally commits one of those acts. Article 40 defines three kinds of criminal accomplices: one who "instigates" (*harada*) the act that constitutes the crime, if the crime occurs on the basis of that instigation; one who agrees with another to commit the crime, if the crime occurs on the basis of that agreement; and one who knowingly gives the perpetrator a tool or other object used to commit the crime or assists the perpetrator in any way in preparing for, committing, or completing the crime. Article 41 states that accomplices are punished equally to principals, with two exceptions: special circumstances that alter the principal's liability do not affect the accomplice's liability if he or she is unaware of those circumstances, and the accomplice is punished according to the nature and degree of his or her own intent or knowledge, even if they are not the nature and degree of the principal's intent or knowledge. Similarly, a defense that exculpates the principal does not necessarily exculpate an accomplice.[31] Accomplices are also liable for crimes they did not intend to be committed if those crimes result from their instigation, agreement, or assistance in a crime they did intend to be committed.[32]

Regarding *mens rea* and causation in unintended crimes (Art. 43), the Court of Cassation has held that accomplices can be liable for all crimes they should have reasonably anticipated as a result of their instigation, agreement, or assistance.[33] Concealing goods that are known to have been obtained from a felony or misdemeanor is a separate crime, punishable by two years' imprisonment or, if the offender knows what precise crime produced the goods and that crime carries a greater punishment, the punishment for that crime.[34]

4. Causation

The Penal Code does not mention causation, but the Court of Cassation has addressed the topic and has held that an offender is liable for crimes that fit in either of the following two categories: (a) foreseeable consequences of an offender's intentional actions, which are also called consequences that are "morally linked" to the offender's actions; and (b) foreseeable consequences of actions taken with disregard for potential harm to others (i.e., recklessness).[35]

B. Defenses

Defenses are listed in a short section of the Penal Code titled "Permissibility Causes [Permissions] and Responsibility Preventives" (*Asbab al-ibahah wa mawani' mas'uliyyah*). This section contains only four articles (Arts. 60–63) and does not list all possible defenses to liability or punishment. The provisions on self-defense, for instance, appear in the Code's special part, just after the provisions that define homicide and other injuries to persons; provisions for discretionary sentence leniency in felony cases and stays of punishment in misdemeanor cases are listed in other sections (see sections II.E.2.i and II.E.2.ii in this chapter); and statutory grounds for pardons and other grounds for remitting punishment (*mawani' 'iqab*, or "penalty preventives") appear ad hoc in provisions on specific crimes. Nor does the section indicate which of the defenses it contains are "permissions," which are "responsibility preventives," or what those terms mean. Commentary, however, which appears to be more abundant than jurisprudence on the topic, makes it clear that the categories of permissions and responsibility preventives correspond roughly with those of justifications and excuses in American law.

Permissions comprise acts that do not cause the harm protected by a criminal statute or that do so in the service of a greater interest. In this category are acts of self-defense (Arts. 245–248); acts by government officials that are performed pursuant to orders of a superior or in the good-faith belief that the acts are lawful executions of their powers (Art.

63); acts performed in the good-faith belief that they are authorized by Islamic law (*sharia*) (Art. 60); and acts of express or implied license, such as in sports, medical treatment, and child discipline. Permissions are said to attach to the act rather than the actor, rendering the act lawful and extending to all participants in the act; neither the actor's free will nor his or her *mens rea* is negated in these defenses. Responsibility preventives, on the other hand, are said to attach to the actor rather than the act, entailing the loss of free will and a consequent negation of the actor's *mens rea*; they thus do not render an act lawful, and they extend only to actors who meet the specified requirements. In this category are infancy, insanity and diminished capacity (Art. 62), involuntary intoxication (Art. 62), and duress (Art. 61 or Art. 62; see section II.D.4). As for the defense of necessity (Art. 61), commentators disagree over whether it is properly characterized as a permission or as a responsibility preventive; the better view appears to be the former, hence its inclusion in that category below (section II.C.1 in this chapter). Defenses of either type appear to negate criminal liability entirely, although other possible consequences might remain, such as institutionalization (for insanity or diminished capacity) or civil liability.

C. Justifications

1. Necessity

Article 61 of the Penal Code sets out the elements of a necessity defense: no punishment applies to an act performed out of necessity (*daruratan*) to prevent the actor or another from imminent and grievous harm, as long as the actor did not create the circumstances that engendered the necessity and had no other means of preventing the harm. Elements of the defense are discussed by commentators, if not yet decided by courts, and the issues are familiar ones—for example, whether the cause of the necessity can be human, as well as natural; what consequences follow a good-faith act that exceeds the limits of the defense; and how necessity differs from duress. Noteworthy in these discussions is what appears to be a majority tendency to lump necessity with duress as a responsibility preventive rather than deeming it a permission, even though it is distinguished from duress and unquestionably shares the features of permissions (and justifications). One authoritative commentator summarizes the debate and argues convincingly that necessity is properly considered a permission.[36]

2. Self-Defense

As noted in section II.B.1, the Penal Code's self-defense provisions do not appear in the Code subsection that is devoted to defenses, but rather in the Code's special part, just after the provisions that define homicide and other injuries to persons. Article 245 states the general proposition that no punishment befalls one who kills or injures another in lawful self-defense, defense of property, or defense of another person's life or property. Article 246 defines lawful self-defense as the use of force necessary to defend oneself against any act that threatens bodily injury and that, if consummated, would constitute a crime under the Code. The same article goes on to reference Code sections that enumerate crimes that, if threatened, allow the use of force in defense of property—namely, crimes of arson, robbery or theft, destruction of property, and burglary or trespass. Article 247 states that there is no right of self-defense when law-enforcement protection is available, and article 248 forbids resisting law-enforcement officers during the good-faith performance of their duties, even if they exceed the scope of their duties, unless a person reasonably fears death or serious bodily injury. In a 1987 opinion the Court of Cassation added another circumstance of lawful force in response to which the defense is unavailable: a citizen's arrest of a *flagrante delicto* offender, which the Code of Criminal Procedure allows. In the same opinion the court said that the policy of self-defense was to ward off unlawful aggression rather than to punish aggressors.[37]

Intentional killing in self-defense is prohibited except in three circumstances: a reasonable fear of death or serious bodily injury, the forcible rape or indecent assault of a woman, and kidnapping.[38] Killing in defense of property is prohibited except to prevent one of four types of crimes: arson, felony robbery or theft, unlawful entry of an inhabited home at night, and an act giving rise to a reasonable fear of death or serious bodily injury.[39] The defense is not available when a person exceeds its lawful limits, but in such a case, if a person has acted in good faith and without intending to commit harm greater than that permitted under the defense, a judge may, if the person has committed an act that constitutes a felony, partially excuse the offender by ordering a jail sentence instead of the prescribed felony punishment.[40]

3. Superior Orders

Article 63 of the Penal Code exempts government employees from criminal liability for acts they undertake in executing orders of superiors that they must obey or believe they must obey, and acts they undertake in the good-faith belief that the acts are required by law or are within the scope of their duties.[41] In both cases the burden is on the accused official to prove that he or she undertook the act only after taking steps to verify its legality, and that he or she reasonably believed that it was legal.[42]

D. Excuses

1. Mistake/Ignorance of Law or Fact

The Penal Code does not expressly provide or proscribe defenses of ignorance or mistake of fact or law. In a 1992 case, however, the SCC articulated the equivalent of a "fair notice" mistake-of-law defense in forbidding the punishment of a ship captain who had navigated into an area of the Red Sea that legislation had designated as a nature preserve and thus off limits to vessels. The officially published version of the pertinent legislation had referred to a map to indicate the protected waters but had failed to include the map. Criminal prohibitions must be clear and unambiguous, the SCC said, and to punish a person absent such clarity would be to deprive him of liberty without due process of law and thus unconstitutional under article 41 of the constitution. For this reason (among others) the SCC forbade the ship captain's punishment.[43]

2. Insanity/Diminished Capacity

As noted in section II.A.1.i in this chapter, article 62 of the Penal Code forbids punishment for acts that are not products of an offender's free will, and it lists among such acts those that result from an offender's insanity or mental infirmity. The Code thus establishes insanity and diminished capacity as formal defenses, and commentary universally deems these defenses responsibility preventives rather than permissions.

3. Intoxication

Intoxication is not mentioned in the Penal Code, but article 62 effectively establishes a responsibility preventive (excuse) of involuntary intoxication by including acts committed under the influence of drugs ingested forcibly or unknowingly in its list of conduct for which punishment is forbidden since it is not a product of the offender's free will (Art. 62; section II.A.1.i. in this chapter). The Court of Cassation has expanded on the Code provision by stating that intoxication, whether voluntary or involuntary, can negate specific intent as a general matter and particularly in the case of willful murder.[44]

4. Duress

Commentary universally recognizes a duress defense and deems it a responsibility preventive. The source of the defense is seen either as article 61, which sets out the necessity defense, or article 62, the provision that forbids punishment for acts that are not products of the defendant's free will (and that expressly lists insanity, diminished capacity, and involuntary intoxication as defenses of that type). The better view appears to be the latter one, for the same reasons that necessity seems best considered a permission rather than a responsibility preventive (see section II.C.1). Details of the defense are well established. Two types of duress are identified, "material coercion" (*ikrah maddi*) and "mental coercion" (*ikrah ma'nawi*); the first is described as the actual physical movement of the defendant's body by the coercer to compel the commission of a crime, while the second involves a threat of harm to the defendant or another to which the defendant accedes by committing the crime. In either case the actor's free will is said to be negated.

E. Sanctions

1. Punishment

The Penal Code lists "primary" punishments (*'uqubat asliyyah*) and "ancillary" punishments (*'uqubat tab'iyyah*). Primary punishments are fines, detention (*habs*), imprisonment (*sijn*), and death.[45] Imprisonment or detention for a year or more also brings mandatory penal servitude (*habs ma'a al-shugl*).[46] Ancillary punishments are of four kinds: (1) deprivation of certain rights and privileges; (2) removal from government employment; (3) probationary supervision by the police; and (4) seizure and confiscation of contraband and fruits or instrumentalities of the crime.[47] All these punishments are discussed in more detail in the following sections.

2. Quantity/Quality of Punishment
   i. Felonies

Felonies include intentional homicide, rape, mayhem, kidnapping, robbery, burglary, arson, and terrorism offenses. Every felony conviction carries one of the following primary punishments: imprisonment (*sijn*), which means a term of three to fifteen years in a "general jail" (*sijn 'umumi*); aggravated imprisonment (*sijn mushaddad*), which means a term of three to fifteen years in a "specialized jail" (*sijn mutakhassis*); life imprisonment (*sijn mu'abbad*), also served in a specialized jail; or the death penalty (*i'dam*).[48] Men over the age of sixty who are sentenced to aggravated or life imprisonment, and all women who receive one of these sentences, serve their terms in a general jail rather than a specialized one.[49] Felony sentences may be reduced if, in the discretion of the sentencing judge, conditions warrant leniency (*ra'fah*): a death sentence can be reduced to life imprisonment or aggravated imprisonment; life imprisonment can be reduced to aggravated imprisonment or (simple) imprisonment; aggravated imprisonment can be reduced to (simple) imprisonment or to the misdemeanor punishment of detention for at least six months; and (simple) imprisonment can be reduced to detention for at least three months.[50]

Every felony conviction also carries two mandatory ancillary punishments and two discretionary ones. First, every convicted felon is deprived of the following rights or privileges: government service; decoration with a rank or medal; testifying in court (for the period of the sentence); managing his or her own funds or property (for the period of the sentence), responsibility for which is instead turned over to a court-appointed trustee; and remaining a member of certain local councils or committees and, if sentenced to life or aggravated imprisonment, ever again serving in one of those groups or serving as an expert or a witness to contracts.[51] Second, any felon who is employed by the government loses that employment and remains ineligible for reappointment to government service for a period of at least one year and not more than six years after completion of the sentence.[52] (A government employee who is convicted of a felony in one of several specified categories—bribery, embezzlement, forgery, torturing a suspect, or otherwise harming civilians by abusing his or her position—but is given a sentence of detention due to judicial leniency [see the preceding paragraph] must be ordered ineligible for government employment for a period of at least twice the length of the detention.)[53] Third, a person sentenced to any term of imprisonment for a felony conviction of any of another list of specified crimes is, after serving the sentence, to be placed under police surveillance for a period of time equal to his or her sentence or for five years, whichever is less; but the sentencing judge can reduce or eliminate this penalty.[54] Convicts under police surveillance must abide by provisions set forth in separate laws that govern such surveillance, and violating those laws brings a penalty of one year's detention.[55] Fourth, the sentencing judge may order the confiscation of fruits or instrumentalities of the crime, and must order the seizure of any such objects the use or possession of which is itself a crime—that is, items that are contraband.[56]

ii. Misdemeanors

Misdemeanors include a wide range of crimes, from simple theft and impersonating a public official to perjury, false imprisonment, aggravated assault, and negligent homicide. Convictions bring detention for up to three years and fines that can exceed £E 100.[57]

Detention is served in a general jail or central jail (*sijn markazi*). Sentences of one year or more include mandatory penal servitude, while sentences of less than one year can include penal servitude or not; in the latter case they are called "simple confinement" (*habs basit*).⁵⁸ Misdemeanor sentences may also include any of the ancillary punishments except one—the deprivation of rights and privileges—but, unlike with felony sentences, none of them are mandatory.⁵⁹

A misdemeanor sentence of a fine or detention for one year or less may be "stayed" (*iqaf*) upon issuance if the sentencing judge finds that, given the defendant's character, background, or age, or the circumstances of the crime itself, the defendant is unlikely to commit any crime again.⁶⁰ The court must state the reasons for the stay in its ruling, and the stay can reach all ancillary penalties and other consequences of the conviction. A stay becomes final after three years—that is, the criminal conviction is then vacated—but it may be canceled before then if (1) the defendant is sentenced to detention for more than one month for an act committed before or after the stay, or (2) the defendant had received such a sentence before the stay, but the judge who issued the stay had not known about it.⁶¹ In the first scenario the staying court may act on its own to cancel the stay, but in the second scenario it may cancel the stay only upon motion of the prosecution and service to the defendant.⁶² The original sentence is imposed upon cancellation of the stay, along with any ancillary punishments and collateral consequences of the conviction.⁶³

iii. Violations

Violations carry fines of not more than £E 100.⁶⁴ Examples of violations are disturbing the peace, unlawful discharge of a firearm, defacing property, and littering public roads or waterways.

iv. Sentence Computations, Commutations, and Pardons

Under the Penal Code, time spent in custody before conviction is counted as part of any sentence of imprisonment or jailing.⁶⁵ If a defendant is detained before trial but, upon conviction, sentenced only to a fine, £E 5 is subtracted from the fine for each day the defendant was in custody; and if a defendant who was detained before trial receives both a fine and a custodial sentence that is shorter than the period of pretrial detention, the same amount is deducted for each day in excess of the sentence the defendant was detained.⁶⁶ The constitution gives the president the authority to grant amnesties and to commute offenders' sentences (Const. Art. 149); the Code too discusses commutations and pardons. Full pardons, partial commutations, and lighter substitute sentences are set out as the three possibilities; ancillary penalties and collateral consequences remain in place unless included in a pardon or commutation order; and five years of police surveillance still follow the pardon or commutation of a life sentence.⁶⁷

3. Death Penalty

The Penal Code specifies hanging as the method of capital punishment.⁶⁸ A death sentence requires the unanimous decision of the three judges who hear the case, and before the sentence is issued, the court must send the case file to the country's highest religious official, the chief mufti (*qadi al-jumhuriyyah*), to seek his opinion.⁶⁹ But the court is not bound by the chief mufti's opinion, and it need not await that opinion longer than ten days before issuing the sentence.⁷⁰ If the chief mufti is unavailable or unable to review the case, the minister of justice is to review it instead.⁷¹ When appeals are exhausted and a death sentence is final, it is submitted to Egypt's president, who has fourteen days to pardon the defendant or commute the sentence.⁷² A commuted death sentence becomes a sentence of life imprisonment.⁷³

III. SPECIAL PART

A. Structure

The Penal Code's special part consists of its Books 2 through 4. Book 2, which is titled "Felonies and Misdemeanors Prejudicial to the Public Interest" and is the longest of the Code's four Books, lists crimes of terrorism, bribery and other wrongdoing by public officials, damage to the country's currency or infrastructure, and other ostensible threats to national security or integrity. Book 3, "Felonies and Misdemeanors Occurring to Individuals," treats crimes of homicide and lesser physical injury, sexual assault, burglary and theft, arson and other damage to personal property, fraud, and other ostensible damage to individuals (including "corruption of morals" and "slander"). Book 4, "Violations," contains a handful of provisions addressing miscellaneous minor wrongdoing in the public sphere, including disturbing the peace, failing to restrain one's dog from passersby, and "snapping rudely at another person for no public reason." Other provisions that were initially listed in Book 4 and addressed wrongdoing such as violations of public health or weights and measurements were abolished and replaced by separate statutes via 1981 legislation.

B. Homicide

Homicide offenses are treated in nine articles that lead off the Penal Code's Book 3, "Felonies and Misdemeanors Occurring to Individuals." Terms analogous to murder or manslaughter are not used in the Code; homicides are instead distinguished and graded according to the offender's *mens rea*.

1. Murder/Manslaughter

Death is the penalty for a killing committed willfully (*'amdan*) and with premeditation (*sabq al-israr*) or by "ambush" (*tarassud*) (Art. 230). Premeditation is defined as the intent, reached before the act (*qasd musammim 'alaihi qabla al-fi'l*), to commit a misdemeanor or felony the purpose of which is to harm a particular person or any person one finds or comes across (*wajadahu au sadafahu*), even if that intent is related to the occurrence of some event or dependent on a condition (Art. 231). Ambush is defined as lying in wait for a person (*tarabbus al-insan*) in one place or several places for a period of time, whether long or short, to kill that person or to harm the person by striking or a similar method (Art. 232). An intentional killing via some substance (*jawhar*)—that is, a drug—is considered poisoning (*qatil bi al-samm*) and is also a capital crime, whether or not death occurs immediately and regardless of how the substance is administered (Art. 233). An intentional killing without premeditation or ambush brings life or aggravated imprisonment unless it occurs in the course of committing another felony, that is, constitutes felony murder, in which case it brings the death penalty; and if it occurs during acts accompanied by a degree of intent that would constitute a misdemeanor, including assisting the perpetrators of a misdemeanor in committing the crime or escaping, either death or life imprisonment is the sentence (Art. 234). Death is also the sentence for any intentional killing committed with a "terrorist purpose" (*tanfidhan li gharad irhabi*) (id.). Accomplices in a murder that carries a mandatory death penalty can receive the same sentence or life imprisonment (Art. 235). As noted in section II.D.3 in this chapter, the Court of Cassation has held that intoxication, whether voluntary or involuntary, can negate the specific intent required for conviction of willful murder.

Unintentional killings that result from intentionally inflicting physical injury or providing a victim harmful materials (*mawadd darrah*) bring three to seven years of simple imprisonment or aggravated imprisonment, that is, in a "general" jail or a "specialized" one (see section II.E.2 in this chapter), or enhanced punishment as follows: if the wrongful act is committed with premeditation or by ambush (still without the intent to kill), the death brings a standard term of simple or aggravated imprisonment, that is, three to fifteen years; the same penalty applies if the wrongful act is committed with a "terrorist purpose"; and if the act that results in unintended death is committed with premeditation or by ambush and with a terrorist purpose, the penalty is aggravated or life imprisonment.[74] An accidental killing caused by one's mistake, negligence, imprudence or carelessness, or failure to observe the law—that is, negligent homicide, or "misdemeanor manslaughter"—brings detention for at least six months and/or a fine of up to £E 200.[75] The penalty increases to one to five years of detention and/or a fine of £E 100 to £E 500 if the death results from a "gross breach" (*ikhlal jasim*) of the norms of one's position, profession, or occupation, or if, when the conduct that causes the death takes place, the actor is intoxicated by liquor or drugs or refrains from assisting the victim or requesting assistance despite being able to do so.[76] The penalty is detention for one to seven years if the conduct results in the death of more than three people; and if the act that causes death is accompanied by one of the aggravating factors just listed, the penalty is detention for one to ten years.[77]

2. Provocation

The Penal Code recognizes only one form of provocation as adequate to mitigate the penalty for unjustifiable homicide: a husband who surprises his wife in the act of adultery and kills her and/or her partner "in the instant" faces detention—the misdemeanor punishment of three years or less in a general jail—instead of either life or aggravated imprisonment (for unpremeditated intentional homicides, Art. 234) or aggravated or basic imprisonment (for unintentional homicides that result from intentional physical injury, Art. 236).[78] Court decisions and commentary have identified various aspects of this defense, including extensions of it and limitations on it. The first requirement is this familiar pair: the provocation must be sudden—the infidelity must truly be a surprise—and the killing(s) must take place in the heat of it. Second, following the text of the Code provision, the mitigation is available only to men—that is, to husbands, but not to wives who kill their husbands (and/or their husbands' adulterous partners) in similar circumstances. Third, the mitigation is not independently available to anyone but the husband himself; a relative or family member of either the husband or the adulterous wife who independently kills the wife or her partner in these circumstances is not entitled to the mitigation. But, fourth, any accomplice of the husband in a qualifying killing is entitled to the mitigation. Finally, a husband need not have witnessed actual intercourse to receive the mitigation; finding his wife with a man in sufficiently suspicious circumstances can constitute adequate provocation for the mitigation.

C. Sex Offenses

1. Rape and Indecent Assault

The Penal Code treats sexual assault in three short provisions. The first of these, article 267, is considered the Code's rape provision, although the Code does not use the formal term for rape (*ightisab*) in this provision or any other. Article 267 says that sexual intercourse with a female without her consent (*waqa'a untha bighair ridaha*) brings a penalty of aggravated or life imprisonment. The provision adds that the penalty is higher, namely mandatory life imprisonment, if any of a list of aggravating factors is present: if the offender is a blood relation of the victim, or is responsible for her upbringing or supervision or has (other) authority over her, or is a paid domestic employee (*khadim*) of the victim or of one of the other persons just described. The second and third provisions, articles 268 and 269, set out punishments for a lesser and different crime, "indecent assault" (*hatk 'ird*, literally "violation of honor"). The Code does not define indecent assault, but court judgments and commentary explain that indecent assault differs from rape in several ways. These will be summarized in the next paragraph; first, the penalties for indecent assault under the two pertinent provisions are as follows. Under article 268, indecent assault by force or threats (or its attempt) brings three to seven years of aggravated imprisonment. As in the rape provision (Art. 267), the penalty is higher if specified aggravating circumstances are present: if (a) the victim is under sixteen years of age, or (b) the perpetrator has one of the special relationships with the victim listed in article 267, the ceiling rises to the maximum felony imprisonment term of fifteen years; and if (c) both aggravating factors are present, the penalty is life imprisonment. Under article 269, indecent assault without force or threats, but of a person who is under eighteen but at least seven years old, brings detention; and the penalty rises to mandatory aggravated imprisonment if the perpetrator is one of the persons described in article 267 or the victim is under seven years old. (Unlike the previous provision, this one does not specify an even higher penalty for cases in which both aggravating factors are present.)

Rape and indecent assault differ, according to court judgments and commentary, in several ways. First, rape—nonconsensual sexual intercourse, forbidden and punished by article 267—is understood to include only vaginal penetration (and its attempt, although the Code provision itself does not say so). Indecent assault, on the other hand, means any other type of penetration, as well as nonconsensual sexual touching that does not involve penetration. Second, given that distinction, rape is considered a crime that can be committed only by males, and only against females; indecent assault covers the other possible gender combinations. Third, a husband cannot be prosecuted for raping his wife, on the rationale that marriage gives him a right to sexual intercourse with his wife; but that right extends only to vaginal intercourse, so a husband can be prosecuted and punished for an act that constitutes indecent assault of his wife.

For both crimes, however, proof of force, the threat of force, or its equivalent is deemed essential to a conviction. The requirement of force or threats is explicit in the text of the indecent-assault provisions; for rape, although it is not in the text of the provision, it is seen as the basis for establishing a woman's nonconsent. But it is not the only such basis: a woman's insanity, mental infirmity, intoxication, or unconsciousness at the time of the act suffices to establish her nonconsent for rape. So does a man's deceit or trickery, as when a man enters a woman's bed as if he is her husband, or a doctor secretly achieves or attempts intercourse while examining a patient.

2. Adultery

Immediately following the Penal Code's provisions on rape and sexual assault comes a series of provisions on adultery. These provisions are noteworthy in several respects. To begin with, a person who is married can be charged with adultery only upon the complaint of his or her spouse (Arts. 273, 277). Next, adultery by a married man is a crime only if it takes place in the marital home, and the penalty for it is detention for up to six months (Art. 277). But adultery by a married woman is a crime wherever it takes place, and it brings a penalty of detention for up to two years for both the offender and the man with whom she commits the offense (Arts. 274, 275). The husband of a convicted offender can stay the execution of his wife's sentence if he consents to maintaining intimate relations with her (Art. 274). If a husband has committed adultery in the marital home, an adultery complaint by him against his wife will not be heard (Art. 273).

3. Public and Private Indecency

Two provisions of the Penal Code treat public and private indecency, which are lesser forms of sexual wrongdoing. The public indecency provision, article 278, criminalizes the performance in public (*'alaniyyatan*) of any "scandalous, indecent act" (*fi'l fadih mukhill bi al-hayah*) and sets a penalty of detention for up to a year and a fine of up to £E 300. A public act of immorality and an accompanying *mens rea* are said to be required for the crime, but whether the "scandalous and indecent" element is satisfied is apparently for the fact finder to decide on a case-by-case basis. Public exposure is one illustration of the crime; so too is kissing or hugging a woman against her will and in a manner that falls short of indecent assault (Arts. 268 and 269), discussed in section III.C.1. Private indecency, in article 279, is defined as the commission of an "indecent act" (*amr mukhill bi al-hayah*) with a woman, in public or private, and it carries the same penalty as public indecency; it too is seen as a lesser version of indecent assault. For both crimes, indecent words alone are said to be insufficient to trigger liability. Another Penal Code provision, article 269(*bis*), prescribes detention for up to one month for anyone who, in a public place, incites passersby to indecency (literally, "depravity," *fisq*) by speech or gestures; a second offense within a year brings detention for up to six months and a fine of up to £E 50. Commentary says that an invitation to a passerby to fornicate is sufficient to constitute this offense.

4. Prostitution and "Debauchery"

Prostitution is criminalized by the 1961 Law Combating Prostitution (the Prostitution Law), which addresses "debauchery" (*fujur*) as well as prostitution (*di'arah*). No statute defines debauchery, but courts and commentators have established its meaning as prostitution by men. Soliciting or facilitating either type of prostitution, or maintaining premises for its purpose, is punished by one to three years of detention and a fine of £E 100 to £E 300 (Arts. 1(a), 8). The maximum penalties increase to five years' detention and a fine of £E 500 in any of four circumstances: the solicitee-victim is under the age of twenty-one; the defendant employs deception, force, or coercion to induce the act; the defendant keeps a person in a place for prostitution against his or her will; or the defendant induces or assists a male under twenty-one or a woman of any age to leave the country to engage in prostitution. (Arts. 1(b), 2, 3.) Publicly advertising for prostitution brings up to three years of detention and a fine of up to £E 300 (Art. 14). Prostitutes themselves, meanwhile, may be punished for "habitual engagement" (*i'tad mumarasah*) in the offense, with detention for three months to three years and a fine of £E 25 to £E 300 (Art. 9(c)). Conviction of any Prostitution Law offense also allows, but does not require, the ancillary penalty of police supervision for a period equal to the length of detention (Art. 15).

The Prostitution Law is also used to prosecute and punish individuals for noncommercial sexual contact that is deemed illicit, such as sodomy, which is not expressly criminalized in Egyptian law. This is because courts and commentators have defined the offense of prostitution, whether committed by a man (and thus called *fujur*) or a woman (*di'arah*), as simply "illicit" or "indiscriminate" sexual contact—that is, fornication, with or without a commercial component. As a result, in recent years dozens of homosexual men have been prosecuted, convicted, and punished under the "habitual engagement in debauchery" provision of the Prostitution Law. Also used for such prosecutions is article 98-F of the Penal Code, which prescribes detention for six months to five years and a fine of £E 25 to £E 300 for anyone who propagates "contempt of religion" or otherwise threatens "national unity or social peace." In the most notorious of these cases, fifty-two men arrested at a Cairo nightclub in 2001 were prosecuted for homosexual conduct under the "habitual debauchery" provision of the Prostitution Law; two of the defendants were also charged with "contempt of religion" under the Penal Code provision. Convictions and sentences of one to two years of detention were handed down for twenty-one of the defendants charged only with debauchery, while the twenty-nine others were acquitted. Of the remaining two defendants, one was convicted of both offenses and sentenced to five years of detention, and the other was acquitted of debauchery but convicted of contempt of religion and sentenced to three years of detention.[79]

D. Theft and Fraud

1. Theft

The Penal Code defines theft (*sariqah*) as taking another's movable property (*ikhtalasa manqul mamluk li ghairihi*), and sets a baseline penalty for it of up to two years of detention (Arts. 311, 318). The penalty is higher—from a mandatory minimum of six months' detention to life imprisonment—when one or more aggravating factors are present. Life imprisonment is the penalty for thefts that are committed when all five of the following factors are proved: the theft was committed at night, by two or more defendants, while armed, by entering a dwelling via breaking and entering or a false claim of official authority, and by using force or the threat of force (Art. 313). Life or aggravated imprisonment is the penalty for thefts that carry some of these five factors and are committed on public roads or transport (Art. 315), and for thefts that are committed by force or threat of force and cause injury (Art. 314). Aggravated imprisonment alone is the penalty for thefts that are committed by force or threat of force but do not cause injury (and have no other aggravating factors), and for thefts committed with three factors in combination (at night, by two or more defendants, while armed) (Arts. 314, 316). Six months to seven years of detention is the penalty for thefts committed with only one aggravating factor of three specified ones (while armed, by entering a dwelling via breaking and entering or a false claim of official authority, or on public roads or transport) (Art. 316(*bis*-3)), [80] and misdemeanor detention with penal servitude is the penalty for thefts committed with one of four other specified aggravating factors (at night, by two or more defendants, by entering a dwelling without breaking and entering or a false claim of authority, or by entering an enclosed nondwelling area) (Art. 317).[81] Further provisions punish the theft of materials used in telecommunications services, utilities, and other public works (felony imprisonment, absent aggravating factors) (Art. 316(*bis*-2)); theft during an air raid (same) (Art. 316(*bis*-4)); and the theft of military weapons or ammunition, which brings aggravated imprisonment or, if aggravating factors are present, life imprisonment (Art. 316(*bis*-1)).

An offender who steals from a spouse or blood relative can be prosecuted only upon the request of the victim (Art. 312). In such a case the victim can also halt a theft prosecution any time after its initiation or stay the execution of sentence after conviction (id.). An individual who finds a lost item or animal and does not return it to its owner or submit it to police or other public officials within three days faces up to two years of detention with penal servitude if the finder intended to take possession of the item; absent that intention, the penalty is £E 100 (Art. 321(*bis*)). A repeat offender who has previously been sentenced to detention for theft can be placed under police surveillance for a period of one to two years (Art. 320).

2. Fraud

The acquisition of money, property, or other items of value from another by fraud (*ihtiyal*) brings the misdemeanor punishment of detention (up to three years in jail) (Art. 336). Unsuccessful attempts bring detention for not more than one year, and repeat offenders can be placed under police surveillance for one to two years (id.). The same penalties attach to writing a check with insufficient funds "in bad faith" (*bi su' niyyah*), withdrawing sufficient funds to cover a check after writing it, or stopping payment on a check (Art. 337).

E. "Victimless" Crimes

1. Drug Offenses

The 1960 Drug Law, as amended periodically (most recently in 2004), regulates the lawful production, distribution, and use of controlled substances, as well as defining and punishing unlawful drug activity. As in U.S. criminal law, a series of schedules in the law classifies controlled substances in categories according to their type, and these categories are used to govern both lawful and unlawful drug activity. The most serious drug crimes carry the death penalty and a fine of between £E 100,000 and £E 500,000. Among these crimes are producing, importing, acquiring, or transporting drugs with the intent to distribute them unlawfully (Arts. 33, 34); maintaining or providing premises for the unlawful use of drugs for pay, when the act is accompanied by any of a list of aggravating factors (Art. 34);[82] and coercing or tricking another person to ingest cocaine, heroin, or any other "Schedule 1" drug (Art. 34(*bis*)). Life imprisonment and a fine of £E 50,000 to £E 100,000 are the penalties for maintaining or providing premises for the unlawful use of drugs without payment, and for unlawfully providing drugs to another without payment (Art. 35). Discretionary sentence reductions under article 17 (see section II.E.2.i) are forbidden for each of these crimes (Art. 36), and any business establishment or other nonresidential location in which any of these crimes occurs is subject to closure (Art. 47). Penalties may be suspended, however, for any participant in one of these crimes who informs the authorities of it before they learn of it on their own, or after they learn of it if the information leads to the arrest of the other participants (Art. 48). The death penalty and a fine are also the penalties for causing a death while resisting the efforts of public officials to implement or enforce the Drug Law (Arts. 40, 41). Meanwhile, on the other end of the penalty spectrum, any person who is present in a place where drugs are unlawfully distributed and knows about the illegality faces one year of detention and a fine of £E 1,000 to £E 3,000; but spouses and relatives of a person who lives in the location are exempted from this provision, as are any other nonoffenders who live there (Art. 39).

A special set of provisions addresses unlawfully obtaining, possessing, or producing marijuana and related plants ("Schedule 5" drugs) for personal use. Article 37 of the Drug Law sets a penalty of aggravated imprisonment and a fine of £E 10,000 to £E 50,000 for these crimes, but it then goes on to authorize courts to suspend sentences and send offenders instead to special clinics (*masahhat*) established by the government for treating convicts in these circumstances. Terms and conditions of this alternative disposition are also set out, including that offenders who violate the terms of their treatment are subject to serving the original sentence (Art. 37/2).

2. Alcohol Offenses

The 1973 Law Forbidding Drinking Alcoholic Beverages prohibits serving or drinking such beverages in public places other than authorized hotels, tourist establishments, and recreational clubs (Art. 2). Violations bring six months of detention for offenders and fines of £E 200 for offenders and offending establishments; repeat offenses bring mandatory closure of offending establishments for one week to six months (Art. 5). Advertising alcoholic beverages is also forbidden, and it brings the same penalties as unlawfully serving or drinking them (Arts. 3, 6). Public drunkenness brings detention for two weeks to six months or a fine of £E 20 to £E 100; detention is mandatory for repeat offenses (Art. 7).

SELECTED BIBLIOGRAPHY

Egyptian Laws, Decrees, and Regulations

Arabic texts of the following codes and statutes, as amended and with annotations of related laws, decrees, and court decisions, are available via subscription to the Legislation and Developments Information Service (LADIS) at www.tashreaat.com.

Dustur Jumhuriyah 'Arabiyyah Masr [Constitution of the Arab Republic of Egypt], 1971. English translation available in *Constitutions of the Countries of the World*, vol. 6, edited by Albert P. Blaustein and Gisbert H. Flanz. New York: Oxford University Press, 2007.

Law No. 58 of 1937, *Qanun al-'Uqubat* [Penal Code]. Unofficial English translation available for purchase from the Middle East Library for Economic Services (MELES) at www.egyptlaws.com.

Law No. 150 of 1950, *Qanun al-Ijra'at al-Jina'iyyah* [Code of Criminal Procedure].

Law No. 162 of 1958, *Qanun bi Sha'n Halah al-Tawari'* [Law Concerning the State of Emergency]. Unofficial English translation on file with author, courtesy of the Law Department at the American University in Cairo.

Law No. 57 of 1959, *Bi Sha'n Halat wa Ijra'at al-Ta'n Amama Mahkamah al-Naqd* [Law of the Conditions and Procedures of Appeal to the Court of Cassation].

Law No. 182 of 1960, *Fi Sha'n Mukaffahah al-Mukhaddarat wa Tandhim Isti'maliha wa al-Ittijar Fiha* [Law Combating Drugs and Regulating Their Use and Trade].

Law No. 10 of 1961, *Qanun Mukaffahah al-Di'arah* [Law Combating Prostitution].

Law No. 25 of 1966, *Qanun al-Ahkam al-'Askariyyah* [Military Justice Law].

Law No. 63 of 1973, *Bi Hadhr Shurb al-Khamr* [Law Forbidding Drinking Alcoholic Beverages].

Law No. 80 of 2002, *Qanun Mukaffahah Ghasl al-Amwal* [Law Combating Money Laundering].

Law No. 95 of 2003, *Bi Insha' Mahakim Amn al-Dawlah wa Ta'dil ba'd Ahkam Qanuni al-'Uqubat wa al-Ijra'at al-Jina'iyyah* [Law Creating State Security Courts and Amending Provisions of the Penal Code and the Code of Criminal Procedure].

Cases Cited

Supreme Constitutional Court, Case No. 22, Judicial Year 8 (4 Jan. 1992).
Supreme Constitutional Court, Case No. 3, Judicial Year 10 (2 Jan. 1993).
Supreme Constitutional Court, Case No. 105, Judicial Year 12 (12 Feb. 1994).
Supreme Constitutional Court, Case No. 20, Judicial Year 15 (1 Oct. 1994).
Supreme Constitutional Court, Case No. 49, Judicial Year 17 (15 June 1996).
Supreme Constitutional Court, Case No. 114, Judicial Year 21 (2 June 2001).

Secondary Sources

Abu 'Amir, Muhammad Zaki. *Qanun al-'Uqubat: Al-Qism al-'Amm* [The Penal Code: The General Part]. Alexandria: Dar al-Jami'ah al-Jadidah li al-Nashr, 1996.

Akida, M. "Criminal Law." In *Egypt and Its Laws*, edited by Nathalie Bernard-Maugiron and Baudouin Dupret, 37–48. London: Kluwer Law International, 2002.

Bernard-Maugiron, Nathalie, and Baudouin Dupret, eds. *Egypt and Its Laws*. London: Kluwer Law International, 2002.

Boyle, Kevin, and Adel Omar Sherif, eds. *Human Rights and Democracy: The Role of the Supreme Constitutional Court of Egypt*. London: Kluwer Law International, 1996.

Brown, Nathan. *The Rule of Law in the Arab World: Courts in Egypt and the Gulf*. Cambridge: Cambridge University Press, 1997.

Cotran, Eugene, and Adel Omar Sherif, eds. *The Role of the Judiciary in the Protection of Human Rights*. London: Kluwer Law International, 1997.

Dupret, Baudouin. "Morality on Trial: Structure and Intelligibility System of a Court Sentence Concerning Homosexuality." *Qualitative Sociology Review* 2 (2006): 98–122.

El-Morr, Awad Mohammed. "Recent Landmark Decisions of the Supreme Constitutional Court of Egypt." In *Democracy, the Rule of Law, and Islam*, edited by Eugene Cotran and Adel Omar Sherif, 239–272. London: Kluwer Law International, 1999.

Fahmy, Khalid, and Rudolph Peters. "Introduction: The Legal History of Ottoman Egypt." *Islamic Law and Society* 6 (1999): 129–135.

Gabr, Hatim Aly Labib. "Recent Judgments of the Supreme Constitutional Court of the Arab Republic of Egypt Upholding Human Rights." In *The Role of the Judiciary in the Protection of Human Rights*, edited by Eugene Cotran and Adel Omar Sherif, 61–68. London: Kluwer Law International, 1997.

Goldschmidt, Arthur. *Modern Egypt: The Formation of a Nation State*. Boulder, CO: Westview Press, 2d ed., 2004.

Hill, Enid. *Mahkama! Studies in the Egyptian Legal System*. London: Ithaca Press, 1979.

Human Rights Watch. *In a Time of Torture: The Assault on Justice in Egypt's Crackdown on Homosexual Conduct*. New York: Human Rights Watch, 2004.

Mahmoud, W. "Civil and Criminal Justice." In *Egypt and Its Laws*, edited by Nathalie Bernard-Maugiron and Baudouin Dupret, 136–180. London: Kluwer Law International, 2002.

Pratt, Nicola. "The Queen Boat Case in Egypt: Sexuality, National Security and State Sovereignty." *Review of International Studies* 33 (2007): 129–144.

Peters, Rudolph. *Crime and Punishment in Islamic Law: Theory and Practice from the Sixteenth to the Twenty-first Century*. Cambridge: Cambridge University Press, 2005.

Reza, Sadiq. "Egypt." In *Criminal Procedure: A Worldwide Study*, edited by Craig M. Bradley, 107–147. Durham, NC: Carolina Academic Press, 2d ed., 2007.

———. "Endless Emergency: The Case of Egypt." *New Criminal Law Review* 10 (2007): 532–553.

Salamah, Ma'mun Muhammad. *Qanun al-'Uqubat: Al-Qism al-'Amm* [The Penal Code: The General Part]. Cairo: Dar al-Fikr al-Arabi, 1979.

Shalakany, Amr A. "Islamic Legal Histories." *Berkeley Journal of Middle Eastern and Islamic Law* 1 (2008): 1–82.

Shawaribi, Abd al-Hamid. *Al-Ta'liq al-Maudu'i 'ala Qanun al-'Uqubat* [Substantive Commentary on the Penal Code]. 4 vols. Alexandria: Munsha'ah al-Ma'arif, 2003.

Sherif, Adel Omar. "The Rule of Law in Egypt from a Judicial Perspective." In *The Rule of Law in the Middle East and the Islamic World: Human Rights and the Judicial Process*, edited by Eugene Cotran and Mai Yamani, 1–34. London: I. B. Tauris, 2000.

Surur, Ahmad Fathi. *Al-Wasit fi Qanun al-'Uqubat, Al-Juz' al-Awwal: Al-Qism al-'Amm* [Nutshell on the Penal Code, Part One: The General Part]. Cairo: Dar al-Nahdah al-Arabiyyah, 1981.

World Bank. "Arab Republic of Egypt: Detailed Assessment Report on Anti-Money Laundering and the Financing of Terrorism." *Middle East and North Africa Financial Action Task Force* (May 2009), http://www.menafatf.org/images/UploadFiles/MER_Egypt_ForPublication.pdf (accessed 25 Oct. 2009).

NOTES

1. References to articles of the Penal Code will hereafter be listed simply as "Art."; references to articles of other laws will be indicated with additional abbreviations: "CCP Art." for the Code of Criminal Procedure, "Const. Art." for the Constitution, and so on. Full citations for all laws cited are in the selected bibliography.

2. Arts. 1–4.

3. CCP Art. 217.

4. CCP Art. 218.

5. CCP Art. 219.

6. Mil. Just. L. Art. 6; Penal Code Arts. 77-102(*bis*-F).

7. Const. Art. 179. This new provision anticipated a new antiterrorism law, which has been promised for several years and has apparently been drafted but has not yet been publicly disclosed. Meanwhile, terrorism is defined and punished in a series of Penal Code provisions that were substantially expanded in 1992 (Arts. 86–90).

8. Const. Arts. 66, 187.

9. SCC Case No. 22, Judicial Year 8 (4 Jan. 1992).

10. SCC Case No. 3, Judicial Year 10 (2 Jan. 1993).

11. SCC Case No. 105, Judicial Year 12 (12 Feb. 1994).

12. The Code originally had 395 articles; many have been deleted and others added over the years. An added article is numbered in one of two ways. The first way is as the "repeat" version—*bis*, in Latin—of the article number that precedes it. Thus, following Art. 86 in the Code is Art. 86(*bis*). In these instances, when more than one article is inserted in succession at the same place in the Code, sequential letters are added to the *bis*; thus, following Art. 86(*bis*) are Art. 86(*bis*-A), Art. 86(*bis*-B), and so on. But inserted provisions may also be numbered with letters alone, without a "*bis*"; thus, Art. 77 of the Code is followed immediately by Art. 77-A, Art. 77-B, and so on. Internally, separate paragraphs of articles are not typically labeled as formal subdivisions of the articles, but they may be indicated in citations by a forward slash. Thus, "Art. 86(*bis*-D)/2" means the second paragraph of Art. 86(*bis*-D), which is the fifth article after Art. 86.

13. Arts. 9–12.

14. See section III.E.1 in this chapter.

15. CCP Art. 215; Penal Code Arts. 11–12.

16. CCP Art. 410.

17. CCP Arts. 216, 283, 382; Penal Code Arts. 10, 14, 16.

18. Cited supra note 10.

19. Cited supra note 10.

20. This ruling is discussed further in subsection II.A.1.iii, "Status," and subsection II.A.2, "Subjective/*Mens Rea*/Mental Element," in this chapter.

21. Examples of the former are Art. 116 (failure to distribute public commodities as required), Art. 116(*bis*-C) (nonperformance or default on contracts for public works), Art. 122 (failure to issue judicial rulings when required), and Art. 377/7 (failure to perform assigned duties such as assisting during disaster or arrest). Examples of the latter are Arts. 284 and 392 (failure to comply with a judicial order or a lawful demand for custody of child) and Art. 293 (failure to pay alimony after a judgment ordering it).

22. SCC Case No. 49, Judicial Year 17 (15 June 1996).

23. W. Mahmoud, "Civil and Criminal Justice," in *Egypt and Its Laws*, ed. Nathalie Bernard-Maugiron and Baudouin Dupret (London: Kluwer Law International, 2002), 156.

24. Id.

25. Mahmoud, "Civil and Criminal Justice," 157.

26. Art. 45.

27. Id.

28. Mahmoud, "Civil and Criminal Justice," 154.

29. Art. 46.

30. SCC Case No. 114, Judicial Year 21 (2 June 2001).

31. Art. 42.

32. Art. 43.

33. Mahmoud, "Civil and Criminal Justice," 155.

34. Art. 44.

35. M. Akida, "Criminal Law," in *Egypt and Its Laws*, ed. Nathalie Bernard-Maugiron and Baudouin Dupret (London: Kluwer Law International, 2002), 45; Mahmoud, "Civil and Criminal Justice," 154.

36. Ahmad Fathi Surur, *Al-Wasit fi Qanun al-'Uqubat, Al-Juz' al-Awwal: Al-Qism al-'Amm* [Nutshell on the Penal Code, Part One: The General Part] (Cairo: Dar al-Nahdah al-Arabiyyah, 1981), 382–385.

37. Mahmoud, "Civil and Criminal Justice," 153.

38. Art. 249.

39. Art. 250.

40. Art. 251.

41. Art. 63.

42. Id.

43. SCC Case No. 20, Judicial Year 15 (1 Oct. 1994).

44. Akida, "Criminal Law," 47; Mahmoud, "Civil and Criminal Justice," 155–156.

45. Arts. 10–23. "Permanent hard labor" and "temporary hard labor" were also possible primary punishments for felonies until 2003, when legislation abolished them and replaced them with, respectively, life imprisonment and aggravated imprisonment. Law 95/2003, Art. 2. But Code provisions that specified one or the other of those now-discontinued punishments for a particular crime have not been individually amended to reflect the change.

46. Art. 20.

47. Art. 24.

48. Arts. 10, 14, 16.

49. Art. 15.
50. Art. 17.
51. Art. 25.
52. Art. 26.
53. Art. 27.
54. Art. 28. The felonies that carry this penalty include crimes against national security, counterfeiting, theft, homicide, the nighttime harming of beasts of burden or fish, and the nighttime destruction of agricultural lands or other flora. Id.
55. Art. 29.
56. Art. 30.
57. Arts. 11, 18.
58. Arts. 19, 20.
59. Arts. 30, 31.
60. Art. 55.
61. Arts. 56, 59.
62. Art. 57.
63. Art. 58.
64. Art. 12.
65. Art. 21.
66. Art. 23.
67. Arts. 74–75.
68. Art. 13.
69. CCP Art. 381/2.
70. Id.
71. CCP Art. 381/3.
72. CCP Art. 370.
73. Art. 75.
74. Art. 236.
75. Art. 238.
76. Id.
77. Id.
78. Art. 237.
79. The twenty-one debauchery-only convictions were subsequently reversed, and all fifty of those defendants were retried; in 2003 convictions again were handed down in twenty-one cases, but the sentences increased to three years of detention and three years of police supervision. On appeal, fourteen of those sentences were reduced to time served and one year of supervision.
80. A term of six months is listed as a mandatory minimum sentence. Note that this penalty straddles the categories of misdemeanor (detention for up to three years) and felony (imprisonment for three to fifteen years).
81. The provision says only "penal servitude," but that is not a stand-alone punishment; given the other theft penalties, the intended penalty appears to be misdemeanor detention with work.
82. These factors include the following: the offender provided the drug to a person under the age of twenty-one, a relative or spouse, or a person under the offender's

guardianship or other authority; the offender is a public official whose duty is to implement or enforce the Drug Law; the offender is a public official who used his or her official authority to commit the crime; the offense occurred in a place of worship, an educational institution, a public club or garden, a health-care facility, a penal institution, or a military facility; the offender paid or forced a person to ingest the drug; the drug involved was cocaine, heroin, or another "Schedule 1" drug; and the offender has a prior conviction under this article or the previous one.

FRANCE

Catherine Elliott

I. Introduction
   A. Historical Sketch
   B. Jurisdiction
   C. Legality Principle
   D. Sources of Criminal Law
   E. Process

II. General Part
   A. Theories of Punishment
   B. Liability Requirements
   C. Defenses
   D. Justifications
   E. Excuses

III. Special Part
   A. Structure
   B. Homicide: Murder and Manslaughter
   C. Sex Offenses
   D. Theft and Fraud

I. INTRODUCTION

A. Historical Sketch

1. Before the Revolution

In the thirteenth century the system of private justice, under which victims and their families played a central role in obtaining justice for criminal wrongs, fell into decline

---

Catherine Elliott is a Senior Lecturer at City University London. Her recent publications include (with Frances Quinn) *Criminal Law* (Pearson Education, 2009) and *French Criminal Law* (Willan, 2001).

as the state became more powerful. Between the sixteenth and eighteenth centuries the sources of criminal law were curiously international.[1] Roman law enjoyed a renaissance, and the Roman Digest, containing the writings of Roman lawyers,[2] was considered to be in force and was followed unless there was a clear provision of custom or a written text.

The criminal law was also influenced by Christianity and canon law. In the Middle Ages the ecclesiastical courts played an important role in society. They had jurisdiction over matters that touched the church's interests in any way.

2. The Evolution of Ideas in the Eighteenth Century

The classical theory of criminal law[3] was born between 1748, the date of the publication of *L'esprit des lois* by Montesquieu, and 1813, when the Bavarian Criminal Code was passed. This classical theory was developed by the writings of the German lawyer Ludwig Feuerbach, the French intellectuals Montesquieu and Jean-Jacques Rousseau, the Italian Cesare Beccaria, and the Englishman Jeremy Bentham. Montesquieu recommended a general softening of punishments, but this philosophy had little influence on the actual law until the sensational success of the work of Beccaria,[4] who in 1764 published in Milan his famous *Treatise on Offenses and Punishments*,[5] which influenced criminal law across the whole of Europe.

3. Revolutionary Law[6]

Translated into French in 1766, the book of Beccaria was received with enthusiasm in France. Influenced by his and Montesquieu's ideas, the Revolutionary Assemblies made considerable reforms to the criminal law. They passed two Acts dated 19–22 July 1791 and 24 September–6 October 1791 that amounted to a criminal code.[7] The sentences were generally reduced, corporal punishments were abolished, and capital punishment was preserved for only a few offenses. The legislation posed the principle of equality and took this to an extreme by imposing fixed sentences and abolishing pardons. In addition, the Declaration of the Rights of Man of 1789 outlawed arbitrary decision making. The principle of legality was included in the Declaration, which stated in article 6: "All that is not forbidden by the law cannot be prevented and no one can be forced to do what it does not order."[8] Article 8 added: "[T]he law can only lay down punishments that are strictly and obviously necessary and a person can only be punished by virtue of a law established and promulgated prior to the wrongful conduct and legally applicable."[9] The Declaration now forms part of the French constitution. As regards criminal procedure, the legislation was inspired by the English accusatorial system, and a jury system was introduced.

4. The Criminal Code of 1810

The Napoleonic Code of 1810 mixed aspects of the revolutionary law with the law that existed before the Revolution. On the one hand, the ideas of Beccaria and Montesquieu, which had directly inspired the revolutionary Criminal Code of 1791, left their traces on the imperial code. Thus the principle of legality was included in the Criminal Code of 1810, and it imposed an egalitarian system founded on the mental responsibility of the offender. On the other hand, the social unrest at the time had given rise to lawless behavior and led to the imposition of a fairly harsh criminal system, which reflected the severity of the prerevolutionary law. The Code was influenced by the work of the English philosopher Bentham, founder of the utilitarian doctrine. He supported the use of severe punishments where these would serve as an effective deterrent. The severity of the system was gradually weakened by subsequent governments, culminating on 9 August 1981 with the abolition of the death penalty.

The Code was adopted in Belgium and Luxembourg and served as a model for criminal codes of other countries in Europe. It was generally accepted that the Criminal Code of 1810 was not the best of the Napoleonic codes. Its structure was criticized as illogical because it dealt with the sentence before defining the offense, and the general defenses were scattered throughout the Code in parts relating to specific substantive offenses. There had been talk of reform ever since 1832, and until 1992 various unsuccessful attempts were made to replace it. Numerous amendments were made to the Code in an effort to modernize and improve it.

5. *The Criminal Code of 1992*

The process of creating a new criminal code started with the Commission for Revision of 1974, which was composed of practicing lawyers and university academics. The new Code was prepared as four Acts of Parliament that were passed on 22 July 1992. A decree was issued on 29 March 1993 containing the minor offenses to be included in the Code.

The Code finally came into force on 1 March 1994. It is divided into two parts, the first legislative and the second regulatory. The substantive offenses concerning major and serious offenses are contained in books II to V of the legislative part. The regulatory part is found in book VI and contains the minor offenses. The numbering of the code has changed. Each article is designated by four numbers. The first corresponds to the relevant book of the Code, the second to the relevant part[10] of the Code, and the third to the chapter where the article can be found. The fourth number refers to the position of the article in the chapter. Thus, the first article in the Code is not article 1 but article 111-1. This method of numbering was preferred because it is easier to insert new articles as the criminal law develops. The letter "R" before the numbers refers to a part of the Code made by regulations.

The main aim of the Code was to group together the criminal law in a form that was accessible to the general public. It does not represent a major reform of the law. Its primary aim was to modernize the drafting and layout of the code by simplifying the language and providing clearer definitions of some of the offenses. The basic principles of the criminal law have remained unchanged. The new Code provided an opportunity for legislation to take into account some of the case-law developments in the field. The major changes made by the Code were to introduce corporate liability and to create a new offense of deliberately putting another in danger.

The Code starts with the general principles of the criminal law, criminal responsibility, and sentencing. It deals with these matters in more detail than the old Code. It then moves on to the study of offenses against the person, property, the nation, the state, and public peace. In following this order, in preference to that of the Napoleonic Code, which had started with offenses against the state before dealing with those against the individual, the new Code seeks to prioritize the value of human life over other interests. Some important legislation remains outside the Code, including the Act of 21 July 1881 on freedom of the press.

B. Jurisdiction

The application of French criminal law is limited in both time and space.

1. Limitations in Time

French legislation is published in *Le Journal officiel* (the Official Journal), both on paper and online at www.legifrance.gouv.fr. There are various ways in which this legislation is brought into force:

- The legislation itself may provide a date when it will come into force.
- If no date is contained in the legislation, then it will come into force on the day after it is published.
- Where some of the provisions in the legislation require certain measures to be taken in order for the legislation to take effect, those provisions will not come into force until those measures have been taken.
- In case of an emergency, legislation can come into effect as soon as it is published where provision is made for this.

2. Territorial Application

French criminal law applies to all offenses committed on French territory. Some criminal conduct has an international aspect. The key legislative provisions that determine the jurisdiction of French criminal law are articles 113-1 to 113-12 of the new Criminal Code. The general principle is that French criminal law applies to offenses committed in France, and this is interpreted broadly to include criminal conduct having indirect links to French territory and where only part of a crime has been committed in France.[11] However, it can sometimes apply to offenses committed abroad. French criminal law can apply to French nationals who commit major or serious crimes abroad, provided the conduct is also a criminal offense in the country where it was committed.[12] French criminal law can also be applied where an imprisonable serious or major offense has been committed abroad against a French national.[13] Criminal conduct abroad that attacks the fundamental interests of the French nation can be the subject of French criminal law.[14] The French criminal courts are treated as having universal jurisdiction for certain international crimes listed in articles 689-2 to 689-10 of the Code of Criminal Procedure, including torture and terrorism.

C. Legality Principle

Under the principle of legality, a person can be subjected to French criminal law only if there is relevant legislation providing for the offense and the sanction is in force before its commission.

The principle of legality is formally proclaimed in the Declaration of the Rights of Man.[15] Today the principle of legality is affirmed in the preamble to the French Constitution, so the principle forms part of the Constitution.[16] Articles 111-2 and 111-3 of the new

Criminal Code also refer to the principle of legality: "No one can be punished for a serious crime or for a major offense whose elements are not defined by an Act or for a minor offense whose elements are not defined by a regulation."[17]

Although in common-law countries key offenses such as murder are frequently the creation of the judiciary and continue to be applied in the absence of any legislative provision, this is not possible in France.

D. Sources of Criminal Law

All criminal law must be in writing. Therefore, custom plays only a very limited role in this context.

1. Legislature

According to the Constitution of 1958, only Acts of Parliament and their equivalent[18] can lay down serious and major crimes and the possible punishments.[19] Article 34 of the Constitution states: "Legislation shall determine the rules concerning . . . the determination of what constitutes a serious crime or a major offense, and the prescribed sentence." The main piece of legislation is the new Criminal Code of 1992, discussed in section I.A.5. In practice, Parliament sometimes delegates this legislative power to the executive under article 38 of the Constitution, particularly to clarify the details of an offense, and the resulting legislation is treated as having the same status as Acts of Parliament, even though it emanates from the executive. To do this, Parliament passes an enabling Act empowering the executive to make ordinances that have the effect of Acts of Parliament when they are ratified.

2. Judiciary

The decisions of judges are not a source of any French law, including French criminal law. The role of the judiciary is restricted by the principle of legality, as a reaction to the arbitrary criminal sanctions imposed by judges under the prerevolutionary system. Because of the principle of legality, judges have to give a strict, narrow interpretation to legislation[20] and cannot extend its scope by analogy to similar but different situations from those referred to by the legislator. The revolutionaries were keen supporters of the principle of the separation of powers and therefore tried to reduce judges' powers to the mere application of the law, which would primarily be found in the new codes, and banned judges from creating law. Judges were simply to decide the case they were hearing by applying the criminal code, rather than to try and establish a precedent for the future and thereby effectively create the law themselves. Judges can never cite a previous judicial decision as the basis for their own judgment.

In light of this approach, judicial decisions are not technically a source of French criminal law because they do not have normative force and merely influence the law's development. In practice, the influence of French case law has been increasing since the immediate backlash of the French Revolution. Initially, after codification, textbooks simply discussed the articles of the Criminal Code and made no reference to any case law. Now textbooks are gradually placing more emphasis on judicial decisions, although still not as much as textbooks on common law do, and often primarily in the footnotes rather than in the main text. A judicial decision can still not be based solely on a previous decision; some other legal source must be cited as the grounds for the judgment. French academic writers and courts still rarely cite a single case as a legal authority, preferring instead to point out that judges consistently decide in a certain way on the same facts, or that conflicting judgments are handed down on a certain issue. Inevitably the decisions of the highest courts carry more weight than those of the lower courts. Although technically a lower court is not bound by a higher court, courts prefer to follow earlier judgments so that like cases are treated alike, allowing justice to be done. What is important in this context is not the factual decision of the court, but the legal reasons on which it relied.

3. Executive

Under article 37 of the Constitution, the executive has the authority only to create minor offenses. Under article R.610-1 of the Criminal Code, minor offenses can be laid down only in a decree of the Conseil d'Etat.[21] Thus the Conseil d'Etat must be consulted during this legislative process. Ordinary executive decrees can be used only to specify sanctions that have been provided for by decrees of the Conseil d'Etat or by legislation.

4. Scholars

The opinions on the criminal law developed by academics in their writing are not strictly a source of law but constitute a powerful influence on its development.

E. Process

1. Adversarial/Inquisitorial

The criminal process can be divided into three stages, with different officials responsible for each stage of the procedure to prevent one individual from becoming too powerful:

- The police investigation and the prosecution
- The judicial investigation
- The trial

The distinction between the first two stages is slightly artificial because in practice the investigating judges delegate most of the tasks of investigation to the police, so the police play a key role during both phases.

The rules of criminal procedure are developed around the distinction between the three categories of offense: serious,[22] major,[23] and minor.[24] In particular, a judicial investigation tends to be used only where a serious offense has been committed.

The first two stages of the French criminal procedure have traditionally been inquisitorial in nature, with particular emphasis being placed on the building up of a written file of the case containing all the statements, expert reports, and records of investigative procedures carried out. Elements of the adversarial process have been added in recent years in an effort to give greater protection to the rights of the citizen. The trial hearing has always mixed elements of the inquisitorial and adversarial system because it usually takes place in public with limited opportunity for the parties to put their case orally, but the written file on the case prepared during the pretrial investigations is central to the hearing.

2. Judge and Jury

Major and minor offenses are tried by professional judges. At the end of the hearing the judge or judges deliberate in private, and verdicts are reached according to their personal conviction.[25] Reasons for the judgment have to be given for major and minor offenses.[26] Thus the judge must justify the verdict by the evidence that was provided in the file and at the hearing. Every judgment consists more or less of a syllogism, which includes a major statement affirming a general legal rule, a minor statement exposing the facts of the case, and the application of the former to the latter, leading to the verdict.

Serious offenses are tried by three professional judges and nine jurors sitting together in the *Cour d'assises*. The judges and the jurors deliberate and vote together on the facts, the law, and the punishment. They are not obliged to give reasons for their decision.

II. GENERAL PART

A. Theories of Punishment

Both the *Conseil constitutionnel* (the constitutional court of France) and the European Court of Human Rights have declared that the label placed on a sanction (disciplinary or administrative, for example) within a country is irrelevant. If the sanction amounts to a punishment, it will be treated as penal and will be subject to the relevant safeguards contained in the Constitution and article 6 of the European Convention on Human Rights guaranteeing a fair trial in criminal matters.[27]

B. Liability Requirements

1. Objective/Actus Reus

The French analyze their offenses as requiring both an *actus reus* (*l'élément matériel*) and a *mens rea* (*l'élément moral*). It has long been established in France that people should not be punished for their thoughts alone, but that these thoughts must have crystallized into some material conduct. The general principle is now expressly provided for in article 121-1 of the new Criminal Code, which states that "a person is criminally responsible only for his conduct."[28]

i. Act

In most cases the *actus reus* consists of a positive act. Criminal liability can be imposed only for voluntary acts.[29]

ii. Omission

The *actus reus* can consist of an omission only if that omission is expressly incriminated by a specific text. In all these cases it is the omission itself that constitutes the offense and that is punishable, whatever may be the consequences of the omission. Liability is analyzed by the academic writers as being imposed for a failure to carry out a particular duty to act. For example, the offense of allowing a military secret to be divulged is based on the duty to protect the military interests of the state.[30]

In the nineteenth century there was no criminal liability for omissions, but this individualistic approach was gradually abandoned. First, offenses for omissions were created to protect the vulnerable in society, such as minors and the disabled. Offenses were therefore created of neglecting a child in 1898 and of abandoning the family in 1924. In the 1940s offenses imposing obligations to act to protect a wider range of people were created, with offenses such as failing to give evidence in favor of an innocent person and failing to prevent the commission of a crime against another. This development reached its height with the new Criminal Code, which created the offense of failing to help a person in danger;[31] it was initially raised as a possible ground for imposing liability on the paparazzi who were accused of failing to assist Princess Diana after the car accident in which she was killed.

But where legislation does not expressly provide for liability by omission, there can be no liability by treating an omission as if it were an action.[32] This approach of the criminal law was highlighted by the case known as the "hostage of Poitiers."[33] In that case the court of Poitiers decided that the crime of intentionally injuring another[34] had not been committed by parents who had left without care, in a dark room, an old and frail person suffering from a mental illness to the point that her life was in danger. It was held that this omission could not be treated as equivalent to an act, and so it fell outside the legal definition of the nonfatal offense.

2. Subjective/Mens Rea/Mental Element

Mens rea in French law is called *l'élément intellectuel*, *l'élément moral*, or *l'élément psychologique*. A basic distinction is drawn in French law between those offenses that require intention and those that do not. Where no intention is required, the *mens rea* requirement can be satisfied on proof of negligence, that a person was deliberately put in danger, or that the conduct was voluntary. Serious crimes are always intentional; major offenses are in principle intentional unless legislation expressly provides that a fault of negligence or of deliberately putting another in danger is sufficient.

Criminal liability can be imposed only for voluntary acts.[35] Minor offenses normally require only that the accused behaved voluntarily, and in this context the mental element is known as *la faute contraventionnelle*. It is recognized that this is a very low threshold of *mens rea*[36] that in the past applied not just to minor offenses but also to a few major offenses.[37] These were abolished by the new Criminal Code.

Each of the different forms of *mens rea* will be considered in turn.

i. Intent

The first paragraph of article 121-3 of the Criminal Code states: "There is no serious crime or major crime in the absence of an intention to commit it."[38] Thus all offenses categorized as serious or major crimes require a mental element of intention even if the Code or another form of legislation defining the offense makes no direct reference to this requirement, while minor offenses will require intention only if specific reference to this is made in the definition of the offense.

An important restriction to the general principle laid down in the first paragraph of article 121-3 is provided by the second paragraph, which states: "However, when the law so provides, a major offense can be committed by imprudence, negligence or by deliberately putting another in danger."[39] Major crimes can therefore be committed without intention if legislation provides that one of the three forms of nonintentional *mens rea* suffices.

The old and new French criminal codes provide no definition of the concept of intention, and it has been left to academics to analyze its meaning. In French criminal law there are in fact two forms of intention, known as *dol général* and *dol spécial*, which will be translated, respectively, as "general intention" and "special intention."

a. General Intention

The classic definition of general intention is provided by the eminent nineteenth-century French criminal lawyer Emile Garçon: "Intention, in its legal sense, is the desire to commit a crime as defined by the law; it is the accused's awareness that he is breaking a law."[40] Thus, according to its classic definition, there are two mental elements that make up general intention: desire and awareness. The concept of awareness simply requires the defendants to be aware that they are breaking the law. Because of the principle *nemo censetur ignorare legem* (no one can be considered to be ignorant of the law) there is a presumption in French law that people know the law, so the existence of this element of general intention will normally be assumed. A legislative exception to this presumption was added by the new Criminal Code under article 122-3, which states: "A person is not criminally liable if he can prove he believed he could legitimately carry out the act, due to a mistake of law that he was not in a position to avoid."[41] The scope of this provision will depend on the interpretation it is given by the courts, but the parliamentary debates that preceded the passing of the new Code suggest that it will be limited to cases where the mistake about the law was induced by a misrepresentation emanating from the civil service.

As to the requirement of desire, this is traditionally interpreted as simply referring to a desire to commit the wrongful act and not a desire to commit the result of that act. Thus, if one takes the factual situation of a person throwing a stone at a victim and the victim dying as a result, to prove that the person has a general intention for the offense of murder, it would merely need to be proved that he or she desired to throw the stone. For the purposes of general intention there would be no requirement to show that the person desired the result of killing the victim.[42]

b. Special Intention

The second form of intention in French criminal law, special intention, requires an intention to cause a result forbidden by the law. For example, the special intention required for murder is the intention to kill. Depending on the definition of special intention for the particular offense, it may not be necessary to prove that the accused desired the result that constitutes the *actus reus*: intention with regard to some lesser result may be sufficient. This is the case where it is not possible for defendants to know precisely what the result of their conduct will be and is known in French as *le dol indéterminé*.[43] The accused does an act seeking a result without being able to foresee exactly what the result will be.

As a result of article 121-3, general intention applies to all serious and major crimes. By contrast, special intention applies only to certain serious and major crimes, usually those that require a particular result.

c. Oblique Intention

There is one major restriction on the meaning of intention for the purposes of French criminal law, and that is in respect of indirect or oblique intention, which in French is called *le dol éventuel*. Here we are concerned with the situation where defendants foresee that they could possibly cause a result, but they do not desire it. In French law this does not amount to specific intention.[44] It may now amount to a lesser fault recognized by the new Criminal Code and treated as an aggravating factor in relation to involuntary murder and nonfatal offenses against the person.[45] It can also now constitute an offense in its own right under article 223-1 of the new Criminal Code where there was an immediate risk of death or serious injury.

ii. Recklessness

The fault of deliberately putting someone in danger[46] is a creation of the new Criminal Code. Until then there had been only the *mens rea* of intention and negligence (and arguably that of voluntary conduct). It was felt that this failed to recognize the different degrees of fault that could exist; in particular, no express provision was made for the person who saw a risk and took it but did not actually intend the result. This situation would be covered in English law by the concept of recklessness and has traditionally been described by French jurists as *dol éventuel*. Before the new Code it did not amount to a specific category of *mens rea*; instead, the defendants would simply be treated as if they had been negligent. The person taking a risk knowingly and causing a harm by this fact gave rise to the same punishment as that of causing a similar harm by negligence, despite the fact that this conduct was extremely dangerous and immoral. This type of situation would occur where, for example, a driver deliberately goes through a red light or overtakes on a bend.

The new fault of deliberately putting another in danger aims to deal with this perceived weakness of the old law. Some clarification about the scope of the concept is provided by the offenses that rely on this *mens rea*.[47] These describe the fault of deliberately putting another in danger as being a "deliberate failing in an obligation of security or care imposed by the law."[48] This fault thus supposes, in the first place, the desire to breach an obligation of security or care. Second, there must have been a breach of the law. In this context breaches of the health and safety regulations are likely to be important because this *mens rea* is intended to cover some accidents at work.

Offenses that have the *mens rea* of deliberately putting another in danger[49] are treated as aggravated offenses of negligence with a higher sentence.

In addition, the fact of deliberately putting another in danger can constitute an offense in its own right under article 223-1 of the Criminal Code, which states that the offense is committed by "directly exposing another to an immediate risk of death or injury leading to a mutilation or permanent infirmity by the manifestly deliberate violation of a particular obligation of security or care imposed by the law."[50] This offense arises whether or not any harm was actually caused by the deliberate risk taking. A sentence of one year's imprisonment or a fine of 15,000 euros can be imposed.

iii. Negligence

Originally article 121-3 simply stated that there was a major offense "where there was carelessness [or] negligence"[51] and provided no definition of the terms. Academics traditionally consider that the existence of negligence is appreciated subjectively (*in concreto*) by the judge.

This statement, however, is misleading because the judge does not take into account the psychology or the particular characteristics of defendants, who cannot thus plead their inexperience or incompetence to escape liability. The element of subjectivity simply stems from the fact that the courts will take into account the actual external circumstances of the defendant. The judge will compare the defendant's conduct with that of a normally prudent and careful individual and, taking into account the circumstances, determine whether the defendant has been negligent. It would thus be more accurate to describe negligence as an objective test.

Article 121-3 was amended by the Act of 13 May 1996 to reassure elected representatives and civil servants that they would not be the subject of an unjust prosecution. This amendment provides that the external circumstances of the individual should be taken into account. Paragraph 3 of article 121-3 now states:

> There is also a major offense, when the law so provides, where there is carelessness, negligence or a failure to fulfill an obligation of care or of security laid down by Acts or regulations, if it has been established that the person has not exercised normal care taking into account, where appropriate, the nature of his mission, functions, and competence, as well as the power and the means at his disposal.[52]

At the same time at which it made changes to article 121-3 of the Criminal Code, the legislation made amendments to the General Code for Local Government Areas[53] and to the Act of 13 July 1983[54] concerning the rights and obligations of civil servants. These provisions specify that local and regional representatives and civil servants cannot be convicted on the basis of the third paragraph of article 121-3 of the Criminal Code for acts that were not intentionally committed in the exercise of their functions unless it is established that they did not exercise normal care, taking into account their competence and the power and the means at their disposal, as well as the difficulties specific to the missions that the law confers on them. These provisions were highly controversial, but the arguments for making specific provision for elected representatives and civil servants were that they were in a different and more vulnerable position than, for example, heads of business. They did not always have a free choice about the people they had to work with and frequently had little control over their budget. They had a wide range of responsibilities, including public security, and because of their limited means they had to prioritize. It was thus felt to be vital that after a death or injury due, perhaps, to a fire or pollution within the constituency of a politician or civil servant, the judge should consider whether that person was personally at fault before imposing criminal liability.[55]

Further reform was made to the legislation on criminal liability for nonintentional offenses by the Act of 10 July 2000.[56] There had been concern, particularly among politicians, that people in public office were continuing to be exposed to criminal liability where there was no real evidence of personal fault. The third paragraph of article 121-3 was amended, and a fourth paragraph was added as follows:

> In the case foreseen by the preceding paragraph, physical people who have not directly caused the harm, but who have created or contributed to creating the situation that has permitted the realization of the harm or who have not taken the measures permitting its avoidance, are criminally responsible if it is established that they have either obviously

deliberately breached a particular obligation of care or security laid down by legislation or regulation, or committed an established fault and who exposed another to a particularly serious risk of which they could not have been unaware.[57]

Thus the Act of 10 July 2000 created a distinction for natural persons (as opposed to legal persons) between where the harm has been directly caused by the accused and where the harm has been indirectly caused by the accused. Where the harm has been directly caused by the accused, the third paragraph of article 121-3 applies. Only minor changes have been made to this paragraph. First, the legislation expressly refers to carelessness, negligence, or the failure to follow an obligation of care or security as a form of "fault" to emphasize the fact that fault is required. Second, the legislation refers to a breach of a "regulation" in the singular rather than in the plural. This change means that when one is looking for a breach of a regulation, only a breach of a decree or an official order[58] is sufficient; breach of a circular or internal company rule is not sufficient. Third, the change in drafting seeks to highlight the fact that it is the responsibility of the prosecution to prove that the accused satisfies the requirement of fault, and the burden of proof is not on the accused to show that he or she lacked this element of fault.

3. Theories of Liability
i. Inchoate Crimes

There are two inchoate offenses in French criminal law: attempts (*la tentative*) and conspiracy (*une association de malfaiteurs*). French academics treat conspiracy as an ordinary autonomous offense rather than expressly categorizing it as an inchoate offense.

a. Attempt

There are three key elements to the existence of an attempt. For the *actus reus*, the defendant must have started to execute the full offense (*le commencement d'exécution*). The *mens rea* requires that the defendant intended to commit the full offense, and the full offense was not committed because of circumstances independent of the will of the defendant (*l'absence de désistement volontaire*). In the words of article 121-5: "An attempt is constituted when the defendant has started to execute the full offense, which was only suspended or failed to achieve its result because of circumstances independent of the will of the defendant."[59]

This is identical to the definition found in the old Criminal Code. There can be two reasons that the full offense was not committed: either the defendant stopped before completing the full offense (known as an "interrupted attempt"),[60] or the defendant did everything necessary for the commission of the full offense, but the result was not attained (known as a "failed attempt").[61]

Actus reus. The defendant must have started to carry out the full offense;[62] mere preparatory acts are insufficient. The *Cour de cassation* treats this as a question of law that is subject to its control.[63] No element of the *actus reus* of the full offense need have been committed. The Criminal Division uses various formulas to identify the point when the *actus reus* has been committed:

- "Acts directly aimed at the commission of the offense"[64]
- "Acts having for direct and immediate consequence the completion of the offense"[65]

- "Any act directly aimed at the commission of the offense when it has been carried out with the intention of committing it"[66]
- "Acts that should have for direct and immediate consequence the completion of the offense, having entered into the stage of executing the offense."[67]

Sometimes the *Cour de cassation* avoids using any formula, simply confirming the existence of the attempt.[68] The approach of the *Cour de cassation* has lacked consistency, but it would appear that it requires a sufficiently close and direct link between the conduct of the defendant and the full offense (an objective element).

Mens rea. The defendant must have an irrevocable intention to commit the full offense. The courts will find an attempt only if the full offense was not committed because of circumstances independent of the will of the defendant. The failure to commit the full offense will be voluntary where defendants freely decide not to proceed with their criminal enterprise. This decision might have been reached because of pity for the victim or because of the fear of being caught. The failure to carry out the full offense will be involuntary where it is solely due to an external factor, for example, if the defendant was prevented from proceeding because the police arrived at the scene[69] or because he or she was unable to open the safe.

The impossible offense. Where the full offense was impossible, the legislation gives no general guidance about the appropriate approach. Following a judgment of 9 November 1928,[70] the *Cour de cassation* appears to have accepted that all attempts to commit impossible offenses can give rise to criminal liability. In this decision the *Cour de cassation* upheld a conviction for abortion where there was an absolute impossibility of committing the full offense because of the method used.

b. Conspiracy

The offense of conspiracy is defined in article 450-1, which states: "A conspiracy consists of any group formed or understanding established with a view to the preparation, evidenced by one or more physical facts, of one or more serious offenses or one or more major offenses punishable by at least five years' imprisonment."[71] A similar definition can be found in article 132-71, which defines an organized gang,[72] but that article does not create an autonomous offense; instead, it establishes an aggravating circumstance for offenses such as theft[73] and rape.[74] Following the Act of 17 June 1998, inserting article 450-4 into the Code, the offense was extended to apply to moral persons.

Under the original drafting of the Criminal Code of 1810, a conspiracy arose only where there was a clear hierarchical structure to the criminal organization,[75] of a type associated with the Italian Mafia. This proved ineffective in the face of anarchic movements in the late 1800s. The Code was therefore amended to cover more loosely organized groups.

In order to establish the existence of a conspiracy, three elements must exist:

- An understanding;
- Aim to prepare certain offenses;
- Intention.

The maximum sentence for this offense is ten years and a fine of 150,000 euros.

ii. Complicity

Article 121-1 of the Criminal Code lays down the fundamental rule that a person is criminally responsible only for his or her own acts.[76] The principal offender is known as *l'auteur matériel* and is defined in article 121-4:

The principal offender is the person who:

1. Commits the criminal conduct;
2. Attempts to commit a serious offense or, in the cases provided for by the legislation, a major offense.[77]

The law will occasionally treat people who cause the commission of a principal offense, but who do not actually personally carry out the *actus reus* of that offense, as the principal offender, known as *l'auteur intellectuel* or *l'auteur moral*[78] (although frequently they will be treated as accomplices). For example, if a child has been abducted, the law will treat as a principal offender not only the person who physically removed the child, but also the person who arranged for the child to be abducted.

As regards accomplices (*les complices*), the key legislative provisions can be found in articles 121-6 and 121-7. These state:

Art. 121-6. The accomplice of the offense, as defined in article 121-7, will be punished as a principal offender.[79]

Art. 121-7. An accomplice to a serious or major offense is the person who knowingly, by help or assistance, facilitated its preparation or commission.

A person is also an accomplice who by gift, promise, threat, order, abuse of authority or power has provoked an offense or given instructions to commit it.[80]

In order to impose criminal liability on a secondary party, a crime must have been committed by a principal offender. Second, there must have been an act of complicity, and third, the accomplice must have the requisite *mens rea*.

Actus reus. A crime must have been committed by the principal offender in order for liability to be imposed on the accomplice. The crime must have been either a serious or a major offense. As regards minor offenses, the new Criminal Code distinguishes according to the form of complicity. Where the complicity took the form of the accomplice instigating the principal offense,[81] liability can be imposed.[82] By contrast, if the complicity simply takes the form of help or assistance, no liability can be imposed.[83] There must exist a sufficiently clear causal link between the conduct of the supposed accomplice and the commission (or the attempted commission) of the principal offense.[84] The principal offense need not have been the subject of a conviction.

Article 121-7 lists the types of conduct that can give rise to liability as an accomplice, and conduct falling outside this widely drawn list cannot give rise to liability. A positive act is usually required. Generally, mere presence at the scene of a crime is not sufficient to constitute complicity.[85] Complicity can consist of helping or assisting the commission of the principal offense or instigating its commission. The instigation, help, or assistance must have been provided before or at the time of the principal offense.[86] An exception exists where assistance was provided after the commission of the offense but had been promised beforehand.[87]

Mens rea. Accomplices must have knowingly participated in the principal offense. They need to have known the criminal intention of the principal offender, although they need not have shared this intention. Problems can arise where the principal offense differs from that which had been foreseen by the potential accomplice. If the offense committed has a different *actus reus* or *mens rea* than that foreseen by the potential accomplice, the latter is not liable.[88]

a. Defense of Withdrawal

Where accomplices, having instigated, helped, or assisted in the commission of a principal offense, subsequently change their mind and wish to abandon the criminal enterprise, they can avoid liability if they take positive action to prevent the commission of the offense.[89]

b. Sentencing

The new Code states that the accomplice will be punished "as a principal offender."[90] In practice, the courts tend to impose lighter sentences on accomplices than on principal offenders.

4. Causation

The problem of causation can arise where an offense is defined as requiring a certain result and it has to be determined whether the defendant caused that harm to the victim. The criminal courts have favored the "equivalence-of-conditions" approach to causation,[91] according to which all the events that have led to the realization of the harm are treated as having equivalent weight, and it is possible to treat each one of them in isolation as the cause of the harm. Thus, in the context of the fatal and nonfatal offenses against the person that do not require intention, the courts regularly state that there need not exist between the fault and the damage "a direct and immediate causal link,"[92] nor that the wrongful conduct of the defendant be the "exclusive cause" of the harm.[93]

C. Defenses

1. Types of Defense

Defenses are laid down in articles 122-1 to 122-8 of the new Criminal Code. French academic writers draw a distinction between objective defenses (sometimes called justifications) and subjective defenses (sometimes called excuses), although this distinction is not expressly referred to by the Code. Justifications are concerned with the surrounding circumstances in which the offense was committed rather than with the defendant. They provide a justification for the criminal conduct, which ceases to be viewed as antisocial.[94] There are four justifications: order of law, order of a legitimate authority, legitimate defense, and necessity. Excuses are defenses directly linked to the defendant. There are four excuses that remove the liability of the individual:[95] mental illness, the defense of being a minor, constraint, and mistake of law.

2. Burden of Proof

In a criminal trial the burden of proof is on the prosecution to prove that the defendant is guilty. When a jury is hearing the case, the jurors must be personally convinced that the defendant is guilty.[96] When the defendant puts forward a defense, this can affect the burden of proof. For example, with the defense of mental incapacity, the courts start with a presumption that the person is sane, and the burden of proof is on the defendant to prove that he or she falls within the defense. If a defendant argues that he or she made a mistake of law, everyone is presumed to know the law,[97] and the burden of proof to displace this presumption lies on the defendant. Where self-defense is argued, the defendant normally has to prove that the conditions of the defense have been satisfied, but where the defendant has been in a particularly dangerous situation, the burden of proof is reversed by article 122-6 of the Criminal Code, which states:

> A person is presumed to have acted in a state of legitimate defense when he carries out the act:
>
> 1. To repel, at night, an entrance by force, violence or fraud into inhabited premises;
> 2. To defend himself against the authors of theft or looting executed with force.[98]

In such circumstances it is up to the prosecution to prove that the individual was not acting in a state of legitimate defense.[99]

D. Justifications

1. Necessity

It was in the 1950s that a court of first instance recognized the defense of necessity. The court acquitted the accused of the charge of building without a permit because he was trying to provide decent living conditions for his family, who had been living in slum accommodation.[100] Soon afterward the *Cour de cassation* formally recognized the defense of necessity.[101] The defense is now expressly provided for in article 122-7 of the Criminal Code, which states: "A person is not criminally liable who, faced with an existing or imminent danger that threatens him, another person or property, carries out a necessary act to safeguard the person or property, except if there is disproportion between the means used and the gravity of the threat."[102]

The defense of necessity is available to all types of offenses, but three conditions must be satisfied in order for it to be applied: there must be an existing or imminent danger, this danger must have necessitated the commission of the offense, and the offense must have been proportionate to the danger. These conditions are very similar to those for the legitimate defense because legitimate defense is really just a special form of the defense of necessity, always requiring that the danger to which the defendant was responding be a criminal offense.

2. Self-Defense

Article 122-5 of the Criminal Code lays down the parameters of self-defense, frequently called legitimate defense. This states:

A person who, faced with an unjustified attack against himself or another, carries out at that time an act required by the necessity of the legitimate defense of himself or another is not criminally liable, except if there is a disproportion between the means of defense used and the gravity of the attack.

A person who, in order to prevent the commission of a serious or major offense against property, carries out an act of defense, other than voluntary homicide, when this act is strictly necessary for the goal sought is not criminally liable when the means used are proportionate to the gravity of the offense.[103]

The traditional concept of self-defense thus falls within this defense, though its parameters are obviously wider than this. The attack that gave rise to the response must be in breach of the law, although it need not pose a threat to a person's life.[104] There must be an actual or imminent attack,[105] and the defendant's response must bear some relation to the intensity of the attack.[106] Where defendants mistakenly believe they are about to be attacked, they will be able to rely on the defense if that mistake was reasonable.[107]

3. Consent

There is no general defense of consent in French criminal law, although the issue of consent can be relevant to the definition of an offense, for example, the offense of rape.

4. Superior Orders

The second paragraph of article 122-4 of the Criminal Code contains the defense of superior orders. It states: "A person who carries out an act ordered by a legitimate authority is not criminally liable, except if this act is obviously illegal."[108] In determining whether the defense applies, the courts need to consider whether the order came from a legitimate authority and whether the order was obviously illegal.

5. Order of Law

Where a person appears to have committed an offense, that person may have a defense if his or her conduct was authorized by another piece of legislation. The Criminal Code states in the first paragraph of article 122-4: "A person is not criminally liable who carries out an act ordered or authorized by legislative or regulatory provisions."[109] Generally the defense will cease to be available if a person has gone beyond what was necessary to satisfy the legal imperatives.[110]

E. Excuses

Subjective defenses do not generally abolish the existence of the offense; they simply remove liability for its commission from the individual. This means that secondary parties can be liable for the offense even where the principal offender has avoided liability by relying on the defense.

1. Mistake/Ignorance of Law or Fact

Article 122-3 of the Criminal Code states: "A person is not criminally liable who proves that he believed, because of a mistake of law which he was not in a position to avoid, that he could legitimately carry out the act."[111]

There was no equivalent defense under the old Criminal Code,[112] and the new defense was considered to be one of the major changes introduced by the new Code. But the defense is very narrowly defined and so is of only limited application. Three conditions must be satisfied for the defense to succeed: the mistake must have been one of law and not of fact, defendants must not have been in a position to avoid the mistake, and they must have thought their conduct was legal.

2. Insanity/Diminished Capacity

The Criminal Code states in article 122-1: "A person is not criminally liable who was affected at the time of the facts, by a psychological or neuropsychological illness that had removed his discernment or his control over his acts."[113]

The courts start with a presumption that the person is sane, and the burden of proof is on the defendant to prove that he or she falls within the defense. Three conditions must be satisfied: the defendant must have been suffering from a mental illness; this must have removed his or her discernment or control over his or her acts; and, last, the illness must have existed at the time of the commission of the offense. Those people who are mentally ill but who are at least partially capable of discerning their wrongdoing or of controlling their conduct fall outside the defense. The partially responsible are now covered by article 122-1, paragraph 2, of the Criminal Code, which keeps the earlier approach. It states: "A person suffering, at the time of the facts, from a psychological or neuropsychological illness that altered his discernment or impeded his control over his acts remains punishable; however, the court takes account of this circumstance when it determines the length and mode of punishment."[114]

3. Intoxication

Intoxication through the consumption of alcohol or drugs can fall within the defense of diminished capacity, discussed in the preceding subsection. Until 1957 the *Cour de cassation* took the view that intoxication could never give rise to a defense. In 1957 the Court abandoned this dogmatic approach and decided that the influence of alcohol on criminal responsibility was a question of fact that could be resolved only by the facts of each case.[115]

4. Duress

Criminal liability will be imposed only if the defendant acted of his or her own free will. The defense of constraint, sometimes known as duress, applies when the defendant had no choice but to commit the offense. Although this is treated as a subjective defense because the defendant was not acting with free will, this state is often brought about by external circumstances. Article 122-2 of the new Criminal Code states: "A person is not criminally liable who acted under the influence of a force or a constraint that he could not resist."[116]

Although the legislation appears to draw a distinction between "force" and "constraint," that distinction was not drawn by the old Code, and force is really just a specific example of a constraint. The law does not recognize internal psychological constraints as a defense. Thus parents whose child died when they failed to seek medical treatment because of their beliefs in the doctrine of a religious sect were successfully prosecuted for not assisting a person in danger.[117]

It must have been absolutely impossible for the defendant to resist the constraint.[118] The constraint must have been unforeseeable.[119]

5. Entrapment

There is no separate defense of entrapment, but if a person has made a mistake of law because of information from a public servant, then his or her conduct could fall within the defense of mistake of law.

6. Superior Orders

In French law superior orders are treated as a justification and are discussed in the section on justifications.

7. Defense of Being a Minor

Article 122-8 of the Criminal Code states:

> Minors capable of knowing right from wrong are criminally responsible for serious, major, or minor offenses for which they have been found guilty, and can be subjected to measures of protection, assistance, supervision, and education in accordance with conditions fixed by a special law.
>
> This law also determines the educative sanctions that can be imposed on minors aged ten to eighteen, as well as the punishments that can be handed down to minors aged thirteen to eighteen, while taking into account their reduced responsibility due to their age.[120]

Young offenders under thirteen can never receive a criminal sanction. They can, instead, be subjected in appropriate cases to educative measures. These can include ordering them to receive professional training, removing them from their parents into the care of the social services, or placing them under supervision.

Minors aged thirteen to eighteen can be punished for committing an offense, although the level of the punishment should take into account the fact that they were only minors at the time of the offense.[121]

III. SPECIAL PART

A. Structure

The analysis of offenses against the person is divided between homicide offenses and nonfatal offenses and between voluntary offenses and involuntary offenses.

B. Homicide: Murder and Manslaughter

Liability for a homicide offence can be rendered more serious where an aggravating circumstance is present and these will be considered first before looking at the specific offences.

Alongside the basic offenses, many homicide and nonfatal offenses can be aggravated in the presence of one of ten aggravating circumstances or a combination of them. For example, article 222-8 provides for an aggravated form of the offense of unintentional killing laid down in article 222-7. Article 222-8 provides:

The offense defined in article 222-7 is punished by twenty years' imprisonment when it is committed:

1. Against a minor under fifteen;
2. Against a person whose particular vulnerability, due to their age, illness, infirmity, physical or mental disability, or pregnancy, is known or apparent to the offender;
3. Against the legitimate or illegitimate parent or on the adoptive mother or father;
4. Against a judge, juror, *avocat, officier public* or *officer ministériel*, a soldier, a member of the national military police, a police officer, a customs officer, a prison officer, or any other holder of public authority, a professional or voluntary fireman, the official caretaker of a block of flats or a group of flats or an agent exercising on behalf of a landlord caretaker or security functions over a block of residential flats in accordance with article L. 127-1 of the Construction and Property Code, in the exercise of his functions or due to the facts of his functions, when the quality of the victim is apparent or known to the perpetrator;

4bis. Against the spouse, the direct ascendants and descendants of the persons mentioned in [paragraph] 4 or against any other person habitually living in their home, by reason of the functions exercised by these persons;

4ter. Against a person employed by a public transport network or any other person carrying out a public service mission or against a health professional, in the exercise of his duties, where the status of the victim is apparent or known to the perpetrator;

5. Against a witness, victim or civil party, either to stop him from denouncing the facts, making a complaint or giving of evidence or because of his denunciation, complaint or evidence;

5bis. Because of the victim's actual or supposed membership or nonmembership of an ethnic group, nation, race or religion;

5ter. Because of the sexual orientation of the victim;

6. By the spouse or cohabitee of the victim or the partner linked to the victim by a civil pact;
7. By a person holding public authority or charged with carrying out a public service in the exercise or during the exercise of their functions or of their mission;
8. By several people acting as principal offenders or as accomplices;
9. With premeditation or involving a trap;
10. With the use or threat of a weapon.[122]

These aggravating circumstances can be grouped into three types: first, those relating to the nature of the victim (who is young or particularly vulnerable); second, those relating to the status of the offender (as a spouse or cohabitee of the victim or a person in public office); and finally, those relating to the way in which the offense was committed (with premeditation, with a weapon, or in a group).

The fourth aggravating circumstance supposes that the guilty person knows the position of the victim and knows that the victim is acting in the context of his or her functions or mission.[123] As regards the last aggravating circumstance, the concept of a weapon is given a broad definition in article 132-75.

1. Voluntary Homicide Offenses

A voluntary homicide is committed when a person kills with the intent to kill. The law draws a distinction between murder, aggravated murder, and certain specific categories of murder. One practical difference between aggravated murder and the specific categories of murder is that when there is an aggravated murder, liability for that offense will also be applied to joint principals whether or not they were aware of the aggravating circumstances. By contrast, for the specific categories of murder, liability for the particular offense extends to joint principals only if they personally satisfy the criteria for that offense.

i. Murder

The offense of murder is committed when a person deliberately kills another. It is defined in article 221-1 of the Criminal Code, which states: "The fact of voluntarily killing another constitutes murder. It is punished by thirty years' imprisonment."[124] The victim must have been born, for murder does not extend to the killing of an unborn child. The offense of murder is not committed when a person takes his or her own life, because suicide has not been criminalized since the Revolution.

A positive act by the defendant is required for the *actus reus* of murder; there is no liability for murder by omission.[125]

It is the *mens rea* of murder that distinguishes it from other homicides. The *mens rea* has two elements: first, a general intention (*dol général*), and second, a specific intention (*dol spécial*), which is the desire to kill. If the defendant had an intention merely to wound, there can be liability only for involuntary homicide.

Murder carries a maximum sentence of thirty years' imprisonment. This sentence was reduced from life by the new Code so that a distinction could be drawn between murder and the aggravated forms of murder. The sentence can be reduced to two years, which can be suspended. In addition, the new Code adds a range of additional punishments that can be added to, but cannot substitute for, the principal sentence.[126] These punishments include a ban on exercising a profession in the course of which the offense was committed, and a ban on carrying a weapon for five years.

ii. Aggravated Murder

Aggravated murder is committed when the murder victim falls within one of nine categories of people who are given special protection by the Code. These people are listed in article 221-4 of the Criminal Code, and the list is very similar to that contained in article 222-8, discussed in section III.B. The only differences are that the paragraph numbering is slightly different, and paragraph 8 refers to an aggravating feature where "several people act as an organized gang" rather than referring to principal offenders and accomplices. All these aggravating circumstances, apart from the one concerned with organized gangs, relate to particular characteristics of the victim and reflect a desire to protect the more vulnerable in society.

Aggravated murders are punished with life imprisonment and can include a minimum time that must be spent in prison. This minimum period is usually eighteen years when a person is given a life sentence, but it can be reduced or increased to twenty-two years by a special decision of the *Cour d'assises*. The additional punishments available for ordinary murder are also available in this context.

iii. Multiple Aggravating Circumstances

The new Code in the second part of article 221-4 gives the court a wider range of powers when a child under fifteen was murdered and the murder was preceded or accompanied by additional aggravating circumstances. These additional aggravating circumstances are that the victim was raped, tortured, or subjected to barbarous acts. When these criteria are satisfied, the court can increase the minimum period that must normally be spent in prison from twenty-two years to thirty years.[127] When a court orders life imprisonment, it can specify that the convicted individuals should not benefit from any leniency in their sentence. This effectively means that they will normally spend the rest of their life in prison and will not benefit from parole.[128]

iv. Specific Murders

There are five specific murders: assassination, murder combined with another serious offense, murder combined with a major offense, poisoning, and habitual violence on a minor or vulnerable person causing death. Assassination is defined in article 221-3 and is committed when there has been a premeditated killing.

2. Involuntary Homicide Offenses

Involuntary offenses are often committed in the context of road and work accidents. An involuntary offense occurs when a person has caused physical harm to another without having wanted to do so, and sometimes without even having foreseen that he or she might do so. Thus, for an involuntary homicide, there will have been no intention to kill. These offenses are described in French as *involontaire* despite the fact that the act itself was voluntary, although the result was not. For example, in a fatal road accident the driver was often voluntarily driving at an excessive speed, although he or she had not wanted to kill. In the absence of a requirement of intention, these offenses can be analyzed as requiring only an *actus reus* that includes the element of fault, or the fault can be treated as the *mens rea*.

i. Ordinary Involuntary Homicide Article 221-6 states:

> The fact of causing, in the conditions and according to the distinctions laid down by article 121-3, by ineptitude, carelessness, inattention, negligence, or a breach of an obligation of security or of care imposed by legislation or regulation, the death of another constitutes an involuntary homicide punishable by three years' imprisonment and a fine of 45,000 euros.
>
> In the case of an obviously deliberate breach of a particular obligation of security or of care imposed by legislation or regulation, the punishments incurred are increased to five years' imprisonment and a fine of 75,000 euros.[129]

The careless conduct must have caused a harmful result. The defendant's act must have been the direct cause of the death.

A detailed analysis of the relevant concepts of fault can be found in section II.B.2 above. The element of fault is determined objectively by comparing the defendant's conduct with that to be expected of a reasonable person.[130] The Criminal Code lists five forms of fault that can give rise to criminal liability. These can be grouped together into five categories:

- Ineptitude (*la maladresse*)[131]
- Carelessness, inattention, or negligence[132]
- Failure to follow rules
- Deliberate breach of an obligation of security or care
- Gross negligence

ii. Unintentional Killing

Article 222-7 provides: "Violence leading to death without the intention of doing so is punished with fifteen years' imprisonment."[133] The Code places this offense in the section on voluntary offenses, but because there is no intention to kill, it seems more appropriate to treat it as an involuntary offense. Where one of the ten aggravating circumstances exists, the punishment is increased to twenty years' imprisonment, and to thirty years' imprisonment when the victim was under fifteen years old and the offender was in a position of authority over the victim.

C. Sex Offenses

Significant reforms were made to the definitions of sexual offenses by the Act of 23 December 1980. One of the main aims of this Act was to remove discrimination in the definition of the offenses based on the sex of the offender or victim. These reforms have largely been included in the new Code. The Code divides sexual offenses between sexual aggressions and sexual violations. The former are committed with the use of violence, constraint, threat, or deception;[134] the latter are committed without the use of one of these means.

Rape is categorized as a sexual aggression. The current definition of the offense is contained in article 222-23:

> Any act of sexual penetration, of whatever nature it may be, committed on another person by violence, constraint, threat or abuse is a rape.
>
> Rape is punished by fifteen years' imprisonment.[135]

1. Actus Reus

The *actus reus* of rape consists of the exercise of violence, constraint, threat, or abuse in order to commit a sexual penetration.

i. Violence, Constraint, Threat, or Abuse

In order for a rape to be committed, the offender must have used either violence, constraint, threat, or abuse[136] to achieve sexual penetration without the consent of the victim. The constraint can be either physical or psychological.[137] Abuse occurs when a person obtains sexual favors by deceiving the victim about the real situation or by taking advantage of the difficulties the victim has in understanding the situation because of his or her age or physical or mental state.[138]

The definition of the offense of rape contains no direct reference to the requirement that the victim was not consenting. Instead, the absence of consent is implied from the presence of one of the four vitiating factors listed in the preceding paragraph.[139] Following a legislative reform in 2006,[140] a new paragraph has been inserted into article 222-22 that states:

> Rape and the other sexual offenses are established when they have been imposed on the victim in the circumstances laid down by the present section, whatever may be the nature of the relations existing between the attacker and his victim, including if they are united by marriage. In this case, the presumption of consent of spouses to sexual intercourse is rebutted upon the submission of evidence to the contrary.[141]

ii. Sexual Penetration

Under the old Code, rape consisted of the penetration by the man's penis of a woman's vagina. The defendant had to be male and the victim female, although a woman could be an accomplice to a rape. The Act of 1980 broadened the definition of rape and made it less gender specific. This reform has been followed by the new Code. A father has been convicted of raping his son[142] and a mother of raping her daughter.[143] Rape now extends to any act of sexual penetration of whatever nature committed on another person. Thus it includes penetration by an object, such as a bottle or a finger, and not just by the penis. It covers oral[144] and anal[145] intercourse. However, in a case where a group of young people put a stick into the anus of their victim in order to extort money from him, the *Cour de cassation* took the view that the appropriate label was not rape.[146] It stated that penetration of the anus would constitute a rape where there was a sexual motive,[147] which is a debatable distinction, because the motive of the offender is normally irrelevant in determining criminal liability. It also ignores the nature of the offense, which is essentially an offense of violence that seeks to humiliate the victim.

In the past a husband could not be liable for raping his wife. The *Cour de cassation* appeared to shift in its position in 1990, but the facts of that case were exceptional.[148] In 1992 the *Cour de cassation* made it clear that the presumption that a spouse has consented to sexual intercourse is rebuttable and this is reflected in the legislative reform of 2006.[149]

2. Mens Rea

Only a general intent, not any special intent, is required for this offense. Defendants must be aware of the illegal character of their actions. The *mens rea* will therefore not exist if they made a genuine mistake and thought that the potential victim was consenting.

3. Sentencing

The ordinary offense of rape is punishable by a maximum sentence of fifteen years' imprisonment. The maximum sentence is increased up to life imprisonment in a number of circumstances.

D. Theft and Fraud

There are three key property offenses in French criminal law: theft (*le vol*), abuse of confidence (*l'abus de confiance*), and fraud (*l'escroquerie*). These offenses are well established in the law and can be found in the original Criminal Code of 1810. Each will be considered in turn.

1. Theft

The legislative provisions relating to theft are contained in articles 311-1 to 311-16 of the new Criminal Code. The classic definition of theft contained in the old Code[150] has remained unchanged in the new Code. Article 311-1 states: "Theft is the appropriation of the thing of another with guilty intent."[151] Thus the offense consists of four elements:

- Appropriation (*la soustraction*)
- A thing (*la chose*)
- Belonging to another (*d'autrui*)
- Guilty intent (*l'intention frauduleuse*)

The first three elements form part of the *actus reus*, and the last the *mens rea*.

   i. Actus *Reus*
     a. Appropriation

The concept of appropriation is not defined by the legislation, and it has been left to the courts to clarify its meaning. Appropriation has traditionally been restricted to cases where there has been a physical removal[152] of an object, but in recent years this has been found to be inadequate to cope with modern criminal activity. It has therefore been extended to include the legal transfer[153] of property. Recent cases have established that there can be an appropriation without a physical taking where there has been instead a legal transfer of the property.[154]

A complication arose for the criminal courts in relation to sale transactions because in civil law, following article 1583 of the Civil Code, a purchaser acquires ownership in the property "as soon as they [the contracting parties] are agreed on the property and the price, even though the thing has not been handed over nor the price paid." This civil principle has effectively been ignored by the criminal courts in determining liability for theft by nonpayment for goods where the transaction required an immediate payment. The criminal courts take the view that the final transfer of the thing is suspended until the price has been paid; until that point there is merely a provisional transfer that does not change the legal rights of the seller.[155] This is the analysis applied in the context of a self-service supermarket. If a person takes an item from a shelf and then fails to pay for it, this amounts to a usurpation of the rights of the owner and constitutes an appropriation. Thus a theft is committed when a person walks past a cash register without paying for goods. If a person is caught in the process of hiding items on his or her person before going past the cash register, this also amounts to an attempted theft.[156] The exception to the general civil law principle does not apply where payment for the goods is not required immediately. If payment can be deferred or staggered over a period of time, then the ordinary civil principles apply. There will be an immediate transfer of ownership in the property once the price and property have been agreed on, and there will be no theft if the purchaser subsequently fails to pay. If the seller later tries to take back the goods that have not been paid for, he or she will be liable for theft.[157]

b. Consent of the Owner

The property must have been removed against the will of its legitimate owner or possessor. Therefore, there is no appropriation when the property has been voluntarily handed over[158] by its owner to the defendant, even when this has occurred by mistake or as the result of dishonesty.[159] There is, therefore, no theft where a person is given too much change by a cashier, or too much cash from a cash machine, and decides to keep it.[160] In this situation there is merely a potential breach of contract, and criminal liability will not normally be imposed.

The courts will find that the property was handed over involuntarily when victims were unable to give genuine consent to the transfer of their property because of their age or intellectual faculties[161] or because they were acting out of fear (where, for example, they had been threatened with a weapon).[162] Thus there can be an appropriation when a person has handed over their property when under the influence of alcohol.

c. Temporary Appropriation

The traditional view was that there could be no theft if the property was handed back to the owner. As a result, there was no theft when a person took a bicycle for a bike ride and then left it by the side of the road.[163] This position had to be reconsidered with the increased problem of joyriding, when cars were taken only temporarily from their owners. The *Cour de cassation* accepted that property could be appropriated temporarily by using it[164] in 1959.[165] The concept of "theft by use" has been applied where documents have been photocopied and the originals returned to the owner.[166]

d. The Thing Appropriated

In the context of theft the legislation refers to a "thing" (*la chose*), while for fraud and abuse of confidence it refers to "property" (*le bien*). The former must have a physical existence and must be movable, but it need not have any economic value. The latter must have economic value but need not have a physical existence. Because a thing need not have pecuniary value, a love letter can be stolen.

e. Belonging to Another

The object of the theft must belong to another. A person cannot steal something that he or she owns, even if someone else has rights over it.[167] If a person agrees to lend someone property and then takes it back before the agreed time of return, he or she may commit a civil wrong, such as a breach of contract, but he or she will not incur criminal liability for theft.

The thing must belong to someone, and certain things belong to no one, such as the sea, rivers, and wildlife. Because a person belongs to no one, he or she cannot be stolen. Wild animals and plants on private property can be stolen.[168] There is no theft where someone has abandoned property,[169] but this must not be confused with property that has merely been lost.

ii. Mens Rea

The mens rea of theft is a guilty intent.

a. General Intention

The defendant must have known that the property belonged to another and must have intended to act against the will of the owner. If the person has made a mistake of fact, he or she may lack this knowledge. There is no theft if the person thought that he or she owned the property, or that nobody owned it.[170] A classic example is accidentally taking another's coat from a cloakroom.

b. Special Intention

Theft requires a special intention that consists in the intention to treat the property as one's own.[171] In practice, it is difficult to distinguish the general intention from the special intention because the two concepts are almost identical. There is no need to intend to permanently deprive the owner of his or her property. It suffices to intend to usurp one of the rights of an owner, such as the right to reproduce documents.[172]

c. Sentence

Article 311-3 of the Criminal Code lays down that ordinary theft is subject to a maximum sentence of three years and a fine of 45,000 euros. Aggravating circumstances are listed in article 311-4 and can give rise to a heavier sentence. The aggravating circumstances can relate to the offender, the victim, the means used to commit the offense, or the place where the offense took place.

2. Fraud

The basic offense of fraud (*l'escroquerie*) is defined in article 313-1 of the Criminal Code:

> Art. 313-1. Fraud is the fact of tricking a physical or moral person, either by the use of a false name, or of a false characteristic, or by abuse of a real characteristic, or by the use of fraudulent tactics, and to induce that person thereby, to his detriment or to the detriment of a third party, to hand over funds, valuables, or any property, to provide a service, or to consent to an act creating an obligation or a discharge of an obligation.
>
> Fraud is punished by five years' imprisonment and a fine of 375,000 euros.[173]

Both theft and fraud involve the appropriation of property belonging to another. The difference in the offenses arises from the means used to appropriate the property. For theft, the property is taken against the owner's will. For fraud, the owner is tricked by the defendant into handing over the property.

i. Actus reus
a. Property

The Criminal Code refers to the owner handing over "funds, valuables or any property," which is the same formula used in the old Code. There is some overlap in the choice of words because funds are also valuables, and both could be described as property.

While theft refers to "a thing," fraud focuses on "property." Immovable property cannot be the subject of the offense.[174] The property need not be tangible, but it must have some pecuniary value. Thus information can be the subject of a fraud offense.

A major innovation of the new Code is that the offense extends to the obtaining of a service. Although under the old Code using someone else's season ticket did not constitute fraud, it would now fall within the offense.

b. Deception

The defendant must have lied or used fraudulent tactics in order to obtain the property. Omissions are not sufficient to give rise to liability, so a person will not be guilty of fraud where he or she has simply failed to reveal a fact to the victim or has allowed the victim to deceive himself or herself. Liability was imposed where a person failed to provide certain information in an application to obtain welfare benefits.[175] A son who continued to receive his father's pension after his father's death was found to have committed a positive act.[176]

The deception must have induced the owner to hand over his or her property,[177] and it must therefore have preceded the handing over of the property.[178] Only certain types of lies are sufficient to constitute the offense.[179] Defendants must have lied about their name or one of their characteristics, or they must have abused the confidence that their real status affords. The latter concept, of abuse of confidence, was not expressly included in the old Code but had been accepted by the case law.

A mere oral or written lie alone is not sufficient, so the simple fact of claiming to have forgotten one's wallet in order to be loaned money or to promise marriage in exchange for the handing over of some property does not constitute fraud.[180] For a lie to become effective for the purposes of the offense, the simple oral or written lie must be accompanied by an external fact or physical act destined to give it force or credit. In practice, some recent decisions have taken a fairly relaxed view about what would be sufficient to constitute this external fact or physical act.[181]

c. Handing Over the Property

The owner of the property must have handed it over to the defendant. This handing over can take a range of forms. It can occur simply in a conversation when the victim provides valuable information to the defendant.[182]

d. Physical or Psychological Harm

The perpetrator need not get any personal benefit from the fraud. Because the harm can consist of psychological harm, defendants can be liable where they have paid the correct price for the property, but the owner would not have handed over the property if he or she had known the true situation.[183]

ii. Mens Rea

The defendant must have intended to defraud the victim. No offense is committed where the defendant mistakenly believed that he or she had a right to use the false name or false characteristic.

iii. Sentencing

Ordinary fraud incurs a maximum sentence of five years' imprisonment and a fine of 375,000 euros. Unlike theft, fraud can never become a serious offense; it is always a major offense. There are five aggravating circumstances for fraud, which increase the maximum sentence to seven years' imprisonment and a fine of 750,000 euros.

SELECTED BIBLIOGRAPHY

Further Reading

Conte, Philippe. *Droit pénal spécial.* Paris: Litec, 2007.
Desportes, Frédéric, and Francis Le Gunehec. *Droit pénal général.* Paris: Economica, 2007.
Elliott, Catherine. *French Criminal Law.* Devon: Willan Publishing, 2001.

Elliott, Catherine, Carole Geirnaert, and Florence Houssais. *French Legal System and Legal Language: An Introduction in French.* London: Longman, 1998.
Elliott, Catherine, Catherine Vernon, and Eric Jeanpierre. *French Legal System.* London: Longman, 2007.
Gattegno, Patrice. *Droit pénal spécial.* Paris: Dalloz, 2007.
Mayaud, Yves. *Code pénal.* Paris: Dalloz, 2008.
Renout, Harald. *Droit pénal général.* Paris: Paradigme, 2007.

Books

Beccaria, Cesare. *Traité des délits et des peines.* Translated by Lucette Khaiat. Paris: Cujas, 1966.
Garçon, Emile. *Code pénal annoté*, Paris: Sirey, 1901.
Gide, André. *La sequestrée de Poitiers.* Paris: Gallimard, 1930.

Articles

Bonfils, Philippe. "Les dispositions relatives au droit pénal des mineurs délinquants dans la loi prévention de la délinquance." *Le Dalloz* no. 15 (12 avril 2007): 1027–1034.
Bouloc, Bernard. "Observations sur Crim. 31 janvier 2007, *Bulletin des Arrêts de la Cour de Cassation* 2007, no. 25, p. 84." *Le Dalloz* no. 26 (5 juillet 2007): 1843–1848.
Jacomella, Sergio. "L'actualité de Cesare Beccaria." *Revue Internationale de Criminologie* (1964): 84.
Larguier, Jean. "La notion d'auteur moral."*Revue de Sciences Criminelles* (1976): Observations 409.
Mayaud, Yves. "Observations sur Crim. 13 février 2007, *Bulletin des Arrêts de la Cour de Cassation* 2007, no. 44, p. 261." *Revue de Science Criminelle et de Droit Pénal Comparé* 2 (avril–juin 2007): 295–297.
Mestre, Jacques, and Bertrand Fages. "Observations sur Crim. 13 septembre 2006, *Bulletin des Arrêts de la Cour de Cassation* 2006, no. 221, p. 784." *Revue Trimestrielle de Droit Civil* 2 (avril–juin 2007): 350–351.
Plawski, Stanislaw. "Le Peletier de Saint-Fargeau, auteur du Code pénal de 1791." *Revue de Science Criminelle* (1957): 619.
Rassat, Michèle-Laure. "Du code pénal en général et de l'article 121-3 en particulier." *Droit Pénal* Chronique (juillet 1996): 28.
Salvage, Philippe. "Le lien de causalité en matière de complicité." *Revue de Science Criminelle* (1981): 25.

Statutes

Act of 2 February 1981
Act of 8 July 1983
Act of 23 December 1980
Act of 13 July 1983
Act of 13 May 1996
Act of 17 June 1998
Act of 10 July 2000

Act of 4 April 2006
Code of Criminal Procedure
Criminal Code 1810
Criminal Code 1992
French Constitution 1958
General Code for Local Government Areas (*Code général des collectivités territoriales*)
Public Highway Code (*Code de la route*)

Cases

Alger, 9 novembre 1953, *Recueil Dalloz*, 1954, 369, note Pageaud.
Civ. 19 décembre 1912, *Recueil Sirey*, 1914.I.249, note Morel.
Conseil Constitutionnel, decision of 19–20 January 1981 relating to the Act of Security and Liberty 1981, *Recueil des Décisions du Conseil Constitutionnel*, p. 15; *Jurisclasseur Périodique* 1981.II.19701, note Franck.
Conseil Constitutionnel, decision of 30 December 1987 relating to the Finance Act for 1988, *Recueil des Décisions du Conseil Constitutionnel*, p. 63.
Crim. 30 novembre 1810, *Bulletin des Arrêts de la Cour de Cassation* no. 154.
Crim. 6 février 1812, *Recueil Sirey*, chroniques.
Crim. 24 février 1820, *Bulletin des Arrêts de la Cour de Cassation* no. 33.
Crim. 27 mars 1846, *Bulletin des Arrêts de la Cour de Cassation* no. 82.
Crim. 12 avril 1850, *Recueil Dalloz*, 1850.I.112.
Crim. 12 février 1864, *Bulletin des Arrêts de la Cour de Cassation* no. 39.
Crim. 27 avril 1866, *Recueil Dalloz*, 1866, jurisprudence, 288.
Crim. 6 juin 1878, *Recueil Dalloz*, 1879.I.482.
Crim. 1er mai 1879, *Recueil Sirey*, 1880.I.233.
Crim. 23 juin 1883, *Bulletin des Arrêts de la Cour de Cassation* no. 161.
Crim. 22 février 1894, *Bulletin des Arrêts de la Cour de Cassation* no. 51.
Crim. 28 décembre 1900, *Recueil Dalloz Périodique*, 1901.I.81, note Le Poittevin.
Crim. 25 juin 1901, *Bulletin des Arrêts de la Cour de Cassation* no. 213.
Crim. 27 mars 1902, *Bulletin des Arrêts de la Cour de Cassation* no. 128.
Crim. 3 avril 1903, *Bulletin des Arrêts de la Cour de Cassation* no. 148.
Crim. 24 juillet 1903, *Recueil Dalloz*, 1903.I.490.
Crim. 26 octobre 1912, *Recueil Sirey*, 1914.I.225, note J. A. Roux.
Crim. 3 janvier 1913, *Affaire dite du faubourg Saint-Honoré*, *Recueil Dalloz*, 1914.I.41, note H. Donnedieu de Vabres; *Recueil Sirey*, 1913.I.281, note J. A. Roux.
Crim. 4 juin 1915, *Recueil Dalloz*, 1921.I.57, note Nast.
Crim. 7 mars 1918, *Recueil Sirey*, 1921.I.89, note Roux.
Crim. 4 juin 1920, *Bulletin des Arrêts de la Cour de Cassation* no. 257.
Crim. 29 janvier 1921, *Recueil Sirey*, 1922.I.185, note Roux.
Crim. 23 juillet 1927, *Recueil Sirey*, 1929.I.73, note J.A. Roux.
Crim. 3 novembre 1927, *Recueil Sirey*, 1929.I.119.
Crim. 9 novembre 1928, Fleury, *Receuil Dalloz*, 1929.I.97, note A. Henry, J. Pradel, and A. Varinard.
Crim. 15 novembre 1934, *Recueil Dalloz Périodique*, 1935.I.11, note Donnedieu de Vabres.

Crim. 16 novembre 1934, *Recueil Dalloz Hebdomadaire*, 1934, p. 183.

Crim. 8 février 1936, *Recueil Dalloz Périodique*, 1936.I.44, note Donnedieu de Vabres.

Crim. 30 octobre 1936, *Recueil Dalloz*, 1936, 590.

Crim. 28 mai 1937, *Gazette du Palais*, 1937.II.336.

Crim. 12 février 1948, *Recueil Dalloz*, 1948, jurisprudence, 242, *Revue de Science Criminelle*, 1948, 534, observations Bouzat.

Crim. 26 mai 1948, *Bulletin des Arrêts de la Cour de Cassation* no. 141.

Crim. 4 août 1949, *Revue de Science Criminelle*, 1950, 47, observations Magnoil.

Crim. 29 décembre 1949, *Jurisclasseur Périodique*, 1950.II.5582, note A. C.

Crim. 5 juillet 1951, *Bulletin des Arrêts de la Cour de Cassation* no. 198.

Crim. 14 janvier 1954, *Bulletin des Arrêts de la Cour de Cassation* no. 14.

Crim. 29 janvier 1956, *Recueil Dalloz*, 1936.I.134.

Crim. 14 avril 1956, *Recueil de Droit Pénal*, 1956.I.191.

Crim. 13 décembre 1956, *Recueil Dalloz*, 1957.I.349, note Marcel Rousselet and Maurice Patin.

Crim. 5 février 1957, *Bulletin des Arrêts de la Cour de Cassation*, 112, observations Ligal; *Revue de Science Criminelle*, 1958, 93.

Crim. 16 octobre 1957, *Bulletin des Arrêts de la Cour de Cassation* no. 636.

Crim. 19 mai 1958, *Bulletin des Arrêts de la Cour de Cassation* no. 395.

Crim. 25 juin 1958, Lesage, *Jurisclasseur Périodique*, 1959.II.10941, note J. Larguier; *Recueil Dalloz*, 1958.I.693, note Marcel Rousselet and Maurice Patin.

Crim. 19 février 1959, *Recueil Dalloz*, 1959.I.161, note Marcel Rousselet and Maurice Patin; *Jurisclasseur périodique*, 1959.II.11112, note Bouzat.

Crim. 28 octobre 1959, *Recueil Dalloz* 1960.I.314, note A. Chavanne.

Crim. 20 juillet 1960, *Recueil Dalloz*, 1961, jurisprudence, 191, note Chavanne; *Jurisclasseur Périodique* 1961.II.11973, note Guyon.

Crim. 25 octobre 1962, *Recueil Dalloz*, 1963.I.221, note Bouzat; *Jurisclasseur Périodique* 1963.II.12985, note Vouin.

Crim. 30 avril 1963, *Bulletin des Arrêts de la Cour de Cassation* no. 157; *Revue de Science Criminelle*, 1964, 134, observations A. Ligal.

Crim. 21 avril 1964, *Bulletin des Arrêts de la Cour de Cassation* no. 121.

Crim. 29 juillet 1967, *Jurisclasseur Périodique*, 1968.II.15377, note J. Pradel.

Crim. 18 juin 1969, *Bulletin des Arrêts de la Cour de Cassation* no. 485.

Crim. 7 october 1969, *Bulletin des Arrêts de la Cour de Cassation* no. 242; *Revue de Science Criminelle* 1970, 398, observations Bouzat.

Crim. 3 décembre 1970, *Bulletin des Arrêts de la Cour de Cassation* no. 325.

Crim. 29 décembre 1970, *Jurisclasseur Périodique*, 1971.II.16770, note Bouzat; *Revue de Science Criminelle*, 1972.I.99, observations Ligal.

Crim. 13 janvier 1971, *Recueil Dalloz*, 1971, jurisprudence 191.

Crim. 27 octobre 1971, *Bulletin des Arrêts de la Cour de Cassation* no. 698.

Crim. 16 mars 1972, *Bulletin des Arrêts de la Cour de Cassation* no. 110.

Crim. 24 octobre 1972, *Bulletin des Arrêts de la Cour de Cassation* no. 306; *Revue de Science Criminelle*, 1973, 417, observations Bouzat.

Crim. 8 novembre 1972, *Bulletin des Arrêts de la Cour de Cassation* no. 329; *Recueil Dalloz*, 1973, sommaires commentés 17.

Crim. 3 janvier 1973, *Gazette du Palais*, 1973.I.290.
Crim. 7 février 1973, *Bulletin des Arrêts de la Cour de Cassation* no. 72.
Crim. 4 mai 1973, *Gazette du Palais*, 1973.I.612.
Crim. 10 juillet 1973, *Bulletin des Arrêts de la Cour de Cassation* no. 322; *Revue de Science Criminelle*, 1974, 594, observations G. Levasseur.
Crim. 5 février 1974, *Bulletin des Arrêts de la Cour de Cassation* no. 54.
Crim. 3 mai 1974, *Bulletin des Arrêts de la Cour de Cassation* no. 157.
Crim. 4 décembre 1974, *Gazette du Palais*, 1974.I.93 sommaires commentés.
Crim. 19 juin 1975, *Gazette du Palais*, 1975.II.660.
Crim. 11 février 1976, *Recueil Dalloz*, 1976, jurisprudence, 295.
Crim. 12 octobre 1976, *Bulletin des Arrêts de la Cour de Cassation* no. 289.
Crim. 14 juin 1977, *Bulletin des Arrêts de la Cour de Cassation* no. 215; *Revue de Science Criminelle*, 1979.I.539, observations J. Larguier.
Crim. 4 novembre 1977, *Bulletin des Arrêts de la Cour de Cassation* no. 330.
Crim. 4 janvier 1978, *Bulletin des Arrêts de la Cour de Cassation* no. 5.
Crim. 18 janvier 1978, *Bulletin des Arrêts de la Cour de Cassation* no. 20.
Crim. 19 mai 1978, *Recueil Dalloz*, 1978, Informations Rapides, 345, observations Roujou de Boubée.
Crim. 8 janvier 1979, *Recueil Dalloz*, 1979.I.509, note P. Corlay.
Crim. 19 juin 1979, *Bulletin des Arrêts de la Cour de Cassation* no. 219; *Revue de Science Criminelle*, 1980, 969, observations J. Larguier.
Crim. 3 novembre 1981, *Bulletin des Arrêts de la Cour de Cassation* no. 289; *Gazette du Palais*, 1982.I.66, sommaires commentés, note J. P. Doucet, observations Larguier; *Revue de Science Criminelle*, 1984, 489.
Crim. 25 janvier 1982, *Bulletin des Arrêts de la Cour de Cassation* no. 29.
Crim. 12 juillet 1982, *Revue de Science Criminelle* 1983, 261, observations Levasseur.
Crim. 3 novembre 1983, *Bulletin des Arrêts de la Cour de Cassation* no. 277.
Crim. 24 novembre 1983, *Recueil Dalloz*, 1984.I.465, note Lucas de Leyssac.
Crim. 22 février 1984, *Bulletin des Arrêts de la Cour de Cassation* no. 71; *Revue de Science Criminelle* 1984, 743, observations Levasseur.
Crim. 5 juin 1984, *Bulletin des Arrêts de la Cour de Cassation* no. 212.
Crim. 4 janvier 1985, *Bulletin des Arrêts de la Cour de Cassation* no. 10; *Revue de Science Criminelle* 1984, 814, observations Levasseur.
Crim. 3 juin 1985, *Bulletin des Arrêts de la Cour de Cassation* no. 211.
Crim. 18 novembre 1985, *Bulletin des Arrêts de la Cour de Cassation* no. 343, observations Levasseur; *Revue de Science Criminelle* 1987, 427.
Crim. 29 avril 1986, *Recueil Dalloz*, 1987.I.131, note Lucas de Leyssac; *Revue de Science Criminelle* 1987.I.701, observations Bouzat.
Crim. 1er juin 1988, *Jurisclasseur Périodique*, 1989.II.21172, note Devoze.
Crim. 8 novembre 1988, *Bulletin des Arrêts de la Cour de Cassation* no. 381.
Crim. 12 janvier 1989, *Bulletin des Arrêts de la Cour de Cassation* no. 14; *Droit de l'Informatique*, 1989, 34, observations Devoze.
Crim. 16 mars 1989, *Gazette du Palais*, 1989.II.379, sommaires commentés, observations Doucet.
Crim. 20 juin 1989, *Droit Pénal* 1989, commentaire no. 60.

Crim. 17 octobre 1989, *Droit Pénal* 1990, no. 122.

Crim. 14 mai 1990, *Bulletin des Arrêts de la Cour de Cassation* no. 187; *Droit Pénal* 1990, commentaire 255.

Crim. 5 septembre 1990, *Bulletin des Arrêts de la Cour de Cassation* no. 313; *Recueil Dalloz*, 1991.I.13, note Angevin; *Jurisclasseur Périodique*, 1991.II.21629, note M.-L. Rassat; *Gazette du Palais*, 1991.I.58, note Doucet; *Revue de Science Criminelle*, 1991, 348, observations Levasseur.

Crim. 24 octobre 1990, *Gazette du Palais*, 1991 sommaire 167; *Bulletin des Arrêts de la Cour de Cassation* no. 335.

Crim. 3 juillet 1991, *Gazette du Palais*, 1992, chronique droit criminel, 39; *Droit Pénal* 1991, commentaire 314.

Crim. 9 juillet 1991, *Bulletin des Arrêts de la Cour de Cassation* no. 294.

Crim. 11 juin 1992, *Bulletin des Arrêts de la Cour de Cassation* no. 228.

Crim. 11 juin 1992, *Bulletin des Arrêts de la Cour de Cassation* no. 232; *Recueil Dalloz*, 1993, 118, note M.-L. Rassat.

Crim. 15 juin 1992, *Droit Pénal* 1992, commentaire 281.

Crim. 4 mai 1993, *Droit Pénal* 1993, commentaire 179.

Crim. 9 décembre 1993, *Bulletin des Arrêts de la Cour de Cassation* no. 383; *Droit Pénal* 1994, sommaires commentés no. 83, observations M. Viron.

Crim. 26 avril 1994, *Droit Pénal* 1994, commentaire 181; *Revue de Science Criminelle*, 1994, 773, observations Giudicellidelage.

Crim. 27 avril 1994, *Bulletin des Arrêts de la Cour de Cassation* no. 157.

Crim. 25 mai 1994, *Bulletin des Arrêts de la Cour de Cassation* no. 203; *Jurisclasseur Périodique, édition générale* 1994, IV, 1962; *Recueil Dalloz*, 1994, *Informations rapides*, 217.

Crim. 23 novembre 1994, *Droit Pénal* 1995, no. 88, observations Véron.

Crim. 8 février 1995, *Droit Pénal* 1995, commentaire no. 171, observations M. Viron.

Crim. 25 octobre 1995, *Droit Pénal* 1995 commentaire no. 63.

Crim. 6 décembre 1995, *Bulletin des Arrêts de la Cour de Cassation* no. 372; *Droit Pénal* 1996, commentaire no. 101.

Crim. 10 janvier 1996, *Droit Pénal* 1996.I.97; *Revue de Science Criminelle*, 1996.I.846, observations Bouloc.

Crim. 21 février 1996, *Bulletin des Arrêts de la Cour de Cassation*, no. 84, observations Bouloc; *Revue de Science Criminelle*, 1996, 849.

Crim. 20 mars 1997, *Droit Pénal* 1997, commentaire 93.

Crim. 5 mai 1997, *Bulletin des Arrêts de la Cour de Cassation* no. 167.

Crim. 8 décembre 1998, *Bulletin des Arrêts de la Cour de Cassation* no. 336; *Revue de Science Criminelle*, 1999, 67, observations R. Ottenhof.

Crim. 16 mars 1999, *Jurisclasseur Périodique, édition générale*, 1999.II.10166, note S. Bouretz.

Crim. 13 septembre 2006, *Bulletin des Arrêts de la Cour de Cassation* 2006 no. 221.

Crim. 31 janvier 2007, *Bulletin des Arrêts de la Cour de Cassation* 2007 no. 25.

Crim. 13 février 2007, *Bulletin des Arrêts de la Cour de Cassation* 2007 no. 44.

European Court of Human Rights, decision of 8 June 1976, *England and Others against the Netherlands,* series A, no. 22.

Orléans, 28 janvier 1896, *Recueil Dalloz*, 97.II.5.

Paris, 16 janvier 1960, *Jurisclasseur Périodique*, 1960.II.11473.
Paris, 24 juin 1965, *Jurisclasseur Périodique, édition générale*, 1966. II. 14700, note Bicourt.
Pau, 18 décembre 1950, *Jurisclasseur Périodique*, 1952.II.6684, note Hubrecht.
Poitiers, 20 novembre 1901, *Recueil Dalloz Périodique*, 1902.II.81, note L. E. Poittevin; *Recueil Sirey*, 1902.II.305, note Himard.
Poitiers, 29 novembre 1901, *Recueil Dalloz*, 1902.II.81, note Le Poittevin; *Recueil Sirey* 1902.II.305, note Himard.
Tribunal correctionnel Colmar, 27 avril 1956, *Recueil Dalloz*, 1956.I.500.
Tribunal correctionnel Saint-Claude, 7 janvier 1954, *Jurisclasseur Périodique, édition générale*, 1954.II.7938, note Chambon.
Tribunal Montpellier, 21 décembre 1970, *Recueil Dalloz*, 1971.I.637, note Chabas.

NOTES

1. For a more detailed analysis of French criminal law, see Catherine Elliott, *French Criminal Law* (Devon: Willan Publishing, 2001). All translations are provided by the author. On the issue of English/ French legal translation, see Catherine Elliott, Carole Geirnaert, and Florence Houssais, *French Legal System and Legal Language: An Introduction in French* (London: Longman, 1998).
2. *Jurisconsultes.*
3. *Le droit pénal classique.*
4. Sergio Jacomella, "L'actualité de Cesare Beccaria," *Revue Internationale de Criminologie* (1964): 84.
5. Cesare Beccaria, *Traité des délits et des peines,* translated by Lucette Khaiat (Paris: Cujas, 1966).
6. *Le droit intermédiaire.*
7. Stanislaw Plawski, "Le Peletier de Saint-Fargeau, auteur du Code pénal de 1791," *Revue de Science Criminelle* (1957): 619.
8. "Tout ce qui n'est pas défendu par la loi ne peut être empêché et nul ne peut être contraint de faire ce qu'elle n'ordonne pas."
9. "La loi ne peut établir que les peines strictement et évidemment nécessaires et nul ne peut être puni qu'en vertu d'une loi établie et promulguée antérieurement au défit et légalement applicable."
10. *Titre.*
11. Criminal Code art. 113-2, para. 2.
12. Ibid. art. 113-6.
13. Ibid. art. 113-7.
14. Ibid. art. 113-10.
15. See section I.A.3 in this chapter.
16. Conseil Constitutionnel, decision of 19–20 January 1981 relating to the Act of Security and Liberty 1981, *Recueil des Décisions du Conseil Constitutionnel*, p. 15; *Jurisclasseur Périodique*, 1981.II.19701, note Franck.
17. "Art. 111-3. Nul ne peut être puni pour un crime ou pour un délit dont les éléments ne sont pas définis par la loi ou pour une contravention dont les éléments ne sont pas définis par le règlement."

18. *La loi.*
19. Constitution art. 34.
20. Criminal Code art. 111-4: "la loi pénale est d'interprétation stricte."
21. *Le décret en Conseil d'Etat.*
22. *Le crime.*
23. *Le délit.*
24. *La contravention.*
25. Code of Criminal Procedure arts. 353 and 427.
26. Ibid. art. 353.
27. Conseil Constitutionnel, decision of 30 December 1987 relating to the Finance Act for 1988, *Recueil des décisions du Conseil Constitutionnel,* p. 63; European Court of Human Rights, decision of 8 June 1976, *England and Others against the Netherlands,* series A, no. 22.
28. "Nul n'est responsable pénalement que de son propre fait."
29. "Toute infraction suppose que son auteur ait agi avec volonté": Crim. 13 décembre 1956, *Recueil Dalloz,* 1957.I.349, note Marcel Rousselet and Maurice Patin.
30. Criminal Code art. 413-10.
31. Ibid. art. 223-6.
32. Crim. 29 janvier 1956, *Recueil Dalloz,* 1936.I.134; see, however, Crim. 27 octobre 1971, *Bulletin des Arrêts de la Cour de Cassation* no. 698, where the defendant had the obligation to oppose what he had allowed to happen; Crim. 25 janvier 1982, *Bulletin des Arrêts de la Cour de Cassation* no. 29.
33. André Gide, *La sequestrée de Poitiers* (Paris: Gallimard, 1930); Poitiers, 20 novembre 1901, *Recueil Dalloz Périodique,* 1902.II.81, note L. E. Poittevin; *Recueil Sirey,* 1902.II.305, note Himard.
34. "Coups et blessures volontaires": old Criminal Code arts. 309 and 311.
35. "Toute infraction suppose que son auteur ait agi avec volonté": Crim. 13 décembre 1956, *Recueil Dalloz,* 1957, 349, note Marcel Rousselet and Maurice Patin.
36. Crim. 7 mars 1918, *Recueil Sirey,* 1921.I.89, note Roux.
37. Known as *délits matériels.*
38. "Il n'y a point de crime ou de délit sans intention de le commettre."
39. "Toutefois, lorsque la loi le prévoit, il y a délit en cas d'imprudence, de négligence ou de mise en danger délibérée de la personne d'autrui."
40. "L'intention, dans son sens juridique, est la volonté de commettre le délit tel qu'il est déterminé par la loi; c'est la conscience, chez le coupable, d'enfreindre les prohibitions légales." Emile Garçon, *Code pénal annoté,* (Paris: Sirey, 1901), art. 1, no. 77.
41. "N'est pas pénalement responsable la personne qui justifie avoir cru, par une erreur sur le droit qu'elle n'était pas en mesure d'éviter, pouvoir légitimement accomplir l'acte."
42. Note that the French offense of murder requires both general and specific intention.
43. Also known as *le dol imprécis.*
44. Crim. 27 mars 1902, *Bulletin des Arrêts de la Cour de Cassation* no. 128.
45. Criminal Code arts. 221-3, 222-19, 222-20, and 223-1.
46. "Mise en danger délibérée de la personne d'autrui."

47. Criminal Code arts. 221-6 and 222-19.

48. "Manquement délibéré à une obligation de sécurité ou de prudence imposée par la loi ou les règlements."

49. Criminal Code arts. 221-6, 222-19, 222-20, R.625-2, and 322-5.

50. "Le fait d'exposer directement autrui à un risque immédiat de mort ou de blessures de nature à entraîner une mutilation ou une infirmité permanente par la violation manifestement délibérée d'une obligation particulière de sécurité ou de prudence imposée par la loi ou le règlement."

51. "En cas d'imprudence [ou] de négligence."

52. "Il y a également délit, lorsque la loi le prévoit, en cas de faute d'imprudence, de négligence ou de manquement à une obligation de prudence ou de sécurité prévue par la loi ou le règlement s'il est établi que l'auteur des faits n'a accompli les dilgences normales compte tenu, le cas échéant, de la nature de ses missions ou de ses fonctions, de ses compétences ainsi que du pouvoir et des moyens dont il disposait." Yves Mayaud, "Observations sur Crim. 13 février 2007, *Bulletin des Arrêts de la Cour de Cassation* 2007, n° 44, p. 261," *Revue de Science Criminelle et de Droit Pénal Comparé* 2 (avril–juin 2007): 295–297.

53. *Code général des collectivités territoriales.*

54. Inserting art. 11bis.

55. For an extremely critical analysis of the 1996 Act, see Michèle-Laure Rassat, "Du code pénal en général et de l'article 121-3 en particulier," *Droit Pénal* (juillet 1996): Chronique 28.

56. Act no. 2000-647.

57. "Dans le cas prévu par l'alinéa qui précède, les personnes physiques qui n'ont pas causé directement le dommage, mais qui ont créé ou contribué à créer la situation qui a permis la réalisation du dommage ou qui n'ont pas pris les mesures permettant de l'éviter, sont responsables pénalement s'il est établi qu'elles ont, soit violé de façon manifestement délibérée une obligation particulière de prudence ou de sécurité prévue par la loi ou le règlement, soit commis une faute caractérisée et qui exposait autrui à un risque d'une particulière gravité qu'elles ne pouvaient ignorer."

58. *Un arrêté.*

59. "La tentative est constituée dès lors que, manifestée par un commencement d'exécution, elle n'a été suspendue ou n'a manqué son effet qu'en raison de circonstances indépendantes de la volonté de son auteur."

60. *Une tentative interrompue.*

61. *Une tentative achevée/une tentative stérile.*

62. *Le commencement d'exécution.*

63. Crim. 1er mai 1879, *Recueil Sirey*, 1880.I.233; Crim. 3 janvier 1913, *Affaire dite du faubourg Saint-Honoré, Recueil Dalloz*, 1914.I.41, note H. Donnedieu de Vabres; *Recueil Sirey*, 1913.I.281, note J. A. Roux.

64. "Les actes tendant directement à l'accomplissement du délit": Crim. 3 mai 1974, *Bulletin des Arrêts de la Cour de Cassation* no. 157; Crim. 5 juin 1984, *Bulletin des Arrêts de la Cour de Cassation* no. 212.

65. "Les actes ayant pour conséquence directe et immédiate de consommer le délit": Crim. 4 juin 1920, *Bulletin des Arrêts de la Cour de Cassation* no. 257; Crim. 3 novembre 1927, *Recueil Sirey*, 1929.I.119.

66. "Constitue un commencement d'exécution tout acte qui tend directement au délit lorsqu'il a été accompli avec l'intention de le commettre."

67. "Les actes devant avoir pour conséquence directe et immédiate de consommer le crime, celui-ci étant entré dans la période d'exécution": Crim. 25 octobre 1962, *Recueil Dalloz*, 1963.I.221, note Bouzat; *Jurisclasseur Périodique*, 1963.II.12985, note Vouin; Crim. 29 décembre 1970, *Jurisclasseur Périodique*, 1971.II.16770, note Bouzat; *Revue de Science Criminelle*, 1972.I.99, observations Ligal; Crim. 5 juin 1984, *Bulletin des Arrêts de la Cour de Cassation* no. 212.

68. Crim. 14 juin 1977, *Bulletin des Arrêts de la Cour de Cassation* no. 215; *Revue de Science Criminelle*, 1979.I.539, observations J. Larguier; Crim. 4 janvier 1978, *Bulletin des Arrêts de la Cour de Cassation* no. 5; Crim. 5 mai 1997, *Bulletin des Arrêts de la Cour de Cassation* no. 167; Crim. 25 octobre 1995, *Droit Pénal* 1995.I.63; Crim. 10 janvier 1996, *Droit Pénal* 1996.I.97; *Revue de Science Criminelle*, 1996.I.846, observations Bouloc.

69. Crim. 5 juillet 1951, *Bulletin des Arrêts de la Cour de Cassation* no. 198; Crim. 19 juin 1979, *Bulletin des Arrêts de la Cour de Cassation* no. 219; *Revue de Science Criminelle*, 1980.I.969, observations J. Larguier.

70. Crim. 9 novembre 1928, Fleury, *Receuil Dalloz*, 1929.I.97, note A. Henry, J. Pradel, and A. Varinard.

71. "Art. 450-1. Constitue une association de malfaiteurs tout groupement formé ou entente établie en vue de la préparation, caractérisée par un ou plusieurs faits matériels, d'un ou plusieurs crimes ou d'un ou plusieurs délits punis d'au moins cinq ans d'emprisonnement."

72. "Art. 132-71. Constitue une bande organisée au sens de la loi tout groupement formé ou toute entente établie en vue de la préparation, caractérisée par un ou plusieurs faits matériels, d'une ou de plusieurs infractions."

73. Criminal Code art. 311-4, para. 1.

74. Ibid. art. 222-24, para. 6.

75. Old Criminal Code arts. 265–268.

76. Criminal Code art. 121-1: "Nul n'est responsable pénalement que de son propre fait."

77. "Est auteur de l'infraction la personne qui:
   1. Commet les faits incriminés;
   2. Tente de commettre un crime ou, dans les cas prévus par la loi, un délit."

78. Crim. 24 octobre 1972, *Gazette du Palais*, 1973.I.218; Crim. 4 décembre 1974, *Gazette du Palais*, 1974.I.93, sommaires commentés; Jean Larguier, "La notion d'auteur moral," *Revue de Sciences Criminelles* (1976): Observations 409.

79. "Sera puni comme auteur le complice de l'infraction, au sens de l'article 121-7."

80. "Est complice d'un crime ou d'un délit la personne qui sciemment, par aide ou assistance, en a facilité la préparation ou la consommation.

"Est également complice la personne qui par don, promesse, menace, ordre, abus d'autorité ou de pouvoir aura provoqué à une infraction ou donné des instructions pour la commettre."

81. *Complicité par instigation*.

82. Criminal Code arts. 121-7, para. 2, and R.610-2.

83. Ibid. art. 121-7, para. 1.

84. Philippe Salvage, "Le lien de causalité en matière de complicité," *Revue de Science*

Criminelle 1981.I.25; Crim. 3 novembre 1981, *Bulletin des Arrêts de la Cour de Cassation* no. 289; *Gazette du Palais*, 1982.I.66, sommaires commentés, note J. P. Doucet, observations Larguier; *Revue de Science Criminelle*, 1984, 489.

85. Crim. 30 novembre 1810, *Bulletin des Arrêts de la Cour de Cassation* no. 154; Crim. 27 mars 1846, *Bulletin des Arrêts de la Cour de Cassation* no. 82; Crim. 26 octobre 1912, *Recueil Sirey*, 1914.I.225, note J. A. Roux.

86. Bernard Bouloc, "Observations sur Crim. 31 janvier 2007, *Bulletins des Arrêts de la Cour de Cassation* 2007, no. 25, p. 84," *Le Dalloz*, no. 26 (5 juillet 2007): 1843–1848; Crim. 23 juillet 1927, *Recueil Sirey*, 1929.I.73, note J. A. Roux.

87. Crim. 30 avril 1963, *Bulletin des Arrêts de la Cour de Cassation* no. 157; *Revue de Science Criminelle*, 1964, 134, observations A. Ligal; Crim. 8 novembre 1972, *Bulletin des Arrêts de la Cour de Cassation* no. 329; *Recueil Dalloz*, 1973.I.17, sommaires commentés.

88. Orléans, 28 janvier 1896, *Recueil Dalloz*, 97.II.5.

89. Crim. 6 février 1812, *Recueil Sirey*, chroniques.

90. Criminal Code art. 121-6.

91. *La théorie de l'équivalence des conditions.*

92. "Un lien de causalité directe ou immédiate": Crim. 20 juin 1989, *Droit Pénal* 1989, commentaire no. 60; Crim. 19 mai 1958, *Bulletin des Arrêts de la Cour de Cassation* no. 395; Crim. 19 mai 1978, *Recueil Dalloz*, 1978, Informations Rapides, 345, observations Roujou de Boubée.

93. "La cause exclusive": Crim. 7 février 1973, *Bulletin des Arrêts de la Cour de Cassation* no. 72.

94. *Faits justificatifs.*

95. *Causes de non-imputabilité.*

96. *Une intime conviction.*

97. "Nul n'est censé ignoré la loi"; Crim. 24 février 1820, *Bulletin des Arrêts de la Cour de Cassation* no. 33.

98. "Est présumé avoir agi en état de légitime défense celui qui accomplit l'acte:
   1. Pour repousser, de nuit, l'entrée par effraction, violence ou ruse dans un lieu habité;
   2. Pour se défendre contre les auteurs de vols ou de pillages exécutés avec violence."

99. Crim. 19 février 1959, *Recueil Dalloz*, 1959.I.161, note Marcel Rousselet and Maurice Patin; *Jurisclasseur périodique*, 1959.II.11112, note Bouzat.

100. Tribunal correctionnel Colmar, 27 avril 1956, *Recueil Dalloz*, 1956.I.500.

101. Crim. 25 juin 1958, Lesage, *Jurisclasseur Périodique*, 1959.II.10941, note J. Larguier; *Recueil Dalloz*, 1958.I.693, note Marcel Rousselet and Maurice Patin.

102. "N'est pas pénalement responsable la personne qui, face à un danger actuel ou imminent qui menace elle-même, autrui ou un bien, accomplit un acte nécessaire à la sauvegarde de la personne ou du bien, sauf s'il y a disproportion entre les moyens employés et la gravité de la menace."

103. "N'est pas pénalement responsable la personne qui, devant une atteinte injustifiée envers elle-même ou autrui, accomplit dans le même temps, un acte commandé par la nécessité de la légitime défense d'elle-même ou d'autrui, sauf s'il y a disproportion entre les moyens de défense employés et la gravité de l'attteinte.

"N'est pas pénalement responsable la personne qui, pour interrompre l'exécution d'un crime ou d'un délit contre un bien, accomplit un acte de défense, autre qu'un homicide volontaire, lorsque cet acte est strictement nécessaire au but poursuivi dès lors que les moyens sont proportionnés à la gravité de l'infraction."

104. Crim. 14 avril 1956, *Recueil de Droit Pénal*, 1956.I.191.

105. Crim. 28 mai 1937, *Gazette du Palais*, 1937.II.336.

106. Crim. 4 août 1949, *Revue de Science Criminelle*, 1950, 47, observations Magnoil.

107. "Raisonnablement croire": Crim. 21 février 1996, *Bulletin des Arrêts de la Cour de Cassation*, 84, observations Bouloc; *Revue de Science Criminelle*, 1996, 849.

108. "N'est pas pénalement responsable la personne qui accomplit un acte commandé par l'autorité légitime, sauf si cet acte est manifestement illégal."

109. "N'est pas pénalement responsable la personne qui accomplit un acte prescrit ou autorisé par des dispositions législatives ou réglementaires."

110. Alger, 9 novembre 1953, *Recueil Dalloz*, 1954.I.369, note Pageaud.

111. "N'est pas pénalement responsable la personne qui justifie avoir cru, par une erreur sur le droit qu'elle n'était pas en mesure d'éviter, pouvoir légitimement accomplir l'acte."

112. Crim. 24 juillet 1903, *Recueil Dalloz* 1903.I.490; Crim. 16 mars 1972, *Bulletin des Arrêts de la Cour de Cassation* no. 110.

113. "N'est pas pénalement responsable la personne qui était atteinte au moment des faits, d'un trouble psychique ou neuropsychique ayant aboli son discernement ou le contrôle de ses actes."

114. "La personne qui était atteinte, au moment des faits, d'un trouble psychique ou neuropsychique ayant altéré son discernement ou entravé le contrôle de ses actes demeure punissable; toutefois, la juridiction tient compte de cette circonstance lorsqu'elle détermine la peine et en fixe le régime."

115. Crim. 5 février 1957, *Bulletin des Arrêts de la Cour de Cassation* no. 112, observations Ligal; *Revue de Science Criminelle*, 1958, 93.

116. "N'est pas pénalement responsable la personne qui a agi sous l'empire d'une force ou d'une contrainte à laquelle elle n'a pas pu résister."

117. Crim. 29 juillet 1967, *Jurisclasseur Périodique*, 1968.II.5377, note J. Pradel.

118. "L'impossibilité absolue de se conformer à la loi": Crim. 8 février 1936, *Recueil Dalloz Périodique*, 1936.I.44, note Donnedieu de Vabres; Crim. 28 décembre 1900, *Recueil Dalloz Périodique*, 1901.I.81, note Le Poittevin.

119. Crim. 29 janvier 1921, *Recueil Sirey*, 1922.I.185, note Roux; Crim. 15 novembre 1934, *Recueil Dalloz Périodique*, 1935.I.11, note Donnedieu de Vabres.

120. "Les mineurs capables de discernement sont pénalement responsables des crimes, délits ou contraventions dont ils ont été reconnus coupables, dans des conditions fixées par une loi particulière qui détermine les mesures de protection, d'assistance, de surveillance et d'éducation dont ils peuvent faire l'objet.

"Cette loi détermine également les sanctions éducatives qui peuvent être prononcées à l'encontre des mineurs de dix à dix-huit ans, en tenant compte de l'atténuation de responsabilité dont ils bénéficient en raison de leur âge."

121. Philippe Bonfils, "Les dispositions relatives au droit pénal des mineurs délinquants dans la loi prévention de la délinquance," *Le Dalloz*, no. 15 (12 avril 2007): 1027–1034.

122. "L'infraction définie à l'article 222-7 est punie de vingt ans de réclusion criminelle lorsqu'elle est commise:
   1. Sur un mineur de quinze ans;
   2. Sur une personne dont la particulière vulnérabilité, due à son âge, à une maladie, à une infirmité, à une déficience physique ou psychique ou à un état de grossesse, est apparente ou connue de son auteur;
   3. Sur un ascendant légitime ou naturel ou sur les père ou mère adoptifs;
   4. Sur un magistrat, un juré, un avocat, un officier public ou ministériel, un militaire de la gendarmerie nationale, un fonctionnaire de la police nationale, des douanes, de l'administration pénitentiaire ou toute autre personne dépositaire de l'autorité publique, un sapeur-pompier professionnel ou volontaire, un gardien assermenté d'immeubles ou de groupes d'immeubles ou un agent exerçant pour le compte d'un bailleur des fonctions de gardiennage ou de surveillance des immeubles à usage d'habitation en application de l'article L. 127-1 du code de la construction et de l'habitation, dans l'exercice ou du fait de ses fonctions, lorsque la qualité de la victime est apparente ou connue de l'auteur;
   4 bis Sur le conjoint, les ascendants et les descendants en ligne directe des personnes mentionnées au [paragraphe] 4 ou sur toute autre personne vivant habituellement à leur domicile, en raison des fonctions exercées par ces personnes;
   4 ter Sur un agent d'un exploitant de réseau de transport public de voyageurs ou toute autre personne chargée d'une mission de service public ainsi que sur un professionnel de santé, dans l'exercice de ses fonctions, lorsque la qualité de la victime est apparente ou connue de l'auteur;
   5. Sur un témoin, une victime ou une partie civile, soit pour l'empêcher de dénoncer les faits, de porter plainte ou de déposer en justice, soit en raison de sa dénonciation, de sa plainte ou de sa déposition;
   5 bis A raison de l'appartenance ou de la non-appartenance, vraie ou supposée, de la victime à une ethnie, une nation, une race ou une religion déterminée;
   5 ter A raison de l'orientation sexuelle de la victime;
   6. Par le conjoint ou le concubin de la victime ou le partenaire lié à la victime par un pacte civil de solidarité;
   7. Par une personne dépositaire de l'autorité publique ou chargée d'une mission de service public dans l'exercice ou à l'occasion de l'exercice de ses fonctions ou de sa mission;
   8. Par plusieurs personnes agissant en qualité d'auteur ou de complice;
   9. Avec préméditation ou avec guet-apens;
   10. Avec usage ou menace d'une arme."

123. Crim. 3 décembre 1970, *Bulletin des Arrêts de la Cour de Cassation* no. 325.

124. "Le fait de donner volontairement la mort à autrui constitue un meurtre. Il est puni de trente ans de réclusion criminelle."

125. Poitiers 29 novembre 1901, *Recueil Dalloz*, 1902.II.81, note Le Poittevin; *Recueil Sirey*, 1902.II.305, note Himard.

126. Criminal Code arts. 221-8, 9, and 10.

127. *La période de sûreté.*

128. But note Code of Criminal Procedure art. 720.4.

129. "Le fait de causer, dans les conditions et selon les distinctions prévues à l'article 121-3, par maladresse, imprudence, inattention, négligence ou manquement à une obligation de sécurité ou de prudence imposée par la loi ou le règlement, la mort d'autrui constitue un homicide involontaire puni de trois ans d'emprisonnement et de 45 000 euros d'amende.

"En cas de violation manifestement délibérée d'une obligation particulière de sécurité ou de prudence imposée par la loi ou le règlement, les peines encourues sont portées à cinq ans d'emprisonnement et à 75 000 euros d'amende."

130. *Le bon père de famille.*

131. Crim. 17 octobre 1989, *Droit Pénal* 1990, no. 122.

132. Crim. 5 février 1974, *Bulletin des Arrêts de la Cour de Cassation* no. 54.

133. "Les violences ayant entraîné la mort sans intention de la donner sont punies de quinze ans de réclusion criminelle."

134. "Art. 222-22: Constitue une agression sexuelle toute atteinte sexuelle commise avec violence, contrainte, menace ou surprise."

135. "Tout acte de pénétration sexuelle, de quelque nature qu'il soit, commis sur la personne d'autrui par violence, contrainte, menace ou surprise est un viol."

"Le viol est puni de quinze ans de réclusion criminelle."

136. "Abuse" is a loose translation of the concept of *la surprise* because there is no directly equivalent concept in English law.

137. Crim. 8 févr. 1995, *Droit Pénal* 1995, commentaire no. 171, observations M. Viron.

138. Crim. 11 juin 1992, *Bulletin des Arrêts de la Cour de Cassation* no. 228.

139. Crim. 10 juillet 1973, *Bulletin des Arrêts de la Cour de Cassation* no. 322; *Revue de Science Criminelle*, 1974, 594, observations G. Levasseur; Crim. 4 mai 1993, *Droit Pénal* 1993, commentaire 179.

140. Act no. 2006-399 of 4 April 2006, art. 11.

141. "Le viol et les autres agressions sexuelles sont constitués lorsqu'ils ont été imposés à la victime dans les circonstances prévues par la présente section, quelle que soit la nature des relations existant entre l'agresseur et sa victime, y compris s'ils sont unis par les liens du mariage. Dans ce cas, la présomption de consentement des époux à l'acte sexuel ne vaut que jusqu'à preuve du contraire."

142. Crim. 3 juillet 1991, *Gazette du Palais*, 1992, chronique droit criminel, 39; *Droit Pénal* 1991, commentaire 314.

143. Crim. 4 janvier 1985, *Bulletin des Arrêts de la Cour de Cassation* no. 10; *Revue de Science Criminelle*, 1984, 814, observations Levasseur.

144. Crim. 22 février 1984, *Bulletin des Arrêts de la Cour de Cassation* no. 71; *Revue de Science Criminelle*, 1984, 743, observations Levasseur; Crim. 9 juillet 1991, *Bulletin des Arrêts de la Cour de Cassation* no. 294.

145. Crim. 27 avril 1994, *Bulletin des Arrêts de la Cour de Cassation* no. 157.

146. Crim. 9 décembre 1993, *Bulletin des Arrêts de la Cour de Cassation* no. 383; *Droit Pénal* 1994, sommaires commentés no. 83, observations M. Viron.

147. Crim. 6 décembre 1995, *Bulletin des Arrêts de la Cour de Cassation* no. 372; *Droit pénal* 1996, commentaire 101.

148. Crim. 5 septembre 1990, *Bulletin des Arrêts de la Cour de Cassation* no. 313; *Recueil Dalloz*, 1991, 13, note Angevin; *Jurisclasseur Périodique*, 1991.II.21629, note M.-L. Rassat; *Gazette du Palais*, 1991.I.58, note Doucet; *Revue de Science Criminelle*, 1991, 348, observations Levasseur.

149. Crim. 11 juin 1992, *Bulletin des Arrêts de la Cour de Cassation* no. 232; *Recueil Dalloz*, 1993, 118, note M.-L. Rassat.

150. Old Criminal Code art. 379.

151. Criminal Code art. 311-1: "Le vol est la soustraction frauduleuse de la chose d'autrui."
152. *Le déplacement matériel.*
153. *Le maniement juridique.*
154. Crim. 21 avril 1964, *Bulletin des Arrêts de la Cour de Cassation* no. 121.
155. Crim. 4 juin 1915, *Recueil Dalloz*, 1921, 1, 57, note Nast.
156. Crim. 3 janvier 1973, *Gazette du Palais*, 1973.I.290.
157. Crim. 12 octobre 1976, *Bulletin des Arrêts de la Cour de Cassation* no. 289.
158. *La remise volontaire.*
159. For decisions to the contrary, see Crim. 24 octobre 1972, *Bulletin des Arrêts de la Cour de Cassation* no. 306; *Revue de Science Criminelle*, 1973, 417, observations Bouzat; Crim. 4 novembre 1977, *Bulletin des Arrêts de la Cour de Cassation* no. 330, which concerned the head of the warehouse of a shop found to be an accomplice of the thief.
160. Crim. 24 novembre 1983, *Recueil Dalloz*, 1984, 465, note Lucas de Leyssac; Crim. 1er juin 1988, *Jurisclasseur Périodique*, 1989.II.21172, note Devoze.
161. Crim. 18 janvier 1978, *Bulletin des Arrêts de la Cour de Cassation* no. 20; Crim. 16 mars 1989, *Gazette du Palais*, 1989.II.379, sommaires commentés, observations Doucet.
162. Crim. 22 février 1894, *Bulletin des Arrêts de la Cour de Cassation* no. 51; Crim. 4 mai 1973, *Gazette du Palais*, 1973.I.612.
163. Tribunal correctionnel Saint-Claude, 7 janvier 1954, *Jurisclasseur Périodique, édition générale*, 1954.II.7938, note Chambon.
164. *Le vol d'usage.*
165. Crim. 28 octobre 1959, *Recueil Dalloz*, 1960.I.314, note A. Chavanne.
166. Crim. 8 janvier 1979, *Recueil Dalloz*, 1979.I.509, note P. Corlay; Crim. 29 avr. 1986, *Recueil Dalloz*, 1987.I.131, note Lucas de Leyssac; *Revue de Science Criminelle*, 1987.I.701, observations Bouzat; Crim. 24 octobre 1990, *Bulletin des Arrêts de la Cour de Cassation* no. 355; Crim. 8 déc. 1998, *Bulletin des Arrêts de la Cour de Cassation* no. 336; *Revue de Science Criminelle*, 1999, 67, observations R. Ottenhof; Crim. 16 mars 1999, *Jurisclasseur Périodique, édition générale*, 1999.II.10166, note S. Bouretz.
167. Crim. 13 janvier 1971, *Recueil Dalloz*, 1971, jurisprudence 191; Pau, 18 décembre 1950, *Jurisclasseur Périodique*, 1952.II.6684, note Hubrecht.
168. Crim. 3 avril 1903, *Bulletin des Arrêts de la Cour de Cassation* no. 148; Crim. 12 février 1948, *Recueil Dalloz*, 1948, jurisprudence 242; *Revue de Science Criminelle*, 1948, 534, observations Bouzat.
169. Crim. 12 avril. 1850, *Recueil Dalloz*, 1850.I.112.
170. Crim. 12 février 1864, *Bulletin des Arrêts de la Cour de Cassation* no. 39; Crim. 25 juin 1901, *Bulletin des Arrêts de la Cour de Cassation* no. 213.
171. *La volonté d'appropriation.*
172. Crim. 24 octobre 1990, *Gazette du Palais*, sommaire 167; *Bulletin des Arrêts de la Cour de Cassation* no. 335.
173. "Art. 313-1. L'escroquerie est le fait, soit par l'usage d'un faux nom ou d'une fausse qualité, soit par l'abus d'une qualité vraie, soit par l'emploi de manoeuvres frauduleuses, de tromper une personne physique ou morale et de la déterminer ainsi, à

son préjudice ou au préjudice d'un tiers, à remettre des fonds, des valeurs ou un bien quelconque, à fournir un service ou à consentir un acte opérant obligation ou décharge

"L'escroquerie est punie de cinq ans d'emprisonnement et de 375 000 euros d'amende."

174. Crim. 15 juin 1992, *Droit Pénal* 1992, commentaire 281.

175. Crim. 26 avril 1994, *Droit Pénal* 1994, commentaire 181; *Revue de Science Criminelle*, 1994, 773, observations Giudicellidelage.

176. Crim. 20 mars 1997, *Droit Pénal* 1997, commentaire 93.

177. Crim. 14 mai 1990, *Bulletin des Arrêts de la Cour de Cassation* no. 187; *Droit Pénal* 1990, commentaire 255.

178. Crim. 8 novembre 1988, *Bulletin des Arrêts de la Cour de Cassation* no. 381.

179. Paris, 16 janvier 1960, *Jurisclasseur Périodique*, 1960.II.11473; Crim. 7 octobre 1969, *Bulletin des Arrêts de la Cour de Cassation* no. 242; *Revue de Science Criminelle*, 1970, 398, observations Bouzat.

180. Crim. 23 juin 1883, *Bulletin des Arrêts de la Cour de Cassation* no. 161; Crim. 20 juillet 1960, *Recueil Dalloz*, 1961, jurisprudence, 191, note Chavanne; *Jurisclasseur Périodique*, 1961.II.11973, note Guyon; Crim. 16 octobre 1957, *Bulletin des Arrêts de la Cour de Cassation* no. 636; Crim. 11 février 1976, *Recueil Dalloz*, 1976, jurisprudence, 295; Crim. 3 novembre 1983, *Bulletin des Arrêts de la Cour de Cassation* no. 277.

181. Crim. 3 juin 1985, *Bulletin des Arrêts de la Cour de Cassation* no. 211.

182. Jacques Mestre and Bertrand Fages, "Observations sur Crim. 13 septembre 2006, *Bulletin des Arrêts de la Cour de Cassation* 2006, no. 221, p. 784," *Revue Trimestrielle de Droit Civil* 2 (avril–juin 2007): 350–351.

183. Crim. 30 octobre 1936, *Recueil Dalloz*, 1936.I.590; Crim. 29 décembre 1949, *Jurisclasseur Périodique*, 1950.II.5582, note A. C.

GERMANY

Thomas Weigend

I. Introduction
    A. Historical Sketch
    B. Jurisdiction
    C. Legality Principle
    D. Sources of Criminal Law
    E. Process

II. General Part
    A. Theories of Punishment
    B. Liability Requirements
    C. Defenses
    D. Justifications
    E. Excuses
    F. Sanctions

III. Special Part
    A. Structure
    B. Homicide
    C. Sex Offenses
    D. Theft and Fraud
    E. "Victimless" Crimes

Thomas Weigend is Professor of Criminal Law at the University of Cologne. His recent publications include "Intent, Mistake of Law, and Co-perpetration in the Lubanga Decision on Confirmation of Charges," 6 *Journal of International Criminal Justice* 471 (2008); and "The Decay of the Inquisitorial Ideal: Plea Bargaining Invades German Criminal Procedure," in John D. Jackson, Máximo Langer, and Peter Tillers (eds.), *Crime, Procedure and Evidence in Comparative and International Context: Essays in Honour of Professor Mirjan Damaska* (Hart, 2008).

I. INTRODUCTION

A. Historical Sketch

The German Penal Code dates from 1871. The unification of criminal law was one of the first legislative projects of the new German empire founded in 1870. The new Penal Code was greatly influenced by the Prussian Criminal Code of 1851. It incorporated liberal ideas of the time and followed a "classical" (mainly retributive) penological approach.

The Penal Code has since been amended numerous times, but its main structure has remained intact. A major reform of the General Part was introduced in 1975, bringing the formulation of general rules up to the state of the art of the 1960s. Sanctions have also been subject to frequent changes. In 1933 measures of security and rehabilitation were added to criminal penalties. In 1949 the death penalty was abolished by the new constitution (Basic Law) of the Federal Republic of Germany. The 1975 reform emphasized the rehabilitative function of criminal sanctions, discouraging the imposition of short-term imprisonment and increasing the scope of applicability of fines, suspended sentences, and other noncustodial measures. In recent decades many new offense categories have been added to take account of new interests to be protected, for example, environmental protection, data security, and a better protection of privacy against unwanted contact (stalking), as well as unauthorized recording of words or images. The Penal Code was repromulgated in 1998[1] but has since been amended again several times.

B. Jurisdiction

German law follows the territoriality principle, which extends its reach to all offenses committed on German territory, as well as German ships and airplanes (§§ 3 and 4 of the Penal Code; hereafter PC). Beyond territoriality, there are several other recognized grounds for establishing the applicability of the German Penal Code, which go hand in hand with giving German courts jurisdiction. Most important, Germany claims jurisdiction over offenses committed by German nationals abroad if the act in question was criminal according to the law of the jurisdiction where it was committed (§ 7 (2) no. 1 PC). The same applies when the victim of an offense committed abroad is a German national (§ 7 (1) PC). For some offenses, the place of commission is deemed irrelevant because the offense is directed against the German national interest, for example, high treason, offenses of a German public servant with relation to that person's official duties, or illegal disclosure of business secrets of a German enterprise (§ 5 nos. 2, 7, 12 PC). For policy reasons, illegal abortions committed abroad by a German woman or doctor also fall under the jurisdiction of German criminal courts (§ 5 no. 9 PC). Finally, Germany claims universal jurisdiction over certain offenses against international criminal law, notably genocide, crimes against humanity, and war crimes (§ 1 International Crimes Code),[2] as well as certain offenses subject to prohibition by international conventions, such as illegal traffic of drugs and pornography, as well as of human beings for the purpose of sexual exploitation (§ 6 nos. 4, 5, 6 PC).

C. Legality Principle

Section 1 of the Penal Code proclaims the principle of legality. An identically worded version of the principle is contained in Art. 103 sec. 2 of the Basic Law, elevating the principle of legality to constitutional rank.[3] Section 1 of the Penal Code and Art. 103 sec. 2 of the Basic Law read: "An act can be punished only if its punishability was determined by law before the act had been committed."

Four subprinciples have been read into this short sentence:[4]

1. Punishability requires a written act of parliament (*lex scripta parlamentaria*) and cannot be based on custom.
2. Criminal prohibitions must "determine" the prohibited conduct; that is, they must not be too vague.
3. Acts cannot be punished retroactively.
4. The wording of the statute denotes the outer limits of punishability; the statutory prohibition thus cannot be extended by analogy to conduct not covered by the ordinary meaning of the words used.

The first two requirements aim to protect a citizen from executive or judicial arbitrariness; they place the responsibility for determining the punishability of any conduct exclusively on the legislature. Germany has always insisted that there can be no unwritten or judge-made "common law" of crimes. For that reason, Germany lodged a reservation with respect to Art. 7 sec. 2 of the European Convention on Human Rights, which provides for the possibility to try and punish a person for an act that was criminal, at the time of its commission, "according to the general principles of law recognized by civilized nations." Germany would not recognize criminality based on unwritten customary international law and therefore, in 2002, passed an International Crimes Code,[5] which defines the core crimes recognized in current international criminal law. Simultaneously, the reservation concerning Art. 7 sec. 2 of the European Convention on Human Rights was withdrawn.

The principle that criminal laws must be "determinate" also has the dual purpose of protecting a citizen from arbitrariness and making the legislature decide the exact delimitation of criminally prohibited behavior.[6] The Federal Constitutional Court has in several instances been called to decide whether individual provisions of the criminal law were sufficiently clear to let a citizen know what conduct was prohibited. Only rarely has the court found a statute too imprecise to meet the constitutional standard.[7] The court has recognized that it is not feasible for the legislature to write laws that are detailed and on the other hand catch the multitude of situations that can occur in real life. The legislature can thus not be expected to exclusively use exact and descriptive terms but can also employ general, evaluative words when describing prohibited conduct. It is sufficient that a citizen can recognize the interest protected by the statute and foresee the state's punitive reaction. In interpreting an unclear statute, a citizen may have to resort to the legislative context and/or long-standing jurisprudence of the courts.[8]

Neither the legislature nor the courts can impose criminal sanctions for acts that were not criminally prohibited at the time when they were done. Nor is it permissible to retroactively increase criminal punishment. An exception applies to measures of rehabilitation and security, the purpose of which is not to sanction past offenses but to prevent future crime. Because prevention of crime should be adapted to the best methods available at any given time, the Penal Code provides that the court shall impose such measures in accordance with law in force at the time of the court's decision (§ 2 (6)). In a controversial decision the Federal Constitutional Court has held that this rule is applicable to security detention (*Sicherungsverwahrung*, § 66 PC) although that measure has very little rehabilitative effect but is designed to keep permanently dangerous offenders incarcerated even beyond the time proportionate to their past crimes.[9]

The strict prohibition of applying criminal laws retroactively led to problems with respect to shootings of persons who had tried to leave the former German Democratic Republic (GDR). Under certain circumstances, GDR law had justified the use of deadly force against fugitives, and after the reunification of Germany, soldiers who were indicted for manslaughter raised the relevant GDR statute as a defense. The Federal Constitutional Court held that laws of another state purporting to justify certain otherwise criminal behavior need not be recognized under all circumstances, and that therefore the defendants could be convicted of manslaughter. An exception to the strict prohibition of the retroactive determination of criminality was thus recognized but was limited to extraordinary situations.[10]

The fourth aspect of the principle of legality prevents courts from extending the reach of a criminal prohibition by analogy to the defendant's detriment. In interpreting and applying criminal laws, courts cannot go beyond the ordinary meaning of the words of the statute even if the defendant's conduct was very similar to what the statute proscribed.[11] Courts sometimes interpret certain terms broadly, but by and large they strive to stay within the limits drawn by everyday usage when interpreting criminal laws. For example, the Federal Court of Appeals ruled that a man who violently assaulted his victim, causing him to lose one kidney, could not be convicted of aggravated wounding (§ 224 CP former version) when the relevant provision of the Penal Code stated as a prerequisite that the victim lose the use of an "important member" of his body. According to ordinary language, the court argued, a kidney is an organ but not a "member" of the body.[12] Similarly, the Federal Constitutional Court found a violation of the principle of legality when a protester who had sat down on a railway track to block transports to a nuclear plant was convicted of coercion (§ 240 PC), which requires "violence or threats." It would go beyond a normal understanding of "violence" to say that a person who does not do more than sit down on a railroad track commits a "violent" act, the court ruled.[13] It should be noted that Germany does not recognize a "rule of leniency"; words of a criminal statute are to be interpreted in accordance with their ordinary meaning, and doubts about a statute's applicability to a given case need not necessarily be resolved in favor of the defendant. On the other hand, the principle of legality does not preclude the courts from establishing or from extending, by analogy, legal norms in favor of the defendant. For example, the voluntary consent of the victim of harmful conduct has—within limits established by the courts—long been recognized as a justification, although the written law does not mention this defense.[14]

D. Sources of Criminal Law

1. Legislature

The German version of the principle of legality requires that criminal prohibitions and sanctions be based on written law. The main body of criminal law is contained in the Penal Code, but numerous legal norms providing for criminal liability can be found in other statutes, for example, in statutes regulating commercial matters, road traffic, or the handling of potentially dangerous drugs. Such statutes typically establish certain duties and requirements and add one or more paragraphs defining as crimes the violation of specified duties.[15] Under the German federal system, the federation is competent to create criminal law (Art. 74 sec. 1 no. 1 Basic Law); only in very few subject matters can individual states pass criminal statutes.

2. Judiciary

Under German constitutional theory, the role of the courts is to interpret the law, not to make it. Judges thus have no power to establish criminal liability without a clear statutory basis. When courts are of the opinion that certain conduct not covered by a statute should be treated as criminal, they cannot extend the reach of the statute. Their only recourse is to acquit the defendant and to write an opinion alerting the legislature to the gap in the present statutory law.

In spite of the clear division of state powers, courts can give statutes a new interpretation as required by new insights or technological development. One well-known instance of judicial reinterpretation of a criminal statute refers to the criminal prohibition of driving under the influence of alcohol. The relevant statute (§ 316 PC) defines as criminal the driving of a vehicle in road traffic although the driver "is not capable of safely driving the vehicle" because of prior consumption of alcohol or another intoxicating substance. On the basis of medical and psychological expertise, the Federal Court of Appeals in 1966 declared that a driver whose blood contains 0.13 percent of alcohol is irrefutably presumed incapable of safely driving a car.[16] In 1990 the Federal Court of Appeals lowered the limit of the presumption to a blood alcohol concentration of 0.11 per cent.[17] In the latter decision the court convicted the defendant of drunken driving although his blood alcohol concentration had been below the limit set by the court earlier; the court claimed that it did not make retroactive law but only applied new scientific insight to the interpretation of an unchanged statutory provision.

In practice, opinions of higher courts greatly influence the application of criminal law. Although lower courts are not formally bound by precedent, they will invariably look for guidance to the jurisprudence of the Federal Court of Appeals and state courts of appeals.[18]

3. Executive

Under German constitutional law, the legislature can authorize the federal government, a state government, or a federal minister to issue regulations. The contents, purpose, and scope of the regulation must be determined by statute (Art. 80 sec. 1 Basic Law), but the executive will be responsible for the details. Regulations are frequently used for technical matters that the legislature wishes to leave to the expertise of a ministry. A regulation can, in principle, contain criminal prohibitions,[19] but the Basic Law (Art. 104 sec. 1 Basic Law) provides that the freedom of a person can be restricted only on the basis of a statute passed by the legislature. Since in practice all criminal prohibitions foresee imprisonment as a sanction, the stricter rule of Art. 104 of the Basic Law applies. According to the jurisprudence of the Federal Constitutional Court, this section of the Basic Law does not rule out a delegation of complementary regulation to the executive, but the statute must describe exactly the conduct that is to be criminally prohibited and the maximum sanction to be imposed.[20]

4. Scholars

Legal scholarship has traditionally played an important role in German jurisprudence. Scholars were prominently involved in the 1960s reform of the Penal Code, which led to the new General Part that entered into force in 1975. In recent years, however, the influence of scholars on criminal policy has diminished markedly, and many amendments of the law have been passed in spite of widespread academic criticism. But even today appellate courts take account of and cite scholarly articles and handbooks when giving reasons for their decisions. Academics still have great influence on the interpretation of criminal statutes through numerous commentaries on the Penal Code, as well as learned treatises, handbooks, and monographs on issues of criminal law.

E. Process

1. Adversarial/Inquisitorial

The structure of the criminal process in Germany is still heavily influenced by the inquisitorial tradition. Although the ancient inquisitorial judicial pretrial procedure was abolished in 1975 and the defense has obtained far-reaching participation rights, especially in the trial phase, the process is a unilateral "search for the truth" conducted by the public prosecutor before trial and again by the court when a formal accusation has been filed. According to the Code of Criminal Procedure (§ 244 (2) Code of Criminal Procedure), the trial court is responsible for gathering all evidence that is needed to arrive at a decision. The parties can, if they so choose, remain passive at the trial stage, and the defense does not have any obligation whatsoever to present evidence. The defendant can instead rely on the presumption of innocence and on the court's effort to bring out the truth.

Since the 1980s the ancient procedural structure has undergone a marked change through the advance of consensual dispositions. Without a basis in written law, in practice a great number of criminal judgments resulted from negotiations between the trial court, the defense, and the prosecution.[21] Typically, the court offered the defendant a lenient sentence if the defendant in turn confessed to the crime charged and thereby made a lengthy (or any) presentation of evidence unnecessary. In 2009 the practice of negotiating criminal sentences was eventually written into a new provision (§ 257c Code of Criminal Procedure), which specifies certain ground rules of the procedure, including the possibility for the defendant to withdraw a confession when the court deviates from the agreed-on sentence.[22] The legal authorization of sentence bargaining does not formally abandon the inquisitorial structure of the criminal process; according to the law, the court remains responsible for determining the relevant facts of the case.[23] But in effect, sentence bargaining often turns issues of substantive criminal into mere bargaining chips, with the defendant offering a carefully worded limited "confession" that allows the court to hand down exactly the sentence that the parties and the presiding judge had agreed on.

2. Jury/Written Opinions

In line with the inquisitorial model, courts are obliged to issue written opinions when they pass judgment. Even first-instance trial courts have to give elaborate reasons for their verdict and sentence, including the evaluation of evidence. The duty to explain the judgment in writing is greatly reduced when all parties have waived their right to appeal (§ 267 (4) Code of Criminal Procedure). That is another reason for the advance of negotiated judgments, because plea bargains often include a tacit agreement not to file an appeal against the judgment.

Although Germany does not have a jury system, laypersons participate in most trials for nonpetty offenses. Offenses expected to be sanctioned by more than two years' imprisonment are tried before mixed panels consisting of professional and lay judges. These mixed panels can have different configurations (one professional judge and two laypersons, two persons of each group, or three professional judges and two lay judges), but under all circumstances lay judges can block a conviction if they vote together.[24] Lay judges serve for terms of five years. They are chosen by a committee elected by the local city or community council. Although deliberations of courts are secret, it is well known that in most cases lay judges go along with what the professional judges suggest. Appellate courts do not have any lay participation.

II. GENERAL PART

A. Theories of Punishment

According to prevailing legal theory, the general purpose of criminal law is the protection of certain individual and collective interests. The threat of punishment is expected to deter potential violators from committing offenses; the general purpose of criminal law is thus to *prevent* crime.[25]

Whenever someone has nevertheless committed a criminal act and the issue of punishing that person arises, the main purpose of imposing a criminal sanction is not preventive but *retributive*. The Penal Code (§ 46 (1)) gives some guidance in this respect: "The offender's culpability [*Schuld*] is the basis for the determination of the sentence. The effect that the sentence can be expected to have on the offender's future life in society shall be taken into account." This provision informs courts' sentencing decisions and at the same time gives an indication of the purposes of criminal punishment. The culpability[26] orientation of criminal sentencing indicates that the main purpose of punishment is retributive, and there is consensus that the amount of punishment the offender "deserves" for the offense is the maximum a court can impose (principle of proportionality).[27] That means that the court cannot give the offender a sentence higher than what he or she "deserves," even if considerations of deterrence or rehabilitation might prompt a longer prison term. According to the courts, guilt proportionality also demarcates the lowest threshold of punishment: even for rehabilitative reasons, the court must not impose a sentence so lenient as to be out of proportion to the seriousness of the offense; the effect of the sentence on the offender's future life shall only "be taken into account," as the Penal Code puts it.[28] German law provides for special sanctions (*Maßregeln der Besserung und Sicherung*, measures of rehabilitation and security) that are not regarded as punitive but as responsive to an offender's continuing dangerousness.[29]

Each statutory crime definition states a sentence range; courts must choose a sentence within that range. Only genocide by killing (§ 6 (1) no. 1 International Crimes Code)[30] and murder (§ 211 PC) prescribe imprisonment for life as the only possible penalty.[31]

B. Liability Requirements

In analyzing criminal liability, German theory distinguishes three (or four) steps. The first step concerns the question whether a person has fulfilled each element of the statutory description of an offense (*Tatbestandsmäßigkeit*). This includes both objective and subjective (e.g., intention or negligence) elements. In the second step, one asks whether the person's conduct was unlawful (*Rechtwidrigkeit*) or was justified because of exceptional circumstances, as when the person acted in legitimate self-defense. The third step of analysis is to ask for the person's individual accountability for the wrongdoing (*Schuld*), which can be excluded, for example, by the person being psychotic or totally drunk at the time of the commission of the offense (see section II.E in this chapter). Most authors recognize a fourth step of analysis at which policy elements of individual punishability are being discussed (*Strafbarkeit*). These include, for example, abandonment of attempt (§ 24 PC) and making wrong statements in court in order to protect oneself from prosecution for a crime (§ 157 PC).

The strict distinction between wrongfulness, on the one hand, and the issues of blameworthiness and punishability, on the other hand, is a characteristic of German law. This distinction is important theoretically because it draws the line between conduct that is normatively acceptable and conduct that is criminally "wrong." Although a person cannot be punished for committing a wrongful act when he or she did not act culpably or is for some policy reason not deemed punishable, the mere existence of a wrongful act is relevant in several respects. For example, for accessory liability, as well as for the crimes of receiving stolen goods and money laundering (§§ 259, 261 PC), it is necessary only that the main actor committed a "wrongful" criminal act (it is not necessary that the person acted culpably). Moreover, a person who committed a wrongful criminal act without having acted culpably can be subjected to a measure of rehabilitation and security, for example, being committed to a psychiatric hospital (§ 63 PC).

1. Objective/Actus Reus
i. Act

Unless an offense is defined as an omission (see section I.B.1.ii in this chapter), an act attributable to the offender is a necessary prerequisite of criminal liability. The definition of an act was a central issue in the debates of the 1950s and 1960s.[32] There is now widespread agreement that a person can be held liable only for voluntary bodily movements (including speech), not for effects brought about by movements beyond his or her control, such as sudden spasms or sleepwalking.[33] A person does not act when he or she is being used by another as a physical instrument, for example, being pushed into a swimming pool and falling on another person who is thereby drowned. But in many cases where an involuntary movement has caused harm, the person can be held liable if he or she omitted to take precautions against doing harm while in an unconscious state. For example, a mother who takes her newborn into her bed and smothers the baby in her sleep can be held criminally liable for negligent manslaughter (or even murder if she acted intentionally) for the prior conduct of taking the baby into her bed without taking care to protect the child from possible harm.

ii. Omission

German criminal law contains several offense definitions that do not require an act but attach liability to remaining passive in a given situation. For example, a person who does nothing in an emergency situation when he or she can reasonably be expected to render assistance to persons in danger is punishable for omitting help (§ 323c PC), and a person who learns of an impending serious crime and refrains from warning the potential victim and from alerting the police is liable for not reporting planned offenses (§ 138 PC). In these instances anyone can be a potential offender by omission, and liability does not require that any negative consequence ensue from the offender's passivity.[34]

A person can also be criminally liable for mere nonfeasance when he or she is under a legal duty to avert a particular harm and neglects to fulfill that duty. In that case the offender is punished according to the statutory provision that is applicable to actively bringing about the harm. For example, a mother who passively watches as her toddler walks into a pool and drowns will be punished for murder by omission. The Penal Code (§ 13) provides: "Whoever omits to avert a consequence that is part of a statutory offense description [*Tatbestand*] is punishable according to that statute only if he is legally responsible for averting that consequence and when the omission is equivalent to actively committing the offense."

The main problem with this statutory definition of commission by omission is the reference to being "legally responsible for averting that consequence." Nowhere does the written law explain under what circumstances such "legal responsibility" arises. The courts have developed four grounds that can give rise to a duty to act when the risk of harm arises: an explicit statutory obligation, a contractual or quasi-contractual obligation, an unlawful creation or increase of risk attributable to the actor, and a social duty based on living together.[35] These are fairly broad categories that can overlap in particular instances, and although there is broad agreement on the existence of a duty to act in several situations,[36] opinions differ with respect to others. Problematic and contested issues include the following: Does an employer have a duty to prevent his employee from committing criminal offenses against customers of his business? Under what conditions does a producer have a duty to recall products that can be harmful to customers?[37] Does one have a duty to actively help a person one has previously injured in legitimate self-defense? To what extent is one obliged to become active to rescue a more distant relative or an estranged spouse?[38] The courts determine these and similar issues on a case-by-case basis, without clear guidance by the legislature.[39]

If a person has violated a legal duty to avert a harm as defined in an offense description, and the harm has occurred, the person is liable only if he or she could have averted the harm by fulfilling the duty to act. If, for example, a mother sitting at the seashore does nothing although she sees that her child swimming outside is close to drowning in the high waves, she cannot be held responsible for "causing"[40] the child's eventual death by her remaining passive when she cannot swim and there was no means available to obtain help from others. Doubts whether a defendant could have averted the harm must—like any factual doubt—be resolved in the defendant's favor.[41]

If liability for omission has been established, the offender is convicted of the offense that he or she should have averted. For example, a husband who knowingly fails to call a doctor to his seriously ill wife and thus brings about her death will be convicted of murder or intentional manslaughter (§§ 211, 212 PC). His sentence can, however, be reduced because of the fact that his wrongful conduct may be less reprehensible than actively killing his wife (§ 13 (2) PC).

iii. Status

A mere status (e.g., being a drug addict) cannot lead to criminal liability. There are, however, offense descriptions that come close to proscribing a status, for example, being a member of a criminal association (§ 129 (1) PC) or illegally possessing narcotics (§ 29 (1) no. 3 Narcotics Law).[42] But in both cases the offender must have brought about the proscribed status by some prior act, for example, by joining the criminal association or buying illegal drugs.

Some offenses require that the offender hold a certain status. For example, accepting bribes (§ 332 PC) is an offense that can be committed only by public servants, and only witnesses and expert witnesses can be guilty of giving false testimony (§ 153 PC). In such cases a person who lacks the required personal capacity can be liable only as an accessory, and the sentence is reduced in relation to that of the main offender (§ 28 (1) PC).

2. *Subjective*/Mens Rea/Mental Element
   i. Intent

According to the Penal Code (§ 15), only intentional commission of a crime is punishable unless the statute explicitly extends liability to negligent conduct. Many offense descriptions, especially those of offenses against property, do not include negligence and thus limit criminal liability to intentional conduct.

Generally, intent has been defined as the will to realize all objective elements of a crime definition, coupled with knowledge that these elements exist.[43] German doctrine distinguishes three forms of intent, namely, intention (*Absicht*), knowledge (*Wissentlichkeit*), and conditional intent (*bedingter Vorsatz*).[44] If the statute does not provide otherwise, any form of intent is sufficient. Sometimes a statute explicitly states that only one or another of these forms suffices to establish criminal liability; for example, obstruction of criminal justice (§ 258 PC) requires that the offender "intentionally or knowingly" renders impossible the deserved punishment of another offender, and to be punishable for malicious libel (§ 187 PC), the offender must spread defamatory information about someone "despite better knowledge" (*wider besseres Wissen*), that is, knowing about the falsehood of the allegation.

Intention is characterized by the fact that it is the offender's primary purpose to achieve what the crime definition describes; it is not necessary that the offender is convinced that he or she will obtain that goal. For example, an assailant acts with the intention to kill his victim if that is the purpose of shooting at him; it does not matter if the actor, because of the great distance at which he shoots, is not certain that he will actually hit the intended victim. In *knowledge*, on the other hand, the cognitive element of intent is dominant: an offender acts with knowledge when he or she is (almost) certain that the act will bring about a certain result; in that case it is irrelevant whether this result is emotionally welcome. Thus a husband who gives a strong poison to his wife, who is suffering from terminal cancer, kills her knowingly even though he may greatly regret her death. The most controversial form of intent is *conditional intent*.[45] In this form of intent, both the cognitive and the volitional element are reduced. Typically, the actor recognizes only the possibility that a certain (prohibited) result will follow from the act and takes the risk (for example, the actor throws a brick from the rooftop onto a street, knowing that pedestrians are passing below). Some writers regard the knowledge of risk as sufficient for intent because by doing the risky act the perpetrator shows that he or she disregards the interests of the (potential or actual) victim.[46] The courts and the majority of writers require an additional volitional element, often defined as "approvingly taking into account" (*billigend in Kauf nehmen*) the possibility of a harmful outcome.[47] In homicide cases the courts sometimes use this formula to declare nonintentional the life-endangering acts of defendants whom they regard as generally hesitant to kill someone.[48] The postulated volitional element of conditional intent thus permits the courts to distinguish between defendants on the basis of their general character and to refrain from convicting those whom they regard as "good guys" of intentional (attempted) homicide.[49]

    ii. Recklessness and Negligence

German law does not recognize recklessness as a separate type of subjective attitude toward the possible consequence of one's act. Many cases that in other jurisdictions are regarded as endangering or causing harm recklessly would in Germany be treated as instances of conditional intent (see section II.B.2.i in this chapter). If, however, the actor lacks the volitional element of "approving" of the result, German courts may find that person guilty only of negligence.[50]

German doctrine has long recognized "conscious" negligence, which occurs when the actor is aware of a risk but thinks (or hopes) that the harmful result will not come about even if he or she performs an act he or she knows to be dangerous. In the example given earlier, the man who threw a brick from the rooftop onto the street below may be deemed to have acted only with conscious negligence when he told himself, "There is a risk that the brick will hit someone, but I don't think it will."[51] "Conscious" negligence is treated as one of two forms of negligence and is thus punishable only when the statute specifically provides for negligence liability.[52]

In general, there are four prerequisites for liability for criminal negligence:

1. The actor can foresee the risk for a protected interest.
2. The actor violates a duty of care with respect to the protected interest.
3. Harm as defined by the statute occurs.[53]
4. The offender could have avoided the harm by careful conduct.

Much has been written about possible sources and standards of due care.[54] But in fact the standard of care in any individual case derives not from general rules but from what risk the actor can foresee. If a situation is such as to alert a careful citizen to potential harm, the actor must do everything necessary and within his or her power to avoid the occurrence of harm.[55] For example, if a small child drives his bicycle in the middle of a highway, the driver of an oncoming car must swerve to the right or to the left in order to save the child from harm, regardless of what road traffic rules have to say about the use of the right or left lane.

The standard of foreseeability, as well as of care, is to be determined on the basis of the defendant's individual capabilities, not by an objective standard. A defendant therefore cannot be convicted of a negligent offense if he or she was, because of some cognitive defect, unable to foresee a risk that an average person could have foreseen. For example, a car driver who suddenly becomes drowsy because of a disease of which he had not previously been aware cannot be held liable for negligent wounding of a cyclist whom the driver was unable to recognize because of his sudden drowsiness.[56] But the subjective standard does not save the driver from criminal responsibility when he was aware of the defect, because in that case he could have foreseen the risk of an accident and should therefore have abstained from driving altogether.[57]

3. Theories of Liability

German law recognizes criminal liability for attempts and complicity, but these are not treated as separate crimes but as special forms of liability for the "main" offense. For example, a person who unsuccessfully tries to kill another will be convicted not of a separate crime of "attempt" but of attempted murder, and the sanction will be taken from the sentence range provided for murder, although the court can impose a less severe sentence (§ 23 (2) PC).

i. Inchoate Crimes
  a. Attempt

Attempts to commit an offense are generally punishable with respect to serious offenses (*Verbrechen*);[58] with respect to less serious offenses, attempt liability exists only when specifically provided by statute (§ 23 (1) PC).[59] To be punishable for attempt, the perpetrator must have had intent with respect to committing the offense and must have immediately set out to commit the offense (§ 22 PC). The attempt offender must thus possess the full *mens rea* as required by the relevant statutory definition of the crime.[60] With respect to the *actus reus*, attempt liability does not presuppose that the actor already completed a part of the activity described in the offense definition, but the actor must have come very close to taking that first step.

The courts often use the formula that an attempt exists when the actor, in accordance with an individual plan, has advanced so far that he or she need not take any further substantial intermediate step before doing what the statute defines as criminal conduct.[61] That formula still needs to be adapted to each individual situation, but it gives an indication that attempt liability should not be extended to mere preparatory acts. Modern jurisprudence has been rather hesitant to establish attempt liability when the actor was not very close to doing the act proscribed. For example, a defendant was acquitted of charges of attempted robbery when he rang at the door of the intended victim's apartment, but the victim did not open the door;[62] and a person who secretly burned an insured object was held not to have committed attempted fraud of the insurance company as long as he did not report the loss to the company.[63]

The fact that it is impossible to commit the offense by the means or at the time chosen by the perpetrator does not exclude attempt liability. Under German law, the would-be thief who reaches into an empty pocket can be convicted of attempted larceny. If the perpetrator's plan was clearly unreasonable (*grober Unverstand*), he or she still remains punishable, but the court can reduce the sentence or refrain from punishment altogether (§ 23 (3) PC). This would apply, for example, to a woman who drinks lots of coffee in the mistaken belief that she could thereby abort her foetus. But any attempt to commit an offense logically requires that there exist a relevant criminal prohibition. Hence a man who thinks that he commits a crime by cheating on his wife cannot be convicted of attempted adultery because adultery is no longer a criminal offense under German law.

The Penal Code provides for impunity for those who voluntarily abandon an attempt (§ 24). Liability for attempt is extinguished when the perpetrator refrains from taking the last steps he or she deems necessary for the completion of the offense or when the perpetrator, after having done everything necessary to bring about the desired consequence, becomes active and prevents the harm from occurring. The first alternative would apply to a burglar who breaks into a house and then retreats without taking anything with him; the second alternative covers the situation of a man who, with the intent to kill his victim, inflicts a life-threatening injury but then rushes the victim to the hospital, where his life is saved. In these cases the actor will be acquitted of an attempt to steal or to kill, respectively, but liability for completed offenses (breaking and entering in the first example, dangerous assault in the second) remains intact. Abandonment is recognized only if it is done voluntarily, that is, without being forced by external factors that make completion impossible or significantly more risky for the offender. The law even grants impunity to a person who, after having committed an attempt, only tries to save the victim when the harmful consequence has in fact been averted by others, or when the victim was never really at risk (§ 24 (1), 2d sent. PC). Thus an arsonist who subsequently calls the fire brigade will not be punished even if others had, unknown to him, already extinguished the flames or the fire had gone out by itself. The courts have interpreted § 24 of the Penal Code very liberally, granting impunity even when the defendant had reached his goal and only refrained from doing "extra" harm. In one case the defendant wished to give a "warning" to his victim and fired a gun at him, voluntarily risking the victim's death. The victim was injured, and the defendant thought that he was sufficiently "warned" and walked away. The Federal Court of Appeals acquitted the defendant of the charge of attempted murder, arguing that he could have fired more shots at the victim and therefore that he voluntarily abandoned his earlier attempt (done with "conditional intent") of killing him.[64]

b. Conspiracy

An agreement of two or more persons to commit a crime is regarded as an inchoate form of committing the crime; the conspirators' sentence is therefore derived from the sentence range provided for the offense they had planned. Agreeing to commit a crime is punishable only with respect to serious offenses with a minimum sentence of one year's imprisonment (§ 30 (2) PC). A conspiracy requires a serious agreement to commit the crime together, that is, as co-perpetrators.[65] It is also punishable to attempt to incite another to commit a serious offense, to offer to commit a serious offense, or to accept such an offer (§ 30 (1) and (2) PC).

A conspirator who prevents the commission of the offense gains impunity (§ 31 no. 3 PC). The same applies when the offense is not carried out for other reasons or is carried out without the participation of the co-conspirator and he or she has tried to prevent its commission (§ 31 (2) PC).

Convictions for conspiracy are rare because liability for conspiracy is superseded by punishability for participation in the completed or attempted offense.

ii. Complicity

German law distinguishes three forms of perpetratorship and two forms of accessorial liability. According to the Penal Code, whoever commits an offense individually or through another person is liable as a perpetrator (§ 25 (1)), and the same applies to two or more persons who jointly commit an offense (§ 25 (2)). Instigators (*Anstifter*) are not regarded as perpetrators but are punished equally (§ 26 PC), whereas mere aiders (*Gehilfen*) receive lesser punishment (§ 27 PC). Instigators and aiders are punishable only if the person with whom they had interacted commits an intentional and wrongful offense;[66] it is not necessary that the main perpetrator have acted culpably.

The distinction between these five forms of complicity is sometimes difficult. Problems arise, in particular, when it becomes necessary to distinguish perpetrators through another from instigators, and co-perpetrators from aiders. The courts have long relied on subjective factors to draw those distinctions: in order to be a perpetrator of any kind, it is necessary, according to long-standing jurisprudence, to have the mind-set of a perpetrator (*animus auctoris*) or the will to commit the offense oneself. The characteristic of a mere accomplice, by contrast, is that person's will to support another (*animus socii*).[67] In recent years the courts have moved away from this strictly subjective approach toward a holistic one, evaluating all objective and subjective elements of the situation.[68] Many academic writers have rejected the courts' subjective distinction between perpetrators and mere accessories and have instead suggested an objective criterion: perpetrators are those who "dominate" the commission of the offense (*Tatherrschaft*), in other words, those who have control over whether and how the offense is carried out. In most cases, both approaches lead to similar results.

The concept of co-perpetratorship (*Mittäterschaft*) covers situations in which none of the persons involved completely fulfills all elements of the offense.[69] If, for example, A forcefully restrains the victim while B takes the victim's wallet out of his jacket, neither A nor B applies force *and* takes away the victim's wallet, but both A and B can be held liable for robbery if they worked together in accordance with a common plan; in that case their respective acts are attributed to each co-perpetrator. Co-perpetratorship requires a common plan shared by all accomplices. That plan can also be developed nonverbally, spontaneously, and even while one offender is already in the process of committing the offense. In accordance with the theory of *Tatherrschaft* (domination of the commission of the offense), a person can be a co-perpetrator only if the common plan assigns to him or her a responsible role so that he or she can codetermine the perpetration of the offense; persons who have only assisting roles cannot be co-perpetrators but only helpers. According to the majority view, it is not necessary for a co-perpetrator to be personally present at the place where the plan is being carried out; even a gang leader who has designed the criminal plan but leaves to others the actual performance can be a co-perpetrator.[70]

Perpetration through another or indirect perpetration (*mittelbare Täterschaft*) also relies on the concept of control over the offense. In this case the perpetrator exercises control by means of another person. Originally the doctrine of indirect perpetration was developed to cover cases that could not be punished as instigation because the person carrying out the criminal act did not act wrongfully or did not act with intent, as required for instigation (§ 26 PC). For example, a doctor who leads a nurse to believe that the medication she is to give the patient is innocuous when the doctor has exchanged it for a poisonous substance cannot be punished as a "direct" perpetrator because he does not administer the poison. Nor is there a common plan that could make the participants liable as co-perpetrators, and the doctor cannot be an instigator because the nurse does not kill the patient with intent. To resolve this doctrinal dilemma, indirect perpetratorship was introduced to make possible the conviction of the evil doctor for murder. Indirect perpetratorship thus requires domination of the perpetrator over the acts of another person who actually performs the criminal act. Domination can be exercised through superior information (in this example the doctor has better information on the qualities of the substance administered to the patient) or psychological control (as in the situation where the doctor holds a gun to the nurse's head and threatens to shoot her unless she administers the poisonous substance to the patient). For a long time, indirect perpetration was equated with the use of a somehow "innocent" agent, that is, a person who is not (fully) punishable for the act he or she performed.[71] In recent years, however, German jurisprudence has recognized a form of indirect perpetration through hierarchical control of the agent, as in the case of a dictatorial regime the leaders of which order soldiers to shoot at innocent fugitives. Although the soldiers can be held liable for murder, the leaders (in that case, the military leaders of the German Democratic Republic) were also convicted of murder committed as indirect perpetrators.[72] More recently, the Federal Court of Appeals has extended this doctrine of perpetration through culpable agents to business leaders[73]—an extension that has met with some criticism in academic literature.[74]

Instigation (*Anstiftung*) resembles indirect perpetration in that the instigator exerts psychological influence on the person who performs the criminal act. But an instigator does not "dominate" or control the perpetration of the offense; he or she only plants the idea in the perpetrator's mind, and it is the latter who decides whether and how exactly to commit the act. According to the majority view, it is not necessary for an instigator to establish direct contact with the perpetrator; creating a situation that provokes another person to commit a particular offense can also be regarded as instigation.[75] The instigator's intent must extend both to the offense to be committed and to the instigation of it. With respect to the offense, it is sufficient that the instigator has a correct notion of the broad contours of the act to be carried out. The instigator need not give the perpetrator precise indications about the proper time and place, but on the other hand, it is not sufficient for criminal instigation just to say, "You might commit a crime in order to obtain money."[76] Finally, instigation requires planting an idea in the perpetrator's mind; it is thus impossible to instigate a crime with someone who is already determined to commit that crime.[77]

A conviction for aiding (*Beihilfe*) in the perpetration of an offense requires that the aider have given some support, knowing that the main perpetrator was going to commit or was in the process of committing an (intentional) offense.[78] There need not be any direct contact between the perpetrator and the aider, and the perpetrator does not even have to know about the support that is given.[79] The aider's act must have facilitated the commission of the offense; however, according to the majority view, the aider's contribution need not have been a *conditio sine qua non* for the success of the criminal enterprise.[80] The courts also treat mere psychological support (e.g., verbal encouragement) of the perpetrator as punishable aiding, although it is difficult in such cases to prove a causal nexus between the aider's words or acts and the commission of the offense. In recent years courts and writers have engaged in a spirited controversy whether "normal" professional conduct can be punished as aiding in an offense. Examples are a bank teller helping the bank's client transfer money to a foreign state in order to hide the funds from tax authorities, or an owner of a hardware store selling a crowbar to a customer when he knows that the customer plans to use the crowbar in a burglary.[81] The Federal Court of Appeals has not recognized a general exception for "professional" activities but has limited liability for aiding in these situations to persons who know (and not only take into account the possibility) that these acts will be used for criminal purposes.[82]

iii. Corporate Criminal Liability

German criminal law provides only for liability of natural persons. According to traditional German doctrine, corporations cannot be subject to criminal punishment because they cannot act, they cannot be blamed, and the morally reprobative element of criminal punishment does not apply to them.[83] But it is possible to impose administrative, non-criminal fines on corporations if one of their representatives or a high-level employee has committed a criminal offense by which a duty of the corporation was violated or the corporation was enriched.[84] Such fines can be as high as 1 million euros (approximately U.S. $1.25 million).

4. Causation

Whenever the definition of an offense includes a harmful consequence (e.g., death or injury of a person, monetary damage), it is necessary to prove that the consequence can be attributed to the offender's act. The primary element of attribution is a causal link between the offender's conduct and the consequence. German criminal courts regard as a cause any act without which the effect would not have come about; they do not distinguish between proximate causes and more remote causes. If two persons have independently acted in such a way that their contributions worked together to bring about the effect (for example, A, as well as B, give X one ounce of poison, and two ounces were necessary to kill X), each contributor is deemed to have caused the effect. In the exceptional case of two independent sufficient causes acting simultaneously to bring about a consequence, each factor is regarded as causal. If, in the example just posed, both A and B independently pour two ounces of poison into X's drink and X dies after drinking the lethal potion in one gulp, both A and B are regarded as having caused X's death.[85] Similarly, each member of a board of directors who supported a unanimous board decision in favor of a criminal undertaking of the company is deemed to have caused the offense; that person cannot claim that a single vote in opposition would not have changed the outcome.[86] Generally, hypothetical alternatives are not taken into account when analyzing causation; if A shoots at B and inflicts a lethal wound from which B dies, A is deemed to have caused B's death even if B was suffering from terminal cancer.[87]

Causation is only the first step toward attributing a consequence to the perpetrator's act. A consequence that the perpetrator has caused cannot be attributed to him or her if that act did not unjustifiably increase a risk (for example, a driver hits a pedestrian when the driver has followed the traffic rules and the pedestrian has unforeseeably slipped and has fallen onto the street), if the consequence was not one to be averted by the rule the perpetrator violated (in the example just given, the driver had been speeding five minutes before the incident; had he stayed within the permissible speed limit, he would not have been at the place when the pedestrian slipped), or if a voluntary act of risk taking on the part of the victim or a third person intervened (in the example here, the pedestrian threw himself before the speeding driver's car in order to commit suicide). Many details of the requirements of "objective attribution" (*objektive Zurechnung*) of harmful consequences are still subject to debate.[88]

C. Defenses

1. Types of Defense

German law does not have a concept of "defenses" in the sense that a defendant would have to come forward with certain grounds that exclude punishability. Rather, a court can convict someone only when it has found that all requirements of punishability exist in that person's case. What other legal systems term *defenses* in Germany are (negative) requirements for conviction, and the court is responsible for making sure that there are no grounds of justification or excuse standing in the way of convicting the defendant.

Although any distinction between the "prosecution case" and "defense case" is thus procedurally irrelevant, German doctrine distinguishes several categories of grounds of nonconvictability. A primary distinction is drawn between substantive and procedural grounds. For example, the expiration of a statute of limitation is considered a procedural limit to conviction, with the consequence that the strict prohibition of retroactive changes to the defendant's disadvantage (Art. 103 sec. 2 Basic Law; see section I.C in this chapter) does not apply.[89] Among substantive grounds that hinder a conviction,[90] the law distinguishes between those that permit the actor to (exceptionally) do what is normally defined as a criminal offense (justification) and those that only make it possible to excuse the actor's wrongful behavior because of individual defects or an unusually stressful situation (excuses). Finally, there exists a rather vaguely defined group of circumstances that exclude punishability for various policy reasons, for example, the averting of harm from the (planned) offense (§ 24 PC) or consideration for the perpetrator's felt need to protect himself or herself from criminal prosecution for another offense (§ 258 (5) PC).

2. Burden of Proof

As mentioned in section I.E.1, the fact that a circumstance has an exonerating rather than an incriminating effect is not relevant for the criminal process. In either case it is up to the court to determine whether the circumstance in question exists because the court is responsible for establishing all facts relevant for its judgment. Likewise, in the process before trial the public prosecutor is obliged to investigate both incriminating and exonerating circumstances (§ 160 (2) Code of Criminal Procedure). The defendant has no burden of proof whatsoever and need not even mention a "defense." For example, the court can investigate the defendant's possible mental illness at the time of the offense even when the defendant claims to have been in perfect mental health. However, courts will in practice pursue certain lines of investigation only if there is some indication that grounds hindering conviction exist. For example, if the defendant is accused of assaulting another man in a bar, the court will not look into the issue of possible self-defense unless there is some factual indication that the defendant might have been attacked first. It is thus factually beneficial for the defendant to alert the court to possible grounds of justification or excuse.

D. Justifications

1. Necessity

The justification of necessity (*Notstand*) is recognized in the Penal Code (§ 34):

> A person who commits an offense in a situation of present risk for life, health, freedom, honor, property, or any other legal interest does not act unlawfully if this risk cannot otherwise be averted, if this person acts in order to avert this risk from himself or herself or another person, and if, upon weighing the conflicting interests, in particular, the legal interests involved and the degree of risk to each of them, the protected interest substantially outweighs the interest affected. This applies only to the extent that committing the offense is an appropriate means for averting the risk.

This complicated formulation, introduced into the Penal Code in 1975, was the result of long scholarly debates. The reason for acknowledging necessity as a ground of justification is not altogether clear. The most plausible explanation refers to an obligation of every citizen to show solidarity to fellow citizens in severe distress; in such a situation one is obliged to tolerate the loss of one's own legally protected interests if that is necessary to avert substantially greater harm from others.[91] The field of application of this defense is very limited because committing an offense must be the only way to resolve a dilemma, and there must be a clear difference of importance between the interest negatively affected and the interest saved. Because the interests of privacy and dignity also form part of the equation, it is questionable whether invasions of an innocent bystander's bodily integrity can ever be justified under the heading of necessity. In any event, necessity does not permit taking a person's life, because one person's life can never "substantially outweigh" the importance of another person's life, regardless of the age and state of health of the persons involved. According to long-standing German philosophical and legal tradition, the inviolability of life holds true even if several lives could be saved by killing a single innocent person. Since human life constitutes the highest value, it cannot be outweighed even by a multitude of other human lives,[92] so that a killing can never be justified under § 34 of the Penal Code.

Opinions differ whether cases of duress by threats can be subsumed under § 34 of the Penal Code. If, for example, A holds a gun to B's head and thereby forces him to beat up C, B would, according to the majority view, be justified because he perpetrates a lesser evil (harming C's health) in order to protect a more important interest (his life).[93] But a minority view claims that intentionally harming an innocent person can never be justified; this view would grant B only the excuse of duress (§ 35 PC; see section II.E.4 in this chapter).[94]

2. Self-Defense

Self-defense (*Notwehr*) has always been recognized as a ground of justification. The Penal Code defines self-defense as "the defense that is necessary to avert a present unlawful attack from oneself or from another person" (§ 32 (2)). This definition includes defense of others, which thus follows the same rules as defense of oneself.[95] The reason behind recognizing self-defense as a justification is twofold: a person must have a right to preserve his or her life, health, and property when he or she has been unlawfully attacked; and the defender represents the interest of the community in upholding the legal order.

Given these strong rationales, the right to self-defense has traditionally been "strong" and aggressive in Germany. Most important, the law does not expect a person to retreat in the face of an imminent unlawful attack. Rejecting the attack thus does not have to be the last resort, but the attacked person can stand his ground even if he could have averted harm to himself, as well as to the aggressor, by retreating. When the law speaks of defense "that is necessary," that restriction only refers to the choice among several available means of (aggressive) defense; for example, the defender must not shoot and kill the aggressor when it would have been sufficient to strike him down with his fist. But in considering the necessity of a certain course of action, the courts emphasize that the defender has the right to use a means that averts the attack reliably and permanently; the defender need not engage in a fight the outcome of which is uncertain.[96]

Nevertheless, there are certain limits to the right to defend oneself or another. For example, a person who has voluntarily or even negligently through unlawful conduct provoked an attack cannot reject that attack with full force but must use other, less harmful means to de-escalate the conflict if such other means are available.[97] Similarly, if the attacker is a child or an insane person, the defender must try to retreat or otherwise avert the attack instead of using potentially fatal means. In such cases the defender cannot (fully) rely on the second "leg" of the rationale for allowing self-defense, namely, the interest of the community in upholding the legal order. Because § 32 of the Penal Code does not provide for any restriction on the right to self-defense, limiting this right might conflict with the principle of legality, because any restriction of the grounds of justification leads to an extension of the criminally prohibited area; but the courts have nevertheless regarded the introduction of restrictions based on "social ethics" as necessary.[98]

A person who goes beyond the limits of necessary self-defense by using excessive force acts unlawfully. But if that person was in a state of confusion, fear, or terror due to the attack, the act will be excused (§ 33 PC).

3. Consent

Although the Penal Code does not mention consent as a justification, it is generally agreed that the consent of a person affected by a harmful act can render that act lawful. In some offense definitions, for example, in rape (§ 177 PC) or breaking and entering (§ 123 PC), acting against the will of the victim is part of the definition; a person who enters a house or has intercourse with another person when that person agrees thus cannot fulfill the definition of the crime. With respect to other offenses, consent can remove the injurious character of the act; if, for example, the owner of a painting agrees that the actor should burn it, the legal definition of "destruction of property" is met, but there is no interest to be protected and hence no use in punishing the actor. Consent thus renders the act of burning lawful.[99]

Consent does not negate unlawfulness in all offenses, however. An individual cannot give valid consent to the violation of communal interests, for example, environmental protection or the safety of road traffic. Nor does the victim's consent permit one to intentionally kill a person. Section 216 of the Penal Code only reduces the punishment for murder and manslaughter in case the perpetrator was motivated to kill by the victim's "serious and express request." In cases of causing bodily harm, the actor is justified by the victim's consent unless the act, regardless of the consent given, violates public morals (*gute Sitten*) (§ 228 PC). The Federal Court of Appeals has interpreted this restriction to apply only to instances of life-threatening or maiming injuries, not to violations of majority moral views as such.[100]

The consent of the person concerned is valid only if it has been given voluntarily and on the basis of full information before the commission of the relevant act. A victim who agrees to being injured or otherwise harmed under duress or under the influence of a mistake about relevant facts cannot be deemed to have consented. According to the majority view, even an error unrelated to the interest affected makes a consent invalid; if, for example, a person agrees to being subjected to painful medical experiments because he has been promised a monetary reward, and the perpetrator never intends to actually give the reward, the perpetrator commits not only fraud but also unlawful bodily assault when he carries out the experiments.[101]

4. Superior Orders

Superior orders as such are not recognized as a grounds of justification or excuse. When a subordinate has been threatened with bodily harm or substantial loss of freedom if he or she refuses to carry out an order to commit a criminal offense, that person may be able to rely on (justifying or excusing) necessity in his or her defense, but the fact that a person has been ordered to commit a crime does not relieve him or her of responsibility.

A special rule applies with respect to military orders in connection with a mistake of law. If a soldier has been ordered to do a criminal act and does not recognize that the act is a criminal offense, he or she will be excused unless it is evident that the act is a criminal offense[102] (§ 5 (1) Military Criminal Law).[103] This rule is somewhat more lenient than the general rule on mistake of law (see section II.E.1 in this chapter).

E. Excuses

1. Mistake/Ignorance of Law or Fact

A mistake of fact with respect to an element of the definition of an offense negates the actor's intent. If, for example, a hunter mistakes a helper for a bear and shoots the helper, he does not have the intent to kill a human being and therefore cannot be punished for intentional homicide. If the mistake resulted from the actor's lack of proper care, that person may well be liable for an offense of negligence (§ 16 (1) PC). If the definition of an offense includes a legal element (for example, theft under § 242 PC requires that the object taken belong to another person, which may depend on rules of property law), the offender acts with intent only if he or she draws correct conclusions with regard to the legal situation.[104]

A factual mistake about an element of a ground of justification technically leaves the actor's intent intact, but German jurisprudence and doctrine treat such mistakes in much the same way as factual mistakes concerning the definition of an offense and therefore do not hold the actor liable for an intentional offense.[105] For example, if A mistakenly believes that B is attacking him and injures B in supposed self-defense, A will not be punished for intentional assault; if his mistake was due to a careless evaluation of the situation, he may be punishable for negligent bodily harm.

Mistakes about factual elements need to be distinguished from pure mistakes of law. In the latter case the perpetrator is fully aware of the factual situation but erroneously assumes that the conduct is not forbidden or is justified. The actor in this situation is deemed to act with intent, since intent does not presuppose a correct evaluation of the legal relevance of one's conduct. But an actor does not act culpably if he or she thought that the behavior was lawful and he or she was unable to avoid this mistake (§ 17 PC).[106] The courts apply fairly strict standards with respect to the possibility of avoiding a mistake of law because they assume that most people learn about the basic rules of socially acceptable conduct as they grow up.[107] If someone violates a more "technical" rule in an area where he or she does business, the courts will often not regard a mistake as unavoidable because the actor may have had the duty to obtain legal advice before entering into a regulated business.[108]

2. Insanity/Diminished Capacity

A person acts without culpability when that person suffers, at the time of committing an offense, from a mental disease, a substantial impairment of consciousness, imbecility, or another mental aberration and is therefore unable to recognize the wrongfulness of his or her conduct or is unable to act according to his or her insight (§ 20 PC). If, for one of the reasons just named, the person's ability to recognize the wrongfulness of his or her conduct or to act according to his or her insight is substantially diminished, that person acts culpably, but the sentence can be reduced (§ 21 PC). This legislative concept leads to a two-step analysis in cases of possible insanity. As a first step, the court has to establish whether the actor suffered from one of the mental defects named in § 20 of the Penal Code; often the court will rely on psychiatric expertise in making a finding on this issue. If the presence of a mental defect has been established, the court must ask whether that defect negated the actor's ability to realize that he or she did wrong or whether he knew that he or she did wrong but was unable to control himself or herself sufficiently to avoid the act. This concept inherently builds on the assumption that a "normal" person has some freedom of will that enables that person to refrain from doing wrong. Most writers justify this assumption as being grounded, regardless of its scientific correctness, in the mutual expectations of people in their social interactions.[109]

It should be noted that a defendant found to have committed a criminal offense in a state of insanity cannot be convicted of the crime but can be committed to a psychiatric hospital as a measure of rehabilitation and security (§ 63 PC).

3. Intoxication

Intoxication as such does not excuse the perpetrator. However, the influence of alcohol or drugs on the perpetrator's mind can be so strong as to be classified as a temporary mental disease, thus permitting a finding of insanity in the sense of §§ 20 and 21 of the Penal Code (see section II.E.2 in this chapter). There is no exact amount of alcohol consumption that leads to temporary insanity,[110] but courts tend to apply § 20 of the Penal Code when a person had, at the time of the offense, a blood alcohol concentration of 0.3 per cent or more. If the perpetrator was unable to control himself or herself or to recognize the wrongfulness of the conduct because of alcohol-induced insanity, the perpetrator will be excused under § 20 of the Penal Code.

The fact that the actor had voluntarily brought about the state of intoxication does not exclude a finding of temporary insanity because § 20 of the Penal Code explicitly refers to the "time of the offense" at which a mental disease must exist to negate culpability. There exists, however, a long-standing doctrine that denies exculpation if the offender had voluntarily intoxicated himself with the intent to commit a (defined) crime at the time when he started to get drunk. German theory speaks of *actio libera in causa* (an act free in its origin). It is questionable, however, whether denying a person the exculpation provided by § 20 of the Penal Code on the basis of an unwritten rule is compatible with the principle of legality.[111] The Federal Court of Appeals has declared the doctrine inapplicable with respect to offense definitions containing a particular act to be performed by the offender (for example, "Whoever drives a vehicle . . ." [§ 316 PC]); in such cases it would violate the principle of legality to maintain that someone who imbibes alcohol in a pub thereby begins to commit the act of "driving a vehicle."[112]

Independently of these considerations, the legislature has created the criminal offense of complete intoxication (*Vollrausch*) (§ 323a PC). Under that statute, it is a criminal offense to intentionally or negligently consume so much alcohol as to reach a state of insanity or diminished responsibility. It is a further condition of punishability that the offender commits an offense in the state of intoxication, but he or she need not even have foreseen this outcome while he or she was still in a culpable state. Under § 323a of the Penal Code, the perpetrator is not punished for the offense committed in the state of intoxication but for the act of intoxication.

4. *Duress*

A person who commits an offense in order to save himself or herself or a relative from an imminent danger will be excused under the following conditions (§ 35 PC):

> A person who commits an unlawful offense acts without culpability when there is a present risk to life, health, or liberty that cannot otherwise be averted and when he or she acts to avert that risk from himself or a relative or another person standing in a close relationship to him or her. This does not apply if the perpetrator could reasonably be expected to accept the risk under the circumstances, especially because the perpetrator had himself caused the risk or because he stood in a special legal relationship.

Like the justification of choice of evils (see section II.D.1 in this chapter), this ground of excuse is called necessity (*Notstand*), but it does not negate the unlawfulness of the act but only provides grounds for negating the actor's criminal responsibility. The reason for this difference lies in the fact that duress applies, in principle, regardless of any proportionality between the interest protected and the interest harmed. For example, a person who kills another in order to protect his own health or liberty could not be justified under § 34 of the Penal Code because the person did not protect the more valuable interest (the victim's life); but he or she can well be excused in accordance with § 35 of the Penal Code. The rationale of duress is society's tolerance for a person acting in a conflict situation where his own or his relative's most important interests are at stake. In such an exceptional situation one may still be expected by the law not to harm others, but one should not be punished if one gives preference to one's selfish interest.

Because of the rather precarious foundation of these grounds of excuse, the legislature has taken care to permit conviction of an offender when equity considerations point toward blaming him or her for the act. Two such considerations have been named in the second sentence of § 35 of the Penal Code: a person who has culpably caused the conflict situation will not be tolerated to resolve the conflict in his or her own favor, sacrificing the interests of an innocent bystander; and a person who has accepted a special duty to deal with certain conflict situations—for example, as a fireman, soldier, or police officer—will not be heard if that person claims that the situation became too risky and that he had to save his own health at the cost of someone else's life. The excuse of duress is also unavailable when the harm done is vastly out of proportion with the interest protected. For example, a person who has mistakenly been arrested cannot rely on § 35 of the Penal Code if that person kills two jail guards in order to escape and thereby avoid a limited loss of liberty.[113]

5. Entrapment

The fact that an offender has been instigated by agents of the state to commit an offense has not been recognized as a defense by German law, but the Federal Court of Appeals has granted a reduction of sentence to a drug dealer who had been put under great pressure by undercover police agents to provide illegal drugs. The actions of these agents were regarded as violative of the principle of fair trial, and the court reduced the offender's sentence as a compensation for not having received a fair trial.[114] A violation of fair-trial principles will be found especially when the dimension of the crime instigated by police agents goes vastly beyond what the offender was suspected to have planned or committed.[115]

F. Sanctions

1. Punishment

German law provides for punishment (*Strafen*) and measures of rehabilitation and security (*Maßregeln der Besserung und Sicherung*). Punishments include imprisonment (§ 38 PC), fines (§ 40 PC), and a temporary prohibition to drive a car (§ 44 PC). Measures of rehabilitation and security, which are to neutralize the offender's continuing dangerousness, include commitment to a psychiatric hospital (§ 63 PC), commitment to an institution for alcohol or drug rehabilitation (§ 64 PC), security detention (§ 66 PC), and revocation of a driver's license (§ 69 PC).

Imprisonment can last from one month to fifteen years or can be for life. Only a few offenses provide for the possibility of life imprisonment, and even when a life sentence has been imposed, the offender can be released on parole after a minimum period of fifteen years (§ 57a PC). Prison terms of up to two years can be suspended; this means that a prison sentence is imposed but will not be executed unless the convict commits new offenses or otherwise violates the conditions of probation (§ 56 PC). German courts make comparatively little use of prison sentences and suspend many of them; in practice, only about 8 percent of convicted defendants actually serve prison sentences.[116]

Fines are imposed in accordance with a day-fine system. The fine imposed is the product of a number of days proportional to the offender's culpability and the amount of a day fine, which depends on the offender's daily income (§ 40 PC). The minimum day fine is one euro; the maximum is 30,000 euros.

Measures of rehabilitation and security can be imposed on persons who have committed an unlawful criminal act and have thereby (and by prior offenses) shown their continuing serious dangerousness. The most severe measure is security detention (*Sicherungsverwahrung*, § 66 PC), which is meant for dangerous recidivists, especially those who committed sexual offenses. Security detention is added to a prison term and can last for the person's natural life. Every two years a court reviews the offender's case and determines whether the person's dangerousness persists (§ 67e (2) PC). Security detention can also be imposed by a court while an offender is serving a prison sentence if new facts become known indicating that the offender, if released after the prison sentence has expired, is likely to commit crimes that cause serious bodily or mental harm (§ 66b PC).

2. Quantity/Quality of Punishment

In determining the sentence, the court[117] must primarily take the offender's blameworthiness into account. The impact of the sentence on the offender's future life in society also has to be considered (§ 46 (1) PC).[118] The statute further lists several factors that should guide the court's sentencing decision, for example, the offender's motivation for committing the crime, the way in which the offense was committed and its consequences, and the prior life and the present living conditions of the offender, as well as the offender's conduct subsequent to the offense, in particular, any effort to compensate the victim (§ 46 (2) PC). These factors are only listed and are not quantified; the court thus remains free to decide how much weight it gives to each factor. A prior criminal record of the defendant is not explicitly listed as a sentencing consideration, but it can be (and normally is) considered under the heading of the offender's "prior life."

In determining the sentence, the court must start from the sentence range that the statute indicates for each offense.[119] The court will then determine whether the case, given all its objective and offender-related factors, is more serious, is less serious, or lies in a middle range compared with "average" cases of the particular offense. The court must accordingly select a sentence close to the top or to the bottom of the sentence range.

German sentencing law discourages the imposition of short prison sentences. According to § 47 of the Penal Code, a prison term of less than six months can be imposed only if special circumstances in the personality of the offender or the need to defend the legal order makes short-term imprisonment necessary. If the court decides to impose a prison sentence of one year or less, there is a presumption that it should be suspended unless considerations of special prevention demand its execution (§ 56 (1) PC).

The court must give reasons in writing for its sentencing decision, and the sentence can be challenged on appeal, both by the defendant and by the prosecution.

3. Death Penalty

The death penalty was abolished in 1949 (Art. 102 Basic Law). It would not be possible to reintroduce the death penalty under the present constitution because its imposition is likely to violate human dignity, and the guarantee of human dignity (Art. 1 sec. 1 Basic Law) cannot be abridged even by constitutional amendment (Art. 79 sec. 3 Basic Law).[120]

III. SPECIAL PART

A. Structure

It is difficult to detect a systemic structure in the Special Part of the German Penal Code. The original concept was to organize the Penal Code around legal interests (*Rechtsgüter*) protected, starting with the interests of the state and moving on to family and then individual interests. Thus, for example, murder and manslaughter (§§ 211, 212 PC) are treated after offenses against the security of the state, as well as offenses against communal interests, such as counterfeiting (§ 146 PC) and perjury (§ 154 PC). Interestingly, within the group of offenses against individual interests, sex offenses (§§ 174–184f PC), as well as violations of personal honor and reputation (§§ 185–187 PC), precede homicide. Offenses against the person are followed by those against property, and toward the end there are again sections that deal with communal interests, for example, arson (§ 306 PC) and environmental offenses (§ 324 PC). In sum, one has to know one's way around the Special Part because there is no clear structure to guide the ignorant.

B. Homicide

1. Murder/Manslaughter

German law distinguishes two forms of intentional homicide, murder (*Mord*, § 211 PC) and manslaughter (*Totschlag*, § 212 PC). Negligent homicide (§ 222 PC) is proscribed separately; the sentence range for that offense (a fine or imprisonment for up to five years) is significantly lower than the sentence range for intentional homicide.

Manslaughter is the intentional killing of another person[121] without aggravating circumstances. Any form of intent (see section II.B.2.i in this chapter) is sufficient for manslaughter, but the perpetrator must at least have willingly taken the risk of causing death. Germany has no felony-murder rule. There is a separate offense of assault with fatal consequences (§ 227 PC), which requires intent to cause bodily harm and negligence as to the death of the victim.

Murder carries a mandatory life sentence. Murder is defined as an intentional homicide aggravated by certain base motives on the part of the offender or by particularly reprehensible means of causing death. The statute (§ 211 PC) lists the following motives, any one of which turns an intentional killing into murder: enjoyment of killing (*Mordlust*), satisfaction of sexual desire, greed, the purpose to make possible or to cover up another offense, or any other base motive. If the killing is committed deviously (*heimtückisch*), cruelly, or with means that endanger third persons, that also turns a homicide into murder. This list of aggravating circumstances has been criticized as arbitrary and overly broad.[122] For example, killing "deviously" has been defined by the courts to cover every situation in which the victim does not expect an attack;[123] this means that regardless of the killer's understandable motivation or other extenuating circumstances, the court must impose life imprisonment if the killer has failed to give the victim advance warning of an impending assault. In spite of the obvious deficiency of the law of homicide in the Penal Code, various reform proposals have been unsuccessful.[124]

2. Provocation

In cases of murder (§ 211 PC), the fact that the offender was provoked by the victim has no influence on the sentence.[125] If the killing is classified as manslaughter, provocation of the offender through an assault or a verbal insult directed at him or her or a relative reduces the sentence to a range between one and ten years' imprisonment if the offender killed the aggressor in the heat of passion (§ 213 PC).

C. Sex Offenses

The Penal Code chapter on sex offenses is built on the idea that it is not the purpose of the criminal law to protect people's views on moral behavior; rather, the aim of prohibiting certain sexual conduct is solely to protect every person's autonomy in the sphere of sexual relations. The core offense is sexual coercion (§ 177 PC). This offense definition covers any act of coercing a person to tolerate sexual acts on his or her[126] body or to perform sexual acts on the offender or another person by force, by threat with an imminent risk for life or health, or by exploiting a situation in which the victim is without protection against the offender's acts. The performance of sexual intercourse under these circumstances (rape) is defined as an aggravated case of sexual coercion (§ 177 (2) no. 1 PC). Children under fourteen years of age are presumed to be incapable of giving valid consent to sexual acts; therefore, any sexual act involving a child is a criminal offense (§ 176 PC). The legislature has also declared criminal the abuse of certain relationships between the offender and the victim for sexual purposes (§§ 174 (1), 174a, 174c PC); in these relationships (for example, teacher/student, warden/prisoner, psychotherapist/patient) the victim typically lacks full autonomy in sexual matters.

Prostitution has been legalized and regulated in Germany. It remains a criminal offense, however, to exploit a prostitute, to supervise and control the prostitute's professional conduct, or to keep the prostitute in a state of organizational dependence (§§ 180a, 181a PC). The rationale of these prohibitions is to safeguard the prostitute's autonomy and to enable him or her to give up prostitution without fear of repercussions. It is also a criminal offense for an adult to perform any sexual act with a person under eighteen years of age in exchange for payment (§ 182 (2) CP).

Pornography as such is not prohibited, but there are numerous limits on its dissemination. There is a general ban on dealing with material that depicts violent sex, sex with animals, or sex with children or juveniles under eighteen years of age (§§ 184a, 184b, 184c PC). With respect to child pornography depicting real or realistic acts, even the mere attempt to obtain or to possess such materials is punishable (§ 184b (4) PC). With respect to other pornography, dissemination to juveniles under eighteen years of age or in such a way that juveniles can easily get access to the materials is prohibited (§ 184 (1) PC).

D. Theft and Fraud

Theft (*Diebstahl*) and fraud (*Betrug*) are separate offense categories under German law.

Theft (§ 242 PC) is the taking of an object against the possessor's will with the intention to unlawfully appropriate the object to oneself or another person. Theft is directed both against property and possession rights, but for the completion of the offense it is sufficient that the perpetrator unlawfully takes possession. In doing so, it must be the offender's purpose to transfer the factual position of an owner to another person (including himself), and he must know that the rightful owner will permanently lose the possibility to exert his proprietary rights over the object. Burglary of a home is an aggravated form of theft (§ 244 (1) no. 3 PC). If a person unlawfully appropriates an object without taking it from someone's possession (for example, the person who has borrowed a book sells it on his own account), that person commits the separate offense of unlawful appropriation (§ 246 PC), which has a lower sentence range than theft. Taking someone else's object only for the purpose of temporarily using it and with the intention of returning it after some time is not a punishable offense except when the object is a motor vehicle or a bicycle (§ 248b PC). It is theft, however, if the object the perpetrator had "borrowed" loses all or much of its value through the extended use. Thus it would be theft to "borrow" a bunch of flowers for three days and then to return them wilted.[127]

The core element of fraud (§ 263 PC) is the deception of the victim, which leads to a self-damaging act (or omission) on the part of the victim resulting in a monetary loss for the victim or a person on whose behalf the victim has acted. Fraud can be committed in a multitude of forms, and many issues concerning this offense are contested. Contrary to theft, a fraud is completed only when the victim has suffered some monetary damage; however, the courts regard a situation where such damage is virtually certain to occur later as completed fraud.[128] For example, if someone takes out a loan from a bank although the debtor knows that he or she will never be able to repay the money, the bank is deemed to have suffered a monetary loss even at the time the loan contract has been made, because the bank's claim for repayment is economically worthless.

A specialty of German law is the offense of violation of trust (*Untreue*, § 266 PC). This offense can be committed by a person who has authority to legally oblige another (natural or legal) person or who has a duty to act in the economic interest of another person. If the trustee violates his duty and thereby causes monetary damage to the other person, he or she is guilty of violation of trust, even if the trustee did not act for his or her own benefit. This offense category has been given a wide field of application. The offense can be committed, for example, by a member of a board of directors of a company who takes an unjustifiable economic risk and thereby causes a loss to the company, or by a city official who orders a plumber employed by the city to make repairs in the perpetrator's private home.

E. "Victimless" Crimes

Many offenses under German law lack an individual victim but affect the community. Examples are environmental crime (§§ 324–330d PC), bribery and taking bribes by public officials (§§ 331–334 PC), and damaging telecommunications or traffic installations (§§ 317, 318 PC). But there are few "morals" offenses that affect only the feelings of persons or attempt to protect people from damaging their own long-term interest.[129] Some of these offenses are said to protect the "public peace"; that is, the prohibited conduct might arouse aggression and could thus eventually lead to violence. Examples are defamation of religious beliefs (§ 166 PC), disturbing a religious service (§ 167 PC), or desecrating graves (§ 168 PC). A similar rationale explains the criminal prohibition of publicly denying or approving of the Holocaust (§ 130 (3) PC).

In the area of sexual morals, few criminal prohibitions still exist that cannot be explained by the need to protect persons from violations of their autonomy in sexual matters (see section III.C in this chapter). One such example may be the punishability of sexual intercourse between siblings (§ 173 (2) PC); the constitutionality of this norm was recently challenged but has been upheld by the Federal Constitutional Court.[130]

The unauthorized possession of narcotics, as well as the production, importation, or selling of narcotic substances, is criminally prohibited (§§ 29–30b Narcotics Law).[131] The alleged rationale of this prohibition is the protection of public health (*Volksgesundheit*). Lower courts have challenged the constitutionality of punishing the possession of soft drugs such as marijuana, but the Federal Constitutional Court did not regard this prohibition as a disproportionate restriction of the freedom of the individual.

SELECTED BIBLIOGRAPHY

Bohlander, Michael. *Principles of German Criminal Law.* Oxford: Hart Publishing, 2009.
Jakobs, Günther. *Strafrecht Allgemeiner Teil,* 2d ed. Berlin: de Gruyter, 1991.
Jescheck, Hans-Heinrich, and Thomas Weigend. *Lehrbuch des Strafrechts: Allgemeiner Teil,* 5th ed. Berlin: Duncker & Humblot, 1996.
Krey, Volker. *German Criminal Law General Part,* vols. 1 and 2. Stuttgart: Verlag W. Kohlhammer, 2002–2003.
Maurach, Reinhart, Friedrich-Christian Schroeder, and Manfred Maiwald. *Strafrecht Besonderer Teil, Teilband 1,* 9th ed. Heidelberg: C. F. Müller Verlag, 2003.
Roxin, Claus. *Strafrecht Allgemeiner Teil,* 4th ed. Munich: Verlag C. H. Beck, 2006.
Strafgesetzbuch: Leipziger Kommentar, ed. Heinrich Wilhelm Laufhütte, Ruth Rissing–van Saan, and Klaus Tiedemann, vols. 1–3, 12th ed. Berlin: de Gruyter, 2006–2008.
Wessels, Johannes, and Michael Hettinger. *Strafrecht Besonderer Teil 1,* 33d ed. Heidelberg: C. F. Müller Verlag, 2009.
Wessels, Johannes, and Thomas Hillenkamp. *Strafrecht Besonderer Teil 2,* 32d ed. Heidelberg, C. F. Müller Verlag, 2009.

NOTES

1. *Strafgesetzbuch,* published in *Bundesgesetzblatt* (Federal Register of Laws) 1998, vol. 1, p. 3322.
2. *Völkerstrafgesetzbuch,* published in *Bundesgesetzblatt* 2002, vol. 1, p. 2254.
3. Under the German system, the Basic Law prevails over any other statute and official act. Any statute that conflicts with the constitution will be ruled void by the Federal Constitutional Court.
4. See 92 *Entscheidungen des Bundesverfassungsgerichts* (Decisions of the Federal Constitutional Court, hereafter BVerfGE) 1 at 11–13 (1995).
5. See *supra* note 2.
6. See Gerhard Dannecker, in *Strafgesetzbuch: Leipziger Kommentar,* ed. Heinrich Wilhelm Laufhütte, Ruth Rissing–van Saan, and Klaus Tiedemann, vol. 1, 12th ed. (Berlin: de Gruyter, 2007), § 1 notes 179–180.
7. For a rare example, see 78 BVerfGE 372 at 383 (1989).
8. For concise summaries of these standards, see, e.g., 48 BVerfGE 48 at 57 (1978); 93 BVerfGE 266 at 291–292 (1995).
9. 109 BVerfGE 133 at 167 (2004). By contrast, the European Court of Human Rights held in 2009 that the retrospective extension of *Sicherungsverwahrung* violated Art. 7 sec. 1 2nd sent. of the European Convention on Human Rights ("Nor shall a heavier penalty be imposed than the one that was applicable at the time of criminal offence was committed."); M. v. Germany, Application 19359/04, Judgment of Dec. 17, 2009.
10. 95 BVerfGE 96 at 133 (1996).The Federal Court of Appeals had argued that the

laws of the GDR were to be interpreted in the light of international human rights standards and therefore deemed these laws not to justify the defendants' shooting at unarmed fugitives; 39 *Entscheidungen des Bundesgerichtshofes in Strafsachen* (Decisions of the Federal Court of Appeals, hereafter BGHSt) 1 at 26–30 (1992).

11. See 71 BVerfGE 198 (1985) (overturning a conviction for "avoiding" the legal duty to be an election helper when the defendant had provoked his dismissal from the election office by wearing a political badge).

12. 28 BGHSt 100 (1978).

13. 92 BVerfGE 1 at 16–17 (1995).

14. See 6 BGHSt 85 at 87–88 (1954) (extending a statutory rule on exculpatory abandonment of attempt to situations not covered by the words of the Code).

15. For example, the *Betäubungsmittelgesetz* (Narcotics Law) of 1981, published in *Bundesgesetzblatt* 1994, vol. 1, p. 358, regulates at length the permits and conditions required for dispensing and transporting narcotic substances. Sections 29–38 of that law provide for heavy criminal sentences for persons dealing in narcotics without having the requisite permits.

16. 21 BGHSt 157 (1966).

17. 37 BGHSt 89 (1990).

18. In criminal matters, state courts of appeals are courts of last instance in criminal matters starting at the level of local courts (which make up the bulk of criminal cases). Serious cases, especially those involving homicide, are brought before district courts; for these cases, the Federal Court of Appeals is the court of last instance. When individual state courts of appeals disagree about the interpretation of a statute, the conflict must be brought before the Federal Court of Appeals, which will then render a final opinion.

19. Cf. 22 BVerfGE 21 at 25 (1967) (upholding a regulation that provides for an obligation to take part in road traffic classes as a consequence of committing a traffic violation).

20. 32 BVerfGE 346 at 363 (1972); 78 BVerfGE 374 at 382 (1988). For a critical assessment of this jurisprudence, see Dannecker (*supra* note 6) § 1 note 127.

21. This practice has been accepted by the appellate courts; see 43 BGHSt 195 (1997); 50 BGHSt 40 (2005).

22. *Gesetz zur Regelung der Verständigung im Strafverfahren*, published in *Bundesgesetzblatt* 2009, vol. 1, p. 2353, amending the Code of Criminal Procedure (*Strafprozessordnung*) of 1987. For details, see Thomas Weigend, "The Decay of the Inquisitorial Ideal: Plea Bargaining Invades German Criminal Procedure," in *Crime, Procedure and Evidence in a Comparative and International Context: Essays in Honour of Professor Mirjan Damaška*, ed. John D. Jackson, Máximo Langer, and Peter Tillers (Oxford; Portland, OR: Hart, 2008).

23. See § 257c (1) Code of Criminal Procedure.

24. A two-thirds majority of the judges is needed for any decision disadvantaging the accused (§ 263 (1) Code of Criminal Procedure), and there are no panels in which professional judges have a two-thirds majority.

25. Some writers maintain that the preventive effect of criminal justice is not achieved mainly through simple deterrence but through symbolically emphasizing and

reinforcing the continuing validity of the norm that the offender had violated. See Günther Jakobs, *Strafrecht Allgemeiner Teil*, 2d ed. (Berlin: de Gruyter, 1991), 6–13; Franz Streng, *Strafrechtliche Sanktionen*, 2d ed. (Stuttgart: Kohlhammer, 2002), 13–14.

26. "Culpability" in practice does not denote an individualized assessment of blameworthiness in accordance with the offender's psychological and social conditions. Rather, "culpability" reflects the seriousness of the offense to the extent that it can be attributed to the offender. For example, the influence of a mental defect (§ 21 PC) or having to act in a situation of strong conflict of interests (§ 35 PC) normally reduces culpability.

27. 45 BVerfGE 187 at 228 (1977); 91 BVerfGE 1 at 31–32 (1994).

28. 43 BGHSt 195 at 209 (1997).

29. For details, see section II.F.1 in this chapter.

30. See *supra* note 2.

31. Even a person sentenced to life imprisonment can be placed on parole after having served a minimum of fifteen years (§ 57a PC).

32. See the summary in Hans-Heinrich Jescheck and Thomas Weigend, *Lehrbuch des Strafrechts: Allgemeiner Teil*, 5th ed. (Berlin: Duncker & Humblot, 1996), 210–222.

33. For a discussion of cases of "automatism," see Grischa Merkel, "Zur Strafwürdigkeit automatisierter Verhaltensweisen," 119 *Zeitschrift für die gesamte Strafrechtswissenschaft* 214 (2007).

34. Thus, even if the planned offense is not being carried out for independent reasons, the person who failed to report it remains punishable under § 138 of the Penal Code, but the court can refrain from imposing punishment (§ 139 (1) PC).

35. See 2 BGHSt 150 at 153 (1952).

36. Typical examples of a duty to act are the following: a police officer must act to prevent crime (statutory duty); a physician must act to prevent a patient from harm (contractual duty); a driver who had negligently injured a pedestrian must act to save the pedestrian from death or more serious physical harm (causing of risk); and a man must actively help the woman with whom he has lived together for some time when there is a risk to her life or health (social duty).

37. See 37 BGHSt 106 at 116 (1990).

38. Cf. Federal Court of Appeals, published in 2003 *Neue Juristische Wochenschrift* 3212.

39. For a discussion of these and other problem cases, see Thomas Weigend, in *Strafgesetzbuch: Leipziger Kommentar*, ed. Heinrich Wilhelm Laufhütte, Ruth Rissing-van Saan, and Klaus Tiedemann, vol. 1, 12th ed. (Berlin: de Gruyter, 2007), § 13 notes 29, 45, 53, 56.

40. There is a philosophical dispute whether passivity can be said to "cause" a harm. It is better here to speak of hypothetical causation: the person *could have* caused the victim to be saved by becoming active.

41. See, e.g., 43 BGHSt 381 at 397 (1997).

42. See *supra* note 15.

43. See 19 BGHSt 295 at 298 (1964).

44. For an overview and discussion of case law, see Joachim Vogel, in *Strafgesetzbuch: Leipziger Kommentar*, ed. Heinrich Wilhelm Laufhütte, Ruth Rissing-van Saan, and Klaus Tiedemann, vol. 1, 12th ed. (Berlin: de Gruyter, 2007), § 15 notes 79–132.

45. In German debate the Latin term *dolus eventualis* is often used for conditional intent.

46. Wolfgang Frisch, *Vorsatz und Risiko* (Cologne: Heymann, 1983), 197; Ingeborg Puppe, in *Strafgesetzbuch Nomos-Kommentar*, ed. Urs Kindhäuser, Ulfrid Neumann, and Hans-Ullrich Paeffgen, vol. 1, 2d ed. (Baden-Baden: Nomos, 2005), § 15 notes 64–71.

47. Federal Court of Appeals in 1981 *Juristenzeitung* 35.

48. 36 BGHSt 1 at 10–12 (1988) (concerning transmitting HIV through sexual intercourse).

49. See Federal Court of Appeals in 1982 *Strafverteidiger* 509 (defendant drove a car in direction of police officer who tried to stop him; held not to be attempted murder); Federal Court of Appeals in 2001 *Neue Zeitschrift für Strafrecht* 475 (offender's personality and his relationship with the victim are used in determining whether he acted with intent).

50. However, the Federal Court of Appeals has declared that one can "approvingly take into account" a result even if one does not wish that result to come about; it is sufficient that the perpetrator foresees the risk and accepts the fact that he or she may cause the result to occur (7 BGHSt 363 at 369 [1955]; two men strangled the victim with a leather belt while robbing him; they had previously agreed that they did not want to kill the victim but were found guilty of murder).

51. See Claus Roxin, *Strafrecht Allgemeiner Teil*, 4th ed. (Munich: Verlag C. H. Beck, 2006), 1086–1088. It cannot be denied that "conscious negligence" describes a psychological self-contradiction: the actor knows that the harmful consequence can occur and at the same time denies it. German doctrine has nevertheless accepted this possibility, most likely as an alternative to liability for intent in cases where that liability would appear too harsh for an actor who was only careless.

52. In most instances the sentence range for a negligent offense is lower than that for a comparable intent offense.

53. Typical offenses of negligence are negligent killing (§ 222 PC) and negligent wounding (§ 229 PC). There are, however, a few offense definitions that do not require the occurrence of a harmful consequence of negligent behavior, for example, negligent false swearing in court (§ 163 PC) and negligent driving under the influence of intoxicants (§ 316 (2) PC). In these cases it is sufficient for liability that the perpetrator could have known that he engaged in prohibited conduct, for example, that he had consumed so much alcohol as to render him unfit to drive.

54. See, e.g., Roxin (*supra* note 51), 1067–1079; for further references see Vogel (*supra* note 44), § 15 notes 164–168.

55. See Gunnar Duttge, *Zur Bestimmtheit des Handlungsunwerts von Fahrlässigkeitsdelikten* (Tübingen: Mohr Siebeck, 2001); Friedrich-Christian Schroeder, in *Strafgesetzbuch: Leipziger Kommentar*, ed. Burkhard Jähnke, Heinrich Wilhelm Laufhütte, and Walter Odersky, vol. 1, 11th ed. (Berlin: de Gruyter, 1994), § 16 notes 127–138.

56. The majority of writers would hold that the driver in this situation acted wrongfully but not culpably; a minority would even deny wrongfulness because the law cannot demand a standard of attention and care that the individual addressee of the norm is unable to provide.

57. Cf. 40 BGHSt 341 (1995) (driver negligent when he drove although he knew that he was prone to epileptic seizures).

58. The Penal Code distinguishes between *Verbrechen* (serious offenses, carrying a minimum punishment of one year's imprisonment) and *Vergehen* (less serious offenses). That distinction resembles the divide between felonies and misdemeanors in U.S. law, but many offenses that would be felonies in the United States are mere *Vergehen* in Germany.

59. In fact, attempts of many common crimes, such as assault, larceny, burglary, fraud, forgery, and destruction of property, have been made punishable by statute.

60. For example, attempted theft (§ 242 PC) requires that the offender have the intent to unlawfully appropriate the item he or she intends to take away. A punishable attempt does not exist when the actor only wishes to go as far as to attempt the offense; for that reason, agents provocateurs are not criminally liable if their plan is to have the main perpetrator arrested while he is still perpetrating the offense.

61. 26 BGHSt 201 at 203 (1975); 28 BGHSt 162 at 163 (1978).

62. Federal Court of Appeals in 1999 *Strafverteidiger* 593; but for a different result in a similar case, see 26 BGHSt 201 (1975).

63. Cf. Oberlandesgericht München in 2006 *Zeitschrift für Wirtschafts- und Steuerstrafrecht (wistra)* 436.

64. 39 BGHSt 221 (1993).

65. Federal Court of Appeals in 2002 *Neue Zeitschrift für Strafrecht Rechtsprechungs-Report* 74. For further detail, see Bernd Schünemann, in *Strafgesetzbuch: Leipziger Kommentar*, ed. Heinrich Wilhelm Laufhütte, Ruth Rissing-van Saan, and Klaus Tiedemann, vol. 1, 12th ed. (Berlin: de Gruyter, 2007), § 30 notes 60, 63.

66. The offense can also be a punishable attempt.

67. This jurisprudence can be traced back to early decisions of the Imperial Court (Reichsgericht), especially 3 *Entscheidungen des Reichsgerichts in Strafsachen* 181 (1881); see also the famous "bathtub case," 74 *Entscheidungen des Reichsgerichts in Strafsachen* 84 (1940), where the Imperial Court regarded as a mere aider a woman who drowned her sister's newborn baby in a bathtub because the baby's unwed mother wished to get rid of the child. The court argued that the woman who actually drowned the baby had no strong interest in the baby's death and only wished to help her sister; therefore, she did not have the mind-set of a perpetrator. The Federal Court of Appeals initially followed the same approach; see 18 BGHSt 87 (1962); Federal Court of Appeals in 1974 *Monatsschrift für deutsches Recht* 547.

68. See 37 BGHSt 289 at 291 (1991) (taking into account the offender's interest in the outcome, his control over the act, and the extent of his participation).

69. For details, see Claus Roxin, *Täterschaft und Tatherrschaft*, 8th ed. (Berlin: De Gruyter Recht, 2006); Schünemann (*supra* note 65), § 25 notes 155–204.

70. Schünemann (*supra* note 65), § 25 note 184.

71. In the examples given in the text, the nurse would not be liable for murder because she lacked intent to kill or was acting under duress (§ 35 PC). A more difficult case arose when an offender A insinuated to a rather gullible young man B that it was necessary that B kill victim V in order to save the world from destruction by an evil spirit. B, who carried out the killing, was held to have killed V intentionally and to have

been influenced by an unreasonable mistake of law (namely, that one was allowed to kill an innocent person in order to save millions of others), which led to a reduced punishment. The Federal Court of Appeals nevertheless convicted A as an indirect perpetrator of V's murder; 35 BGHSt 347 (1988).

72. 40 BGHSt 218 at 236 (1994).

73. *Dictum* in 40 BGHSt 218 at 237; *held* in 48 BGHSt 331 at 342 (2003) and 49 BGHSt 147 at 163 (2004).

74. See Thomas Rotsch, "Tatherrschaft kraft Organisationsherrschaft?" 112 *Zeitschrift für die gesamte Strafrechtswissenschaft* 518 (2000); Claus Roxin, "Mittelbare Täterschaft kraft Organisationsherrschaft," 2002 *Neue Zeitschrift für Strafrecht* 52.

75. See examples in Schünemann (*supra* note 65), § 26 note 51.

76. Cf. 34 BGHSt 63 (1986).

77. See Schünemann (*supra* note 65), § 26 notes 17–20. But note that with respect to serious offenses, even attempting to instigate an offense is punishable (§ 30 (1) PC).

78. According to the definition of aiding in § 27 PC, there can be no liability for aiding in a *negligent* offense.

79. An example is the man who learns about a planned burglary of his neighbor's house and secretly kills the neighbor's watchdog in order to make it easier for the burglar to break in.

80. 8 BGHSt 390 (1956), citing earlier decisions of the Imperial Court.

81. For an overview of the discussion, see Hans Kudlich, *Die Unterstützung fremder Straftaten durch berufsbedingtes Verhalten* (Berlin: Duncker & Humblot, 2004).

82. 46 BGHSt 107 (2000). Persons who have only "conditional intent" (see section II.B.2.i in this chapter) with respect to the crime to be committed are thus normally not punishable.

83. For an English-language summary of the discussion, see Thomas Weigend, "Societas delinquere non potest? A German Perspective," 6 *Journal of International Criminal Justice* 927–945 (2008).

84. § 30 *Gesetz über Ordnungswidrigkeiten* (Law on Violations of the Order) of 1987 (*Bundesgesetzblatt* 1987, vol. 1, p. 602).

85. See 39 BGHSt 195 (1993); Roxin (*supra* note 51), 361–362.

86. 37 BGHSt 107 at 129 (1990).

87. Cf. 2 BGHSt 20 (1951).

88. For a good overview, see Roxin (*supra* note 51), 371–421.

89. 25 BVerfGE 269 (1969); see also 46 BGHSt 310 at 317 (2001) (concerning the retroactive elimination of a requirement that the victim specifically request criminal prosecution).

90. See section II.B. in this chapter.

91. For a detailed explanation, see Michael Pawlik, *Der rechtfertigende Notstand* (Berlin: de Gruyter, 2002), 57–80.

92. See 115 BVerfGE 118 at 153–154 (2006) (concerning a statute authorizing the shooting down of airplanes abducted by terrorists); 35 BGHSt 347 at 350 (1988).

93. Volker Erb, in *Münchener Kommentar zum Strafgesetzbuch*, ed. Bernd von Heintschel-Heinegg, vol. 1 (Munich: Beck, 2003), § 34 note 140; Roxin (*supra* note 51), 755–757; Frank Zieschang, in *Strafgesetzbuch: Leipziger Kommentar*, ed. Heinrich

Wilhelm Laufhütte, Ruth Rissing–van Saan, and Klaus Tiedemann, vol. 2, 12th ed. (Berlin: de Gruyter, 2006), § 34 note 69a.

94. Theodor Lenckner and Walter Perron, in *Strafgesetzbuch Kommentar*, ed. Adolf Schönke and Horst Schröder, 27th ed. (Munich: Beck, 2006), § 34 note 41b.

95. Defense of others is not permissible, however, when the person under attack does not wish to be defended.

96. Federal Court of Appeals, 1998 *Neue Zeitschrift für Strafrecht* 508.

97. Cf. 24 BGHSt 356 (1972); 42 BGHSt 97 (1996).

98. For an overview, see Lenckner and Perron (*supra* note 94), § 32 notes 43–61b.

99. There is some argument on the theoretical question whether consent works to negate the *Tatbestand* (commission of the offense) or the unlawfulness of the act; see Roxin (*supra* note 51), 536–554.

100. 49 BGHSt 166 (2004) (concerning sadomasochistic practices).

101. See Thomas Rönnau, in *Strafgesetzbuch: Leipziger Kommentar*, ed. Heinrich Wilhelm Laufhütte, Ruth Rissing–van Saan, and Klaus Tiedemann, vol. 2, 12th ed. (Berlin: de Gruyter, 2006), vor § 32 notes 199–202.

102. *Wehrstrafgesetz*, published in *Bundesgesetzblatt* 1974, vol. 1, p. 1213.

103. The Federal Court of Appeals held that it was "evident" to a soldier of the German Democratic Republic that it was a criminal act to shoot at fugitives who tried to escape from the GDR; 39 BGHSt 1 at 33–34 (1992).

104. For example, if A takes away a television set belonging to B because A mistakenly believes that he has acquired property of the television set through an oral sales agreement, A cannot be convicted of theft because he failed to recognize the offense element "belonging to another person."

105. 3 BGHSt 105 (1952). For an extensive discussion, see Roxin (*supra* note 51), 622–632.

106. This rule is based on the principle of culpability: It would violate that rule to recognize the maxim *error iuris nocet* (an error of law is injurious) and to hold a person responsible when that person was unable to know about the relevant prohibition (cf. 2 BGHSt 194 [1952]). If the offender mistakenly thought that his or her conduct was lawful and could have avoided this mistake, the sentence can be mitigated (§ 17 2nd sent. PC).

107. 4 BGHSt 236 at 242–243 (1953).

108. 21 BGHSt 18 at 20–21 (1966).

109. See, for example, Hans Joachim Hirsch, "Das Schuldprinzip und seine Funktion im Strafrecht," 106 *Zeitschrift für die gesamte Strafrechtswissenschaft* 746 at 759–764 (1994); Roxin (*supra* note 51), 868–875.

110. 43 BGHSt 66 (1997).

111. For a good discussion of this problem, see Michael Hettinger, *Die "actio libera in causa": Strafbarkeit wegen Begehungstat trotz Schuldunfähigkeit?* (Berlin: Duncker & Humblot, 1988).

112. 42 BGHSt 235 (1996).

113. Cf. Roxin (*supra* note 51), 986.

114. 45 BGHSt 321 (1999).

115. 47 BGHSt 44 (2001).

116. For an English-language account of German sentencing law, see Thomas Weigend, "Sentencing and Punishment in Germany," in *Sentencing and Sanctions in Western Countries*, ed. Michael Tonry and Richard S. Frase (Oxford: Oxford University Press, 2001), 188.

117. Sentencing is done by the whole court, including lay judges if they sit together with professional judges (see section I.E.2 in this chapter).

118. See also section II.A in this chapter.

119. For example, for simple larceny the sentence range is from a fine (with a minimum of five day fines) to five years' imprisonment (§ 242 PC); for aggravated assault, the sentence range is from three months' to ten years' imprisonment (§ 224 PC).

120. Cf. Jescheck and Weigend (*supra* note 32), 752–753.

121. Suicide is not covered by the definition of homicide. Germany has no criminal prohibition of instigating or assisting suicide.

122. For a constitutional challenge of § 211 PC, see 45 BVerfGE 187 (1977).

123. 2 BGHSt 60 (1951).

124. For a recent proposal, see Arbeitskreis AE, "Alternativ-Entwurf Leben," in 2008 *Goldammer's Archiv für Strafrecht* 193.

125. In extreme cases, the Federal Court of Appeals has permitted courts to impose a lower sentence for murder, although the Penal Code does not provide for such mitigation; 30 BGHSt 105 at 120 (1981).

126. All sexual offenses are now defined in a gender-neutral way; the only exception is exhibitionism, which is punishable only for men (§ 183 PC).

127. For a discussion of such cases, see Karl Lackner and Kristian Kühl, *Strafgesetzbuch: Kommentar*, 26th ed. (Munich: Verlag C. H. Beck, 2007), § 242 notes 23, 24.

128. See 34 BGHSt 394 (1987).

129. For an incisive discussion of such offenses, see Tatjana Hörnle, *Grob anstößiges Verhalten* (Frankfurt am Main: Klostermann, 2005).

130. 120 BVerfGE 224 (2007).

131. See *supra* note 15.

INDIA

Stanley Yeo

I. Introduction
   A. Historical Sketch
   B. Jurisdiction
   C. Legality Principle
   D. Sources of Criminal Law
   E. Process

II. General Part
   A. Theories of Punishment
   B. Liability Requirements
   C. Defences
   D. Justifications
   E. Excuses
   F. Sanctions

III. Special Part
   A. Structure
   B. Homicide
   C. Sex Offences
   D. Theft and Fraud
   E. "Victimless" Crimes
   F. Offences Involving Cruelty to Wives and Dowry Deaths
   G. Voluntary Active Euthanasia and Physician-Assisted Suicide

---

Stanley Yeo is Professor of Law at the National University of Singapore. His recent publications include (with Mark Findlay and Stephen Odgers) *Australian Criminal Justice* (Oxford, 4th ed., 2009) and (with Neil Morgan and Chan Wing Cheong) *Criminal Law in Malaysia and Singapore* (LexisNexis, 2007).

I. INTRODUCTION

A. Historical Sketch

The criminal law of India is governed principally by the Indian Penal Code of 1860 (hereinafter the Code). Before its advent the prevailing criminal law in India was a patchwork of Muslim and Hindu law. The Code's authors drew their inspiration from several sources, notably the English criminal law, the French Penal Code, and Edward Livingston's Code for Louisiana. When they were drafting the Code, they were very clear in their goal of making it exhaustive.

The Code's authors proposed a scheme whereby ambiguities or gaps in the Code were to be referred to Parliament, which should decide the point and, if necessary, amend the Code. Regrettably, this proposal was not adopted in India, so the courts have had to undertake the tasks of determining the meaning to be given to an ambiguous provision and' filling a gap left by the Code.

Two points from legal history are worth noting because they provide useful background from which to consider the Code. The first is that English criminal law when the Code was drafted was in a state of chaos, and serious efforts at reforming the law were being made. Second, the Code's authors were heavily influenced by the individualistic libertarian philosophy of Jeremy Bentham. This philosophy imbued the Code with a utilitarian base and cast *mens rea* in largely subjective terms, in contrast to the prevailing retributionism and frequently objectively based *mens rea* of nineteenth-century English criminal law.

B. Jurisdiction

The Code specifies the extent of criminal jurisdiction over offences committed within and outside India. India's territory comprises its land, internal waters, territorial coastal waters, and airspace above its land and waters. Section 2 makes the Code applicable to every person irrespective of rank, caste, creed, or nationality. Section 108A also provides that a person who in India instigates the commission of an offence outside India is liable to be punished under the Code. Foreign nationals who commit a crime in India cannot plead ignorance of Indian law. It has also been held that a foreign national who in India instigates the commission of a crime outside India is also liable to punishment under the Code.[1]

Certain people are exempt from the criminal jurisdiction of the courts by virtue of the constitution of India, statutory provisions, or rules of international law. They include the president of India, the governor of an Indian state, Supreme Court and High Court judges, and foreign sovereigns and ambassadors.

Extraterritorial jurisdiction is afforded by section 3 of the Code, which stipulates that any person may be tried for an offence committed by him or her outside India provided he or she is liable to be punished for it by Indian law as if he or she had committed it within India. This section therefore postulates the trial of Indian citizens for crimes committed abroad even though their conduct may not be recognized as a crime in the place where it was committed.

Also, the section applies to foreigners who are covered by special laws bringing them under Indian jurisdiction.[2] Additionally, section 4 provides that the Code applies to any offence committed by any Indian citizen in any place outside India and to any person on any ship or aircraft registered in India, wherever it may be at the time of the offence.

There is no statute of limitations for the prosecution of offences mentioned in the Code. However, some offences created by special laws may be subject to a limitation period prescribed by those special laws.[3]

C. Legality Principle

Although the legislature has the power to enact both prospective and retrospective laws, those laws are subject to the maxim *nulla poena sine lege* (no punishment without law). This maxim is enshrined in article 20 of the constitution, which consists of two parts. The first proclaims that "no person shall be convicted of any offence except for a violation of law in force at the time of the commission of the act charged as an offence." The second declares that no person shall "be subjected to a penalty greater than that which might have been inflicted under the law in force at the time of the commission of the offence." Hence, if a trial is held with respect to a law which came into force after the date when the offence was committed, article 20 requires the court to consider whether the penalty imposed is higher than the penalty which could have been imposed under the previous law.[4] Article 20 would not be infringed if the court imposed a penalty which was not greater than the one prescribed under the previous law.

These two constitutionally entrenched limitations do not prevent the legislature from enacting retrospective procedural laws. Consequently, the Supreme Court has held that a trial under a procedure different from that which obtained at the time of the commission of the offence is not in itself unconstitutional.[5]

D. Sources of Criminal Law

1. Legislature

The general principles of criminal liability and major offences are contained in the Code. There are also various statutes enacted by the central and state legislatures criminalizing conduct which may apply generally,[6] specially,[7] or locally.[8] A special law is applicable to the particular subject, while a local law applies to a particular part of India. The defences provided for in the Code are available to persons charged with an offence under special or local laws.[9]

2. Judiciary

The courts have an important role in interpreting the provisions of the Code and other penal statutes and applying them to the case at hand. Since the legislature has not been forthcoming in clarifying or resolving many ambiguities or gaps in the Code, this task has fallen on the courts. Moreover, the courts have often displayed ingenuity in interpreting Code provisions in ways which accommodate the social, cultural, and religious diversity of Indian society. It would therefore be correct to assert that the criminal law of India comprises statute law as interpreted and applied by a large body of case law which has been built up over time.

3. Executive

The executive cannot enact offences; that power belongs to the legislature. However, the legislature occasionally provides the executive with a range of powers to regulate activities which may be subjected to criminal sanction. For example, under special laws like the Unlawful Activities (Prevention) Act 1967 and the Armed Forces (Special Powers) Act 1958, wide powers are conferred on the executive to declare an organization "unlawful" or an area a disturbed area. Similarly, the Police Act 1861 confers on the police wide powers of surveillance over persons whom the police have reasonable grounds to believe are leading a life of crime.

4. Scholars

Several voluminous and long-standing commentaries on the Code have been edited by distinguished Indian jurists and judges of higher courts.[10] They are occasionally referred to in judgments. Recent editions of these commentaries have tended toward becoming mere repositories of case summaries.

E. Process

1. Adversarial/Inquisitorial

The Indian criminal justice process has inherited and maintained the English adversarial model with its underlying premise that a person is presumed innocent until he or she is proved guilty. The judge's role is more than that of a mere umpire; he or she takes an active interest in the proceedings by putting questions to witnesses to ascertain the truth.[11] As the state's representative, the prosecution assists the trier of fact to arrive at the truth. In doing so, the prosecutor is disallowed from urging an argument which in his or her opinion does not carry weight, nor can he or she exclude legal evidence which supports the interests of the defendant. Counsel for the defence, if there is one, is required to do everything he or she ethically can to protect the interest of the defendant. Criminal proceedings are held in open court and may be reported in the press, and judgments are accessible to the public.

2. Jury/Written Opinions

Under colonial rule, the British administration introduced a jury system very much like the one operating in England at the time. However, the system did not work well, largely because it was difficult in such a diverse country as India to find sufficient numbers of people with similar status and backgrounds to sit in judgment of their peers. This resulted in a modification of the jury system which effectively overrode the jury verdict by vesting in the judge the power to set aside verdicts of acquittal by juries. Jury trials were eventually abolished by the legislature in 1960 on the ground that they were susceptible to media and public influence.

II. GENERAL PART

A. Theories of Punishment

None of the penal statutes, including the Code, expressly specify the theories of punishment. The Benthamite philosophy with its emphasis on utilitarianism has had a strong influence on the Code's approach to punishment. This is evident in the types of punishment which the Code recognized when it was first enacted, namely, the death penalty, transportation, imprisonment, whipping, and fines of sizable amounts. Likewise, the severe maximum penalties imposed for most offences in the Code attest to the view that the meting out and threat of punishment are essential for the control and prevention of crime.

Courts and commentators have suggested that the main theories of punishment are deterrence, retribution, and rehabilitation. The deterrent theory of punishment aims to deter the particular offender from reoffending and also to deter prospective offenders from committing the type of crime for which the offender was convicted.[12] The retributive theory views punishment as necessary to satiate the desire of crime victims and other members of society for vengeance. However, "[N]o sentence should ever appear to be vindictive [since] an excessive sentence defeats its own object and tends to further undermine respect for the law."[13] The rehabilitative theory of punishment seeks to make offenders harmless by curing them of those drawbacks which caused them to commit crime. Proponents of rehabilitation regard the punishment structure of the Code as brutal and harsh and a relic of former regressive times. They contend that in modern Indian society, sentencing should be seen as a process of reshaping a person who has degenerated into criminality. As a leading commentary has colorfully put it, "[A] therapeutic rather than an 'in terrorem' outlook should prevail in our criminal courts since brutal incarceration of the person merely produces laceration of his mind."[14]

Although these various theories of punishment may appear incompatible, they have in common the general aim of social defence. The Supreme Court endorsed this view when it dictated that the "sentence should bring home to the guilty party the consciousness that the offence committed by him was against his own interest and also against the interest of the society of which he happens to be a member."[15]

B. Liability Requirements

1. *Objective*/Actus Reus
i. Act

The word *act* is not defined in the Code. The courts have advised interpreting it in a commonsensical way by stating that "['act'] must necessarily be something short of a transaction which is composed of a series of acts ... it means the action taken as a whole and not the numerous separate movements involved."[16]

There is a fundamental principle of criminal law which declares that, where the physical elements of the crime include conduct (whether an act or an omission), such conduct must be voluntary. This is implicit in all the offence-creating provisions of the Code. Where conduct is involuntary, the defendant cannot be held criminally liable for the crime charged. Voluntariness comprises the will or ability of the person to control his or her conduct.[17]

In cases where the defendant has performed a series of acts, it may be important to determine when the conduct element of the crime in question is concluded. This will be so in relation to *mens rea* crimes which require the defendant to have possessed the requisite mental element during the commission of the conduct element of the crime. For instance, if D has strangled V with the intention of killing him and, wrongly believing him to be dead, hangs V from a tree, is D liable for murder? This type of case raises the issue of the need for concurrence between the *actus reus* and the *mens rea* of a crime before D may be held liable. The courts have dealt with this issue by holding that D is liable if his or her subsequent act was morally congruent with his or earlier act.[18] Thus, in the example given, D would be liable for murder if his act of hanging V was prompted by D's desire to conceal his or her previous act of strangulation which was done with the requisite *mens rea* for that offence.

ii. Omission

The general rule is that criminal liability is attached to conduct comprising positive activity by the defendant, but not to his or her failure to act. However, the law recognizes exceptions to this general rule. Section 43 of the Code confines these exceptions to omissions which are "illegal," by which is meant "everything which is an offence or which is prohibited by law, or which furnishes a ground for a civil action." Briefly stated, "[A]n illegal omission would apply to omissions of everything which [a person] is legally bound to do."[19]

There are three types of circumstances described in section 43 which render omissions illegal for the purposes of criminal liability. The first is omissions which are expressly made offences by the Code or other penal statutes. The second circumstance envisaged by section 43 is where the omission was prohibited by law. What is "prohibited by law" certainly includes omissions which are expressly made offences, but the term is not restricted to these offences. For example, shipping legislation may impose a duty on a captain to provide medical treatment to sick persons on board. Although the legislation does not make a captain's failure to discharge this duty an offence, it does prohibit such failure, which would therefore constitute an illegal omission under section 43.[20]

The third circumstance requires a court to determine whether the particular defendant's omission would attract civil liability. Failures to act which furnish ground for a civil action are most commonly related to tort law, in particular, the tort of negligence. Like criminal law, tort law has a general rule imposing a legal duty of care in respect of positive activity which might harm others, and it imposes such a duty of care for omissions in exceptional situations. Civil law imposes a legal duty to act where a special relationship exists between the defendant and the person injured by the defendant's omission. Examples include the relationship between a parent and his or her young child, or when a person voluntarily assumes responsibility for a physically and mentally infirm adult who is incapable of looking after himself or herself. Civil law also imposes a duty of care in respect of omissions when the defendant has negligently created the dangerous situation. Besides tort law, a failure to act may furnish ground for a civil action based on contract law.

iii. Status

There are some offences which base criminal liability on the defendant's status, that is, relationship with a specified state of affairs, which may be a circumstance or an event. These offences are invariably created by statute and are relatively minor in nature. An example is provided in section 3 of the Public Gambling Act 1867 of being the occupier of any premises used as a common gaming house. The crime is established upon proof that the defendant was the occupier of the premises fitting the specified description, and there is no formal requirement of an act or omission by him or her. Furthermore, the defendant cannot escape liability on the ground of ignorance.

As in the case of omissions, criminal law is circumspect in imposing criminal liability based merely on status, for otherwise, freedom of individuals to be connected to a circumstance or an event would be greatly stifled. Such a form of liability is therefore limited to persons who have responsibility for, or are in control of, the proscribed situation. Thus, in the example just given, the statute creating the offence confines liability to the occupier of the premises used as a common gaming house and does not extend it to other occupants or visitors who have no control over the state of affairs of those premises.

2. Subjective/Mens Rea/Mental Element
i. Intent

The term *intention* is not defined in the Code, and the task of doing so is thus left to the courts. The Supreme Court has held that it comprises "a conscious state in which mental faculties are aroused into activity and summoned into action for the purpose of achieving a conceived end. It means shaping of one's conduct so as to bring about a certain event."[21] It is uncertain whether the meaning of intention extends beyond its purposive sense to include knowledge of the virtual certainty of an event occurring (sometimes described as "oblique" or "indirect" intention). Against such an extension is the fact that many Code offences include, besides intention, the *mens rea* of knowing the likelihood of the proscribed result. For these offences, oblique intention would more than satisfy this type of knowledge.

The courts have ruled that the concept of intention is distinguishable from desire. Desire introduces an emotional or motivational element that may or may not be present in intention. Similarly, intention is not to be confused with motive.[22] Motive is the emotional force behind the defendant's conduct and is distinguished from intention, which is a technical concept denoting a mental state in which the defendant acts with the purpose to bring about a result.

ii. Recklessness

Although the term *reckless* does not appear in the Code, this type of *mens rea* is expressed in other ways in the Code insofar as it denotes advertence to a risk. The most common expression of this nature in the Code is "knows to be likely" to cause a proscribed result, an instance of which is section 299(3) concerning the offence of culpable homicide. Another expression used by the Code is "rashness," which is the *mens rea* for the crime of causing death by a rash act under section 304A. This term has been judicially interpreted as "acting with the consciousness that mischievous and illegal consequences may follow, but with the hope that they will not and often with the belief that the actor has taken sufficient precautions to prevent their happening."[23] The difference between "rash" and "knows to be likely" is one of degree, with the former requiring only knowledge that the proscribed harm was possible, while the latter requires knowledge that a harm was probable.[24] Clearly, oblique intention will satisfy either of these forms of recklessness.

iii. Negligence

There are some offences in the Code which are based on negligence.[25] The Code does not define the term *negligence*, and it has been left to the courts to do so. It has been held that "[c]riminal negligence is the gross and culpable neglect or failure to exercise that reasonable and proper care and precaution to guard against injury . . . , which having regard to all the circumstances out of which the charge has arisen, it was the imperative duty of the defendant person to have adopted."[26] A gross degree of negligence is required before criminal liability will lie.[27]

The defendant's conduct is measured against what a reasonable person, judged according to the knowledge, experience, and skill expected of such a person, would have done in the same or similar circumstances as those of the defendant. The courts have been prepared to partially subjectivize this objective standard of care by taking into account the mental incapacity of a particular defendant which prevented him or her from appreciating the danger at the material time.[28]

Although the concept of "good faith" as used in the Code is not strictly a form of *mens rea*, it is closely related to that of negligence. Section 52 of the Code states that "[n]othing is said to be done or believed in good faith which is done or believed without due care and attention."

3. *Theories of Liability*
   i. Inchoate Crimes
   a. Attempt

The Code provisions on attempt comprise a general provision[29] coupled with specific provisions[30] for the punishment of attempt. All these provisions serve only to regulate the extent of punishment for an attempt and do not contain a definition of what constitutes an attempt. Consequently, the courts have had to pronounce on the elements of attempt.

In relation to the *actus reus*, the courts have applied several tests. One is that the defendant's conduct must have gone beyond the stage of preparation and have been sufficiently proximate to the substantive offence. However, this does not require such conduct to have been the last act which the defendant was capable of doing.[31] Another test is whether the defendant's conduct was such as to unequivocally indicate his or her intention to commit the offence.[32]

With respect to the *mens rea*, the courts have held that, insofar as the general provision on attempt is concerned, criminal liability requires nothing less than an intention by the defendant to commit the substantive offence.[33] The words appearing in the general provision, "Whoever attempts . . . to cause such an offence to be committed," make it possible to convict a person of attempting to abet, or attempting to conspire with, another person to commit an offence. This is because abetment and conspiracy are recognized as offences in their own right by the Code. Conviction for attempt will lie even if the person abetted or conspired with does not proceed to commit the substantive offence.

The courts have ruled that a person may be liable for attempt even if what he or she had set out to do was factually impossible to achieve.[34] Supporting this ruling are the illustrations accompanying section 511 of the Code, which show that a person may be guilty of attempting to steal from an empty receptacle.

   b. Conspiracy

The Code defines the offence of criminal conspiracy as constituting an agreement by two or more persons to do or cause to be done an illegal act, or an act which is not illegal by illegal means.[35] Furthermore, where the agreement is not to commit an offence, an overt act done by one or more of the parties in pursuance of the agreement is required. The *actus reus* of criminal conspiracy is the agreement which involves a meeting of minds and unity of purpose between the conspirators.[36] There need not be a physical meeting of the parties, nor does a person have to be a party to the agreement from the start.[37] A person may be convicted of criminal conspiracy even though the other party involved is still at large, dead, unknown, or has been acquitted on a technical ground.[38] The Code does not explicitly exclude agreements between spouses or with the intended victim of the offence from the scope of criminal conspiracy.

The *mens rea* of criminal conspiracy consists of an intention by the parties to carry out the object of the agreement. Such an intention is absent from a party who merely pretends to join a criminal conspiracy but does not share the object of the scheme. Each party to the agreement is not required to know all the details of the scheme.[39]

People may be liable for criminal conspiracy whose object was factually impossible to achieve, provided the agreement was to commit an offence. Thus, in one case, two men who had agreed with each other to kill their intended victim by witchcraft were held liable for criminal conspiracy to commit murder, since they had agreed to commit murder and not merely to perform acts of witchcraft.[40]

ii. Complicity

The Code contains a number of provisions dealing with complicity, which is described as "abetment." The main provision is section 107, which provides for three types of abetment: by instigation, by conspiracy, and by intentional aiding. Abetment is recognized as an offence in its own right and, subject to one qualification, is not dependent on the person abetted committing the substantive offence.[41] The courts have held that this is true for cases of abetment by instigation and abetment by conspiracy. The qualification is that, for abetment by aiding, the person abetted must be proved to have committed the offence since the word *aid* suggests that the act aided was committed.[42] The Code recognizes a double inchoate crime by stipulating that "[t]he abetment of an offence being an offence, the abetment of such an abetment is also an offence."[43]

Regarding the *actus reus*, abetment by instigation requires the defendant to have actively suggested or stimulated the commission of the substantive offence.[44] As for abetment by conspiracy, the abettor must have engaged with one or more persons in a conspiracy, the conspiracy must be for the doing of the act abetted, and an act or illegal omission must have taken place in pursuance of the conspiracy and in order to the doing of the act abetted. A person cannot be convicted of abetment by conspiracy if the charges against all the other alleged conspirators have failed.[45] Regarding abetment by aiding, "aid" involves facilitating the commission of the act[46] and, therefore, must have been given before or at the time of the commission of the act. It has been held that mere presence at or near the scene of the crime does not itself amount to abetment by aiding.[47]

In relation to the *mens rea*, the general position is that the defendant must have intended that the person abetted carry out the conduct abetted, and must have known that such conduct amounted to a crime.[48] The law does not require the person abetted to have any guilty intention or knowledge or even to be capable of committing the crime.[49]

The Code has provisions dealing with cases where the person abetted committed an offence which differed from that intended by the abettor. Section 111 provides that when an act was abetted but a "different act" was done, the abettor is liable for that act provided it was "a probable consequence of the abetment and was committed under the influence of the instigation, or with the aid or in pursuance of the conspiracy which constituted the abetment." Section 113 provides that when the act abetted causes a "different effect" than that which was intended by the abettor, the abettor is liable for the effect caused, provided he or she "knew that the act abetted was likely to cause that effect." It has been observed that the test for criminal liability under section 111 is objective, while that under section 113 is subjective.

The Code also specifies the law in relation to joint criminal liability. The main provision is section 34, which states that "[w]hen a criminal act is done by several persons, in furtherance of the common intention of all, each of such persons is liable for that act in the same manner as if the act were done by him alone." The offence for which the secondary offender may be liable on the basis of section 34 is that which was committed by the principal offender; they cannot be liable for different offences. Participation in some form or other in the criminal act constitutes the main feature of section 34. For participation to be made out, the defendant must have been physically or constructively present when the offence occurred.[50]

The term *common intention* in section 34 refers to the common design of two or more persons acting together and signifies the reason for doing the acts collectively forming the "criminal act."[51] The phrase "in furtherance of a common intention" contained in this section enables criminal liability for collateral offences to be imputed to persons acting in concert even though those offences may not have formed part of the common design. Case authorities recognize three situations when this could occur. The first is the act which was intended by all the parties;[52] the second is the act which, though not intended, was known by the parties to be a possible consequence of the criminal enterprise; and the third is the act which any one of the parties commits "in order to avoid or remove any obstruction or resistance put up in the way of the proper execution of the common intention."[53]

iii. Corporate Criminal Liability

In spite of its antiquity, the Code does criminalize and punish corporations for offences having a *mens rea* element. For example, a corporation can be liable for certain offences of personal violence, including culpable homicide, by virtue of the particular definitions given to these offences, read with section 11 of the Code. That section provides that the word *person* appearing in the Code includes a company, association, or body of persons, whether incorporated or not. However, other offences such as rape and perjury are excluded because the wording of these offences shows that they can be committed only by a natural person.[54]

A difficulty arises in establishing the *mens rea* element of an offence where a corporate entity is involved. Since the Code is silent on this issue, the courts have adopted the doctrine of identification developed by English common law.[55] Under this doctrine, a corporation will be held criminally liable if its "directing mind" (which could be an individual person or the board of directors of the corporation) possessed the requisite *mens rea*.[56] Where individuals are concerned, they have to be sufficiently high up in the organizational hierarchy of the corporation to satisfy this test.[57]

Since a corporation is a fictitious entity, it is incapable of receiving bodily punishments such as imprisonment. Consequently, a corporation can be prosecuted for offences which are punishable only by a fine.[58] There is also case authority holding that corporations may be prosecuted for offences where a fine and imprisonment term are mandatory, in which case it would be punished only by a fine.[59]

4. Causation

The authors of the Code considered prescribing general rules on causation but eventually decided that the infinite variety of cases made the rules a matter for the courts to develop. Although the Code's authors chose not to devise general principles on causation, they thought it necessary to include specific provisions on causation in respect of the offence of culpable homicide. The relevant provisions appear as explanations to section 299 (the section on culpable homicide) and read as follows:

> *Explanation 1*
> A person who causes bodily injury to another who is labouring under a disorder, disease, or bodily infirmity, and thereby accelerates the death of that other, shall be deemed to have caused his death.
>
> *Explanation 2*
> Where death is caused by bodily injury, the person who causes such bodily injury shall be deemed to have caused the death, although by resorting to proper remedies and skilful treatment the death might have been prevented.

The courts have generally applied a two-stage inquiry to the issue of causation.[60] The first stage involves inquiring whether the defendant caused the proscribed result in fact. This is resolved by applying the "but-for" test, which, if met, shows that the defendant's conduct was a *causa sine qua non* (a necessary or indispensable condition) of the victim's harm. The second stage involves inquiring whether the defendant's conduct had caused the victim's harm as a matter of law (a *causa causans*). This involves a value judgment whether the defendant was sufficiently blameworthy for causing the harm to warrant conviction and punishment. The courts have occasionally applied the test of "a substantial cause" in relatively straightforward cases of causation. However, the judicial preference appears to be for a test of reasonable foresight by the defendant of the harm. For example, it was held in a murder case that "any act is said to cause death . . . when the death results either from the act itself or from some consequences necessarily or naturally flowing from that act, and reasonably contemplated as its result."[61]

In many cases the defendant's conduct would have been the primary or even sole cause of the proscribed result. However, there will be other cases where a subsequent causal act or event occurs (a *novus actus interveniens*), thereby raising the question whether the defendant's conduct continued to play a causal role or merely formed part of the factual background. The Indian courts have, in many cases, used the reasonable-foresight test to resolve these more complicated cases of causation.[62]

C. Defences

1. Types of Defence

The principal defences are contained in the Code. They consist of the "general exceptions" contained in part IV[63] of the Code, which apply to offences found within[64] the Code, as well as without,[65] unless excluded by statute. In addition, there are the "special exceptions" to murder as spelled out in section 300 of the Code. These various exculpatory defences can be categorized into three types. The first denies personal responsibility for what occurred, such as the defences of mistake of fact and accident. The second type is where the offence elements are proved, but the broader context in which the conduct transpired offers a justification or excuse which negates criminal liability. Examples of justificatory defences are consent, self-defence, necessity (choice of evils), and superior orders. Excusatory defences include duress, mistake, and provocation. The third type of exculpatory defences has mental impairment as its core. Although evidence of mental impairment may be used to deny an offence element such as knowledge or intent, such evidence can support an independent defence. For example, mental impairment can prevent a person from having the capacity to judge the rightness or wrongness of his or her conduct or can affect his or her capacity to control conduct. Examples include the defences of unsoundness of mind, intoxication, and infanticide.

2. Burden of Proof

There are a number of broad principles which are applicable to all criminal trials. The first is that it is the responsibility of the prosecution to prove its case beyond a reasonable doubt. If it fails to do so, the defendant is entitled to be acquitted on the basis that he or she is presumed innocent of the crime charged unless proved otherwise. Once the prosecution has proved beyond a reasonable doubt facts which, if unanswered, would establish the charge against the defendant, it is the responsibility of the defendant who seeks to be exculpated to adduce evidence in support of one of the legally recognized defences. The court decides on the case after taking into consideration the evidence as a whole.

The Indian Evidence Act 1872 contains two provisions which endorse these broad principles. The first is section 101, the relevant parts of which provide that "[w]hoever desires any court to give judgment as to any legal right or liability, dependent on the existence of facts which he asserts, must prove that those facts exist," and that "[w]hen a person is bound to prove the existence of any fact, it is said that the burden of proof lies on that person." This section clearly provides that in a criminal trial the legal burden of proving that the defendant is guilty of the crime charged lies throughout with the prosecution.

The second provision is section 105, which stipulates that the defendant bears the burden of proving a full or partial defence. The Supreme Court has interpreted this provision to mean that the defendant bears the burden, as in a civil case, of raising some evidence in support of a defence.[66] In other words, the court will presume the absence of circumstances which bring the case under one of the recognized defences, and it will cast the burden on the defendant to rebut this presumption by adducing evidence showing that the preponderance of probabilities is in favor of his or her plea. Should this occur, the prosecution has to rebut the evidence supporting a defence beyond a reasonable doubt, in keeping with the prosecution's obligation to discharge the legal burden of proof that the defendant is guilty of the crime as charged.

D. Justifications

1. Necessity

Section 81 of the Code recognizes a defence of necessity which is available to all offences, including murder. The requirements of the defence are contained in the rather sparsely worded section and the explanation and illustrations accompanying it.

Although no mention is made of a requirement of proportionality, this is evidenced by the illustrations. Illustration (a) is of a ship captain who chooses to run the risk of running down a boat with two passengers on board in order to avoid inevitably colliding with a boat holding thirty passengers. The illustration declares that the captain is not guilty of any offence if he runs down the first boat, provided he satisfies all the requirements of section 81. The "choice-of-evils" doctrine is apparent here, with the defendant justified in risking the lives of a few to save many. To the same effect, illustration (b) is of a defendant who pulls down houses in order to stop a great fire from spreading and causing loss of human life and property.

Besides the requirement of proportionate response, section 81 requires the defendant to have lacked any "criminal intention" to cause the harm. The meaning of this provision is unclear. It is likely to refer to the defendant's objective in committing the proscribed conduct; if the objective was to prevent other harm, the defendant's intention would not have been "criminal." Another requirement is that the defendant must have incurred the risk "in good faith" (i.e., "with due care and attention") for the purpose of preventing or avoiding "imminent"[67] harm. This may be contrasted with the more demanding test of "instant" harm for the closely related defence of duress.[68] It has also been noted that section 81 does not specify the types of threatened harms, leaving them open ended. Third, the defendant must have been "without any fault or negligence"[69] in creating the circumstances of necessity.

2. Self-Defence

The provisions dealing with the defence of person and of property are spelled out in great detail in the Code.[70] Two preconditions have to be met before the right of self-defence arises. The first is that an offence affecting the human body or property was being committed against the defendant or some other person.[71] A supplementary provision specifies circumstances when the law will recognize the right of self-defence even though the act confronting the defendant was not an offence. These circumstances include the aggressor's youth, want of maturity of understanding, unsoundness of mind, intoxication, and mistake of fact.[72] The second precondition is that there must not have been time for the defendant or person threatened to have recourse to the protection of the public authorities.[73]

If the preconditions are met, there are certain other requirements that have to be satisfied for the defence to succeed. One requirement is that the defendant must have reasonably apprehended the particular danger which he or she claims compelled him or her to take defensive action. In relation to defence of the person, the Code expressly provides that the right to self-defence extends to the causing of death if the defendant reasonably apprehended a threat of death or grievous hurt or, in the case of an assault for the purpose of wrongful confinement, reasonably apprehended that he or she would be unable to have recourse to the public authorities for his or her release.[74] With regard to defence of property, fatal force may be used against certain specified threats, such as where the defendant reasonably apprehended death or grievous hurt to be a consequence of theft, mischief, or house trespass.[75] The duration of the right of self-defence is commensurate with the duration of the danger as reasonably apprehended by the defendant.[76]

A further requirement of self-defence is that the defendant must not have inflicted "more harm than it is necessary to inflict for the purpose of defence."[77] When dealing with this requirement, the courts have held that the force used by the defendant "should not be weighed in golden scales."[78] A person need not wait till the attack has commenced to exercise his or her right of self-defence. Depending on the circumstances, such a preemptive strike could satisfy the requirement of necessary harm.[79] There is also no legal duty to retreat; although having an opportunity to retreat may tell against the defendant in respect of satisfying the requirement of necessary harm, it is not conclusive about that requirement.

3. *Consent*

The Code devotes several sections to outlining different sets of circumstances when consent would be a full defence.[80] The term *consent* is not defined in the Code. The courts have held that for consent to be valid, the giver must have fully understood the nature and consequences of the conduct consented to, and that mere submission or passivity is not consent.[81] Furthermore, section 90 provides that consent is vitiated if it was given by a person under fear of injury or under a misconception of fact, or of unsound mind or intoxicated so as not to understand what he or she consented to, or who was under twelve years of age. The Code adopts the individualistic libertarian stance that the criminal law should intervene only where there was harm to others. Accordingly, where a "victim" consents to harm and no other person is hurt, the criminal law should not intervene, whether on moral, paternalistic, or utilitarian grounds.

The main provisions of the defence of consent are sections 87 and 88. Section 87 embraces most fully the individualistic libertarian philosophy concerning consensual harm. It provides that so long as the consenting party was above eighteen years of age, the doer is not criminally responsible for the harm consented to which the doer intentionally caused or knew he or she was likely to cause to the consenting party. There is no requirement that the harm-causing act have been beneficial in some way to the consenting party. The only restriction imposed by section 87 is that the doer must not have intended or known that death or grievous hurt would be caused.

The other main provision, section 88, differs materially from section 87 in several important respects. First, section 88 applies so long as the consenting party is twelve years of age or above,[82] whereas section 87 imposes the eighteen-year age restriction. Additionally, the doer under section 88 can intentionally or knowingly cause harm short of death. The explanation for this wider scope of section 88 is due to yet another difference between them, which is that under section 88, the act causing the harm must have been done for the benefit of the consenting party. The Code does not define the meaning of the term *benefit* other than that it excludes "mere pecuniary benefit."[83] The individualistic libertarian premise of the defence lets the doer and consenting party decide whether the harm-causing act had been done for the consenting party's benefit. However, the doer of the harm-causing act must have "in good faith" (i.e., with "due care and attention") intended the consenting party to benefit from that act.

4. Superior Orders

The defence of superior orders is recognized under section 76 of the Code, the relevant part of which reads: "Nothing is an offence which is done by a person who is . . . bound by law to do it." One of the accompanying illustrations is of a soldier who, in conformity with the law, obeys the order of his superior officer to fire at a mob. The soldier commits no offence by virtue of this provision. For these types of cases, it is immaterial whether the defendant believed that the order was lawful.[84] Such a belief is relevant only where the superior's order was found to have been unlawful, in which event the case will attract the excusatory defence, to be described in section II.E.6 in this chapter, that the subordinate mistakenly believed as a matter of fact that he or she was bound by law to obey the order.

Civil legislation will generally dictate what orders can be lawfully issued by a superior officer. During states of emergency or a period of martial law, the duties and attendant extraordinary powers exercised by police or military personnel will have received the endorsement of the civil law. Accordingly, an order which is authorized by the emergency legislation or martial law will be lawful for the purposes of the defence of superior orders.

A member of the police or armed forces should refuse to obey an order which he or she knows would result in a breach of the criminal law, even if such refusal may render him or her subject to military discipline. The judicial explanation for this stance is that "military discipline, while it regulates the conduct of a soldier in military matters, is made subject to a higher law in favor of public safety, when the act which the military discipline attempts to enforce or to justify is one which affects the person or property of another."[85]

E. Excuses

1. Mistake/Ignorance of Law or Fact

The primary Code provision on mistake is section 79, which concerns a person who, under a mistake of fact, believes that he or she was justified by law in committing an offence. The expression *justified by law* requires only that the actor's conduct have been lawful, while the term *law* denotes the general municipal law of the land. Section 79 expressly declares that mistake of law is not a defence. It imposes a blanket rule preventing mistakes of law from operating as a defence to a criminal charge. The strictness of this exclusionary rule is exemplified by a judicial ruling that a person who had accepted the decision of a court as a guide to his or her conduct was liable for a technical offence if that decision had subsequently been held not to express the correct law.[86] Mistake of law is, however, recognized as a mitigating factor in sentencing.[87]

The term *mistake* is not defined in the Code. It has been suggested that a mistake of fact consists of "an unconsciousness, ignorance, or forgetfulness of a fact, past or present, material to the transaction, or in the belief of the present existence of a thing material to the transaction, which does not exist, or in the past existence of a thing which has not existed."[88] Section 79 requires that the defendant's mistake pertain to a factual matter, as opposed to a legal one. A mistake of mixed fact and law has been treated by the courts as a mistake of fact for the purposes of these provisions.[89]

Section 79 requires the defendant to have "in good faith" (i.e., with "due care and attention") believed himself or herself to be bound or justified by law in doing a criminal act. The element "in good faith" under section 79 relates to the defendant's perception of the factual circumstances rather than to his or her performance of the criminal act. Furthermore, that perception must have led the defendant to believe that he or she was justified by law in doing the thing complained of. Certainly a defendant's careful performance of conduct would often support his or her belief that he or she was justified by law in doing it. But the inquiry into "in good faith" under section 79 does not stop at the defendant's conduct but proceeds from there to consider his or her belief. Although the concept "in good faith" is appraised objectively, account will be taken of certain personal characteristics of the defendant, together with the particular circumstances he or she experienced.[90]

2. Insanity/Diminished Capacity

The defence of insanity or diminished capacity, known as "unsoundness of mind," is contained in section 84 of the Code. It has been modeled after the principal rule pronounced in *M'Naghten's Case*,[91] the leading English common law authority on the defence of insanity. The Code does not define the term *unsoundness of mind* contained in section 84, and the courts have not elaborated upon it. The suggestion has been made that the term is wider than "disease of the mind" under the M'Naghten rules. Although *unsoundness of mind* is a legal term with a clinical component, it is finally the responsibility of the court to determine its application in any particular case.

A person is not exempt from criminal liability simply because he or she was of unsound mind at the time of the alleged offence. It must be shown that the unsoundness of mind was of a kind and severity which rendered the defendant "incapable of knowing the nature of the act or that he is doing what is either wrong or contrary to law."

The meaning of "nature of an act" is not elaborated in section 84. The courts have interpreted the expression as signifying the mental impairment of either the surface features of the act (such as cutting a person's throat believing it to be a loaf of bread) or the harmful consequences to the victim (such as causing his or her death). Under this interpretation, a defendant who was capable of knowing the surface features of his or her act but was too mentally disordered to be capable of knowing the harmful consequences of that act would be covered by the section 84 defence.

It has been held that the word *wrong* appearing in the phrase "either wrong or contrary to law" in section 84 refers to moral wrongness as opposed to legal wrongness (i.e., contrary to law).[92] The defence will apply where the defendant knew that his or her act was contrary to law but thought that it was morally right to do the act, and vice versa.[93]

3. Intoxication

The defence of intoxication is very narrowly circumscribed under section 85 of the Code. For the defence to succeed, the intoxication must have been involuntary; the relevant words of the provision state that "the thing which intoxicated him was administered to him without his knowledge or against his will." The defence is therefore limited to cases where the defendant was mistaken about the nature of the drink or drugs, or else the defendant's drink or medication was spiked or had been forced on him or her.

Even if this was the case, the defendant must go on to prove that his or her intoxicated condition was so severe as to have incapacitated his or her cognitive faculties in the same way and degree as that required for the defence of unsoundness of mind (i.e., insanity). The relevant part of section 85 states that "[n]othing is an offence which is done by a person who, at the time of doing it, is, by reason of intoxication, incapable of knowing the nature of the act, or that he is doing what is either wrong, or contrary to law." Since the form of incapacity is the same for both the defences of intoxication and unsoundness of mind, what distinguishes them is the cause of the incapacity. In respect of intoxication, it is drink or drugs, whose effect is transient by nature, compared with the cause of unsoundness of mind, which is of a longer-lasting nature.

Section 86 of the Code provides that in cases of voluntary intoxication, the same liability may be imposed on the defendant as could be imposed on a sober person who may have the knowledge to foresee the consequences of his or her conduct. With regard to crimes whose *mens rea* consists of an intention by the defendant to achieve the consequences of his or her conduct, voluntary intoxication could be a defence if the degree of intoxication was so severe as to negate that intention.[94]

4. Duress

The Code provides for the defence of duress under section 94, but murder and offences against the state punishable by death are excluded from its scope of operation. Section 94 unequivocally specifies that nothing short of a threat of instant death to the defendant will suffice. Thus the defence will be unavailable in cases where the threat was of some lesser harm, was not immediate, or was directed at a third party.

Another requirement of the defence is that the threat must have "reasonably cause[d] the apprehension" of instant death, so that it is not simply the defendant's belief but what he or she reasonably believed to be the nature of the threat. There is also a proviso in section 94 which requires that the defendant "did not of his own accord . . . place himself in the situation by which he became the subject" of the threat. The example given in the Code is that of a person who voluntarily joins a gang of robbers with knowledge of their character. He is not entitled to the benefit of the defence should he subsequently be compelled by his associates to do anything which is an offence. The wording of the proviso is also capable of being interpreted so as to require the defendant to have taken a reasonable opportunity to escape from his or her threatener.

5. Entrapment

The Code does not have a provision recognizing entrapment as a defence, and the courts have refused to do so, treating the issue as an evidentiary matter. The courts have drawn a distinction between so-called legitimate and illegitimate traps. The former consists of cases where the offence was going to be committed in any event, and the trap was laid in order for the offence to be detected. The latter involves cases where there was no thought of committing an offence, and a temptation was offered to see if an offence would be committed in succumbing to it.

In respect of a legitimate trap, the law-enforcement officer taking part in the trap and witnesses to the trap are not accomplices in any sense, and their evidence will not require corroboration, although prudence will require that the evidence be carefully scrutinized and accepted as true before a conviction can be secured.[95] With regard to an illegitimate trap, the evidence obtained will be admissible only if it is corroborated. Furthermore, the persons participating in the trap will be guilty of an offence unless such entrapment was authorized by the legislature.[96]

6. Superior Orders

The Code recognizes that there may be instances where a subordinate mistakenly believed that he or she was bound by law to obey an order which turned out to be unlawful. This recognition is afforded by section 76, the relevant part of which states that "[n]othing is an offence which is done by a person . . . who by reason of a mistake of fact and not by reason of a mistake of law in good faith believes himself to be bound by law to do it." Where the subordinate knew that the order was unlawful, he or she is prevented from pleading section 76.

This defence comes into play only where the subordinate did not know that the order was unlawful. It is crucial to determine just what the subordinate did not know concerning the legality of the order. If the subordinate thought that the superior officer had legal authority to make the order when he or she did not, this is a mistake of law and therefore falls outside the operation of section 76. It is only where the subordinate mistakenly believed that the factual circumstances warranted giving the order and that he or she was therefore bound to obey it that the defence under section 76 is applicable. The defendant will be acquitted of any offence if he or she had "in good faith" (i.e., with "due care and attention") believed that the circumstances were such as to make the order lawful.[97] Although some judgments have described unlawful orders attracting section 76 as being "manifestly unlawful,"[98] this concept should not be regarded separately from the wording and tenor of section 76 with its focus on the reasonableness of the subordinate's mistake concerning the lawfulness of the order.

F. Sanctions

1. Punishment

As noted in section II.A, the strong utilitarian underpinnings of the Code gave no room for the theory of rehabilitation. In recent times there has been a move to humanize punishment by considering not only the criminal conduct but the offender as a person. Some results of this shift are the abolition of whipping as a type of punishment on account of its brutality, and the introduction of probation as an alternative to imprisonment.

There are five types of punishment available: the death penalty, life imprisonment, imprisonment, forfeiture, and fine. The death penalty is discussed in section II.F.3. Life imprisonment means rigorous (as opposed to simple) imprisonment for the remainder of an offender's life. Although the executive is empowered to commute the sentence, an embargo is imposed on the lifer to serve at least fourteen years of imprisonment.[99] There are two kinds of imprisonment, rigorous and simple. An offender sentenced to rigorous imprisonment is required to perform hard labor, such as digging earth and grinding corn, whereas one who is undergoing simple imprisonment does not have to do any kind of work. A court which imposes a sentence of imprisonment is required to state its reasons for not extending the benefit of probation to the offender.[100]

The punishment of forfeiture used to be available for quite a number of offences but is now confined to three offences in which the offender has to give up specific property. They are depredations on the territories of any power in alliance or at peace with the government of India (s. 126), knowingly receiving property taken by war or depredations under section 126 (s. 127), and a public servant unlawfully buying property which the public servant by virtue of his or her office is prohibited from buying (s. 169). Fines are forfeitures of a sum of money by way of penalty. They may be imposed as the sole punishment, as an alternative punishment, or as an additional punishment.

2. Quantity/Quality of Punishment

The sentencing decision is generally left entirely to the discretion of the judge. In deciding the appropriate punishment, the judge will consider the nature and magnitude of the offence, as well as the need for the penalty to be proportionate to the offence.[101]

Judges are empowered to impose concurrent or consecutive sentences and are inclined to have sentences run concurrently where the ends of justice are met. There are also statutory provisions which limit the amount of punishment. For example, section 71 of the Code protects an offender against multiplicity of punishment by providing that where he or she intended to commit an offence the commission of which involved perpetration of acts which are themselves punishable, the offender shall not be punished for them separately.

Except for a few offences, only the maximum punishments are prescribed for offences; the rationale is that the imposition of minimum punishments unduly restrains the sentencing judge from tailoring the penalty to fit the offender. The practice of the courts has been to impose the maximum punishment, whether of imprisonment or a fine, only in extreme cases.

The Code does not distinguish between positive activity and an omission in specifying the penalty to be imposed on an offender. Persons convicted of abetment are liable for the same penalty as that prescribed for the substantive offence.[102] Those convicted of attempt are generally liable for up to one-half the maximum term of imprisonment provided for the complete offence.[103]

Life imprisonment aside, the maximum term of imprisonment that a court can impose is fourteen years,[104] and the lowest term actually provided for a given offence is twenty-four hours. The judge has discretion to impose either rigorous or simple imprisonment unless otherwise directed by the law. Some offences, such as armed robbery or attempting such robbery, attract a minimum term of imprisonment. The amount of a fine may be limited or unlimited, depending on the offence. Some provisions specify that the convict "shall be punished with imprisonment and shall also be liable to fine." This has been judicially interpreted to mean that a sentence of imprisonment must be imposed, but that the court has discretion whether to add a fine.[105]

3. Death Penalty

The death penalty may be imposed for a small number of offences—murder, robbery accompanied by murder, attempted murder by a person serving a life sentence if hurt is caused, waging war against the government of India, abetting mutiny actually committed, and giving false evidence upon which an innocent person suffers death.

The courts have upheld the constitutionality of the death penalty and have affirmed the view that hanging by the neck until death ensues is scientific and one of the least painful methods of execution.[106] Furthermore, they have striven to confine the imposition of the death penalty to the gravest cases of extreme culpability. In particular, the Supreme Court has declared that life imprisonment is the rule and the death penalty the exception and that any mitigating factors should be given their full weight.[107]

III. SPECIAL PART

A. Structure

The Code has chapters which classify offences according to the interests protected, namely, those of the state, the state apparatus, the public, the person, and property. Offences against the state aim to prevent the state's legal authority from being undermined. They include treasonable offences and seditious conduct causing hatred, contempt, or disaffection toward the state. Offences against the state apparatus protect the processes of justice and prohibit the corruption of public servants. Examples are obstructing public servants in the discharge of their duties, fabricating false evidence, and bribing a public servant. The use of criminal sanctions to protect the state and the state apparatus seeks to preserve the security of the social order.

Offences against the public seek to maintain public tranquility, public health, and public morals. Examples are unlawful assembly, rioting, affray, promoting disharmony between racial or religious groups, selling adulterated food, spreading infectious diseases, and the sale, publication, or distribution of obscene materials with a view to corrupting the morals of susceptible persons.

Offences against the person and property aim to protect the human body and the proprietary interests of individuals. Examples of offences against the person are culpable homicide, causing hurt, rape, criminal force, endangering human life or personal safety, and wrongful confinement. Offences against property include theft, cheating, criminal breach of trust, extortion, robbery, criminal trespass, housebreaking, and receiving stolen property.

B. Homicide

1. Murder/Manslaughter

The Code uses the term *culpable homicide* to describe killings involving a very high degree of culpability. There are two types of culpable homicide: murder and culpable homicide not amounting to murder. The Code commences with a definition of culpable homicide (s. 299), which is followed by a definition of murder (s. 300). Under this structure, culpable homicide not amounting to murder is what is left of section 299 which does not overlap with murder. The various types of *mens rea* for murder and culpable homicide not amounting to murder can be categorized as intention-based and knowledge-based. These types of *mens rea* fit into a structure where the degrees of fault are carefully graded in comparison with one another.

In relation to intention-based *mens rea*, the Code structure places at the apex the paradigm mental element of murder, that of an intention to cause death (s. 300(1)). Below this is an intention to cause such bodily injury as the offender knows to be likely to cause the death of the person to whom the harm is caused (s. 300(2)). This comes very close to the paradigm mental element for murder, given that the offender intended the bodily harm knowing that it was likely to cause death. Consequently, he or she deserves to be convicted of murder. Next in order of degree of culpability is an intention to cause bodily injury to any person, where the injury intended is sufficient in the ordinary course of nature to cause death (s. 300(3)). This is a hybrid subjective/objective form of *mens rea*, with the offender intending to cause the bodily injury which is objectively appraised to "most probably"[108] cause death. Therefore, it is not as culpable as the offence in section 300(2) but nevertheless comes close to it and therefore warrants liability for murder. Where an offender intends to cause bodily injury which is objectively appraised to be "likely" (that is, "probably" as opposed to "most probably") to cause death, he or she is regarded as not displaying the *mens rea* required for murder but for culpable homicide not amounting to murder (s. 299(2)).

With regard to knowledge-based *mens rea*, an offender who does an act knowing that it is so imminently dangerous that it must in all probability cause death or such bodily injury as is likely to cause death and who lacks any excuse for incurring the risk is regarded by the Code as displaying the fault for murder (s. 300(4)). Although knowledge is generally not in the same league as intention, knowledge of the virtual certainty[109] of causing death or bodily injury likely to cause death is comparable in degree of culpability with the forms of intentional murder under section 300(3). Where an offender does an act knowing that it is "likely" (i.e., "probable" as opposed to virtually certain) to cause death, this lesser degree of knowledge compared with section 300(4) warrants him or her being convicted of culpable homicide not amounting to murder (s. 299(3)). Where an offender has done an act knowing that it could possibly (as opposed to "be likely to/probably") cause death, he or she has not displayed the *mens rea* required for culpable homicide under the Code. Consequently, such an offender is guilty of the much less serious crime of causing death by a rash act (s. 304A).

Cases of negligent killings do not constitute culpable homicide but the much less serious offence of causing death by a negligent act under section 304A of the Code.[110] The *mens rea* for this offence consists of a gross departure from the standard of care expected of a reasonable person.[111]

A defendant charged with murder may seek to have his or her offence reduced to culpable homicide not amounting to murder by relying on one of the "special exceptions" (i.e., partial defences) to section 300. These exceptions are provocation,[112] exceeding the exercise of self-defence,[113] exceeding the exercise of legal powers,[114] sudden fight,[115] and consent.[116] Provocation is dealt with in section III.B.2 in this chapter. Exceeding self-defence is made out in two situations. The first is where the defendant honestly, albeit mistakenly and unreasonably, apprehended that the nature of the attack was of a type[117] against which the Code permitted the use of fatal force. The second situation is where the defendant honestly believed that the fatal force used was necessary when it was not. The Code is also prepared to partially excuse public servants who had exceeded their powers by using fatal force in circumstances which did not warrant their doing so. They would be liable for culpable homicide not amounting to murder if they believed in good faith that their act was lawful and necessary for the due discharge of their duty as a public servant, and without ill will toward the victim.

The partial defence to murder of sudden fight requires that the defendant have killed his or her victim in a sudden fight in the heat of passion upon a sudden quarrel, without premeditation and without the defendant having taken undue advantage or acted in a cruel or unusual manner. With respect to consent, it was noted in section II.D.3 in this chapter that sections 87 and 88 of the Code expressly exclude cases where the doer intended his or her act to cause death to the consenting party or else knew that it was likely to cause death.[118] Exception 5 to section 300 of the Code provides that in such a case the defendant is liable only for culpable homicide not amounting to murder if the victim was above the age of eighteen years and had consented to suffer death or take the risk of death. This defence has been successfully pleaded by survivors of suicide pacts and in cases of mercy killings.

2. Provocation

Provocation is covered in exception 1 to section 300 of the Code and, if successfully pleaded, reduces the offence of murder to culpable homicide not amounting to murder. For the defence to succeed, the offender must have been deprived of his or her power of self-control as a result of grave and sudden provocation offered by the deceased, which caused the offender to kill the deceased. The provocation can constitute conduct or words, and there is case authority which recognizes hearsay provocation provided the defendant had reasonable grounds to believe that the provocation had actually occurred.[119] Furthermore, the provocation need not have been directed at the defendant but could have been aimed at someone else.[120]

Although the exception does not specify an objective test, the courts have read one into the exception by requiring that for the defence to succeed, "a reasonable man, belonging to the same class of society to which the defendant belongs, and placed in the situation in which the defendant was placed, would be so provoked as to lose his self-control."[121] On this basis, there have been cases which have held that a defendant's ethnic background can be taken into account when applying the objective test, both in relation to its effect on the gravity of the provocation and with regard to the power of self-control expected of the reasonable person.[122]

A proviso accompanying the exception disallows the defence where the provocation was "sought or voluntarily provoked by the offender as an excuse for killing or doing harm to any person." A second proviso renders the defence unavailable where the provocation consisted of conduct performed by a public servant in the lawful exercise of his or her powers, and a third does the same in respect of conduct involving the lawful exercise of the right of self defence.

C. Sex Offences

The Code recognizes several sex offences, which can be categorized into those based on the victim's lack of consent and those where conduct is criminal irrespective of consent. The major offences under the first category are rape and assault with intent to outrage modesty. Those in the second category include carnal intercourse against the order of nature, incest, and sexual conduct involving children.

Rape occurs when a man penetrates a woman's vagina with his penis without her consent.[123] The offence is therefore gender specific and excludes penetration of other bodily orifices by the penis, as well as penetration of the vagina by another object. The Code does not define the term *consent* but assumes that its meaning is clear and then refers to circumstances when consent is vitiated.[124] The provision on rape supplements these circumstances by stipulating that the victim has not consented when the defendant has put her in fear of bodily injury, and also when the defendant knew that the victim had mistakenly believed him to be her husband.[125] The prosecution does not need to prove that the defendant knew that the victim was not consenting to sexual intercourse with him. Rather, it is for the defendant to contend that he lacked such knowledge by relying on the defence of mistake of fact provided for under the Code.[126] This requires the defendant to show that he had "in good faith" (i.e., with "due care and attention") believed that the victim had consented. Consequently, the defendant's belief must have been reasonable if it is to relieve him of liability. A husband can be convicted of raping his wife only if she was under fifteen years of age. The Code also makes it an offence for a husband to have sexual intercourse with his wife without her consent if she is living separately from him under a decree of separation.[127]

The offence of assaulting or using criminal force with intent to outrage the modesty of a woman can be committed by both men and women.[128] For the charge to be established, the prosecution must prove that the defendant used or threatened to use force on the victim without her consent, and that the defendant intended to outrage modesty or knew that his or her conduct was likely to outrage modesty. The Code does not define the meaning of the term *modesty*; the likely reason is that the concept can vary over time and depends on the context in which the conduct occurs. The Supreme Court has stated that "the quality of being modest in relation to women means 'womanly propriety of behavior, scrupulous chastity of thought, speech and conduct.'"[129] Because of the focus of the offence on the defendant's intention or knowledge, a person charged with outraging modesty could contend that he or she lacked the *mens rea* of the offence because he or she honestly (albeit unreasonably) believed that the victim had consented.[130]

The offence of carnal intercourse against the order of nature is committed when the defendant penetrates a person's anus or mouth with his penis.[131] It follows that the offence can be committed only by a male, although the "victim" can be either a male or a female. All such acts are covered by the offence, including those which were consensual and performed in private. If the act was consensual, the "victim" can be charged with abetting the offence.

D. Theft and Fraud

Theft is defined in section 378 of the Code as follows: "Whoever, intending to take dishonestly any movable property out of the possession of any person without that person's consent, moves that property in order to such taking is said to commit theft." The physical element of the offence is that the defendant must have moved (however slightly) the victim's movable property, and it is unnecessary for the property to have been removed from the victim's possession. The explanations accompanying section 378 show that movement can occur indirectly, such as where the defendant has caused an animal to move so that the item of the alleged theft is also moved, or where the defendant has removed obstacles to the subject matter's movement.[132] The Code defines "movable property" as "corporeal property of every description, except land and things attached to the earth, or permanently fastened to anything which is attached to the earth."[133] It has been observed that the offence of theft protects possessory rather than ownership interests. Consequently, a person can be held criminally liable for stealing his or her own property, provided that it can be proved that he or she acted dishonestly.

The *mens rea* of theft is that the defendant must have intended to take the property dishonestly out of the victim's possession without his or her consent. The Code defines "dishonestly" in terms of a person "intending to cause wrongful gain or wrongful loss."[134] "Wrongful gain" is in turn defined as "gain by unlawful means of property to which the person gaining is not legally entitled," and "wrongful loss" constitutes "loss by unlawful means of property to which the person losing it is legally entitled."[135] In particular, the courts have held that the concept of wrongful loss is broad enough to cover short-term as well as longer-term deprivations. It is unnecessary to prove any actual loss or gain—what is material is that the defendant intended to cause wrongful loss or gain. Accordingly, other forms of *mens rea*, such as knowledge, rashness, or negligence, will not suffice.

There is some judicial uncertainty whether the issue of consent forms part of the *actus reus* or *mens rea* elements of theft.[136] However, if one takes into account the syntax and punctuation in section 378, it is clear that lack of consent forms part of the *mens rea*. Accordingly, the issue is not whether the victim consented to the taking but whether the defendant intended to take without consent.

Cases of fraud are dealt with under the offence of cheating, which is provided for under section 415 of the Code. For the *actus reus* of cheating to be made out, the prosecution must prove that the defendant deceived the victim and thereby induced him or her (1) to deliver property to any person; (2) to consent to another person retaining property; or (3) to do or omit to do something which caused or was likely to cause damage or harm to that person in body, mind, reputation, or property. The *mens rea* for (1) and (2) is "fraudulently" or "dishonestly," and for (3) it is "intentionally."

Unlike theft, cheating is not limited to movable property, nor is it an offence against possession or ownership; it relates simply to the delivery or retention of property. Deception and dishonesty are separate elements of the offence, so that it is incumbent on the prosecution to particularize the deception and not merely to allege dishonesty. An explanation accompanying section 415 states that a "dishonest concealment of facts" can constitute deception.

The meaning of "dishonestly" has been dealt with in the discussion of theft. "Fraudulently" is defined unhelpfully by the Code as follows: "A person is said to do a thing fraudulently if he does that thing with intent to defraud but not otherwise."[137] The courts have held that a person acts with intent to defraud if he or she intends that some person be deceived and that, through such deception, an advantage should accrue to him or her, or that injury, loss, or detriment should befall some other person.[138] Therefore, in contrast to dishonesty, fraudulence can exist even where there was no intention to cause any property gain or loss or a detriment that can be measured in financial terms. It appears to be sufficient that the defendant intended to cause some advantage or to imperil another person's interests in some way.

E. "Victimless" Crimes

Many of the common forms of victimless crimes are also found in India, such as the failure to wear seat belts in motor vehicles or crash helmets when riding motorcycles.[139] It is also an offence to engage in gambling other than the forms of gambling authorized by the state.[140] Another example is the use of prohibited drugs except for medical or scientific purposes.[141] Furthermore, homosexual intercourse between consenting adults is covered by the offence of "carnal intercourse against the order of nature" under the Code.[142] Although engaging in prostitution voluntarily is legal, it is an offence to solicit or loiter in or near public places.[143]

Other offences falling within the description of victimless crimes are those against public order and morals which, by their nature, may annoy or cause affront (as opposed to physical injury) to members of the public in general. One example is the offence of public nuisance, which is committed when a person "does any act which causes annoyance to the public,"[144] such as urinating in a public place. Another is the sale of obscene material, which is defined as "tend[ing] to deprave and corrupt persons who are likely to read, see or hear" the material.[145]

To these offences may be added specifically political offences recognized by the Code which are directed against the body politic, so that no individuals are injured as such. Examples are flag desecration, treason, abuse of political power which does not involve specific persons, and electoral fraud.

F. Offences Involving Cruelty to Wives and Dowry Deaths

The phenomenon of wives in northern Indian communities being killed by their husbands or in-laws, or committing suicide on account of their cruelty, has frequently caught the attention of both the national and the international media. The problem became so acute in the 1980s that legislation was enacted creating new offences and making their prosecution easier. Section 498A of the Code makes both physical and mental cruelty by husbands or their relatives for the purpose of obtaining the wife's dowry an offence punishable by three years' imprisonment and a fine. The offence has been designated as cognizable (arrestable without a warrant) and non-bailable to provide the wife immediate relief from such cruelty.

Additionally, section 304B of the Code creates the offence of "dowry death." It provides that where the death of a woman is caused by burns or bodily injury or occurs otherwise than under normal circumstances within seven years of her marriage and this occurrence is preceded by cruelty or harassment by the husband or his relatives in connection with the demand for the dowry, the husband or his relatives shall be deemed to have caused the death. Accordingly, the normal rules of causation do not apply; it is sufficient that there was a connection between the death and the cruelty or harassment. The offence is punishable by imprisonment for not less than seven years but may extend to life imprisonment.

Section 498A of the Code and section 113A of the Evidence Act raise a rebuttable presumption that the husband or his relatives have abetted the suicide of his wife if she died within seven years of her marriage under suspicious circumstances.[146] This provision is attracted whenever there is evidence that the deceased woman had been subjected to cruelty by her husband or his relatives, who then have to prove their innocence.

Although these initiatives are commendable, they have been criticized for not going far enough to protect battered wives. In particular, they fail to protect wives who are subjected to beatings and cruelty by their husbands and relatives for reasons unconnected with the obtaining of dowries. For these types of cases, the usual Code offences of causing hurt or grievous hurt apply. A problem with these offences is that they are concerned only with bodily injury and not with mental harm. Also, because they are bailable offences, they enable the offender to be released immediately upon furnishing bail, which poses a grave risk to the wife's personal safety.

G. Voluntary Active Euthanasia and Physician-Assisted Suicide

Suicide is not an offence, but attempted suicide is under section 309 of the Code. The Law Commission of India in its *42nd Report, Penal Code* recommended the repeal of this offence on the ground that it was harsh and unjustifiable to punish a person who had already found life so unbearable.[147] The recommendation was accepted by the government but has yet to become law.[148] Abetting (or assisting) suicide is an offence under section 306 of the Code. So too is abetting attempted suicide by virtue of section 309 read with section 107 (the main provision on abetment) of the Code.

These various provisions criminalize both voluntary active euthanasia and assisted suicide performed by physicians on their patients. What role, if any, does the law give to the patient's consent in such cases? If voluntary active euthanasia and assisting suicide are regarded as acts of mercy killing, reference may be made to section 88 of the Code, which states in part that "nothing . . . is an offence by reason of any harm which it may cause, or be intended by the doer to cause . . . to any person for whose benefit it is done in good faith, and who has given consent . . . to suffer that harm."[149] However, this provision is unavailable to a person performing voluntary active euthanasia or assisting suicide because it expressly excludes cases where the accused "intended to cause death." In this regard, it has been observed that section 88 could be relied on by a physician who engages in the accepted medical practice of withdrawing treatment from a terminally ill patient to hasten the process of dying from a disease.[150] The physician does not intend to cause his or her patient's death as such, although he or she knows that the termination of treatment will cause the patient to die more quickly. The same may be said of a physician who administers strong doses of pain-relieving drugs to a patient knowing that a side effect of these drugs is to hasten the patient's death. In both cases the physician could invoke section 88 because he or she had withdrawn the treatment or administered the pain relieving drugs in good faith for the benefit of the patient, because the patient (who had consented to the medical procedure) was relieved from suffering prolonged and severe pain. Insofar as cases of voluntary active euthanasia by physicians are concerned, consent of the patient is given some significance by reducing what would otherwise be the crime of murder to the lesser offence of culpable homicide not amounting to murder.[151]

There have been several challenges before the Supreme Court to the constitutional validity of the offence of abetting suicide under section 306 of the Code. The leading decision is the Supreme Court case *Gian Kaur v. State of Punjab*,[152] which involved an appeal by the appellants against their convictions for abetting the commission of suicide by one Kulwant Kaur on the basis that the offence under section 306 was unconstitutional. The court held unanimously that section 309 and, consequently, section 306 did not violate article 21 of the constitution, which embodies the fundamental right to "protection of life."[153] The appellants had argued that this right included both the positive and negative aspects so that the right to live includes the right not to live, that is, the right to die or to end one's life.[154] Accordingly, section 309 violated article 21 by criminalizing attempted suicide. The court rejected this argument by noting that "by no stretch of imagination can 'extinction of life' be read to be included in 'protection of life.'"[155]

On the basis of *Gian Kaur*, the constitutional validity of the offence of abetting suicide under section 306 can safely be put to rest. However, this does not in any way prevent the legislature from abolishing or qualifying that offence. Although the constitutional basis for the offence may be sound, it is the prerogative of Parliament to decide whether the offence should remain or be qualified in some way. The beginning of the twenty-first century has witnessed India's economy growing as never before, making an increasingly sizable portion of the society able both to afford and to demand medical treatment and services which will prolong life. It will be a matter of time before this social phenomenon spawns the debate, occurring elsewhere, concerning the prohibition of assisted suicide and voluntary active euthanasia conducted by physicians.

SELECTED BIBLIOGRAPHY

(* Revised by these persons.)
Banerjee, T. K. *Background to Indian Criminal Law*. Bombay: Orient Longmans, 1963.
*Chandra Chud, Y. V., V. R. Manoher, and Avtar Singh. *Ratanlal and Dhirajlal's The Indian Penal Code*. 31st ed. Nagpur: Wadha & Co., 2006.

Dube, Dipa. *Rape Laws in India*. New Delhi: LexisNexis, 2008.
Indian Law Institute. *Essays on the Indian Penal Code*. Rev. ed. New Delhi: Indian Law Institute, 2005.
Law Commission of India. *42nd Report, Penal Code*. New Delhi: Government of India, 1971.
Nigam, Ramesh Chandra. *Law of Crimes in India*. Vol. 1, *Principles of Criminal Law*. Bombay: Asia Publishing House, 1965.
Raju, Vadrevu Bhadir. *Commentaries on the Penal Code*. 4th ed. Delhi: Eastern Book Co., 1982.
Saxena, Shobha. *Crime against Women and Protective Laws*. New Delhi: Deep & Deep Publications, 1995.
*Singh, B. P., and G. S. Sharma. *RA Nelson's The Indian Penal Code*. 8th ed. Allahabad: Law Book Co., 1996.
*Srivastava, A. B. *HS Gour's The Penal Law of India*. 11th ed. Allahabad: Law Publishers, 2000.
*Thakker, C. K., and M. C. Thakker. *Ratanlal and Dhirajlal's Law of Crimes*. 26th ed. New Delhi: Bharat House, 2007.

NOTES

1. *Emperor v. Chhotalal Babar* (1912) ILR 36 Bom 524.
2. For example, the Indian Army Act 1950.
3. For example, the Indian Merchandise Marks Act 1889, s. 15.
4. *Satwant Singh v. State of Punjab* AIR 1960 SC 266.
5. *Rao Shiv Bahadur Singh v. State of Uttar Pradesh* 1953 SCR 1188.
6. The General Clauses Act 1897, s. 8(38), reads: "'Offence' shall mean any act or omission made punishable by any law for the time being in force."
7. Penal Code, s. 41.
8. Ibid., s. 42.
9. Ibid., s. 40.
10. Some of the major ones appear in the selected bibliography in this chapter.
11. *Ram Chander v. State of Haryana* 1981 SCC (Cri) 683.
12. *State v. Bhalchandra Waman Pethe* AIR 1966 Bom 122 at 126.
13. *Dulla v. State* AIR 1958 All 198 at 203.
14. Y. V. Chandra Chud, V. R. Manoher, and Avtar Singh, *Ratanlal and Dhirajlal's The Indian Penal Code*, 31st ed. (Nagpur: Wadha & Co., 2006), 236.
15. *Modiram v. State of Madhya Pradesh* AIR 1972 SC 2438 at 2439.
16. *Emperor v. Bhogilal Chimanal Nanavati* AIR 1931 Bom 409 at [5]. Likewise, s. 3 of the Code states that the word *act* denotes as well a series of acts.
17. *Emperor v. Bhogilal Chimanal Nanavati* AIR 1931 Bom 409.
18. *Emperor v. Kaliappa Goundan* AIR 1933 Madras 798; *Emperor v. Nebal Mahto* (1939) ILR Pat 485.
19. Ramesh Chandra Nigam, *Law of Crimes in India*, vol. 1, *Principles of Criminal Law,* (Bombay: Asia Publishing House, 1965), 43.
20. *D'Souza v. Pashupati Nath Sarkar* 1968 Cri LJ 405.

21. *Jai Prakash v. State (Delhi Administration)* 1991 2 SCC 32 (Cri) at 42.
22. *Basdev v. State of Pepsu* AIR 1956 SC 488.
23. *In re. Nidarmati Nagabhushanam* (1872) 7 MHCR 119 at 120.
24. *Empress of India v. Idu Beg* (1881) 3 All 776 at 780.
25. Examples are s. 304 (causing death by negligent act); s. 284 (negligent conduct in respect to a poisonous substance); and s. 336 (negligently endangering human life or personal safety).
26. *Empress of India v. Idu Beg* (1881) 3 All 776 at 780.
27. *Bala Chandra v. State of Maharashtra* AIR 1968 SC 1319.
28. *Emperor v. Waryam Singh* 1927 Cri LJ 39.
29. Penal Code, s. 511.
30. For example, Penal Code, s. 307 (attempted murder); s. 308 (attempted culpable homicide not amounting to murder).
31. *Abhayanand Mishra v. State of Bihar* AIR 1961 SC 1698.
32. *State of Maharashtra v. Mohd Yakub* AIR 1980 SC 1111.
33. *Om Prakash v. State of Punjab* AIR 1961 SC 1712.
34. *Asgarali Pradhania v. Emperor* (1933) ILR 61 Cal 54.
35. Penal Code, s. 120A.
36. *Ajay Aggarwal v. Union of India* 1993 SCC (Cri) 961.
37. *Saleem-Ud-Din v. State* (1971) ILR 1 Delhi 432.
38. *Pradumna Shriniwas Auradkar v. State of Maharashtra* 1981 Cri LJ 1873.
39. *Yash Pal Mittal v. State of Punjab* AIR 1977 SC 2433.
40. *Emperor v. Shankaraya Gurushiddhayya Hiremath* AIR 1940 Bom 365.
41. Penal Code, explanation 2 to s. 108.
42. *Jamuna Singh v. State of Bihar* AIR 1967 SC 553.
43. Penal Code, explanation 4 to s. 108.
44. *Girjashankar v. State of Madhra Pradesh* 1989 Cri LJ 242.
45. *Harachan Chakrabarty v. Union of India* 1990 SCC (Cri) 280.
46. Penal Code, explanation 2 to s. 107.
47. *Harji v. State of Rajasthan* 1978 Raj LW 1.
48. *Mohd Jamal v. Emperor* AIR 1930 Sind 64.
49. Penal Code, explanation 3 to s. 108.
50. *Noor Mohammad Mohd Yusuf Momin v. State of Maharashtra* 1971 AIR SC 885. In *Jaikrishnadas Manohardas Desai v. State of Bombay* AIR 1960 SC 899 it was held that physical presence, though evidential of participation, was not invariably required.
51. *Bashir v. State* AIR 1953 All 668.
52. This first situation is subscribed to in several decisions of the Supreme Court, e.g., *Hardev Singh v. State of Punjab* AIR 1975 SC 179. However, there are lower-court case authorities which support the other two situations described in the text.
53. C. K. Thakker and M. C. Thakker, *Ratanlal and Dhirajlal's Law of Crimes*, 26th ed. (New Delhi: Bharat House, 2007), 143.
54. *State of Maharashtra v Syndicate Transport Co Ltd* AIR 1964 Bom 195.
55. First developed from the civil case of *Lennard's Carrying Company Ltd v. Asiatic Petroleum Company Ltd* [1915] AC 705.

56. *Gopal Khaitan v. State* AIR 1969 Cal 132.

57. *Dharma Pratishtan v. B Mandal* (1988) 173 ITR 487, following the English case *Tesco Supermarkets v. Nattrass* [1972] AC 153.

58. *Girdharilal v. Lalchand* AIR 1970 Raj 145.

59. *Municipal Corporation of Delhi v. JB Bottling Company Private Limited* 1975 Cri LJ 1148.

60. For example, see *Rangawalla v. State of Maharashtra* AIR 1965 SC 1616.

61. *Yohanan v. State* AIR 1958 Ker 207 at 210, cited by several commentators.

62. For example, *Yohanan v. State* AIR 1958 Ker 207; *Nga Moe v. The King* AIR Rang 141; *Nandkumar Natha v. State* 1988 Cri LJ 1313.

63. Constituting ss. 76 to 106 of the Penal Code.

64. Penal Code, s. 6.

65. Ibid., s. 40.

66. *James Martin v. State of Kerala* (2004) 2 SCC 203.

67. This element is found in the explanation to s. 81.

68. Penal Code, s. 94. Duress is discussed in section II.E.4 in this chapter.

69. This requirement is found in illustration (a) of s. 81.

70. Penal Code, ss. 96–106. The term "self-defence" is used here to cover both defence of person and of property.

71. Ibid., s. 97.

72. Ibid., s. 98.

73. Ibid., s. 99(3).

74. Ibid., s. 100.

75. Ibid., s. 103.

76. Ibid., s. 102.

77. Ibid., s. 99(4).

78. *Jai Dev v. State of Punjab* AIR 1963 SC 612 at 617.

79. *Govindan v. State* AIR 1960 Ker 258.

80. Penal Code, ss. 87–92.

81. *Dalip Singh v. State of Bihar* (2005) SCC 88.

82. By virtue of Penal Code, s. 90(d).

83. Penal Code, explanation to s. 92.

84. See *State of West Bengal v. Shew Mangal Singh* AIR 1981 SC 1917.

85. *Niamat Khan v. Empress* (1883) PR No. 17 of 1883 at 29.

86. *State v. Krishna Murari* 1955 Cr LJ 1025.

87. *State of Maharashtra v. Mayer Hans George* AIR 1965 SC 722.

88. Thakker and Thakker, *Ratanlal and Dhirajlal's Law of Crimes*, 276.

89. *State of Bombay v. Jaswantlal Manilal Akhaney* AIR 1956 SC 575.

90. *Chirangi v. State* AIR 1952 Nag 282.

91. (1843) 10 Cl. & Fin. 200.

92. *Shivraj Singh v. State* 1975 Cr LJ 1458.

93. *Ashiruddin Ahmed v. The King* AIR 1949 Cal 182.

94. *Basdev v. State of Pepsu* AIR 1956 SC 488.

95. *PP v. A Thomas* AIR 1959 Mad 166.

96. *Ramjanam Singh v. State of Bihar* AIR 1956 SC 643.

97. The requirements of mistake of fact and good faith are the same as for the closely related defence under Penal Code, s. 79, discussed in section II.E.1 in this chapter, of mistake of fact that one was justified by law in doing an act.

98. For example, see *Queen Empress v. Subba Naik* (1898) 21 Mad 249 at 251.

99. Criminal Procedure Code 1973, s. 433A.

100. Probation of Offenders Act 1958, s. 361.

101. *Sham Sunder v. Puran* AIR 1991 SC 8.

102. Penal Code, s. 109.

103. Ibid., s. 511.

104. Criminal Procedure Code, s. 31(2)(a).

105. *Emperor v. Durg* AIR 1929 All 260.

106. *Deena v. Union of India* AIR 1983 SC 1155.

107. *Machhi Singh v. State of Punjab* AIR 1983 SC 957.

108. Paraphrasing the words "sufficient in the ordinary course of nature to cause death" appearing in Penal Code, s. 300(3).

109. Paraphrasing the words "so imminently dangerous that it must in all probability cause death" appearing in Penal Code, s. 300(4).

110. The maximum penalty is two years' imprisonment.

111. *State v. Lazarus AW* AIR 1953 All 72.

112. Penal Code, exception 1 to s. 300.

113. Ibid., exception 2 to s. 300.

114. Ibid., exception 3 to s. 300.

115. Ibid., exception 4 to s. 300.

116. Ibid., exception 5 to s. 300.

117. These are specified in Penal Code, ss. 100 and 103.

118. See the discussion under the subheading "Consent," section II.D.3 in this chapter.

119. *Gohra v. Emperor* (1890) PR No. 7 of 1890; *Chanan Khan v. Emperor* 1943 Cri LJ 595.

120. *Indreswar Kalita v. State* 1981 Cri LJ 1887.

121. *Nanavati v. State of Maharashtra* AIR 1962 SC 605 at 630.

122. *Jamu Majhi v. State* 1989 Cri LJ 753; *Atma Ram v. State* 1967 Cri LJ 1697.

123. Penal Code, s. 375.

124. Ibid., s. 90. See the discussion under the subheading "Consent," section II.D.3 in this chapter.

125. Penal Code, s 375, fourth limb.

126. Ibid., s. 79. See the discussion of this plea under the subheading "Mistake/Ignorance of Law or Fact," section II.E 1 in this chapter.

127. Penal Code, s. 376A.

128. Ibid., s. 354. The offences of assault and criminal force are defined in ss. 351 and 350, respectively, of the Code.

129. *Rupan Deol Bajaj v. KPS Gill* AIR 1996 SC 309 at [14], quoting from the *Shorter English Dictionary*, 3d ed. (Oxford: Oxford University Press, 1944).

130. In contrast to the offence of rape, the difference being that the definition of rape does not include the intention or knowledge of the defendant pertaining to the victim's consent.

131. Penal Code, s. 377.
132. Ibid., explanations 3 and 4 to s. 378.
133. Ibid., s. 22.
134. Ibid., s. 24.
135. Ibid., s. 23.
136. For a case example favoring the former, see *KN Mehra v. State of Rajasthan* AIR 1957 SC 369; and for a case favoring the latter, see *Packeer Ally v. Svarimuttu* (1926) 2 CWR 216.
137. Penal Code, s. 25.
138. *Dr Vimla v. The Delhi Administration* AIR 1963 SC 1572.
139. Motor Vehicles Act 1988.
140. Public Gambling Act 1867.
141. Narcotic Drugs and Psychotropic Substances Act 1985.
142. Penal Code, s. 377.
143. Immoral Traffic (Prevention) Act 1956.
144. Penal Code, s. 268.
145. Ibid., s. 292.
146. Abetment of suicide is an offence under s. 306 of the Code.
147. Law Commission of India. *42nd Report, Penal Code* (New Delhi: Government of India, 1971), at [16.33].
148. The Law Commission of India has again recently recommended abolition; see *Report No. 210, Humanization and Decriminalization of Attempt to Suicide* (New Delhi: Government of India, 2008).
149. See further the discussion of this provision in the subheading "Consent," section II.D.3 in this chapter.
150. This is a form of passive euthanasia; see *Airedale National Health Authority Trust v. Bland* [1993] AC 789, referred to with approval by the Supreme Court of India in *Gian Kaur v. State of Punjab* AIR 1996 SC 1257 at [40].
151. Penal Code, Exception 4 to s. 300. See further the discussion of this partial defence to murder under the subheading "Murder/Manslaughter," section III.B.1 in this chapter.
152. AIR 1996 SC 1257.
153. Article 21 reads: "*Protection of life and personal liberty*: No person shall be deprived of his life or personal liberty except according to procedure established by law."
154. Relying on the judgment of the Supreme Court of India in *Rathinam* v. *Union of India* AIR 1994 SC 1844, which had held on this basis that s. 309 violated article 21 of the constitution.
155. *Gian Kaur v. State of Punjab* AIR 1996 SC 1257 at [22], thereby overruling *Rathinam* on this issue. See also *State of Maharashtra v. Maruti Shripati Dubal* AIR 1997 SC 411.

IRAN

Silvia Tellenbach

I. Introduction
   A. Historical Sketch
   B. Jurisdiction
   C. Legality Principle
   D. Sources of Criminal Law
   E. Process

II. General Part
   A. Theories of Punishment
   B. Liability Requirements
   C. Defenses
   D. Justifications
   E. Excuses
   F. Sanctions

III. Special Part
   A. Structure
   B. Homicide
   C. Sex Offenses
   D. Theft and Fraud
   E. "Victimless" Crimes
   F. Other Offenses

Silvia Tellenbach is Head of the Turkey, Iran and the Arab States section at the Max Planck Institute for Foreign and International Criminal Law in Freiburg, Germany. Her recent publications include "The Legality Principle in Iranian Constitutional and Criminal Law," 121 *Zeitschrift für die gesamte Strafrechtswissenschaft* 1054 (2009); and Silvia Tellenbach (ed.), *The Role of Honor in Criminal Law* (Duncker & Humblot, 2007).

I. INTRODUCTION

A. Historical Sketch

"All civil, penal, financial, economic, administrative, cultural, military, political and other laws and regulations must be based on Islamic criteria."[1] This principle, laid down in article 4 of the constitution of the Islamic Republic of Iran, adopted in 1979, is one of the basic principles of the new state that was founded after the breakdown of the shah's regime in the Islamic Revolution of 1979. As a consequence, in the first years of the Islamic Republic many laws of the former state were abolished. One of these was the General Criminal Code of 1926, the first Iranian penal code, which had been strongly influenced by the French Code Napoléon. It was replaced by four new laws in 1982 and 1983 that reflected the structure of classical Islamic criminal law. Because Islamic law categorizes crimes according to the punishments provided for them, the new Iranian laws contained four categories of crimes: crimes punished by fixed divine punishments (*hadd,* pl. *hodud*); crimes punished by retaliation (*qisas*); crimes punished by blood money (*diya*, pl. *diyat*); and crimes punished by chastisement (*ta'zir* penalties, pl. *ta'zirat*). Crimes punished by hadd penalties are the core of Islamic criminal law. They consist of a limited number of offenses for which the punishments are regarded as having been fixed by God in the Qur'an—the death penalty or severe corporal punishments. According to the Shi'i Dja'fari school, these offenses are theft, fighting against God and corruption on earth, unlawful sexual intercourse, homosexual and lesbian acts, pandering, defamation of having committed unlawful sexual intercourse, drinking alcohol, rebellion, and apostasy. In the Iranian penal code, however, rebellion is to a certain degree treated as part of fighting against God, and apostasy is not mentioned.[2] The chapter titled "Qisas" comprises the provisions regarding intentional homicide and bodily injury. The chapter titled "Diyat" refers to the blood money that has to be paid in cases of nonintentional crimes against life and bodily integrity when the blood avengers waive their claim to retaliation or in other cases prescribed by law.[3] Crimes punished by ta'zir penalties were hardly discussed by the Islamic jurists because they were regarded more or less as a matter of administration. It was left to the discretion of judges to punish any act that seemed to require a punishment according to the general principles of Islamic law. This concept gives Islamic law a remarkable flexibility and makes it able to react to the necessities of a particular space and time. Because of the concept of ta'zirat, Iran's new law on general provisions and the law on ta'zirat penalties continued to be influenced by French law. The laws of 1982 were revised in 1991 and united in one criminal code; the revised law of ta'zirat and *bazdarande* (deterrent) penalties was joined with the code in 1996.

The current Iranian Penal Code, known as the Islamic Penal Code (IPC), consists of five books. The general part (arts. 1–62) contains provisions referring to general concepts, such as the distinction between perpetrators and accessories, attempt, punishments, and so on. Unlike the penal codes of most countries, however, these provisions do not necessarily apply to all the crimes of the special part. Each provision has to be examined in order to determine whether it is applicable to all crimes or whether it is applicable only to ta'zirat and deterrent crimes. The special part is divided into four books: hadd (arts. 63–203), qisas (arts. 204–293), diyat (arts. 294–497), and ta'zirat and deterrent punishments,[4] a newly created category of offenses that is designed to protect public order and the interests of society (arts. 498–729). The last book contains the overwhelming majority of the offenses punishable in Iran.

The Islamic Penal Code of 1991 and 1996 is the most important law, but it is not the only law that refers to offenses in Iran. Offenses are also found in many pre- and postrevolutionary laws, such as the Anti-Drugs Act of 1988.

The IPC is under revision again, and a new draft has been presented to Parliament and passed to its committee on legal affairs. After having been examined by the Council of Guardians, which has lodged many objections, the draft has been returned to the committee again. It is not yet clear if or when it will replace the code that is currently in force.[5]

B. Jurisdiction

Criminal jurisdiction is regulated in detail in articles 3–8 of the IPC. As a rule, every crime committed in Iran is punished according to Iranian criminal law. In this sense, Iran means Iranian territory, Iranian waters, and Iranian airspace (art. 3 IPC). If part of the crime is committed in Iran and the result occurs abroad, or vice versa, the crime is regarded as having been committed in Iran (art. 4 IPC). Every Iranian and every foreigner who commits one of the crimes contained in article 5 of the IPC (most of them crimes against the interests of the Islamic Republic) outside Iran and is found in or extradited to Iran will be punished according to Iranian law. The same applies to every national or foreigner who is employed by the Iranian government, as well as every Iranian diplomat or cultural or consulate attaché enjoying diplomatic immunity (art. 6). Furthermore, every Iranian citizen who commits a crime abroad and is found in Iran is punished in accordance with Iranian criminal law (art. 7). Finally, the perpetrator of a crime that, according to international conventions or special laws, must be prosecuted in the country where he or she is found will be prosecuted according to Iranian law (art. 8). The current IPC does not apply the *ne bis in idem* rule,[6] which contains the prohibition of double jeopardy, in cases in which a perpetrator has been judged and punished abroad before being brought before an Iranian court.[7]

C. Legality Principle

The role of the principle of legality is not absolutely clear in Iranian criminal law. On the one hand, article 169 of the constitution provides that no act or omission can be regarded as a crime under a law that has been adopted after the commission of that act or omission. Similarly, article 36 of the constitution says that no criminal judgment can be pronounced except by a competent court on legal grounds. On the other hand, article 167 of the constitution states that although the judge is obliged to pronounce a judgment in any case brought before him according to the written laws, if he[8] cannot find such a law, he has to pronounce judgment on the basis of authoritative Islamic sources and fatwas. Iranian lawyers try to solve this seeming contradiction in different ways, of which two examples may be given here. According to one position, article 167 of the constitution has to be understood in the sense that the judge cannot create new legal provisions but can use authoritative Islamic sources and fatwas to interpret notions and concepts in the written law that are not explained clearly enough. Those sources are thus understood as means of interpretation.[9] Another position holds that an authoritative Islamic source and a fatwa have to be regarded as laws in the sense of articles 169 and 36 of the constitution.[10]

In Iranian scholarship, most authors defend the principle of legality in the sense of written law as a requirement for punishment. But there are some laws that seem intended to give the judge the power to derive a basis for punishment from authoritative Islamic sources and fatwas if there is a lacuna in the written law, as is pointed out, for example, in article 214 of the Code of Criminal Procedure, which describes the requirements of a judgment.[11] Note 1 to article 42 of the ordinance on the Special Court for the Clergy of 1990 (1369) goes a step further, saying that in exceptional cases a judge can pronounce a judgment based on his own opinion if there is no punishment provided in the religious law (*shar'*) or in the positive law.

Article 11 of the IPC contains the principle against retroactivity. Punishments, security measures, and educational measures have to be based on laws that were passed before the commission of the crime. No act or omission can be punished as a crime by virtue of a law *ex post*, except when the regulation in question favors the defendant. The principle against retroactivity does not apply, however, to the hadd and the qisas and diya laws. Because they are regarded as divine orders, it is assumed that they have been in force from the beginning of Islam.[12]

D. Sources of Criminal Law

1. Legislature

The most important legislative institution is the Parliament, called the Islamic Consultative Assembly. The Council of Guardians has to review laws adopted by the Parliament for conformity to the constitution and to Islamic precepts (art. 94 of the constitution). If the Council of Guardians holds that there is a violation of either, it returns the law to Parliament. The law can then be amended in accordance with the opinion of the Council of Guardians and passed again. If Parliament declines to amend the law and passes it again, the Expediency Council[13] has to provide a definitive resolution to the matter.

The Islamic Consultative Assembly is not the only lawgiver in Iran. First, it can delegate its legislative powers to commissions of Parliament that are empowered to enact laws for a limited time (for instance, for five or ten years). In such cases final approval rests with Parliament (art. 85 of the constitution). Famous examples of this type of lawgiving are the criminal laws of 1982 and 1983 and the first four books of the Penal Code of 1991.[14] In extremely important economic, political, social, and cultural matters, a law can also be enacted by a referendum (art. 58 of the constitution). The Expediency Council derives legislative authority from article 110, no. 8, which says that a religious leader can solve problems that cannot be solved by conventional methods through the Expediency Council.[15] But this claim is not uncontested.[16] Finally, there are some institutions that were empowered to make laws during a limited time in the history of the Islamic Republic. Examples include the decrees enacted by the Revolutionary Council in the first months after the Islamic Revolution, when the Parliament did not yet exist.

2. Judiciary

The courts have to apply the laws by rendering judgments, and the Supreme Court plays the most important role in this regard. Although most of the Supreme Court's decisions are not binding, they provide direction to the lower courts. There is, however, one type of judgment that almost has the function of a law, namely, a judgment that unifies the application of a law by the general courts. This type of judgment is pronounced by the Plenary Assembly if two divisions of the Supreme Court or two lower courts make contradictory decisions in similar cases.[17] It must be mentioned, however, that this kind of judgment cannot create new offenses; it can only give a binding interpretation of a certain legal problem that arises within the framework of a legal provisions adopted by the lawgiver.

Judges and prosecutors may also turn to the Law Office of the Judiciary for advice on legal problems. The opinions of the Law Office are not binding, but in practice they play a considerable role in providing direction to the judiciary. Finally, the head of the judiciary[18] can pass circulars *(bakhshname)* to the courts in which he prescribes how they should deal with and decide certain questions that arise in their proceedings.[19]

3. Executive

As provided in the constitution, the executive can enact ordinances for "performing its administrative duties, ensuring the implementation of laws" (art. 138 para. 1). Neither the government nor a single ministry, however, can enact provisions that impose criminal punishment. Nevertheless, the history of the Islamic Republic shows that there are exceptions to this rule, such as when the religious leader authorizes the executive to enact provisions that also create criminal offenses. This happened in 1987/1988 (1366/1367), when the executive was authorized by Ayatollah Khomeini to enact ordinances that contained a number of provisions concerning economic crimes (the so-called governmental ta'zirat offenses, *ta'zirat-e hukumati*). Another important ordinance enacted in that manner is the ordinance concerning the special courts for the clergy of 1990 (1369).[20]

4. Scholars

There are many voluminous and thorough commentaries on Islamic criminal law and on the Islamic Penal Code of Iran. Khomeini's famous work *Tahrir al-Wasila* must be mentioned first because it influenced a number of provisions in the IPC and is regarded as an absolutely authoritative source when used for solving a legal problem. There are also a number of famous classic scholars whose commentaries are used in courts and universities. Furthermore, there are many textbooks and monographs published by modern authors, most of whom teach in one of the Iranian universities. Many of them are familiar with Western law, especially French law, and the structure of their textbooks mostly follows the classical French theory of crime that distinguishes between a crime's legal element, material element *(actus reus)*, and moral element *(mens rea)*.

E. Process

1. Adversarial/Inquisitorial

The Iranian criminal process is still influenced by its French heritage, but the new Code of Criminal Procedure (CCP) of 1999 brought important changes and introduced a number of Islamic elements. Today the proceedings are a mixture of adversarial and inquisitorial procedures. Crimes are divided into three groups: those violating the rights of God (hadd crimes), those violating the rights of humans (e.g., homicide and bodily injury), and a group newly developed in Shi'i legal thinking, crimes violating the rights of the public and public order. The group to which a crime belongs determines the way in which proceedings must be started. In the case of a violation of the rights of God or the rights of the public or public order, the proceedings must begin with a public claim. In the case of a violation of the rights of humans, they must begin with a private claim. In cases in which a crime violates both kinds of rights, both types of claims are admissible. In cases based on public claims, the proceedings are merely inquisitorial; in cases based on private claims, there are adversarial elements as well.

The court has a strong inquisitorial role in the proceedings. It has to conduct the trial and, if necessary, to ensure that the investigations are completed. The court is responsible for questioning witnesses; cross-examination is not allowed (arts. 197 and 199 CCP). The court must also assess a defendant's confession, which is not itself sufficient to convict; it must be clear and confirmed by other means of proof without leaving reason for doubt (art. 194 CCP). The most important adversarial element in a criminal trial lies in the fact that in cases of homicide and bodily injury, the victim or the victim's blood avengers are free to ask retaliation, to settle with the perpetrator regarding blood money, or even to pardon the perpetrator.

2. Jury/Written Opinions

An Iranian court is normally composed of one or more judges who fulfill the conditions prescribed in the 1982 (1361) law concerning the election of judges. Apart from personal requirements, judges have to complete their legal studies in one of the institutions mentioned in the law. As a rule, therefore, there are no laymen and no juries in ordinary Iranian courts. The only exception is provided by article 168 of the Iranian constitution, which prescribes a jury for political and media crimes. There are some provisions referring to juries in the Press Law, and several laws about juries were adopted in 2000, 2004, and 2005. In practice, however, juries in proceedings for political offenses do not exist.

II. GENERAL PART

A. Theories of Punishment

Theories of punishment are not dealt with expressly in the IPC. Commentaries regard punishment as characterized by inflicting an evil and by restricting the rights of the criminal (e.g., the right to freedom if he or she is put in prison). Punishments protect important social values, such as life, bodily integrity, freedom, and property. Modern commentators hold that the aims of punishment are individual and general deterrence, retribution, and rehabilitation. Deterrence aims at preventing the general public from following the example of the offender and preventing the offender from committing a crime again. Retribution pleads for the satisfaction of the victim and of society. Rehabilitation aims at reintegrating the perpetrator into society by educating him or her to be a responsible citizen. In some crimes, all of these aims can be pursued at the same time; in other crimes, only one or two of these aims can be pursued. In the category of crimes punished by retaliation (killing, bodily injury) the satisfaction of the victim and/or his or her blood avengers—retribution—is essential.

B. Liability Requirements

1. Objective/Actus Reus

i. Act

The meaning of the term *act* is not defined in the IPC. Iranian jurisprudence defines an act as the "movement of a part of a human body," as an external activity,[21] or as conduct that influences or changes the world around us.[22] Conduct can have legal meaning only if it is guided by human will. In most criminal provisions the act that is required to cause a certain result is not described in a detailed manner. A provision forbids killing a person, for example, but is indifferent to the way in which this is done.

ii. Omission

Most crimes are committed by a positive act (*fi'l*) of the perpetrator. In some cases, however, the law specifically creates crimes that can be committed by the omission of a due act (*tark-e fi'l*). A husband who violates his obligation to pay alimony to his wife (art. 642 IPC), for example, commits a crime by failing to act in a manner required by law.

A special form of omission is "commission by omission" (*djara'im-e fi'l nashi az tark-e fi'l*). This expression means that a crime that is normally committed by a positive act may, in special circumstances, be committed by an omission. A famous example in Islamic law is the mother who kills her baby by not caring for it, who will be punished for murder.[23] There is no general provision in the IPC that prescribes the conditions under which an omission is equivalent to a positive act. Scholars also disagree about whether it is possible to speak of commission by omission in Iranian law.[24] Supporters of such commission refer to specific provisions, such as abandonment (art. 633 IPC), not to a general rule.[25]

iii. Status

In some cases criminal liability is not based on an act but on a status (*halat*), in the sense of a relationship of the offender to a certain situation. Article 16 of the Anti-Drugs Act punishes the psychical status of being a drug addict (*halat-e ma'nawi*), and article 712 of the IPC punishes vagrancy as a reproachable lifestyle (*halat-e idjtima'i*). Membership in certain criminal organizations is also regarded as a status (arts. 499 and 510 IPC).[26]

2. Subjective/Mens Rea/Mental Element

As reflected in the third and fourth books of the IPC, Islamic law divides mental states into three categories (intention, semi-intention, and mere inadvertency) for purposes of crimes against life and bodily integrity,. This section will thus briefly discuss the three mental states, leaving a fuller examination of them to the section on murder and manslaughter.[27] Otherwise, the law does not define mental states, such as intention or recklessness, in the general provisions. The Iranian literature distinguishes only between intentional and nonintentional crimes.

i. Intent

The IPC does not define criminal intent. According to the definitions in the literature, criminal intent consists of the intention of the perpetrator to commit the crime as it is defined in the law. This intent is composed of two elements: (1) the knowledge of the criminal nature of the act and (2) the will to commit the unlawful act and to bring about a result that violates the commands and prohibitions of the law. The literature distinguishes between general intent and specific intent,[28] between definite intent and indefinite intent,[29] and between direct intent and indirect intent (*dolus eventualis*).[30] The notion of motive is understood as an emotional force that drives the perpetrator to commit the act; it is not considered part of criminal intent.

ii. Recklessness

Recklessness, as a special category between intent and negligence that refers to the actor's advertence to a risk, is not defined in Iranian criminal law. However, the law does recognize situations that are covered by the notion of recklessness in common law. If the perpetrator knows that an act is likely to bring about a criminal result but commits the act anyway, he or she acts with *dolus eventualis* (*qasd-e ehtemali*). Iranian authors discuss *dolus eventualis* in chapters about intention but describe it as a kind of intention that lies on the borderline between intentional and nonintentional crimes.[31] Some authors,[32] in fact, take the position that it should be regarded as a case of nonintentional crime.[33]

In Iranian criminal law the legal consequences of *dolus eventualis* are not always the same. On the one hand, *dolus eventualis* as a kind of mental relation to the act is known in Islamic criminal law and finds expression in the IPC's regulations about retaliation, especially in article 206 lit b). According to this article, a murder is regarded as intentional if the murderer intentionally commits an act that is inherently deadly, even if the murderer does not intend to kill the victim. It is understood that a perpetrator who uses a deadly weapon must have accepted the foreseeable result of his or her action. The murder is therefore placed in the same category as intentional homicide and is punished by retaliation.

Dolus eventualis is regarded as a kind of intention in some special laws as well. Iranian authors often quote the law against sabotage in the oil industry of 1957 (1336), which provides that acts of sabotage should be punished by the death penalty if the perpetrator could have known that the crime could lead to the death of other persons. On the other hand, Iranian authors cite the case of arson (art. 689 IPC) as an example of a situation in which *dolus eventualis* is considered nonintentional: if persons die or are injured as a result of the arson, the punishment is retaliation or blood money, depending on the circumstances of the case. From this wording it is deduced that perpetrators who did not have the intention to kill but recognized the danger of a lethal result are punished for a nonintentional crime, and blood money is the typical sanction.[34]

iii. Negligence

Negligence as a general notion is not defined in the general part of the IPC. In the literature it is understood as the disregard of a legal duty of care either by carelessly failing to foresee an objectively foreseeable result or by carelessly believing that a foreseen result could be averted.[35] In the IPC four different forms of negligence are specifically mentioned: imprudence, carelessness, lack of experience, and disregard of regulations. They are found in several articles in the fourth book (diyat) and the fifth book (ta'zirat and bazdarande punishments), mostly with regard to crimes against life and bodily integrity. The most severe religious crimes (hadd), however, are always intentional crimes.

In article 295 of the IPC there are two kinds of nonintentional acts that do not exactly correspond to the notion of negligence in Western criminal law. The first occurs when the criminal neither intended to commit the crime nor intended to commit the act that caused the prohibited result (mere inadvertency, *khata-ye mahz*). An example is given in the provision itself: a person tries to shoot his or her prey but hits someone else instead. In the second situation the perpetrator commits an act that is not inherently deadly and does not intend to kill a person. Again, this is explained by an example: a person beats another person to correct him or her in a manner that is not inherently deadly, but the victim dies incidentally. In Islamic law this kind of act is called semi-intentional (*shibh 'amd*).

3. Theories of Liability
i. Inchoate Crimes
a. Attempt

The Islamic Penal Code includes a general provision on attempt (art. 41). According to that provision, a perpetrator who intends to commit an offense but does not successfully carry it out will be punished only if the actions done are themselves offenses (art. 41). There are, however, some provisions that criminalize attempting to commit specific offenses, such as homicide or theft. These provisions stipulate that the attempt is punishable and provide a punishment that is more lenient than the punishment for the completed crime. They do not, however, define what constitutes an attempt. Therefore, the literature and the courts have had to define the elements of attempt.

As to the *actus reus*, there is agreement that the act has to go beyond the stage of preparation, which is generally not punished. There are, however, different views concerning the dividing line between preparation and attempt. According to one view, an attempt requires the materialization of at least one element of the attempted crime. The opposite opinion holds that it is sufficient if an act shows the firm intention of the perpetrator to commit the offense. A third group, which tries to find a compromise between the first two positions, takes the view that the act must show that it is beyond all doubt that the actor intends to commit the crime. This normally requires that the act have a proximate and unequivocal relation to the offense.[36]

The *mens rea* of attempt requires that the perpetrator intended to commit the completed offense and failed to complete it only because of circumstances that were independent of his or her will.

b. Conspiracy

In Iranian law, conspiracy is not treated as an inchoate offense, but there are two ordinary offenses in the special part that relate to conspiracy. The first is article 610, which provides: "Whenever two or more persons associate and conspire to commit a crime against the internal or external security of the state . . . they shall be imprisoned from two to five years, provided that they are not regarded as *muharib*."[37] It is clear from this wording that mere agreement between the conspirators is sufficient to fulfill all the elements of the crime. It is not necessary that any further action take place.

The second provision relating to conspiracy is article 611: "Whenever two or more persons associate and conspire to attack honor, life or property of others they shall be imprisoned from 6 months to two years, provided that they took some preliminary steps towards the accomplishment of the crime, but their actions were brought involuntarily to naught."[38] In this case the punishment is more lenient, and it must be proved that steps beyond the criminal agreement must have been taken that did not complete the crime or, in some cases, constitute a punishable attempt to commit a crime.

ii. Complicity

The provisions of the IPC usually start from the fact that a crime is committed by a single perpetrator who directly commits or attempts to commit a crime with the required mental state. In some cases, however, a crime is committed by two or more persons who act as coperpetrators or as principals and accessories.

a. Joint Preparation

In Iranian criminal law, joint perpetration is regulated in the general part of the IPC (art. 42), but this provision is applicable only to the category of ta'zir crimes; crimes falling under the other categories are regulated by norms of the special part or by the Islamic legal literature as a means of interpretation. Article 42 provides that everyone who knowingly and intentionally participates with one or more persons in the commission of a ta'zir crime shall be regarded as a coperpetrator and shall be punished as a sole perpetrator, provided that the crime is attributable to the acts of all of them. Consequently, it is not necessary for every coperpetrator to carry out every element of the crime; it is sufficient that all the acts together constitute the crime, provided that the requirement of attributability is met. It is also not necessary that the different actions have the same influence on the result. If the action of a coperpetrator is of minor significance, the court can mitigate his or her punishment by assessing the extent of the contribution to the crime (art. 42, note 1). Remarkably, article 42 also applies these regulations to unintentional crimes that result from the negligence of two or more persons, thus accepting coperpetration for nonintentional crimes.

In the category of qisas crimes, article 215 of the IPC contains a provision regarding the coperpetration of homicide that is identical to article 42. In the case of bodily injury and the categories of diya and hadd crimes, there is no equivalent regulation, and the decision is thereby left to judges, who have to deliver their judgment, according to article 167 of the constitution, on the basis of authoritative Islamic sources and fatwas. In the case of bodily injury, the majority of Islamic jurists hold that each coperpetrator must commit all the elements of the crime, contrary to the regulation for homicide in article 215 of the IPC.[39] In the category of diya, first and foremost referring to unintentional crimes against life and bodily integrity, article 365 of the IPC provides that all people who act together to cause harm to a person are equally liable.

There is no regulation that is applicable to all hadd crimes. Sexual crimes, such as unlawful sexual intercourse or homosexual acts, require two participants, but those participants are considered sole perpetrators, not joint principals whose intention is directed toward a third-party victim. For some hadd crimes, such as drinking alcohol or accusations of unlawful sexual intercourse, coperpetration is not possible for logical reasons: every perpetrator completes the crime on his or her own. The provision on hadd theft alludes to coperpetration when enumerating the elements of this crime: "The thief should alone or together with others break into the safe custody." On the other hand, it means that only the person who breaks into the safe custody and takes the property can be regarded as the perpetrator or the coperpetrator of a hadd theft.[40] If the thief only removes the property, he or she cannot be sentenced for hadd theft, only theft under the fifth book (ta'zirat).

The classical hadd crime of *muharaba* has been well developed in the IPC. Today it is a crime that covers many forms of political, economic, and other activities against the government, including terrorism. Furthermore, in this special case the distinction between perpetrators, coperpetrators, and even accessories has actually disappeared, as will be explained later.[41]

b. Accessoryship

The punishability of an accessory depends on the existence of an unlawful act. If there is any ground of justification, neither the principal nor the accessory is liable to prosecution. By contrast, the existence of an excuse in favor of the principal does not affect the guilt of the accessory. Article 43 of the IPC enumerates the groups of accessories:

1. Everyone who instigates, encourages, intimidates, or allures another to commit a crime, or who causes the commission of crime through plotting and deception

2. Everyone who knowingly and intentionally prepares the instrumentalities of committing a crime, or who, knowing the intention of the perpetrator, guides him to commit it

3. Everyone who knowingly and intentionally facilitates the commission of the crime

The accessory has to commit a positive act; there is no accessorial participation by omission. In light of explanatory note 1, in which a common purpose between the accessory and the principal is required, the accessory must know that the act of the perpetrator constitutes a crime, and he or she must act with the intention to assist the perpetrator.

According to article 43, accessories are to be punished by a ta'zir punishment. However, it is necessary to examine this regulation more closely. The wording of the article seems to leave the determination of punishment to the discretion of the judge, but the study of other articles of the IPC shows that the range of the judge's discretion is very limited in this case. As to ta'zir crimes, the amendment of the IPC of 1996 stipulated in article

726 that "anybody who acts as an accessory in ta'zirat crimes shall according to the case be punished with the minimum limit of punishment provided for the principal crime." For the category of qisas crimes, specific provisions ensure that the punishment of the accessory is more lenient than the punishment of the principal (arts. 207, 208, and 269 IPC). The nature of diya crimes as unintentional crimes[42] means that there is no place for accessoryship.[43] Finally, for hadd crimes, the IPC contains specific provisions for the punishment of an accessory to theft (imprisonment for one to three years, note 2 of art. 201 IPC) and drinking alcohol (up to seventy-four lashes, art. 175 IPC). This means that the ta'zir punishment provided for in article 43 is applicable only to the other hadd crimes (unlawful sexual intercourse, homosexual acts, pandering, and accusation of unlawful sexual intercourse). In the case of ta'zir punishments, the judge has significant discretion when the lawgiver has not defined its their limits in the law. The scope of discretion is limited only by a principle of Islamic jurisprudence that says that ta'zir punishments must be less severe than hadd.[44]

To sum up, the punishment of accessories is more lenient than the punishment of principals. This holds true for the instigator of a crime, as well, who in criminal codes of many other countries is punished like a principal.

iii. Corporate Criminal Liability

The IPC does not contain any provisions regarding corporate criminal liability. Courts have taken the position that criminal responsibility of legal entities is unacceptable because the text of the criminal provisions is directed at "persons," which means natural persons. There are, however, some exceptions in special laws, mostly regarding economic crimes, in which legal entities may be held criminally responsible and punished by closure or a fine.[45]

4. Causation

In Islamic law, although the problem of causation has been thoroughly dealt with in the categories of qisas and diya crimes, it has played no role in the other categories of crimes (hadd, ta'zir). This may explain why causation is regulated in detail in the third and fourth books (qisas and diyat) of the IPC but not in the general part. Thus the application of theories of causality to hadd and ta'zir crimes has been left to the literature and the courts.

The main distinction in the field of causality in Islamic law is the distinction between a direct cause (*mubashirat*) and an indirect cause (*sabab*). The criminal law contains legal definitions of both concepts. Mubashirat means that the crime is directly carried out by the perpetrator (art. 317 IPC), whereas sabab is defined as a situation in which an individual causes the killing or injury of another person but does not directly commit the crime—for example, where someone digs a pit and another person falls into it (art. 318). If a direct and an indirect cause coincide to create a result, the person who is responsible for the direct cause will be liable unless the indirect cause was stronger than the direct cause (art. 363). If two persons indirectly but independently cause a result, the liability lies with the person whose action had an effect on the result first (art. 364). A large number of casuistic provisions deal with specific cases of direct and indirect causes or cases in which different direct and indirect causes coincide at the same time or one after the other (arts. 323–362).[46]

There are no legal provisions concerning causation for hadd and taʿzir crimes. In the literature, Iranian authors endorse theories known in Europe, such as the theory of "but-for" cause and the theory of adequate causation.

C. Defenses

1. Types of Defense

The general part of the IPC contains a number of defenses in a chapter titled "Limits of Criminal Liability." There are also other provisions containing defenses, particularly in the second book (hadd) and in the fifth book (taʿzirat and bazdarande punishments). Although the IPC does not clearly distinguish justifications and excuses, the distinction between "does not constitute a crime" and "is not to be punished," which is found in a number of provisions, shows that the law, as well as the literature, reflects the fact that Iranian criminal law treats justifications and excuses differently. Following the French model, cases of justification are often labeled objective grounds of nonliability; cases of excuse are often labeled subjective grounds of nonliability. Whereas in the case of justification, the act is not unlawful and accessories cannot be punished, in the case of excuses, the act as such remains unlawful, and accessories will be punished according to their own guilt.

Apart from the defenses to be dealt with in this chapter, it should be mentioned that in Islamic criminal law there are further grounds for an exemption from punishment, especially in hadd crimes. Because God almighty cannot be damaged by humans, it is not necessary for him to punish them for violating his rights. The application of hadd penalties is thus limited not only by narrow interpretations of the jurists and stringent requirements of proof but also by the concept of *shubha*, which means that an unlawful act that resembles in any way a lawful one excludes the application of a hadd penalty. Furthermore, a hadd penalty can be avoided by withdrawing a confession to the crime or in some crimes by repentance.

2. Burden of Proof

In general, the prosecutor has the burden of proof for all the elements of a crime, while the defendant who pleads a defense has to prove the facts that verify its existence. In the book on hadd, however, there are a number of legal presumptions in favor of the defendant, especially in the provisions on unlawful sexual intercourse. On the other hand, there is also a case in which the burden of proof is reversed: the member of an organization planning acts against the security of the country has to prove that he or she did not know the aims of the organization (art. 499 IPC).

D. Justifications

1. Necessity

Necessity as a ground of justification is already recognized in a famous passage of the Qurʾan (2, 173) that allows eating dead meat and pork when necessary for survival. In the IPC, necessity is regulated by article 55 and by some special provisions, such as article 198, number 12 (theft in a year of famine). There is, however, no agreement among Iranian authors about the legal nature of necessity. Some consider it a justification,[47] others an excuse.[48] Some even make a distinction between situations in which necessity functions as a justification and other situations in which it constitutes an excuse.[49]

According to article 55 of the IPC, necessity requires the fulfillment of four conditions. First, a great danger to the life or property of the perpetrator or another person, such as a fire or a flood, must exist. Second, the commission of the crime must be necessary to avert the danger. Third, the perpetrator must not have intentionally caused the danger. Finally, the crime committed in order to avert the danger must have been proportionate to the danger. This is generally understood to require that the object of the act of necessity be of a higher value than the object violated by the act. In Islamic criminal law, for example, the killing of a person in order to save the life of another person is never recognized as a case of necessity (art. 211 IPC).

2. Self-Defense

Self-defense is the right of every person to defend himself or herself against an unlawful attack. In Islamic law self-defense is even understood as a kind of religious duty.[50] According to article 61 of the IPC, a person who acts in a way that fulfills the elements of a crime is not punished if he or she acts in order to repel an unlawful attack on the life, honor, property, or physical liberty of himself or herself or a third party. Both the attack and the act of defense must fulfill certain conditions. First, the unlawful attack must be present or immediately impending. As soon as the attack is finished, self-defense is no longer possible. Second, the defense must be necessary to repel the attack. If there is, for instance, a possibility of being helped by the authorities, self-defense is not necessary.[51] Third, the defense must be proportionate to the attack. Finally, the defender must choose the minimum means of defense. As often pronounced by decisions of the Iranian Supreme Court, however, there is no obligation to take flight even if this would be the easiest way to avoid the attack.[52]

These rules are repeated in the book of the ta'zirat crimes in the chapter dealing with crimes against persons. They concern cases in which the defense ends in killing or injuring the aggressor. It must be mentioned that article 627 provides that the defender must act out of fear for life, honor, or property and that the fear must be based on reasonable grounds, a subjective state of mind that is not found in the rules of the general part.

Article 62 expressly provides that defense against security and military forces fulfilling their duties is not regarded as legitimate defense, except when those forces overstep their authority and there are signs that their actions may lead to killing, injuring, or attacking the honor of a citizen.

3. Consent

The defense of consent is not regulated in a general provision in the first book of the IPC. It is discussed in the literature, but the limits of consent as a ground of justification are rather restricted. Above all, in most cases consent refers to the elements of a crime, not to the defense of justification. In such cases the consent of the victim makes the criminal provision inapplicable. The person who takes away the property of another person, for example, cannot be a thief if the other person agrees. In the remaining cases consent must fulfill a number of conditions to have legal consequences. First and foremost, if the legal interest is strictly personal, the consenting person must have the right to dispose of that interest. If it is an interest that (also) concerns the public, the individual person's consent is irrelevant. For instance, no one can consent to be killed, because in Islam life is regarded as God-given. Euthanasia and suicide, therefore, are forbidden in Islam. Crimes concerning sexual relations are also regarded as belonging to the public sphere of societal and family life, not as a private matter. Thus consent to unlawful sexual intercourse (*zina'*) and homosexual acts does not have any legal effect.

In the IPC there are only two cases in which consent is regulated in special situations: in cases of medical interventions and in sport (art. 59 nos. 2 and 3). To be valid, consent must be given before or at the latest during the act, and the consenting person must be of age, sane, and acting out of free will. Both provisions also contain other requirements that must be fulfilled. A doctor must act in accordance with the rules of the medical or surgical profession. In sport, the activity must not violate the principles of the Shari'a.

4. Superior Orders

Article 56 of the IPC recognizes two situations in which superior orders are a ground for justification, provided that the necessary requirements are fulfilled: the command of the law and the order of a superior. In the first case, the crime must be committed to promote a law that is more important than the law governing the crime. For example, a doctor must not breach professional secrecy but is nevertheless obliged to inform the Ministry of Health of certain infectious diseases. In the second case, the order must have been given by a lawful superior and must not violate the Shari'a.[53]

The specific problem that arises in the case of an unlawful order is dealt with in article 57. In this case both the superior and the subordinate are punished in accordance with the law. If the subordinate carries out the order believing on acceptable grounds that it is lawful, however, a punishment will be meted out that consists (in case of homicide or bodily injury) of blood money and damages. This shows that carrying out an unlawful order is not an excuse but under certain circumstances may be a ground of mitigation. A subordinate cannot believe in the lawfulness of the order on acceptable grounds if the order was—in the language of the Rome Statute of the International Criminal Court—manifestly unlawful.[54]

E. Excuses

1. Mistake/Ignorance of Law or Fact

There is no general provision in the IPC about mistake or ignorance of law or fact. Some regulations, however, exclude hadd penalties in specific cases of hadd crimes, such as unlawful sexual intercourse (arts. 64, 65), drinking of wine (note 1 to art. 166), and theft (art. 198 nos. 5 and 6). Iranian jurists generally hold that the general part's silence concerning mistake does not mean that mistakes cannot be recognized. Mistake and ignorance are thus generally discussed in the chapter dealing with excuses.[55] As a rule, every citizen is expected to know the law. Ignorance or mistake of law, therefore, does not constitute an excuse. This principle is based on both Islamic and Western law. There may be an exception in rare cases, such as in the hadd crimes mentioned earlier in this paragraph. Some authors also distinguish between simple mistake or ignorance of law and inevitable mistake or ignorance of law and want to recognize the latter as an excuse.[56]

Mistake or ignorance of fact can have different effects. If it involves an element of a crime, it will usually constitute an excuse that entails exemption from punishment. If there is a parallel crime that can be committed by negligence (for instance, intentional homicide and nonintentional homicide), however, the perpetrator will be considered guilty of the corresponding negligent crime. If the mistake or ignorance refers to a ground that increases the severity of a crime, the perpetrator will be punished for the less severe crime. For instance, A insults B, not recognizing that B is one of the public figures whose insult entails a more severe punishment (art. 609) than the insult of an average citizen (art. 608). A is punished only under article 608.

Other cases that deserve to be mentioned are the following: (1) A fires on B in order to kill him but hits C, who dies (*aberratio ictus*). In this case, article 296 provides that the act is to be regarded as "mere inadvertency" (*khata-ye mahz*) and is punished by blood money. (2) A wants to kill B. After the crime has been committed, it turns out that the victim is not B but C (*error in persona*). This case is not expressly regulated in the law. The Supreme Court, basing its judgment on fatwas of high-ranking religious jurists, has held that the perpetrator is to be sentenced for semi-intentional homicide entailing the payment of blood money, not retaliation.[57] The solution in both of these cases is criticized by many Iranian authors, who take the view that the perpetrator should be punished for intentional homicide.[58]

2. Insanity/Diminished Capacity
According to article 51 of the IPC, madness (*djunun*) in whatever degree is considered an excuse. Moreover, in the book of hadd crimes, the sanity requirement is expressly mentioned in the description of the elements of a crime punished by a hadd penalty. The question discussed among Iranian scholars is whether madness comprises all mental illnesses or is limited to cases of loss of reason (*'aql*). In practice, this question is resolved by requiring a medical specialist in psychiatry to give an advisory opinion about the mental state of the defendant.

Article 49 of the IPC provides that a child is not responsible for the crimes he or she has committed. The court may order only educational measures. The only exception concerns homicide, where the IPC stipulates that intentional homicide or bodily injury committed by a child is treated as equivalent to mere inadvertency (arts. 221 and 272) and is punished by blood money. Neither article 49 nor other articles in the IPC deal with the definition of a child. Article 49, note 1, merely makes the statement that a person is of age if he or she has reached physical maturity (*bulugh*). To understand this notion, one has to refer to article 1210 of the Civil Code. This provision indicates that a girl is considered to have reached the age of maturity at nine lunar years (about eight years, nine months, in solar years) and a boy at fifteen lunar years (about fourteen years, seven months, in solar years).[59] Apart from the unique difference in coming of age for boys and girls, this provision imposes full criminal responsibility at a very early age. This age is highly discussed in Iran, all the more because there are different opinions in Islamic law concerning the age of full criminal responsibility.[60]

In practice, courts reduce the punishments for young convicts as far as possible by applying the mitigating ground of special circumstances in the life of the defendant (art. 22 IPC). This provision is applicable only to crimes punishable with ta'zirat or deterrent punishments. For qisas crimes, the court may only try to influence the blood avengers to take blood money instead of insisting on retaliation. As in hadd crimes, the criminal must be mentally sane, must understand the meaning of his or her act and the fact of its prohibition, and must act out of free will. The court can avoid applying a hadd punishment only by questioning whether these requirements were fulfilled by the child who committed the crime in question.

Islamic criminal law also distinguishes between children not yet capable of understanding the wrongfulness of their acts (*ghair mumayyiz*) and children capable of understanding them (*mumayyiz*). This distinction is reflected in some of the provisions of the IPC, such as article 211, notes 1 and 2, which provide that a child incapable of understanding who is forced to kill somebody else is not responsible at all, while a child who is capable of understanding his or her 'aqila[61] must pay blood money. According to Iranian authors, a child under seven years of age is always regarded as criminally not responsible (ghair mumayyiz).[62] Otherwise, the IPC does not contain a general provision that distinguishes between children who are not yet responsible and children who are partly responsible.

3. Intoxication

Intoxication as such is not regulated in the IPC. There are, however, two provisions dealing with drunkenness and its consequences, articles 53 and 224. Article 53 holds that if a perpetrator loses his or her free will under the influence of alcohol and commits a crime, he or she will be punished for drinking alcohol, as well as for committing the other crime, if it is proved that he or she drank the alcoholic beverage in order to have the courage to commit the crime. Article 224 refers to homicide in the state of complete drunkenness. In principle, retaliation has to take place unless it is proved that the perpetrator completely lost the ability to form an intention and did not get drunk in order to commit the crime. If the case involves a violation of public order or the danger of recidivism or imitation by others, however, the perpetrator is sentenced to imprisonment for from three to ten years, the same punishment that is provided if the blood avengers renounce their right to retaliation. Article 224 also provides that complete drunkenness may under certain circumstances be recognized in mitigation. In the literature, a person who is addicted to alcohol is sometimes considered to be mad, thus opening the way to an excuse.[63] The vast majority of Iranian authors, by contrast, do not recognize drunkenness as an excuse;[64] on the contrary, drunkenness may even be an aggravating ground, for example, in traffic offenses (art. 718).

There is no provision in the IPC that refers to the use of drugs when committing a crime. Some scholars propose regarding drug addicts as mad persons.[65] Apart from that opinion, it has to be mentioned that acting under the influence of drugs may be regarded as a special circumstance in the person of the defendant, which is one of article 22's mitigating grounds for offenses punished by ta'zir and deterrent punishments. But this is fully within the discretion of the judge.

4. Duress

Article 54 of the IPC defines duress as the commission of a crime punished by ta'zir or deterrent punishments under a constraint that is usually irresistible. In this case the person who exerts pressure on the perpetrator will be punished for the crime, not the person who commits the crime under constraint. Most hadd crimes require that the perpetrator have acted of his or her free will as part of the elements of the crime.[66] Consequently, somebody who commits a hadd crime under constraint will not be punished by a hadd penalty. In the case of homicide, however, constraint does not constitute an excuse. If somebody kills another person under constraint, he or she will be punished by retaliation, while the person who exerted the pressure is sentenced to life imprisonment. There are only two exceptions to this rule. A person who exerts pressure on a mad person or a child who is not yet capable of understanding the wrongfulness of the act will be punished by retaliation (note 1 to art. 211). If the child was already capable of understanding the wrongfulness of the act, his or her family has to pay blood money to the family of the victim, while the person who exerts pressure is sentenced to life imprisonment (note 2 to art. 211).

5. Entrapment

Entrapment is not discussed as an excuse in Iranian criminal law. It may only constitute a mitigating ground according to article 22 of the IPC or, in the case of drug crimes, article 38 of the Anti-Drugs Act.

6. Superior Orders

As explained earlier,[67] a subordinate who carries out an unlawful order of a superior on reasonable grounds will receive a mitigated punishment.

F. Sanctions

1. Punishment

The punishments provided in the IPC are divided into five categories:

1. *Hadd* (pl. *hodud*) is a punishment whose kind and extent are fixed by the Shari'a for a limited number of crimes. The punishments include crucifixion, stoning, the death penalty, chopping off limbs, whipping, imprisonment, and banishment.

2. *Qisas* is a punishment that is equal to the result of an intentional offense (retaliation). Possible punishments include the death penalty and, for instance, chopping off limbs or blinding.

3. *Diya* (pl. *diyat*) is blood money that has to be paid in cases of nonintentional offenses against the life or bodily integrity of the victim or in cases of intentional offenses against life or bodily integrity if the victim or the blood avengers and the perpetrator agree. Blood money may consist of money, animals, or clothes (art. 297). In practice, it is an amount that is fixed every year by a governmental commission that takes into account the changing value of money. In semi-intentional crimes it is the perpetrator who has to pay the blood money; in cases of mere inadvertency, the blood money has to be paid by the 'aqila.[68]

4. *Ta'zir* (pl. *ta'zirat*) is a punishment whose kind and extent are not fixed by the Shari'a. It applies to acts that are criminalized on the basis of general principles of Islamic law. In earlier times the judge had to determine both the elements of the offense and the punishment within the framework of Islamic law. Today the crimes punished by ta'zir penalties are provided in the Iranian Penal Code, and the judge has to determine the punishment within the statutory range. Punishments may consist of sanctions such as imprisonment, fines, or whipping. The number of lashes, however, is limited by the rule that it has to be less than for hadd crimes (art. 16). Because the lowest number of lashes for a hadd crime is 75 (art. 138), the regulation in article 16 is the reason that the IPC rather often provides a punishment of "up to 74 lashes."

5. *Mudjazat-e bazdarande* (deterrent punishment) was created by the Iranian lawgiver in 1991. It refers to a punishment for offenses provided in state regulations that safeguard social order and the interests of society. Punishments may include imprisonment, fines, closure of enterprises, withdrawal of licenses, or the deprivation of rights (art. 17).

In cases involving children and mad persons, the court can order educational or security measures against those persons (arts. 49 and 52 ICP).

2. Quantity/Quality of Punishment

Hadd punishments are fixed punishments that the judge is required to impose. There is only one exception in the IPC, the crime of fighting against God and corruption on earth.[69] In its original form, this crime could be committed in four different ways, each carrying its own penalty: crucifixion, the death penalty, chopping off the right hand and the left foot, and banishment. Later, following a minority opinion by the Shi'i school of law, the Iranian lawgiver severed the link between a certain way of committing a crime and a certain punishment and permitted judges to choose the punishment that they believed was most appropriate for the perpetrator. Thus the punishment of crucifixion has never been applied in the Islamic Republic of Iran.

As for the application of retaliation and blood money, it is up to the blood avengers, not the judge, to decide which punishment they prefer. In practice, although retaliation for death may sometimes be chosen, it is normally much more attractive for the blood avengers to take the blood money. In the case of bodily injury, retaliation is extremely rare.

Ta'zir punishments and deterrent punishments are meted out at the discretion of the judge within the statutory range of punishment. Whereas in the ta'zirat law of 1983 fines and imprisonment were replaced by whipping for a large number of provisions, the fifth book of ta'zirat and deterrent punishments passed in 1996 are more cautious in this regard. Many regulations provide imprisonment, fines, or whipping alternatively to avoid corporal punishment. The judge can even mitigate these punishments if one of the conditions provided in article 22 of the IPC is fulfilled, such as provocation or special circumstances in the person or the earlier life of the defendant. Under certain circumstances the judge can also suspend the execution of a sentence with probation (arts. 25–37).

3. Death Penalty

The IPC provides the death penalty for a relatively high number of crimes, especially those involving state security. The death penalty often is provided by the words that "the perpetrator is punished as a fighter against God (muharib)" or "if the perpetrator is a fighter against God."[70] The death penalty is also provided in special laws such as the Drugs Law. Iran is one of the top five countries in the world in numbers of executions.[71]

III. SPECIAL PART

A. Structure

Islamic criminal law distinguishes between violations of the rights of God and violations of the rights of humans. Rights of God are violated by offenses such as drinking alcohol. Rights of humans are violated by offenses such as homicide. In some cases the offense is of a mixed nature, violating both the rights of God and the rights of humans. The defamation of unlawful sexual intercourse (arts. 139–164) is an example.[72] A rough description of both types of rights is that the rights of God are violated when public interests are involved, while the rights of humans are violated when private interests are involved. In the new Iranian Code of Criminal Procedure, which entered into force in 1999, a third type of offenses was created: crimes against society and public order.

Another distinction is between the types of punishment associated with particular offenses: hadd penalties, retaliation (qisas), blood money (diyat), or ta'zir punishments. The general part of the IPC also provides another type of punishment, called deterrent (bazdarande) punishment. This type of punishment refers to offenses that were criminalized by the government (*hukumat*) with a view to maintaining public order and protecting the interests of society (art. 17).

According to Islamic scholars, the crimes punished by hadd, retaliation, or blood money must protect the most important legal interests, the necessary conditions of life (*darurat*): religion, life, reason, origin, and property. Religion is protected by the crime of apostasy;[73] life by retaliation and blood money; reason by the prohibition of alcohol; origin by the sexual crimes; and property by the crime of theft.

B. Homicide

1. Murder/Manslaughter

Homicide is one of the crimes that play a central role in Islamic criminal law. It was punished by retaliation on a large scale as early as pre-Islamic Arabia. The Qur'an regulated and restricted the limits of retaliation (qisas). In Islamic law the prosecution and punishment of homicide are initially a matter of the blood avengers of the victim, not of the authorities. They are free to choose among retaliation, blood money, or even pardon. The role of the state is limited to conducting criminal proceedings on the demand of the blood avengers and to passing the judgment that allows the blood avengers to execute the punishment against the perpetrator. Only if the blood avengers waive their claim of retaliation does the state, in a case involving a violation of public order or a danger of recidivism or imitation by others, have the right to punish the perpetrator (art. 208).[74]

The provisions on homicide in Iranian law are to be found in the third book (qisas) and the fourth book (diyat), with some additional provisions in the fifth book (ta'zirat). The law distinguishes between intentional, semi-intentional, and negligent homicide (art. 204). Manslaughter is considered to be voluntary in three situations: (1) if the manslaughter is committed with the intention to kill a certain person or to kill a person who is part of a certain group; (2) if the perpetrator intentionally commits an act that is inherently deadly even if he or she did not have the intention to kill; (3) if the perpetrator does not have the intention to kill the victim and the act is not inherently deadly, but the act resulted in the death of the victim because of special circumstances in the person of the victim that were known to the perpetrator (art. 206)—for instance, if the victim is a hemophiliac for whom the lightest bleeding may lead to death.

As a rule, voluntary manslaughter is punished by retaliation. There are, however, other requirements for retaliation that are not a consequence of the crime itself but result from the position of the perpetrator and/or the victim. The first requirement is based on the principle of equal values. Originally, the clan of the perpetrator would lose a member who had the same value for it as the victim had for the other clan. If the victim did not have the same value for the clan, retaliation had to be replaced by blood money. In practice, this meant that retaliation was possible only if the victim had the same religion, the same sex, and the same sanity of mind as the perpetrator. The provisions of the IPC adhere to this system. Article 207 says that retaliation takes place if a Muslim is killed. Retaliation also takes place if a Christian, Jew, or Zoroastrian non-Muslim kills another non-Muslim adhering to one of these religions (art. 210). Retaliation does not take place, therefore, when a Muslim kills a non-Muslim. If a Muslim man (art. 209) or a non-Muslim man (art. 210) kills a woman who adheres to his religion, retaliation is possible only if the blood avenger of the female victim pays the perpetrator half the blood money paid for a man before executing the retaliation. If a sane person kills an insane person, retaliation is not possible; instead, the perpetrator has to pay blood money (art. 222). Blood money is also due if an insane person or a minor kills a person, because in these cases the crime is always regarded as negligent homicide. Retaliation is also commuted to blood money if the perpetrator is the father or the paternal grandfather of the victim (art. 220). Finally, in the case of two or more perpetrators, retaliation is possible against all the perpetrators. But if there are two perpetrators, the blood avengers pay half the blood money to each of them before retaliation. In the case of three perpetrators, the blood avengers pay two-thirds of the blood money to each of them, and so on (art. 212). Apart from all these regulations, the blood avengers may always make a deal with the perpetrator commuting the retaliation to blood money or even to pardon (art. 257).

Semi-intentional (shibh 'amd) homicide refers to a situation in which the perpetrator lacks the intention to kill and commits an act that is not inherently deadly but nevertheless causes the death of the victim because of unfortunate circumstances. An example is where the perpetrator beats a person moderately, but for some unknown reason the victim dies (art. 295).[75] According to note 2 of article 295, a homicide is also considered semi-intentional if it is caused by imprudence, negligence, lack of experience, or disregard of legal regulations, situations that many other criminal law systems would regard as involuntary homicide. In the case of semi-intentional killings, the perpetrator has to pay blood money.

Blood money is also due in cases of mere inadvertency (khata-ye mahz), but it has to be paid by the 'aqila of the perpetrator, not by the perpetrator himself or herself. Mere inadvertency constitutes a different category of homicide, often but not necessarily resulting from inadvertence (for example, arts. 295 lit a) and 296).

Because of an amendment of the IPC in 2004, blood money for Muslims and Christian, Jewish, or Zoroastrian non-Muslims[76] is now the same (note 2 to art. 297). Blood money for women is half the blood money for men (art. 300). Although the law speaks only of Muslim women, the same rule applies to non-Muslim women as well.[77]

In the book of ta'zirat crimes, additional provisions refer to voluntary manslaughter in cases where retaliation does not take place and to involuntary manslaughter. In cases involving a breach of public order and safety or the risk of encouraging the perpetrator or a third party to commit the crime again, a principal of voluntary manslaughter is punished by three to ten years' imprisonment (art. 612), and an accessory to voluntary manslaughter is punished by one to five years' imprisonment (note to art. 612). A special provision referring to attempted voluntary manslaughter provides a sentence of six months to three years' imprisonment (art. 613). Involuntary manslaughter is punished by one to three years' imprisonment, in addition to the blood money that has to be paid to the blood avengers (art. 616). There is also a special provision referring to involuntary homicide in traffic situations (art. 714). The main difference between these two provisions is the minor punishment imposed by article 714, which is limited to six months' imprisonment.

2. Provocation

Provocation does not generally constitute an excuse for committing a homicide. There is, however, a special case in which the perpetrator will be exempt from punishment. When a husband catches his wife committing adultery, he can kill her and/or the man with whom she is committing adultery without being punished. If his wife is raped, the husband can kill the rapist without being punished (art. 630 IPC).

C. Sex Offenses

The main principle of Islamic criminal law underlying the whole system of sex offenses is that sexual relations are lawful only within a valid marriage. Every sexual relation outside a valid marriage, whether with or without the consent of the participants, and whether heterosexual or homosexual, is considered unlawful and a basis for punishment. Whereas in the Sunni school only unlawful heterosexual intercourse (zina') is punished by a hadd penalty, in the Shi'i school—and consequently in Iranian penal law—homosexual acts, as well as pandering, are also regarded as hadd crimes (arts. 63–138).

In the fifth book (ta'zirat), some acts that are not considered sexual offenses punishable with a hadd penalty are nevertheless considered criminal because they create circumstances that facilitate the commission of a sexual offense,. For example, article 637 punishes acts such as kissing or staying in the same bed if the persons involved are not married to one another.

The basic sexual offense is zina', unlawful sexual intercourse. Zina' refers to sexual intercourse between persons who are not married to one another. Adultery, defined as sexual intercourse by a married person with a third party even though he or she can have sexual intercourse with his or her spouse,[78] is an aggravating circumstance. Unlawful sexual intercourse between unmarried people is punished by 100 lashes; adulterers are sentenced to stoning (art. 83).[79] Aggravating circumstances that entail the death penalty for unlawful sexual intercourse are the following: (1) if there is a bar to marriage based on the prohibition of marriage between relatives; (2) if a man has sexual intercourse with the wife of his father;[80] (3) if a non-Muslim man has sexual intercourse with a Muslim woman; and (4) if a person uses force to have sexual intercourse (art. 82). The unlawful sexual intercourse has to be proved by a confession before the judge that is made four times, by the testimony of four honest[81] male witnesses, or by three honest male witnesses and two honest female witnesses (art. 74). If the crime is punished only by lashes, the testimony of two honest men and four honest women is sufficient (art. 75). The pregnancy of an unmarried woman is not accepted as proof of unlawful sexual intercourse (art. 73), because she may have been raped. If a man and a woman who had sexual intercourse claim that they were mistaken concerning the law or the circumstances of the sexual intercourse (for example, they believed that they were legally married), this claim is accepted without any further proof if it is possible that the defendants are sincere (art. 66). Even more favorable to the defendant is article 67, which holds that the claim of having been forced to commit the unlawful sexual intercourse must be accepted if the contrary is not clearly proven. Finally, if the defendant confesses the unlawful sexual intercourse and later retracts the confession, a sentence of death or stoning will no longer be possible (art. 71). This applies in a similar way if the defendant repents before the testimony of the witnesses is offered. In this case, no hadd punishment is possible (art. 81).

Iranian criminal law punishes homosexual acts, not homosexual orientation. Homosexual intercourse, completed by the introduction of the penis into the body of another man, is punished by the death penalty (arts. 108 and 110). All other homosexual acts between men entail 100 lashes, while lesbian acts entail a punishment of up to 100 lashes. In all cases of homosexual acts between men, the offenses have to be proved by four valid confessions before the judge (arts. 114 and 116), by four honest male witnesses (art. 117), or by the knowledge of the judge (art. 120). The same applies to lesbian acts (art. 128); the testimony of female witnesses is not admitted to prove such acts. If the defendant repents before the statements of the witnesses, hadd penalties become inapplicable (arts. 126 and 132). Finally, the punishment for pandering is 75 lashes; a man who panders is additionally banished for three months to one year (arts. 135–138).

D. Theft and Fraud

In Islamic criminal law the ability to punish theft as a hadd crime is based on a Qur'an verse that holds that the hand of the thief, whether man or woman, must be chopped off. Starting from this verse, Islamic jurists, over the course of centuries, developed a detailed theory of the requirements that have to be fulfilled to punish a thief with a hadd punishment. These requirements refer to the elements of the crimes, as well as to certain circumstances that must be present during or after the commission of the crime. They demonstrate the efforts of Islamic jurists to avoid applying a hadd punishment for theft wherever possible.

The doctrine of theft is reflected in articles 197–203 of the second book (hadd) of the IPC. A thief must fulfill more than twenty requirements before being subjected to a hadd punishment. A lack of one or more of these requirements does not necessarily mean, however, that the thief goes unpunished: cases of theft that are not punished according to the hadd provisions are regulated in the fifth book (ta'zirat) (arts. 651–656, 658, 661, 666, 667).

Theft is defined as the clandestine taking away of the property of somebody else (art. 197). The law expressly enumerates that the thief must be of age, sane, and acting intentionally when the crime is committed. Furthermore, he or she must know and must be conscious of the fact that the stolen object belonged to somebody else and that taking the object away is forbidden. The thief must not have acted under any constraint. The stolen property must have a minimum value of 1.6 grams of gold and must be kept in safe custody (hirz). The thief must break the safe custody and take the stolen object (alone or together with other coperpetrators) out of it; if the safe custody itself is taken away by the thief and opened later, the requirement is not fulfilled. There is no hadd punishment if the theft is committed in a year of famine. There is also no hadd punishment if the stolen object was the property of the state, a religious foundation, or a similar institution. Finally, there is no punishment of hadd if the thief returns the property to the owner, acquires ownership of the stolen object by gift, purchase, or other legal acts before the judgment, or if the stolen property belonged to a child of the thief (arts. 198 and 200).

Theft punished by a hadd penalty must be proved either by two honest men or by a confession of the perpetrator to the judge that is made twice. At the moment of confession, the perpetrator must be of age, sane, and acting intentionally and out of free will. The theft can also be proved by the knowledge of the judge (art. 199), which allows the use of modern methods of investigation.

The hadd punishment for theft is chopping off four fingers of the thief's right hand, leaving one finger and the palm. If the thief is a recidivist, half of the left foot of the thief is removed; a third hadd theft results in life imprisonment. If the thief does not stop stealing in prison, the punishment is the death penalty (art. 201).

If the requirements for a hadd punishment are not satisfied, a thief can be subjected to a ta'zir punishment. A theft without any aggravating circumstances is punished by imprisonment of three months and one day up to two years and 74 lashes (art. 661). The law also contains a detailed system of aggravating circumstances, for example, commission at night, commission by two or more persons, bearing arms, or climbing up walls. The ta'zir punishment is scaled according to the type and the number of aggravating circumstances in a way that still seems to be influenced by the French model (arts. 651–656, 658–660, 666) and may result in up to twenty years' imprisonment and 74 lashes if five of the aggravating circumstances enumerated in article 651 are present at the same time.

Fraud is regulated not by the IPC itself, but in the law of December 6, 1988 (15.9.1367) concerning the aggravation of punishments for those who have committed bribery, embezzlement, or fraud. Articles 1 and 2 of this law deal with fraud in a very casuistic way that reflects the influence of the earlier French law. Any person who uses deceptive means—such as feigning the existence of trade companies, suggesting hope or fear of imaginary events, or assuming a false name or title—to obtain money, documents of legal value, or objects that belong to another is sentenced to one to seven years' imprisonment and fined. If any of the numerous circumstances that aggravate the punishment are present (such as the use of mass media, or if the perpetrator is an employee of the state or an institution that depends on the state), the punishment is two to ten years' imprisonment, a fine, and removal from office, if applicable.

E. "Victimless" Crimes

The concept of a victimless crime is not discussed in Iranian criminal law. There are, however, some offenses that can be regarded as victimless crimes, such as driving without a license (art. 723).

F. Other Offenses

1. Fighting against God and Corruption on Earth (Muharaba *and* Ifsad fi'l-'ard) *(Articles 183–196)*

The legal elements of the crime of fighting against God and corruption on earth are set out in articles 183–188 and result from a recent development in Shi'i criminal law. The original form of fighting against God, which is based on the Qur'an (5, 33), is described as unsheathing a weapon in order to terrify the people and to deprive them of their freedom and security (art. 183). Consequently, every armed thief and every highway robber who interferes with public security and terrifies the people is a muharib (art. 185). The other articles, however, deal with elements of crimes that in classical Islamic law meant the crime of rebellion against the Islamic government (bagj), which most scholars regarded as crimes that had to be punished by the more lenient ta'zir punishments. These crimes have now been incorporated into the more severe hadd crimes and take a form that reflects modern constellations of opposition to the state. According to article 186, as long as the center of the group or organization is active, all members and followers of a group or an organization that carries out an armed rebellion against the Islamic state are fighters against God. It is necessary and sufficient for a fighter against God to know the (ideological) position of the organization and to engage in any activity supporting the organization's aims, and this is true even if the person is not an accessory to the military branch of the organization. Articles 187 and 188 punish a number of accessorial and even preparatory acts as fighting against God, abandoning the general distinction between principals and accessories. For example, every person who provides arms or explosives to a group planning the overthrow of the Islamic government is considered a fighter against God and a person who brings corruption on earth. The same applies to persons who knowingly and voluntarily put considerable financial means, instruments, or arms at the disposal of such a group (art. 187). Everyone who agrees to play a crucial role in planning the overthrow of the Islamic government is regarded as a muharib if that willingness actually plays a role in the planned overthrow (art. 188).

The crime of fighting against God and corruption on earth is proved by one confession before a judge or by two honest male witnesses (art. 189). The punishment, determined according to the judge's discretion, is the death penalty, crucifixion, amputation of the right hand and the left foot, or banishment (art. 190).[82]

Another reason that these provisions are important is that many other provisions refer to them in different ways,[83] such as "Who commits... is regarded as a muharib" (art. 504), or "if he or she is not regarded as a muharib, he or she will be punished with... imprisonment" (art. 508). The other provisions leave the distinction between muharib and non-muharib to the discretion of the judge.[84]

2. Ta'zir Crimes against Religion

In Islamic criminal law apostasy is generally regarded as a serious crime. Many Islamic jurists even consider it a hadd crime. According to the Shi'i Dja'fari doctrine that is ruling in Iran, men have to be sentenced to death for apostasy and women to life imprisonment. Nevertheless, there is no provision in the IPC dealing with apostasy.[85] It is mentioned in article 26 of the Press Law, according to which the sentence of apostasy applies to anyone who by means of the press insults Islam or one of its holy values. It should also be mentioned that the draft for a new IPC[86] contained a detailed article on apostasy, which was, however, removed from the draft in the course of summer 2009, for reasons as to which we can only conjecture.

Other provisions in the IPC refer to religion, the result of a 1996 amendment to the the fifth book (ta'zirat). Article 513 holds that every person who insults the holy values of Islam, one of the revered prophets, one of the sinless Imams, or the Truthful and Pure will be punished by death if the act meets the requirements of disparaging the Prophet Mohammad. Otherwise, the perpetrator will be punished by one to five years' imprisonment. "Holy values" (muqaddasat) is a broad concept; it includes sanctuaries, persons, rituals, ideas, and other items that are of great importance to the religion of Islam and its believers. As to the revered prophets, there is discussion whether this means all the prophets or only the 100 prophets whose names are mentioned in the Qur'an, such as Mohammad, Jesus, and Moses.[87] The sinless Imams are the twelve Imams in the Twelver Shi'i school who are regarded as sinless. The "Truthful and Pure" is Fatima, the daughter of the prophet Mohammad and wife of 'Ali, the first of the twelve Shi'i Imams.

Article 514 contains a provision imposing punishment of six months to two years' imprisonment on anyone who in any way insults Imam Khomeini, the founder of the Islamic Republic.

3. Drinking of Alcohol (Articles 165–182, 701–704)

The consumption of alcohol is forbidden in Islam. It is one of the crimes punished by a hadd punishment and thus belongs to the central regulations of Islamic criminal law. In the IPC it is regulated in the second book (hadd), joining some additional provisions in the fifth book (ta'zirat and deterrent punishments).

The IPC provides that a person who drinks alcohol is punished by a hadd punishment of 80 lashes. At the moment of consumption, the perpetrator must have been of age, sane, acting out of his or her free will, and conscious of the fact that the liquid was alcohol and that drinking alcohol is forbidden (arts. 165, 174). A non-Muslim is punished by this hadd punishment only if the crime was committed in public (note to art. 174). The drinking of alcohol must be proved by a confession of the perpetrator made twice or by two honest male Muslim witnesses (arts. 168–172). Further provisions of this chapter once again demonstrate that the lawgiver seeks to avoid imposing hadd punishments. If the defendant claims not to have known the rule forbidding the consumption of alcohol or not to have known what he or she was drinking, this defense is accepted if it seems possible (note 1 to art. 166). The confession or the testimony can be the basis of a hadd sentence only if there is no reasonable possibility that there may be an excuse for the crime (art. 173). If somebody is required to drink alcohol in order to save his or her life or to be cured of a disease and drinks no more than is necessary, no hadd sentence will be imposed (art. 167).

Articles 701 to 704 contain additional provisions regarding the consumption of alcohol. Those provisions apply to both Muslims and non-Muslims. Article 701 provides a ta'zir punishment of imprisonment (two to six months) for drinking alcohol in public. Articles 702 and 703 punish the production, import, transport, offering for sale, selling, or buying of alcohol or placing alcohol at the disposal of another person. Article 704 prohibits opening a place where alcohol can be consumed and encouraging people to visit this place.

4. Interest (Riba, *Article 595*)

Article 595 gives a precise definition of what *riba* means in the legal sense: an agreement of any kind between two or more persons (as, for example, purchase, loan, and the like) concerning a certain object in which something of the same kind will be joined to that object or in which an amount of money must be paid that is higher than the initial amount. Consequently, it does not matter whether there is any disproportionality between the value of the object of the agreement and the value of the objects added. In other word, the agreement is not required to be usurious. Both parties, as well as any intermediary, are punished by six months to two years' imprisonment, up to 74 lashes, and a fine. Moreover, the objects or the amount of money that was added to the original object of the agreement must be returned to the original owner.

There are some interesting exemptions from punishment. A person will not be punished if it is proved that he or she paid the interest under constraint to do so (note 2). Article 595 will also not be applied if the contract is concluded between a father and his son or between wife and husband, or if a Muslim takes interest from an unbeliever (*kafir*) (note 3).

SELECTED BIBLIOGRAPHY

Ardébili, Muhammad Ali. *Hoquq-e djaza-ye 'omumi* [The General Part of Criminal Law]. Vol. 1. 18th ed. Tehran: Nashr-e Mizan, 2007 (1386).

Ardébili, Muhammad Ali. *Hoquq-e djaza-ye 'omumi* [The General Part of Criminal Law]. Vol. 2. 16th ed. Tehran: Nashr-e Mizan, 2007 (1386).

Golduziyan, Iradj. *Bayeste-ha-ye hoquq-e djaza-ye 'omumi* [The Essentials of the General Part of Criminal Law]. 10th ed. Tehran: Nashr-e Mizan, 2005 (1384).

Golduziyan, Iradj. *Hoquq-e djaza-ye 'omumi-ye Iran* [The General Part of Iranian Criminal Law]. Vol. 1. 10th ed. Tehran: Entesharat-e Daneshgah-e, 2007 (1386).

Golduziyan, Iradj. *Muhashsha-ye qanun-e mudjazat-e islami* [Commentary to the Islamic Penal Code]. 8th ed. Tehran: Entesharat-e Majd, 2007 (1386).

Hashemi, Sayyid Mohammad. *Hoquq-e asasi-ye jomhuri-ye eslami-ye Iran* [Constitutional Law of the Islamic Republic of Iran]. Vol. 2. 8th ed. Tehran: Nashr-e Mizan, 2004 (1383).

Najafi, Ali-Hossein, "The Iranian Penal Policy between the Minister of Justice and the Head of the Judiciary." *European Journal of Crime, Criminal Law and Criminal Justice* 9 (2001): 299–308.

Rahmdel, Mansour. "The *Ne Bis in Idem* Rule in Iranian Criminal Law." *Journal of Financial Crime* 11 (2004): 277–281.

Rezaei, Hassan, and Hussein Aghababaei. "Iranian Criminal Law on Political Opposition." *Yearbook of Near and Middle Eastern Law* 12 (2005/2006): 97–109.

Sadr Touhid-khaneh, Mohammad. "Participation in Crime: Criminal Liability of Leaders of Criminal Groups and Networks in Iran." In *Masterminds and Their Minions: Punishing Participants in Complex Criminal Structures—Täter hinter Tätern: Strafbare Beteiligung in komplexen kriminellen Strukturen*, vol. 5: *Africa and Asia*, ed. Ulrich Sieber, Hans-Georg Koch, and Jan Michael Simon, 310–386. Berlin/Freiburg: Duncker & Humblot/Max-Planck-Institut für ausländisches und internationales Strafrecht, forthcoming.

Shambayati, Houshang. *Hoquq-e djaza-ye 'omumi* [The General Part of Criminal Law]. Vol. 1. 11th ed. Tehran: Entesharat-e Majd, 2003 (1382).

Shambayati, Houshang. *Hoquq-e djaza-ye 'omumi* [The General Part of Criminal Law]. Vol. 2. 11th ed. Tehran: Entesharat-e Majd, 2003 (1382).

Walidi, Mohammad Saleh. *Bayeste-ha-ye hoquq-e djaza-ye 'omumi* [The Essentials of. the General Part of Criminal Law]. Tehran: Entesharat-e Khorshid, 2003 (1382).

Zira'at, Abbas. *Hoquq-e djaza-ye 'omumi* [The General Part of Criminal Law]. Vol. 1. 3d ed. Tehran: Entesharat-e Qoqnus, 2007 (1386).

NOTES

1. Iranian Parliament, http://mellat.majlis.ir/CONSTITUTION/ENGLISH.HTM, accessed on 11 August 2008.

2. See sections III.F.1 and III.F.2 in this chapter.

3. See section III.B.1 in this chapter.

4. See section II.F.1 in this chapter.

5. For the draft, see the homepage of the Iranian parliament. http://www. http://tarh.majlis.ir/?Report&RegId=127&dore=8, accessed on 8 June 2010.

6. For further information, see Mansour Rahmdel, "The *Ne Bis in Idem* Rule in Iranian Criminal Law," *Journal of Financial Crime* 11 (2004): 277–281.

7. In the draft of a new Islamic criminal code, the *ne bis in idem* principle is recognized and dealt with in detail.

8. In Iran, women are not allowed to act as judges in criminal matters except as investigative judges in the prosecutor's office.

9. Muhammad Ali Ardébili, *Hoquq-e djaza-ye 'omumi* [The General Part of Criminal Law], vol. 1, 18th ed. (Tehran: Nashr-e Mizan, 2007 [1386]), 141–142; Iradj Golduziyan, *Hoquq-e djaza-ye 'omumi-ye Iran* [The General Part of Iranian Criminal Law], vol. 1, 10th ed. (Tehran: Entesharat-e Daneshgah-e, 2007 [1386]), 212–216.

10. See Abbas Zira'at, *Hoquq-e djaza-ye 'omumi* [The General Part of Criminal Law], vol. 1, 3d ed. (Tehran: Entesharat-e Qoqnus, 2007 [1386]), 69–70.

11. Art. 214 CCP, phrase 2: The court is obliged to find the judgment in every case in the written laws, and if there is no law concerning the case it has to deliver its judgment on the basis of authoritative Islamic sources and fatwas.

12. Judgment of the Supreme Court to unify the application of law in general courts; see Ardébili, *Hoquq-e djaza-ye 'omumi*, vol. 1, 160–172.

13. This council, apart from its role in the lawgiving process, must consider any issue forwarded to it by the religious leader or conferred on it by the constitution; art. 112 of the constitution.

14. Only the fifth book (ta'zirat and deterrent punishments) was adopted by Parliament directly in 1996.

15. Sayyid Mohammad Hashemi, *Hoquq-e asasi-ye jomhuri-ye eslami-ye Iran* [Constitutional Law of the Islamic Republic of Iran], vol. 2, 8th ed. (Tehran: Nashr-e Mizan, 2004 [1383]), 552–553.

16. Ardébili, *Hoquq-e djaza-ye 'omumi*, vol. 1, 133.

17. Golduziyan, *Hoquq-e djaza-ye 'omumi-ye Iran*, 149–151.

18. The head of the judiciary, appointed by the religious leader, is responsible for establishing an appropriate judicial structure, for drafting judiciary bills, and for the employment of judges (arts. 157 and 158 of the constitution).

19. For more information, see Ali-Hossein Najafi, "The Iranian Penal Policy between the Minister of Justice and the Head of the Judiciary," *European Journal of Crime, Criminal Law and Criminal Justice* 9 (2001): 306.

20. Ardébili, *Hoquq-e djaza-ye 'omumi*, vol. 1, 134–136.

21. Zira'at, *Hoquq-e djaza-ye 'omumi*, 143–144.

22. Ardébili, *Hoquq-e djaza-ye 'omumi*, vol. 1, 209.

23. Mohammad Saleh Walidi, *Bayeste-ha-ye hoquq-e djaza-ye 'omumi* [The Essentials of. the General Part of Criminal Law] (Tehran: Entesharat-e Khorshid, 2003 [1382]), 225.

24. Negative: Ardébili, *Hoquq-e djaza-ye 'omumi*, vol. 1, 211; affirmative: Golduziyan, *Hoquq-e djaza-ye 'omumi-ye Iran*, 371–374.

25. See Iradj Golduziyan, *Bayeste-ha-ye hoquq-e djaza-ye eslami* [The General Part of Iranian Criminal Law], 10th ed. (Tehran: Nashr-e Mizan, 2005 [1384]), 159.

26. Ardébili, *Hoquq-e djaza-ye 'omumi*, vol. 1, 211–212.

27. See section III.B.1 in this chapter.

28. For instance, it is a matter of specific intent whether the perpetrator who hits somebody else wants to kill or to hurt that other person.

29. For instance, a perpetrator puts a bomb in a public place knowing that it will kill a number of persons but not knowing how many persons and whom the bomb will kill.

30. See section II.B.2.ii in this chapter.

31. Ardébili, *Hoquq-e djaza-ye 'omumi*, vol. 1, 245.

32. For instance, Walidi, *Bayeste-ha-ye hoquq-e djaza-ye 'omumi*, 257–259.

33. This may be due to the familiarity of most of the authors with French law, which regards *dolus eventualis* as a kind of negligence.

34. Ardébili, *Hoquq-e djaza-ye 'omumi*, vol. 1, 244; Zira'at, *Hoquq-e djaza-ye 'omumi*, 200.

35. See, for instance, Ardébili, *Hoquq-e djaza-ye 'omumi*, vol. 1, 244; Zira'at, *Hoquq-e djaza-ye 'omumi*, 205.

36. Ardébili, *Hoquq-e djaza-ye 'omumi*, vol. 1, 219–223.

37. See section III.F.1 in this chapter.

38. Mohammad Sadr Touhid-khaneh, "Participation in Crime: Criminal Liability of Leaders of Criminal Groups and Networks in Iran," in *Masterminds and Their Minions: Punishing Participants in Complex Criminal Structures—Täter hinter Tätern: Strafbare Beteiligung in komplexen kriminellen Strukturen*, vol. 5, *Africa and Asia*, ed. Ulrich Sieber, Hans-Georg Koch, and Jan Michael Simon (Berlin/Freiburg: Duncker & Humblot/Max-Planck-Institut für ausländisches und internationales Strafrecht, forthcoming), 368–369.

39. Ibid., 328.

40. It should be mentioned here that in some cases Islamic criminal law recognizes the notion of the indirect perpetrator: if a thief lets a little child or a mad person take the stolen object out of its safe custody, this is regarded as if the thief had taken the object himself or herself (note 2 to art. 198).

41. See section III.F.1 in this chapter.

42. Of course, accessories can be punished in cases in which an intentional homicide or bodily injury is not punished by qisas but is commuted to a diya by the agreement of the parties involved or by provisions of the law concerning specific cases.

43. Sadr Touhid-khaneh, "Participation in Crime," 353.

44. See section II.F.1 in this chapter for details.

45. See Muhammad Ali Ardébili, *Hoquq-e djaza-ye 'omumi* [The General Part of Criminal Law], vol. 2, 16th ed. (Tehran: Nashr-e Mizan 2007 [1386]), 20–26.

46. For more information, see Zira'at, *Hoquq-e djaza-ye 'omumi*, 157–159.

47. See, for instance, Ardébili, *Hoquq-e djaza-ye 'omumi*, vol. 1, 174–179.

48. See, for instance, Zira'at, *Hoquq-e djaza-ye 'omumi*, 250–255.

49. See, for instance, Golduziyan, *Bayeste-ha-ye hoquq-e djaza-ye eslami*, 131–135. He distinguishes between external factors as enumerated in article 55, which treat necessity as a justification, and internal factors resulting from personal considerations (such as hunger), which result in necessity being considered an excuse (art. 198 no. 12).

50. Ardébili, *Hoquq-e djaza-ye 'omumi*, vol. 1, 197.

51. See note 3 of art. 61.

52. Ardébili, *Hoquq-e djaza-ye 'omumi*, vol. 1, 203.

53. The texts speaks of the *shar'*, the Islamic religious law, but according to prevailing opinion this is to be understood in a broader sense as law in general.

54. See, for instance, Golduziyan, *Hoquq-e djaza-ye 'omumi-ye Iran*, 288–292.
55. Zira'at, *Hoquq-e djaza-ye 'omumi*, 190–196, regards them as part of the *mens rea*.
56. Ardébili, *Hoquq-e djaza-ye 'omumi*, vol. 1, 99.
57. For a detailed description of this case, see Houshang Shambayati, *Hoquq-e djaza-ye 'omumi* [The General Part of Criminal Law], vol. 2, 11th ed. (Tehran: Entesharat-e Majd, 1382 [2003]), 113–116.
58. See, for instance, Ardébili, *Hoquq-e djaza-ye 'omumi*, vol. 1, 102–103; Zira'at, *Hoquq-e djaza-ye 'omumi*, 194; Golduziyan, *Hoquq-e djaza-ye 'omumi-ye Iran*, 561.
59. This means that young men and women who are regarded as minor offenders in most of the states of the world are considered in Iran as being of age. Amnesty International, "Executions of Juveniles since 1990," http://www.amnesty.org/en/death-penalty/executions-of-child-offenders-since-1990, accessed on 11 August 2008.
60. See Ardébili, *Hoquq-e djaza-ye 'omumi*, vol. 2, 111–114; Zira'at, *Hoquq-e djaza-ye 'omumi*, 231–234; Shambayati, *Hoquq-e djaza-ye 'omumi*, vol. 2, 31–61. Article 141-1 of the draft of a new Iranian Criminal Code sets a limit of age of eighteen solar years for young criminals. It contains some special rules for hadd crimes, in which the age of full criminal responsibility continues to be nine years for girls and fifteen years for boys, but it requires courts to carefully examine whether there is any legal way to avoid a hadd penalty (art. 141-4 of the draft).
61. See section II.F.1 in this chapter.
62. See Ardébili, *Hoquq-e djaza-ye 'omumi*, vol. 2, 111.
63. Ibid., p. 90.
64. For the opposite opinion, see Zira'at, *Hoquq-e djaza-ye 'omumi*, 243.
65. Ardébili, *Hoquq-e djaza-ye 'omumi*, vol. 2, 90.
66. Unlawful sexual intercourse (art. 64), homosexual acts (art. 111), lesbian acts (art. 130), pandering (art. 136), defamation of having committed unlawful sexual intercourse (art. 146), drinking alcohol (art. 166), and theft (art. 198).
67. See section II.D.4 in this chapter.
68. The 'aqila consists of the male paternal relatives who would inherit from the perpetrator in case of his or her death. They are obliged to pay their share of the blood money for the crime in the same degree as their right of inheritance.
69. See section III.F.1 in this chapter.
70. See section III.F.1 in this chapter.
71. See Amnesty International, "The Death Penalty in 2009," http://www.amnesty.org/en/death-penalty/death-sentences-and-executions-in-2009?utm_source=supporters&utm_medium=banner&utm_content=globe_2009_320_250_en&utm_campaign=death_penalty, accessed on 26 May 2010.
72. The protected right of humans is the honor of the victim; the protected right of God is the order of society.
73. Apostasy at the moment is not punishable in Iran; see section III.F.2 in this chapter.
74. The punishment is three to ten years' imprisonment.
75. This is called *dol dépassé* in French law.
76. The relevant provision speaks of adherents to religions recognized in article 12 of the constitution.

77. Iradj Golduziyan, *Muhashsha-ye qanun-e mudjazat-e islami* [Commentary to the Islamic Penal Code], 8th ed. (Tehran: Entesharat-e Majd 2007 [1386]), 183.

78. Such a person is called *muhsin* (feminine *muhsina*), but in Shi'i law this notion is much narrower than in Sunni law, where it denotes an adult free Muslim who has previously been married regardless of whether the marriage still exists at the time of the crime. As examples of the impossibility of having sexual intercourse, the law explicitly mentions travel, imprisonment, or absence for similar reasons (art. 86).

79. In 2002 the head of the judiciary announced a moratorium on stoning. Nonetheless, information indicates that several stonings have taken place during the last few years. Amnesty International, "Iran: Announcement of Suspension of Stoning a Welcome Step if Carried Out," http://www.amnesty.org/en/for-media/press-releases/iran-announcement-suspension-stoning-welcome-step-if-carried-out-2008080, accessed on 26 May 2010.

80. In this case the woman is to be punished for adultery but not the man, provided he is not married to another woman.

81. "Honest" implies that the witness is a Muslim.

82. See section II.F.2 in this chapter.

83. Especially in the field of military, economic, and drug crimes. See Sadr Touhidkhaneh, "Participation in Crime," 330, 365–367.

84. For more information about this crime, see Hassan Rezaei and Hussein Aghababaei, "Iranian Criminal Law on Political Opposition," *Yearbook of Near and Middle Eastern Law* 12 (2005/2006): 97–109.

85. It seems that the lawgiver did not include such a provision in the IPC for political reasons.

86. See section I.A in this chapter.

87. See Golduziyan, *Muhashsha-ye qanun-e mudjazat-e islami*, 251.

ISRAEL

Itzhak Kugler

I. Introduction
   A. Historical Sketch
   B. Legality Principle
   C. Interpretation
   D. Temporal Application of Criminal Enactments
   E. Categories of Offenses
   F. Process

II. General Part
   A. Theories of Punishment
   B. Liability Requirements
   C. Defenses
   D. Sanctions

III. Special Part
   A. Structure
   B. Homicide
   C. Sex Offenses

I. INTRODUCTION

A. Historical Sketch

In 1936 the British Mandatory legislature enacted the Criminal Code Ordinance of 1936 (hereafter the CCO). This code contained a General Part and a Special Part. The State of Israel was established in 1948, and the Israeli legislature decided that the CCO would re-

---

Itzhak Kugler is the Ivan C. Rand Senior Lecturer in Criminal Law at the Hebrew University of Jerusalem. His recent publications include *Direct and Oblique Intention in the Criminal Law: An Inquiry into Degrees of Blameworthiness* (Ashgate, 2002) and "Two Concepts of Omission," 14 *Criminal Law Forum* 421–447 (2003).

main in force. Although the CCO was translated into Hebrew, the English version was the binding text. In 1977 the sections of the CCO that were still in force were officially translated into Hebrew; from that point onward, the Hebrew version of these sections was the binding text. Several laws that had been enacted by the Knesset (the Israeli parliament) since 1948 were added to these provisions. The product was a new and consolidated law—the Penal Law, 1977. Most of the General Part of this law and big portions of its Special Part contained sections that had originally been enacted in 1936 (although from time to time amendments had been made, especially with respect to specific offenses). In the 1990s it was decided to enact a new General Part. In 1994 the Knesset enacted Amendment no. 39 to the Penal Law, 1977. This amendment replaced all the sections of the General Part (except for the sections dealing with penalties) with new sections. Sections 1–17 of the Penal Law presently form the Preliminary Part, and sections 18–90B form the General Part. The Amendment came into force in 1995, but the whole law is still called the Penal Law, 1977. Thus the Preliminary and General Parts consist of legislation that came into force in 1995 (except for those sections of the General Part that deal with penalties). It should be noted that the framers of Amendment no. 39 were influenced and inspired not only by Anglo-American law but also by Continental law, and therefore some of the sections of Amendment no. 39 have been influenced by Continental law. Amendment no. 39 did not change the Special Part of the Penal Law, and it remained as it was before 1995. Of course, from time to time, specific amendments to certain sections of the Special Part are made. The new Preliminary and General Parts apply not only to offenses that have been enacted since 1995, but also to the old Special Part of the Penal Law, 1977. In addition, these new parts apply not only to the offenses included in the Penal Law, 1977, but also to criminal offenses included in other laws.

B. Legality Principle

Section 1 of the Penal Law, 1977, provides that "there shall be no offense and no penalty unless determined by Law or according to it."[1] This section establishes the principle of legality, according to which offenses and penalties are to be set only in legislation. The main offenses appear in primary legislation (laws of the Knesset), but offenses can appear also in secondary legislation, that is, in regulations enacted, for example, by a minister.[2] Courts are not allowed to create offenses, and therefore there are no common-law offenses in Israel. Section 1 is interpreted as also prohibiting the use of analogy, which means that judges are not allowed to broaden the scope of an offense by way of analogy. Conviction of an offense is legitimate only in cases that are covered by the wording of the statute.[3]

C. Interpretation

The courts interpret the law. The interpretation adopted by the Supreme Court and its other decisions bind the lower courts. The courts are sometimes influenced by the academic literature.

The courts are allowed to create criminal defenses.[4] The courts are also entitled to "read into" the definition of an offense a certain condition for conviction that does not appear in the language of the statute. This means that in certain cases that are covered by the wording of the offense a conviction will not be obtained because of considerations of justice and policy. The main context in which this method of interpretation is used is when the defendant's action is covered by the wording of a certain offense, but it does not harm or endanger the interest protected by the offense. In such a case the court may acquit the defendant.[5] But the court may exclude from the scope of an offense even certain types of cases in which the protected interest is harmed or endangered when this seems justified to the court on the basis of considerations of justice or policy. This would be the case, for example, when the court wishes to limit the scope of the infringement on freedom of speech produced by the existence of a given offense.[6]

If the language of the law can be interpreted in two or more ways, the law should be interpreted according to its purpose. If, even after the law's purpose is taken into account, two or more interpretations remain reasonable, the court should adopt the interpretation that is most favorable to the accused (section 34U).

D. Temporal Application of Criminal Enactments

According to sections 3 and 5, an enactment that either creates a new offense, broadens the scope of an existing offense, or increases the penalty for a certain offense does not apply to actions performed before the date the enactment came into force. In contrast, an enactment that either repeals an offense, narrows its scope, or reduces the applicable penalty applies even to actions performed before the date the new enactment came into force (sections 4–5).[7]

E. Categories of Offenses

Section 24 divides criminal offenses into three categories. A *felony* is an offense whose maximum penalty is higher than three years of imprisonment. A *misdemeanor* is an offense whose maximum penalty is higher than three months' imprisonment but does not exceed three years' imprisonment. A *contravention* is an offense whose maximum penalty does not exceed three months' imprisonment.[8] The classification has practical implications for certain issues of substantive criminal law and criminal procedure.

F. Process

1. Adversarial/Inquisitorial

The Israeli criminal justice system is adversarial.

2. Jury/Written Opinions

There is no jury in Israel, and all cases are tried by professional judges. Cases are tried before a single judge or a panel of three judges (according to the provisions of the Courts Law, 1984). The first stage is devoted to the question whether to convict or acquit the accused. If the decision is to convict the accused, then a sentencing hearing is held, at the conclusion of which the judge (or panel of judges) imposes the sentence. A decision to convict or acquit a defendant, as well as the sentencing decision, must be given in writing and must specify the reasons for the decision.

The prosecutor may appeal an acquittal or a sentence that he or she thinks is too lenient, and the offender may appeal his or her conviction and/or a sentence that he or she thinks is too harsh.

II. GENERAL PART

A. Theories of Punishment

The legislature has not specified the purposes of punishment. The courts recognize as legitimate the commonly accepted purposes of punishment, including retribution, general and specific deterrence, incapacitation, rehabilitation, denunciation, and education of the public.

B. Liability Requirements

1. Objective/Actus Reus/Physical Element
  i. Components of the Physical Element

Section 18 clarifies that the physical element of an offense consists of the conduct, the circumstances, and the result that are required by the definition of the offense.

  ii. Omission

Section 18 also deals with omissions. In the context of result crimes like "causing the death of another person" (i.e., result crimes that do not include specific conditions relating to conduct or circumstances), it is possible to convict not only in cases of a positive action but also in cases where the result was caused by an omission of the defendant, provided (in cases of omission) that the defendant was under a duty to act.

Section 18(c) states that the source of the duty to act may be "any law or a contract." The words "any law" clarify that the duty to act may be found not only in the criminal law but also in other branches of the law, like civil law or administrative law. In fact, the law's reference to a contract is redundant because the duty to fulfill one's contractual obligations applies by virtue of the civil law.

Duties to act may be found, first of all, in sections 322–326. These sections define a number of situations in which certain individuals are made subject to a duty to act, and they clarify that the individuals concerned shall be held to have caused any harmful consequences to the life or health of another person that occur as a result of a failure on their part to fulfill the duty in question. These sections are not independent offenses; therefore, they do not provide for any penalty. Rather, the sole objective of these sections is to create and supply duties to act for the purpose of obtaining a conviction (in cases of omissions) as regards offenses that appear in other sections. Sections 322–326 supply duties to act only for the purpose of convicting of an offense against the person, like the offense of causing the death of another person or causing bodily harm to another person. These sections establish, for example, that the parent of a child under eighteen who shares the same household with him or her has the duty to provide the child with necessities of life and to take care of his or her health; and that a person who has in his or her charge or under his or her control a dangerous thing has the duty to use reasonable care to prevent that thing from causing bodily harm to another person or causing the death of another person.

However, according to section 18(c), a duty to act may also be found outside sections 322–326. A duty to act may be found in a "simple crime of omission," like the offense defined in section 362. This section provides, inter alia, that if a person is unable to provide for his or her own needs, and if the parent of that person does not supply him or her with food, clothes, bedding, and other essentials of life to the extent required to preserve his or her well-being and health, the parent commits a criminal offense, subject to a maximum punishment of three years' imprisonment. This offense is a "simple crime of omission," and therefore there is no need to find a duty to act outside the offense in order to convict. It should also be noted that liability for this offense applies even if no bodily harm materializes. But if the omission of the defendant establishes liability under the said offense and, in addition, it caused the death of the victim (and the defendant was reckless with regard to this result), then he or she may be convicted of the offense of manslaughter (subject to a maximum punishment of twenty years' imprisonment), based on the duty to act found in section 362.

A duty to act may also be found in a noncriminal enactment. For example, if the defendant failed to perform a certain act and this failure to act generates (under a civil enactment) an obligation to pay compensation that grounds the conclusion that there was a duty to act, then the civil enactment can be used as a source of a duty to act for the purpose of convicting the defendant of the result crime concerned. This can be done with respect to an omission that establishes, for example, a breach of contract or a tort.

Two issues are in dispute in Israeli criminal law literature concerning the sources of the duty to act. The first question is whether the duty to act required for a conviction of a result crime must appear in an enactment. This question asks whether judges may create a duty to act directly for the purpose of the result crime with which they are dealing, without finding any enactment that establishes the said duty to act. According to one approach, judges are not allowed to create duties to act because this is akin to judges creating a criminal offense, which is forbidden according to the principle of legality.[9] According to a second approach, judges should be allowed to create duties to act in spite of the conflict with the principle of legality. In order to sufficiently protect the interests protected by criminal offenses, the argument runs, the law must be enabled to develop. The legislature cannot provide alongside each result crime (of the kind discussed here) a closed list of all the situations in which a duty to act applies (nor can it foresee in advance all cases where it would be desirable to impose a duty to act). In any case, thus far the legislature has not provided the courts with such closed lists. Even relying on all existing enactments does not ensure that a conviction will be obtained in all cases in which such an outcome is justified. Thus a rule to the effect that the duty to act must appear in an enactment will improperly reduce the scope of protection given to the interests protected by the criminal law. Therefore, judges should be allowed to create duties to act in appropriate cases.[10] The Supreme Court has held that judges do have the power to create a duty to act directly for the purpose of the result crime with which they are dealing.[11]

The second question is whether the fact that a certain enactment entails a duty to act (i.e., in the framework of a simple crime of omission or in the framework of the civil law) automatically dictates that this duty also be used for the purpose of convicting a defendant of the result crime concerned. According to one approach, the rationale of the requirement of a duty to act is that of refraining from overly limiting the freedom of the citizen. But when a simple crime of omission applies in a certain context, the legislature has already determined that in this context the citizen is required to act because the value of freedom is outweighed in this context by other values. If this is the case, then the desire not to overly limit the liberty of the citizen is not relevant anymore in this context; therefore, the defendant should be convicted of the result crime concerned. In the same vein, when there is a civil enactment that imposes on a person the obligation to pay compensation in a given case of omission on his or her part, this enactment implies that this person was obliged to act. If this is the case, then the desire not to overly limit the liberty of the citizen is not relevant anymore in this context; therefore, the defendant should be convicted of the result crime concerned.[12]

According to a second approach, enactments should not be automatically adopted as sources of duties to act. There are certain simple crimes of omission that should not serve as sources of a duty to act for the purpose of result crimes. One argument is that a simple crime of omission can serve as a source of a duty to act for the purpose of result crimes only if this simple crime of omission is based on a special connection between the defendant and the victim or the defendant and the source of the danger. For the sake of illustration, I will use the "Good Samaritan" offense that exists in Israel.[13] According to the approach under discussion, if the defendant does not help the person in danger (and does not notify the authorities), foreseeing the possibility that this person might die because of his or her omission, and this outcome actually occurs, the defendant may be convicted only of the Good Samaritan offense, and not of manslaughter, because the duty to act that is imposed by the Good Samaritan law is not based on a special connection to the victim or to the source of the danger.[14] A further argument against the use of the Good Samaritan offense as a source of a duty to act for the purpose of convicting a defendant of manslaughter is that the punishment prescribed by the legislature for this offense is only a fine, and it is not fair or logical that, because the death of the victim has materialized, the defendant be held liable for an offense that is subject to a maximum penalty of twenty years' imprisonment (the punishment for manslaughter in Israel). Similar arguments have been raised with regard to civil law enactments as well. The fact that in the civil law context the legislature required that a person perform a certain act and also provided that failure to perform this act should generate an obligation to pay compensation does not necessarily lead to the conclusion that this omission should generate a criminal conviction. It may be the case that the said omission is not sufficiently serious to justify the stigma attached to a criminal conviction and the imposition of the penalties that exist in criminal law. Therefore, according to the approach under discussion, judges should be granted discretion to decide whether to use a given criminal or noncriminal enactment that imposes an obligation to act as a source for the duty to act required to convict a person of the result crime concerned. The Supreme Court has not yet decided which of the two approaches to adopt.[15]

2. *Subjective*/Mens Rea/*Mental Element*
   i. Criminal Thought
      a. *The General Rule: A Requirement of Criminal Thought*

The position of the legislature is that the general rule should be that an offense is committed only when the actor acts with a subjective mental state ("criminal thought"). Accordingly, section 19 states that a person commits an offense only if he or she acts with criminal thought unless the definition of the offense states that negligence suffices for conviction (and unless the offense is a strict liability offense). Thus criminal-thought offenses are offenses whose definition contains a requirement of criminal thought and offenses whose definition does not mention the required mental state. If the definition of a certain offense does not mention the required mental state, courts cannot interpret the offense as an offense of negligence. Negligence offenses are exceptional, and it must be specifically stated in the definition of the offense that negligence suffices for conviction.[16] The conclusion is that most criminal offenses require criminal thought.

b. Criminal Thought with Respect to the Nature of the Conduct and the Circumstances
Section 20(a) defines "criminal thought." Criminal thought exists when the actor is aware of the nature of the conduct, of the existence of the circumstances, and of the possibility that his or her conduct will bring about the result (when the conduct, circumstances, and result are ingredients of the *actus reus* of the offense). Criminal thought is internally divided only in relation to the result, based on the volitional attitude of the actor toward the result.

Criminal thought with respect to the conduct and circumstances is defined only in cognitive terms. With respect to the conduct and circumstances, the law does not refer at all to the volitional attitude of the actor.

I will now examine in greater detail criminal thought concerning circumstances. The discussion here applies to the nature of the conduct as well, because the definition of criminal thought with respect to the nature of the conduct and the circumstances is identical.

At first glance, it might be thought that criminal thought exists only when the actor knows for sure that the relevant circumstance exists, but this is not the case. Section 20(c)(1) states that for the purpose of section 20, a person who suspects the possibility that a circumstance exists and refrains from investigating the suspicion is deemed to be aware of the existence of the circumstance (the same applies to the nature of the conduct).

The explanatory notes to the Penal Law Bill[17] refer to the rule appearing in section 20(c)(1) as the rule of "willful blindness," and the courts, too, use this terminology. It should be noted, however, that the Israeli rule of willful blindness applies to a wider scope of cases than the Anglo-American rule of willful blindness (as it is generally understood). The Israeli concept of willful blindness is more akin to the English concept of "subjective recklessness" with respect to circumstances. According to section 20(c)(1), to establish willful blindness, it is sufficient that the actor have realized the mere possibility that the circumstance existed; there is no requirement of belief of a higher degree of probability that the circumstance existed. In addition, the motives of the actor for not investigating the suspicion are irrelevant, and the application of the rule is not made dependent on the fact that it was easy to find out whether the circumstance existed. In all cases where it was possible to find out the truth, but the actor refrained from investigating and remained in doubt, criminal thought with regard to the circumstance exists. The wide scope of this rule is justified because, according to section 19, the mental state required in offenses that do not specify the mental state required (i.e., most offenses) is criminal thought. In England the rule is that subjective recklessness with regard to the circumstances is generally sufficient for conviction of a criminal offense; similarly, in Israel the rule is that willful blindness with respect to the circumstances is generally sufficient.

I have explained that the Israeli concept of willful blindness is akin to the English concept of subjective recklessness. However, for two reasons, I refrained from stating that the two are identical. The first reason has to do with the fact that the Israeli provision requires that the actor refrain from investigating the suspicion. The question arises whether the rule of willful blindness applies even in a case where, before the defendant acted, there was no way to find out the truth, and, for that reason, the actor simply could not have found out whether the relevant circumstance existed. If in such a case the actor acted in spite of his or her suspicion that the circumstance existed, may he or she be convicted? It seems that from a linguistic perspective, in such a case the condition that the actor refrained from investigating is not fulfilled, such that criminal thought does not exist and the actor should be acquitted. However, from a policy point of view, it seems that in many cases we would want a person who suspects that a certain circumstance exists to refrain from acting even if there is no way to find out whether the circumstance actually exists. Considerations of deterrence thus support the idea that in such cases the actor should be convicted. From the point of view of desert, it also seems that because the person in such cases acted in spite of the suspicion, it is generally just to convict and punish him or her.[18] If we take into account that section 20(c)(1) determines the minimal state of mind required for conviction for most offenses, it seems logical to convict in such cases. The Supreme Court has not ruled on this point yet, but in my view the rule of willful blindness should apply even in cases where the actor could not have found out whether the relevant circumstance existed. If this view is adopted, then section 20(c)(1) should be understood as simply stating that criminal thought is present not only when the actor is sure that the relevant circumstance exists, but also when he or she knowingly takes a risk that it exists. If this is the case, then, the concept that appears in section 20(c)(1) could be considered as almost identical to the English concept of subjective recklessness. However, I am still refraining from suggesting that the two concepts are completely identical for a reason that will be noted now.

The definition of the term *recklessness* in Anglo-American law also contains an objective component: that the taking of the risk was unreasonable (or, in another formulation, unjustifiable). The Israeli legislature recognizes this component in the definition of recklessness with respect to the result (section 20(a)(2)), but (in contrast to the usual practice in Anglo-American law) it does not mention the concept of "reasonable risk" at all with respect to circumstances (or with respect to conduct). If section 20(c)(1) is interpreted according to its plain language, the conclusion follows that in every case where a person knowingly took a risk that the relevant circumstance existed, criminal thought exists (at least in cases where there was a way to find out the truth), and the actor can never be exempted from criminal liability by virtue of the claim that it was reasonable to take the risk. It can be argued that this is not justified, because even in cases where the option to investigate in order to find out the truth is present, it is sometimes reasonable or justifiable not to investigate but to take the risk that the relevant circumstance exists. For example, in the context of the offense of receiving stolen property, sometimes the investigation whether the article is stolen costs a lot of money or takes so much time that the actor will in the meantime lose the rare opportunity to buy an article that is very important to him or her. Of course, permission to take reasonable risks is needed even more if the rule of willful blindness is interpreted as applying even in cases where there is no way to find out the truth, for it is logical to assume that in some cases where there is no way to find out the truth concerning the existence of a certain circumstance, it will be reasonable to take the risk that the circumstance in question actually exists. Therefore, it may be argued that in spite of the language of section 20(c)(1) the courts should exempt a person from criminal liability in cases where the taking of the risk was reasonable (in other words, the concept of willful blindness should be interpreted as requiring, inter alia, that it was unreasonable to take the risk that the relevant circumstance exists). The Supreme Court has not ruled on this point yet, but in my view it should recognize that sometimes it is reasonable, and therefore permitted, to take a risk that a certain circumstance exists. If my position is accepted concerning the two issues I have discussed here, the conclusion that follows is that with respect to circumstances, the Israeli concept of willful blindness is identical to the English concept of subjective recklessness.

As I mentioned earlier, the law concerning the mental element with respect to the nature of conduct is identical to the law concerning the mental element with respect to the circumstances. For example, the offense of assault is established when, inter alia, a person touches another person without his or her consent (section 378). If A touches B without B's consent, and at the time of the act A suspects that he or she is touching B, the rule of willful blindness will apply, because in this case there is a suspicion on the part of A concerning the nature of his or her conduct. Another example is where a person suspects that his or her act *hinders* a public servant in the exercise of his or her duty (section 288A).

Section 20 does not mention at all the possibility that offenses may exist that are not subject to the rule of willful blindness (i.e., offenses that are established only if the actor is sure that the relevant circumstance exists). However, the definition of a number of offenses enacted before Amendment no. 39 included the requirement that the actor act "knowingly" with respect to the circumstances. In some judicial decisions rendered before the enactment of Amendment no. 39, some judges adopted the view that in such offenses conviction is dependent on the actor being sure that the relevant circumstance exists, i.e., that the general rule—that suspicion that the relevant circumstance exists suffices for conviction—does not apply to these offenses. Some judges and scholars did not agree with this view. What is the law concerning these offenses after the enactment of Amendment no. 39? Section 90A(3), which came into force the same day as Amendment no. 39, provides that wherever a legislative provision enacted before the entry into force of Amendment no. 39 defines the mental element of an offense using the term *knowingly* (or a term of similar meaning), the term should be interpreted as criminal thought as defined in section 20(a). Subsequent to section 20(a), section 20(c)(1) clarifies that criminal thought as defined in section 20(a) exists even in cases of mere suspicion. The conclusion follows that the rule of willful blindness does apply to offenses enacted before Amendment no. 39 that use the term *knowingly* or similar terms.[19] This means that if the law is interpreted according to its wording, the sweeping conclusion follows that there is no offense (enacted before

Amendment no. 39) with respect to which suspicion concerning the existence of a relevant circumstance does not suffice for conviction.

However, the Supreme Court has decided not to follow the language of the law. In Israel there is an offense of "failure to prevent a felony" that was enacted before Amendment no. 39, the maximum punishment for which is two years' imprisonment (section 262). The offense is established when "[a] person ... knowing that a person designs to commit a felony, fails to use all reasonable means to prevent the commission or completion thereof." The question arose whether the rule of willful blindness applies to this offense with respect to the circumstance element pertaining to the other person's designing to commit a felony. The Supreme Court noted that from the perspective of the language of the law, the rule of willful blindness should be applied to this offense in spite of its use of the term *knowing*, because of the rule set forth in section 90A(3). Nonetheless, the court decided not to apply the rule of willful blindness to this offense because this would be unjustified from the perspective of policy and justice.[20] The court took into consideration the fact that the said offense relates to all felonies, and that the rule of willful blindness applies even in cases where only a low probability exists that the relevant circumstance is present. Therefore, if the rule of willful blindness were to be applied to the offense in question, it would entail that whenever a person has the slightest suspicion that another person is planning to commit a felony of any sort, and he or she does not manage to find out whether as a matter of fact the person actually possesses such an intention, he or she has to inform the police about his or her suspicion concerning the other person (even if that person is his or her friend or relative). This interpretation imposes too heavy a burden on citizens and overly infringes on their personal liberty. The implementation of a duty to inform the police in any case of suspicion and in the context of any felony may also cause much harm to the actor's relations with friends and relatives. The court also indicated that we do not want every person who suspects that another person (including his or her relative or friend) is planning to commit a felony to start gathering information about this person, shadow him or her, and pry into his or her affairs in an effort to find out whether he or she is really planning to commit a felony. The fact that liability for the said offense is established by omission, the court explained, adds weight to the considerations militating against overly extending the scope of the offense. In light of these arguments, the court concluded that the said offense is established only in cases where the defendant is sure that the other person plans to commit a felony, and not in cases of mere suspicion.[21] In light of this decision it is possible that in the future the Supreme Court will also decide, in the context of other specific offenses, that the rule of willful blindness does not apply.[22]

c. Criminal Thought with Respect to the Result

Criminal thought with respect to a result element of the offense is established when the actor foresees the possibility that the result, which forms part of the *actus reus* of the offense, will be brought about by his or her conduct (section 20(a)). With respect to the result, the code divides criminal thought into different categories based on the volitional attitude of the actor. The main division is between "intention" and "recklessness," with intention being considered a more serious state of mind than recklessness. Intention is established when the actor acts with the purpose of causing the result.[23] Recklessness is established when the actor foresees the possibility that the result will be brought about, and this foresight is not accompanied by a desire that the result occur. When an offense is silent concerning the required mental state, recklessness is sufficient for conviction. Only when the legislative definition of the offense requires intention is intention required for conviction.

ii. Intention

When the actor acts in order to cause the result, intention is established even if he or she foresees that there is only a low probability that the result will occur. A further point is that it is not necessary for the actor to desire the result as an end in itself. Intention is established even if the actor only needs the result to occur as a means to another end.[24]

I will now turn to the issue of "oblique intention." Section 20(b) provides that a person who is almost certain that the result will occur is considered to have acted with the intent to cause the result. Thus intention is established even in a case where there was no purpose to cause the result, provided that the actor foresaw that the result was almost certain to occur (i.e., the actor had oblique intention). The rule that appears in section 20(b) is called in Israel "the foresight rule." The main question concerning this rule that has been debated by the courts is whether this rule applies without exception to all "intention crimes," or whether there are intention crimes to which this rule does not apply, that is, offenses in the context of which oblique intention (as opposed to direct intention) does not suffice for conviction.

Before Amendment no. 39 the concept of intention was not defined by the legislature, and the issue of oblique intention was dealt with only in case law. The courts rejected the view that the foresight rule should automatically apply to all intention crimes. The Supreme Court ruled that a court may decide that in the context of a given intention crime the foresight rule does not apply and that only direct intention suffices to convict, on the basis of the legislature's intent or considerations of justice and policy.[25] In reality, in most cases where the Supreme Court had to decide whether to apply the foresight rule to a given offense, the court decided to apply the rule. The court has decided not to apply the rule in the context of only two offenses. The first is the offense of murder with premeditation. The main form of murder in Israel is that of causing death with premeditation. It requires, inter alia, that the actor intend to cause the death of the victim.[26] The punishment for murder is mandatory life imprisonment. If the actor is only reckless with respect to the death of the victim, he or she is guilty of manslaughter, which is subject to a maximum penalty of twenty years' imprisonment. The Supreme Court has held that in order to convict a person of murder with premeditation it is required, inter alia, that the actor have wanted to cause the death of the victim. If the actor's performance of the act was not accompanied by such a desire, the actor may be convicted only of manslaughter, even if at the time of the act he or she was almost sure (or even sure) that the death would occur. The court gave two reasons for its decision. First, only those who want to cause death (as opposed to those who act with mere oblique intention) deserve to be stigmatized as murderers. Second, a mandatory sentence of life imprisonment is appropriate only for actors who want to kill; some actors who cause death with mere oblique intention do not deserve the harsh penalty of life imprisonment.[27]

The second offense to which the Supreme Court decided that the foresight rule does not apply is defamatory libel. To convict a person of this offense, it is required that the actor have published the defamation with intent to injure the reputation of the victim.[28] The Supreme Court held that the foresight rule does not apply to this offense. Only a person who published the defamation out of a desire to injure the reputation of the victim may be convicted of this offense. If the act of publication was not accompanied by such a desire, the actor cannot be convicted of this offense even if he or she was almost sure (or even sure) that the publication would cause injury to the victim's reputation. In fact, the result is that in such a case the actor cannot be convicted of any offense.[29]

As was mentioned earlier in this section, the foresight rule now appears in section 20(b). At first glance it appears that this section establishes a sweeping rule that applies to all intention crimes. Therefore, the question has been raised whether, after the enactment of section 20(b), the courts still have the power to declare that the said rule does not apply to a certain offense. The Supreme Court ruled on this point in a case concerning the offense of defamatory libel.[30] In this case the argument was raised that after the enactment of section 20(b) courts no longer have the discretion to decide to which offenses the foresight rule applies, such that they are obliged to apply it to every intention crime, including the offense of defamatory libel. Two of the nine judges accepted this argument. However, seven judges rejected it. The latter judges made a distinction between "result crimes of intention" (i.e., intention crimes in which the intended result is part of the *actus reus*) and offenses of "ulterior intent" (i.e., offenses in which an intention to cause X is required, but X is not part of the *actus reus* of the offense, so that conviction of the offense is not dependent on the occurrence of X). The majority reasoned that the structure and language of section 20 suggest that the definition of intention, as well as the foresight rule, that appear in this section relate only to result crimes of intention. Indeed, in the context of these crimes the sweeping rule that appears in section 20(b) applies. But section 20 does not deal at all with the concept of intention that appears in offenses of ulterior intent. Therefore, in the context of offenses of ulterior intent the law remains as it was before Amendment no. 39—that courts have the power to determine that in the context of some of these offenses the foresight rule does not apply. Because the offense of defamatory libel is an ulterior-intent offense, courts have discretion to decide whether to apply this rule to this offense. The seven judges decided to consider anew the question whether the foresight rule should apply to this offense. Six of them decided that considerations of justice and policy lead to the conclusion that the foresight rule should not apply to this offense. Thus they decided to preserve the law concerning this offense as it was before Amendment no. 39.[31] As a result, the foresight rule does not apply to defamatory libel today.

It is clear that the main reason that motivated the majority to reject sweeping application of the foresight rule to all intention crimes was their belief that in the context of certain offenses considerations of justice and policy may lead to the conclusion that the foresight rule should not apply. The distinction made between result crimes and ulterior-intent offenses was merely a formal device enabling them to reach the desired conclusion. However, in the context of result crimes they yielded to the clear wording of the statute, from which they did not wish (for the time being, at least) to deviate.[32]

Another question raised after the enactment of Amendment no. 39 was whether the foresight rule applies at the present time to the crime of murder with premeditation. This question was addressed by the courts in some cases in obiter dicta. Some judges stated that in light of the sweeping rule set forth in section 20(b) concerning result crimes, the law now is that the foresight rule applies to this offense because it is a result crime.[33] But other judges who were of the view that the reasons given for refraining from applying the foresight rule to this offense before Amendment no. 39 are strong and still hold true found a formal way to avoid applying section 20(b) to this offense. They contended that section 20(b) speaks of "intention" without referring at all to "premeditation." Therefore, they reasoned that this section does not apply to murder with premeditation, and that as a result, the law as it was before Amendment no. 39—that the foresight rule does not apply to this offense—should be preserved.[34]

Thus far the offense of defamatory libel constitutes the only ulterior-intent offense with respect to which the Supreme Court has decided that the foresight rule does not apply. All other ulterior-intent offenses regarding which the court had to decide whether to apply the foresight rule were made subject to the rule. For example, the foresight rule has been applied to the offenses of threats, indecent acts, criminal trespass, and certain offenses against state security. However, there is one ulterior-intent offense, namely, the offense of obstructing the course of justice (section 244), to which a novel rule was applied that differs from prior common practice in the area of oblique intention. This offense is established whenever a person "does anything with intent to prevent or obstruct a judicial proceeding or to cause perversion of justice." When investigated by the police as a witness, the defendant lied. His conduct was not motivated by a desire to obstruct the course of justice, but he knew that lying would almost certainly cause such an obstruction. The question arose whether to apply the foresight rule to this ulterior-intent offense and convict the defendant. The Supreme Court reasoned that because the *actus reus* of this offense is very broad ("does anything"), so that the offense covers a great variety of cases, it is difficult to give a uniform answer to the question whether the foresight rule should be applied to this offense, for the answer should be context sensitive. On the other hand, it is problematic from the perspective of legal certainty to adopt a very flexible rule and declare that in each concrete case the judge should decide whether to apply the foresight rule according to the specific circumstances of the case. Therefore, the solution adopted by the court was to set a less flexible rule and declare that in the context of this offense, the law concerning oblique intention will vary according to types of cases. In some types of cases the foresight rule will apply, and in others it will not.[35] The court did not take it on itself in this case to determine the types of cases in which the foresight rule should apply and the types of cases in which it should not. It only defined one category of cases in which the foresight rule applies, stating that cases where the defendant lies to the police belong to this category. Therefore, the defendant was convicted. It is possible that in the future the rule adopted in this case will be applied to certain other offenses as well. The conclusion is that in Israel there are now three types of ulterior-intent offenses: offenses to which the foresight rule applies, offenses to which this rule does not apply, and offenses to which the more flexible rule that was adopted concerning section 244 applies. Courts have discretion to decide to which type the offense they are dealing with belongs. It should also be added that after the legislature learned of the Supreme Court's decision conferring discretion on courts to decide whether to apply the foresight rule to ulterior-intent offenses even after Amendment no. 39, it expressly specified in the definition of some newly enacted ulterior-intent offenses that the foresight rule applies.[36]

iii. Recklessness

As indicated in section II.B.2.i.c in this chapter, as regards result crimes that are silent concerning the mental state required, recklessness with respect to the result is sufficient for conviction. According to section 20, recklessness with respect to the result exists when the actor foresees the possibility that the result will be brought about by his or her action. From the volitional point of view, it does not matter whether the actor hoped that the result would not ensue or whether he or she did not care whether it would ensue. In both cases recklessness is established. Consequently, when discussing whether to convict a defendant of an offense in which recklessness suffices for conviction, there is no need to examine the question of the nature of the actor's volitional attitude toward the result.[37]

However, recklessness does not exist in every case where the result is foreseen as possible. Recklessness has an objective component as well. For a person who knowingly takes a risk that a result will occur to be considered reckless, it is required that the taking of the risk be unreasonable (section 20(a)(2)(b)). Thus the Israeli concept of recklessness with respect to results is identical to the English concept of subjective recklessness with respect to results.

In spite of what has been said in the first paragraph of this subsection, section 20(a)(2) divides recklessness with respect to the result into two categories. The first category is "indifference." Indifference exists when the actor does not care whether the result will ensue. The second category encompasses cases in which the actor hopes that the result will not occur. This category is called in Hebrew *kalut daat*. The structure of the section makes it clear that the first category is considered more serious, but the code does not specify at all the practical implications of the distinction made between these two categories. At the present time there is no offense in Israel that requires indifference for conviction. For all the result crimes that require criminal thought without specifying a requirement of intention in their definition, recklessness is sufficient for conviction. This means that *kalut daat* suffices to convict for all these offenses. Therefore, it may be argued that the legislature should not have distinguished between these two categories in the General Part.[38]

iv. Negligence

Section 21 defines the term *negligence*. Negligence is considered a kind of mental state, albeit an objective one. Negligence with respect to a result is established when the actor is not aware of the possibility that the result will ensue but a reasonable person, in the same circumstances, would have been aware of it. There are differences of viewpoint concerning the model of the reasonable person to be used for purposes of this test. According to one approach, the question is whether an ordinary average person would have foreseen the possibility of the result occurring. According to another approach, the reasonable person is a prudent and careful person, a person who is prudent to the desirable degree, a person who always foresees what a citizen should foresee. According to the latter approach, in certain cases the court may find the defendant negligent in spite of the fact that under the circumstances of the case an ordinary person would not have foreseen the possibility of the result occurring, because in those circumstances a reasonable person would have foreseen it. The second approach thus broadens the scope of negligence in comparison with the first one. The reason given for adopting the second approach is that it raises the degree of general deterrence. The argument is that if this approach is adopted, more people will think before they act, and, in turn, more people will gain awareness of the possible results of their actions. As a result, the number of dangerous actions performed will diminish. There is still no binding decision of the Supreme Court concerning this matter rendered after the enactment of Amendment no. 39, but it seems that the court is inclined toward adopting the second approach, that is, the one according to which the scope of negligence is broader.[39] The approach that broadens the scope of negligence may alternatively be based on a different line of reasoning than that just presented. It may be suggested that attention should focus on the exact words of the code. The code does not state that the test is whether a reasonable person, in the circumstances, would have foreseen the possibility of the result occurring. Rather, it states that the test is whether a reasonable person, in the circumstances, could have foreseen this possibility. Therefore, courts can accept that the reasonable person is an ordinary person and can convict even in those cases where an ordinary person would not have foreseen the possibility of the result occurring, by relying on the claim that in spite of the fact that in the circumstances an ordinary person would not have foreseen the said possibility, he or she could have foreseen it.[40]

Another question is whether judges should attribute to the model of the reasonable person some of the special characteristics of the defendant. Sometimes the defendant has a special disability or characteristic because of which he or she did not foresee an outcome that would have been foreseen by a reasonable person. In such cases it may sometimes be claimed that the fact that the defendant did not foresee an outcome that would have been foreseen by a reasonable person does not evince culpability on the part of the defendant. This is the case, for example, when the defendant is very young, has a low intelligence level, or lacks life experience. It would be unjust to convict the defendant when the reason that the defendant did not foresee the possibility that a result would ensue is that he or she has a low intelligence level, even if an average person with normal intelligence would have done so. Similarly, when a driver (or doctor or soldier) who is a beginner did not foresee an outcome that an experienced driver (or doctor or soldier) would have foreseen, and his or her failure to foresee it stems only from lack of experience (and the activity in which he or she was engaged was one in which he or she was obliged or permitted to engage in spite of his or her lack of experience), it is not just to convict him or her. Therefore, some scholars suggest that the special characteristics of the defendant be attributed to the model of the reasonable person and that the inquiry should focus on whether a reasonable person who has these characteristics would have foreseen the possibility of the result occurring. The code does not expressly recognize this possibility. However, the code states that the question that should be asked concerning negligence is whether a reasonable person *in the circumstances* would have foreseen the possibility of the result occurring. In the legal literature it has been suggested that the special characteristics of the defendant should be considered part of the "circumstances," and therefore they may be attributed to the model of the reasonable person.[41] According to this approach, in the case of the driver who was a beginner, the question should be whether a reasonable driver who is a beginner would have foreseen the possibility of the result occurring. The Supreme Court has not decided yet which of the special characteristics of the defendant, if any, should be attributed to the model of the reasonable person.

Thus far I have discussed negligence as a mental state; however, negligence has an additional component, namely, that the risk was unreasonable. Thus, if the act was done in circumstances in which a person who would have foreseen the possibility of the occurrence of the result would have been permitted to take the risk that it might occur because taking such a risk would have been reasonable, the actor is not negligent.

The legislature defines negligence also with respect to the circumstances and the nature of the conduct. Negligence with respect to a circumstance is established when the actor is not aware of the existence of the circumstance, but a reasonable person, in the circumstances, would have been aware of it. An identical definition applies to the nature of the conduct.

Section 21(b) states that it may be provided that negligence suffices for conviction only with respect to offenses that are not felonies. This section gives expression to the outlook that the degree of blameworthiness of the negligent actor is not very high, and that it cannot justify a punishment higher than three years' imprisonment. Indeed, the maximum penalty for negligently causing the death of another person is three years' imprisonment (section 304).

v. Strict Liability

Section 22 deals with strict liability. Before Amendment no. 39 there were offenses of "absolute liability" in Israel. In order to convict a person of those offenses, it was sufficient that the actor performed the *actus reus* of the offense. Even if his or her action was not accompanied by a mental state of either criminal thought or negligence with respect to the *actus reus*, he or she was convicted. This legal situation was heavily criticized because it contradicted the principle that it is justified to convict and punish a person only if he or she is blameworthy. Therefore, Amendment no. 39 abolished absolute liability and replaced it with "strict liability." In strict liability offenses the prosecution is not required to prove any mental element. Nonetheless, the defendant is entitled to an acquittal if he or she proves (on a balance of probabilities) that he or she acted without criminal thought or negligence and that he or she did everything possible to prevent the offense. It should be noted that to escape liability, it is not sufficient to prove the absence of criminal thought and negligence. In order to be acquitted, the actor is required to also prove that he or she did everything possible to prevent the offense.[42]

The code states that an offense X can be considered a strict liability offense only if the legislature itself states that X is such an offense. This means that if offense X does not mention any mental state, it cannot be interpreted as being a strict liability offense. Rather, it must be understood as requiring criminal thought. However, this rule applies only to offenses enacted after the coming into force of Amendment no. 39. A different rule applies to offenses enacted before the coming into force of Amendment no. 39. Before Amendment no. 39 courts were allowed to interpret an offense that was silent concerning the mental state required either as requiring criminal thought or as being an absolute liability offense. Indeed, some of the offenses that were silent concerning the mental state required were interpreted as being absolute liability offenses. In order to prevent Amendment no. 39 from converting these offenses into criminal-thought offenses, the legislature declared in section 22(a) that if an offense X was interpreted by the courts (before Amendment no. 39) as being an absolute liability offense, this offense does not become a criminal-thought offense by virtue of Amendment no. 39. Such an offense becomes a strict liability offense.

Section 22(c) concerns strict liability offenses for which imprisonment is available as a penalty. According to this section, in cases where the prosecution does not prove beyond a reasonable doubt that the actor acted with either criminal thought or negligence, the actor shall not be sentenced to imprisonment in spite of the fact that he or she was convicted. In such cases only other penalties, like a fine, can be imposed. Only in cases where the prosecution proves beyond a reasonable doubt the existence of criminal thought or negligence can imprisonment be imposed.

3. *Theories of Liability*
   i. Inchoate Crimes
      a. *Attempt*

The physical and mental elements of criminal attempt are defined in section 25. The physical element of attempt exists when the actor performs an act that is more than merely preparatory to the commission of the substantive offense. The mental state required for conviction of an attempt is an intention to commit the substantive offense. Hence, with regard to the result of the substantive offense, the actor has to act with the purpose of causing the result. The Supreme Court ruled that oblique intention with respect to the result is sufficient.[43] In cases of incomplete attempts, a requirement of "future conduct intention" also applies: it is required that the actor intend (plan) to perform the act that constitutes the "conduct element" of the substantive offense. As to the circumstances of the substantive offense, willful blindness is sufficient for conviction.[44] Section 26 clarifies that an impossible attempt is punishable. This section relates to cases in which the commission of the offense is impossible owing to a state of things of which the actor is not aware or about which he or she is mistaken (e.g., when A, in order to kill B, gives B a drink, mistakenly thinking that it contains poison, or when the actor mistakenly believes that a certain circumstance that forms part of the *actus reus* of the substantive offense exists). The code does not address cases of mistake about the criminal law, for example, when a person commits adultery, believing mistakenly that adultery is a criminal offense. The legislative history indicates clearly that the legislature intended that criminal liability not apply in such cases. Another case the code does not expressly address is that of the superstitious attempt (e.g., when the actor attempts to kill by invoking black magic). It is not clear whether such cases are punishable.

The maximum punishment for an attempt is the same as that of the substantive offense (section 34D). If the punishment prescribed for an offense is mandatory, then in cases of attempt the punishment represents only the maximum limit. If a minimum sentence is set for a certain offense, it does not apply in cases of attempt (section 27). An attempt can be committed by omission (section 25 in conjunction with section 18(b)). The code recognizes the defense of renunciation (section 28). In order to be acquitted, the defendant has to prove (on a balance of probabilities) that the elements of the defense are present. An attempt to commit a contravention is not punishable (section 34C).

b. Conspiracy

A conspiracy to commit a felony or a misdemeanor is a criminal offense. This offense appears in the Special Part (section 499). Certain other cases of conspiracy appear in section 500.

ii. Complicity

a. Introduction

The legislature recognizes four forms of liability for complicity. "Coperpetration" and "perpetration by means of another," which give rise to principal liability, are the most serious forms of complicity. The law concerning these forms of complicity is the same as the law that applies in cases where an offender acts alone. The less serious forms of complicity are "instigation" and "aiding," which give rise to secondary liability.

One of the differences between principal liability and secondary liability concerns the applicable punishment. The penalty for coperpetration or perpetration by means of another is the same as the penalty for the principal offense. The penalty for attempted coperpetration or attempted perpetration by means of another is the same as the penalty for an attempt to commit the principal offense. In contrast, the penalty for aiding an offense is lower than the penalty for the principal offense, and the penalty for attempted instigation is lower than the penalty for an attempt to commit the principal offense.

Another difference is that liability for coperpetration and perpetration by means of another applies with respect to contraventions, whereas criminal liability does not apply to cases of aiding or instigating a contravention. In addition, the law concerning responsibility for "further offenses" (see section II.B.3.ii.f in this chapter) is harsher for coperpetrators than it is for aiders and instigators.

Instigation is considered more serious than aiding. While the penalty for instigation is the same as the penalty applicable to the principal offense, the maximum penalty for aiding is half the maximum penalty of the principal offense. Another difference is that attempt to instigate is punishable, while attempt to aid is not.

b. Aiding

Aiding is the least serious form of complicity. The definition of aiding appears in section 31. The maximum penalty for aiding is half the maximum penalty for the principal offense (section 32).[45] In order to convict a person of aiding, it is required that the principal offender commit the principal offense. If the principal commits a robbery, the aider may be convicted of aiding robbery. If the principal commits an attempted robbery, the aider is guilty of aiding an attempted robbery. In case the aided person did not act at all toward the commission of the offense or only performed preparatory acts short of an attempt, the aided person does not commit an offense, and therefore the aider cannot be convicted of aiding. He or she cannot be convicted of attempting to aid either, because there is no such offense. In such a case the aider is fully exempted from criminal liability.[46]

The commonly accepted view is that in order to convict a person of aiding, it is required that in principle the principal be susceptible of being convicted of the principal offense, that is, that the principal must have acted with the mental state required for conviction of the said offense and must not have a criminal defense. In cases where the principal actor is exempted from criminal liability because the mental element is lacking or a criminal defense applies, the aider may, in certain cases, be convicted of perpetration by means of another.

As regards the physical element of aiding, it is not required that the act of the aider actually facilitate the commission of the crime. It is sufficient that the act could have potentially facilitated the commission of the crime.[47] The contribution of the aider may be physical (like supplying an instrument) or psychological (like strengthening with words the morale of the principal).[48]

As regards the mental state required, section 31 states that the aider must act in order to facilitate the commission of the offense. Various views appeared in case law concerning the interpretation of this requirement. Finally, the Supreme Court held that it is not required that the aider have wanted the principal offense to be committed, nor is it required that he or she have wanted the conduct appearing in the definition of the principal offense to be performed. It is sufficient that the aider foresaw the possibility that the principal offender would commit the principal offense (i.e., recklessness with regard to all the elements of the principal offense is sufficient).[49] The requirement of the code that the actor act with the purpose of facilitating the crime relates only to the contribution of the aider; that is, it is required that he or she want his or her act to *facilitate* the commission of the offense.[50] The Supreme Court also ruled that oblique intention is sufficient in this respect. Thus, in the case where the aider was almost certain that his or her act would facilitate the commission of an offense, the aider may be convicted in spite of the fact that he or she did not desire to facilitate the commission of the offense.[51] A subsequent decision of the court clarified that a precondition for finding that an aider was "almost certain that his act would facilitate the commission of the offense" is that the aider was almost certain that the principal offense would actually be committed.[52]

The Supreme Court has also ruled that it is not required that the aider have acted with every special mental state required for conviction of the principal offense. Thus, for example, in the context of offenses that require an intention to cause a certain result, the aider may be convicted of aiding the commission of such an offense even if he or she personally did not want the result to be caused by the acts of the principal. I will use the crime of murder for the sake of illustration. The offense of murder with premeditation requires, inter alia, that the actor want the death of another person to occur. In order to convict a person of aiding this offense, it is not required that the aider have wanted the death of another person to be caused by the acts of the principal. It is sufficient that the aider have foreseen the possibility that the principal would cause the death of another person and that the principal's actions would be performed with the mental state required for conviction of murder with premeditation, and that the aider also have wanted to facilitate the commission of the offense.[53]

The code recognizes the defense of abandonment (section 34). Aiding to commit a contravention is not punishable (section 34C). The issue of liability for further offenses will be dealt with later (section II.B.3.ii.f in this chapter).

The Special Part of the code contains a specific offense of facilitation. Liability for this offense is established when a person "gives to another any tools, materials, money, information or any other means, knowing that the same may directly or indirectly be used for the commission or to facilitate the commission of a felony" (Section 498(a)). Foresight of the possibility that a felony will be committed and that the said provision of means will enable or facilitate the commission of the felony is sufficient for conviction. This offense does not require that the felony be committed or attempted. The offense is completed at the moment the means are given. The maximum penalty for this offense is three years' imprisonment.

c. Instigation

Instigation is considered a more serious form of liability than aiding. The definition of instigation appears in section 30. The penalty for instigation is the same as the penalty prescribed for the principal offense (section 34D).

In order to convict a person of instigation, it is required that the principal offender commit the principal offense. If the principal commits a robbery, the inciter may be convicted of instigating robbery. If the principal commits an attempted robbery, the inciter may be convicted of instigating attempted robbery.

In contrast to "attempt to aid," "attempt to instigate" is punishable. If A convinces B to commit a specific offense, but B does not act at all toward the commission of the offense or performs only preparatory acts short of an attempt, B does not commit either the substantive offense or an attempt, and therefore A cannot be convicted of instigation. However, in these cases A may be convicted of attempt to instigate. Other examples of attempt to instigate are when A speaks to B and tries, but fails, to convince B to commit the offense; or when A sends a letter to B in which A asks B to commit a specific offense, but the letter does not reach B. The maximum penalty for an attempt to instigate is only half the maximum penalty for the principal offense,[54] in spite of the fact that the maximum penalty for an attempt is the same as the maximum penalty for the substantive offense and the maximum penalty for instigation is the same as the maximum penalty for the principal offense.

The commonly accepted view is that in order to convict a person of instigation, it is required that in principle the principal be susceptible of being convicted of the principal offense, that is, that the principal act with the mental state required for conviction of the said offense, and that he or she not have a criminal defense. In cases where the principal actor is exempted from criminal liability because the mental element is lacking or because a criminal defense applies, the instigator may, in certain cases, be convicted of perpetration by means of another.

In order to be convicted of instigation, it is required that the words uttered by the inciter to the principal constitute a *causa sine qua non* of the decision of the principal to commit the offense and its actual commission.[55]

Section 30 does not specify the mental state required. The Supreme Court has decided that to be convicted of instigation, the instigator must have wanted to persuade the principal to commit the offense and must have wanted the offense to be committed.[56] The court did not address the question whether oblique intention is sufficient for conviction.

Instigating a contravention is not an offense (section 34C). Abandonment is a defense to a charge of instigation or attempt to instigate (section 34). The issue of liability for further offenses will be dealt with later (section II.B.3.ii.f in this chapter).

d. Perpetration by Means of Another

When a person who perpetrates the *actus reus* of an offense is exempted from criminal liability (e.g., because of infancy or because the required criminal thought is lacking), the person who aided or instigated him or her cannot be convicted of aiding or instigation. In such cases the aider or instigator may, in certain circumstances, be convicted of "perpetration by means of another." This form of complicity gives rise to principal liability. Therefore, the penalty is the same as the penalty prescribed for the standard case of perpetration of the principal offense (section 29(a)), and perpetration by means of another of a contravention is punishable. An attempt to commit perpetration by means of another is punishable, and the penalty is the same as the penalty for a standard attempt to directly perpetrate the principal offense.

According to section 29(c), "perpetration by means of another" exists in the case where A contributes to the commission of the act [of the offense] by B, while B serves as a tool in the hands of A. The use of the term *contributes* suggests that the section covers not only cases of instigation but cases of aiding as well. The code requires that B serve as a tool in the hands of A and provides several examples of this. The list of examples includes, inter alia, cases in which B is an infant or insane, and cases in which B acts without criminal thought or under duress. The list is not exhaustive.

The section does not specify the mental state required for the conviction of A. The language of the section, which speaks of B being used as a tool, implies the requirement that A want the *actus reus* of the offense to be perpetrated by B.[57] On the other hand, it may be argued that considerations of justice and policy justify the conclusion that recklessness should suffice for conviction (where it is sufficient to convict in cases of direct perpetration of the principal offense).

Section 29(d) clarifies that when an offense can be committed, according to its definition, only by a person who has a certain personal characteristic (e.g., when it can be committed only by a public officer), A may be convicted of perpetration of this offense by means of another even if he does not have this characteristic, provided that B has it. This means, inter alia, that a bachelor can perpetrate bigamy by means of another (married) person.[58]

e. Coperpetration

Coperpetration is considered a form of complicity that gives rise to principal liability. Consequently, the penalty is the same as the penalty prescribed for perpetration of the principal offense by a lone offender (section 29(a)), and coperpetration of a contravention is punishable. Attempted coperpetration of an offense is punishable, and the penalty is the same as the penalty prescribed for an attempt to commit the principal offense by an offender acting alone.

The definition of coperpetration appears in section 29(b). The first condition for coperpetration is the presence of an agreement between the parties to commit the offense (a common plan to commit the offense). The second condition is that each party to the agreement performs an act or acts for the commission of the offense. The problem is that the code does not clarify when the acts done for the commission of the offense amount to coperpetration, as opposed to mere aiding. It is clear that the liability is merely for aiding in cases where there is no agreement between the parties, but difficulties arise in cases where there is an agreement: what additional elements are needed, besides the agreement, to establish coperpetration? The question whether the defendant is guilty of aiding or coperpetration is important not only because the punishment prescribed for coperpetration is higher than the punishment prescribed for aiding, but also because the law concerning liability for further offenses is harsher with respect to coperpetrators than it is with respect to aiders (as will be explained in section II.B.3.ii.f in this chapter).[59]

From this point onward, I will assume that A and B have agreed to commit a certain offense. If each of them personally perpetrated the whole *actus reus*, it is clear that they are coperpetrators. It is also clear that they are coperpetrators if each of them performed part of the *actus reus*, and their acts combined fulfill the complete *actus reus*. However, the legislative history indicates clearly that the legislature intended that the doctrine of coperpetration extend to additional situations and that personally committing part of the *actus reus* not form a necessary condition for being convicted as a coperpetrator. Indeed, the courts have adopted this position. Therefore, the difficult question presents itself as follows: in cases where B personally commits the whole *actus reus* (he or she performs all the actions in the definition of the offense, and in the case of a result crime he or she also personally causes the result), and A contributes to the completion of the offense by doing acts that are not part of the *actus reus*, what is needed in order to convict A of coperpetration, as opposed to mere aiding? There is no consensus on this question. It seems that the explanatory notes to the Penal Law Bill adopt the view that A should be classified as a coperpetrator only if A's act was necessary for the completion of the offense (i.e., A's contribution was so important that in its absence the offense could not have been completed), and A's act was committed at an advanced, nonpreparatory stage of the enterprise. But courts have not always adhered to these lines of demarcation and have generally conceived coperpetration as broader in scope. The courts have said, in a general fashion, that the stronger the physical contribution of A, the easier it should be to classify A as a coperpetrator. In addition, it has sometimes been said that if A belongs to the "inner" circle of the enterprise, A should be classified as a coperpetrator, whereas if A belongs to the "outer" circle, A should be convicted of merely aiding. Some decisions have provided more concrete tests. For example, according to one view, two factors should be taken into account: (1) on the physical plane, how strong was the contribution of A to the commission of the offense? (2) on the mental plane, to what degree did A regard the criminal project "as his own"? If the result of the calculation is that A was strongly involved in the commission of the offense, A should be classified as a coperpetrator. Of course, if the contribution on the physical plane was very strong, less is required on the mental plane, and vice versa. However, there is a minimal contribution required on the physical plane, without which A cannot be considered a coperpetrator even if A's mental involvement was very strong.[60] According to another view that broadens the scope of coperpetration even further, whenever there is an agreement between A and B to commit the offense that involves an allocation of tasks, and each of the parties subsequently fulfills his or her part according to the plan, A should be classified as a coperpetrator, irrespective of whether A's contribution was important or not, and irrespective of the degree to which A regarded the enterprise as "his own."[61] I will not describe here all the various positions found in case law. I will only add that some of them are vague or inconsistent. The conclusion is that it is difficult at the present time to give a conclusive and widely accepted answer to the following question: what is the test for distinguishing between coperpetration and aiding (in cases in which there was an agreement between A and B)? The general impression, however, is that the courts tend increasingly to broaden the scope of coperpetration.

As regards the mental state required for conviction of coperpetration, the Supreme Court has decided that it is required, inter alia, that the defendant have acted with the mental state required for conviction of the principal offense (for example, to be convicted of coperpetration of murder with premeditation, it is required, inter alia, that A act with intent that the victim die).[62]

f. Liability for Further Offenses

Section 34A deals with liability for "further offenses." The principle on which this section is based is that when A participates in the commission of offense X by B, and in the course of the commission of X, B commits an additional offense Y, A may (in certain circumstances) bear liability for Y even if A does not fulfill all the standard conditions required for conviction of complicity in the commission of Y.

As is clear from the discussion above (sections II.B.3.ii.b and II.B.3.ii.c), negligence is not sufficient to convict a person of aiding or instigation. However, in the case where A fulfilled all the requirements to convict him or her of aiding the commission of X (including an intention to facilitate and foresight of the possibility that X might be committed), and A also was negligent with respect to the possibility that in the course of committing X, B would also commit Y, A may also be held liable for Y (if, in fact, Y is committed). However, A shall bear liability for Y only "as an offense of negligence" (section 34A(a)(2)). It does not matter whether B committed Y intentionally, recklessly, or negligently. In any event, the responsibility of A (who was only negligent) is only for an offense of negligence. Of course, it is possible to convict A only if there is a negligence offense with the same physical elements as offense Y. The same rules apply in the case where A instigated the commission of X.

However, the law is harsher with respect to coperpetrators. According to section 34A(a)(1), a coperpetrator A may be convicted of an offense of "criminal thought" even though A was only negligent with respect to the possibility that it might be committed. In the case where A and B are coperpetrators of offense X, and in the course of the commission of X, B commits offense Y (which is a criminal-thought offense), A may be convicted of Y (as a criminal-thought offense) even if A was only negligent with respect to the possibility that Y would be committed.[63] This rule is very problematic because it deviates from a basic principle of criminal law: every person should be convicted and punished only in accordance with the degree of his or her personal blameworthiness. The rule in section 34A(a)(1) allows a person to be convicted of an offense of criminal thought in spite of the fact that he or she was only negligent. In addition, section 21(b) provides that the maximum penalty for offenses of negligence cannot be higher than three years' imprisonment. In this provision the legislature expressed its view that the level of blameworthiness of the negligent actor cannot justify a sentence in excess of three years' imprisonment. Indeed, the maximum penalty for causing death negligently is three years' imprisonment. In spite of that, according to section 34A(a)(1), negligent actors may be convicted of offenses of criminal thought and thus may be held liable, in certain cases, to a maximum penalty of twenty years' imprisonment. Indeed, section 34A(a)(1) has been strongly criticized in the legal literature.[64]

Section 34A(a)(1) was subjected to constitutional challenge in the *Silgado* case.[65] A and B were coperpetrators of an attempted robbery. In the course of the attempt B shot his pistol. The shot killed the victim. B was convicted of murder by causing the death of another person in the commission of an offense.[66] In this variation of murder, recklessness with respect to the death of another person is sufficient for conviction. A, who was negligent with respect to the possibility that B might recklessly cause the death of another person in the course of the robbery, was convicted of murder based on section 34A(a)(1). In the appeal A argued that section 34A(a)(1) contradicts the Basic Law: Human Dignity and Liberty and therefore should be declared unconstitutional by the court.[67] The Supreme Court rejected this argument and held that this section is constitutional. The decision was based mainly on consideration of general deterrence, and it can be argued that the court did not pay enough attention to the principle that every person should be convicted and punished only in accordance with the degree of his or her personal blameworthiness.

The code does not address the question of liability for further offenses in cases of perpetration by means of another. This is a lacuna.

4. Causation

Section 18, which deals with the physical element of an offense, refers, inter alia, to a result that is caused by the conduct. The code does not determine a test for establishing the existence of a causal connection. According to case law, the test to establish factual causation is that of *causa sine qua non*.[68] The test for legal causation is that of reasonable foreseeability. If the actor had the mental state required for conviction, but his or her action brought about the result in a manner that was not objectively foreseeable (i.e., the chain of causation was objectively unforeseeable), he or she is not guilty of the result crime concerned, because legal causation is absent.[69] According to one approach found in case law, in cases where the actor acted with intention or indifference with respect to the result (as opposed to acting merely with *kalut daat* or negligence with respect to the result), he or she may be convicted of the result crime concerned even if the manner in which the result was actually brought about was unforeseeable. There is no final decision on this point yet.[70]

Another question is whether there is a separate and independent rule that an intervening act by a third party (or the victim) that is the immediate cause of the prohibited result breaks the causal connection between the defendant's act and the prohibited result. If A's action was followed by the free and informed action of B (a third party or the victim, who was not insane or an infant), and B's action was the immediate cause of the result, does B's intervening act break the chain of causation from A's act in spite of the fact that B's action and the manner in which B caused the result were foreseeable, or even actually foreseen, by A, and in spite of the fact that A's action was a *causa sine qua non* of the prohibited result? The Supreme Court has declared that no such independent rule applies. The court has specified that the foreseeability test is the only relevant test, and it applies even to cases of intervening acts.[71] However, it seems that there is a hidden inconsistency in the decisions of the Supreme Court concerning this issue. In cases where A performed an act that enabled B to commit, say, murder, A is commonly convicted merely of aiding murder and not of murder, even if A had the mental state required for murder and even if A's act was a *causa sine qua non* of the death of the victim (provided that the requirements for conviction as a coperpetrator are not fulfilled). In cases where A instigated B to commit murder, A is commonly convicted merely of instigating murder and not of murder, in spite of the fact that the act of convincing B to act was a *causa sine qua non* of the commission of the murder, and A acted with the mental state required for murder. Thus the question arises: in these cases, why is A not convicted of murder? The courts have not provided an explanation, but it seems that the only possible answer is that B's action breaks the causal connection between A's action and the death of the victim. We will have to wait and see how the Supreme Court rules once it is directly confronted with this contradiction.[72]

C. Defenses

1. Types of Defenses
The code does not distinguish between justifications and excuses. All defenses appear in the same chapter, without a division into justifications and excuses. In addition, the language of the law concerning the implications of having a defense does not help classify the various defenses according to the distinction just mentioned, because the legislature uses the same exact words in the context of all defenses—that the result of having a defense is that the actor "shall bear no criminal liability."[73]

2. Burden of Proof
There is a presumption that an act is performed in circumstances in which a criminal defense does not apply (section 34E). However, if there is evidence supporting the application of a certain defense, the existence of the defense must then be negated beyond a reasonable doubt by the prosecution (section 34V(b)). This rule applies to all the general defenses, including insanity.[74]

3. Self-Defense
Self-defense appears in section 34J. It relates to cases in which the act was required in order to repel an attack creating a tangible danger of injury to the life, freedom, body, or property of the actor or another person. It is not required that the harm was about to materialize immediately. Rather, it is only required that the action of the defendant was immediately required to repel the attack. It is also required that the act of the defendant was

reasonable, in the circumstances, for the purpose of preventing the injury (section 34P). The defense does not apply when the defendant brought about the attack by his or her own improper behavior, foreseeing that things might develop in this direction (section 34J). In 2008 the Knesset added section 34J1 to the code. The new section deals with a special case of self-defense: that in which the action of the defendant was immediately required to repel someone entering a dwelling house, a place of business, or a fenced farm with intent to commit a crime. The scope of this special defense is broader than that of general self-defense appearing in section 34J. The main difference is that whereas the application of general self-defense is precluded whenever the action of the defendant was unreasonable, in the circumstances, for the purpose of preventing the injury, the application of the special defense appearing in section 34J1 is precluded only if the action of the defendant was *manifestly* unreasonable, in the circumstances, for the purpose of repelling the person who was entering the property concerned.

4. Necessity and Duress

The defense of necessity appears in section 34K, and that of duress appears in section 34L. The difference between them is that in the case of duress the source of the danger is the threat made by a person ordering the defendant to act, whereas in the case of necessity the source of the danger is a given set of circumstances.

i. Necessity

Since the code does not contain a separate defense of "choice of evils," it is difficult to know whether the necessity defense is a justification or an excuse, or whether it covers both cases of justification and cases of excuse.[75] The necessity defense applies to cases in which the defendant committed an act that was required to save his or her, or another's life, freedom, body, or property from a tangible danger of severe injury deriving from a given set of circumstances, provided that he or she had no other alternative but to commit the act in question. There is no requirement that the harm was about to materialize immediately; it is only required that the defendant's action was immediately required to prevent the harm. It is also required that the act of the defendant was reasonable, in the circumstances, for the purpose of preventing the injury (section 34P).[76] The defense does not apply where the defendant is required by law or by virtue of his or her office to face the danger (section 34O). In addition, the defense does not apply where the defendant placed himself or herself, by voluntary and improper behavior, in the dangerous situation.[77]

ii. Duress

The defense of duress applies where the actor committed an act that he or she was ordered to perform under a threat involving a tangible danger of severe injury to his or her, or another's, life, freedom, body, or property, because of which he or she was coerced to perform the act. The law concerning this defense is similar to the law concerning necessity (sections 34L, 34N, 34O, 34P).

5. Justification

Section 34M deals with a defense called "justification." This section deals with five situations. Section 34M(1) declares that an actor does not bear criminal liability for an act that was required or authorized by law. Sections 34M(3) and 34M(4) deal with medical treatment, and section 34M(5) deals with sports. Section 34M(2) deals with superior orders. A person (like a soldier) bears no criminal liability for an act done in obedience to the order of a competent authority whom he is bound by law to obey, even if the order is unlawful. However, the defense does not apply in a case where the order is *manifestly* unlawful.

6. Mistake of Fact

Section 34R deals with mistake of fact. Section 34R(a) establishes the principle that the actor is entitled to be judged on the basis of the facts as he or she believed them to be. For example, if A mistakenly thought that he or she was attacked by B, and in order to defend himself or herself he or she harmed B, A is not guilty of the criminal-thought offense concerned, even if A's mistake was unreasonable (provided that if the facts had been as A believed them to be, A would have been entitled to an acquittal by virtue of the doctrine of self-defense).[78] However, section 34R(b) provides that in cases in which A's mistake was unreasonable, A is guilty of an offense of negligence (of course, the conviction is possible only if there is a relevant negligence offense whose *actus reus* was performed by the defendant).[79]

7. Mistake of Law

Section 34S deals with mistake of criminal law. The general rule is that mistake of criminal law is no defense. However, the actor has a defense if the mistake was not reasonably avoidable. The Supreme Court has ruled that in certain circumstances the defense is available to an actor who relied on the advice of a private attorney.[80] Mistake of civil law is considered a mistake of fact.[81]

8. Intoxication

Section 34I deals with intoxication. Involuntary intoxication exempts from criminal liability when, because of the state of intoxication, the actor did not have control over his or her acts or lacked criminal thought. In a case of voluntary intoxication, the fact that the actor did not have control over his or her acts or lacked criminal thought does not exempt him or her from criminal liability with respect to standard criminal-thought offenses. In such cases, however, the actor cannot be convicted of an offense that requires an intention to cause a certain result unless he or she caused the state of intoxication in order to commit the offense.[82]

9. Lack of Control

A person bears no criminal liability for an act done by him or her under circumstances where he or she did not have control over his or her bodily movements, as in the case of a reflex action or an act done in a state of sleep or hypnosis (section 34G). However, the defense does not apply if the actor placed himself or herself, by improper and controlled behavior, in the condition whereby he or she lacked control over bodily movements.[83]

10. Insanity

Section 34H deals with the defense of insanity. A person bears no criminal liability for an act done by him or her if at the time of the act, because of a mental illness or mental retardation, he or she was not able to understand what he or she was doing or that the act was wrong, or to refrain from doing the act (the latter case is known as the case of "irresistible impulse").

11. Infancy

A person bears no criminal liability for an act done when he or she was under the age of twelve years (section 34F).

12. De Minimis

The defense of *de minimis* is dealt with in section 34Q. It provides that a person bears no criminal liability for a trivial act.

13. Protection of Judicial Officers

A judicial officer bears no criminal liability for an act done in the exercise of his or her judicial functions, even if he or she acts in excess of his or her authority (section 34T).

14. Consent

The defense of consent does not appear in the code. Of course, there are some offenses (like rape or assault) in which the lack of consent of the victim constitutes a circumstance of the *actus reus*, but the code does not contain a defense of consent that applies to other offenses. However, it should be noted that the code deals with sports activities and medical treatment in the framework of the defense called "justification" (see section II.C.5 in this chapter), and that in cases in which consent negates the harm or danger to the interest protected by the relevant offense, the court may acquit the defendant following the standard principles of interpretation (see section I.C in this chapter). The fact that Israeli law has not yet formally recognized a separate defense of consent has not given rise to any difficulties in practice because in cases where a consensus exists that the act should be permitted, the prosecution uses its discretion not to prosecute.

15. Entrapment

Entrapment is not a criminal defense in Israel. However, it is possible that in the future courts will decide, in extreme circumstances, to dismiss a prosecution because of abuse of process.

16. Chastisement of Children

The defense of chastisement of children does not appear in the code. The Supreme Court has decided that the legal rule, which was developed in the past by the courts, allowing parents to use a reasonable amount of force on children for educational purposes is not valid anymore. Consequently, there is, in principle, an absolute prohibition on the physical punishment of children.[84]

D. Sanctions

1. Punishment

The main penalties imposed in Israel are imprisonment, suspended imprisonment, fines, probation, and community service. In most offenses the legislature sets only maximum penalties, but there are several offenses with respect to which the legislature has prescribed a minimum or mandatory sentence. However, even in the context of an offense for which a minimum or mandatory sentence is prescribed, the judge is allowed to impose a lighter penalty if the offense was committed in special mitigating circumstances (section 35A(a)). But for some offenses that carry a mandatory sentence, the judge is not allowed to impose a lighter sentence. These offenses are listed in section 35A(b) and include the offense of murder, which carries a mandatory sentence of life imprisonment.[85] A committee of the Knesset is currently examining the option of adding to the code several sections to make judicial discretion in sentencing more structured than it is at the present time.

2. Death Penalty

The death penalty is the maximum penalty for a small number of offenses, but in fact it is not imposed. The only person to have been executed in Israel was the Nazi Adolf Eichmann, who was put to death in 1962.

III. SPECIAL PART

A. Structure

The offenses that appear in the Special Part of the Penal Law, 1977, are gathered in separate chapters, mainly according to the interests protected by the various offenses. These chapters are titled "State Security, Foreign Relations and Official Secrets" (sections 91–132); "Offenses against the Political and Social Order" (sections 133–235); "Offenses Relating to Public Authority and the Administration of Justice" (sections 236–297); "Offenses against the Person" (sections 298–382); "Offenses Relating to Property" (sections 383–460); "Forgery of Money and Stamps" (sections 461–488); "Minor Offenses" (sections 489–496); and "Preparatory Offenses and Conspiracy" (sections 497–500).[86] Many criminal offenses appear outside the Penal Law, 1977 (in other enactments), for example, drug offenses, money laundering, financing of terrorism, defamatory libel, the Good Samaritan offense, and sexual harassment.

B. Homicide

There are three degrees of homicide: murder, manslaughter, and causing death negligently. The punishment for murder is mandatory life imprisonment (section 300(a)). The maximum penalty for manslaughter is twenty years' imprisonment (section 298), and the maximum penalty for causing death negligently is three years' imprisonment (section 304).

There are four forms of murder. The main form is murder with premeditation, which will be discussed later in this section (recklessness with respect to the death of the other person is not sufficient for conviction of this form of murder). The other three forms of murder are established in these cases: (a) where a person causes the death of his father, mother, grandfather, or grandmother (section 300(a)(1)); (b) where a person causes the death of another person in the course of the commission of an offense or in the course of engaging in acts preparatory to its commission, or in order to facilitate its commission (section 300(a)(3)); and (c) where, once an offense has been committed, a person causes the death of another person in order to secure his or her escape or avoidance of punishment in connection with the offense committed, or that of a participant therein (section 300(a)(4)). In these three forms of murder, recklessness with respect to the death of the other person is sufficient for conviction.[87]

As was mentioned in the preceding paragraph, the main form of murder is murder with premeditation, which is established where a person causes the death of another person with premeditation (section 300(a)(2)). The legislature defines premeditation in section 301. It provides that killing with premeditation is established where the actor decided to kill the victim, and killed him in cold blood without immediate provocation, and after having prepared himself to kill him or after having prepared the instrument with which he killed him.

The first element of premeditation is a "decision to kill." This element is interpreted by the courts as an "intention to kill." It is established where the actor acts with a desire that the victim will die.[88] Recklessness with respect to the death of the victim is not sufficient for conviction, and the same holds true for a desire to cause grievous bodily harm. The question whether oblique intention with respect to the death of the victim is sufficient for conviction is open.[89] The two other elements of premeditation, namely, "preparation" and "the absence of provocation," will not be discussed here.[90]

As was mentioned earlier, the penalty for murder is mandatory life imprisonment. However, section 300A provides that a court is allowed to impose a lighter penalty than life imprisonment where the offense of murder was committed in one of three situations: (1) where because of a severe mental disorder or because of mental retardation, the actor's ability to understand what he or she was doing or that his or her act was wrong, or to refrain from doing the act, was grossly diminished (but not to the point where the full defense of insanity that appears in section 34H is established); (2) where the defendant's action slightly deviated from the reasonableness standard required (under section 34P) for the application of self-defense, necessity, or duress (sections 34J, 34K and 34L); or (3) where the defendant was in a state of severe mental distress as a result of severe and lasting abuse suffered by him or her or a family member of him or her at the hands of the person whom he or she killed.

Manslaughter is established where a person causes the death of another person recklessly; that is, recklessness with respect to the death of the other person is required for conviction.[91] Where a person who causes death is negligent with respect to the death of the other person, he or she is guilty of causing death negligently.

Suicide and attempted suicide are not criminal offenses. However, there is an offense of instigating or assisting suicide, the maximum penalty for which is twenty years' imprisonment (section 302).

C. Sex Offenses

The offense of rape is defined in section 345. The maximum penalty for rape is sixteen years' imprisonment. Rape is established where a person penetrates the vagina of a female with a part of his (or her) body or with an object, in one of five situations. The main form of rape is constituted where the penetration is committed without the woman's free consent. The other four situations are where the consent of the woman was obtained by deception about the nature of the act or about the person committing it; where the female was under the age of fourteen (even if she consented to the act); where the actor exploited the fact that the female was unconscious or was in another condition that made her unable to consent freely; and where the actor exploited the fact that that the female suffered from a mental disease or mental retardation (if, because of her mental condition, her consent to the act was not given freely). The minimum penalty for rape is four years' imprisonment, but a court is allowed to impose a lighter penalty on special grounds that must be specified in the reasons for judgment (section 355(a)).[92]

Where a person penetrates the anus of another person (male or female) with a part of his (or her) body or with an object (or where he penetrates the mouth of another person with his penis) in circumstances that are similar to those establishing the offense of rape, one of the forms of the offense called "act of sodomy" is established. The penalties that apply to rape apply to this form of act of sodomy (section 347(b)).[93]

In addition to the offenses discussed here, there are other sex offenses, including, for example, indecent act[94] and sexual harassment.[95]

SELECTED BIBLIOGRAPHY

Bein, Dan. "Mistake of Law." *Israel Law Review* 30 (1996): 214–221.
Enker, Aaron. "Duress, Self-Defence and Necessity in Israeli Law." *Israel Law Review* 30 (1996): 188–206.
Feller, S. Z., and Mordechai Kremnitzer. "Proposal for a General Part of a New Penal Law—Introduction." *Israel Law Review* 30 (1996): 36–59.
Ghanayim, Khalid, Mordechai Kremnitzer, and Boaz Shnoor. *The Law of Libel*. Jerusalem: Sacher Institute and Israel Democracy Institute, 2005 (in Hebrew).
Gur-Arye, Miriam. "Can Freedom of Expression Survive Social Trauma: The Israeli Experience." *Duke Journal of Comparative and International Law* 13 (2003): 155–202.
Gur-Arye, Miriam. "Reliance on a Lawyer's Mistaken Advice—Should It Be an Excuse from Criminal Liability?" *American Journal of Criminal Law* 29 (2002): 455–480.
Kannai, Ruth. "The Judge's Discretion in Sentencing: Israel's Basic Laws and Supreme Court Decisions." *Israel Law Review* 30 (1996): 276–315.
Kremnitzer, Mordechai. "Constitutional Principles and Criminal Law." *Israel Law Review* 27 (1993): 84–99.
Kremnitzer, Mordechai, and Re'em Segev. "The Legality of Interrogational Torture: A Question of Proper Authorization or a Substantive Moral Issue?" *Israel Law Review* 34 (2000): 509–559.
Kugler, Itzhak. *Direct and Oblique Intention in the Criminal Law: An Inquiry into Degrees of Blameworthiness*. Aldershot: Ashgate, 2002.
Lederman, Eliezer. "Aspects of Negligence in Israeli Criminal Law." *Israel Law Review* 30 (1996): 126–139.
Levy, Yuval. "Criminal Intent: A Comment on 'Foreseeability', 'Probability', 'Purpose' and 'Knowledge.'" *Israel Law Review* 30 (1996): 106–125.
Sangero, Boaz. *Self-Defence in Criminal Law*. Oxford: Hart Publishing, 2006.
Shachar, Yoram. "Wresting Control from Luck: The Secular Case for Aborted Attempts." *Theoretical Inquiries in Law* 9 (2008): 139–164.
Shapira, Ron, and Avi Sagi. "Civil Disobedience and Conscientious Objection." *Israel Law Review* 36 (2002): 181–217.
Shapira-Ettinger, Keren. "The Two Dimensions of Consciousness." *Mechkarey Mishpat* 14 (1997): 179–207 (in Hebrew).

NOTES

1. Unless indicated otherwise, all statutory provisions mentioned in this chapter are from the Penal Law, 1977. Hereafter this law is referred to as "the code." An unofficial English translation of Amendment no. 39 may be found in *Israel Law Review* 30 (1996): 5–27.

2. Section 2 provides that the authority to make regulations for the implementation of a Law includes the authority to establish offenses and penalties. It also provides that where a penalty of imprisonment is prescribed by a regulation, its length shall not exceed six months; and that regulations that prescribe offenses and penalties require approval of a committee of the Knesset. The rule in section 1 that an offense can be determined "according to Law" relates to the enactment of offenses in regulations. It means that the authority to enact regulations that include offenses and penalties must be provided for in primary legislation.

3. The rule in section 1 that offenses and penalties can be determined "according to Law" is not meant to permit the imposition of criminal liability based on analogy. As was explained in note 2, this rule refers to regulations.

4. C.F.H. 1042/04 *Biton v. State of Israel* (not yet published).

5. C.F.H. 8613/96 *Gabarin v. State of Israel* 54(5) PD 193; C.A. 6696/96 *Kahana v. State of Israel* 52(1) PD 535; C.A.P. 9140/99 *Romano v. State of Israel* 54(4) PD 349. See Mordechai Kremnitzer, "Interpretation in Criminal Law," *Israel Law Review* 21 (1986): 358, 378–384.

6. C.A. 6696/96 *Kahana v. State of Israel* 52(1) PD 535; C.F.H. 1789/98 *State of Israel v. Kahana* 54(5) PD 145; C.A. 2831/95 *Elba v. State of Israel* 50(5) PD 221; C.A. 697/98 *Susatzkin v. State of Israel* 52(3) PD 289.

7. Also, an enactment creating a new defense or broadening the scope of an existing defense applies retroactively, in contrast to an enactment that repeals a defense or narrows its scope. The rules according to which enactments in favor of the actor apply retroactively do not apply to offenses under "temporary enactments" (section 6).

8. Section 24 also determines when an offense the penalty for which is only a fine will be considered a misdemeanor and when it will be considered a contravention.

9. See S. Z. Feller, *Elements of Criminal Law*, vol. 1 (Jerusalem: Sacher Institute, 1984), 400–402 (in Hebrew); and S. Z. Feller, *Elements of Criminal Law*, vol. 3 (Jerusalem: Sacher Institute, 1992), 156 (in Hebrew).

10. See Itzhak Kugler, "Criminal Omissions," *Mechkarey Mishpat* 20 (2003): 201–288 (in Hebrew). In order not to deviate from the principle of fair warning, I suggested in this article that at least in cases in which the creation of the duty to act was not reasonably foreseeable, the court that creates the new duty should declare that the duty is valid only for omissions that take place after the creation of the duty by the court, that is, that the court not apply the duty retroactively. This means, inter alia, that when the court decides to create the new duty to act, the decision reached in this respect will not influence the court's judgment whether to convict the specific defendant concerned. I also suggested the following alternative: that in appropriate cases where a court decides to create a new duty to act, the court determine whether the specific defendant concerned, who thought at the time of his omission that the duty did not exist, committed

a mistake that could not have been reasonably avoided, and, if so, acquit him in virtue of the defense of mistake of law according to section 34S (ibid., 254–258).

To illustrate the problem that may arise if judges are not allowed to create duties to act, I used the doctrine of "creating a dangerous situation." The criminal law of many countries recognizes the principle that a person who created a dangerous situation by his or her action, when the action was not accompanied by *mens rea*, and afterward became aware that he or she created the danger must act to neutralize the danger, and if he or she does not do so, and the result occurs, he or she may be convicted of the result crime concerned. This doctrine does not appear in any Israeli enactment. Therefore, if judges are not allowed to create this important doctrine, they will not be able to use it. However, S. Z. Feller contends that this doctrine can be adopted through the tort of negligence. The tort of negligence appears in Israel in an enactment, and within the framework of this tort, judges may create the duty to act in cases of "creating a dangerous situation." Once the duty is created within the tort of negligence, it will in fact be anchored in an enactment, and therefore it will be permitted to import it into the criminal law. See Feller, above note 9, vol. 1. However, I think that this approach is not consistent because it forbids judges to create duties to act directly for the purposes of criminal law and at the same time allows them to create duties for the purposes of tort law and then to import them into the criminal law. Furthermore, Feller's solution does not help in contexts in which the tort of negligence does not apply, such as the context of a person who causes suffering to an animal that is not his or another's property or that of offenses against state security. See Kugler, "Criminal Omissions," 270–273.

11. C.A. 119/93 *Lawrence v. State of Israel* 48(4) PD 1, 30–32; C.A.P. 3626/01 *Veitzman v. State of Israel* 56(3) PD 187. However, a subsequent decision implies that the question is still open. See C.A. 70/04 *Poriadin v. State of Israel* (not yet published).

12. However, in exceptional contexts the fact that there is an obligation to pay compensation does not imply that there was an obligation to act. In such contexts the civil enactment should not serve as a source of a duty to act for the purpose of result crimes.

13. The "Thou Shalt Not Stand against the Blood of Thy Neighbour" Law (1998). Generally speaking, this law provides that a person is required to extend aid to a person before him or her whose life, physical integrity, or health is in serious and immediate danger due to a sudden event. The law also provides that a person who notifies the authorities, or calls on another person who can provide the necessary aid to intervene, will be deemed to have extended aid. The punishment for breaching this duty is only a fine.

14. See Mordechai Kremnitzer, "Amendment No. 39 to the Penal Law," in Eli Lederman (ed.), *Directions in Criminal Liability* (Tel-Aviv: Raphael Taubenschlag Institute of Criminal Law and Israel Bar Publishing, 2001), 55, 66–67 (in Hebrew).

15. In *Veitzman* the court stated, in an obiter dictum, that the second approach is the correct one, and that therefore the "Good Samaritan" offense should not serve as a source of a duty to act for the purpose of convicting a person of other crimes (see *Veitzman*, above note 11, at 215–216). However, in a subsequent case the question was raised again and left open. See C.A. 70/04 *Poriadin v. State of Israel* (not yet published).

16. Strict liability offenses are exceptional as well. However, for historical reasons, offenses that were enacted before Amendment no. 39 came into force in 1995 and do not

mention any mental state in their definition can sometimes be considered strict liability offenses. This point will be clarified in the discussion of strict liability (in section II.B.2.v in this chapter).

17. Explanatory Notes to the Penal Law Bill (Preliminary Part and General Part) 1992, hereafter cited as the explanatory notes to the Bill.

18. Of course, conviction of the relevant offense is conditioned on the fact that at trial it is proved that the relevant circumstance did actually exist, because otherwise the *actus reus* is not established. This means that after the defendant acted, a way to learn the truth became available. It may be argued that in cases in which there is no way to find out the truth, there are some cases in which it is reasonable to take the risk that the relevant circumstance exists. But this point should not lead to a sweeping exemption in all cases in which the truth cannot be found out, but only to the recognition of the principle that it is permitted to act when the taking of the risk is reasonable (a principle that can apply even in some of the cases in which there is a way to find out the truth). I will refer to this principle later in this section.

19. The legislative history clearly supports this conclusion.

20. C.A. 3417/99 *Har-Shefi v. State of Israel* 55(2) PD 735, 756–768.

21. Miriam Gur-Arye is of the view that the court's decision is justified. See Miriam Gur-Arye, "A Failure to Prevent Crimes—Should It Be Criminal?" *Criminal Justice Ethics* 20, no. 2 (2001): 3, 21. Others criticize the decision, arguing that it leads to undesired consequences in the context of serious offenses. For example, the decision means, inter alia, that a person who knows that there is an 80 percent chance that his neighbor intends to murder his wife within an hour does not have to notify the police even anonymously and also does not have to tell the woman about her husband's intentions. Cf. Mordechai Kremnitzer, "On the Offense of Misprision of Felony," *Hamishpat* 11 (2007): 55–78 (in Hebrew). However, it should be borne in mind that there are countries that do not have an offense of failure to prevent a felony. It should also be noted that if the legislature's definition of willful blindness had included the requirement that the taking of the risk was unreasonable, it is possible that the court would have applied the rule of willful blindness to this offense and at the same time would have allowed for flexibility in its application to concrete cases according to factors such as the seriousness of the planned felony and the degree of probability that the other person plans to commit it.

22. In light of the fact that the decision in *Har-Shefi* (above note 20) is based on considerations of policy and justice and not on the fact that the term *knowing* appears in the definition of the discussed offense, it seems that in the future the decision not to apply the rule of willful blindness to a certain offense may be taken even with respect to an offense whose definition does not specify the mental state required. Another point is that it remains to be seen whether Israeli case law will develop a rule of willful blindness in the strict (Anglo-American) sense of the rule, one that will apply to offenses to which the broad Israeli willful blindness does not apply (like the offense defined in section 262). Such a rule could extend such offenses, for example, to cases in which the actor believes that there is a high probability that a relevant circumstance exists. The decision in *Har-Shefi* does not refer to such a possibility.

23. The issue of oblique intention will be discussed in section II.B.2.ii in this chapter.
24. C.A. 3338/99 *Pakovitz v. State of Israel* 54(5) PD 667, 694–695.
25. C.A. 63/58 *Ajami v. Attorney General* 13(1) PD 421, 431–432.
26. Generally speaking, the other three forms deal with causing the death of a father, mother, grandfather, or grandmother; causing the death of another in the commission of an offense; and causing death in order to secure escape after committing an offense. See sections 300–301. In these forms of murder, recklessness with regard to the death of the other person is sufficient for conviction. It should be noted that a special committee that has been appointed by the Ministry of Justice is currently working on a report on the law of homicide. It seems that the report will call for widespread reform in this area of the law.
27. C.A. 552/68 *Iluz v. State of Israel* 23(1) PD 377, 390.
28. Prohibition of Defamation Law (1965), section 6.
29. C.A. 677/83 *Borochov v. Yefet* 39(3) PD 205.
30. C.A.P. 9818/01 *Biton v. Sultan* 59(6) PD 554.
31. The judges stressed the importance of narrowing the scope of this offense in order not to overly limit freedom of expression. They also stated that the appropriate way to deal with cases in which there is no purpose on the part of the actor to injure the reputation of the victim is by using the civil law of defamation (in the context of which liability is not dependent on the existence of an intent to injure the reputation of the other person). Some judges stated that protection of the reputation of individuals is meant to be achieved by the civil law of defamation and that the purpose of the criminal offense of defamatory libel is to protect the public peace. They added the argument that a substantial danger to the public peace exists mainly in cases in which the publication was motivated by the actor's desire to injure the reputation of the victim (in contrast to cases of oblique intention), and therefore the existence of such a desire is required for conviction. For a discussion of a possible rationale for the requirement of intent to injure in the Israeli offense of defamatory libel, see Itzhak Kugler, *Direct and Oblique Intention in the Criminal Law* (Aldershot: Ashgate, 2002), 213–214, 225–226.
32. It should be noted, however, that some of the judges tried to suggest a principled reason for the distinction they made between the two types of offenses. They said that because of the fact that ulterior-intent offenses cover even cases in which the harm did not occur, there is more justification for refraining from applying the foresight rule to some of these offenses than for refraining from applying it to result crimes, which cover only cases in which the harm occurred.
33. C.A. 4317/97 *Poliakov v. State of Israel* 53(1) PD 289 (Englard J.).
34. C.A. 5446/99 *Elimelech v. State of Israel* 56(4) PD 49 (Matza J.).
35. C.A.P. 7153/99 *Elgad v. State of Israel* 55(5) PD 729, 745–753.
36. See, for example, section 8 of the Prohibition of Terror Financing Law (2005).
37. Of course, if in the context of a recklessness offense, another offense with the same *actus reus* exists that is more serious and in which intention with respect to the result is required, the question whether the actor desired that the result occur is important to decide whether there are grounds to convict him or her of this offense of greater seriousness.
38. However, it is possible that the legislature wanted to clear the path for enacting other offenses that require indifference. It may be argued that the distinction is important

because when a judge considers which penalty to impose on an offender, he or she may take into account whether the case is one of indifference or one of *kalut daat*. However, this can be done anyway even if the distinction did not appear in the definitions of mental states in the code. It should also be noted that according to one approach, there is a practical ramification of this distinction with respect to the issue of "legal causation." But the subject of legal causation is not dealt with at all in the code. (For a discussion of legal causation, see section II.B.4 in this chapter). A further point is that the requirement that the risk taken be unreasonable appears in the code only in the definition of *kalut daat* (section 20(a)(2)(b)); it does not appear in the definition of indifference (section 20(a)(2)(a)). If we interpret the code according to its wording, a person who performed a routine and common action that is considered to amount to a reasonable risk might be convicted if at the time of the action he or she did not care whether the result might occur, and the result in fact ensued. This outcome seems undesirable, and therefore it is reasonable to assume that if the courts were to be faced with such a case, they would rule that the taking of a reasonable risk precludes a conviction even in cases of indifference.

39. See C.A. 7832/00 *Yaakubov v. State of Israel* 56(2) PD 534, 543–547; C.A. 7193/04 *Yakirevitz v. State of Israel* (not yet published).

40. This way of reasoning appears in the explanatory notes to the Bill.

41. See Mordechai Kremnitzer, "On Criminal Negligence," *Mishpatim* 24 (1994): 71, 94 (in Hebrew).

42. The requirement that the defendant did everything possible to prevent the offense should not be understood literally. The explanatory notes to the Bill explain that what is intended is that in the context of strict liability offenses the standard of care required from the actor is higher than the standard that is required in the context of offenses of negligence. The Supreme Court has not yet clarified the meaning of this "higher standard of care."

43. C.A. 1599/08 *Levinshtein v. State of Israel* (not yet published).

44. This question is not expressly dealt with in the code, but the Supreme Court has decided that "willful blindness" suffices for conviction. See C.A. 1282/07 *Ben Abu v. State of Israel* (not yet published). As was explained in section II.B.2.i.b in this chapter, the Israeli notion of willful blindness is akin to the English notion of subjective recklessness. In addition, there is an obiter dictum of the Supreme Court indicating its inclination to view willful blindness as sufficient even in the context of impossible attempts. According to this view, a person who smokes a legal substance while suspecting that it is marijuana should be convicted of an attempt to use an illegal drug. See C.A.P. 7560/01 *CMP v. Shubin Dimitri* 59(3) PD 931.

45. This section also determines the punishment for aiding in contexts in which the principal offense carries a mandatory or minimum sentence.

46. However, in certain circumstances the aider may be convicted of the specific offense of facilitation according to section 498(a) of the code (see later in this section).

47. C.A. 320/99 *Plonit v. State of Israel* 55(3) PD 22, 31.

48. However, if the words uttered formed a *causa sine qua non* for the decision to commit the offense and its actual commission, then the case turns into a case of instigation, which is a more serious form of liability.

49. If there is mere negligence with respect to even one of the elements of the principal offense, there cannot be a conviction of aiding.

50. *Plonit*, above note 47, at 32–39. The implication of the court's decision is that if the aider believes that the principal will commit the principal offense and acts in order to facilitate the commission of the offense, he or she may be convicted of aiding in spite of the fact that he or she has no interest in the commission of the offense. It seems that in a case where the aider only foresees the possibility of the commission of the principal offense, the aider may be convicted if it is his or her desire that should the offense actually be committed, his or her act will facilitate its commission.

51. *Plonit*, above note 47, at 32–39.

52. C.A. 7580/02 *Gaber v. State of Israel* (not yet published). The implication is that if the aider wants to facilitate the commission of the offense, recklessness with respect to commission of the principal offense is sufficient. But where there is no desire to facilitate the commission of the offense, conviction is dependent on the finding that the aider was almost certain that the principal offense would be committed and that his or her act would facilitate its commission.

53. *Plonit*, above note 47, at 32–39. One of the reasons given by the Court for this rule was that the penalty for aiding an offense is lower than the penalty prescribed for the principal offense.

54. Section 33. This section also determines the penalty for an attempt to instigate in cases where the principal offense carries a mandatory or minimum sentence.

55. Section 30. See also C.A. 8469/99 *Eskin v. State of Israel* 55(2) PD 65, 78–79. The condition of *causa sine qua non* is fulfilled not only in the case where the instigator plants the idea of committing the offense in the mind of the principal, but also when the principal is deliberating independently whether to commit the offense and the instigator persuades him or her to do so. In cases where the condition of *causa sine qua non* is not fulfilled, there cannot be a conviction of instigating, but there may still be a conviction of aiding based on the secondary's psychological contribution, as when a principal who already decided to commit the crime is encouraged to do so by another person who strengthens his or her morale or stiffens his or her resolution.

56. *Eskin*, above note 55, 81–83. One of the reasons given by the court for this decision was that the penalty for instigation is the same as the penalty prescribed for the principal offense.

57. When the relevant offense is a result crime that does not include a specific course of conduct in its definition (like the offenses of manslaughter or negligently causing the death of another person), and the act of A is a *causa sine qua non* for the act of B (who is an infant or insane) that causes the relevant result, A may be convicted of the said offense according to the standard principles of causation, without the help of the doctrine of "perpetration by means of another." It is clear that in such cases the mental state that suffices for conviction of the principal offense (for example, recklessness or negligence) should suffice for the conviction of A.

58. This example appears in the explanatory notes to the Bill.

59. The distinction between coperpetration and aiding has further implications. For example, attempt to aid is not an offense, but attempted coperpetration is an offense.

Also, coperpetration of a contravention is punishable, but aiding a contravention is not punishable.

60. C.A. 8573/96 *Markado v. State of Israel* 51(5) PD 481 (Goldberg J.).

61. C.A. 2801/95 *Korakin v. State of Israel* 52(1) PD 791 (Kedmi J.); C.F.H. 1294/96 *Meshulam v. State of Israel* 52(5) PD 1 (Kedmi J.). Actually, it seems that according to Kedmi, A may be classified as a coperpetrator even if his or her "physical" contribution amounts only to giving instructions to the other participants. For a criticism of Kedmi's approach, see Miriam Gur-Arye, "Complicity in Criminal Law," in Lederman, above note 14, at 83, 96–97 (in Hebrew).

62. C.A. 2796/95 *Plonim v. State of Israel* 51(3) PD 388, 402. Of course, in the context of liability for further offenses, different rules apply, as will be explained in section II.B.3.ii.f in this chapter.

63. However, the code alleviates the harshness of the law in two ways. First, if Y is an offense that requires an intention to cause a certain result, A cannot be convicted of Y; rather, A may be convicted only of an offense that deals with the same *actus reus* as that of Y, but in which recklessness with respect to the result is sufficient for conviction. Second, if A is convicted of Y (a criminal-thought offense) based on A's negligence with respect to Y, and Y is an offense for which a mandatory penalty is prescribed, the court may impose a lighter penalty on A.

64. See Miriam Gur-Arye, "Deviations from the Requirement of Culpability," *Mechkarey Mishpat* 13 (1996): 129, 134–137 (in Hebrew). For a defense of the code, see Mordechai Kremnitzer, "Justified Deviations from the Requirement of Mens Rea," *Mechkarey Mishpat* 13 (1996): 109, 120–125 (in Hebrew). On section 34A, see also Daniel Ohana, "The Natural and Probable Consequence Rule in Complicity: Section 34A of the Israeli Penal Law (Part I)," *Israel Law Review* 34 (2000): 321–351; and Daniel Ohana, "The Natural and Probable Consequence Rule in Complicity: Section 34A of the Israeli Penal Law (Part II)," *Israel Law Review* 34 (2000): 453–508.

65. C.A. 4424/98 *Silgado v. State of Israel* 56(5) PD 529.

66. Section 300(a)(3).

67. Section 5 of the Basic Law says: "There shall be no deprivation or restriction of the liberty of a person by imprisonment, arrest, extradition or otherwise." Section 2 says that there shall be no violation of the life, body, or dignity of any person. Section 8 (known as "the limitation clause") says: "There shall be no violation of rights under this Basic Law except by a law befitting the values of the State of Israel, enacted for a proper purpose, and to an extent no greater than is required, or by a regulation enacted by virtue of express authorization in such a law." A argued that section 34A(a)(1) deviates unjustifiably from the principle that a person will be convicted and punished only according to his or her personal degree of blameworthiness, and therefore it violates sections 2 and 5 while not fulfilling the requirements determined in section 8.

68. C.A. 9723/03 *State of Israel v. Blazer* 59(2) PD 408, 415.

69. Ibid., 423–426. However, it seems that where there was only a slight deviation from the foreseeable manner of causation, the defendant may be convicted.

70. See ibid., 424–425; C.A. 341/82 *Belker v. State of Israel* 41(1) PD 1, 42–51. It may be that those who adopt the position that in cases of intention or indifference the actor

may be convicted even in cases where the manner of causation was unforeseeable believe that in such cases it is possible to convict only if a further condition is fulfilled: that in the case under discussion there was a "unified set of events" (*Blazer*, above note 68, 424). Another possibility is that instead of the previously mentioned further condition one requires that in the case under discussion the manner in which the result was brought about was not *extremely* extraordinary (C.A. 5870/01 *Hseyn v. State of Israel* 57(1) PD 221, 232–233).

71. C.A. 402/75 *Elgavish v. State of Israel* 30(2) PD 561, 574–577. This decision was applied in subsequent cases. In one case the defendant, who played Russian roulette with another person, was convicted of causing his death, in spite of the fact that the victim, who killed himself in the course of the game, was apparently reckless with respect to his death (*Lawrence*, above note 11). Another case is *Yaakubov*. In this case the victim was a battered woman. Once, after being beaten and threatened by her husband, the victim, out of despair, committed suicide by jumping out of the window of their apartment. The Supreme Court convicted the husband of negligently causing the death of another person, stating that in the circumstances, a reasonable person could have foreseen the possibility that the wife would kill herself, and therefore the wife's action did not break the chain of causation in spite of the fact that she jumped with intent to kill herself. See *Yaakubov*, above note 39, at 545.

72. In September 2005 the Supreme Court gave a decision that deviates from its usual practice of convicting the aider merely of aiding rather than perpetration. See C.A. 7580/02 *Gaber v. State of Israel* (not yet published). In this case the defendant drove a suicide bomber to a mall in the center of a city, where the latter activated the bomb and killed five people. The defendant was prosecuted for aiding murder. The Supreme Court decided that the driver did not *know* that the passenger was a terrorist who was on his way to commit murder, but he suspected that this might be the case. On the basis of these facts the court decided that the mental state required for aiding murder did not exist because the driver had neither a direct intention (desire) to facilitate the murder nor an oblique intention (for he was not almost sure that a murder would be committed; see section II.B.3.ii.b in this chapter). The driver only foresaw the possibility that the passenger might commit murder and that his actions would facilitate the commission of the crime. Therefore, the court acquitted the driver of aiding murder. However, the court held that the driver might be viewed as a perpetrator of manslaughter. The action of driving the passenger was a *causa sine qua non* of the death of the victims, and the driver foresaw the possibility that his action would cause the death of human beings. The court concluded that the *actus reus* and *mens rea* of manslaughter existed and convicted the driver of manslaughter (note that the driver was convicted of manslaughter as a direct perpetrator, not as a coperpetrator; this was not a case of coperpetration, first of all because there was no agreement to murder). However, the court did not address at all the fact that its decision deviated from its common practice, nor did it address at all the doctrine that the intervening act of a third party breaks the chain of causation even when the intervening act is foreseen as possible by the first actor. Therefore, the decision in *Gaber* cannot be viewed as the final decision concerning this doctrine.

73. However, the distinction between justification and excuse is recognized and discussed in the Israeli legal literature. See, for example, Aaron Enker, "Duress, Self-Defence and Necessity in Israeli Law," *Israel Law Review* 30 (1996): 188–206.

74. There may be exceptions to this rule in the context of defenses that apply to specific contexts. There are two such contexts in the General Part of the code, in which the defendant has to prove the elements of a defense on a balance of probabilities. See section II.B.2.v in this chapter concerning strict liability, and section II.B.3.i.a concerning the defense of renunciation (in the context of attempt).

75. See Enker, above note 73, at 205.

76. The meaning of the requirement of reasonableness depends on how the defense is understood: as a justification, as an excuse, or as a defense that covers both cases of justification and cases of excuse. See Enker, above note 73, at 205.

77. Section 34N. In order to negate the application of the defense with respect to standard criminal-thought offenses, it is sufficient that the defendant have been negligent with respect to the possibility that he or she might perform the prohibited act in a situation of necessity. Only if the actor placed himself or herself in the dangerous situation in order to commit the offense may he or she be convicted of an offense that requires an intention to cause a certain result. The defense is not negated because the actor placed himself or herself in a situation of necessity if his or her act was committed in order to save the interest of a third party.

78. The requirement appearing in section 34P that the defendant's act in cases of self-defense, necessity, or duress, be reasonable does not contradict the rule that A is not guilty even in cases of an unreasonable mistake, for section 34P should be understood as relating to other issues, such as the requirement of proportionality between the harm done and the harm prevented.

79. In the context of a strict liability offense, the principles of strict liability apply.

80. C.A. 845/02 *State of Israel v. Tnuva* (not yet published); C.A. 5672/05 *Tagar v. State of Israel* (not yet published).

81. The explanatory notes to the Bill; C.A. 5672/05 *Tagar v. State of Israel* (not yet published).

82. Intoxication exists not only in cases in which the person is under the influence of alcohol, but also in cases in which he or she is under the influence of a dangerous drug or other intoxicating substance.

83. Section 34N. In order to negate this defense with respect to standard criminal-thought offenses, it is sufficient that the actor have been negligent with respect to the possibility that he or she might commit the offense in a condition whereby he or she lacked control over his or her bodily movements. In order to convict the actor of an offense that requires an intention to cause a certain result, it is required that the actor place himself or herself in such a condition in order to commit the offense. For criticism of the rule in the code providing that negligence is sufficient in this context to convict a person of a criminal-thought offense, see Gur-Arye, above note 64, at 130–131. For a defense of the code, see Kremnitzer, above note 64, at 125–127.

84. In 1998 the Supreme Court abolished the rule allowing teachers to use force. See C.A. 5224/97 *State of Israel v. Sdeh Or* 52(3) PD 374. In 2000 the court abolished the rule

allowing parents to use force. See C.A. 4596/98 *Plonit v. State of Israel* 54(1) PD 145, 172–187. The fact that the defense of chastisement of children does not appear in the new General Part is mentioned by the court as supporting its position that this defense does not exist anymore. It should be noted, however, that in *Plonit* the court clarified that there are mechanisms that may prevent convictions in trivial cases, such as the exercise of prosecutorial discretion not to prosecute, and the defense of *de minimis* (*Plonit*, 187).

85. However, section 300A provides an exhaustive list of cases in which the judge may impose a lighter penalty than life imprisonment on an offender convicted of murder.

86. The last chapter of the Special Part of the code is titled "Miscellaneous Provisions" and does not contain offenses.

87. See section 90A(1); C.A. 4577/98 *Dayan v. State of Israel* 55(2) PD 405, 421; C.A. 5728/96 *Golan v. State of Israel* (not yet published).

88. C.A. 396/69 *Benno v. State of Israel* 24(1) PD 561, 567.

89. See above notes 33–34 and accompanying text.

90. It should be noted that a special committee that has been appointed by the Ministry of Justice is currently working on a report on the law of homicide. It seems that the report will call for widespread reform in this area of the law.

91. In most cases of manslaughter there is mere recklessness, as opposed to intention, with respect to the death of the other person. However, in cases of provocation the defendant is convicted of manslaughter, rather than murder, in spite of the fact that he or she intended (wanted) to kill the victim. At the present time, in all (or almost all) other cases of causing death (by a positive act) in which the actor wanted to kill the victim, a murder conviction applies because of the way the Supreme Court interprets the element of "preparation."

As was explained earlier, there are three special situations in which recklessness with respect to the death of the other person is sufficient for conviction of murder. A further point is that in these three situations conviction of murder applies even in a case of provocation.

It should also be noted that section 303 provides that where a woman causes (by an act or omission) the death of her child who is under the age of twelve months, and at the time of her act or omission the balance of her mind was disturbed by reason of her not having fully recovered from the effect of giving birth to the child or by reason of the effect of breast-feeding subsequent to the birth of the child, she is liable to a maximum penalty of five years' imprisonment, notwithstanding the fact that in the circumstances of the case the elements of murder or manslaughter exist.

92. Where certain aggravating circumstances that are listed in section 345(b) and in section 351(a) exist (for example, where the victim is both under the age of eighteen and a member of the actor's family), the maximum penalty for rape is twenty years' imprisonment, and the minimum penalty is five years' imprisonment (here also the court may impose a lighter penalty on the basis of special reasons).

93. Homosexual relations between consenting adults are not prohibited.

94. Section 348.

95. The Prevention of Sexual Harassment Law, 1998, sections 3–5.

JAPAN

John O. Haley

I. Introduction
   A. Historical Sketch
   B. Jurisdiction
   C. Legality Principle
   D. Sources of Criminal Law
   E. Process

II. General Part
   A. Theories of Punishment
   B. Liability Requirements
   C. Defenses
   D. Justifications
   E. Excuses
   F. Sanctions

III. Special Part
   A. Structure
   B. Homicide
   C. Sex Offenses
   D. Theft, Embezzlement, Robbery, and Fraud
   E. "Victimless" Crimes
   F. Crimes of Negligence

John O. Haley is the William R. Orthwein Distinguished Professor of Law Emeritus at Washington University in St. Louis. His recent publications include "Why Study Japanese Law?" 58 *American Journal of Comparative Law* 1 (2010); and "Comment on Using Criminal Punishment to Serve Both Victim and Social Needs," 72 *Law and Contemporary Problems* 219 (2009). He is currently on the faculty of the Vanderbilt University School of Law.

I. INTRODUCTION

A. Historical Sketch

Japanese criminal law is governed by the Penal Code of 1907[1] (hereafter the Code), the Code of Criminal Procedure of 1948,[2] and various special statutes. Historically, Japanese criminal law reflected the formative influence of imperial Chinese law, notably the Tang Code in the seventh-century *ritsuryō* and the Ming Code in the eighteenth-century *Osadamegaki*. More significant were the edicts of nearly five centuries of warrior rulers. Criminal law in Japan, however, was never as prominent or as severe as in imperial China. For much of Japanese history, the vast majority of the population has been subject less to formal legal controls than to informal community sanctions. The continuing strength of informal social sanctions functioning in tandem with formal law enforcement has long been a distinguishing feature of Japanese criminal justice.

The reforms based on European law of the later half of the Meiji period (1868–1912) transformed all areas of law. The predominant influence was German. The 1907 Code thus reflects the prevailing policies and conceptions of late nineteenth- and early twentieth-century German criminal jurisprudence. German law and legal science continue to exert strong influence. Remarkably, the Code has remained largely unchanged despite repeated efforts both before and after World War II to replace it. The Allied Occupation authorities carefully reviewed the 1907 Code to ensure conformity with the 1947 constitution. They considered it to be highly progressive, and, except for the lèse-majesté provisions and a few technical changes, revision was deemed to be unnecessary. In 1995 (Law No. 91) the Diet modernized the grammar and written forms to make the Code more accessible to contemporary readers, again without significant change in content. More recently, in 2004 (Law No. 156) the Diet enacted more extensive amendments. Gang rape (*shudan gōkan*) was added as a separate and more serious crime than rape (art. 178-2). Japan's criminal jurisdiction was extended to cover major Code offenses against Japanese nationals committed outside Japan by non-Japanese. Prison terms for felonies were lengthened. The maximum and minimum amounts of fines were revised upward to reflect current yen values more accurately. Proscriptive periods for prosecution (statutes of limitations) were increased. Included also were additional rights for victims.

B. Jurisdiction

Crimes subject to Japanese jurisdiction include those committed by persons within Japanese territory, including crimes committed on Japanese vessels and aircraft (art. 1). The Code does subject to Japanese criminal jurisdiction certain crimes committed by persons outside of Japan (art. 2). They include the crimes of insurrection; instigation of foreign aggression; counterfeiting, forging, or passing counterfeit or forged currency, state documents, securities or seals; and making false statements to officials upon entry into Japan. As noted in the preceding section, a new article 3-2 added in 2004 subjects to Japanese criminal jurisdiction major Code offenses committed outside Japan by non-Japanese nationals against Japanese nationals. These crimes range from homicide, rape, and robbery to kidnapping, unlawful arrest, and confinement. Japanese nationals are also subject to criminal prosecution for a long list of crimes even though they are committed or attempted outside Japan (art. 3). They include arson; rape and other sexual offenses; homicide; bodily injury; unlawful arrest and confinement; kidnapping and abduction; defamation; larceny; robbery; fraud; extortion; embezzlement; destruction of negotiable instruments, promissory notes, and similar private documents and computer records; and forgery or passing of forged private documents, as well as causing damage by flooding to buildings, mines, or railway cars while occupied. Otherwise, criminal jurisdiction applies solely to criminal acts committed within the territory of Japan.

C. Legality Principle

Japan has long adhered to the twin principles of legality of continental European law (*nullum crimen sine lege* and *nulla poena sine lege*) that all crimes and criminal penalties require express legislative authorization and definition. Under article 23 of the 1889 constitution, for example, no Japanese national could be "arrested, detained, tried or punished, unless according to statute [*hōritsu*]," and under article 9 no ordinance or regulation could alter an existing statute. An 1890 statute did provide for minor criminal penalties for administrative infractions,[3] but pre–World War II judicial decisions invalidated as *ultra vires* criminal penalties provided by regulation rather than statute.[4] Even during the most repressive periods of the prewar era, Japanese judges and enforcement authorities punctiliously honored these mandates. Article 31 of the 1946 constitution is even more explicit. It provides that "[n]o person shall be deprived of life or liberty, nor shall any other criminal penalty be imposed, except according to procedure established by statute [*hōritsu*]." Article 73(6) of the constitution further expressly prohibits the inclusion of penal provisions in cabinet orders without legislative authorization. A 1952 Grand Bench decision construed this provision to proscribe any comprehensive legislative authorization of crimes or penalties to be detailed by regulation. The constitution requires, by this decision, a specific statutory basis for crimes.[5]

The legality principles also restrict judicial interpretation of statutory provisions. Courts and scholars have long rejected interpretation of penal provisions by analogy contrary to the interests of those charged with a crime. For example, in a 1956 decision the Supreme Court held that Molotov cocktails did not satisfy the definition of "explosives" under an 1884 penal statute.[6] In contrast, on the ground that computerized records are written documents, in 1983 the Supreme Court affirmed the charge that falsification of a digitized record of a notarial deed constituted the crime of falsifying such a deed under article 157 of the Criminal Code.[7] In this decision the Supreme Court stated that computerized records of automobiles satisfied the definition of "original document of a notarial deed." In 1987 the Diet amended the Code to include computer-related crimes (chapter 18-2, arts. 163-2 to 163-5). The case reflects the courts attempt to construe the language of penal provisions as reasonably as is allowed under the legality principles, especially if the language is vague, in view of the social purpose of the particular proscription, technological changes, and societal norms as perceived by judges. Thus, for instance, "electricity" was held to constitute a "thing" under the pre-Code proscription of theft,[8] and a diesel-powered train was construed to be covered in the crime of negligently endangering the passage of a "steam- or electric-powered train" of article 129 of the Code.[9]

A notable exception to Japan's observance of the legality principles in particular and the influence of German law in general is the rejection of mandatory prosecution. Prosecutorial discretion, especially discretion to suspend prosecution of convictable offenders, has long been a distinguishing and very prominent feature of Japanese criminal process and practice. On average, as indicated in section I.E.1 in this chapter, procurators annually suspend prosecution of roughly one-third of all convictable offenders. Similarly, the Code grants judges considerable discretion, albeit subject to well-defined parameters, to reduce penalties or to suspend execution. Annually, on average, judges similarly suspend execution for over half of all convicted defendants.

D. Sources of Criminal Law

1. Legislature

Since 1889 constitutional mandates incorporating European legality principles, as indicated above, have required specific statutory provision for all crimes and penal sanctions. The Criminal Code sets out the basic principles of criminal liability, as well as all major crimes. In addition to the Code of Criminal Procedure, supplementing the Criminal Code are special statutes for juvenile offenses and minor crimes, as well as various regulatory statutes, such as Japan's Antimonopoly Law, that make certain violations a crime with specified penalties.

2. Judiciary

The provisions of the Code and special statutes are subject to judicial interpretation and application. As a matter of general consensus and legal practice, decisions by both the full, fifteen-justice Supreme Court (Grand Bench) and each of the three panels of five justices (Petty Bench) that hear most appeals are recognized, at least as a matter of practice, as establishing controlling precedent as binding interpretations of law. Decisions by the lower courts (district and high courts) do not establish binding precedent, but if they are consistent, they do indicate exemplary judicial outcomes. Decisions by the highest prewar court, the Great Court of Cassation (Taishin'in), are also accorded deference.

The size and organization of the judiciary, as well as the widely accepted commitment by judges to consistency and certainty to a degree matched by few, if any, judicial systems, contribute to judicial adherence to past decisions by courts at all levels. Japan has a unified national judiciary with fewer than 3,000 career judges who are assigned generally for three-year terms to courts at all levels throughout the nation. Under current practice, career judges, commencing their careers as assistant judges, are assigned by the General Secretariat in the Supreme Court for three-year terms either to the Tokyo District Court or the Osaka District Court, the two largest. Most are subsequently posted to a district or family (and juvenile) court, frequently in a different region. Some are subsequently assigned to the Ministry of Justice or other administrative offices, including the General Secretariat of the Supreme Court. Training programs for overseas study and work in private companies are also available. The pattern varies afterward, but before their reappointment as "regular" judges after ten years of service, they will have gained wide experience on courts at all levels, although not all have experience on one of the high courts, and in various urban and rural areas of the country. This pattern of judicial posting throughout a judge's career produces a high degree of nationwide consistency in adjudication. The Japanese judiciary also has a globally unparalleled record of integrity.

3. Executive

The Ministry of Justice and particularly the career procuracy within the ministry have significant influence on the formation, as well as the implementation, of policy. All proposals for legislation pertaining to criminal law are subjected to painstaking review within the ministry with the active participation of the Office of the Procurator-General. Most legislative proposals are produced by advisory committees organized under the auspices of the ministry. All government bills are drafted under the supervision of the Cabinet Legislation Bureau (Naikaku Hōsei Kyoku), whose members include highly respected, legally trained officials seconded (i.e., loaned) from various ministries. All government bills are also subject to final review by the Bureau.

4. Scholars

As in other civil law jurisdictions, scholars have long played a leading role in drafting legislation, including the codes, as well as legal interpretation. Generally accepted scholarly theory (*tsūsetsu*) is regarded at least as an authoritative source of interpretation. Thus leading scholarly commentaries are commonly treated as sources of law. Scholarly research and writings have also long served as a conduit for the reception of European—particularly German—legal theory and practice both in the interpretation of existing codes and statutes influenced by European models and in drafting new legislation. Illustrative are the pioneering contributions of such scholars as Makino Eiichi (1878–1970) and Ono Seiichirō (1891–1986). In addition to their written work, leading scholars are frequently also sources of new ideas and policies as active participants on commissions and committees that develop and propose legislative reforms.

E. Process

1. Adversarial/Inquisitorial

Although adversarial features were intentionally introduced in the 1948 Code of Criminal Procedure, with respect to the roles of judges and procurators, the criminal justice process continues to conform to European antecedents as predominantly inquisitorial. All persons are presumed innocent until proved guilty. No one may be convicted solely on the basis of a plea or confession of guilt. All convictions require credible evidence of guilt presented to a presiding judge or panel of three judges. The overriding function of the judge as finder of fact is to ascertain the truth. Thus in contested cases the judge plays a leading role in putting questions to the defendant and witnesses. The procurator (*kensatsukan*, often translated as "public prosecutor") is responsible, however, for presentation to the court of the evidence of guilt. Defense counsel may also present and examine witnesses. Under article 37 of the postwar constitution, every defendant has the constitutional rights to "a speedy and public trial by an impartial tribunal," "full opportunity to examine all witnesses," access to "compulsory process for obtaining witnesses on his behalf at public expense," and "assistance of competent counsel who shall, if the accused is unable to secure the same by his own efforts, be assigned to his use by the State."

Procurators in effect make a preliminary determination of guilt. Under prewar procedures the process involved a formal examination made in camera, followed, if guilt was determined, by a judicial trial, often, particularly if not contested, based on the written dossier of the preliminary examination. The procedure was similar to the preliminary examination by investigating magistrates in France, Italy, Spain, and several other systems. Concern by U.S. lawyers over the lack of a full, adversarial judicial trial led to its abolition during the Allied Occupation.[10] However, Japanese procurators in practice continue to share with judges a self-perceived "truth"-seeking responsibility and are generally reluctant to indict anyone unless they are certain of both guilt and conviction.[11] Moreover, as noted in section I.C in this chapter, procurators routinely suspend prosecution in a significant number of cases where guilt is not at issue. In addition to the nature of the offense, the critical factors include acknowledgment by offenders of wrongdoing, their acceptance of accountability, particularly with respect to victim reparation, usually negotiated informally by intermediaries, and the willingness of the victim either to withdraw any required complaint (see section II.D.3) or to express a willingness to pardon. The percentages vary considerably depending on the offense, but on average prosecution is suspended annually for one-third of all convictable offenders. These factors, along with the high percentage of uncontested trials, contribute to relatively high conviction rates in Japan.

2. Jury/Written Opinions

A 1923 statute[12] (not put into effect until 1928)[13] created a modified jury system that failed to function as originally intended and atrophied. In 1943 it was formally suspended.[14] Pursuant to the recommendation of the 1999 Judicial Reform Commission,[15] in 2004 the Diet enacted a special statute to create a system of "lay assessors" (*saiban'in*) in cases involving serious offenses.[16] The system went into effect in May 2009. The lay assessors are selected by lot from the pool of voters in the judicial district. Excluded are lawyers and other legal professionals. Depending on the seriousness of the offense, the court is composed of three judges and six lay assessors or one judge and four lay assessors. Both career judges and lay assessors are collectively responsible for findings of fact to determine guilt, as well as sentencing. A simple majority is required for conviction and sentencing, with, however, a consenting vote by at least one career judge and one lay assessor. The participation of lay assessors are limited, however, to cases involving offenses punishable by death or life imprisonment with or without labor, such as homicide and intentional burning of an inhabited building, judicial panel cases in which a person has been killed as a consequence of an intentional criminal act, such as rape, robbery, or unsafe driving resulting in death, and serious cases involving certain special statutory offenses, such as violations of firearms or drug-control laws. The Ministry of Justice estimates that law assessors will participate in about 3,000 cases each year.[17]

II. GENERAL PART

A. Theories of Punishment

Japanese law-enforcement authorities—police, procurators, and judges—have long adhered in practice to a correctional theory of punishment based on the restoration of community relationships and the reintegration of offenders into society. Incarceration, especially long-term imprisonment, has generally been perceived, albeit rarely explicitly, as a socially detrimental option that should be avoided unless it is necessary for public safety. Deterrence is achieved primarily by detection and exposure through effective policing and conviction. Retribution is rejected as a socially beneficial response.

B. Liability Requirements

1. Objective/Actus Reus

i. Act

The Code defines crimes in terms of acts. Excluded are acts committed involuntarily. An action while sleeping is not an "act" under the Code. The constituent requirements of criminal acts comprise both objective and subjective elements. Criminal acts must be unlawful as statutorily defined, as well as culpable or blameworthy.

ii. Omission

With the exception of crimes of negligence (discussed in section III.F in this chapter), the Code is silent with respect to crimes of omission or nonfeasance. If omissions or failures to act result from bad faith or are deemed culpable, however, they may constitute crimes, as provided by statute. Similarly, if a defendant has an obligation to act, omission may be deemed an act. For example, if parents did not feed their baby and the baby died, their omission could be considered the act of homicide. Both scholarly opinion and judicial decisions tend to treat the problem in terms of culpability and the duty of the defendant to prevent the harm. Thus in the first of two often-cited decisions,[18] in 1932 the Great Court of Cassation held that a son engaged in a life-and-death struggle with his adoptive father was guilty of the crime of setting fire to an inhabited building (art. 108) for failing to put out a fire caused by burning wood the father had thrown at him.[19] Six years later the Supreme Court held that the failure to extinguish a fallen candle that caused a fire that burned down a house did not constitute the crime of arson despite the fact that it had been lit by the defendant.[20] In this case the court deemed that the omission of the defendant to extinguish a fire did not constitute the crime of arson. The determinative fact appears to be the degree of culpability as determined initially by procurators and ultimately by the courts.

iii. Status

The 1947 constitution guarantees the equality of all citizens and expressly prohibits "discrimination in political, economic, or social relations because of race, creed, sex, social status, or family origin" (art. 14). Applying this provision in a landmark decision in 1973, the Supreme Court ruled unconstitutional the Code provision of article 200 imposing a more severe penalty for the crime of homicide in cases involving lineal ascendants.[21] As will be noted in section III.F, Japanese law does impose greater duties of care on persons engaged in occupations and activities that involve public health and safety. The constituent elements of some crimes do include the status of the offender, the victim, or, in the case of bribery, a third party. For example, the crime of disclosure of confidential information depends on the occupational status of the offender (art. 134). Similarly, the crime of embezzlement in the course of a business requires that the embezzled property be in the possession of the offender in the course of business (art. 253), and the crime of bribery requires that the person bribed have the status of a public officer (art. 197). Personal status also allows exculpation for receipt of stolen property. Article 257 provides that persons who receive stolen property belonging to a spouse, lineal relative, or relatives living together or a spouse of such relatives are to be exonerated.

2. *Subjective*/Mens Rea/Mental Element
   i. Intent

Article 38 of the Code makes "intent" (*ishi*) a prerequisite for any punishable criminal act. It provides that acts "performed without the intent to commit a crime" are not punishable "unless specially provided by statute." The provision leaves open the possibility of explicit provision for prosecution of unintentional criminal acts; however, none, other than crimes of negligence, have been enacted. The Code does not define intent, but the term is generally understood to require evidence of an awareness or acknowledgment of the objective facts constituting the crime. Conscious intentionality is not necessary. A Takamatsu High Court decision, for example, held the defendant criminally liable for intent to kill "buried within the depth of consciousness," as in the case of rage or excessive anger.[22] Japanese criminal law distinguishes intent from responsibility. Thus both temporary and permanent mental incapacity preclude conviction because of lack of responsibility, not intent. Motive or desire that the constituent facts come into being is not necessary. The intent requirement is satisfied so long as the actor is aware of constituent facts. For example, if Z intentionally stabs Y with a knife, evidence of awareness of the possibility that the wound would cause death is sufficient. Proof of a desire to inflict a fatal wound is not necessary.[23] Similarly, both courts and scholars accept what Shigemitsu Dando termed a theory of "statutory overlapping"[24] that a mistake of fact about object may still constitute a crime of intent. For example, if Z actually intends to kill Y but mistakenly and fatally stabs X, the crime of intentional homicide is established.[25] Also noteworthy is article 38(2) of the Code, which provides: "When a person who commits a crime is not aware at the time of its commission of the facts constituting a greater crime, the person shall not be punished for the greater crime."

   ii. Recklessness

Recklessness is not an independently relevant concern under Japanese criminal law. Except with respect to crimes of negligence, recklessness is not a constituent element of any crime. The notion of recklessness is instead treated as a form of intent called "ill-considered intention" (*mihitsu no koi*) or as a form of negligence called "cognitive negligence" (*ninshiki aru kashitsu*), that is, negligence of the awareness of the possibility of a result. The distinction between *mihitsu no kōi* and *ninshiki aru kashitsu* is ambiguous and thus the subject of multiple explanations. Actors who recognize or acknowledge the probable consequences of their actions are generally deemed to have intent, but not actors who doubt or disbelieve, albeit erroneously, that their actions would produce such results. Whether reckless or not, disregard of the constituent facts of an intentional crime does not preclude a finding of intent.

iii. Negligence

As described later (section III.F), a number of crimes set out in the Code are based on negligence, including many of the most frequently prosecuted. The crimes of negligence include acts that in most jurisdictions would incur only civil liability as torts. In fact, the most common is negligent driving, a category that has for many years comprised over a quarter of all reported crimes.

3. *Theories of Liability*
   i. Inchoate Crimes
      a. *Attempt*

For an attempt to constitute a punishable offense, the Code requires express provision for each crime and further allows reduction of the statutory punishment for voluntary interruption of the commission of a crime (art. 44). The Code does, however, explicitly include as punishable offenses attempts to commit most serious crimes, such as attempts to commit the crimes of homicide (art. 203), arson (art. 112), breaking into a residence (art. 132), obstructing traffic (art. 128), and kidnapping (art. 228). Article 43 of the Code permits reduction of punishment for offenders who have commenced but not completed criminal acts and, in addition, possible exculpation or, perhaps more accurately, impunity for those who voluntarily (intentionally) abandon their commission. Japanese scholars and courts have construed these provisions to necessitate evidence (1) of the requisite intent to commit the criminal act and (2) that at least some of the constituent elements of the crime have been performed. Courts have thus required that acts of perpetration have commenced. For example, the crime of attempted theft (in contrast to the separate crime of attempted breaking into a residence) requires that the offender not only enter the residence but also begin to look for property.[26] Of course, if all the constituent elements of the crime have been completed, the crime itself, not its attempt, has been committed.

   b. *Conspiracy*

No provision in the Code makes "conspiracy" to commit a crime a separate offense. Instead, as in other civil law systems, Japan relies on notions of complicity to deal with crimes committed by more than one actor.

   ii. Complicity

Persons are criminally liable for complicity in the commission of criminal acts under Japanese law as coprincipals, as instigators (or inducers), or as accessories. Article 60 defines as principals all persons who jointly commit a crime. Similarly, article 61 provides that persons who induce others to commit a crime or who induce others to induce a crime are to be sentenced as principals. Under article 62, persons who aid principals are deemed accessories with, under article 63, reduced punishment. The central issue of complicity is to distinguish the criminal liability of an actor as principal, as coprincipal, as instigator, or as accessory. Because complicity as a coprincipal requires joint commission of a crime, if two or more persons independently commit identical criminal acts even at the same time and place, their actions are construed as separate, simultaneous crimes and thus are not treated as complicity in the same crime. Thus the first requirement is concurrence of intent or collusion to act together to commit a criminal act. Common purpose and tacit understandings suffice.[27] The second requirement is joint acts of perpetration. For this purpose evidence of sequential acts[28] is sufficient.

Instigation of a crime requires evidence that the defendant has expressly suggested the commission of a specific criminal act, although its manner and means or even the victim need not be mentioned.[29] Causation between the acts of instigation and the perpetration of the crime also must be established.

For a person to be deemed an accessory, evidence of intent to aid a principal is required, and the crime must have been committed. The principal need not be aware, however, that he or she is being assisted physically or mentally. Nor does it matter whether the assistance is given in preparation or in the actual commission of the crime.[30]

iii. Corporate Criminal Liability

Corporate entities as juridical persons are not subject to criminal liability under the Code. Special legislation is necessary.[31] However, a variety of regulatory statutes, such as the Antimonopoly Law and the Trade Association Law, do impose criminal liability on corporate entities, as well as unincorporated associations. Needless to say, the only applicable sanction is a fine.

4. Causation

Influenced largely by German scholarship, Japanese criminal law scholars have introduced and debated several theories of causation.[32] All are premised on a finding that "but for" the act the harm would not have occurred. In other words, the act is a necessary condition of the harm (*conditio sine qua non*). Simple application of this approach—referred to as the "equivalency theory" (*Äquivalenztheorie*)—is rejected by scholars and the courts for lack of a second determination or value judgment about the criminality of the act in terms of both the constituent elements of the crime in question and its societal context. Two closely related approaches prevail. The first, called the "prerequisite" (*jōken*) principle, focuses on the constituent elements of the crime in question in terms of both the illegality of the act and the culpability of the actor. The second, also based on German scholarship, is generally referred to as the "theory of adequate causation" (*Theorie der adäquaten Verursachung*). Theoretical differences do not appear to matter in most cases. The requisite causation may be found to exist under both theories despite intervening actions by other persons or natural occurrences. However, in cases where the harm results from or is aggravated by some preexisting condition of the victim, the adequacy principle would ordinarily require consideration of its foreseeability and frequency of occurrence. In a frequently cited 1967 decision the Supreme Court expressly referred to the adequacy theory and, contrary to the lower courts, found no causation on the ground that the defendant could not possibly have foreseen that his negligence would lead to the victim's death.[33] However, the court did not reverse the judgment of the lower court because the Code provision under which the defendant had been convicted (art. 211) covered causing injury, as well as death through negligence.

In cases where lack of foreseeability would have exonerated the defendant, the courts more frequently impose criminal liability via what scholars view as the application of the prerequisite theory.[34] In so doing, the judges appear to be making a value judgment with respect to culpability, as frequently expressed in other cases, in terms of their view of the "common sense of society" (*shakai tsūnen*).

C. Defenses

1. Types of Defense

Aside from the basic defenses related to the constituent elements of an alleged crime, for example, that the criminal act was not committed or that, even if it was committed, it did not cause the harm, the Code explicitly excludes from criminal liability otherwise proscribed acts on several grounds. They include defenses related to intent, justification, and excuse. Each of the principal defenses in these categories is discussed in the following sections.

2. Burden of Proof

No person may be convicted of a criminal offense under Japanese law unless the prosecution proves "beyond a reasonable doubt" that he or she has committed the alleged offense. Otherwise the defendant must be acquitted. The prosecution must accordingly present evidence to the court that establishes as fact beyond such doubt each and all of the constituent elements of the alleged crime. The standard for establishing facts that are beyond "reasonable doubt," as most recently articulated by the Supreme Court,[35] is relatively expansive. The prosecution need not establish facts beyond any question but only provide evidence that excludes doubt based on "sound social common sense." Since the judges, along with lay assessors in cases of serious offenses (since 2009), are the fact finders, evidence of guilt must be sufficient to convince the judges. Noteworthy too is the provision of article 319(2) of the Code of Criminal Procedure, which precludes conviction solely on the basis of the defendant's confession even if made in open court.

Closely related to the burden of proof are three other features of Japanese law and practice. The first is the continental European law "principle of free evaluation of evidence" (*jiyū shinshō shugi*). This principle, codified in article 318 of the Code of Criminal Procedure, mandates that judges freely determine the credibility and probative value of all evidence. Second, in contrast to purely adversarial proceedings, as finders of fact, judges also have a duty to clarify evidence. Thus, although the burden of proof is on the prosecution, the court may, if necessary, take the initiate to gather and examine evidence. Moreover, as noted in section I.E.1 in this chapter, prosecutors rarely, if ever, prosecute if they have any doubt about the likelihood of conviction.

D. Justifications

1. Necessity

Article 37(1) of the Code exonerates persons who commit criminal acts "unavoidably" in order "to avert a present danger to the life, body, liberty, or property of oneself or any other person." The defense of "urgent avoidance" (*kinkyū hinan*) under the first paragraph of article 37 parallels that of self-defense (see section II.D.2 in this chapter). The coverage of the provision is somewhat broader, however, in that it applies to any "present danger" (*genzai no kinan*), which includes both human actions and natural phenomena, as in the case of a defendant who successfully used the defense where he had illegally destroyed a wooden floodgate to prevent the destruction of his rice seedlings by a flood.[36] The defense also requires a balancing of the affected interests inasmuch as the article explicitly allows the defense only when the injury caused by the otherwise criminal act does not exceed the averted harm. Nor does the defense necessarily apply where the danger arises from the defendant's own culpable conduct. This point was established in a 1924 decision of the Great Court of Cassation in which the defense was denied to a motorist whose reckless driving had forced him to swerve to avoid one accident, only to hit another automobile, killing the driver.[37]

The second paragraph of article 37 precludes the defense of necessity if the actor was subject to a special professional or occupational duty that would require that the defendant bear the risk. Special statutory exemptions have been considered necessary for police and firefighters to allow them the benefit of the defense for injury to persons and property in fulfilling their otherwise protective duties.[38]

2. Self-Defense

The first paragraph of article 36 of the Code similarly exempts otherwise criminal acts "unavoidably" committed "to protect the rights" of the actor or any other person "against imminent and unlawful infringement." The first set of preconditions for the defense of self-defense thus includes an "imminent and unlawful infringement" of the "rights" of the defendant or some other person. The second requirement is that the commission of the act be "reasonable" or "appropriate." The Japanese term *yamu wo enai* is ambivalent in that it translates as "unavoidable" in cases involving "necessity," but for self-defense, it translates as "reasonable" or "appropriate."[39] This provision requires that several conditions be satisfied. The first is that harm to a protected legal interest is threatened. In addition to threats to life and bodily injury, threatened harm to property is at least theoretically included. However, in such cases not only the availability of civil redress for damage to property but also, more significantly, the comparison of the act to the threat and the interest the actor seeks to protect make it difficult to satisfy the requirements of imminence and reasonableness.[40] In general, an "imminent danger" (*kyūhaku no shingai*) is a present risk of harm that necessitates immediate action to prevent the injury from occurring. In turn, the harm may be avoided if future legal redress is available. The defense is also available in cases of threats to third persons.

Under the second paragraph of article 36, an act in excess of these requirements may result in either a reduction of the penalty or full exoneration.

3. Consent/Victim Complaint Required

Except for abortions committed without consent (art. 215), the Code is silent with respect to consent as a defense. The Code explicitly excludes consent as a defense in cases of assisted suicide (art. 202) and abortion with consent, which, needless to say, incurs a lesser penalty than abortion without consent (art. 213). In the case of rape (*gokan*, literally "coerced intercourse") under article 177, consent is an implicit defense if the victim is at least thirteen years of age but not if the victim is younger. Consent in such cases must be free and voluntary, precluding various forms of coercion, manipulation, or misrepresentation to induce consent. Similarly, lack of victim consent is an implicit element for most property and personal injury crimes.

For prosecution of certain crimes, however, the Code requires that the victim lodge a formal complaint, thereby making ongoing consent an effective defense. These crimes include rape (art. 180), criminal breaches of a duty of confidentiality (art. 135), criminal defamation and injury to reputation (art. 232), damage to documents for private use or property (art. 264), and kidnapping (art. 229) unless committed for profit or involving threat to the life or body of the victim. Of note is the proviso to article 229 that if the victim has married the defendant, the effectiveness of the complaint is suspended so long as the marriage remains in effect.

4. Superior Orders

A defense of "superior orders" is recognized under article 35 of the Code, which excludes from criminal liability any act committed in accordance with statutory law or administrative orders or in pursuit of "lawful business activity." In principle, acts committed in the execution of official duties or the exercise of private rights lack the requisite illegality to constitute crimes. However, actions that exceed the legitimate bounds of the public duty or right are considered to constitute an abuse of right (*kenri no ran'yō*) and, if the elements of a crime are established, become subject to criminal sanction. For example, a 1934 Great Court of Cassation decision affirmed the criminal liability of a creditor who improperly threatened to seize flooring and fixtures from a debtor's home if he did not agree to conciliation of the claim. More recently, the Supreme Court disallowed the defense in the well-known case of the *Mainichi* newspaper reporter who in the context of an illicit affair with a Ministry of Foreign Affairs secretary obtained and subsequently disclosed a secret cable related to covert funds Japan paid the United States upon reversion of Okinawa.[41]

E. Excuses

1. Mistake/Ignorance of Law or Fact

As indicated in section II.B.2.i in this chapter, mistake of fact may be a defense to the extent that the defendant is deemed as a result to lack the requisite intent to commit a crime. Mistakes of law have not been considered to constitute a defense for lack of intent under the express provision of article 38(2), although the punishment may be reduced. Casting some doubt on the prevailing view, at least in the context of regulatory crimes, is the Tokyo High Court acquittal of two individual defendants in the 1980 petroleum production restriction case,[42] the first of two related oil cartel decisions. The court reasoned that the reasonableness of the defendants' erroneous belief that their actions were legal precluded their criminal liability. The decision was not appealed, however, leaving the issue unresolved.

2. Insanity/Diminished Capacity

Article 39 of the Code provides that acts of "mentally deranged persons" (*shinshin sōshitsusha*) are not punishable, and those of psychologically enfeebled or "mentally weak persons" (*shinshin mojakusha*) receive reduced punishment. Japanese courts have tended to interpret these terms to exonerate persons found to have diminished cognitive and volitional capacity. Thus the defense of mental abnormality encompasses a wide variety of mental disorders and conditions, not limited to medically recognized mental illnesses. Moreover, the distinction between mental derangement and mental weakness is significant in term of liability. For example, extreme paranoia may be considered mental derangement, but mental retardation is generally treated as mental weakness.

3. Intoxication

Intoxication has long been deemed an exculpating defense in terms of responsibility, as well as a form of mental weakness.[43]

4. Duress

Despite the lack of any explicit provision in the Code, duress is considered a defense if sufficient to preclude intent in terms of free will and culpability.

5. Entrapment

The Code is also silent about entrapment, which is treated as a matter of criminal procedure. At least in the context of narcotics control, the courts have dismissed it as a defense.[44]

F. Sanctions

1. Punishment

Article 9 of the Code lists seven allowable categories of punishment: the death penalty, imprisonment with labor, imprisonment without labor, fines, misdemeanor detention, petty fines, and forfeiture as a supplementary penalty. Only rarely, however, do convicted offenders receive any significant formal punishment. The vast majority of cases involve theft or professional negligence in traffic accidents with uncontested, expedited proceedings that subject offenders to relatively minor fines. The aim, as noted at the outset, is to correct and to reintegrate offenders, not merely to punish them. The police are estimated to fail to report over one-third of all identified offenders in the exercise of their discretion not to report "minor crimes." Similarly, as indicated in section I.E.1 in this chapter, prosecutors suspend prosecution in about one-third of all Code offenses (with significant variation depending on the nature of the offense), and judges routinely suspend sentences overall for nearly 60 percent of those convicted of Code offenses, with similar variation depending on the offense. Moreover, prison terms tend to be relatively short, and parole is common.[45] These well-embedded features of criminal policy and practice combine with relatively low crime rates to allow Japan to enjoy the lowest per capita incarceration rate of any industrial democracy, the Nordic countries included.[46]

2. Quantity/Quality of Punishment

Sentencing is a discretionary duty of the judge, limited by the types and ranges of penalties prescribed by the relevant provisions of the Code. Articles 68 through 71 (chapter 13 of the Code), for example, set out the rules governing the reduction of sentences. These rules are applied in combination with other provisions of the Code. Thus in cases involving homicide, a court imposing the minimum penalty of incarceration for a term of not less than five years under article 199 can, if mitigating circumstances are found, as in the case of a "mentally weak" person, reduce that sentence to a minimum of two and one-half years.

3. Death Penalty

The Code provides for the death penalty (by hanging) for a limited number of serious offenses: those related to sedition and treason, arson, causing a flood to damage an inhabited building, homicide, and cases in which the perpetrator has caused a death in the course of committing another crime, such as robbery. The number of executions decreased steadily during the second half of the twentieth century from an annual average of just over twenty-four in the 1950s to fewer than five in the 1980s. Because four successive ministers of justice either refused or were "unable" to sign the requisite death warrants, no executions occurred from November 1989 to March 1993. Executions resumed in November 1993 with four signed warrants and have increased somewhat since then.

III. SPECIAL PART

A. Structure

Part 2 of the Code currently comprises 209 articles on specific crimes in 40 chapters. One entire chapter (4 articles) on crimes against the emperor and the imperial family (the lèse-majesté provisions) was deleted, as noted in section I.A, under the Allied Occupation. Since 1907 only 10 other articles have been repealed. In contrast, one entirely new chapter (18-2) on computer-related crimes and 27 additional crimes have been added. Each chapter covers a separate category of offenses, beginning with "Crimes Related to Insurrection" in chapter 2 and ending with "Crimes of Construction and Concealment" in chapter 40. Their order of appearance tends to relate to the legislative priority of the protected interests rather than the perceived societal gravity of the offense, with crimes against the state and state-related interests preceding those involving persons, property, and other private interests. The specific articles rarely, if ever, define a crime but instead merely prescribe the penalties and their allowable range for persons who commit the specified "act." For example, persons who "give, offer or promise to give" bribes are to be punished by imprisonment with labor for not more than three years or a fine of not more than 2.5 million yen (art. 198). The definition of "bribery" and what constitutes the acts "giving, offering or promising" are left to be resolved by a combination of generally accepted scholarly theory and judicial construction. As noted in section I.D.1, special regulatory statutes add to the number of specific crimes. All, of course, are subject to the requirements of the general provisions (part 1) of the Code.

B. Homicide

1. Murder/Manslaughter

Chapter 26 of the Code contains four articles on crimes of homicide (*satsujin no tsumi*). The first provides that a person who "kills" another is to be punished by the death penalty or imprisonment with labor for a period of not less than five years. What constitutes the crime of "killing" under article 199 is resolved, as in other instances, by a combination of prevailing scholarly theory and judicial construction. The criminal act is the intentional taking of the life of another natural person by whatever means. Of note is the exclusion of suicide. Under article 202, "killing" a person at his or her request or with consent also constitutes the crime of homicide with a lesser penalty of imprisonment with or without labor for a period of not less than six months but not more than seven years, applicable also for the crime of "inducing or aiding" a person to commit suicide.

Article 201 and 203 include preparing to commit homicide and attempted homicide as criminal offenses with considerably lighter penalties. (The penalty for attempted homicide is left to the discretion of the court.)

Japan has one of the lowest per capita rates of homicide in the world. In 2007, for example, only 1,309 cases of homicide were reported.[47] As is the case with most violent crimes, the number of reported homicides has decreased almost steadily since 1955. In that year 3,269 homicides were reported, the highest number of reported homicides in modern Japanese history.[48]

2. Provocation

The Code does not provide for a specific defense of provocation in the case of homicide or any other crime. A defense of "provocation" is available only to the extent that the actions of the victim, as well as the offender, satisfy the previously discussed requirements for either self-defense under article 36 or averting danger under article 37 of the Code.

C. Sex Offenses

The Code in chapter 22 (arts. 174–184) subjects nine sexually related acts to criminal penalties. The most serious are rape (art. 177), forcible indecency (art. 176), and gang rape (art. 178-2). Also included are the crimes of public indecency (art. 174), bigamy (art. 184), as well as distribution, sale, or display of pornographic objects and material (art. 175). In addition, article 181 sets out the penalties in cases where the rape or forcible indecency resulted in the death of the victim. Article 178 provides separately for cases where an indecent act or sexual intercourse occurs in cases where the offender has taken advantage of the inability of the victim to resist because of a loss of consciousness or other circumstances. The crime of forcible indecency requires the use of some degree of force for the purpose of satisfying a sexual desire against the will of another person.[49] For rape, commencement is sufficient. Actual penetration is not a requirement. With respect to commencement, forcible assault with the intent to have sexual intercourse has been held sufficient.[50]

The offenses also tend to be gender specific. Article 176 subjects to criminal penalties persons who forcibly commit an "indecent act" on either a male or female. Under article 177, however, the victim of rape must be female, although persons of either gender may be offenders.[51]

In 2006 only 1,948 cases of rape and 8,326 cases of forcible indecency were reported. The highest number of reported rape cases in postwar Japan within a five-year period occurred in 1965 (8,444).[52]

D. Theft, Embezzlement, Robbery, and Fraud

The most frequently committed Criminal Code offenses are property crimes. In 2006 over half of all Criminal Code offenses involved theft (*settō*, sometimes translated as "larceny").[53] Fraud and embezzlement are also among the most frequently committed Criminal Code offenses, surpassed only by "professional" negligence in traffic accidents (discussed in section III.F in this chapter) and criminal vandalism or "malicious mischief" causing damage to household and other miscellaneous objects (*kibutsu*). The relevant provisions of the Code are found in chapter 36 (arts. 235–245) on theft and robbery and chapter 37 on fraud and extortion (arts. 246–255).

Both theft and robbery involve the unlawful taking of property of another person, but robbery requires assault or intimidation. Although early judicial decisions required ownership of the property in question,[54] more recent decisions have construed the crime of theft (and presumably robbery as well) to include property in the possession of the victim, even where such possession was prohibited by law.[55] Article 235-2 (added by Law No. 83, 1960) makes the unlawful possession of the real property of another a separate crime.

Embezzlement is the intentional misappropriation of property in one's possession, thereby infringing the property rights of another. It can be viewed as either a violation of trust and good faith or merely as unlawful appropriation of property entrusted to the offender.

E. "Victimless" Crimes

Aside from various safety regulations and occupational licensing requirements backed by criminal sanctions, the principal "victimless" crimes in Japan relate to the sale, possession, and use of narcotics under the Narcotics Control Law.[56] Under the Code, gambling and sale of lottery tickets (arts. 185–187) and, as noted in section III.C in this chapter, the distribution, sale, or display of pornography (art. 175) are also prohibited, although these provisions are rarely enforced. In a consistent line of cases beginning with a 1957 decision upholding the criminal conviction of a prominent publisher and novelist for translation and publication of D. H. Lawrence's *Lady Chatterley's Lover*,[57] the Supreme Court has held that the guarantee of freedom of expression in article 21 of the 1947 constitution does not apply to criminal obscenity.[58]

F. Crimes of Negligence

Japanese criminal law is noteworthy for subjecting a wide variety of negligent conduct to criminal as well as civil liability. In addition to special regulatory statutes, as well as particular

Code provisions, the Code includes three articles (in chapter 28) that impose criminal sanctions for a broad scope of negligent misconduct. Article 209, "Causing Injury through Negligence," imposes a criminal fine of not more than 300,000 yen in cases of personal injury caused by negligence (but only upon complaint). Article 210, "Causing Death through Negligence," increases the criminal fine to a maximum of 500,000 yen in cases involving wrongful death. Finally, article 211, "Causing Death or Injury through Negligence in the Pursuit of Occupational Activities," provides in the first paragraph that anyone "who fails to exercise due care required in the pursuit of their occupational activities and thereby causes the death or injury of another shall be punished by imprisonment with or without labor for not more than 5 years or a fine of not more than 1,000,000 yen." The penalty also applies to a person "who through gross negligence causes the death or injury of another." The second paragraph of article 211 additionally subjects anyone who "fails to exercise due care required in driving a vehicle and thereby causes the death or injury of another" to "imprisonment with or without labor for not more than 7 years or a fine of not more than 1,000,000 yen." A provision allows impunity of a minor in "light of [extenuating] circumstances." The standards for negligence are the same for the purposes of both criminal and civil liability, with a higher duty of care required for activities with the greatest risks to health and safety.

Crimes under these categories—especially those under article 211(2) arising from traffic accidents—account annually for over two-thirds of all reported Code offenses. Prosecution is suspended in the vast majority of cases (84 percent in 2007).[59] Over half of the remaining cases are prosecuted in uncontested expedited proceedings, with a minor fine as the maximum penalty. In the vast majority of cases, the offenders pay agreed-on reparations to any victims, who in return indicate to the authorities, in effect, their pardon of the offender. The prosecution is thereupon suspended. This use of the threat of criminal liability is thus used effectively to ensure victim compensation. Less than 1 percent of these cases are formally prosecuted in regular public trial proceedings. Although the number of cases remains small, the provision for criminal liability for occupational negligence under article 211(1) has been used in an increasing number of medical malpractice cases. Coupled with the legal duty of physicians to report any "unnatural death" under article 21 of the Medical Practitioners [Physicians] Law,[60] these cases raise the issue of self-incrimination under article 38(1) of the 1947 constitution. The Supreme Court has upheld the reporting requirement against such challenges.[61]

SELECTED BIBLIOGRAPHY

Dando Shigemitsu. *The Criminal Law of Japan: The General Part*. Trans. B. J. George. Littleton, CO: Fred Rothman Co., 1997.

Maeda Masahide. *Keihō Kakuron Kōgi* [Lectures on Particular Principles of Criminal Law]. Tokyo: University of Tokyo Press, 1989.

Maeda Masahide. *Keihō Sōron Kōgi* [Lectures on General Principles of Criminal Law]. Tokyo: University of Tokyo Press, 1989.

Nishida Noriyuki, Yamaguchi Atsushi, and Saeki Hitoshi, eds. *Hanrei Keihō Kakuron* [Judicial Precedents on the Special Part of the Criminal Code]. Tokyo:Yūhikaku, 2006.

Nishida Noriyuki, Yamaguchi Atsushi, and Saeki Hitoshi, eds. *Hanrei Keihō Sōron* [Judicial Precedents on the General Part of the Criminal Code]. Tokyo: Yūhikaku, 2002.

Ōtsuka Hitoshi and Kawabata Hiroshi, eds. *Shin-Hanrei Konmentaru: Keihō* [New Judicial Precedents Commentary: Criminal Law]. 6 vols. Tokyo: Sanseidō, 1996.

Ōtsuka Hitoshi, Kawakami Kazuo, Satō Fumiya, and Furuta Yūki, eds. *Dai Konmentaru Keihō* [Great Criminal Law Commentary]. 13 vols. and supplement. 2d ed. Tokyo: Seirin Shoin, 1999–2006.

Tanaka, Hideo. *The Japanese Legal System*. Tokyo: University of Tokyo Press, 1976.

Zong Uk Tjong and Paul Eubel. "Strafrecht." In Paul Eubel, ed., *Das japanische Rechtssystem*. Frankfurt am Main: Alfred Metzner Verlag, 1979, 205–254.

NOTES

1. *Keihō* (Law No. 45, 1907).
2. *Keiji Soshō Hō* (Law No. 131, 1948).
3. *Meirei no Jōkō Ihan ni kansuru Keibatsu no Ken* [Cases of Criminal Punishment for Violations of the Provisions of Administrative Orders] (Law No. 84, 1890).
4. See, e.g., Satō v. Japan, 16 *(Taihan) Keishū* 193 (Gr. Ct. Cass., Dec. 3, 1936).
5. Oda v. Japan, 6 *Keishū* 1346 (Sup. Ct., G.B., Dec. 24, 1952).
6. Japan v. Saitō, 10 *Keishū* 921 (Sup. Ct., G.B., June 27, 1956), partially translated in *The Japanese Legal System* (Tokyo: University of Tokyo Press, 1976), 99–102.
7. Arai v. Japan, 37 *Keishū* 1538 (Sup. Ct., 1st P.B., Nov. 24, 1983).
8. Fujimura v. Japan, 9 *Daihan Keiroku* 874 (Gr. Ct. Cass., May 21, 1903), partially translated in Hideo Tanaka, *The Japanese Legal System* (Tokyo: University of Tokyo Press, 1976), 105–106. With this case in mind, the drafters of the 1907 Code expressly provided in article 245 that electricity constitutes property.
9. Egawa v. Japan, 19 *Daihan Keishū* 540 (Gr. Ct. Cass., Aug. 22, 1940), partially translated in Hideo Tanaka, *The Japanese Legal System* (Tokyo: University of Tokyo Press, 1976), 106–107.
10. See Richard B. Appleton, "Reforms in Japanese Criminal Procedures under Allied Occupation," 24 *Washington Law Review* (1949), 401–430.
11. See David T. Johnson, *The Japanese Way of Justice: Prosecuting Crime in Japan* (Oxford: Oxford University Press, 2002), 97–98.
12. *Baishin Hō* [Jury Law] (Law No. 50, 1923)
13. *Chokurei* [Imperial Order] No. 165, 1928.
14. *Baishin Hō no Teishi ni kansuru Hōritsu* [Law Concerning the Suspension of the Jury Law] (Law No. 88, 1943).
15. See Office of the Prime Minister of Japan, http://www.kantei.go.jp/foreign/judiciary/2001/0612report.html (accessed May 17, 2010).
16. *Saiban'in no Sanka suru Keijisaiban ni kansuru Hōritsu* [Law Concerning the Participation of Lay Assessors in Criminal Trials] (Law No. 63, 2004).
17. Research and Training Institute, Ministry of Justice, Japan, *White Paper on Crime 2004* (Tokyo: Ministry of Justice, 2004). White Papers on Crime available at Mnistry of Justice of Japan, http://hakusyo1.moj.go.jp/en/53/nfm/mokuji.html.

18. See Dando, *Criminal Law of Japan*, 61.

19. X v. Japan, 24 *Keiroku* 1558 (Gr. Ct. Cass., Dec. 18, 1932).

20. Akagawa v. Japan, 17 *Daihan Keishū* 237 (Gr. Ct. Cass., Mar. 11, 1938). See also Yoshida v. Japan, 12 *Keishū* 2882 (Sup. Ct., G.B., Sept. 9, 1958).

21. Aizawa v. Japan, 27 *Keishū* 256 (Sup. Ct., G.B., April 4, 1973). The provision was finally repealed in 1995 (Law No. 91).

22. *Kōsai Keiji Saiban Tokuhō* (No. 230) 984 (Takamatsu High Ct., Oct. 16, 1956), cited in Dando, *Criminal Law of Japan*, 151.

23. See Yoshida v. Japan, 35 *Keishū* 911 (Sup. Ct., 1st P.B., Dec. 21, 1981); Konishi v. Japan, 38 *Keishū* 1961 (Sup. Ct., 3rd P.B., Mar. 6, 1984).

24. Dando, *Criminal Law of Japan*, 159.

25. Koretomo v. Japan, 4 *Keishū* 1261 (Sup. Ct., 2nd P.B., July 11, 1950).

26. Umemura v. Japan, 13 *Daihan Keishū* 1473 (Gr. Ct. Cass., Oct. 19, 1934).

27. Sumiyoshi v. Japan, 4 *Keishū* 1096 (Sup. Ct., 3rd P.B., June 17, 1950).

28. Akagawa v. Japan, 17 *Daihan Keishū* 788 (Gr. Ct. Cass., Oct. 28, 1938).

29. See Terazaki v. Japan, 7 *Keishū* 510 (Sup. Ct., 1st P.B., Mar. 5, 1953).

30. Ishigaki v. Japan, 23 *Daihan Keiroku* 789 (Gr. Ct. Cass., July 5, 1917).

31. See Shōwa Kinyū K.K. v. Japan, 14 *Keishū* 1217 (Gr. Ct. Cass., Nov. 25, 1935).

32. For fuller discussion in English, see Dando, *Criminal Law of Japan*, 62–70.

33. Furorini [in katakana] v. Japan, 21 *Keishū* 1116 (Sup. Ct., 3rd P.B., Oct. 24, 1967).

34. See, e.g., Dando, *Criminal Law of Japan*, 67.

35. Tōjō v. Japan, 61 *Keishū* 677 (Sup. Ct., 1st P.B., Oct. 16, 2007).

36. Munemura v. Japan, 12 *Daihan Keishū* 2160 (Gr. Ct. Cass., Nov. 30, 1933).

37. See X v. Japan, 3 *Daihan Keishū* 867 (Gr. Ct. Cass., Dec. 12, 1924).

38. See, e.g., article 7 (on use of weapons) of the *Keisatsukan Shokumu Shikkō Hō* [Police Duties Law] (Law No. 136, 1948), translated in Dando, *Criminal Law of Japan*, 117 n. 138.

39. See Kobayashi v. Japan, 23 *Keishū* 1573 (Sup. Ct., Dec. 4, 1969).

40. See Matsue v. Japan, 13 *Kōsai Keishū* 240 (Osaka High Ct., Mar. 30, 1960), rejecting the defense of necessity in a case involving criminal prosecution for damage to a building.

41. Nishiyama v. Japan, 32 *Keishū* 457 (Sup. Ct., 1st P.B., May 31, 1978).

42. Japan v. Seikyu Renmei et al. *Hanrei Jihō* (No. 983) 22 (Tokyo High Ct., Sept. 26, 1980). For comment and translation of the official summary of the case, see J. Mark Ramseyer, "The Oil Cartel Criminal Cases: Translations and Postscript," 15 *Law in Japan: An Annual* 57 (1982).

43. See, e.g., Tamabashi v. Japan, *Hōritsu Shinbun* (No. 3320) 4 (Tokyo Ct. App., Sept. 22, 1931).

44. See Shin v. Japan 7 *Keishū* 482 (Sup. Ct., 1st P.B., Mar. 5, 1953).

45. See generally Elmer H. Johnson and Carol H. Johnson, *Linking Community and Corrections in Japan* (Carbondale: Southern Illinois University Press, 2000), esp. pp. 63–116 on adult probation and parole.

46. King's College London, World Prison Brief, http://www.kcl.ac.uk/depsta/law/research/icps/worldbrief/wpb_stats.php (accessed May 17, 2010).

47. Hōmusho [Ministry of Justice], *Heisei 19 Nenkan Hanzi Hakusho* [2007 White Paper on Crime] (Tokyo: Saeki Insatsu K.K., 2007), 5; also available at Ministry of Justice of Japan, http://www.moj.go.jp/HOUSO/2007/hk1_2.pdf (accessed Aug. 13, 2008).

48. From data from 1910 through 2007 collected from Ministry of Justice white papers on crime.

49. See Yokobi v. Japan, 24 *Keishū* 1 (Sup. Ct., Jan. 29, 1970).

50. Tajima v. Japan, 7 *Keishū* 529 (Sup. Ct., 2nd P.B., Mar. 13, 1953). See also Mitsunari v. Japan, 24 *Keishū* 585 (Sup. Ct., 3rd P.B., July 28, 1970).

51. Misawa v. Japan, 19 *Keishū* 125 (Sup. Ct., 3rd P.B., Mar. 30, 1965). The case involved a man and a woman as coprincipals. Both were convicted. The woman appealed on the basis that the crime of rape could not be committed by a woman. The court ruled otherwise.

52. From data between 1910 and 2007 collected from Ministry of Justice white papers on crime.

53. A total of 1,534,528 cases of theft were reported out of the total of 2,877,027 Criminal Code offenses. 2007 White Paper on Crime, 5.

54. See, e.g., Murata v. Japan, 24 *Daihan Keiroku* 121 (Gr. Ct. Cass., Sept. 25, 1919).

55. See Matsumoto v. Japan 5 *Keishū* 1744 (Sup. Ct., 1st P.B., Aug. 9, 1951)

56. *Kakuseizai Torishimari Hō* (Law No. 252, 1951).

57. Koyama v. Japan, 11 *Keishū* 997 (Sup. Ct., G.B. Mar. 13, 1957), translated in John M. Maki, *Court and Constitution in Japan* (Seattle: University of Washington Press, 1964), 3–37.

58. See, in English, Lawrence Ward Beer, *Freedom of Expression in Japan: A Study in Comparative Law, Politics, and Society* (Tokyo: Kodansha International, 1984), 335–361.

59. Hōmusho [Ministry of Justice], *2007 White Paper on Crime*, 10.

60. *Ishi Hō* (Law No. 201, 1948).

61. See, e,g., Okai v. Japan, 58 *Keishū* 247 (Sup. Ct., 3rd P. B., April 13, 2004). For an English translation, see Supreme Court of Japan, http://www.courts.go.jp/english/judgments/text/2004.04.13-2003-A-No.1560.html (accessed May, 17, 2010).

RUSSIA

Stephen C. Thaman

I. Introduction
   A. Historical Sketch
   B. Jurisdiction
   C. Legality Principle
   D. Sources of Criminal Law
   E. Process

II. General Part
   A. Theories of Punishment
   B. Liability Requirements
   C. Defenses
   D. Justifications
   E. Excuses
   F. Sanctions

III. Special Part
   A. Structure
   B. Homicide
   C. Sex Offenses
   D. Theft and Fraud
   E. "Victimless" Crimes: Drug and Narcotics Offenses
   F. Other Offenses

Stephen C. Thaman is Professor of Law at Saint Louis University. His recent publications include *Comparative Criminal Procedure: A Casebook Approach* (Carolina Academic Press, 2d ed. 2008), and "The Two Faces of Justice in the Post-Soviet Legal Sphere: Adversarial Procedure, Jury Trial, Plea-Bargaining and the Inquisitorial Legacy," in John Jackson, Máximo Langer, and Peter Tillers (eds.), *Crime, Procedure and Evidence in Comparative and International Context: Essays in Honour of Professor Mirjan Damaska* (2008).

I. INTRODUCTION

A. Historical Sketch

The earliest evidence of Russian criminal law is found in the eleventh-century Russkaia Pravda (Russian truth), which provides rules for compensation for harm caused by wrongful conduct that would today be classified as criminal. With Moscovy's Ulozhenie of 1649, one can see a more imperial, inquisitorial cast to criminal law and procedure, with an emphasis on crimes against the church and state and the heavy use of torture and death penalties.[1] By 1832 the Russian Digest of Laws included the first modern notion of a crime as an "act in breach of the law," but this and the later 1845 code still gave priority to crimes against the state and state property over crimes against the individual and private property. The judicial reforms of Alexander II in 1864, which led to the introduction of jury trial, adversarial procedure, and an independent judiciary and bar, were not nearly as successful in the area of substantive criminal law, largely because of attempts on the life of Alexander II, which were eventually successful.[2]

The Bolshevik Revolution in 1917 eventually led to the abolition of all prerevolution criminal law, which was replaced with decrees and "socialist legal consciousness." In 1919 Soviet law simply defined crime as "any act or omission dangerous to the given system of social relations." The concept of crime as socially dangerous activity proved to be long lived. The Criminal Code that followed in 1922 allowed for punishment based on undefined socially dangerous acts that were analogous to those listed in the code. Under the subsequent 1926 code a finding of "social dangerousness" replaced any finding of individual guilt or blameworthiness, and "social protective measures" replaced retributive punishment as the goal of the criminal law. An offense whose elements were provable could be dismissed or not charged if the crime (or the criminal) was not, or was no longer, socially dangerous.[3]

The 1960 Criminal Code of the Russian Socialist Federated Soviet Republic (UK-1960) replaced the 1926 code. It abolished the use of analogy but failed to comply with international human rights standards by punishing religious and political dissidents and entrepreneurs for, inter alia, "anti-Soviet agitation and propaganda," "parasitism," "hooliganism," and any economic entrepreneurial activity. Crimes against the state and state property still had priority over those against individual rights.[4]

After the collapse of the Soviet Union in December 1991, the 1960 code was subjected to thoroughgoing amendments, including the elimination of the section protecting socialist property. A new constitution, the Constitution of the Russian Federation (hereafter Const. RF), was passed by referendum in December 1993 that largely brought Russia into line with international standards in the area of human rights as they affect criminal law and procedure. Finally, the new Criminal Code of the Russian Republic (UK) was adopted in June 1996 and went into effect in 1997.[5]

The UK was amended by 65 different laws from May 27, 1998, through February 13, 2009. The most comprehensive reforms were signed into law by President Vladimir Putin on December 8, 2003, which added 26 new articles and amended some 250 sections.

B. Jurisdiction

Pursuant to section 11, the UK asserts jurisdiction according to the territorial principle over all crimes committed on Russian territory, airspace, waters, continental shelf, exclusive economic zones, or Russian flagships. Pursuant to the active-personality principle, Russian law also exercises jurisdiction in cases where a Russian citizen (or permanent resident) commits a crime abroad that violates interests protected by the code and the person has not been punished according to the law of the state in whose territory the crime was committed (s. 12(1)). Russian law also recognizes the passive-personality principle and exercises jurisdiction when a foreigner commits a crime against a Russian citizen or against "the interests of the Russian Federation [RF]" (s. 12(3)).

C. Legality Principle

In Russia the criminal nature of an act and its punishability are determined exclusively by the UK, and the use of analogy is specifically prohibited (s. 3). A law criminalizing conduct must be in force at the time the criminal act is committed (Art. 54 Const., s. 9), but statutes that decriminalize an act or reduce the threatened punishment have retroactive force (s. 10). A crime is defined as a "socially dangerous act" made punishable by the UK (s. 14(1)), and even if the act committed contains all the elements of a crime, it is not deemed to be criminal if it presents no danger to society (s. 14(2)). This substantive "concrete" approach to crime is a vestige of the Soviet approach to criminal law, which still enjoys strong support in Russia.

Russian law, therefore, nearly always requires that concrete harm result before criminal liability is imposed, or that, minimally, a situation of concrete endangerment to life, human health, or property has been created. Rarely in the UK does one find the prohibition of conduct that only theoretically affects protected legal interests. This lack of abstract endangerment offenses thus places a substantial burden on criminal investigators to prove the harmful consequences of wrongful conduct and guilty *mens rea* in relation thereto, arguably making them more susceptible to corruption.[6]

The principle of legality in European criminal procedure is also meant to limit prosecutorial discretion in charging provable crimes. Russian law provides that "in each case of uncovering of the elements of a crime" all law-enforcement officials will "take measures provided in this Code to establish the facts of the crime and to discover the person or persons guilty of the commission of the crime" (s. 21(2) Ugolovno-protsessual'nyy kodeks Rossiyskoy Federatsii [UPK]). The requirement of social dangerousness, however, gives the prosecutor some discretion not to charge clearly provable criminal conduct, which would seem to undermine the legality principle (or principle of mandatory prosecution).

D. Sources of Criminal Law

1. Legislature

The UK is the sole statutory source of criminal law in Russia, and any new criminal laws, provisions, or amendments must be included therein (s. 1(1)). However, some sections of the UK dealing with public health and welfare offenses criminalize the violation of provisions contained in noncriminal legislation.

2. Judiciary

According to article 126 Const. RF, the Supreme Court of the Russian Federation (SCRF) is the highest judicial organ in criminal cases and gives "explanations" (*raz"iasneniia*, hereafter SCRF-Expl.) relating to judicial practice in criminal cases, which are binding on the lower courts. It is disputed whether these explanations are exercises of statutory interpretation or independent normative sources of law.[7] The SCRF also periodically publishes summaries of decisions in individual cases that are not considered as precedent. They are published regularly in the SCRF's monthly bulletin (*Biulleten' Verkhovnogo Suda Rossiyskoy Federatsii*, hereafter SCRF Bulletin).

The Constitutional Court of the Russian Federation (CCRF) was established in 1991 and was intended to be the ultimate arbiter of the constitutionality of Russian legislation, but in October 1995 the SCRF issued an opinion claiming that the lower courts and the SCRF had independent power to examine the constitutionality of legislation without referring the issue to the CCRF (SCRF-Expl.: Constitutional Application).[8] Thus a bifurcated system has developed, with the CCRF and the SCRF acting as parallel arbiters of the constitutionality of statutes.

3. Executive

The violation of certain executive (administrative) regulations can constitute an element of one of the public health and safety crimes in the Special Part of the UK.

4. Scholars

There is a plethora of scholarly treatises on the criminal law used in Russian law schools and commentaries on the UK produced by well-known criminal law scholars, often associated with particular law faculties, legal institutes, or even the SCRF. However, the SCRF and CCRF seldom, if ever, mention scholarly writings as authorities in their opinions or explanations, so it is difficult to assess the actual influence of Russia's scholarly output.

E. Process

1. Adversarial/Inquisitorial

Soviet criminal procedure was mixed, characterized by an inquisitorial, secret preliminary investigation, supervised by a legally trained investigative official, and a public trial, dominated by a judge with inquisitorial powers who sat with two lay assessors, who were known for their lack of independence, thus earning them the nickname "nodders." The judge questioned all the witnesses, could introduce evidence *sua sponte*, and could also remand a case to the investigative stage to avoid an acquittal. Acquittals were thus virtually nonexistent.

Reforms were initiated during Mikhail Gorbachev's *perestroyka* but bore fruit during the presidency of Boris N. Yeltsin with the passage of a jury law and a new constitution in 1993 that guaranteed adversarial procedure and equality of arms[9] (art. 123(3)), the right to jury trial (art. 123(4)), the presumption of innocence (art. 49), the right to remain silent (art. 51(1)), and the exclusion of evidence gathered in violation of the law or the constitution (art. 50(2)).[10] These positive reforms were finally codified in the new UPK of 2001. The UPK also introduced a type of guilty plea, actually more like a plea of *nolo contendere*, in which the accused expresses his or her "agreement with the charges." If this plea is accepted (the public prosecutor and the victim have a veto, which thus opens the door for plea bargaining), the judge may sentence the accused to no more than two-thirds of the maximum term. The procedure originally applied to charges punishable by up to five years' deprivation of liberty, but the law was amended in 2003 to extend the new procedure to crimes punishable by up to ten years' deprivation of liberty.[11] A federal law was passed on June 29, 2009, which amended the UK and added a new chapter to the UPK (chapter 40.1) to allow for "pretrial co-operation agreements" between the prosecution and defense, which can lead to dismissal of the defendant's charges if the defendant aids the prosecution in solving more serious cases (arts. 317.1–317.9 UPK).

2. Jury/Written Opinions

Jury trial is available for aggravated murder cases and select other serious felonies. The jury court consists of twelve jurors presided over by one professional judge. The jury verdict is made up of a special verdict consisting of a list of questions. The three main questions ask whether the crime was committed, whether the defendant was the perpetrator, and whether he or she was guilty of its perpetration. Questions also may deal with justifications, excuses, and aggravating and mitigating circumstances. A simple majority of seven of the twelve jurors is required to prove a fact disadvantageous to the defendant. Jury acquittals are appealable. Once the jury answers the questions in the special verdict, the professional judge must issue a written judgment giving reasons for the legal qualification of the acts found proved by the jury and is theoretically bound by the answers given in the jury's special verdict. Such reasons are required in nonjury cases as well.

The jury law requires that the judge instruct the jury on the substantive criminal law before it decides the guilt question. The fact that the jury can affirmatively answer that the defendant committed acts fulfilling all the statutory elements of the crime, but return a verdict of not guilty, also seems to affirm the Russian jury's power to nullify the law, a power that was unquestioned in the prerevolution jury court.

But the SCRF has undermined the jury's role in deciding guilt in two ways. First, it has interpreted the finding of "guilt" to be limited to whether the defendant committed a series of acts, thus leaving to the professional judge the decision whether those facts constitute the charged crime. The SCRF has also decided that the mental element of a crime, *mens rea*, is a "legal question" that falls to the judge, not the jury, to decide. Thus it is the judge, not the jury, who determines whether the defendant acted intentionally, recklessly, or under heat of passion. In addition, virtually uncontrolled powers of review exercised by the SCRF allow it to overturn any decision it does not like, including the majority of all acquittals. As a result, the jury's right to nullify the law has effectively been nullified by the SCRF's interpretation of the jury law.[12]

When a jury does convict, the jurors may make a finding of "lenience," which eliminates the death penalty, prevents the judge from sentencing to more than two-thirds of the maximum punishment (s. 65), and can even lead to a sentence to less than the minimum under "extraordinary circumstances."

II. GENERAL PART

A. Theories of Punishment

The UK lists as its goals "the protection from criminal infringements of the rights and freedoms of the human being and citizen, property, social order and social security, the environment, the constitutional structure of the RF, and the guarantee of peace and security of humanity, as well as the deterrence of crimes" (s. 2(1)).

Punishment is imposed in Russia in order to "restore social justice" and to "correct the convicted person and prevent the commission of new crimes" (s. 43(2)). This is a departure from the UK-1960, which emphasized retribution as the primary goal of criminal punishment. The UK dispenses with the socialist goal of reeducation and does not differentiate between general and special deterrence. Punishment must be "just" in the sense that it is "proportional to the character and level of social dangerousness of the crime, the circumstances of its commission and the personal characteristics of the guilty person" (s. 6(1)). The code also proclaims a "principle of humanism," aimed at preventing "the infliction of physical suffering or the denigration of human dignity" (s. 7). This "humanism" is reflected in the fact that there is now a presumption that the least restrictive punishment must be imposed unless the goals of punishment cannot be achieved without meting out a more severe punishment (s. 60(1)).

B. Liability Requirements

1. *Objective*/Actus Reus
   i. Act

The basis for criminal liability in Russia is the "commission of an act containing all the elements of the criminal offense" (s. 8). More specifically, it must be a "guiltily committed socially dangerous act" prohibited by the code (s. 14(1)). An act containing all the elements of a criminal offense, however, is still not a "crime" if it is *de minimis* and does not present any danger to society (s. 14(2)). There is a dispute in the legal literature whether social dangerousness is an additional "element" of the crime that must be proved by the prosecution, or whether all acts criminalized in the UK are per se "socially dangerous," and *de minimis* crimes should be treated like decriminalized administrative violations. The modern notion of "social dangerousness" limits the reach of the penal law, whereas the early Soviet approach, coupled with the use of analogy, expanded its scope.[13]

   ii. Omission

Russian law punishes socially dangerous omissions (s. 5(1)). Some crimes may be committed only by omission, such as the failure of a ship's captain to come to the rescue of persons in danger (s. 270). The UK limits liability for omissions, unless otherwise provided by law, to cases where the suspect has a familial, contractual, or other duty to render aid. For instance, the knowing failure to help a person "in a situation dangerous to life or health and deprived of the possibility of taking measures of self-preservation" is punishable only if the defendant's acts placed the person in the situation or he or she had a duty to help (s. 125). This is a departure from both Soviet law (s. 127 UK-1960) and the 1845 tsarist code, which required citizens to aid those in need if they could do so "without serious danger to the accused or others." This elimination of a venerable "Good Samaritan" tradition is likely a reflection of the move from a social welfare state ideology to laissez-faire capitalism.

iii. Status

Because an act or omission is required, status punishment is not permitted under the UK.

2. Subjective/Mens Rea/Mental Element

The UK firmly establishes the principle of "guilt" as the subjective side of the crime. All forms of *mens rea* in Russia are conceived in relation to the social dangerousness of the *actus reus* and result elements of the crime. Today the focus of "guilt" is psychological, rather than the ideologically laden ethical or sociopolitical content that prevailed in socialist times and facilitated the repression of innocent persons.[14]

i. Intent

For a person to be guilty of a crime in Russia, the act must have been committed either intentionally or "through carelessness" (*po neostorozhnosti*) (s. 24(1)). "Intentional" crimes may be committed with either "direct intent" or "indirect intent" (s. 25(1)). Direct intent is proved "if the person recognized the social dangerousness of his or her acts (omissions), foresaw the possibility or inevitability of the occurrence of the socially dangerous result and desired its occurrence" (s. 25(2)).

ii. Recklessness

Indirect intent, on the other hand, is proved "if the person recognized the social dangerousness of his acts (omissions), foresaw the possibility of the occurrence of the socially dangerous result, did not desire, but consciously allowed for this result or was indifferent to it" (s. 25(3)). This mental state is similar to "recklessness" as understood in U.S. law, although in section 2.02(2)(c) of the Model Penal Code (MPC) the risk must be "substantial and unjustifiable" and relate to the mere presence of an element of the crime, and not to the broader notion of "social dangerousness."

iii. Negligence

Carelessness may be the subjective basis for guilt only if this is specifically provided in the Special Part of the code (s. 24(2)). Only five offenses explicitly allow for a finding of guilt based on carelessness, the most prominent of which is the "careless causing of death" (s. 109). The law distinguishes between two types of carelessness. The more egregious type borders on recklessness and could be translated as "thoughtlessness" (*legkomyslie*), where "the person foresaw the possibility of the occurrence of a socially dangerous result of his acts (omissions), but without sufficient reason, arrogantly calculated that he could prevent these results" (s. 26(2)). The second type of carelessness (*po nebrezhnosti*) can be translated as "negligence" and exists "if the person did not foresee the possibility of the occurrence of the socially dangerous result of his acts (omissions), but with necessary care and prudence should have and could have foreseen these results" (s. 26(3)).

Russian law subjectivizes the standard for "negligent" crimes more than most U.S. jurisdictions by providing that the actor is not guilty if he or she "did not recognize and under the circumstances of the case could not have recognized the social dangerousness of his acts (omissions) or did not foresee the possibility of the occurrence of a socially dangerous result and under the circumstances of the case neither should nor could have foreseen it" (s. 28(1)). A similar subjectivization occurs in relation to "thoughtless" crimes.

Reflecting the UK's focus on social dangerousness, most crimes in the UK require a harm, a loss, or a specified grave result, often laid out in a sequence of aggravating factors rising from the least serious result to the most serious. In such cases the UK requires "two forms of guilt" (s. 27), that is, a guilty *mens rea* in relation to the act (omission) and one in relation to the result. The defendant must act in a "careless" manner in relation to the result for it to be proved. There is thus no strict liability for results caused by criminal conduct. If a result element does not allow explicitly for a finding of guilt based on "carelessness," then the defendant must have acted with either direct or indirect intent.

3. *Theories of Liability*
   i. Inchoate Crimes
      a. *Preparation and Attempt*

Inchoate or "incomplete" crimes in Russia are separated into those of preparation and attempt (s. 29(2)). "Preparation," which is punishable only in relation to grave or especially grave crimes, consists in "looking for, preparing or adapting the means or weapon to commit the crime, looking for co-participants in the crime, conspiring to commit the crime or in any other intentional creation of the conditions for the commission of the crime, if the crime was not completed due to circumstances independent of the will of the actor" (s. 30(1, 2)). A "preparatory" act must be something more than an act that merely reveals the actor's criminal intent; that is, it must be socially dangerous in itself.

"Attempt," on the other hand, is described as an "intentional act (omission) of a person, directly aimed at the commission of the crime, if the crime was not completed due to circumstances independent of this person" (s. 30(3)). In comparison with preparation, an attempt constitutes an enhanced state of social dangerousness because the actor has begun to create a substantive danger that the crime will be carried out. For an act to be an attempt, one must have taken a step in the commission of the *actus reus* of the crime. For instance, if one enters a building with intent to commit a "secret theft" (*krazha*), one has already engaged in the commission of the "secret" aspect of the theft and thus would be guilty of attempted secret theft, whereas if one enters a house to commit a homicide, one would be guilty only of preparation of murder, because entering the house does not constitute any part of the *actus reus* of homicide.

To be guilty of attempted murder in Russia, one must have the direct intent to kill. Indirect intent (recklessness) will not suffice (¶ 2, SCRF-Expl.: Murder). Furthermore, if a person forges documents to use in a fraud but does not use them because of circumstances beyond his or her control, he or she is guilty of counterfeiting (s. 327(1)) and of preparation to commit fraud (s. 159). If, on the other hand, he or she presents the forged documents but does not obtain the desired property through fraud, the acts would amount to an attempted fraud (¶ 6, SCRF-Expl.: Fraud).

Russian theory distinguishes between "completed" attempts, where the actor does all he or she sought to do, for instance, shoots the victim, but the victim does not die, and "incompleted" attempts, where, because of reasons independent of his or her will, the actor could not commit all the acts he or she intended and that were necessary to cause the criminal result. Both are attempts, but the law distinguishes only between the relative social dangerousness of the two variants. An example of a completed attempt in Russia is when the police engage in a controlled buy of narcotics from a suspect. Although such an act would constitute a completed sale in the United States, it is considered to be an attempt because the drugs are taken out of circulation by the police (¶ 13, SCRF-Expl.: Narcotics).

Finally, Russian law provides for impunity if the actor, who has already committed acts that constitute preparation or attempt, "voluntarily abandons the crime." Abandonment applies to all preparation, but also to attempts, if the person "recognized the possibility of carrying out the crime to its end" but "voluntarily and conclusively" refused to carry it out (s. 31(1, 2)). If, however, the acts already committed constitute a lesser criminal offense, then the person will still be guilty of that offense (s. 31(3)).

Punishment for preparation of a crime cannot exceed one-half the maximum punishment prescribed for the completed crime, and that for attempt may not exceed three-fourths thereof. When in Russia, for instance, a thief intends to commit "open theft" of a "large amount" of money (punishable by from 2 to 7 years) but succeeds only in stealing a smaller amount (punishable by no more than 4 years) (on "open theft," see section III.D *infra*), then the defendant is guilty of attempted theft of a large amount, punishable by a maximum of three-quarters of 7 years, that is, 5.5 years, that is, longer than he could get for the crime he actually completed (¶ 25, SCRF-Expl.: Theft).

b. Conspiracy

There is no inchoate crime of "conspiracy" in Russian law. Instead, the fact that more than one person combine to commit a crime is a statutory aggravating factor for many completed offenses (s. 35(7)).

The UK lists four group aggravators, from the least to the most serious. A crime is committed by a "group of persons" (s. 35(1); hereafter "group") when one or more persons participate in a crime without a prior conspiracy. Otherwise, section 35(2) applies to crimes committed by a "group of persons pursuant to a preceding conspiracy" (hereafter "group conspiracy"). A crime is committed by an "organized group" (s. 35(3); hereafter "orggroup") when a "steadfast" (*ustoychivaia*) group conspired to commit it or several crimes. Finally, a crime is committed by a "criminal society (organization)" (s. 35(4); hereafter "crimorg") if the group is "solid" (*splochennaia*) and was "created for the commission of grave and especially grave crimes, or is a unification of organized groups created for the same goals."

According to the SCRF, "solidness" is defined as the "presence among managers and participants of a unified intent to commit grave or especially grave crimes," coupled with their "creation of general goals for the functioning of the crimorg." There must be an organized managerial structure and a material and financial base into which the proceeds of crime are paid. There must be a hierarchy, discipline, and division of labor. A crimorg may include special structures, such as a director, a board of directors, and specialized branches. Solidness is evidenced by planning of criminal activities over a long period of time, the corrupting of public officials, or other acts aimed at neutralizing representatives of law enforcement and other state organs (¶ 3, SCRF-Expl.: Crimorg).

Russian law does, however, punish as substantive crimes the creation of, and membership in, an "illegal armed formation" (s. 208(1)), a "steadfast armed group with intent to attack citizens" ("banditism," s 209(1, 2)), a "crimorg" (s. 210(1, 2)), and an "extremist organization" whose members plan any of a number of specified crimes based on "ideological, political, racial, nationalistic or religious hatred or ill-will in relation to any social group" (ss. 282.1, 282.2). The confusing, intertwined definitions of the various forms of criminal organization have made prosecution under these provisions quite difficult.[15]

A person is guilty of creation of a crimorg (s. 210(1)) when conditions exist that evince the readiness of the organization to realize its criminal aims, whether or not the participants have yet committed the planned crimes. This may be proved by showing that tools for the commission of crimes have been distributed, turf has been divided among the members, or agreements to commit certain crimes have been forged (¶ 4, SCRF-Expl.: Crimorg). Guilt for "management" of a crimorg, also punishable under section 210(1), may be based on the realization of organizational or managerial functions during commission of particular crimes and in guaranteeing the general functioning of the crimorg. Examples are the creation of goals, working out general plans, preparing grave or especially grave crimes, dividing roles among participants, organizing the material-technical bases for commission of the crimes, providing for security measures, or dividing the spoils. On the guilt of creators and managers for crimes committed by the crimorg, see section II.B.3.ii in this chapter.

A member of a crimorg becomes guilty of "participation" by fulfilling tasks determined by the group in organizing grave or especially grave crimes (such as looking for victims, developing plans, or contacting public officials), participating in meetings of organizers, directors, or other representatives, or directly participating in fulfilling functional duties that contribute to the efficiency of the crimorg, such as financing, maintaining organizational unity, gathering information, and keeping records (¶ 10, SCRF-Expl.: Crimorg).

ii. Complicity

Complicity in the commission of a crime is described as "intentional mutual participation by two or more persons in the commission of an intentional crime" (s. 32). Section 33 differentiates between four types of accomplice liability: (1) an "executor," who "directly commits the crime or directly participates in its commission with other persons (coexecutors), and also a person who commits a crime by using other persons who do not incur criminal liability because of age, insanity, or other circumstances provided in this code"; (2) an "organizer," who "organizes the commission of the crime or manages its execution, as well as a person who creates an orggroup or crimorg or manages it"; (3) an "instigator," who "induces another person to commit a crime through persuasion, purchase, threats or other means"; and (4) an "aider," who "influences the commission of the crime by counsel, orders, providing information, means or tools to commit the crime, as well as a person who in advance promises to hide the criminal, means or tools of committing the crime, evidence of the crime or objects gained in a criminal manner, as well as a person who in advance promised to obtain or sell such objects."

The accomplice must intend and desire the commission of the acts committed by the executor or at least recklessly allow them to take place. "Where the executor commits a crime not encompassed by the intent of the other accomplices," the other accomplices will not be liable for such "excess," that is, the commission of the greater crime (s. 36). Thus, if an aider intends only to burglarize a residency, but the executor kills the resident, the aider is guilty only of burglary.[16]

Russian law also requires that the accomplice actually aid in causing the crime. If the would-be executors do not carry out the crime because of circumstances beyond their control, the other coparticipants incur criminal responsibility for either preparation or attempt. A person who, independent of his or her will, was not able to induce other people to commit the crime incurs responsibility for preparation of crime (s. 34(5)).

Although "executors" of a crime are sentenced solely for the offense they committed (s. 34(2, 3)), the other accomplices are sentenced on the basis of the type of their complicity as specified by section 33, whereby the court takes into consideration "the character and level of factual participation, the importance of this participation to the achievement of the criminal goal, and its influence on the character and level of the possible harm" (s. 67(1)). Aggravating or mitigating circumstances relating to one accomplice are not per se applicable to other coparticipants (s. 67(2)). True "accomplices after the fact" are punished for "covering up the crime" only in relation to especially dangerous crimes not committed by one's spouse or close relatives (s. 316).

When a person is found guilty of "creating" or "managing" an orggroup or crimorg, he or she is then guilty of all crimes committed by its members in carrying out the plans of the organization (s. 35(5)). Members or participants in such organizations incur liability, however, for criminal acts committed by the organization only when they actually participate in their preparation or commission or share the precise criminal purpose (s. 35(5)). Thus the SCRF reversed an attempted murder conviction of participants who, although properly found guilty of "banditism" (s. 209(2)), claimed that they were surprised that their copartner had a gun and silencer and that, when they asked him why he had brought it, he had said that he was only going to "scare" the victims (Decision (Oct. 30, 2008), SCRF Bulletin 9 (2009)).

Someone who knowingly aides a crimorg without being a member thereof, for example, by giving it credit, selling weapons, or providing information, is guilty as an accomplice both to the acts he or she actually aids (s. 33(5)) and to the crime of management of the crimorg (s. 210(1)) (¶ 12, SCRF-Expl.: Crimorg).

iii. Corporate criminal liability

The UK explicitly limits criminal responsibility to "sane, physical persons" who are of age (s. 19). Thus corporate criminal liability is excluded.

4. Causation

Because of the plethora of crimes requiring a socially dangerous result, principles of causation are very important in Russian law. Nevertheless, they are nowhere articulated in the code. From the legal literature, however, it is quite clear that Russian law strictly eschews any notion of strict liability in relation to harmful results of an otherwise criminal act.

To find causation, there must be an unlawful act, a necessary link between act and harmful (socially dangerous) result, and a guilty *mens rea* in relation to the result element of the crime. The actor must intend the result, be reckless about whether it will ensue (indirect intent), or be "careless" (negligent or thoughtless) in relation thereto; that is, the resultant harm must be reasonably foreseeable and not merely accidental. Thus a truck driver who was violating the law by driving without a valid license would not be guilty of homicide if a boy unexpectedly fell under his truck. Russian law naturally has to deal with results that have more than one cause, either multihuman causes or combinations of human and natural causes. In Russia intervening medical malpractice will not break causation when the inflictor of a life-threatening wound is prosecuted for homicide.[17]

C. Defenses

1. Types of Defense

Justifications, listed in chapter 8 of the UK under the rubric "circumstances excluding the criminality of the act," include extreme necessity, necessary defense, infliction of harm during arrest, physical and psychic coercion, justified risk, and carrying out an order. Other than being underage, that is, under sixteen years of age for normal crimes and fourteen for murder and a few other serious felonies (s. 20), insane, or suffering from diminished capacity, one finds few true excuses in Russian law.

However, the UK does set out certain factors leading to "liberation from criminal responsibility" (hereafter "liberation") that would not be considered "defenses" in U.S. law, but rather reasons for a prosecutor to exercise his or her discretion not to charge. For countries like Russia that do not recognize the "opportunity principle," or unlimited prosecutorial discretion, circumstances that potentially "liberate from criminal responsibility" give a substantive criminal law basis for not charging, much like the decriminalization of *de minimis* offenses because of lack of social dangerousness.

In relation to crimes of slight or average gravity, a first offender "can be liberated from criminal responsibility if, after committing the crime he voluntarily turned himself in, facilitated the solving of the crime, made restitution or in another way compensated for the harm caused by the crime, and due to active remorse ceased being socially dangerous." Such "active remorse" led to dismissal in a case of a pensioner who in 1997 fraudulently received a pass to use the trains, resulting in a loss of 117,800 rubles to the state, but who made restitution.[18] A person charged with a more serious crime may also be subject to liberation from criminal responsibility, but only if this is allowed in the offense description in the Special Part (s. 75(1, 2)).

Liberation is often allowed for grave or especially grave crimes where the suspect/accused ensures, in statutorily specified ways, that the crime is not successfully completed. This applies to the first-time human trafficker (s. 127.1), those charged with assisting terrorism (s. 205.1), hostage takers (s. 206) and even those involved in high treason, espionage, attempting to overthrow the government, or attempts on the life of state officials (ss. 275–278). Liberation, however, does not mean that the suspect may not be prosecuted for lesser offenses he or she has committed. It appears that the more disastrous the results of a crime, the more likely the UK will trade impunity for protecting lives or other crucial state or social interests.

A person who has committed for the first time a crime of slight or average gravity may also be liberated if he or she conciliates with the victim of the crime (s. 76).

2. Burden of Proof

Although article 49(2) of the constitution declares that the "defendant is not obligated to prove his innocence," and the UK places no explicit burden on the defendant to prove justifications or excuses, commentators believe that such a burden exists. For instance, a defendant pleading "justified risk" under section 41 would have the burden to show that he or she was pursuing socially useful goals and took measures to avoid harm with his or her conduct, whereas the prosecutor would have to prove that the defendant acted at least with a negligent mental state.[19]

D. Justifications

1. Necessity

The UK provides that it is "not a crime," and is therefore justified, "to inflict harm to interests protected by the criminal law in a situation of extreme necessity, that is, to eliminate danger immediately threatening the person or rights of that person or other person, or interests of society or the state protected by law, if this danger cannot be eliminated by other means." The law further provides that the "limits of extreme necessity have been exceeded when the infliction of harm clearly does not correspond to the character and level of the threatened danger and the circumstances under which the danger was eliminated, when the aforementioned interests suffered a harm which was equal to or more significant than the harm avoided. Such excess incurs criminal responsibility only in cases of intentional infliction of harm" (s. 39).

"Extreme necessity" existed in the UK-1960 but applied if the harm avoided was equal to that inflicted by the act. The current rendition, however, requires that the evil avoided be greater than the harm inflicted by the actor, thus making it a true choice-of-evils justification.

The justification of extreme necessity incorporates some of the aspects of the defense of duress, which is usually considered an excuse in U.S. law. Although Russian law provides for an excuse of coercion (s. 40(1)), it applies only when the coercion deprives the actor of free will. If free will is still present and the coerced person violates a legally protected interest, then the conduct will be evaluated according to the test for extreme necessity.

A novelty in the UK, somewhat related to necessity, is the provision that decriminalizes violations of interests protected by the criminal law when the actor takes a "justified risk toward the achievement of socially useful goals." To be justified, the risk must be necessary, that is, if the socially useful goals "could not be achieved with acts (omissions) not associated with the risk and the person, allowing the risk, took sufficient measures to prevent the harm to the interests protected by the criminal law." Furthermore, the risk must not threaten the "life of many persons" or an "ecological catastrophe or community disaster" (s. 41(1–3)).

This provision was inspired by the turn from the Communist administrative-command economy, where the criminal law was routinely used to punish managers of state enterprises who took risks that injured employees, to the capitalist economy, where risk taking is encouraged. Although some commentators see the section as applicable to banking, investment, or speculative ventures,[20] the language of the section would seem to exclude risks taken solely in the search for personal profit unless they were connected with achievement of socially useful ends. Memories of the primacy of the social element still shine through this justification inspired by the turn to capitalist economics.

In a sense, this novel justification is a defense in cases of crimes of indirect intent (recklessness) or thoughtlessness (*legkomyslie*) (see II.B.2.ii–iii *supra*). In other words, the actor was aware of a risk that the legally protected interests would be infringed in the risk taking, but the risk would have been "justified" by the socially useful goal of the acts and the fact that harm to interests protected by the criminal law did not occur through "arrogant" miscalculation and despite the exercise of necessary care. Since the actor may not run a risk of death to many persons or a catastrophe or disaster, the defense would not have applied, for instance, in the storming of the Moscow theater on October 26, 2002, to free hostages in the hands of Chechen terrorists, which resulted in 129 deaths. Apparently the defense has not yet been pleaded.[21]

2. Self-Defense

"Necessary defense" in the UK is broader than typical U.S. self-defense provisions because it stamps as "noncriminal" the "infliction of harm on the attacker" not only to defend oneself or others but also to defend "social or state interests protected by the law" in the event of the use or threat of use of deadly force. In the case of an attack with less than deadly force, the response must be proportional and must not "exceed the limits of necessary defense," thus explicitly excluding "intentional acts clearly not corresponding to the character and dangerousness of the attack" (s. 37(1, 2)).

The 2003 amendments provide for complete justification despite the actor's use of excessive force "if due to the sudden nature of the attack he or she could not evaluate the level and character of the dangerousness of the attack" (s. 37(2.1)). They also extend the standard rules to "all persons independent of their special preparation or official position" (thus including police officers). There is also explicitly no duty to retreat or appeal to others for help before using deadly force (s. 37(3)).

Under the UK-1960, a person who negligently used excessive force in self-defense was not responsible for the killing. The UK, however, specifically punishes "murder, committed in exceeding the limits of necessary defense" (s. 108(1)), and if the original aggressor does not die, it punishes "infliction of grave or medium harm to health in exceeding the limits of necessary defense" (s. 114(1)).

3. Consent

The General Part of the UK contains no generic provisions dealing with consent as a defense to any crimes. Consent is discussed in theoretical treatises on the criminal law but was excluded from the code. It is not a defense to homicide or infliction of any injuries but slight ones, and since cases involving slight injuries are strictly subject to private prosecution, a "consenting" victim has the right not to prosecute.

4. Superior Orders

A justification for following superior orders, although previously recognized in Russian jurisprudence, was codified for the first time in the UK. It is "not a crime," and therefore is justified, to "inflict harm to interests protected by the criminal law, when acting to carry out an order or directive which is mandatory. The criminal responsibility for inflicting that harm is incurred by the person who gave an illegal order or directive." However, the commission of an intentional crime "in carrying out a clearly illegal order or directive" will lead to criminal responsibility "under ordinary conditions" (s. 42(1, 2)). Thus the SCRF reversed the acquittal of an employee who was ordered by his employer to split a bribe because the order was clearly illegal.[22]

5. *Law Enforcement (Effecting Lawful Arrest)*

In Russian law it is "not a crime," and is therefore justified, to inflict harm on a person committing a crime when one is making an arrest, turning him or her over to law-enforcement officials, or preventing him or her from committing new crimes, "if other means of arresting that person did not appear possible and the necessary means for this measure were not exceeded" (s. 38(1)). Such means are "excessive" when there is a "clear incommensurability with the character and level of social dangerousness of the crime committed by the arrested person and the circumstances of the arrest, when the person without necessity inflicts clearly excessive harm not called for under the circumstances. This excess leads to criminal responsibility only when the harm is intentionally inflicted" (s. 38(2)).

E. Excuses

1. *Mistake/Ignorance of Law or Fact*

The authors of the UK rejected a section dealing directly with mistakes of law and fact, but the topic is well known in the legal literature and jurisprudence. Russian law recognizes the doctrine *ignorantia legis neminem excusat*, which provides that mistake about whether certain conduct is criminal is no defense. However, voices in the legal literature support a requirement that those charged with some of the new economic crimes, often with elements referring to complex regulations in other normative acts, should know that their conduct is prohibited.[23]

If a person makes a factual error about the social dangerousness of his or her acts or omissions and is incapable of a correct assessment thereof, then that person would be not guilty (s. 28(1)). If a person errs about an attendant circumstance that would make the crime more serious, then that person is guilty of the lesser crime actually committed and of an attempted commission of the more serious crime. Errors about results or causation are punished in a similar way. Thus, if one man beats another, thinks that he is dead, and then throws him into the river to get rid of the body, and the man actually dies from drowning, the first man would be guilty of careless causing of death (s. 109) and attempted murder.

Russian law also applies "transferred intent" and would find a person guilty of murder if he or she intends to take the life of one person but mistakenly takes the life of another. In addition, if a person intends to cause a "large amount of damage" and mistakenly causes "an especially large amount," he or she would be guilty of the greater offense.[24]

2. *Insanity/Diminished Capacity*

In general, excuses in Russian law have been seen as variants on imputability related either to intellectual underdevelopment, nervous disorders, or states of unconsciousness, all of which must normally be corroborated by scientific or medical evidence.[25]

In Russia insanity is defined in cognitive and volitional terms. "A person is not subject to criminal responsibility, who at the time of commission of the socially dangerous act was in a state of insanity, that is, could not realize the factual character and social dangerousness of his acts (omissions) or act accordingly due to chronic psychic disturbance, temporary psychic disturbance, mental retardation or other sickly psychic condition" (s. 21(1)).

Once it appears that a person may be insane within the terms of the code, the case is dismissed and diverted to the "procedure for application of coercive medical procedures" (s. 97(1)(a, b, v); s 433(1) UPK). The decision to institute proceedings to apply coercive medical procedures is made by the judge, who also decides whether the charged acts were committed in a condition of insanity (ss. 440(1, 2), 442(3, 5) UPK). Thus, unlike before the revolution, juries do not decide the issue of insanity in cases that would otherwise be within their jurisdiction.[26]

A person found insane and dangerous following coercive procedures of a medical nature may be given ambulatory treatment or locked in a mental institution (s. 99(1)(a, b)). The fact that these proceedings are dominated by professional judges and doctors is disturbing in light of the history of the use of coercive psychiatric commitment of dissidents in the Soviet Union and some indications that such practices still occur today.

For the first time in Russian history, an excuse of diminished capacity/responsibility due to mental illness has been codified. It has two prongs whose interrelationship is a bit confusing. On the one hand, the UK provides for mitigation of sentence in relation to a "sane person, who at the time of commission of the crime, due to psychic disturbance could not completely recognize the factual character and social dangerousness of his acts (omissions) nor conduct himself accordingly," but at the same time it permits the application of coercive medical measures in such cases (s. 22). On the other hand, the code provides a complete defense if an actor could not have recognized the social dangerousness of his or her acts or, "while foreseeing the possibility of the occurrence of socially dangerous results of his acts (omissions), could not prevent their occurrence due to the incommensurateness of his psychophysiological characteristics with the demands of the extreme conditions or neuropsychic burdens" (s. 28(1, 2)).

3. Intoxication

Section 23 proclaims: "A person, who has committed a crime in a condition of drunkenness, caused by use of alcohol, narcotic substances or other hallucinating substances, is subject to criminal responsibility."

Because of the centuries-long Russian penchant for excessive consumption of vodka, Russian criminal law has struggled with how to assess the effect of alcohol on *mens rea*. Before the Bolshevik Revolution tsarist juries viewed the drunken criminal with sympathy if they felt that the perpetrator would not have committed the crime in a sober state, and they often acquitted or returned verdicts of guilt for lesser offenses. At the same time, the law treated drunkenness as an aggravating factor in sentencing if the perpetrator drank with the intent of summoning up courage to commit the crime.[27] The UK-1960 also provided that drunkenness was an aggravating factor at the time of sentencing if the actor, in a state of drunkenness, used a "source of increased dangerousness," that is, a weapon (s. 39(10) UK-1960).

The Russian legal literature struggles with how to characterize a crime committed by a person who intentionally drinks to summon up the courage or to disinhibit himself or herself to commit a particular crime. Should the actor be guilty of the commission of the crime even though he or she is unconscious or, in Russian terms, unable to recognize the social dangerousness of the act at the time of its commission? One view is that such a person would be guilty only of attempt because of the lack of imputability at the time the crime was carried out, but that a person who was actually unable to appreciate the wrongfulness of the act or unable to conform his or her conduct to the law because of mental illness caused by pathological drunkenness would be found not guilty under section 28.[28]

The aggravating factor of drunkenness has been eliminated from the UK, but it remains an aggravating factor to induce a person in a state of drunkenness to participate in a crime (s. 63(d)).

Although the UK does not have the substantive crime of "complete drunkenness" (*Vollrausch*) that one finds in Germany, which serves as a fallback crime for actors who are nonimputable for the crime they have committed while intoxicated, it does have a crime called "hooliganism" that has traditionally captured many crimes committed by the intoxicated (see III.F.3 *infra*).

4. Duress

The Russian version of duress, literally, "physical or psychic coercion," is treated as a justification, not an excuse. The inclusion of this justification is a first in Russian law. Under the Soviet-era code, the commission of a crime because of a threat or coercion qualified only as a mitigating factor (s. 38(3) UK-1960). A similar mitigating factor also exists in section 61(1)(e). It is "not a crime," and is therefore justified, to inflict harm "to interests protected by law" when it "is the result of physical coercion or if due to such coercion the person could not control his acts (omissions)" (s. 40(1)). On the treatment of duress when the actor still "maintains the "possibility of controlling his acts," under the justification of "extreme necessity," see II.D.1 *supra*.

5. Entrapment

Entrapment is not mentioned in the UK as an excuse for crime.

6. Superior Orders

The defense of superior orders per section 42 is treated as a justification. See II.D.4 *supra*.

F. Sanctions

1. Punishment

In the early nineteenth century, Russian law recognized ten types of punishment and divided them between "punitive" and "corrective" sanctions, but the distinction between punitive and corrective punishments gradually became meaningless and was dropped. The Russian codes, however, continued to maintain a "staircase of punishments," which in the old days was a "down staircase," beginning with the most severe, the death penalty, and descending to hard labor (*katorga*), exile, and finally to short-term imprisonment and a fine.[29] The current staircase, in contrast, for the first time is an ascending one, beginning with the least intrusive punishment and culminating in the death penalty, in accordance with the principle that a more severe punishment should be imposed only if a less severe one will not fulfill the goals of punishment (s. 60(1)). One climbs this staircase from a fine to professional prohibition, deprivation of military or other ranks or state awards, obligatory labor, corrective labor, limitation of military duty, limitation of freedom, short-term detention, incarceration in a disciplinary military barracks, deprivation of liberty for a determinate period, life imprisonment, and finally the death penalty (s. 44). No other punishments may be imposed.

The punishments from obligatory labor up to the death penalty may be imposed only as the main punishment, whereas a fine and professional prohibition may be imposed as either the main or a supplementary punishment. Deprivation of ranks and awards, however, may only be a supplementary punishment (s. 45).

The threatened punishment also determines whether a crime falls into one of the four categories recognized by Russian law: (1) crimes of slight gravity, punishable by up to two years' deprivation of liberty; (2) crimes of average gravity, punishable by more than two years; (3) grave crimes, the punishment for which does not exceed ten years; and (4) especially grave crimes, punishable by more than ten years or the death penalty (s. 15).

2. Quantity/Quality of Punishment

Under the 2003 amendments, fines may be imposed in amounts of from 2,500 to 1,000,000 rubles (for several years the value of one U.S. dollar has hovered around 30 rubles) or from a two-week to a five-year pro rata portion of one's earnings. Fines higher than 500,000 rubles or three years' income may be imposed only for grave or especially grave crimes. If a person in bad faith fails to pay a fine, then any of the other more severe punishments may be imposed (s. 46(2, 5)).

Professional prohibition can extend to government service, work in municipal organs, or the right to practice a profession or "other activity." This punishment may be imposed for from one to five years as a main punishment and from six months to three years as a supplementary form of punishment (s. 47(1, 2)).

Obligatory labor consists of from 60 to 240 hours of unpaid "socially useful labor" performed outside one's normal work or school hours (s. 49(1, 2)). Corrective labor, on the other hand, is for persons who are otherwise unemployed. They are assigned to a work station in the district where they live and work under the supervision of local authorities for a term of from two months to two years. Corrective labor is compensated, but the state may withhold from 5 to 20 percent of the income for expenses (s. 50(1, 3)).

Limitation of liberty consists of the commitment of the convicted person to a special institution without isolation from society, where he or she can be supervised, and applies to persons without a criminal record sentenced for intentional crimes to one to three years or for "careless" (negligent) crimes to a period of one to five years (s. 53(1, 2)). Short-term detention consists of a sentence to extreme isolation from society for a period of from one to six months (s. 54(1)) and was meant to be a short, stern reminder to the criminal about what punishment is, in order to deter future criminal conduct. It should be applied to a first offender convicted of a crime of slight or average gravity.

Deprivation of liberty for a determinate term (in various types of institutions from work colonies of various levels of security to locked prisons) may be imposed for any period from two months to twenty years for a single crime (s. 56(1, 2)). In the case of conviction of more than one crime and the imposition of cumulative punishments, the term of deprivation of liberty may rise to thirty years (ss. 56(4), 70(3)) but in no case may exceed 1.5 times the maximum punishment for the most serious crime (s. 69(3)). The 2003 amendments by and large eliminated mandatory minimum sentences. The maximum sentence for deprivation of liberty under the old code was fifteen years (s. 24 UK-1960).

Life imprisonment did not exist in the 1960 code until it was amended in 1992 to provide an alternative to the death penalty following a presidential commutation. In the new code it may be imposed only for grave crimes against life or public security and may not be imposed on women or on men who are under eighteen years of age or who have reached sixty years of age (s. 57). A person serving a life term, however, may be eligible for conditional release after twenty-five years (s. 79(5)).

The choice of punishment and its magnitude depend on an assessment of mitigating and aggravating circumstances. The statutory mitigating circumstances are listed in the following subsections of section 61(1): (a) first-offense crime of slight gravity due to an accidental occurrence of circumstances; (b) minor age; (v)[30] pregnancy; (g) having care of small children, if they were not the victims of the crime (¶ 8, SCRF-Expl.: Punishment); (d) crime committed because of "difficult life circumstances or a motive of compassion"; (e) crime committed as a result of physical or psychic coercion or because of a material, service, or other dependence; (zh) exceeding the proportionality requirements in the course of otherwise justified conduct (necessary defense, necessity [choice of evils], making an arrest, justified risk, or carrying out an order); (z) illegal or immoral conduct of the victim creating a reason for the crime; (i) turning oneself in and confessing, actively facilitating the uncovering of crimes, identifying other co-participants in the crime, and finding property stolen as a result of crime; and (k) giving the victim medical or other help directly after committing the crime, voluntary restitution of property or moral loss (i.e., pain and suffering) caused by the crime, and other acts aimed at mitigating the harm caused by the crime (s. 61(1)). The court may take into account any other mitigating circumstance not listed in the UK (s. 61(2)). If the court finds the presence of subsection (i) or (k), and there are no aggravating circumstances, then the punishment may not exceed three-fourths of the maximum punishment (s. 62).

The mitigating circumstance of turning oneself in and admitting guilt (s. 61(1)(i)) does not apply when one confesses after being arrested on the basis of probable cause unless one then confesses to other crimes of which the police had no prior knowledge (¶ 7, SCRF-Expl.: Punishment).

The UK provides for an exhaustive list of aggravating circumstances in the following subsections of section 63(1): (a) recidivism; (b) grave results of the crime; (v) committing the crime as a group, orggroup, crimorg, or group conspiracy; (g) extremely active role in commission of the crime; (d) inducing a person who suffers from serious psychic disturbances, is drunk, or is too young to incur criminal responsibility to commit the crime; (e) motive of national, racist, or religious hatred or animosity or hatred or animosity against any social group; (e-1) motive of revenge for illegal acts of other people, or of covering up a crime or facilitating its commission; (zh) crime committed against a person or family of a person who is fulfilling a social duty or working in government service; (z) commission of the crime in relation to a woman known to be pregnant, or in relation to a child or other defenseless or helpless person or a person in a relationship of dependence on the guilty person; (i) commission of the crime with exceptional cruelty, sadism, or violence or causing the victim to suffer; (k) using a gun, grenade, explosive material, or explosive device, poison, or radioactive substances, medicine, or other chemical-pharmacological preparations, or using physical or psychic coercion; (l) commission of the crime during a state of emergency or other type of social disaster or during mass disorder; (m) taking advantage of trust placed in the guilty person because of his or her public office or an agreement; and (n) using an official uniform or official documents (s. 63(1)).

Russian law specifically prohibits "double counting" of an aggravating circumstance if it is already included as an element of a crime or an aggravated version of a crime (s. 63(2)).

Judges also have discretion to impose less than the statutory minimum prison sentence or to impose a less serious form of punishment "in the presence of exceptional circumstances connected with the goals and motives of the crime, the role of the guilty person, his conduct during and after commission of the crime, and other circumstances which substantially mitigate the level of social dangerousness of the crime, or by active contribution of a member of a group to solve a group crime" (s. 64). Even recidivists may be sentenced below the statutory minimum of at least one-third of the maximum term of imprisonment (s. 68(2)) in "exceptional circumstances" (s. 68(3, 4)). On the effect of a jury's verdict of "lenience," see I.E.2 *supra*. Judges may also sentence below the minimum in cases where the defendant enters a plea of *nolo contendere* (see I.E.1 *supra*), which limits the punishment in itself to two-thirds of the maximum sentence, taking into account mitigating circumstances. Thus, if the defendant pleads *nolo contendere* to a crime and has "turned himself in" per section 63(1)(i) or has given medical aid to the victim or made restitution per section 63(1)(k), then the maximum sentence would be two-thirds of three-fourths of the maximum sentence, or one-half of the maximum (¶ 37, SCRF-Expl.: Sentencing) (see s. 64 *supra*).

The UK provides for "conditional conviction," which is really the suspension of the imposition of sentence as a condition of completing a period of probation. It applies to any crimes punishable by up to eight years' deprivation of liberty (s. 73(1)). Terms of probation range from a minimum of six months to a maximum of three years for crimes punishable by less than one year's deprivation of liberty and up to five years for more serious crimes (s. 73(3)). The UK provides a nonexhaustive list of conditions that may be imposed, such as not to change place of residence, work, or schooling without notifying the authorities, not to visit certain places, to undergo treatment for alcoholism, drug addiction, or venereal diseases, and to support one's family (s. 73(5)).

A conviction is completely expunged from one's record upon successful completion of probation (s. 86(2)). Those actually sentenced to deprivation of liberty may also have their conviction expunged within three years in the case of crimes of slight or medium gravity, within six years in the case of grave crimes, and within eight years in the case of especially grave crimes (s. 86(3)).

Russian law also provides for complete and partial relief from punishment following a judgment of guilt, that is, a type of parole. Most important, this may occur following a conviction of a crime of slight or average seriousness "if the person or the crime committed is no longer socially dangerous" (s. 80.1). Convicted persons may be partially relieved of their sentences if the court recognizes that completion of the sentence is not needed for correctional purposes (s. 79(1)). The person must have served one-third of the sentence for crimes of slight or average gravity and two-thirds for grave crimes. Judges may base a refusal of parole neither solely on the fact that the prisoner violated parole or prison rules or has failed to make restitution because of economic inability, nor on any reasons not listed in the statute, such as the mildness of the punishment imposed or the failure of the prisoner to accept guilt. The court must engage in an "all-sided accounting of information about his conduct during the entire period of punishment in relation to the question whether further incarceration is necessary for rehabilitation" (¶¶ 2, 5–7, SCRF-Expl.: Parole).

With the decriminalization of minor theft and drug crimes and the increased use of probation, Russia's prison population, which was second per capita in the world at 700 per 100,000 population in 1998 (behind Rwanda), fell in 2003 to 614 per 100,000, less than that of the United States, whose prison population had risen to 680 per 100,000. However, the prison population increased by almost 50,000 in 2006 and was increasing by 6,000 per month in early 2007, so it is unclear whether the decrease was merely a politically engineered short-term achievement or a long-term trend.

3. Death Penalty

Russia has always had an ambivalent attitude toward the death penalty, with tsars (Empress Elizabeth, for instance, in 1753) and the Communist Party abolishing it for brief periods, only to have it come back with a vengeance.[31] This ambivalence is reflected in article 20 of the constitution, which provides for the death penalty "until its abolition" for especially grave crimes against life as long as the defendant has had the right to a jury trial.

The UK-1960, at its most repressive, provided for the death penalty for seventeen different offenses, including some economic offenses.[32] Executions reached a high of 2,000 a year in the 1960s and then dropped to 1,000 per year from the early 1970s to the mid-1980s.[33]

After the collapse of the USSR the death penalty was eventually eliminated for all nonviolent crimes. Even though the death penalty continued on the books for aggravated murder and a few other crimes, a clemency commission established in 1991 by President Yeltsin began commuting the lion's share of death sentences. The entry of Russia into the Council of Europe in February 1996 and its signing of the European Convention on Human Rights, however, led to a moratorium on executions, of which there have been none since August 1996, although Amnesty International has reported that the separatist Chechen Republic carried out executions from 1996 through 1999.[34]

Despite Russia's promises to the Council of Europe, the death penalty was included in the 1996 code for "especially grave crimes against life," but it may not be imposed on women or on men under eighteen or over sixty years of age (s. 59(1, 2)). The death penalty threatens those convicted of aggravated murder (s. 105(2)) and genocide (s. 357), but it also applies to attempts on the lives of state officials (s. 277), persons involved in the administration of justice (s. 295), and law-enforcement officers (s. 317). This seems to contradict section 66(2, 4), which says that the death penalty or life imprisonment may not be imposed for an attempt. The death penalty may be imposed only when the court determines the "high level of social dangerousness of the act" and "extremely negative information characterizing the guilty person as a person presenting an exceptional danger to society" (¶ 20, SCRF-Expl.: Murder).

On February 2, 1999, the CCRF declared that the death penalty could no longer be imposed on equal-protection grounds. Inasmuch as article 20 of the constitution guarantees the right to jury trial for anyone facing the death penalty and the jury system functioned at the time in only nine Russian regions and territories, the CCRF held that no death sentences could be imposed anywhere until jury trial was available throughout Russia. Although jury trials were extended to the rest of Russia, excluding Chechnya, by 2004, and should soon be in operation there, death penalty opponents hope that Russia will not risk its membership in the Council of Europe by lifting the execution moratorium.

III. SPECIAL PART

A. Structure

The 1996 code reflects the move from socialism to a democratic, liberal capitalist system in the interests that it seeks to protect. The UK-1960 was based on class principles, the priority of socialist ideology, and subjugation of the criminal law to the administrative-command economy. The UK-1960 prioritized the protection of state and social interests over individual interests. The UK, however, turns these priorities on their head.[35] The Special Part of the UK includes, in the following order, crimes against the person (part VII), crimes in the economic sphere (part VIII), crimes against social security and social order (part IX), crimes against state power (part X), crimes against military service (part XI), and crimes against the peace and security of humankind (part XII).

B. Homicide

1. Murder/Manslaughter

Murder (*ubiystvo*) is defined as "intentionally causing the death of another person" and is punished by deprivation of liberty for from six to fifteen years (s. 105(1)). Nonaggravated murders are meant to be those that take place during a fight or are motivated by jealousy, revenge, envy, ill feelings, hatred, or other human emotions falling short of "heat of passion," and that lack the aggravating circumstances listed in section 105(2) (¶ 4, SCRF-Expl.: Murder). "Intentionality" in Russian law encompasses both direct and indirect intent (recklessness) (see II.B.2.ii *supra*).

Aggravated murder is punishable by from eight to twenty years' deprivation of liberty, life imprisonment, or death. Section 105(2) lists the aggravated forms of murder in the following subsections: murder (a) of two or more persons; (b) of a person or his or her relatives in connection with the carrying out of official duties or fulfillment of a social duty; (v) of a person obviously in a helpless state, a kidnap victim, or a hostage; (g) of a woman known to be pregnant; (d) with exceptional cruelty; (e) committed by a means dangerous to many; (e-1) committed on the basis of blood revenge; (zh) committed by a group, group conspiracy, or orggroup; (z) for financial gain, or by hire, or connected with robbery, extortion, or banditism; (i) with hooliganistic motivation; (k) in order to conceal another crime or to facilitate its commission or connected with rape or violent acts of a sexual character; (l) based on national, racist, or religious hatred or animosity, hatred or animosity towards any social group, or blood revenge; and (m) to use organs or skin of the victim.

It should first be noted that a killing based on blood revenge, which is still customary law in some parts of the Russian Caucasus, constitutes an aggravated murder, whereas one based on personal revenge does not. This could be interpreted as an unequal application of the law to these Caucasian ethnicities, but this is clearly a policy decision aimed at preventing the killing of innocent persons and the hatching or continuing of blood feuds, which were traditionally one of the historical reasons for state-imposed criminal law in the first place.

The aggravating factor of "hooliganistic motivation" is peculiarly Russian (on the crime of "hooliganism," see III.F.3 *infra*). Murder with hooliganistic motivation, according to the SCRF, is murder "based on clear disrespect for society and generally accepted norms of morality, when the conduct of the guilty person is an open challenge to social order and based on the desire to confront those around one, demonstrating a contemptuous relationship to them (such as the intentional causing of death without a clear reason or using an insignificant reason as a pretext for murder)." For trial judges, it is thus extremely important to clearly distinguish murders with "hooliganistic motivation" from nonaggravated murders arising from an argument or a fight. If the deceased provoked the fight or argument, then the killing is not with "hooliganistic motivation," whereas it might be if the defendant provoked the fight to provide a pretext to kill (¶ 12, SCRF-Expl.: Murder).

The overwhelming majority of killings with hooliganistic motivation have been by intoxicated persons. Thus Russian law has indirectly found a way to use intoxication as an aggravating factor when the killer's cognitive capacities have not been reduced to a state of inability to realize that he or she is committing a life-endangering act, but to an extent where insignificant reasons may trigger the desire to kill.

The aggravating factor of exceptional cruelty (s. 105(2)(d)) relates both to the means of killing and to attendant circumstances. Examples are torturing or mocking the victim during the murderous assault, or using a means that causes exceptional suffering, such as inflicting a large number of bodily wounds, administering slow-acting, pain-inducing poison, burning alive, or prolonged deprivation of food and water. But exceptional cruelty may also be proved when the murder is in the presence of close relatives or friends of the victim and causes them great suffering. Mocking or desecrating the body or dismembering it to conceal the crime is not, however, exceptional cruelty, although desecration can be punished separately under section 244 of the UK (¶ 8, SCRF-Expl.: Murder).

The aggravating factor consisting of the "intent to conceal another crime or facilitate its commission" or murders "connected with rape or other violent acts of a sexual nature" (s. 105(2)(k)) may not be charged along with other aggravating factors, such as hooliganistic motivation or financial gain (¶ 13, SCRF-Expl.: Murder).

The UK also has three mitigated forms of ubiystvo, all of which might fall under the rubric of "voluntary manslaughter" in some U.S. states. The first is murder by a mother of her newborn child during or immediately after birth, or "under conditions of a psychotraumatic situation" or "psychic disturbance not excluding insanity," which is punished by deprivation of liberty for up to five years (s. 106). The second is murder in a condition of "affect" (see III.B.2 *infra*). The third is "murder committed in exceeding the limits of necessary defense," punishable by a maximum of two years' deprivation of liberty, and "murder committed in exceeding the measures necessary to arrest a person who has committed a crime," punishable by up to three years' deprivation of liberty (s. 108).

Finally, Russian law punishes "causing death through carelessness," with a maximum punishment of two years' deprivation of liberty, unless the death was caused "as a result of an improper fulfillment by the person of his professional duties," in which case the punishment rises to a maximum of three years (s. 109).

Not surprisingly, Russia does not bootstrap deaths caused during the commission of another crime into murder or manslaughter, as is done in the United States through use of the felony-murder or misdemeanor-manslaughter (unlawful-act) rules. But if, during the performance of a large number of crimes listed in the Special Part, a person's death "carelessly" results, then the defendant is punished for an aggravated form of the crime he or she was in the process of committing. Thus strict liability with regard to fatal results of otherwise serious crimes is also avoided.

In some cases the resultant punishment rises to the same magnitude as that provided for nonaggravated murder, thus achieving a result similar to felony murder without distorting the doctrinal underpinnings of the principle of guilt and guilty *mens rea*. Thus a person could be convicted of an aggravated form of "intentional infliction of grave harm to health" that "negligently caused the death of the victim" and be punished by from five to fifteen years' deprivation of liberty (s. 111(4)). Punishments similar in length to those for aggravated murder (eight to twenty years' deprivation of liberty) may result from negligently caused deaths in the course of a kidnapping or forcible rape or other sexual assaults (ss. 126(3)(v), 131(1, 3(a)), 132(1, 3(a))). Similar enhancements apply to deaths caused negligently during the commission of human trafficking, the taking of hostages, hijacking, piracy, and inducement to use narcotic or psychotropic substances.

When deaths are negligently caused as a result of less grave crimes, the punishments may be similar to those achieved by use of the U.S. misdemeanor-manslaughter rule. Thus an illegal abortion performed by someone without a medical degree is punished by corrective labor at most, but if a death or grave harm to health negligently ensues, it is punished by up to five years' deprivation of liberty (s. 123(1, 3)). The fatality aggravator can also apply to false imprisonment, illegal commitment to a locked psychiatric facility (a practice often used in Soviet times against dissidents), intentional destruction of property, and other crimes.

Russian law provides for a wide swath of concrete endangerment regulatory criminal offenses (*mala prohibita*), designed to enforce worker and environmental safety, as well as good business practices. These crimes are good examples of the employment of a staircase of aggravation, where the most aggravated forms relate to the negligent causing of death. Some of these will be dealt with in III.F *infra*.

Russian law also punishes "inducing a person to commit suicide or to attempt suicide through threats, cruel treatment or systematic denigration of human dignity of the victim" as a separate offense, not ubiystvo, with a maximum punishment of five years' deprivation of liberty (s. 110).

2. Provocation

An ubiystvo "committed in a condition of suddenly arising strong psychic emotion (affect) caused by violence, taunting, grave insult from the person of the victim or any other illegal or immoral acts (omissions) of the victim, as well as a lengthy psychotraumatic situation arising in connection with systematic illegal or immoral conduct of the victim," is punished by three years' deprivation of liberty if one person is killed and five years if more than one person is killed (s. 107). If the victim does not die but incurs "grave or medium grave damage to health," then section 113 threatens a lesser punishment of up to two years' deprivation of liberty.

Although the provocation must arise from the victim, the victim's conduct can be either of a substantive physical nature, such as a beating, or of a psychic nature, such as harassment over time, cynical degradation, or grave insults. Thus there is no "mere-words" exception that would eliminate this lesser form of ubiystvo. Long-term harassment may be connected with acts that violate legal norms, such as property rights, or moral norms, for example, fraud or treachery by a close friend, or it could be systematic minor physical attacks or insults or denigrations that, in their totality, give rise to heat of passion.[36]

C. Sex Offenses

The UK punishes all forcible sexual crimes in an identical manner as either rape, described simply as "sexual intercourse" (s. 131(1)), or "violent acts of a sexual nature," which include "homosexual sodomy [*muzhelozhstvo*] lesbianism, or other acts of a sexual character" (s. 132(1)). In the last Soviet-era code all acts of consensual homosexual sodomy were punished by deprivation of liberty for up to five years (s. 121 UK-1960).

These acts must be accompanied by the "application of force or threats of its application against the aggrieved party or another person or in taking advantage of the powerless condition of the aggrieved party" and are punished by deprivation of liberty for from three to six years. The two sections have identical aggravating factors. Deprivation of liberty for from four to ten years is triggered under the following subsections of sections 131(2) and 132(2): when the acts (a) are committed by a group, group conspiracy, or orggroup; (b) are accompanied by a threat of murder or infliction of grave harm to health or with exceptional cruelty in relation to the aggrieved party or other persons; (v) caused infection with venereal disease; or (g) were knowingly committed against a juvenile. The punishment can rise to from eight to fifteen years, pursuant to the following subsections of sections 131(3) and 132(3), if the acts (a) caused the death of the aggrieved party through negligence; (b) caused grave harm to health, infection with HIV, or another grave result; or (v) were committed by a person who knew he was victimizing a child who was under fourteen years of age. For convenience, I will use the term *rape* to refer to both sections.

Nowhere does the code describe in detail what physical acts constitute "rape," "homosexual sodomy," "lesbianism" or "other acts of a sexual nature." Even the commentaries, perhaps because of an instinctual Russian prudery, do not utter words such as "penetration," "anus," "vagina," "oral copulation," or "foreign object." The SCRF only indicates that "sexual intercourse" is limited to a sexual act between a man and a woman and that *muzhelozhstvo* refers to sexual contact between males, and that "lesbianism" means sexual contact between women (¶¶ 1, 5, SCRF-Expl.: Rape).

To prove "force" or "threats of its application," the intentional causing of even minor harm to health during the rape is sufficient. If a person's consent is achieved through deceit, abuse of trust, or, for instance, a false promise to marry, this is not rape because the acts are not viewed as crimes against sexual inviolability and sexual freedom. It must also be proved that the force used was not accidental but was intended by the defendant to accomplish intercourse. Russia does not punish each sexual penetration as a separate act of rape but sees penetrations as one continuing crime as long as they were interrupted only for a short time and the circumstances of their commission evidence a single intent of the guilty person to commit the same acts (¶¶ 2, 5, 8, 15, SCRF-Expl.: Rape).

Rape achieved by taking advantage of the "powerless state of the victim" includes cases where the victim, because of his or her physical or psychic condition (mental retardation, psychic disturbance, physical inadequacies, illness, or unconsciousness) or his or her young age or senility, could not understand the character and significance of the acts committed or resist the defendant. The prosecution must prove that the defendant was aware of this state of powerlessness as well. If the powerlessness is caused by intoxication, the level thereof, whether from drugs or alcohol, must be such as to deprive the victim of the possibility of resisting the aggressor. It is also irrelevant whether the defendant gave the victim alcohol, narcotics, sleeping pills, or other drugs, or whether the victim was in the condition independent of any acts of the defendant (¶ 3, SCRF-Expl.: Rape).

The aggravating circumstance consisting in a threat of death or infliction of serious harm to health, which can be proved by the defendant's words or brandishing of a weapon, is triggered only if the threat was actually the means of overcoming the resistance of the victim. If the threats were made after the consummation of the sexual act in order to deter the victim from reporting the crime, then the threats may be punished separately under section 119. The aggravating circumstance of exceptional cruelty, as in murder cases (see III.B.1 *supra*), exists when the defendant tortures or mocks the victim while performing the actual act or performs it in the presence of the victim's family or close friends (¶¶ 11, 12, SCRF-Expl.: Rape).

Russian law further punishes "coercion" of a person to submit to rape "through blackmail, threats of destruction, damage or confiscation of property, or taking advantage of the material or other dependency of the aggrieved party" with up to one year's deprivation of liberty (s. 133). Statutory rape exists when a person eighteen years of age or older engages in sexual intercourse or "other acts of a sexual nature" with a person whom the defendant knew had not reached sixteen years of age. It is punished by up to four years' deprivation of liberty (s. 134). A lesser form of illegal sexual conduct with minors is the commission of "depraved acts" without application of force against a person whom the defendant knew had not reached sixteen years of age. It is punished by deprivation of liberty of up to three years (s. 135).

Russian law does not allow strict liability with regard to the age of a victim of a sex crime, whether the victim is under sixteen and has engaged in consensual sex or is under fourteen years of age and the victim of rape. Guilt is shown in relation to victims under fourteen years of age only when the defendant credibly knew the age of the victim (he or she was a relative, neighbor, or the like) or "when the external appearance of the victim clearly showed his or her age." If the defendant in good faith believed that an older victim was of age because of the "acceleration" of his or her maturation, then this is a complete defense (¶ 14, SCRF-Expl.: Rape).

The UK also punishes the infection of another with a venereal disease when the actor had knowledge that he or she had contracted the disease. The punishment is at most three to six months' short-term detention unless more than one person is infected, in which case the maximum punishment rises to two years' deprivation of liberty (s. 121). Knowingly putting another person at risk of being infected with HIV is punished by a maximum sentence of one year's deprivation of liberty, but actually infecting a person is punishable by up to five years, and the punishment rises to a maximum of eight years if more than one person is infected (s. 122(1–3)).

To be subject to the aggravating circumstances in the rape statutes, mentioned earlier, the rapist who infects the victim with a venereal disease must have been aware that he was suffering from it and must have foreseen the possibility or inescapability of infecting the victim and wanted or allowed this infection to happen (purpose or recklessness). The rapist who infects with HIV must only be careless about the possibility of infection (¶ 13, SCRF-Expl.: Rape).

D. Theft and Fraud

Theft crimes are listed under "crimes in the economic sphere" in part VII. It is odd to think of a strong-arm robbery as a "crime in the economic sphere." Theft (*khishchenie*) is an illegal taking of personal property of another with intent to permanently (*bezvozmezdno*) deprive the person of ownership thereof and causing actual property loss. Russian law differentiates between two types of theft.

The "secret taking of another's property" (*krazha*) is committed when the owner or possessor of the property taken either is not present or is present and unaware of the taking. Even if bystanders observe the taking, it is still krazha as long as the actor believes that he or she is accomplishing the theft secretly or if the bystanders are close relatives of the thief and he or she believes they will not resist the taking (¶¶ 2, 3, SCRF-Expl.: Theft). Krazha triggers a stepladder of punishments from a fine of 80,000 rubles up to two years' deprivation of liberty (s. 158(1)).

The "open taking of another's property" (*grabezh*) is a theft in the presence of the owner or possessor of the property (a krazha can become a grabezh if the victim suddenly becomes aware of it) or in the presence of other bystanders where the thief realizes that the bystanders comprehend the illegal nature of his or her conduct (e.g., , by telling him or her not to do so), whether or not they take measures to prevent the taking (¶¶ 3–5, SCRF-Expl.: Theft). Grabezh is punished by corrective labor, short-term detention, or up to four years' deprivation of liberty (s. 161(1)).

Both types of theft are completed when the thief has secured a real possibility of using or selling the stolen property at his or her discretion. Thus in the *Gunchev* case in Moscow, it was proved that the defendant broke into a store, took an expensive fur coat, and then left the store, but was confronted by Yershova, who demanded that he give up the coat. The defendant tried to flee but was arrested by the police. A conviction for a completed open theft was reduced to an attempt because Gunchev did not have the possibility to actually use or sell the coat.[37]

Secret theft has three levels of aggravation, of which the most aggravated is punishable by deprivation of liberty for from five to ten years. The first level of aggravation applies if the theft is committed by group conspiracy; through burglary of a building; with infliction of significant harm to a citizen (not less than 2,500 rubles); or from the clothing, suitcase, or other hand luggage carried by the victim. The second level of aggravation applies if the theft is committed through burglary of a dwelling; from a gas or oil pipeline; or in a large amount (more than 250,000 rubles). In Russian law, burglary is not an autonomous offense, but exists solely as a factor which aggravates the punishment in cases of theft. The third level of aggravation applies if the theft is committed by an orggroup or in an especially large amount (more than 1 million rubles) (s. 158(24)). Minor petty thefts of property were decriminalized in 2003 and are now prosecuted as administrative offenses.

Open theft, on the other hand, has two aggravated forms, with terms of imprisonment for from six to twelve years. The first level applies if the theft is committed by group conspiracy; burglary of a dwelling or other building; with use of force not dangerous to life or health or threat of such force; or in a large amount. The most aggravated level applies if the theft is committed by an orggroup or in especially large amounts (s. 161(2, 3)).

Robbery (*razboy*) is described as an attack with the aim of stealing another's property committed with the use of force dangerous to life or health or a threat thereof. A robbery is complete at the moment of the attack with intent to steal. It is not required that anything actually be stolen (¶ 6, SCRF-Expl.: Theft). Simple robbery is punished by deprivation of liberty for from three to eight years. There are three aggravated forms of robbery. The first applies when the robbery is committed by group conspiracy or with the use of a weapon. The second applies when the robbery is committed following burglary of a dwelling or other building or in a large amount. Finally, the superaggravated form applies when the robbery is committed by an orggroup, with intent to steal especially large amounts, or with infliction of grave harm to the health of the victim and is punishable by from eight to fifteen years' deprivation of liberty (s. 162(1–4)).

Aggravated open theft and robbery are distinguished by the character of the force or threats used. The use of force "not dangerous to life or health" that aggravates the punishment for open theft includes a beating or other violent acts connected with infliction of physical pain or limitation of freedom (such as binding the hands of the victim, using handcuffs, or locking him or her in a room), whereas the force "dangerous to life and health" required for robbery means force that caused mild, grave, or moderately grave harm to health or harm that impaired the victim's ability to work. If the grave harm to health actually results in death (and there was no intent to kill), then the defendant is guilty of superaggravated robbery. If, however, the limitation of freedom imposed during an open theft constitutes a significant harm to health (being tied up in a cold room without possibility of calling for help), then the acts could qualify as robbery. If the thief brandishes an unloaded, unworkable, or toy gun without intent to use it to inflict serious injury, the theft should still be qualified as robbery unless the victim knew that the weapon was not dangerous, in which case the offense would be characterized as open theft (¶¶ 21, 23, SCRF-Expl.: Theft).

If more than one person engages in a conspiracy to commit an aggravated robbery with the use of a weapon, then all are guilty even though only one uses the weapon. If the conspiracy is to commit a secret theft, however, and one or more of the executors commit an open theft or a robbery, then all conspirators are guilty of open theft or robbery, aggravated through the group conspiracy (¶ 14, SCRF-Expl.: Theft).

Thieves and robbers are not subject to aggravated punishment because of recidivism, but they may be sentenced in the aggregate for a series of thefts, but to no more than 1.5 times the punishment for the most serious crime (s. 69(2, 3)). But if a thief engages in a "continuous theft," that is, the repeated taking of property from one and the same source united by a single larcenous intent, then the thief is guilty of only one offense (¶ 16, SCRF-Expl.: Theft).

As noted earlier, burglary is not an autonomous offense but an aggravated form of theft or robbery. The actor must have the intent to steal at the time of entering the building or dwelling but is also guilty if he or she is able to remove the stolen items from the building without crossing its threshold. If the intent to steal was formed after the person entered a building with consent of a friend or relative, or entered a commercial showroom or a store, then there is no burglary (¶¶ 18, 19, SCRF-Expl.: Theft).

Extortion of property or money may be committed "through threat of application of force or destruction or damaging of another's property, or through threat of disseminating information which puts the aggrieved party or his close relatives into disrepute or other information which can cause substantial damage to the rights or legal interests of the aggrieved party or his close relatives." It is punished in its nonaggravated form like open theft. Two further levels of aggravation, similar to those applying to other forms of theft, can raise the deprivation of liberty to from seven to fifteen years (s. 163(1–3)).

Fraud (*moshennichestvo*), misappropriation (*prisvoenie*), and embezzlement (*rastrata*) are punished in their nonaggravated forms like secret theft, and two levels of aggravation, similar to those outlined earlier, can raise the maximum punishment to from five to ten years (ss. 159(1–4), 160(1–4)).

Fraud is committed through the use of deception or abuse of trust that causes the owner of property or another with authority over the property to transfer rights to the property to another or to fail to stop the acquisition of such rights by another. Such deception can consist in knowingly reporting clearly false information or keeping quiet about true facts, or offering falsified commodities, or committing other acts that lead the property owner into confusion. Abuse of trust can be based on circumstances like work position or personal or family relationships between the guilty person and the victim. It can also take place by taking on duties one does not intend to fulfill in order to obtain property without payment, such as obtaining credit, an advance on work to be done, or prepayment for delivery of goods. Fraud may also be committed through illegal receipt of social payments or subsidies; use of the documents of others, such as a pension guarantee, a certificate that a baby was born, or a bank deposit book; or by presenting clearly false information to executive organs or public agencies or concealing information (¶¶ 1-3, 11, SCRF-Expl.: Fraud).

The SCRF has upheld findings of intent to steal in fraud cases based on circumstantial evidence, such as the clear lack of real financial means to fulfill the contractual obligations, lack of the necessary license to carry on the activity, use of fictitious charter documents or letters of guarantee, the concealment of information about the existence of debts or liens on property, or the creation of a shell enterprise (¶ 5, SCRF-Expl.: Fraud).

Aggravated forms of theft have been articulated in separate sections of the UK based on the importance of the item stolen, such as theft of (1) "objects having special historical, scientific, artistic or cultural value" (s. 164(1, 2)); (2) weapons, explosives, or materials used to manufacture weapons of mass destruction (s. 226(1-4)); and (3) narcotic or psychotropic substances (s. 229(1-3)). Each of these offenses has typical and sometimes not-so-typical aggravating factors that increase the already-substantial punishment.

E. "Victimless" Crimes: Drug and Narcotics Offenses

Drug abuse has skyrocketed since the collapse of the USSR, and the SCRF recently proclaimed that it was threatening national security, especially because of its effect on children and youth (preamble, SCRF-Expl.: Drugs). Nonetheless, the 2003 amendments succeeded in decriminalizing the most "victimless" forms of these crimes, that is, the possession of small amounts of narcotics and the sale of narcotics in amounts not exceeding ten times the amount needed for a single dose.

The illegal acquisition, possession, transportation, preparation, or mixing of narcotic or psychotropic substances or their analogues (hereafter "drugs") without intent to sell is criminally punished only if it involves "large amounts," and the maximum punishment is deprivation of liberty for up to three years. In the case of especially large amounts, the punishment rises to from three to ten years (s. 228(1, 2)). Drug traffickers can, however, liberate themselves from criminal responsibility if they voluntarily turn over their drugs (if this is not done as a result of being arrested or successfully searched) and work actively with law enforcement (s. 228, note 1) (see II.C.1 *supra*). Although illegal transfer of drugs can be in the form of a gift, satisfaction of a loan, and even an injection, when a person injects another with that person's own drugs or with drugs purchased for mutual use, then the conduct is not punishable (¶ 5, SCRF-Expl.: Drugs).

Illegal production, sale, or transport of drugs, however, is punished by deprivation of liberty for from four to eight years. Two levels of aggravation exist, with the maximum punishment reaching to from eight to twelve years. The lower level exists when the crime is committed by group conspiracy, in large amounts, or by an adult in relation to a person known to be a juvenile. The superaggravated sentences apply when the crime is committed by an orggroup, by exploiting one's public office, in relation to children known to be under fourteen years of age, or in especially large amounts (s. 228.1(1-3)). The transportation of drugs across international borders is punished in a separate section of the Special Part as *kontraband* by three to seven years' deprivation of liberty, with enhancements for using one's "official position," using force, or committing the crime as an orggroup (s. 188(2–4)).

Illegal cultivation of plants that contain narcotic substances is punished by up to two years' deprivation of liberty in its nonaggravated form, but by from three to eight years if committed by group conspiracy, orggroup, or in large amounts (s. 231(1, 2)).

Drug crimes can, however, claim victims, and, as can be expected under the Russian concrete approach to crime, the penalties rise accordingly. Inducing another to use drugs is punished by deprivation of liberty for up to five years, escalating to from three to eight years if committed by group conspiracy or orggroup, in relation to two or more persons, or by use of force or threat of force, and to from six to twelve years if a person dies as a negligent result of the inducement or there are "other grave consequences" (s. 230(1–3)). "Other grave consequences" include suicide, attempted suicide, development of addiction, and infection with HIV. A person can be guilty of inducement to drug use by performing an act only once that is "aimed at awakening in another person the desire to use the illegal drugs," even if the person "induced" does not actually use the drugs (¶¶ 27, 28, SCRF-Expl.: Drugs).

A surprisingly stiff punishment of up to four years' deprivation of liberty is provided for organizing or maintaining a den for the use of narcotics, which can rise to from three to seven years if the act is committed by an orggroup (s. 232(1, 2)). "Organizing" a den includes the acts of "searching for, financing, obtaining, renting, or repairing of premises" with the intent that it be used for consumption of drugs by more than one person. "Maintaining" a den could consist in paying the rent, using the space, charging for its use, or providing security as long as the den is actually used either twice by one person or once by more than one person (¶ 32, SCRF-Expl.:Drugs).

The code does not articulate a separate offense for selling "bunk," that is, selling a noncontrolled substance in lieu of illegal drugs. The SCRF, however, characterizes the acts of the seller as "fraud" (s. 159) and those of the buyer as attempted illegal acquisition of drugs (ss. 30(3), 228) (¶ 16, SCRF-Expl.: Drugs).

F. Other Offenses

1. Economic Crimes

Some of the most radical changes in the UK are contained in part VIII, "Crimes in the Economic Sphere." Under Soviet law all types of private enterprise were illegal and, at times, severely punished. Article 8(2) Const. RF guarantees the "free movement of goods, services and financial resources, support for competition and freedom of economic activity," and article 34(1) Const. RF guarantees the right of everyone to free use of his or her capabilities and property for entrepreneurial and other economic activities not prohibited by law. Part VIII has responded by including criminal offenses that can be separated, generally, into nine groups: (1) crimes of public officials in regulating economic activity; (2) violations of laws regulating entrepreneurial activity; and crimes in the area of (3) credit relations; (4) monopoly and unfair competition; (5) monetary circulation and securities; (6) customs; (7) currency; (8) bankruptcy; and (9) taxes.[38]

Here, as in other areas, there is a complete absence of abstract endangerment provisions, and a concrete harmful result is required for violations of regulations and rules to be criminally punishable. Thus "illegal entrepreneurialism," which includes conducting business in violation of registration or permit rules, is punishable by a fine, obligatory labor, or short-term detention for from four to six months only if it caused great loss to citizens, organizations, or the state or was connected with receipt of income in large amounts. Further aggravation applies for larger amounts or when an orggroup is involved (s. 171(1, 2)). For one to be guilty of illegal entrepreneurialism, one's activity must be aimed at obtaining a systematic profit from using property, selling commodities, doing work, or providing services and must be realized independently at one's own risk, without having registered under the procedure provided by law in the quality of an "individual entrepreneur." The SCRF recognizes an exception for property purchased, inherited, or obtained as a gift that is temporarily rented at a profit at a time when it is not personally used by the owner (¶¶ 1, 2, SCRF-Expl.: Illegal Entrepreneurialism and Money Laundering).

Some violations, such as false labeling (s. 171.1(1, 2)) and currency violations (s. 194(1, 2)), are criminalized only if they are committed in "large amounts." An exception is made for trafficking in precious metals, stones, or gems, which is punishable upon mere violations of the rules by short-term detention of up to six months. Deprivation of liberty of up to seven years, however, may be imposed if "large amounts" are involved (s. 191(1, 2)).

Other violations are punished criminally only if they result in "large or exceptionally large losses." Examples are (1) illegal banking (s. 172(1)), (2) creating of shell companies (s. 173), (3) fraudulent receipt of credit (s. 176(1)), (4) hindrance of market competition (s. 178(1)), (5) securities fraud (s. 185(1)), and (6) bankruptcy violations (ss. 195, 196, 197).

Although conducting an unlicensed medical or pharmaceutical practice is punished under chapter 25 dealing with crimes against public health and morals when harm to health or a death is caused through carelessness (s. 235), the SCRF has indicated that it is to be punished as "illegal entrepreneurialism" (s. 171(1, 2)) if it caused "large losses" to citizens or resulted in "a large income" for the guilty parties. However, if more specific sections of the code cover certain types of illegal business, such as the illegal sale of firearms or narcotics, then the crimes should not be prosecuted under section 171. Furthermore, if a person engages in illegal entrepreneurial activity by producing or trading in falsified commodities, such as alcoholic beverages or medicines, as if they were genuine and thus demanding a price far in excess of the value of the item sold, then the conduct should be punished as fraud, not under section 171 (¶¶ 5, 18, SCRF-Expl.: Illegal Entrepreneurialism and Money Laundering).

Where a legal entity (business or corporation) that is not otherwise subject to criminal sanctions in Russia (see II.B.3 *supra*) is in violation of section 171 because it is unlicensed, punishment is limited to those who permanently, temporarily, or factually fulfill managerial functions or have the right without power of attorney to act in the name of the legal entity. Workers or other employees not in managerial positions who carry out acts of the legal entity that constitute illegal entrepreneurialism are not subject to punishment (¶¶ 10, 11, SCRF-Expl.: Illegal Entrepreneurialism and Money Laundering).

The "legalization (laundering) of monetary instruments or other property (hereafter 'assets') obtained by criminal means" was criminalized as part of the 2003 amendments. In its nonaggravated form, one is subject to no punishment greater than a fine if one commits "financial operations or other deals" with assets, "knowing that they were obtained by others through criminal means... with the intent of giving their possession, use or distribution a legal appearance" (s. 174), or commits the same acts in relation to assets one has oneself obtained through criminal means or uses them in entrepreneurial or economic activities (s. 174.1). However, three levels of aggravation relating to group activity or using official position can lead to punishment of up to twelve years' deprivation of liberty in relation to assets acquired by others criminally and up to ten to fifteen years in relation to assets one has oneself obtained through criminal means (ss. 174(1–4), 174.1(1–4)). The aggravating factor of "official position" can apply to officials in a private enterprise or corporation if they are carrying out managerial functions, and a notary who certifies a transaction knowing that its purpose is laundering illegal gains can be guilty as an accomplice of money laundering (ss. 33(5), 174) (¶¶ 23, 24, SCRF-Expl.: Illegal Entrepreneurialism and Money Laundering).

The SCRF has explained that "financial operations or other deals" include contracts to obtain credit, making a bank deposit, and investing in economic projects. "Other deals" may include transfer through gift or inheritance. Only one financial operation or deal is sufficient for liability to ensue. Mere sale of illegally acquired property does not qualify as money laundering because there is no intent to give the property a legal appearance. However, if a person who illegally obtains property enters into a contract with another to sell the property, and the purchaser knows that the property was obtained criminally and intends to give the property a legal appearance, the purchaser is guilty under section 174 and the seller under section 174-1 (¶¶ 19, 20, 25, 26, SCRF-Expl.: Illegal Entrepreneurialism and Money Laundering). The use of money obtained from the sale of narcotics to buy a gold ring does not constitute a violation of section 174-1 because the defendant was using it for his or her own personal needs, not to disguise its character.[39]

2. Environmental Crimes

Article 42 of the constitution guarantees the right to a "favorable environment, credible information as to its condition, and compensation for harm caused to health and property by ecological law violations." The UK punishes seventeen "ecological" crimes. These crimes can be divided into three main categories: (1) violations of rules dealing with improper handling of dangerous substances, such as biological agents, toxins, and radioactive materials; (2) acts infringing on specific environmental resources: water, atmosphere, soil, forest, subsoil, continental shelf, and specially protected natural territories and objects; and (3) acts infringing on flora and fauna, biological diversity, and preservation of the biosphere..[40]

The need for strong environmental protection laws in Russia stems from an acute awareness among the population and the legislature of the devastating effects of Soviet industrialization, which included not only the Chernobyl disaster in 1986 but a similar nuclear leak in Chelyabinsk region in 1957, massive oil spills in the Russian north, and the disappearance of the Aral Sea in Soviet central Asia, just to name a few. As of 1995, 40 percent of all Russian inland waters were polluted.

Because the great bulk of environmental offenses require a concrete, harmful result or at least concrete danger to the environment or human health, "the establishment of causation between the acts committed and the resulting harmful consequences or the incidence of threats of significant damage to the environment and human health takes on special significance" (¶ 2, SCRF-Expl.: Ecological Crimes).

The crimes in this area are classically crimes with two forms of guilt, one relating to the *actus reus*, the other to the result. The *actus reus*, however, is either the violation of rules relating to environmentally dangerous activity that are fixed in nonpenal environmental protection legislation, or acts of "pollution" of an environmental resource. Normally, the actor must act with "intent" (direct or indirect) in relation to the violation of the rules or the act of pollution and in relation to the result (unless "carelessness" is specifically provided for in the provision).[41] Thus "air pollution," for which the maximum nonaggravated punishment is short-term detention for up to three months, is described as a "violation of the rules of emission into the atmosphere of polluting substances or violation of the exploitation of rigs, structures or other objects if these acts caused pollution or other changes to the natural properties of the air." Since no mental state is mentioned, intent must be proved in relation to the result. Two forms of aggravation, however, permit "careless" (negligent) liability for "harm to human health," punishable by up to two years' deprivation of liberty, and "the death of a person," punishable by up to five years (s. 251(1–3)). The SCRF has defined "harm to human health" as the deterioration of health so as to cause a temporary or permanent inability to work, or the infliction of from mild to grave damage to the health of one or more persons (¶ 4, SCRF-Expl.: Ecological Crimes).

"Water pollution," subject to the same punishments in its nonaggravated form as air pollution, does not refer to rules but is defined as "polluting, obstructing, exhausting of the surface or underground waters, sources of drinking water or causing changes of their natural characteristics, if these acts caused substantial harm to the animal or plant world, fish stocks, forests or agriculture." If the defendant intentionally causes harm to human health or massive death of animals or commits the offense in specially protected zones (e.g., national parks, ecological disaster areas), he or she can face up to two years' deprivation of liberty. Negligently causing a death is punished the same as with air pollution (s. 250(1–3)).

Punishments for illegal hunting, fishing, and cutting of timber, sources of great profits in Russia, include aggravating factors similar to those applied to economic crimes. The results are also not related to danger to human health but rather to economic aims (ss. 256, 258, 260, 261). An example is "illegal poaching of fish, marine or river animals or algae," where the maximum nonaggravated punishment is from three to six months' short-term detention if the actor inflicts a "large loss," uses a means of massive destruction of animals or plants, such as explosives or electricity, or commits the crime in breeding grounds or migrational pathways or in specially protected areas. The aggravated form, punishable by up to two years' deprivation of liberty, is applicable if the actor exploited his or her official position or was part of a group conspiracy or orggroup (s. 256 (1–3)).

The most severe form of environmental crime, ecocide, described as the "mass destruction of the plant or animal world, poisoning of atmosphere or water resources or other acts capable of calling forth an ecological catastrophe," is included in the chapter on crimes against humanity and is punishable by twelve to twenty years' deprivation of liberty (s. 358). It clearly requires direct or indirect intent.

3. Hooliganism

The crime of "hooliganism" (*khuliganstvo*) takes its name from the drunken exploits of Irish seamen, but it is now a peculiarly Soviet-Russian crime. It first appeared in the 1922 Soviet Russian criminal code as a crime against "life, health and dignity" and reappeared in the 1926 code as a crime against "administration." In the 1960 Soviet code it was finally placed in the section of crimes against social security, where it has remained. It originally began as an offense aimed at conduct that in the United States could be called "disturbing the peace" or being "drunk and disorderly." Hooliganism traditionally involved rowdy drunkenness that escalated into personal injury or property destruction, and nearly all those prosecuted were intoxicated at the time of the offense. Traditionally, "hooliganism" was described as "gross mischief and drunken boldness, and striving in an acute way to show one's power and strength, a desire to show disdain to those around one, to draw attention to oneself with one's cynical behavior."[42]

In the last Soviet code "hooliganism" was described as "intentional acts that grossly violate social order and express a clear disrespect for society." An aggravated form, "malicious hooliganism," applied to those with prior hooliganism convictions, those who acted against representatives of the state or social organizations, or whose conduct "distinguishes itself by its unmistakable cynicism or audacity" (s. 206 UK-1960).

The definition of petty hooliganism was taken directly from the last Soviet code, but the crime has gone through several permutations and has today become a crime of concrete endangerment. In the original 1996 version of the UK it was limited to cases involving force used against citizens, but pursuant to amendments in 2003 and 2007, hooliganism may be punished as a crime only if it is committed either "with the use of a weapon or objects used like a weapon" or "for reasons of political, ideological, racial, national or religious hatred or animosity or for reasons of hatred or animosity in relation to any social group" (hereafter "extremist motivation"), and it is punishable by up to five years' deprivation of liberty. An aggravated form, punishable by up to seven years, applies to acts committed by a group conspiracy or orggroup or coupled with opposition to a representative of state power or another person carrying out functions of preserving the public peace (s. 213(1, 2)). Petty hooliganism has been decriminalized and is treated as an administrative violation.

Because of the inherent vagueness of the definition of petty hooliganism, confusion arises when a charge of hooliganism is coupled with other conduct that clearly violates more precise sections of the UK. For instance, the SCRF has noted that one might injure someone as a result of "extremist motivation," but the act might not reflect a "gross violation of social order, giving rise to clear disrespect of society." In such a case the conduct should thus be qualified as the aggravated intentional infliction of midlevel harm to health based on extremist motivation (s. 112(2)(e)) (¶ 12, SCRF-Expl.: Hooliganism).

Critics have pointed out the absurdity of such holdings and maintain that serious crimes, such as attacks based on extremist motivation, torture, or desecration of a corpse, indeed, most intentional crimes, are per se "gross violation[s] of social order expressing a clear disrespect for society."[43] For instance, vandalism with extremist motivation constitutes aggravated vandalism and is punished by deprivation of liberty for up to three years (s. 214(2)), but if it is also coupled with hooliganism, then the acts should be qualified as hooliganism (s. 213(1)(b)). One must also intend to commit hooliganism and simultaneously intend to do it out of extremist motivation. But there is a separate section of the UK that punishes "acts, aimed at awakening hatred or animosity, or at denigrating the dignity of a person or group of persons due to reasons of sex, race, nationality, language, origin, relation to religion, or belonging to any social group, committed publicly or by using means of mass communication" (s. 282).

The SCRF also tries to distinguish "normal" criminal assaults, motivated, for example, by insults, personal animosity, or improper acts by the victim, from those inflicted "without any reason at all or due to an insignificant reason" (¶¶ 12, 13, SCRF-Expl.: Hooliganism). This also leads to bizarre formulations such as the following in a 2002 case: "Lopukhov, not desiring to violate social order [i.e., without hooliganistic motivation] followed them [the victims] to the door of the house where, feeling animosity toward them, drew, a cigarette lighter-pistol, decided to scare them, and then hit R several times with the cigarette lighter-pistol, as a result of which a fight started."[44]

The SCRF has directed judges, in handling cases of hooliganism, to take into account the means, time, and place of its commission and its intensity, duration, and other circumstances. The acts may be committed in relation to a concrete person or an undifferentiated group of people. "Clear disrespect of society" is reflected, according to the SCRF, in "the intentional violation of universally recognized norms and rules of conduct, dictated by the desire of the guilty person to confront those surrounding him, to demonstrate a disrespectful relation to them" (¶ 1, SCRF-Expl.: Hooliganism). Thus hooliganism is still an aggravated variant of disturbing the public peace, for there are decisions that require that the conduct take place in public.[45]

Although critics have called for the abolition of the independent crime of hooliganism and leaving "hooliganistic motivation" only as an aggravating circumstance for certain crimes,[46] this vague, protean version of drunken and disorderly conduct, which long ago would have been declared unconstitutionally vague in the United States, persists, likely as a sentimental vestige of Soviet criminal law, much as felony murder persists, despite its irrationality, because of nostalgic attachment to the common law.

SELECTED BIBLIOGRAPHY

Books

Burnham, William, Peter B. Maggs, and Gennady M. Danilenko. *Law and Legal System of the Russian Federation*. 3d ed. New York: Parker School of Foreign and Comparative Law, Columbia University, 2005.
Butler, William E. *Russian Law*. 2d ed. Oxford: Oxford University Press, 2003.
Kudriavtsev, V. N., V. V. Luneev, and A. V. Naumov, eds. *Ugolovnoe pravo Rossii: Osobennaia chast'* [Criminal Law of Russia: Special Part]. Moscow: Yurist', 2006.
Kuznetsova, N. F., and I. M. Tiazhkova, eds. *Ugolovnoe pravo Rossii: Obshchaia chast'* [Criminal Law of Russia: General Part]. Moscow: Zertsalo, 2005.

Lebedev, V. V., and S. V. Borodin, eds. *Sudebnaia praktika k ugolovnomu kodeksu Rossiyskoy Federatsii* [Judicial Practice Based on the Criminal Code of the Russian Federation]. Moscow: Spark, 2001.

Naumov, A. V., ed. *Kommentariy k ugolovnomu kodeksu Rossiyskoy Federatsii* [Commentary to the Criminal Code of the Russian Federation]. 3d ed. Moscow: Yurist', 2004.

Nethercott, Frances. *Russian Legal Culture before and after Communism*. London: Routledge, 2007.

Smith, Gordon B. *Reforming the Russian Legal System*. Cambridge: Cambridge University Press, 1996.

Chapters

Schroeder, Friedrich-Christian. Introduction to *Strafgesetzbuch der Russischen Föderation*, ed. Friedrich-Christian Schroeder. Berlin: Duncker & Humblot, 2007, 1–47.

Thaman, Stephen C. "Comparative Criminal Law and Enforcement: Russia." In *Encyclopedia of Crime and Justice*, ed. Joshua Dressler. Farmington Hills, MI: Macmillan Reference, 2001, 207–217.

Thaman, Stephen C. "The Two Faces of Justice in the Post-Soviet Legal Sphere: Adversarial Procedure, Jury Trial, Plea Bargaining and the Inquisitorial Legacy." In *Crime, Procedure and Evidence in International and Comparative Context: Essays in Honour of Professor Mirjan Damaska*, ed. John Jackson, Máximo Langer, and Peter Tillers. Oxford: Hart, 2008, 99–118.

Articles

Agapov, P. V. "Poniatie i priznaki prestupnogo soobshchestva (prestupnoy organizatsii) po ugolovnomu pravu Rossii: Problemy zakonodatel'noy reglamentatsii" [Understanding and Elements of a Criminal Association (Organization) in the Criminal Law of Russia]. *Gosudarstvo i pravo* no.12 (2007): 47–54.

Baburin, V. V. "Differentsiatsiia ugolovnoy otvetstvennosti za neobosnovannyy risk" [The Differentiation of Criminal Responsibility for Unjustifiable Risk]. *Gosudarstvo i pravo*, no. 3 (2008): 46–53.

Barry, Donald D., and Eric J. Williams. "Russia's Death Penalty Dilemmas." *Criminal Law Forum* 8 (1997): 231–258.

Ivanov, I. G. "Khuliganstvo kak prestuplenie: Kriticheskiy vzgliad" [Hooliganism as a Crime: A Critical View]. *Gosudarstvo i pravo* no. 6 (2009): 53–61.

Krug, Peter. "Departure from the Centralized Model: The Russian Supreme Court and Constitutional Control of Legislation." *Virginia Journal of International Law* 37 (1997): 725–787.

Muradov, Ye. "Oshibki pri kvalifikatsii ekonomicheskikh prestupleniy" [Errors in Qualifying Economic Crimes]. *Rossiyskaia yustitsiia*, no. 1 (2004): 45–46.

Naumov, Anatoliy V. "The New Russian Criminal Code as a Reflection of Ongoing Reforms." *Criminal Law Forum* 8 (1997): 191–230.

Thaman, Stephen C. "The Nullification of the Russian Jury: Lessons for Jury-Inspired Reform in Eurasia and Beyond." *Cornell International Law Journal* 40 (2007): 357–428.

Thaman, Stephen C. "The Resurrection of Trial by Jury in Russia." *Stanford Journal of International Law* 31 (1995): 61–274.

Legislation

Ugolovno-protsessual'nyy kodeks Rossiyskoy Federatsii [Criminal Procedure Code of the Russian Federation]. Moscow: INFRA-M, 2005 (UPK).

Ugolovnyy kodeks Rossiyskoy Federatsii. Federal Law 63-F3, June 13, 1996. In *Ugolovnyy kodeks Rossiyskoy Federatsii* [Criminal Code of the Russian Federation]. Moscow: Prospekt, 2009 (cited in the text as UK, with sections indicated by "s").

Ugolovnyy kodeks RSFSR [Criminal Code of the RSFSR], October 27, 1960. In *Zakony RSFSR i postanovleniia Verkhovnogo Soveta RSFSR* [Laws of the RSFSR and Resolutions of the Supreme Soviet of the RSFSR], 58–158. Moscow: Supreme Soviet RSFSR, 1960 (UK-1960).

Court Opinions

Biulleten' Verkhovnogo Suda Rossiyskoy Federatsii (SCRF Bulletin). http://www.supcourt.ru/vscourt_detale.

Obzor nadzornoy praktiki sudebnoy kollegii po ugolovnym delam Verkhovnogo suda Rossiyskoy Federatsii za 2008 god (SCRF-Criminal Review Practice-2008). http://www.supcourt.ru/vscourt_detale.php?id=5921.

Postanovlenie Plenuma Verkhovnogo Suda Rossiyskoy Federatsii [Resolution of the Plenum of the Supreme Court of the Russian Federation], no. 8 (October 31, 1995): "O nekotorykh voprosakh primeneniia sudami Konstitutsii Rossiyskoy Federatsii pri osushchestvlenii pravosudiia" [On Some Questions on the Courts' Application of the Constitution of the Russian Federation in the Administration of Justice] (SCRF-Expl.: Constitutional Application).

Postanovlenie Plenuma Verkhovnogo Suda Rossiyskoy Federatsii, no. 14 (November 5, 1998, with changes from February 6, 2007): "O praktike primeneniia sudami zakonodatel'stva ob otvetstvennosti za ekologicheskie pravonarusheniia" [On the Practice of the Courts' Application of the Legislation on Responsibility for Ecological Law Violations] (SCRF-Expl.: Ecological Crimes). http://www.supcourt.ru/vscourt_detale.php?id=971.

Postanovlenie Plenuma Verkhovnogo Suda Rossiyskoy Federatsii, no. 1 (January 17, 1999): "O sudebnoy praktike po delam ob ubiystve" [On Judicial Practice in Cases of Murder] (SCRF-Expl.: Murder). http://www.supcourt.ru/vscourt_detale.php?id=984.

Postanovlenie Plenuma Verkhovnogo Suda Rossiyskoy Federatsii, no. 29 (December 27, 2002): "O sudebnoy praktike po delam o krazhe, grabezhe i razboe" [On Judicial Practice in Cases of Secret Theft, Open Theft and Robbery] (SCRF-Expl.: Theft). http://www.supcourt.ru/vscourt_detale.php?id=1132.

Postanovlenie Plenuma Verkhovnogo Suda Rossiyskoy Federatsii, no. 11 (June 15, 2004): "O sudebnoy praktike po delam o prestupleniiakh, predusmotrennykh stat'iami 131 i 132 Ugolovnogo kodeksa Rossiyskoy Federatsii"[On Judicial Practice in Cases of Crimes Provided for in Articles 131 and 132 of the Criminal Code of the Russian Federation] (SCRF-Expl.: Rape). http://www.supcourt.ru/vscourt_detale.php?id=1547.

Postanovlenie Plenuma Verkhovnogo Suda Rossiyskoy Federatsii, no. 23 (November 18, 2004): "O sudebnoy praktike po delam o nezakonnom predprinimatel'stve i legalizatsii (otmyvanii) denezhnykh sredstv ili inogo imushchestva, priobretennykh pretupnym putem" [On Judicial Practice in Cases of Illegal Entrepreneurialism and the Legalization (Laundering) of Money or Other Property Obtained by Criminal Means] (SCRF-Expl.: Illegal Entrepreneurialism and Money Laundering). http://www.supcourt.ru/vscourt_detale.php?id=1559.

Postanovlenie Plenuma Verkhovnogo Suda Rossiyskoy Federatsii, no. 14 (June 15, 2006): "O sudebnoy praktike po delam o prestuplenniakh, sviazannykh s narkoticheskimi sredstvami, psikhotropnymi, sil'nodeystvuiushchimi i yadovitymi veshchestvami" [On Judicial Practice in Cases of Crimes Connected with Narcotic, Psychotropic, Virulent or Poisonous Substances] (SCRF- Expl.: Drugs). http://www.supcourt.ru/vscourt_detale.php?id=4348.

Postanovlenie Plenuma Verkhovnogo Suda Rossiyskoy Federatsii, no. 45 (November 13, 2007): "O sudebnoy praktike po ugolovnym delam o khyliganstve i inykh prestupleniiakh sovershennykh iz khuliganstikh pubuzhdeniiy" [On Judicial Practice in Criminal Cases of Hooliganism or Other Crimes Committed with Hooliganistic Motivation] (SCRF-Expl.: Hooliganism). http://www.supcourt.ru/vscourt_detale.php?id=5066.

Postanovlenie Plenuma Verkhovnogo Suda Rossiyskoy Federatsii, no. 51 (December 27, 2007): "O sudebnoy praktike po delam o moshennichestve, prisvoenii i rastrate" [On Judicial Practice in Cases of Fraud, Misappropriation and Embezzlement] (SCRF-Expl.: Fraud). http://www.supcourt.ru/vscourt_detale.php?id=5120.

Postanovlenie Plenuma Verkhovnogo Suda Rossiyskoy Federatsii, no. 8 (June 10, 2008): "O sudebnoy praktike rassmotreniia ugolovnykh del ob organizatsii prestupnogo soobshchestva (prestupnoy organizatsii)" [On Judicial Practice in Hearing Criminal Cases Concerning the Organization of a Criminal Association (Criminal Organization] (SCRF-Expl.: Crimorg). http://www.supcourt.ru/vscourt_detale.php?id=5334

Postanovlenie Plenuma Verkhovnogo Suda Rossiyskoy Federatsii, no. 8 (April 21, 2009): "O sudebnoy praktike uslovnogo dosrochnogo osvobozhdeniia ot otbyvaniia nakazaniia, zameny neotbytoy chasti nakazaniia bolee miagkim vidom nakazaniia" [On Judicial Practice of Conditional Early Release from Serving a Sentence, and Substitution of the Part of a Sentence not Served for a Milder Form of Punishment] (SCRF-Expl.: Parole). http://www.supcourt.ru/vscourt_detale.php?id=5747.

NOTES

1. Gordon B. Smith, *Reforming the Russian Legal System* (Cambridge: Cambridge University Press, 1996), 2–5.

2. Frances Nethercott, *Russian Legal Culture before and after Communism* (London: Routledge, 2007), 2, 25.

3. Friedrich-Christian Schroeder, introduction to *Strafgesetzbuch der Russischen Föderation*, ed. Friedrich-Christian Schroeder (Berlin: Duncker & Humblot, 2007), 1–47, 7–10.

4. Anatoliy V. Naumov, "The New Russian Criminal Code as a Reflection of Ongoing Reforms," *Criminal Law Forum* 8 (1997): 191–230, 192–193.

5. Stephen C. Thaman, "Comparative Criminal Law and Enforcement: Russia," in *Encyclopedia of Crime and Justice*, ed. Joshua Dressler (Farmington Hills, MI: Macmillan Reference, 2001), 207–217, 207, 214.

6. Schroeder, introduction, 29.

7. Peter Krug, "Departure from the Centralized Model: The Russian Supreme Court and Constitutional Control of Legislation," *Virginia Journal of International Law* 37 (1997): 725–787, 735–736.

8. Full citations of the various SCRF-Expls. are given in the Selected Bibliography.

9. *Equality of arms* is a term used in human rights conventions to mean that both sides have equal procedural rights.

10. Stephen C. Thaman, "The Resurrection of Trial by Jury in Russia," *Stanford Journal of International Law* 31 (1995): 61–274, 61–70.

11. Stephen C. Thaman, "The Two Faces of Justice in the Post-Soviet Legal Sphere: Adversarial Procedure, Jury Trial, Plea Bargaining and the Inquisitorial Legacy," in *Crime, Procedure and Evidence in International and Comparative Context: Essays in Honour of Professor Mirjan Damaska*, ed. John Jackson, Máximo Langer, and Peter Tillers (Oxford: Hart, 2008), 99–118, 110–111.

12. Stephen C. Thaman, "The Nullification of the Russian Jury: Lessons for Jury-Inspired Reform in Eurasia and Beyond," *Cornell International Law Journal* 40 (2007): 357–428, 397–402.

13. William Burnham, Peter B. Maggs, and Gennady M. Danilenko, *Law and Legal System of the Russian Federation*, 3d ed. (New York: Parker School of Foreign and Comparative Law, Columbia University, 2005), 549–610, 550–554.

14. Anatoliy V. Naumov, ed., *Kommentariy k ugolovnomu kodeksu Rossiyskoy Federatsii*, 3d ed. (Moscow: Yurist', 2004), 84–85.

15. P. V. Agapov, "Poniatie i priznaki prestupnogo soobshchestva (prestupnoy organizatsii) po ugolovnomu pravu Rossii: Problemy zakonodatel'noy reglamentatsii," *Gosudarstvo i pravo* 12 (2007): 47–54.

16. Naumov, *Kommentariy k ugolovnomu kodeksu Rossiyskoy Federatsii*, 123.

17. N. F. Kuznetsova and I. M. Tiazhkova, eds., *Ugolovnoe pravo Rossii: Obshchaia chast'* (Moscow: Zertsalo, 2005), 198–202.

18. Naumov, *Kommentariy k ugolovnomu kodeksu Rossiyskoy Federatsii*, 186.

19. Burnham, Maggs, and Danilenko, *Law and Legal System of the Russian Federation*, 584.

20. Ibid.

21. V. V. Baburin, "Differentsiatsiia ugolovnoy otvetstvennosti za neobosnovannyy risk," *Gosudarstvo i pravo*, no. 3 (2008): 46–53, 46–47.

22. Burnham, Maggs, and Danilenko, *Law and Legal System of the Russian Federation*, 585.

23. Ye. Muradov, "Oshibki pri kvalifikatsii ekonomicheskikh prestupleniy," *Rossiyskaia yustitsiia* 1 (2004): 45–46, 45.

24. Ibid., 46.

25. Nethercott, *Russian Legal Culture before and after Communism*, 33.

26. Thaman, "Nullification of the Russian Jury," 396.

27. Ibid., 399–400.

28. Naumov, *Kommentariy k ugolovnomu kodeksu Rossiyskoy Federatsii*, 83.

29. Nethercott, *Russian Legal Culture before and after Communism*, 33–34.

30. The Russian alphabet, as transliterated from Cyrillic into the Latin alphabet, proceeds as follows: a, b, v, g, d, e, zh, z, i, k, l, m, n, o, p, r, s, t, etc. I have used the transliterated Russian Cyrillic letters in this text.

31. Burnham, and Maggs, and Danilenko, *Law and Legal System of the Russian Federation*, 600.

32. Donald D. Barry and Eric J. Williams, "Russia's Death Penalty Dilemmas," *Criminal Law Forum* 8 (1997): 231–258, 233.

33. Burnham, Maggs, and Danilenko, *Law and Legal System of the Russian Federation*, 601.

34. Barry and Williams, "Russia's Death Penalty Dilemmas," 239–243; Amnesty International, "Abolitionist and Retentionist Countries," http://www.amnesty.org/en/death-penalty/abolitionist-and-retentionist-countries#practice.

35. Naumov, *Kommentariy k ugolovnomu kodeksu Rossiyskoy Federatsii*, 15.

36. V. N. Kudriavtsev, V. V. Luneev, and A. V. Naumov, eds., *Ugolovnoe pravo Rossii: Osobennaia chast'* (Moscow: Yurist', 2006), 52–53.

37. V. V. Lebedev and S. V. Borodin, eds., *Sudebnaia praktika k ugolovnomu kodeksu Rossiyskoy Federatsii* (Moscow: Spark, 2001), 103.

38. Kudriavtsev, Luneev, and Naumov, *Ugolovnoe pravo Rossii*, 186.

39. Obzor nadzornoy praktiki sudebnoy kollegii po ugolovnym delam Verkhovnogo suda Rossiyskoy Federatsii za 2008 god [Survey of the Review Practice of the Judicial Panel for Criminal Cases of the SCRF for 2008].

40. Kudriavtsev, Luneev, and Naumov, *Ugolovnoe pravo Rossii*, 344.

41. Ibid., 343–373.

42. Ibid., 275.

43. I. G. Ivanov, "Khuliganstvo kak prestuplenie: Kriticheskiy vzgliad," *Gosudarstvo i pravo* 6 (2009): 53–61, 56–57.

44. Ibid., 57.

45. Ibid., 55.

46. Ibid., 61.

SOUTH AFRICA

Jonathan Burchell

I. Introduction
   A. Historical Sketch
   B. Jurisdiction
   C. Legality Principle
   D. Sources of Criminal Law
   E. Process

II. General Part
   A. Theories of Punishment
   B. Liability Requirements
   C. Defences
   D. Justifications
   E. Excuses
   F. Sanctions

III. Special Part
   A. Protected Interests
   B. Homicide
   C. Sex Offences
   D. Theft and Fraud
   E. "Victimless" Crimes
   F. Selected Crimes with a Distinctive South African Definition

---

Jonathan Burchell is Professor of Law at the University of Cape Town. His recent publications include the coauthored *Principles of Criminal Law*, 3d ed. (Juta and Co., 2005); and *South African Criminal Law and Procedure*, vol. 1, *General Principles of Criminal Liability*, 3d ed. (Juta and Co., 1997).

I. INTRODUCTION

A. Historical Sketch

The Roman-Dutch and English roots of South African criminal law produced a hybrid or mixed system. These roots were firmly planted in South African soil by the Dutch settlers who arrived at the Cape of Good Hope in 1652 and by the British in the late eighteenth and early nineteenth centuries.

The reception of aspects of English criminal law was greatly facilitated by the Transkeian Penal Code of 1886 (applicable only to the region then known as Transkei and now only of historical interest). The English adversarial model of criminal procedure prevailed from an early stage, and trial by jury remained until 1969. Although the courts resisted the subtle English distinctions between felonies and misdemeanors, assault and battery,[1] and burglary and housebreaking, English law nevertheless exerted its influence on definition and detail of the criminal law. The basic system of criminal law remained Roman-Dutch, but the English influence was significant, at least initially, in both form and substance. This amalgam of Roman-Dutch and English law gradually spread to the other provinces of South Africa.

During the second half of the twentieth century, South African criminal law, particularly in its statutory form, was used by successive governments to promote racial segregation and oppression under the notorious policy of apartheid. Draconian security laws reinforced by emergency regulations, racially based penal provisions, and use of the death penalty evoked widespread political resistance. Substantial resistance from within and outside South Africa ultimately led, in the last years of the twentieth century, to the termination of the state of emergency, the unbanning of the African National Congress, the introduction of democratic government, the removal of racially based crimes from the statute book, and the adoption of a constitution with a bill of rights.

Legal research in criminal law has been influenced by both English and Continental sources (especially Dutch and, more recently, German). The interpretation by South African writers of theories from Germany and England has helped shape South African criminal law, while the courts have also, at times, developed peculiarly South African solutions to problems. The English and German theories that have influenced the shape of the general principles of South African criminal law will be documented in this chapter.

The present system of criminal law in South Africa is a truly mixed system, blending Roman-Dutch, English, German, and uniquely South African elements, which all require testing against the norms and values of the justiciable Bill of Rights. The indisputable fact that all criminal prosecutions inevitably involve state action means that the quintessential private-law dispute regarding the extent of the horizontal application of the Bill of Rights in South Africa is not reflected in criminal law. Principles of law, whether derived from common law, customary law, or statute, have to pass the litmus test of constitutionality. The postconstitutional ethos not only provides the catalyst for the reevaluation even of hallowed principles of statutory or common law on crime but also facilitates the continuing influence of customary law, nonstate systems of justice, and restorative justice on fundamental principles of fairness.

B. Jurisdiction

The courts that adjudicate criminal trials in South Africa are the district magistrate's courts, which can hear all criminal cases other than treason, murder, and rape and impose sentences of up to three years' imprisonment and a fine not exceeding R60,000; the regional magistrate's courts, which can try all criminal cases except treason and impose life sentences (if this punishment falls within the framework of the minimum sentence legislation referred to in this chapter; see sections IIA and II.F.2) and a maximum fine of R300,000; the High Courts, which have original jurisdiction in respect of all offences, can impose penalties up to and including life imprisonment, and can hear appeals; the Supreme Court of Appeal, which hears appeals; and the Constitutional Court, which hears constitutional challenges and has the final decision on these matters.

The territorial principle forms the basis for criminal jurisdiction in South Africa, but certain statutes, particularly in the fields of corruption, organised crime, and terrorism,[2] provide for extraterritorial jurisdiction.

Under section 18 of the Criminal Procedure Act,[3] the right to institute prosecutions for certain crimes (murder, treason committed when the Republic is in a state of war, robbery with aggravating circumstances, kidnapping, child stealing, rape, genocide, crimes against humanity, and war crimes) does not prescribe (that is, is not subject to a statute of limitations). For other crimes not listed, the period of prescription is twenty years unless another period is expressly provided.

The Diplomatic Immunities and Privileges Act[4] sets out the immunities and privileges for diplomatic missions and consular posts and for members of such missions and posts.

C. Legality Principle

Under the influence of eighteenth- and nineteenth-century European criminal theory and writing, South Africa adopted the fundamental principle of legality, which in essence requires that the criminal law should be reasonably certain in its definition, that it should not be retrospective in its operation, and that the courts, as opposed to the legislature, should not be empowered to create new crimes. The essential aspects of the principle of legality are also entrenched in sections 35(3)(*l*) and (*n*) of the Constitution of the Republic of South Africa of 1996. The South African constitution enjoins the courts to develop the common law (including criminal law) in ways that are compatible with the constitution, and so the hallowed principle of legality has to accommodate this development.[5]

D. Sources of Criminal Law

South African criminal law is found in the common law (judicial judgments), legislation (penal statutes enacted by Parliament), regulations made by the executive giving substance to these legislative provisions, and criminal offences created by subordinate legislatures such as provincial and municipal bodies. All laws (from whatever source) must comply with the constitution, and the Constitutional Court has power to invalidate rules of law that do not comply with constitutional principles.

1. Legislature

South African criminal law is not codified, but the details of certain specific crimes are contained in acts of Parliament. The legislature has enacted comprehensive statutes governing criminality in the following fields: drugs, corruption, organized crime, terrorism, and sexual offences. Provincial legislatures are granted concurrent and exclusive legislative competence over certain matters set out in the constitution.

2. Judiciary

The bulk of the general principles of the criminal law and most of the definitions of serious crimes in South Africa can be found in judicial decisions.

3. Executive

Criminal statutes often confer powers on members of the executive to promulgate regulations giving substance to broad legislative provisions.

4. Scholars

Because South African law is based on Roman-Dutch law, the writings of certain Roman-Dutch scholars of criminal law (such as Antonius Matthaeus II, Dionysius Godefridus van der Keessel, and Johannes van der Linden) exerted special influence on the development of South African criminal law in its formative phase. Modern South African writers on criminal law are also referred to in court judgments.[6]

E. Process

1. Adversarial/Inquisitorial

Rules relating to the criminal process are set out in the Criminal Procedure Act,[7] and certain fundamental procedural rights of arrested, detained, and accused persons are protected in section 35 of the Constitution of the Republic of South Africa (subject to the limitations clause contained in section 36).

Criminal proceedings are predominantly accusatorial or adversarial (a term that extends wider than the criminal process), but there are some inquisitorial influences, particularly in plea procedures. Plea and sentence agreements, which in the past were in practice entered into between the state and accused persons or their legal representatives, were formally recognized and regulated by an amendment to the Criminal Procedure Act in 2001.

2. Jury/Written Opinions

Juries in criminal trials were abolished in 1969 by the Abolition of Juries Act.[8] Magistrates and judges reach decisions on fact and law but have discretion to appoint assessors to assist in factual findings and, in the case of magistrates, where the imposition of a community-based sentence is possible.

II. GENERAL PART

A. Theories of Punishment

Courts have invoked the traditional theories of punishment, that is, retribution, prevention, deterrence (general and individual), and reformation. Courts have taken the gravity of the crime and the interests of the criminal and society into account as factors affecting sentence. More recently the restorative-justice theory has gained some prominence, especially in regard to the treatment of young offenders.[9] The legislature has also opted for minimum sentences for certain offences, with an option to depart from the prescribed sentence in "substantial and compelling circumstances."[10]

B. Liability Requirements

For criminal liability to result, the prosecution (the state) must prove, beyond reasonable doubt, that the accused has committed (i) *voluntary conduct* that is *unlawful* (sometimes referred to as *actus reus*), and that this conduct was accompanied by (ii) *criminal capacity* and (iii) *fault* (sometimes referred to as *mens rea*).

1. Objective/Actus Reus
i. Act

In essence, the criminal law punishes the conduct of human beings. However, a person may be held liable for using an animal to inflict harm on another, and in certain statutorily defined instances an artificial person (such as a company) may incur criminal liability.[11]

Criminal conduct must be *voluntary* in the sense that it is controlled by the accused's conscious will. Involuntary conduct during sleep, concussion, heavy intoxication, provocation, or severe emotional stress, for instance, is not considered by the courts to be "conduct" for the purposes of criminal liability. Automatism may also result from mental illness (insane, as opposed to sane, automatism).

However, even if an accused person acts in a state of automatism, he or she may nevertheless be criminally liable for such conduct if there was prior voluntary conduct, combined with antecedent fault, that is causally linked to the unlawful consequence committed in a state of automatism. This form of liability, which has a resonance in German jurisprudence, is based on the *actio libera in causa* (or prior conduct and fault) principle.

Courts in South Africa have warned that evidence of automatism must be carefully scrutinized and that there is a presumption that, in normal circumstances, persons act voluntarily.

In certain circumstances the criminal law punishes a "state of affairs," such as being found in possession of prohibited matter or being drunk in a public place.

ii. Omission

As a general rule, conduct must constitute doing something (a positive act) or not doing something (an omission). There is no general duty for individuals to act, but, depending on the legal convictions of the community, there may be criminal liability for a failure to act.

The legal convictions of the community have crystallized into judicial recognition that exceptional legal duties may arise in the following circumstances: where there is prior conduct on the part of the accused creating a legal duty to act (the so-called *omissio per commissionem* rule); where the accused is in control of a potentially dangerous thing or animal, which imposes on him or her a legal duty to act to prevent that thing or animal from causing harm to others; where the accused is in a protective relationship with the person harmed so as to be under a legal duty to prevent that person from suffering harm;

where the accused occupies a public or quasi-public office vis-à-vis the victim; and where either statute or contract requires a legal duty to act. The courts have affirmed that these categories do not constitute a closed list and are not watertight. Further categories or factors can be added, provided these new circumstances do not overturn the fundamental rule of no liability and remain within the constraints of the principle of legality. The Constitutional Court has emphasized that the approach of the common-law courts to the development of circumstances giving rise to a legal duty to act must be informed by and developed in accordance with constitutional norms and values.[12]

iii. Unlawfulness

The accused's conduct must be unlawful in order to lead to criminal liability. Usually this means that there must be no defence excluding unlawfulness available to the accused. The general defences excluding the unlawfulness of conduct are private defence (or self-defence), necessity, impossibility, obedience to superior orders, consent, public authority, disciplinary chastisement, *de minimis non curat lex* (the law does not concern itself with trifles), and *negotiorum gestio* (unauthorized administration). These defences are discussed in sections II.C and II.D in this chapter.

Whether entrapment is a defence has not been authoritatively decided in South African criminal law, but a 1997 High Court decision[13] rejected the defence of entrapment in South African law. However, the courts can regulate any potential abuse of state power by declaring evidence obtained as a result of an abuse of state power inadmissible in court, or by requiring that the state must come to the court "with clean hands."

2. Subjective/Mens Rea/Mental Element

i. The Concept of Capacity

In 1967 a Commission of Inquiry into the Responsibility of Mentally Deranged Persons and Related Matters (under the chairmanship of Justice F. L. H. Rumpff) recommended that the question of criminal responsibility of the insane accused be tested in terms of criminal capacity, like that of the responsibility of young children and insane persons in Roman law. Capacity means the capacity to appreciate the wrongfulness of conduct (cognitive function of the mind) and the capacity to act in accordance with that appreciation (conative function of the mind). The prosecution must prove criminal capacity beyond reasonable doubt, except in the case of pathological incapacity (insanity) (see subsection b in this section).

Criminal capacity must be present in the prosecution both of crimes based on intention and of those for which negligence is sufficient. Capacity is tested subjectively rather than objectively.

a. Youthfulness

In South Africa children under the age of ten are not criminally liable.[14] There is an irrebuttable presumption that a child under ten years of age is not criminally responsible (i.e., lacks criminal capacity) for his or her actions.

With regard to children between the ages of ten and fourteen,[15] there is a presumption that they are not criminally responsible for their conduct, but this presumption is rebuttable, and the presumption's effect weakens as the child approaches the age of fourteen. Criminal responsibility of children above the age of fourteen is assessed in the same way as that of an adult.

b. Insanity (or Pathological Incapacity)

The only common-law exception to the rule placing the onus on the state to prove the elements of criminal liability (including capacity) beyond reasonable doubt is in the context of the defence of insanity. When the defence of insanity is raised, the accused (under the influence of English law) has to prove on a balance of probabilities that he or she was suffering from a legally recognized pathological condition (mental illness or mental defect) at the time he or she committed the prohibited conduct and that this condition impaired criminal capacity.[16] Placing a burden of proof on the accused to prove insanity on a balance of probabilities is arguably an unjustifiable and unreasonable infringement of the constitutionally entrenched presumption of innocence that requires the prosecution to prove the elements of criminal liability (including criminal capacity) beyond reasonable doubt.

c. Intoxication

The leading judgment of the Appellate Division (now the Supreme Court of Appeal) in *S v Chretien*[17] rejected the application of the English specific-intent rule relating to intoxication in South Africa and affirmed that self-induced intoxication, depending on its degree, could be a complete defence excluding the voluntariness of the accused's conduct, criminal capacity, or intention. Although this judgment in 1981 opened up the opportunity for lack of capacity to succeed as a defence[18] in a case of self-induced intoxication under the common law, the legislature subsequently intervened (albeit unsuccessfully) to try to fill the gap created by *Chretien*. By enacting section 1(1) of the Criminal Law Amendment Act,[19] a vain attempt to reflect public sentiment on intoxication, the legislature has simply compounded the problems.

In essence, section 1(1) of the Criminal Law Amendment Act, modeled on section 330a1 of the German Penal Code, created a special statutory offence of committing a prohibited act while in a state of criminal incapacity induced by the voluntary consumption of alcohol. The section requires the prosecution to prove beyond reasonable doubt that the accused is not liable for a common-law offence because of lack of capacity resulting from self-induced intoxication, thus requiring the prosecution to engage in an unfamiliar volte- face. If the intoxication, leading to an acquittal of the common-law offence, is only sufficient to impair intention (as on the facts of *Chretien*), rather than sufficient to impair capacity, then no liability can result under section 1(1), because lack of capacity resulting from intoxication has to be proved for a conviction under section 1(1). The section is in need of reform or replacement with a more appropriately worded section.

d. Provocation or Emotional Stress

Roman and Roman-Dutch law did not regard anger, jealousy, or other emotions as an excuse for any criminal conduct, but only as a factor that might mitigate sentence if the anger (emotion) was justified by provocation. The Rumpff Commission of Inquiry into Responsibility of

Mentally Deranged Persons and Related Matters (1967) did not regard the affective functions of the mind, which regulate emotions, such as hatred, love, and jealousy, as relevant to the legal inquiry into criminal capacity, as opposed to punishment.

South African law might well have followed Roman and Roman-Dutch law on provocation had it not been for the introduction of the mandatory death penalty for murder in 1917. However, the courts did not follow Roman-Dutch law and the advice of the Rumpff Commission, initially inclining toward the policy-based partial-excuse rule for provoked killing (leading to a middle verdict of culpable homicide) under the influence of section 141 of the Transkeian Penal Code of 1886: homicide that would otherwise be murder could be reduced to culpable homicide if the person who caused the death did so in the heat of passion occasioned by sudden provocation and where an ordinary person would also have lost the power of self-control.

However, this partial-excuse rule was ultimately rejected in favor of a novel approach developed in the last three decades of the twentieth century, when the South African courts acknowledged that evidence of provocation was relevant not only to the existence of intention but also to a finding of criminal capacity. Under the influence of the development of the overarching subjective concept of capacity, the courts acknowledged that any factor, whether intoxication, provocation, or emotional stress, could serve to impair this criminal capacity, assessed essentially subjectively. The courts began to distinguish between the concept of "non-pathological incapacity" and that of insanity or "pathological incapacity."

In three High Court decisions and one Supreme Court of Appeal decision[20] an accused who raised the defence of non-pathological incapacity to a charge of murder was completely acquitted. The basis of the decisions was that the evidence adduced on the provocation/emotional stress experienced by the accused at the time of, or before, the killing led to a conclusion that criminal capacity had not been proved beyond reasonable doubt. The courts did not even consider the appropriateness of a conviction of culpable homicide, based on a deviation from the standard of the reasonable person, because a preliminary subjective finding of capacity was required for such a conviction as well. This approach had no obvious parallel in Anglo-American jurisprudence, and some courts were not happy with an open-ended defence of non-pathological incapacity.

The most recent pronouncement of the Supreme Court of Appeal on the matter of provocation is *S v Eadie*,[21] where the decision of the High Court, that the accused could not successfully raise the defence of non-pathological incapacity on the facts, was affirmed. The accused had battered another to death in an alleged road-rage incident. Both the High Court and the Supreme Court of Appeal in *Eadie*, drawing a pragmatic distinction between loss of control and loss of temper, held that a defence of non-pathological incapacity could not succeed.

Judge of Appeal Navsa in *Eadie* reviewed the jurisprudence on provocation and emotional stress and clearly indicated that although the test of capacity appears to remain subjective in principle, the application of this test must be approached with caution. Courts must not too readily accept the *ipse dixit* of the accused regarding provocation or emotional stress and are entitled to draw legitimate inferences from objective circumstances.

Equating the second part of the capacity inquiry with that into the voluntariness of the conduct, Judge of Appeal Navsa held that provocation would be a defence only when it led to involuntary conduct (or automatism). It is not entirely clear whether this limitation on the scope of a defence of provocation to cases of automatism applies also to instances of intoxication and domestic abuse.

ii. Intent

The overriding principle of South African criminal law is enshrined in the maxim *actus non facit reum nisi mens sit rea*—an act is not unlawful unless there is a guilty mind. Although a handful of regulatory and other statutory offences are based on strict (or no-fault) liability, the general rule is that fault is required for criminal liability and that the fault element may take the form of either intention or, in some cases, negligence. The Constitutional Court has indicated a strong antipathy toward strict liability,[22] and the Supreme Court of Appeal has shown a firm preference for the presence of negligence in the case of statutory offences.[23]

All common-law crimes are based on intention with two exceptions—culpable homicide and contempt of court by a newspaper editor—for which negligence is sufficient for liability. Even in the context of statutory criminal provisions the presumption is that fault is required for liability, and the Constitutional Court has affirmed the preeminence of fault as a requirement for criminal liability.

Fault may take two broad forms—intention (*dolus*) or negligence (*culpa*). Although there is some debate about whether negligence is a form of fault or an assessment of conduct, it seems to be accepted that failure to measure up to notional standards of reasonableness can be seen as a type of fault.

a. *Forms of Intention*

Intention is divided into four varieties—*dolus directus*, *dolus indirectus*, *dolus eventualis*, and *dolus indeterminatus*. All forms of intention are assessed subjectively, and *dolus eventualis* is a sufficient form of intention for all crimes based on intention. Motive is not equivalent to intention.

Dolus directus is intention in its ordinary grammatical sense and refers to the accused's aim and object to perpetrate the unlawful conduct or cause the unlawful consequence.

Dolus indirectus is present where the accused foresaw the unlawful conduct or consequence as certain or substantially certain to occur.

Dolus eventualis exists where the accused foresaw the possibility that the prohibited consequence might occur, in substantially the same manner as that in which it actually did occur, or the accused foresaw the possibility that the prohibited circumstance might exist, and he or she accepted this possibility into the bargain. There has been much debate on whether the foresight of even a remote possibility may be sufficient for this type of intention. There is a strong argument for restricting the scope of criminality to foresight of a real or substantial possibility and regarding foresight of any possibility short of a real or substantial one as at most satisfying the first part of a test for conscious negligence.[24] Nevertheless, in 1985 the then Appellate Division in *S v Ngubane*[25] preferred a different approach. In principle, *dolus eventualis* could extend to foresight of even a remote possibility, but the likelihood of the possibility eventuating would have a bearing on whether the accused accepted the possibility into the bargain (the so-called volitional element of *dolus eventualis*).

Dolus directus, indirectus, and *eventualis* may be general (*indeterminatus*) if the accused does not have a particular object or person in mind, for instance, if he or she throws a bomb into a crowd of people or derails a train.

b. Knowledge of Unlawfulness

If the accused genuinely does not know, or does not foresee, the possibility of the unlawfulness of his or her conduct, then he or she cannot be held to have the required guilty mind in the form of intention. Thus in South African criminal law genuine ignorance of the law may be an excuse. Unlike German law, which requires that the lack of knowledge of unlawfulness be unavoidable to be excusable, in South African law intention is lacking if there is a genuine (even unreasonable or avoidable) lack of knowledge of unlawfulness. The current South African approach to knowledge of unlawfulness was established in 1977 when the highest court in South Africa rejected the English presumption that everyone is presumed to know the law and that ignorance of the law is not an excuse, holding that this maxim was out of keeping with the concept of intention in South Africa.[26] In this context, no distinction in principle is drawn between mistake or ignorance of law or fact.

c. Mistake Regarding the Causal Sequence

Intention, at least in the form of foresight, must extend to every element of the crime, including unlawfulness, and also, where a consequence crime is involved, to the general manner in which the unlawful consequence occurs. For instance, on a murder charge, if a marked difference existed between the actual way in which death occurred and the foreseen way in which death might occur, then the accused would be entitled to an acquittal on grounds of mistake regarding the causal sequence.[27] Where, however, the accused's aim and object was to bring about an unlawful consequence (i.e., *dolus directus* was present), in general, his or her mistake or ignorance of the causal sequence would not be a defence.

d. Defences and Putative Defences Excluding Intention

Any of the factors serving to exclude a finding of criminal capacity or voluntariness (namely, youthfulness, insanity, intoxication, and provocation or emotional stress) can also serve to exclude intention. Furthermore, where there is evidence that the accused genuinely believed that a defence excluding unlawfulness was available to him or her,[28] whereas in fact such a defence was not available, he or she can successfully raise a defence excluding intention in the form of a putative defence. An accused who genuinely believes that he or she is acting in self-defence, whereas in fact and in law he or she is exceeding the bounds of this defence, will be able to raise putative self-defence (not actual self-defence) as a defence excluding fault in the form of intention. A putative or supposed defence can arise where lack of knowledge of unlawfulness relates to the existence of any defence excluding unlawfulness, namely, putative necessity, putative obedience to orders, putative disciplinary chastisement, putative public authority, and putative consent.

Where the blow intended by X for Y goes astray (the so-called *aberratio ictus* situation) and kills Z, X's genuine ignorance or mistake about the presence of the ultimate victim might be a defence excluding intention.

iii. Negligence

Negligence is sufficient for the fault element of culpable homicide, contempt of court by a newspaper editor, and numerous statutory offences. A person will be held negligent where his or her conduct falls short of the standard of the reasonable person. The deviation from the standard of the reasonable person does not have to be gross in order to give rise to criminal liability.

In a multicultural society such as South Africa, much academic and some judicial discussion has focused on the definition of the "reasonable-person" standard. For instance, can the law, in determining whether the accused satisfied the standard of reasonable conduct, take account of the fact that the accused genuinely believes in superstition? In *S v Ngema*,[29] Judge Hugo took the view that belief in superstition could be taken into account in the essentially objective test of negligence, thus departing from the outdated Eurocentric approach to the unreasonableness of belief in the supernatural taken in *R v Mbombela*[30] in 1933. The subjective inquiry into criminal capacity (discussed in section II.B.2.i in this chapter), which is a preliminary investigation preceding the examination into negligence, can assist in alleviating certain potential injustices in a multicultural society by accommodating subjective factors such as youthfulness, lack of education, or belief in the supernatural.

The standard of the reasonable person is raised to accommodate an accused who has special knowledge above the norm or who is a person who possesses or professes skill in the area in which potential liability arises, for example, a reasonable doctor or a reasonable lawyer.

The operation of the test of negligence can best be seen in culpable homicide cases, which are considered in section III.B.1.[31]

In negligence-based crimes, if the accused does not know or did not foresee the possibility of the unlawfulness of his or her conduct, such ignorance or mistake must be reasonable in order to excuse. If the accused works in a particular sphere of activity, then he or she ought to know the law relating to that sphere of activity and will be adjudged negligent if he or she does not know the appropriate legal provisions.

Normally, negligence consists of "inadvertent" conduct, but the South African Appellate Division[32] has accepted that the existence of subjectively assessed intention does not necessarily preclude a finding of advertent negligence: Although intention postulates foreseeing, negligence does not necessarily postulate not foreseeing. In terms of this judicial acknowledgment, a person may foresee the possibility of death, for example, but be found to be negligent if a reasonable person in his position would have taken steps to guard against this consequence and the accused did not take the required steps. This is called "conscious" or "advertent" negligence.

3. Theories of Liability
i. Inchoate Crimes
a. Attempt

In South African criminal law a person can be liable for an attempt to commit a crime. A distinction is drawn between a completed attempt (where the accused has done everything he or she can toward the completion of the crime but has failed to commit the crime) and an uncompleted attempt (where the accused has not done everything toward the completion of the crime). Both completed and uncompleted attempts can lead to liability for attempt in South African law, but in the first-mentioned instance the proximity of the accused's conduct to the completed crime does not have to be investigated, while in the second instance the court has to determine whether the accused's conduct was close enough to the completion of the crime to amount to an attempt, rather than preparation, to commit the crime. In certain circumstances there can even be liability for an attempt to commit a physically or factually impossible act.

b. Conspiracy

An agreement to commit a crime constitutes a conspiracy in South African statutory law (s 18(2)(a) of the Riotous Assemblies Act 17 of 1956) and under common law.

c. Incitement

Inciting another to commit a crime is an offence in South African statutory law (s 18(2)(b) of the Riotous Assemblies Act 17 of 1956) and under common law.

ii. Complicity

a. Participation before the Completion of the Crime

A distinction is drawn in South African criminal law between coperpetrators and accomplices. A perpetrator (or coperpetrator) is someone who satisfies the definitional elements of a particular crime. An accomplice is someone who knowingly associates himself or herself with the commission of the crime by the perpetrator and furthers the commission of the crime.

A controversial rule in South African criminal law concerns common-purpose cases whereby the conduct of the perpetrator may, in certain circumstances, be attributed or imputed to the other participants in the common purpose. By means of this process of imputation, all those who actively associate in the common purpose with the requisite guilty mind will be coperpetrators. South African courts have drawn a distinction between, on the one hand, common-purpose cases arising out of a mandate or prior agreement to commit a crime or series of crimes and, on the other hand, a common purpose arising out of active association in the common purpose where no mandate or prior agreement exists. Where common-purpose liability is based on the unlawful conduct of "active association" alone, there are special additional requirements (such as presence at the scene of the crime) for liability to be imposed on the participants in the common purpose.[33]

The common-purpose rule relieves the prosecution of the burden of proving, on the part of remote parties in a common purpose, the essential element of causation in consequence crimes. However, the Constitutional Court has affirmed that the common-purpose rule, as formulated by South African courts, is constitutional.[34]

The common-purpose rule, unlike the felony-murder rule in other countries, does not obviate the need for the prosecution to prove the fault element of each individual participant in the common purpose. The general principles governing fault liability (stated in sections II.B.2.ii and iii in this chapter) apply, and so certain participants may be guilty of murder by virtue of the common-purpose principle, while others are merely guilty of culpable homicide, depending on their respective degrees of fault.

Even though the prosecution is relieved of proving the causal element of each participant in the common purpose, it does have to prove beyond reasonable doubt that at least one party to the joint venture caused, in fact and in law, the unlawful consequence. Furthermore, the remote parties to a common purpose to whom the causal conduct of the actual perpetrator is attributed can nevertheless avail themselves, in appropriate circumstances, of the rule that a mistake regarding the causal sequence may be relevant to their liability.

The South African Appellate Division, in the majority judgment in *S v Nkwenja*,[35] held that the correct moment for assessing the fault element of parties to a common purpose is when the common purpose is formulated. The minority in this case was of the view that the correct moment for assessing the fault element is when the unlawful conduct forming the essence of the common purpose is perpetrated. The minority opinion appears to be preferable because it allows for subsequent changes in mind after the common purpose is formulated.

The joint-enterprise rule in England, which is the foundation of the development of the South African common-purpose rule, is different in its effect from its South African counterpart. The English rule regards participants in the joint enterprise as accomplices, not coperpetrators.

The existing common-purpose rule in South Africa regards participants in a common purpose as coperpetrators by a process of imputing or attributing the causal conduct of the actual perpetrator to the others in the common purpose. This form of liability has been found in cases of homicide, treason, public violence, assault, and housebreaking. The prosecution in common-purpose cases can also rely on a range of alternative charges: accomplice liability, conspiracy, incitement, attempt, and public violence.

b. Participation after the Completion of the Crime

A person who intentionally assists the perpetrator after the completion of the crime is not an accomplice because he or she does not further the commission of the crime. Such a person may, however, be liable as an accessory after the fact (or for defeating, or attempting to defeat, the administration of justice).

iii. Corporate Criminal Liability

Section 332(1) of the Criminal Procedure Act[36] removes the obstacle to fixing criminal liability on an artificial person that because it has no mind, it cannot be found guilty of a crime requiring fault. In terms of the subsection, where a corporation is charged with such a crime, the fault of the director or employee ("servant") who committed the crime will be imputed to the corporation. Thus in *R v Bennett & Co (Pty) Ltd*[37] the negligence of an employee was imputed to the company, resulting in a conviction of the latter for culpable homicide.

Liability of the corporation in terms of section 332(1) extends to crimes based on intention, negligence, and even strict liability. The fact that the scope of corporate liability in section 332(1) is broad enough to include crimes based on negligence and strict liability was emphasized in *Ex parte Minister van Minister van Justisie: In re S v Suid-Afrikaans Uitsaaikorporasie*.[38] Where, however, a statute specifically confines liability to natural persons, corporate liability cannot result.[39]

Section 332(1) expressly renders the corporate body liable where, in committing the crime, the director or servant acted beyond his or her powers or duties but while "furthering or endeavouring to further the interests of" the corporation. Liability under this section, therefore, extends beyond the normal limits of vicarious responsibility, where the principal or master is liable only if the agent or servant acted within the scope of his or her authority or employment.

In South Africa the theory behind corporate responsibility and the translation of this theory into a realistic form of corporate responsibility are in need of review. The organizational theory of collective responsibility, founded on both the outward manifestation of the policy of the corporation and an evaluation of whether this policy is actually adhered to in practice, would seem to hold the key to future development.

4. Causation

In crimes that involve an unlawful consequence, as opposed to an unlawful circumstance, there must be a causal link between the initial act or omission and the ultimate unlawful consequence. Both factual and legal causation are required for liability.

The *sine qua non* test for determining factual causation is favored by the South African courts, and a theoretical distinction is drawn between causation by a positive act (involving a notional elimination of the positive act from the sequence of events) and causation by an omission (involving a notional addition to the sequence of events of the act legally required of the accused). In either inquiry, if the consequence of the act or omission in question disappears after engagement in the notional inquiry, then the conduct is a cause in fact of the particular consequence. To put the inquiry in its more traditional way: if the consequence would not have resulted but for the conduct of the accused, the conduct of the accused is a factual cause of the consequence.

A smorgasbord approach to legal causation allows the courts to weigh in the balance a variety of policy factors in order to limit the scope of liability for factual causes. In particular, the following inquiries are used by the courts to limit liability on the grounds of legal policy: was the consequence in question a direct consequence of the conduct of the accused, or did an abnormal act or event (*novus actus* [or *nova causa*] *interveniens*) break the causal sequence; and, in the light of human experience, would this type of conduct normally lead to this type of consequence (the adequate theory of causation)? The unifying feature of these inquiries is the examination of what is normal or abnormal in the light of human experience. If the occurrence of an intervening act or event was foreseen or foreseeable, the act or event is not considered abnormal in nature.

C. Defences

1. Types of Defence

South African criminal law distinguishes between defences to criminal liability on the basis of the element of criminal liability that is excluded by the defence, that is, defences excluding the unlawfulness of the conduct (grounds of justification), defences excluding capacity (see section II.B.2.i in this chapter), and defences and putative defences excluding intention (section II.B.2.ii.d). South African law does not specifically make the distinction between justification and excuse drawn in German law, but it does recognize the concept of defences excluding intention and knowledge of unlawfulness. For such a defence excluding knowledge of unlawfulness to be available where negligence is sufficient for criminal liability, the absence of knowledge of unlawfulness must be reasonable, as well as bona fide and genuine.

2. Burden of Proof

There is no burden of proof on the accused to establish defences excluding unlawfulness, since the prosecution bears the overall onus of proving the unlawfulness of conduct beyond reasonable doubt. The state is required to negate the existence of any defence introduced by an accused beyond reasonable doubt. The only recognized exception to this rule is in the context of the insanity defence, where, according to common law and statute, the accused bears the burden of proving mental illness or defect leading to lack of capacity on a balance of probabilities.[40] If there is insufficient evidence to support the finding of the existence of every element of a defence excluding the unlawfulness of the conduct in order to create the reasonable doubt necessary for acquittal, there may, nevertheless, be sufficient evidence to support the conclusion that the accused's moral blameworthiness in the circumstances was reduced sufficiently to impose a lesser sentence or to find "substantial and compelling reasons" to depart from the minimum prescribed sentence.

D. Justifications

1. Necessity

Necessity will be a defence where a person, faced with human threats (compulsion) or overwhelming force of surrounding circumstances, contravenes the norms of the criminal law by inflicting harm on an innocent third party or the latter's property. For many years legal systems have had to grapple with the difficult ethicolegal question whether necessity or compulsion can justify or excuse the intentional killing of another human being or human beings. The South African solution to this dilemma is to acknowledge that the criminal law requires reasonable conduct from the ordinary person rather than a "blueprint for saintliness," as does the English law. Under South African criminal law, necessity or compulsion may, in principle, be a defence to all crimes, including murder, provided a reasonable person would not have been able to resist the threats implicit in the necessity or compulsion situation. An exception to the rule that, in principle, necessity or compulsion can be a complete defence even to a charge of murder is that a person who voluntarily and deliberately joins a criminal gang knowing, or at least foreseeing, that the violent code of vengeance of the gang might lead to such compulsion cannot successfully raise the defence of compulsion if such threats are exerted by the gang. This exception is also recognized in English law.

South African criminal law does not draw a distinction between necessity (or compulsion) as a ground of "justification" and an "excuse" in the jurisprudential sense of the German Penal Code, but it does distinguish between a defence of necessity (or compulsion) as a defence excluding unlawfulness and putative necessity (or compulsion) as a defence excluding fault (see section II.B.2.ii.d in this chapter).

2. Private Defence

The term *private defence* is used in preference to *self-defence* because the former term is wide enough to include legitimate defence of a third party. The term also stresses the essence of the distinction between "private" defence and publicly sanctioned use of force, such as the use of force by persons effecting an arrest or apprehending a fleeing suspect.

Private defence will be a defence where it becomes necessary for a person faced with an imminent or commenced unlawful attack on his or her or a third party's legal interests to take the law into his or her own hands by using reasonable force to repel the unlawful attack. There is authority to the effect that in special circumstances a person may kill in defence of property, but this authority, dating back to the 1960s, can be challenged on the basis that it unjustifiably undermines the preeminence given to the right to life (as opposed to property) in the constitution. A 2005 High Court decision[41] extended the concept of an imminent attack to include an "inevitable" attack in the context of a "pattern" or "cycle" of domestic abuse.

3. Consent

The principle *volenti non fit injuria* (an injury is not done to one who consents) applies to a limited extent in the criminal law. Strictly speaking, a person cannot validly consent to be killed, because the state has an interest in the preservation of life. However, support is emerging in the High Court for a limited exception to this rule in a medical context where the subject is in a persistent vegetative state, lacks basic quality of life, and has no reasonable prospect of recovery.[42] The courts in South Africa have not yet pronounced on the validity of what is colloquially called the "living will," although the South African Law Commission has urged legal recognition of such documents.

Consent may be a valid defence to what would otherwise constitute an assault in the context of, for example, therapeutic medical treatment or lawful sporting activities.

The circumstances in which a complainant in a rape trial does not voluntarily or without coercion agree to an act of sexual penetration are mentioned in section III.C.1 in this chapter.

4. Superior Orders

The defence of superior orders arises in the context of military or police commands. Obedience to certain orders may be a defence under South African criminal law. However, this defence will not be available where the order was manifestly unlawful. For instance, a command issued by a military superior to a subordinate to kill or rape innocent civilians will be regarded as manifestly unlawful. The defence of superior orders has not been recognized beyond the scope of commands issued by legally acknowledged military or police authorities.

5. Impossibility

If it is physically impossible for the accused to comply with a positive obligation imposed by law, he or she may escape liability for failing to comply with this obligation. For instance, it may be physically impossible for a taxpayer to submit an income tax return as required by law if the taxpayer has been declared insane and committed to a mental institution for treatment.

6. Public Authority

The state is authorized by statute (s 49 of the Criminal Procedure Act)[43] to use force, including deadly force, on a person who flees or resists arrest. The courts[44] and the legislature[45] have redefined the scope of legitimate deadly force that can be used by police officers and others in preventing a suspect from fleeing arrest. The courts have specifically required a balancing of the nature of the crime that the fugitive is suspected of having committed against the threat or potential threat of physical harm to the arrester and others.

It is clear that under the current law, an arrester who has attempted to arrest an unarmed youth for stealing an apple is not entitled to shoot to kill the fleeing youth, even if the obligatory warning shot has been fired. Contrary to perceptions that fueled police resistance to this enactment before it came into force, the power of arresters to protect themselves and others against violent criminals is not curtailed by recent court decisions or the legislative reform of section 49. In essence, the public authority granted to certain persons to use force against fleeing suspects is, notwithstanding some subtle differences, based on the normal constraints on the use of force in private defence.

The issue of onus of proof in section 49 situations remains disputed. Case law interpreting the pre-1998 definition of the scope of deadly force that can legitimately be used by arresters in apprehending fleeing suspects placed the onus on the arrester to prove that his or her actions fell within the framework of section 49. This judicially sanctioned shifting of the onus onto the accused (the arrester) to prove the existence of a defence excluding unlawfulness was clearly an infringement of the presumption of innocence, which requires the prosecution to prove guilt (including the unlawfulness of the accused's conduct) beyond reasonable doubt. This infringement of the fundamental rule of criminal law was arguably justified on the policy grounds of constraining a statutory provision that was couched in overly broad terms. The revised (1998) version of section 49, unlike its predecessor, is not as widely defined or open to abuse, and so, it is claimed, the courts should interpret this new provision in such a way that it does not infringe the fundamental rule that the prosecution must prove all the elements of criminal liability (including the unlawfulness of conduct) beyond reasonable doubt.

7. Disciplinary Chastisement

i. The Past

Parents and guardians of children were, by common law dating back to the early twentieth century, authorized to inflict moderate corporal chastisement for educational purposes on young persons in their charge. Twentieth-century legislation provided for teachers and prefects, acting *in loco parentis*, to inflict similar moderate corporal chastisement on male pupils in their charge. The Criminal Procedure Act 51 of 1977 permitted courts to use corporal punishment as a sentencing option.

ii. The Present

In *S v Williams* (1995)[46] the Constitutional Court held that the judicial imposition of corporal punishment in South Africa was unconstitutional—juvenile whipping as a sentencing option violated human dignity and the right not to be subjected to cruel, inhuman, and degrading punishment. The infringements of these rights could not be justified in terms of the limitations clause of the constitution.[47]

Section 10 of the South African Schools Act 84 of 1996 outlawed the use of corporal punishment on a learner, and the Constitutional Court[48] has held that this provision extends to both public (state) and private schools. The court did not deal specifically with the last vestige of disciplinary chastisement—chastisement of children by parents and guardians in the privacy of the family home.

iii. The Future

Logically, the same reasoning regarding the degrading nature of corporal punishment in schools should also apply to corporal punishment in the domestic context, although the practical problem of monitoring abusive parents' conduct in the privacy of the home can not be ignored. It is possible that South African courts might in the future take the approach that all forms of corporal punishment, except those that could be classified as *de minimis* or where the discretion to prosecute is declined, might fall foul of the constitution.[49] If South African courts do opt for criminalizing all forms of corporal punishment except those instances falling within these limits, it might be appropriate to deal with punishable cases of corporal punishment within the domestic environment by diversionary and restorative-justice techniques rather than through the ordinary criminal process.

8. De Minimis Non Curat Lex *(The Law Does Not Concern Itself with Trifles)*

A particular instance of a crime may be so insignificant in nature that the law may disregard it as too trivial to warrant criminal liability.

9. Negotiorum Gestio *(Unauthorized Administration)*

Where a person performs an otherwise unlawful act in the interest of another person with the intention of benefiting that other person, but without the latter's knowledge or consent, we refer to the situation as one of *negotiorum gestio*. The conduct of the *negotiorum gestor* (the unauthorized administrator) may be regarded as lawful in certain circumstances.

E. Excuses

South African criminal law does not draw the German distinction between "justification" and "excuse," although it does distinguish between defences excluding unlawfulness (see sections II.B.1.iii and II.C and D), defences excluding capacity (see section II.B.2.i) and defences excluding fault (see section II.B.2.ii).

F. Sanctions

1. Punishment

Punishment remains the distinctive feature of the criminal, as opposed to the civil, process in South Africa.[50] However, section 300 of the Criminal Procedure Act[51] provides for victims of crimes against property to be compensated for their loss by the criminal culprits. A restorative-justice model is gaining support, especially in the context of child justice and as a result of a greater awareness of the meaning of *ubuntu*.[52]

2. Quantity/Quality of Punishment

In 1998 legislation[53] came into force prescribing minimum sentences for certain offences and stipulating that judicial officers could impose a lesser sentence only if they were satisfied that "substantial and compelling circumstances" existed to justify this lesser sentence. This minimum-sentence legislation is still operational.[54]

Capital[55] and corporal punishment[56] are no longer regarded as legitimate sentencing options in South Africa. The main forms of punishment for crimes in South Africa are imprisonment (including life imprisonment),[57] monetary fines, correctional supervision,[58] and community service.[59]

3. Death Penalty

Capital punishment for murder was mandatory from 1917 to 1935 in South Africa. Thereafter judges were given discretion to impose a lesser sentence if the killing was accompanied by "extenuating circumstances," and in 1990 this discretion became an unfettered one.[60] Between 1990 and 1995 there was a moratorium on the carrying out of any death sentence. Ultimately, the Constitutional Court in *S v Makwanyane* (1995)[61] decided conclusively that capital punishment, as a sentence for any crime,[62] was unconstitutional because it was a "cruel, inhuman and degrading punishment."

III. SPECIAL PART

A. Protected Interests

South African criminal law protects a variety of interests:

Human life, essentially by the crime of homicide

Person, essentially by the crimes of assault, rape, and related offences,[63] *crimen injuria*,[64] and kidnapping

Family life, by the crimes of abduction,[65] bigamy, and incest[66]

Property, by the crimes of theft and related offences (including robbery),[67] extortion,[68] fraud, forgery and uttering,[69] malicious damage to property,[70] arson, and housebreaking[71]

Community interests, by the crimes of public violence, public indecency, and blasphemy

Sexual morality, by the crime of prostitution[72]

Collective welfare, by statutory crimes of terrorism,[73] racketeering, money laundering and other organised criminal offences,[74] corruption,[75] substance abuse,[76] road traffic offences,[77] firearms offences,[78] human trafficking,[79] and so on

Maintenance of government, by the crimes of treason and sedition

Administration of justice, by the crimes of defeating or obstructing the administration of justice, contempt of court, perjury, and compounding[80]

B. Homicide

1. Murder and Culpable Homicide

South African criminal law draws a basic distinction between intentional killing (murder) and negligent killing (culpable homicide). Murder is defined as the unlawful, intentional killing of another. Culpable homicide is the unlawful, negligent killing of another. By adopting this essentially Roman-Dutch dichotomy between intentional and negligent killing, South African law has shunned both the English categorisation of killing into premeditated murder, on the one hand, and voluntary and involuntary manslaughter, on the other hand, and the American terminology of first- and second-degree murder and voluntary manslaughter. Adherence to the basic distinction between intentional and negligent killing has an attractive simplicity, but it also means that South African law regards "murder" as including a killing where death was merely foreseen as a possibility, as well as the archetypal case of murder, where the killing was premeditated.

2. Suicide and Assisted Suicide

In 1970 the Appellate Division in *Ex parte Minister of Justice: In re S v Grotjohn*[81] held that although suicide is not a crime in South African law, knowingly assisting another to commit suicide nevertheless constituted the factual and legal cause of death, despite the fact that "the last act is committed by the non-criminal hand" of the person committing suicide. The essence of this case dealt with the issue of causation, but the court did state that in principle, assisting another to commit suicide could be murder if the assistance was unlawful and intentional, or culpable homicide if the killing was merely negligent. The court did, however, use the term *accessory* to describe the role of the assistant in another's suicide and, by emphasising that the conduct must be both intentional and unlawful, left open the door for future courts to take account of changing attitudes to death and dying.

However, in 1975 the Cape Provincial Division of the High Court in *S v Hartmann*[82] emphasized that a medical practitioner who hastened the death of his father, suffering from cancer and already close to death, by injecting pentothal into his drip was nevertheless guilty of murder, despite his compassionate motive. This decision underscored the state's interest in the preservation of life and the rule that it is murder to hasten a person's death, even when the person is terminally ill. However, this broad principle may need to be qualified.

In the light of the decision of the Natal Provincial Division of the High Court in *Clarke v Hurst NO*,[83] it is now considered ethically and legally permissible for artificial nasogastric feeding to be withheld from a patient whose brain has "permanently lost the capacity to induce a physical and mental existence at a level which qualifies as human life."[84] According to the court, the legal convictions of the community did not require that the patient should be kept alive in these circumstances.

The factual circumstances in both *Grotjohn* and *Hartmann* involved positive conduct (in the first case, handing a shotgun to a person threatening to commit suicide, and in the second case, injecting a substance into another's medical drip). These forms of positive conduct and, in the case of *Grotjohn*, nonmedical conduct can be distinguished from *Clarke*, which involved the withholding of treatment (omission) in a controlled medical environment.

The general defences excluding the unlawfulness element and the attitude of the courts to the causal problem in homicide have been considered in sections II.C and D and II.B.4 in this chapter, and the only aspect of the crime of murder not yet considered is defining the moment of death.[85] The traditional legal approach to the moment of death is to determine whether breathing or heartbeat is absent. Medical science, more accurately, places the focus on irreversible damage to the brain stem, and the courts should, in the future, opt for a criterion of death that is linked to irreversible brain stem injury

Unlike other Anglo-American and some African[86] systems of law, for a conviction of culpable homicide in South Africa, the negligence does not have to be "gross" in nature. Negligence is assessed objectively according to the standard of the reasonable person. The debate surrounding the extent of limited, subjectively assessed personal characteristics of an individual accused that can legitimately be taken into account in determining whether he or she has been negligent has not yet been fully resolved.[87]

For a conviction of culpable homicide, death (not merely bodily injury) must have been reasonably foreseeable, a reasonable person would have taken steps to guard against this consequence, and the accused must have failed to take such steps.

C. Sex Offences

1. Rape

According to South African common law, rape was defined as "unlawful, intentional sexual intercourse with a woman without her consent." As a result of a comprehensive evaluation of the common-law definitions of sexual offences starting in 1996, new definitions of rape and other sexual offences have been included in the Criminal Law (Sexual Offences and Related Matters) Amendment Act 32 of 2007. However, the state's delay in passing and implementing this piece of legislation resulted in the Constitutional Court in *Masiya v DPP, Pretoria*[88] anticipating the legislation by prospectively extending the common-law definition of rape to cover anal penetration of females.[89]

Section 3 of the Criminal Law (Sexual Offences and Related Matters) Amendment Act now defines the crime of rape in the following terms: "Any person ('A') who unlawfully and intentionally commits an act of sexual penetration with a complainant ('B'), without consent of B, is guilty of the offence of rape." Under this new legislation, rape ceases to be an offence committed only by a man against a woman. Men are also recognized as victims of rape. Sexual penetration by genital organs of one person into the genital organs, anus, or mouth of another is classified as rape.[90] Rape is perpetrated by sexual penetration of nongenital parts of the body or sexual penetration by objects into the genital organs or anus of another person or penetration of the genital organs of an animal into the mouth of another person.[91] Even women can be found guilty of "sexual penetration," and not just as accomplices to someone else's crime of penetration, as in the past.

Consent in the context of sexual penetration is defined in the legislation as "voluntary or uncoerced agreement," and various factors that could impair consent—such as force or intimidation, threat of harm, abuse of power or authority, false pretences or fraudulent means, or incapacity—are specifically identified. According to both common law and the new legislation, fraud leading to *error in negotio* (error as to the nature of the act) or *error personae* (error as to the identity of the person participating in the conduct) can nullify consent. Children under twelve years of age and persons who are mentally disabled are incapable of consenting to sexual acts. Consensual sexual penetration or sexual violation of children between the ages of twelve and sixteen[92] (subject to certain defences),[93] sexual exploitation of children and mentally disabled persons,[94] and sexual grooming of children and mentally disabled persons[95] are punished in the legislation.

By recognizing that compelled rape of a third party is sufficient to constitute the crime of rape itself,[96] rape ceases to be a crime that can be committed only personally. Similarly, the provision on compelled sexual assault[97] and compelled self-sexual assault[98] indicates that sexual assault also ceases to be a crime that has to be committed personally.

A distinction is drawn between nonpenctrative sexual violation (called "sexual assault" and covering the domain of the crime of "indecent assault" under common law) and sexual penetration (rape).

2. Sexual Assault (Replacing the Common-Law Definition of "Indecent Assault")

A person (A) who unlawfully and intentionally sexually violates a complainant (B) without the consent of B is guilty of the offence of sexual assault. Similarly, a person (A) who unlawfully and intentionally inspires the belief in a complainant (B) that B will be sexually violated is guilty of the offence of sexual assault.[99]

D. Theft and Fraud

1. Theft

Theft is defined as the unlawful appropriation with intent to steal of property capable of being stolen.

i. Unlawfulness

The consent of the owner is the most important defence excluding the unlawfulness of the taking. This consent of the owner may not be "real" if it is induced by fear, force, or fraud. Thus a hijacker who threatens a wealthy traveler with the words "your money or your life" is truly a robber (and hence guilty of theft) if the taking of the money is induced by the threat.[100]

ii. Appropriation

The Roman law concept of *contrectatio* has been defined as an "assumption of control" of a thing. This assumption of control requires that the accused must deal in some way with the property, but that an actual removal of the property is not required. The true nature of the *contrectatio* element of theft helps distinguish the completed crime of theft from an attempt, and the central issue becomes whether the accused has deprived the owner of control.

The problem is highlighted by the classic case of removing an object from a shelf in a self-service store and, with intent to steal, concealing the object on one's person before reaching the checkout point. Although some decisions hold the person who acts in this way guilty of only attempted theft, there are other cases[101] where a conviction of theft has been entered on these facts. These cases indicate that even if the owner retains some control over the object in his or her store until the shopper passes through the checkout point, the shopper nevertheless unlawfully appropriates sufficient control by surreptitiously hiding the object before approaching the checkout.

Modern writers on theft, therefore, favor a concept of *appropriation* rather than *contrectatio*. Appropriation is regarded as assuming the rights of the owner and excluding the owner from his or her property. This approach to the "taking element" of theft is one that can accommodate the dishonest transfer of money, electronically or otherwise. This concept of appropriation also coincides with the intention element of theft, that is, the intention to deprive the owner permanently of the benefits of ownership. The Supreme Court of Appeal in *S v Boesak*[102] defined theft in terms of appropriation.

iii. Property Capable of Being Stolen

Some property is absolutely incapable of being stolen, and other property is only relatively incapable of being stolen. Property that is absolutely incapable of being stolen includes immovable property, incorporeals, such as an idea or design, and things that are common to all (*res communes*), such as air, water of the sea, and public streams. Property that is relatively incapable of being stolen includes things unowned but capable of ownership (*res derelicta*), one's own property (*res sua*), and wild animals (*fera natura*) that have not been sufficiently enclosed.[103]

Special rules relate to the theft of money that is handed over by A to B to be used by B for the benefit of A (i.e., trust money). It is no defence in the case of theft of trust money that the accused intended to return an equivalent amount, but the fact that the accused held an equivalent liquid fund available to cover the liability may be an important factor in determining whether the accused had knowledge of the unlawfulness of his or her conduct.[104]

iv. Intention to Steal

The intent to steal exists where the accused (i) intentionally effects an appropriation of property (ii) intending to deprive the owner permanently of his or her property or control over property and (iii) knowing that he or she is acting unlawfully in taking it. Intent to steal does not require intent to benefit from the property stolen.

The definition of intent to steal was established in *R v Sibiya*.[105] In this case the accused and M, employees at a garage, took the complainant's car, which had been parked in the garage, on a joy ride. They were convicted of theft in the trial court even though they had always intended to return the car to the garage. Acting Chief Justice Schreiner, delivering the majority judgment and upholding the appeal against conviction and sentence, held: "I have come to the conclusion that the law requires for the crime of theft, not only that the thing should have been taken without belief that the owner . . . had consented or would have consented to the taking, but also that the taker should have intended to terminate the owner's enjoyment of his rights or, in other words, to deprive him of the whole benefit of his ownership." This intention may be inferred, for instance, in circumstances showing recklessness about what becomes of the property.

Sibiya therefore confirmed that *furtum usus* (unauthorized borrowing) was not to be criminal at common law. Shortly after *Sibiya* the legislature stepped in and enacted section 1(1) of the General Law Amendment Act,[106] which sought, according to the long title of the Act, to "declare the unlawful appropriation of the use of another's property an offence." The legislature did not succeed in its aim. The unlawful use of property by someone who already happens to be in possession of it is apparently not punishable. The emphasis, in terms of the wording of the statute, is not on use but on removal from control in order to use. However, the Supreme Court of Appeal in S v Rheeder[107] has now reinterpreted the word *control* of the owner to cover not just physical control but complete control over the use of the property, thus including an extracontractual user within the purview of section 1(1).

In certain instances the unauthorized borrower will not only contravene section 1(1) but will also be guilty of common-law theft, for instance, if he or she abandons the thing with reckless disregard about whether it will be found, or if he or she borrows what is called a fungible (something that is consumed by use, such as gasoline) and uses it, even though he or she intends to return an equivalent amount of gasoline to the owner.

Judge of Appeal Van den Heever in *Sibiya* suggested that a motorcar, like a candle, is consumed by use. If the accused uses a nonfungible, such as a car, it is a matter of degree whether the car's economic value has been consumed by use.

The motive of the accused (for instance, to annoy the complainant) must be distinguished from the intention to steal. Neither a motive of gain nor a motive to prejudice the complainant is required.

The accused must know or foresee the possibility that the property is capable of being stolen. In South African law an accused does not have intent to steal unless the state proves that he or she knew (or foresaw the possibility) that he or she was not lawfully entitled to take the property. For instance, the accused might escape liability for theft if he or she genuinely believed that the property was abandoned or that the owner consented or would have consented to the taking. It is even a defence, as decided in S v De Blom,[108] that he or she genuinely but erroneously thought that he or she was entitled in law to take the property. In other words, knowledge of unlawfulness is part of intention. The mistake or ignorance does not have to be reasonable, as well as bona fide, to exclude knowledge of unlawfulness, although the unreasonableness of the belief might lead to an inference of such knowledge.

Theft is a "continuing crime." This means that a theft continues as long as the stolen property is in the possession of the thief, or of someone who was a party to the theft, or of some person acting on behalf of or even, possibly, in the interests of the original thief or party to the theft. This rule has implications for jurisdiction and parties in theft cases. Even though the original appropriation took place outside the court's jurisdiction, the thief may be tried at the place where he or she is found with the property. Furthermore, the person who assists the thief while the theft continues is not merely an accessory after the fact but is guilty of theft itself.

A crime of theft by false pretences has been recognised by South African courts in the past, but this crime straddles theft and fraud, and its continued existence can be questioned.

2. *Theft-Related Offences*
   i. Receiving Stolen Property

The common-law crime of receiving stolen property consists in unlawfully receiving possession of stolen property that one knows has been stolen. Receiving is regarded as punishable because it facilitates theft. There would be few thieves if there were no "fences" or receivers to whom the stolen goods could be passed.

One of the major difficulties encountered by the state in securing a conviction for this common-law offence is in proving that the alleged receiver knew or foresaw that the goods were stolen. This difficulty prompted the legislature to provide that in certain circumstances it is possible to achieve a conviction for receiving even though the *mens rea* for common-law receiving (namely, intention) has not been established.[109] This legislative form of receiving also contained a reverse onus, which the majority of the Constitutional Court struck down as contrary to constitutional norms.[110] The majority of the Constitutional Court read into the section an evidential onus, while the minority delivered a dissent upholding the reverse onus.

  ii. Unexplained Possession of Goods Suspected of Having Been Stolen

The South African legislature has also punished the unexplained possession of goods reasonably suspected of having been stolen.[111] This legislative provision will become even more important now that the Constitutional Court has taken the sting out of the statutory receiving provision. The essence of the unexplained-possession provision is the emphasis on the inability of the accused to give a satisfactory account of his or her possession of goods suspected of having been stolen, and the Constitutional Court has upheld its validity in terms of both the presumption of innocence and the right to remain silent.[112]

  3. Fraud and Forgery

Fraud in South African criminal law is punished in terms of a general common-law offence. The offence of fraud consists in unlawfully making, with intent to defraud, a misrepresentation that causes actual prejudice or is potentially prejudicial to another.

In the early twentieth century South African courts extended the ambit of this crime to cover both potential and nonproprietary prejudice. Potential prejudice would arise where there was a risk of prejudice that was not too remote or fanciful. Nonproprietary prejudice might arise where, for instance, the accused laid a false charge with the police and so caused them unnecessary investigation. The extension of the crime to potential prejudice serves to blur the line between fraud and attempted fraud.

The ultimate, broad definition of fraud that emerged in South African law has been challenged on the grounds of alleged vagueness, but in *S v Friedman (1)*[113] the current definition of fraud managed to survive the challenge.

The intent-to-defraud element of the offence has been interpreted to require not just an intention to deceive but also an intention to defraud in the sense that the intention is to induce the victim of the fraud to alter or abstain from altering his or her position.

Forgery is a special form of fraud committed by a person who unlawfully makes, with intent to defraud, a false document that causes actual prejudice or is potentially prejudicial to another. If the document is communicated (or "put off"), the crime becomes forgery and uttering.

E. "Victimless" Crimes

South African criminal law punishes certain so-called victimless offences, such as prostitution,[114] drug abuse,[115] and contraventions of antismoking legislation.[116]

F. Selected Offences with a Distinctive South African Definition

1. Crimen Injuria

Both the law of delict (civil law) and the criminal law seek to protect the personality interest of dignity. Dignity is protected by the crime of *crimen injuria*. This crime is derived from Roman law and was developed in South African common law.

Prosecution for criminal *injuria* (the unlawful, intentional impairment of a person's dignity) is sometimes used to protect individuals from serious impairments of dignity or invasions of privacy. Although there have not been many prosecutions of this nature, those that have taken place have usually involved some element of sexual impropriety (for instance, watching a stranger undressing).

"Dignity" includes a person's self-respect, self-esteem, personal autonomy, and privacy and is assessed both subjectively and objectively: the complainant's dignity must have been actually impaired (subjective inquiry), and a person of ordinary sensibilities must regard the conduct as offensive (objective inquiry). The impairment of dignity has to be "serious" in order to be considered criminal.

2. Corruption, Organised Crime, Terrorism, and International Crimes

At the beginning of the twenty-first century the South African democratic government enacted a raft of legislation punishing corruption, organised crime, and terrorism.

i. Corruption

In 2004 South Africa enacted comprehensive legislation punishing corruption. A fundamental purpose of the Prevention and Combating of Corrupt Activities Act 12 of 2004 (which came into force on 27 April 2004), which is designed to give effect to South Africa's obligations under the United Nations Convention against Corruption, is the "unbundling" of the offence of corruption. The Act provides for a general offence of corruption and also punishes a variety of specific forms of corruption. The essence of the general and the specific offences of corruption is the unlawful giving or accepting of "gratification," a term that is defined widely to include not merely money but also, inter alia, any office, honor, employment, right, privilege, vote, consent, influence, benefit of any kind, or avoidance of loss. The Act imposes a duty to report corrupt practices[117] and establishes a register in order to place certain restrictions on persons and enterprises convicted of corrupt activities relating to tenders and contracts.

ii. Organised Crime

A feature of almost every modern society is the emergence of organised criminal enterprises that transcend national boundaries and whose conduct involves some element of continuity. Although certain manifestations of organised crime are adequately punished within the parameters of existing common-law and statutorily defined crimes, the legislature in South Africa, to some extent impelled by international pressure, enacted the Prevention of Organised Crime Act 121 of 1998, which came into operation on 21 January 1999.

This piece of legislation specifically criminalizes racketeering, money laundering, and certain gang activities and introduces a dual system of recovery of criminal assets based on both postconviction confiscation and civil forfeiture, without requiring conviction.

The effective implementation of the Prevention of Organised Crime Act is reinforced by the implementation of the Financial Intelligence Centre Act 38 of 2001.[118] The implications of a number of the provisions of the Prevention of Organised Crime Act have been decided by the Supreme Court of Appeal and the Constitutional Court.[119]

iii. Terrorism

The Protection of Constitutional Democracy against Terrorist and Related Activities Act[120] punishes, inter alia, terrorism and other offences associated or connected with terrorist activities. Under section 2 of the Act, "Any person who engages in a terrorist activity is guilty of the offence of terrorism."

"Terrorist activity" is defined as including the systematic or repeated use of violence; systematic or repeated release into the environment of a harmful substance; endangering life; violating physical integrity; causing serious risk to health or safety; destruction or substantial damage to property, natural resources, or environmental or cultural heritage; conduct designed or calculated to cause serious interference with or disruption of an essential service, facility, or system; causing major economic loss or extensive destabilization of an economic system or substantial devastation of the national economy of a country; or creating a serious public emergency or general insurrection. The definition of "terrorist activity" covers harm suffered inside and outside the Republic of South Africa.

The crime of "terrorism" requires intention[121] with specific objectives: to threaten unity and territorial integrity; to intimidate or induce feelings of insecurity (including economic insecurity); to cause or spread "feelings of terror, fear or panic"; or to unduly force a person, a government, the general public or a segment of the public, or a domestic or international body to do or abstain from doing any act or holding any standpoint. Furthermore, the intention of the accused must be to do an act that is "committed, directly or indirectly, in whole or in part, for the purpose of the advancement of an individual or collective, political, religious, ideological or philosophical motive, objective, cause or undertaking."

Section 2 of the Act provides for a duty to report a person suspected of intending to commit an offence under the legislation.

iv. International Crimes

South Africa ratified the Rome Statute that created the International Criminal Court, which came into operation on 1 July 2002 after the lodging of the sixtieth ratification. The South African legislature also passed the International Criminal Court Act,[122] which ensures that South Africa complies with its obligations as a state party to the Rome Statute. By this piece of legislation South Africa incorporated the international definitions of genocide, crimes against humanity, and war crimes into domestic law.

SELECTED BIBLIOGRAPHY

Burchell, E. M., and P. M. A. Hunt. *South African Criminal Law and Procedure.* Vol. 1, *General Principles of Liability.* 3d ed. by Jonathan Burchell. Cape Town: Juta and Co., 1997.

Burchell, Jonathan, and John Milton. *Cases and Materials on Criminal Law.* 3d ed. by Jonathan Burchell. Cape Town: Juta and Co., 2007.

Burchell, Jonathan, and John Milton. *Principles of Criminal Law.* 3d ed. Cape Town: Juta and Co., 2005, revised reprint 2006.

Hunt, P. M. A. *South African Criminal Law and Procedure.* Vol. 2, *Common-Law Crimes.* 3d ed. by John Milton. Cape Town: Juta and Co., 1996.

Milton, J. R. L., and M. G. Cowling. *South African Criminal Law and Procedure.* Vol. 3, *Statutory Offences.* Cape Town: Juta and Co., 1988.

Snyman, C. R. *Criminal Law.* 5th ed. Pretoria: Butterworths Lexis-Nexis, 2008.

NOTES

1. Common assault in South Africa consists in unlawfully and intentionally (i) applying force to the person of another or (ii) inspiring a belief in that other that force is immediately to be applied to him or her. Both forms of conduct are labeled "assault," and no distinction is drawn between "assault" and "battery."

2. See section III.F in this chapter.

3. Act 51 of 1977.

4. Act 37 of 2001.

5. In *Masiya v Director of Public Prosecutions, Pretoria and Another (Centre for Applied Legal Studies and Another, Amici Curiae)* 2007 (5) SA 30 (CC) the majority of the Constitutional Court extended the common-law crime of rape to include anal penetration of a female. The minority agreed on this point but, emphasizing dignity and equality, held that the common law should be further extended to cover anal rape of males as well.

6. See the selected bibliography.

7. 1 of 1977.

8. 4 of 1969.

9. The Child Justice Act 75 of 2008 (which came into force on 1 April 2010) entrenches the notion of restorative justice in the criminal justice system in respect of children in conflict with the law and provides for the diversion of young offenders away from mainstream criminal justice (see chapters 6, 7, and 8 and Schedules 1, 2, and 3 of the Act).

10. See section II.F.2 in this chapter.

11. See section II.B.3.iii in this chapter.

12. *Carmichele v Minister of Safety and Security* (2001) 10 BCLR 995 (CC); *Minister of Safety and Security v Van Duivenboden* 2002 (6) SA 431 (SCA); and *Van Eeden v Minister of Safety and Security* 2003 (1) SA 389 (SCA).

13. *S v Hassen* 1997 (1) SACR 247 (T).

14. Section 7 of the Child Justice Act 75 of 2008 (above n. 9). Under the common law the lower age limit was seven.

15. At the time of the commission of the offence.

16. The presumption of sanity and the shifting of the onus onto the accused to prove insanity, where he or she raises the issue, are now entrenched in South African criminal law by section 5 of the Criminal Matters Amendment Act 19 of 1998, which amends section 78 of Act 51 of 1977. This amendment came into force on 28 February 2002.

17. 1981 (1) SA 1097 (A).

18. The approach of the Supreme Court of Appeal in *S v Eadie* 2002 (1) SACR 663 (SCA) limiting the defence of provocation to cases of automatism (see section II.B.2.i.d) could have a similar effect of limiting the common-law defence of intoxication to instances of automatism.

19. 1 of 1988.

20. *S v Arnold* 1985 (3) SA 256 (C); *S v Nursingh* 1995 (2) SACR 331 (D); *S v Moses* 1996 (1) SACR 701 (C); and *S v Wiid* 1990 (1) SACR 561 (A) (in this case, however, there was evidence that the accused suffered from concussion and so may have acted involuntarily).

21. 2002 (1) SACR 663 (SCA).

22. *S v Coetzee* 1997 (3) SA 527 (CC).

23. See the majority judgment of the Appellate Division in *Amalgamated Beverage Industries Natal (Pty) Ltd v Durban City Council* 1994 (3) SA 170 (A).

24. See section II.B.2.iii in this chapter.

25. *S v Ngubane* 1985 (3) SA 677 (A).

26. *S v De Blom* 1977 (3) SA 513 (A).

27. *S v Goosen* 1989 (4) SA 1013 (A) (invoking, inter alia, German jurisprudence).

28. See sections II.B.2.ii.b and II.B.2.ii.d in this chapter.

29. 1992 (2) SACR 651 (D).

30. 1933 AD 269.

31. See section III.B.1 in this chapter.

32. See *S v Ngubane* supra n. 25 at 685A–B.

33. *S v Mgedezi* 1989 (1) SA 687 (A) at 705–706.

34. *S v Thebus* 2003 (6) SA 505 (CC); 2003 (2) SACR 319 (CC), unanimous judgment of the Constitutional Court, delivered by Moseneke J, affirming (at para. 50) the rule set out in *Mgedezi* regarding "active association" common purpose.

35. 1985 (2) SA 560 (A).

36. Act 51 of 1977. The Companies Act 71 of 2008 (which has not yet come into force) provides for civil (delictual) liability of directors and prescribed officers of companies (section 77), criminal liability of persons for false statements, reckless conduct and non-compliance (section 214), and general civil liability for anyone contravening provisions of the Act (section 218(2)).

37. 1941 TPD 194.

38. 1992 (4) SA 804 (A) at 807.

39. See *S v Sutherland* 1972 (3) SA 385 (N), where it was held that, under the terms of the liquor legislation, only a natural person could hold a liquor license, not a company.

40. See section II.B.2.i.b in this chapter.

41. *S v Engelbrecht* 2005 (2) SACR 41 (W) at para. 349.

42. See further section III.B in this chapter.

43. Act 51 of 1977, as amended.

44. *Govender v The Minister of Safety and Security* 2001 (4) SA 273 (SCA) and *Ex parte Minister of Safety and Security: In re S v Walters* 2002 (2) SACR 105 (CC).

45. An amendment of the scope of section 49 of the Criminal Procedure Act 51 of 1977 was effected by section 7 of the Judicial Matters Second Amendment Act 122 of

1998. The amended section 49 came into force on 18 July 2003. Apparently a further amendment to the wording of section 49 is imminent, but the text of this new amendment is not available at the time of writing.

46. 1995 (3) SA 632 (CC).

47. Then section 33 of the Interim Constitution, Act 200 of 1993, now section 36 of the Final Constitution, Act 108 of 1996.

48. *Christian Education SA v Minister of Education* 2000 (10) BCLR 1051 (CC).

49. The Israeli Supreme Court in *Plonit v. State of Israel* (2000) 54(1) PD 145 indicated that even the last vestige of corporal punishment in the privacy of the family home may not be immune from criminal prosecution. The direction of this and other foreign precedents could influence the direction of South African society, where child abuse has reached alarming proportions.

50. Theories of punishment are mentioned briefly in section II.A in this chapter.

51. Act 51 of 1977.

52. *Ubuntu* is an African concept encompassing the essence of being "human" and emphasizing that we are "human through others." On the Child Justice Act, see n. 9 above.

53. Criminal Law Amendment Act 105 of 1997.

54. The validity of this legislation was affirmed by the Supreme Court of Appeal in *S v Malgas* 2001 (1) SACR 469 (SCA) and the Constitutional Court in *S v Dodo* 2001 (3) SA 382 (CC). Suggestions, however, have been advanced for a new sentencing framework that would move South Africa away from the rigidity of mandatory minimum sentences toward sentencing guidelines developed by a Sentencing Council. See the recommendations of the South African Law Commission in a report (project 82), *A New Sentencing Framework* (Pretoria: South African Law Commission, November 2000).

55. Infra nn. 61 and 62.

56. *S v Williams* 1995 (3) SA 632 (CC).

57. Since the abolition of capital punishment in 1995 (see section II.F.3) and the implementation of minimum sentence legislation in 1998 (see section II.F.2), the imposition of life sentences has increased considerably.

58. Under section 276(1)(*h*) of the Criminal Procedure Act 51 of 1977. Correctional supervision requires placing the sentenced person under supervision of a correctional officer. The sentence can be served at home and may include community service.

59. Under section 297 of the Criminal Procedure Act 51 of 1977.

60. Between 1911 and 1988, 4,226 convicted persons were executed, 1,904 of these between 1968 and 1988 (an average of 95 a year). The highest number of executions in a year was in 1987, when 164 persons were executed. See (1989) 2 *SACJ* 251.

61. 1995 (3) SA 391 (CC).

62. With the possible exception of treason in a state of war (supra n. 61 at para. 149; 452F–G).

63. Under the recently enacted Criminal Law (Sexual and Related Matters) Amendment Act 32 of 2007.

64. A description of this unique, Roman-law-based South African offence is included in section III.F.1 in this chapter.

65. Abduction consists in unlawfully taking a minor out of the control of his or her custodian *with the intention of enabling someone to marry or to have sexual intercourse with that minor.* The italicized portion of this definition distinguishes abduction from kidnapping.

66. The common-law crime of incest was codified in the Criminal Law (Sexual Offences and Related Matters) Amendment Act 32 of 2007.

67. Robbery consists in theft of property by intentionally using violence or threats of violence to induce submission to the taking of it from another.

68. Extortion consists in obtaining from another some advantage by unlawfully and intentionally subjecting that person to pressure that induces submission to the taking. The common-law definition of this crime was restricted to the obtaining of a pecuniary advantage, but legislation in 1992 extended the nature of the advantage to a nonpecuniary advantage as well (see s 1 of the Criminal Law Amendment Act 139 of 1992).

69. South African criminal law recognizes "uttering" (the act of communicating the forged document to someone) as a distinct crime.

70. The overarching crime of malicious damage to property is not ideally suited to damage to intangible property, and so the legislature has intervened to proscribe unauthorised access to computer systems and altering computer data (see chapter XIII of the Electronic Communications and Transactions Act 25 of 2002).

71. Strictly speaking, the crime of housebreaking in South Africa is the common-law crime of "housebreaking *with intent*" to commit a crime.

72. See *S v Jordan (Sex Workers Education and Advocacy Task Force and Others as Amici Curiae)* 2002 (6) SA 642 (CC) and section 11 of the Criminal Law (Sexual Offences and Related Matters) Amendment Act 32 of 2007.

73. Protection of Constitutional Democracy against Terrorist and Related Activities Act 33 of 2004; see section III.F.2.iii in this chapter.

74. Prevention of Organised Crime Act 121 of 1998 and the Financial Intelligence Centre Act 38 of 2001, see section III.F.2.ii in this chapter.

75. Prevention and Combating of Corrupt Activities Act 12 of 2004; see section III.F.2.i in this chapter.

76. Drugs and Drug Trafficking Act 140 of 1992.

77. National Road Traffic Act 93 of 1996.

78. Firearms Control Act 60 of 2000.

79. See various provisions of the Criminal Law (Sexual Offences and Related Matters) Amendment Act 32 of 2007 (especially Chapter 7 Part 6 (sections 70 and 71), Chapter 8 of the Child Care Act 74 of 1983, and the common-law crimes of abduction and kidnapping.

80. Compounding consists of unlawfully and intentionally agreeing for reward not to prosecute a crime which is punishable otherwise than by fine only. The victim of a crime is punished for not reporting the crime.

81. 1970 (2) SA 355 (A).

82. 1975 (3) SA 532 (C).

83. 1992 (2) SACR 676 (D).

84. Above n. 83 at 702d–f.

85. *S v Williams* 1986 (4) SA 1188 (A) at 1194E–F.

86. See, for instance, Kwame Frimpong and Alexander McCall Smith, *The Criminal Law of Botswana* (Cape Town: Juta and Co., 1992), 20, where it is stated that criminal negligence must be of "a sufficiently serious nature."

87. See section II.B.2.iii in this chapter.

88. *Masiya v DPP, Pretoria and Another (Centre for Applied Legal Studies and Another, Amici Curiae)* 2007 (5) SA 30 (CC).

89. Langa and Sachs JJ (dissenting on this point) were prepared to extend the common-law definition to include anal penetration of males as well.

90. Criminal Law (Sexual Offences and Related Matters) Amendment Act 32 of 2007, section 1(1).

91. Ibid.

92. Ibid., section 15.

93. Ibid., sections 56(2)(*a*) and (*b*).

94. Ibid., sections 17 and 23, respectively.

95. Ibid., sections 18 and 24, respectively.

96. Ibid., section 4.

97. Ibid., section 6.

98. Ibid., section 7.

99. Ibid., section 5.

100. *Ex parte Minister of Justice: In re R v Gesa; R v De Jongh* 1959 (1) SA 234 (A).

101. *S v M* 1982 (1) SA 309 (O); *S v Dlamini* 1984 (3) SA 196 (N).

102. 2000 (1) SACR 633 (SCA) at para. 97.

103. The Game Theft Act 105 of 1991.

104. *S v Visagie* 1991 (1) SA 177 (A).

105. 1955 (4) SA 247 (A).

106. 50 of 1956.

107. 2000 (2) SACR 558 (SCA).

108. 1977 (3) SA 513 (A).

109. Section 37 of the General Law Amendment Act 62 of 1955.

110. *S v Manamela* 2000 (1) SACR 414 (CC).

111. Section 36 of the General Law Amendment Act 62 of 1955. Cf. the unexplained possession of stock or produce suspected of having been stolen: section 2 of the Stock Theft Act 57 of 1959.

112. *Osman v Attorney-General for the Transvaal* 1998 (4) SA 1224 (CC).

113. 1996 (1) SACR 181 (W).

114. The Constitutional Court affirmed the criminality of sexual intercourse for reward in *S v Jordan* 2002 (6) SA 642 (CC), and section 18 of the Criminal Law (Sexual Offences and Related Matters) Amendment Act 32 of 2007 punishes a person who engages the services of another for reward for the purposes of engaging in a sexual act.

115. The Drugs and Drug Trafficking Act 140 of 1992.

116. Tobacco Products Control Act 83 of 1993, as amended by the Tobacco Products Control Amendment Act 23 of 2007. These amendments came into force on 21 August 2009.

117. Prevention and Combating of Corrupt Activities Act 12 of 2004, section 20.

118. The International Co-operation in Criminal Matters Act 75 of 1996 facilitates the provision of evidence, execution of sentences in criminal cases, and the confiscation and transfer of proceeds of crime between South Africa and foreign states.

119. The Supreme Court of Appeal decided on matters pertaining to retrospectivity in *National Director of Public Prosecutions v Carolus* 1999 (2) SACR 607 (SCA); the definition of "instrumentality of an offence" in *National Director of Public Prosecutions v R O Cook Properties (Pty) Ltd; National Director of Public Prosecutions v 37 Gillespie Street Durban (pty) Ltd and Another; National Director of Public Prosecutions v Seevnarayan* 2004 (2) SACR 208 (SCA); and *Singh v NDPP* [2007] SCA 82 (RSA); and proportionality in *NDPP v Vermaak* [2007] SCA 150 (RSA). The Constitutional Court has pronounced on the scope of section 38 of the Prevention of Organised Crime Act dealing with preservation orders: see *National Director of Public Prosecutions v Mahomed (1)* 2002 (4) SA 843 (CC) and *NDPP v Mahomed (2)* 2003 (4) SA 1 (CC); the nature of arbitrary deprivation of property in *First National Bank of SA Ltd t/a Wesbank v Commissioner, South African Revenue Service; First National Bank of SA Ltd t/a Wesbank v Minister of Finance* 2002 (4) SA 768 (CC); the proportionality of the asset forfeiture to the offence and the objectives of the organised crime legislation in *Mohunram v National Director of Public Prosecutions (Law Review Project as Amicus Curiae)* 2007 (2) SACR 145 (CC); and the purposes and ambit of the criminal confiscation provisions (chapter 5) in *Shaik v The State* 2008 (8) BCLR 834 (CC).

120. Act 33 of 2004.

121. The form of intention would seem to be *dolus directus* (see section II.B.2.ii.a in this chapter), in that the accused's aim and object must be to do certain things, even if these objectives are not achieved.

122. Act 27 of 2002.

SPAIN

Carlos Gómez-Jara Díez and Luis E. Chiesa

I. Introduction
   A. Historical Sketch
   B. Jurisdiction
   C. Principles of Punishment
   D. Sources of Criminal Law
   E. Process

II. General Part
   A. Theories of Punishment
   B. Liability Requirements
   C. Defenses
   D. Justifications
   E. Excuses
   F. Sanctions

III. Special Part
   A. Structure
   B. Homicide
   C. Sex Offenses
   D. Larceny and Robbery
   E. False Pretenses and Embezzlement

Carlos Gómez-Jara Díez is Professor at the Universidad Autónoma de Madrid (cgj@corporatedefense.es). His recent publications include "Financial Crisis and Executive Compensation," *Indret* (February 2009) and "Corporations as Victims of Mismanagement," 28 *Pace Law Review* 795 (2008).

Luis E. Chiesa is Associate Professor of Law at Pace Law School (lchiesa@law.pace.edu). His recent publications include "Beyond Torture: The Nemo Tenetur Principle in Borderline Cases," 30 *Boston College Third World Law Journal* 35 (2009), and "Why Is It a Crime to Stomp on a Goldfish? Harm, Victimhood and the Structure of Anti-cruelty Offenses," 78 *Mississippi Law Journal* 1 (2008).

F. Business Crimes
G. "Victimless" Crimes
H. Terrorism Offenses

I. INTRODUCTION

A. Historical Sketch

Modern Spanish criminal law developed as a result of the reform movement of the late eighteenth and early nineteenth centuries. Therefore, it was influenced by the humanist and utilitarian ideals of the Enlightenment and, more specifically, by Cesare Beccaria's *Dei delitti e delle pene* (1764). The Spanish constitution of 1812 required the enactment of a penal code reflecting the principles of the nineteenth-century European liberal tradition of codification. Because the drafters of the first code (1822) were greatly influenced by the ideas of Jeremy Bentham and Beccaria, they attempted to limit judicial discretion in sentencing and to curb the imposition of disproportionate punishments. The rapidly changing social environment that followed led to a series of reforms that culminated in the enactment of the Penal Code in 1870, which was supposed to be in force only for a short time. Although it was dubbed the "Summer Code" in light of its transitory nature, it was ironically still in force in 1928.[1] The Spanish Civil War that erupted in 1936 led to a period of social and political unrest that lasted for three years. Although the post–Civil War era brought about minor changes to the criminal law and several reforms to the Penal Code, it was not until 1995 that the Spanish Parliament enacted the Spanish Penal Code (SPC) presently in force.[2]

Although most criminal legislation is included within the Spanish Penal Code of 1995, some criminal provisions are found in specific statutes like the Substantive and Procedural Criminal Law Regulating Air Navigation (Ley Penal y Procesal de la Navegación aérea), the Smuggling Repression Act (Ley Orgánica de Represión del Contrabando), and the General Electoral System Act (Ley del Régimen Electoral General).[3] It should also be noted that the Spanish criminal laws were reformed on several occasions (1980, 1983, 1989, 1992) with the aim of achieving a "Penal Code of the Democracy" that would be compatible with the social and democratic values that inspired the enactment of the Spanish constitution of 1978.[4] The commitment to forge links between the criminal law and the higher values of the constitution led to a reaffirmation of the validity of suprastatutory fundamental principles of criminal law, such as the *ultima ratio* principle (i.e., that criminal law should be used as a last resort only if noncriminal sanctions are inadequate).[5]

B. Jurisdiction

The Spanish Penal Code does not specify the rules providing for criminal jurisdiction because they are contained within other laws, such as the Judiciary Act (Ley Orgánica del Poder Judicial) and the Rules of Criminal Procedure (Ley de Enjuiciamiento Criminal). The chief ground for exercising criminal jurisdiction is the territorial principle. According to this principle, embodied in article 23.1 of the Judiciary Act, Spanish criminal law applies to events that occur within Spanish borders. This area includes not only Spain's land but also its waters and airspace, which are defined by legislation. Furthermore, under the flag principle, Spanish criminal law applies to events that take place in vessels or crafts flying the Spanish flag[6] unless otherwise provided by international treaties.

Article 23 of the Judiciary Act also provides for jurisdiction pursuant to the passive and active nationality principles and the principle of protective jurisdiction; that is, Spain has jurisdiction over events that might harm interests of the Spanish state. Furthermore, it provides for the exercise of jurisdiction on the basis of the universality principle—one of the major innovations of twentieth century international criminal law. Spanish courts have appealed to the principle of universal jurisdiction in a number of cases. As a result, they have jurisdiction over crimes such as genocide, terrorism, piracy, currency counterfeiting, prostitution, and drug trafficking, regardless of where these offenses were committed.

Cases arising out of the application of the universality principle are prosecuted in the Audiencia Nacional (National Court), which has jurisdiction over only a limited number of crimes, including, but not limited to, terrorism and high-profile cases of white-collar crime and organized crime. In recent years the Audiencia Nacional has assumed jurisdiction over cases involving human rights violations in Chile, Guatemala, Argentina,[7] and Tibet.[8] Members of the international legal community have expressed concern over the interventionist approach adopted by Spanish courts in these cases. The Spanish Supreme Court tried to limit this interventionist trend by reversing some decisions of the Audiencia Nacional.[9] However, the Spanish Constitutional Court[10] subsequently upheld the approach adopted by the Audiencia Nacional, and the Supreme Court has now followed suit.[11]

C. Principles of Punishment

1. Legality Principle

Following the tradition of many civil law jurisdictions, the legality principle is now firmly entrenched in article 25.1 of the Spanish constitution. The requirements of the leglality principle are usually expressed by way of the Latin maxim *nulla poena sine lege praevia, scripta, et stricta* (no punishment without a previous, written and accurate law). This principle requires that punishment be imposed only for the violation of a criminal law previously enacted by the legislature. This guarantees that citizens will not be punished for conduct that has not been previously declared wrongful by the people.[12] This is a consequence of the so-called self-legislation paradigm: citizens must abide by and endure the consequences of legal rules as long as they had the opportunity to participate in the process that led to their enactment.

The first legal safeguard deriving from the legality principle is the prohibition of retroactivity. This requires the state to warn the actor in advance about the consequences of his or her actions. *Ex post facto* criminal provisions are therefore forbidden. Moreover, if a subsequent amendment of a criminal law provision is more lenient to the defendant than the one in effect at the time of the commission of the offense, the defendant has the right to ask the court to be tried under the more lenient provision.[13] The legality principle also requires that Spanish criminal law be statutory law. Therefore, there is no such thing as a Spanish criminal common law. It should also be noted that an act of Parliament adopted by a qualified majority—more than two-thirds of the Parliament—is required for a criminal provision to be enforceable. The executive has no authority to enact criminal statutes.[14] This will be more closely examined when we address the sources of criminal law. A third consequence of the principle of legality is the requirement that laws be drafted in a clear and precise manner and that the courts abstain from expanding the scope of criminal statutes by way of analogy. Some commentators have argued that the principle of legality also requires that if various interpretations of the law are available, the court must choose the interpretation that is more favorable to the defendant. Others, however, believe that the court is free to choose among competing interpretations as long as they do not analogically expand the scope of the criminal statute.[15]

Given that the prohibition of analogy is a rule of constitutional stature, defendants often point to violations of this rule when they are challenging their convictions in the Constitutional Court. This has raised important conflicts between the Constitutional Court and the Supreme Court, because matters of statutory interpretation are said to be jurisdictional questions for which the Supreme Court should have the last word. However, the Constitutional Court defers to the Supreme Court only if certain constitutional limits on the interpretation of criminal statutes are strictly observed.

2. Culpability Principle

The culpability principle is a fundamental tenet of modern Spanish criminal law. Respect for the principle entails that there should be no punishment if the actor did not act with a culpable *mens rea*. More generally, it also requires that only conduct that is worthy of condemnation (i.e., culpable or blameworthy) may be legitimately punished by the state.[16]

Culpability functions both as a prerequisite for and as a limit to punishment. As to the former, no person can be punished if he or she does not understand the nature of his or her wrongdoing. No strict or absolute liability is permitted under Spanish criminal law. Regarding the latter, the culpability principle requires that the punishment imposed on the offender not exceed his or her just deserts, regardless of whether imposing additional punishment enhances social utility.

Most scholars believe that the culpability principle protects human dignity and can thus be grounded in article 10 of the Spanish constitution. For them, respect for human dignity precludes the state from inflicting more pain than the person deserves even if doing so would be socially beneficial.[17] Other commentators have argued that the culpability principle protects free speech and participation in the public square. For them, an offense not only affects the physical world but also calls into question certain community and societal values.[18] According to this theory, the offender is culpable because he or she could have questioned those values by way of the legal mechanisms that the state provides to its citizens to voice their discontent. Therefore, the actor's culpability is a function of his or her decision to express his or her views through the commission of an offense against legal rules.

3. Ultima Ratio *Principle*

The state should make use of the criminal law only as a last resort. Thus punishment should not be imposed for conduct that can be adequately dealt with by imposing noncriminal sanctions. As a result, civil fraud cases and cases involving the infraction of administrative rules should not be treated as criminal matters.[19] The *ultima ratio* principle is often invoked by courts to dismiss cases for lack of criminal jurisdiction when the charged conduct is not sufficiently serious to warrant the imposition of penal sanctions.[20] It should be noted, however, that—as the frequent prosecution of business and tax crimes demonstrates—the state often fails to abide by this principle.[21]

In the 1990s Winfried Hassemer, a leading German criminal theorist, advanced an interesting proposal that has found support among some Spanish scholars. Hassemer suggests that we gravitate toward a "minimalist" criminal law that intervenes only when a core offense has been committed (e.g., homicide, rape, assault). All other offenses, such as business and tax crimes, should be dealt with by creating a new type of law that subjects the offender to lesser punishment but would make a conviction easier to obtain by relaxing the procedural and substantive hurdles to prosecution and conviction.[22]

4. Double Jeopardy

No person shall be punished twice for the same offense. Double jeopardy, or, as it is called in civil law jurisdictions, *non bis in idem*, is a chief principle of criminal law. According to the Spanish Constitutional Court, this principle can be derived in part from the legality principle.[23] The doctrine of double jeopardy bars imposing multiple punishments on the same person on the basis of identical facts and legal grounds. Double jeopardy prohibits not only the imposition of multiple punishments but also the imposition of penal and administrative sanctions for the same offense.[24] Contrary to the practice in common-law jurisdictions, it does not preclude prosecutors from appealing acquittals. However, courts have recently barred the initiation of new prosecutions against the same person for the same facts and on the same grounds in order to avoid risking the conviction of previously acquitted defendants.[25]

As a result of the Spanish approach to double jeopardy, the state cannot simultaneously conduct civil and criminal investigations of the same conduct. Once an administrative agency believes that the investigated conduct may have criminal implications, it must give notice to the prosecutors' office and stop the investigation. Nonetheless, if the criminal proceedings end without a conviction, the administrative agency may recommence its investigation. This happens often in cases involving offenses related to employee safety, tax crimes, and other crimes typically investigated by administrative agencies.[26]

Pursuant to article 54 of the Schengen Treaty, the *non bis in idem* principle has a European dimension. European Court of Justice (ECJ) case law has expanded the double-jeopardy doctrine not only to bar the imposition of multiple punishments but also to prohibit retrying offenders after acquittals grounded on the expiration of a statute of limitations.[27] The commencement of new criminal proceedings grounded on the same facts is also prohibited by ECJ case law.[28] Final criminal judgments by a court of a member state of the European Union (EU) are not only binding domestically but also bind other member states. An EU citizen cannot be tried or sanctioned twice for the same conduct in the EU.[29] Needless to say, developments in this area represent a step toward the harmonization of substantive and procedural European criminal law.

D. Sources of Criminal Law

1. Legislature

The chief source of Spanish criminal law is the Penal Code of 1995. Although the country is made up of various statelike administrative regions—*comunidades autónomas*—there is only one penal code for the entire territory. It is important to note that criminal laws may be enacted only by parliamentary act—so-called organic act (*ley orgánica*)—that require a special majority.[30] Nevertheless, Parliament sometimes expressly or tacitly makes reference to nonpenal legislation enacted by the comunidades autónomas in order to supplement the content of criminal statutes. This is the case, for example, with environmental crimes that make reference to specific regulations that are enacted by each comunidad autónoma, such as those dealing with species that ought to be considered endangered. The Spanish Constitutional Court has ruled that this is permissible as long as the core prohibited conduct is fleshed out in the Penal Code.[31]

Additional problems have arisen since Spain became a member of the European Union. Although it is debatable whether the EU has the authority to enact penal legislation that is directly enforceable in the different member states (European Regulations), the EU can undoubtedly enforce certain pieces of legislation, such as its guidelines and framework decisions.[32] These statutes, which are enacted by the European Parliament and the European Council, play an increasingly important role in shaping Spanish criminal law.[33] As the EU consolidates its power over member states, European scholars are noting that the process of creating supranational federal criminal law resembling the federal/state system in the United States of America is under way.[34]

2. Judiciary

Although Spanish courts do not abide by the common-law doctrine of *stare decisis*, the rulings handed down by the Supreme Court and the Constitutional Court provide guidance for lower courts. Certain qualifications in this regard are in order, however. First, cases in the Supreme Court are assigned to different panels of justices, and therefore the court sometimes hands down contradictory judgments on the same issue. Second, the Constitutional Court is also a court of last instance, although it may only entertain constitutional claims.[35] Nevertheless, constitutional issues sometimes overlap with matters concerning the interpretation of criminal statutes. Constitutional rulings on such matters sometimes conflict with the doctrines put forth by the Supreme Court (for example, their respective interpretations of the statute of limitations diverge radically). Third, certain convictions cannot be appealed to either court. Therefore, the rulings of each of the fifty-two Spanish courts of appeals are sometimes considered final.[36]

Additionally, the case law of the ECJ also influences the way in which member states interpret EU-related criminal provisions in their regional courts.[37] In theory, when a state court has doubts regarding the proper interpretation of a certain statute in light of European legislation, it should ask for a ruling from the ECJ. This is especially true in the context of business crimes and environmental crimes, because many laws creating such offenses are enacted by the European Union. The Spanish Constitutional Court has recognized that

Spanish citizens have a constitutional right to demand a European interpretation of state law provisions that might affect their case.[38]

3. Executive

The executive has no authority to enact criminal laws. However, certain executive decisions indirectly affect Spanish criminal law. The executive branch's regulation of financial institutions, for example, might end up determining whether a bank employee has aided or abetted in the commission of a money-laundering offense.[39] Additionally, the interpretation of criminal provisions is sometimes dependent on regulations promulgated by administrative agencies.

4. Scholars

Scholarly writings play an important role in the interpretation of criminal statutes. Although barely mentioned in court rulings, Spanish scholars have undoubtedly shaped the interpretation of many criminal law doctrines of the General Part. Scholarly opinion is particularly important when there is no prior case law that sheds light on the issue facing the court. The interpretation of tax and insider-trading offenses, for example, has been heavily influenced by academic writings because there is little case law on the subject.[40] The fact that many judges are also professors contributes to some citation of scholarly writings in judicial opinions.

E. Process

1. Adversarial/Inquisitorial

Following the French tradition, Spanish criminal procedure is divided into two stages—the investigative phase and the trial phase. An examining magistrate presides over the investigative phase. Therefore, it is chiefly inquisitorial in nature, although the prosecutors and the police have an initial, albeit limited, authority to investigate before submitting their findings to the examining magistrate. The trial phase is presided over by a single judge or a three-judge panel, depending on whether the potential offense is punishable by less or more than five years of imprisonment. The examining magistrate does not participate in the trial phase in order to eschew any bias when deciding the case. The investigative phase is not public. However, the information gathered as a result of the investigation is usually, though not always, available to the parties. The trial phase, on the contrary, is held in open court.[41]

During the trial the prosecution has the burden of proof, given that the defendant is presumed innocent until proved guilty. Although the prosecution has no duty to reveal all exculpatory evidence, it must seek an acquittal if it believes that the defendant is not guilty. Furthermore, the defendant may seek constitutional relief if the evidence presented before the trial court was insufficient to ground a conviction.[42]

Due process considerations forbid the usage of illegally obtained evidence before and during the trial proceedings.[43] Although there is no specific formal motion to suppress such evidence, the defendant may request suppression at any given time. Furthermore, Spanish courts exclude evidence that has been obtained as a result of the exploitation of other illegally obtained evidence. However, the evidence is not suppressed if the link between the evidence and the governmental illegality is sufficiently attenuated.

2. Parties

A distinctive feature of Spanish criminal law is that there are various types of prosecutors who may initiate the process against the defendant. Public prosecutors represent the government and normally bear the brunt of prosecuting the defendant. Private prosecutors, on the other hand, represent the victims of crime and also have the authority to prosecute the offenders directly. If the victim is the state, the state attorneys have standing to prosecute the suspect. In some cases so-called popular prosecutors also have the authority to initiate a process against the offender. Popular prosecutors represent organizations that have an interest in the outcome of the trial, such as nongovernmental organizations (NGOs) that represent victims in terrorism-related cases. It should also be pointed out that victims may exercise their civil actions against defendants within the criminal proceedings.

Since civil claims are also adjudicated in the criminal trial, any person who might be held civilly liable as a result of the defendant's conduct may participate in the criminal proceedings. It should be noted, however, that his or her role is limited to aspects of the case that might affect his or her civil liability. Those who have unknowingly reaped economic benefits as a result of the defendant's conduct may also participate in the proceedings.

3. Jury/Written Opinions

Jury trials were not authorized in Spain until 1995, when the Jury Trial Act was enacted pursuant to article 125 of the Spanish constitution. This law allowed for the trial by jury of defendants accused of committing certain crimes, such as homicide, criminal threats, trespass, bribery, and certain types of arson. The Spanish jury is composed of nine laypeople, and the procedures are similar to those followed by common-law juries. Because their function is to serve as fact finders, the presiding magistrate instructs them about the legal issues that are pertinent to the case. However, the Spanish Supreme Court has held that if one of the counts with which the defendant is charged is not a crime listed in the Jury Trial Act, a bench trial is mandatory.[44] This has greatly diminished the impact of jury trials in Spain, which now account for only a small percentage of trials held in the country.

4. Civil Liability

Contrary to recent trends in Europe, civil claims may be exercised in Spain within the criminal proceedings.[45] This is usually justified by pointing out that it is cost efficient to adjudicate criminal and civil responsibility in a single proceeding. It is also a natural consequence of the formal standing afforded to victims in the criminal process. As private prosecutors, the victims not only charge the defendant with the commission of an offense but also seek monetary relief through restitution, compensation, or indemnification. However, the rules of criminal procedure enable prosecutors to waive the right to pursue a civil action within the criminal proceeding and to commence civil litigation within the civil jurisdiction. This course of action is rarely initiated because the civil courts cannot impose civil liability for conduct that amounts to a criminal offense unless a criminal court has determined that a crime was actually committed. It is possible to settle the civil claim within the criminal proceeding and still face the prospect of criminal responsibility. It is also worth mentioning that the perpetrator's decision to pay restitution to the victim requires a mandatory mitigation of punishment according to article 21.5 of the Penal Code.

The rules for determining the civil liability of the defendant for conduct that amounts to a commission of a criminal offense are fleshed out in section V of the Penal Code. Article 116 of the Code holds all perpetrators and accomplices jointly liable for damages to the victim. The civil liability of accomplices is, however, subsidiary to the liability of perpetrators. The Code also states that insurance companies are jointly and directly liable for any criminal events covered by the insurance policy. The criminal court can hold the defendant liable for damages even if it concludes that the person is not guilty of the criminal charges by reason of insanity, diminished capacity, or intoxication. Corporations are only secondarily liable for the actions perpetrated by their employees.

The allocation of civil responsibility arising out of criminal cases is extremely important when the perpetrator's conduct has caused physical injury. Spanish courts make use of a table in order to determine the amount of damages that should be awarded for different kinds of injuries. The imposition of civil liability does not preclude the imposition of monetary fines on the defendant if such a course of action is authorized by statute. If the insurance company ends up compensating the victim, it can recover from the defendant if—as is usually the case in criminal cases—he or she acted in bad faith.

5. *Statute of Limitations*

The statutes of limitations governing criminal actions are regulated in articles 132 and 133 of the Code.[46] Initially the rules related to statutes of limitation were considered procedural. However, recent case law has suggested that these rules are substantive in nature. The purpose of these rules is to prohibit punishing conduct that is no longer in need of punishment because of the passage of time.

The specific length of the applicable statute of limitations varies according to the severity of the offense. Minor offenses are usually governed by a three-year statute of limitations, whereas offenses punished by up to five, ten, and fifteen years of imprisonment are governed by five-, ten-, and fifteen-year limitation periods, respectively. Genocide and crimes against humanity have no statute of limitations.

The statute of limitations may be interrupted either when the prosecutor files the criminal complaint against the defendant or when the judge grants a petition authorizing the investigation of the offense. Pursuant to an important decision handed down by the Constitutional Court on March 14, 2005,[47] the limitation period should be interrupted only when the judge initiates the investigation. However, the Supreme Court has continued to suggest that the prosecutor's filing of the complaint interrupts the term.[48] Most Spanish scholars agree with the Constitutional Court's approach to this problem.

II. GENERAL PART

A. Theories of Punishment

Although the Penal Code does not adopt a specific theory of punishment, article 25.2 of the Spanish constitution states that the main goal of criminal punishment is the rehabilitation of the offender. Additionally, the suspension or mitigation of imprisonment sanctions is sometimes dependent on whether the convict has been rehabilitated. In spite of this, the Constitutional Court has held that rehabilitation is not the sole aim of punishment in Spain, although it should be taken into account by the legislature when enacting criminal laws.[49]

This interpretation is compatible with so-called combined theories of punishment, which hold that it is coherent and desirable that punishment serve different purposes.[50] In addition to rehabilitation, for example, courts have taken into account theories of retribution in order to determine the legitimacy of punishment. Thus both the Supreme Court and the Constitutional Court have ruled that the punishment imposed may not be disproportionate to the punishment deserved by the offender under a retributive theory of punishment.[51]

A distinctive feature of Spanish criminal law is that it allows for the imposition of two distinct types of penal sanctions, namely, punishment and security measures.[52] Punishment may be imposed only on those who have committed an offense without justification or excuse. Security measures, on the other hand, may be imposed on dangerous individuals who have engaged in wrongful but excusable conduct. The imposition of security measures seeks to prevent possible future harmful conduct instead of exacting retribution for past acts. Thus these measures are prospective in nature.

Many Spanish criminal theorists argue that the aim of punishment should be to achieve so-called positive general deterrence.[53] According to the theory of positive general deterrence, punishment should not be conceived as a means to deter future criminals from engaging in harmful conduct (negative deterrence), but rather as a mechanism that reinforces the expectations of law-abiding citizens that the criminal laws will be enforced. This normative (positive) approach to punishment, which is grounded in recent developments in the fields of sociology and social psychology, is increasingly favored by commentators over the more traditional coercive (negative) justification for punishment. This theory treats offenders not as "animals" that fear "sticks" and pursue "carrots," but as rational beings who understand both the meaning of their actions and the duties that they have assumed as a result of living in society. The supporters of the theory of general positive deterrence sometimes conceive punishment as a way of reinforcing law-abiding attitudes in the offender, or as a vehicle for reassuring the trust that fellow citizens have in the legal system, or as a way of reaffirming the validity of the legal system itself. Regardless of how the theory is conceived, however, there is agreement that punishment should be viewed as a positive stimulus rather than a negative reaction. The theory of positive general deterrence also stresses the importance of the expressive meaning of crime and punishment and of recent studies that highlight the expressive nature of law.[54]

B. Liability Requirements

1. Objective/Actus Reus
i. Act

It is a bedrock principle of Spanish criminal law that liability should be imposed for what the perpetrator does, not for who he or she is. Thus it is often stated that criminal law is concerned with "acts," not "actors."[55] Although the importance of this proposition is seldom questioned, there is significant disagreement about how to define what actually amounts to an act. Some defend a mechanistic concept of action that defines an act as a "willed bodily movement."[56] Others endorse a teleological theory of action that conceives of an act as a bodily movement that is intentionally directed toward achieving a desired goal.[57] In recent decades some commentators have adopted a "social" conception of acts according to which an action is "an instance of socially relevant conduct."[58] Finally, an increasing number of scholars defend an "expressive" concept of action that conceives of an act as "conduct that is intersubjectively perceived as an instance of meaningful and relevant behavior."[59]

In spite of the theoretical differences that exist between these different conceptions of action, everyone agrees that the involuntariness of the actor's conduct negates the existence of an act that is relevant for the criminal law. As a result, an act that is compelled by the employment of irresistible physical force against the defendant is not "voluntary" and, therefore, not punishable.[60] The force is irresistible only if it completely overbears the actor's will. On the other hand, force that substantially reduces but does not completely eliminate the actor's volition does not negate the voluntariness of the conduct.[61] Given that such force can be resisted, it does not impair the actor's volition to the extent that it renders his or her conduct irrelevant for the criminal law. It could, however, generate a full or partial excuse for the conduct.[62]

Bodily movements that are the product of a reflex are also irrelevant for the criminal law because of their lack of voluntariness. Consequently, a person who strikes another as a result of an epileptic seizure has not performed an act that may trigger the imposition of penal responsibility. Spanish theorists distinguish between conduct that is the product of a reflex and conduct that is the result of a controllable impulse. Whereas volition is totally absent in the case of a reflex, impulsive conduct is reflective of some volition, albeit significantly diminished. An example of an impulsive act that falls short of a reflex is that of a driver who runs over someone after losing control of his car when he swats at a bee that entered the vehicle through the driver's side window. Although the driver's conduct is certainly abrupt and spontaneous, it cannot be said to be entirely involuntary. Consequently, the driver's conduct qualifies as an act that is relevant for the criminal law. However, the impulsive nature of his conduct might be taken into consideration when determining whether the driver's wrongful act should be fully or partially excused.

Unconsciousness can also negate the voluntariness of the defendant's conduct. Thus a Spanish court held that a guard who unlawfully fired his weapon while sleepwalking should not be held criminally liable because of the lack of voluntariness of his act.[63] Defendants who injure third parties when they fall asleep while driving have frequently argued that they should not be held liable for the harms that their conduct has caused because they were "unconscious" at the time that the accident took place. Although such conduct is, in principle, not voluntary, the Spanish Supreme Court has repeatedly held that drivers who cause harm when they fall asleep at the wheel should generally be held liable on the basis of negligence, because they usually have time to pull over when the first signs of sleepiness set in.[64]

ii. Omission

According to article 10 of the Spanish Penal Code, both acts and omissions may trigger the imposition of criminal liability. Generically, an omission can be defined as the failure to perform an act that is required by law. Although omissions may involve the nonperformance of conduct (e.g., a lifeguard who idly stands by while a child is drowning in a pool), they may also involve the performance of an act that is different from the one prescribed by law (e.g., stepping on the gas instead of braking before a stop sign).

There are two distinct types of punishable omissions. On the one hand, an actor may be held liable when he or she fails to perform an act that the criminal law requires to be performed regardless of whether the failure to act produces a harmful result. These types of omissions are called "pure" omissions. Examples of crimes of pure omission are failing to file a tax return, failing to stop at a red light, and failing to pay child support. These failures to act are punishable even when no one is harmed as a result of the omission.

On the other hand, sometimes an actor is held liable for an omission only when his or her failure to act produces a harmful result. These kinds of omissions are called "impure" omissions. It is said that impure omissions give rise to liability for a crime of "commission by omission" because the failure to act generates liability for the harm caused as if it had been committed by way of an affirmative act. Examples of instances of commission by omission include a parent who kills his or her child by failing to feed the child and a nurse who kills his or her patient by refusing to turn on the patient's respirator.

According to article 11 of the Spanish Penal Code, omissions should give rise to liability for a crime of harmful consequences only when the defendant's failure to act has brought about the wrongful result as if he or she had caused it by way of a positive act. Sometimes it is difficult to determine whether the omission caused the result in a way that is equivalent to it having been produced by way of affirmative conduct. Article 11 provides that when courts are determining whether the result caused by an omission should be deemed equivalent to the result having been caused by an act, they should take into account whether the actor had a special legal or contractual duty to act. A special duty to act may arise as a result of the existence of close familial ties. Thus a mother has a special duty to take care of her newborn child. If a breach of this duty results in the death of the child, the mother would be held liable for homicide under a theory of commission by omission. The Spanish Supreme Court has also held that adult children are under a duty to take care of their elderly parents.[65] It also seems that those who voluntarily decide to partake in a dangerous enterprise assume a reciprocal duty to render aid to those who participate in the activity. An oft-cited example of this type of case is that of a group of hikers who decide to go on an alpine expedition. If one of the hikers gets injured during the expedition, the other hikers have a duty to aid him or her. Similarly, those who have voluntarily assumed the obligation to aid others in need are under a duty to do so. The paradigmatic example is that of the lifeguard who voluntarily assumes the duty to rescue swimmers who are in danger of drowning.

Article 11 also provides that defendants who engage in acts that create a risk of harm to a legally protected interest have an obligation to impede the materialization of such harm. As a result, a person who lights a fire in a forest to keep himself warm has a duty to control the fire from spreading throughout the forest. His failure to do so might give rise to liability for the harms caused by the fire.

A particularly vexing problem arises when an actor has negligently created the risk but intentionally omitted to aid the person put at risk by his or her imprudent conduct. Take, for example, the case of a driver who contributed to the death of a pedestrian by failing to provide him assistance after he negligently ran the pedestrian over with his car. Some have argued that such omissions are of "intermediate gravity" because they are less serious than those that are preceded by an intentional creation of the risk (intentionally running over the pedestrian) but more serious than a failure to render aid to someone who was not put at risk by the omitter's conduct (someone who was not involved in the accident failed to assist the pedestrian).[66] In light of the intermediate gravity of these failures to act, there are good reasons to punish them more severely than pure omissions but less severely than full-fledged cases of commission by omission.[67] The Spanish Supreme Court, however, has not directly addressed this question.

The obligation to control sources of risk or the conduct of third parties under one's supervision could also give rise to a duty to act that might generate responsibility for a crime of commission by omission. Thus the owner of an animal with a violent disposition who fails to control the creature might be held criminally liable for the harms caused by the animal. Similarly, a person who has an obligation to supervise the conduct of third parties may be responsible for the harmful results caused by an individual who was under his or her supervision. A typical case is that of the responsibility of the personnel in charge of patients in mental institutions for the harmful acts committed by a dangerous mentally deranged patient.[68]

iii. Status

In Spain, as in most jurisdictions, being in possession of a certain object is sometimes considered criminal. Consequently, the Spanish Penal Code punishes the unlawful possession of weapons,[69] drugs,[70] and child pornography,[71] among other objects. Several scholars have called into question the legitimacy of criminalizing such conduct in light of the fact that being in possession of something amounts to a status that is neither an act nor an omission.[72]

It seems that this criticism is misplaced, however, because it is sensible to conceive of possession crimes as offenses of omission. According to this conception of possession offenses, the prohibited conduct is the actor's failure to terminate the possession of the object in circumstances where the law required him or her to do so.[73] Such a failure to act, of course, amounts to a punishable omission.

As a general rule, the state cannot legitimately criminalize a person's status. Thus it would be illegitimate for the state to punish people for being drunkards or for being beggars. This flows naturally from the general principle discussed at the outset of this section that an actor should be punished only for what he or she does, not for who he or she is. One possible exception to this general rule, however, is the offense of "being a member of a criminal organization."[74] Determining the reasons that legitimize the criminalization of such conduct and the scope of application of the offense has been a notoriously elusive task for both courts and commentators. Some have suggested that belonging to a criminal organization is criminalized in order to neutralize the members of the organization before they engage in concrete acts that are harmful to third parties.[75]

Others contend that certain acts of gaining membership in a criminal association should be punished because they make the individual complicit in the illegal acts of the organization.[76] Regarding the scope of application of these offenses, proponents of both theories agree that belonging to an unlawful association should be criminalized only when the defendant has engaged in acts of membership that clearly demonstrate the actor's desire to belong to the organization permanently.[77] As a result, passive acts of integration into the organization that do not reveal the actor's clear commitment to furthering the aims of the association should not trigger the imposition of liability pursuant to this offense.[78]

2. Subjective/Mens Rea/Mental Element

Pursuant to articles 5 and 10 of the Penal Code, there can be no criminal liability without culpability. Therefore, there can be no strict or absolute liability under Spanish law. However, the meaning of the term *culpability* has long been debated by Spanish scholars. For most of the twentieth century a majority of courts and commentators argued in favor of the so-called psychological theory of culpability. According to this theory, an offender acts culpably if he or she *desires* to commit an offense and *knows* that his or her acts will culminate in the commission of a crime.[79] However, during the last two decades courts and criminal theorists have increasingly focused on the cognitive element of culpability (knowledge) at the expense of the volitive element (desire) of guilt. This has resulted in a normative approach to *mens rea* that focuses primarily on examining whether the offender was aware of the risk he or she was creating and of the possibility that his or her risky conduct might result in actual harm.[80] The leading case regarding this matter is a Spanish Supreme Court products-liability decision handed down on April 23, 1992. The question presented to the court was whether the defendant intended to kill hundreds of people and injure thousands more. The court convicted the defendant because it concluded that he had knowledge of the risk that he created when he sold industrial oil for the purpose of human consumption.[81]

This does not mean that the volitive element plays no role in the interpretation of criminal statutes. Some offenses do refer to terms such as intent (e.g., articles 270.2, 275, 277, 408, 605 SPC) or malice (e.g., article 459 SPC). When discussing the meaning of these mental states, courts and commentators make reference to well-established categories that bear some resemblance to the Model Penal Code's section 2.02 distinctions between purpose, knowledge, recklessness, and negligence:

1. *Dolus* in the first degree (purpose)—the offender desires the final outcome of his criminal action,
2. *Dolus* in the second degree (knowledge)—the offender knows that the commission of the crime is a natural consequence of his conduct,
3. *Dolus eventualis* (recklessness)—the offender is aware that it is probable that his actions might bring about a crime,
4. Negligence—the offender should have known that his conduct unjustifiably created a risk of producing a criminal result.

Although these mental states are not defined in the Spanish Penal Code, their scope and meaning have been fleshed out by Spanish case law and scholarship.[82]

3. *Theories of Liability*
   i. Inchoate Crimes
      a. *Attempt*

Article 16 of the Penal Code defines the conduct that amounts to a criminal attempt and distinguishes between acts of execution and acts of preparation. Pursuant to article 15, acts of preparation are not punishable as criminal attempts. Scholars have advanced a number of objective, subjective, and mixed objective-subjective theories to explain and justify the punishment of attempts.[83] The law of attempts raises four vexing problems: (1) drawing the line between acts of preparation and acts of execution, (2) distinguishing between complete and incomplete attempts, (3) differentiating between impossible and possible attempts, and (4) determining when an actor has voluntarily abandoned his or her criminal attempt.

The *actus reus* of a criminal attempt is satisfied when the offender has commenced the *execution* of the crime. In order to determine what amounts to an act of execution, Spanish case law has adopted a standard that combines objective (the dangerousness of the conduct) and subjective (the actor's plan for committing the offense) features of the act.[84] Furthermore, courts have employed a "proximity test" that leads to punishing an actor for a criminal attempt only if his or her acts are objectively dangerous and proximately close to producing a criminal harm. Additionally, the Code requires that the offender's actions be, from an objective point of view, ideal or adequate to produce the result, that is, that no substantial intermediate steps need to be taken by the actor in order for the result to occur. The *mens rea* of criminal attempts is the intent to commit the crime. Therefore, there is no attempt liability for negligent acts. The Code also requires that the actor's failure to consummate the offense be the product of forces beyond the control of the actor.

In sum, an actor has engaged in a criminal attempt if (1) he or she intended to commit a crime, (2) he or she took substantial steps to produce the criminal harm, (3) his or her acts were proximately close to producing the result, and (4) the harm did not occur because of reasons that had nothing to do with the actor's original intention.[85] This last element raises important questions about the doctrine of voluntary abandonment as a defense to attempt liability. Pursuant to this doctrine, an actor will not be held liable if he or she voluntarily abandons his or her criminal attempt either by not performing the remaining acts of execution needed to consummate the offense or by taking affirmative steps to prevent the result from taking place after the acts of execution have been completed. Abandonment of the criminal attempt that is the product of third-party intervention or the victim's resistance does not bar liability. Spanish courts have illustrated the distinction between voluntary and involuntary abandonment by citing the following famous passage authored by a famous German criminal theorist, Reinhardt Frank: "An actor may claim to have voluntarily abandoned his attempt when he can say that 'I could have reached the finish line had I wanted to'. Contrarily, an actor has not voluntarily abandoned his attempt when he can only say that 'I could not have reached the finish line, even if I wanted to.'"[86]

Spanish criminal law distinguishes between complete and incomplete attempts.[87] An attempt is complete when the offender has engaged in all the acts that are necessary to produce the result. On the other hand, an attempt is incomplete if the actor has performed only some of the acts that are needed for the harm to take place. Case law[88] defines an incomplete attempt as an attempt that has been thwarted, whereas completed attempts have been defined as instances when the offender has finished performing the acts that would ideally lead to the causation of the harm. Pursuant to article 62 of the Code, incomplete attempts should be punished less severely than completed attempts.

Finally, it should be noted that an actor sometimes attempts to commit a crime in circumstances where it is impossible to consummate the offense. This raises the problem of the punishability of so-called impossible attempts. As a general rule, Spanish criminal law does not punish impossible attempts. However, recent case law has limited the scope of this general rule by contending that impossible attempts should be punished when an *ex ante* evaluation of the actor's conduct would lead a reasonable person to believe that the consummation of the offense was possible even though an *ex post* examination of the act reveals that it was impossible for the actor to consummate the offense.[89]

b. Conspiracy

Pursuant to article 17 of the Penal Code, a criminal conspiracy takes place when two or more persons agree to commit a crime and decide to go forward with their criminal plan.[90] Therefore, an accord to commit a crime does not in and of itself amount to criminal conspiracy, because the crime is consummated only when the parties decide to act on their plans to carry out the offense. As soon as an act of execution amounting to a punishable attempt is performed, conspiracy gets absorbed by the attempt offense and cannot be punished separately, pursuant to article 8.3 of the Code. According to Spanish case law,[91] conspiracy is an anticipated form of joint coperpetration of a crime. Therefore, conspirators can be punished only when they are planning to be coperpetrators of the offense, as opposed to being mere accomplices to the crime. Furthermore, an actor is guilty of conspiracy only if he or she has firmly manifested his or her intention to carry out the offense.

The existence of a conspiracy is sometimes considered an aggravating factor at the sentencing stage. Furthermore, whether the actor conspired to commit an offense may also be relevant to determining whether he or she should be found guilty of committing the offense of "belonging to an unlawful association."[92] The crime of being a member of a criminal organization is committed if the following four requirements are met: (1) the actor joins an association consisting of three or more persons, (2) the association has a hierarchical and well-delineated organizational structure, (3) the organization has existed for some time, and (4) the main goal of the association is to commit crimes.[93]

ii. Perpetration

A person is considered a perpetrator if he or she makes a substantial contribution to the commission of the offense. In order to determine whether the actor's contribution is substantial, courts and commentators rely on the so-called control-over-the-event theory (*teoría del dominio del hecho*).[94] Pursuant to this theory, only those who have control or dominion over the criminal conduct can be considered perpetrators. An actor has control or dominion over the criminal conduct in three circumstances:

1. *Direct perpetration*—when he or she produces the result by way of his or her own acts or omissions
2. *Perpetration by means*—when the actor has control over an innocent person who is used by him or her as an instrument for the commission of the offense (e.g., ordering a hypnotized person to commit an offense)
3. *Joint perpetration or coperpetration*—when he or she has joint control over the criminal conduct

The first form of perpetration is self-explanatory. The second form of perpetration entails gaining control over an "innocent" person in order to commit the offense. In such cases it is said that the person who controls the acts of the innocent person is the "perpetrator behind the perpetrator" because he or she is the force that put in motion the events that led to the commission of the crime. A common case is that of an actor who gains control over an inculpable person (e.g., a child or someone who is insane) who is used as a means to perpetrate the crime. A more controversial case, although still considered an instance of perpetration by means, arises when someone who is under duress is used as an instrument to commit the offense. Recently, scholars have argued that the theory of perpetration by means should be employed in the corporate context to enable punishing low-level employees as direct perpetrators and higher-level corporate executives and officers as perpetrators by means who have used the lower-level employees as instruments for the commission of the offense.[95]

The third form of perpetration entails the joint execution of the offense by two or more persons.[96] The coperpetrators must have agreed to help each other commit the offense. The agreement to commit the crime need not be express. An implicit agreement based on a tacit mutual understanding suffices. An agreement reached through third parties who served as intermediaries between the different coperpetrators is also sufficient.

iii. Complicity

Complicity is defined in negative terms: an accomplice is someone who aids or abets the perpetrator without having executed the actual offense. Accomplices are punished because their help increases the probability that the perpetrator will successfully commit the offense. Therefore, accomplices are punished only if they rendered actual physical or psychological assistance to the perpetrator. Thus attempted complicity is not punishable. An actor must have knowledge of the perpetrator's criminal plan in order to be held liable as an accomplice.

If the offense would not have been perpetrated without the accomplice's help, the accomplice will be punished as severely as the perpetrators.[97] However, if the accomplice's conduct facilitated the commission of the offense but was not necessary for its consummation, the accomplice will be punished less severely than the perpetrators. The difference between complicity and joint perpetration is that accomplices do not have control over the criminal conduct, whereas coperpetrators share control over the criminal event.[98]

iv. Corporate Criminal Liability

Spanish criminal law does not allow for the imposition of corporate criminal liability per se. However, corporations may be subjected to various types of noncriminal sanctions and civil liability. Before we examine these sanctions in more detail, it is worth noting that a vigorous debate is currently taking place in Spain about whether it would be appropriate to impose criminal liability on corporations.[99] Those who oppose holding corporations criminally liable argue that corporate entities are incapable of engaging in conduct, of possessing a criminal mental state, or of suffering the physical pain associated with punishment. On the other hand, modern advocates of corporate criminal responsibility contend that corporations are indeed capable of organizing themselves in a way that is relevant to the criminal law, that they do possess a certain organizational awareness that meets the *mens rea* standard of knowledge, and that corporations may suffer the pain associated with social stigma. The most recent proposal for amending the Code allowed for the imposition of corporate criminal responsibility based on notions of vicarious liability, but it was eventually rejected by Parliament.

With regard to noncriminal liability, there are two principal grounds for subjecting corporations to civil liability. Pursuant to article 120.3 of the Code, corporations are civilly liable for the harm resulting from the commission of an offense within their commercial establishment if at the time of the offense the corporation was not abiding by applicable regulations. Furthermore, article 120.4 of the Code holds corporations responsible in tort for the actions of their employees within the scope of their employment. In such cases the corporate entity is held strictly liable, and there is thus no need to show that the harm took place as a result of negligence.

Corporations are also subject to the so-called derivative consequences of punishment prescribed in article 129 of the Code for certain type of offenses. The sanctions that may be imposed pursuant to this provision include the closing of corporate plants, a freeze on their business activities, and the liquidation of their assets (i.e., the corporate death penalty). The first two sanctions can be imposed as preemptive measures. These sanctions are seldom imposed by Spanish courts, and when they are, it is usually for conduct related to environmental crimes.[100] Scholars have long debated the nature and meaning of these sanctions.[101] Most commentators tend to view them as administrative sanctions that are imposed on dangerous corporations.

Finally, article 31.2 of the Code was recently amended to require corporations to pay the criminal fine imposed on an offender who acted on behalf of, or for the benefit of, the corporation.[102] It remains to be seen whether this sanction will apply to all types of offenses or only to offenses in which the corporation itself is the addressee of the provisions (i.e., corporate income tax provisions), but the actual person in charge of fulfilling these duties is a natural person (i.e., a corporate tax director). Given that article 31.2 does not seem to allow for defenses that would defeat the imposition of the sanctions on the corporation, the corporate entity will be held liable regardless of whether it acted culpably.

4. Causation

Liability for a crime of harmful consequences may be imposed only when it has been determined that the defendant's conduct was the cause of the harm. The Spanish Penal Code does not contain rules regarding the issue of causation. It has thus been up to courts and commentators to develop a conceptual framework to deal with the problem. For most of the twentieth century, case law followed the "but-for" rule to determine causation (the *conditio sine qua non* rule). According to this rule, an actor's conduct is the cause of the victim's harm if it constitutes a condition without which the harm would not have taken place. Relying solely on this test may lead to unfair results, especially in cases involving multiple intervening causes. Therefore, scholars attempted to supplement the "but-for" rule with the so-called theory of adequate causation. Causation would be established under this theory if an *ex ante* evaluation of the actor's conduct would lead a reasonable person to believe that harm to the victim was a foreseeable consequence of the act.[103]

Subsequently, courts and commentators abandoned the theory of adequate causation and replaced it with the so-called theory of objective imputation.[104] The theory of objective imputation requires that courts engage in a normative assessment of the facts surrounding the act in order to determine whether the harmful result that ensued should be *imputed* or *attributed* to the defendant. As a general rule, a result will be attributed to the defendant if the following two conditions are met: (1) his or her conduct created an unjustifiable risk of producing a criminal harm, and (2) the harm was produced as a result of the unjustifiable risk created by the defendant's conduct.[105]

The theory of objective imputation will frequently lead to the same results that would be obtained by employing the common-law theory of proximate or legal causation. However, the theory of objective imputation sometimes bars the imposition of punishment in cases that would usually be punished pursuant to proximate-cause theories. Scholars have identified four instances in which the theory of objective attribution bars the imposition of liability on the defendant:

1. The harmful result will not be attributed to the defendant when the conduct that brought about the harm was lawful. Take the case of driving as an example. Driving is a lawful, albeit risky, activity. Therefore, according to the theory of objective attribution, a person who drives in accordance with traffic regulations cannot be held liable for harmful events that occur as a result of performing this activity. However, if the person is driving in violation of traffic regulations—by speeding, for example—any harm that occurs as a direct result of such conduct will be objectively attributed to the driver.

2. The harmful result will not be attributed to the defendant when it was brought about by the performance of a task that the actor was supposed to perform in light of his or her social role at the time of the event. Suppose, for example, that a cab driver takes a person from point A to point B, and the passenger happens to commit a robbery afterward. Given that the cab driver adequately performed the task that he was expected to perform in light of his social role at the time (taking the passenger to his destination), the harm that ensued (robbery) cannot be objectively attributed to the cab driver, regardless of whether he had knowledge of the passenger's plans. However, if the cab driver engages in conduct that goes beyond what he is supposed to do in light of his occupation (attempting to escape

from a police patrol that is trying to detain the passenger), he becomes complicit in his passenger's conduct.

3. The harmful result will not be attributed to the defendant when it was brought about by the negligent conduct of a third party to whom the defendant had entrusted the performance of a task. Thus, if a surgeon entrusts an anesthesiologist with the task of anesthetizing the patient, any harm brought about by the negligent administration of the anesthetic will not be attributed to the surgeon.

4. The harmful result will not be attributed to the defendant when it was brought about by the victim's voluntary decision to engage in a dangerous joint enterprise. Therefore, if a person decides to have sex with prostitutes and he or she gets infected with a sexually transmitted disease, the harm that ensues will be attributed to the client, not the prostitute.

C. Defenses

1. Types of Defense

Criminal law defenses in Spain can be divided into three main categories: absent-element defenses,[106] justification defenses,[107] and excuse defenses.[108] Absent-element defenses negate the existence of an element of the offense charged. The paradigmatic example of this type of claim is the mistake-of-fact defense, for such mistakes negate the subjective element or *mens rea* of the crime charged. Justification defenses, on the other hand, negate the wrongfulness of the act without negating the elements of the offense. Thus a person who justifiably kills another in self-defense does not act wrongfully (i.e., unlawfully) even though his or her conduct satisfies the elements of the offense of homicide (intentionally killing a human being). In contrast to justifications, excuses do not negate the wrongfulness of the act. They do, however, exclude the actor's culpability for having engaged in the admittedly wrongful act. Take, for example, the case of an insane assailant who kills an innocent person. Although his act is wrongful because it satisfies the elements of the offense of homicide without justification, the insane actor will not be punished because his mental impairment negates his culpability for having engaged in the act.

Article 20 of the Code lists the principal claims of justification and excuse available to the defendant. Article 14 deals with the defenses of mistake of fact and law. Finally, there seems to be agreement regarding the fact that several defenses might relieve the defendant of liability, although they are not expressly included in the Code.

2. Burden of Proof

In light of the *in dubio pro reo* principle,[109] the judge must acquit if he or she has reasonable doubts about the guilt of the defendant. Given that justifications and excuses negate guilt,[110] reasonable doubt about whether the defendant's conduct was justified or excused should lead to an acquittal. It should be noted, however, that the defendant has the initial burden of producing evidence of justification or excuse. Once the defendant produces such evidence, however, the prosecution should attempt to dispel any reasonable doubts about the justifiable or excusable nature of the act.

D. Justifications

1. Necessity

An act that satisfies the elements of an offense is justified by virtue of the necessity defense if the evil inflicted is not greater than the evil averted by the conduct. Take, for example, the case of a person who breaks the window of a stranger's car in order to save the life of a child who is suffocating inside the vehicle. Although the actor's conduct satisfies the elements of the offense of criminal damages (intentionally damaging the property of another), his act will be considered justified because the evil averted (death of the child) is greater than the harm inflicted (damage to property).

Pursuant to article 20.5 of the Code, an actor's use of force can be justified under the necessity defense only if the following requirements are met:

1. A legally protected interest is in imminent danger of harm.
2. The only way to save the legally protected interest from harm is by causing harm to a different legally protected interest.
3. The harm caused must not be greater than the harm averted.
4. The situation of necessity must not have been intentionally provoked by the actor.

Regarding the first requirement, the Spanish Supreme Court has repeatedly held that the necessity defense can be invoked only when it is practically certain that harm will take place if the defendant does not act.[111] Mere probability of harm is not sufficient to trigger the defense.[112] Furthermore, force is not considered justified if it is preemptively employed in order to avoid a future harm. By the same token, conduct will be considered unjustified if it takes place after the harm has occurred.[113] It is also worth mentioning that, in contrast with the approach adopted in most common-law jurisdictions, the necessity defense may be invoked regardless of whether the danger to be averted emanates from a human or a natural threat. Ultimately, the determinative factor is whether the harm inflicted by the actor was not greater than the harm averted rather than the source of the threat.

In light of the second requirement, an actor may plead necessity only if the infliction of harm to a legally protected interest is necessary in order to avoid the causation of harm to a different legally protected interest. Therefore, the defense may not be invoked if there was a less harmful way of averting the threatened harm.

The most problematic aspect of the necessity defense is the requirement that the harm caused not be greater than the harm averted. Although it is generally believed that conduct that causes a lesser harm than the one avoided is justified,[114] there is considerable disagreement regarding whether conduct that causes the same harm as the one averted should also be justified. An oft-cited example is the case of a shipwrecked sailor who drowns a fellow sailor in order to gain control over a plank that would allow him to float safely to shore. Some have argued that justification should not follow in such cases, for such defenses should be reserved for instances in which the actor has chosen the lesser evil. Given that the lives of the sailors are of equal value, it would be inadequate for the criminal law to favor the life of one sailor over the other. Thus the appropriate solution would be to excuse the sailor's conduct, not justify it by way of the lesser-evils principle. Others, however, argue that the state has no reason to disapprove of the sailor's decision to save his life over the life of a fellow sailor. Although such conduct may not be commendable, it is unclear whether it is worthy of condemnation. Consequently, it would be sensible to justify an actor when his or her conduct causes the same harm as the one averted.[115]

The comparison of evils is also made difficult by the heterogeneous nature of the interests that might be in conflict. It is not easy, for example, to compare the value of human dignity with the value of life. This would be crucial in a case in which an actor alleges that he tortured someone in order to save many lives (e.g., the ticking-time-bomb scenario). In order to deal with many of these problems, it has been suggested that the necessity defense may not be invoked when the harm caused is the violation of a person's fundamental human rights, regardless of the benefits that might be reaped by engaging in such conduct.[116] It should be noted, however, that the text of article 20.5 does not impose such a limitation on the scope of the defense.

Finally, an actor forfeits his or her right to plead necessity if he or she intentionally caused the conditions of his or her own defense. Thus a defendant who purposely sets fire to a forest loses his right to invoke the necessity defense as a justification for burning down a row of buildings in order to erect a firewall so that the people living in a nearby town may be spared from the fire.

2. Self-Defense

An actor may justifiably use force against the person or property of another in order to protect his or her interests or the interests of others from a wrongful attack. According to article 20.4 of the Code, the defense can be successfully invoked if the following requirements are met:

1. A wrongful attack threatens to cause imminent harm to the actor's personal or property interests or the personal and property interests of others.
2. The actor's use of force was necessary in order to repel the wrongful aggression.
3. The actor did not provoke the defensive situation.

In light of the first requirement, force in self-defense is justified only when it is used in response to a wrongful attack. An aggression is considered wrongful if it satisfies the elements of an offense without justification.[117] Thus self-defense may not be invoked against justified aggression. Take, for example, the case of a fleeing felon who uses force against a police officer in order to avoid being arrested. Such force is not lawful pursuant to self-defense, given that the police officer's use of force to arrest the fleeing felon is justified. Furthermore, the right to use force in self-defense can be triggered only by conduct that is reflective of human agency. Consequently, natural threats and aggressions that originate in the acts of nonhuman animals cannot be repelled in self-defense. By the same token, attacks that are the product of involuntary human conduct that does not satisfy the "act requirement" do not generate a right to use force in self-defense to avert the aggression. This does not mean, however, that these kinds of threats cannot be justifiably warded off, for the actor may repel such nonwrongful aggressions pursuant to the defense of justifiable necessity.

In addition to being wrongful, the attack that triggers a justifiable response in self-defense must also place the interests of the actor in imminent danger of harm. As a result, self-defense may not be invoked in order to neutralize a future attack or after the aggression has been consummated.

The means employed by the actor must be necessary in order to ward off the attack. This usually means that the actor should not cause more harm than that which is necessary in order to neutralize the aggressor. Any unnecessary harm caused by the defender is unjustified and thus wrongful. Nevertheless, the actor is under no obligation to retreat when faced with a wrongful attack.[118] In such circumstances the defender is entitled to hold his ground and repel the aggression. One should be careful not to confuse necessity with proportionality. Although the Code requires that the force used to repel the attack be necessary, it contains no proportionality requirement. Consequently, it has generally been held that defensive force will be deemed justified if it was necessary to avert the aggression even if the harm caused by the offender is disproportionate to the one threatened by the wrongful aggressor. In spite of this, an increasing number of commentators have called for conditioning the availability of the justification of self-defense to instances in which the harm caused by the defender was not grossly disproportionate to the harm threatened.[119]

An actor loses his or her right to use force in self-defense if he or she has provoked the aggressor's wrongful attack. Pursuant to the Code, the defender's conduct will bar him or her from justifiably repelling the aggression in self-defense only if it amounts to "sufficient" provocation. It has been suggested that the actor's provocation should be considered sufficient if the aggressor's wrongful attack was a reasonably foreseeable consequence of the defender's conduct.[120] Intentionally provoking the wrongful attack clearly amounts to sufficient provocation.

3. Consent

The Code does not recognize consent as a general justification defense. However, consent functions as an absent-element defense whenever the victim's nonconsent is an essential element of the offense. Thus the victim's consent to engage in sexual intercourse relieves the defendant of responsibility, given that the victim's nonconsent negates one of the offense elements of rape.[121] Similarly, an actor will not be held criminally liable for taking the property of another if the owner acquiesced to the taking, because theft is an offense only if the actor obtains the good "against the will of the owner."[122]

In view of the Code's silence regarding the matter, it is unclear whether consent can justify conduct that satisfies the elements of an offense. A particularly controversial case arises when the victim consents to physical harm. Pursuant to article 155 of the Code, the victim's consent to physical harm warrants a mandatory mitigation of punishment. It does not, however, fully relieve the defendant of responsibility for the harm caused. Nevertheless, article 156 justifies the causation of physical harm when it is inflicted pursuant to "organ transplants, sex change operations and sterilization procedures." This article has been rightly criticized because it does not seem to afford exculpatory force to the patient's consent in the context of aesthetic surgeries, such as breast-augmentation procedures or face-lifts. As a result of the shortcomings of the Code, scholars have suggested that consent to physical harm in such contexts justifies the doctor's conduct in light of article 10 of the Spanish constitution, which recognizes an individual's right to the "free development of personality." This right must surely include a person's right to seek aesthetic surgery. Some scholars have gone as far as suggesting that article 10 also encompasses a person's right to consent to physical harm in the nonmedical context, particularly when the harm caused is not grave.[123]

Finally, it should be noted that consent is not a defense to homicide, because the right to life cannot be waived under Spanish law. As a result, the Code punishes both mercy killings[124] and assisted suicide.[125] Nonetheless, such offenses are punished less severely than homicides in which the victim has not acquiesced to being killed.[126]

4. Superior Orders

According to article 20.7 of the Code, a person may justifiably engage in conduct that satisfies the elements of an offense if he is under a legal duty to do so. As a general rule, a person who receives an order to act from a superior is under a legal duty to do as he or she is told. Take, for example, the case of a police officer who is ordered to detain a suspect pursuant to an arrest warrant secured from a magistrate. Although the detention of the suspect interferes with his freedom, it is justified because the officer was under a legal duty to effectuate the arrest.

Justifying the conduct of someone who is following the orders of a superior is unproblematic when the order is lawful. Problems arise, however, when the superior's orders are unlawful. At first glance, one might be tempted to conclude that following an unlawful order cannot be considered justified. Upon closer inspection, however, one can see why following some orders should be considered justified even if they turn out to be unlawful. The reasons for this are pragmatic in nature. In a complex society we should discourage governmental actors from second-guessing the lawfulness of the orders of their superiors unless, of course, the orders are manifestly unlawful. As a result, conduct carried out in pursuance of the orders of a superior will be considered justified if the following requirements are met:

1. There is a superior-subordinate relationship between the parties.
2. The superior reasonably appears to have the authority to issue the order.
3. The order is specific and express, and it appears that the procedures and legal formalities required for its issuance have been complied with.
4. The order is not manifestly unlawful.[127]

It is sometimes difficult to determine whether the subordinate is not under a legal duty to comply with the order because it is "manifestly unlawful." Whereas orders to engage in certain types of acts are clearly unlawful (e.g., orders to commit homicide or torture), orders to engage in other types of conduct are less obviously illegal (e.g., orders to shred documents or to wiretap phone communications). When faced with orders of the latter type, how are we to determine whether the subordinate is under a duty to comply with his or her superior's demands? As was previously stated, the lawfulness of the order is not determinative, for subordinates have a duty to comply with unlawful orders as long as their illegality is not evident. It seems that the best approach would be to ask whether a reasonable person in the subordinate's position would have believed the order to be lawful.[128] If a reasonable person would have believed the order to be lawful, the subordinate's compliance with the order will be deemed justified, even if it is later proved that the order was unlawful.[129]

E. Excuses

1. Mistake/Ignorance of Law or Fact

i. Mistakes of Fact and Law in General

Mistake of fact is not truly an excuse but rather an absent-element defense that negates the subjective element or *mens rea* of the offense. Thus mistakes of fact are dealt with in the section of the Code dedicated to defining the elements of punishable offenses rather than in the section dealing with general defenses to criminal liability. Mistakes of law, on the other hand, are true excuses that negate the actor's culpability without negating the elements of the offense or the wrongfulness of the conduct.

It is sometimes difficult to distinguish between mistakes of fact and mistakes of law. A mistake of fact arises when the actor is aware that conduct X is prohibited but is unaware that his or her conduct amounts to X. Thus an actor who shoots at a person mistakenly believing that he is shooting at a quail acts under a mistake of fact because he is aware that "shooting at a human being" is prohibited, but he is not aware that his conduct amounts to "shooting at a human being" (because he believes that he is shooting at a quail). On the other hand, a mistake of law arises when the actor is aware that his or her conduct amounts to X but is unaware that engaging in X is prohibited. Consequently, an actor who shoots at a human being believing that doing so is lawful acts under a mistake of law because he is aware that he is "shooting at a human being," but he is unaware that "shooting at a human being is prohibited."

ii. Mistakes of Fact

Mistakes of fact negate intent regardless of whether the mistake is reasonable or unreasonable. Intent entails not only the purpose of engaging in the conduct constitutive of the *actus reus* of the offense but also the knowledge of the attendant circumstances that make the conduct a crime. Mistakes of fact negate the knowledge of such attendant circumstances. Take, for example, the case of a person who mistakenly takes the coat of another, believing it to be his own. Although the person has purposely taken a coat that does not belong to him, his mistaken belief about the ownership of the coat negates his knowledge of the fact that the coat belongs to another person. This is true even if the belief is unreasonable. As a result, mistakes of fact preclude punishing the actor for intentional crimes, regardless of their reasonableness. Therefore, given that the offense of theft is committed only if the defendant intentionally takes the property of another, an actor's reasonable or unreasonable mistake of fact about the ownership of the property would relieve him or her of liability.

On the other hand, an actor's unreasonable mistake of fact will not relieve him or her of liability for a crime of negligence. This can be illustrated by way of the following example.

Suppose that Harry the hunter shoots and kills Jeff, mistakenly believing him to be a bear. Harry's mistake of fact precludes convicting him of an intentional homicide because it negates his knowledge of an essential element of the offense (i.e., that he was killing a human being). If his mistake is reasonable, it also precludes convicting him of negligent homicide because reasonable mistakes are, by definition, not negligent. If, however, his mistake is unreasonable, he may properly be convicted of negligent homicide, given that unreasonableness is the touchstone of negligence.

iii. Mistakes of Law

Unlike mistakes of fact, mistakes of law do not negate the subjective element or *mens rea* of the offense. Thus a person who acts under a mistake of law has intentionally engaged in the conduct that is prohibited by the offense. Take, for example, the case of a parent who savagely beats his son, believing that it is lawful for him to do so in order to discipline his child. It would be wrong to claim that his mistake of law (mistakenly believing that savagely beating his son in order to discipline him is lawful) negates the fact that he "intentionally" beat his son. His mistake would, at the most, reduce or negate his culpability or blameworthiness for having intentionally beaten his son, not negate his intent to engage in the conduct.

According to the Code, mistakes of law relieve the actor of criminal liability only if they are reasonable. Unreasonable mistakes of law, on the other hand, do not preclude convicting the offender. Furthermore, because such mistakes do not negate intent, the unreasonably mistaken actor will be convicted of a full-fledged intentional offense, not of a less severe crime of negligence. Although unreasonable mistakes of law do not lead to an acquittal, they do warrant a mandatory mitigation of punishment.

2. Insanity/Diminished Capacity

According to article 20.1 of the Code, an actor will be excused from criminal responsibility if because of mental disease or defect he or she was not able to comprehend the illegality of his or her act or to conform his or her conduct to the mandates of the law. As a result, insanity leads to an acquittal of the defendant only if his or her mental disease impaired his or her capacity for cognition (awareness of the nature of his or her act) or volition (ability to control his or her acts). The excuse applies regardless of whether the volitional or cognitive impairment is the product of a permanent or a transitory illness.[130] Actors who are acquitted because of their insanity may be subjected to treatment in a mental institution if the court believes this to be in the interests of the individual and society.[131]

Because insanity exculpates the defendant even in cases in which it is the product of a mental "defect," proof of psychological disease need not be offered in order to relieve the actor of responsibility. Thus mental handicaps such as oligophrenia may trigger the application of the insanity defense even if, strictly speaking, they fail to qualify as "diseases" of the mind from a psychological perspective. The Spanish Supreme Court has held that only profound oligophrenia may lead to the defendant's acquittal.[132]

Insanity is a defense only if it completely hindered the defendant's ability to appreciate the unlawfulness of his or her conduct or to control his or her acts. If the disease or defect does not produce such effects, it may still be considered a mitigating factor in the sentencing stage. Thus the Supreme Court has asserted that the punishment imposed on a mentally handicapped individual who suffers from nonprofound oligophrenia should be mitigated in light of Art. 21.1 of the Code.[133]

According to the Supreme Court, the insanity defense is not available to psychopathic offenders.[134] This conclusion is grounded on the fact that psychopathies seldom, if ever, affect the defendant's capacity to comprehend the criminality of his or her acts or to control his or her conduct.[135]

3. Intoxication

Unlike in common-law jurisdictions, in Spain intoxication may generate an excuse for the commission of an offense. There is no defense, however, if the actor intentionally provoked his or her intoxication in order to commit the offense (to build up his or her courage, for example). Similarly, intoxication does not relieve the actor of responsibility if it was foreseeable that his or her inebriation was going to lead to the perpetration of a crime. In such cases the actor may be punished for the commission of a negligent offense.

The Code affords exculpatory effect to the actor's intoxication if it hindered his or her ability to comprehend the unlawfulness of his or her conduct or to conform his or her acts to the mandates of the law. Furthermore, it provides that drug or alcohol addicts who have developed "abstinence syndrome" may be excused provided that they demonstrate that they lacked control over their conduct or awareness of the illegality of their actions as a result of their intoxication.[136] As in the case of insanity, intoxication that does not produce such effects may nonetheless generate a partial mitigation of punishment. If the effects of the intoxication are light or moderate, unmitigated punishment may be imposed on the actor.

Intoxication may excuse wrongdoing regardless of its voluntary or involuntary nature. Thus an actor who voluntarily ingests alcohol will be excused if at the time of the commission of the offense he or she lacked the capacity to understand the unlawfulness of his or her act or to control his or her conduct because of intoxication. There is no defense, however, if the actor voluntarily became intoxicated with the intent to commit an offense while under the effects of the intoxicant.

4. Duress

Strictly speaking, duress is not a freestanding defense under the Code because it is considered to be a species of either the necessity defense or the insurmountable-fear defense. An actor's decision to cause harm to the interests of an innocent party in order to avoid suffering harm to his or her own interests is justified pursuant to the necessity defense if the evil averted is greater than the one inflicted. Suppose, for example, that Harry threatens to kill Charlie if he does not steal Jerry's car. Charlie's decision to steal Jerry's car in order to avoid being killed by Harry is justified by virtue of the necessity defense because the harm averted (loss of life) is greater than the one caused (taking of property).

On the other hand, the actor is not justified if he or she decides to avert the threat by causing more harm than the one threatened. Suppose that this time Harry threatens to rape Charlie's daughter if he refuses to kill Jerry. Charlie's decision to kill Jerry in order to avoid the rape of his daughter is not justified pursuant to the necessity defense because the harm averted (rape of his daughter) is not greater than the one inflicted (killing of an innocent person). It may, however, give rise to an excuse pursuant to article 20.6 of the Code. According to this provision, a defendant should be relieved of responsibility if an "insurmountable" fear led him or her to commit the offense. The defense can be successfully invoked if two requirements are met. First, it must be proved that the defendant was moved to action by the fear of suffering harm. Second, it must be demonstrated that the actor's fear was "insurmountable." The insuperability of the fear is to be determined objectively. Therefore, a defendant's fear will be considered insuperable if a reasonable person would not have been able to overcome the fear.[137] As a result, Charlie's killing of Jerry would be excused pursuant to the defense of insurmountable fear if a reasonable person would choose to kill an innocent third party in order to prevent the threatened harm from taking place.

5. *Entrapment*

There is no entrapment defense under the Code. However, courts have crafted a rule that bars the imposition of liability when the commission of the crime has been "provoked" by governmental agents. In order for this judicially crafted defense to apply, it must be shown that the governmental agents induced the defendant to commit a crime that he or she otherwise would not have committed.[138] It must also be demonstrated that the governmental conduct was motivated by a desire to lure the actor into committing the offense so that criminal charges could be filed against him or her.[139]

Courts have taken care to distinguish cases in which the police act with the purpose of obtaining evidence of crimes that have already been perpetrated or are in the process of being consummated from instances where the police actively seek to provoke the commission of an offense that was not contemplated by the actor. Police provocation is a defense to liability in the latter type of cases, but not in the former. This is of particular importance in the context of drug offenses because the government typically makes use of undercover agents to infiltrate drug rings. The Supreme Court has held that such tactics are generally permissible, given that the purpose of the police conduct is not to lure someone into committing an offense that he or she would otherwise not have perpetrated but rather to obtain evidence about what appears to be an ongoing criminal activity.[140] Thus, as a general rule, a defendant will not be held liable if his or her decision to commit the crime was brought about by the police conduct. There is generally no defense, however, when the defendant had freely and voluntarily decided to perpetrate the offense before he or she was contacted by the police.[141]

6. *Superior Orders*

As noted in section II.D.4 in this chapter, a person who engages in conduct that satisfies the elements of an offense is justified if he or she acts pursuant to the orders of his or her superior as long as the order is not manifestly unlawful. Therefore, superior orders provide a justification for conduct, not an excuse. A subordinate who follows a manifestly unlawful order may be excused, however, if it can be proved that he or she committed the offense under duress. A subordinate may also have a valid mistake-of-law claim if it can be demonstrated that he or she believed that the order was lawful and it is deemed that the belief is objectively reasonable.

F. Sanctions

1. Punishment

The Code contemplates three different types of punishment: deprivation of liberty, deprivation of other rights, and fines.[142] Although the paradigmatic example of punishment that deprives the actor of his or her liberty is imprisonment, the judge may choose to impose home detention as punishment for the commission of petty crimes. Punishment may also consist of the deprivation of other rights, such as the right to hold public office or the right to have custody of one's children (this is generally imposed as punishment for crimes involving abuses of minors).[143] The actor's punishment may also consist in working for the benefit of the community without being remunerated.[144] Such punishment may not be imposed without the consent of the actor because the Spanish constitution prohibits the use of "forced labor" as punishment.[145] Finally, punishment may consist in the payment of a monetary fine.

2. Quantity/Quality of Punishment

The legislature adopted a determinate sentencing framework in the Code. Thus the sentence imposed by the judge must fall within the range of punishment prescribed statutorily for the crime committed. The judge may, however, make downward or upward adjustments in punishment as long as the sentence imposed remains within the statutory range. Such adjustments are made by taking into account the aggravating and mitigating factors spelled out in articles 65–68 of the Code. On some occasions the judge is required by law to make certain adjustments in punishment. Thus, for example, mandatory mitigation of punishment is warranted if the defendant demonstrates that his or her conduct should be partially excused pursuant to article 21.1 of the Code. Sometimes, however, the judge has discretion to make adjustments in punishment as long as he or she selects a sentence that is within the statutorily prescribed range.[146]

A set of special rules for the determination of punishment applies when the defendant's conduct gives rise to the commission of two or more offenses. In general terms, the rules are as follows:

1. Lesser included offenses merge into the greater offense (e.g., "theft" merges into "robbery").[147]

2. Crimes other than lesser included offenses merge into a greater offense when the commission of the greater offense usually, though not necessarily, entails the commission of the other crimes (e.g., the offense of "criminal damages" merges with "burglary," although a burglary may be perpetrated without damaging the burglarized property).[148]

3. When the defendant engages in a single act that gives rise to the commission of multiple crimes that do not merge into a greater offense, he or she should be punished only for the gravest of the perpetrated offenses. For example, D attempts to impede the lawful arrest of his daughter by punching the arresting officer in the face. Since his conduct satisfies the elements of the offenses of "assault" and "resisting arrest," he should be punished only for the graver of the two crimes.[149]

4. When the defendant commits a crime as a means to commit another crime, he or she should be punished only for the gravest of the perpetrated offenses (e.g., a defendant who forges a document in order to commit the offense of theft by false pretenses should be punished for the graver of the two crimes).[150]

With regard to the quantity of punishment, prison sentences range from days to years depending on the gravity of the offense. However, punishment may never exceed forty years of imprisonment. The Code also requires that accomplices be punished less severely than perpetrators[151] and that consummated crimes be punished more severely than attempted offenses.[152]

3. Death Penalty

The Spanish constitution forbids the imposition of the death penalty unless otherwise provided by military law for times of war.[153] Public outcry over the constitutional proviso led to the enactment of a law in 1995 forbidding the practice even in times of military conflict.[154]

4. Suspension and Substitution of Imprisonment Sanctions

The law provides that imprisonment sanctions of two years or less may be suspended. However, if the convict commits a crime while his or her imprisonment sanction is suspended, he or she will have to serve out the full term of both sentences. Only first-time offenders who have satisfied the civil obligations generated by the crime are eligible to receive a suspended sentence. Instead of suspending the sentence to be imposed on such offenders, courts may decide to substitute fines or community service for the imprisonment sanctions. A previously determined monetary amount or a day of community service may be substituted for each day of imprisonment. In order to determine whether a sentence should be suspended or substituted with fines or community service, courts take into account both the dangerousness of the convict and the existence of other criminal proceedings pending against him or her. It is also worth mentioning that a foreigner who is not a legal resident of the EU who commits an offense punishable by up to six years of imprisonment may be punished by being expelled from Spain.

III. SPECIAL PART

A. Structure

The Special Part of the Code is divided into twenty-four sections. The first five sections list crimes against born and unborn life. Section 6 contains various offenses against freedom, whereas section 7 lists several crimes against human dignity, including torture. Crimes against sexual autonomy and other sex-related offenses are included in section 8 of the Code. The next four sections punish certain types of omissions and crimes against privacy and the family.

Section 13 includes a wide array of crimes against property. Most commentators agree that the Code places too much emphasis on the protection of property.[155] Given that the Code criminalizes conduct against property that may arguably be adequately dealt with by the imposition of noncriminal sanctions, some scholars have argued that certain property offenses should be decriminalized.

The remaining sections of the Code protect so-called collective interests,[156] such as the environment, the rights of workers, national security, and the administration of justice. These offenses criminalize conduct that interferes with collective interests (e.g., the environment) in order to prevent future harm to individual interests (e.g., death from drinking polluted water).

B. Homicide

1. Murder

Section 1 of the Special Part criminalizes negligent and intentional homicide (arts. 138 and 142), murder (art. 139), and inducing, facilitating, or assisting suicide (art. 143).[157] Pursuant to article 138, a person who kills another human being should be punished by imprisonment ranging from ten to fifteen years in the absence of aggravating or mitigating factors. Spanish courts have held that this provision criminalizes only the killing of born human beings.[158] Therefore, the killing of a fetus satisfies the elements of the offense of abortion rather than homicide.

The offense of attempted homicide is sometimes difficult to distinguish from the crime of aggravated assault. Ultimately, a defendant will be held liable for attempted homicide if he or she grievously injured the victim with the intent to kill him or her. On the other hand, if the actor inflicted the injuries with the intent to harm but not to kill the victim, he or she will be found guilty of aggravated assault rather than homicide. Spanish courts have stated that judges should consider how the defendant behaved before,[159] during,[160] and after[161] he or she assaulted the victim in order to determine whether he or she intended to kill the victim or not.

An actor will be convicted of the felony of negligent homicide only if he or she acted with gross negligence. If his or her conduct amounted to ordinary but not gross negligence, he or she will be convicted of a misdemeanor. The defendant's driver's license or professional license may be revoked if he or she negligently killed the victim while driving or practicing his or her profession.

Murder is a form of aggravated homicide that is punishable by a term of imprisonment of fifteen to twenty years. A homicide is punished as murder if any of the following conditions applies:

1. The defendant was compensated to kill the victim.
2. The victim was tortured.
3. The defendant employed means or took advantage of circumstances that substantially increased the chances that the victim would die. Examples include shooting at the victim at point-blank range, attacking the victim from behind, killing a helpless person such as a child or an elderly person, premeditating the commission of the offense, and attacking at night.

Double-jeopardy problems arise in assessing the criminal responsibility of a person who offered compensation to the person who actually committed the murder. Given that the compensation is the means to induce the actual perpetrator to kill the victim, the payment of such compensation should not aggravate the accomplice's liability.

2. Abortion

The traditional justification for the criminalization of abortion stems from the general right to life afforded by article 15 of the Spanish constitution. As a result of changing societal attitudes, the Code has been amended to decriminalize certain types of abortions. The Spanish Constitutional Court has ruled that these amendments are compatible with the constitutional right to life. Pursuant to these amendments, an abortion may lawfully be performed if the pregnancy was the result of a rape, if the fetus suffers from severe physical or mental defects, or to save the life of the mother. An abortion will be considered lawful only if it is performed by a doctor in a certified abortion clinic and with the mother's previous and informed consent. The concurrence of one of these special circumstances must be confirmed by an independent doctor. In 2004, according to the Institute of Family Policy, 84,985 legal abortions were performed in Spain. Close to 88 percent of them took place during the first twelve weeks of pregnancy. Almost all of them were conducted in private clinics.

C. Sex Offenses

The Code lists various crimes against sexual autonomy. At their core, these offenses prohibit engaging in nonconsensual sexual intercourse.[162] Therefore, the victim's consent negates an element of the offense and typically bars the imposition of liability. However, under Spanish law, minors and the mentally disabled are deemed incapable of consent. Consequently, their acquiescence does not provide a defense to a charge of sexual assault.

The basic offense of sexual assault consists of interfering with the victim's sexual freedom by way of violence or intimidation. Violence is defined as a "force that is capable of overbearing the victim's will."[163] Intimidation is defined as instilling fear in the victim by way of threats.[164] This offense is punishable by imprisonment of one to four years. If, however, the defendant engages in nonconsensual vaginal, anal, or oral intercourse with the victim or forcibly penetrates the vagina or anus of the victim with his/her fingers or foreign objects, he is guilty of rape. Rape is punishable by six to twelve years of imprisonment.

According to the Spanish Supreme Court,[165] a person may engage in nonconsensual sexual intercourse either by forcibly penetrating the victim or by forcing the victim to penetrate him or her. Pursuant to recent amendments to the Code, it is now clear that prostitutes, spouses, and men can be victims of rape. It should also be noted that the victim does not need to actively resist the offender's assault. Although the victim's resistance usually reveals his or her lack of consent, the nonconsensual nature of the sexual act can be established in other ways. The following aggravating factors increase the punishment for rape to twelve to fifteen years of imprisonment:

1. The rape was perpetrated in an especially degrading or humiliating manner.
2. The victim was raped by two or more perpetrators.
3. The victim was especially vulnerable because of his or her age, physical or mental conditions, or other circumstances.
4. The perpetrator was a close relative of the victim.
5. A deadly weapon was used to perpetrate the rape.

D. Larceny and Robbery

Pursuant to article 234 of the Code, larceny is defined as the nonconsensual taking of the property of another with intent to profit from the taking.[166] Larceny is punishable by six to eighteen months of imprisonment. Scholars have vigorously debated whether theft offenses protect property or possessory interests. This is of particular relevance when a person takes property from a thief, because the thief possesses the property but does not rightfully own it. The *actus reus* of the offense consists in obtaining control over the victim's property. Therefore, the crime is not consummated until the perpetrator has enough control over the property to be able to dispose of it if he or she is so inclined. The *mens rea* of the crime requires that the actor be aware that the property belongs to another and that the owner has not consented to the taking. The taking of property worth less than 400 euros is a misdemeanor that is punishable only by the imposition of a fine.

Robbery is the taking of property by using force against the victim's property or person. Article 238 of the Code lists several uses of force against the victim's property that amount to robbery: trespassing into the victim's property; breaking walls, windows, floors, or containers in order to obtain the property; picking locks or using duplicate keys to open doors or containers; and tampering with alarm systems to disable them.

E. False Pretenses and Embezzlement

The crime of false pretenses is defined in article 248 of the Code as obtaining property from another by way of fraud with the intent to profit from the conduct.[167] The crime of false pretenses is punishable by a term of imprisonment ranging between six months and three years and/or the imposition of a fine.

Only fraudulent misrepresentations that would be believed by a reasonable person give rise to liability for false pretenses. Thus falsely claiming the authority to sell the Eiffel Tower for 1,000 euros is not a criminally relevant instance of fraud, given that a reasonable person should know that it is impossible to buy the Eiffel Tower for this amount. According to Spanish courts, the reasonable-person standard should take into account the victim's specialized knowledge. It would be unreasonable, for example, for a financial institution to grant a loan without verifying whether the information provided by the loan applicant is accurate. Therefore, the applicant's fraudulent misrepresentation of his or her income or his assets will not give rise to liability for theft by false pretenses if the bank could have easily corroborated the information and failed to do so. The actor's fraud must be the actual and proximate cause of the transfer of property from the victim to the perpetrator.

There are two distinct types of embezzlement offenses.[168] One type criminalizes the embezzlement of movable goods, while the other criminalizes the embezzlement of money. The embezzlement of movable goods takes place when the perpetrator is in lawful possession of the movable property and later wrongfully converts it. The embezzlement of money, on the other hand, takes place when the perpetrator has legal access to the victim's money and wrongfully diverts it for unauthorized use. Some have suggested that the scope of this type of embezzlement offense is too broad. It has also been pointed out that actors who commit this offense are often guilty of committing the crime of "corporate mismanagement" as well. Given that embezzlement is punished more severely than corporate mismanagement, the punishment imposed on a perpetrator who commits both offenses should not exceed the maximum punishment for the crime of embezzlement.

F. Business Crimes

The Code lists several business crimes whose criminalization seeks to protect diverse interests of economic importance.[169] Criminalization of some of these offenses seeks to preserve the integrity of bankruptcy proceedings (e.g., making false accounts in a bankruptcy proceeding, filing a false bankruptcy procedure to defraud others, or concealing assets). Other provisions aim to protect intellectual and industrial property rights. Provisions on some business crimes seek to protect consumers and investors from unfair practices, such as insider trading and false advertising. Finally, provisions on some offenses, such as those that criminalize the false filing of financial statements or the denial of shareholder voting rights, aim to protect the rights of corporate stakeholders and investors.

G. "Victimless" Crimes

The Code contains provisions on several victimless crimes that prohibit conduct that interferes with collective interests, such as the economy, public safety, public health, and the environment. These offenses are "victimless" because they involve conduct that does not entail the causation of harm to a concrete individual. Spanish scholars have called into question the legitimacy of these types of offenses by pointing out that it is difficult, if not impossible, to determine when a single act has meaningfully interfered with a collective interest, such as the "public health" or the "environment." They also claim that victimless offenses are overbroad because they sometimes criminalize arguably innocuous activity for the sake of protecting abstract collective interests. In spite of these criticisms, it is unlikely that victimless crimes will be abolished in Spain.[170]

The most widely prosecuted victimless crimes in Spain are offenses related to drug possession and trafficking. This should come as no surprise because Spain is one of the main European entry ports of illegal narcotics. As a result, these offenses are prosecuted far more often than other types of crimes.[171] Spanish criminal laws prohibit the cultivation and possession of drugs for nonpersonal consumption. Punishment is aggravated if the possessed drug is especially harmful to human health (e.g., cocaine, heroine, LSD). Other aggravating factors include whether the amount of drugs possessed exceeds a certain threshold, whether the perpetrator was a member of a drug-trafficking organization, and whether the drugs were distributed to minors. Given the broad scope of these statutes, the traditional rules for distinguishing between perpetration and complicity are not applied. Therefore, every single person who contributes to the commission of a drug-related crime is considered a perpetrator.

H. Terrorism Offenses

It is well known that Spain has had to deal with terrorism for several decades.[172] Therefore, it should come as no surprise that terrorism-related offenses figure prominently in the

Spanish Penal Code. Not only is the punishment imposed for these offenses uncommonly high, but the rules governing the manner in which the convict will serve his or her term of imprisonment also differ from rules that apply to other crimes. It is also worth mentioning that it is a crime either to belong to or to aid or abet a terrorist organization. Furthermore, it is an offense to justify or praise the commission of a terrorist offense.

The increasingly repressive nature of provisions on terrorism offenses has generated an impassioned debate in Continental legal circles about the nature and legitimacy of these crimes.[173] One of Germany's leading criminal theorists, Günther Jakobs,[174] has contended that such offenses respond to the logic of "enemy criminal law." Enemy criminal law is characterized by three chief features: (1) the punishment of conduct well before it harms a legally protected interest, (2) the imposition of punishment that is disproportionate to the harm caused, and (3) the reduction of the procedural rights of the defendant. Whereas the purpose of citizen criminal law is to communicate with the perpetrator, the aim of enemy criminal law is to fight against the offender, even if this means that we should simply get rid of him or her. Although many scholars, including the authors, have called into question the legitimacy of making use of enemy criminal law in a democratic and liberal society, they also recognize that the state needs to have the tools to adequately combat internal and external threats. Whether the state can do so without making recourse to enemy criminal law is unclear.

SELECTED BIBLIOGRAPHY

Álvarez Pastor, Daniel, and Eguidazu Palacios. *Manual de prevención del blanqueo de capitales*. Madrid: Marcial Pons, 2007.

Arnull, Anthony. *The European Court of Justice*. 2d ed. London: Oxford University Press, 2006.

Bacigalupo, Enrique. *Principios de derecho penal: Parte general*. 5th ed. Madrid: Akal, 1998.

Cancio Meliá, Manuel. "Delitos contra la Libertad Sexual." In *Comentarios al Código penal*, ed. Gonzalo Rodríguez Mourullo, 514–552. Madrid: Civitas, 1998.

Cancio Meliá, Manuel. "Victim Behavior and Offender Liability: A European Perspective." 7 *Buffalo Criminal Law Review* 541–544 (2004).

Cancio Meliá, Manuel. "The Wrongfulness of Crimes of Unlawful Association." 11 *New Criminal Law Review* 563 (2008).

Cerezo Mir, José. *Curso de derecho penal: Parte general*. Vol. 1. 5th ed. Madrid: Civitas, 1998.

Cerezo Mir, José, *Curso de derecho penal: Parte general*. Vol. 2. 6th ed. Madrid: Tecnos, 2002.

Chiesa, Luis E., and Francisco Muñoz Conde. "The Act Requirement as a Basic Concept of Criminal Law." 28 *Cardozo Law Review* 2461 (2007).

Cobo del Rosal, Manuel, and Tomas S. Vives Antón. *Derecho penal: Parte general*. 5th ed. Valencia: Tirant lo Blanch, 1999.

Corstens, Geert, and Jean Pradel. *European Criminal Law*. New York: Kluwer, 2002.

Dopico Gómez Aller, Jacobo. "Criminal Omissions: A European Perspective." 11 *New Criminal Law Review* 419 (2008).

Dubber, Markus D. "The Promise of German Criminal Law: A Science of Crime and Punishment." 6 *The German Law Journal* 1049 (2005).
Feijoo Sánchez, Bernardo. *Retribución y prevención general: Un estudio sobre las teorías de la pena y las funciones del derecho penal*. Madrid and Buenos Aires: BdF, 2008.
Feijoo Sánchez, Bernardo. *Sanciones para empresas por delitos contra el medio ambiente*. Madrid: Civitas, 2002.
Gómez-Jara Díez, Carlos. "Constitución Europea y Derecho penal: ¿Hacia un Derecho penal federal europeo?" In *Política transnacional y derecho penal*, 153–201. Barcelona: Atelier, 2005.
Gómez-Jara Díez, Carlos. *La culpabilidad penal de la empresa*. Madrid: Marcial Pons, 2005.
Gómez-Jara Díez, Carlos. "Enemy Combatants v. Enemy Criminal Law." 11 *New Criminal Law Review* 529 (2008).
Gómez-Jara Díez, Carlos. "Teoría de sistemas y Derecho penal" In *Teoría de sistemas y derecho penal*, 390–425. Granada: Comares, 2005.
Gracia Martín, Luis. *Prolegómenos para la lucha por la modernización y expansión del derecho penal y para la crítica del discurso de resistencia*. Valencia: Tirant lo Blanch, 2003.
Hörnle, Tatiana. "Offensive Behavior and German Law." 5 *Buffalo Criminal Law Review* 256 (2001).
Instituto de Ciencias Criminales de Franfurt. *La insostenible situación del derecho penal*. Granada: Comares, 1995.
Jakobs, Günther. "Imputation in Criminal Law." 7 *Buffalo Criminal Law Review* 491 (2004).
López Barja de Quiroga, Jacobo. *Tratado de derecho procesal penal*. Navarra: Thomson/Aranzadi, 2007.
Luzón Peña, Diego Manuel. *Curso de derecho penal: Parte general*. Vol. 1. Madrid: Editorial Universitaria SA, 1996.
Márquez de Prado Pérez, Julio. *La responsabilidad civil ex delicto*. Madrid: Consejo General Poder Judicial, 2005.
Martínez-Buján Pérez, Carlos. *Derecho penal económico: Parte especial*. 2d ed. Valencia: Tirant lo Blanch, 2005.
Martínez-Buján Pérez, Carlos. *Derecho penal económico: Parte general*. 2d ed. Valencia: Tirant lo Blanch, 2007.
Mata Barranco, Norberto de la. *Tutela penal de la propiedad y delitos de apropiación*. Barcelona: PPU, 1994.
Mir Puig, Santiago. *Derecho penal: Parte general*. 7th ed. Barcelona: Reppetor, 2004.
Mir Puig, Santiago. *El derecho penal en un estado social y democrático de derecho*. Barcelona: Ariel, 1994.
Muñoz Conde, Francisco. *Derecho penal: Parte especial*. 16th ed. Valencia: Tirant lo Blanch, 2007.
Muñoz Conde, Francisco, and Mercedes García Arán. *Derecho penal: Parte general*. 6th ed. Valencia: Tirant lo Blanch, 2004.
Nieto Martín, Adán. *Fraudes comunitarios: Derecho penal económico europeo*. Barcelona: Praxis, 1996.

Ortells Ramos, Manuel, et al. *El proceso penal en la doctrina del Tribunal Constitucional [1981-2004]*. Navarra: Thomson/Aranzadi, 2005.

Palermo, Omar. *Legítima defensa: Una revisión normativista*. Barcelona: Bosch, 2006.

Pastor Muñoz, Nuria. *Los delitos de posesión y los delitos de estatus: Una aproximación politico-criminal y dogmática*. Barcelona: Atelier, 2005.

Pastor Muñoz, Nuria. *La determinación del engaño típico en la estafa*. Madrid: Marcial Pons, 2004.

Peñaranda Ramos, Enrique. "Asesinato." In *Compendio de derecho penal: Parte especial*, ed. Miguel Bajo Fernández, vol. 1, 175-232. Madrid: CEURA, 1998.

Pérez Tremps, Pablo. *El recurso de amparo*. Valencia: Tirant lo Blanch, 2004.

Quintero Olivares, Gonzalo, Morales Prats Fermín, and José Miguel Prats Canut. *Manual de derecho penal*. Navarra: Thomson/Aranzadi, 1999.

Ragués i Vallés, Ramón. *La prescripción: Fundamento y aplicación*. Barcelona: Bosch, 2005.

Sanz Morán, Ángel. *Las medidas de corrección y de seguridad en el derecho penal*. Madrid: Lex Nova, 2003.

Silva Sánchez, Jesús María. "Criminal Omissions: Some Relevant Distinctions." 11 *New Criminal Law Review* 452 (2008).

Varona Gómez, Daniel. *El miedo insuperable: Una reconstrucción de la eximente desde una teoría de la justicia*. Granada: Comares, 2000.

Vervaele, John E. "Fundamental Rights in the European Space for Freedom, Security and Justice: The Praetorian Ne Bis In Idem Principle of the Court of Justice."*In Criminal Proceedings in the European Union: Essential Safeguards*, ed. Montserrat de Hoyos Sancho, 77-100. Madrid: Lex Nova, 2008.

Vives Antón, Tomás. *Fundamentos del sistema penal*. Valencia: Tirant lo Blanch, 1996.

NOTES

SCCS = Spanish Constitutional Court Sentence; SNCS = Spanish National Court Sentence; SPC = Spanish Penal Code; SSCS = Spanish Supreme Court Sentence.

1. For an excellent historical account of this period, see José Cerezo Mir, *Curso de derecho penal: Parte general*, vol. 1 (Madrid: Civitas, 1998), 112-122.

2. Ibid., 123-143.

3. Ibid., 145-149.

4. For a more detailed analysis of the relationship between the Spanish constitution and the criminal law, see the groundbreaking essays contained in Santiago Mir Puig, *El derecho penal en un estado social y democrático de derecho* (Barcelona: Ariel, 1994).

5. See section II.C.3 in this chapter.

6. Refer to Santiago Mir Puig, *Derecho penal: Parte general*, 7th ed. (Barcelona: Reppetor, 2004), 63-67, for a list of more references.

7. SNCS April 19, 2005, available at www.westlaw.es, Ref: ARP 2005\132318.

8. SNCS January 10, 2006, available at www.westlaw.es, Ref: ARP 2005\771.

9. SSCS February 25, 2003, available at www.westlaw.es, Ref: RJ 2003\2147.

10. SCCS September 26, 2005, available at www.westlaw.es, Ref: RJ 2005\237; SCCS October 22, 2007, available at www.westlaw.es, Ref: RTC 2007\227.

11. SSCS June, 20 2006, available at www.westlaw.es, Ref: RJ 2006\5184.
12. Mir Puig, *supra* note 6 at 114–115; Manuel Cobo del Rosal and Tomas S. Vives Antón, *Derecho penal: Parte general*, 5th ed. (Valencia: Tirant lo Blanch, 1999), 67–80.
13. Francisco Muñoz Conde and Mercedes García Arán, *Derecho penal: Parte general* 6th ed. (Valencia: Tirant lo Blanch, 2004), 136–146; Gonzalo Quintero Olivares, Morales Prats Fermín, and José Miguel Prats Canut, *Manual de derecho penal* (Navarra: Thomson/Aranzadi, 1999), 161–173.
14. Quintero Olivares, Prats Fermín, and Prats Canut, *supra* note 13 at 70–77.
15. Diego Manuel Luzón Peña, *Curso de derecho penal: Parte general*, vol. 1 (Madrid: Editorial Universitaria SA, 1996), 161–176 (presents an interesting take on this discussion).
16. SSCS July 5, 1991, available at www.westlaw.es, Ref: 1991\5634 (stating that respect for the culpability principle requires more than abiding by the slogan that there should be no punishment without culpability).
17. Santiago Mir Puig, *supra* note 6 at 132–136.
18. Carlos Gómez-Jara Díez, *Teoría de sistemas y derecho penal* (Granada: Comares, 2005), 390–425; Günther Jakobs, "Imputation in Criminal Law," 7 *Buffalo Criminal Law Review* 491 (2004).
19. Quintero Olivares, Prats Firmín, and Prats Canut, *supra* note 13 at 103–109.
20. Barcelona Court of Appeals decision, July 6, 2004, available at www.westlaw.es, Ref: AAP 2004\219205.
21. Carlos Martínez-Buján Pérez, *Derecho penal económico: Parte general*, 2d ed. (Valencia: Tirant lo Blanch, 2007), 60–71.
22. For a thorough discussion of these principles, see Instituto de Ciencias Criminales de Frankfurt, *La insostenible situación del derecho penal* (Granada: Comares, 1995).
23. SCCS January 30, 1981, available at www.westlaw.es, Ref: RTC 1981\2; SCCS July 10, 1990, available at www.westlaw.es, Ref: RTC 1990\154.
24. SSCS April 8, 2008, available at www.westlaw.es, Ref: RJ 2008\1852.
25. SCCS January 16, 2003, available at www.westlaw.es, Ref: RTC 2003\2; SSCS April 22, 2003, available at www.westlaw.es, Ref: RJ 2005\1415.
26. Martínez-Buján Pérez, *supra* note 21 at 132–145.
27. ECJ, Case 467/04 (Gasparini), September 2006.
28. ECJ, Case 288/05 (Kretzinger), July 18, 2007; ECJ, Case 367/05 (Kraaijenkrik), July 18, 2007.
29. John E. Vervaele, "Fundamental Rights in the European Space for Freedom, Security and Justice: The Praetorian Ne Bis In Idem Principle of the Court of Justice," in*Criminal Proceedings in the European Union: Essential Safeguards*, ed. Montserratde Hoyos Sancho, 77–100. Madrid: Lex Nova.
30. Luzón Peña, *supra* note 15 at 131–142.
31. The case law and scholarly writings are summarized ibid., 146–180.
32. Geert Corstens and Jean Pradel, *European Criminal Law* (New York: Kluwer, 2002), 469–485.
33. Adán Nieto Martín, *Fraudes comunitarios: Derecho penal económico europeo* (Barcelona: Praxis, 1996), 82–132.
34. Carlos Gómez-Jara Díez, "Constitución Europea y Derecho penal," in *Política transnacional y derecho penal* (Barcelona: Atelier, 2005), 153–201.

35. Pablo Pérez Tremps, *El recurso de amparo* 22-48 (Valencia: Tirant lo Blanch, 2004), 22–48.
36. Jacobo López Barja de Quiroga, *Tratado de derecho procesal penal* (Navarra: Thomson/Aranzadi, 2007), 132–211.
37. Anthony Arnull, *The European Court of Justice*, 2d ed. (London: Oxford University Press, 2006), 35–48.
38. SCCS June 19, 2006, available at www.westlaw.es, Ref: RTC 2006\194.
39. An updated overview in Daniel Álvarez Pastor and Eguidazu Palacios, *Manual de prevención del blanqueo de capitales* (Madrid: Marcial Pons, 2007).
40. Madrid Court of Appeals, February 14, 2006, available at www.westlaw.es, Ref: ARP 2006\211.
41. López Barja de Quiroga, *supra* note 36 at 435–489.
42. Manuel Ortells Ramos et al., *El proceso penal en la doctrina del Tribunal Constitucional [1981–2004]* (Navarra:Thomson/Aranzadi, 2005). The authors include an analysis of the constitutional case law.
43. López Barja de Quiroga, *supra* note 36 at 567–601.
44. SSCS March 22, 2006, available at www.westlaw.es, Ref: RJ 2006\2282.
45. See generally Julio Márquez de Prado Pérez, *La responsabilidad civil ex delicto* (Madrid: Consejo General Poder Judicial, 2005).
46. See generally Ramón Ragués i Vallés, *La prescripción: Fundamento y aplicación* (Barcelona: Bosch, 2005).
47. SCCS March 14, 2005, available at www.westlaw.es, Ref: RTC 2005\63.
48. SSCS May 19, 2005, available at www.westlaw.es, Ref: RJ 2005\4138.
49. SCCS October 19, 1988, available at www.westlaw.es, Ref: RTC 1988\194.
50. Mir Puig, *supra* note 6 at 97–102; Bernardo Feijoo Sánchez, *Retribución y prevención general: Un estudio sobre las teorías de la pena y las funciones del derecho penal* (Madrid and Buenos Aires: BdF, 2008) (includes a comprehensive examination of these issues).
51. SCCS July 4, 1991, available at www.westlaw.es, Ref: RTC1991\150/1991; SCCS December 14, 1991, available at www.westlaw.es, Ref: RJ 1991\9313.
52. Feijoo Sánchez, *supra* note 50 at 334–435.
53. Markus D. Dubber, "The Promise of German Criminal Law: A Science of Crime and Punishment," 6 *German Law Journal* 1049 (2005) (contains an excellent overview of these theories).
54. For further references, see Gómez-Jara Díez, *supra* note 18 at 414–432.
55. Mir Puig, *supra* note 6 at 134.
56. For a list of commentators who defend this position, see ibid. at 183–184.
57. See generally José Cerezo Mir, *Curso de derecho penal: Parte general*, vol. 2, 6th ed. (Madrid: Tecnos, 2002).
58. Mir Puig, *supra* note 6 at 189.
59. Tomás Vives Antón, *Fundamentos del sistema penal* (Valencia: Tirant lo Blanch, 1996), 55–72; Luis E. Chiesa and Francisco Muñoz Conde, "The Act Requirement as a Basic Concept of Criminal Law," 28 *Cardozo Law Review* 2461 (2007) (for a thorough discussion of this theory in English).

60. Muñoz Conde and García Arán, *supra* note 13.

61. SSCS September 23, 1983, available at www.westlaw.es, Ref: RJ 1983\4571.

62. Mir Puig, *supra* note 6 at 218.

63. Zaragoza Court of Appeals, July 7, 1999, available at www.westlaw.es, Ref: RJ 1999\2816.

64. SSCS November 16, 1976; December 14, 1981, available at www.westlaw.es, Ref: RJ 1981\5001; March 31 1982, available at www.westlaw.es, Ref: RJ 1982\2046].

65. Mir Puig, *supra* note 6 at 321.

66. Jesús María Silva Sánchez, "Criminal Omissions: Some Relevant Distinctions," 11 *New Criminal Law Review* 451 (2008).

67. Jacobo Dopico Gómez Aller, "Criminal Omissions: A European Perspective," 11 *New Criminal Law Review* 419 (2008).

68. Mir Puig, *supra* note 6 at 327.

69. SPC Art. 563 (1995 revised).

70. SPC Art. 368 (1995 revised).

71. SPC Art. 189.2 (1995 revised).

72. See authorities cited in Nuria Pastor Muñoz, *Los delitos de posesión y los delitos de estatus: Una aproximación politico-criminal y dogmática* (Barcelona: Atelier, 2005), 49–61

73. Ibid., 39–43.

74. SPC Art. 516.2 (1995 revised).

75. See, for example, Pastor Muñoz, *supra* note 72 at 108–109.

76. See generally Manuel Cancio Meliá, "The Wrongfulness of Crimes of Unlawful Association," 11 *New Criminal Law Review* 563 (2008).

77. Ibid., 568

78. Ibid., 570; Pastor Muñoz, *supra* note 72 at 87.

79. For a psychological interpretation of the *mens rea* element in Spanish criminal law, see Santiago Mir Puig, *supra* note 6 at 258–270.

80. Enrique Bacigalupo, *Principios de derecho penal: Parte general*, 5th ed. (Madrid: Akal, 1998), 223–232.

81. SSCS April 23, 1992, available at www.westlaw.es, Ref: RJ 1992\6783.

82. Ragués i Vallés, *supra* note 46.

83. Mir Puig, *supra* note 6 at 336–339.

84. SSCS February, 7, 2007, available at www.westlaw.es, Ref: RJ 2007\1921.

85. Mir Puig, *supra* note 6 at 351–353.

86. SSCS December 19, 2007, available at www.westlaw.es, Ref: RJ 2008\343.

87. Mir Puig, *supra* note 6 at 353–356.

88. SSCS November 2, 2007, available at: www.westlaw.es, Ref: RJ 2008\543.

89. SSCS February 16, 2007, available at www.westlaw.es, Ref: RJ 2007\2381.

90. Mir Puig, *supra* note 6 at 341.

91. SSCS November 29, 2002, available at www.westlaw.es, Ref: RJ 2002\10874.

92. See generally Cancio Meliá, *supra* note 76.

93. SSCS July 16, 2004, available at www.westlaw.es, Ref: RJ 2004\5127.

94. Mir Puig, *supra* note 6 at 372–373.

95. Muñoz Conde and García Arán, *supra* note 13 at 473–479.

96. Ibid., 451–454.

97. Ibid., 462–464.

98. SSCS September 2, 2003, available at www.westlaw.es, Ref: 2004\459.

99. For additional references, see Carlos Gómez-Jara Díez, *La culpabilidad penal de la empresa* (Madrid: Marcial Pons, 2005), 82–133.

100. Bernardo Feijoo Sánchez, *Sanciones para empresas por delitos contra el medio ambiente* 152-187 (Madrid: Civitas, 2002), 152–187.

101. Ibid., 69 74.

102. Gómez-Jara Díez, *supra* note 99 at 73–74.

103. See Mir Puig, *supra* note 6 242–254.

104. For a brief explanation of this theory in English, see Manuel Cancio Meliá, "Victim Behavior and Offender Liability: A European Perspective," 7 *Buffalo Criminal Law Review* 541–544 (2004).

105. Mir Puig, *supra* note 6 at 254–259.

106. These defenses are generally referred to in Spanish as *causas de atipicidad*.

107. These defenses are generally referred to in Spanish as *causas de justificación*.

108. These defenses are generally referred to in Spanish as *causas de exculpación*. A fourth category, nonexculpatory defenses (*causas de exclusion de la punibilidad* in Spanish), will not be discussed here.

109. Roughly translated, *in dubio pro reo* means "in case of doubt one should rule in favor of the defendant."

110. Although defendants who act justifiably or excusably are not guilty of committing an offense, the reasons underlying their acquittal are different. A defendant who acts justifiably should be acquitted because justified conduct is not wrongful. On the other hand, a defendant who is excused should be acquitted because he or she did not perform the admittedly wrongful conduct in a blameworthy manner.

111. For example, refer to SSCS September 29, 1978, and SSCS February 14, 1978.

112. For example, refer to SSCS December 5, 1994, available at www.westlaw.es, Ref: RJ 1994\9366.

113. Mir Puig, *supra* note 6 at 455.

114. Ibid. (arguing that conduct should be considered justified only if the harm averted is considerably greater than the harm inflicted).

115. For example, Muñoz Conde and García Arán, *supra* note 13 at 393.

116. See, e.g., Mir Puig, *supra* note 6 at 463–464.

117. Omar Palermo, *Legítima defensa: Una revisión normativista* (Barcelona: Bosch, 2006) 233–258 (arguing that the right to use force in self-defense should be triggered by an unjustified and culpable attack).

118. See, e.g., Mir Puig, *supra* note 6 at 437.

119. See, e.g., ibid.

120. Muñoz Conde and García Arán, *supra* note 13 at 327.

121. SPC (1995 revised) Arts. 178–179.

122. SPC (1995 revised) Art. 234.

123. Francisco Muñoz Conde, *Derecho penal: Parte especial*, 16th ed. (Valencia: Tirant lo Blanch, 2007), 125–126.

124. SPC Art. 143.4 (1995 revised).

125. SPC Art. 143.1 (1995 revised).

126. Compare the punishment contemplated for incitement to suicide (4 to 8 years of imprisonment), assisted suicide (2 to 5 years of imprisonment), and mercy killings (2 to 8 years of imprisonment) with the punishment for homicide (10 to 15 years of imprisonment); SPC Arts. 138 and 143 (1995 revised).

127. Muñoz Conde and García Arán, *supra* note 13 at 342–344.

128. Mir Puig, *supra* note 6 at 494.

129. Ibid.

130. Ibid., 560.

131. SPC Art. 101 (1995 revised).

132. SSCS December 6, 1982, available at www.westlaw.es, Ref: RJ 1982\7379; SSCS October 24, 2001, available at www.westlaw.es, Ref: RJ 2001\1977.

133. SSCS June 20, 1990, available at www.westlaw.es, Ref: RJ 1990\5001.

134. SSCS May 12, 1975.

135. SSCS December 6, 1982, available at www.westlaw.es, Ref: RJ 1982\7379.

136. SPC Art. 20.2 (1995 revised).

137. Daniel Varona Gómez, *El miedo insuperable: Una reconstrucción de la eximente desde una teoría de la justicia* (Granada: Comares, 2000).

138. SSCS April 18, 1972.

139. SSCS June 22, 1950.

140. SSCS December 27, 2001, available at www.westlaw.es, Ref: RJ 2001\1561.

141. STS May 20, 1997, available at www.westlaw.es, Ref: RJ 1997\4263.

142. SPC Art. 32 (1995 revised).

143. SPC Art. 39 (1995 revised).

144. SPC Art. 39(i) (1995 revised).

145. Spanish Constitution Art. 25.2.

146. SPC Art. 66.6 (1995 revised).

147. SPC Art. 8.1 (1995 revised).

148. SPC Art. 8.3 (1995 revised).

149. SPC Art. 77.1 (1995 revised). Although the sentence imposed on the defendant will consist only of the punishment for the graver offense, the fact that the defendant committed more than one offense is considered an aggravating factor that requires the judge to make an upward sentence adjustment.

150. SPC Art. 77.1 (1995 revised). Although the sentence imposed on the defendant will consist only of the punishment for the graver offense, the fact that the defendant committed an offense to facilitate the commission of another crime is considered an aggravating factor that requires the judge to make an upward sentence adjustment.

151. SPC Art. 63 (1995 revised).

152. SPC Art. 62 (1995 revised).

153. Spanish Constitution Art. 15.

154. LO 11/1995.

155. Martínez-Buján Pérez, *supra* note 21 at 75–78.

156. Tatjana Hörnle, "Offensive Behavior and German Law," 5 *Buffalo Criminal Law Review* 256–260 (2001).

157. Enrique Peñaranda Ramos, "Asesinato," in *Compendio de derecho penal: Parte especial*, vol. 1, ed. Miguel Bajo Fernández (Madrid: CEURA, 1998), 175–232.

158. SSCS November 29, 2001, available at www.westlaw.es, Ref: 2252\2001.

159. Previous acts that might be relevant to this determination include past interactions between the victim and the offender.

160. The severity, location, and number of injuries inflicted on the victim might be relevant in determining whether there was an intent to kill. The weapon used might also be relevant.

161. The intent to kill may also be established by making reference to the defendant's attitudes and conduct after the injuries were inflicted.

162. Manuel Cancio Meliá, "Delitos contra la libertad sexual," in *Comentarios al Código penal*, ed. Gonzalo Rodríguez Mourullo (Madrid: Civitas, 1998), 514–552.

163. SSCS September 23, 2002, available at www.westlaw.es, Ref: RJ 8167\2002.

164. SSCS May 28, 1998, available at www.westlaw.es, Ref: RJ 1998\5001.

165. SSCS May 25, 2005, available at www.westlaw.es, Ref: RJ 2005\7140.

166. Muñoz Conde, *supra* note 123 at 140–155.

167. See generally Nuria Pastor Muñoz, *La determinación del engaño típico en la estafa* (Madrid: Marcial Pons, 2004).

168. Norberto de la Mata Barranco, *Tutela penal de la propiedad y delitos de apropiación* (Barcelona: PPU, 1994).

169. Carlos Martínez-Buján Pérez, *Derecho penal económico: Parte especial*, 2d ed. (Valencia: Tirant lo Blanch, 2005).

170. Luis Gracia Martín, *Prolegómenos para la lucha por la modernización y expansión del derecho penal y para la crítica del discurso de resistencia* (Valencia: Tirant lo Blanch, 2003).

171. Muñoz Conde, *supra* note 123 at 322–356.

172. Cancio Melia, *supra* note 162 at 1364–1395.

173. Carlos Gómez-Jara Díez, "Enemy Combatants v. Enemy Criminal Law," 11 *New Criminal Law Review* 530 (2008).

174. For a review of Günther Jakobs's works on this subject, see ibid.

UNITED KINGDOM

Andrew J. Ashworth

I. Introduction
   A. Historical Sketch
   B. Legality Principle
   C. Sources of Criminal Law
   D. Process

II. General Part
   A. Theories of Punishment
   B. Liability Requirements
   C. Defences
   D. Justifications
   E. Excuses
   F. Sanctions

III. Special Part
   A. Structure
   B. Homicide
   C. Sex Offences
   D. Theft and Fraud
   E. "Victimless" Crimes
   F. Regulatory Offences

Andrew J. Ashworth is the Vinerian Professor of English Law at the University of Oxford and a Fellow of All Souls College, Oxford. His recent publications include *Principles of Criminal Law*, 6th ed. (Oxford University Press, 2009), and *Sentencing and Criminal Justice*, 5th ed. (Cambridge University Press, 2010).

I. INTRODUCTION

The first important point is that there is very little "criminal law of the United Kingdom" because the United Kingdom is composed of several separate jurisdictions. This chapter describes the criminal law of England and Wales, the most populous jurisdiction. It does not describe the criminal law of Scotland, a vibrant legal system with a separate history and separate principles.[1] Nor does it describe the criminal laws of Northern Ireland, Jersey, Guernsey, or other smaller jurisdictions. All these separate systems have some principles in common with English law, and some that differ.

A. Historical Sketch

English criminal law has a rich history, from which three recent phases may be identified. First, in the seventeenth and eighteenth centuries the criminal law was largely systematized, rationalized, and indeed influenced by the writings of several institutional writers, including Sir Edward Coke and Sir William Blackstone.[2] These writers typically discussed judicial decisions and then elaborated on them. Second, in the nineteenth century there was a move toward consolidation of criminal law legislation that led to major statutes such as the Offences against the Person Act 1861 (most of which is still in force today) and the Malicious Damage Act 1861. Third, in the second half of the twentieth century there were the beginnings of a drive to codify English criminal law. The Law Commission was created in 1965 and had codification of the criminal law as one of its objectives. Progress toward the creation of a single criminal code has been slow, but there has been major legislation to reform the criminal law in the last half century, including the Theft Act 1968, the Criminal Damage Act 1971, the Criminal Attempts Act 1981, the Sexual Offences Act 2003, the Fraud Act 2006, and others mentioned later. However, the vast majority of rules relating to the general part of the criminal law remain governed by the common law and therefore by judicial decisions, as will be evident from sections II.B, II.C, II.D, and II.E in this chapter.

B. Legality Principle

English criminal law had only a shadowy engagement with the principle of legality for many centuries. As recently as 1962 the House of Lords was able to create the offence of conspiracy to corrupt public morals and to convict the defendant of that offence,[3] even though no lawyer would have advised him that the offence existed if he had inquired beforehand. No less controversial was the decision of the House of Lords in 1992 to abolish a husband's immunity from conviction for the rape of his wife;[4] this decision clearly extended the law, and many believed that only the legislature could do this, but the European Court of Human Rights held that this did not violate the principle of legality because it was a foreseeable continuation of a perceptible development in the law.[5] In other respects, however, the enactment of the Human Rights Act 1998 (bringing the European Convention on Human Rights [ECHR] into English law) has served to increase awareness of the principle of legality, which is enshrined in article 7 of the Convention. Thus, for example, when the House of Lords had to determine the ambit of the common-law offence of public nuisance, it proceeded by way of an analysis of the principle of legality and the requirements of certainty of definition that it entails.[6] There is now high authority for the proposition that judges should not extend the criminal law.[7]

C. Sources of Criminal Law

1. Legislature

In the nineteenth century there were major consolidating statutes in criminal law, but numerically the greatest legislative activity was in new regulatory offences. These offences, concerned with such matters as the operation of railways, the purity of foods, and public health, were typically crimes of strict liability, often crimes of omission, and sometimes crimes that could be committed by companies (on the ground that they omitted to provide x). The twentieth century saw increasing legislative activity in the criminal law, and all indications are that this trend will continue in the twenty-first century as governments reach for the criminal law to create new offences in response to all manner of social problems.

In the nineteenth century there were several abortive attempts to codify English criminal law. Some of those codifiers were successful elsewhere—for example, India and some of the Australian states—but not in the United Kingdom. The resurgence of interest in a criminal code for England and Wales led a team of academic lawyers to produce a draft code in 1985,[8] adopted in a revised form by the Law Commission in 1989.[9] More than twenty years later there is still no sign of the criminal code, and the Law Commission has formally abandoned codification as an ongoing project.[10] It has produced reports on several aspects of criminal law, some of which have led to legislation, and its intention is to continue to propose reforms of particular areas of English criminal law. There are difficulties and ambiguities about the process, however. The reform of sexual offences law (see section III.C in this chapter) was given to an ad hoc committee rather than to the Law Commission; and although the reform of the law of homicide was given to the Law Commission (see section III.B in this chapter), it was then taken over by the Ministry of Justice, with further consultations.

2. Judiciary

Judicial decisions have been a major source of development of English criminal law for centuries, and judicial precedents continue to have this central role. Significant parts of the criminal law are still predominantly the creatures of common law rather than legislation—for example, the law of homicide and most of the general part of the criminal law. Moreover, the judiciary takes charge of the interpretation of legislation on criminal law and also of the application of the Human Rights Act to both legislation and common law. As will be evident in the remainder of this chapter, the approach taken by the two appellate courts, the Court of Appeal and ultimately the House of Lords (replaced from 2009 by the Supreme Court), continues to exert considerable influence on the direction taken by English criminal law.

3. Executive

The direct influence of the executive appears not to be great, but it is important to recognize that many new criminal offences are created by government ministers under powers granted to them by statute. For example, it has been estimated that some 3,000 criminal offences were created by legislation during the first ten years of the Labour government (1997–2007), but only 1,300 of these were created by primary legislation, and the majority of new offences were created by the executive acting under powers delegated by Parliament.[11]

4. Scholars

The tremendous influence of institutional writers in the formative years of English criminal law was mentioned in the historical sketch (see section I.A). Scholars continue to exert an influence to this day, but often in a rather more indirect way than in continental European systems, for example. The Law Commission often acknowledges academic contributions in its reports on reform of the criminal law; but although the arguments of scholars are often put to appellate courts, the judgments are not punctilious in referring to those sources. Sometimes a judgment will discuss a relevant academic contribution—a book, an article, or a case note—but on other occasions there will be no specific discussion, even though it is obvious that the argument has been put to the court. The final quarter of the twentieth century was marked by a burgeoning of scholarly writings on the philosophy of criminal law in the United Kingdom, as in many other parts of the common-law world. These significant intellectual developments are filtering into textbooks and occasionally into the work of the Law Commission.

D. Process

1. Adversarial/Inquisitorial

In general terms the system of criminal justice in England and Wales remains an exemplar of the adversarial approach. However, modifications are being introduced all the time, and most of them involve movements, however slight, away from pure adversarialism. For example, prosecutors are being given greater powers (such as the power to issue conditional cautions that include conditions such as the payment of a fine or compensation),[12] legislation and sentencing guidelines provide for significant reductions in sentence for early pleas of guilty,[13] and judges at pretrial reviews have a case-management role that can be regarded as inquisitorial.[14]

2. Jury/Written Opinions

For procedural purposes, English offences are divided into three categories: those triable only on indictment, those triable only summarily, and those triable either way. The final quarter of the twentieth century saw a gradual reduction in the number of offences triable by jury, that is, those in the first or third categories. For example, the Criminal Justice Act 1988 made several common offences triable only summarily, ostensibly for reasons of cost but also, one suspects, to improve the conviction rate by taking certain cases away from juries and placing them in the hands of magistrates. Summary trials are held in magistrates' courts: some of those courts have a district judge presiding, but the majority have three lay magistrates advised by a legally trained clerk. There are some 30,000 lay magistrates in England and Wales, selected from local people and receiving some training, usually sitting in court one day a fortnight. Opinions differ about whether they function genuinely as a form of community justice or whether they are a historical relic, retained only because they cost little.

Offences triable only on indictment go to the Crown Court, as does any offence triable either way that either the magistrates' court or the defendant decides should be tried there. Homicides, robbery, and many serious sexual offences are triable only on indictment; the category of offences triable either way includes many offences of burglary and fraud but also any theft, however small the amount involved, and any assault occasioning bodily harm. Sentences are usually higher in the Crown Court, but around two-thirds of defendants committed for trial to the Crown Court plead guilty. Thus only one-third experience jury trial, and the acquittal rate is around 40 percent. The Criminal Justice Act 2003 provides for trial by judge alone where the length or complexity of the trial would make it unduly burdensome for a jury.[15]

II. GENERAL PART

A. Theories of Punishment

The Criminal Justice Act 1991 gave pride of place to the "desert" or retributive approach to sentencing, with proportionality as the key concept. However, for a variety of reasons this statute fell out of favor, and section 142 of the Criminal Justice Act 2003 now provides that a court should "have regard to" five purposes of sentencing: punishment, crime reduction (including deterrence), rehabilitation, public protection, and reparation. Following this bewildering array of possibilities, the next section of the Act restates the proportionality principle, and this (rather than a free choice among purposes) is the touchstone of English sentencing guidelines. This does not mean that the other purposes are irrelevant, but rather that they are expected to operate within the parameters of the proportionality principle. For example, if a court wishes to pursue rehabilitation, it should not exceed the proportionate sentence. The only exception to this is public protection: the Criminal Justice Act 2003 (as amended) provides for sentences of "imprisonment for public protection" and life imprisonment, with an indefinite duration that may well exceed the proportionate sentence.[16]

B. Liability Requirements

1. Objective/Actus Reus
i. Act

It is often stated that there must be a voluntary act as the foundation of any criminal liability in English law. However, there is no legislation on this matter, and the requirements have developed in the happenstance manner typical of common law. Leaving out of account omissions (discussed in section II.B.1.ii), the principle appears to be that unless the prosecution can prove that the defendant's act was voluntary, no criminal conviction is possible. In practice, of course, the defence has to raise the matter by adducing some evidence of involuntariness. This is typically described as "the defence of automatism," and it includes cases where the accused was totally or partly unconscious and/or was unable to control bodily movements, for example, because of physical compulsion by another person or because of a hypoglycemic episode. The courts have striven to restrict the scope of the doctrine of automatism, largely by two methods. First, they have held that any involuntariness that originates in an "internal factor" (rather than something external, such as concussion or taking medication) is deemed to be a "disease of the mind" and therefore a form of insanity, to be dealt with as such.[17] This has had the effect of designating conditions such as sleepwalking and epilepsy as insanity and means that few defendants persist in their plea of not guilty in those circumstances. The distance of this distinction from medical science is shown by the inclusion of hyperglycemia as an internal condition, while hypoglycemia (resulting from the taking of insulin to correct diabetes) is classified as an external factor and therefore as automatism.[18] Second, the courts have held that if the automatism stemmed from the accused's own fault, it cannot form the basis of an acquittal on ground of involuntariness.[19]

ii. Omission

The common-law position is that a person cannot be convicted on the basis of an omission unless there was a duty to act in the relevant situation. Statute has now created a wide range of duties, some obvious (such as that of a parent to care for a child) and some less so. However, uncertainty remains about the scope of other duties, recognized only at common law. This uncertainty becomes particularly important in areas such as the law of manslaughter, where the key issue is often whether there was a recognized duty of the defendant to take steps to avoid what happened.[20] There is also uncertainty about what amounts to an omission, as distinct from an act. In one case the House of Lords held that the discontinuance of artificial feeding of a patient in a persistent vegetative state would be an omission, and that since there was no duty to continue the feeding when it was no longer in the patient's best interests, no offence would be committed by the discontinuation.[21] Whether this characterization is applicable throughout the criminal law, or only as an expedient in medical cases, remains to be decided.

iii. Status

There is no doctrinal barrier against status crimes in English law, and their numbers are proliferating. The offence of being drunk in charge of a motor vehicle is long standing, and there are some instances of vicarious liability (but no developed doctrine).[22] More prominent in recent times have been offences such as belonging or professing to belong to a proscribed organization, contrary to the Terrorism Act 2000. A particular difficulty is the proliferation of offences of possession, because they are not normally accompanied by any requirement to prove intent, and indeed the concept of possession is broad enough to encompass a person who has a container without knowing what is in it, and a person who has things in a house but has not investigated their contents.[23]

2. *Subjective*/Mens Rea/Mental Element

i. Intent

Many of the most serious offences require proof of intent or knowledge—usually, intent with regard to causing the proscribed consequences and/or knowledge of the proscribed circumstances, insofar as that distinction can be drawn. There is no statutory definition of intention, and so the courts have developed it themselves. Intention clearly includes cases where it is the defendant's purpose to bring about the proscribed result, but beyond that the law is not crystal clear. The authoritative formulation is that a jury is "entitled to find" intention if it is satisfied that the defendant foresaw that the consequence was virtually certain to result;[24] this appears to mean that a jury is not required to regard such foresight as intention, and thus that liability for oblique intent is possible but not inevitable. Juries are left with some discretion, an unsatisfactory position when liability for a serious crime (including murder) can turn on this. In relation to knowledge of circumstances, it may be assumed that parallel definitions apply, but the courts have not explored this in detail.

ii. Recklessness

Recklessness is a sufficient fault element for some serious crimes (such as unlawful wounding) and some less serious crimes (such as common assault). The leading judicial decision on the meaning of recklessness holds that a person is reckless if he or she "has foreseen that the particular kind of harm might be done, and yet has gone on to take the risk of it."[25] Although this notion of the conscious taking of an unjustified risk remains authoritative, during two recent decades the courts broadened the definition of recklessness to include defendants who created an obvious risk without giving thought to it.[26] That broader definition resulted in the conviction of some defendants who, by reason of youth or mental disturbance, were unaware of the risk they had created. The subjective definition has now been restored, and it probably applies also to reckless knowledge where that is an element of the crime.

iii. Negligence

Although negligence is rarely found as a requirement in serious crimes, it does feature in some such offences. The offences of careless driving and causing death by careless driving both turn on whether the defendant drove without due care and attention or inconsiderately. The more serious offences of dangerous driving and causing death by dangerous driving turn on whether the defendant's driving fell "far below what would be expected of a competent and careful driver."[27] The latter requirement is higher than mere negligence and comes close to the standard of gross negligence, which is a requirement for the offence of manslaughter (see section III.B in this chapter). Other negligence requirements are sprinkled throughout the criminal law, particularly in the form "knowing or having reason to suspect," which is a sufficient fault element for the crime of dealing in counterfeit goods (with a maximum sentence of ten years' imprisonment).[28]

iv. Strict Liability

A large number of offences in English criminal law have no fault element at all (strict liability) or provide only a defence such as "without reasonable excuse." Many of these strict liability offences have only low penalties, but elements of strict liability are to be found where substantial penalties are possible. Thus, as will be seen in section III.C.3 in this chapter, the Sexual Offences Act imposes strict liability with regard to age when a child victim is under thirteen[29] for offences for which life imprisonment is the maximum sentence. It is barely a decade since the House of Lords proclaimed "no liability without fault" to be a constitutional principle,[30] but there is a long history of courts finding exceptions to any such principle.[31]

3. Theories of Liability

i. Inchoate Crimes

English law contains two general inchoate offences: attempt and conspiracy. A third inchoate offence at common law, incitement, has recently been abolished.[32] The two remaining inchoate offences have been the subject of modern legislative restatement, resulting from reports by the Law Commission. Thus the Criminal Attempts Act 1981 lays down three broad principles for attempted crimes.

a. Attempt

First, a person commits an attempt only where the act done is "more than merely preparatory" to the commission of the full crime.[33] Several Court of Appeal judgments have tried to draw the line between "merely preparatory" acts and "more than merely preparatory" acts, but it remains hard to identify. In *R v. Campbell*[34] the defendant had in his possession a demanding note, dark glasses, and an imitation firearm, and he had been seen walking up and down past the post office; but he was arrested before he entered the post office, and it was held that he had not yet passed the point of preparation because he had not "gained the place" where the offence was to be perpetrated. He had not yet attempted to rob. The distinction, as put by the Lord Chief Justice, Lord Bingham, in *R v. Geddes*,[35] falls between doing an act "which shows that he has actually tried to commit the offence" and doing something that suggests that "he has only got ready or put himself in a position or equipped himself to do so." Applying this distinction to different sets of facts is problematic. Second, the act must be done with intent to commit the full crime. Third, the impossibility of committing the full crime by the means chosen is not relevant.

b. Conspiracy

The Criminal Law Act 1977 (as amended) lays down three somewhat similar principles for the crime of statutory conspiracy: first, two or more people must agree that a "course of conduct will be pursued which, if the agreement is carried out in accordance with their intentions, will necessarily amount to or involve the commission of an offence." This wording seems very demanding in its requirement that the parties should agree on a course of conduct that will "necessarily" involve the commission of an offence, but the courts have not adopted a strict interpretation. In a case where the defendants agreed to shoot in the leg a man who was on trial for burglary in order to provide him with mitigation if he were convicted, the Court of Appeal upheld the conviction for conspiracy to pervert the course of justice on the basis that the agreement would necessarily have led to the commission of the offence if the contingency (the conviction for burglary) had occurred.[36] Second, the alleged conspirators must intend that the full offence be committed, in full knowledge of the relevant circumstances; and third, the impossibility of committing the full crime by the agreed means is not relevant. The offence of statutory conspiracy has led to difficulties of interpretation, and the Law Commission has recommended changes to the legislation on attempts and on conspiracies.[37] However, there are two particular difficulties with the offence of conspiracy. One is that the offence is often charged where the substantive offence has actually been committed (e.g., conspiracy to rob may be charged when a group of people have robbed a bank), in order to take advantage of evidential rules favorable to the prosecution. The other difficulty is that some forms of common-law conspiracy still exist, including the notorious offence of conspiracy to corrupt public morals;[38] their abolition has been proposed but, for fear of leaving gaps in the law, never implemented. Indeed, the Fraud Act 2006 contains a range of new offences of fraud (see section III.D in this chapter), but the government insisted that the broad common-law offence of conspiracy to defraud should be retained.[39]

The common-law offence of incitement was abolished by part 2 of the Serious Crime Act 2007, which introduced a new offence of intentionally doing an act capable of encouraging or assisting the commission of an offence (section 44). This is supported by two other offences, that of encouraging or assisting an offence in the belief that it will be committed (s. 45) and encouraging or assisting offences believing that one or more of a number of contemplated offences will be committed (s. 46). It is anticipated that these offences will be used not only in incitement cases but also in place of the offences of aiding, abetting, counselling, or procuring an offence (see section II.B.3.ii in this chapter), although those offences remain good law. The new offences are all defined in inchoate terms (e.g., "doing an act with intent"), and the maximum sentence is set by the offence assisted or encouraged.

ii. Complicity

English law on accessorial criminal liability is in a state of flux. Section 8 of the Accessories and Abettors Act 1861 provides that "whosoever shall aid, abet, counsel or procure the commission of any indictable offence . . . shall be liable to be tried, convicted and indicted as a principal offender." The four key words—*aid*, *abet*, *counsel*, and *procure*—have been subjected to considerable judicial interpretation.[40] It appears that one can be convicted of aiding and abetting an offence by applauding or encouraging that offence, or by signifying approval by saying "Oh good."[41] Where a person has the power to control another, for example, as the owner of a company, a house, or a car, that person can be liable for aiding and abetting an offence for omitting to tell the other not to commit the offence.[42] The term *counselling* includes the giving of advice or information to a principal offender. *Procuring* means bringing about an offence, as by deceiving another so that the other commits the offence. Complicity requires proof of intention, not purpose, and it seems possible that advertent recklessness will be sufficient in some cases.[43] However, there has been great debate over one aspect of the common law of complicity—the doctrine of joint enterprise. According to that doctrine, where it is evident that two or more defendants acted with a common purpose, and where one of them went beyond that purpose and committed a more serious offence, the others are liable to conviction for that more serious offence if they realized that this was a possible consequence of their joint enterprise.[44] This test usually turns on whether the others knew that one of the group was carrying a deadly weapon. There is broad judicial support for the doctrine, and the Law Commission has recommended that it be put in statutory form.[45]

iii. Corporate Criminal Liability

Judicial decisions in the nineteenth century imposed criminal liability on companies for failing to meet certain statutory requirements, but these were usually strict liability offences.

It was not until 1944 that the courts held that a company could be convicted of an offence requiring a form of subjective fault.[46] The basis of liability lies in the identification doctrine, under which the intention or knowledge of an officer who can fairly be regarded as the "directing mind and will" of the company is imputed to the company, a doctrine that effectively restricts corporate liability to small companies or to the rare cases where a senior manager of a large corporation can be proved to have the necessary fault.[47] However, a different and broader conception of corporate liability has now been introduced in fatal cases by the Corporate Manslaughter and Corporate Homicide Act 2007. No court has yet interpreted the Act, but essentially there are five elements to liability: (1) an "organization" (including a corporation, hospital trust, charity, or police force, for example) must (2) owe a relevant duty of care, and (3) the way in which the activities of the organization were managed must amount to a gross breach of that duty of care, (4) a substantial element in that gross breach being the way in which the organization's activities were organized by senior management, and (5) death must have been caused as a result of the way the activities were organized or managed.[48]

4. Causation

There is no legislation on causation in English criminal law, and it is therefore a matter of distilling some principles from judicial decisions in a range of particular cases. The general principle is that the defendant will be said to have caused a particular event if his or her voluntary conduct was the last significant contributory act,[49] but for which the event would not have occurred. This has recently been reaffirmed by the House of Lords.[50] On the question of when an intervening human act will not be treated as relieving the defendant of causal responsibility, three major principles have support from case law.

First, if the intervening act cannot be described as "voluntary," it will not be held to have severed the causal connection between the defendant's act and the prohibited consequence. Nonvoluntary conduct would include the acts of persons deceived by the defendant, or the acts of a child or insane person,[51] or acts done in necessary self-defence.[52] On this principle the deliberate act of a trespasser (assuming that person to be of full age and sound mind) should have relieved the owners of an oil tank of liability for causing pollution in *Environment Agency v. Empress Cars Ltd.*,[53] but the House of Lords held otherwise, largely on the ground that the trespasser's act could not be regarded as "abnormal and extraordinary." However, that decision was almost distinguished out of existence in a subsequent House of Lords judgment.[54]

Second, if the intervening act is bona fide and nonculpable medical treatment that occurs before the original wound has ceased to be life threatening, it will not sever the causal chain. The decisions distinguish between cases where the original wound has begun to heal and grossly negligent treatment is then administered that causes death,[55] and others where the original wound was still life threatening when wrong treatment was administered;[56] cases in the second group have been held not to break the causal chain.

Third, if the intervening conduct is that of the victim, this should not relieve the defendant of causal responsibility unless it is wholly abnormal. Thus where a driver begins to make sexual advances to his passenger and she jumps out of the moving car, injuring herself, her conduct may not be considered so abnormal as to remove the driver's responsibility for causing her injury.[57] However, in *R v. Blaue*[58] the victim of a stabbing refused to have a blood transfusion because of her religion, even though she was advised that she would die without one. The Court of Appeal upheld the defendant's conviction for murder, stating the principle that a wrongdoer must "take his victim as he finds her," both physically and spiritually. This brief discussion of the cases shows that the courts are often more concerned with moral judgments and public policy outcomes than with strict causal principles, and it is doubtful whether codification, important as it would be for other reasons, would stifle this tendency.

C. Defences

1. Types of Defence

There is no legal or doctrinal distinction between justifications and excuses in English criminal law. Defences to liability have been developed piecemeal at common law, with little attention to overarching principles of the kind embodied in many continental European codes. Indeed, even the draft criminal code for England and Wales proceeded without a doctrinal distinction between justification and excuse,[59] although it did deal separately with "incapacity and mental disorder," "defences," and "fault" (which includes cases of mistake and of intoxication).

2. Burden of Proof

It was famously declared in 1935 that "throughout the web of English criminal law one golden thread is always to be seen—that it is the duty of the prosecution to prove the prisoner's guilt."[60] Two exceptions were recognized: the defence of insanity and statutory offences where Parliament has placed the burden on the defence. In practice Parliament reversed the burden of proving defences in many statutory offences, but the enactment of the Human Rights Act 1998 has led to judicial reassessment of some of these reverse-onus provisions. The courts have taken article 6(2) of the European Convention on Human Rights to require any reverse onus to be supported as a "proportionate and justifiable response" in view of the maximum penalty for the offence, the danger of convicting the innocent, and ease of proof by either party.[61] Thus some reverse-onus provisions have been allowed to stand, placing on the defendant the burden of proving a defence on a balance of probabilities, while other reverse-onus provisions have been "read down" by the courts and reinterpreted as placing merely an evidential burden on the defendant.

D. Justifications

1. Necessity

There is no legislative recognition of a general defence of necessity, but on a small number of occasions the courts have encountered powerful arguments of this kind. The most famous case is *R v. Dudley and Stephens*,[62] where three people had been drifting in a boat for many days without food and the two defendants killed and ate the cabin boy in order to save their own lives. The courts refused to allow them a defence on these facts, largely because of the difficulty of structuring and confining any such justification. Whether this approach would be taken if the sacrifice of one life would save many remains to be seen. On very different facts in *Re A (Conjoined Twins: Surgical Separation)*,[63] a majority of the Court of Appeal held that it would be justifiable to carry out an operation that separated conjoined twins and caused the death of the weaker twin so as to save the life of the stronger one. It was accepted that both twins would have died soon if the surgeons had not operated, and the Court adopted a "balance-of-evils" justification as supplying a defence to what would otherwise have been murder. Given the circumstances of medical cases,[64] it seems unlikely that this approach would be applied more widely in the criminal law.

2. Self-Defence

Self-defence is a long-standing defence to crime at common law. Section 3 of the Criminal Law Act 1967 provides that "a person may use such force as is reasonable in the prevention of crime," a formulation that is capable of extending to many self-defence cases, but in practice the courts continued to rely on the common-law defence. This has two elements, necessity and reasonableness (or proportionality). Section 76 of the Criminal Justice and Immigration Act 2008 sets out to clarify what amounts to "reasonable force" for the purposes of self-defence at common law or the prevention of crime under section 3 of the Criminal Law Act. The new law says nothing about the requirement that the use of force be necessary because its sole concern is the element of reasonableness. The common law on necessity therefore remains: formerly a person had a duty to retreat before using force, but the possibility of avoiding conflict is now described merely as a factor in deciding whether the force was truly defensive or merely retaliatory.[65] The right to make a preemptive strike is recognized in situations where an attack is imminent.[66] As to reasonableness, section 76(6) of the 2008 Act makes it clear that the use of force will not be reasonable if it is disproportionate. However, the new law reiterates the common law's indulgence toward citizens who react "honestly and instinctively" to a sudden attack.[67] What the new law does not do is reflect the interpretation of article 2 of the ECHR by the Strasbourg Court, which has held that in fatal cases the use of force must be "absolutely necessary" to preserve an individual's safety and "strictly proportionate" to the (threatened) attack.[68] Although there has been some softening of the Strasbourg approach in recent cases,[69] the European decisions clearly require that any mistake be based on reasonable grounds, whereas section 76(3) of the 2008 Act endorses the common law's insistence that a defendant should be judged on the facts as he or she believed them to be.

3. Consent

There is little evidence of a general doctrine of consent in English criminal law, and, where it is relevant, its absence is more usually treated as a core element of the wrong rather than regarding its presence as a defence. Thus section 74 of the Sexual Offences Act 2003 provides that "a person consents if he agrees by choice, and has the freedom and capacity to make that choice" (see section III.C in this chapter). Consent is also relevant to offences against property, but its most extensive discussion has been in relation to nonfatal offences, such as assaults and woundings. There are many relevant judicial decisions, and brief mention may be made of three issues that have troubled the courts. First, what counts as consent? The courts have decided, in the context of consent to sex with someone who is HIV-positive, that only fully informed consent will suffice if the defendant wishes to rely on the complainant's consent.[70] Second, to what offences is consent available as a defence? English law has settled on the rather hazy borderline between common assault (consent can be a defence) and assault occasioning actual bodily harm and more serious crimes of violence (to which consent is irrelevant).[71] Third, are there any circumstances in which consent may be a defence even though the conduct involves actual bodily harm or some more serious consequence? One exception covers properly conducted sport: the legality of boxing remains contested, but in English football (and presumably rugby) it appears that players are taken to consent to a certain amount of bodily harm, leaving it possible that consent may be impliedly withdrawn or legally inoperative where a player uses a degree of force going well beyond what is expected.[72] Attempts to gain recognition for an exception for cases of consensual sadomasochism have been unsuccessful; the courts have held that there is no public interest in such "violence" and "cruelty."[73] However, the English courts have recognized an exception for "rough and undisciplined play" in schools or in the armed forces, where injuries are inflicted recklessly (and not intentionally) in the course of pranks.[74] A review by the Law Commission led to further controversy,[75] and the matter has been left to the drift of the common law.

4. Superior Orders

There is no developed law on a defence of superior orders, and it seems unlikely that any such doctrine will be recognized by the courts.[76]

E. Excuses

1. Mistake/Ignorance of Law or Fact

The leading decision on mistake of fact is *Director of Public Prosecutions v. Morgan*,[77] where the House of Lords held that as a matter of "inexorable logic" mistake of fact is not a defence as such, but is merely a colloquial way of indicating that the defendant is challenging the prosecution to prove the knowledge of facts or circumstances required for conviction of the offence. From this it follows that there is no general requirement that a mistake of fact must be based on reasonable grounds. That remains the general principle, and it has been applied to cases of mistaken belief in circumstances giving rise to a justification.[78] However, a growing number of statutory provisions expressly require a relevant belief to have been based on reasonable grounds. Prominent among these, as will be discussed in section III.C in this chapter, are the provisions in the Sexual Offences Act 2003; for example, the definition of rape includes the requirement that the defendant did not "reasonably believe" that the complainant was consenting.

English law generally subscribes to the principle that ignorance of the criminal law is no excuse, but the facts of cases involving mistakes of law have tested the courts' adherence to this principle. Conflicting decisions have been reached in cases where a citizen has tried to ascertain the lawfulness of a course of conduct, has been informed by an official that it is lawful, and has subsequently been prosecuted.[79] At least one statutory provision creates a defence of reasonable mistake of law where an official's advice has been sought,[80] but in general these issues have not yet been resolved by statute or by case law.

2. Insanity/Diminished Capacity

The defence of insanity at common law applies to all offences but is narrowly circumscribed. If successful, the defence of insanity leads to a special verdict of "not guilty by reason of insanity" and to a medical disposal. In *M'Naghten's Case* in 1843[81] the judges held that the insanity offence is available only where the defendant proves that he was suffering from a such a "defect of reason," arising from "disease of the mind," as not to know the nature and quality of the act or, if he did know, not to know that it was against the law. This definition would appear to capture only gross forms of mental disorder affecting cognition, but in the second half of the twentieth century the courts expanded it to encompass such conditions as epilepsy,[82] sleepwalking,[83] and diabetes leading to hyperglycemia.[84] This expansion was for reasons of social defence, ensuring that such persons did not achieve a complete acquittal but were brought within the special verdict of insanity, which empowers the courts to make certain orders for treatment. The result of this expanded definition is that few defendants raise such arguments. The consequence is that such people, as well as many other mentally disturbed defendants who fall outside the narrow confines of the *M'Naghten* doctrine, plead guilty and then try to ensure that they receive a constructive response from the court at the sentencing stage. Only for murder is there a possibility of pleading a form of diminished capacity. Section 2 of the Homicide Act 1957 introduced a partial defence of diminished responsibility, now revised by section 58 of the Coroners and Justice Act 2009. The offence committed by a person charged with murder may be reduced to manslaughter if that person was suffering from a form of mental disorder that substantially impaired the capacity to understand the nature of his or her conduct, to form a rational judgment, or to exercise self-control.[85]

3. Intoxication

The courts have taken a restrictive view of the potential of intoxication to provide a defence to crime. Even where it is evident that the defendant was so intoxicated as not to realize what he or she was doing, the approach of the leading case *Director of Public Prosecutions v. Majewski*[86] is that such evidence is not admissible unless the offence is one of "specific intent" rather than of "basic intent." This doctrine of specific intent, which has no other application in English criminal law, is designed to ensure that intoxication (however acute) rarely leads to an acquittal. Thus the crimes that have been held to require "specific intent" are mostly crimes such as murder and wounding with intent, which have beneath them other offences (respectively, manslaughter and unlawful wounding) that ensure that the defendant is still convicted of a serious offence.[87] The absence of a rationale became apparent again when the Court of Appeal held that crimes of specific intent require purpose,[88] which is clearly not true of murder. In reality, pragmatism has produced this judicial doctrine of social defence, in response to the fear that simply allowing intoxication to operate in the same way as mistake (i.e., negating the fault required for the offence) might lead to many acquittals of people who are dangerous when drunk or high on drugs. The courts have held that the same approach applies to people who become intoxicated involuntarily (e.g., by the surreptitious act of another), stating that only Parliament can create a wider defence of involuntary intoxication.[89] That is one of many recommendations in a recent Law Commission report.[90]

4. Duress

There is a long-standing defence of duress at common law. Its ambit has varied over the years, but the decision of the House of Lords in *R v. Hasan*[91] aimed to tighten the requirements of the defence. The defence applies only if there is a threat that death or serious bodily harm will follow immediately or almost immediately on the failure to comply, and the threat may be to the defendant or "towards somebody for whom he reasonably regarded himself as responsible."[92] The threat must be such as to affect "a sober person of reasonable firmness sharing the characteristics of the defendant,"[93] implying that unusually timid defendants should receive no concession, but those with physical or psychiatric conditions should. The defence is unavailable if the defendant has voluntarily associated with criminals in circumstances where the risk of threats being made ought to have been anticipated.[94]

In recent years the courts have developed the kindred defence of "duress of circumstances," applicable where the defendant committed the offence because he or she had good cause to believe that there was a danger of death or serious harm to himself or herself or another if he or she did not do so. This has typically been applied in cases of dangerous driving or driving while disqualified, where the defendant has advanced reasons such as a belief that two men approaching his car would harm him, or a belief that his wife would commit suicide.[95] The tighter requirements articulated in *R v. Hasan* also apply to this form of the defence. This new variation on the defence would seem to encompass most cases of excusing necessity; however, if a court were presented with a different form of excusing necessity, the likelihood is that it would adopt the same set of requirements and restrictions.

5. Entrapment

There is no defence of entrapment in English law. However, there is a procedural bar that is even more powerful than a defence. If an official or agent provocateur instigates or incites the commission of an offence—as distinct from merely providing the defendant with an "unexceptional opportunity" to commit the offence—then the court may stay the prosecution for abuse of process.[96] The rationale for invoking this powerful procedural bar is that state-created crime is so objectionable that a person who has been entrapped should not be tried at all.[97]

F. Sanctions

1. Range of Sanctions

Each offence has a statutory maximum sentence, except for a small number of common-law offences for which there is no fixed maximum. The statutory maxima have been created and/or adjusted at different points in history and in consequence do not form a coherent scheme. For serious offences the maximum is invariably expressed as a term of so many years' imprisonment. In the hierarchy of sanctions, suspended sentences of imprisonment come beneath imprisonment; then come community sentences (including such requirements as the performance of unpaid work, drug treatment, or undertaking specified activities); fines are the most frequently used sentence, mostly for lower-level offences; and then courts can also make a range of other orders, for example, compensation orders, reparation orders, or conditional discharges. The principal statutes are the Powers of Criminal Courts (Sentencing) Act 2000 and the Criminal Justice Act 2003, but both statutes have been much amended. The different range of sanctions for young offenders has been restructured by part I of the Criminal Justice and Immigration Act 2008.

2. Sentencing Guidance and Guidelines

There are very few mandatory minimum sentences in English criminal law. The normal approach is for Parliament to set the maximum sentence, and for judges or magistrates to exercise their judgment in deciding on the appropriate sentence within the lawful limits. There has been a system of appeals against sentence since at least 1907, and appellate judgments have given authority to certain principles of sentencing. In the 1980s the Lord Chief Justice began to give occasional "guideline judgments," suggesting starting points for sentencing across various forms of a particular offence.[98] In the same decade the Magistrates' Association, a voluntary association to which most lay magistrates and some district judges belong, prepared a set of sentencing guidelines for magistrates' courts. In 1998 the Sentencing Advisory Panel was created to research, prepare, and consult on draft sentencing guidelines for particular offences;[99] its guidelines were in the form of advice to the Court of Appeal, which the court usually adopted (with occasional modifications) in issuing a guideline judgment. This system was modified in 2003 with the creation of the Sentencing Guidelines Council, a predominantly judicial body to which the Sentencing Advisory Panel reported.[100] The council had an obligation to consult relevant government ministers and a committee of Parliament and then had the power to issue definitive sentencing guidelines, to which the courts must have regard. The Sentencing Guidelines Council issued a substantial set of Magistrates' Court Sentencing Guidelines and guidelines on a broad range of more serious crimes. Provisions in the Coroners and Justice Act 2009 replaced the Panel and the Guidelines Council with a single Sentencing Council,[101] and so sentencing guidelines are firmly entrenched in English criminal law. However, they take a rather different form than that in most U.S. jurisdictions. There are no sentencing grids, the guidelines are narrative, and they are not as strongly presumptive. In terms of punishment levels, England and Wales have one of the highest proportionate imprisonment rates in Europe, substantially higher than France or Germany, but at around 150 per 100,000 the rate remains less than one-quarter of the U.S. imprisonment rate.

3. Death Penalty

Capital punishment was effectively abolished in 1969. Opinion polls suggest that there is still widespread popular support for some use of capital punishment, but there has been no serious political pressure for change, and there is a strong European sentiment against the death penalty.

III. SPECIAL PART

A. Structure

Because there is no criminal code for England and Wales (nor a code of criminal procedure), there is no overarching structure to the offences that form the special part. These offences derive mostly from particular legislation dealing with particular types of offending (homicide, sexual offences, and road traffic offences), together with a few isolated offences created by statutes dealing chiefly with other matters (such as the offence of carrying a bladed instrument in public). The separate origins of the many offences will be mentioned in the brief survey here.

B. Homicide

The Law Commission has recommended significant changes to the structure of the English law of homicide,[102] and the Ministry of Justice has consulted on a revised and pared-down set of proposals for reform.[103] Only the requirements of "voluntary manslaughter" have been reformed by the Coroners and Justice Act 2009, and the law of homicide is otherwise unchanged. The definition of murder remains a matter of common law: in essence, it is the unlawful killing of a living person with "malice aforethought." The latter concept will be discussed later, but the conduct element for murder applies equally to manslaughter and other forms of homicide. A child comes within the protection of the law of homicide only if it is born alive,[104] but if a child who is born alive dies subsequently from injuries inflicted before birth, that can amount to criminal homicide.[105]

English law does not employ degrees of homicide as such, but the common-law structure (with statutory amendments) does yield a threefold gradation. Murder is the most serious form of homicide; then come those homicides known as "voluntary manslaughter" (killings that would have been murder but for the application of a partial defence); and third, there is "involuntary manslaughter," encompassing homicides with a lower level of culpability, such as gross negligence, corporate manslaughter, and causing death by dangerous driving.

1. Murder

The fault element requirement for murder, "malice aforethought," is an intention to kill or to cause really serious bodily harm. The meaning of intention, already discussed in section II.B.2.i in this chapter, extends not only to cases where killing or causing serious injury was the defendant's purpose, but also to cases where the defendant foresaw such a consequence as virtually certain to result. However, English law has an element of constructive liability in its most serious offence, since all that need be proved for a murder conviction is that the defendant intended to cause really serious harm.[106] Since the definition of really serious harm includes breaking another's arm or leg, it is arguable that this head of liability is too wide. That argument may be strengthened by the fact that conviction for murder attracts a mandatory penalty of life imprisonment, with the judge setting a minimum term by applying statutory guidelines,[107] and release is dependent on the Parole Board's judgment of risk to the public. The Law Commission originally proposed that there should be a new offence of first-degree murder that would be confined to an intention to kill, but the Commission subsequently retreated to the broader category of intent to kill or an intent to cause serious injury coupled with awareness of the risk of death,[108] and in any event the government appears to have dropped reform of the law of murder from its legislative agenda.

2. Voluntary Manslaughter and "Loss of Control"

There are three partial defences that may reduce to manslaughter an offence that fulfils the requirements for murder: "loss of control," diminished responsibility, and suicide pacts. The partial defence of "loss of control" was introduced by the Coroners and Justice Act 2009, replacing the common-law doctrine of provocation which had been partly amended by section 3 of the Homicide Act 1957. "Loss of control" has various subjective and objective elements. First, there is the subjective requirement that the acts that caused death must have resulted from the defendant's loss of control; that requirement is not further defined, but actions done with a "considered desire for revenge" are excluded. Second, the loss of control must have had one of two qualifying triggers—either fear of serious violence, or something said or done that was "extremely grave" and which caused the defendant to have a "justifiable sense of being seriously wronged." Third, there is a further objective requirement: that a person of the defendant's sex and age, with a normal degree of tolerance and self-restraint and in the circumstances of the defendant, might have reacted in the same or a similar way. It remains to be seen how this law is interpreted.[109]

There are two further partial defences to murder. Section 4 of the Homicide Act 1957 deals with killing in pursuance of a suicide pact. Mention has already been made, in section II.E.2 in this chapter, of the doctrine of diminished responsibility, introduced by section 2 of the Homicide Act 1957 as a partial defence to murder. The Coroners and Justice Act 2009 has revised the wording of the doctrine of diminished responsibility so as to broaden its ambit, as stated in section II.E.2. The consequence of all three partial defences is to reduce the offence from murder to manslaughter and to avoid the mandatory sentence for murder. The maximum sentence for manslaughter is imprisonment for life, and guidelines have been established for sentencing cases of manslaughter upon provocation.[110]

3. Involuntary Manslaughter

There are two forms of "involuntary manslaughter" at common law. The first is manslaughter by an unlawful and dangerous act, sometimes called constructive manslaughter. Its requirements are that the defendant committed a criminal act against the victim, that this was a dangerous act (i.e., one that would foreseeably cause some harm, not necessarily death), and that this caused death.[111] These requirements are met when the original act was merely a minor assault that was likely to cause some harm, and so this variety of manslaughter is an egregious form of constructive criminal liability. Second, there is manslaughter by gross negligence: this requires that the defendant breached a duty of care, that in doing so the defendant was grossly negligent with regard to the risk of death, and that the death was caused by the breach of duty.[112] It seems that the scope of duties for this purpose is wider than that in the law of negligence; thus in *R v. Wacker*,[113] where fifty-eight would-be immigrants suffocated in a container lorry, their consent to this illegal operation would have removed the duty in tort law but was held irrelevant to the lorry driver's criminal liability.

4. Corporate Manslaughter

At common law there were occasional prosecutions of companies for manslaughter, but the restrictiveness of the identification doctrine (see section II.B.3.iii in this chapter) meant that convictions of larger companies were very rare. As mentioned in that section, a new offence of corporate manslaughter has been introduced by the Corporate Manslaughter and Corporate Homicide Act 2007. The definition, discussed in that section, focuses on senior management failure, and evidence of "corporate culture" in matters of safety is made admissible by the Act. It remains to be seen how this definition will applied in practice.

5. Infanticide

The little-used offence of infanticide is committed where a mother kills a child under twelve months old while her mind is disturbed as a result of giving birth.[114] Conviction is usually followed by a rehabilitative sentence. It is arguable that the offence should be extended to other causes of disturbance or subsumed under a wider concept of diminished responsibility, but provisions in the Coroners and Justice Act 2009 retain infanticide, with only small amendments.

6. Causing Death on the Roads

English law has a considerable number of offences of causing death by driving. In addition to the basic offence of causing death by dangerous driving, there is also an offence of causing death by careless driving while under the influence of alcohol or drugs. Recently Parliament added two further offences: causing death by careless driving and causing death by driving while disqualified, uninsured, or unlicensed.[115] As is evident from the sentencing guidelines,[116] the first two offences are regarded as more serious than many cases of manslaughter. However, the two new offences have much lower maximum penalties (five and two years, respectively), and the basis of liability for causing death by careless driving is an offence (careless driving) that itself is nonimprisonable. This places enormous emphasis on the chance occurrence of resulting harm.

C. Sex Offences

The Sexual Offences Act 2003 is a major reform of the law. It seeks to modernize the law, making it gender neutral in most respects and increasing the number and reach of the offences committed against vulnerable people (notably, children and the mentally disordered).[117] Unfortunately, the Act contains a large number of overlapping criminal offences, and certain key terms are not well defined, giving the law a rather untidy appearance. Three aspects of the legislation are discussed here: the most serious offence, rape; the other three major offences; and offences against children.

1. Rape

Section 1 of the 2003 Act extends the definition of rape beyond vaginal and anal intercourse to include oral penetration with a penis, and the maximum sentence is imprisonment for life. It must be proved that the complainant did not consent to the penetration. Absence of consent can be proved by reliance on two irrebuttable presumptions in section 76, in cases of impersonation or of deception with regard to the purpose of the penetration; alternatively, there can be reliance on one of six rebuttable presumptions set out in section 75, covering such matters as threats of immediate violence, administration of alcohol or drugs, or the complainant being asleep or otherwise unconscious at the time; or the court may have resort to the general statutory definition of consent in section 74, that "a person consents if he agrees by choice, and has the freedom and capacity to make that choice." This definition rests on four contested concepts—agreement, choice, freedom, and capacity—and it remains to be seen how it will be interpreted by the courts. In the case *R v. Bree*[118] the Court of Appeal made the important point that if the victim was so intoxicated that she had lost her capacity to consent, then she was not consenting.

In addition to proving the absence of consent by one of these three routes, the prosecution must also prove that the defendant did not "reasonably believe" that the complainant was consenting. The same presumptions may be invoked here, and it is to be noted that although the requirement of reasonableness introduces an objective standard, the court may have regard to "all the circumstances, including any steps" taken to ascertain whether the complainant was consenting. It remains to be seen how much these "circumstances" are individualized to defendants as the courts interpret the legislation. It is likely that the defendant's drunken beliefs would be left out of account, following the general approach to intoxication.

2. Other Serious Sexual Offences

The Act creates three other general sexual offences, apart from rape. Section 2 creates the offence of "assault by penetration," with a maximum penalty of life imprisonment, which extends to the sexual penetration of another's vagina or anus without consent when the defendant does not reasonably believe that the complainant is consenting. The meanings of consent and reasonable belief are the same as for rape. The same two concepts are also elements of the general offence of sexual assault created by section 3, which consists of an intentional sexual touching of another. In the same vein, section 4 creates an offence of causing another person to engage in a sexual activity without consent. The Court of Appeal has held that sexual assault is an offence of basic intent, thus ruling out any purported defence of intoxication, even though it requires an "intentional touching."[119] For these and all other offences in the Act, there are sentencing guidelines.[120]

3. Protecting Children

Not only does the 2003 Act contain some fourteen offences aimed at protecting mentally disordered persons, but it also contains a scheme of offences aimed at those who have sexual activity with children.[121] In brief, sections 5 to 8 of the Act contain parallel offences to those in sections 1 to 4, except that sections 5 to 8 are offences against children under thirteen and have no requirement of absence of consent; consent is irrelevant. Sections 9 to 16 contain further child sex offences, mostly relating to children aged thirteen to fifteen (the age of consent is sixteen). While the focus is to penalize abuse by adults, the offences are so general as to criminalize children under sixteen who kiss each other or engage in any other sexual activity. Whereas Scots law has now followed the prevailing European approach by creating a defence where two young people are close in age,[122] the English government's intention was that the breadth of the child sex offences would be restricted in practice by the operation of a sensitive prosecution policy. However, the dangers of this approach became apparent in the case *R v. G.*[123] A boy aged fifteen had sex with a girl aged twelve and was charged with rape of a child under thirteen (section 5), the most serious child sex offence. It then emerged that the girl had told him that she was fifteen and had consented to the sex. Under normal circumstances, if those facts had been known at the outset, the boy would not have been charged with an offence, or, if he had been prosecuted, the offence would have been one of sexual activity with a child (maximum penalty five years' imprisonment, compared with life imprisonment for section 5). However, all the elements of the offence under section 5 were present in the case, since consent is irrelevant when the complainant is under thirteen. The House of Lords upheld the boy's conviction of this very serious offence, dismissing the argument that the conviction was a disproportionate interference with his rights under article 8 of the European Convention on Human Rights and upholding the imposition of strict liability with regard to age.

D. Theft and Fraud

Theft and fraud are also areas of English law where statute predominates, and where both the principal statutes derived from work by law-reform bodies. The Theft Act 1968 is probably the closest English approximation to codifying legislation, although it covers only one discrete area. It includes a range of theft-related offences, including blackmail, handling stolen goods, false accounting, and going equipped to steal. But the principal offence is theft, and its elements also form part of the separate offences of robbery and burglary.[124]

1. Theft

The definition of theft has five elements. There must be (1) an appropriation of (2) property that (3) belongs to another, and this must be done (4) with the intention of permanent deprivation and (5) dishonestly. The concept of appropriation extends to any assumption of the rights of an owner (Theft Act 1968, section 3), and the courts have interpreted this to mean that almost any act in relation to another's property satisfies the requirement of appropriation, even a lawful act.[125] The result of this is to throw considerable weight on the concept of dishonesty, discussed in the following paragraph. The circumstances in which property is taken to belong to another are extended by section 5 of the Act to cover the owners of a range of equitable and legal rights in property, including money received on another's account. Section 6 of the Act extends the definition of an intention permanently to deprive another of the property so as to cover cases where a person treats property as his or hers to dispose of, or where it is dealt with in a way that is known to risk its loss.

The definitions of the first four elements of theft are technical and have been the subject of much interpretation by the courts since 1968, but most cases of theft turn on the fifth element, the requirement of dishonesty. This concept is defined partly but not wholly in the Act. Thus section 2 identifies three cases in which conduct is not dishonest: where the defendant believes (a) that he has a legal right to it, or (b) that the owner would have consented if he had known of the circumstances, or (c) that the owner cannot be discovered by taking reasonable steps. Section 2 then specifies that a person may be held to be dishonest even if he is willing to pay for the property. Because these are the only provisions on dishonesty, the Act effectively left the courts to develop the concept of "dishonesty at large." The result of the judicial decisions is that there are now three matters for the court to consider: first, the defendant's motivation for the taking; second, whether a taking in those circumstances with that motivation would be considered dishonest "according to the current standards of ordinary decent people"; and third, whether the defendant believed that the conduct was not dishonest according to those standards.[126] Only if the answer to the second question is yes, and to the third is no, should the court find dishonesty.

2. Fraud

Several offences of deception in the Theft Acts of 1968 and 1978 have now been replaced by offences under the Fraud Act 2006. The principal offence of fraud is created by section 1 of the Fraud Act, and it may be committed in one of three ways specified in sections 2, 3, and 4. The essence of the section 2 offence is dishonestly making a false representation in order to make a gain or cause a loss. The essence of the section 3 offence is the dishonest failure to disclose information to another, when under a legal obligation to do so, in order to make a gain or to cause a loss. The essence of the section 4 offence is the dishonest abuse of a position of trust in relation to property, in order to make a gain or to cause a loss. The concept of dishonesty, common to all three varieties of the offence, bears the same meaning as "dishonesty at large" developed in relation to theft (see section III.D.1). The structure of offences under the Fraud Act is unusual in that the forms of the offence are defined so as to penalize the dishonest conduct irrespective of whether it actually results in a gain or loss. There are sentencing guidelines for offences of fraud, including those under the 2006 Act.[127]

E. "Victimless" Crimes

There is no category of "victimless" crimes in English criminal law, and of course the concept itself is fraught with difficulty. Some would say that drug offences fall into this category, and certainly the Misuse of Drugs Act 1971 contains several offences that make no reference to a victim or a complainant. The Act penalizes the importation,[128] supply, possession with intent to supply, and the mere possession of drugs in classes A, B, or C (class A drugs being considered the most dangerous and class C drugs the least dangerous). There are also offences of producing or cultivating drugs and of permitting premises to be used for taking drugs. Although offences of possession for personal use tend to result in a caution or a low penalty, long sentences of imprisonment are often imposed for importation and for supply, particularly in relation to class A drugs. English law also contains a wide range of other offences of possession that (at least in their definition) may be termed victimless. Under the Firearms Act 1968 there are several offences of possessing firearms, some with ulterior intent. The Prevention of Crime Act 1953 created the crime of possession of an offensive weapon. The Forgery and Counterfeiting Act 1981 criminalizes the possession of implements for forgery. There are many other examples of this form of criminalization.

F. Regulatory Offences

Although the offences discussed in sections III.A to III.E in this chapter are those most discussed by lawyers and include those that attract the greatest censure and longest sentences, the greatest number of offences are to be found elsewhere. Sometimes these are called "regulatory" offences, but the difficulty with that appellation is that some of them are serious offences dealing with matters of great public concern—notably, offences under the Environment Act 1990. However, if the term *regulatory* is confined to a smaller group of offences designed to perform the function of reinforcing regulatory frameworks of different kinds, we find that the offences typically have some of the following four features. First, many of them are offences of omission, along the lines of "failing without reasonable excuse to comply with" a particular notice[129] or "failing with reasonable excuse to notify" the regulator of a relevant conviction.[130] Second, some are offences of giving false information, such as giving a false name or address in response to a lawful requirement.[131] Third, there are also some offences of obstruction, such as obstructing an officer without reasonable cause.[132] Fourth, some of the offences purport to place the burden of proving a defence on the defendant,[133] although the courts must then decide whether such a reverse burden is compatible with the presumption of innocence (see section II.C.2 in this chapter). It is also a feature of many of these regulatory offences that they do not require intention or recklessness but impose strict liability (see section II.B.2.iv in this chapter), although sometimes with a defence such as "without reasonable excuse."

SELECTED BIBLIOGRAPHY

Books

Ashworth, Andrew. *Principles of Criminal Law*. Oxford: Oxford University Press, 2009.
Ashworth, Andrew. *Sentencing and Criminal Justice*. 5th ed. Cambridge: Cambridge University Press, 2010.
Ashworth, Andrew, and Michael Redmayne. *The Criminal Process*. 4th ed. Oxford: Oxford University Press, 2010.
Blackstone, William. *Commentaries on the Laws of England*. Book IV. 1769.
Chalmers, James, and Fiona Leverick. *Criminal Defences and Pleas at Bar of Trial*. Edinburgh: W. Green, 2006.
Coke, Edward. *Institutes of the Lawes of England*. 1618–1624.
East, Edward Hyde. *Pleas of the Crown*. 1803.
Farmer, Lindsay. *Criminal Law, Tradition and Legal Order*. Cambridge: Cambridge University Press, 1997.
Foster, Michael. *Crown Law*. 1762.
Gordon, Gerald, and Michael Christie. *Criminal Law of Scotland*. Edinburgh: Scottish Universities Law Institute; W. Green, 2001.
Hale, Matthew. *Pleas of the Crown*. 1678.
Hart, H. L. A., and Tony Honoré. *Causation in the Law*. Oxford: Clarendon Press, 1985.
Leverick, Fiona. *Killing in Self-Defence*. Oxford: Oxford University Press, 2006.
McSherry, Bernadette, Alan Norrie, and Simon Bronitt, eds. *Regulating Deviance*. Oxford: Hart Publishing, 2008.
Ormerod, David, and David Huw Williams. *Smith's Law of Theft*. Oxford: Oxford University Press, 2007.
Rook, Peter, and Robert Ward. *Sexual Offences: Law and Practice*. Oxford: Hart, 2004.

Simester, Andrew, and G. R. Sullivan. *Criminal Law: Theory and Doctrine*. Oxford: Hart Publishing, 2007.

Sprack, John. *A Practical Approach to Criminal Procedure*. Oxford: Oxford University Press, 2009.

Wells, Celia. *Corporations and Criminal Responsibility*. Oxford: Oxford University Press, 2001.

Articles

Ashworth, Andrew. "Criminal Law, Human Rights and Preventive Justice." In Bernadette McSherry, Alan Norrie, and Simon Bronitt, eds., *Regulating Deviance*. Oxford: Hart Publishing, 2008, 87–108.

Ormerod, David, and Richard Taylor. "The Corporate Manslaughter and Corporate Homicide Act 2007." [2008] *Criminal Law Review* 589–611.

Smith, A. T. H. "Judicial Law-making in the Criminal Law." (1984) 100 *Law Quarterly Review* 46–73.

Spencer, John. "Child and Family Offences." [2004] *Criminal Law Review* 347–360.

Wasik, Martin. "Sentencing Guidelines in England and Wales—State of the Art?" [2008] *Criminal Law Review* 253–263.

Cases

Airedale NHS Trust v. Bland [1993] A.C. 789.
Attorney General for Jersey v. Holley [2005] UKPC 23.
Attorney-General's Reference No. 1 of 1980 [1981] Q.B. 715.
Attorney-General's Reference No. 3 of 1994 [1998] A.C. 245.
Attorney General's Reference No. 3 of 2000 (Looseley) [2001] 1 W.L.R. 2060.
Attorney-General's Reference No. 4 of 2002; Sheldrake v. Director of Public Prosecutions [2004] UKHL 43.
B. v. Director of Public Prosecutions [2000] 2 A.C. 428.
Beckford v. R [1988] 1 A.C. 130.
Blakely and Sutton v. Chief Constable of West Mercia [1991] R.T.R. 405.
Bubbins v. United Kingdom (2005) 41 E.H.R.R. 458.
Cambridgeshire and Isle of Ely C.C. v. Rust [1972] 1 Q.B. 426.
Coppen v. Moore (No. 2) [1898] 2 Q.B. 306.
Director of Public Prosecutions v. Kent and Sussex Contractors Ltd. [1944] K.B. 146.
Director of Public Prosecutions v. Majewski [1977] A.C. 443.
Director of Public Prosecutions v. Morgan [1976] A.C. 182.
Director of Public Prosecutions v. Newbury and Jones [1977] A.C. 500.
Du Cros v. Lambourne [1907] 1 K.B. 40.
Environment Agency v. Empress Cars Ltd [1999] 2 A.C. 22.
Gammon v. Attorney General for Hong Kong [1985] A.C. 1.
Gul v. Turkey (2002) 34 E.H.R.R. 719.
Laskey v. United Kingdom (1997) 24 E.H.R.R. 39.
Maxwell v. Director of Public Prosecutions for Northern Ireland [1978] 3 All E.R. 1140.
McCann v. United Kingdom (1996) 21 E.H.R.R. 97.

M'Naghten's Case (1843) 10 Cl. & Fin. 200.
Nachova v. Bulgaria (2004) 39 E.H.R.R. 37.
Norris v. Government of the United States of America [2008] UKHL 16.
Palmer v. R. [1971] A.C. 814.
Postermobile plc v. Brent L.B.C., The Times, 8 December 1997.
R v. Adomako [1995] 1 A.C. 171.
R v. Aitken (1992) 95 Cr. App. R. 304.
R v. Alford Transport [1997] 2 Cr. App. R. 326.
R v. Aramah (1982) 4 Cr. App. R. (S) 407.
R v. Bailey [1983] 1 W.L.R. 760.
R v. Barnes [2005] 1 W.L.R. 910.
R v. Bingham [1991] Crim. L.R. 433.
R v. Bird [1985] 1 W.L.R. 816.
R v. Blaue [1975] 1 W.L.R. 1411.
R v. Bowen [1997] 1 W.L.R. 372.
R v. Brown [1994] 1 A.C. 212.
R v. Burgess [1991] 2 Q.B. 92.
R v. Byrne [1960] 2 Q.B. 396.
R v. Caldwell [1982] A.C. 341.
R v. Campbell (1991) 93 Cr. App. R. 350.
R v. Cato [1976] 1 W.L.R. 110.
R v. Cheshire [1991] 1 W.L.R. 844.
R v. Clegg [1995] 2 A.C. 355.
R v. Conway (1988) 89 Cr. App. R. 159.
R v. Cunningham [1957] 2 Q.B. 396.
R v. Cunningham [1982] A.C. 566.
R v. Deyemi and Edwards [2008] 1 Cr. App. R. 25.
R v. Dica [2004] Q.B. 1257.
R v. Dudley and Stephens (1884) 14 Q.B.D. 273.
R v. Feely [1973] Q.B. 530.
R v. G. [2003] UKHL 50.
R v. G. [2008] UKHL 37.
R v. Geddes [1996] Crim. L.R. 894.
R v. Ghosh [1982] Q.B. 1053.
R v. Gianetto [1997] 1 Cr. App. R. 1.
R v. Gomez [1993] A.C. 442.
R v. Hasan [2005] UKHL 22.
R v. Heard [2008] Q.B. 43.
R. v. Hennessy [1989] 1 W.L.R. 287.
R v. Hinks [2001] 2 A.C. 241.
R v. Jackson [1985] Crim. L.R. 442.
R v. Jones (1986) 83 Cr. App. R. 375.
R v. Jones [2007] 1 A.C. 136.
R v. Jordan (1956) 40 Cr. App. R. 152.

R v. K. [2002] 1 Cr. App. R. 121.
R v. Kennedy (No. 2) [2008] 1 A.C. 269.
R v. Kingston [1995] 2 A.C. 355.
R v. Konzani [2005] 2 Cr. App. R. 13.
R v. Lewis (1988) 87 Cr. App. R. 270.
R v. Michael (1840) 9 C. & P. 356.
R v. Muhamad [2003] Q.B. 1031.
R v. Pagett (1983) 76 Cr. App. R. 279.
R v. Powell [1999] A.C. 1.
R v. Quick [1973] Q.B. 910.
R v. R. [1992] 1 A.C. 599.
R. v. Rimmington and Goldstein [2006] 1 A.C. 459.
R v. Roberts (1972) 56 Cr. App. R. 95.
R v. Smith [1959] 2 Q.B. 35.
R v. Smith (Morgan) [2001] 1 A.C. 146.
R v. Sullivan [1984] 1 A.C. 156.
R v. Tosti [1997] Crim. L.R. 746.
R v. Van Dongen [2005] Crim. L.R. 971.
R v. Wacker [2003] Q.B. 1203.
R v. Willer (1986) 83 Cr. App. R. 225.
R v. Woollin [1999] 1 A.C. 82.
Re A (Conjoined Twins: Surgical Separation) [2001] Fam. 147.
Scott v. Metropolitan Police Commissioner [1975] A.C. 819.
Shaw v. Director of Public Prosecutions [1962] A.C. 220.
Sheldrake v. Director of Public Prosecutions [2004] UKHL 43.
S.W. and C.R. v. United Kingdom (1995) 21 E.H.R.R. 363.
Teixeira de Castro v. Portugal (1999) 28 E.H.R.R. 101.
Tesco Supermarkets v. Nattrass [1972] A.C. 153.
Warner v. Metropolitan Police Commissioner [1969] 2 A.C. 256.
Wilcox v. Jeffrey [1951] 1 All E.R. 464.
Woolmington v. Director of Public Prosecutions [1935] A.C. 462.

Legislation

Clean Neighbourhoods and Environment Act 2005.
Commissioners for Revenue and Customs Act 2005.
Control of Pollution Act 1974.
Coroners and Justice Act (2009).
Crime and Disorder Act 1998 (U.K.).
Criminal Justice Act 2003.
Criminal Justice and Immigration Act 2008.
Customs and Excise Management Act 1979.
Education Act 2005.
Gambling Act 2005.
Infanticide Act 1938.
Infant Life Preservation Act 1929.

Road Safety Act 2006, amending the Road Traffic Act 1988.
Road Traffic Act 1988 (ss. 1–3), as amended by the Road Safety Act 2006.
Serious Crime Act 2007.
Sexual Offences Act 2003.
Trade Marks Act 1994.

Law Commission

Law Com. No. 143. *Codification of the Criminal Law: A Report to the Law Commission.* London: The Stationery Office, 1985.
Law Com. No. 177. *A Criminal Code for England and Wales.* 2 vols. London: The Stationery Office, 1989.
Law Commission Consultation Paper No. 139. *Consent in the Criminal Law.* London: The Stationery Office, 1995.
Law Commission Consultation Paper No. 177. *A New Homicide Act for England and Wales?* London: The Stationery Office, 2005.
Law Commission Consultation Paper No. 183. *Conspiracy and Attempts: A Consultation Paper.* London: The Stationery Office, 2007.
Law Com. No. 307. *Murder, Manslaughter and Infanticide.* London: The Stationery Office, 2007.
Law Com. No. 311. *Tenth Programme of Law Reform.* London: The Stationery Office, 2008.
Law Com No. 314. *Intoxication and Criminal Liability.* London: The Stationery Office, 2009.
Law Com No. 318. *Conspiracy and Attempts.* London: The Stationery Office, 2009.

Sentencing Guidelines Council

Sentencing Guidelines Council. *Manslaughter by Reason of Provocation: Definitive Guideline.* London: Sentencing Guidelines Council, 2005.
Sentencing Guidelines Council. *Sexual Offences.* London: Sentencing Guidelines Council, 2006.
Sentencing Guidelines Council. *Reduction in Sentence for Guilty Plea: Revised Guideline.* London: Sentencing Guidelines Council, 2007.
Sentencing Commission Working Group. *Sentencing Guidelines in England and Wales: An Evolutionary Approach.* London: Sentencing Guidelines Council, 2008.
Sentencing Guidelines Council. *Causing Death by Driving.* London: Sentencing Guidelines Council, 2008.
Sentencing Guidelines Council. *Sentencing for Fraud: Statutory Offences.* London: Sentencing Guidelines Council, 2009.

SUGGESTED FURTHER READING

Among the many criminal law textbooks, the following three can be recommended:

Ashworth, A. *Principles of Criminal Law.* 6th ed. Oxford: Oxford University Press, 2009.
Ormerod, D. *Smith and Hogan's Criminal Law.* 12th ed. Oxford: Oxford University Press, 2008.

Simester, A. P., and G. R. Sullivan. *Criminal Law: Theory and Doctrine*. 3d ed. Oxford: Hart Publishing, 2007.

There are many monographs on criminal law theory, of which four can be selected:

Duff, R. A. *Answering for Crime*. Oxford: Hart Publishing, 2007.
Gardner, J. *Offences and Defences*. Oxford: Oxford University Press, 2007.
Horder, J. *Excusing Crime*. Oxford: Oxford University Press, 2004.
Norrie, A. *Punishment, Responsibility and Justice*. Oxford: Oxford University Press, 2000.

In addition, the many consultation papers and reports from the Law Commission for England and Wales are a splendid resource for analysis of the current law, as well as proposals for reform. They can be accessed at www.lawcom.gov.uk.

NOTES

1. For a historical appraisal, see Lindsay Farmer, *Criminal Law, Tradition and Legal Order* (Cambridge: Cambridge University Press, 1997); the leading texts are Gerald Gordon and Michael Christie, *Criminal Law of Scotland* (Edinburgh: Scottish Universities Law Institute; W. Green, 2001); and James Chalmers and Fiona Leverick, *Criminal Defences and Pleas at Bar of Trial* (Edinburgh: W. Green, 2006).
2. For example, Sir Edward Coke's *Institutes of the Lawes of England* (1618–1624); Sir Matthew Hale's *Pleas of the Crown* (1678); Sir Michael Foster's *Crown Law* (1762); Sir William Blackstone's *Commentaries on the Laws of England*, Book IV (1769); and Sir Edward Hyde East's *Pleas of the Crown* (1803).
3. *Shaw v. Director of Public Prosecutions* [1962] A.C. 220; for analysis of the retreat from this kind of judicial activism in criminal law, see A. T. H. Smith, "Judicial Lawmaking in the Criminal Law" (1984) 100 *Law Quarterly Review* 46, 69–73.
4. *R v. R* [1992] 1 A.C. 599.
5. *S.W. and C.R. v. United Kingdom* (1995) 21 E.H.R.R. 363.
6. *R v. Rimmington and Goldstein* [2006] 1 A.C. 459.
7. *R v. Jones* [2007] 1 A.C. 136, per Lord Bingham at [29].
8. Law Com. No. 143, *Codification of the Criminal Law: A Report to the Law Commission* (London: The Stationery Office, 1985).
9. Law Com. No. 177, *A Criminal Code for England and Wales*, 2 vols. (London: The Stationery Office, 1989).
10. Law Com. No. 311, *Tenth Programme of Law Reform* (London: The Stationery Office, 2008).
11. See Andrew Ashworth, "Criminal Law, Human Rights and Preventive Justice," in Bernadette McSherry, Alan Norrie, and Simon Bronitt, eds., *Regulating Deviance* (Oxford: Hart Publishing, 2008), 95.
12. Criminal Justice Act 2003, ss. 22–27.
13. Criminal Justice Act 2003, s. 144, and Sentencing Guidelines Council, *Reduction in Sentence for a Guilty Plea: Revised Guideline* (London: Sentencing Guidelines Council, 2007).

14. For further discussion of criminal procedure in general, see John Sprack, *A Practical Approach to Criminal Procedure* (Oxford: Oxford University Press, 2009).

15. For fuller discussion of the matters in this section, see Andrew Ashworth and Michael Redmayne, *The Criminal Process* (Oxford: Oxford University Press, 2005), ch. 11.

16. For fuller discussion of these issues, see Andrew Ashworth, *Sentencing and Criminal Justice*, 5th ed. (Cambridge: Cambridge University Press, 2010).

17. E.g., *R v. Sullivan* [1984] 1 A.C. 156; *R v. Hennessy* [1989] 1 W.L.R. 287. See further section II.E.2 in this chapter.

18. Cf. *R v. Hennessy* (above, n. 17) with *R v. Bingham* [1991] Crim. L.R. 433.

19. E.g., *R v. Quick* [1973] Q.B. 910; *R v. Bailey* [1983] 1 W.L.R. 760.

20. See section III.B in this chapter.

21. *Airedale NHS Trust v. Bland* [1993] A.C. 789; cf. *Re A (Conjoined Twins: Surgical Separation)* [2001] Fam. 147.

22. E.g., *Coppen v. Moore (No. 2)* [1898] 2 Q.B. 306.

23. The leading decision is still *Warner v. Metropolitan Police Commissioner* [1969] 2 A.C. 256; it was applied doubtfully in *R v. Lewis* (1988) 87 Cr. App. R. 270 and was challenged in *R v. Deyemi and Edwards* [2008] 1 Cr. App. R. 25.

24. *R v. Woollin* [1999] 1 A.C. 82.

25. *R v. Cunningham* [1957] 2 Q.B. 396.

26. The broader definition was introduced by the House of Lords in *R v. Caldwell* [1982] A.C. 341 and was overruled by the same court in *R v. G.* [2003] UKHL 50.

27. Road Traffic Act 1988, ss. 1–3, as amended by the Road Safety Act 2006.

28. Trade Marks Act 1994, s. 92.

29. Sexual Offences Act 2003, ss. 5–8, and *R v. G.* [2008] UKHL 37.

30. *B. v. Director of Public Prosecutions* [2000] 2 A.C. 428; *R v. K.* [2002] 1 Cr. App. R. 121.

31. Two examples are *Gammon v. Attorney General for Hong Kong* [1985] A.C. 1 and *R v. Muhamad* [2003] Q.B. 1031.

32. Serious Crime Act 2007, s. 59; see section II.B.3.i.b below.

33. This phrase has been the subject of considerable judicial analysis, without a clear definition resulting: see Andrew Simester and G. R. Sullivan, *Criminal Law: Theory and Doctrine* (Oxford: Hart Publishing, 2007), ch. 9; and Andrew Ashworth, *Principles of Criminal Law* (Oxford: Oxford University Press, 2009), ch. 11.

34. (1991) 93 Cr. App. R. 350.

35. [1996] Crim. L.R. 894.

36. *R v. Jackson* [1985] Crim. L.R. 442.

37. For its initial proposals, see Law Com No. 318, *Conspiracy and Attempts* (London: The Stationery Office, 2009).

38. See n. 3 above.

39. The leading authority is *Scott v. Metropolitan Police Commissioner* [1975] A.C. 819, but the principle of legality (see section I.C in this chapter) was applied in *Norris v. Government of United States of America* [2008] UKHL 16 to restrict the scope of the offence.

40. On which see Simester and Sullivan (above, n. 33), ch. 7, or Ashworth (above, n. 33), ch. 10.

41. *Wilcox v. Jeffrey* [1951] 1 All E.R. 464; *R v. Gianetto* [1997] 1 Cr. App. R. 1.

42. *Du Cros v. Lambourne* [1907] 1 K.B. 40; *R v. J.F. Alford Transport Ltd* [1997] 2 Cr. App. R. 326.

43. E.g., *Blakely and Sutton v. Chief Constable of West Mercia* [1991] R.T.R. 405. See also the controversial decision in *Maxwell v. Director of Public Prosecutions for Northern Ireland* [1978] 3 All E.R. 1140.

44. *R v. Powell* [1999] A.C. 1.

45. Law Com. No. 307, *Murder, Manslaughter and Infanticide* (London: The Stationery Office, 2007), pt. 4.

46. *Director of Public Prosecutions v. Kent and Sussex Contractors Ltd.* [1944] K.B. 146.

47. *Tesco Supermarkets v. Nattrass* [1972] A.C. 153; see generally Celia Wells, *Corporations and Criminal Responsibility* (Oxford: Oxford University Press, 2001).

48. For analysis of the new offence, see David Ormerod and Richard Taylor, "The Corporate Manslaughter and Corporate Homicide Act 2007," [2008] *Criminal Law Review* 589–611.

49. As the Court of Appeal put it in *R v. Cato* [1976] 1 W.L.R. 110, more than a "*de minimis*" contribution.

50. *R v. Kennedy (No. 2)* [2008] 1 A.C. 269.

51. *R v. Michael* (1840) 9 C. & P. 356; see generally H. L. A. Hart and Tony Honoré, *Causation in the Law* (Oxford: Clarendon Press, 1985).

52. *R v. Pagett* (1983) 76 Cr. App. R. 279.

53. [1999] 2 A.C. 22.

54. *R v. Kennedy (No. 2)* [2008] 1 A.C. 269.

55. *R v. Jordan* (1956) 40 Cr. App. R. 152.

56. *R v. Smith* [1959] 2 Q.B. 35.

57. *R v. Roberts* (1972) 56 Cr. App. R. 95.

58. [1975] 1 W.L.R. 1411.

59. Law Com. No. 177, *A Criminal Code for England and Wales*, vol. 1.

60. *Woolmington v. Director of Public Prosecutions* [1935] A.C. 462, per Viscount Sankey L.C.

61. The leading decision is *Attorney-General's Reference No. 4 of 2002; Sheldrake v. Director of Public Prosecutions* [2004] UKHL 43.

62. (1884) 14 Q.B.D. 273.

63. [2001] Fam. 147.

64. Cf. the different approach taken in *Airedale NHS Trust v. Bland* [1993] A.C. 789.

65. *R v. Bird* [1985] 1 W.L.R. 816.

66. *Beckford v. R* [1988] 1 A.C. 130.

67. Section 76(7), reflecting *Palmer v. R.* [1971] A.C. 814.

68. E.g., *McCann v. United Kingdom* (1996) 21 E.H.R.R. 97; *Gul v. Turkey* (2002) 34 E.H.R.R. 719.

69. *Bubbins v. United Kingdom* (2005) 41 E.H.R.R. 458.

70. *R v. Dica* [2004] Q.B. 1257; and *R v. Konzani* [2005] 2 Cr. App. R. 13.

71. *Attorney-General's Reference No. 1 of 1980* [1981] Q.B. 715.

72. *R v. Barnes* [2005] 1 W.L.R. 910.

73. *R v. Brown* [1994] 1 A.C. 212; the Strasbourg Court held that the convictions did not violate the applicants' article 8 rights in *Laskey v. United Kingdom* (1997) 24 E.H.R.R. 39.

74. *R v. Jones* (1986) 83 Cr. App. R. 375; and *R v. Aitken* (1992) 95 Cr. App. R. 304.

75. Law Commission Consultation Paper No. 139, *Consent in the Criminal Law* (London: The Stationery Office, 1995).

76. *R v. Clegg* [1995] 2 A.C. 355.

77. [1976] A.C. 182.

78. Recently reasserted by the Criminal Justice and Immigration Act 2008, s. 76(3).

79. Compare *Cambridgeshire and Isle of Ely C.C. v. Rust* [1972] 1 Q.B. 426 with *Postermobile plc v. Brent L.B.C., The Times*, 8 December 1997.

80. Control of Pollution Act 1974, s. 3(4).

81. (1843) 10 Cl. & Fin. 200.

82. *R v. Sullivan* [1984] 1 A.C. 156.

83. *R v. Burgess* [1991] 2 Q.B. 92.

84. *R v. Hennessy* [1989] 1 W.L.R. 287.

85. For analysis, see R. D. Mackay, "The New Diminished Responsibility Plea," [2010] *Criminal Law Review* 290–302.

86. [1977] A.C. 443.

87. *R v. Heard* [2008] Q.B. 43, a decision that stretches the concept of "basic intent" to crimes (such as sexual assault) that require proof of intention only.

88. See n. 87 above.

89. *R v. Kingston* [1995] 2 A.C. 355.

90. Law Com. No. 314, *Intoxication and Criminal Liability* (London: The Stationery Office, 2009).

91. [2005] UKHL 22.

92. Ibid., at [21].

93. *R v. Bowen* [1997] 1 W.L.R. 372.

94. *R v. Hasan* [2005] UKHL 22, at [38].

95. *R v. Willer* (1986) 83 Cr. App. R. 225; *R v. Conway* (1988) 89 Cr. App. R. 159.

96. *Attorney General's Reference No. 3 of 2000 (Looseley)* [2001] 1 W.L.R. 2060.

97. A doctrine developed in European human rights law; see *Teixeira de Castro v. Portugal* (1999) 28 E.H.R.R. 101.

98. The first judgment of this kind set out guidelines for the sentencing of drug offences: *R v. Aramah* (1982) 4 Cr. App. R. (S) 407.

99. Crime and Disorder Act 1998 (U.K.), ss. 80–81.

100. The statutory framework may be found in the Criminal Justice Act 2003, ss. 167–173. For discussion of the system, see Martin Wasik, "Sentencing Guidelines in England and Wales—State of the Art?" [2008] *Criminal Law Review* 253.

101. For analysis, see A. Ashworth, "Sentencing Guidelines and the Sentencing Council," [2010] *Criminal Law Review* 389–401.

102. Law Com. No. 307, *Murder, Manslaughter and Infanticide*.

103. Ministry of Justice, *Murder, Manslaughter and Infanticide: Proposals for Reform of the Law*, Consultation Paper CP19/08 (2008).

104. There are other offences protecting unborn children, such as the offence of child destruction under the Infant Life Preservation Act 1929.

105. *Attorney-General's Reference No. 3 of 1994* [1998] A.C. 245.

106. Confirmed by the House of Lords in *R v. Cunningham* [1982] A.C. 566.

107. Criminal Justice Act 2003, schedule 21.

108. Law Commission Consultation Paper No. 177, *A New Homicide Act for England and Wales?* (London: The Stationery Office, 2005); Law Com. No. 307, *Murder, Manslaughter and Infanticide*.

109. For analysis, see A. Norrie, "Loss of Control," [2010] *Criminal Law Review* 275–289.

110. Sentencing Guidelines Council, *Manslaughter by Reason of Provocation: Definitive Guideline* (London: Sentencing Guidelines Council, 2005).

111. The leading case is probably *Director of Public Prosecutions v. Newbury and Jones* [1977] A.C. 500.

112. *R v. Adomako* [1995] 1 A.C. 171.

113. [2003] Q.B. 1203.

114. Infanticide Act 1938.

115. Road Safety Act 2006, amending the Road Traffic Act 1988.

116. Sentencing Guidelines Council, *Causing Death by Driving* (London: Sentencing Guidelines Council, 2008).

117. See Peter Rook and Robert Ward, *Sexual Offences: Law and Practice* (Oxford: Hart, 2004).

118. [2007] EWCA Crim 804.

119. *R v. Heard* [2008] Q.B. 43.

120. Sentencing Guidelines Council, *Sexual Offences* (London: Sentencing Guidelines Council, 2006).

121. For a strong critique of these offences, see John Spencer, "Child and Family Offences," [2004] *Criminal Law Review* 347.

122. Sexual Offences (Scotland) Act 2009, s. 39(3).

123. [2008] UKHL 37.

124. David Ormerod and David Huw Williams, *Smith's Law of Theft* (Oxford: Oxford University Press, 2007).

125. *R v. Gomez* [1993] A.C. 442; *R v. Hinks* [2001] 2 A.C. 241.

126. *R v. Feely* [1973] Q.B. 530; *R v. Ghosh* [1982] Q.B. 1053.

127. Sentencing Guidelines Council, *Sentencing for Fraud—Statutory Offences* (London: Sentencing Guidelines Council, 2009).

128. See also the Customs and Excise Management Act 1979, s. 170.

129. Clean Neighbourhoods and Environment Act 2005, s. 20.

130. Gambling Act 2005, s. 138(3).

131. E.g., Clean Neighbourhoods and Environment Act 2005, s. 28(8).

132. E.g., Commissioners for Revenue and Customs Act 2005, s. 31(1).

133. E.g., Education Act 2005, s. 109(2) and s. 111(3).

UNITED STATES

Paul H. Robinson

I. Introduction
II. The Structure of American Criminal Law
    A. Source and Form
    B. The Legality Principle
III. A Brief Summary of the American Criminal Justice Process
    A. Investigation and Accusation
    B. Pretrial
    C. Trial and Post-Trial
IV. Liability Requirements
    A. Objective Offense Requirements
    B. Offense Culpability Requirements
    C. Doctrines of Imputation
    D. Inchoate Liability
V. General Defenses
    A. Types of Defenses
    B. Justification Defenses
    C. Excuse Defenses
    D. Nonexculpatory Defenses
VI. Specific Offenses
    A. Overview
    B. Homicide

Paul H. Robinson is the Colin S. Diver Professor of Law at the University of Pennsylvania Law School. His recent publications include *Distributive Principles of Criminal Law: Who Should Be Punished How Much?* (Oxford University Press, 2008) and (with Michael Cahill) *Law without Justice: Why Criminal Law Doesn't Give People What They Deserve* (Oxford University Press, 2005).

C. Sex Offenses
D. Theft Offenses

I. INTRODUCTION

This chapter provides a very brief summary of the central features of American criminal law. Section II describes its source and current form, which is almost exclusively statutory, embodied in the criminal codes of each of the fifty American states and (to a lesser extent) the federal criminal code. Section III sketches the typical process by which a case moves through an American criminal justice system, from the report of a crime through trial and appellate review. Section IV summarizes the most basic objective and culpability requirements necessary to establish liability for an offense and the doctrines that sometimes impute those elements when they do not in fact exist. Section V describes the general defenses that may bar liability, even if the offense elements are satisfied or imputed. Finally, section VI describes the general organization of a typical American criminal code's definition of offenses and gives highlights concerning a few of the most common offenses.

II. THE STRUCTURE OF AMERICAN CRIMINAL LAW

A. Source and Form

In the eighteenth century, English criminal law was generally uncodified. This "common law" was developed by—and embodied in—judicial opinions. The American colonies adopted the common law of England as it existed at the time of American independence. The period's most popular treatise, William Blackstone's *Commentaries on the Laws of England*, became a highly influential work in America not because of anything particularly distinguished about the four volumes, but simply because its popularity coincided with American independence. Volume 4 provided a useful summary of the then-existing body of common-law criminal jurisprudence.[1] American courts then took on the role of further refining and developing the law, thereby creating differences with English law. Today's courts generally no longer have the role of refining and developing the criminal law; that function has been taken over by legislatures. Nearly every state has a criminal code as its primary source of criminal law. Courts interpret the code but generally have no authority to create new crimes or change the definition of existing crimes. The reasons for the shift from common-law, judicially defined offenses to criminal codes are found chiefly in the rationales offered in support of what is called the *legality principle*, discussed in section II.B in this chapter.

1. Modern Criminal Code Reform

Although there were some heroic efforts, little criminal code reform occurred in the United States before the 1960s. Most early codes were less a code and more a collection of ad hoc statutory enactments, each triggered by a crime or a crime problem that gained significant public interest for a time. The major contribution of early codifiers frequently was to put the offenses in alphabetical order. The greatest catalyst of modern American criminal law codification was the Model Penal Code, which was promulgated by the American Law Institute (ALI) in 1962. Since its introduction, the Model Penal Code has served as the basis for wholesale replacement of existing criminal codes in almost three-quarters of the states. Some states adopted the Code with only minor revisions, while others—especially those that adopted it early—borrowed the Model Penal Code's style and form but only some of its content in the course of reworking their existing doctrine.

2. The Model Penal Code

The American Law Institute, which drafted the Model Code, is a nongovernmental, broad-based, and highly regarded group of lawyers, judges, professors, and others that undertakes research and drafting projects designed to bring rationality and enlightenment to American law. The Institute's Restatements of the Law have been influential in bringing clarity and uniformity to many fields, such as tort law and contract law. Although a criminal law project was undertaken by the Institute in 1953, it was concluded that the criminal law of the various states had become too disparate to permit a "restatement," and, in any case the existing law was too unsound and ill considered to merit restating. What was needed instead was a model criminal code. After nine years of work and a series of *Tentative Drafts*, the Institute approved an *Official Draft* in 1962. Later, the original commentary contained in the various Tentative Drafts was consolidated, revised, and finally in 1985 published along with the 1962 text as a six-volume set.[2]

3. Continuing Reform Efforts

About one-quarter of the states have not yet adopted a modern criminal code. The federal system is the most unfortunate example of frustrated reform. Congress has been engaged in an effort to reform the federal criminal code since 1966. At one point a modern code bill passed in the Senate but did not pass in the House. Criminal code reform is always difficult because it touches highly political issues, but the lack of a modern federal criminal code is a matter of some embarrassment in a country whose states lead the world in enlightened criminal law codification. The present federal criminal code is not significantly different in form from the alphabetical listing of offenses that was typical of the original American codes in the 1800s. Fortunately, the U.S. Constitution vests the criminal law power in the states, not in the federal government, which has jurisdiction over only uniquely federal offenses.

4. Central Features of Modern American Codes

Modern American codes stand apart from many other modern codes because they are designed to include a comprehensive and self-contained statement of all the rules required to adjudicate all criminal cases. They try not to depend on other sources of law, academic or judicial. Modern codes have a general part containing general provisions that apply to the specific offenses defined in the code's special part. General provisions include such things as general rules for the definition and interpretation of offenses; a collection of definitions for commonly used terms; general liability doctrines concerning omission liability, complicity, and voluntary intoxication; and general defenses, such as self-defense, insanity, and time limitations. In the special part of a code, offenses are defined and organized as conceptually related groups and are formulated and consolidated to minimize overlaps among offenses and gaps between them. A significant practical effect of reform is that code sections can no longer be read in isolation. To fully understand each offense definition in the special part, several provisions in the general part must be consulted.

B. The Legality Principle

In its original Latin dress the legality principle was expressed as *nullum crimen sine lege, nulla poena sine lege*, meaning roughly, "no crime without law, nor punishment without law." In its modern form it means that criminal liability and punishment can be based only on a prior legislative enactment of liability rules expressed with adequate precision and clarity. The principle is not itself a legal rule, but rather a legal concept embodied in a series of legal rules and doctrines.

1. Legality Doctrines

Two of the doctrines that make up the legality principle include the rules in modern American criminal codes that abolish common-law crimes and prohibit the judicial creation of offenses. In contrast, in 1962 the English House of Lords approved prosecution of a common-law offense of "conspiracy to corrupt public morals."[3] American jurisdictions typically would bar prosecution for such an uncodified offense because it is undefined by statute. In addition, the legality principle is embodied in the constitutional prohibition of vague statutes, the rule requiring strict construction of penal statutes, and the constitutional prohibition of application of *ex post facto* laws.

The vagueness prohibition, rooted in the Constitution's Due Process Clause, requires that a criminal statute give "sufficient warning that men may conform their conduct so as to avoid that which is forbidden."[4] A statute is not unconstitutionally vague, however, merely because one of its elements calls for a matter of judgment. Rather, an offense provision is *vague* if it does not adequately define the prohibited conduct. If an offense definition defines the prohibited conduct with some specificity but is subject to two or more interpretations, then it is termed *ambiguous*, which is not necessarily unconstitutional. When faced with an ambiguity, the law traditionally applies a special rule for interpreting criminal statutes. The rule of strict construction, as it is called, directs that an ambiguity in a penal statute be resolved against the state and in favor of the defendant.[5] For this reason, it is also called the *rule of lenity*.

One final legality doctrine is the constitutional prohibition against *ex post facto* laws.[6] This has been interpreted to invalidate "[e]very law that makes an action done before the passing of the law, and which was innocent when done, criminal; and punishes such action. Every law that aggravates a crime, or makes it greater than it was, when committed. Every law that changes the punishment, and inflicts a greater punishment, than the law annexed to the crime, when committed."[7]

2. Legality Principle Rationales

The American devotion to the legality principle arises from rationales unrelated to, and often in conflict with, blameworthiness. Although not all the rationales may be applicable in all situations, the rationales most commonly offered in support of the legality principle include the following.

i. Procedural Fairness

Fairness requires that a person have at least an opportunity to find out what the criminal law commands. Actual notice is not required for liability; it is enough that the prohibition has been lawfully enacted. Similarly, a defendant's actual knowledge that the conduct is prohibited and punished does not vitiate a legality-based defense. The concern of the legality principle is procedural fairness, not blamelessness.

ii. Criminalization as a Legislative Function

In a democracy the legislature—the most representative branch of government—is generally thought to be the proper body to exercise the criminalization decision. This rationale directly supports the prohibition of judicial creation of offenses and the abolition of judicially created offenses. It also has application in less obvious ways to support the invalidation of vague statutes and the disapproval of ambiguous statutes. Courts applying such statutes provide the specificity the legislature has not—a de facto delegation of criminalization authority to the courts.

iii. Rules of Conduct and Principles of Adjudication

The rationales noted so far—procedural fairness and reserving the criminalization function to the legislature—concern the rule-articulation function of the criminal law, understood as its obligation to communicate the governing rules to all members of society. The rationales reflect the American preference for how that rule-articulation function ought to be performed: the legislature should set the rules, and the formulations should be calculated to give adequate notice to deter effectively and properly and to condemn a violation fairly. But the criminal law also serves an adjudication function, with which several rationales in support of the legality principle are associated.

iv. Inconsistency and Abuse of Discretion

Consistency in the treatment of similar cases is possible only with a sufficiently clear and precise definition of an offense, one that does not call for discretionary judgments. With individual discretion inevitably comes disparity based on the inherent differences among decision makers. Also, the exercise of discretion can allow the operation of malevolent influences, such as racism, sexism, and the like. An unclear prohibition, therefore, can create a potential for abuse of discretion by police officers, prosecutors, and others with decision-making authority. In *Papachristou v. City of Jacksonville*, for example, police officers arrested "mixed" couples (of blacks and whites), charging them with a variety of vague offenses such as "vagrancy," "loitering," and "disorderly loitering on street." The Supreme Court reversed the convictions finding that the vagueness of the statutes encouraged arbitrary convictions, as well as arbitrary arrests.[8]

III. A BRIEF SUMMARY OF THE AMERICAN CRIMINAL JUSTICE PROCESS

The authority to define and punish crimes is vested primarily in the states, not in the federal government (except for offenses relating to a special federal interest). Thus there are fifty-two American criminal justice systems (including the federal and District of Columbia systems), and each is different from the others in some way. Below is a brief description of a procedural process that is typical in most American criminal justice systems.

A. Investigation and Accusation

1. Report and Investigation

The criminal justice process usually begins with a report of a crime by a citizen or a police officer. Typically an investigation follows to determine whether a crime has in fact been committed and, if so, by whom. Once a suspect has been identified, the investigation may continue in order to collect evidence for use in prosecution.

2. Arrest and Booking

When a police officer believes that there exists "probable cause" to think that a crime was committed and that a particular suspect committed it, the officer may arrest that suspect. Sometimes the evidence is presented to a magistrate beforehand and a judicial warrant to arrest is obtained, but most arrests are made without a warrant. An arrest is essentially a taking of physical control over the person and usually includes a search of the person for weapons, contraband, and evidence relating to the crime. The arrestee is then taken to the police station, where he or she is "booked." This procedure consists of entering the arrestee's name, the time, and the offense charged in a police log. The arrestee is photographed and fingerprinted, informed of the charge, and allowed to make a telephone call. Those charged with minor offenses are allowed to post cash security as "station-house bail," which allows them to leave the police station with a promise to appear before a magistrate at a specified date. Persons who are arrested for more serious offenses or who are unable to post station-house bail are sent to a "lockup" after another more careful search, including an inventory of their personal possessions.

3. Precharge Screening

The first of many reviews of the charging decision is frequently made at this point. A higher-ranking police officer may reduce or drop the charges for which a suspect was booked. This may occur either because the evidence is insufficient to proceed or because an informal disposition—perhaps including a lecture and warning—is more appropriate. Ten to 20 percent of all cases are dropped from the system at this point. A member of the prosecutor's office also may screen the cases during this stage, although this frequently occurs only in felony cases.

4. Filing Complaint

If it is determined that the prosecution will proceed, formal charges are filed with the court via a "complaint." This document briefly describes the facts of the case and is sworn to by the complainant, likely to be either the victim or the investigating officer. The affiant (or person giving the affidavit) can swear only to the facts known to him or her, of course, so a complaint by the investigating officer is likely to contain only claims about what the officer believes or what others reported. A magistrate will review the complaint *ex parte* (without the presence or participation of the parties) to determine whether probable cause exists to believe that the "defendant," as he or she is now called, committed the offense charged. If the magistrate is not satisfied that there is probable cause, he or she will dismiss the complaint, but without prejudice—that is, the prosecutor may amend and refile the complaint in the future. Where an arrest warrant was previously obtained on the basis of a complaint, this step will, of course, already be complete; the defendant will be taken directly from booking to the initial appearance.

5. Initial Appearance

Soon after a person is arrested and booked, unless released on station-house bail, he or she is brought before a magistrate. The magistrate confirms that the arrestee is the person named in the complaint and informs the arrestee of his or her constitutional rights, including the right to remain silent, the right to have counsel, and the right to have counsel appointed if he or she cannot afford one. Frequently, counsel is appointed at this stage.

6. Bail

The magistrate at the initial appearance also reviews any bail conditions previously set at the station house and sets bail for those arrestees who did not previously have it set. High bail amounts typically require the services of a professional bondsman to ensure the defendant's appearance, to whom the defendant must pay a nonrefundable or only partially refundable fee. Increasingly, defendants have been allowed to pay, in cash, an amount equal to 10 percent of the total bail amount, which is then refundable if the defendant appears as directed.

B. Pretrial

1. Preliminary Hearing

For felony cases, another judicial screening decision is made within a week or two of the initial appearance. Unlike the *ex parte* review at the complaint stage, this screening involves an adversarial process where the prosecution presents witnesses and the defendant, now represented by counsel, may cross-examine. The defendant may present his or her own evidence but in practice rarely does so, preferring instead to learn as much as possible about the prosecution's case without divulging his or her own defense. The magistrate may dismiss the charges or may allow only a lesser charge than that alleged in the complaint.

2. Grand Jury Indictment and Prosecutorial Information

Another screening stage for felonies is grand jury review to determine whether an indictment should be returned against a defendant. The federal system and about half the states give felony defendants a right to grand jury review. A grand jury is made up of citizens who are called to meet regularly to review cases during a set term of perhaps several months. The traditional size is twenty-three people, of whom a majority of twelve must agree in order to indict a defendant. This majority corresponds to the standard size of a trial jury. The grand jury review procedure is significantly different from trial and from the preliminary hearing; it is in fact more akin to a magistrate's review of a complaint. Only the prosecution presents witnesses; the hearing is held in secret; and the defendant has no right to be present.

3. Arraignment

If the defendant is indicted by the grand jury, the indictment substitutes for the complaint as the formal charging document. The defendant is arraigned in the general trial court on this document and is asked to plead guilty, not guilty, or, where permitted, *nolo contendere*. A date is then set to hear pretrial and trial matters.

4. Plea Bargaining

From the point of filing the complaint, and sometimes before, until trial, the defense counsel and prosecutor may engage in plea negotiations. This may involve either an agreement to dismiss some charges if the defendant will plead guilty to others or, in some jurisdictions, a promise of a lenient sentence or a recommendation for one in exchange for a plea of guilty. Challenges to the institution of the prosecution (such as challenging the makeup of the grand jury) or the sufficiency of the charging instrument, as well as requests for discovery and motions to suppress evidence, typically are made before trial. These motions may produce a dismissal for a defendant without the need for a plea bargain.

C. Trial and Post-Trial

1. The Trial

After a defendant has been arrested and charged with a crime, if there has not been a dismissal (on a pretrial motion) and the defendant has not entered a guilty plea, the case goes to trial. Several features distinguish the American criminal system from the civil system. These include (1) the presumption of a defendant's innocence, (2) the requirement of proof beyond a reasonable doubt, (3) the right of the defendant not to take the stand, (4) the exclusion of evidence obtained by the state in an illegal manner, and (5) the more frequent use of incriminating statements of defendants as evidence.

An American trial uses an adversarial process. The defendant is represented by an advocate representing his or her position, while the state's prosecutors represent the state's interest in punishing offenders. The sides argue in front of an impartial decision maker. In all fifty-two jurisdictions the defendant has a right to a jury trial for all felony offenses and for misdemeanors punishable by more than six months' imprisonment. Most states also provide a jury trial for lesser misdemeanors as well. The right to a jury trial can be waived in favor of a bench trial.

2. Sentencing

If a defendant is convicted at trial or pleads guilty before a trial takes place, the court will set a date for a sentencing hearing at which both sides will present evidence relating to the appropriate sentence. While a few jurisdictions allow for sentencing by a jury in noncapital cases, most assign the sentence determination to the court. Typically, three different types of sanctions can be used: financial sanctions (e.g., fines, restitution orders); some form of release into the community (e.g., probation, unsupervised release, house arrest, drug rehabilitation); and incarceration in a jail (for lesser sentences) or a prison (for longer sentences). The most severe form of punishment is the death penalty, the availability of which is determined by each individual state. The legislature typically sets the maximum penalty available for an offense. It sometimes also narrows the sentencing options for an offense by excluding community release or by setting a mandatory minimum term of imprisonment. Increasingly, court sentencing decisions are restricted by guidelines that suggest a guideline sentence for offenders of a particular sort committing offenses of a particular sort. Some guideline systems are more binding than others.

3. Appeal

A defendant generally has a right to appeal a conviction to the next higher court in the particular system's judicial hierarchy. For misdemeanors tried in a magistrate court, this may mean a new trial in the general trial court. The right to appeal is not necessarily limited to those convicted at trial, however; a defendant who pleads guilty but who receives a more severe sentence than he or she expected, for example, may be able to appeal, challenging his or her plea. Appellate review of the appropriateness of the sentence is generally not permitted, although review of a deviation from sentencing guidelines may be. The most common objections on appeal concern admission of evidence claimed to be improperly obtained (generally the most successful claim), insufficient evidence to support the conviction, incompetent counsel, improper identification procedures, and improper admission of a defendant's confession or incriminating statements.

4. Postconviction Remedies

After exhausting possibilities for appellate review, a convict who has not gained release may seek relief through postconviction remedies, sometimes called *collateral attacks* on conviction. Sometimes this is done through the writ of habeas corpus, but it is commonly governed by a more modern statutory procedure. After exhausting postconviction remedies in state court, state prisoners who have a constitutional claim may present the same claim for review by the federal courts under federal postconviction remedy procedures. In both state and federal systems the process of appellate review of a denial of a postconviction petition follows the same appellate course that the direct appeal did.

IV. LIABILITY REQUIREMENTS

Offense definitions are typically made up of three kinds of objective elements—conduct, circumstance, and result elements—each accompanied by a corresponding culpability requirement of purpose, knowledge, recklessness, or negligence. Some doctrines will allow a defendant to be treated as if he or she satisfies a required element that is not in fact present, if the defendant does satisfy the requirements of a doctrine of imputation. For example, a defendant may be liable for an offense that requires conduct that the defendant did not commit if the conduct, performed by another person, is imputed to the defendant by the complicity doctrine. Finally, a defendant who is apprehended or stops before completing an offense may be held liable for an inchoate offense on the basis of his or her intention to commit or encourage conduct toward the commission.

A. Objective Offense Requirements

Offense definitions consist of two kinds of elements: objective elements (conduct, circumstance, or result elements) and culpability elements (typically purpose, knowledge, recklessness, or negligence). Each objective offense element has a corresponding culpability element, and the culpability level may be different with respect to different objective elements of the same offense.

1. Conduct, Circumstance, and Result Elements

The Model Penal Code's drafters constructed a useful system for the precise definition of offenses. Section 1.13(9), defining "elements of an offense," distinguishes between (i) conduct, (ii) attendant circumstances, and (iii) a result of conduct. These are the objective building blocks for offense definitions. Each offense definition typically has at least one conduct element, which satisfies the act requirement inherent in all criminal offenses. Most offense definitions include one or more circumstance elements as well, defining the precise nature of the prohibited conduct (e.g., having intercourse with a person under fourteen years old) or the characteristic of a prohibited result (e.g., causing the death of another human being). A minority of offenses contain a result element. Homicide offenses, personal injury offenses, and property destruction offenses are examples of this minority of offenses; they require a resulting physical harm in order to sustain a conviction for the offense. Other offenses, such as endangerment, indecent exposure, and falsification, may require the person to cause a risk of harm or to cause an intangible harm, such as alarm or a false impression.[9]

2. Causation Requirement

Whenever an offense definition includes a result element (e.g., homicide requires a death), a causation requirement also is implied. That is, it must be shown that the person's conduct caused the prohibited result. This required relation between the defendant's conduct and the result derives from American notions of causal accountability. The rules of the causation doctrine are the means by which the law attempts to define the conditions under which such causal accountability exists.

i. Requirements of Causation

Establishing a causal connection between a defendant's conduct and a result typically has two independent requirements. First, the conduct must be a "but-for" cause of the result. That is, in the language of Model Penal Code section 2.03(1)(a), the conduct must be "an antecedent but for which the result in question would not have occurred." This is sometimes called the *factual cause* requirement. Second, the strength and nature of the causal connection between the conduct and the result must be sufficient. *Legal cause*, or *proximate cause*, as this is sometimes called, requires that the resulting harm be "not too remote or accidental in its occurrence to have a [just] bearing on the actor's liability or on the gravity of his offense." This language, from Model Penal Code sections 2.03(2)(b) and (3)(b), is sometimes supplemented by an additional requirement that the resulting harm "not be too . . . dependent on another's volitional act."[10]

ii. Factual Cause

Conduct is a factual (but-for) cause of a result if the result would not have occurred but for the conduct. In other words, the conduct is a factual cause if it was necessary for the result to occur. The factual cause inquiry is essentially a scientific and hypothetical one. It asks what the world would have been like had the defendant not performed his or her conduct.

Specifically, would the result still have occurred when it did? If the answer is no, then the defendant's conduct was necessary for, and thus was a but-for cause of, the result.

iii. Proximate (Legal) Cause

In contrast to the scientific inquiry of the factual cause requirement, the proximate (legal) cause requirement presents essentially a normative inquiry. Deciding whether a result is "too remote or accidental in its occurrence" or "too dependent on another's volitional act" obviously calls for an exercise of intuitive judgment. The inquiry cannot be resolved by examining the facts more closely or having scientific experts analyze the situation. Ultimately, the decision maker must determine how much remoteness is "too remote" or how much dependence on another's volitional act is "too dependent" for the result to have a just bearing on the defendant's liability. Typically the foreseeability of the result following from the defendant's conduct is a highly influential factor in a determination of proximate cause.

B. Offense Culpability Requirements

Modern American codes typically follow Model Penal Code section 2.02(1) in providing that "a person is not guilty of an offense unless he acted purposely, knowingly, recklessly, or negligently, as the law may require, with respect to each material element of the offense." This provision reflects the criminal law's commitment to requiring not only a breach of society's objective rules of conduct but also a defendant's culpability with regard to the conditions that make the conduct a breach. A defendant's conduct may be harmful; the victim may have a claim in tort; and fairness and utility both may suggest that the defendant rather than the victim should bear the loss for the injury. But without culpability in the defendant, causing the injury may be seen as lacking sufficient blameworthiness to deserve the condemnation and reprobation of criminal conviction.

1. Shift to Element Analysis

Model Penal Code section 2.02(1) makes clear that the Code requires culpability "with respect to each material element of the offense."[11] In other words, it is not just that different offenses may have different culpability requirements. With this section the Model Penal Code makes clear that different objective elements within a single offense may have different culpability requirements than all or some of the other objective elements of the offense.

2. Culpability Levels under the Model Penal Code

In place of the plethora of common-law terms—*wantonly, heedlessly, maliciously,* and so on—the Code defines four levels of culpability: purposely, knowingly, recklessly, and negligently. Ideally, all offenses are defined by designating one of these four levels of culpability with regard to each objective element. If the objective elements of an offense require that a person take the property of another, the culpability elements might require, for example, that the person know that he or she is taking property and that he or she be at least reckless about it being someone else's property. An offense also may require culpability with regard to a circumstance or result beyond what the objective elements of the offense require. Thus theft may require a purpose to permanently deprive the owner of his or her property, although it need not be shown that the owner was permanently deprived.

3. Purpose

Under the Code, a person acts "purposely" with respect to a result if his or her conscious object is to cause such a result.[12] This is a demanding requirement that is often difficult to prove. The offense of indecent exposure, for example, requires more than showing that the defendant exposed himself or herself to another, knowing that it would alarm the person; it must be proved that the conduct was motivated by a desire to gain sexual gratification or arousal by the conduct. Doing it just to annoy or alarm the victim would not satisfy the offense's gratification purpose requirement, even if the offender did experience unplanned-for gratification.[13]

4. Purposely versus Knowingly

A person acts "purposely" with respect to a result if it is his or her conscious object to cause the result. A person acts "knowingly" with respect to a result if it is not his or her conscious object, but he or she is practically certain that the conduct will cause that result.[14] An antiwar activist who sets a bomb to destroy a draft board's offices may be practically certain that the bomb will kill the night watchman, but may wish that the watchman would go on a coffee break so that he would not be killed. The essence of the narrow distinction between these two culpability levels is the presence or absence of a positive desire to cause the result; purpose requires a culpability beyond the knowledge of a result's near certainty. In the broader sense this distinction divides the vague notion of "callousness" from the more offensive "maliciousness" or "viciousness." The latter may simply be an aggressively ruthless form of the former.

5. Knowingly versus Recklessly

A person acts "knowingly" with respect to a result if he or she is nearly certain that his or her conduct will cause the result. If he or she is aware only of a substantial risk, he or she acts "recklessly" with respect to the result.[15] The narrow distinction between knowledge and recklessness lies in the degree of risk—"practically certain" versus "substantial risk"—of which the defendant is aware. The distinction between recklessness (and lower levels of culpability) and the two higher levels of culpability (purposely and knowingly) is that we tend to scold a reckless person for being "careless," while we condemn an offender who falls within one of the higher culpability categories for "intentional" conduct.

6. Purpose as Independent of Likelihood

While knowing and reckless culpability focus on the likelihood of causing the result—"practically certain" versus "substantial risk"—purposeful culpability pays no regard to the likelihood of the result. This characteristic of the purpose requirement reflects an instinct that trying to cause the harm, whatever the likelihood, is more condemnable than acting with the belief that the harm will or might result without desiring it. The practical effect of this is that reckless conduct, as manifested in risk taking, can be elevated to purposeful conduct if the defendant hopes that the risk will come to fruition. This characteristic of purpose also illustrates how specially demanding it is. A requirement of a particular belief is something a jury might logically deduce from other facts: the defendant "must have known" the certainty or the risk of harm if he or she knew this fact or that. A purpose requirement requires the jury to determine a defendant's object or goal, a somewhat more complex psychological state. To find this, a jury may have to dig deeper into the defendant's psyche and his or her general desires and motivations to reach a conclusion. If a jury is conscientious in adhering to the proof-beyond-a-reasonable-doubt standard constitutionally required for offense elements, this may be a difficult conclusion to reach.

7. Recklessly versus Negligently

A person acts "recklessly" with respect to a result if he or she consciously disregards a substantial risk that his or her conduct will cause the result; he or she acts only "negligently" if he or she is unaware of the substantial risk but should have perceived it.[16] The recklessness issue focuses not on whether he or she should have been aware of the risk, but instead on whether he or she was, in fact, aware (and whether it was culpable for him or her to disregard the risk).

8. Recklessness as Conscious Wrongdoing

The narrow distinction between recklessness and negligence lies in the defendant's awareness of risk. The difference between negligence and the three higher levels of culpability is one of the most critical distinctions in U.S. criminal law. A person who acts purposely, knowingly, or recklessly is aware of the circumstances that make his or her conduct criminal or is aware that harmful consequences may result and is therefore both blameworthy and deterrable. A defendant who acts negligently, in contrast, is unaware of the circumstances or consequences and therefore, some writers argue, is neither blameworthy nor deterrable. Although writers disagree over whether negligence ought to be adequate to support criminal liability, it is agreed that negligence represents a lower level of culpability than, and is qualitatively different from, recklessness in that the negligent person fails to recognize, rather than consciously disregards, the risk. For this reason, recklessness is considered the norm for criminal culpability, while negligence typically is punished in American jurisdictions only in exceptional situations, such as where a death is caused.

9. Negligence as Normative Assessment

A person who fails to appreciate the risk that his or her conduct will cause a result is "negligent" with regard to the result if the failure "involves a gross deviation from the standard of care that a reasonable person would observe in the actor's situation."[17] Thus, unless he or she grossly deviates from the standard of care that a reasonable person would observe, a person is not negligent and, at least in the eyes of the criminal law, is without cognizable fault. If a person is not aware of the risk of death, should he or she have been? Would a reasonable person in his or her situation have been aware that a risk of death existed? Was his or her failure to perceive the risk a gross deviation from the attentiveness to the possibility of risk that the reasonable person in his or her situation would have had? These are the issues that a jury considers in assessing whether the person ought to be liable for negligent homicide. They are not factual but rather normative issues. The jury is asked to judge whether the person's failure to perceive the risk was, under the circumstances, a blameworthy failure.

10. Negligently versus Faultlessly

Liability imposed for faultless conduct is termed *absolute* or *strict* liability. The distinction between negligence and strict liability focuses on whether the defendant's unawareness of the risk constituted a failure to meet the standard of the reasonable person. The broader distinction between the four categories of culpability and faultlessness is the distinction between a blameworthy and a blameless defendant. The objections to strict liability stem from an understandable reluctance to punish conduct that is not unreasonable.

11. Concurrence Requirement

When an offense definition requires a particular level of culpability for a particular element, it means that the required culpability for the element must exist at the time of the conduct constituting the offense. This concurrence requirement, as it is called, reflects the law's interest in judging the culpability of the act rather than the general character of the defendant. The required concurrence between act and culpability is implicit in the Model Penal Code's culpability definitions in section 2.02(2).[18] It is neither necessary nor sufficient that the culpability exist at the later time of the result of the conduct. Changing one's mind after setting a bomb, for example, does not bar liability for deaths caused by the blast, even if the intent to kill no longer exists at the time the bomb explodes or the victims die.

C. Doctrines of Imputation

Typically a person is liable for an offense if and only if the person satisfies the elements of an offense definition. There are two exceptions to this rule. First, a person may be liable for an offense even though he or she does not satisfy all offense elements, if a rule or doctrine imputes the missing element. Second, a person may escape liability even though the person does satisfy the elements of an offense, if he or she satisfies the conditions of a general defense. General defenses are discussed in section V; this section examines doctrines of imputation.

1. Imputation Principles as Independent of Offense

A legislature conceivably could include inculpatory (and exculpatory) exceptions to the offense paradigm within the offense definition. For example, Tennessee defines the offense of arson to include not only setting the fire but also assisting another in doing so.[19] More typically, however, doctrines of imputation such as complicity are drafted in a form independent of offense definitions—a form that applies to all offenses. This approach harnesses the benefits of drafting efficiency, as well as encouraging conceptual clarity. Like general defenses—such as insanity, duress, and law-enforcement authority, which are separate and apart from any offense definition—the rules of imputation represent principles of liability independent of any single offense. An additional point of similarity with general defenses arises because most of the doctrines of imputation, at least theoretically, can impute a required element for any offense defined in the code's special part. Some doctrines of imputation may tend to apply most frequently to certain recurring factual situations. Transferred intent, for example, appears most commonly in bad-aim murder cases. This, however, is a factual rather than a theoretical limitation of the principle.

2. Doctrines Imputing Objective Elements

American criminal law permits the imputation of both objective and culpability elements of an offense. The most obvious and common instances of imputing objective elements are found in the rules governing complicity, discussed in section III.C.3 in this chapter. But complicity is only one of several doctrines that impose liability even though the person does not satisfy the objective elements of an offense. Where a person exercises control over an innocent or irresponsible person, the latter's satisfaction of the objective elements of an offense may be imputed to the former as an instance of "causing crime by an innocent."[20] Similarly, various statutory and judicial presumptions permit the imposition of liability even though the evidence adduced at trial would not establish the objective elements of the offense. Finally, rules imposing liability for a person's omissions, even when the offense charged is defined only in terms of affirmative conduct, also may be viewed as instances of imputed conduct.

3. Complicity

Complicity is not an offense in itself, as are conspiracy and solicitation (discussed in section III.C.4), for example. Rather, it is a theory of liability by which an accomplice is held liable for an offense committed by the perpetrator.[21] An offense definition typically requires that the person have performed certain conduct, but a person may be held liable for the offense, although the person has not performed the required conduct, if he or she is legally accountable for the actual perpetrator's conduct. At common law, complicity liability required that the accomplice assist the perpetrator in committing the offense. The assistance need not be necessary for successful commission of the offense, nor need it be substantial. Indeed, the accomplice need not assist in a physical sense at all; encouragement is recognized as a form of assistance. On the other hand, the Model Penal Code, in section 2.06(3)(a)(ii), extends complicity liability to those instances in which the person simply "agrees or attempts to aid" the principal. Actual assistance, even in the form of psychological assistance through encouragement, is not required. The drafters intended that what constitutes an adequate "attempt to aid" will be determined by reference to the definition of the general inchoate offense of attempt.

4. Doctrines Imputing Culpability Elements

Just as a variety of rules and doctrines can impute an unsatisfied objective element of the offense charged, another group of doctrines can impute a required culpability element. The most common of these doctrines governs cases of voluntary intoxication. Even though a person does not have the awareness of risk required by the offense definition, for example, the required recklessness can be imputed to him or her by the voluntary intoxication rules.[22] Because the person voluntarily intoxicated himself or herself, the reasoning goes, he or she can properly be treated as if he or she had the awareness of risk that he or she would have had if he or she had not intoxicated himself or herself at all.

Another doctrine that can impute a culpable state of mind is the doctrine of transferred intent, which imputes the required culpability to a person who intends to harm one person but actually harms another. Imputation also is accomplished through a device that may be termed *substituted culpability*. This doctrine uses a person's culpability for the offense the person thought he or she was committing as the basis for imputing to the person the intention required for the offense actually committed. Thus a person who commits statutory rape but who, because of his mistake about the true identity of his partner, believes that he is instead committing incest can nonetheless be held liable for statutory rape. His missing culpability with respect to his partner being underage is imputed to him on the grounds that he thought that he was committing another offense, namely, incest. His intention to commit incest is transferred to satisfy the intent required for statutory rape. Another doctrine of imputation is apparent in those cases where courts permit suspension of the requirement of concurrence between act and intent: a person's earlier intention to commit an act that the person believes is the offense, but is not, is relied on to impute the required intention during the later conduct that actually constitutes the offense. Finally, as with objective elements, a variety of statutory and judicial presumptions effectively impute culpability elements upon proof of a logically related fact.

5. Corporate Criminal Liability

Because an organization can neither act nor think except through its agents and officers, it cannot satisfy the elements of an offense except through imputation. Thus, if criminal liability for organizations is to be provided, the criminal law must specify the rules for imputation of conduct and culpability to an organization. Under current American law, two forms of liability against organizations are common and accepted. First, liability is permitted where the offense consists of an omission to perform a specific duty imposed on the organization by law.[23] This requires no imputation and no application of special rules for liability, because liability follows directly from an organization's failure to perform the affirmative duty placed on it by relevant legislation.

Most jurisdictions also permit organizational criminal liability for standard offenses based on an affirmative act of an agent or an omission of an agent to perform a legal duty not expressly imposed on the organization. Most jurisdictions permit corporate liability for a serious offense under certain circumstances—even for offenses carrying a significant penalty and requiring culpability. In *State v. Christy Pontiac-GMC, Inc.*, for example, a salesman for the Christy Pontiac car dealership swindled two customers out of cash rebates and kept the money for the corporation. Under the rules of organizational liability used in *Christy*, the criminal acts of a corporation's agents are imputed to the corporation if they are (1) performed within the scope of employment, (2) in furtherance of the interests of the corporation, and (3) authorized, tolerated, or ratified by corporate management.[24] Because the corporation received the swindled funds and the conduct was ratified, if not authorized, by the corporation's president, the corporation was held liable for the employee's criminal act.

Some jurisdictions follow the Model Penal Code in extending liability beyond conduct authorized or ratified by corporate management to offense conduct "recklessly tolerated" by such actors.[25] This doctrine seeks to prevent management from simply turning a blind eye to violations because the violations further the corporate interest. Most jurisdictions provide a defense where upper management exercised due diligence to prevent commission of the offense.[26]

D. Inchoate Liability

American criminal law recognizes three general inchoate offenses: attempt, conspiracy, and solicitation. Where a person attempts, conspires with another, or solicits another to commit an offense, but the offense is never committed, the person nonetheless may be liable for one of these inchoate offenses.

1. Attempt

At some point in the chain of events from thinking about committing an offense to completing it, a person's conduct becomes criminal. This point typically is described as the moment at which *mere preparation* becomes a *criminal attempt*. Defining this point is an important part of attempt liability because it demarcates both when a person becomes criminally liable and when authorities lawfully may intervene. Attempt is significantly different from other offenses under American law because even after this point is reached and all the elements of attempt (or other inchoate offense) are satisfied, a person typically may escape liability if he or she voluntarily and completely renounces the attempt. Absent such renunciation, the failure to complete an offense only prevents liability for the full offense; it does not relieve the person from liability for the attempt.

The most common American objective requirement for attempt is that the person take a "substantial step" toward commission of the offense.[27] Rather than focusing on how close to the end of the chain the person has come—the approach of the "proximity" test used at common law—this approach focuses on how far from the beginning of the chain the person has gone. The Code gives seven illustrations of what "shall not be held insufficient as a matter of law" to constitute a substantial step.

Current American law commonly elevates the culpability required for an offense when it is charged in its inchoate form.[28] Thus, although recklessness with respect to causing injury may be sufficient for aggravated assault, in many jurisdictions attempted aggravated assault may require purpose or knowing with regard to causing injury. There is disagreement over whether this is wise policy. It may well be that attempt should require proof of a purpose to complete the conduct constituting the offense, but that the normal culpability levels for the offense elements ought not to be elevated.

2. Conspiracy

Conspiracy typically requires an agreement between two or more conspirators that at least one of them will commit a substantive offense.[29] The agreement need not be an act in a strict sense. Speaking, writing, or nodding can signal agreement, but one also can agree through silence where, under the circumstances or custom, silence is meant and understood to mean positive agreement. At common law, and currently in some jurisdictions without modern codes, the agreement requirement is taken to require actual agreement on both sides—an actual "meeting of the minds." Thus, for the person to be liable for conspiracy, the other conspirator must actually be agreeing, not just pretending to agree (as an undercover police officer would, for example). Modern American codes have adopted a unilateral agreement requirement, which permits conspiracy liability as long as the person agrees with another person, without regard for whether the other person is returning the agreement. Perhaps because conspiracy's agreement requirement is so slim a conduct requirement, an overt act is typically also required of one of the conspirators in furtherance of the agreement in order to sustain a conviction.

3. Solicitation

Solicitation is essentially an attempt to commit conspiracy by encouraging or requesting another person to do what would constitute an offense or an attempt.[30] As with conspiracy, the offense focuses on the person's subjective view of the world. The solicitation need not be successfully communicated; it is sufficient that the solicitor's "conduct was designed to effect such communication."[31] Unlike attempt, where the person's conduct may be ambiguous with respect to its criminal purpose, the solicitation offense includes no special requirement that the person's conduct strongly corroborate his or her criminal purpose.

V. GENERAL DEFENSES

In casual language anything that prevents conviction of a person is called a *defense*, but this term includes doctrines that are very different from one another. The legal doctrines that we refer to as defenses typically are of five sorts: absent-element defenses, offense modifications, justifications, excuses, or nonexculpatory defenses.

A. Types of Defenses

1. Absent-Element Defenses

Some doctrines that are called defenses are nothing more than the absence of a required offense element. If a person takes an umbrella, believing it to be his or her own, he or she may claim a mistake defense, but this defense derives not from a special defense doctrine about mistake as to ownership, but rather from the elements of the theft offense itself. The definition of theft includes a requirement that the person know that the property taken is owned by another. If a person mistakenly believes that the umbrella taken is his or her own, he or she does not satisfy the required culpability element of knowledge that it belongs to another.[32] Such a mistake defense is called an *absent-element defense* (or a *failure-of-proof defense*) because it derives from the inability of the state to prove a required element. The person is claiming that the prosecution cannot prove all the elements of the offense. It is within accepted casual usage to call such claims defenses, but they are simply another way of talking about the requirements of an offense definition.

2. Offense-Modification Defenses

Some defenses are indeed independent of the offense elements but in fact concern criminalization issues closely related to the definition of the offense. They typically refine or qualify the definition of a particular offense or group of offenses. Voluntary renunciation, for example, can provide a defense to inchoate offenses like attempt or conspiracy.[33] Consent is recognized as a defense to some kinds of assault.[34] Such a consent defense helps define what we mean by the offense of assault, just as renunciation helps refine the definitions of inchoate offenses (as including only unrenounced criminal plans). Indeed, assault frequently is defined as an unconsented-to touching. That is, the absence of consent sometimes is included as an element of the offense. As the practice illustrates, the difference between absent-element defenses and offense-modification defenses is one more of form than of substance. An offense-modification defense can as easily be drafted as a negative element of the offense, for each defines in part what the offense is not.

3. Criminalization Defenses versus General Defenses

Because both absent-element and offense-modification defenses serve to refine the offense definition, they tend to apply to a single offense or group of offenses. Justifications, excuses, and nonexculpatory defenses, in contrast, are unrelated to a particular offense; they theoretically apply to all offenses and therefore are called *general defenses*. The recognition of each general defense rests on reasons extraneous to the criminalization goals and policies of the offense. A general defense is provided not because there is no criminal wrong, but rather despite the occurrence of a legally recognized harm or evil. The offense's harm or evil may have occurred, but the special conditions establishing the defense suggest that the violator ought not to be punished.

4. Justifications

Justification defenses such as lesser evils, self-defense, and law-enforcement authority exculpate on the theory that the person's otherwise criminal conduct avoided a greater harm or evil. That is, although a person satisfies the elements of an offense, his or her offense is tolerated or even encouraged because it does not cause a net societal harm. A person who burns a firebreak on another's land may thereby commit arson but also may have a justification defense (of lesser evils) because, by the burning, the person saves innocent lives threatened by the fire. The commonly available doctrines of justification are the lesser-evils defense, the *defensive-force defenses* of self-defense, defense of others, defense of property, and defense of habitation, and the *public authority defenses* of law-enforcement authority, authority to maintain order and safety, parental authority, benevolent custodial authority, medical authority, authority to prevent a suicide, judicial authority, military authority, and general public authority.[35]

5. Excuses

Excuse defenses such as insanity and duress exculpate under a different theory. The defendant has admittedly acted improperly—has caused a net societal harm or evil—but the defendant is excused because he or she cannot properly be held responsible for his or her offense conduct. Note the difference in focus between justifications and excuses: a defendant's conduct is justified, a defendant is excused. Excuses are of two sorts: *disability excuses*, which include insanity, involuntary intoxication, duress, and immaturity (the defense for involuntary conduct also serves this purpose), and *mistake excuses*, which include mistake about a justification, reliance on an official misstatement of law, and unreliable law.[36]

6. Nonexculpatory Defenses

A final group of general defenses does not exculpate a person but does provide an exemption from liability. Even if the person's conduct is criminal and unjustified and the person is fully responsible for it, such *nonexculpatory defenses* are made available because each furthers important societal interests. Thus diplomatic immunity may provide a defense, without regard to the guilt or innocence of the person, because by doing so a country's diplomats are protected from interference when abroad, and diplomatic communications among nations can be established and maintained. Other common nonexculpatory defenses in American codes include statutes of time limitation; judicial, legislative, and executive immunities; and immunity after compelled testimony or pursuant to a plea agreement.[37] Further, many constitutional principles function as nonexculpatory defenses, such as the double-jeopardy clause and the exclusionary rule,[38] as well as the legality principle doctrines discussed earlier.

B. Justification Defenses

1. Lesser-Evils Defense

The lesser-evils defense—sometimes called *choice of evils* or *necessity*, or simply the *general justification defense*—is formally recognized in about half of American jurisdictions.[39] It illustrates the structure and operation of justification defenses generally by relying explicitly on the rationale inherent in all justifications: although the person may have caused the harm or evil of an offense, the justifying circumstances suggest that his or her conduct avoided a greater harm or evil than it caused. In the language of the Model Penal Code, a person's conduct is justified if it is "necessary to avoid a harm or evil to himself or to another . . . provided that: the harm or evil sought to be avoided by such conduct is greater than that sought to be prevented by the law defining the offense charged."[40]

The triggering of a lesser-evils defense, like that of all other justifications, does not give a person unlimited authority. His or her response must be both necessary and proportionate. The necessity requirement has two components: the conduct must be necessary in time and in the amount of harm caused. The lesser-evils defense, like all other justifications, requires proportionality between the harm or evil caused by the person's conduct and the harm or evil avoided. Indeed, the defense contains a more explicit statement than does any other justification. While most other justifications require proportionality through a general requirement that the person's conduct be "reasonable," the lesser-evils requirement might be seen as being more demanding. It is not enough for the defense that the harmfulness of the person's conduct is generally proportionate to the harm threatened. The person's conduct must be shown to have been less harmful than the harm threatened.

2. Defensive-Force Justification

Defensive-force justifications are triggered when an aggressor unjustifiably threatens harm. The triggering conditions for defensive force are considerably more specific than those of the lesser-evils defense; defensive force requires an unlawful, aggressive use or threat of force. That the person against whom the defendant uses force is acting unlawfully is not sufficient to trigger a defensive-force justification. Smoking on a bus or refusing to get out of the way of an emergency vehicle may be unlawful conduct that justifies the use of force against the violator, but a justification defense other than defensive force must be relied on. For defensive force, active physical aggression is required. In order to trigger a defensive-force justification, the aggressor must unjustifiably threaten harm to the defendant. Thus, when a police officer uses justified force to effect an arrest, the arrestee has no right of self-defense, and others may not lawfully use defensive force on his or her behalf. Similarly, where a person unjustifiably attacks another and his or her victim then uses justified defensive force to repel the attacker, the initial aggressor has no right of self-defense against the justified defensive response. On the other hand, where the intended victim uses unnecessary or disproportionate force in response, the initial aggressor gains a right to use defensive force.

3. Public Authority Justifications

Public authority justifications are available when a person has been specifically authorized to engage in conduct otherwise constituting an offense that is necessary to protect or further a societal interest. Unlike defensive-force justifications, the person's authority is not limited to defensive action. He or she may act affirmatively to further a public interest, even one that is entirely intangible. These justification defenses most commonly are distinguished from one another according to the specific interests they foster: different defenses authorize the use of force for law-enforcement purposes, medical purposes, military purposes, judicial purposes, to maintain order and safety on public carriers or in other public places of assembly, or for use by parents or guardians. A catchall public authority justification commonly provides a defense for performing public duties other than those for which a special defense is provided.

The common structure of public authority justifications is thus that special authorization and evoking conditions trigger a person's right to use necessary and proportional force. The authorization and evocation elements as triggering conditions act together to describe the factors and circumstances that will give rise to an authority to act. For example, a police officer and a bus driver are both given authorizations to act, but in different situations and with different limitations on their use of force. The necessity and proportionality requirements—the response elements—describe the nature of the conduct that is justified once the authority to act is triggered.

C. Excuse Defenses

The common rationale of excuse defenses—to exculpate the blameless—gives rise to common requirements: a disability or reasonable mistake must cause an excusing condition. The disability and mistake excuses generate the same conclusion of blamelessness in different ways. In disability excuses, the disabling abnormality, such as insanity or involuntary intoxication, sets the person apart from the general population. The mistake excuses seem to do the opposite: they argue that the person should not be punished because in fact he or she has made a mistake that anyone else would have made in the same situation. That is, the person's mistake was reasonable; any reasonable person would have made the same mistake.

1. Mistake Excuses

Several types of mistakes are commonly allowed as grounds for a general excuse defense (as distinguished from mistakes that provide an absent-element defense by negating an element of the offense). Reliance on an official misstatement of law and mistake due to the unavailability of a law are two such general mistake excuses. A mistake about whether one's conduct is justified also is commonly recognized as an excuse. (A fourth commonly recognized mistake excuse is reliance on unlawful military orders, essentially a special subclass of a mistake about a justification excuse, where the justification is the public authority of lawful military orders.)[41]

2. Exceptions to "Ignorance of Law Is No Excuse"

The common law adhered to the maxim that "ignorance or mistake of law is no excuse," but states following the lead of the Model Penal Code recognize two exceptions to it. A general defense is commonly available to a person whose ignorance or mistake of law results because the law violated was not made reasonably available or because the person reasonably relied on an official misstatement of the law. In a few jurisdictions the maxim is simply rejected, and a general excuse is given for a reasonable mistake of law.[42]

3. Mistake with Regard to Justification

Every jurisdiction recognizes a defense for some form of mistake with regard to a justification. The often-unpredictable and confrontational nature of justifying circumstances makes such mistakes particularly understandable. This is especially true for defensive-force justifications, where the person must make the decision to act under an impending threat of harm. Most jurisdictions provide the mistake defense by including the word *believes* or the phrase *reasonably believes* in the definition of the justification defense (or by giving a defense if the person acts with a proper justifying "purpose").[43] This means that a person will get the defense if he or she believes that the conduct is justified, even if it is not. A popular alternative means of providing an excuse for mistake with regard to a justification—and one with some advantages—is to define justifications objectively, without the "believes" language, and to provide a separate general excuse defense for mistakes with regard to a justification.

4. Disability Excuses

Similarly, disability excuses share a common internal structure: a disability causes a recognized excusing condition. The disability is an abnormal condition of the person at the time of the offense, such as insanity, intoxication, subnormality, or immaturity. Each is a real-world condition with a variety of observable manifestations apart from the conduct constituting the offense. It may be a long-term or even permanent condition, such as subnormality, or a temporary state, such as intoxication, somnambulism, automatism, or hypnotism. Its cause may be internal, as in insanity, or external, as in coercion from another person (duress).

Having a recognized disability does not itself qualify a person for an excuse, for it is not the disability that is central to the reason for exculpating the person. A person is not excused because he or she is intoxicated, but rather because the effect of the intoxication is to create a condition that renders the person blameless for the conduct constituting the offense. The requirement of an excusing condition, then, is not an element independent of the person's disability but rather is a requirement that the person's disability cause a particular result—a particular exculpating mental or emotional condition in relation to the conduct constituting the offense.

5. Mental Disease or Defect as Disability

The disability requirement of the insanity defense is a mental disease or defect. What constitutes a mental disease or defect is a question for the jury. It is a legal concept, not a medical one,[44] but the members of the jury will no doubt be influenced by the expert witnesses they hear.

i. M'Naghten Test

In *M'Naghten's Case* the House of Lords held that a person has a defense of insanity if, "at the time of committing the act, the party accused was laboring under such a defect of reason, from disease of the mind, as *not to know the nature and quality of the act he was doing, or, if he did know it, [he] did not know he was doing what was wrong.*"[45] This test is in use in many American jurisdictions today.[46]

ii. Irresistible-Impulse Test

As early as 1887 the *M'Naghten* test was criticized as failing to reflect then-modern advances in the behavioral sciences. To permit a defense in cases where the person involved suffers a loss of the power to choose, a "control prong" was introduced by adding the *irresistible-impulse* test to *M'Naghten*. Under this modification, a person is given an insanity defense if he or she satisfies the requirements of the *M'Naghten* defense or (1) if, by reason of the duress of such mental disease, he or she had so far lost the power to choose between right and wrong, and to avoid doing the act in question, that his or her free agency was at the time destroyed; (2) and if, at the same time, the alleged crime was so connected with such mental disease, in the relation of cause and effect, as to have been the product of it *solely*.[47] This formulation remains popular in the United States as an addition to the *M'Naghten test*.[48]

iii. American Law Institute Test

The most modern test is that contained in the American Law Institute's Model Penal Code § 4.01(1): "A person is not responsible for criminal conduct if at the time of such conduct as a result of mental disease or defect he *lacks substantial capacity either to appreciate the criminality [wrongfulness] of his conduct or to conform his conduct to the requirements of law*" (emphasis added). This formulation conceives that there are degrees of impairment possible and requires as a minimum that the person must "lack substantial capacity." The ALI test follows the structure of the *M'Naghten*-plus-irresistible-impulse test in specifically noting that the dysfunction may affect either cognitive or control capacities. It differs from *M'Naghten*-plus-irresistible-impulse, however, in that those tests appear to require absolute dysfunction: the absence of knowledge of criminality or the loss of power to choose. The ALI test, in contrast, requires only that the person lack "substantial capacity" to "appreciate" the criminality or to conform his or her conduct to the requirements of the law. The test has gained wide acceptance,[49] rivaling or surpassing the popularity of the *M'Naghten* and *M'Naghten*-plus-irresistible-impulse formulations.

iv. Federal Insanity Test

Some jurisdictions that previously adopted the ALI test have recently cut back on it. The new federal insanity statute, for example, uses the "appreciates" language of the ALI, rather than the *M'Naghten* "know" language and thereby implies that there are degrees of cognitive dysfunction short of complete loss that nonetheless may exculpate. On the other hand, the new federal statute drops the "lacks substantial capacity" language, which makes it closer to the apparently absolute requirement of *M'Naghten*. Most important, the federal formulation drops the control prong of the defense; it reverts to the single cognitive prong of *M'Naghten*, adopting a position that was criticized more than 100 years ago.[50]

6. Involuntary Intoxication

The involuntary intoxication excuse has a disability of intoxication and the same excusing conditions as the insanity defense—a cognitive or a control dysfunction. That is, a person's involuntary intoxication provides an excuse if it causes the same level of dysfunction required by the jurisdiction's insanity defense (*M'Naghten* test, *M'Naghten*-plus-irresistible-impulse test, or ALI test, for example). Voluntary intoxication, even when severe enough to cause an excusing condition, will not provide an excuse defense.[51]

7. Duress

The duress defense typically requires that the person committed the offense while under coercion to do so. The defense does not require, however, that the coercion cause in the person a "substantial lack of capacity to conform his conduct to the requirements of law" or another similar description of the degree of control impairment that the excusing conditions for insanity or involuntary intoxication require. Instead, the duress defense requires that the person's disability, which is in this case the state of coercion, come from a particular cause: a threat of force that "a person of reasonable firmness ... would have been unable to resist."[52] The Model Penal Code's duress formulation permits a court to take account of a person's individual circumstances and characteristics by allowing a partial individualization of the reasonable-person standard. The seriousness of the threat is to be assessed against the kind of threat that would coerce "a person of reasonable firmness *in [the actor's] situation*" (emphasis added).

D. Nonexculpatory Defenses

Nonexculpatory defenses, which give a defense even though the person's conduct may be wrongful and the person blameworthy, include such defenses as statutes of time limitation; diplomatic immunity; judicial, legislative, and executive immunities; immunity after compelled testimony or pursuant to a plea agreement; and incompetency to stand trial. Each of these forms of immunity furthers an important societal interest. Overriding nonexculpatory public policy interests also serve as the basis for many constitutional defenses. The double-jeopardy clause of the Fifth Amendment, for example, may foreclose the trial of even a blameworthy and convictable offender by barring the state from making repeated attempts to convict him or her. Notions of procedural fairness are said to demand that the state not subject a person to the embarrassment, expense, and ordeal of trial more than once for the same offense, nor compel him or her to live in a continuing state of anxiety and insecurity. Dismissals based on the operation of the exclusionary rule or on prosecutorial misconduct also may be nonexculpatory in nature, especially if the dismissals are unrelated to the reliability of the evidence in the fact-finding process. The public policies served by nonexculpatory defenses may be as broad as protecting all members of society from unlawful searches, or they may narrowly focus on assuring fairness in the treatment of individual defendants.

The nonexculpatory entrapment defense furthers societal interest in deterring police misconduct. Where a police officer or agent has had some hand in having a person commit an offense, the person may be entitled to an entrapment defense.[53] The United States is one of the few countries that recognize such a defense, and within the United States, jurisdictions disagree over how the defense should be formulated. "Objective" formulations of the entrapment defense focus on the impropriety of the police conduct. The defense is available, even if the person was predisposed to commit the offense, if the police conduct is such that it "creates a substantial risk that such an offense will be committed by persons other than those who are ready to commit it."[54] "Subjective" formulations of the entrapment defense focus on the degree to which the entrapping conduct, rather than the person's own choice, is responsible for commission of the offense. Under this formulation, the defense is given "because the wrongdoing of the officer originates the idea of the crime and then induces the other person to [commit the offense] when the other person is not otherwise disposed to do so."[55]

The objective formulation is clearly nonexculpatory: it uses the threat of acquittal of the defendant as a means of deterring improper police conduct. The blameworthiness of the defendant is not relevant. A subjective formulation, in contrast, might appear to be an excuse similar to duress that exculpates the defendant because he or she is coerced to commit an offense. However, the subjective formulation does not require that the inducement to commit the offense be one that a "person of reasonable firmness would have been unable to resist," as the duress excuse does. Instead, it gives the defense even if we could well have expected the defendant to have resisted the temptation. The subjective formulation is a nonexculpatory defense like the objective formulation, but one that seeks to exclude career criminals from the defense in order to limit the costs it accrues in trying to deter overreaching on the part of police.

VI. SPECIFIC OFFENSES

A. Overview

Most modern American codes are typically divided into two sections common in modern codes around the world. The general part sets out those doctrines that are applicable to all specific offenses, such as the definitions of culpability level, theories of imputation, inchoate offenses, and general defenses, as previously discussed. The special part enumerates the liability requirements for each specific offense. Most American codes follow the Model Penal Code's approach of grouping offenses by subpart and article according to the interest they concern:

Offenses Involving Danger to the Person
    Article 210. Criminal Homicide
    Article 211. Assault; Reckless Endangering; Threats

Article 212. Kidnapping and Related Offenses; Coercion

Article 213. Sexual Offenses

Offenses against Property

Article 220. Arson, Criminal Mischief, and Other Property Destruction

Article 221. Burglary and Other Criminal Intrusion

Article 222. Robbery

Article 223. Theft and Related Offenses

Article 224. Forgery and Fraudulent Practices

Offenses Against the Family

Article 230. Offenses against the Family

Offenses against Public Administration.

Article 240. Bribery and Corrupt Influence

Article 241. Perjury and Other Falsifications in Official Matters

Article 242. Obstructing Governmental Operations; Escape

Article 243. Abuse of Office

Offenses against Public Order and Decency

Article 250. Riot, Disorderly Conduct, and Related Offenses

Article 251. Public Indecency

The general rules for defining offenses have been discussed in sections IV.A and IV.B in this chapter. Details on a few of the more important offenses are given here.

B. Homicide

1. Murder

With some important exceptions, an intentional killing is murder. Model Penal Code section 210.1(1)(a) defines murder as "criminal homicide ... committed purposely or knowingly." Thus either causing the death must be the person's "conscious object" or he or she must be "practically certain" that his or her conduct will cause the death.[56] Although all objective elements of an offense need not have the same level of culpability, in this instance the "purposely or knowingly" requirement appears to apply both to causing the result (death) and to the requirement that the victim be a human being (and not just a fetus, for example). Thus it also must be shown that the person "believed or hoped" that the victim was a human being.[57]

2. Manslaughter and Negligent Homicide

The paradigm for murder is an intentional (knowing) killing; the paradigm for manslaughter is a reckless killing. The Model Penal Code provides that "criminal homicide constitutes manslaughter when it is committed recklessly,"[58] by which the Code means a killing for which the person is reckless about causing death and is reckless about the victim being a human being. Where a person is not aware of a substantial risk that a death will result from his or her conduct, but should have been aware of such a risk, he or she is negligent about causing the death and is liable for negligent homicide.

3. Mitigation for Extreme Emotional Disturbance

The Model Penal Code provides for a mitigation from murder to manslaughter where "murder is committed under the influence of extreme mental or emotional disturbance for which there is reasonable explanation or excuse. The reasonableness of such explanation or excuse shall be determined from the viewpoint of a person in the actor's situation under the circumstances as he believes them to be."[59] The mitigation has two components. First, the killing must have been committed under the influence of extreme mental or emotional disturbance. If most people would have experienced such a disturbance under the same circumstances, but the person in fact did not, he or she is not eligible for the mitigation. Second, if the person is acting under the influence of extreme mental or emotional disturbance, there must be a reasonable explanation or excuse for the disturbance. No mitigation is available if the person's reaction to the situation is unreasonable or peculiar to the person.

4. Aggravation for Extreme Indifference to the Value of Human Life

Although a reckless killing is normally manslaughter, homicide doctrine typically deviates from the paradigm to aggravate a reckless killing to murder in circumstances judged to be egregious. At common law, this doctrine of aggravation was called *depraved and malignant heart* or *abandoned and malignant heart* murder. The Model Penal Code carries forward the common law's recognition of a reckless form of murder but bases the aggravation on the person's "extreme indifference to the value of human life."[60] The Code allows a killing in the course of certain enumerated felonies to trigger a presumption of the recklessness and extreme indifference required for this aggravation. It offers this as a substitute for a felony-murder rule, which it does not otherwise recognize.

5. Felony Murder

Most American jurisdictions adopt a felony-murder rule, although there are many varieties of the rule in operation. The traditional felony-murder rule has two components. First, it imposes liability for murder for any killing, even one that is entirely accidental, that occurs in the course of an attempt of, commission of, or flight from a felony. Second, the traditional rule holds accomplices in the original felony accomplices in the murder. Nearly every jurisdiction limits the felony-murder rule in one or more of the following ways: the killing frequently must be a "probable consequence of the unlawful act"; the underlying felony must be a *malum in se* offense (an offense that is inherently wrong or evil, as opposed to an offense that is wrong only because it is prohibited); or the underlying offense must be inherently dangerous.

C. Sex Offenses

Rape and related sexual offenses have engendered some of the greatest controversy in the definition of specific offenses. This has occurred in part because of changing views of women and toward women, changing social mores concerning sexual relations among consenting adults generally, and increased awareness of the harm of unwanted intrusions on personal bodily autonomy.

Traditional sexual offense statutes are concerned with intercourse induced by force or threat of force. Current statutes tend to go further and criminalize many lesser forms of conduct, often including any unconsented-to intercourse. In this area the Model Penal

Code's liability requirements for sexual offenses are often viewed as outdated. First, the Code's continuation of the common law's spousal exception is commonly dropped in modern American statutes. Second, in both its rape and statutory rape offenses the Model Penal Code follows the common-law rule of limiting liability to males who victimize females. Current statutes, in contrast, are commonly gender neutral. Statutory rape provisions have also been expanded in most states. States commonly apply a two-level approach to this offense: sexual intercourse with a very young girl remains punishable at the level of rape; intercourse with a girl over a certain age but under another age (especially if the male is older than the female by a specified number of years) is a felony of a lesser degree.

Another shift from traditional to modern sexual offense statutes is the advent of rape shield statutes. Defendants traditionally sought to present evidence regarding the alleged victim's sexual history and character. However, almost every state now denies a defendant the opportunity to cross-examine the alleged victim without good cause and prevents the introduction of evidence regarding the alleged victim's prior sexual activity.

D. Theft Offenses

The recent trend in modern code development has been to consolidate traditional common-law theft offenses, such as larceny, embezzlement, and false pretenses, into a single theft offense. The differences between the offenses were relatively insignificant because there was no meaningful difference between the offenses in terms of the culpability of the defendants, their dangerousness, or the seriousness of the harm caused. The Model Penal Code creates a single theft offense that can be committed in a variety of ways, such as theft by unlawful taking or disposition, theft by deception, theft by extortion, and theft of property lost, mislaid, or delivered by mistake.[61] The consolidation avoids problems of pleading and proof by allowing the prosecutor simply to allege that the defendant stole and to support this at trial with evidence of any form of theft.

SELECTED BIBLIOGRAPHY

Dressler, Joshua. *Understanding Criminal Law*. 5th ed. Newark, NJ: LexisNexis, 2009.
LaFave, Wayne R. *Criminal Law*. 5th ed. St. Paul, MN: West, 2010.
Model Penal Code and Commentaries (Official Draft and Revised Comments). Philadelphia, PA: American Law Institute, 1980, 1985.
Robinson, Paul H. *Criminal Law*. New York: Aspen Publishers, 1997 (2d ed. forthcoming 2011)
Robinson, Paul H. *Structure and Function of Criminal Law*. Oxford: Oxford University Press, 1997.

NOTES

1. William Blackstone, *Commentaries on the Laws of England*, vol. 4 (Boston: Beacon Press, 1962).
2. *Model Penal Code Proposed Official Draft* was published by the American Law

Institute in 1962. *Model Penal Code Official Draft & Explanatory Notes* was published by the American Law Institute in 1985.

3. *Shaw v. Director of Public Prosecutions*, [1962] A.C. 220 (H.L.).

4. *Rose v. Locke*, 423 U.S. 48, 50 (1975) (statutory phrase "crime against nature" gave adequate notice that forced cunnilingus was prohibited).

5. *Rewis v. United States*, 401 U.S. 808, 812 (1971).

6. U.S. Const. art. I, § 9, cl. 3 ("No bill of attainder or *ex post facto* law shall be passed"); U.S. Const. art I, § 10, cl. 1 ("No State shall . . . pass any bill of attainder, *ex post facto* law").

7. *Calder v. Bull*, 3 U.S. (3 Dall.) 386, 390 (1798) (emphasis omitted).

8. *Papachristou v. City of Jacksonville*, 405 U.S. 156, 162 (1972).

9. Model Penal Code §§ 211.2, 213.5, 241.3(1)(b) (Official Draft 1962).

10. *See, e.g.*, N.J. Stat. Ann. § 2C:2-3 (West 2009).

11. Model Penal Code § 2.02(1) (Official Draft 1962).

12. *Ibid.* § 2.02(2)(a)(i).

13. *See, e.g., ibid.* § 213.5 (requiring "purpose of arousing or gratifying sexual desire").

14. *Ibid.* § 2.02(2)(b)(ii).

15. *Ibid.* § 2.02(2)(c).

16. *Ibid.* § 2.02(2)(d).

17. *Ibid.* Parallel language appears in the definition of recklessness in § 2.02(2)(c). In that context, however, the language concerns whether a "law-abiding" person would have consciously disregarded the risk that the defendant disregarded.

18. *See* Model Penal Code § 2.02 cmt. 1 at 229 (Official Draft and Revised Comments 1985).

19. Tenn. Code Ann. § 39-3-202 (1982).

20. *See, e.g.*, Model Penal Code § 2.06(2)(a) (Official Draft 1962).

21. *See, e.g., ibid.* § 2.06(3).

22. *See, e.g., ibid.* § 2.08(2).

23. *See ibid.* § 2.07(1)(b).

24. *State v. Christy Pontiac-GMC, Inc.*, 354 N.W.2d 17, 18–20 (Minn. 1984).

25. Model Penal Code § 2.07(1)(c) (Official Draft 1962).

26. *See ibid.* § 2.07(5).

27. *Ibid.* § 5.01(1)(c).

28. *See, e.g., ibid.* § 5.01(1).

29. *See, e.g., ibid.* § 5.03(1).

30. *See, e.g., ibid.* § 5.02(1).

31. *Ibid.* § 5.02(2).

32. *See, e.g., ibid.* § 2.04(1).

33. *See, e.g., ibid.* § 5.01(4).

34. *See, e.g., ibid.* § 2.11(2).

35. *See, e.g., ibid.* §§ 3.01–3.11.

36. *See, e.g., ibid.* §§ 2.04; 2.08; 2.09; 3.09; 4.01–4.10.

37. *See, e.g., ibid.* §§ 2.13; 4.04.

38. *See, e.g., ibid.* §§ 1.08–1.10.

39. *See* Paul H. Robinson, *Criminal Law Defenses*, vol. 2 (St. Paul, MN: West, 1984), § 124(a).

40. Model Penal Code § 3.02(1)(a) (Official Draft 1962).

41. The excuse and the justification of lawful military orders commonly are treated together under "defense of military orders." *See, e.g., ibid.* § 2.10.

42. *See, e.g.,* N.J. Stat. Ann. § 2C:2-4(c)(3) (West 2009).

43. The "purpose" formulation is most common in justifications for persons with special responsibilities.

44. For an interesting discussion of the legal concept of "mental disease or defect," *see State v. Guido*, 191 A.2d 45 (N.J. 1963).

45. *M'Naghten's Case*, (1843) 8 Eng. Rep. 718, 722 (H.L.) (appeal taken from Eng.) (emphasis added).

46. *See* authorities collected at Robinson, *Criminal Law Defenses*, § 173(a) n. 1.

47. *Parsons v. State*, 2 So. 854, 866–867 (Ala. 1887) (emphasis in original).

48. *See* authorities collected at Robinson, *Criminal Law Defenses*, § 173(a) n. 2.

49. *See ibid.*

50. *See, e.g., Parsons*, 2 So. 854.

51. *See, e.g.,* Model Penal Code § 2.08(4), (5) (Official Draft 1962) (requiring both involuntary intoxication and resulting dysfunction similar to insanity).

52. *See, e.g., ibid.* § 2.09(1).

53. *See* authorities collected at Robinson, *Criminal Law Defenses*, § 209 n. 1.

54. Model Penal Code § 2.13(1)(b) (Official Draft 1962). An officer also entraps if he or she "[makes] knowingly false representations designed to induce the belief that such conduct is not prohibited." *Ibid.* § 2.13(1)(a).

55. Del. Code Ann. tit. 11, § 432 (2009).

56. *See* Model Penal Code § 2.02 (2)(a)(i) & (b)(ii) (Official Draft 1962) (defining purposely and knowingly as to a result).

57. *See ibid.* § 2.02(2)(a)(ii) & (b)(i) (defining purposely and knowing as to a circumstance).

58. *Ibid.* § 210.3(1)(a).

59. *Ibid.* § 210.3(1)(b).

60. *Ibid.* § 210.2(1)(b).

61. *See, e.g.,* Model Penal Code art. 223 (Official Draft 1962).

THE ROME STATUTE OF THE INTERNATIONAL CRIMINAL COURT

Kevin Jon Heller

I. Introduction
   A. Historical Sketch
   B. Jurisdiction
   C. Legality Principle
   D. Sources of Criminal Law
   E. Process

II. General Part
   A. Theories of Punishment
   B. Liability Requirements
   C. Defenses
   D. Sanctions

III. Special Part
   A. Structure
   B. Genocide
   C. Crimes against Humanity
   D. War Crimes
   E. Aggression

I. INTRODUCTION

A. Historical Sketch

The Rome Statute of the International Criminal Court (ICC, also the Court) entered into force on 1 July 2002, less than four years after 120 countries voted in favor of its adoption.[1]

Kevin Jon Heller is a Senior Lecturer at Melbourne Law School. His recent publications include "The Cognitive Psychology of Mens Rea," 99 *Journal of Criminal Law and Criminology* 317 (2009), and "Mistake of Legal Element, the Common Law, and Article 32 of the Rome Statute: A Critical Analysis," 6 *Journal of International Criminal Justice* 419 (2008).

The Statute has been described as a "major step forward for substantive international criminal law,"[2] and with good reason: unlike the minimalist statutes of earlier international courts, such as the Nuremberg Tribunal and the International Criminal Tribunals for the former Yugoslavia and Rwanda, the Rome Statute provides detailed definitions of the core international crimes, the possible modes of participation in those crimes, and the permissible grounds for excluding criminal responsibility. The Statute thus represents the international community's most ambitious attempt to create a special and general part of international criminal law.

Although one of the founders of the International Committee for the Red Cross proposed creating a permanent international court as early as 1872, the international community did not take the idea seriously until the end of World War I. In 1920, following aborted calls to create temporary international courts to prosecute those responsible for committing war crimes during the war—including Kaiser Wilhelm II himself—the Advisory Committee of Jurists that was appointed by the League of Nations to create the Permanent International Court of Justice proposed establishing a "High Court of International Justice" that would "be competent to try crimes constituting a breach of international public order or against the universal law of nations."[3] That court never materialized, but the interest in international criminal justice it generated ultimately led the League of Nations to adopt the Convention pour la Création d'une Cour Pénale Internationale in 1937. Unfortunately, although thirteen states signed the Convention, it never went into effect.[4]

The international community renewed its efforts to create a permanent international court after the International Military Tribunal at Nuremberg (IMT) convicted nineteen high-ranking Nazis of various war crimes, crimes against humanity, and crimes against peace (now known as crimes of aggression). In 1947 the United Nations General Assembly asked the International Law Commission (ILC) to draft a Code of Offenses against the Peace and Security of Mankind based on the Nuremberg Charter.[5] The following year the General Assembly adopted the Convention for Prevention and Punishment of the Crime of Genocide, which established genocide as an independent international crime—the IMT had considered it a crime against humanity—and requested that the ILC study the desirability and feasibility of creating the "international penal tribunal" contemplated by article VI of the Convention.[6]

The ILC made substantial progress on the two projects over the next few years. In 1951, following a favorable report by the ILC, a General Assembly subcommittee submitted a Draft Statute for an International Criminal Court.[7] A second draft of the Statute was submitted to the General Assembly in 1953, in response to comments by member states. The ILC also submitted a Draft Code of Offenses that year.[8] The General Assembly quickly suspended work on both the Draft Statute and the Draft Code, however, because of concerns about how to define the crime of aggression.[9]

The General Assembly finally adopted a definition of aggression in 1974,[10] and in 1981 the ILC resumed work on the Draft Code of Offenses.[11] Nevertheless, the General Assembly did not ask the ILC to resume work on the Draft Statute until 1989, when Trinidad and Tobago suggested creating a specialized international court to deal with drug trafficking.[12] The ILC submitted a final version of the Draft Statute in 1994; in addition to dealing with various organizational and procedural matters, the Statute gave the contemplated court jurisdiction over "treaty crimes" like drug trafficking and terrorism, as well as over the so-called core crimes of international criminal law: war crimes, crimes against humanity, genocide, and aggression.[13]

Despite the completion of the Draft Statute, many states were not yet ready to conclude a treaty creating a permanent international criminal court. The General Assembly thus convened an Ad Hoc Committee to further the ILC's work.[14] In 1995 the Committee submitted its report, which contained both procedural and substantive provisions, thereby putting an end to the ILC's fifty-year tradition of dividing the two into a Draft Statute and a Draft Code.[15] That report led the General Assembly to create a Preparatory Committee on the Establishment of an International Criminal Court, which produced, after a number of revisions, a final Draft ICC Statute in 1998.[16] In addition to coming from very different legal systems, the majority of the delegates at PrepCom, as it is known, were diplomats "who lacked expertise in international criminal law, comparative criminal law, or comparative criminal procedure." Indeed, most of the delegates "had no criminal practical experience of any kind."[17]

The Draft ICC Statute, which contained 116 different articles, 1,400 bracketed additions, and nearly 200 options,[18] served as the basis for the five-week Diplomatic Conference that was held in Rome in 1998. More than 160 states participated in the Conference. The final provisions of the Rome Statute were adopted "by general agreement"; votes on the different proposals were not taken. Procedural issues proved the most difficult to resolve, particularly concerning the relationship between the Security Council and the Court, the scope of the Court's jurisdiction over nationals of nonparty states, and whether the Prosecutor would be able to initiate investigations *proprio motu*—in the absence of a state or Security Council referral.[19] Substantive issues, by contrast, proved relatively uncontroversial, especially once the Diplomatic Conference agreed to exclude treaty crimes from the Court's jurisdiction. The one exception was the crime of aggression: like the ILC before it, the Conference was unable to agree on a definition of the crime. States thus compromised, including aggression within the Court's jurisdiction but conditioning that jurisdiction on the Assembly of States Parties eventually adopting a workable definition.[20]

On 17 July 1998 the Diplomatic Conference met to approve the Rome Statute. One hundred twenty states voted in favor of the Statute, 21 states abstained, and 7 states voted against: the United States, Israel, Iraq, China, India, Vietnam, and Qatar.[21] The Rome Statute then entered into force on 1 July 2002, a few months after it received its required 60th ratification.[22] As of this writing, 111 states are members of the ICC: 30 from Africa, 25 from the Americas, 14 from Asia and the Pacific Islands, 41 from Europe and Central Asia, and 1 from the Middle East.

B. Jurisdiction

1. Subject-Matter Jurisdiction

The ICC has subject-matter jurisdiction over four crimes: genocide, crimes against humanity, war crimes, and aggression.[23] The Rome Statute variously describes these crimes as "the most serious crimes of concern to the international community as a whole," "unimaginable atrocities that deeply shock the conscience of humanity," and "international crimes." The last, most prosaic, expression is the most accurate because it foregrounds the fact that the four crimes entail individual criminal responsibility under international law itself; their status under domestic criminal law is irrelevant.[24] As the IMT said in rejecting the argument that international law only binds states, "[C]rimes against international law are committed by men, not abstract entities, and only by punishing individuals who commit such crimes can the provisions of international law be enforced.... [I]ndividuals have international duties which transcend the national obligations of obedience imposed by the individual state."[25]

As reflected in the ILC's 1994 Draft Statute, many states advocated including treaty crimes in the ICC's jurisdiction, particularly terrorism and drug trafficking. The Diplomatic Conference ultimately rejected proposals to that effect, with some states believing that treaty crimes were less serious than the so-called core crimes and others insisting that their inclusion in the Rome Statute would interfere with existing international and transnational suppression efforts.[26]

2. Temporal Jurisdiction

The ICC's temporal jurisdiction is purely prospective: it can only prosecute crimes committed after 1 July 2002, the date the Rome Statute entered into force.[27] If a state ratifies the Rome Statute after that date, the ICC has jurisdiction over crimes committed by its nationals or on its territory (see section I.B.3) only after the Statute enters into force for that state, although the state can file a declaration with the Court accepting jurisdiction retroactive to 1 July 2002.[28]

The ICC's inability to exercise retroactive jurisdiction has been widely criticized. "The answer to this objection is entirely pragmatic. Few States—even those who were the Court's most fervent advocates—would have been prepared to recognize a court with such an ambit."[29]

3. Personal and Territorial Jurisdiction

The ICC has personal jurisdiction over nationals of states parties who are accused of committing crimes within the subject-matter jurisdiction of the Court, regardless of where those crimes are committed.[30] The Court can also prosecute nationals of nonparty states in two situations: where the nonparty state accepts the jurisdiction of the Court on an ad hoc basis,[31] and where the Security Council refers a situation to the Court under chapter VII of the United Nations Charter.[32] Personal jurisdiction was the least controversial form of jurisdiction during the Diplomatic Conference, although there was substantial debate concerning article 26 of the Rome Statute, which excludes perpetrators who were under eighteen at the time of the offense from the Court's jurisdiction.[33]

Similar principles apply to the Court's territorial jurisdiction. The Court has jurisdiction over any crime that is committed on the territory of a state party, regardless of the nationality of the perpetrator(s).[34] It also has territorial jurisdiction over crimes committed on the territory of a nonstate party that either accepts the Court's jurisdiction on an ad hoc basis[35] or is the subject of a Security Council referral under chapter VII.[36]

It is worth noting that many states wanted to give the Court universal jurisdiction over the four core crimes, allowing it to prosecute any international crime regardless of whether it was committed on the territory of or by a national of a state party.[37] Proposals to that effect were ultimately rejected, however, largely because it was felt that universal jurisdiction would discourage too many states from ratifying the Statute.[38]

C. Legality Principle

The Rome Statute provides for both aspects of the principle of legality: *nullum crimen sine lege* and *nulla poena sine lege*. At least in theory, each principle is strictly guaranteed in all four of the forms commonly discussed in the civilian tradition: *lex scripta*, *lex certa*, *lex stricta*, and *lex praevia*.[39]

The *nullum crimen sine lege* principle is contained in articles 22 and 24. Article 22(1) provides that "[a] person shall not be criminally responsible under this Statute unless the conduct in question constitutes, at the time it takes place, a crime within the jurisdiction of the Court"—*lex scripta*. Agreement on the importance of *lex scripta* explains the detailed definitions of crimes in article 5: the drafters did not believe that the ILC's 1994 Draft Statute, which enumerated but did not define the crimes within the jurisdiction of the court, satisfied the principle.[40] Article 22(2) guarantees *lex certa* and *lex stricta*, as well as their corollary, the principle of lenity: "The definition of a crime shall be strictly construed and shall not be extended by analogy. In case of ambiguity, the definition shall be interpreted in favour of the person being investigated, prosecuted or convicted." Finally, article 24(1) guarantees *lex praevia*, providing that "[n]o person shall be criminally responsible under this Statute for conduct prior to the entry into force of the Statute."

Nulla poena sine lege is the subject of article 23, which provides that "[a] person convicted by the Court may be punished only in accordance with this Statute." Article 77, in turn, states that the Court may impose a maximum sentence of thirty years' imprisonment unless the "extreme gravity of the crime and the individual circumstances of the convicted person" justify a life sentence. Read together, articles 23 and 77 only partially comply with the strict legality approach to the *nulla poena* principle found in most national legal systems: although the articles satisfy *lex scripta* and *lex praevia*, they "certainly do not comply with the standards of certainty and strictness of penalties common to national criminal law, since they do not specify distinct sanctions depending on the offenses within the jurisdiction of the Court."[41] That said, international criminal law has traditionally adopted a much more liberal interpretation of *nulla poena* that requires only a general norm for penalties.[42] The Rome Statute's sentencing provisions more than satisfy that requirement.

D. Sources of Criminal Law

Because the Rome Statute is a multilateral treaty, its ultimate source of authority is the consent of the states parties themselves. By ratifying the Statute, those states have agreed to permit the Court to apply the Rome Statute's substantive and procedural provisions to criminal acts committed by their nationals and on their territory.[43]

Article 21 governs the specific legal sources that the Court applies—the first codification of the sources of international criminal law.[44] The article divides those sources into three tiers, which must be applied hierarchically: (1) the Rome Statute itself, along with the Elements of Crimes and the Rules of Procedure and Evidence; (2) applicable treaties and the principles and rules of international law; and (3) general principles of law derived from the world's legal systems.

1. Statute, Elements, Rules

"In the first place," the Court shall apply the provisions of the Rome Statute, the Elements of Crimes, and the Rules of Procedure and Evidence.[45] Article 21 does not rank the three primary sources, but article 9(3) provides that "[t]he Elements of Crimes ... shall be consistent with the Statute," and article 51(5) states that "[i]n the event of conflict between the Statute and the Rules of Procedure and Evidence, the Statute shall prevail."

The Elements of Crimes were drafted after the adoption of the Rome Statute and were approved in 2000 by the Assembly of States Parties—the Court's "legislature," in which each state party has one vote. They specify with great precision the essential elements of every war crime, crime against humanity, and act of genocide within the jurisdiction of the Court; the drafting committee specifically decided not to define article 25's modes of participation in a crime or the Statute's grounds for excluding criminal responsibility.[46] The Elements are not binding on the Court, even if they are consistent with the Statute; instead, they "shall assist the Court" in interpreting the various crimes.[47] That language represents a compromise between the United States, which insisted that the *nullum crimen* principle required binding elements, and the substantial number of states that thought the Elements themselves were unnecessary.[48]

2. Treaties, Principles, and Rules

"In the second place, where appropriate," the Court may apply "applicable treaties and the principles and rules of international law, including the established principles of the international law of armed conflict."[49] The "where appropriate" language makes clear that reference to this second tier of sources is within the Court's discretion.

The scope of all three sources is difficult to determine, given article 21's thin drafting history. To begin with, it is unclear whether the category of "applicable treaties" is limited to treaties that are specifically referenced in the Rome Statute, such as the 1949 Geneva Conventions,[50] or also includes treaties that are not referenced but concern legal issues germane to the interpretation of the Statute, such as the International Covenant on Civil and Political Rights. The more restrictive interpretation is probably better, given that the drafters specifically rejected proposals that would have substituted "relevant" for "applicable."[51]

The "principles ... of international law" are even murkier. The Statute is silent concerning how those principles differ from the "general principles of law derived by the Court from national laws of the legal systems of the world," the third-tier source, discussed in section II.D.3. That silence has led one scholar to suggest that, in fact, the category is simply a "verbal tic" in the drafting that has no meaning.[52]

Finally, it is not clear whether the "rules of international law" refer to the rules of customary international law or to something else. Most scholars agree that, at a minimum, the category includes customary rules, which are international law's "oldest and original source."[53] That conclusion should not be accepted too uncritically, however, given that the drafters almost certainly omitted the word *custom* from article 21 for a reason—perhaps because "the concept of gradually evolving custom was considered too imprecise for the purposes of international *criminal* law."[54]

3. General Principles

If reference to sources in the second tier fails, the Court may apply the "general principles of law derived by the Court from national laws of the legal systems of the world, including, as appropriate, the national laws of the States that would normally exercise jurisdiction over the crime."[55] This provision, which is the most controversial aspect of article 21, reflects a compromise between two blocs of states: those that believed that interpretive questions should be resolved by reference to the applicable national law, and those that wanted to sever the connection between international criminal law and national law entirely.[56] Whether the compromise makes sense is debatable: "There is of course a certain contradiction between the idea of deriving general principles, which indicates that this process could take place before a certain case is adjudicated, and that of looking also to particular national laws of relevance to a certain case."[57] The Court itself will ultimately have to determine when it is "appropriate" to take the latter path.

Scholars disagree—and article 21 is of no help—concerning how widely accepted a legal principle must be to qualify as a "general principle of law." Some believe that a representative majority of the world's legal systems is enough; others insist that near unanimity is required.[58]

E. Process

1. Adversarial/Inquisitorial

The Court's procedural regime is a hybrid of the adversarial and inquisitorial traditions that finds no analogue either in so-called mixed adversarial/inquisitorial national systems or in previous international tribunals, such as the International Criminal Tribunal for the former Yugoslavia (ICTY) and the International Criminal Tribunal for Rwanda (ICTR). This was a conscious decision on the part of the Rome Statute's drafters; indeed, "their innovative spirit is reflected even in their use of terminology. Technical terms such as *indictment*, *juge d'instruction* (investigating judge), or *cross-examination* have been replaced by neutral terms . . . to avoid a language carrying too much baggage from one particular legal family."[59]

i. Investigation

The Court's hybrid procedural regime is particularly evident in the role the Pre-Trial Chamber plays during the investigative phase of a case. Following the adversarial tradition, the prosecution and defense are responsible for collecting evidence and preparing their cases; the Pre-Trial Chamber does not examine witnesses or request experts to prepare reports on important issues. Nevertheless, the Pre-Trial Chamber plays a much more inquisitorial role during the investigation than is typical in the adversarial tradition: the prosecution can initiate an investigation *proprio motu*—one not referred by a state party or the Security Council— only with the approval of the Pre-Trial Chamber;[60] the Pre-Trial Chamber may act on its own initiative to ensure that evidence essential for the defense will remain available at trial;[61] and all of the evidence reciprocally disclosed between the defense and the prosecution prior to trial must be communicated to the Pre-Trial Chamber for inclusion in a dossier.[62] Whether the Trial Chamber has access to that dossier, however, will have to be decided by the Court itself —one of many examples of the "constructive ambiguity" in the Statute and Rules necessitated by the difficulty of reconciling very different legal traditions.[63]

ii. Trial

The trial phase is also primarily adversarial: the prosecution and defense present their own evidence, call their own witnesses, and conduct their own cross-examinations.[64] That said, the adversarial nature of the trial is tempered by a number of more inquisitorial procedures: the Trial Chamber has "the authority to request the submission of all evidence that it considers necessary for the determination of the truth";[65] a defendant is entitled to make an unsworn statement to the court, even if he or she chooses not to testify;[66] and both the judges[67] and victims[68] can question witnesses, the former even before the parties have examined them. The trial phase also includes procedures that are uncommon in both adversarial and inquisitorial systems, such as rule 140 of the Rules of Procedure and Evidence, which permits the prosecution and defense to determine jointly "the order and manner in which the evidence shall be presented to the Trial Chamber."

iii. Evidence

Consistent with the international tribunals that preceded it, the Court applies the "free-proof" evidentiary regime that is normally found in inquisitorial systems.[69] According to rule 63 of the Rules of Procedure and Evidence, the Trial Chamber has the authority "to assess freely all evidence submitted in order to determine its relevance or admissibility." Both hearsay and character evidence are thus admissible, although the Rome Statute exhibits a strong aversion to the former, prohibiting the use of prerecorded witness statements at trial unless the opposing party previously had the opportunity to cross-examine the witness,[70] a limitation that is similar to U.S. Federal Rule of Evidence 804(b)(1).

iv. Appeal

The appellate phase is perhaps the most clearly inquisitorial aspect of the Court's procedural regime. In contrast to most adversarial systems, the prosecution is always permitted to appeal an acquittal.[71] Not surprisingly, this was a very contentious issue during the drafting of the Rome Statute.[72] The prosecution is also entitled to appeal a conviction or sentence on behalf of the defendant,[73] a right rarely found in adversarial systems.

2. Jury/Written Opinions

International criminal tribunals have never used juries, and the ICC is no exception. The Trial Chamber sits in panels of three judges;[74] although the Rome Statute encourages panels to reach unanimous decisions, two votes are sufficient to convict.[75] Regardless of outcome, the Trial Chamber is required to deliver a written decision that contains "a full and reasoned statement of [its] findings on the evidence and conclusions."[76] That decision must be based exclusively on the evidence presented at trial,[77] although the ICC's Regulations of the Court entitle the Trial Chamber to modify the legal characterization of facts—convicting a defendant charged with committing war crimes, for example, of crimes against humanity instead. That right is common in inquisitorial systems but generally foreign to adversarial ones.[78]

II. GENERAL PART

Part 3 of the Rome Statute, titled "General Principles of Criminal Law," has been described as an "unsystematic conglomeration from a variety of legal traditions."[79] That description has a superficial plausibility, because the drafters deliberately avoided tradition-specific terminology, particularly that of the common law: the Statute defines crimes in terms of required "material elements" and "mental elements," not in terms of *actus reus* and *mens rea*; and it provides "grounds for excluding criminal responsibility" instead of defenses. In general, however, it is clear that the Statute's "two-pronged concept of crime"[80] is patterned after the common law, not the civil law. First, "it does not distinguish between the subjective/mental element of the offense, in the sense of a *Tatvorsatz* (*dolus*) and the blameworthiness of the act belonging to a separate and autonomous (third) level of culpability (*Schuld*)."[81] Second, the system "does not distinguish between wrongfulness/justification and culpability/excuse as the two- or three-fold structure of an offense as applied in the Germanic systems."[82]

A. Theories of Punishment

The Preamble to the Rome Statute affirms that "the most serious crimes of concern to the community must not go unpunished" and states the determination of the states parties "to put an end to impunity for the perpetrators of these crimes and thus to contribute to the prevention of such crimes." Retribution and deterrence, therefore, are the Court's primary sentencing objectives.

In giving meaning to these objectives, the ICC's judges will no doubt be guided by the sentencing practices of previous international tribunals. Those tribunals have consistently emphasized the importance of retribution,[83] although they have been careful to insist that punishment imposed for retributive purposes "is not to be understood as fulfilling a desire for revenge, but as duly expressing the outrage of the international community at these crimes."[84] A sentence must, therefore, always be proportionate to the seriousness of the crime.[85]

International tribunals have also recognized the importance of deterrence.[86] They have normally insisted, however, that the deterrent effect of punishment "must not be accorded undue prominence" in sentencing decisions, because punishment is supposed to deter by "bringing about the development of a culture of respect for the rule of law and not simply the fear of the consequences of breaking the law."[87] Promoting deterrence through retributively disproportionate sentences is thus unacceptable.[88]

B. Liability Requirements

1. Objective/Actus Reus

As noted earlier, the drafters of the Rome Statute made a conscious decision to refer to "material elements" instead of to an *actus reus*. There is no general provision in the Statute concerning material elements; instead, following the Model Penal Code, article 30 of the Statute ("Mental Element") simply refers to conduct elements, consequence elements, and circumstance elements.[89] The material elements of a crime are thus "those characteristics . . . of the actor's behavior that, when combined with the appropriate level of culpability, will constitute the offense."[90]

A *conduct* element specifies the positive act or omission prohibited by the crime in question. The war crime of unlawful deportation or transfer, for example, requires the perpetrator to have "deported or transferred one or more persons to another State or to another location."[91]

A *consequence* element specifies the required result of the prohibited conduct. That result may involve either actual harm, such as the crime against humanity of torture's requirement that "[t]he perpetrator inflicted severe physical or mental pain or suffering upon one or more persons,"[92] or simply the possibility of harm, such as the war crime of biological experiment's requirement that an experiment "seriously endangered the physical or mental health or integrity" of the victim.[93]

A *circumstance* element specifies an additional state of affairs that must exist for the prohibited conduct and consequence to be criminal. That state of affairs can be either factual or legal. For example, the war crime of using child soldiers requires the children to have been "under the age of 15 years,"[94] a factual circumstance, while the war crime of denying a fair trial requires the defendant to have been "protected under one or more of the Geneva Conventions of 1949,"[95] a legal circumstance.

i. Act

The Rome Statute does not specify what qualifies as an "act" for purposes of a conduct element. Nevertheless, because article 30 defines intent in relation to conduct as "mean[ing] to engage in the conduct," it is clear that a conduct element is satisfied as long as the person voluntarily committed the prohibited act.[96] Involuntary actions, such as those committed in a state of automatism, do not qualify.[97]

ii. Omission

Various provisions in the Rome Statute and the Elements of Crimes criminalize specific omissions. The war crime of starvation as a method of warfare, for example, prohibits "depriv[ing] civilians of objects indispensable to their survival."[98] Similarly, a military commander (or civilian superior) can be punished for failing to prevent his subordinates from committing international crimes or for failing to punish those crimes once they are brought to his attention.[99]

General liability for omissions, however, proved to be one of the most controversial issues during the drafting of the Rome Statute. Article 28 of the 1998 Draft ICC Statute, then still titled "Actus Reus," provided that "conduct for which a person may be criminally responsible and liable for punishment can constitute either an act or an omission, or a combination thereof." Most states supported the provision, but a "small minority," particularly France, insisted that liability for omissions should be limited to specific crimes. The Preparatory Committee initially compromised by replacing references to "an act or an omission" with the more vague "conduct." When even that compromise met with resistance, the

Diplomatic Conference decided to drop the *actus reus* article entirely.[100] It is will thus be up to the Court to determine—keeping in mind article 22's prohibition of extending the definition of crimes by analogy—whether omissions other than those specified in the Rome Statute and the Elements of Crimes are criminal.[101]

iii. Status

There are no status crimes in the Rome Statute, but the concept is not foreign to international criminal law. Control Council Law no. 10, enacted by the Allies after World War II, declared that "[m]embership in categories of a criminal group or organization declared criminal by the International Military Tribunal is recognized as a crime." A number of defendants in the various war-crimes trials held pursuant to Law No. 10 were later convicted of membership in the Schutzstaffel (SS), the Gestapo, or the Leadership Corps of the Nazi Party.[102]

2. *Subjective*/Mens Rea/*Mental Element*

The mental element of a crime is determined by article 30 of the Rome Statute, which provides in paragraph 1 that "unless otherwise provided, a person shall be criminally responsible and liable for punishment for a crime within the jurisdiction of the Court only if the material elements are committed with intent and knowledge." Article 30 thus takes an "element analysis" approach to *mens rea* that is similar to, and almost certainly based on, the approach taken by the Model Penal Code.[103]

Despite the plain language of paragraph 1, however, article 30 does not actually apply the default "intent and knowledge" requirement to every kind of material element. As discussed in the following subsections, paragraphs 2 and 3 of article 30 make clear that the intent requirement applies only to conduct and consequence elements, while the knowledge requirement applies only to consequence and circumstance elements. Intent and knowledge are thus both required only for consequence elements.[104]

i. Intent

Article 30(2) defines intent differently depending on whether the material element in question involves conduct or a consequence. A perpetrator acts with intent in regard to a conduct element when he or she "means to engage in the conduct."[105] This definition, with its volitional emphasis, is functionally equivalent to "purpose" in the Model Penal Code[106] and to *dol général* in French criminal law.[107]

A perpetrator acts with intent in regard to a consequence element, by contrast, when he or she either "means to cause that consequence" or "is aware that it will occur in the ordinary course of events.[108] The first definition is explicitly volitional and corresponds to "purpose" and the civil law's *dolus directus* in the first degree.[109]

The correct interpretation of article 30's second definition of intent, which is cognitive instead of volitional, is controversial. Textually, the definition is equivalent to "knowledge" in the Model Penal Code, to the common law's "oblique intent," and to the civil law's *dolus directus* in the second degree, all of which require the perpetrator to recognize that it is virtually certain that his or her conduct *will* lead to the prohibited consequence.[110] The question is whether the definition also includes *dolus eventualis*, which is satisfied if the perpetrator reconciles himself or herself to the possibility that his or her conduct *may* lead to the prohibited consequence.[111] The Pre-Trial Chamber has held that article 30's cognitive definition of intent includes *dolus eventualis*,[112] and a number of scholars agree.[113] That position, however, contradicts the plain language of the article: "[I]t is not enough for the perpetrator to merely anticipate the possibility that his conduct would cause the consequence. This follows from the words 'will occur'; after all, it does not say 'may occur.'"[114]

Finally, it is important to note that a number of crimes in the Rome Statute also require the perpetrator to act with specific intent or *dolus specialis*. Some of these "otherwise provided" requirements modify article 30's default "intent and knowledge" requirement with regard to a material element. A perpetrator is guilty of hostage taking, for example, only if he or she specifically intends his or her act to "compel a State . . . to act or refrain from acting as an explicit or implicit condition for the safety or the release of such person or persons";[115] knowledge of that consequence is not enough. Others supplement article 30 because they do not apply to the material elements of a crime. To commit the crime of genocide, for example, the perpetrator must not only have acted with intent and knowledge regarding the material elements of the crime, such as killing members of a protected group, but must also have acted with the specific intent "to destroy" that group "in whole or in part."[116]

ii. Knowledge

Article 30(3) provides two different definitions of knowledge. The first definition, which concerns consequence elements, is the same as article 30(2)'s definition of intent with regard to consequences: "awareness that . . . a consequence will occur in the ordinary course of events." The fact that both intent and knowledge are required for circumstance elements is thus effectively meaningless; in practice, knowledge is all that is required.

The second definition concerns knowledge in relation to circumstance elements. Here knowledge is defined as "awareness that a circumstance exists." This is a very high threshold, going beyond the Model Penal Code's definition of knowledge, which is satisfied as long as the perpetrator is "aware of a high probability of [a circumstance's] existence, unless he actually believes it doesn't exist."[117] It also seems to exclude willful blindness, even in Glanville Williams's restrictive formulation: "He suspected the fact; he realized its probability; but he refrained from obtaining the final confirmation because he wanted in the event to be able to deny knowledge."[118]

iii. Recklessness

With one exception, common-law recklessness is never sufficient for criminal responsibility under the Rome Statute. Earlier drafts of article 30 included a definition of recklessness, but that provision was deleted when the drafters realized that the word *reckless* did not appear in any of the definitions of crimes.[119] Moreover, most of the states that were involved in drafting the article were reluctant to base criminal responsibility for serious international crimes on recklessness.[120]

The one exception concerns the responsibility of civilian superiors, a form of complicity. Article 28(b)(1) provides that a civilian superior is responsible for failing to prevent and/or punish crimes committed by subordinates if he or she "knew, or consciously disregarded information which early indicated, that the subordinates were committing or about to commit such crimes." Scholars agree that the "consciously disregarded" language is equivalent to recklessness.[121]

iv. Negligence

The drafters of part 3 were equally reluctant to base criminal responsibility on negligence, in either its common-law or its civil law form.[122] Nevertheless, negligence appears both in the Rome Statute and in the Elements of Crimes as an "otherwise provided" mental element. Article 28(a)(1) of the Statute provides that a military commander is responsible for failing to prevent and/or punish crimes committed by his subordinate forces if he "knew or, owing to the circumstances at the time, should have known, that the forces were committing or about to commit such crimes." Moreover, the Elements apply a common-law negligence standard to a number of factual circumstances required by various war crimes. The war crime of improperly using the distinctive emblems of the Geneva Conventions, for example, requires that the perpetrator "knew or should have known of the prohibited nature of such use."[123]

3. Causation

There is no specific causation provision in the Rome Statute. The 1998 Draft Statute provided that "[a] person is only criminally responsible under this Statute for committing a crime if the harm required for the commission of a crime is caused by and [accountable] [attributable] to his or her act or omission," but that provision was deleted prior to the Diplomatic Conference.[124] Most scholars agree, however, that a causation requirement is implicit in the Rome Statute whenever a crime contains a consequence element.[125] Indeed, article 30 initially defined intent with regard to a consequence as "mean[ing] to cause that consequence." Causation requirements are also explicitly required by certain crimes, such as genocide by causing serious bodily or mental harm[126] and the war crime of willfully causing great suffering.[127]

4. Theories of Liability

Article 25 of the Rome Statute provides a comprehensive list of the possible modes of participation in the crimes within the jurisdiction of the Court. The article thus represents a significant advance over previous international tribunals, which "did not pay much attention to distinguishing different modes of participation . . . but rather applied a so-called unified perpetrator model. The guiding principle was that any support or promotion of the crime was to be considered criminal participation."[128] The Nuremberg Military Tribunals, for example, routinely convicted defendants because they were "principals in, accessories to, ordered, abetted, took a consenting part in, were connected with plans and enterprises involving, [or] were members of organizations or groups connected with, atrocities."[129]

Article 25 divides modes of participation into four categories: (1) commission,[130] (2) ordering and instigating,[131] (3) assistance,[132] and (4) contribution to a group crime.[133] Modes of participation in category 1 are forms of principal liability; modes in categories 2–4 are forms of accessory liability. What distinguishes principals from accessories is "control over the crime": principal perpetrators either "physically carry out the objective elements of the offense" or "control or mastermind its commission."[134] The Rome Statute thus rejects both the common law's objective approach to principal liability, which emphasizes "presence" at the crime, and the subjective approach of the ad hoc tribunals, which emphasizes shared intent to commit the crime, in favor of the objective/subjective "act dominion" (*Tatherrschaft*) approach of German criminal law.[135]

i. Commission

The first category includes direct perpetration ("as an individual"), coperpetration ("jointly with another"), and perpetration by means ("through another person").

a. Direct Participation

A perpetrator who commits the material elements of a crime with the requisite mental state commits that crime "as an individual." Scholars have noted that this description is imprecise because it fails to make clear that the direct perpetrator acts alone, without the assistance of another person.[136]

b. Coperpetration

When two or more perpetrators exercise "joint control" over the commission of a crime, each individual is responsible for that crime as a coperpetrator. According to the Pre-Trial Chamber in *Lubanga*, coperpetration has two objective and three subjective elements:

1. *Agreement or common plan.* Because coordinated criminal activity is the hallmark of coperpetration, the crime must be committed pursuant to an agreement or common plan between two or more persons.[137]

2. *Essential contribution.* To qualify as a coperpetrator, a person must have "joint control" over the commission of the crime. A person has such control if he or she makes an "essential" contribution to the common plan. A contribution is essential if the crime could not be committed without it—if, in other words the person has "the power to frustrate the commission of the crime by not performing" his or her task.[138]

3. *Required mental state.* A coperpetrator must make his or her essential contribution to the common plan with the mental state required for the underlying crime, including any requisite *dolus specialis*.[139]

4. *Awareness and acceptance of the crime.* A coperpetrator must also be "aware of the risk that implementing their common play may result in the realization of the objective elements of the crime" and "accept such a result" by reconciling with or consenting to its possibility.[140] That awareness and acceptance, according to the Pre-Trial Chamber, justifies holding each coperpetrator liable for the completed crime.[141]

5. *Awareness of joint control.* Finally, a coperpetrator must be aware that his or her contribution to the common plan is essential—that the plan cannot succeed but for his or her participation in it.[142]

c. Perpetration by Means

A perpetrator who uses another person as a tool to commit a crime commits that crime "through another person." Although many national legal systems recognize perpetration by means, the Rome Statute marks its first explicit appearance in international criminal law.[143] Unlike some national systems, however, article 25(3)(a) of the Rome Statute provides that a perpetrator by means is responsible for the crime committed by the direct perpetrator "regardless of whether that other person is criminally responsible."[144]

The Pre-Trial Chamber applied perpetration by means in the *Katanga* case, relying specifically on German criminal law.[145] According to the Pre-Trial Chamber, this form of participation is particularly relevant when the perpetrator behind the perpetrator—*Täter hinter dem Täter*—commits an international crime through another by means of his or her "control over an organized apparatus of power."[146] Objectively, such control has four elements. First, the apparatus must be "based on hierarchical relations between superiors and subordinates."[147] Second, the apparatus must be "composed of sufficient subordinates to guarantee that superiors' orders will be carried out, if not by one subordinate, then by another."[148] Third, each superior must exercise sufficient "authority and control" over the apparatus—normally because of his or her capacity to "hire, train, impose discipline, [or] provide resources"—that his or her orders will automatically produce their desired results.[149] Fourth, each superior must actually mobilize his or her authority and control over the apparatus to commit a crime within the jurisdiction of the Court.[150] Subjectively, perpetrators by means must not only act with the mental state necessary for the underlying crime[151] but must also "be aware of the character of their organizations, their authority within the organization, and the factual circumstances enabling near-automatic compliance with their orders."[152]

   ii. Ordering and Instigating
      a. *Ordering*

Article 25(3)(b) holds criminally responsible a person who "[o]rders . . . the commission of such a crime which in fact occurs or is attempted." Ordering presumes the existence of a superior-subordinate relationship: the superior uses his or her position of command to compel the subordinate to commit the crime.[153]

By virtue of its placement in paragraph b, ordering is a form of accessory liability. A number of scholars, however, have suggested that ordering is better understood as a form of perpetration by means, given that "exploiting a hierarchical power structure in terms of organizational predominance is typical of such intermediary perpetration."[154] Categorizing ordering as a form of accessory liability also fails to reflect the fact that the superior's culpability for the crime is greater than the subordinate's, because the superior not only violates his or her duty to control the subordinates but also misuses his or her power in order to ensure that the crime is committed.[155]

      b. *Soliciting and Inducing*

Article 25(3)(b) also holds criminally responsible a person who "solicits or induces the commission of such a crime which in fact occurs or is attempted." No superior-subordinate relationship is necessary for soliciting or inducing; an instigator is simply someone who "prompts" another to commit an international crime,[156] usually by means of psychological pressure.[157] A causal link between the instigation and the crime is necessary, but it is sufficient if the instigation "substantially" contributes to the direct perpetrator's decision to act.[158] Subjectively, under article 30, the instigator must either intend that the direct perpetrator commit the crime or recognize that the crime will be committed "in the ordinary course of events."

iii. Assistance

Article 25(3)(c) holds criminally responsible a person who, "[f]or the purpose of facilitating the commission of such a crime, aids, abets or otherwise assists in its commission or its attempted commission, including providing the means for its commission." This category of accessory liability covers assistance that does not rise to the level of ordering and instigating but is more significant than mere contribution to a group crime. It includes, according to the ICTY, any "practical assistance, encouragement, or moral support which has a substantial effect on the perpetration of the crime."[159] Article 25(3)(c) does not itself require a "substantial effect," but most scholars believe that the requirement is implicit in the paragraph, given that the ILC's 1996 Draft Code of Crimes explicitly included it.[160]

Subjectively, the assistance must not only be intentionally provided, as required by article 30, but must also be provided "for the purpose" of facilitating the crime. This "otherwise provided" specific-intent requirement, which is borrowed from the Model Penal Code,[161] means that the perpetrator must have consciously intended the direct perpetrator to commit the crime[162]—a much higher standard than the one applied by the ICTY and the ICTR, which have held that aiding and abetting only requires the perpetrator to know that his or her assistance will facilitate the direct perpetrator's commission of the crime.[163]

iv. Contribution

Finally, article 25(3)(d) holds criminally responsible a person who "[i]n any other way contributes to the commission or attempted commission of such a crime by a group of persons acting with a common purpose." This provision, which is copied almost verbatim from the International Convention on the Suppression of Terrorist Bombings of 1997, resulted from contentious debates during the drafting over whether to include conspiracy in the Rome Statute.[164] It is a residual form of accessory liability that applies "to indirect forms of assistance—such as financing the group—that do not warrant liability for either co-perpetration or aiding and abetting, as they have no substantial effect on the commission of the crime under international law."[165] Subjectively, such assistance must be made either "with the aim of furthering" the group's criminal activity or "in the knowledge of the intention of the group to commit the crime."[166] The difference seems to be that the second standard requires the prosecution to prove that the person knew the specific crime the group intended to commit, whereas the first standard requires it to prove only that the person intended to further the group's general criminal activity.[167]

v. Inchoate Crimes

a. Conspiracy

Conspiracy is not criminal under the Rome Statute. Earlier versions of the Statute oscillated between the traditional common-law approach to conspiracy, which views conspiracy as an inchoate crime, and the civil law approach, which views conspiracy as a mode of participation in a crime.[168] The difficulty of reconciling those traditions ultimately led the drafters to compromise by replacing conspiracy with the idea of contribution to a group crime, art. 25(3)(d) of the Statute.[169]

b. Incitement to Genocide

Article 25(3)(e) holds criminally responsible a person who, "[i]n respect of the crime of genocide, directly and publicly incites others to commit genocide." This provision, which is borrowed from the Genocide Convention, is a purely inchoate crime: the incited genocide need not be carried out or even attempted.[170] A perpetrator incites "publicly" by "communicating the call for criminal action to a number of individuals in a public place or to members of the general public at large," usually through radio or television.[171] A perpetrator incites "directly" by "specifically urging another individual to take immediate criminal action rather than making a vague or indirect suggestion."[172] The later qualification obviously blurs the line between incitement and other forms of accessorial liability, such as solicitation and inducement.

Scholars agree that, subjectively, a perpetrator must intend to incite his or her listeners to commit an act of genocide, such as killing members of a protected group, with the specific intent to destroy that group in whole or in part.[173] They disagree, however, concerning whether the perpetrator must also possess that specific intent, as is the norm in national criminal codes.[174] It is difficult to imagine a situation in which a perpetrator who does not have genocidal intent would intentionally try to incite that intent in others. Nevertheless, because incitement to genocide does not "otherwise provide" a specific-intent requirement, unlike aiding and abetting and contributing to a group crime, the perpetrator would likely be guilty of incitement in such a situation.[175]

c. Attempt

Article 25(3)(f) holds criminally responsible a person who "[a]ttempts to commit such a crime by taking action that commences its execution by means of a substantial step, but the crime does not occur because of circumstances independent of the person's intentions." General criminal responsibility for attempts is an innovation of the Rome Statute; previously, "neither a duly generalized nor an adequate concept of attempt" existed in international criminal law.[176]

Objectively, article 25(3)(f) represents an amalgamation of French law (*commencement d'exécution*) and the Model Penal Code ("substantial step").[177] Preparatory acts do not qualify as substantial steps because they do not represent a "commencement of execution." The perpetrator is not required, however, to fulfill one of the physical elements of the crime; most scholars agree that the attempt provision is patterned after German criminal law's concept of attempt, which equates commencement with acts committed "immediately proceeding to the accomplishment of the elements of the offense" (*unmittlebares Ansetzen zur Tatbestandverwirklichung*).[178]

d. Abandonment

Article 25(3)(f) also provides that "a person who abandons the effort to commit the crime or otherwise prevents the completion of the crime shall not be liable for punishment under this Statute for the attempt to commit that crime if that person completely and voluntarily gave up the criminal purpose." Although abandonment is likely a general principle of criminal law, it was included in the Rome Statute only at the last minute. The provision is based on the Model Penal Code[179] and is thus, by requiring the perpetrator to both physically abandon the attempt and renounce his or her criminal intention, more strict than many national criminal codes.[180]

vi. Superior Responsibility

Superior responsibility is "an original creation of international criminal law."[181] At the broadest level, it holds military commanders and civilian superiors criminally responsible for failing to prevent their subordinates from committing international crimes or for failing to punish those crimes once they are brought to their attention.

The nature of superior responsibility is controversial. Some national legal systems treat it as a form of complicity, while others consider it an independent crime of omission akin to dereliction of duty.[182] Article 28 of the Rome Statute adopts the former approach, providing that a superior who fails to prevent or punish crimes committed by his or her subordinates "shall be criminally responsible" for those crimes.[183]

According to article 28, superior responsibility involves four elements. First, a superior-subordinate relationship must exist. The essence of that relationship is the superior's "effective control" over the direct perpetrators, understood as the "material ability to prevent and punish commission of the offenses."[184] Military commanders often possess effective control de jure, by virtue of their rank. Some civilian superiors, such as government officials, also exercise de jure control over their subordinates. De facto effective control is sufficient, however, in both the military and civilian contexts.[185]

Second, the superior must have the requisite mental element concerning his or her subordinates' crimes. Unlike the statutes of previous international tribunals, the Rome Statute holds military commanders and civilian superiors to different standards. A military commander is criminally responsible if he or she "either knew or, owing to the circumstances at the time, should have known that the forces were committing or about to commit such crimes"[186]—a negligence-like standard that asks whether the commander, "in the proper exercise of his duties, would have gained knowledge" of the crimes.[187] A civilian superior, by contrast, is criminally responsible only if he or she "either knew, or consciously disregarded information which clearly indicated, that the subordinates were committing or about to commit such crimes"[188]—a standard that seems to include both recklessness and willful blindness.[189]

Third, the superior must have failed to take "necessary and reasonable measures" to either prevent or punish his or her subordinate's crimes. What measures qualify as necessary and reasonable must be determined on a case-by-case basis, taking into account the degree of the superior's effective control: the greater the control, the greater the superior's obligation to take preventive or punitive measures. Typical prevention measures include teaching subordinates about the principles of international humanitarian law and creating effective systems of supervision, reporting, and sanctioning. With regard to punishment, the Rome Statute specifically mentions submitting subordinates' crimes "to the competent authorities for investigation and prosecution."[190]

Fourth, and finally, the subordinates' crimes must "result" from the superior's failure to exercise proper control over them.[191] This is clearly a negative causality requirement: the superior can only be held responsible for his or her subordinates' crimes insofar as, "but for his failure to fulfill his duty to act, the acts of his subordinates would not have been committed."[192]

vii. Corporate Criminal Liability

Article 25(1) of the Rome Statute provides that "[t]he Court shall have jurisdiction over natural persons pursuant to this Statute." Legal persons, therefore, cannot be held criminally responsible for crimes within the jurisdiction of the Court. This exclusion was a relatively late development: earlier versions of article 25 included an option to extend the Court's jurisdiction to legal as well as to natural persons.[193] That option was ultimately deleted at the Diplomatic Conference, largely because the idea of corporate criminal liability was simply alien to a number of national legal systems.[194]

C. Defenses

1. Types of Defense

As noted earlier, because they wanted to avoid tradition-specific language, the drafters of the Rome Statute chose to refer to "grounds for excluding criminal responsibility" instead of to "defenses." The Statute approaches those grounds in three different ways. First, articles 31–33 make certain defenses specifically available to a defendant. Some, such as self-defense, are traditionally categorized as justifications; others, such as mental disease or defect, are traditionally categorized as excuses. The Rome Statute, however, does not distinguish between the two.[195] Indeed, article 31(1)(d) collapses a justification (necessity) and an excuse (duress) into a single ground.

Second, article 31(2) provides that "[t]he Court shall determine the applicability of the grounds for excluding criminal responsibility provided for in this Statute to the case before it." If this provision simply authorizes the Court to prevent a defendant from raising a ground that is not supported by sufficient evidence, it is unproblematic. The provision will clearly run afoul of the principle of legality, however, if it authorizes the Court to exclude a ground for nonevidentiary reasons of "justice" or "fairness."[196] Unfortunately, the drafting history seems to support the latter interpretation.[197]

Third, and finally, article 31(3) gives the court the right to "consider a ground for excluding criminal responsibility other than those referred to ... where such a ground is derived from applicable law as set forth in article 21." Such grounds will normally be found in customary international law.[198]

2. Burden of Proof

Article 66(2) of the Rome Statute provides that "[t]he onus is on the Prosecutor to prove the guilt of the accused." The relevant burden is—as it has been at every international tribunal since Nuremberg—proof beyond a reasonable doubt.[199] In addition, article 67(1)(i) guarantees a defendant the right "[n]ot to have imposed on him or her any reversal of the burden of proof or any onus of rebuttal." The latter provision is particularly important, because it implies that the Rome Statute follows the Model Penal Code in requiring the prosecution to disprove the existence of grounds for excluding criminal responsibility proffered by the defendant, at least insofar as those grounds are supported by sufficient evidence.[200] That is the position taken by Roger Clark,[201] one of the most important drafters of the Rome Statute, although he acknowledges that "[c]onfused discussion during the drafting of the Elements demonstrated that there are some very different conceptions across legal systems on how the burden of proof issues will eventually play out."[202]

3. Mental Disease or Defect/Diminished Capacity

Article 31(1)(a) excludes from criminal responsibility a person who, at the time of the crime, "suffers from a mental disease or defect." That defect must destroy either the "capacity to appreciate the unlawfulness or nature of his or her conduct" or the "capacity to control his or her conduct to conform with the requirements of law."[203]

The Rome Statute does not recognize the defense of diminished capacity. Diminished capacity is, however, a mitigating factor at sentencing.[204]

4. Intoxication

Article 31(b) excludes from criminal responsibility a person who lacks either of the capacities mentioned earlier because of an involuntary state of intoxication. Voluntary intoxication can also exclude criminal responsibility, but in much more limited circumstances: the defense is not available if "the person has become voluntarily intoxicated under such circumstances that the person knew, or disregarded the risk, that, as a result of the intoxication, he or she was likely to engage in conduct constituting a crime."[205] This limitation represents a compromise between national legal systems (primarily those applying Islamic law) that view voluntary intoxication as an aggravating factor and those that view it either as a mitigating factor or as a complete defense.[206]

5. Self-Defense

Article 31(1)(c) excludes from criminal responsibility a person who acts in self-defense. The self-defensive situation must be based on the "imminent and unlawful use of force," which includes both physical and psychological threats.[207] If such a situation exists, the defensive measures must be both objectively reasonable and proportionate to the threatened harm. The perpetrator must also have genuinely acted with the intent to defend himself or herself.[208]

Thus understood, the Rome Statute's definition of self-defense does not differ substantially from most national definitions. There is, however, one major difference: in addition to permitting force to be used in defense of self or others, article 31(1)(c) permits the use of force to defend "property which is essential for the survival of the person or another person or property which is essential for accomplishing a military mission." This extension, which was advocated most strongly by Israel and the United States, was a "real cliffhanger" during the drafting. States ultimately compromised by limiting the defense of property to cases involving war crimes; the defense is not available if the defendant is charged with genocide or crimes against humanity.[209]

6. Duress/Necessity

Article 31(1)(d) collapses the defenses of duress and necessity into one uniform duress defense. Duress excludes criminal responsibility if four requirements are satisfied. First, the defendant's criminal act must have been "caused by duress resulting from a threat of imminent death or of continuing or imminent serious bodily harm against that person or another person." The threat can either be "made by other persons" (traditional duress) or "constituted by circumstances beyond that person's control" (traditional necessity). In keeping with the Model Penal Code, a threat to others can create excusable duress even in the absence of a special relationship between the defendant and those others.[210]

Second, the defendant must have acted "necessarily and reasonably" to avoid the threat. An action is "necessary" if there was no other way to avoid the threat and "reasonable" if it was not disproportionate to the threat. Article 31(1)(d) thus permits a person to use deadly force in response to an imminent threat of death, a position that is consistent with both the common law and the civil law but was controversially rejected by the ICTY in the *Erdemovic* case.[211]

Third, the defendant must have acted with the intent to avoid the threat, but without the intent "to cause a greater harm than the one sought to be avoided." The latter subjective proportionality requirement, which supplements the objective one, is "unprecedented in comparative law" and represents an artifact of the drafting process.[212]

Finally, when the defendant acted to avoid a natural threat, the threat must have resulted from "circumstances beyond that person's control." Some scholars believe that this requirement applies both to human-made and to natural threats.[213] As a textual matter, however, it applies only to the latter.

7. Mistake

Article 32 of the Rome Statute provides that a mistake of fact or a mistake of law will exclude criminal responsibility if it "negates the mental element required by . . . a crime." The article thus follows the common-law approach to mistake, because "most civil law systems regard mistake as an excuse bearing on culpability, which does not necessarily imply lack of *mens rea*."[214] This means that even unreasonable mistakes normally exclude criminal responsibility: an unreasonable mistake negates both knowledge and intent, article 30's default mental elements.[215] By contrast, even a reasonable mistake concerning a ground for excluding criminal responsibility is not exculpatory: textually, article 32 applies only to elements required by "a crime." A number of scholars have criticized this limitation,[216] which is at odds with both the common law[217] and the Model Penal Code.[218] Finally, and equally controversially,[219] article 32 does not recognize unavoidable mistakes of law, such as where the perpetrator reasonably but erroneously relied on an official statement of the law.[220]

8. Superior Orders

Article 33 of the Rome Statute recognizes a limited version of the defense of superior orders. In general, "[t]he fact that a crime within the jurisdiction of the Court has been committed by a person pursuant to an order of a Government or of a superior, whether military or civilian, shall not relieve that person of criminal responsibility."[221] Moreover, the defense of superior orders is categorically prohibited for crimes against humanity and genocide.[222] The defense of superior orders is thus available only with regard to war crimes.

Three requirements must be satisfied for superior orders to exclude criminal responsibility for a war crime. First, the defendant must have been legally obligated to obey the order "of the government or the superior in question,"[223] a fact that must be determined—

unusually, for the Rome Statute—with reference to the defendant's national legal system.[224] It is an open question whether the defense is available to civilian subordinates, such as members of rebel groups and employees of private corporations, who are normally not under a legal obligation to obey orders. Some scholars believe that article 33 applies to rebels but not to civilian subordinates,[225] while others believe that it applies to both.[226] In either case, the superior issuing the order must exercise the kind of de facto effective control over the defendant that would suffice for superior responsibility.[227]

Second, the defendant must not have actual knowledge that the order was unlawful.[228]

Third, the order must not have been "manifestly unlawful."[229] What determines whether an order is manifestly unlawful is controversial; the most famous definition, and one that is quite restrictive, is found in the *Eichmann* case: "The distinguishing mark of a 'manifestly unlawful order' should fly like a black flag above the order given . . . [n]ot formal unlawfulness, hidden or half-hidden, nor unlawfulness discernible only to the eyes of legal experts, but a flagrant and manifest breach of the law."[230] It is another open question whether the test, which is nominally objective, should be subjectivized to take into account the rank and experience of the defendant.[231]

D. Sanctions

1. Punishment

The Rome Statute's sentencing provisions are very general. Pursuant to article 77, the Court may sentence a convicted defendant to a maximum of thirty years' imprisonment unless "the extreme gravity of the crime and the individual circumstances of the convicted person" warrant a life sentence.[232] The Court may also fine the defendant or order forfeiture of the "proceeds, property and assets derived directly or indirectly from" his or her crime, but only "in addition to" imprisonment.[233] Forfeiture cannot include the instrumentalities of a crime; proposals to that effect were considered and rejected during the drafting.[234]

Article 78 instructs the Court to take into account the gravity of the crime and the circumstances of the offender when determining sentence.[235] Rule 145 of the Rules of Procedure and Evidence adds that the Court should additionally take into account, inter alia, the extent of the damage caused by the defendant, particularly to the victims and their families; the degree of the defendant's participation in the crime and the degree of his or her intent; and the defendant's age, education, and social/economic situation.[236] Rule 145 also specifies a number of relevant mitigating and aggravating factors: in mitigation, diminished capacity, duress, and postcrime assistance; in aggravation, prior criminal convictions, abuse of power, a defenseless victim, particular cruelty, multiple victims, and discriminatory motive.[237]

2. Death Penalty

The Court cannot sentence a defendant to death, although a number of states—the Arab and Islamic states, along with the English-speaking Caribbean states and a few others—ardently supported including the death penalty in the Rome Statute.[238] No international tribunal since World War II has imposed capital punishment.[239]

III. SPECIAL PART

A. Structure

1. Protected Interests

As reflected in the Preamble to the Rome Statute, the ICC's primary goal[240] is to protect the fundamental values of the international community: the "peace, security, and well-being of the world."[241] That goal explains why the Court's jurisdiction is limited to genocide, crimes against humanity, war crimes, and aggression: because those crimes each "presume a context of systematic or large-scale use of force,"[242] they pose a far greater threat to the world's peace, security, and well-being than "ordinary" domestic crimes. For genocide, the disruption of world peace lies in an (intentional) attack on the physical or social existence of a particular group. For crimes against humanity, the threat to peace, security, and the well-being of the world consists of the systematic or widespread violation of the fundamental human rights of the civilian population. For war crimes, criminalizing violations of the laws of war is intended to minimize the effects of armed conflict as much as possible and help prevent escalation. Armed conflicts between states generally disrupt world peace; the criminality of aggression thus depends on whether behavior can be found to have brought about aggressive war.[243]

At the same time, the Court also seeks to protect "the legal values of individuals."[244] This subsidiary goal is reflected in the specific acts of genocide, crimes against humanity, and war crimes that are within the Court's jurisdiction. For example, the war crime of willful killing[245] protects the individual's right to life; the crimes against humanity of rape and forced pregnancy[246] protect the individual's right to bodily integrity; and the war crime of humiliating and degrading treatment[247] protects the individual's right to human dignity.

2. Double Structure

All of the crimes within the jurisdiction of the Court possess a "double-layered" structure.[248] First, there must be a prohibited individual act. That act normally constitutes a criminal offense under domestic law, such as murder, rape, or theft. Some acts, however, are unique to international criminal law, such as declaring that no quarter will be given[249] or employing weapons that cause unnecessary suffering.[250] Second, the prohibited individual act must be committed in the context of collective violence—what is known as the crime's "contextual element."[251] War crimes, for example, can be committed only during an armed conflict. The presence of that contextual element is what elevates "ordinary" domestic crimes into "serious crimes of concern to the international community."[252]

All of the material elements of the act underlying genocide, a crime against humanity, or a war crime must be committed with "intent and knowledge" unless otherwise provided. It is an open question, however, whether article 30's default rule also applies to contextual elements, such as the existence of an armed conflict for war crimes. The issue was contentious during the drafting of the Elements of Crimes: some states took the position that contextual elements were material elements to which article 30 applied; others insisted that they were jurisdictional elements to which it did not.[253] The drafters ultimately compromised, categorizing the contextual elements as material elements, but "otherwise providing" a mental element for each of them that is lower than intent and knowledge.

B. Genocide

Article 6 of the Rome Statute defines genocide as the commission of "any of the following acts ... with the intent to destroy, in whole or in part, a national, ethnical, racial or religious group, as such":

1. Killing members of the group
2. Causing serious bodily or mental harm to members of the group
3. Deliberately inflicting on the group conditions of life calculated to bring about its physical destruction in whole or in part
4. Imposing measures intended to prevent births within the group
5. Forcibly transferring children of the group to another group

As interpreted by the Elements of Crimes, genocide consists of four elements: the individual act; the victims' membership in a protected group; the perpetrator's intent to destroy the group; and a pattern of conduct against the group.

1. Individual Acts

The list of prohibited acts in article 6, which is based on the Genocide Convention, is exclusive; no other act can qualify as genocide. The drafters of the Genocide Convention considered but ultimately rejected proposals to prohibit two other kinds of acts: cultural genocide, the destruction of a protected group's historical, cultural, or religious heritage; and ethnic cleansing, the forcible removal of members of a protected group from their homes.[254]

i. Killing Members of the Group

Killing members of the group is the most serious form of genocide. According to the Elements, "killing" is synonymous with "causing death."[255] Causing the death of even one member of a protected group is sufficient.[256]

ii. Causing Serious Bodily or Mental Harm to Members of the Group

The ICTR defines "serious bodily harm" as harm that "seriously injures the health, causes disfigurement or causes serious injury to the external or internal organs or senses."[257] The use of machetes to hack limbs off Tutsis during the Rwandan genocide is an example. "Serious mental harm" includes but is not limited to "acts of torture, rape, sexual violence or inhuman or degrading treatment."[258] Such harm must cause "grave and long-term disadvantage to a person's ability to lead a normal and constructive life."[259]

iii. Deliberately Inflicting on the Group Conditions of Life Calculated to Bring About Its Physical Destruction in Whole or in Part

The third form of genocide, which is based on the treatment of the Jews during the Holocaust, prohibits "extermination through slow death"—measures that are not immediately lethal but will inevitably lead to death over the long term.[260] Qualifying measures include depriving members of a group of food, water, medicine, or shelter.[261] The Elements of Crimes also include "systematic expulsion from homes"—ethnic cleansing—but scholars agree that such expulsion would have to be combined with other slow-death measures to qualify as genocide.[262] The term *calculated* indicates that the deliberately inflicted conditions do not actually have to cause death.

iv. Imposing Measures Intended to Prevent Births within the Group

Measures intended to prevent births within the group include "sexual mutilation, the practice of sterilization, forced birth control, separation of the sexes, and prohibition of marriages."[263] Rape also qualifies if its object is to change the ethnic composition of the victim's group.[264] Only one victim is required, as the Elements make clear.[265]

v. Forcibly Transferring Children of the Group to Another Group

Forcible transfer borders on cultural genocide but is better understood as a "subtle form" of biological genocide, because forcibly transferred children will normally not reproduce within their own group.[266] The removal must be permanent and forcible, although the Elements provide that "forcibly" refers both to physical force and to the "threat of force or coercion."[267]

2. *Protected Groups*

Genocide can be committed only against the four groups protected by the Genocide Convention and specified in article 6: national, ethnical, racial, and religious. Attempts were made during PrepCom to expand article 6 to include social and political groups, but the Committee ultimately decided to follow the drafters of the Genocide Convention and exclude them.[268]

The ICTR's *Akayesu* decision provides the clearest definitions of the four groups, although they are not completely satisfactory. A *national group* is "a collection of people who are perceived to share a legal bond based on common citizenship, coupled with reciprocity of rights and duties." An *ethnic group* is "a group whose members share a common language or culture." A *racial group* is "based on the hereditary physical traits often identified with a geographical region, irrespective of linguistic, cultural, national or religious factors." A *religious group* is "one whose members share the same religion, denomination or mode of worship."[269]

If the ICC follows the jurisprudence of the ad hoc tribunals, a person can qualify as a member of a protected group either objectively or subjectively. In other words, even if a person is not a member of a protected group from a physical or anthropological perspective, he or she qualifies for protection if the perpetrator perceived him or her to be a member of that group at the time of the genocidal act.[270]

3. *Specific Intent*

The prohibited act must be committed with the "intent to destroy, in whole or in part, a national, ethnical, racial or religious group, as such." This is a specific-intent or *dolus specialis* requirement: the perpetrator must act with "the aim, goal, purpose or desire to destroy part of a protected group."[271] As the "in part" language of article 6 indicates, a perpetrator does not possess the requisite specific intent if he or she intends to destroy only a small number of group members; he or she must at least intend to destroy a "substantial" part of the group.[272] Moreover, the perpetrator must select his or her victims because of their membership in the group; an indiscriminate attack that has the effect of destroying a substantial part of a protected group does not satisfy the specific-intent requirement. That is the meaning of the "as such" requirement.[273]

4. Pattern of Conduct

Finally, according to the Elements of Crimes, the prohibited act must have been committed "in the context of a manifest pattern of similar conduct directed against that group or was conduct that could itself effect such destruction." This is the contextual element of genocide; it was included in the Elements in response to the *Jelisic* decision, in which the ICTY held that killings committed by an individual perpetrator are sufficient "to establish the material element of the crime of genocide" because "it is *a priori* possible to conceive that the accused harboured the plan to exterminate an entire group without this intent having been supported by any organization in which other individuals participated."[274] The contextual element indicates that individual genocidal acts rise to the level of international crimes only if they are part of a larger genocidal plan or at least achieve a certain scale.

C. Crimes against Humanity

Article 7 of the Rome Statute defines a crime against humanity as the commission of one of a number of prohibited acts "as part of a widespread or systematic attack directed against any civilian population, with knowledge of the attack." A crime against humanity thus consists of two elements: the contextual element and the prohibited individual act.

1. Contextual Element

An individual act prohibited by article 7 becomes a crime against humanity when it is knowingly committed as part of a widespread or systematic attack on a civilian population. As the "as part of" language makes clear, the widespread or systematic attack is a collective phenomenon; the perpetrator's act does not itself have to qualify as widespread or systematic. There must, however, be a sufficient nexus between the perpetrator's act and the overall attack: "The fundamental language is that the acts must not be...capable of being characterized as the isolated and random conduct of an individual acting alone."[275]

This contextual element can be broken down into four separate requirements. First, the act must be directed against "any civilian population." This does not mean that the attack must target the population of an entire territory or area; the expression simply foregrounds the collective element of the crime, thereby ruling out attacks against individual civilians.[276] Crimes against humanity can be committed either in peacetime or during war.[277]

Second, the attack must be either widespread or systematic. An attack is "widespread" if it involves a large number of victims, whether because small numbers of victims are attacked over a wide geographic area (such as rapes of civilians in a number of different villages) or because a single attack is particularly lethal (such as the destruction of the World Trade Center).[278] An attack is "systematic" if it is committed "pursuant to a preconceived plan or policy."[279]

Third, regardless of whether the attack is widespread or systematic, it must be carried out "pursuant to or in furtherance of a State or organizational policy to commit such attack."[280] This "policy element" was included in article 7 at the insistence of states that wanted to limit crimes against humanity to attacks that were both widespread and systematic.[281] The disjunctive language of article 7 thus appears to have little meaning: in practice, the prosecution will be required to prove that even a "widespread" attack had systematic aspects.

Fourth, and finally, the perpetrator must commit the underlying act "with knowledge" of the widespread and systematic attack. This mental element does not require "proof that the perpetrator had knowledge of all characteristics of the attack or the precise details of the plan or policy of the State or organization";[282] general awareness that the broader attack is taking place is sufficient.

2. Individual Acts

Eleven different acts qualify as crimes against humanity when they are committed as part of a widespread or systematic attack on a civilian population. What follows is an overview of some of the most important.

i. Murder

Murder is the prototypical crime against humanity. There is some ambiguity concerning the mental element required for this crime, however, because the Elements of Crimes equate "murder" with "causing death"[283]—similar to killing as an underlying act for the crime of genocide—and "causing death" can be viewed as either a conduct or a consequence element. Indeed, the drafters of the Elements disagreed concerning which one it was.[284] If "causing death" is a conduct element, the perpetrator must have meant to cause death, but if it is a consequence element, the perpetrator must only have caused harm with the awareness that death would occur in the ordinary course of events.

ii. Extermination

Extermination is murder committed on a large scale, involving at least "part of a population."[285] Unlike genocide, the victims of extermination do not have to be members of a protected group or possess any common sociological characteristics. The perpetrator does not have to personally kill a large number of people; killing "one or more persons" in the context of the broader program of extermination is sufficient.[286]

iii. Deportation or Forcible Transfer

Article 7(2)(d) of the Rome Statute defines deportation or forcible transfer as the "forced displacement of the persons concerned by expulsion or other coercive acts from the area in which they are lawfully present, without grounds permitted under international law." Ethnic cleansing is often prosecuted as the crime against humanity of deportation or forcible transfer.[287] "Deportation" refers to displacement across a national border, while "transfer" means displacement within a state. Either form of displacement must be forcible, although physical force is not required—any involuntary displacement, such as through the threat of force or psychological oppression, is sufficient.[288] Finally, the displacement must violate international law, which means that it is not criminal to forcibly transfer a population for legitimate reasons of national security, public order, or public health.[289]

iv. Torture

Article 7(2)(e) defines torture as "the intentional infliction of severe pain or suffering, whether physical or mental, upon a person in the custody or under the control of the accused." This definition is based on the 1984 Convention against Torture,[290] but it differs from the Convention definition in two important respects. First, the crime against humanity of torture does not require that the severe pain and suffering be inflicted "by or at the instigation of... a public official."[291] Torture can thus be committed by rebels, paramilitaries, and even private citizens.[292] Second, the crime against humanity of torture does not require that the severe pain and suffering be inflicted "for such purposes as obtaining from him or a third person information or a confession."[293] Purely sadistic acts of torture thus also qualify, as long as they are knowingly committed in the context of a widespread or systematic attack.

v. Sexual Violence

Article 7(1)(g) provides that a number of different forms of sexual violence can qualify as crimes against humanity: "[r]ape, sexual slavery, enforced prostitution, forced pregnancy, enforced sterilization, or any other form of sexual violence of comparable gravity." This article represents a significant advance over earlier international instruments prohibiting or criminalizing sexual violence, which normally treated such violence as violations of a woman's honor or dignity, not her physical and psychological integrity.[294]

a. Rape

The Elements define rape as "penetration, however slight, of any part of the body of the victim or of the perpetrator with a sexual organ, or of the anal or genital opening of the victim with any object or any other part of the body," when committed "by force, or by threat of force or coercion."[295] This definition of rape, although most indebted to the common law, significantly expands the common law's narrow conception of coercion to include "fear of violence, duress, detention, psychological oppression or abuse of power."[296] It also makes the victim's consent an affirmative defense instead of an element of the crime, a "welcome departure" from the common-law position.[297]

b. Sexual Slavery

Sexual slavery is defined as using "any or all of the powers attaching to the right of ownership over" a person to cause that person "to engage in one or more acts of a sexual nature."[298] Japanese "comfort stations" during World War II and Serbian "rape camps" during the Yugoslav conflict are examples of this form of sexual violence.

c. Enforced Prostitution

Enforced prostitution is a less serious form of sexual slavery in which a person is compelled to engage in an act of a sexual nature by force or the threat of force. It differs from rape in that either the perpetrator or another person must obtain or expect to obtain "pecuniary or other advantage in exchange for or in connection with" the sexual act.[299]

d. Forced Pregnancy

Forced pregnancy is defined as "the unlawful confinement of a woman forcibly made pregnant, with the intent of affecting the ethnic composition of any population or carrying out other grave violations of international law."[300] This provision was extremely controversial because some states feared that it would criminalize national laws prohibiting abortion. The definition thus requires both forced pregnancy and unlawful confinement, although the perpetrator need not have personally impregnated the victim.[301] In addition, article 7(2)(f) specifies that the provision cannot be interpreted "as affecting national laws relating to pregnancy."

e. Enforced Sterilization

Enforced sterilization is defined as depriving "one or more persons of biological reproductive capacity" when that deprivation "was neither justified by the medical or hospital treatment of the person or persons concerned nor carried out with their genuine consent."[302] The medical experiments conducted by the Nazis in concentration camps are prototypical examples of this form of sexual violence.

f. Other Sexual Violence

Article 7(1)(g) also prohibits acts that are comparable in gravity to the five specified forms of sexual violence. Forcing a female student to strip naked and perform gymnastics before a large crowd is an example.[303]

vi. Other Inhumane Acts

Finally, article 7(1)(k) prohibits "[o]ther inhumane acts of a similar character intentionally causing great suffering, or serious injury to body or to mental or physical health." This catch-all provision was deemed necessary because the drafters recognized that it is impossible to specify in advance every act that deserves to be punished as a crime against humanity.[304] Such acts must be comparable in "nature and gravity" to one of the enumerated acts in article 7;[305] nevertheless, one important scholar has described article 7(1)(k) as a "classic example of punishment by analogy in contradiction to the *lex stricta* requirement under Article 22(2)" of the Rome Statute.[306]

D. War Crimes

Article 8 divides war crimes into four categories. The first two apply only in international armed conflict: article 8(2)(a), which prohibits grave breaches of the Geneva Conventions; and article 8(2)(b), which prohibits "other serious violations of the laws and customs applicable in international armed conflict." The second two apply only in noninternational armed conflict: article 8(2)(c) prohibits serious violations of common article 3 of the Geneva Conventions; and article 8(2)(e) prohibits "other serious violations of the laws and customs applicable in non-international armed conflict." The list of war crimes in international armed conflict is far more comprehensive than the list of war crimes in noninternational armed conflict, an asymmetry that reflects states' unwillingness to limit their ability to use armed force to combat rebellions and insurrections.[307]

1. Contextual Element

All war crimes must be committed "in the context of" and be "associated with" armed conflict. This contextual element has three components: the existence of an armed conflict, a nexus between the perpetrator's act and the armed conflict, and the perpetrator's knowledge of the armed conflict.

i. Armed Conflict

An *international armed conflict* exists whenever a state uses armed force against the internationally protected territory of another state. The magnitude of the attack is irrelevant, although the mere threat of force does not qualify.[308] Some nominally internal conflicts also qualify as international armed conflicts, such as wars of national liberation and internal conflicts in which a rebel group is effectively controlled by another state.[309]

A *noninternational armed conflict* exists whenever "there is protracted armed conflict between governmental authorities and organized armed groups or between such groups." What constitutes "protracted" armed conflict is defined negatively, as excluding "situations of internal disturbances and tensions, such as riots, isolated and sporadic acts of violence or other acts of a similar nature."[310] In other words, a conflict that is not between two states qualifies as a noninternational conflict only if it is comparable to an international armed conflict in its organization and intensity.[311]

ii. Nexus

It is not enough for the perpetrator's act to be committed during an armed conflict; there must also be a sufficient nexus between the armed conflict and the act.[312] In general, this means that the armed conflict must have played a "substantial part in the perpetrator's ability to commit it, the manner in which it was committed, or the purpose for which it was committed."[313] Acts committed by an individual whose actions are attributable to one of the belligerent parties—for example, a soldier, a member of a militia or volunteer corps, or a government official involved in the war effort—satisfy the requirement.[314] Acts committed by civilians also satisfy the nexus as long as they are ordered or tolerated by a belligerent party.[315]

iii. Knowledge

Finally, at the time of the act, the perpetrator must have been aware "of the factual circumstances that established the existence of an armed conflict."[316] This is a minimal requirement: the perpetrator must simply have known that fighting was taking place when he or she committed the act. "There is no requirement for a legal evaluation by the perpetrator as to the existence of an armed conflict or its character as international or non-international."[317]

2. Individual Acts

As noted at the beginning of this section, article 8 categorizes war crimes by the type of conflict to which they apply and by the international humanitarian law source from which they derive. This structure has been severely criticized as a "hodge-podge"[318] that exhibits "little apparent logic."[319] It is thus useful to consider war crimes not by type of conflict or by source, but by the type of conduct they criminalize.

i. Crimes against Noncombatants

Crimes against noncombatants—civilians, prisoners of war, sick and wounded soldiers—are the most common kind of war crimes. These crimes fall into two basic categories: those involving violence and mistreatment; and those affecting other basic rights, such as liberty and mobility. The first category includes the war crimes of murder,[320] willfully causing great suffering or serious injury,[321] torture and inhuman treatment,[322] biological experimentation,[323] sexual violence,[324] and outrages upon personal dignity.[325] The second category includes such war crimes as the taking of hostages,[326] unlawful deportation or transfer in an international armed conflict,[327] and depriving a noncombatant of a fair trial.[328]

ii. Attacks on Prohibited Targets

One of the fundamental principles of international humanitarian law is that belligerents are required to "direct their operations only against military objectives,"[329] a category that includes combatants and objects that, "by their nature, location, purpose, or use make an effective contribution to military action."[330] A number of important war crimes thus involve violations of this "principle of distinction": directing attacks against civilians[331] or civilian objects;[332] attacking undefended towns, dwellings, and buildings;[333] directing attacks against buildings dedicated to "religion, education, art, science or charitable purposes," as well as historic monuments and hospitals;[334] and directing attacks against buildings, transports, and personnel using the distinctive emblems of the Geneva Conventions, such as the Red Cross.[335]

iii. Attacks Inflicting Excessive Damage

Even if an attack is consistent with the principle of distinction, it must not cause damage to civilian objects or the natural environment that is "clearly excessive in relation to the concrete and direct overall military advantage anticipated."[336] Criminalizing excessive environmental damage is unprecedented in international criminal law.[337] There are, however, two significant problems with the war crime of excessive damage. First, it applies only in international armed conflicts, despite the fact that noninternational conflicts are now far more common.[338] Second, because the drafters of the Rome Statute rejected assessing proportionality from the standpoint of the reasonable military commander in favor of a purely subjective test,[339] very few clearly excessive attacks will be criminal: a commander will commit a war crime only if he or she launches an attack despite consciously recognizing that it will be clearly excessive.[340]

iv. Crimes against Property

A number of war crimes involve acts committed against property. Examples include the "[e]xtensive destruction and appropriation of property, not justified by military necessity,"[341] which is unique to international criminal law, and pillaging,[342] which is similar to the domestic crime of theft in that it refers to the appropriation of property for personal, as opposed to military, use.[343]

v. Prohibited Means of Warfare

In the context of an international armed conflict, it is a war crime to use certain kinds of weapons that cause unnecessary suffering or are not capable of distinguishing between combatants and noncombatants: poison or poisoned weapons;[344] asphyxiating, poisonous, or other gases;[345] and bullets that flatten or expand on impact (so-called dumdum bullets).[346] Proposals to criminalize the use of biological, chemical, and nuclear weapons failed because developed states refused to include nuclear weapons ("the rich man's weapons of mass destruction"), while developing states refused to include biological and chemical weapons ("the poor man's weapons of mass destruction").[347]

vi. Prohibited Methods of Warfare

The use of certain methods of warfare is also a war crime. It is criminal in both international and noninternational armed conflicts to declare that no quarter will be given to captured enemy combatants[348] or to "treacherously" kill or wound an enemy combatant.[349] Examples of the latter method, commonly known as "perfidy," include using a white flag to feign surrender, feigning sickness, or feigning protected status by using emblems such as the Red Cross.[350] In international armed conflict it is also criminal to use human shields[351] and to kill a combatant who is hors de combat.[352]

vii. Violations of Other Values

Finally, two war crimes in article 8 protect other kinds of values. First, it is a war crime for an occupying power to transfer parts of its civilian population into the territory it occupies.[353] Israel has refused to ratify the Rome Statute primarily because of this provision.[354] Second, it is a war crime to conscript, enlist, or use child soldiers.[355] A child soldier is defined as a boy or girl under fifteen years of age.[356]

E. Aggression

The IMT described aggression as "the supreme international crime ... in that it contains within itself the accumulated evil of the whole."[357] Article 5 of the Rome Statute gives the ICC jurisdiction over the crime of aggression,[358] but it conditions that jurisdiction on the Assembly of States Parties adopting a provision "defining the crime and setting out the conditions under which the Court shall exercise jurisdiction" over it.[359] This conditional jurisdiction reflects the fact that because of the inherently political nature of aggression, states were unable to agree on a definition of the crime during the drafting of the Rome Statute.[360]

SELECTED BIBLIOGRAPHY

Ambos, Kai. *Der Allgemeine Teil des Völkerstrafrechts*. Berlin: Dunker & Humblot, 2002.

Ambos, Kai. "General Principles of Criminal Law in the Rome Statute." 10 *Crim. L.F.* 1 (1999).

Badar, Mohamed Elewa. "The Mental Element in the Rome Statute of the International Criminal Court: A Commentary from a Comparative Criminal Law Perspective." 19 *Crim. L.F.* 473 (2008).

Boon, Kristin. "Rape and Forced Pregnancy under the ICC Statute: Human Dignity, Autonomy, and Consent." 32 *Colum. Hum. Rts. L. Rev.* 625 (2001).

Clark, Roger S. "The Mental Element in International Criminal Law." 12 *Crim. L.F.* 291 (2001).

Crycr, Robert, et al. *An Introduction to International Criminal Law and Procedure*, 2d ed. Cambridge: Cambridge University Press, 2010.

Orie, Alphons. "Accusatorial v. Inquisitorial Approach in International Criminal Proceedings." In Otto Triffterer (ed.), *Commentary on the Rome Statute of the International Criminal Court*, 2d ed. Munich: C. H. Beck, 2008.

Schabas, William A. *An Introduction to the International Criminal Court*, 3d ed. Cambridge: Cambridge University Press, 2007.

Werle, Gerhard. "Individual Criminal Responsibility in Article 25 ICC Statute." 5 *J. Int'l Crim. Just.* 953 (2007).

NOTES

1. Twenty-one countries abstained and seven voted against the treaty: the United States, Israel, Iraq, China, India, Vietnam, and Qatar. Edward M. Wise et al. (eds.), *International Criminal Law* 787 (Newark, NJ: Lexis-Nexis, 2007). *But cf.* Antonio Cassese, *International Criminal Law* 330 (Oxford: Oxford University Press, 2d ed. 2008) (providing a different list that includes Libya, Syria, and the Sudan instead of India, Vietnam, and Qatar).
2. Gerhard Werle, *Principles of International Criminal Law* 24 (The Hague: T. M. C. Asser Press, 2005).
3. *See* Cassese, *supra* note 1, at 319.
4. Werle, *supra* note 2, at 18–19.
5. Cassese, *supra* note 1, at 323.
6. Study by the International Law Commission of the Question of an International Criminal Jurisdiction, GA Res. 216 B (III).
7. Report of the Committee on International Criminal Court Jurisdiction, UN Doc. A/2135 (1952).
8. Report of the Committee on International Criminal Court Jurisdiction, UN Doc. A/2645 (1954).
9. GA Res. 897(IX) 1954.
10. GA Res. 3314 (XXIX) (1974).
11. *See* GA Res. 36/106 (1981).
12. GA Res. 44/89 (1989).
13. *See* Robert Cryer et al., *An Introduction to International Criminal Law and Procedure* 120 (Cambridge: Cambridge University Press, 2007).
14. UN Doc. A/RES/49/53 (1994).
15. *See* Werle, *supra* note 2, at 20.
16. *See, e.g.*, UN Doc. A/CONF.183/2/Add.1 (1998).
17. M. Cherif Bassiouni, "Negotiating the Treaty of Rome on the Establishment of an International Criminal Court," 32 *Cornell Int'l L.J.* 443, 460 (1999).
18. Werle, *supra* note 2, at 21.
19. *See* William A. Schabas, *An Introduction to the International Criminal Court* 20 (Cambridge: Cambridge University Press, 3d ed. 2007).
20. *See* Werle, *supra* note 2, at 21.
21. *Ibid.* at 22.
22. *See* Rome Statute, art. 126 [hereinafter RS].
23. *Ibid.*, art. 5.
24. *See, e.g.*, Werle, *supra* note 2, at 25.
25. "Judgment of the International Military Tribunal," 41 *Am. J. Int'l L.* 172, 221 (1947).
26. *See* Schabas, *supra* note 19, at 89.
27. RS, art. 11(1).

28. *Ibid.*, art. 11(2).
29. Schabas, *supra* note 19, at 68.
30. RS, art. 12(2)(b).
31. *Ibid.*, art. 12(3).
32. *Ibid.*, art. 13(b).
33. *See* Schabas, *supra* note 19, at 71–72.
34. RS, art. 12(2)(a).
35. *Ibid.*, art. 12(3).
36. *Ibid.*, art. 13(b).
37. *See, e.g.*, Werle, *supra* note 2, at 21.
38. *See* Schabas, *supra* note 19, at 62.
39. *See* Cassese, *supra* note 1, at 37–38.
40. *See* Bruce Broomhall, "Article 22," in Otto Triffterer (ed.), *Commentary on the Rome Statute of the International Criminal Court* 714 (Munich: C.H. Beck, 2d ed. 2008).
41. Kai Ambos, "General Principles of Criminal Law in the Rome Statute," 10 *Crim. L.F.* 1, 6 (1999).
42. *Ibid.*
43. Schabas, *supra* note 19, at 59.
44. Margaret McAuliffe deGuzman, "Article 21," in Triffterer, *supra* note 40, at 703.
45. RS, art. 21(1).
46. *See* Roger S. Clark, "The Mental Element in International Criminal Law," 12 *Crim. L.F.* 291, 319 (2001).
47. RS, art. 9(1).
48. *See* deGuzman, *supra* note 44, at 705.
49. RS, art. 21(1)(b).
50. *See, e.g.*, RS, art. 8(2)(a).
51. *See* deGuzman, *supra* note 44, at 705.
52. Alain Pellet, "Applicable Law," in Antonio Cassese et al. (eds.), *The Rome Statute of the International Criminal Court: A Commentary* 1072 (2002).
53. Robert Jennings and Arthur Watts (eds.), *Oppenheim's International Law* 25 (Oxford: Oxford University Press, 9th ed. 1992).
54. DeGuzman, *supra* note 44, at 707.
55. RS, art. 21(1)(c).
56. *See* Per Saland, "International Criminal Law Principles," in Roy S. Lee (ed.), *The International Criminal Court: The Making of the Rome Statute* 214 (The Hague: Kluwer Law International,1999).
57. *Ibid.* at 215.
58. *See* deGuzman, *supra* note 44, at 707.
59. Claus Kress, "The Procedural Law of the International Criminal Court in Outline: Anatomy of a Unique Compromise," 1 *J. Int'l Crim. Just.* 603, 605 (2003).
60. RS, art. 15(3).
61. *Ibid.*, art. 56(3).
62. Rules of Procedure and Evidence, r. 121(2)(c) [hereinafter RPE].
63. Kress, *supra* note 59, at 612.
64. RPE, r. 140.

65. RS, art. 69(3).
66. *Ibid.*, art. 67(1)(h).
67. RPE, r. 140(2)(c).
68. *Ibid.*, r. 91(3)(a).
69. Alphons Orie, "Accusatorial v. Inquisitorial Approach in International Criminal Proceedings," in Triffterer, *supra* note 40, at 1485.
70. RPE, r. 68(a).
71. RS, art. 81(1).
72. *See* Schabas, *supra* note 19, at 306.
73. RS, art. 81(1)(b).
74. *Ibid.*, art. 39(2)(b)(ii).
75. *Ibid.*, art. 74(3).
76. *Ibid.*, art. 74(5).
77. *Ibid.*, art. 74(2).
78. *See* Carsten Stahn, "Modification of the Legal Characterization of Facts in the ICC System," 16 *Crim. L.F.* 1, 1 (2005).
79. Albin Eser, quoted in Werle, *supra* note 2, at 91.
80. *Ibid.* at 92.
81. Kai Ambos, "Remarks on the General Part of International Criminal Law," 4 *J. Int'l Crim. Just.* 660, 665 (2006).
82. *Ibid.*
83. Prosecutor v. Aleksovski, Case No. IT-95-14/1-A, Judgment, para. 185 (Mar. 24, 2000).
84. *Ibid.*
85. *Ibid.*
86. *Ibid.*
87. Prosecutor v. Momir Nikolic, Case No. IT-02-60/a-S, Sentencing Judgment, para. 89 (Dec. 2, 2003).
88. *Ibid.*
89. *See* Albin Eser, "Mental Elements—Mistake of Fact and Mistake of Law," in Cassese et al., *supra* note 52, at 909.
90. Model Penal Code, §2.02, comment 1, note 1 [hereinafter MPC].
91. Elements of Crimes, art. 8(2)(a)(vii)-1, element 1 [hereinafter Elements].
92. *Ibid.*, art. 7(1)(f), element 1.
93. *Ibid.*, art. 8(2)(a)(ii)-3, element 2.
94. *Ibid.*, art. 8(2)(b)(xxxvi), element 2.
95. *Ibid.*, art. 8(2)(a)(vi), element 2.
96. *See* Eser, *supra* note 89, at 913.
97. *See* Werle, *supra* note 2, at 104.
98. Elements, art. 8(2)(b)(xxv), element 1.
99. *See* RS, art. 28(a)(ii).
100. Clark, *supra* note 46, at 303–304.
101. *See* Saland, *supra* note 56, at 212–213.
102. *See* Nina H. B. Jorgensen, "A Reappraisal of the Abandoned Nuremberg Concept of Criminal Organizations in the Context of Justice in Rwanda," 12 *Crim. L.F.* 371, 395 (2001).

103. *See* Mohamed Elewa Badar, "The Mental Element in the Rome Statute of the International Criminal Court: A Commentary from a Comparative Criminal Law Perspective," 19 *Crim. L.F.* 473, 476 (2008).

104. *See* Werle, *supra* note 2, at 103.

105. RS, art. 30(2)(a).

106. *See* MPC, §2.02(2)(a).

107. Eser, *supra* note 89, at 913 n. 122.

108. RS, art. 30(2)(b).

109. *See* Badar, *supra* note 103, at 483.

110. *See ibid.* at 485.

111. *See* Werle, *supra* note 2, at 113.

112. Prosecutor v. Lubanga, Case No. ICC-01/04-01/06, Decision on the Confirmation of Charges, para. 438 (Jan. 29, 2007).

113. *See* Werle, *supra* note 2, at 114 n. 134.

114. *Ibid.* at 104; *see also* Ambos, *supra* note 41, at 21–22.

115. Elements, art. 8(2)(a)(viii), element 3.

116. RS, art. 6.

117. MPC, §2.02(7).

118. Glanville Williams, *Criminal Law: The General Part* 159 (London: Stevens & Sons, 2d ed. 1961). *But cf.* Badar, *supra* note 103, at 496 (arguing that such willful blindness does satisfy article 30(3)'s knowledge requirement).

119. *See* Saland, *supra* note 56, at 205.

120. *See* Clark, *supra* note 46, at 301.

121. *See* Saland, *supra* note 56, at 206.

122. *See* Clark, *supra* note 46, at 301.

123. Elements, art. 8(2)(b)(vii)-4.

124. *See* Clark, *supra* note 46, at 304.

125. *See ibid.* at 304 n. 42; Werle, *supra* note 2, at 98.

126. Elements, art. 6(b).

127. *Ibid.*, art. 8(2)(a)(iii).

128. Gerhard Werle, "Individual Criminal Responsibility in Article 25 ICC Statute," 5 *J. Int'l Crim. Just.* 953, 955 (2007).

129. United States v. Otto Ohlendorf et al., reprinted in IV *Trials of War Criminals before the Nuremberg Military Tribunals under Control Council Law No. 10* (Washington, DC: United States Government Printing Office, 1949), Indictment (*Einsatzgruppen Case*).

130. RS, art. 25(3)(a).

131. *Ibid.*, art. 25(3)(b).

132. *Ibid.*, art. 25(3)(c).

133. *Ibid.*, art. 25(3)(d).

134. *Lubanga*, para. 330.

135. *See* Badar, *supra* note 103, at 505.

136. *See* Kai Ambos, "Article 25," in Triffterer, *supra* note 40, at 747.

137. *Lubanga*, para. 343.

138. *Ibid.*, para. 347.

139. *Ibid.*, para. 349.

140. *Ibid.*, para. 361.
141. *Ibid.*, para. 362.
142. *Ibid.*, para. 366.
143. *See* Werle, *supra* note 2, at 964.
144. RS, art. 25(3)(a); *cf.* MPC, §2.06(2) (limiting perpetration by means to those who cause "an innocent or irresponsible person" to commit a crime).
145. *See* Prosecutor v. Katanga, Case No. ICC-01/04-01/07, Decision on the Confirmation of Charges, para. 496 (Sept. 30, 2008).
146. *Ibid.*, para. 510.
147. *Ibid.*, para. 512.
148. *Ibid.*
149. *Ibid.*, para. 513.
150. *Ibid.*, para. 514.
151. *Ibid.*, para. 527.
152. *Ibid.*, para. 534.
153. *See* Eser, *supra* note 89, at 796.
154. *Ibid.* at 797.
155. *Ibid.* at 796.
156. *See* Prosecutor v. Kordic and Cerkez, Case No. IT-95-14/2-A, Judgment, para. 27 (Dec. 17, 2004).
157. Eser, *supra* note 89, at 796.
158. *Ibid.*
159. Prosecutor v. Furundzija, Case No. IT-95-17/1-T, Judgment, para. 231 (Dec. 10, 1998).
160. *See, e.g.*, Eser, *supra* note 89, at 800.
161. MPC, §2.06(3)(a).
162. *See* Badar, *supra* note 103, at 507.
163. *See* Ambos, *supra* note 136, at 757; Eser, *supra* note 89, at 801. *But cf.* Werle, *supra* note 2, at 969 (arguing that the standards are the same).
164. *See, e.g.*, Eser, *supra* note 89, at 802.
165. Werle, *supra* note 2, at 970–971.
166. RS, arts. 25(3)(d)(i) and 25(3)(d)(ii).
167. *See* Ambos, *supra* note 136, at 760.
168. *See* Eser, *supra* note 89, at 802.
169. *See* Saland, *supra* note 56, at 199–200.
170. *Ibid.* at 804. Eser notes that because direct and public incitement is limited to genocide, the provision seems misplaced in part 3's "General Principles of Criminal Law." It would have been better placed in article 6, which defines the crime of genocide. Eser, *supra* note 89.
171. *Ibid.* at 805.
172. *Ibid.*
173. *Ibid.* at 806; Werle, *supra* note 2, at 972.
174. Werle, *supra* note 2, at 972 (mentioning the German Criminal Code as an example).
175. Eser, *supra* note 89, at 806.
176. *Ibid.* at 808.

177. *See* Ambos, *supra* note 136, at 763.
178. *See, e.g., ibid.*
179. *See* MPC, §5.01(4).
180. *See* Eser, *supra* note 89, at 817.
181. Kai Ambos, *Der Allgemeine Teil des Völkerstrafrechts* 667 (2002).
182. *See* Cryer et al., *supra* note 13, at 328–329.
183. RS, art. 28(a).
184. Prosecutor v. Delalic et al., Case No. IT-96-21-A, Judgment, para. 256 (Feb. 20, 2001).
185. Ambos, *supra* note 181, at 675.
186. RS, art. 28(a)(i).
187. Werle, *supra* note 2, at 134.
188. RS, art. 28(b)(i).
189. *See* Werle, *supra* note 2, at 134.
190. RS, arts. 28(a)(ii) and 28(b)(iii).
191. *Ibid.*, arts. 28(a) and 28(b).
192. Cited in Cryer et al., *supra* note 13, at 327.
193. *See* Andrew Clapham, "The Question of Jurisdiction under International Criminal Law over Legal Persons," in Menno T. Kamminga and Saman Zia-Zarifi (eds.), *Liability of Multinational Corporations under International Law* 144 (The Hague: Kluwer, 2000).
194. *See ibid.* at 157.
195. Antonio Cassese, "Justifications and Excuses in Criminal Law," in Cassese et al., *supra* note 52, at 954.
196. *See* Cryer et al., *supra* note 13, at 333.
197. *See* Saland, *supra* note 56, at 208–209.
198. *See* Cryer et al, *supra* note 13, at 346–348.
199. RS, art. 66(3).
200. MPC, §1.12(2)(a).
201. Clark, *supra* note 46, at 304 n. 44.
202. *Ibid.* at 309 n. 62.
203. RS, art. 31(a).
204. *See* RPE, r. 145(2)(a)(i).
205. RS, art. 31(b).
206. *See* Kai Ambos, "Other Grounds for Excluding Criminal Responsibility," in Cassese et al., *supra* note 52, at 1030.
207. *See ibid.* at 1032.
208. *See* Werle, *supra* note 2, at 142.
209. Ambos, *supra* note 206, at 1033.
210. *Ibid.* at 1038.
211. *See ibid.* at 1042–1045.
212. *Ibid.* at 1041.
213. *See, e.g., ibid.* at 1038–1039.
214. E. van Sliedregt, *The Criminal Responsibility of Individuals for Violations of International Humanitarian Law* 312 (The Hague: T. M. C. Asser Press, 2003).

215. *See, e.g.*, Kenneth W. Simons, "Mistake and Impossibility, Law and Fact, and Culpability: A Speculative Essay," 81 *Nw. J. Crim. L. & Criminology* 447, 466 (1990).
216. *See*, e.g., Eser, *supra* note 89, at 939–940.
217. *See*, *e.g.*, Williams, *supra* note 118, at 213.
218. *See* George P. Fletcher, *Rethinking Criminal Law* 689 (New York: Oxford University Press, 2000). As Fletcher notes, the MPC does not even require mistakes regarding a justification to be reasonable. *Ibid.*
219. *See, e.g.*, Werle, *supra* note 2, at 152 (arguing that this limitation violates the principle of legality).
220. *Cf.* MPC, §2.04(3)(b).
221. RS, art. 33(1).
222. *Ibid.*, art. 33(2).
223. *Ibid.*, art. 33(1)(a).
224. *See* Andreas Zimmerman, "Superior Orders," in Cassese et al., *supra* note 52, at 969.
225. *See, e.g., ibid.*
226. *See, e.g.*, Otto Triffterer, "Article 33," in Triffterer, *supra* note 40, at 924.
227. *Ibid.* at 925.
228. RS, art. 33(1)(b).
229. *Ibid.*, art. 33(1)(c).
230. Attorney General of Israel v. Eichmann, 36 ILR 277 (Isr. Sup. Ct., 1962).
231. *See* Cryer et al., *supra* note 13, at 345–346.
232. RS, art. 77(1).
233. *Ibid.*, art. 77(2).
234. *See* Schabas, *supra* note 19, at 318.
235. RS, art. 78(1).
236. RPE, r. 145(1)(c).
237. *Ibid.*, r. 145(2).
238. Schabas, *supra* note 19, at 315–316.
239. Cryer et al., *supra* note 13, at 394.
240. *See, e.g.*, Otto Triffterer, "Preliminary Remarks," in Triffterer, *supra* note 40, at 23.
241. RS, Preamble, para. 3.
242. Werle, *supra* note 2, at 29.
243. *Ibid.*
244. Triffterer, *supra* note 240, at 23.
245. RS, art. 8(2)(a)(i).
246. *Ibid.*, art. 7(1)(g).
247. *Ibid.*, art. 8(2)(c)(ii).
248. Cassese, *supra* note 1, at 54.
249. RS, art. 8(2)(b)(xii).
250. *Ibid.*, art. 8(2)(b)(xx).
251. *See* Ambos, *supra* note 81, at 663.
252. Werle, *supra* note 2, at 28.
253. *See, e.g.*, Clark, *supra* note 46, at 326–327.
254. William A. Schabas, "Article 6," in Triffterer, *supra* note 40, at 150–151.

255. Elements, art. 6(a)(1).
256. *Ibid.*, art. 6(a), element 1, n. 2.
257. Prosecutor v. Kayishema and Ruzindana, Case No. ICTR-95-1-T, Judgment, para. 109 (May 21, 1999).
258. Elements, art. 6(b), element 1, n. 3.
259. Prosecutor v. Krstic, Case No. ICTY-98-33-T, Judgment, para. 513 (Aug. 2, 2001).
260. Frank Selbmann, *Der Tatbestand dez Genozids im Völkerstrafrecht* 161 (Leipzig: Leipziger Universitätsverlag, 2002).
261. Claus Kress, "The Crime of Genocide under International Law," 6 *Int'l Crim. L. Rev.* 461, 482 (2006).
262. *See, e.g., ibid.*
263. Prosecutor v. Akayesu, Case No. ICTR-96-4-T, Judgment, para. 507 (Sept. 2, 1998).
264. *Ibid.* at 508. This would be the case, for example, in a society in which a child's ethnicity is determined by the father.
265. Elements, art. 6(d), element 1.
266. *See* Kress, *supra* note 261, at 484.
267. Elements, art. 6(e), element 1 n. 5.
268. *See* Schabas, *supra* note 254, at 149.
269. *Akayesu* Trial Judgment, paras. 512–515.
270. *See, e.g., Krstic* Trial Judgment, para. 557.
271. Kress, *supra* note 261, at 493.
272. *Kayishema and Ruzindana* Trial Judgment, para. 96.
273. *See* Cryer et al., *supra* note 13, at 181.
274. Prosecutor v. Jelisic, Case No. IT-95-10-T, Judgment, para. 400 (Dec. 14, 1999).
275. Christopher K. Hall, "Article 7," in Triffterer, *supra* note 40, at 176.
276. *Ibid.*
277. *See* Werle, *supra* note 2, at 221–222.
278. *See* 1 Y.B. ILC 47 (1996).
279. *Ibid.*
280. RS, art. 7(2)(a).
281. *See* Werle, *supra* note 2, at 226.
282. Elements, art. 7, Introduction, para. 2.
283. *Ibid.*, art. 7(1)(a), element 1, n. 7.
284. *See* Clark, *supra* note 46, at 325.
285. Elements, art. 7(1)(b), element 1.
286. *Ibid.*
287. *See* Schabas, *supra* note 19, at 105.
288. Elements, art. 7(1)(d), element 1, n. 12.
289. *See* Werle, *supra* note 2, at 241.
290. Convention against Torture and Other Cruel, Inhuman or Degrading Treatment or Punishment, A/RES/39/46, art. 1 (December 10, 1984).
291. *See ibid.*, art. 1.
292. *See* Cryer et al., *supra* note 13, at 207.
293. Convention against Torture, *supra* note 290, art. 1.

294. *See* Hall, *supra* note 275, at 208.
295. Elements, art. 7(1)(g)-1, elements 1, 2.
296. *Ibid.*, art. 7(1)(g)-1, element 2.
297. *See* Kristin Boon, "Rape and Forced Pregnancy under the ICC Statute: Human Dignity, Autonomy, and Consent," 32 *Colum. Hum. Rts. L. Rev.* 625, 648 (2001).
298. Elements, art. 7(1)(g)-2, elements 1, 2.
299. *Ibid.*, art. 7(1)(g)-3, elements 1, 2.
300. RS, art. 7(2)(f).
301. *See* Cryer et al., *supra* note 13, at 211–212.
302. Elements, art. 7(1)(g)-5, elements 1, 2.
303. *See Akayesu* Trial Judgment, para. 598.
304. *See* Werle, *supra* note 2, at 264.
305. Elements, art. 7(1)(k), element 2, n. 30.
306. Ambos, *supra* note 81, at 670.
307. *See* Cryer et al., *supra* note 13, at 229–232.
308. *See* Werle, *supra* note 2, at 287–288.
309. *See* Cryer et al., *supra* note 13, at 234–235.
310. RS, art. 8(2)(f).
311. *See* Cryer et al., *supra* note 13, at 236–237.
312. Michael Cottier, "Article 8," in Triffterer, *supra* note 40, at 293.
313. Prosecutor v. Kunarac et al., Case No. IT-96-23 & IT-96-23/1-A, Judgment, para. 58 (June 12, 2002).
314. *See* Werle, *supra* note 2, at 294–295.
315. *Ibid.* at 296.
316. Elements, art. 8, Introduction.
317. *Ibid.*, art. 8, Introduction.
318. Michael Bothe, "War Crimes," in Cassese et al., *supra* note 52, at 396.
319. Cottier, *supra* note 312, at 296.
320. RS, art. 8(2)(a)(i).
321. *Ibid.*, art. 8(2)(a)(iii).
322. *Ibid.*, art. 8(2)(a)(ii). Unlike torture as a crime against humanity, torture as a war crime requires that the pain and suffering be inflicted for the purpose of obtaining a confession or information. Elements, art. 8(2)(a)(ii)-1, element 2.
323. RS, art. 8(2)(b)(x).
324. *Ibid.*, art. 8(2)(b)(xxii).
325. *Ibid.*, art. 8(2)(b)(xxi). Examples include desecration of corpses and forcing prisoners of war to violate the tenets of their religion. *See* Cryer et al., *supra* note 13, at 244.
326. RS, art. 8(2)(a)(viii).
327. *Ibid.*, art. 8(2)(a)(vii). In a noninternational armed conflict it is a war crime to displace civilians for reasons unrelated to the conflict. *Ibid.*, art. 8(2)(e)(viii).
328. *Ibid.*, art. 8(2)(a)(vi).
329. Protocol Additional to the Geneva Conventions of 12 August 1949, and Relating to the Protection of Victims of International Armed Conflicts (Protocol I), art. 48 (June 8, 1977).

330. *Ibid.*, art. 52(2).
331. RS, art. 8(2)(b)(i).
332. *Ibid.*, art. 8(2)(b)(ii).
333. *Ibid.*, art. 8(2)(b)(v).
334. *Ibid.*, art. 8(2)(b)(ix).
335. *Ibid.*, art. 8(2)(b)(vii).
336. *Ibid.*, art. 8(2)(b)(iv).
337. *See* Jessica C. Lawrence and Kevin Jon Heller, "The First Ecocentric Environmental War Crime: Article 8(2)(b)(iv) of the Rome Statute," 20 *Geo. Int'l Env. L. Rev.* 61 (2007).
338. *Ibid.* at 85.
339. *See* Cryer et al., *supra* note 13, at 252.
340. *See* Lawrence and Heller, *supra* note 337, at 83.
341. RS, art. 8(2)(a)(iv).
342. *Ibid.*, art. 8(2)(b)(xvi).
343. *See* Cryer et al., *supra* note 13, at 254.
344. RS, art. 8(2)(b)(xvii).
345. *Ibid.*, art. 8(2)(b)(xviii).
346. *Ibid.*, art. 8(2)(b)(xix).
347. *See* Cryer et al., *supra* note 13, at 255.
348. *See, e.g.*, RS, art. 8(2)(b)(xii).
349. *See, e.g.*, RS, art. 8(2)(b)(xi).
350. *See* Cryer et al., *supra* note 13, at 257.
351. RS, art. 8(2)(b)(xxiii).
352. *Ibid.*, art. 8(2)(b)(vi).
353. *Ibid.*, art. 8(2)(b)(viii).
354. *See* Cryer et al., *supra* note 13, at 259.
355. RS, art. 8(2)(e)(vii).
356. *Ibid.*
357. Judgment, United States v. Goering et al., International Military Tribunal, 1 Oct. 1946, *Nazi Conspiracy and Aggression: Opinion and Judgment* 186 (Washington, DC: United States Government Printing Office, 1947).
358. RS, art. 5(1)(d).
359. *Ibid.*, art. 5(2).
360. *See* Cryer et al., *supra* note 13, at 259.

INDEX

A (Conjoined Twins: Surgical Separation), Re, 542
Abandonment defense, 30; in Argentine criminal law, 23–24; complicity and, 62; in German criminal law, 264; in Israeli criminal law, 370–371; in Rome Statute, 609–610; in Russian criminal law, 422. *See also* Attempt; Complicity; Discontinued crimes, in Chinese criminal law
Abetting. *See* Complicity
Abolition of Juries Act of 1969 (South Africa), 458
Abortion: in Argentine criminal law, 35, 37; in German criminal law, 253; in Spanish criminal law, 519
Absent-element defenses: in American criminal law, 580; in Spanish criminal law, 507
Absicht, 261. See also *Dolus*
Absolute liability; in Australian criminal law, 64; in Israeli criminal law, 367–368; in Spanish criminal law, 491, 501. *See also* Strict liability
Accessories: in Australian criminal law, 61–62; in Iranian criminal law, 330–331; in South African criminal law, 474; to suicide, 474; in United Kingdom (England and Wales) criminal law, 539
Accessories and Abettors Act 1861 (England), 539
Accomplice liability. *See* Complicity
Act for Punishing Counterrevolutionaries of 1951 (China), 138

Act for the Punishment of Corruption of 1952 (China), 138
Actio libera in causa, 459
Active-personality principle, 416
Act requirement: in Argentine criminal law, 21–22; in Australian criminal law, 57; in Canadian criminal law, 103–105; in Chinese criminal law, 147; in Egyptian criminal law, 186; in French criminal law, 215; in German criminal law, 259–260; in Indian criminal law, 292–293; in Iranian criminal law, 326; in Japanese criminal law, 399; in Rome Statute, 602; in Russian criminal law, 419; in South African criminal law, 459; in Spanish criminal law, 497–498; in United Kingdom (England and Wales) criminal law, 535–536
Actus reus: accomplice liability and, 33; in Argentine criminal law, 21–24, 33; in Australian criminal law, 53, 56, 57–58; in Canadian criminal law, 103–106; in Chinese criminal law, 147–148; in Egyptian criminal law, 186–187; in French criminal law, 215–216; in German criminal law, 259–261; in Indian criminal law, 292–294; in Iranian criminal law, 326; in Israeli criminal law, 355–357; in Japanese criminal law, 399–400; in Rome Statute, 601–603; in Russian criminal law, 419–420; in South African criminal law, 459–460; in Spanish criminal law, 497–501; in United Kingdom (England and Wales) criminal law, 535–536

Adultery, in Egyptian criminal law, 199
African National Congress, 456
Aggression, in Rome Statute, 624
Aiding. *See* Complicity
Akayesu, 3, 617
Alcohol offenses: in Egyptian criminal law, 202; in Iranian criminal law, 336, 345–346. *See also* Intoxication
Alexander II, 415
ALI. *See* American Law Institute
Ali, Muhammad, 180
American Convention on Human Rights, 20
American criminal law, 2, 3, 8; absent-element defenses in, 580; American Law Institute test in, 585; attempted crimes in, 579; causation in, 572–573; common law in, 2–3, 566; complicity in, 577; concept of, 2; concurrency requirement in, 576; consent in, 580; conspiracy in, 579–580; corporate criminal liability in, 578; culpability requirements in, 573–576; defenses in, 580–587; defensive-force justification in, 582–583; disability excuses in, 584; doctrines of imputation in, 576–578; double jeopardy in, 582, 586; duress defense in, 586; embezzlement in, 590; excuses in, 581, 583–586; federal insanity test in, 585–586; homicide in, 588–589; ignorance of fact/law defense in, 584; inchoate crimes in, 579–580; insanity defense in, 581, 584, 585; intoxication in, 577, 584, 586; investigation/accusation process in, 568–569; justifications in, 581, 582–583; legality principle in, 566–567; lesser-evils defense in, 582; liability requirements in, 571–587; mistake of fact/law defense in, 581, 583–584; mistake of justification in, 584; necessity defense in, 582; negligence in, 575–576; nonexculpatory defenses in, 581–582, 586–587; objective offense requirements in, 571–573; offense-modification defenses in, 580–581; plea bargaining in, 570; pretrial processes in, 569–570; process of, 567–571; public authority defense in, 581, 583; purpose in, 574; recklessness in, 574, 575; reform efforts in, 564–565; self-defense in, 581; sex offenses in, 578, 589–590; solicitation in, 580; sources/form of, 564–566; specific offenses in, 587–590; statutory rape in, 578; strict liability in, 576; substituted culpability in, 577–578; theft in, 590; trial/post-trial processes in, 570–571
American Law Institute (ALI), 565
American Law Institute test, 585. *See also* Insanity defense
Anglo-American criminal law, 1, 9, 359. *See also* American criminal law; United Kingdom (England and Wales) criminal law
Answer to Several Issues on the Specific Application of Handling Hooligan Cases (China), 167
Anti-Drugs Act of 1988 (Iran), 322, 326, 337
Antimonopoly Law (Japan), 402
Antonius Matthaeus II, 458
Apostasy, 345
Appeals Law of 1959 (Egypt), 183
Arancibia-Clavel, 16–17
Argentine constitutional law, 14–15
Argentine criminal law, 4, 12–41; abandonment defense in, 23–24; abortion in, 35, 37; act requirement in, 21–22; *actus reus* in, 21–24, 33; attempted crimes in, 29–31; complicity in, 31–34; constitutional law and, 14–15; corporate criminal liability in, 34–35; culpability principle in, 24; defenses, 35–37; *dolus* v. negligence in, 25–27; failed attempts in, 29–31; federalism and, 15–16; historical background, 13–14; homicide, 19, 23, 28, 38–39; insanity defense in, 19, 35–36; juries in, 15; jurisdiction, 15–16; legality principle, 16–18; liability requirements, 21–35; *mens rea* in, 24–28; mental element in, 24–28; necessity defense in, 35; negligence clauses in, 25; omissions in, 22–24; outweighing rights defense in, 36–37; pornography in, 40; property offenses, 40–41; prostitution in, 40; punishment schedule, 14; self-defense in, 35; sex offenses, 39–40; special part, 37–41; strict liability and, 24; structure of special part, 37–38; theories of punishment, 18–21
Armed conflict, 622
Arrest and Detention Act of 1954 (China), 138

Arson, 7, 117, 120, 160, 164, 175, 188, 191–193, 196, 264, 277, 327, 395, 399, 401, 407, 473, 495, 576, 581, 588
Assistance, in Rome Statute, 608. *See also* Complicity
Assisted suicide: in Canadian criminal law, 126; in Chinese criminal law, 156–157; in Indian criminal law, 313–314; in Israeli criminal law, 381; in South African criminal law, 474–475. *See also* Voluntary euthanasia
Attempt: abandonment defense for, 264; aiding/instigating and, 371; in American criminal law, 579; in Argentine criminal law, 29–31; in Australian criminal law, 59–60; in Canadian criminal law, 110–111; in Chinese criminal law, 150; in Egyptian criminal law, 189; in French criminal law, 220–221; in German criminal law, 263–265; in Indian criminal law, 295; in Iranian criminal law, 328; in Israeli criminal law, 368–369; in Japanese criminal law, 401; in Russian criminal law, 421–422; in Rome Statute, 609; in South African criminal law, 465–466; in Spanish criminal law, 502–503; in United Kingdom (England and Wales) criminal law, 538. *See also* Inchoate crimes
Attempted suicide: in Indian criminal law, 313; in Israeli criminal law, 381
Australian criminal law, 4, 50–82; accessories in, 61–62; act requirement in, 57; *actus reus* in, 53, 56, 57–58; attempted crimes in, 59–60; burden of proof in, 65; causation in, 63–64; complicity in, 61–62; consent in, 68–69; conspiracy in, 60–61; corporate criminal liability in, 62–63; death penalty in, 76; defenses, 64–65; duress defense in, 73–74; entrapment in, 74; excuses, 69–75; fraud in, 80; historical background, 50–51; homicide in, 63–64, 78–79; insanity defense in, 70–72; intent in, 58–59; intoxication in, 72–73; jurisdiction, 51–52; justifications, 65–69; legality principle, 52–53; liability requirements, 56–64; mistake/ignorance of law defense in, 69–70; mistake of fact defense in, 69–70; necessity defense in, 65–67; negligence in, 59; omission in, 57; process of, 54–55; punishment in, 75–76; recklessness in, 59; sanctions, 75–76; self-defense in, 67–68; sex offenses in, 79–80; sources of, 53–54; special part, 77–82; status crimes and, 58; superior orders in, 69, 74–75; terrorism and, 53, 81–82; theft in, 80; theories of punishment, 55–56
Australian Criminal Reports, 54
Automatism: in Australian criminal law, 57, 72; in Canadian criminal law, 114, 118; in South African criminal law, 459, 463; in United Kingdom (England and Wales) criminal law, 535–536

Bad Samaritan statute, 22, 24
Balance-of-evils defense. *See* Choice-of-evils defense
Barton v. The Queen, 55
Bavarian Criminal Code (1813), 4, 13, 210
Beard, Director of Public Prosecutions v., 119
Beccaria, Cesare, 8, 210, 489
Bennett & Co. (Pty.) Ltd., R v., 467
Bentham, Jeremy, 210, 211, 289, 489
Beyond a reasonable doubt: in American criminal law, 570, 575; in Canadian criminal law 101, 103, 108, 111, 114, 119; in Egyptian criminal law, 186; in Indian criminal law, 299–300; in Israeli criminal law, 368, 376; in Japanese criminal law, 403; in Rome Statute, 611. *See also* Burden of proof; *In dubio pro reo*
Bill of Rights (South Africa), 456
Blackstone, William, 532, 564
Blaue, R v., 541
Blood money, 7, 336, 339–341
Bolshevik Revolution, 138, 415, 429
Bree, R v., 550
Bribery, 5, 84, 138, 162, 164, 172, 194, 196, 279, 344, 400, 407, 495, 588
Burden of proof, 8; in Australian criminal law, 65; in Chinese criminal law, 153; in Egyptian criminal law, 186; in French criminal law, 224; in German criminal law, 269; in Indian criminal law, 299–300; in Iranian criminal law, 332; in Israeli criminal law, 376; in Japanese criminal law, 403; in Rome Statute,

Burden of proof (*continued*)
611–612; in Russian criminal law, 426; in South African criminal law, 469; in Spanish criminal law, 494, 507; in United Kingdom (England and Wales) criminal law, 541. *See also* Beyond a reasonable doubt; *In dubio pro reo*

Business crimes, in Spanish criminal law, 521. *See also* Corporate criminal liability

Campbell, R v., 538

Canadian Charter of Rights and Fundamental Freedoms, 79, 98, 100

Canadian criminal law, 4–5; act requirement in, 103–105; *actus reus* in, 103–106; assisted suicide in, 126; attempted crimes in, 110–111; burden of proof, 114–115; causation in, 105–106; common law in, 99–100, 103; complicity in, 111–113; consent in, 116–117; conspiracy in, 111; corporate criminal liability in, 113–114; death penalty in, 122; defenses, 114–115; duress defense in, 120–121; entrapment in, 121; excuses, 117–121; historical background, 98; homicide in, 123–124; inchoate crimes in, 110–111; insanity defense in, 117–119; intent in, 107–108; intoxication defense in, 119–120; jurisdiction, 98–99; justifications, 115–117; knowledge/willful blindness in, 108; legality principles/codification of, 99–100; liability requirements, 103–114; *mens rea* in, 106–110; mistake/ignorance of law/fact in, 117; necessity justification in, 115, 120–121; negligence in, 109–110; omissions in, 105; process in, 101–102; provocation defense in, 124; punishment in, 121–122; recklessness in, 108–109; sanctions, 121–122; self-defense in, 115–116; sex offenses in, 124–125; sources of, 100–101; special part, 122–129; status crimes in, 58; superior orders in, 121; Supreme Court interpreting, 128–129; terrorism and, 127–129; theft/fraud in, 125–126; theories of punishment, 102–103; uniformity of, 128–129; victimless crimes in, 126–127

Canadian Supreme Court, 3

Capital punishment: in American criminal law, 570; in Argentine criminal law 4, 13, 20–21; in Australian criminal law, 76, 93–94; in Canadian criminal law, 122; in Chinese criminal law, 159, 161–164; in Egyptian criminal law, 195–196; in French criminal law, 210; in German criminal law, 253, 277; in Indian criminal law, 306, 307; in Iranian criminal law, 339; in Israeli criminal law, 380; in Japanese criminal law, 407; in Rome Statute, 614; in Russian criminal law, 434–435; in South African criminal law, 473, 484; in Spanish criminal law, 517; in United Kingdom (England and Wales) criminal law, 546

Case of Huang Jingqiu: The Crime of Subverting the State Power (China), 171

Caste system, 6

Causa. *See* Negligence

Causation: in American criminal law, 572–573; in Australian criminal law, 63–64; in Canadian criminal law, 105–106; in Chinese criminal law, 152–153; in Egyptian criminal law, 190; in French criminal law, 223; in German criminal law, 268; in Indian criminal law, 298–299; in Iranian criminal law, 331–332; in Israeli criminal law, 375–376; in Japanese criminal law, 402–403; in Rome Statute, 605; in Russian criminal law, 424–425; in South African criminal law, 468; in Spanish criminal law, 505–507; in United Kingdom (England and Wales) criminal law, 540–541

Causing death by driving, 549

Chastisement of children defense: in Israeli criminal law, 379; in South African criminal law, 471–472

Chinalawinfo.com, 171

Chinese Communist Party, 5, 138, 171

Chinese constitutional law, 141

Chinese criminal law, 5; act requirement in, 147; *actus reus* in, 147–148; assisted suicide in, 156–157; attempted crimes in, 150; burden of proof in, 153; causation in, 152–153; complicity in, 151; consent in, 156–157; corporate criminal liability in, 152;

crime preparation in, 150; death penalty in, 159, 161–164; defense counsel rights in, 142–143; defenses, 153; deprivation of political rights in, 159–160; discontinued crimes in, 150; excuses in, 157–158; fraud in, 169; historical background, 138–139; homicide in, 165–166; imprisonment in, 159; inchoate crimes in, 150; insanity defense in, 158; interpretations of, 141; judicial structure, 139–140; juries v. people's assessors in, 143–144; jurisdiction, 139–140; justifications in, 153–157; liability requirements, 146–153; matching punishment with crime in, 145–146; *mens rea* in, 148–150; necessity defense in, 155–156; no presumption of guilt until judgment in, 142; omissions in, 147; political crimes in, 170; prescribed punishments principle in, 145; pretrial discovery in, 144; process, 142–144; provocation in, 166; punishment in, 158–161; sanctions, 158–164; sex offenses in, 166–168; sources, 140–142; special part, 164–171; status in, 148; subjects of crime in, 148; superior orders in, 157; theft in, 141, 168–169; theories of punishment, 144–146; unavoidable/unforeseeable circumstances in, 149; underage criminals in, 157–158; victimless crimes in, 169–170

Chinese Patriotic and Democratic Party, 171

Choice-of-evils defense, 35, 155, 274, 299–300, 377, 426, 432, 542, 582. *See also* Duress defense; Necessity defense

Chretien, S v., 461

Christy Pontiac-GMC, Inc., State v., 578

Civil law, 9

Civil liability, 495–496; corporate, 505

Civil Procedure Law (China), 139

Clark, Roger, 611

Clarke v. Hurst NO, 474

Code for Louisiana (Livingston), 289

Code of Criminal Procedure (Egypt), 183, 184–185

Code of Criminal Procedure (Germany), 257, 258

Code of Criminal Procedure (Iran), 323, 325, 339

Code of Criminal Procedure (Japan), 394

Code of Offenses against the Peace and Security of Mankind (1947), 594

Código Penal (CP), 4, 13–16, 18–20, 22–27, 29–41. *See also* Argentine criminal law

Coke, Edward, 532

Commentaries on the Laws of England (Blackstone), 564

Common law, 2, 3, 9, 50; in American criminal law, 2–3, 566; in Australian criminal law, 4; in Canadian criminal law, 99–100, 103; complicity and, 61–62; in criminal law of Commonwealth countries, 4; defenses from, 128; duress defense in, 73, 128; intoxication and, 72–73, 119; necessity defense and, 120; negligence in, 59

Common-law crimes. *See* Legality principle

Common-law misdemeanors. *See* Legality principle

Common-purpose rule, 466, 467

Commonwealth Constitution (Australia), 51

Commonwealth countries, 3

Commutation of sentence: for death penalty, 196; in Egyptian criminal law, 195, 196

Comparative analysis, 3; as critical theory, 2

Comparative criminal law, project of, 1–4

Complicity: abandonment defense for, 62; aiding, 369–371; in American criminal law, 577; in Argentine criminal law, 31–34; in Australian criminal law, 61–62; in Canadian criminal law, 111–113; in Chinese criminal law, 151; common law and, 61–62; in Egyptian criminal law, 189–190; external dependence in, 33; in French criminal law, 222–223; in German criminal law, 265–267; in Indian criminal law, 296–297; internal dependence in, 33–34; in Iranian criminal law, 329–331; in Israeli criminal law, 369–375; in Japanese criminal law, 401–402; recklessness and, 112; in Russian criminal law, 423–424; in South African criminal law, 466–467; in Spanish criminal law, 504; in United Kingdom (England and Wales) criminal law, 539; withdrawal and, 62, 223

Concurrency requirement, in American criminal law, 576

Conditional intent, 261–262
Conscious negligence, 27
Consensual dispositions, 257
Consent: in American criminal law, 580; in Australian criminal law, 68–69; in Canadian criminal law, 116–117; in Chinese criminal law, 156–157; in French criminal law, 225; in German criminal law, 255, 271; in Indian criminal law, 301–302; in Iranian criminal law, 333–334; in Israeli criminal law, 379; in Japanese criminal law, 405; in Russian criminal law, 427; in South African criminal law, 470; in Spanish criminal law, 510–511; in United Kingdom (England and Wales) criminal law, 542–543
Conspiracy: in American criminal law, 579–580; in Australian criminal law, 60–61; in Canadian criminal law, 111; in Egyptian criminal law, 189; in French criminal law, 221; in Indian criminal law, 295–296; in Iranian criminal law, 329; in Israeli criminal law, 369; in Japanese criminal law, 401; in Rome Statute, 608; in Russian criminal law, 422–423; in South African criminal law, 466; in Spanish criminal law, 503; in United Kingdom (England and Wales) criminal law, 538–539. *See also* Inchoate crimes
Constitution, Australian, 75; victimless crimes in, 80–81. *See also* Commonwealth Constitution
Constitution, French, 210, 212
Constitution, U.S., 14, 565, 566
Constitutional law: Argentine, 14–15; Chinese, 141; German, 256
Constitution of the Russian Federation, 415
Contempt of court, 99–100, 103, 463, 465, 473
Contempt of religion, 200
Contempt toward the state, 307
Contemptuous relationship to others, 436
Contraventions: in Australian criminal law, 94; in French criminal law, 243; in Israeli criminal law, 354, 369, 371–372, 383, 389. *See also* Regulatory offenses
Contribution, in Rome Statute, 608
Controlled Drugs and Substance Act (Canada), 99

Control-over-the-event theory, 503
Convention for Prevention and Punishment of the Crime of Genocide, 594
Convention pour la Création d'une Cour Pénale Internationale (1937), 594
Cook, James, 50
Coperpetration: in Argentine criminal law, 33; in German criminal law, 265–266; in Iranian criminal law, 329; in Israeli criminal law, 369, 372–374; in Rome Statute, 606; in Spanish criminal law, 504. *See also* Complicity; Joint perpetration
Coroners and Justice Act 2009 (England), 544, 547, 548, 549
Corporal punishment, 471–472, 473
Corporate civil liability, 505
Corporate criminal liability: in American criminal law, 578; in Argentine criminal law, 34–35; in Australian criminal law, 62–63; in Canadian criminal law, 113–114; in Chinese criminal law, 152; in German criminal law, 267; in Indian criminal law, 297–298; in Iranian criminal law, 331; in Japanese criminal law, 402; in Rome Statute, 611; in Russian criminal law, 424; in South African criminal law, 467–468; in Spanish criminal law, 505; in United Kingdom (England and Wales) criminal law, 539–540
Corporate manslaughter, 540, 548–549
Corporate Manslaughter and Corporate Homicide Act 2007 (England), 540, 549
Corruption, in South African criminal law, 480
Corruption on earth, 344–345
Counterrevolution, 170–171
CP. *See* Código Penal
Crabbe, 78
Crimen injuria, 480
Crimes against humanity, 3; contextual element of, 618–619; in German criminal law, 253; individual acts in, 619–621; in Rome Statute, 618–621
Crimes against Humanity and War Crimes Act (Canada), 121
Crimes against religion, 345
Crimes of Undermining the Socialist Market Economic Order (China), 169

Crime type, in Argentine criminal law, 25–26
Criminal Attempts Act 1981 (England), 532, 538
Criminal capacity, in South African criminal law, 460
Criminal Code (Canada), 98–100, 102–103, 105–106, 111–113, 115–117, 119–125, 128–129
Criminal Code (China), 140–141, 144–153, 157, 159, 162–170
Criminal Code (France), 5, 210–236
Criminal Code (Soviet Union), 415
Criminal Code Act 1995 (Australia), 53
Criminal Code of the Russian Republic (UK), 415–449
Criminal Code Ordinance (Israel), 352–353
Criminal Damage Act 1971 (England), 532
Criminal Exchange Act (Argentina), 17
Criminal Justice Act 1988 (England), 534
Criminal Justice Act 1991 (England), 535
Criminal Justice Act 2003 (England), 535, 546
Criminal Justice and Immigration Act 2008 (England), 542, 546
Criminal law: critical theory of, 2; minimalist, 492; systems of, 1; universal theory of, 3; world, 8
Criminal Law Act 1967 (England), 542
Criminal Law Act 1977 (England), 538
Criminal Law Amendment Act (South Africa), 461, 475
Criminal Law Journal (Australia), 54
Criminal organizations, in Russian criminal law, 423–424
Criminal Procedure Act (South Africa), 457, 458, 471
Criminal Procedure Law (China), 139, 153, 158, 163, 164
Crimorgs, 423–424
Cruelty to wives, in Indian criminal law, 312–313
Culpa, 10. *See also* Negligence
Culpability principle: in Argentine criminal law, 24; in Spanish criminal law, 491
Culpability requirements, in American criminal law, 573–576. See also *Mens rea*
Culpable homicide, in South African criminal law, 473–475

Cultural Revolution, 145
Customs Act of 1987 (China), 152

Dando, Shigemitsu, 400
Daviault, R v., 119
Davidson, R v., 66
Death penalty. *See* Capital punishment
Decision on Banning Cult Organizations, and Guarding against and Punishing Cult Activities (China), 140
Decisions of Severely Punishing the Criminals Who Seriously Disturbed the Social Order (China), 138, 146
Decisions of Severely Punishing the Criminals Who Seriously Undermine the Economy (China), 138
Declaration of the Rights of Man (France), 210, 212
Defamation: in Argentine criminal law, 36–37, 47; in German criminal law, 262, 279 (of religious beliefs); in Iranian criminal law, 321, 339, 350; in Israeli criminal law, 363–364, 380, 386; in Japanese criminal law, 395, 405. *See also* Libel; Slander
Defenses: in American criminal law, 580–587; in Argentine criminal law, 35–37; in Canadian criminal law, 114–115; in Chinese criminal law, 153; in Egyptian criminal law, 190–191; in French criminal law, 223–224; in German criminal law, 268–269; in Indian criminal law, 299–300; in Iranian criminal law, 332; in Israeli criminal law, 376–379; in Japanese criminal law, 403; in Rome Statute, 611–614; in Russian criminal law, 425–426; in South African criminal law, 464, 468–469; in Spanish criminal law, 507; in United Kingdom (England and Wales) criminal law, 541. *See also specific defenses*
Delalic, 3
De l'esprit des lois (Montesquieu), 210
Dei delitti e delle pene (Beccaria), 8, 210, 489
De minimis: in Canadian criminal law, 106; in Israeli criminal law, 379, 392; in Russian criminal law, 419, 425; in South African criminal law, 460, 472; in United Kingdom (England and Wales) criminal law, 560

Deng Xiaoping, 138
Deportation/forcible transfer, as crime against humanity, 619
Deterrence. *See* Punishment, theories of
Digest of Laws (Russia), 415
Diminished capacity. *See* Insanity defense
Diminished responsibility. *See* Insanity defense
Diplomatic Immunities and Privileges Act (South Africa), 457
Diplomatic immunity, 581–582, 586
Disability excuses, in American criminal law, 584
Disciplinary chastisement defense, 471–472
Discontinued crimes, in Chinese criminal law, 150. *See also* Abandonment defense
Disease of the mind. *See* Insanity defense; Mental disease or defect
Dol éventuel, 5, 218. *See also Mens rea*
Dol général, 217, 229, 603. *See also Mens rea*
Dol indéterminé, 217. *See also Mens rea*
Dolus, 10; in Argentine criminal law, 25–27; attempt liability and, 29; fraud and, 41; larceny and, 41; negligence v., 25–27; in Spanish criminal law, 501. *See also Mens rea*
Dolus directus, 463, 603. *See also Mens rea*
Dolus eventualis, 7, 26–27; in Iranian criminal law, 327; in Rome Statute, 603–604; in South African criminal law, 463–464; in Spanish criminal law, 501. *See also Mens rea*
Dolus indeterminatus, 463–464. *See also Mens rea*
Dolus indirectus, 463. *See also Mens rea*
Dolus specialis, 604. *See also Mens rea*
Double jeopardy: in American criminal law, 582, 586; in Iranian criminal law, 322; in Spanish criminal law, 492, 518
Dowry deaths, in Indian criminal law, 313
Drug-related offenses: in Argentine criminal law, 17, 22, 28, 44; in Australian criminal law, 51, 58, 74, 78, 80; in Canadian criminal law, 99, 101, 108, 117; in Chinese criminal law, 154, 164, 170; in Egyptian criminal law, 182, 184, 187, 196, 201–208; in German criminal law, 256, 261, 275, 280; in Indian criminal law, 312; in Iranian criminal law, 322, 326, 336–337, 339; in Israeli criminal law, 380; in Japanese criminal law, 398; in Rome Statute, 594–596; in Russian criminal law, 434, 443–444; in South African criminal law, 458, 479; in Spanish criminal law, 500, 514–515, 521; in United Kingdom (England and Wales) criminal law, 552
Dudley and Stephens, R v., 541
Duress defense: in American criminal law, 586; in Australian criminal law, 73–74; in Canadian criminal law, 120–121; common law and, 73, 128; in Egyptian criminal law, 193; in French criminal law, 226–227; in German criminal law, 275–276; in Indian criminal law, 304; in Iranian criminal law, 337; in Israeli criminal law, 377; in Japanese criminal law, 406; in Rome Statute, 612–613; in Russian criminal law, 430; in Spanish criminal law, 514–515; in United Kingdom (England and Wales) criminal law, 545. *See also* Choice-of-evils defense; Necessity defense
Duty of care. *See* Omission liability
Duty to act. *See* Omission liability

Eadie, S v., 462
ECHR. *See* European Convention on Human Rights
ECJ. *See* European Court of Justice
Economic crimes, in Russian criminal law, 444–446
Egyptian criminal law, 5; act requirement in, 186; *actus reus* in, 186–187; adversarial/inquisitorial process in, 184–185; alcohol offenses in, 202; attempted crimes in, 189; bench trials in, 185; burden of proof in, 186; causation in, 190; complicity in, 189–190; conspiracy in, 189; death penalty in, 195–196; defenses in, 190–191; drug offenses in, 201–202; duress defense in, 193; excuses in, 192–193; felonies in, 193–194; fraud in, 201; historical background, 180–181; homicide in, 196–198; inchoate crimes in, 189; insanity defense and, 192–193; intent in, 188; intoxication in, 193; jurisdiction, 181–182; justifications in, 191–192; legality principle, 182; liability requirements in,

186–190; *mens rea* in, 187–189; misdemeanors in, 194–195; mistake of law/fact defense and, 192; necessity defense in, 191; negligence in, 188; omissions in, 186–187; permissions in, 190–191; presumption of innocence in, 185; process of, 184–186; prostitution in, 200; provocation defense in, 197–198; punishment in, 193–195; recklessness in, 188; responsibility preventives in, 190–191; sanctions in, 193–196; self-defense in, 191–192; sentence computations/commutations/pardons, 195; sex offenses in, 198–200; sources of, 182–184; special part of, 196–202; status in, 187; strict liability in, 188–189; superior orders in, 192; theft in, 200–201; victimless crimes in, 201–202; violations in, 195

Eichmann, Adolf, 380

Element-negating defenses. *See* Absent-element defenses

Embezzlement, 5; in American criminal law, 590; in Argentine criminal law, 19, 28, 40–41; in Chinese criminal law, 138, 160–162; in Egyptian criminal law, 194; in Iranian criminal law, 344; in Japanese criminal law, 395, 400, 409; in Russian criminal law, 442; in Spanish criminal law, 520–521

Emergency Law of 1958 (Egypt), 181, 183

Emotional stress, in South African criminal law, 461–463

Empress Cars Ltd., *Environmental Agency v.*, 540

Enemy criminal law (*Feindstrafrecht*), 522

Enforced prostitution, 620

Enforced sterilization, 621

Entrapment: in American criminal law, 587; in Australian criminal law, 74–75, 93; in Canadian criminal law, 115, 121, 128; in Chinese criminal law, 157; in French criminal law, 227; in German criminal law, 275; in Indian criminal law, 305; in Iranian criminal law, 337; in Israeli criminal law, 379; in Japanese criminal law, 406; in Russian criminal law, 430; in South African criminal law, 460; in Spanish criminal law, 515; in United Kingdom (England and Wales) criminal law, 545

Environment Act 1990 (England), 553

Environmental crimes: in Australian criminal law, 53; in Canadian criminal law, 101; in German criminal law, 253, 271, 277, 279; in Russian criminal law, 437, 446–448; in Spanish criminal law, 493, 505

Equivalency theory, 402

Ethnic groups, 617

European Convention on Human Rights (ECHR), 8, 215, 254, 532, 541, 542, 551

European Court of Human Rights, 215

European Court of Justice (ECJ), 492

Excuses: in American criminal law, 581, 583–586; in Australian criminal law, 69–75; in Canadian criminal law, 117–121; in Chinese criminal law, 157–158; in Egyptian criminal law, 192–193; in French criminal law, 225–227; in German criminal law, 272–275; in Indian criminal law, 302–305; in Iranian criminal law, 334–337; in Japanese criminal law, 405–406; in Russian criminal law, 428–430; in South African criminal law, 472; in Spanish criminal law, 507, 512–515; in United Kingdom (England and Wales) criminal law, 543–545

Ex post facto. *See* Legality principle

Extermination, as crime against humanity, 619

Extortion: in Argentine criminal law, 40; in Indian criminal law, 307; in Japanese criminal law, 395, 409; in Russian criminal law, 436, 442

Extreme emotional disturbance. *See* Provocation defense

Facilitation: in Argentine criminal law, 33, 38, 40; in Canadian criminal law, 104, 127, 136; in Egyptian criminal law, 200; in German criminal law, 267; in Indian criminal law, 296; in Iranian criminal law, 330, 341; in Israeli criminal law, 370–371, 374, 380, 387–388, 390; in Rome Statute, 608; in Russian criminal law, 433, 436; in Spanish criminal law, 504, 518, 529. *See also* Complicity; Inchoate crimes

Failure of proof defense, 580
False pretenses: in American criminal law, 590; in Argentine criminal law, 31; in Spanish criminal law, 517, 520
Federal Constitutional Court (Germany), 6
Federalism, 15–16
Federal Rule of Evidence, U.S., 600
Felonies: in American criminal law, 569–570; in Australian criminal law, 77; in Egyptian criminal law, 184–185, 190, 192–195; in Israeli criminal law, 354, 361, 371, 385
Felony murder: in American criminal law, 589; in Australian criminal law, 78–79, 94; in Canadian criminal law, 123; in German criminal law, 277; in Russian criminal law, 437, 449; in South African criminal law, 466
Feuerbach, P. J. A., 2, 3, 13
Fighting against God, 344–345
Financial Intelligence Centre Act 38 of 2001 (South Africa), 481
Finta, R v., 121
Fletcher, George, 3
Forced pregnancy, 620–621
Force majeure, 149
Foresight rule (Israel), 362–364
Forfeiture: in Indian criminal law, 306; in Japanese criminal law, 406; Rome Statute, and, 614; in South African criminal law, 480, 487
Forgery: in American criminal law, 588; in Argentine criminal law, 22; in Australian criminal law, 77; in Egyptian criminal law, 181, 194; in German criminal law, 284; in Israeli criminal law, 380; in Japanese criminal law, 395; in South African criminal law, 473, 479; in United Kingdom (England and Wales) criminal law, 552
Forgery and Counterfeiting Act 1981 (England), 552
Fraud: in Argentine criminal law, 41; in Australian criminal law, 80; in Canadian criminal law, 125–126; in Chinese criminal law, 169; in Egyptian criminal law, 201; in French criminal law, 235–236; in German criminal law, 279; in Indian criminal law, 311–312; in Iranian criminal law, 344; in Japanese criminal law, 409; in Russian criminal law, 442–443; in South African criminal law, 479; in United Kingdom (England and Wales) criminal law, 552
Fraud Act 2006 (England), 532, 539, 552
Freedom of speech, 36–37
French criminal law, 5–6; act requirement in, 215; *actus reus* in, 215–216; adversarial/inquisitorial process in, 214; attempted crimes in, 220–221; burden of proof in, 224; causation in, 223; complicity in, 222–223; consent in, 225; conspiracy in, 221; defenses in, 223–224; duress defense in, 226–227; entrapment in, 227; excuses in, 225–227; fraud in, 235–236; historical background, 209–212; homicide in, 227–231; impossibility defense in, 221; inchoate crimes in, 220–221; insanity defense in, 226; intent in, 216–218; intoxication in, 226; juries/written opinions in, 215; jurisdiction of, 212; justifications in, 224–225; legality principle in, 212–213; liability requirements, 215–223; *mens rea* in, 216–220; minors in, 227; mistake/ignorance of fact/law in, 225–226; necessity defense in, 224; negligence in, 218–220; omissions in, 215–216; order of law in, 225; process of, 214–215; recklessness in, 218; self-defense in, 224–225; sex offenses in, 231–232; sources of, 213–214; special part, 227–236; superior orders in, 225, 227; theft in, 233–235; theories of punishment, 215
French Penal Code, 6
Friedman, S v., 479

G, R v., 550
Gang of Four, 140
Garçon, Emile, 217
Gazette of the SPC (Supreme People's Court), 142
GDR. *See* German Democratic Republic
Geddes, R v., 538
General Criminal Code (Iran), 6, 321
Geneva Conventions, 3
Genocide: extermination v., 619; individual acts in, 616–617; pattern of conduct in, 618; protected groups in, 617; in Rome Statute, 616–618; specific intent in, 617–618

Genocide Convention, 609, 616; protected groups specified by, 617
German constitutional law, 256
German criminal law, 2, 3, 6, 9; abandonment defense in, 264; abortion in, 253; act requirement in, 259–260; *actus reus* in, 259–261; adversarial/inquisitorial process in, 257–258; attempted crimes in, 263–265; burden of proof in, 269; causation in, 268; complicity in, 265–267; consent in, 255, 271; corporate criminal liability in, 267; crimes against humanity in, 253; death penalty in, 253, 277; defenses in, 268–269; duress in, 275–276; entrapment in, 276; excuses in, 272–275; fraud in, 279; historical background, 253; homicide in, 277; impossibility defense in, 264; insanity defense in, 273; instigation in, 267; intent in, 261–262; international criminal law and, 253; intoxication in, 273–274; juries/written opinions in, 258; jurisdiction of, 253; justifications in, 269–272; knowledge in, 261–262; legality principle of, 254–255; liability requirements, 259–268; *mens rea* in, 261–263; mistake/ignorance of fact/law defense in, 272; necessity justification in, 269–270; negligence in, 262–263; omissions in, 260–261; pornography in, 278; process of, 257–258; prostitution in, 278; provocation in, 277; punishment in, 258–259, 276–277; recklessness in, 262–263; sanctions in, 253, 275–276; sex offenses in, 277–278; sources of, 256–257; special part of, 276–280; status in, 261; superior orders in, 272; theft in, 278–279; theories of punishment in, 258–259; victimless crimes in, 279–280; violation of trust in, 279; war crimes in, 253. *See also* Bavarian Criminal Code (1813)
German Democratic Republic (GDR), 6
German Penal Code, 2, 6
Gestapo, 603
Gian Kaur v. State of Punjab, 314
Giorgianni, 61
Gorbachev, Mikhail, 417
Grand jury: in American criminal law, 569–570; in Australian criminal law, 55

Griffith, Samuel, 50
Griffith Code, 50
Grotjohn, Ex parte Minister of Justice: In re S v., 474

Handicap Protection Law (China), 167
Harm principle (Mill), 21
Hartmann, S v., 474
Hasan, R v., 545
Hassemer, Winfried, 492
Haughton v. Smith, 60
Homicide, 6, 9; aggravation for extreme indifference to value of human life, 589; in American criminal law, 588–589; in Argentine criminal law, 19, 23, 28, 38–39; attempted, 29; in Australian criminal law, 63–64, 78–79; in Canadian criminal law, 123–124; causation and, 63–64; in Chinese criminal law, 165–166; in Egyptian criminal law, 196–198; in French criminal law, 227–231; in German criminal law, 277; in Indian criminal law, 308–310; in Iranian criminal law, 339–341; in Israeli criminal law, 380–381; in Japanese criminal law, 408; mitigation for emotional disturbance, 589; negligence and, 465; in Russian criminal law, 435–438; in South African criminal law, 465, 473–475; in Spanish criminal law, 518–519; in United Kingdom (England and Wales) criminal law, 547–549
Homicide Act 1957 (England), 544, 548
Hooliganism, 436, 448–449
Humanism principle (Russia), 419
Human rights, 16; in Spanish criminal law, 490
Human Rights Act 1998 (England), 8, 532, 541

ICC. *See* International Criminal Court
ICTR. *See* International Criminal Tribunal for Rwanda
ICTY. *See* International Criminal Tribunal for the former Yugoslavia
Ifsad fi'l-'ard, 344–345
Ignorance of law. *See* Mistake of fact or law
Illegal armed formations, 423
Illegal encroachment, 154
Illegal entrepreneurism, 445

Impossibility defense: in Argentine criminal law, 31; in Australian criminal law, 60, 87–88; in Canadian criminal law, 111; in French criminal law, 221; in German criminal law, 264; in South African criminal law, 460, 470; in United Kingdom (England and Wales) criminal law, 538

Imprisonment Administration Act of 1996 (Argentina), 20

Imputability. *See* Imputation

Imputation: in American criminal law, 571, 576–578, 587; in Argentine criminal law, 26; in French criminal law, 246; objective, 506; in Russian criminal law, 428, 430; in South African criminal law, 466; in Spanish criminal law, 506

IMT. *See* International Military Tribunal

Incapacitation. *See* Punishment, theories of

Incest, 11; in American criminal law, 578; in Australian criminal law 80; in Canadian criminal law, 117; in Indian criminal law, 310; in South African criminal law, 473, 485

Inchoate crimes: in American criminal law, 579–580; in Argentine criminal law, 29–31; in Australian criminal law, 59–61; in Canadian criminal law, 110–111; in Chinese criminal law, 150; conspiracy, 60–61; in Egyptian criminal law, 189; in French criminal law, 220–221; in Indian criminal law, 295–296; in Iranian criminal law, 328–329; in Israeli criminal law, 368–369; in Japanese criminal law, 401; in Rome Statute, 608–610; in Russian criminal law, 421–423; in South African criminal law, 465–466; in Spanish criminal law, 502–503; in United Kingdom (England and Wales) criminal law, 538–540

Incitement: in Canadian criminal law, 110; in Egyptian criminal law, 199; in German criminal law, 265; in Israeli criminal law, 371; in Rome Statute, 609; in South African criminal law, 466; in Spanish criminal law, 529; in United Kingdom (England and Wales) criminal law, 538–539, 545

Incomplete offenses. *See* Inchoate crimes

Indecent assault, in Egyptian criminal law, 198–199

Indian criminal law, 6; act requirement in, 292–293; *actus reus* in, 292–294; adversarial/inquisitorial process in, 291; assisted suicide in, 313–314; attempted crimes in, 295; attempted suicide in, 313; burden of proof in, 299–300; causation in, 298–299; complicity in, 296–297; consent in, 301–302; conspiracy in, 295–296; corporate criminal liability in, 297–298; cruelty to wives in, 312–313; death penalty in, 306, 307; defenses in, 299–300; dowry deaths in, 313; duress defense in, 304; entrapment in, 305; excuses in, 302–305; fraud in, 311–312; historical background, 289; homicide in, 308–310; inchoate crimes in, 295–296; insanity defense in, 303–304; intent in, 294; intoxication in, 304; juries/written opinions in, 291; jurisdiction, 289–290; justifications in, 300–302; legality principle in, 290; liability requirements in, 292–299; mistake/ignorance of law/fact defense in, 302–303; necessity defense in, 300; negligence in, 294–295; omission in, 293; process of, 291; provocation in, 309–310; punishment in, 305–307; recklessness in, 294; sanctions in, 305–307; self-defense in, 300–301; sex offenses in, 310–311; sources of, 290–291; special part of, 307–314; status in, 293–294; superior orders in, 302, 305; theft in, 311–312; theories of punishment in, 291–292; victimless crimes in, 312; voluntary euthanasia in, 313–314

Indian Evidence Act 1872, 299, 313

Indian Penal Code, 6

Indirect perpetration, 266–267

In dubio pro reo, 507. *See also* Beyond a reasonable doubt; Burden of proof; Legality principle

Inducement. *See* Complicity; Inchoate crimes

Infancy: in Chinese criminal law, 157–158; in Egyptian criminal law, 191; in Israeli criminal law, 372, 379; in South African criminal law, 460–461

Infanticide: in Canadian criminal law, 124; in United Kingdom (England and Wales) criminal law, 549

Insanity defense: in American criminal law, 581, 584, 585; in Argentine criminal law, 19, 35–36; in Australian criminal law, 70–72; in Canadian criminal law, 118; in Chinese criminal law, 158; in Egyptian criminal law, 192–193; in French criminal law, 226; in German criminal law, 273; in Indian criminal law, 303–304; in Iranian criminal law, 335–336; in Israeli criminal law, 378; in Japanese criminal law, 406; non-pathological incapacity v., 462; in Rome Statute, 612; in Russian criminal law, 428–429; safety measures and, 19; in South African criminal law, 461; in Spanish criminal law, 513–514; in United Kingdom (England and Wales) criminal law, 544

Instigation. *See* Complicity; Inchoate crimes

Intent: in Australian criminal law, 59; in Canadian criminal law, 107–108; conditional, 261–262; in Egyptian criminal law, 188; in French criminal law, 216–218; in genocide, 617–618; in German criminal law, 261–262; in Indian criminal law, 294; intoxication and, 72; in Iranian criminal law, 327; in Israeli criminal law, 362–365; in Japanese criminal law, 400; in Rome Statute, 603–604; in Russian criminal law, 420; in South African criminal law, 463–464, 477–478; terrorism and, 481; theft and, 477–478; in United Kingdom (England and Wales) criminal law, 536–537

Interest, in Iranian criminal law, 346

Interim Act of Customs (China), 138

International Committee for the Red Cross, 594

International Convention on the Non-applicability of Statutory Limitations to War Crimes and Crimes against Humanity, 16–17

International Covenant on Civil and Political Rights, 19–20, 598

International Criminal Court (ICC), 3, 8, 481, 593–624

International Criminal Court Act (South Africa), 481

International criminal law, 3, 17; German criminal law and, 253; historical background, 593–595; jurisdiction, 595–597; legality principle in, 597; sources of, 597–599; South African criminal law and, 481

International Criminal Tribunal for Rwanda (ICTR), 3, 8, 594, 599, 617

International Criminal Tribunal for the former Yugoslavia (ICTY), 3, 8, 594, 599, 608, 613

International Military Tribunal (IMT), 594, 603

Interpretation of How to Apply Law When Adjudicating Theft Cases (China), 141

Intoxication: in American criminal law, 577, 584, 586; in Australian criminal law, 72–73; in Canadian criminal law, 119–120; common law and, 72–73, 119; in Egyptian criminal law, 193; in French criminal law, 226; in German criminal law, 273–274; hooliganistic motivation and, 436; in Indian criminal law, 304; intent and, 72; involuntary, 586; in Iranian criminal law, 336; in Israeli criminal law, 378; in Japanese criminal law, 406; in Rome Statute, 612; in Russian criminal law, 429–430; in South African criminal law, 461; in Spanish criminal law, 514; in United Kingdom (England and Wales) criminal law, 544

Involuntary manslaughter: in Chinese criminal law, 165; in Iranian criminal law, 341; in South African criminal law, 474; in United Kingdom (England and Wales) criminal law, 547–548

Iranian criminal law, 6–7; accessories in, 330–331; act requirement in, 326; *actus reus* in, 326; adversarial/inquisitorial process in, 325; alcohol offenses in, 336, 345–346; apostasy in, 345; attempted crimes in, 328; burden of proof in, 332; causation in, 331–332; complicity in, 329–331; consent in, 333–334; conspiracy in, 329; corporate criminal liability in, 331; corruption on earth in, 344–345; crimes against religion in, 345; death penalty in, 339; defenses in, 332; *dolus eventualis* in, 327; duress defense in, 337; entrapment in, 337; excuses in, 334–337; fighting against God in, 344–345; fraud in, 344; historical background, 321–322;

Iranian criminal law (*continued*)
homicide in, 339–341; inchoate crimes in, 328–329; insanity defense in, 335–336; intent in, 327; interest in, 346; intoxication in, 336; juries/written opinions in, 325; jurisdiction of, 322; justifications in, 332–334; legality principle of, 322–323; liability requirements, 326–332; *mens rea* in, 326–328; mistake/ignorance of law/fact in, 334–335; necessity defense in, 332–333; negligence in, 328; omission in, 326; process of, 325; provocation in, 341; punishment in, 337–338; recklessness in, 327; rights of God v. rights of humans in, 339; sanctions in, 337–339; self-defense in, 333; sex offenses in, 341–342; sources of, 323–324; special part of, 339–346; status in, 326; superior orders in, 334, 337; theft in, 342–343; theories of punishment in, 325–326; victimless crimes in, 344

Iranian Penal Code, 6–7

Irresistible impulse test: in American criminal law, 585–586; in Argentine criminal law, 36; in Israeli criminal law, 378. *See also* Insanity defense

Islamic criminal law, 321

Islamic Penal Code (Iran), 321–346

Islamic Revolution, 6, 321

Israeli criminal law, 7; abandonment defense in, 370–371; *actus reus* in, 355–357; aiding in, 369–371; assisted suicide in, 381; attempted crimes in, 368–369; attempted suicide in, 381; burden of proof in, 376; categories of offenses in, 354; causation in, 375–376; chastisement of children defense in, 379; complicity in, 369–375; consent in, 379; conspiracy in, 369; coperpetration in, 369, 372–374; criminal thought in, 357–362; death penalty in, 380; defenses in, 376–379; *de minimis* in, 379; duress defense in, 377; entrapment in, 379; failure to prevent felony in, 361; historical background, 352–353; homicide in, 380–381; inchoate crimes in, 368–369; infancy defense in, 379; insanity defense in, 378; intent in, 362–365; interpretation of, 353–354; intoxication in, 378; juries/written opinions in, 354–355; justification defense in, 377–378; lack of control defense in, 378; legality principle, 353; liability for further offenses in, 374–375; liability requirements, 355–376; *mens rea* in, 357–368; mistake of fact/law in, 378; murder in, 364, 380–381; necessity defense in, 377; negligence in, 365–367; omissions in, 355–357; perpetration by means of another in, 369, 372; process of, 354–355; protection of judicial officers in, 379; punishment in, 355, 379–380; recklessness in, 365; sanctions in, 379–380; self-defense in, 376–377; sex offenses in, 381–382; special part of, 380–382; strict liability in, 367–368; temporal application of criminal enactments in, 354; theories of punishment in, 355

Israeli Penal Law, 7

Italian Criminal Code, 4, 13

Japanese criminal law, 7; act requirement in, 399; *actus reus* in, 399–400; adversarial/inquisitorial process in, 397–398; attempted crimes in, 401; burden of proof in, 403; causation in, 402–403; complicity in, 401–402; consent in, 405; conspiracy in, 401; corporate criminal liability in, 402; crimes of negligence in, 409–410; death penalty in, 407; defenses in, 403; duress defense in, 406; embezzlement in, 409; entrapment in, 406; excuses in, 405–406; fraud in, 409; historical background, 394; homicide in, 408; inchoate crimes in, 401; insanity defense in, 406; intent in, 400; intoxication in, 406; juries/written opinions in, 398; jurisdiction of, 394–395; justifications in, 404–405; legality principle of, 395–396; liability requirements in, 399–403; mistake/ignorance of fact/law in, 405–406; necessity defense in, 404; negligence in, 400–401; omission in, 399; process of, 397–398; provocation defense in, 408; punishment in, 399, 406–407; recklessness in, 400–401; robbery in, 409; sanctions in, 406–407; self-defense in, 404; sex offenses in, 408–409; sources of, 396–397; special part of, 407–410; status in, 399–400; superior orders in, 405; theft in,

409; theories of punishment in, 399; victim complaint requirement in, 405; victimless crimes in, 409
Jobidon, R v., 104, 116
Joint-enterprise rule, 467
Joint perpetration: in Iranian criminal law, 329–330; in Spanish criminal law, 504. *See also* Complicity; Coperpetration
Le journal officiel (France), 212
Judicial review, in Argentine criminal law, 14–15
Judiciary Act (Spain), 489–490
Jurisdiction: in Argentine criminal law, 15–16; in Australian criminal law, 51–52; in Canadian criminal law, 98–99; in Chinese criminal law, 139–140; in Egyptian criminal law, 181–182; in French criminal law, 212; in German criminal law, 253; in Indian criminal law, 289–290; in international criminal law, 595–597; in Iranian criminal law, 322; in Japanese criminal law, 394–395; in Rome Statute, 595–597; in Russian criminal law, 416; in South African criminal law, 457; in Spanish criminal law, 489–490
Jury: in American criminal law, 569–570; in Argentine criminal law, 15; in Chinese criminal law, 143–144; in French criminal law, 215; in German criminal law, 258; in Indian criminal law, 291; in Iranian criminal law, 325; in Israeli criminal law, 354–355; in Japanese criminal law, 398; in Rome Statute, 600–601; in Russian criminal law, 418; in South African criminal law, 458; in Spanish criminal law, 495; in United Kingdom (England and Wales) criminal law, 534–535
Justice Act 2009 (England), 548
Justifications: in American criminal law, 581, 582–583; in Australian criminal law, 65–69; balance-of-evils, 542; in Canadian criminal law, 115–117; in Chinese criminal law, 153–157; in Egyptian criminal law, 191–192; in French criminal law, 224–225; in German criminal law, 269–272; in Indian criminal law, 300–302; in Iranian criminal law, 332–334; in Israeli criminal law, 377–378; in Japanese criminal law, 404–405; in Rome Statute, 601, 611, 621, 623; in Russian criminal law, 426–428; in South African criminal law, 469–472; in Spanish criminal law, 507, 508–512; in United Kingdom (England and Wales) criminal law, 541–543
Juvenile Code of 1974/1996 (Egypt), 183
Juvenile offenders. *See* Infancy

Kaur, Kulwant, 314
Keihō, 7
Khomeini (Ayatollah), 324
Knowledge: in American criminal law, 571–574; in Canadian criminal law, 108; in German criminal law, 261–262; in Rome Statute, 604; in South African criminal law, 464; of unlawfulness, 464; war crimes and, 622. See also *Mens rea*

Lack of control defense, in Israeli criminal law, 378. See also *Actus reus*
Lady Chatterley's Lover (Lawrence), 409
Larceny: in American criminal law, 590; in Argentine criminal law, 19, 28, 40–41; in Australian criminal law, 80; in German criminal law, 264, 284, 287; in Japanese criminal law, 395, 409; in Spanish criminal law, 520. *See also* Theft
Law Combating Drugs and Regulating Their Use and Trade of 1960 (Egypt), 182, 184, 201–202
Law Combating Money Laundering of 2002 (Egypt), 183
Law Combating Prostitution of 1961 (Egypt), 183, 200
Law Forbidding Drinking Alcoholic Beverages of 1973 (Egypt), 183, 202
League of Nations, 594
Legality principle, 9; in American criminal law, 566–567; in Argentine criminal law and, 16–18; in Australian criminal law, 52–53; in Egyptian criminal law, 182; in French criminal law, 212–213; in German criminal law, 254–255; in Indian criminal law, 290; in Iranian criminal law, 322–323; in Israeli criminal law, 353; in Japanese criminal law, 395–396; in Rome Statute, 597; in Russian

Legality principle (*continued*)
criminal law, 416; in South African criminal law, 457; in Spanish criminal law, 490–491; in United Kingdom (England and Wales) criminal law, 532–533
Legal science, 2
Legislativity. *See* Legality principle
Lenity, rule of. *See* Strict construction
Lergesner v. Carroll, 69
Lesser-evils defense, in American criminal law, 582. *See also* Necessity defense
Lex certa, 16, 18, 597
Lex praevia, 16–17, 597
Lex scripta, 16–17, 254, 597
Lex stricta, 16, 18, 23, 597
Libel: in Argentine criminal law, 36; in German criminal law, 262; in Israeli criminal law, 363–364, 380, 286. *See also* Defamation; Slander
Life imprisonment: in Argentine criminal law, 19–20, 38–39; in Australian criminal law, 58, 81; in Canadian criminal law, 123; in Chinese criminal law, 139–140, 153, 158–159, 162, 165, 167–169, 176; in Egyptian criminal law, 189, 194, 196–198, 200–202, 206; in French criminal law, 230, 232; in German criminal law, 275, 277, 282; in Indian criminal law, 306–307, 313; in Iranian criminal law, 337, 343, 345; in Israeli criminal law, 362, 380–381, 392, 398; in Rome Statute, 614; in Russian criminal law, 431–432, 435; in South African criminal law, 457, 473; in United Kingdom (England and Wales) criminal law, 535, 547, 550–551
Livingston, Edward, 289
Loughnan, R v., 66
Louisiana Penal Code (Livingston draft), 6

Majewski, Director of Public Prosecutions v., 544
Makwanyane, S v., 473
Malice, 58, 501; aforethought, 165, 187, 547. *See also Mens rea*
Malicious Damage Act 1861 (England), 532
Manslaughter, 6, 408; in American criminal law, 588; in Australian criminal law, 78–79;
in Canadian criminal law, 106, 123–124; in Chinese criminal law, 165–166; corporate, 548–549; in Egyptian criminal law, 196–197; in German criminal law, 277; in Indian criminal law, 308–309; involuntary, 548; in Iranian criminal law, 339–341; in Israeli criminal law, 381; in Russian criminal law, 435–438; in United Kingdom (England and Wales) criminal law, 548; voluntary, 548. *See also* Homicide
Mao Zedong, 138
Masiya v. DPP, Pretoria, 475
Mayer v. Marchant, 64
Mbombela, R v., 465
Mens rea, 3, 5, 7, 8, 9; in American criminal law, 573–576; in Argentine criminal law, 24–28; in Australian criminal law, 53, 56, 58–59; in Canadian criminal law, 103, 106–110; in Chinese criminal law, 148–150; in Egyptian criminal law, 187–189; in French criminal law, 216–220; in German criminal law, 261–263; in Iranian criminal law, 326–328; in Israeli criminal law, 357–368; in Japanese criminal law, 400–401; in Rome Statute, 603–605; in Russian criminal law, 420–421; in South African criminal law, 460–465; in Spanish criminal law, 501–502; in United Kingdom (England and Wales) criminal law, 536–537
Mental disease or defect. *See* Insanity defense
Mental state. See *Mens rea*
Military Justice Law of 1966 (Egypt), 181, 183
Mill, John Stuart, 21
Ming Code, 394
Misdemeanors: in Australian criminal law, 77; in Chinese criminal law, 146; in Egyptian criminal law, 181, 183–186, 194–195; in German criminal law, 284; in Israeli criminal law, 354
Mistake of fact or law: in American criminal law, 581, 583–584; in Argentine criminal law, 24, 26, 27–28; in Australian criminal law, 69–70; in Canadian criminal law, 117; in Egyptian criminal law, 192; in French criminal law, 225–226; in German criminal law, 272; in Indian criminal law, 302–303; in

Iranian criminal law, 334–335; in Israeli criminal law, 378; in Japanese criminal law, 405–406; in Rome Statute, 613; in Russian criminal law, 428; in Spanish criminal law, 507, 512–513; in United Kingdom (England and Wales) criminal law, 543

Misuse of Drugs Act 1971 (England), 552

M'Naghten rules, 70–71, 118, 544, 585–586. *See also* Insanity defense

Model Criminal Code (Australia), 4, 50–51, 52, 53, 57, 58, 59, 60, 61, 64, 65, 66, 68, 71, 74, 75, 77, 79

Model Penal Code (U.S.), 2, 8, 50–51, 59, 100, 420, 565, 572, 573, 576, 577, 578, 584, 585, 586, 588, 589, 603, 604, 608, 611

Mode of Culpability. See *Mens rea*

Money laundering, 183, 259, 380, 445–446, 473, 480, 494

Montesquieu, 210

Moreno, Rodolfo, 13

Moreno Code, 13

Morgan, Director of Public Prosecutions v., 543

Motive, 30, 58, 81, 87, 127, 149, 165, 232, 277, 294, 327, 358, 400, 432–433, 463, 474, 478, 481, 614

Muharaba, 330, 344–345

Murder, 3, 4, 5, 6; in American criminal law, 588, 589; in Australian criminal law, 78–79; in Canadian criminal law, 123–124; in Chinese criminal law, 165–166; as crime against humanity, 619; in Egyptian criminal law, 196–197; extermination as, 619; felony, 589; in French criminal law, 229–230; in German criminal law, 277; in Indian criminal law, 308–309; in Iranian criminal law, 339–341; in Israeli criminal law, 364, 380–381; in Japanese criminal law, 408; premeditation, 364, 380–381; provocation defense, 124; in Russian criminal law, 435–438; in South African criminal law, 473–475; in Spanish criminal law, 518; in United Kingdom (England and Wales) criminal law, 547. *See also* Homicide

Napoleonic Code, 5, 6–7, 210, 211, 321

Narcotics Control Law (Japan), 409

National Customs Code (Argentina), 31

Nazi Party, 603

Ne bis in idem. See Double jeopardy

Necessity defense: in American criminal law, 582; in Argentine criminal law, 35; in Australian criminal law, 65–67; in Canadian criminal law, 115, 120–121; in Chinese criminal law, 155–156; common law and, 120; in Egyptian criminal law, 191; in French criminal law, 224; in German criminal law, 269–270; in Indian criminal law, 300; in Iranian criminal law, 332–333; in Israeli criminal law, 377; in Japanese criminal law, 404; in Rome Statute, 612–613; in Russian criminal law, 426–427; in South African criminal law, 469; in Spanish criminal law, 508–509; in United Kingdom (England and Wales) criminal law, 541–542. *See also* Choice-of-evils defense; Duress defense

Negligence, 5, 9; in American criminal law, 575–576; in Argentine criminal law, 25–27; in Australian criminal law, 59; in Canadian criminal law, 109–110; conscious, 27; death by, 308–309; *dolus* v., 25–27; in Egyptian criminal law, 188; in French criminal law, 218–220; in German criminal law, 262–263; homicide and, 465; in Indian criminal law, 294–295; in Iranian criminal law, 328; in Israeli criminal law, 365–367; in Japanese criminal law, 400–401, 409–410; recklessness as, 400–401; in Rome Statute, 605; in Russian criminal law, 420–421; in South African criminal law, 465; in Spanish criminal law, 501; in United Kingdom (England and Wales) criminal law, 537. *See also Culpa*

Negotiorum gestio, in South African criminal law, 472

Nette, R v., 106

Ngema, S v., 465

Ngubane, S v., 463

Nkwenja, S v., 467

Notice of Strike-Hard on Robbery and the Other Related Crimes (China), 146

Nulla poena sine lege, 9. *See also* Legality principle

Nuremberg Charter, 594

Nuremberg Tribunal, 8, 594, 605, 611. *See also* International Military Tribunal
Nydam test, 59

Oblique intention, 4, 7, 94, 218, 294; in Israeli criminal law, 362, 364, 368, 370, 372, 381
Obscenity: in Argentine criminal law, 40, 43; in Canadian criminal law, 126; in Chinese criminal law, 148; in Indian criminal law, 307, 312; in Japanese criminal law, 409
O'Connor, R v., 72
Of Crimes and Punishments (Beccaria), 8, 210
Offense-modification defenses, in American criminal law, 580–581
Offenses against the Person Act 1861 (England), 532
Omission liability: in Argentine criminal law, 22–24; in Australian criminal law, 57–58; in Canadian criminal law, 105; in Chinese criminal law, 147; in Egyptian criminal law, 186–187; in French criminal law, 215–216; in German criminal law, 260–261; in Indian criminal law, 293; in Iranian criminal law, 326; in Israeli criminal law, 355–357; in Japanese criminal law, 399; in Rome Statute, 602–603; in Russian criminal law, 419–420; in South African criminal law, 459–460; in Spanish criminal law, 498–500; in United Kingdom (England and Wales) criminal law, 536
Opinion on Taking Further Steps to Ensure the Quality of Handling Death Penalty Cases According to Law (China), 163
Ordering crimes, in Rome Statute, 607
Order of a legitimate authority, in French criminal law, 225. *See also* Justifications
Order of law, in French criminal law, 225. *See also* Justifications
Organic Law of the People's Courts (China), 139, 144, 164
Organized crime, in South African criminal law, 480–481
Osadamegaki, 394
Osland, 62
Outweighing rights defense, in Argentine criminal law, 36–37. *See also* Necessity defense

Papachristou v. City of Jacksonville, 567
Pardons: in Egyptian criminal law, 195; in French criminal law, 210; in Iranian criminal law, 325, 339–340; in Japanese criminal law, 398, 410
Parole: in Argentine criminal law 13, 18; in French criminal law, 230; in German criminal law, 275, 282; in Japanese criminal law, 406; in Russian criminal law, 434; in United Kingdom (England and Wales) criminal law, 547
Passive-personality principle, 416. *See also* Jurisdiction
Penal Code (Egypt), 5, 180–193, 195–201
Penal Code (France), 289
Penal Code (Germany), 253–266, 269–279
Penal Code (India), 289–314
Penal Code (Japan), 394
Penal Law (Israel), 353, 358
People's assessor system, 143–144
Perestroyka, 417
Perka, R v., 115
Permissions, in Egyptian criminal law, 190–191
Perpetration. *See* Complicity; Coperpetration; Joint perpetration
Peters v. The Queen, 59
Plea bargaining: in American criminal law, 570; in Chinese criminal law, 161; in German criminal law, 258, 281; in Russian criminal law, 418
Police Authority Law of 1971 (Egypt), 183
Police misconduct, 587
Police power, 1–2
Political crimes, in Chinese criminal law, 170–171
Political rights, deprivation of, 159–160, 170
Popular prosecutors, 495
Pornography: in Argentine criminal law, 40; in Australian criminal law, 80; in German criminal law, 278. *See also* Obscenity
Positive general prevention, 497. *See also* Punishment, theories of
Possession: in Argentine criminal law, 21–22; in Canadian criminal law, 99, 104, 126; in Chinese criminal law, 172; in Egyptian

criminal law, 185, 194; in German criminal law, 279; in Indian criminal law, 409; in Russian criminal law, 443; in South African criminal law, 459, 479, 486; in Spanish criminal law, 500, 521; in United Kingdom (England and Wales) criminal law, 536, 552. See also *Actus reus*; Property offenses; Status

Powers of Criminal Courts (Sentencing) Act 2000 (England), 546

Premeditation, 7, 38, 115, 166, 188, 196–197, 228, 230, 248, 309, 362, 364, 370, 374, 380–381, 474, 518. See also *Mens rea*; Murder

Preparation for crimes. *See* Attempt

Prerequisite (*jōken*) principle, 402

Press Law (Iran), 325

Pretrial discovery, in Chinese criminal law, 144

Prevention of Crime Act 1953 (England), 552

Prevention of Organized Crime Act 121 of 1998 (South Africa), 480–481

Prison: in Argentine criminal law, 18–19, 21; in Australian criminal law, 75–76; in Canadian criminal law, 122; in Chinese criminal law, 159

Private defense, in South African criminal law, 470. *See also* Self-defense

Private indecency, in Egyptian criminal law, 199

Private prosecutors: in Russian criminal law, 427; in Spanish criminal law, 495

Prohibited means of warfare, 623

Prohibited methods of warfare, 624

Property offenses: in American criminal law, 590; in Argentine criminal law, 40–41; in Canadian criminal law, 125; in Chinese criminal law, 168; in Egyptian criminal law, 200; in French criminal law, 232; in German criminal law, 278; in Indian criminal law, 311; in Iranian criminal law, 342; in Japanese criminal law, 409; in Rome Statute, 623; in Russian criminal law, 440; in South African criminal law, 476; in Spanish criminal law, 520; in United Kingdom (England and Wales) criminal law, 551

Proportionality: in criminalization, 123, 126, 280; in definition of interest (Iranian criminal law), 346; in ECHR, 541, 551; in punishment, 102, 104, 107, 121, 255, 258–259, 306, 419, 487, 489, 497, 522, 535, 601; in self-defense, 8, 35, 67–68, 225, 391, 427, 432, 510, 542, 612–613; in necessity/duress, 120–121, 224, 274, 300, 333, 391, 432, 582–583

Prospectivity. *See* Legality principle

Prostitution: in Argentine criminal law, 40; in Canadian criminal law, 126; in Chinese criminal law, 162–163, 170; death penalty and, 162–163; in Egyptian criminal law, 200; enforced, 620; in German criminal law, 278; organizing, 162–163

Protection of Constitutional Democracy against Terrorist and Related Activities Act (South Africa), 481

Proudman v. Dayman defense, 69–70

Provisional Act for Punishment of Crimes That Endanger State Currency of 1951 (China), 138

Provocation defense: in American criminal law, 589; in Australian criminal law, 79; in Canadian criminal law, 103, 109, 114, 124; in Chinese criminal law, 166; in Egyptian criminal law, 197–198; in German criminal law, 277; in Indian criminal law, 309–310; in Iranian criminal law, 341; in Israeli criminal law, 381, 392; in Japanese criminal law, 408; in Russian criminal law, 438; in South African criminal law, 461–463, 483; in Spanish criminal law, 510; in United Kingdom (England and Wales) criminal law, 548

Prussian Criminal Code (1851), 253

Public authority defense: in American criminal law, 581, 583; in South African criminal law, 471. *See also* Justifications

Public Gambling Act of 1867 (India), 293

Public indecency: in American criminal law, 588; in Egyptian criminal law, 199; in Japanese criminal law, 408; in South African criminal law, 473

Publicity. *See* Legality principle

Public surveillance, 158–159

Punishment, theories of: in Argentine criminal law, 18–21; in Australian criminal law, 75–76; in Canadian criminal law, 102–103, 121–122; in Chinese criminal law, 158–161; in Egyptian criminal law, 193–195; in German criminal law, 258–259, 276–277; in Indian criminal law, 291–292, 305–307; in Iranian criminal law, 325–326, 337–338; in Israeli criminal law, 355, 379–380; in Japanese criminal law, 399, 406–407; in Rome Statute, 601; in Russian criminal law, 419, 430–434; in South African criminal law, 458–459, 472–473; in Spanish criminal law, 490–492, 496–497, 516–517; in United Kingdom (England and Wales) criminal law, 535, 545–546
Punishments. *See* Sanctions
Purpose, in American criminal law, 574
Putin, Vladimir, 415

Qanuns, 180
Qur'an, 321

Radford, R v., 71
Rape, 3, 9; in American criminal law, 578, 589–590; in Argentine criminal law, 39; in Australian criminal law, 79; in Chinese criminal law, 166–167; as crime against humanity, 620; in Egyptian criminal law, 198–199; in French criminal law, 231–232; in Indian criminal law, 310; in Israeli criminal law, 381–382; in Japanese criminal law, 408–409; in Russian criminal law, 438–440; in South African criminal law, 475–476; in Spanish criminal law, 519; statutory, 189, 578; in United Kingdom (England and Wales) criminal law, 549–550
Rechtsgut, 10, 276
Recklessness, 9; in American criminal law, 574, 575; in Anglo American law, 359; in Australian criminal law, 59; in Canadian criminal law, 108–109; complicity and, 112; in Egyptian criminal law, 188; in French criminal law, 218; in German criminal law, 262–263; in Indian criminal law, 294; in Iranian criminal law, 327; in Israeli criminal law, 365; in Japanese criminal law, 400–401; in Rome Statute, 604–605; in Russian criminal law, 420; subjective, 358–360; in United Kingdom (England and Wales) criminal law, 537
Reclusion, in Argentine criminal law, 18–19. *See also* Prison
Red Cross, 624
Regulatory offenses: in Argentine criminal law, 17; in Australian criminal law, 53, 77, 94; in Canadian criminal law, 99, 101, 105, 113; in French criminal law, 211; in Japanese criminal law, 396, 402, 405, 407, 409; in Russian criminal law, 437; in South African criminal law, 463; in United Kingdom (England and Wales) criminal law, 533, 552–553. *See also* Contraventions
Rehabilitation. *See* Punishment, theories of
Religious groups, 617
Renunciation. *See* Abandonment defense
Resocialization. *See* Punishment, theories of
Restatements of the Law (ALI), 565
Retaliation: as form of punishment (Iranian criminal law), 7, 321, 325–327, 335–342; as subjective offense element, 148–149
Rethinking Criminal Law (Fletcher), 3
Retribution. *See* Punishment, theories of
Retroactivity. *See* Legality principle
Righi, Esteban, 29
Riotous Assemblies Act 17 of 1956 (South Africa), 466
Ritsuryo, 394
Robbery: in American criminal law, 588; in Argentine criminal law, 19, 32–33, 39–41, 46; in Australian criminal law, 73; in Canadian criminal law, 112, 119–120; in Chinese criminal law, 146, 148, 155, 161, 164, 175; in Egyptian criminal law, 191–193; in German criminal law, 264, 266; in Indian criminal law, 307; in Israeli criminal law, 369, 371, 375; in Japanese criminal law, 394, 409; in Russian criminal law, 440–442; in South African criminal law, 457, 473, 485; in Spanish criminal law, 520; in United Kingdom (England and Wales) criminal law, 535, 551

Rodriguez v. British Columbia, 116
Roman-Dutch criminal law, 456, 458, 461–462
Rome Statute, 3, 8; abandonment defense in, 609–610; act requirement in, 602; *actus reus* in, 601–603; adversarial/inquisitorial process in, 599–600; aggression in, 624; assistance in, 608; attempted crimes in, 609; burden of proof in, 611–612; categories of criminal participation in, 605–611; causation in, 605; conspiracy in, 608; contribution in, 608; coperpetration in, 606; corporate criminal liability in, 611; crimes against humanity in, 618–621; death penalty and, 614; defenses in, 611–614; *dolus directus* in, 603; *dolus eventualis* in, 603–604; double-layered structure of crimes in, 615–616; duress defense in, 612–613; genocide in, 616–618; historical background of, 593–595; inchoate crimes in, 608–610; incitement to genocide in, 609; insanity in, 612; intent in, 603–604; intoxication in, 612; juries/written opinions in, 600–601; jurisdiction of, 595–597; knowledge in, 604; legality principle of, 597; liability requirements in, 601–611; *mens rea* in, 603–605; mistake of fact/law defense in, 613; necessity defense in, 612–613; negligence in, 605; omissions in, 602–603; ordering crimes in, 607; perpetration by means in, 606–607; perpetration in, 606–607; process of, 599–601; protected interests in, 615; punishment in, 601; recklessness in, 604–605; sanctions in, 614; self-defense in, 612; soliciting/inducing crimes in, 607–608; sources of, 597–599; special part of, 615–624; status in, 603; superior orders in, 610–611, 613–614; theories of punishment in, 601; war crimes in, 621–624
Rousseau, Jean-Jacques, 210
Rule of law, 2, 52
Rules of Criminal Procedure (Spain), 489
Rumpff, F. L. H., 460, 461
Russian criminal law, 7–8; abandonment defense in, 422; act requirement in, 419; *actus reus* in, 419–420; adversarial/inquisitorial process of, 417–418; attempted crimes in, 421–422; burden of proof in, 426; causation in, 424–425; complicity in, 423–424; consent in, 427; conspiracy in, 422–423; corporate criminal liability in, 424; criminal organizations in, 423–424; death penalty in, 434–435; defenses in, 425–426; drug-related offenses in, 443–444; duress defense in, 430; economic crimes in, 444–446; embezzlement in, 442; entrapment in, 430; environmental crimes in, 446–448; excuses in, 428–430; extortion in, 442; fraud in, 442–443; historical background, 415; homicide in, 435–438; hooliganism in, 436, 448–449; inchoate crimes in, 421–423; insanity defense in, 428–429; intent in, 420; intoxication in, 429–430; juries/written opinions in, 418; jurisdiction of, 416; justifications in, 426–428; legality principle of, 416; liability requirements in, 419–425; liberation from criminal responsibility in, 425–426; *mens rea* in, 420–421; mistake/ignorance of fact/law in, 428; necessity defense in, 426–427; negligence in, 420–421; omissions in, 419–420; preparation for crimes in, 421–422; process of, 417–418; provocation defense in, 438; punishment in, 419, 430–434; recklessness in, 420; robbery in, 441–442; sanctions in, 430–435; self-defense in, 427; sex offenses in, 438–440; sources of, 416–417; special part of, 435–449; status in, 420; superior orders in, 427–428, 430; theft in, 440–441; theories of punishment in, 419; victimless crimes in, 443–444
Russkaia Pravda, 415

Sanctions: in Australian criminal law, 75–76; in Canadian criminal law, 121–122; in Egyptian criminal law, 193–196; in German criminal law, 253, 275–276; in Israeli criminal law, 379–380; in Japanese criminal law, 406–407; in Rome Statute, 614; in Russian criminal law, 430–435; in South African criminal law, 472–473; in Spanish criminal law, 516–517; in United Kingdom (England and Wales) criminal law, 545–546

Schengen Treaty, 492
Schloss v. Maguire, 69
Schools Act 84 of 1996 (South Africa), 472
Security Administration Punishment Act of 1957 (China), 138
Security measures (Spanish criminal law), 497
Selected Opinions of People's Courts (Supreme People's Court), 142
Self-defense, 8; in American criminal law, 581; in Argentine criminal law, 35; in Australian criminal law, 67–68; in Canadian criminal law, 115–116; in Egyptian criminal law, 191–192; in French criminal law, 224–225; in German criminal law, 270–271; in Indian criminal law, 300–301; in Iranian criminal law, 333; in Israeli criminal law, 376–377; in Japanese criminal law, 404; in Rome Statute, 612; in Russian criminal law, 427; in South African criminal law, 470; in Spanish criminal law, 509–510; in United Kingdom (England and Wales) criminal law, 542
Sentence bargaining, 257–258
Serious Crime Act 2007 (England), 539
Sex offenses: in American criminal law, 578, 589–590; in Argentine criminal law, 39–40; in Australian criminal law, 79–80; in Canadian criminal law, 124–125; in Chinese criminal law, 166–168; as crimes against humanity, 620–621; in Egyptian criminal law, 198–200; in French criminal law, 231–232; in German criminal law, 277–278; in Indian criminal law, 310–311; in Iranian criminal law, 341–342; in Israeli criminal law, 381–382; in Japanese criminal law, 408–409; *mens rea* for, 125; in Russian criminal law, 438–440; in South African criminal law, 475–476; in Spanish criminal law, 519; in United Kingdom (England and Wales) criminal law, 549–551
Sexual Offences Act 2003 (England), 8, 532, 537, 542, 543, 549, 550
Sexual slavery, 620
Sharia, 180, 191
Shi'i Dja'fari school, 321
Silgado, 375

Slander: in Argentine criminal law, 36, 47; in Egyptian criminal law, 196. *See also* Defamation; Libel
Smithers, R v., 106
Smuggling, in Argentine criminal law, 31
Solicitation: in American criminal law, 580; in Canadian criminal law, 110, 112, 126; in Egyptian criminal law, 200; in Indian criminal law, 312; in Rome Statute, 607–608. *See also* Inchoate crimes
South African criminal law, 8; accessories in, 474; act requirement in, 459; *actus reus* in, 459–460; adversarial/inquisitorial process in, 458; attempted crimes in, 465–466; automatism in, 459; burden of proof in, 469; capital punishment in, 473; causation in, 468; complicity in, 466–467; consent in, 470; conspiracy in, 466; corporal punishment in, 473; corporate criminal liability in, 467–468; corruption in, 480; *crimen injuria* in, 480; criminal capacity in, 460; death penalty in, 473; defenses in, 464, 468–469; *de minimis* in, 472; disciplinary chastisement defense in, 471–472; English criminal law and, 456; excuses in, 472; forgery in, 479; fraud in, 479; historical background of, 456; homicide in, 465, 473–475; impossibility defense in, 470; inchoate crimes in, 465–466; incitement in, 466; insanity in, 461; intent in, 463–464, 477–478; international criminal law and, 481; intoxication in, 461; juries/written opinions in, 458; jurisdiction of, 457; justifications in, 469–472; knowledge of unlawfulness in, 464; legality principle of, 457; liability requirements in, 459–468; *mens rea* in, 460–465; mistake of causal sequence in, 464; necessity defense in, 469; negligence in, 465; *negotiorum gestio*, 472; omissions in, 459–460; organized crime in, 480–481; private defense in, 470; process of, 458; protected interests in, 473; provocation/ emotional stress in, 461–463; public authority defense in, 471; punishment in, 458–459, 472–473; receiving stolen property in, 478–479; Roman-Dutch criminal law and, 456, 458, 461–462; sanctions in,

472–473; self-defense in, 470; sex offenses in, 475–476; sources of, 457–458; special part of, 473–481; suicide/assisted suicide in, 474–475; superior orders in, 470; terrorism in, 481; theft in, 476–478; theft-related offenses in, 478–479; theories of punishment in, 458–459; unlawfulness in, 460, 476; victimless crimes in, 479; war crimes in, 481; youthfulness in, 460–461

Sovereignty, 1, 121

Spanish Civil War, 489

Spanish criminal law, 8; abortion in, 519; absent-element defenses in, 507; act requirement in, 497–498; *actus reus* in, 497–501; adversarial/inquisitorial process in, 494; attempted crimes in, 502–503; burden of proof in, 494, 507; business crimes in, 521; causation in, 505–507; civil liability in, 495–496; complicity in, 504; consent in, 510–511; conspiracy in, 503; corporate criminal liability in, 505; culpability principle in, 491; death penalty in, 517; defenses in, 507; *dolus* in, 501; *dolus eventualis* in, 501; double jeopardy in, 492, 518; duress defense in, 514–515; embezzlement in, 520–521; entrapment in, 515; excuses in, 507, 512–515; false pretenses in, 520; historical background, 489; homicide in, 518–519; human rights in, 490; inchoate crimes in, 502–503; insanity defense in, 513–514; juries/written opinions in, 495; jurisdiction of, 489–490; justifications in, 507, 508–512; larceny in, 520; legality principle in, 490–491; liability requirements in, 497–507; *mens rea* in, 501–502; mistake/ignorance of fact/law defense in, 512–513; mistake of fact/law defense in, 507; necessity defense in, 508–509; omissions in, 498–500; parties to, 495; perpetration in, 503–504; positive general deterrence in, 497; principles of punishment in, 490–492; process of, 494–496; punishment in, 496–497, 516–517; robbery in, 520; sanctions in, 516–517; security measures in, 497; self-defense in, 509–510; sex offenses in, 519; sources of, 493–494; in Spanish criminal law, 514; special part of, 517–522; *stare decisis* in, 493; status in, 500–501; statute of limitations in, 496; superior orders in, 511–512, 515; terrorism in, 521–522; theories of punishment in, 496–497; theory of adequate causation in, 506; theory of objective imputation in, 506; types of prosecutors in, 495; *ultima ratio* principle in, 491–492; victimless crimes in, 521

Spanish Penal Code (SPC), 489, 493, 495–496, 498–503, 505, 507–508, 510–511, 513–522

Spigelman, J. J., 56

Stare decisis, 1; in Spanish criminal law, 493

State: police power of, 1–2; punishment by, 2

Status: in Australian criminal law, 58; in Canadian criminal law, 105; in Chinese criminal law, 148; in Egyptian criminal law, 187; in German criminal law, 261; in Indian criminal law, 293–294; in Iranian criminal law, 326; in Japanese criminal law, 399–400; in Rome Statute, 603; in Russian criminal law, 420; in Spanish criminal law, 500–501; in United Kingdom (England and Wales) criminal law, 536. See also *Actus reus*

Statute of limitations, in Spanish criminal law, 496

Statutory rape: in American criminal law, 578; in Egyptian criminal law, 189

Stephen, James Fitzjames, 99

Strict construction: in American criminal law, 566; in Canadian criminal law, 103–104

Strict liability, 8; in American criminal law, 576; in Argentine criminal law, 24; in Australian criminal law, 53, 69–70, 79, 82; in Egyptian criminal law, 188–189; in Israeli criminal law, 358, 367–368, 384–385, 387, 391; in Russian criminal law, 421, 424, 437, 440; in South African criminal law, 463, 467; in United Kingdom (England and Wales) criminal law, 533, 537, 539, 551, 553

Substituted culpability, in American criminal law, 577–578

Suid-Afrikaans Uitsaaikorporasie, Ex parte Minister van Justisie: In re S. v., 467

Superior orders: in Australian criminal law, 69, 74–75; in Canadian criminal law, 121; in Chinese criminal law, 157; in Egyptian criminal law, 192; in French criminal law, 225, 227; in German criminal law, 272; in Indian criminal law, 302, 305; in Iranian criminal law, 334, 337; in Japanese criminal law, 405; in Rome Statute, 610–611, 613–614; in Russian criminal law, 427–428, 430; in South African criminal law, 470; in Spanish criminal law, 511–512, 515; in United Kingdom (England and Wales) criminal law, 543

Supplementary Rules of Punishing the Crimes of Embezzlement and Bribery (China), 138

Supplementary Rules of Punishing the Crimes of Revealing National Secrets (China), 138

Supplementary Rules of Punishing the Crimes of Smuggling (China), 138

Tahrir al-Wasila (Khomeini), 324

Tang Code, 394

Tejedor Code, 13

Terra nullius, 50

Territoriality principle: in Argentine criminal law, 15; in Australian criminal law, 51, 78, 81, 83; in French criminal law, 212; in German criminal law, 253; in Indian criminal law, 289; in Russian criminal law, 416; in South African criminal law, 457; in Spanish criminal law, 489. *See also* Jurisdiction

Terrorism: Australian criminal law and, 51, 53–54, 58, 77, 81–83, 87, 95–96; Canadian criminal law and, 110, 123, 127–128, 135–136; in Egyptian criminal law, 181–182, 193, 196–197, 205; in French criminal law, 212; in German criminal law, 285; in Iranian criminal law, 330; in Israeli criminal law, 380, 390; in Rome Statute, 595–596; in Russian criminal law, 425; in South African criminal law, 457–458, 473, 480–481; in Spanish criminal law, 490, 495, 521–522; in United Kingdom (England and Wales) criminal law, 536

Terrorism Act 2000 (England), 536

Theft, 9; in American criminal law, 590; in Australian criminal law, 80; in Canadian criminal law, 125–126; in Chinese criminal law, 141, 168–169; in Egyptian criminal law, 200–201; in French criminal law, 233–235; in German criminal law, 278–279; in Indian criminal law, 311–312; intent in, 477–478; in Iranian criminal law, 342–343; in Japanese criminal law, 409; in Russian criminal law, 440–441; in South African criminal law, 476–478; in United Kingdom (England and Wales) criminal law, 551–552; of vehicles, 16. *See also* Larceny

Theft Act 1968 (England), 8, 532, 552

Theft Act 1978 (England), 552

Toonen v. Australia, 81

Tort law, 293, 384, 548, 565

Torture, 32, 212, 439, 517–518; in Rome Statute, 616, 620

Trade Association Law (Japan), 402

Transkeian Penal Code, 456, 462

Ugolovno-protsessual'nyy kodeks Rossiyskoy Federatsii (UPK), 416, 418, 429

Ugolovnyy kodeks Rossiyskoy Federatsii (UK), 7

UK. *See* Criminal Code of the Russian Republic; Ugolovnyy kodeks Rossiyskoy Federatsii

Ultima ratio principle, 489, 491–492

United Kingdom (England and Wales) criminal law: accessories in, 539; act requirement in, 535–536; *actus reus* in, 535–536; adversarial/inquisitorial process in, 534; attempted crimes in, 538; automatism in, 535–536; burden of proof in, 541; causation in, 540–541; causing death by driving in, 549; complicity in, 539; consent in, 542–543; conspiracy in, 538–539; corporate criminal liability in, 539–540; death penalty in, 546; defenses in, 541; drug-related offenses in, 552; duress defense in, 545; entrapment in, 545; excuses in, 543–545; forgery in, 552; fraud in, 552; historical background, 532; homicide in, 547–549; inchoate crimes in, 538–540; infanticide in, 549; insanity defense in, 544; intent in, 536–537; intoxication in, 544;

juries/written opinions in, 534–535; justifications in, 541–543; legality principle in, 532–533; liability requirements in, 535–541; loss of control in, 548; *mens rea* in, 536–537; mistake/ignorance of fact/law in, 543; necessity defense in, 541–542; negligence in, 537; omissions in, 536; process of, 534–535; provocation in, 548; punishment in, 535, 545–546; recklessness in, 537; regulatory offenses in, 552–553; sanctions in, 545–546; self-defense in, 542; sex offenses in, 549–551; sources of, 533–534; special part of, 546–553; status in, 536; strict liability in, 537; superior orders in, 543; theft in, 551–552; theories of punishment in, 535; victimless crimes in, 552

United Nations, 51, 594

United Nations Charter, 596

United Nations Convention on the Rights of the Child, 162

Universal theory of criminal law, 3

Unlawful act (manslaughter), 123, 437, 548

Unlawfulness (justification), 8, 65, 67, 74–75, 115–116, 121, 192, 259, 269–271, 302, 305, 334, 378, 404, 460, 464, 468–471, 507, 511, 513–515, 582, 612, 614. *See also* Justifications

Unlawfulness (offense element), 187, 195, 202, 260, 278, 284, 291, 306, 307, 311, 321, 333, 341–342, 409, 475–480, 500, 502–503, 537, 590, 602, 620, 623

Unlawful purpose (conspiracy), 111–112

UPK. *See* Ugolovno-protsessual'nyy kodeks Rossiyskoy Federatsii

U.S. criminal law. *See* American criminal law

Utilitarianism, 291, 305

Vagueness. *See* Legality principle

Van der Keesel, Dionysius Godfridus, 458

Van der Linden, Johannes, 458

Vicarious liability: in Argentine criminal law 34; in Australian criminal law, 63; in South African criminal law, 468; in Spanish criminal law, 505; in United Kingdom (England and Wales) criminal law, 536. *See also* Corporate criminal liability

Vicarious responsibility. *See* Vicarious liability

Victimless crimes, 9; in Australian criminal law, 80–81; in Chinese criminal law, 169–170; in Egyptian criminal law, 201–202; in German criminal law, 279–280; in Indian criminal law, 312; in Iranian criminal law, 344; in Japanese criminal law, 409; in Russian criminal law, 443–444; in South African criminal law, 479; in Spanish criminal law, 521; in United Kingdom (England and Wales) criminal law, 552

Victims: civil claims within criminal proceedings by, 8; complaints, in Japanese criminal law, 405

Violation of trust, in German criminal law, 279

Violations: in Egyptian criminal law, 181, 183–185, 195, 196; in Russian criminal law, 419. *See also* Regulatory offenses

Violations of rights of God (Iranian criminal law), 339

Voluntary-act requirement. *See Actus reus*

Voluntary euthanasia: in Australian criminal law, 51; in Indian criminal law, 313–314; in Iranian criminal law, 334; in South African criminal law, 470. *See also* Assisted suicide

Vorsatz, 261. *See also Dolus*

War crimes: in Canadian criminal law, 121; contextual element of, 621–622; in German criminal law, 253; individual acts in, 622–624; knowledge in, 622; noncombatants and, 622–623; prohibited means of warfare, 623; prohibited methods of warfare, 624; prohibited targets in, 623; in Rome Statute, 621–624; in South African criminal law, 481

Ward v. The Queen, 51

Wilhelm II (Kaiser), 594

Williams, S v., 471

Willful blindness: in Australian criminal law, 61; in Canadian criminal law, 78, 107–108, 125; in Israeli criminal law, 358–361, 368, 385, 387; in Rome Statute, 604, 610, 628

Wissentlichkeit, 261. *See also Dolus*

Withdrawal. *See* Abandonment defense

World Criminal Law, 9

World War II, 121, 394

Yeltsin, Boris, 417
Young offenders. *See* Infancy

Zaffaroni, Eugenio Raúl, 29, 34
Zanardelli, Giuseppe, 4, 13
Zanardelli Code, 13
Zecevic v. DPP, 67
Zhang Shuancheng: Manslaughter Due to Negligence (China), 149
Zina', 342